THE ST. MARTIN'S GUIDE TO WRITING

Seventh Edition

THE ST. MARTIN'S GUIDE TO WRITING

Rise B. Axelrod
UNIVERSITY OF CALIFORNIA, RIVERSIDE

Charles R. Cooper
UNIVERSITY OF CALIFORNIA, SAN DIEGO

BEDFORD/ST. MARTIN'S
BOSTON ■ NEW YORK

For Bedford / St. Martin's

Senior Developmental Editor: John Elliott
Senior Production Editor: Harold Chester
Senior Production Supervisor: Dennis J. Conroy
Art Director: Lucy Krikorian
Copy Editor: Rosemary Winfield
Photo Research: Alice Lundoff, Joan Scafarello
Text and Cover Design: Anna George
Composition: Monotype Composition Company, Inc.
Printing and Binding: R.R. Donnelley & Sons Company

President: Joan E. Feinberg
Editorial Director: Denise B. Wydra
Editor in Chief: Nancy Perry
Director of Marketing: Karen Melton Soeltz
Director of Editing, Design, and Production: Marcia Cohen
Managing Editor: Erica T. Appel

Library of Congress Control Numbers: 2003107892 (with Handbook)
2003107893 (without Handbook)

Manufactured in the United States of America.

9 8 7 6 5 4
f e d c b a

For information, write: Bedford / St. Martin's, 75 Arlington Street, Boston, MA 02116 (617-399-4000)

ISBN: 0-312-40052-7 (with Handbook)
0-312-40053-5 (without Handbook)

Acknowledgments

Acknowledgments and copyrights appear at the back of the book on pages A1–A2, which constitute an extension of the copyright page.

Advisory Board

We owe an enormous debt to all the rhetoricians and composition specialists whose theory, research, and pedagogy have informed *The St. Martin's Guide to Writing*. We would be adding many pages if we were to name everyone to whom we are indebted.

The members of the Advisory Board for the seventh edition, a group of dedicated composition instructors from across the country, have provided us with extensive insights and suggestions for the chapters in Part One and have given us the benefit of their advice on new features, in many cases testing them in their own classrooms. *The St. Martin's Guide to Writing* has been greatly enhanced by their contributions.

Jeffrey T. Andelora
Mesa Community College

Lawrence Barkley
Mt. San Jacinto College–Menifee

Sandie McGill Barnhouse
Rowan-Cabarrus Community College

Helen Deese
University of California–Riverside

Elizabeth M. Gardner
Millersville University

Gregory Glau
Arizona State University

Maurice Hunt
Baylor University

Michael A. Miller
Longview Community College

Scott Payne
The University of Findlay

Sharran S. Slinkard
Des Moines Area Community College

Rachelle Smith
Emporia State University

Kim Stallings
University of North Carolina at Charlotte

Rosemary Winslow
Catholic University of America

Preface

When we first wrote *The St. Martin's Guide to Writing,* we took what we had learned from classical rhetoric as well as from contemporary composition theory and research and did our best to make it accessible to students. We aimed to demystify writing and authorize students as writers. We wanted to help students learn to commit themselves to writing projects, communicate effectively with chosen readers, and question their own certainties. We also wanted them to understand that knowledge of writing comes both from analyzing published and student writing and from working seriously on their own writing and giving and getting advice on work in progress.

The response from instructors and students has been overwhelmingly positive ever since the first publication of *The Guide* in 1985. That first edition immediately became the most widely adopted text of its kind in the nation, and the book has maintained that position through six editions, with the number of copies sold increasing over the years. Although *The Guide* has changed in many ways since we wrote the first draft in 1983, our basic goals for this seventh edition remain the same.

AN OVERVIEW OF THE BOOK

As a rhetoric and reader, *The St. Martin's Guide* can serve as a comprehensive introduction to many genres of writing. It comprises several parts:

Part One, Writing Activities, presents nine different essay assignments, all reflecting actual writing situations that students may encounter both in and out of college, genres of writing that they should learn to read critically and to write intelligently. Among the types of essays included are narrating a remembered event, explaining a concept, taking and supporting a position, proposing a solution to a problem, and interpreting a short story.

You may choose among these chapters and teach them in any sequence you wish, though they are sequenced here to move students from writing based on personal experience and observation to writing based on established information or on continuing debates over arguable issues, problems, and questions.

Each chapter follows the same organizational plan.

Chapter Organization for Part One

- Six brief **scenarios** identifying the genre covered in the chapter and suggesting the range of occasions when such writing is done—in other courses, in the community, and in the workplace
- A **collaborative activity** that gets students working with the genre
- A set of four **readings** accompanied by a **critical apparatus** designed to help students explore connections to their culture and experience and to analyze writing strategies used in the genre
- A summary of the **purpose and audience** and the **basic features** of the genre
- A flexible **guide to writing,** tailored to the particular genre, that escorts students through a process of invention, planning, drafting, and revising, including a critical reading guide for peer review of drafts
- **Editing and proofreading guidelines,** based on our nation-wide study of error in first-year college students' writing in nine genres, to help students check for one or two sentence-level problems likely to occur in a genre.
- A look at one **writer at work,** focusing on some aspect of the process of writing the student essay featured in the chapter
- A box exploring how writers work on **document design,** expanding on one of the scenarios presented at the beginning of the chapter
- A trio of **critical thinking activities** designed to help students reflect on and consolidate what they learned about writing and reading and consider the social dimensions of the genre taught in the chapter

Part Two, Critical Thinking Strategies, collects in two separate chapters practical heuristics for invention and reading. The catalog of invention strategies includes clustering, looping, dramatizing, and questioning, while the catalog of reading strategies includes annotating, summarizing, exploring the significance of figurative language, and evaluating the logic of an argument.

Part Three, Writing Strategies, looks at a wide range of writers' strategies: paragraphing and coherence, logic and reasoning, and the familiar methods of presenting information, such as narrating, defining, and classifying. Examples and exercises have been drawn from a wide range of contemporary publications as well as reading selections appearing in Part One. Because of the extensive cross-referencing between Parts One and Three, instructors will find it easier to teach writing strategies as students work on full essays.

Part Four, Research Strategies, discusses field as well as library and Internet research and includes thorough, up-to-date guidelines for using and documenting sources, with detailed examples of the Modern Language Association (MLA) and American Psychological Association (APA) documentation styles. An annotated sample student research paper models ways students can integrate citations into their own work in accordance with the MLA documentation style.

Part Five, Writing for Assessment, covers essay examinations, showing students how to analyze different kinds of exam questions and offering strategies for writing answers. It also addresses portfolios, helping students select, assemble, and present a representative sample of their writing.

Part Six, Writing and Speaking to Wider Audiences, helps students design written and online documents and prepare oral presentations. This part of The Guide also includes chapters on collaborative learning and service learning, designed to help students work together on individual and joint writing projects and to write in and for their communities.

The Handbook offers a complete reference guide to grammar, word choice, punctuation, mechanics, common ESL problems, sentence structure, and usage. We have designed the Handbook so that students will find the answers that they need quickly, and we have provided student examples from our nation-wide study so that students will see errors similar to the ones in their own essays. In addition to the section on ESL problems, boxes throughout the rest of the Handbook offer specific support for ESL students.

Proven Features

Since the first edition, two central features have made *The St. Martin's Guide to Writing* such an effective textbook: the practical guides to writing different genres and the systematic integration of reading and writing.

Practical Guides to Writing. We do not merely talk about the composing process; rather, we offer practical, flexible guides that escort students through an entire process, from invention through revision and self-evaluation. Commonsensical and easy to follow, these writing guides teach students to assess a rhetorical situation, identify the kinds of information they will need, ask probing questions and find answers, and organize writing to achieve a particular purpose for chosen readers.

Systematic Integration of Reading and Writing. Because we see a close relationship between the ability to read critically and the ability to write intelligently, *The St. Martin's Guide* combines reading instruction with writing instruction. Each chapter in Part One introduces one genre, which students are led to consider both as readers and as writers. Each reading is accompanied by carefully focused critical apparatus. First is a response activity, Connecting to Culture and Experience, that relates a central theme of the reading to students' cultural knowledge and personal experience. The two sections following, Analyzing Writing Strategies and a brief Commentary, examine how each writer makes telling use of some of the basic features and strategies typical of the genre. Taken together, these analytical activities and commentaries provide students with a comprehensive rhetorical introduction that prepares them to write an essay of their own in a genre. Finally, in Considering Topics for Your Own Essay, students approach the most important decision they have to make with a genre-centered assignment: choosing a workable topic that inspires their commitment to two or three weeks of thinking and writing.

Continuing Attention to Changes in Composition

With each new edition, we have tried to respond to new thinking and new issues in the field of composition and to continue our tradition of turning current theory and research into practical classroom activities—with a minimum of jargon. As a result, from the first to the sixth editions the *Guide* incorporated a number of added features that have contributed to its continued effectiveness, including activities that promote group discussion and inquiry and encourage students to reflect on what they have learned as well as material on document design, oral presentations, and writing in the community.

Collaborative Activities. *The St. Martin's Guide* offers multiple opportunities for group work throughout each Part One chapter. At the start of each chapter is a collaborative activity that invites students to try out some of the thinking and planning they will be engaged in as they complete the chapter's assignment. The Connecting to Culture and Experience section that follows each reading is designed to provoke thoughtful responses about the social and political dimensions of the reading. The Guide to Writing contains another collaborative activity that invites students to discuss their work in progress with one another, along with a Critical Reading Guide, which guides students as they read and comment on each other's drafts. Finally, a discussion activity invites students to explore the social dimensions of the genre they have been learning to write. Each activity includes questions and prompts to guide students to work productively together. In addition to these activities in Part One, the book also includes a variety of small group acivities in the chapters in Part Three and an entire chapter in Part Six (Chapter 27) on working with others on individual and joint writing projects.

Critical Thinking Activities. Each chapter in Part One concludes with three metacognitive activities to help students become aware of what they have learned about the process of writing, about the influences of reading on writing, and about the social and political dimensions of the genres they have written. These activities are based on research showing that reflecting on what they have learned deepens students' understanding and improves their recall.

Attention to Document Design, Oral Presentations, and Writing in the Community. Responding to concerns voiced by many instructors, in the previous (sixth) edition we added full chapters in Part Six on each of these current issues in composition, as well as material in the rest of the book related to document design and service learning.

Changes in the Seventh Edition

In this new edition, we have set as our central goal to ensure that the *Guide* fully reflects the ongoing computerization of all aspects of writing and research. We have done so in a variety of ways, from providing new electronic writing tools to making many technology-related changes and additions to the book. In addition, continuing our efforts to make the *Guide* even more appealing and useful, we have made other significant changes and additions to the Guides to Writing and the coverage of research and documentation, as well as adding a substantial number of new readings.

Web Activities in Every Writing Guide. Recognizing that many students turn to the World Wide Web when given a writing assignment, we have added to the Invention section in every Part One chapter a new activity that suggests ways students can use the Web selectively and productively. For example, Chapter 2, Remembering Events, encourages students who are having difficulty choosing a significant event of their own to look at the kinds of events other people consider significant enough to post on the Web; Chapter 6, Arguing a Position, directs students to other position essays on the same issue to help them develop an informed counterargument. To offer useful suggestions that would not waste students' time, we have tried to provide advice that is as specific as possible, suggesting particular sites, keywords, or other search strategies.

Current, Concrete Advice on Technology throughout the Book. Both the Guides to Writing and the rest of the text have been thoroughly revised to reflect the many diverse ways that both students and instructors now rely on computers, ranging from the keyword-searching, editing-tracking, and cutting-and-pasting capabilities of word processors to the use of chat rooms, online collaboration and peer review, and other aspects of the increasingly electronic classroom. New "sidebars" in the assignment chapters in Part One provide concise information and advice about technological topics such as grammar- and spellcheckers and software-based commenting tools.

Free Writing Guide Software. Because most students today write their papers on computers, we now include a free copy of the book's award winning Writing Guide Software with each copy of the text. The software, which wraps around the word-processing program of the student's computer, provides an online version of much of the content in the Guide to Writing in each chapter in Part One, so that students can work through the assignment in the online format in which most of them are now most comfortable. A guide on the gold-bordered pages in the back of the book explains how to use the software, and cross-references thoughout the book systematically direct students to it, extending a clear invitation to move seamlessly between reading the book and working online. The Instructor's Resource Manual includes a new chapter on introducing the software to students and helping them understand its relation to the text.

Easier Access to Interactive Online Exercises. To encourage students to take advantage of Exercise Central, Bedford/St. Martin's database of more than 7,000 exercise items covering grammar, punctuation, and other sentence-level issues, new cross-references in the Editing and Proofreading section of most of the Writing Guides and in the section headings throughout the Handbook direct students to URLs that will take them directly to exercises on the topics covered in that section.

Sentence Strategies for Each Genre. To provide students with practical help to increase their rhetorical prowess, we have introduced in every Part One chapter new material explaining and illustrating certain sentence patterns writers typically use when composing in a particular genre. In the Drafting section of each Guide to Writing, a new subsection titled Sentence Strategies explains two sentence-level strategies that are rhetorically important for that genre—that is, likely to help students fulfill their purpose for their readers—and illustrates them with examples from the chapter's readings. For example, Chapter 2, Remembering Events, shows students how short sentences can be used to heighten suspense, point out autobiographical significance, and summarize action and also how placing references to time at the beginning of a sentence helps to orient readers in a narrative. Chapter 6, Taking a Position, demonstrates ways of making a concession to an opposing position but then immediately refuting it and also shows how conjunctions can indicate explicitly and precisely the logical relationships between clauses and sentences.

Revised Guides to Writing Profiles and Concept Explantions. As a consequence of our wider reading of reportage and efforts to better understand students' problems writing profiles, we have redefined the basic features of profiles in Chapter 4—the first time we have revised the basic features of a genre in any of our assignment chapters—and reorganized the Chapter 4 Guide to Writing accordingly. The Chapter 5 Guide has been revised to reflect the two distinctive stages of research in writing about a concept: getting an initial quick overview of information in order to find a focus to write about and then researching this focus in depth.

Engaging New Readings. In the seventh edition, we have replaced fourteen of the reading selections, more than a third of the total, with new authors including Mary Karr, Barbara Ehrenreich, David Brooks, and Natalie Angier. Many of the new readings provide students with provocative perspectives on subjects recently in the news, from a debate on same-sex marriage and a proposal stemming from the child-abuse scandals in the Roman Catholic Church to an analysis of the reasons that Americans resist political proposals to redistribute wealth. Some new selections, including reviews of a recently released movie and computer game, show students ways that writers of the genre can make good use of visuals such as photographs and charts.

More Detailed Advice on Paraphrasing. In response to requests from instructors, we have added more explanation and examples to the discussion of paraphrase in Chapter 22 to help students see more clearly how to integrate source materials successfully into their essays and to show them that plagiarism can involve borrowing either words or sentence structures.

Up-to-Date Coverage of Electronic Research and Documentation. Chapters 21 and 22 have been updated to reflect the latest aspects of electronic research—from the increasing intermeshing of online and library research to the most useful search tools and strategies—as well as the most recent MLA and APA documentation guidelines.

ADDITIONAL RESOURCES

Numerous resources, both print and electronic, accompany *The St. Martin's Guide to Writing.*

The Instructors Resource Manual, by Rise B. Axelrod, Charles R. Cooper, and Lawrence Barkley of Mount Saint Jacinto College–Menifee, includes a catalog of helpful advice for new instructors (by Alison M. Warriner of California State University, Hayward), guidelines on common teaching practices such as assigning journals and setting up group activities, guidelines on responding to and evaluating student writing, course plans, detailed chapter plans, an annotated bibliography in composition and rhetoric, and a selection of background readings. New to this edition is a chapter on teaching with the Writing Guide Software.

Sticks and Stones and other student essays, Fifth Edition, edited by Rise B. Axelrod, Charles R. Cooper, and Lawrence Barkley of Mount San Jacinto College–Menifee, is a collection of essays written by students across the nation using *The St. Martin's Guide.* The ten chapters in the book correspond to those in Part One of *The Guide.* The book includes forms for the submission of students essays so that we may consider them for possible publication in future editions.

Who Are We? Readings in Identity and Community and Work and Career, prepared by Rise B. Axelrod and Charles R. Cooper, contains selections that expand on themes foregrounded in *The St. Martin's Guide to Writing.* Full of ideas for classroom discussion and writing, the readings offer students additional perspectives and thought-provoking analysis.

The St. Martin's Guide for Writing in the Disciplines: A Guide for Faculty, by Richard Bullock of Wright State University, is a handy reference for faculty, with ideas for using writing in courses across the curriculum. Among the topics covered are designing assignments that get students writing, using informal writing activities to help students to learn, assigning portfolios, and responding to student writing.

Additional Resources for Teaching with The St. Martin's Guide to Writing supports classroom instruction with over fifty transparency masters including lists of important features for each genre, critical reading guides, collaborative activities, and checklists, all adapted from the text, and more than fifty exercises designed to accompany the Handbook section of *The Guide.* All the pages are perforated for easy removal and copying.

The St. Martin's Guide companion Web site <bedfordstmartins.com/theguide> provides additional information for students and instructors. Here instructors can access sample syllabi, an exercise gradebook, and a form for electronically submitting student essays for possible use in future editions of the *Guide* or *Sticks and Stones,* among other resources. Students can access electronic versions of the book's Critical Reading Guides and collaborative activities, tutorials to help them practice recognizing and using the sentence strategies presented in Part One of the book, and a variety of resources for research and documentation, as well as the TopLinks and Exercise Central databases discussed below.

TopLinks is a database of topical links accessible through *The St. Martin's Guide to Writing* Web site. Students can search by topic or link to sites relevant to specific chapters in *The St. Martin's Guide.*

Exercise Central, available through *The St. Martin's Guide* Web site, offers a collection of grammar, punctuation, and word choice exercises with customized feedback so that students can work at their own speed. Exercise Central also offers instructors a reporting feature that allows them to monitor their students' progress.

Our content cartridge for WebCT and Blackboard makes it simple for instructors using this online learning architecture to build a course around *The St. Martin's Guide.* The content is drawn from the book and its ancillaries and includes activities, models, reference materials, and links to the interactive editing exercises in Exercise Central.

Comment, a powerful and easy-to-use Web-based tool, allows instructors and students to comment on writing quickly and easily, making the drafting and peer review processes more visible and shareable. Comment with *The St. Martin's Guide* offers the *Guide's* complete Handbook online, so reviewers can include direct links to specific parts of the Handbook.

ACKNOWLEDGMENTS

We owe an enormous debt to all the rhetoricians and composition specialists whose theory, research, and pedagogy have informed *The St. Martin's Guide to Writing.* We would be adding many pages to an already long book if we were to name everyone to whom we are indebted; suffice it to say that we have been eclectic in our borrowing.

We must also acknowledge immeasurable lessons learned from all the writers, professional and student alike, whose work we analyzed and whose writing we used in this and earlier editions.

So many instructors and students have contributed ideas and criticism over the years. Charles acknowledges the valuable contributions of many instructors in the first-year writing and core-course programs that he directed at Marshall College (formerly Third College) of the University of California, San Diego. We are still benefiting from the astute insights of M. A. Syverson, Kate Gardner, Kristin Hawkinson, Michael Pemberton, Irv Peckham, Keith Grant-Davie, Evelyn Torres, Gesa Kirsch, and James Degan. Charles also acknowledges the support of members of the English Department at Sacramento City College, where he has tutored their students, and of Steven Tchudi, Susan Tchudi, and Katherine Boardman of the English Department, University of Nevada, Reno, who have invited him to teach summer-session writing courses for first-year students. Rise similarly acknowledges the many instructors and students both at University of California, Riverside, where she currently teaches and directs the composition program and at California State University, San Bernardino, where she previously taught.

The members of the advisory board for the seventh edition, a group of dedicated composition instructors from across the country, have provided us with extensive insights and suggestions for the chapters in Part One and have given us the benefit of their advice on new readings and other new features. For all of their many contributions, we would like to thank Jeffrey T. Andelora, Mesa Community College; Lawrence Barkley, Mt. San Jacinto College–Menifee; Sandie McGill Barnhouse, Rowan-Cabarrus Community College; Helen Deese, University of California–Riverside; Elizabeth M. Gardner, Millersville University; Gregory Glau, Arizona State University; Maurice Hunt, Baylor University; Michael A. Miller, Longview Community College; Scott Payne, The University of Findlay; Rachelle Smith, Emporia State University; Sharran S. Slinkard, Des Moines Area Community College; Kim Stallings, University of North Carolina–Charlotte; and Rosemary Winslow, Catholic University of America.

Many other instructors have also helped us improve the book. For responding to detailed questionnaires about the sixth edition, we thank Melanie J. Abrams, California State University–San Bernadino; Susan B. Achziger, Community College of Aurora; Deborah M. Alvarez, Bowling Green State University; Cathryn Amdahl, Harrisburg Area Community College, Jeffrey Andelora, Mesa Community College; Linda Austin, McLennan Community College; Ken Autrey, Francis Marion University; Greg Barnhisel, University of Southern California; Melissa Batai, Triton College; Jennifer Berne, Oakland Community College; Eileen Blasius, Community College of Aurora; Diana Bowling, Arizona State University; Daniel Breazeale, Arizona State University; Melissa Bregenzer, Danville Area Community College; Mark Browning, Johnson County Community College; Lou Caton, Auburn University; Patricia Cearley, South Plains College; Maggie Christensen, University of Nebraska–Omaha; Maria A. Clayton, Middle Tennessee State University; Carol Dillon, University of Nebraska–Omaha; Joyce Anne Dvorak, Longview Community College; David Furniss, University of Wisconsin–River Falls; Michele Griegel, University of Cincinnati; Ann C. Hall, Ohio Dominican College; Peggy Jolly, University of Alabama–Birmingham; Melvin Richard Jones, South Suburban College; Steven R. Luebke, University of Wisconsin–River Falls; Sam Martinez, Mesa Community College; Phillip Paul Marzluf, University of Okalahoma; Becky Jo McShane, Weber State University; Terrance Lane Millet, Linn-Benton Community College; Patricia Murphy, Arizona State University; Sarah O'Hara, Pima Community College; Mike Pennell, Purdue University; Michael Pettengell, Kansas City Kansas Community College; Michael D. Quigley, California State University–Ponoma; Elizabeth Rankin, University of North Dakota; Sharon Rankin, Abilene Christian University; Kent Rogers, California State University–San Bernadino; Rachelle M. Smith, Emporia State University; and Bryce Warren, Northern Kentucky University.

For this new edition of *The Guide,* we also gratefully acknowledge the special contributions of four people. Tom Greene, who taught writing at the University of Massachusetts at Amherst and now works at Kaplan Test Prep and Admissions, provided extensive advice on technology and Internet resources for students and also wrote the new Instructor's Resource Manual chapter on using the Writing Guide Software. Debora A. Person, a librarian at the University of Wyoming, reviewed Chapter 21, Library and Internet Research, and suggested updates and other revisions. Mark Gallaher, who has made many creative contributions to *The Guide* from the beginning, both as a St. Martin's editor and as a teacher of an early draft of a

Guide chapter, updated the examples and exercises in Part 2 and Part 3 and the MLA and APA documentation guidelines and examples and the student essay in Chapter 22. Grateful thanks are likewise due to Larry Barkley of Mt. San Jacinto College–Menifee, our co-editor for *The Guide's* ancillary collection of student essays, *Sticks and Stones and other student essays,* and for the Instructor's Resource Manual. Finally, we are especially grateful to the student authors for allowing us to reprint their work in *Sticks and Stones* and in *The Guide.*

We want to thank many people at Bedford/St. Martin's, especially John Elliott, who ushered us through the editorial process with considerable skill and caring. Thank you, John, for your patience and professionalism. You are a fine writer and editor. We also are grateful to our production team of Harold Chester, Erica Appel, and Dennis Conroy. Harold, thanks for your skillful juggling during the final stages of the process. Rosemary Winfield, thanks for your faultless copyediting. We owe a special debt to Greg Johnson for his masterful managing of the *Sticks and Stones* revision and also for his coordinating of all the revisions to the software and the Web site and updating of many of the examples in Chapter 25, Document Design. Without Denise Wydra's and Nick Carbone's expertise and leadership, the electronic supplements to *The Guide* would not have been possible. Our gratitude also goes to Sandy Schechter, Fred Courtright, and Joan Scafarello for their hard work clearing permissions, Kristy Bredin for her invaluable assistance throughout the project, and Alice Lundoff for her imaginative photo research. We wish finally to express our appreciation to Nancy Perry for helping us to launch *The Guide* successfully so many years ago and continuing to stand by us, to Joan Feinberg and Denise Wydra for their adroit leadership of Bedford/St. Martins, and to Karen Melton Soeltz and Linda Sax—along with the extraordinarily talented and hardworking sales staff—for their tireless efforts on behalf of *The Guide.*

Charles dedicates this edition to his three grandchildren, Abigail Cooper Douglas, James Blackburn Douglas, and Lily Isabel Taggart, three late-in-life loves, and to his wife Mary Anne, ever-present, ever-engaged, the decades-long love. Rise dedicates *The Guide* to the person who has been her guiding light, her beloved mother, Edna Borenstein.

A Brief Contents

PART FOUR RESEARCH STRATEGIES

PART FIVE WRITING FOR ASSESSMENT

PART SIX WRITING AND SPEAKING TO WIDER AUDIENCES

Contents

10 Interpreting Stories 507

PART TWO CRITICAL THINKING STRATEGIES

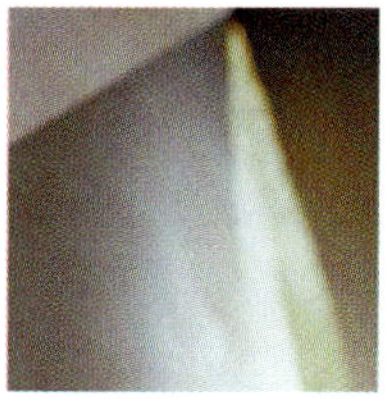

PART THREE WRITING STRATEGIES

PART FIVE WRITING FOR ASSESSMENT

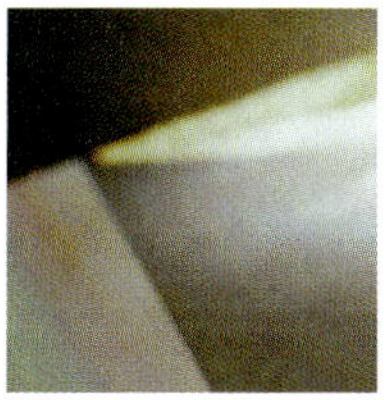

PART SIX WRITING AND SPEAKING TO WIDER AUDIENCES

THE ST. MARTIN'S GUIDE TO WRITING

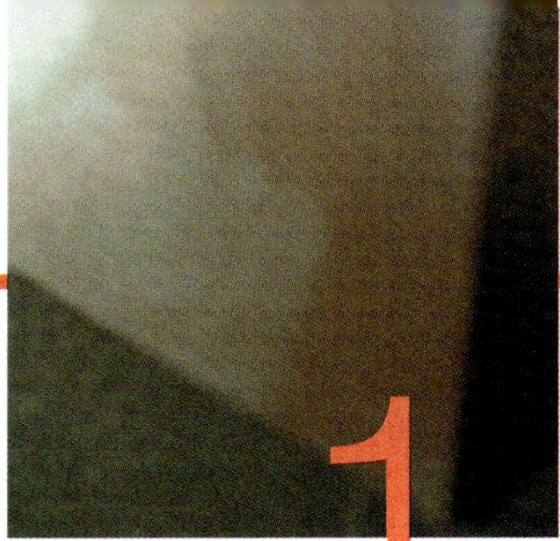

1

Introduction

"Why should learning to write well be important to me? What is the connection between writing and thinking? How will reading help me learn to write better? How can I learn to write more effectively and efficiently?" These are some of the questions you may be asking as you begin this writing course. Read on—for *The St. Martin's Guide to Writing* offers some answers to these and other questions you may have.

WHY WRITING IS IMPORTANT

Writing has wide-ranging implications for the way we think and learn as well as for our chances of success, our personal development, and our relationships with other people.

Writing Influences the Ways We Think

First, the very act of writing encourages us to be creative as well as organized and logical in our thinking. When we write sentences, paragraphs, and whole essays, we generate ideas and connect these ideas in systematic ways. For example, by combining words into phrases and sentences with conjunctions such as *and, but,* and *because,* we can create complex new ideas. By grouping related ideas into paragraphs, we develop their similarities and differences and anchor our general ideas in specific facts and concrete examples.

By writing essays for different purposes and readers, we learn to develop our thinking in different ways. For example, writing about an important event in our lives develops our ability to select significant details and organize them into a meaningful narrative. Writing an explanation of a concept develops categorical thinking, as we connect new information to what we and our readers already know. Speculating about causes develops causal reasoning, proposing solutions develops problem solving, and arguing positions develops logical thinking.

> Some of the things that happen to us in life seem to have no meaning, but when you write them down, you find the meanings for them. . . .
>
> – Maxine Hong Kingston

> Those who are learning to compose and arrange their sentences with accuracy and order are learning, at the same time, to think with accuracy and order.
>
> –HUGH BLAIR

Writing Contributes to the Ways We Learn

Writing helps us learn by making us active, critical thinkers. When we take notes in class, for example, writing helps us identify and remember what is important. Writing in the margins as we read encourages us to question the reading's ideas and information in light of our experience and other reading. Writing in a journal frees us to explore our understanding of and response to what we are learning.

Writing essays of various kinds helps us to organize and present what we have learned and, in the process, to clarify and extend our own ideas. Writing an explanatory essay, for example, helps us better understand the concept or idea we are explaining. Researching a controversial issue helps us both learn from and question others' points of view.

> The mere process of writing is one of the most powerful tools we have for clarifying our own thinking. I am never as clear about any matter as when I have just finished writing about it.
>
> –JAMES VAN ALLEN

> Writing keeps me from believing everything I read.
>
> –GLORIA STEINEM

Writing Fosters Personal Development

In addition to influencing the ways we think and learn, writing can help us grow as individuals. We are led to reflect deeply on our personal experience, for example, when we write to understand the significance of a particular person in our life. Writing about a controversial issue can make us examine critically some of our most basic assumptions. Writing an evaluation requires that we think about what we value and how our values compare to those of others. Writing about stories invites us to reflect on how we understand ourselves and others. Perhaps most important, becoming an author confers authority on us; it gives us confidence to assert our own ideas and feelings.

> In a very real sense, the writer writes in order to teach himself, to understand himself, to satisfy himself. . . .
>
> –ALFRED KAZIN

> Writing has been for a long time my major tool for self-instruction and self-development.
>
> –TONI CADE BAMBARA

Writing Connects Us to Others

It is easier now than ever before to connect with others via email and the Internet. We can use writing to keep in touch with friends and family, take part in academic discussions, and participate actively in democratic debate and decision making. By writing about our experiences, ideas, and observations, we reach out to readers, offering them our own point of view and inviting them to share theirs in return. Writing an argument on a controversial issue, for example, we not only assert our position on the issue but also give readers an opportunity to assert theirs. Moreover, when we respond constructively to each other's writing, we can clarify our differences, reexamine our reasoning, and ultimately influence each other's opinions. Similarly, writing a proposal requires us to work collaboratively with others to invent new, creative ways of solving complex problems.

> Writing is the act of saying *I*, of imposing oneself upon other people, of saying *listen to me, see it my way, change your mind.*
>
> –JOAN DIDION

> I think writing is really a process of communication. . . . It's the sense of being in contact with people who are part of a particular audience that really makes a difference to me in writing.
>
> –SHERLEY ANNE WILLIAMS

Writing Promotes Success in College and at Work

As students, you are probably most aware of the many ways writing can contribute to your success in school. Students who learn to write for different readers and purposes do well in courses throughout the curriculum. No doubt you have been able to use writing to demonstrate your knowledge as well as to add to it. Eventually, you will need to use writing to advance your career by writing persuasive application letters for jobs or graduate school admission. Many businesses and professions expect people to write effective email messages, formal letters, and reports that present clear explanations, convincing evaluations, or constructive proposals.

> The aim of school is to produce citizens who are able to communicate with each other, to defend points of view, and to criticize. . . .
>
> –ALBERT SHANKER

> People think it's sort of funny that I went to graduate school as a biologist and then became a writer. . . . What I learned [in science] is how to formulate or identify a new question that hasn't been asked before and then to set about solving it, to do original research to find the way to an answer. And that's what I do when I write a book.
>
> –BARBARA KINGSOLVER

Exercise 1.1

Think of an occasion when writing helped you accomplish something important. For example, you may recall a time when writing helped you better understand a difficult subject you were studying, when you used writing to influence someone else, when writing helped you achieve a goal, when you expressed your feelings or worked through a problem by writing, or when you used writing for some other worthwhile purpose.

Write a page or two describing what happened on this particular occasion. Describe how you came to write and what you wrote about. Then explain how you used writing on this occasion and what you wanted your writing to accomplish. For example, did you use it to help you learn something, express yourself, or connect to others?

HOW WRITING IS LEARNED

Writing is important. But can it be learned? This question is crucial because writing traditionally has been veiled in mystery. Some people believe that writers are born, not made. They assume that people who are good at writing do not have to spend a lot of time learning to write—that they just naturally know how to do so. Others may assume that if you have to spend time working on your writing—planning, rewriting, or editing—then you might as well give up and do something else. After all, "real" writers write perfectly the first time, every time, dashing off an essay with minimal effort. Their first draft is the last draft. They may need to spell-check their work, but nothing major needs to be clarified, developed, or corrected.

Exercise 1.2

List some of your ideas about writers and writing. Then write a few sentences speculating about where these ideas come from—from personal experience, teachers, textbooks, the media, or elsewhere.

Writers' testimonies, together with extensive research on how people write and learn to write, show that writing can—indeed must—be learned. Some writers may be more skilled than others. Some may find writing easier and more satisfying. But no one is born knowing how to write. Everyone must learn how to write.

> However great a [person's] natural talent may be, the art of writing cannot be learned all at once.
>
> –JEAN JACQUES ROUSSEAU

> Learning to write well takes time and much effort, but it can be done.
>
> –MARGARET MEAD

The St. Martin's Guide to Writing, now in its seventh edition, has helped many students learn how to become effective, confident writers. Using *The St. Martin's Guide,* you will read and write several different kinds of essays. From reading these essays, you will learn how other writers make their texts work for their particular readers. From writing the kinds of essays you are reading, you will learn to compose texts that work effectively for your readers. To take full advantage of what you are learning by reading and writing, *The Guide* will also help you become self-reflective as a reader and writer. From thinking critically about your learning, you will be better able to remember and apply what you have learned, thereby earning a greater sense of confidence and control.

Reading

This section shows how reading texts that work well for their readers helps you learn to write texts for your own readers and how *The St. Martin's Guide* supports your learning from reading.

How Written Texts Work. How a text works depends on what purpose and what audience it is written for. A text's purpose and audience can be used to define the kind of writing it is, what we call its *genre*.

You may be familiar with genres as categories for literature (novel, poem, play) or film (science fiction, western, film noir, romance). College students read and write many different genres, such as lab reports in biology, ethnographies in anthropology, literary analyses or interpretations in English, or research reviews in education. Academic disciplines rely on certain genres that have become established ways of making meaning and communicating among students and specialists in the field. The same is true of writing in business (where genres include résumés and job-application letters, marketing reports, proposals, and personnel evaluations) and the professions (lawyers, for example, write briefs, appeals, closing arguments, and wills).

As these examples show, genres are shared by groups of people with common interests. Some genres are highly specialized and technical; to understand a biologist's lab report or a lawyer's brief, readers have to know the terminology and have to be able to judge the reliability of the lab report's research methods or the credibility of the brief's arguments. Many genres, however, are widely shared and therefore do not require specialized knowledge. For example, because of our shared experience, we can all read and understand most news reports, opinion essays, autobiographies, profiles, and advertisements we encounter in general audience publications such as newspapers, magazines, and Web sites.

Genres develop in different communities to serve particular purposes. Biologists use lab reports to inform readers interested in biology about the results of their research and to enable other researchers to duplicate their experiments. Lawyers use briefs to convince judges that certain points of law apply to their case. Reporters write about news events to inform readers. Columnists write opinion essays to persuade readers to adopt their views. Advertisers write ads to persuade readers to buy their clients' products.

A text's effectiveness—how well it achieves its purpose with its readers—depends on many factors, including how well it fulfills readers' expectations for the genre. Readers expect texts within a particular genre to have distinctive features, use specific strategies, and contain certain types of content. A remembered-event essay, for example, has several basic features: a well-told story about the event, a vivid presentation of the people involved in the event and of the place where it occurred, and an indication of the event's significance. Writers of such essays use strategies of narration and description to help readers imagine what happened and understand the event's significance. Readers expect the content of autobiographical writing to be about events they consider important, such as events that have had some lasting impact—changing, challenging, or complicating the writer's sense of self or connection with others.

Although individual texts within the same genre vary (no two proposals, even those arguing for the same solution, will be identical), they nonetheless follow a general pattern using distinctive basic features, strategies, and kinds of content to accomplish their purposes. This patterning allows for a certain amount of predictability, without which communication would be difficult, if not impossible. Language—whether spoken or written—is a system of social interaction. Everyone who speaks the same language learns to recognize certain patterns—how words should be ordered to make sentences comprehensible, how sentences can be related to one another to make coherent paragraphs, how examples can be used to explain new ideas, how arguments can be supported with quotations from authorities, and so forth. These language patterns, also called *conventions,* make communication possible.

To learn to write genres for particular groups of readers, we need to pay attention to how texts work for their readers. We have to understand also that writing in a genre need not be mechanical or formulaic. Each genre's basic features, strategies, and kinds of content represent broad frameworks within which writers are free to be creative. Most writers, in fact, find that working within a framework allows them to be more creative, not less so. Some even blur the boundaries between genres and invent new genres for new media such as Web sites. And as groups change, developing new interests and new ways of adding to their knowledge, genre conventions also change.

> You would learn very little in this world if you were not allowed to imitate. And to repeat your imitations until some solid grounding . . . was achieved and the slight but wonderful difference—that made *you* and no one else—could assert itself.
>
> –MARY OLIVER

How *The Guide* Helps You Write Texts That Work. To learn the conventions of a particular genre, you need to read examples of that genre. At the same time, you should also practice writing in the genre.

> Read, read, read. . . . Just like a carpenter who works as an apprentice and studies the master. Read!
>
> –WILLIAM FAULKNER

Reading is crucial. As you read examples of a genre, you begin to recognize its predictable patterns as well as the possibilities for innovation. This knowledge is stored in your memory and used both when you read and when you write in that genre.

Experienced writers read and learn from positive examples as well as negative ones. Sometimes, they focus on a particular problem—how to write realistic-sounding dialogue or how to refute someone else's argument effectively, for example. They do not look for answers in a single example. Instead, they sample many texts to see how different writers work with a certain feature of the genre. This sampling is not slavish imitation but education. Like artists and craftspeople, writers have always learned from others. *The St. Martin's Guide to Writing* presents a variety of examples in each genre accompanied by questions and commentary to help you see how writers use the conventional features and strategies of the genre to achieve their own purposes.

> I practiced writing in every possible way that I could. I wrote a pastiche of other people. Just as a pianist runs his scales for ten years before he gives his concert: because when he gives that concert, he can't be thinking of his fingering or of his hands, he has to be thinking of his interpretation. He's thinking of what he's trying to communicate.
>
> –KATHERINE ANNE PORTER

How *The Guide* Helps You Design Texts That Work. Writers have long recognized that no matter how well organized, well reasoned, or compelling a piece of writing may be, how it looks on the page influences to some extent how it works for readers. Today, writers have many more options for designing their documents than ever before. Recent advances in computer technology, digital photography and scanning, and integrated word processing and graphics programs make it relatively easy for writers to heighten the visual impact of the page. For example, they can change type fonts and add colors, charts, diagrams, and photographs to written documents. To construct multimedia Web pages or CD-ROMs, writers can add sound, moving images, and hyperlinks.

> Design is a funny word. Some people think design means how it looks. But of course, if you dig deeper, it's really how it works.
>
> –STEVE JOBS

These multiple possibilities, however, do not guarantee a more effective document. Writers need to learn to design effective texts by studying texts in their everyday lives that capture readers' attention and enhance understanding. As someone who has grown up watching television shows and videos, playing computer games, and looking at the photos, advertisements, cartoons, tables, and graphs in magazines, newspapers, and other sources, you are already a sophisticated visual consumer who has learned many of the conventions of document design for different genres and writing situations. This book will help you become aware of what you already know and help you make new discoveries about document design that you may be able to use in your own writing.

Exercise 1.3

Make two lists—one of the genres you have *read* recently, such as explanations of how to do something, stories, news reports, opinion pieces, and movie reviews, and the other of the genres you have *written* recently, both for college courses and for other purposes. Then write a few sentences speculating about how your reading influences your writing and the design of your texts.

Writing

This section shows how your writing process can become a more productive process of *thinking and writing* and how *The St. Martin's Guide* helps you develop a process to meet the demands of different writing situations.

How to Make Your Writing Process Work. When you reflect on how you write, you probably think of the steps you take: First you read the writing assignment, next you decide which points to cover, then you begin writing the opening paragraph, and so forth. For familiar writing situations—when you know the subject well and feel confident writing in the genre for your particular readers—the process that works best may involve minimal planning and only one draft, followed by a little rewriting, spell-checking, and proofreading. But for most writing situations, you have to figure out what you can say about the subject to your particular readers and how to communicate effectively in the genre. In these situations, the writing process itself becomes a tool for discovery and not just a sequence of steps you take to produce a written text.

> I don't see writing as a communication of something already discovered, as "truths" already known. Rather, I see writing as a job of experiment. It's like any discovery job; you don't know what's going to happen until you try it.
>
> –William Stafford

To make writing a true process of discovery, you need to recognize that the process of writing is a process of thinking—not simply a sequence of steps. Using writing as a process of discovery means that you do not think and then write but that the writing helps you think.

Few writers begin writing with a complete understanding of a subject. Most use writing as a way to learn about the subject, recording ideas and information they have collected, exploring connections and implications, letting the writing lead them to greater understanding. As they develop ideas and plan a draft, writers set goals for their writing: goals for the whole essay (to confront readers or inspire them, for example) and goals for particular passages (to make a sentence emphatic or include details in a paragraph).

> When I start a project, the first thing I do is write down, in longhand, everything I know about the subject, every thought I've ever had on it. This may be twelve or fourteen pages. Then I read it through, for quite a few days . . . then I try to find out what are the salient points that I must make. And then it begins to take shape.
>
> –Maya Angelou

While writing, most writers pause occasionally to reread what they have written. They often reread with their readers in mind to see whether they can make their writing more effective. Rereading sometimes leads to further discovery—filling in a gap in the logic of an argument, for example—and frequently it leads to substantial rethinking and revising: cutting, reorganizing, rewriting.

> I think the writer ought to help the reader as much as he can without damaging what he wants to say; and I don't think it ever hurts the writer to sort of stand back now and then and look at his stuff as if he were reading it instead of writing it.
>
> –James Jones

> The writer must survey his work critically, coolly, as though he were a stranger to it. At the end of each revision, a manuscript may look . . . worked over, torn apart, pinned together, added to, deleted from, words changed and words changed back.
>
> –Eleanor Estes

Rereading your own writing with a critical eye is necessary, but many writers also share their ideas and writing with others, actively seeking constructive critical comments from friends and colleagues. Playwrights, poets, and novelists often join writers' workshops to get help from other writers. F. Scott Fitzgerald depended on his editor, Maxwell Perkins. When Perkins criticized the way the title character was being introduced in an early version of the novel *The Great Gatsby,* Fitzgerald made significant changes in five chapters and completely rewrote two others.

Writers also sometimes write collaboratively. Engineers, business executives, and research scientists usually write proposals and reports in teams. Graduate students and professors in many fields do research together and cowrite conference papers and journal articles. This book is the product of extensive collaboration between the coauthors and numerous composition instructors, student writers, and editors over many years. Your instructor may ask you to try some of *The Guide*'s collaborative activities with other students in your class.

> [Ezra Pound] was a marvelous critic because he didn't try to turn you into an imitation of himself. He tried to see what you were trying to do.
>
> –T. S. Eliot

> I like working collaboratively from time to time. I like fusing ideas into one vision. I like seeing that vision come to life with other people who know exactly what it took to get there.
>
> –Amy Tan

The continual shifting of attention—from setting goals to choosing words, from discovering new ideas to rereading to anticipate readers' likely objections, from adding supporting examples to reorganizing—characterizes the dynamic thinking that underlies the writing process. Although writing may seem to progress in a linear, step-by-step fashion—thinking about what to say and writing it down and then perhaps revising—discovery does not stop when drafting begins. It continues throughout drafting and revising. Most writers plan and revise their plans, draft and revise their drafts, write and read what they have written, and then write some more. This rereading and rethinking is what we mean when we describe the writing process as recursive rather than linear. Instead of progressing in a straight line from the first sentence to the last, from opening paragraph to conclusion, the experience of writing is more like taking a steep trail with frequent switchbacks; it appears that you are retracing old ground, but you are really rising to new levels.

Seasoned writers depend on this recursiveness to lead them to new ideas and to develop their insights. Many writers claim that it is only by writing that they can figure out what they think.

> How do I know what I think until I see what I say?
>
> –E. M. Forster

> As a writer I would find out most clearly what I thought, and what I only thought I thought, when I saw it written down.
>
> –Anna Quindlen

Even writers who plan extensively in their heads eventually have to work out their plans by writing them down. The advantage of writing down ideas is not only that writing makes a record you can review later but also that the process of writing itself can help you articulate and develop your ideas.

> You have to work problems out for yourself on paper. Put the stuff down and read it—to see if it works.
>
> –Joyce Cary

Inexperienced writers or those writing in a new genre or on a difficult subject especially benefit from writing outlines of where they are and where they hope to go so that they can then focus on how to get there. But outlines should not be written in stone; they must be flexible if the writer is to benefit from the recursiveness of the writing process.

> Somebody starting to write should have a solid foundation to build on. . . . When I first started to write I used to do two- or three-page outlines.
>
> –Lillian Hellman

> I began [*Invisible Man*] with a chart of the three-part division. It was a conceptual frame with most of the ideas and some of the incidents indicated.
>
> –Ralph Ellison

> You are always going back and forth between the outline and the writing, bringing them closer together, or just throwing out the outline and making a new one.
>
> –Annie Dillard

Sometimes the hardest part of writing is getting down to work. Writers may procrastinate, but they learn to deal with procrastination. Many writers make writing a habit by setting a time to write and trying to stick to their schedule. Most important, they know that the only way to make progress on a writing project is to keep at it. They work at their writing, knowing it takes time and perseverance.

> I have to write every day because, the way I work, the writing generates the writing.
>
> –E. L. Doctorow

> It's a matter of piling a little piece here and a little piece there, fitting them together, going on to the next part, then going back and gradually shaping the whole piece into something. . . . You don't rely on inspiration—I don't anyway, and I don't think most writers do.
>
> –Dave Barry

Once immersed in figuring out what they want to say about the subject, contemplating what readers already think about it, and so forth, most writers find that they continue making discoveries even when away from their desks. Taking a walk or playing a game can be a productive part of the process rather than a means of procrastinating. Diverting a tired mind and body can help writers see connections or solve problems that had stymied them earlier.

> Often I write by not writing. I assign a task to my subconscious, then take a nap or go for a walk, do errands, and let my mind work on the problem.
>
> –Donald Murray

Like most creative activities, writing is a form of problem solving. As they work on a draft, most writers continually discover and try to solve writing problems—how to bring a scene to life, how to handle objections, whether to begin with this point or that. The more writers know about their subjects, genres, and readers, the better they can anticipate and solve problems as they write.

Experienced writers develop a repertoire of strategies for solving problems they are likely to encounter. *The St. Martin's Guide to Writing* will illustrate for you the strategies that will help you write well in several quite different genres.

How *The Guide* Helps You Develop a Writing Process That Works. As a student learning to write, you need to develop a writing process that is flexible and yet systematic. It should be a process that neither oversimplifies nor overwhelms, one that helps you learn about a subject and write a successful essay. The Guides to Writing in Part One of this book, which you will find on the pages bordered in green, are designed to meet this need. These guides, which are also provided (in a slightly briefer version) in the Writing Guide Software that accompanies this book, suggest what you need to think about for each different writing situation. The first few times you write in a new genre, you can rely on these guides. They provide a scaffolding to support your work until you become more familiar with each genre.

> To see the software version of one of the Guides to Writing, click on
> ▶ **Remembering Events**
> ▶ **Write**

When engaging in any new and complex activity—driving, playing an instrument, skiing, or writing—we have to learn how to break down the activity into a series of manageable tasks. In learning to play tennis, for example, you can isolate lobbing from volleying or work on your backhand or serve. Similarly, in writing about an autobiographical event, you can work first on recalling what happened, imagining the scene, or reflecting on the event's significance. What is important is focusing on one aspect at a time. Dividing the process in this way enables you to tackle a complex writing project without oversimplifying it.

> You know when you think about writing a book, you think it is overwhelming. But, actually, you break it down into tiny little tasks any moron could do.
>
> –ANNIE DILLARD

Exercise 1.4

Write a page or two describing the process you followed the last time you wrote something that took time and effort. Use the following questions to help you recall what you did, but feel free to write about any other aspects of your writing process that you remember.

- What initially led you to write? Who were you writing for, and what was the purpose of your writing?

- What kinds of thinking and planning did you do, if any, before you began writing the first draft?
- If you discussed your ideas and plans with someone, how did discussing them help you? If you had someone read your draft, how did getting a response help?
- If you rewrote, moved, added, or cut anything in your first draft, describe what you changed.

Thinking Critically

This section shows how thinking critically about your learning can help you make your writing more effective and how *The St. Martin's Guide* helps you think critically about your reading, your writing process, and the genres you are using.

How to Think Critically about Your Learning. Thinking critically means becoming self-aware or conscious of your own thinking and learning processes.

When writing, you will find that many of your decisions do not require conscious effort. You can rely on familiar strategies that usually produce effective writing for you in the genre. But there will nearly always be occasions as you write when you become aware of problems that require your full attention. Some problems may be fairly easy to remedy, such as an inappropriate word choice or a confusing sequence of events. Other problems may require considerable rethinking and writing—for example, if you discover that your readers' likely objections seriously undermine your argument.

After you have completed a final draft, reflecting on how you identified and tried to solve such problems can be a powerful aid to learning. Understanding the problem may enable you to anticipate similar problems in the future. It may also give you a firmer grip on the standards you need to apply when rereading your drafts. Most important, reflecting on a problem you solved should enhance your confidence as a writer, helping you realize that problems are not signs of bad writing but that problem-solving signifies good writing.

> That's what a writer is: someone who sees problems a little more clearly than others.
>
> –Eugene Ionesco

To think critically about your learning, it also helps to reflect on what you have learned from reading texts in the genre you are writing. Much of our language and genre-learning comes from modeling. As young children, for example, we learn from hearing our parents and peers tell stories and from watching stories portrayed on television and in film. We learn ways of beginning and ending, strategies for building suspense, techniques for making time sequences clear, how to use dialogue to develop character, and so on. As an adult, we can reinforce and increase our repertoire of storytelling patterns by analyzing how stories that we admire work and by consciously trying out in our own writing the strategies we have seen work in those stories.

> I went back to the good nature books that I had read. And I analyzed them. I wrote outlines of whole books—outlines of chapters—so that I could see their structure. And I copied down their transitional sentences or their main sentences or their clos-

> ing sentences or their lead sentences. I especially paid attention to how these writers made transitions between paragraphs and scenes.
>
> –ANNIE DILLARD

Finally, contemplating what you have learned about writing different genres can help you understand how genres are used to make possible certain kinds of social actions and ways of knowing while discouraging others. Concept explanations, for example, enable the efficient exchange of established knowledge, but they also discourage critical questioning about how certain kinds of knowledge, and not other kinds, get established as authoritative and by whom. Similarly, writing about remembered events enables self-presentation and perhaps even self-knowledge, but it discourages critical questioning about the social construction of identity and the idea of a single true or essential self.

> You leave out a lot, and emphasize this and not that. Your actual experience is a complete flux . . . [and yet] you want the readers to say, this is true . . . to believe [they are] getting the real Robert Lowell.
>
> –ROBERT LOWELL

How *The Guide* Helps You Think Critically. Thinking critically about your reading and writing experiences is not difficult. It simply requires that you shift focus from *what* you are reading and writing to *how* you are reading and writing.

The St. Martin's Guide to Writing helps you talk and write about the hows of reading and writing different genres by providing a shared vocabulary of words and phrases that you can easily learn and others of which you already know. Words like *significance, narrating,* and *thesis,* for example, will help you identify the features and strategies of essays you are reading in different genres. Words and phrases like *invention, setting goals,* and *revising* will help you describe what you are doing as you write your own essays in these genres. Phrases like *established knowledge* and *essential self* will help you examine the social dimensions of genres you are reading and writing.

Each writing assignment chapter in Part One includes many opportunities for you to think critically about your understanding of the genre and to reflect on your writing process. A section entitled Thinking Critically about What You Have Learned concludes each chapter, giving you an opportunity to look back and reflect on these three aspects of your learning:

1. How writing worked for you as a creative problem-solving process
2. How your reading of other essays in the genre helped you write your own essay
3. How you understand the social dimensions of writing in the genre

Exercise 1.5

Read the following quotes to see how writers use similes ("Writing is like ________") and metaphors ("Writing is ________") to describe the processes and products of writing.

> Writing is like exploring . . . as an explorer makes maps of the country he has explored, so a writer's works are maps of the country he has explored.
>
> –LAWRENCE OSGOOD

Writing is manual labor of the mind: a job, like laying pipe.

—John Gregory Dunne

Write two or three similes or metaphors of your own that express aspects of your experience as a writer. Then write a page or so explaining and expanding on the ideas and feelings expressed in your similes and metaphors.

USING THIS BOOK

The St. Martin's Guide to Writing is divided into six major parts.

Part One presents writing assignments for nine important genres: autobiographical events, firsthand biography, profile, explanation, position paper, proposal, evaluation, causal analysis, and literary interpretation. Each of these writing assignment chapters provides readings that demonstrate how written texts of that genre work and a Guide to Writing that will escort you through a process to help you write an effective essay in the genre for your particular purpose and audience. Each chapter also includes a discussion of possible purposes and audiences for the genre, a summary of the genre's basic features and strategies, a narrative showing a Writer at Work on one of the readings in the chapter, and a section on designing documents in the genre. As we have mentioned, a section titled Thinking Critically about What You Have Learned concludes each of these chapters.

Parts Two through Five provide illustrations and practice using strategies for invention and critical reading, writing, and research. Also included are up-to-date guidelines for writing research papers, using a wide range of sources (library sources, the Internet, and your own field research), taking essay exams, and assembling a portfolio of your writing.

Part Six presents four brief chapters that will help you in writing and speaking for audiences beyond your first-year composition classroom, covering the diverse topics of service learning (writing in the community), collaborative learning (consulting and writing with others), print and electronic document design, and oral presentation.

Exercise 1.6

Preview each of the writing assignments in Part One (Chapters 2–10) of *The St. Martin's Guide*. Begin by reading the opening paragraphs of the chapter, which introduce the genre, and skimming the examples of Writing in Your Other Courses, Writing in the Community, and Writing in the Workplace. Then turn to the Guide to Writing in the chapter (easily identified by the green border around the pages), read the Writing Assignment, and skim the Invention activity immediately following the assignment to see examples of possible subjects for essays in the genre, including those listed under Identity and Community and Work and Career. (As you will see, Chapter 10, Interpreting Stories, omits some of these sections.)

List at least two genres you would like to work on in this class. For each genre you list, write a few sentences explaining why you want to work on it.

The Part One Readings

Each Part One chapter includes readings, some written by professional writers and others by students who have used earlier editions of this book. All of the readings have been selected to reflect a wide range of topics and strategies. If you read these selections with a critical eye, you will see many different ways writers use a genre.

Each reading selection (except for those in Chapter 10) is accompanied by the following groups of questions, activities, and commentary to help you learn how essays in that genre work:

> ***Connecting to Culture and Experience*** invites you to explore with other students an issue or question raised by the reading.
>
> ***Analyzing Writing Strategies*** helps you examine closely the reading's basic features or writing strategies.
>
> ***Commentary*** points out important features of the genre and strategies the writer uses in the essay.
>
> ***Considering Topics for Your Own Essay*** suggests subjects related to the reading that you might write about in your own essay.

Most of the assignments in this book provide opportunities to explore your connections to the world. When you are choosing a topic to write about, you might consider suggestions listed under Identity and Community and under Work and Career in the Guides to Writing. These topics enable you to explore your personal connections to the various communities of which you are a part, visit and learn more about places in your community, debate issues important to your community, examine your ideas and attitudes about work, and consider issues related to your future career.

The Part One Guides to Writing

Each Part One assignment chapter provides detailed suggestions for thinking about your subject and purpose as well as your readers and their expectations. These Guides to Writing will help you develop a truly recursive process of discovery that will enable you to write an effective essay in the genre for your particular purpose and audience.

To make the process manageable, the Guide to Writing is divided into sections: the Writing Assignment, Invention and Research, Planning and Drafting, a Critical Reading Guide, Revising, and Editing and Proofreading. The color-coded "menu" preceding the Writing Assignment shows you at a glance the sections and the headings under each section. But to understand how the activities in the Guide to Writing will help you do the kinds of thinking you need to do, you must look closely at the types of activities included in each section.

The Writing Assignment. Each Guide to Writing begins with an assignment that defines the general purpose and basic features of the genre you have been studying in the chapter. The assignment does not tell you what subject to write about or who your readers will be. You will have to make these decisions, guided by the invention activities in the next section.

Invention and Research. Every Guide to Writing includes invention activities, and most also include suggestions for observational, library, or Internet research. The Invention and Research activities are designed to help you find a topic, discover what you already know about it, consider your purpose and audience, research the subject further to see what others have written about it, explore and develop your ideas, and compose a tentative thesis statement to guide your planning and drafting.

Remember that invention is not a part of the writing process you can skip. It is the basic, ongoing preoccupation of all writing. As writers, we cannot choose *whether* to invent; we can only decide *how.*

You can use the Invention activities before, during, and after you have written a first draft. However, the sequence of invention activities can be especially helpful before drafting because it focuses systematically on the basic genre features and writing strategies. The sequence reminds you of questions you need to think about as you collect, analyze, and synthesize ideas and information in light of your particular subject, purpose, and readers. A sequence of invention activities may take only two or three hours to complete. But it works best when spread over several days, giving yourself time to think. So if at all possible, begin the invention process far enough ahead of the deadline to let your thinking develop fully. Here is some general advice to keep in mind as you do the invention activities:

> ***Use Writing to Explore Your Ideas.*** You can use writing to gather your thoughts and see where they lead. As you approach each invention activity, try to refrain from censoring yourself. Simply try writing for several minutes. Explore your ideas freely, letting one idea lead to another. Later, you can reread what you have written and select the most promising ideas to develop.
>
> ***Focus on One Issue at a Time.*** Explore your topic systematically by dividing it into its component parts and exploring them one at a time. For example, instead of trying to think of your whole argument, focus on one reason and the support you would give for it, or focus on how you might refute one objection to your argument.

Exercise 1.7

Preview the Invention section of one of the Guides to Writing. First choose an assignment chapter that interests you (Chapters 2–10). Then find the Invention (or Invention and Research) section, and skim it from beginning to end. Notice the headings and subheadings, but also look closely at some of the activities to see what they ask you to do and think about.

Planning and Drafting. To get you started writing the first draft of your essay, each Guide to Writing includes suggestions for planning. You set goals and try to implement them as you plan and write the draft. While drafting, you may make notes about new ideas or additional information you need to research, but you try to keep your focus on the ideas and information you have already discovered in order to work out their meanings.

The section is divided into four parts:

Seeing What You Have involves reviewing what you have discovered about your subject, purpose, and audience.

Setting Goals helps you think about your overall purpose as well as your goals for the various parts of your essay.

Outlining suggests some of the ways you might organize your essay.

Drafting launches you on the writing of your first draft.

As you begin your first draft, keep in mind the following practical points, many of which assist professional writers as they begin drafting:

Choose the Best Time and Place. You can write a draft anytime and anyplace. As you probably already know, people write under the most surprising or arduous conditions. Drafting is likely to go smoothly, however, if you choose a time and place ideally suited for sustained and thoughtful work. Many professional writers have a place where they can concentrate for a few hours without repeated interruptions. Writers often find one place where they write best, and they return there whenever they have to write. Try to find such a place for yourself.

Make Revision Easy. If possible, compose your draft on a word processor. If you usually write with pen or pencil and paper, consider making the change to word processing for the ease of drafting and revising, as well as for the sake of long-term speed and efficiency. Even if you do not touch-type or if it seems strange at first, you may find, like most students, that you adjust relatively quickly to writing directly on the keyboard. If you do choose to compose on paper, leave plenty of space in the margins to make notes and revisions.

Do the Easy Parts First. Divide your task into manageable portions and do the easy parts first. Just aim to complete a small part of the essay—one section or paragraph—at a time. Try not to agonize over difficult parts, such as the first paragraph or the right word. Start with the part you understand best.

Lower Your Expectations—for the Time Being. Be satisfied with less than perfect writing in a first draft, and do not be overly critical of what you are getting down on paper at this stage. Remember, you are working on a draft that you will revise later. For now, try things out. Follow digressions. Let your ideas flow. Later you can go back and cross out a sentence, rework a section, or make other changes. Now and then, of course, you will want to reread what you have written, but do not reread obsessively. Return to drafting new material as soon as possible. Avoid editing or proofreading during this stage.

Take Short Breaks—and Reward Yourself. Drafting can be hard work, and you may need to take a break to refresh yourself. But be careful not to wander off for too long, or you may lose momentum. By setting small goals and rewarding yourself regularly, you will make it easier to complete the draft.

Critical Reading Guide. Each Guide to Writing includes a Critical Reading Guide that will help you get a good critical reading of your draft as well as help you read others' drafts. Once you have finished drafting your essay, you will want to make every effort to have someone else read the draft and comment on how to improve it. Experienced writers often seek out such advice from critical readers to help them see their drafts as others do.

Ask whether your critical reader would prefer an electronic version of your draft or a hard copy. Even a reader who is going to comment on the draft electronically may prefer to read a hard copy.

When you are asked to evaluate someone else's draft, you need to read it with a critical eye. You must be both positive and skeptical—positive in that you want to identify what is workable and promising in the draft, skeptical in that you need to question the writer's assumptions and decisions.

Here is some general advice on reading any draft critically:

Make a Written Record of Your Comments. Although talking with the writer about your reading of the draft can be useful and even fun, you will be most helpful if you put your ideas into writing. When you write down your comments and suggestions—either within an electronic or hard copy of the draft or in a separate electronic or paper document—you leave a record that can be used later when the writer revises the material.

Read First for an Overall Impression. On first reading, try not to be distracted by any errors in spelling, punctuation, or word choice. Look at the big issues: clear focus, compelling presentation, forcefulness of argument, novelty and quality of ideas. What seems particularly good? What problems do you see? Focus on the overall goal of the draft and how well it is met. Write just a few sentences expressing your initial reaction.

Read Again to Analyze the Draft. For this second reading, focus on individual parts of the draft, bringing to bear what you know about the genre and the subject.

When you read the draft at this level, you must shift your attention from one aspect of the essay to another. Consider how well the opening paragraphs introduce the essay and prepare the reader for what follows. Pay attention to specific writing strategies, like narration or argument. Notice whether the parts seem logically sequenced. Look for detailing, examples, or other kinds of support.

As you analyze, you are evaluating as well as describing, but a critical reading involves more than criticism of the draft. A good critical reader helps a writer see how each part of an essay works and how all the parts work together. By describing what you see, you help the writer view the draft more objectively, a perspective that is necessary for thoughtful revising.

Offer Advice, but Do Not Rewrite. As a critical reader, you may be tempted to rewrite the draft—to change a word here, correct an error there, add your ideas everywhere. Resist the impulse. Your role is to read carefully, to point out what you think is or is not working, to make suggestions and ask questions. Leave the revising to the writer.

In turn, the writer has a responsibility to listen to your comments but is under no obligation to do as you suggest. "Then why go to all the trouble?" you might ask. There are at least two good reasons. First, when you read someone else's draft critically, you learn more about writing—about the decisions writers make, about how a thoughtful reader reads, about the constraints of particular kinds of writing. Second, as a critical reader you embody for the writer the abstraction called "audience." By sharing your reactions with the writer, you complete the circuit of communication.

Exercise 1.8

Preview the Critical Reading Guide in the assignment chapter you chose for Exercise 1.7. Find the section and skim it. Then look closely at item 2 or 3 in the numbered list to get a sense of what you are being asked to think about when reading and responding to another writer's draft. If you have participated in draft workshops before, compare your previous experience as a reader to the experience you think you would have by following this Critical Reading Guide. Also compare the usefulness of the response you got in the past from readers of your draft to the kind of response you could expect from readers following this guide.

Revising. Each Guide to Writing includes a Revising section to help you get an overview of your draft, chart a plan for revision, consider critical comments, and carry out the revisions. Productive invention and smooth drafting rarely result in the essay a writer has imagined. Experienced writers are not surprised or disappointed, however, because they expect revision to be necessary. They know that revising will bring them closer to the essay they really want to write. When writers read their drafts thoughtfully and critically—and perhaps reflect on the advice of critical readers—they are able to see many opportunities for improvement. They may notice sentence-level problems such as misspelled words or garbled syntax, but more important, they discover ways to delete, move, rephrase, and add material in order to develop their ideas and say what they want to say more clearly.

Here is some general advice on revising:

Reflect on Your Purpose and Audience. Remind yourself of what you are trying to accomplish in this essay. If someone has read and responded to your draft, you may now have a better understanding of your readers' likely interests and concerns. You may also have refined your purpose. Keep your purpose and audience in mind as you reread the essay and revise in stages. Do not try to do everything at once.

Look at Major Problems First. Identify any major problems preventing the draft from achieving its purpose. Major problems might include a lack of awareness of your audience, inadequate development of key parts, missing sections, or the need for further invention or research. Trying to solve these major problems will probably lead to some substantial rethinking and rewriting, so do not get diverted by sentence-level problems at this time.

Focus Next on Organization and Coherence. Look at the introductory section of the essay to see how well it prepares readers for the parts that follow. It may help to make a paragraph-by-paragraph scratch outline to help you see at a glance what each paragraph does in the essay. If you have difficulty identifying the function of any paragraph, you may need to add an appropriate transition to clarify the paragraph's connection to the previous paragraphs or write a new topic sentence that better announces the subject of the paragraph. Or you may need to do some more extensive rewriting or reorganization.

Then Consider the Details. As the saying goes, the devil is in the details. The details have to be selected for a specific purpose, such as to convey significance, support an argument, or provide a concrete example of an abstract idea. If any details seem unrelated to your larger purpose, you need to make the connections explicit. If your essay lacks details, you can review your invention notes or do some additional research to come up with the details you need.

Editing and Proofreading. Once you have finished revising your essay, your next step is to edit and proofread it carefully. You want to make sure that every word, phrase, and sentence is clear and correct. Using language and punctuation correctly is an essential part of good writing. Errors will distract readers and lessen your credibility as a writer.

Be sure to save editing until the end—after you have planned and worked out a revision. Too much editing too early in the writing process can limit, or even block, invention and drafting.

Here are some other suggestions:

Proofread on Hard Copy. If your essay exists only in electronic form, print out a copy and proofread that version. Electronic text is difficult and fatiguing to read, and you can easily miss errors that are obvious on the printed page.

Keep a List of Your Common Errors. Note the grammatical and spelling errors you discover in your own writing. You will probably start to recognize error patterns to check for as you edit your work. Many word-processor grammar checkers allow you to customize, to some extent, what kinds of errors they call your attention to. If you find that you consistently make a particular error, cultivate the habit of using your word processor's Find function to locate instances of that error in the late stages of every piece of writing.

To use the Writing Guide Software to keep track of errors, click on
▶ **Error Log**

Begin Proofreading with the Last Word. To focus your attention on word errors, it may help to read backward word for word, beginning with the last word of your essay. When you read backward, it is harder to pay attention to content and thus easier to recognize spelling and keying errors.

Exchange Drafts with Another Student. Because it is usually easier to see errors in someone else's writing than in your own, consider trading essays with a classmate and proofreading one another's writing. If you do this, check whether your classmate would prefer an electronic version of your essay or a hard copy.

Thinking Critically about What You Have Learned. Each chapter in Part One concludes with a set of activities to help you think about what you have learned studying the genre in that chapter. There are three different activities:

> ***Reflecting on Your Writing*** asks you to consider how you solved problems writing that particular kind of essay.
>
> ***Reviewing What You Learned from Reading*** helps you discover what specific influences your reading had on your writing.
>
> ***Considering the Social Dimensions*** of the genre leads you to explore how thinking and writing in a particular genre reflect the social and cultural contexts in which thinking and writing occur.

Thinking and writing about what you have learned not only reinforce your learning by helping you remember what is important but also help you apply what you have learned to new situations. If you are compiling a portfolio of your coursework that will be assessed at the end of the term, these activities may help you decide what to include in your portfolio as well as help you write a reflective essay on the work you select for the portfolio. Finally, thinking critically about the social dimensions of genres may help you become a more perceptive cultural critic and constructive participant in conversations with others in school, at work, and in the larger community.

USING THE WRITING GUIDE SOFTWARE

Most of you who are using this book will be doing a substantial portion of your writing on computers. Some of you are in classes that meet in a networked computer lab; others have instructors who use course Web sites, email discussion lists, and other online tools. Nearly all of you will, at the very least, turn to a word processor to prepare the final drafts of your essays. Because so much of the writing and other coursework you do will be done on a computer, we have added a new feature to *The St. Martin's Guide*—free Writing Guide Software—which you will find on a CD-ROM inside the back cover of the book.

Throughout the book you will find reminders about the Writing Guide Software and suggestions on how you can use it to complete the writing assignments presented in the book. We have also included a full user's guide as an appendix to this book—the pages with gold edges just before the index. What we want to do here is give you just a brief overview of why we have included the software and how you can use it to help you with your writing.

The Writing Guide Software takes the key advice for completing each assignment in Part One of the book and makes it available on your computer screen, so that while you are writing, you can refer to the book's advice, examples, definitions, sample student essays, critical reading guides, and more, just by clicking on a button. Each writing guide in the software follows the same organization as the corresponding guide in this book. You can use the software all the way from your first thinking about your topic to your final proofreading of the essay or at any point in between. For example, if you are just starting an assignment, the software offers advice on brainstorming and a list of questions from the book that you can use to jump-start your thinking. When you are ready to have someone else give your draft a critical reading, the software provides an electronic template of the book's critical reading guide to make things easier for both you and your reader. Because when you write you often need to revisit an earlier stage in the composing process, the software lets you click back or forward to any stage at any time. Most important, the software does all this in conjunction with your own word processor so that you write with the program that you know best.

In addition to making the book's writing guides available on screen, the software also offers

- an electronic journal where you can keep notes, responses to readings, invention writing, and so on
- a diagnostic test and tutorials to help you identify and correct any grammatical problems in your writing
- a log where you can keep track of the kinds of errors you tend to make
- a sample student essay from each of the book's assignment chapters with pop-up annotations pointing out choices the writers made
- direct links to World Wide Web resources developed for student writers, including interactive exercises on many topics and tutorials on useful sentence strategies for each genre of writing and on plagiarism

Taken altogether, the Writing Guide Software brings the most important parts of this book to your computer screen, so that the help you need in writing is right there with you, when and where you need it most. We hope it will go a long way toward making your own writing process even more efficient and effective.

Part One

WRITING ACTIVITIES

Remembering Events

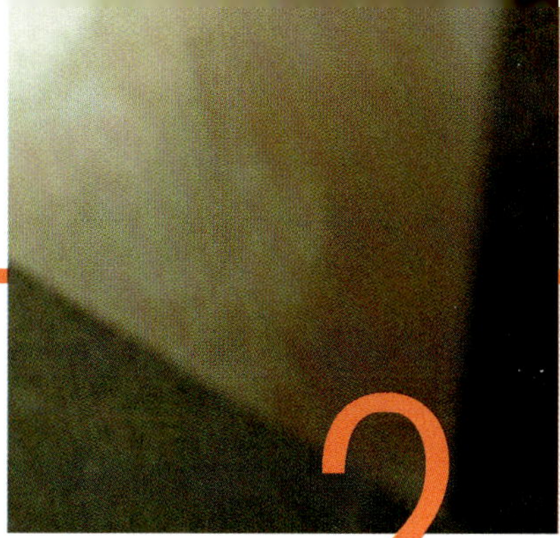

2

When you write about remembered events in your life, you produce autobiography, a genre of writing that is very popular with both readers and writers. Autobiography is popular because reading as well as writing it leads people to reflect deeply on their own lives. When you reflect on the meaning of experience, you examine the forces within yourself and within society that have shaped you into the person you have become.

When you write about a remembered event, your purpose is to present yourself to readers by telling a story that discloses something significant about your life. Autobiographical writers do not just pour out their memories and feelings. Instead, they shape those memories into a compelling story that conveys the meaning and importance of an experience—what can be called its autobiographical significance.

Writing about your life for others to read is not the same as writing for yourself. As a writer, you must remember that autobiography is public, not private. While it requires self-presentation, it does not require you to make unwanted self-disclosures. You choose the event to write about and decide how you will portray yourself.

As you work through this chapter, you will learn to tell a story that entertains readers and lets them know something important about how you came to be the person you are now. You also will learn to describe people and places vividly so that readers can see what makes them memorable for you. As you learn to write well about a remembered event, you will be practicing two of the most basic writing strategies—narration and description. These strategies can play a role in almost every kind of writing. As you will see in Chapters 4–10, narration and description can contribute to explanatory reports and persuasive arguments, in addition to playing an essential role in the remembered-event assignment for this chapter.

You will encounter writing about a remembered event in many different contexts, as the following examples suggest.

Writing in Your Other Courses

- For an assignment in a psychology course, a student tests against her own experience an idea from the developmental psychologist Erik Erikson: "[Y]oung people . . . are sometimes preoccupied with what they appear to be in the eyes of others as compared with what they feel they are." The student recounts a time when she cared tremendously about what the other members of her high school soccer team thought about her. Then she explains how her teammates' reactions influenced her feelings and sense of self.

- For a linguistics course, a student is asked to write about current research on men's and women's conversational styles. One researcher, Deborah Tannen, has reported that women and men have different expectations when they talk about problems. Women expect to spend a lot of time talking about the problem itself, especially about their feelings. Men, in contrast, typically want to cut short the analysis of the problem and the talk about feelings; they would rather discuss solutions to the problem. Applying Tannen's findings to her own experience, the student recounts a conversation about a family problem with her brother, who is one year older. She reconstructs as much of the conversation as she can remember and explains which parts constitute feelings talk and which indicate problem-solving talk. She concludes that her conversation with her brother well illustrates Tannen's findings.

Writing in the Community

- As part of a local history project in a small western ranching community, a college student volunteers to help an elderly rancher write about some of his early experiences. One experience seems especially dramatic and significant—a time in the winter of 1938 when a six-foot snowstorm isolated the rancher's family for nearly a month. The student tape-records the rancher talking about how he and his wife made preparations to survive and ensure the health of their infant sons and how he snowshoed eight miles to a logging train track, stopped the train, and gave the engineer a message to deliver to relatives in the nearest town explaining that they were going to be okay. On a second visit, the student and the rancher listen to the tape recording and afterward talk about further details that might make the event more complete and dramatic for readers. The rancher then writes a draft of the remembered event, and the student later helps him revise and edit the essay. The student copies an old snow-day photograph from the nearby town's newspaper files, and the rancher selects a photograph of his young family from a family photo album. The essay and photographs are published in a special supplement to the newspaper.

For more details on the decisions these writers make about document design, see pp. 77–78.

- To commemorate the retirement of the city's world-famous symphony orchestra conductor, a radio program director invites the conductor to talk about his early experiences with the orchestra. Aware of his tendency to ramble and digress in interviews, the conductor decides to write down a story about the first time he asked the orchestra members to play a never-before-performed modern composition noted for its lack of familiar tones, progressions, and rhythms. He describes how he tried to prepare the orchestra members for this experience and how they went about the hard, slow work of mastering the difficult music. The conductor expresses regret over posing this challenge so early in his experience of working with the orchestra members, but he proudly asserts that their great success with the music gave them the confidence to master any music they played together.

For the radio program, he alternates reading this remembered event aloud with playing brief recorded excerpts from the orchestra's polished performance.

Writing in the Workplace

- As part of an orientation manual for new employees, the founder of a highly successful computer software company describes the day she spent with the Silicon Valley venture capitalists who lent her the money to start the company. She describes how other venture capitalists had turned her down and how desperately anxious she was for this group to fund her company. The meeting had barely begun when she spilled her coffee across the top of the gleaming conference table. She describes some of the questions and her answers and traces her rising and falling hopes during the discussion. She left dejected and resigned to giving up the dream of founding her own company. The next morning a member of the group who had not asked any questions at the meeting phoned her to praise her proposal and announce that his group would fund her company. He invited her to a celebratory lunch with the group at the best restaurant in town, where she was careful not to tip over her long-stemmed wine glass.
- The highway department offices of a large midwestern state have recently been the site of violence and threats of violence. One worker has killed another, and several managers have been threatened. To keynote a statewide meeting of highway department managers seeking solutions to this problem, a manager writes a speech that describes an incident when he was confronted in his office by an employee who was unhappy about an overtime assignment. The employee came into the manager's office without knocking and would not sit down. He talked loudly, waved his arms, and threatened to harm the manager and his family. He would not leave when asked to. The manager reflects on his fear and on his frustration about not knowing what to do when the employee finally left. The department's published procedures seemed not to apply to this case. He acknowledges his reluctance to report the incident to the state office because he did not want to appear to be ineffective and indecisive.

Practice Remembering an Event: A Collaborative Activity

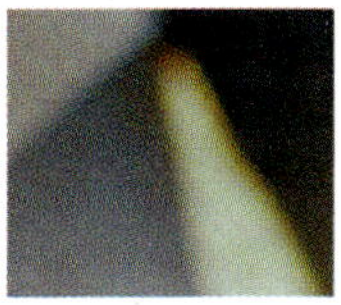

The preceding scenarios suggest some occasions for writing about events in one's life. Think of an event in your life that you would feel comfortable describing to others in your class. The only requirements are that you remember the event well enough to tell the story and that the story lets your classmates learn something about you. Your instructor may schedule this collaborative activity as a face-to-face in-class discussion or ask you to conduct an online real-time discussion in a chatroom. Whatever the medium, here are some guidelines to follow:

Part 1. Consider several events, and choose one you feel comfortable telling in this situation. Then, for two or three minutes, make notes about how you will tell your story.

Now, get together with two or three other students, and take turns telling your stories. Be brief: Each story should take only a few minutes.

Part 2. Take ten minutes to discuss what happened when you told about a remembered event:

- Tell each other how you chose your particular story. What did you think about when you were choosing an event? How did your purpose and audience—what you wanted your classmates to know and think about you—influence your choice?
- Review what each of you decided to include in your story. Did you plunge right into telling what happened, or did you first provide some background information? Did you decide to leave any of the action out of your story? If so, what did you leave out and why? Did you include a physical description of the scene? Did you describe any of the people, including yourself, or mention any specific dialogue? Did you tell your listeners how you felt at the time the event occurred, or did you say how you feel now looking back on it?
- What was the easiest part of telling a story about a remembered event in your life? What was the most difficult part?

READINGS

No two essays remembering an event are alike, and yet they share defining features. Together, the four readings in this chapter reveal a number of these features, so you will want to read as many of them as possible. If time permits, complete the activities in the Analyzing Writing Strategies section that follows each selection, and read the Commentary. Following the readings is a section called Basic Features: Remembering Events (p. 50), which offers a concise description of the features of writing about remembered events and provides examples from the four readings.

Annie Dillard *won the Pulitzer Prize for nonfiction writing with her first book,* Pilgrim at Tinker Creek *(1974). Since then, she has written nine books in a variety of genres, including the essay collections* Teaching a Stone to Talk *(1988) and* For the Time Being *(1999); a novel,* The Living *(1993); poetry,* Mornings Like This *(1996); literary theory,* Living by Fiction *(1988); and an account of her work as a writer,* Writing Life *(1990). Dillard also wrote an autobiography of her early years,* An American Childhood *(1987), from which the following reading comes.*

Dillard is a professor of English and writer in residence at Wesleyan College. In Writing Life*, she describes her writing as a process of discovery: "When you write, you lay out a line* *of words. The line of words is a miner's pick, a woodcarver's gouge, a surgeon's probe. You wield it, and it digs a path you follow. Soon you find yourself in new territory." Through this process, she explains, the writing "changes from an expression of your notions to an epistemological tool." In other words, the very act of writing helps her learn more about herself and others.*

The reading that follows relates an event that occurred one winter morning when the seven-year-old Dillard and a friend were chased relentlessly by an adult stranger at whom they had been throwing snowballs. Dillard admits that she was terrified at the time, and yet she asserts that she has "seldom been happier since." As you read, think about how this paradox helps you grasp the autobiographical significance of this experience for Dillard.

An American Childhood

Annie Dillard

Some boys taught me to play football. This was fine sport. You thought up a new strategy for every play and whispered it to the others. You went out for a pass, fooling everyone. Best, you got to throw yourself mightily at someone's running legs. Either you brought him down or you hit the ground flat out on your chin, with your arms empty before you. It was all or nothing. If you hesitated in fear, you would miss and get hurt: you would take a hard fall while the kid got away, or you would get kicked in the face while the kid got away. But if you flung yourself wholeheartedly at the back of his knees—if you gathered and joined body and soul and pointed them diving fearlessly—then you likely wouldn't get hurt, and you'd stop the ball. Your fate, and your team's score, depended on your concentration and courage. Nothing girls did could compare with it. 1

Boys welcomed me at baseball, too, for I had, through enthusiastic practice, what was weirdly known as a boy's arm. In winter, in the snow, there was neither baseball nor football, so the boys and I threw snowballs at passing cars. I got in trouble throwing snowballs, and have seldom been happier since. 2

On one weekday morning after Christmas, six inches of new snow had just fallen. We were standing up to our boot tops in snow on a front yard on trafficked Reynolds Street, waiting for cars. The cars traveled Reynolds Street slowly and evenly; they were targets all but wrapped in red ribbons, cream puffs. We couldn't miss. 3

I was seven; the boys were eight, nine, and ten. The oldest two Fahey boys were there—Mikey and Peter—polite blond boys who lived near me on Lloyd Street, and who already had four brothers and sisters. My parents approved Mikey and Peter Fahey. Chickie McBride was there, a tough kid, and Billy Paul and Mackie Kean too, from across Reynolds, where the boys grew up dark and furious, grew up skinny, knowing, and skilled. We had all drifted from our houses that morning looking for action, and had found it here on Reynolds Street. 4

It was cloudy but cold. The cars' tires laid behind them on the snowy street a complex trail of beige chunks like crenellated castle walls. I had stepped on some earlier; they squeaked. We could not have wished for more traffic. When a car came, we all popped it one. In the intervals between cars we reverted to the natural solitude of children. 5

I started making an iceball—a perfect iceball, from perfectly white snow, perfectly spherical, and squeezed perfectly translucent so no snow remained all the way through. (The Fahey boys and I considered it unfair actually to throw an iceball at somebody, but it had been known to happen.) 6

I had just embarked on the iceball project when we heard tire chains come clanking from afar. A black Buick was moving toward us down the street. We all spread out, banged together some regular snowballs, took aim, and, when the Buick drew nigh, fired. 7

A soft snowball hit the driver's windshield right before the driver's face. It made a smashed star with a hump in the middle. 8

Often, of course, we hit our target, but this time, the only time in all of life, the car pulled over and stopped. Its wide black door opened; a man got out of it, running. He didn't even close the car door. 9

He ran after us, and we ran away from him, up the snowy Reynolds sidewalk. At the corner, I looked back; incredibly, he was still after us. He was in city clothes: a suit and tie, street shoes. Any normal adult would have quit, having sprung us into flight and made his point. This man was gaining on us. He was a thin man, all action. All of a sudden, we were running for our lives. 10

Wordless, we split up. We were on our turf; we could lose ourselves in the neighborhood backyards, everyone for himself. I paused and considered. Everyone had vanished except Mikey Fahey, who was just rounding the corner of a yellow brick house. Poor Mikey, I trailed him. The driver of the Buick sensibly picked the two of us to follow. The man apparently had all day. 11

He chased Mikey and me around the yellow house and up a backyard path we knew by heart: under a low tree, up a bank, through a hedge, down some snowy steps, and across the grocery store's delivery driveway. We smashed through a gap in another hedge, entered a scruffy backyard and ran around its back porch and tight between houses to Edgerton Avenue; we ran across Edgerton to an alley and up our own sliding woodpile to the Halls' front yard; he kept coming. We ran up Lloyd Street and wound through mazy backyards toward the steep hilltop at Willard and Lang. 12

He chased us silently, block after block. He chased us silently over picket fences, through thorny hedges, between houses, around garbage cans, and across streets. Every time I glanced back, choking for breath, I expected he would have quit. He must have been as breathless as we were. His jacket strained over his body. It was an immense discovery, pounding into my hot head with every sliding, joyous step, that this ordinary adult evidently knew what I thought only children who trained at football knew: that you have to fling yourself at what you're doing, you have to point yourself, forget yourself, aim, dive. 13

Mikey and I had nowhere to go, in our own neighborhood or out of it, but away from this man who was chasing us. He impelled us forward; we compelled him to follow our route. The air was cold; every breath tore my throat. We kept running, block after block; we kept improvising, backyard after backyard, running a frantic course and choosing it simultaneously, failing always to find small places or hard places to slow him down, and discovering always, exhilarated, dismayed, that only bare speed could save us—for he would never give up, this man—and we were losing speed. 14

15 He chased us through the backyard labyrinths of ten blocks before he caught us by our jackets. He caught us and we all stopped.

16 We three stood staggering, half blinded, coughing, in an obscure hilltop backyard: a man in his twenties, a boy, a girl. He had released our jackets, our pursuer, our captor, our hero: he knew we weren't going anywhere. We all played by the rules. Mikey and I unzipped our jackets. I pulled off my sopping mittens. Our tracks multiplied in the backyard's new snow. We had been breaking new snow all morning. We didn't look at each other. I was cherishing my excitement. The man's lower pants legs were wet; his cuffs were full of snow, and there was a prow of snow beneath them on his shoes and socks. Some trees bordered the little flat backyard, some messy winter trees. There was no one around: a clearing in a grove, and we the only players.

17 It was a long time before he could speak. I had some difficulty at first recalling why we were there. My lips felt swollen; I couldn't see out of the sides of my eyes; I kept coughing.

18 "You stupid kids," he began perfunctorily.

19 We listened perfunctorily indeed, if we listened at all, for the chewing out was redundant, a mere formality, and beside the point. The point was that he had chased us passionately without giving up, and so he had caught us. Now he came down to earth. I wanted the glory to last forever.

20 But how could the glory have lasted forever? We could have run through every backyard in North America until we got to Panama. But when he trapped us at the lip of the Panama Canal, what precisely could he have done to prolong the drama of the chase and cap its glory? I brooded about this for the next few years. He could only have fried Mikey Fahey and me in boiling oil, say, or dismembered us piecemeal, or staked us to anthills. None of which I really wanted, and none of which any adult was likely to do, even in the spirit of fun. He could only chew us out there in the Panamanian jungle, after months or years of exalting pursuit. He could only begin, "You stupid kids," and continue in his ordinary Pittsburgh accent with his normal righteous anger and the usual common sense.

21 If in that snowy backyard the driver of the black Buick had cut off our heads, Mikey's and mine, I would have died happy, for nothing has required so much of me since as being chased all over Pittsburgh in the middle of winter—running terrified, exhausted—by this sainted, skinny, furious redheaded man who wished to have a word with us. I don't know how he found his way back to his car.

Connecting to Culture and Experience: Childhood Play

"The point," Dillard tells us near the end, "was that he had chased us passionately without giving up" (paragraph 19). What seems to fascinate her is not that the man chased the kids to bawl them out, but that an adult could still do what she thought only children knew how to do: "you have to fling yourself at what you're doing, you have to point yourself, forget yourself, aim, dive" (paragraph 13). In fact, she explains at the beginning of the essay that in teaching her to play football, the neighborhood boys taught her something that few girls learned about: the joy of flinging yourself wholeheartedly, fearlessly, into play or, indeed, into anything you do in life.

With other students in your class, discuss what you have learned from childhood play about how to live your life. You might begin by telling one another about a particular kind of play you enjoyed as a child—something you did with others or alone such as team sports, computer games, playing a musical instrument, dancing, listening to music, or reading. Then, explore together what the kinds of play you enjoyed taught you about being yourself, facing challenges, getting along with others, or understanding your own body and mind or your attitude toward life.

Analyzing Writing Strategies

1. At the beginning of this chapter, we make several assertions about remembered-event essays. Consider which of these are true of Dillard's essay:
   - It tells an entertaining story.
   - It is vivid, letting readers see what makes the event as well as the people and places memorable for the writer.
   - It is purposeful, trying to give readers an understanding of why this particular event was significant in the writer's life.
   - It includes self-presentation but not unwanted self-disclosures.
   - It can lead readers to think in new ways about their own experiences or about how other people's lives differ from their own.

For more on the describing strategies of naming and detailing, see Chapter 15.

2. **Visual description**—naming objects and detailing their colors, shapes, sizes, textures, and other qualities—is an important writing strategy in remembered-event essays. To see how writers use **naming** and **detailing** to create vivid word pictures or images, let us look closely at Dillard's description of an iceball: "I started making an iceball—a perfect iceball, from perfectly white snow, perfectly spherical, and squeezed perfectly translucent so no snow remained all the way through" (paragraph 6). Notice that she names two things: *iceball* and *snow*. She adds to these names descriptive details—*white* (color), *spherical* (shape), and *translucent* (appearance)—that help readers imagine more precisely what an iceball looks like. She also repeats the words *perfect* and *perfectly* to emphasize the color, shape, and appearance of this particular iceball.

   To analyze Dillard's use of naming and detailing to present scenes and people, reread paragraphs 10–13, where she describes the man and the neighborhood through which he chases her and Mikey. As you read these paragraphs, underline the names of objects and people (nearly always nouns), and put brackets around all of the words and phrases that modify the nouns they name. Here are two examples from paragraph 10 to get you started: "[snowy] Reynolds sidewalk" and "[city] clothes."

   Notice first how frequently naming and detailing occur in these paragraphs. Notice also how many different kinds of objects and people are named. Then consider these questions: Does naming sometimes occur without any accompanying detailing? How do you think the naming helps you as a reader visualize the scene and people? What do you think the detailing contributes?

Commentary: Organizing a Well-Told Story

An American Childhood is a **well-told story**. It provides a dramatic structure that arouses readers' curiosity, builds suspense, and concludes the action in a rather surprising way.

Writers of remembered-event essays usually begin at the beginning or even before the beginning. That is how Annie Dillard organizes *An American Childhood*—opening with two introductory paragraphs that give readers a context for the event and prepare them to appreciate its significance. Readers can see at a glance, by the space that separates the second paragraph from the rest of the essay, that the first two paragraphs are meant to stand apart as an introduction. They also are general, broad statements that do not refer to any particular incident.

In contrast, paragraph 3 begins by grounding readers in specifics. It is not any "weekday morning" but "one" in particular, one morning "after Christmas" and after a substantial snowfall. Dillard goes on to locate herself in a particular place "on a front yard on trafficked Reynolds Street," engaged in a particular set of actions with a particular group of individuals. She has not yet begun to tell what happened but is giving us the cast of characters (the "polite blond" Fahey boys, "tough" Chickie McBride) and setting the scene ("cloudy but cold"). The narrative, up to this point, has been moving slowly, like the cars making their way down Reynolds Street. But in paragraph 9, when the driver of the Buick "got out of it, running," Dillard's narrative itself suddenly springs into action, moving at breakneck speed for the next seven paragraphs until the man catches up with the kids in paragraph 15.

We can see this simple narrative organization in the following paragraph-by-paragraph scratch outline:

1. explains what she learned from playing football
2. identifies other sports she learned from boys in the neighborhood
3. sets the scene by describing the time and place of the event
4. describes the boys who were playing with her
5. describes what typically happened: a car would come down the street, they would throw snowballs, and then they would wait for another car
6. describes the iceball-making project she had begun while waiting
7. describes the Buick's approach and how they followed the routine
8. describes the impact of the snowball on the Buick's windshield
9. describes the man's surprising reaction: getting out of the car and running after them
10. narrates the chase and describes the man
11. explains how the kids split up and the man followed her and Mikey
12. narrates the chase and describes how the neighborhood looked as they ran through it
13. continues the narration, describing the way the man threw himself into the chase
14. continues the narration, commenting on her thoughts and feelings

15. narrates the ending or climax of the chase, when the man caught the kids
16. describes the runners trying to catch their breath
17. describes her own physical state
18. relates the man's words
19. explains her reactions to his words and actions
20. explains her later thoughts and feelings
21. explains her present perspective on this remembered event

For more on scratch outlining, see Chapter 12.

From this simple scratch outline, we can see that Dillard's essay focuses on the chase. This focus on a single incident that occurred in a relatively short span of time is the hallmark of the remembered-event essay. A chase is by nature dramatic because it is suspenseful: Readers want to know whether the man will catch the kids and, if he does, what will happen. Dillard heightens the drama in a couple of ways. One strategy she uses is identification: She lets us into her point of view, helping us to see what she saw and feel what she felt. In addition, she uses surprise. In fact, Dillard surprises us from beginning to end. The first surprise is that the man gets out of the car. But the fact that he chases the kids and that he continues to chase them beyond the point that any reasonable person would do so ratchets up the suspense. We simply cannot know what such a man is capable of doing. Finally, the story reaches its climax when the man catches Mikey and Dillard. Even then, Dillard surprises readers by what the man says and doesn't say or do. All he says is, "You stupid kids" (paragraph 18). Moreover, Dillard tells us, he says it "perfunctorily," as if it is something he is supposed to say as an adult "in his ordinary Pittsburgh accent with his normal righteous anger and the usual common sense" (paragraph 20). Dillard's language here is ironic because it is obvious that she feels that the man's behavior was anything but *ordinary*, *normal*, or *usual*—which is, of course, precisely what Dillard wants us to appreciate.

Considering Topics for Your Own Essay

Dillard writes about throwing yourself body and soul into a sport, a chase, or whatever you are doing. Dillard explains that she learned "concentration and courage" (paragraph 1) from the boys who taught her to play football. What do you think you learned from playing or watching other kids play? Recall your own experiences at play as a child and as a young adult. List any sports events, school projects, musical performances, computer games, or other occasions that would enable you to reflect on your own ideas about play, commitment, or working with others or working alone to achieve a goal.

To use the Writing Guide Software to record your ideas, click on
▶ **Journal**

***Tobias Wolff** is probably best known for his short-story collections* Back in the World *(1985),* In the Garden of the North American Martyrs *(1981), and* The Night in Question *(1996) and for his novel* The Barracks Thief *(1984), which won the PEN/Faulkner Award in 1985. Wolff has also written two autobiographies. The first,* A Boy's Life *(1989), won the* Los Angeles Times *Book Award for biography and was made into a movie (1993) in which Wolff was played by Leonardo DiCaprio. The second autobiography,* In Pharaoh's Army: Memories of the Lost War *(1994), about his experience serving as a Green Beret in the Vietnam War, was a finalist for a National Book Award and a* Los Angeles Times *Award for biography. In addition to his fiction and autobiography, Wolff has also edited several short-story collections, including* The Best American Short Stories. *Wolff has taught creative writing at Syracuse University and is currently the Ward W. and Priscilola B. Woods Professor at Stanford University, where he also has directed the creative writing program.*

In this selection from A Boy's Life, *Wolff tells the story of an experience he had when he was ten years old. He and his mother had just moved west from Florida to Salt Lake City, followed by Roy, his divorced mother's boyfriend. "Roy was handsome," Wolff writes, "in the conventional way that appeals to boys. He had a tattoo. He'd been to war and kept a silence about it that was full of heroic implication." As you read, notice how the young Wolff is motivated, at least in part, by a desire to be the kind of self-sufficient man he associates with soldiers and cowboys.*

On Being a Real Westerner

Tobias Wolff

Just after Easter Roy gave me the Winchester .22 rifle I'd learned to shoot with. It was a light, pump-action, beautifully balanced piece with a walnut stock black from all its oilings. Roy had carried it when he was a boy and it was still as good as new. Better than new. The action was silky from long use, and the wood of a quality no longer to be found. 1

The gift did not come as a surprise. Roy was stingy, and slow to take a hint, but I'd put him under siege. I had my heart set on that rifle. A weapon was the first condition of self-sufficiency, and of being a real Westerner, and of all acceptable employment—trapping, riding herd, soldiering, law enforcement, and outlawry. I needed that rifle, for itself and for the way it completed me when I held it. 2

My mother said I couldn't have it. Absolutely not. Roy took the rifle back but promised me he'd bring her around. He could not imagine anyone refusing him anything and treated the refusals he did encounter as perverse and insincere. Normally mute, he became at these times a relentless whiner. He would follow my mother from room to room, emitting one ceaseless note of complaint that was pitched perfectly to jelly her nerves and bring her to a state where she would agree to anything to make it stop. 3

After a few days of this my mother caved in. She said I could have the rifle if, and only if, I promised never to take it out or even touch it except when she and Roy were with me. Okay, I said. Sure. Naturally. But even then she wasn't satisfied. She plain didn't like the fact of me owning a rifle. Roy said he had owned several rifles by the time he was my age, but this did not reassure her. She didn't think I could be trusted with it. Roy said now was the time to find out. 4

For a week or so I kept my promises. But now that the weather had turned warm Roy was usually off somewhere and eventually, in the dead hours after school when I found myself alone in the apartment, I decided that there couldn't be any harm in taking the rifle out to clean it. Only to clean it, nothing more. I was sure it would be enough just to break it down, oil it, rub linseed into the stock, polish the octagonal barrel and then hold it up to the light to confirm the perfection of the bore. But it wasn't enough. From cleaning the rifle I went to marching around the apartment with it, and then to striking brave poses in front of the mirror. Roy had saved one of his army uniforms and I sometimes dressed up in this, together with martial-looking articles of hunting gear: fur trooper's hat, camouflage coat, boots that reached nearly to my knees. 5

The camouflage coat made me feel like a sniper, and before long I began to act like one. I set up a nest on the couch by the front window. I drew the shades to darken the apartment, and took up my position. Nudging the shade aside with the rifle barrel, I followed people in my sights as they walked or drove along the street. At first I made shooting sounds—kyoo! kyoo! Then I started cocking the hammer and letting it snap down. 6

Roy stored his ammunition in a metal box he kept hidden in the closet. As with everything else hidden in the apartment, I knew exactly where to find it. There was a layer of loose .22 rounds on the bottom of the box under shells of bigger caliber, dropped there by the handful the way men drop pennies on their dressers at night. I took some and put them in a hiding place of my own. With these I started loading up the rifle. Hammer cocked, a round in the chamber, finger resting lightly on the trigger, I drew a bead on whoever walked by—women pushing strollers, children, garbage collectors laughing and calling to each other, anyone—and as they passed under my window I sometimes had to bite my lip to keep from laughing in the ecstasy of my power over them, and at their absurd and innocent belief that they were safe. 7

But over time the innocence I laughed at began to irritate me. It was a peculiar kind of irritation. I saw it years later in men I served with, and felt it myself, when unarmed Vietnamese civilians talked back to us while we were herding them around. Power can be enjoyed only when it is recognized and feared. Fearlessness in those without power is maddening to those who have it. 8

One afternoon I pulled the trigger. I had been aiming at two old people, a man and a woman, who walked so slowly that by the time they turned the corner at the bottom of the hill my little store of self-control was exhausted. I had to shoot. I looked up and down the street. It was empty. Nothing moved but a pair of squirrels chasing each other back and forth on the telephone wires. I followed one in my sight. Finally it stopped for a moment and I fired. The squirrel dropped straight into the road. I pulled back into the shadows and waited for something to happen, sure that someone must have heard the shot or seen the squirrel fall. But the sound that was so loud to me probably seemed to our neighbors no more than the bang of a cupboard slammed shut. After a while I sneaked a glance into the street. The squirrel hadn't moved. It looked like a scarf someone had dropped. 9

When my mother got home from work I told her there was a dead squirrel in the street. Like me, she was an animal lover. She took a cellophane bag off a loaf of bread and we went outside and looked at the squirrel. "Poor little thing," she said. She stuck 10 her hand in the wrapper and picked up the squirrel, then pulled the bag inside out away from her hand. We buried it behind our building under a cross made of popsicle sticks, and I blubbered the whole time.

I blubbered again in bed that night. At last I got out of bed and knelt down and did an imitation of somebody praying, and then I did an imitation of somebody receiving divine reassurance and inspiration. I stopped crying. I smiled to myself and forced a feeling of warmth into my chest. Then I climbed back in bed and looked up at the ceiling with a blissful expression until I went to sleep. 11

For several days I stayed away from the apartment at times when I knew I'd be alone there. 12

Though I avoided the apartment, I could not shake the idea that sooner or later I would get the rifle out again. All my images of myself as I wished to be were images of myself armed. Because I did not know who I was, any image of myself, no matter how grotesque, had power over me. This much I understand now. But the man can give no help to the boy, not in this matter nor in those that follow. The boy moves always out of reach. 13

Connecting to Culture and Experience: Role Playing

Wolff shows us that he took great delight in playing the role of a soldier—looking at himself in the mirror dressed in camouflage and "striking brave poses" (paragraph 5). The word *brave* suggests that the young Wolff wanted to see himself as possessing certain traits, like bravery, that we often associate with soldiers. Another part of the attraction of playing soldier, he admits, is the sense of power he experienced holding a rifle.

With other students in your class, discuss the roles you played as children. What personal and cultural factors influenced the roles that you and your classmates imagined for yourselves? You might begin by comparing your own childhood imaginings with Wolff's desire to play soldier. In addition to having firsthand experience with Roy, a soldier who impressed him with his masculine authority and power, Wolff grew up during World War II, when children were bombarded by media images of brave soldiers fighting heroic wars and lone cowboys bringing justice to the Wild West. What media images—from television, film, the Internet, and computer games—do you think influenced the kinds of role play that you engaged in as a child or young adult?

Analyzing Writing Strategies

1. Writers convey the **significance** of autobiographical events by telling how they felt at the time the event occurred and by telling how they feel now as they look back on the event. Skim paragraphs 7, 8, and 13, noting where Wolff expresses his feelings and thoughts about the event. Try to distinguish between what he remembers thinking and feeling at the time and what he thinks and feels as he looks back on the event. What impression do you get of the young Wolff? What does the adult Wolff seem to think about his younger self?

2. Good stories show people in action—what we call **specific narrative action**—people moving or gesturing. Analyze paragraphs 7 and 9 by underlining the narrative actions and then putting brackets around the verb or verbal in each narrative action that specifically names the action. (A verbal is the *-ing* or *to* form of a verb: *laughing, to laugh.*) For example, here are the narrative actions (underlined) with their action verbs or verbals (in brackets) in paragraph 6:

   [set up] a nest, [drew] the shades, [took up] my position, [nudging] the shade aside, [followed] people, [walked] or [drove], [made] shooting sounds—kyoo! kyoo!, [started cocking] the hammer, [letting] it [snap] down.

   Now that you have completed your analysis of paragraphs 7 and 9, how do you think specific narrative action contributes to autobiographical stories?

3. Like other autobiographers, Wolff sometimes uses relatively short sentences. To understand why he might do so, compare the short and long sentences in the most dramatic and revealing action in the event. Begin by underlining every sentence of nine words or fewer (in paragraph 9). Then put brackets around the relatively long sentence at the end of paragraph 7 and the three relatively long sentences beginning "I had been aiming," "I pulled back," and "But the sound" in paragraph 9. Compare what the long and short sentences contribute to the action. How do their contents differ? What effect do the short sentences have on you as a reader?

For more on the role of short sentences in remembered-event essays, turn to Sentence Strategies, pp. 62–64.

Commentary: Narrative Cueing in a Well-Told Story

This is a gripping story. The subject makes it inherently dramatic: Putting a rifle in a child's hands immediately alerts readers to the possibility that something dreadful could happen. Thus the potential for suspense is great. Contributing to the drama is Wolff's use of narrative strategies that move the action through time and help readers keep track of what happened.

If we look closely at Wolff's narration, we can see how two **narrating strategies**—**verb tenses** and **temporal transitions**—create the impression of time passing. These strategies serve as cueing devices because, like road signs, they enable readers to follow the action.

Verb Tenses. Verb tenses signal when the action occurred—in the past, present, or future. Because remembered-event essays tell about past events, most of the verbs are in the past tense. Looking at the verbs in Wolff's essay, we can find several different kinds of past tense. In the first sentence of the essay, for example, Wolff shows an action that occurred at one point in the past (underlined) together with an action that was already completed (in brackets): "Just after Easter Roy gave me the Winchester .22 rifle [I'd learned to shoot with]." ("I'd learned" is a shortened form of "I had learned.") A second example shows an earlier action that was still going on (in brackets) when the more recent action occurred (underlined): "One afternoon I pulled the trigger. I [had been aiming] at two old people . . ." (paragraph 9).

Our final example is a little more complicated: "Roy took the rifle back but promised me [he'd bring] her around" (paragraph 3). This example presents three past actions. Whereas the first two actions (underlined) occurred at roughly the same time, the third (in brackets) predicts a future action that occurred after the first two actions were completed. (Here "he'd" is a short form of "he would.")

You probably do not know the technical names for these tenses, nor do you need to know them. However, you do need to know what the different verb tenses mean and how to use them. In your remembered-event essay, you will want to be sure that the verb tenses you use accurately indicate the time relations among various actions in your story.

Temporal Transitions. In addition to using verb tense to show time, writers use transitions to move the narrative action forward in time and thereby keep readers oriented. Wolff uses many transitional words and phrases to locate an action at a particular point in time or to relate an action at one point in time to an action at another time. He uses four in the first paragraph alone: *just after, when, still,* and *no longer.* Time markers may appear at the beginning of a sentence or within a sentence. Notice how many paragraphs in Wolff's story include such a transition in the opening sentence: "Just after" (paragraph 1), "After a few days" (4), "For a week or so" (5), "before long" (6), "One afternoon" (9), "When" (10), "again" (11), and "For several days" (12). This extensive use of temporal transitions is not unusual in remembered-event essays. You will want to use them liberally in your own essay to orient readers and propel your narrative through time.

For more on temporal relationships, see Chapter 13, p. 622, and Chapter 14, pp. 630–31.

Considering Topics for Your Own Essay

In this selection, Wolff describes experiencing what he calls the "ecstasy of my power" to inflict harm on others (paragraph 7). Try to recall two or three incidents when you were in a position to exercise power over another person or when you were subject to someone else's power. You may have been in such relationships for long periods of time, but select only those relationships that can be well illustrated by one key incident that occurred within a day or two. Pick one such incident. Think about how you would present it, explaining what you did and how you felt.

To use the Writing Guide Software to record your ideas, click on
▶ **Journal**

Rick Bragg *was twenty when he began working as a journalist for his hometown newspaper, the* Anniston *(Alabama)* Star. *After honing his writing skills at several small southern newspapers, he joined the staff of the* St. Petersburg Times, *where he became Miami bureau chief, and eventually the* Los Angeles Times *and the* New York Times. *Bragg won the Pulitzer Prize for feature writing in 1996, the American Society of Newspaper Editors' Distinguished Writing Award twice, and more than fifty other awards. His journalism has been collected in a book titled* Somebody Told Me: The Newspaper Stories of Rick Bragg *(2000). In addition,* *he has written two autobiographical books:* All Over but the Shoutin' *(1997), about his small-town Alabama childhood, and* Ava's Man *(2001), about the grandfather he never met. Bragg, who has taught writing at the University of South Florida, Boston University, and Harvard, says he learned storytelling "at the knees of some of the best storytellers—back-porch talkers."*

The following selection from All Over but the Shoutin' *tells what happened the summer before Bragg was a senior in high school. As you read about this remembered event, pay attention to Bragg's vivid descriptions. For example, notice how he helps readers virtually see the car and also appreciate his feelings for it when he describes it in loving detail, down to the orange houndstooth-pattern upholstery and the eight-track* Eagles' Greatest Hits *tape.*

100 Miles per Hour, Upside Down and Sideways

Rick Bragg

Since I was a boy I have searched for ways to slingshot myself into the distance, faster and faster. When you turn the key on a car built for speed, when you hear that car rumble like an approaching storm and feel the steering wheel tremble in your hands from all that power barely under control, you feel like you can run away from anything, like you can turn your whole life into an insignificant speck in the rearview mirror. 1

In the summer of 1976, the summer before my senior year at Jacksonville High School, I had the mother of all slingshots. She was a 1969 General Motors convertible muscle car with a 350 V-8 and a Holley four-barreled carburetor as long as my arm. She got about six miles to the gallon, downhill, and when you started her up she sounded like Judgment Day. She was long and low and vicious, a mad dog cyclone with orange houndstooth interior and an eight-track tape player, and looked fast just sitting in the yard under a pine tree. I owned just one tape, that I remember, *The Eagles' Greatest Hits.* 2

I worked two summers in the hell and heat at minimum wage to earn enough money to buy her and still had to borrow money from my uncle Ed, who got her for just nineteen hundred dollars mainly because he paid in hundred-dollar bills. "You better be careful, boy," he told me. "That'un will kill you." I assured him that, Yes, Sir, I would creep around in it like an old woman. 3

I tell myself I loved that car because she was so pretty and so fast and because I loved to rumble between the rows of pines with the blond hair of some girl who had yet to discover she was better than me whipping in the breeze. But the truth is I loved her because she was my equalizer. She raised me up, at least in my own eyes, closer to where I wanted and needed to be. In high school, I was neither extremely popular nor one of the great number of want-to-bes. I was invited to parties with the popular kids, I had dates with pretty girls. But there was always a distance there, of my own making, usually. 4

That car, in a purely superficial way, closed it. People crowded around her at the Hardee's. I let only one person drive her, Patrice Curry, the prettiest girl in school, for exactly one mile. 5

That first weekend, I raced her across the long, wide parking lot of the TG&Y, an insane thing to do, seeing as how a police car could have cruised by at any minute. It 6 was a test of nerves as well as speed, because you actually had to be slowing down, not speeding up, as you neared the finish line, because you just ran out of parking lot. I beat Lyn Johnson's Plymouth and had to slam on my brakes and swing her hard around, to keep from jumping the curb, the road and plowing into the parking lot of the Sonic Drive-In.

It would have lasted longer, this upraised standing, if I had pampered her. I guess I should have spent more time looking at her than racing her, but I had too much of the Bragg side of the family in me for that. I would roll her out on some lonely country road late at night, the top down, and blister down the blacktop until I knew the tires were about to lift off the ground. But they never did. She held the road, somehow, until I ran out of road or just lost my nerve. It was as if there was no limit to her, at how fast we could go, together. 7

It lasted two weeks from the day I bought her. 8

On Saturday night, late, I pulled up to the last red light in town on my way home. Kyle Smith pulled up beside me in a loud-running Chevrolet, and raced his engine. I did not squall out when the light changed—she was not that kind of car—but let her rpm's build, build and build, like winding up a top. 9

I was passing a hundred miles per hour as I neared a long sweeping turn on Highway 21 when I saw, coming toward me, the blue lights of the town's police. I cannot really remember what happened next. I just remember mashing the gas pedal down hard, halfway through that sweeping turn, and the sickening feeling as the car just seemed to lift and twist in the air, until I was doing a hundred miles per hour still, but upside down and sideways. 10

She landed across a ditch, on her top. If she had not hit the ditch in just the right way, the police later said, it would have cut my head off. I did not have on my seat belt. We never did, then. Instead of flinging me out, though, the centrifugal force—I had taken science in ninth grade—somehow held me in. 11

Instead of lying broken and bleeding on the ground beside my car, or headless, I just sat there, upside down. I always pulled the adjustable steering wheel down low, an inch or less above my thighs, and that held me in place, my head covered with mud and broken glass. The radio was still blaring—it was the Eagles' "The Long Run," I believe—and I tried to find the knob in the dark to turn it off. Funny. There I was in an upside-down car, smelling the gas as it ran out of the tank, listening to the tick, tick, tick of the hot engine, thinking: "I sure do hope that gas don't get nowhere near that hot manifold," but all I did about it was try to turn down the radio. 12

I knew the police had arrived because I could hear them talking. Finally, I felt a hand on my collar. A state trooper dragged me out and dragged me up the side of the ditch and into the collective glare of the most headlights I had ever seen. There were police cars and ambulances and traffic backed up, it seemed, all the way to Piedmont. 13

"The Lord was riding with you, son," the trooper said. "You should be dead." 14

My momma stood off to one side, stunned. Finally the police let her through to look me over, up and down. But except for the glass in my hair and a sore neck, I was fine. Thankfully, I was too old for her to go cut a hickory and stripe my legs with it, but I am sure it crossed her mind. 15

The trooper and the Jacksonville police had a private talk off to one side, trying to decide whether or not to put me in prison for the rest of my life. Finally, they informed my momma that I had suffered enough, to take me home. As we drove away, I looked back over my shoulder as the wrecker dragged my car out of the ditch and, with the help of several strong men, flipped it back over, right-side up. It looked like a white sheet of paper someone had crumpled up and tossed in the ditch from a passing car. 16

"The Lord was riding with that boy," Carliss Slaughts, the wrecker operator, told my uncle Ed. With so many people saying that, I thought the front page of the *Anniston Star* the next day would read: LORD RIDES WITH BOY, WRECKS ANYWAY. 17

I was famous for a while. No one, no one, flips a convertible at a hundred miles per hour, without a seat belt on, and walks away, undamaged. People said I had a charmed life. My momma, like the trooper and Mr. Slaughts, just figured God was my copilot. 18

The craftsmen at Slaughts' Body Shop put her back together, over four months. My uncle Ed loaned me the money to fix her, and took it out of my check. The body and fender man made her pretty again, but she was never the same. She was fast but not real fast, as if some little part of her was still broken deep inside. Finally, someone backed into her in the parking lot of the Piggly Wiggly, and I was so disgusted I sold her for fourteen hundred dollars to a preacher's son, who drove the speed limit. 19

Connecting to Culture and Experience: Social Status

Bragg worked hard and saved his money for two years when he was a teenager in high school to buy the convertible. Probably he had several motives for doing so; but after he started driving the car, he came to think of it as "my equalizer," which "closed" the distance between the most popular students and himself and gave him immediate "upraised standing" (paragraphs 4, 5, 7).

With other students, discuss this concern with standing or status in high school. Was it a concern of yours personally? If not, speculate about the reasons. If so, what did you try to do, if anything, to raise (or maintain) your status? Why do you think you made this effort?

Analyzing Writing Strategies

For more on comparing strategies, including similes and metaphors, see Chapter 15, pp. 647–48. For more on creating a dominant impression, see Chapter 15, pp. 653–54.

1. One important strategy used for describing people, places, and objects in autobiographical writing is **comparing**—using similes and metaphors to help readers imagine what happened. Similes use *like* or *as* to make explicit comparisons: "you hear that car rumble like an approaching storm" (paragraph 1). Metaphors are implied comparisons: "Since I was a boy I have searched for ways to slingshot myself into the distance, faster and faster" (paragraph 1). Here Bragg implies a comparison between himself and a stone launched from a hand-held slingshot; the stone speeds into space as Bragg hopes to speed into the future, to get to any place other than the place where he was at the time of this event. Comparisons are not a requirement of successful remembered-event essays, but they can con-

tribute to readers' understanding if they are not merely decorative but instead help readers understand the significance of the event to the writer.

There are several comparisons in paragraph 1 and one each in paragraphs 3, 7, 9, 13, and 16. Locate and underline the comparisons in these paragraphs. Choose one comparison that you think works especially well, and explain briefly why you think so. Then consider the comparisons as a group. What impression do these comparisons give you of the young Bragg and the event he is writing about?

2. In the central incident (paragraphs 9–16), the defining element of a remembered-event essay, Bragg narrates a compelling story. To understand more fully how Bragg organizes the incident, make a paragraph **scratch outline** of it. Does the order of events make sense? Are there further details you need to know to follow easily what happens? What does Bragg do to arouse your curiosity and build suspense?

For an example of a paragraph scratch outline, turn to the Commentary following Annie Dillard's essay on p. 29. For more information on scratch outlining, see Chapter 12, p. 594.

Commentary: Autobiographical Significance

Bragg's essay illustrates the two main ways writers convey the **autobiographical significance** of a remembered event: showing and telling. Bragg shows the event's significance through details and action. For example, he shows us how the car raised his status by describing its power and imposing appearance and the girls he took for rides in it. He shows the importance of the car by recounting how terribly hard he worked to buy it and then to have it repaired after the wreck. He reveals perhaps his resigned acceptance that the car would not change his life by selling it after it was dented in a parking lot. The least Bragg must do to succeed is to show consistently through details and action what the remembered event meant to him. Bragg also tells readers what he believes the autobiographical significance might be, and he does so in two ways: by telling his remembered thoughts and feelings from the time of the event as well as by giving his present perspective on the event.

Bragg's **remembered thoughts and feelings** frame his essay. In the first paragraph, he remembers thinking that owning a powerful car makes "you feel like you can run away from anything, like you can turn your whole life into an insignificant speck in the rearview mirror." In the final paragraphs, he remembers his temporary fame for surviving the accident and his disgust when someone damaged his car in a parking lot. These remembered thoughts and feelings reveal perhaps a change of values, from materialism to some yet-to-be-defined values, from Bragg's relying on a car for status to his parting with it readily for far less money than he had invested in it.

Bragg's **present perspectives** on this remembered event occur in paragraphs 4–7, between the time he bought the car and had the accident. From his perspective in his midthirties, as he was writing *All Over but the Shoutin'*, Bragg writes, "I tell myself I loved that car because she was so pretty and so fast. . . . But the truth is I loved her because she was my equalizer" (paragraph 4). He acknowledges that as a high school student he wanted the car because it made him popular, "upraised" his social "standing" (paragraph 7). But he also admits that he loved the feeling the car gave him that he could "run away from anything" (paragraph 1). By inserting these present-perspective comments, Bragg reflects on desires that are contradictory but all too familiar: the wish to be accepted socially and, at the same time, the need to feel free and powerful. From his adult perspective, he knows that racing was "an insane thing to do" (paragraph 6). But instead of moralizing about the recklessness of his wild ride, he tries to give readers a sense of the joy he felt when he would "slingshot" himself "into the distance, faster and faster" (paragraph 1), as well as the amazement he felt later that he had lived to tell the tale.

Considering Topics for Your Own Essay

Bragg has focused on a particular incident that tells us something about himself both as an adolescent and as the man he would become by his midthirties. Think of incidents early in your life (before you were eleven or twelve years old) that are particularly revealing about you, both as a child and as a person of your present age. You might try to think of incidents that tested or challenged you or incidents in which you behaved either typically or atypically in relation to the way you remember yourself to have been or think of yourself now. Perhaps you experienced a dreadful disappointment or an unexpected delight. Perhaps you were in danger, or you accomplished something you now think you were unprepared for.

To use the Writing Guide Software to record your ideas, click on
▶ **Journal**

Jean Brandt *wrote this essay as a first-year college student. In it, she tells about a memorable event that occurred when she was thirteen. Reflecting on how she felt at the time, Brandt writes, "I was afraid, embarrassed, worried, mad." As you read, look for places where these tumultuous and contradictory remembered feelings are expressed.*

To see this essay with pop-up annotations in the software, click on
▶ **Remembering Events**
▶ **Read**

Calling Home
Jean Brandt

As we all piled into the car, I knew it was going to be a 1
fabulous day. My grandmother was visiting for the holidays; and she and I, along with my older brother and sister, Louis and Susan, were setting off for a day of last-minute Christmas shopping. On the way to the mall, we sang Christmas carols, chattered, and laughed. With Christmas only two days away, we were caught up

with holiday spirit. I felt light-headed and full of joy. I loved shopping—especially at Christmas.

The shopping center was swarming with frantic last-minute shoppers like ourselves. We went first to the General Store, my favorite. It carried mostly knickknacks and other useless items which nobody needs but buys anyway. I was thirteen years old at the time, and things like buttons and calendars and posters would catch my fancy. This day was no different. The object of my desire was a 75-cent Snoopy button. Snoopy was the latest. If you owned anything with the Peanuts on it, you were "in." But since I was supposed to be shopping for gifts for other people and not myself, I couldn't decide what to do. I went in search of my sister for her opinion. I pushed my way through throngs of people to the back of the store where I found Susan. I asked her if she thought I should buy the button. She said it was cute and if I wanted it to go ahead and buy it. 2

When I got back to the Snoopy section, I took one look at the lines at the cashiers and knew I didn't want to wait thirty minutes to buy an item worth less than one dollar. I walked back to the basket where I found the button and was about to drop it when suddenly, instead, I took a quick glance around, assured myself no one could see, and slipped the button into the pocket of my sweatshirt. I hesitated for a moment, but once the item was in my pocket, there was no turning back. I had never before stolen anything; but what was done was done. A few seconds later, my sister appeared and asked, "So, did you decide to buy the button?" 3

"No, I guess not." I hoped my voice didn't quaver. As we headed for the entrance, my heart began to race. I just had to get out of that store. Only a few more yards to go and I'd be safe. As we crossed the threshold, I heaved a sigh of relief. I was home free. I thought about how sly I had been and I felt proud of my accomplishment. 4

An unexpected tap on my shoulder startled me. I whirled around to find a middle-aged man, dressed in street clothes, flashing some type of badge and politely asking me to empty my pockets. Where did this man come from? How did he know? I was so sure that no one had seen me! On the verge of panicking, I told myself that all I had to do was give this man his button back, say I was sorry, and go on my way. After all, it was only a 75-cent item. 5

Next thing I knew, he was talking about calling the police and having me arrested and thrown in jail, as if he had just nabbed a professional thief instead of a terrified kid. I couldn't believe what he was saying. 6

"Jean, what's going on?" 7

The sound of my sister's voice eased the pressure a bit. She always managed to get me out of trouble. She would come through this time too. 8

"Excuse me. Are you a relative of this young girl?" 9

"Yes, I'm her sister. What's the problem?" 10

"Well, I just caught her shoplifting and I'm afraid I'll have to call the police." 11

"What did she take?" 12

"This button." 13

"A button? You are having a thirteen-year-old arrested for stealing a button?" 14

"I'm sorry, but she broke the law." 15

The man led us through the store and into an office, where we waited for the police officers to arrive. Susan had found my grandmother and brother, who, still shocked, didn't say a word. The thought of going to jail terrified me, not because of jail itself, but because of the encounter with my parents afterward. Not more than ten minutes later, two officers arrived and placed me under arrest. They said that I was to be taken to the station alone. Then, they handcuffed me and led me out of the store. I felt alone and scared. I had counted on my sister being with me, but now I had to muster up the courage to face this ordeal all by myself. 16

As the officers led me through the mall, I sensed a hundred pairs of eyes staring at me. My face flushed and I broke out in a sweat. Now everyone knew I was a criminal. In their eyes I was a juvenile delinquent, and thank God the cops were getting me off the streets. The worst part was thinking my grandmother might be having the same thoughts. The humiliation at that moment was overwhelming. I felt like Hester Prynne being put on public display for everyone to ridicule. 17

That short walk through the mall seemed to take hours. But once we reached the squad car, time raced by. I was read my rights and questioned. We were at the police station within minutes. Everything happened so fast I didn't have a chance to feel remorse for my crime. Instead, I viewed what was happening to me as if it were a movie. Being searched, although embarrassing, somehow seemed to be exciting. All the movies and television programs I had seen were actually coming to life. This is what it was really like. But why were criminals always portrayed as frightened and regretful? I was having fun. I thought I had nothing to fear—until I was allowed my one phone call. I was trembling as I dialed home. I didn't know what I was going to say to my parents, especially my mother. 18

"Hi, Dad, this is Jean." 19

"We've been waiting for you to call." 20

"Did Susie tell you what happened?" 21

"Yeah, but we haven't told your mother. I think you should tell her what you did and where you are." 22

"You mean she doesn't even know where I am?" 23

"No, I want you to explain it to her." 24

There was a pause as he called my mother to the phone. For the first time that night, I was close to tears. I wished I had never stolen that stupid pin. I wanted to give the phone to one of the officers because I was too ashamed to tell my mother the truth, but I had no choice. 25

"Jean, where are you?" 26

"I'm, umm, in jail." 27

"Why? What for?" 28

"Shoplifting." 29

"Oh no, Jean. Why? Why did you do it?" 30

"I don't know. No reason. I just did it." 31

"I don't understand. What did you take? Why did you do it? You had plenty of money with you." 32

"I know but I just did it. I can't explain why. Mom, I'm sorry." 33

"I'm afraid sorry isn't enough. I'm horribly disappointed in you." 34

Long after we got off the phone, while I sat in an empty jail cell, waiting for my parents to pick me up, I could still distinctly hear the disappointment and hurt in my mother's voice. I cried. The tears weren't for me but for her and the pain I had put her through. I felt like a terrible human being. I would rather have stayed in jail than confront my mom right then. I dreaded each passing minute that brought our encounter closer. When the officer came to release me, I hesitated, actually not wanting to leave. We went to the front desk, where I had to sign a form to retrieve my belongings. I saw my parents a few yards away and my heart raced. A large knot formed in my stomach. I fought back the tears. 35

Not a word was spoken as we walked to the car. Slowly, I sank into the back seat anticipating the scolding. Expecting harsh tones, I was relieved to hear almost the opposite from my father. 36

"I'm not going to punish you and I'll tell you why. Although I think what you did was wrong, I think what the police did was more wrong. There's no excuse for locking a thirteen-year-old behind bars. That doesn't mean I condone what you did, but I think you've been punished enough already." 37

As I looked from my father's eyes to my mother's, I knew this ordeal was over. Although it would never be forgotten, the incident was not mentioned again. 38

Connecting to Culture and Experience: Shame and Social Disapproval

In paragraph 17, Brandt gives us a vivid portrait of how excruciating the feeling of shame can be: "I sensed a hundred pairs of eyes staring at me. My face flushed and I broke out in a sweat." Shame, as this description indicates, involves a desire for people's approval or a dread of their disapproval. (The words *shame* and *guilt* are often used interchangeably, but they have different connotations: Shame involves anxiety about social acceptance, whereas guilt is a more private, inward-looking emotion associated with morality.) We know that Brandt is feeling shame because of her emphasis on other people's opinions of her.

Identify one occasion when you felt ashamed. With other students, take turns briefly explaining what happened, who was ashamed of you, and why you felt shame. Then, keeping in mind that the social goal of shame is to constrain individuals' behavior, discuss what you think groups—families, friends, teams, employees—gain from creating fear of social disapproval among their members. Consider also what individuals might lose from undue pressure of social disapproval.

Analyzing Writing Strategies

1. Reread the essay, paying particular attention to Brandt's use of **dialogue**—reconstructed conversation from the time of the event. What do you learn about

the author from what she says and how she says it? What do you learn about her relationship with her parents?

2. The story begins and ends in a car, with the two car rides framing the story. **Framing**, a narrative device, echoes something from the beginning in the ending. Review what happens in each car ride. The writer assumes that you might think of the beginning as you are reading the ending. What effect might this awareness have on your response to the ending car ride?

3. The Writer at Work section on pp. 71–77 includes some of Brandt's invention notes and her complete first draft. These materials show how her focus shifts gradually from the theft and subsequent arrest described in her first draft to her emotional confrontation with her parents described in the final version.

   Read over her notes and first draft, and then comment on this shift in focus. Why do you think Brandt decides to stress her confrontation with her parents? Why do you think she decides, against the advice of the student who commented on her draft, to cut the scenes in the police car and station? Notice, in particular, that she leaves out of the final version the vivid image of herself handcuffed to the table (see p. 76, paragraph 5).

Commentary: A Vivid Presentation of Places and People

To present the people involved in the event and especially to dramatize her relationship with her parents, Brandt depends on dialogue. We can see from her use of dialogue the two ways that writers typically present remembered conversations: **quoting** and **summarizing**. Compare the two examples that follow. In the first example, Brandt quotes a brief exchange between herself and her sister as they were leaving the store (paragraphs 3 and 4):

> A few seconds later, my sister appeared and asked, "So, did you decide to buy the button?"
>
> "No, I guess not." I hoped my voice didn't quaver.

In this second example, Brandt summarizes what the store manager said to her as she left the store (paragraphs 5 and 6):

> An unexpected tap on my shoulder startled me. I whirled around to find a middle-aged man, dressed in street clothes, flashing some type of badge and politely asking me to empty my pockets. . . .
>
> Next thing I knew, he was talking about calling the police and having me arrested. . . .

As these examples indicate, writers usually summarize rather than quote when they need to give only the gist of what was said. Brandt apparently decides that the manager's actual words and way of speaking are not important for her purpose. However, presenting her response to her sister's question is important because it shows how she felt at the time. When you write a remembered-event essay, you too will have to decide in light of your overall purpose what to summarize and what to quote.

For more on dialogue, see Chapter 14, p. 635.

Considering Topics for Your Own Essay

Think of a few occasions when you did something uncharacteristic. Perhaps you acted on impulse or took a chance you would not ordinarily take. The events do not have to be reckless, dangerous, or illegal; they can be quite harmless or even pleasant. Pick one occasion you might like to write about. What would you want your readers to recognize about you on the basis of reading your story?

To use the Writing Guide Software to record your ideas, click on
▶ **Journal**

PURPOSE AND AUDIENCE

Writing autobiography, writers relive moments of pleasure and pain, and they also gain insight, learning who they are now by examining who they used to be and the forces that shaped them. Because autobiographers write to be read, though, they are as much concerned with self-presentation as with self-discovery. Writers present themselves to readers in the way they want to be perceived. The rest they keep hidden, though readers may read between the lines.

We read about others' experiences for much the same reason that we write about our own—to learn how to live our lives. Reading autobiography can validate our sense of ourselves, particularly when we see our own experience reflected in another's life. Reading about others' lives can also challenge our complacency and help us appreciate other points of view.

BASIC FEATURES: REMEMBERING EVENTS

A Well-Told Story

An essay about a remembered event should tell an interesting story. Whatever else the writer may attempt to do, he or she must shape the experience into a story that is entertaining and memorable. This is done primarily by building suspense, leading readers to wonder, for example, whether the driver of the Buick will catch Annie Dillard, Tobias Wolff will shoot the rifle, or Jean Brandt will get caught for shoplifting. The principal technique for propelling the narrative and heightening suspense is specific narrative action with its action verbs and verbals. Suspense increases, for instance, when Wolff gives a detailed close-up of his play with the rifle. In addition, writers use temporal transitions to cue readers and move the narrative through time, as when Rick Bragg begins paragraphs with "In the summer of 1976," "That first weekend," and "On Saturday night." Finally, writers often use dialogue to convey immediacy and drama, as Brandt does to dramatize her confrontation with her mother on the phone.

A Vivid Presentation of Places and People

Instead of giving a generalized impression, skillful writers attempt to re-create the place where the event occurred and let us hear what people said. Vivid language and specific details make the writing memorable. By moving in close, a writer can name specific objects at a place, such as when Brandt catalogs the store's knickknacks, calendars, and buttons. A writer may also provide details about some of the objects, as when Brandt describes the coveted "75-cent Snoopy button." Finally, writers use similes and metaphors to draw comparisons and thereby help readers understand the point. For example, when Brandt says she felt "like Hester Prynne being put on public display" (paragraph 17), readers familiar with *The Scarlet Letter* can imagine how embarrassed Brandt must have felt.

To present people who played an important role in a remembered event, autobiographers often provide some descriptive details and a snatch of dialogue. They may detail the person's

appearance, as Annie Dillard does by describing the man who chased her "in city clothes: a suit and tie, street shoes" as "a thin man, all action" (paragraph 10). Dialogue can be an especially effective way of giving readers a vivid impression of someone. Wolff, for example, describes his mother by combining specific narrative actions with her empathetic words: "She took a cellophane bag off a loaf of bread and we went outside and looked at the squirrel. 'Poor little thing,' she said. She stuck her hand in the wrapper and picked up the squirrel, then pulled the bag inside out away from her hand" (paragraph 10).

An Indication of the Event's Significance

There are two ways a writer can communicate an event's autobiographical significance: by showing us that the event was important or by telling us directly what it meant. Most writers do both. Showing is necessary because the event must be dramatized for readers to appreciate its importance and understand the writer's feelings about it. Seeing the important scenes and people from the writer's point of view naturally leads readers to identify with the writer. We can well imagine what that "unexpected tap on [the] shoulder" (paragraph 5) must have felt like for Brandt, how Dillard felt when the man chased her and Mikey "silently over picket fences, through thorny hedges, between houses, around garbage cans, and across streets" (paragraph 13), and what Bragg was thinking as he hung upside down in his overturned car.

Telling also contributes to a reader's understanding, so most writers comment on the event's meaning and importance. Readers expect to understand the significance of the event, but they do not expect the essay to begin with the kind of thesis statement typical of argumentative writing. Instead, as the story moves along, writers tell us how they felt at the time or how they feel now as they look back on the experience. Often writers do both. Wolff, for example, tells us some of his remembered feelings when he recalls feeling "like a sniper" and delighting in the "ecstasy" of power. He also tells us what he thinks looking back on the experience: "Because I did not know who I was, any image of myself, no matter how grotesque, had power over me. This much I understand now" (paragraph 13). Telling is the main way that writers interpret the event for readers, but skillful writers are careful not to append these reflections artificially, like a moral tagged on to a fable.

GUIDE TO WRITING
Remembering Events

THE WRITING ASSIGNMENT

THE WRITING ASSIGNMENT

Write an essay about an event in your life that will be engaging for readers and that will, at the same time, help them understand the significance of the event. Tell your story dramatically and vividly.

INVENTION

INVENTION
- Finding an Event to Write About
- Describing the Place
- Recalling Key People
- Sketching the Story
- Testing Your Choice
- Exploring Memorabilia
- Reflecting on the Event's Significance
- Defining Your Purpose for Your Readers
- Formulating a Tentative Thesis Statement

PLANNING AND DRAFTING

PLANNING & DRAFTING
- Seeing What You Have
- Setting Goals
- Outlining
- Drafting

CRITICAL READING GUIDE

CRITICAL READING GUIDE
- First Impression
- Storytelling
- Vivid Description
- Autobiographical Significance
- Memorabilia
- Organization
- Final Thoughts

REVISING

REVISING
- A Well-Told Story
- A Vivid Presentation of Places and People
- Autobiographical Significance
- Organization

EDITING AND PROOFREADING

EDITING & PROOFREADING
- Checking for Missing Commas after Introductory Elements
- Checking for Fused Sentences
- Checking Your Use of the Past Perfect
- A Common ESL Problem

GUIDE TO WRITING

THE WRITING ASSIGNMENT

Write an essay about an event in your life that will be engaging for readers and that will, at the same time, help them understand the significance of the event. Tell your story dramatically and vividly.

> To use the Writing Guide Software for this assignment, click on
> ▶ **Remembering Events**
> ▶ **Write**

INVENTION

The following invention activities will help you choose an appropriate event, recall specific details, sketch out the story, test your choice, and explore the event's autobiographical significance. Each activity is easy to do and takes only a few minutes. If you can spread out the activities over several days, it will be easier for you to recall details and to reflect deeply on the event's meaning in your life. Keep a written record of your invention work to use when you draft the essay and later when you revise it.

Finding an Event to Write About

To find the best possible event to write about, consider several possibilities rather than choosing the first event that comes to mind.

Listing Remembered Events. *Make a list of significant events from your past. Include only those events about which you can recall detail about what happened, where and when it happened, and the people involved.* Begin your list now, and add to it over the next few days. Include possibilities suggested by the Considering Topics for Your Own Essay activities following each reading in this chapter. Make your list as complete as you can. The following categories may give you some more ideas:

- An occasion when you realized you had a special skill, ambition, or problem
- A time when you became aware of injustice, selflessness, heroism, sexism, racism
- A difficult situation, such as when you had to make a tough choice, when someone you admired let you down (or you let someone else down), or when you struggled to learn or understand something hard
- An occasion when things did not turn out as expected, such as when you expected to be praised but were criticized or ignored or when you were convinced you would fail but succeeded

- An incident charged with strong emotion, such as love, fear, anger, embarrassment, guilt, frustration, hurt, pride, happiness, or joy
- An incident that you find yourself thinking about frequently or occasionally or one you know you will never forget

Listing Events Related to Identity and Community. Whenever you write about events in your life, you are likely to reveal important aspects of your sense of identity and your relationships with others. The suggestions that follow, however, will help you recall events that are particularly revealing of your efforts to know yourself and to discover your place in the communities to which you belong.

- An event that shaped you in a particular way or revealed an aspect of your personality you had not seen before, such as your independence, insecurity, ambitiousness, or jealousy
- An incident that made you reexamine one of your basic values or beliefs, such as when you were expected to do something that went against your better judgment or when your values conflicted with someone else's values
- An occasion when others' actions led you to consider seriously a new idea or point of view
- An incident that made you feel the need to identify yourself with a particular community, such as an ethnic group, a political or religious group, or a group of coworkers
- An event that made you realize that the role you were playing did not conform to what was expected of you as a student, as a male or female, as a parent or sibling, as a believer in a particular religious faith, or as a member of a particular community
- An incident in which a single encounter with another person changed the way you view yourself or changed your ideas about how you fit into a particular community

Listing Events Related to Work and Career. The following suggestions will help you think of events involving your work experiences as well as your career aspirations.

- An event that made you aware of your capacity for or interest in a particular kind of work or career or an event that convinced you that you were not cut out for a particular kind of work or career
- An incident of harassment or mistreatment at work
- An event that revealed to you other people's assumptions, attitudes, or prejudices about you as a worker, your fitness for a particular job, or your career goals
- An incident of conflict or serious misunderstanding with a customer, a fellow employee, a supervisor, or someone you supervised

Finding an Event to Write About: An Online Activity

Exploring Web sites where other people write about their own life experiences might inspire you by triggering memories of similar events in your own life and by suggesting a broad range of possibilities for the kinds of remembered events people find significant.

- If you do a search for remembered-event essays in Google (www.google.com) or Yahoo! Directory (dir.yahoo.com), you will find essays written by students in other composition classes throughout the country.
- Sites such as citystories.com and storypreservation.com where people post brief stories about their lives may suggest significant events in your own life.

Add to your list of possibilities any events suggested by your online research. But do not be disappointed if other people's stories do not help you think of events in your own life that you could write about.

Choosing an Event. *Look over your list of possibilities, and choose one event that you think will make an interesting story.* You should be eager to explore the significance of the event and comfortable about sharing the event with your instructors and classmates, who will be your first readers. You may find the choice easy to make, or you may have several equally promising possibilities from which to choose.

It may help you in choosing an event if you tentatively identify your ultimate readers, the people with whom you most want to share the story. They could include, for example, your personal friends, members of your family, people you work with, members of a group with which you identify or of an organization to which you belong, your classmates, an instructor, or even the public at large.

Make the best choice you can now. If this event does not work out, you can try a different one later.

Describing the Place

The following activities will help you decide which places are important to your story and what you remember about them. Take the time now to explore your memory and imagination. This exploration will yield descriptive language you can use in your essay.

Listing Key Places. *Make a list of all the places where the event occurred, skipping some space after each entry on your list.* Your event may have occurred in one or more places. For now, list all the places you remember without worrying about whether they should be included in your story.

Describing Key Places. *In the space after each entry on your list, make some notes describing each place.* As you remember each place, what do you see (excluding people for the moment)? What objects stand out? Are they large or small, green or brown, square or oblong? What sounds do you hear? Do you detect any smells? Does any taste come to mind? Do you recall anything soft or hard, smooth or rough?

Recalling Key People

These activities will help you remember the people who played a role in the event—what they looked like, did, and said.

Listing Key People. *List the people who played more than a casual role in the event.* You may have only one person to list, or you may have several.

Describing Key People. *Write a brief description of the people who played major roles in the event.* For each person, name and detail a few distinctive physical features or items of dress. Describe the person's way of talking or gesturing.

Re-Creating Conversations. *Reconstruct any important conversations you had during the event.* Also try to recall any especially memorable comments, any unusual choice of words, or any telling remarks that you made or were made to you. You may not remember exactly what was said during an entire conversation, but try to re-create it so that readers will be able to imagine what was going on.

The Writing Guide Software provides an electronic version of each chapter's writing guide. The software wraps around your own word-processing screen, and you click on links or buttons for advice or models. This student can get help re-creating a conversation by clicking on the Reconstruct link in the instructions.

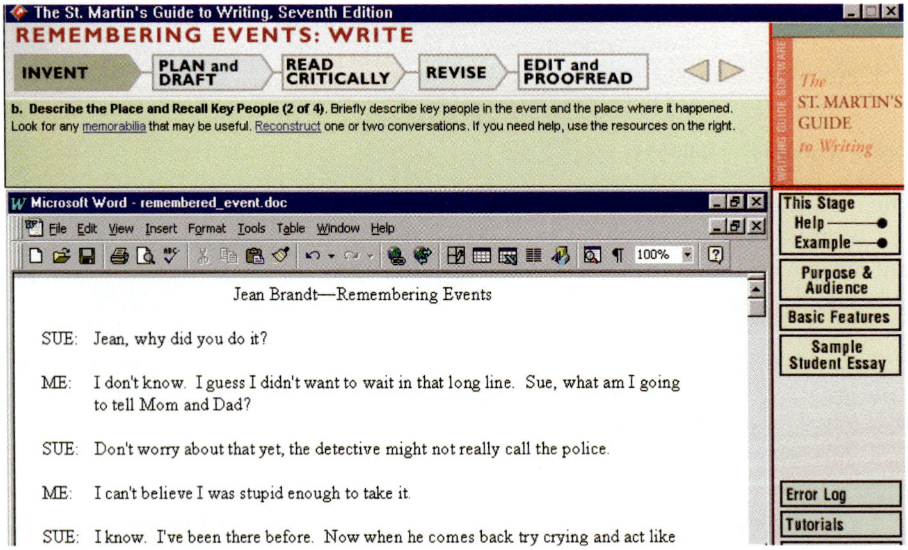

Sketching the Story

Write for a few minutes, telling what happened. You may find it easier to outline what happened rather than writing complete sentences and paragraphs. Any way you can put the main action into words is fine. Over the next few days, you may want to add to this rough sketch.

Testing Your Choice

Now you need to decide whether you recall enough detail to write a good story about this particular event. Reread your invention notes to see whether your initial memories seem promising. If you can recall clearly what happened and what the important scenes and people were like, then you have probably made a good choice. If at any point you lose confidence in your choice, return to your list, and choose another event.

Testing Your Choice: A Collaborative Activity

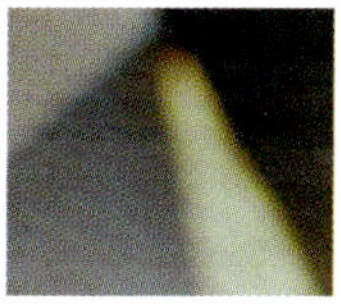

At this point, you will find it useful to get together with two or three other students to try out your story. Your instructor may ask you to do this collaborative activity in class or online using a chatroom. Their reactions to your story will help you determine whether you have chosen an event you can present in an interesting way.

Storytellers: Take turns telling your story briefly. Try to make your story dramatic (by piquing your listeners' curiosity and building suspense) and vivid (by briefly describing the place and key people).

Listeners: Briefly tell each storyteller what you found most intriguing about the story. For example, were you eager to know how the story would turn out? Were you curious about any of the people? Were you able to identify with the storyteller? Could you imagine the place? Could you understand why the event is so memorable and significant for the storyteller?

Exploring Memorabilia

Memorabilia are visual images, sounds, and objects that can help you remember details and understand the significance of an event. Examples include photographs, newspaper or magazine clippings, recordings of popular music, souvenirs, medals or trophies, and even items not necessarily designated as mementoes (restaurant menus and movie, theater, or concert stubs and programs). *If you can obtain access to relevant memorabilia, take time to do so now. Add to your invention notes any details about the period, places, or people the memorabilia suggest.*

For further information on including visuals in a document, see pp. 824–31. For an illustration of memorabilia in a remembered-event essay and for suggestions for choosing and placing memorabilia in your writing, turn to the box on pp. 78–78.

Consider including one or more pieces of memorabilia in your essay. You can simply append photographs or other items to your printed-out essay, or if you have the capability, you can scan them into your electronic document. If you include visual memorabilia in your essay, you should label and number them as Figure 1, Figure 2, and so on, and include captions identifying them.

Reflecting on the Event's Significance

You should now feel fairly confident that you can tell an interesting story about the event you have chosen. The following activities will help you to understand the meaning that the event holds in your life and to develop ways to convey this significance to your readers.

Recalling Your Remembered Feelings and Thoughts. *Write for a few minutes about your feelings and thoughts during and immediately after the event.* The following questions may help stimulate your memory:

- What were my expectations before the event?
- What was my first reaction to the event as it was happening and right after it ended?
- How did I show my feelings? What did I say?
- What did I want the people involved to think of me? Why did I care what they thought of me?
- What did I think of myself at the time?
- How long did these initial feelings last?
- What were the immediate consequences of the event for me personally?

Pause now to reread what you have written. *Then write another sentence or two about the event's significance to you at the time it occurred.*

Exploring Your Present Perspective. *Write for a few minutes about your current feelings and thoughts as you look back on the event.* These questions may help you get started:

- Looking back, how do I feel about this event? If I understand it differently now than I did then, what is the difference?
- What do my actions at the time of the event say about the kind of person I was then? How would I respond to the same event if it occurred today?
- Can looking at the event historically or culturally help explain what happened? For example, did I upset gender expectations? Did I feel torn between two cultures or ethnic identities? Did I feel out of place?
- Do I now see that there was a conflict underlying the event? For example, did I struggle with contradictory desires within myself? Did I feel pressured by others or by society in general? Were my desires and rights in conflict with someone else's? Was the event about power or responsibility?

Pause now to reflect on what you have written about your present perspective. *Then write another sentence or two, commenting on the event's significance as you look back on it.*

Defining Your Purpose for Your Readers

Write a few sentences, defining your purpose in writing about this particular event for your readers. Use these questions to focus your thoughts:

- Who are my readers? (Remember that in choosing an event, you considered several possible readers: your personal friends, members of your family, people you work with, members of a group with which you identify or of an organization to which you belong, your classmates, an instructor, even the public at large.)
- What do my readers know about me?
- What do my readers expect when they read autobiography?
- How do I expect my readers to understand or react to the event?
- How do I want my readers to feel about what happened? What is the dominant impression or mood I want my story to create?
- What specifically do I want my readers to think of me? What do I expect or fear they might think?

It is unlikely, but you may decide at this point that you feel uncomfortable disclosing this event. If so, choose another event to write about.

Formulating a Tentative Thesis Statement

Review what you wrote for Reflecting on the Event's Significance, and add another two or three sentences, not necessarily summarizing what you already have written but extending your insights into the significance of the event, what it meant to you at the time, and what it means now. These sentences must necessarily be speculative and tentative because you may not fully understand the event's significance in your life.

Keep in mind that readers do not expect you to begin your essay with the kind of explicit thesis statement typical of argumentative or explanatory writing. If you do decide to tell readers explicitly why the event was meaningful or significant, you will most likely do so as you tell the story, by commenting on or evaluating what happened, instead of announcing it at the beginning. Keep in mind that you are not obliged to tell readers the significance, but you should show it through the way you tell the story.

PLANNING AND DRAFTING

This section will help you review your invention writing and get started on your first draft.

If you are using the Writing Guide Software, click on
▶ **Planning and Drafting**

Seeing What You Have

You have now done a lot of thinking and writing about the basic elements of a remembered-event essay: what happened, where it happened, who was involved, what was said, and how you felt. You have also begun to develop your understanding of why the event is so important to you. If you have done your invention writing on the computer, you may have sentences or whole paragraphs that can be copied and pasted into your draft. Reread what you have written so far to see what you have. Watch for specific narrative actions, vivid descriptive details, choice bits of dialogue. Note also any language that resonates with feeling or that seems especially insightful. Highlight any writing you think could be used in your draft.

Then ask yourself the following questions:

- Do I remember enough specific details about the event to describe it vividly?
- Do I understand how the event was significant to me?
- Does my invention material provide what I need to convey that significance to my readers?
- Does my present perspective on this event seem clear to me?
- Does the dominant impression I want to create in my essay seem relevant?

If you find little that seems promising, you are not likely to be able to write a good draft. Consider starting over with another event.

If, however, your invention writing offers some promising material, the following activities may help you develop more:

- To remember more of what actually happened, discuss the event with someone who was there or who remembers having heard about it at the time.
- To recall additional details about a person who played an important role in the event, look at any available photographs or letters, talk with the person, or talk with someone who remembers the person. If that is impossible, you might imagine having a conversation with the person today about the event: What would you say? How do you think the person would respond?
- To remember how you felt at the time of the event, try to recall what else was happening in your life during that period. What music, television shows, movies, sports, books, and magazines did you like? What concerns did you have at home, school, work, play?
- To develop your present perspective on the event, try viewing your experience as a historical event. If you were writing a news story or documentary about the event, what would you want people to know?

- To decide on the dominant impression you want your story to have on readers, imagine that you are making a film based on this event. What would your film look like? What mood or atmosphere would you try to create? Alternatively, imagine writing a song or poem about the event. Think of an appropriate image or refrain. What kind of song would you write—blues, hip-hop, country, ranchera, rock?

Setting Goals

Before starting to draft, set goals that will help you make decisions and solve problems as you draft and revise. Here are some questions that will help you set your goals:

Your Purpose and Readers

- What do I want my readers to think of me and my experience? Should I tell them how I felt and what I thought at the time of the event, as Dillard does? Should I tell them how my perspective has changed, as Bragg does?
- If my readers are likely to have had a similar experience, how can I convey the uniqueness of my experience or its special importance in my life? Should I tell them more about my background or the particular context of the event, as Bragg does? Should I give them a glimpse, as Dillard does, of its impact years later?
- If my readers are not likely to have had a similar experience, how can I help them understand what happened and appreciate its importance? Should I reveal the cultural influences acting on me, as Wolff and Bragg do?

The Beginning

- What can I do in the opening sentences to arouse readers' curiosity? Should I begin with a surprising announcement, as Wolff does, or should I establish the setting and situation, as Dillard and Brandt do?
- How can I get my readers to identify with me? Should I tell them a few things about myself, as Bragg does?
- Should I do something unusual, such as begin in the middle of the action or with a funny bit of dialogue?

The Story

- What should be the climax of my story—the point that readers anticipate with trepidation or eagerness?
- What specific narrative actions or dialogue would intensify the drama of the story?
- Should I follow strict chronological order? Or would flashback (referring to an event that occurred earlier) or flashforward (referring to an event that will occur later) make the narrative more interesting?
- How can I use vivid descriptive detail to dramatize the story?

The Ending

- If I conclude with some reflections on the meaning of the experience, how can I avoid tagging on a moral or being too sentimental?
- If I want readers to think well of me, should I conclude with a philosophical statement, as Wolff does? Should I end with a paradoxical statement, like Dillard? Should I be satirical? Should I be self-critical to avoid seeming smug?
- If I want to underscore the event's continuing significance in my life, can I show that the conflict was never fully resolved, as Brandt does? Could I contrast my remembered and current feelings and thoughts?
- Should I frame the essay by echoing something from the beginning to give readers at least a superficial sense of closure, as Brandt does by setting the last scene, like the first, in a car?

Outlining

For an example of a paragraph scratch outline, turn to the Commentary following Annie Dillard's essay on p. 33. For more information on scratch outlining, see Chapter 12, p. 594.

The goals you have set should help you draft your essay, but first you might want to make a quick scratch outline to refocus on the basic story line. You could use the outlining function of your word processing program. In your outline, list the main actions in order, noting where you plan to describe the place, introduce particular people, present dialogue, and insert remembered or current feelings and thoughts. Use this outline to guide your drafting, but do not feel tied to it. As you draft, you may find a better way to sequence the action and integrate these features.

Drafting

General Advice. Start drafting your essay, keeping in mind the goals you have set for yourself, especially the goal of telling the story dramatically. Turn off your grammar checker and spelling checker at this stage if you find them distracting. Don't be afraid to skip around in your story. Jump back and fill in a spontaneous idea, or leap ahead and write a later section first if you find that easier. Refer to your outline to help you sequence the action. If you get stuck while drafting, either make a note of what you need to fill in later or see if you can use something from your invention writing.

As you read over your first draft, you may see places where you can add new material to make the story dramatic. Or you may even decide that after this first draft you can finally see the story you want to write and set out to do so in a second draft.

Sentence Strategies. As you draft a remembered-event essay, you will be trying to help readers feel the suspense of your story and recognize its significance. You will also need to orient readers to the time sequence of all the various actions in your narrative. In thinking about how to achieve these goals, you can often benefit by paying attention to how long your sentences are and where you place references to time.

Use short sentences to heighten the drama or suspense, point out autobiographical significance, and summarize action. Experienced writers of autobiography usually use both short and long sentences, as a glance at any reading in this chapter demonstrates. They write short sentences not to relieve the monotony or effort of writing long sentences but to achieve certain purposes they cannot achieve as easily with long sentences.

To dramatize actions or heighten suspense:

Finally, I felt a hand on my collar. (Rick Bragg, paragraph 13)

He caught us and we all stopped. (Annie Dillard, paragraph 15)

To emphasize the significance of the event to the writer:

I wanted the glory to last forever. (Annie Dillard, paragraph 19)

The humiliation at that moment was overwhelming. (Jean Brandt, paragraph 17)

To summarize actions:

One afternoon, I pulled the trigger. (Tobias Wolff, paragraph 9)

Short sentences are not the only way to achieve these purposes, but they do so notably well. Note, though, that most of these writers use short sentences infrequently. Because short sentences are infrequent, they attract the reader's attention: They seem to say, "Pay close attention here." But short sentences achieve this effect only in relation to long sentences, in context with them. (Some of the Sentence Strategies presented in other chapters of this book illustrate ways that writers construct and purposefully deploy relatively long, complex sentences.) See how Dillard uses a series of longer sentences to build suspense that she brings to a peak with a short one:

For more on using short sentences, go to www.bedfordstmartins.com/theguide and click on Sentence Strategies.

> On one weekday morning after Christmas, six inches of new snow had just fallen. We were standing up to our boot tops in snow on a front yard on trafficked Reynolds Street, waiting for cars. The cars traveled Reynolds Street slowly and evenly; they were targets all but wrapped in red ribbons, cream puffs. We couldn't miss. (paragraph 3)

Place references to time toward the front of your sentences. Because your remembered-event essay is organized narratively—that is, it tells readers a story—you must regularly give them cues about when various actions occur. Without these time cues, readers may not know in which decade, year, or season the event occurred; whether it unfolded slowly or quickly; or in what sequence the various actions took place. When experienced writers of autobiography use these cues, they nearly always place them at the beginnings of sentences (or main clauses), as Annie Dillard does in this sentence from *An American Childhood:*

On one weekday morning after Christmas, six inches of new snow had just fallen. (paragraph 3)

Placing these two important times cues—day of the week and time of the year—at the beginning of a sentence may not seem noteworthy, but in fact time cues can usually be placed nearly anywhere in a sentence. Consequently, Dillard might have written

Six inches of new snow had just fallen *on one weekday morning after Christmas.*

Or she could have written

After Christmas, six inches of new snow had just fallen *one weekday morning.*

For more on placing time cues, go to www.bedfordstmartins.com/theguide and click on Sentence Strategies.

Why might Dillard decide to locate these time cues at the beginning of the sentence, as she does with nearly all the time cues in her essay? Why not begin the sentence with the subject or main idea, in this case *six inches of snow?* The answer is that experienced writers of autobiography give highest priority to keeping readers oriented to time, specifically to the time of each action in the sequence of actions that make up a remembered event. To do so, they can rely on words, phrases, or clauses:

> Slowly, . . . (Deborah Brandt, paragraph 36)
>
> For a week or so . . . (Tobias Wolff, paragraph 5)
>
> A few seconds later, . . . (Deborah Brandt, paragraph 3)
>
> As we drove away, . . . (Rick Bragg, paragraph 16)

In addition to using short sentences and locating explicit time cues at the beginning of sentences, you can strengthen your autobiographical writing with other kinds of sentences as well, and you may want to preview the discussions of sentences that feature participial phrases (pp. 119–120) and adjectives before nouns (pp. 118–19). Autobiographical writing can also be enriched by a kind of sentence that is important in observational writing—absolute phrases (p. 182).

CRITICAL READING GUIDE

Now is the time to get a good critical reading of your draft. Your instructor may schedule readings of drafts as part of your coursework—in class or online. If not, ask a classmate, friend, or family member to read your draft. You could also seek comments from a tutor at your campus writing center. The guidelines in this section can be used by anyone reviewing an essay about a remembered event. (If you are unable to have someone read your draft, turn ahead to the Revising section, where you will find guidelines for reading your own draft critically.)

If you are using the Writing Guide Software, click on
▶ **Critical Reading Guide**

▶ **If You Are the Writer.** To provide focused, helpful comments, your reader must know your essay's intended audience, your purpose, and a problem in the draft that you need help solving. Briefly write out this information at the top of your draft.

- ***Readers:*** Identify the intended readers of your essay.
- ***Purpose:*** What do you hope to achieve in writing this remembered-event essay? What features of your story do you hope will most interest readers? What do you want to disclose about yourself?
- ***Problem:*** Ask your reader to help you solve the single most important problem with your draft. Describe this problem briefly.

▶ **If You Are the Reader.** Use the following guidelines to help you give critical comments to others on remembered-event essays.

1. ***Read for a First Impression.*** Begin by reading the draft quickly, to enjoy the story and to get a sense of its significance. Then, in just a few sentences, describe your first impression. If you have any insights about the meaning or importance of the event, share your thoughts.

   Next, consider the problem the writer identified, and respond briefly to that concern now. (If you find that the problem is covered by one of the other guidelines listed below, respond to it in more detail there if necessary.)
2. ***Analyze the Effectiveness of the Storytelling.*** Review the story, looking at the way the suspense builds and resolves itself. Point to any places where the drama loses intensity—perhaps where the suspense slackens, where specific narrative action is sparse or action verbs are needed, where narrative transitions would help readers, or where dialogue could be added to dramatize people's interactions.
3. ***Consider How Vividly the Places and People Are Described.*** Point to any descriptive details, similes, or metaphors that are especially effective. Note any places or people that need more specific description. Also indicate any descriptive details that seem unnecessary. Identify any quoted dialogue that might be summarized instead or any dialogue that does not seem relevant.
4. ***Assess Whether the Autobiographical Significance Is Clear.*** Explain briefly what you think makes this event significant for the writer. Point out any places in the draft where the significance seems so overstated as to be sentimental or so understated as to be vague or unclear. If the event seems to lack significance, speculate about what you think the significance could be. Then point to one place in the draft where you think the significance could be made clearer by telling the story more fully or dramatically or by stating the significance.
5. ***Assess the Use of Memorabilia.*** If the writer makes use of memorabilia, evaluate how successfully each item is used. How is it relevant? Does it seem integrated into the narrative or merely appended? Is it placed in the most appropriate location? Does it make a meaningful contribution to the essay?
6. ***Analyze the Effectiveness of the Organization.*** Consider the overall plan, perhaps by making a scratch outline. Pay special attention to temporal transitions and verb tenses so that you can identify any places where the order of the action is unclear. Also indicate any places where you think the description or background information interrupts the action. If you can, suggest other locations for this material.

   - Look at the beginning. If it does not arouse curiosity, point to language elsewhere in the essay that might serve as a better opening—for example, a bit of dialogue, a striking image, or a remembered feeling.

Making Comments Electronically
Most word processing software offers features that allow you to insert comments directly into the text of someone else's document. Many readers prefer to make their comments in this way because it tends to be faster than writing on a hard copy and space is virtually unlimited; from the writer's point of view, it also eliminates the problem of deciphering handwritten comments. Even where such special comment features are not available, simply typing comments directly into a document in a contrasting color can provide the same advantages.

- Look at the ending. Indicate whether the conflict in the story is too neatly resolved at the end, whether the writer has tagged on a moral, or whether the essay abruptly stops without really coming to a conclusion. If there is a problem with the ending, try to suggest an alternative ending, such as framing the story with a reference to something from the beginning or projecting into the future.

7. ***Give the Writer Your Final Thoughts.*** What is the draft's strongest part? What part is most in need of further work?

REVISING

Now you have the opportunity to revise your essay. Your instructor or other students may have given you advice. You may have begun to realize that your draft requires not so much revising as rethinking. For example, you may recognize that the story you told is not the story you meant to tell. Or maybe you realize only now why the incident is important to you. Consequently, you may need to reshape your story radically or draft a new version of it, instead of working to improve the various parts of your first draft. Many students—and professional writers—find themselves in this situation. Often a writer produces a draft or two and gets advice on them from others and only then begins to see what might be achieved.

However, if instead you feel satisfied that your draft mostly achieves what you set out to do, you can focus on refining the various parts of it. Very likely you have thought of ways to improve your draft, and you may even have begun revising it. This section will help you get an overview of your draft and revise it accordingly.

If you are using the Writing Guide Software, click on
▶ **Revising**

Getting an Overview

Consider the draft as a whole, following these two steps:

1. ***Reread.*** If at all possible, put the draft aside for a day or two. When you do reread it, start by reconsidering your purpose. Then read the draft straight through, trying to see it as your intended readers will.
2. ***Outline.*** Make a quick scratch outline on paper, or use the headings and outline or summary functions of your word processor.

Planning for Revision. Resist the temptation to dive in and start changing your text until you have a comprehensive view of what needs to be done. Using your outline as a guide, move through the document, using the change-highlighting or commenting tools of your word processor to note comments received from others and problems you want to solve (or mark on a hard copy if you prefer).

Analyzing the Basic Features of Your Own Draft. Turn to the Critical Reading Guide on the preceding pages (pp. 64–66). Using this guide, reread the draft to identify problems you need to solve. Note the problems on your draft.

Turn to pp. 50–51 to review the basic features.

Studying Critical Comments. Review all of the comments you have received from other readers and add to your notes any that you intend to act on. For each comment, refer to the draft to see what might have led the reader to make that particular point. Try to be objective about any criticism. Ideally, these comments will help you to see your draft as others see it (rather than as you hoped it would be) and to identify specific problems.

Carrying Out Revisions

Having identified problems in your draft, you now need to figure out solutions and—most important—to carry them out. Basically, there are three ways to find solutions:

1. Review your invention and planning notes for material you can add to your draft.
2. Do additional invention writing to provide material you or your readers think is needed.
3. Look back at the readings in this chapter to see how other writers have solved similar problems.

The following suggestions, which are organized according to the basic features of remembered-event essays, will get you started solving some writing problems that are common in them.

A Well-Told Story

- ***Is the climax difficult to identify?*** Check to be sure your story has a climax. Perhaps it is the point when you get what you were striving for (Dillard), when you do what you were afraid you might do (Wolff), when something frightening happens (Bragg), or when you get caught (Brandt). If you cannot find a climax in your story or reconstruct your story so that it has one, then you may have a major problem. If this is the case, you should discuss with your instructor the possibility of starting over with another event.
- ***Does the suspense slacken instead of building to the climax?*** Try showing people moving or gesturing, adding narrative transitions to propel the action, or substituting quoted dialogue for summarized dialogue. Remember that writers of autobiography often use short sentences to summarize action and heighten suspense, as when Dillard writes "We couldn't miss" and "He didn't even close the car door."

A Vivid Presentation of Places and People

- ***Do any places or people need more specific description?*** Try naming objects and adding sensory details to help readers imagine what the objects look, feel, smell, taste, or sound like. For people, describe a physical feature or mannerism that shows the role the person plays in your story.
- ***Does any dialogue seem irrelevant or poorly written?*** Eliminate any unnecessary dialogue, or summarize quoted dialogue that has no distinctive language or dramatic purpose. Liven up quoted dialogue with faster repartee to make it more dramatic. Instead of introducing each comment with the dialogue cue "he said," describe the speaker's attitude or personality with phrases like "she gasped" or "he joked."
- ***Do any descriptions weaken the dominant impression?*** Omit extraneous details or reconsider the impression you want to make. Add similes and metaphors that strengthen the dominant impression you want your story to have.
- ***Do readers question any visuals you used?*** Might you move a visual to a more appropriate place or replace an ineffective visual with a more appropriate one? Could you make clear the relevance of a visual by mentioning it in your text?

An Indication of the Event's Significance

- ***Are readers getting a different image of you from the one you want to create?*** Look closely at the language you use to express your feelings and thoughts. If you project an aspect of yourself you did not intend to, reconsider what the story reveals about you. Ask yourself again why the event stands out in your memory. What do you want readers to know about you from reading this essay?
- ***Are your remembered or current feelings and thoughts about the event coming across clearly and eloquently?*** If not, look in your invention writing for more expressive language. If your writing seems too sentimental, try to express your feelings more directly and simply, or let yourself show ambivalence or uncertainty.
- ***Do readers appreciate the event's uniqueness or special importance in your life?*** If not, consider giving them more insight into your background or cultural heritage. Also consider whether they need to know what has happened since the event took place to appreciate why it is so memorable for you.

The Organization

- ***Is the overall plan ineffective or the story hard to follow?*** Look carefully at the way the action unfolds. Fill in any gaps. Eliminate unnecessary digressions. Add or clarify temporal transitions. Fix confusing verb tenses. Remember that writers of autobiography tend to place references to time at the beginnings of sentences—"*When a car came,* we all popped it one"—to keep readers on track as the story unfolds.
- ***Does description or other information disrupt the flow of the narrative?*** Try integrating this material by adding smoother transitions. Or consider removing the disruptive parts or placing them elsewhere.
- ***Is the beginning weak?*** See whether there is a better way to start. Review the draft and your notes for an image, a bit of dialogue, or a remembered feeling that might catch readers' attention or spark their curiosity.

Checking Sentence Strategies Electronically

To check your draft for a sentence strategy especially useful in remembered-event essays, use your word processor's highlighting function to mark references to time. Then look at where each one appears in its sentence, and think about whether moving any of them closer to the beginning of the sentence would make it easier for readers to follow the sequence of actions in your narrative. For more on placement of time references, see p. 63.

- ***Does the ending work?*** If not, think about a better way to end—with a memorable image, perhaps, or a provocative assertion. Consider whether you can frame the essay by referring back to something in the beginning.

EDITING AND PROOFREADING

Now is the time to check your revised draft for errors in grammar, punctuation, and mechanics and to consider matters of style. Our research has identified several errors that occur often in essays about remembered events: missing commas after introductory elements, fused sentences, and misused past-perfect verbs. The following guidelines will help you check your essay for these common errors. This book's Web site also provides interactive online exercises to help you learn to identify and correct each of these errors; to access the exercises for a particular error, go to the URL listed in the margin next to that section of the guidelines.

A Note on Grammar and Spelling Checkers
These tools are good at catching certain types of errors, but currently there's no replacement for a good human proofreader. Grammar checkers in particular are extremely limited in what they can usually find, and often they only give you summary information that isn't helpful if you don't already understand the rule in question. They are also prone to give faulty advice for fixing problems and to flag correct items as wrong. Spelling checkers cause fewer problems but can't catch misspellings that are themselves words, such as *to* for *too.*

> If you are using the Writing Guide Software, click on
> ▶ **Editing and Proofreading**

Checking for Missing Commas after Introductory Elements. Introductory elements in a sentence can be words, phrases, or clauses. A comma tells readers that the introductory information is ending and the main part of the sentence is about to begin. If there is no danger of misreading, you can omit the comma after single words or short phrases or clauses, but you will never be wrong to include the comma. Remembered-event essays require introductory elements, especially those showing time passing. The following sentences, taken from drafts written by college students using this book, show several kinds of introductory sentence elements that should have a comma after them.

For practice, go to bedfordstmartins.com/theguide/commas

▶ **Through the nine-day run of the play, the acting just kept getting better and better.**

▶ **Knowing that the struggle was over, I felt through my jacket to find tea bags and cookies the robber had taken from the kitchen.**

▶ **As I stepped out of the car, I knew something was wrong.**

Checking for Fused Sentences. Fused sentences occur when two independent clauses are joined with no punctuation or connecting word between them. When you write about a remembered event, you try to re-create a scene. In so doing, you might write a fused sentence like this one:

Sleet glazed the windshield the wipers were frozen stuck.

There are several ways to edit fused sentences:

- Make the clauses separate sentences.

  ▶ **Sleet glazed the windshield. ~~the~~ The wipers were frozen stuck.**

- Join the two clauses with a comma and *and, but, or, nor, for, so,* or *yet.*

  ▶ **Sleet glazed the windshield, and the wipers were frozen stuck.**

- Join the two clauses with a semicolon.

  ▶ **Sleet glazed the windshield; the wipers were frozen stuck.**

For practice, go to bedfordstmartins.com/theguide/csplice

- Rewrite the sentence, subordinating one clause.

  ▶ **~~Sleet~~ As sleet glazed the windshield, the wipers ~~were~~ became frozen stuck.**

Checking Your Use of the Past Perfect. Verb tenses indicate the time an action takes place. As a writer, you will generally use the present tense for actions occurring at the time you are writing (we *see*), the past tense for actions completed in the past (we *saw*), and the future tense for actions that will occur in the future (we *will see*). When you write about a remembered event, you will often need to use various forms of the past tense: the past perfect to indicate an action that was completed at the time of another past action (she *had finished* her work when we saw her) and the past progressive to indicate a continuing action in the past (she *was finishing* her work). One common problem in writing about a remembered event is the failure to use the past perfect when it is needed. For example:

For practice, go to bedfordstmartins.com/theguide/verbs

▶ **I had three people in the car, something my father had told me not to do on several occasions.**

In the following sentence, the meaning is not clear without the past perfect:

▶ **Coach Kernow told me I ~~ran~~ had run faster than ever before.**

A Common ESL Problem. It is important to remember that the past perfect is formed with *had* followed by a past participle. Past participles usually end in *-ed, -d, -en, -n,* or *-t: worked, hoped, eaten, taken, bent.*

For practice, go to bedfordstmartins.com/theguide/everb

▶ **Before Tania went to Moscow last year, she had not really ~~speak~~ spoken Russian.**

A WRITER AT WORK

FROM INVENTION TO DRAFT TO REVISION

In this section, we look at the writing process that Jean Brandt follows in composing her essay, "Calling Home." You will see some of her invention writing and her complete first draft, which you can then compare to the final draft printed on pp. 44–47.

Invention

Brandt's invention work produced about nine pages, but it took her only two hours, spread out over four days, to complete. Here is a selection of her invention writings. She begins by choosing an event and then recalling specific sensory details of the scene and the other people involved. She writes two dialogues, one with her sister Sue and the other with her father. Following is the dialogue between her and her sister:

Re-Creating Conversations

SUE: Jean, why did you do it?

ME: I don't know. I guess I didn't want to wait in that long line. Sue, what am I going to tell Mom and Dad?

SUE: Don't worry about that yet, the detective might not really call the police.

ME: I can't believe I was stupid enough to take it.

SUE: I know. I've been there before. Now when he comes back, try crying and acting like you're really upset. Tell him how sorry you are and that it was the first time you ever stole something, but make sure you cry. It got me off the hook once.

ME: I don't think I can force myself to cry. I'm not really that upset. I don't think the shock's worn off. I'm more worried about Mom.

SUE: Who knows? Maybe she won't have to find out.

ME: God, I hope not. Hey, where's Louie and Grandma? Grandma doesn't know about this, does she?

SUE: No, I sort of told Lou what was going on so he's just taking Grandma around shopping.

ME: Isn't she wondering where we are?

SUE: I told him to tell her we would meet them in an hour.

ME: How am I ever going to face her? Mom and Dad might possibly understand or at least get over it, but Grandma? This is gonna kill her.

SUE: Don't worry about that right now. Here comes the detective. Now try to look like you're sorry. Try to cry.

This dialogue helps Brandt to recall an important conversation with her sister. Dialogues are an especially useful form of invention, for they enable writers to remember their feelings and thoughts.

Brandt writes this dialogue quickly, trying to capture the language of excited talk, keeping the exchanges brief. She includes a version of this dialogue in her first revision but excludes it from the final essay printed earlier in this chapter (pp. 44–47). The dialogue with her father does not appear in any of her drafts. Even though she eventually decides to feature other completely different conversations, these invention dialogues enable her to evaluate how various conversations would work in her essay.

Next, Brandt makes her first attempt to bring the autobiographical significance of the event into focus. She explores her remembered as well as her current feelings and thoughts about the experience:

> Being arrested for shoplifting was significant because it changed some of my basic attitudes. Since that night I've never again considered stealing anything. This event would reveal how my attitude toward the law and other people has changed from disrespectful to very respectful.

Brandt begins by stating tentatively that the importance of the event was the lesson it taught her. Reading this statement might lead us to expect a moralistic story of how someone learned something the hard way. As we look at the subsequent invention activities and watch the draft develop, however, we will see how her focus shifts to her relations with other people.

Recalling Remembered Feelings and Thoughts

> I was scared, humiliated, and confused. I was terrified when I realized what was happening. I can still see the manager and his badge and remember what I felt when I knew who he was. I just couldn't believe it. I didn't want to run. I felt there wasn't anything I could do--I was afraid, embarrassed, worried, mad that it happened. I didn't show my feelings at all. I tried to look very calm on the outside, but inside I was extremely nervous. The nervousness might have come through in my voice a little. I wanted the people around me to think I was tough and that I could handle the situation. I was really

disappointed with myself. Getting arrested made me realize how wrong my actions were. I felt very ashamed. Afterward I had to talk to my father about it. I didn't say much of anything except that I was wrong and I was sorry. The immediate consequence was being taken to jail and then later having to call my parents and tell them what happened. I hated to call my parents. That was the hardest part. I remember how much I dreaded that. My mom was really hurt.

Brandt's exploration of her first reaction is quite successful. Naming specific feelings, she focuses on the difference between what she felt and how she acted. She remembers her humiliation at being arrested as well as the terrible moment when she had to tell her parents. As we will see, this concern with her parents' reaction, more than her own humiliation, becomes the focus of her remembered feelings and thoughts.

In exploring her first response to the event, Brandt writes quickly, jotting down memories as they come to mind. Next, she rereads this first exploration and attempts to state briefly what the incident really reveals about her:

I think it reveals that I was not a hard-core criminal. I was trying to live up to Robin Files's (supposedly my best girlfriend) expectations, even though I actually knew that what I was doing was wrong.

Stopping to focus her thoughts like this helps Brandt see the point of what she has just written in her longer pieces of exploratory writing. Specifically, it helps her connect diverse invention writings to her main concern: discovering the autobiographical significance of the event. She reflects on what her remembered feelings of the event reveal about the kind of person she was at the time: not a hard-core criminal. She identifies a friend, who will disappear from the writing after one brief mention. Next, she looks at her present perspective on the event.

Exploring Present Perspectives

At first I was ashamed to tell anyone that I had been arrested. It was as if I couldn't admit it myself. Now I'm glad it happened, because who knows where I'd be now if I hadn't been caught. I still don't tell many people about it. Never before have I written about it. I think my response was appropriate. If I'd broken down and cried, it wouldn't have helped me any, so it's better that I reacted calmly. My actions and responses show that I was trying to be tough. I thought that that was the way to gain respectability. If I were to get arrested now (of course it wouldn't be for shoplifting), I think I'd react the same way because it doesn't do any good to get emotional. My current feelings are ones of appreciation. I feel lucky because I was set straight early. Now I can look back on it and laugh, but at the same time know how serious it was. I am emotionally distant now because I can view the event objectively rather than subjectively. My feelings are settled now. I don't get upset thinking about it. I don't feel angry at the manager or the police. I think I was more upset about my parents than about what was happening to me. After the first part of it was over I mainly worried about what my parents would think.

By writing about her present perspective, Brandt reassures herself that she feels comfortable enough to write for class about this event. Having achieved a degree of emotional distance, she no longer feels humiliated, embarrassed, or angry. Reassessing her reaction at the time, she is obviously pleased to recall that she did not lose control and show her true feelings. Staying calm, not getting emotional, looking tough—these are the personal qualities Brandt wants others to see in her. Exploring her present perspective seems to have led to a new, respectable self-image she can proudly display to her readers:

My present perspective shows that I'm a reasonable person. I can admit when I'm wrong and accept the punishment that was due me. I find that I can be concerned about others even when I'm in trouble.

Next, Brandt reflects on what she has written to express the meaning of the event for her.

Defining the Event's Autobiographical Significance

The event was important because it entirely changed one aspect of my character. I will be disclosing that I was once a thief, and I think many of my readers will be able to identify with my story, even though they won't admit it.

After the first set of invention work, completed in about forty-five minutes on two separate days, Brandt is confident she has chosen an event with personal significance. She knows what she will be disclosing about herself and feels comfortable doing it. In her brief focusing statements she begins by moralizing ("my attitude . . . changed") and blaming others ("Robin Files") but concludes by acknowledging what she did. She is now prepared to disclose it to readers ("I was once a thief"). Also, she thinks readers will like her story because she suspects many of them will recall doing something illegal and feeling guilty about it, even if they never got caught.

The First Draft

The day after completing the invention writing, Brandt reviews her invention and composes her first draft on a word processor. It takes her about an hour to write the draft, and she writes steadily without doing a lot of rearranging or correcting of obvious typos and grammatical errors. She knows this will not be her only draft.

Before you read Brandt's first draft, reread the final draft, "Calling Home," in the Readings section of this chapter (p. 44). Then, as you read the first draft, consider what part it plays in the total writing process.

It was two days before Christmas and my older sister and brother, my grandmother, and I were rushing around doing last-minute shopping. After going to a few stores we decided to go to Lakewood Center shopping mall. It was packed with other frantic shoppers like ourselves from one end to the other. The first store we went to (the first and last for me) was the General Store. The General Store is your typical gift shop. They mainly have the cutesy knick-knacks, posters, frames and that sort. The store is decorated to resemble an old-time western general store but the appearance doesn't quite come off. 1

We were all browsing around and I saw a basket of buttons so I went to see what the different ones were. One of the first ones I noticed was a Snoopy button. I'm not sure what it said on it, something funny I'm sure and besides I was in love with anything Snoopy when I was 13. I took it out of the basket and showed it to my sister and she said "Why don't you buy it?" I thought about it but the lines at the cashiers were outrageous and I didn't think it was worth it for a 75 cent item. Instead I figured just take it and I did. I thought I was so sly about it. I casually slipped it into my pocket and assumed I was home free since no one pounced on me. Everyone was ready to leave this shop so we made our way through the crowds to the entrance. 2

My grandmother and sister were ahead of my brother and I. They were almost to the entrance of May Co. and we were about 5 to 10 yards behind when I felt this tap on my shoulder. I turned around already terror struck, and this man was flashing some kind of badge in my face. It happened so fast I didn't know what was going on. Louie finally noticed I wasn't with him and came back for me. Jack explained I was being arrested for shoplifting and if my parents were here then Louie should go find them. Louie ran to get Susie and told 3 her about it but kept it from Grandma. By the time Sue got back to the General Store I was in the back office and Jack was calling the police. I was a little scared but not really. It was sort of exciting. My sister was telling me to try and cry but I couldn't. About 20 minutes later two cops came and handcuffed me, led me through the mall outside to the police car. I was kind of embarrassed when they took me through the mall in front of all those people.

When they got me in the car they began questioning me, while driving me to the police station. Questions just to fill out the report--age, sex, address, color of eyes, etc. 4

Then when they were finished they began talking about Jack and what a nuisance he was. I gathered that Jack had every single person who shoplifted, no matter what their age, arrested. The police were getting really fed up with it because it was a nuisance for them to have to come way out to the mall for something as petty as that. To hear the police talk about my "crime" that way felt good because it was like what I did wasn't really so bad. It made me feel a bit relieved. When we walked into the station I remember the desk sergeant joking with the arresting officers about "well we got another one of Jack's hardened criminals." Again, I felt my crime lacked any seriousness at all. Next they handcuffed me to a table and questioned me further and then I had to phone my mom. That was the worst. I never was so humiliated in my life. Hearing the disappointment in her voice was worse punishment than the cops could ever give me. 5

Brandt's first draft establishes the main sequence of actions. About a third of it is devoted to the store manager, an emphasis that disappears by the final draft. What ends up having prominence in the final draft—Brandt's feelings about telling her parents and her conversations with them—appears here only in a few lines at the very end. But mentioning the interaction suggests its eventual importance, and we are reminded of its prominence in Brandt's invention writing.

Brandt revises this first draft for another student to read critically. In this revised draft, she includes dialogues with her sister and with the police officers. She also provides more information about her actions as she considered buying the Snoopy button and then decided to steal it instead. She includes visual details of the manager's office. This draft is not much different in emphasis from the first draft, however, and still ends with a long section about the police officers and the station. The parents are mentioned briefly only at the very end.

The reader tells Brandt how much he likes her story and admires her frankness. However, he does not encourage her to develop the dramatic possibilities in calling her parents and meeting them afterward. In fact, he encourages her to keep the dialogue with the police officers about the manager and to include what the manager said to the police.

Brandt's final revision shows that she does not take her reader's advice. She reduces the role of the police officers, eliminating any dialogue with them. She greatly expands the role of her parents: The last third of the essay is now focused on her remembered feelings about calling them and seeing them afterward. In terms of dramatic importance, the phone call home now equals the arrest. When we recall Brandt's earliest invention writings, we can see that she was headed toward this conclusion all along, but she needed invention, a first draft with many changes and refinement, a critical reading, and about two weeks to get there.

DESIGNING YOUR WORK

As the student and rancher were working on the text of the local history project described earlier in this chapter (see p. 26), they considered design elements appropriate to writing about remembered events, including black-and-white and color photographs, other memorabilia, and quotations from the rancher's tape-recorded story.

Selecting Visuals

To begin, they discussed what visuals might accompany the final written piece and how photographs could enhance the telling of the rancher's story. The student found old snow-day photographs from the local newspaper's archives, and the rancher selected a family photograph taken the spring following the great snowstorm of 1938. As alternatives to these visuals, the student and the rancher also considered including a painting of an isolated homestead and an early snapshot that the rancher had taken of his house in 1941. For their final product, they narrowed their selections to pictures that gave readers the strongest basis for becoming involved in and imagining the rancher's story. They decided that black-and-white photographs would

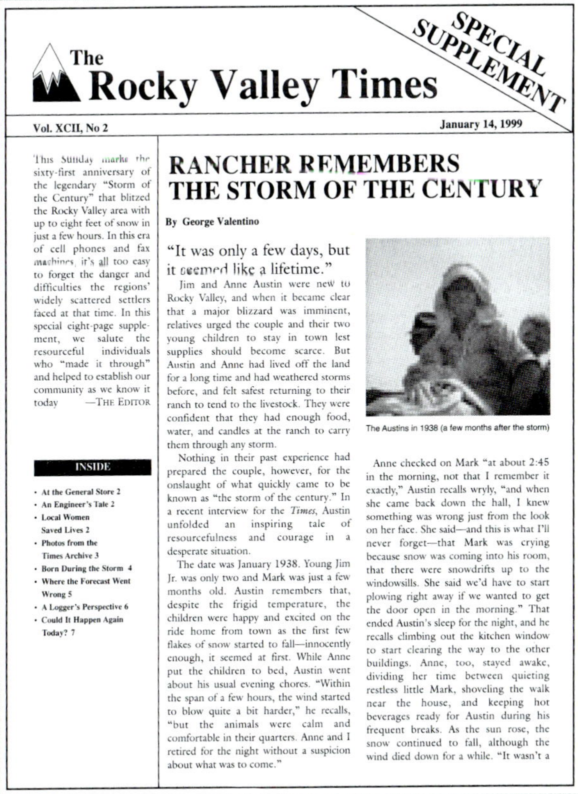

The Rocky Valley Times

SPECIAL SUPPLEMENT

Vol. XCII, No 2 — January 14, 1999

This Sunday marks the sixty-first anniversary of the legendary "Storm of the Century" that blitzed the Rocky Valley area with up to eight feet of snow in just a few hours. In this era of cell phones and fax machines, it's all too easy to forget the danger and difficulties the regions' widely scattered settlers faced at that time. In this special eight-page supplement, we salute the resourceful individuals who "made it through" and helped to establish our community as we know it today —THE EDITOR

INSIDE

- At the General Store 2
- An Engineer's Tale 2
- Local Women Saved Lives 2
- Photos from the Times Archive 3
- Born During the Storm 4
- Where the Forecast Went Wrong 5
- A Logger's Perspective 6
- Could It Happen Again Today? 7

RANCHER REMEMBERS THE STORM OF THE CENTURY

By George Valentino

"It was only a few days, but it seemed like a lifetime."

Jim and Anne Austin were new to Rocky Valley, and when it became clear that a major blizzard was imminent, relatives urged the couple and their two young children to stay in town lest supplies should become scarce. But Austin and Anne had lived off the land for a long time and had weathered storms before, and felt safest returning to their ranch to tend to the livestock. They were confident that they had enough food, water, and candles at the ranch to carry them through any storm.

Nothing in their past experience had prepared the couple, however, for the onslaught of what quickly came to be known as "the storm of the century." In a recent interview for the *Times*, Austin unfolded an inspiring tale of resourcefulness and courage in a desperate situation.

The date was January 1938. Young Jim Jr. was only two and Mark was just a few months old. Austin remembers that, despite the frigid temperature, the children were happy and excited on the ride home from town as the first few flakes of snow started to fall—innocently enough, it seemed at first. While Anne put the children to bed, Austin went about his usual evening chores. "Within the span of a few hours, the wind started to blow quite a bit harder," he recalls, "but the animals were calm and comfortable in their quarters. Anne and I retired for the night without a suspicion about what was to come."

The Austins in 1938 (a few months after the storm)

Anne checked on Mark "at about 2:45 in the morning, not that I remember it exactly," Austin recalls wryly, "and when she came back down the hall, I knew something was wrong just from the look on her face. She said—and this is what I'll never forget—that Mark was crying because snow was coming into his room, that there were snowdrifts up to the windowsills. She said we'd have to start plowing right away if we wanted to get the door open in the morning." That ended Austin's sleep for the night, and he recalls climbing out the kitchen window to start clearing the way to the other buildings. Anne, too, stayed awake, dividing her time between quieting restless little Mark, shoveling the walk near the house, and keeping hot beverages ready for Austin during his frequent breaks. As the sun rose, the snow continued to fall, although the wind died down for a while. "It wasn't a best emphasize that the event took place in a time and place without modern conveniences. In choosing the pictures of the dramatic snowstorm and the rancher's family, the student writer and the rancher hoped to show readers the central idea of the story—the importance of community in the face of adversity.

Remember that visuals do not have to be photographs, drawings, or graphics but may also be any objects that can be connected to the remembered event being described. The rancher and the student also might have included a previously published copy of the weather forecast from the day of the storm or a schedule for the train that ran through the rancher's town.

Pulling Revealing Quotations

Chapter 22, Using and Acknowledging Sources, offers guidelines on selecting quotations for research essays.

After reviewing what they had written, the student and the rancher recommended to the newspaper two quotes from the story to highlight. They wanted to pull short passages that would capture readers' attention and convey some of the story's drama. The idea was not to summarize the rancher's story in these quotes but to emphasize to readers the significance of the event as well as to leave readers with a good understanding of the event as they finished reading the piece.

THINKING CRITICALLY ABOUT WHAT YOU HAVE LEARNED

Now that you have worked extensively in autobiography—reading it, talking about it, writing it—take some time to reflect on what you have learned: What problems did you have while you were writing, and how did you solve them? How did reading about events in other people's lives help you write about a remembered event in your own life? Finally, you might stop to think critically about autobiography as a genre of writing: How does it influence the way we think about ourselves?

Reflecting on Your Writing

Write a page or so telling your instructor about a problem you encountered in writing your essay and how you solved it. Before you begin, gather all of your writing—invention and planning notes, outlines, drafts, critical comments, revision plans, and final revision. Review these materials as you complete this writing task.

1. ***Identify one problem you needed to solve as you wrote about a remembered event.*** Do not be concerned with grammar and punctuation; concentrate on problems unique to writing a story about your experience. For example: Did you puzzle over how to present a particular place or person? Was it difficult to structure the narrative so it held readers' interest? Did you find it hard (or uncomfortable) to convey the event's autobiographical significance?

2. ***Determine how you came to recognize the problem.*** When did you first discover it? What called it to your attention? Did you notice it yourself, or did another reader point it out? Can you now see hints of it in your invention writing, your planning notes, or an earlier draft? If so, where specifically?
3. ***Reflect on how you went about solving the problem.*** Did you work on a particular passage, cut or add details, or reorganize the essay? Did you reread one of the essays in the chapter to see how another writer handled similar material? Did you look back at the invention guidelines? Did you discuss the problem with another student, a tutor, or your instructor? If so, how did talking about it help, and how useful was the advice you got?
4. ***Write a brief explanation of the problem and your solution.*** Be as specific as possible in reconstructing your efforts. Quote from your invention notes or early drafts, from readers' comments, from your revision plan, and from your final revision to show the various changes your writing underwent as you worked to solve the problem. Taking the time now to think about how you recognized and solved a real writing problem will help you become more aware of what works and does not work, making you a more confident writer.

Reviewing What You Learned from Reading

Write a page or so explaining to your instructor how the readings in this chapter influenced your final draft. Your own essay about a remembered event has no doubt been influenced by the essays you have read in this chapter. These readings may have helped you decide which of your own experiences would seem significant to your readers, or they may have given you ideas about how to evoke a vivid sense of place or how to convey your feelings about the event. Before you start writing, take some time to reflect on what you have learned from the four reading selections.

1. ***Reread the final revision of your essay; then review the selections you read before completing your own essay, looking for specific influences.*** If you were impressed, for example, with the way one of the readings described a place, used dialogue, dramatized the action, or conveyed autobiographical significance, look to see where you might have been striving for similar effects in your own essay. Look also for ideas you got from your reading: writing strategies you were inspired to try, specific details you were led to include, effects you sought to achieve.
2. ***Write a page or so explaining these influences.*** Did a single reading selection influence you, or were you influenced by several selections? Quote from the selections and your final revision to show how your essay was influenced by the other essays. If, in reviewing the selections, you have found another way to improve your own essay, indicate briefly what you would change and which of the selections inspired the change.

Considering the Social Dimensions of Essays about Remembered Events

Writing about events that have special significance for you can lead you to recognize personal strengths and weaknesses and to clarify your beliefs and values. At the same time, reading others' autobiographical writing can help forge connections between you and other people. Another person's life often reflects our own experience, enabling us to identify and empathize. Just as often, however, another person's life does not resemble ours, and we learn that people can have radically different experiences, even within the same society. Although reading about other people's lives may not completely bridge these differences, it can help us better understand one another and the circumstances affecting all of us. (Wolff's experience, for example, gives us insight into how the American myth of the cowboy has defined manliness partly in terms of guns and power.) Likewise, striving as writers to forge connections with other people is important, but so is respecting and acknowledging the differences.

These ideas about autobiographical writing lead to some basic questions about how we understand ourselves and our relationships with others.

Autobiography and Self-Discovery. If autobiography leads to self-discovery, what do we mean by the "self"? Should we think of the self as our "true" essence or as the different roles we play in different situations?

If we accept the idea of an essential self, autobiographical writing helps us in the search to discover who we truly are. Given this idea of the self, we might see Tobias Wolff, for example, as searching to understand whether he is the kind of person who shoots squirrels or the kind of person who cries over dead animals. If, on the other hand, we accept the idea that the various roles we play are what create the self, then autobiographical writing allows us to reveal the many sides of our personalities. This view of the self assumes that we present different self-images to different people in different situations. Given this idea, we might see Wolff as presenting his sympathetic side to his mother but keeping his aggressive, "manly" side hidden from her.

1. ***Consider how your remembered-event essay might be considered an exercise in self-discovery.*** Planning and writing your essay, did you see yourself as discovering your true self or examining how you reacted in a particular situation? Do you think your essay reveals your single, essential, true self, or does it show only one aspect of the person you understand yourself to be?
2. ***Write a page or so explaining your ideas about self-discovery and truth in remembered-event essays.*** Connect your ideas to your own essay and to the readings in this chapter.

Ways of Interpreting Our Experience. How might we interpret autobiography? Should we view it psychologically, in terms of personal feelings, relationships, conflicts, and desires, or more publicly, in terms of the social, political, and cultural conditions of our lives? You can understand these different perspectives by applying them to the selections in this chapter. Wolff's essay, for example, could be seen in psychological terms as the story of an adolescent boy trying to assert his manhood. Or it could be seen in political terms as a critique of power and war. Brandt's essay could be interpreted psychologically, either in terms of her childish desire to have what she wants when she wants it, or socially in terms of her relationship with her mother.

1. ***Consider how you have generally interpreted other people's essays about remembered events.*** Have you understood the essays primarily in personal, psychological terms? Or in social or possibly political terms? Or in some of both? When you read Annie Dillard's essay, for example, you may have wondered why she thought of the man who chased her as "sainted"? If you interpreted Dillard's essay in psychological terms, you may have thought that the man represented a father figure, or even a Christ figure, someone who would make great sacrifices to teach her an important lesson. If, on the other hand, you tended to interpret the essay in social terms, perhaps you noted that the young Dillard preferred to play with boys rather than with girls. Or you may have noticed a socioeconomic or ethnic bias in Dillard's distinction between the "polite blond" Fahey brothers who lived on her street and the boys who lived "across Reynolds," who she describes as *dark, furious, skinny,* and *knowing.* She makes the point that her parents "approved" of the polite boys, but she lets us imagine what they thought of the others.
2. ***Reflect on whether you adopted a primarily psychological or primarily social perspective when you were writing about your own life.*** How did you think about your experience? Did you see yourself as being motivated more by personal needs or fears, or by external forces?
3. ***Write a page or two about whether you find yourself interpreting autobiography more psychologically or more socially.*** Neither is preferred over the other; they are simply quite different perspectives. Try to connect your ideas to readings in the chapter and to your experience writing your essay. What do you think we gain or lose by looking at experience in these different ways?

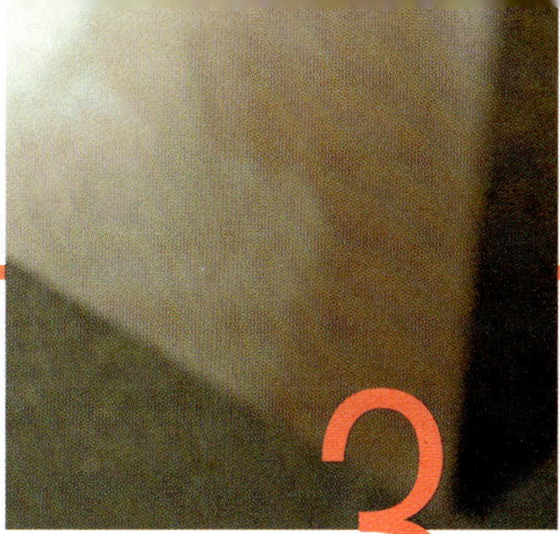

3 *Remembering People*

When you describe someone who played an important role in your life, you very likely have two aims: to portray the person vividly so that readers can imagine what he or she was like and to give readers insight into the person's significance in your life. To give readers a vivid impression of the person, you need to describe the person's physical appearance, mannerisms, ways of speaking, and typical behavior toward you and others. To convey the person's significance in your life, you need to relate specific anecdotes that illustrate the person's character and reveal the nature of your relationship.

A temptation in writing about others is to oversimplify, to remember only the very best or the very worst about people. Consequently, when you search your memory for descriptive details and illustrative anecdotes, you should strive to portray your subject as a complex individual with both shortcomings and strengths. As you do so, you may discover qualities in the person you had overlooked and better understand your own contribution to the relationship.

You will encounter writing about a remembered person in many different contexts, as the following examples suggest.

Writing in Your Other Courses

- For an education class, a student writes about an unusually effective high school literature teacher. He describes the teacher as so enthusiastic about her teaching and about literature that she is able to win over even the most resistant students. To show how the teacher inspires her students, he relates what happened when the class compared key scenes in two film versions of *Romeo and Juliet* and then staged its own versions of the same scenes from the printed text of the play.
- For a history paper on immigration, a student interviews her grandfather and then writes an essay about his experience coming to the United States as a young boy. She begins by describing the major waves of Eastern European immigration during the late nineteenth and early twentieth centuries. Then she relates several anecdotes her grandfather told her. One anecdote tells how her grandfather, who attended school and learned English, had to act as an interpreter for his mother

when he got in trouble at school. Another anecdote illustrates the family tensions caused by the grandfather's efforts to assimilate and hide his ethnic roots by simplifying the spelling of the family name. She concludes with the observation that recent immigrants from places around the world face many of the same problems her grandfather did nearly a century earlier.

Writing in the Community

- As part of a community service project, a student volunteers to help an eighty-year-old man write an essay about his grandfather for his grandchildren who live in another state. The student tape-records the man's stories and later transcribes them on the computer. He also uses a computer scanner to create images of old photographs and war medals. At a later visit, the two of them work together to organize and revise the essay, which they decide to put up on the student's homepage so that the grandchildren can access it.
- For a branch library display about residents who have helped shape the neighborhood, a volunteer helps a woman write about a diner owner she used to work for as a waitress. In a meeting with the woman, he takes notes as she tells him about the diner and about what was memorable about the owner. He later uses her remembrances to write a description of the restaurant as a popular gathering place for high school kids, a place where the woman used to hang out with friends before getting a job there. The writer includes several anecdotes to show that the owner was a tyrant to kids he did not like but a friend and mentor to those he did like, including the woman who worked for him when she was in high school.

For more details on the decisions that these writers made about document design, see pp. 131–32.

Writing in the Workplace

- Invited to contribute an article on someone who influenced her career to a theater program, the lead actor in the play decides to write about her high school drama teacher. She focuses the essay on her first encounters with the teacher, who had a reputation for being brilliant but harsh. She tells what happened when she tried out for her first role, got the part, and then struggled with the teacher, who she thought was squelching her talent. Only after opening night did she realize how much she had learned from the drama instructor.
- For their manager's retirement celebration, several employees write brief essays about their most memorable experiences working with her. One male employee writes about the difficulties he had when he first started working for her, explaining that he had never worked for a woman before. He writes humorously about what happened and how she quickly helped him fit in.

Practice Remembering a Person: A Collaborative Activity

The preceding scenarios suggest some occasions for writing about a remembered person. Think of someone important in your life, someone you would feel comfortable describing to your classmates. The only requirements are that you remember the person well enough to write a description and that your relationship with the person seems important to you now as you look back on it. Your instructor may schedule this collaborative activity as a face-to-face in-class discussion or may ask you to conduct an online real-time discussion in a chatroom. Whatever the medium, here are some guidelines to follow:

Part 1. Consider the possibilities and choose a person. Then make notes about what you could say in only a few minutes to give others a sense of what this person was like and why your relationship was important.

Now get together with two or three other students, and take turns presenting the person you have chosen. Each of you should take just three or four minutes to present your person.

Part 2. As a group, spend ten to fifteen minutes discussing what happened when you presented a remembered person:

- Take turns telling each other what impression you wanted your classmates to get of the person and of your relationship with the person. Then see whether group members got those impressions or different ones.
- Review the kinds of details, events, and other memories each of you decided to include in your brief presentation.
- Conclude by reflecting on what each of you sees as the easiest part and the hardest part of presenting a remembered person—and why

READINGS

No two essays remembering a person are alike, and yet they share defining features. Together, the four readings in this chapter reveal a number of the possibilities, so you will want to read as many of them as possible. If time permits, complete the activities in the Analyzing Writing Strategies section that follows each selection, and read the Commentary. Following the readings is a section called Basic Features: Remembering People (p. 106), which offers a concise summary of the features and strategies commonly used in writing about remembered people and provides examples from the four readings.

***Maya Angelou** is a Renaissance woman: poet, autobiographer, essayist, newspaper editor, director, actor, singer, dancer, and more. She has taught at several universities, including UCLA and the University of Kansas, and is currently the Reynolds Professor of American Studies at Wake Forest University. Nominated for Emmy Awards in acting and screenwriting as well as a Pulitzer Prize and a National Book Award, Angelou has written and produced several television documentaries, including* Afro-Americans in the Arts, *an award-winning PBS special. She also served as the northern coordinator of the Southern Christian Leadership Conference, the civil rights organization led by Martin Luther King Jr., and has served on several presidential commissions.*

The author of many books, she has written five volumes of poetry, including The Complete Collected Poems of Maya Angelou *(1994); two children's books, most recently* Even the Stars Look Lonesome *(1997); two books of essays, including* Wouldn't Take Nothing for My Journey Now *(1993); and a series of six autobiographies, beginning with the National Book Award nominee* I Know Why the Caged Bird Sings *(1970) and ending with her most recent work,* A Song Flung Up to Heaven *(2002). In an interview, Angelou offered this advice to young writers: "I'll tell you my secret about writing and my encouragement to young men and women: READ. If you want to write, read."*

Angelou grew up during the 1930s in the small Arkansas town of Stamps, where she lived with her brother Bailey; her grandmother, the "Momma" mentioned in this selection; and her Uncle Willie. Momma and Willie operated a small grocery store. In this selection, from I Know Why the Caged Bird Sings *(1969), Angelou writes about her childhood memories of her uncle from her perspective as an adult of forty. As you read, notice how she describes him and tells brief stories about him to reveal their relationship.*

Uncle Willie

Maya Angelou

When Bailey was six and I a year younger, we used to rattle off the times tables with the speed I was later to see Chinese children in San Francisco employ on their abacuses. Our summer-gray pot-bellied stove bloomed rosy red during winter, and became a severe disciplinarian threat if we were so foolish as to indulge in making mistakes. 1

Uncle Willie used to sit, like a giant black Z (he had been crippled as a child), and hear us testify to the Lafayette County Training Schools' abilities. His face pulled down on the left side, as if a pulley had been attached to his lower teeth, and his left hand was only a mite bigger than Bailey's, but on the second mistake or on the third hesitation his big overgrown right hand would catch one of us behind the collar, and in the same moment would thrust the culprit toward the dull red heater, which throbbed like a devil's toothache. We were never burned, although once I might have been when I was so terrified I tried to jump onto the stove to remove the possibility of its remaining a threat. Like most children, I thought if I could face the worst danger voluntarily, and triumph, I would forever have power over it. But in my case of sacrificial effort I was thwarted. Uncle Willie held tight to my dress and I only got close enough to smell the clean dry scent of hot iron. We learned the times tables without understanding their grand principle, simply because we had the capacity and no alternative. 2

The tragedy of lameness seems so unfair to children that they are embarrassed in 3
its presence. And they, most recently off nature's mold, sense that they have only narrowly missed being another of her jokes. In relief at the narrow escape, they vent their emotions in impatience and criticism of the unlucky cripple.

Momma related times without end, and without any show of emotion, how Uncle 4
Willie had been dropped when he was three years old by a woman who was minding him. She seemed to hold no rancor against the baby-sitter, nor for her just God who allowed the accident. She felt it necessary to explain over and over again to those who knew the story by heart that he wasn't "born that way."

In our society, where two-legged, two-armed strong Black men were able at best to 5
eke out only the necessities of life, Uncle Willie, with his starched shirts, shined shoes and shelves full of food, was the whipping boy and butt of jokes of the underemployed and underpaid. Fate not only disabled him but laid a double-tiered barrier in his path. He was also proud and sensitive. Therefore he couldn't pretend that he wasn't crippled, nor could he deceive himself that people were not repelled by his defect.

Only once in all the years of trying not to watch him, I saw him pretend to himself 6
and others that he wasn't lame.

Coming home from school one day, I saw a dark car in our front yard. I rushed in to 7
find a strange man and woman (Uncle Willie said later they were school teachers from Little Rock) drinking Dr. Pepper in the cool of the Store. I sensed a wrongness around me, like an alarm clock that had gone off without being set.

I knew it couldn't be the strangers. Not frequently, but often enough, travelers pulled 8
off the main road to buy tobacco or soft drinks in the only Negro store in Stamps. When I looked at Uncle Willie, I knew what was pulling my mind's coattails. He was standing erect behind the counter, not leaning forward or resting on the small shelf that had been built for him. Erect. His eyes seemed to hold me with a mixture of threats and appeal.

I dutifully greeted the strangers and roamed my eyes around for his walking 9
stick. It was nowhere to be seen. He said, "Uh . . . this this . . . this . . . uh, my niece. She's . . . uh . . . just come from school." Then to the couple—"You know . . . how, uh, children are . . . th-th-these days . . . they play all d-d-day at school and c-c-can't wait to get home and pl-play some more."

The people smiled, very friendly. 10

He added, "Go on out and pl-play, Sister." 11

The lady laughed in a soft Arkansas voice and said, "Well, you know, Mr. Johnson, 12
they say, you're only a child once. Have you children of your own?"

Uncle Willie looked at me with an impatience I hadn't seen in his face even when 13
he took thirty minutes to loop the laces over his high-topped shoes. "I . . . I thought I told you to go . . . go outside and play."

Before I left I saw him lean back on the shelves of Garret Snuff, Prince Albert and 14
Spark Plug chewing tobacco.

"No, ma'am . . . no ch-children and no wife." He tried a laugh. "I have an old 15
m-m-mother and my brother's t-two children to l-look after."

I didn't mind his using us to make himself look good. In fact, I would have pre- 16
tended to be his daughter if he wanted me to. Not only did I not feel any loyalty to my

own father, I figured that if I had been Uncle Willie's child I would have received much better treatment.

17 The couple left after a few minutes, and from the back of the house I watched the red car scare chickens, raise dust and disappear toward Magnolia.

18 Uncle Willie was making his own way down the long shadowed aisle between the shelves and the counter—hand over hand, like a man climbing out of a dream. I stayed quiet and watched him lurch from one side, bumping to the other, until he reached the coal-oil tank. He put his hand behind that dark recess and took his cane in the strong fist and shifted his weight on the wooden support. He thought he had pulled it off.

19 I'll never know why it was important to him that the couple (he said later that he'd never seen them before) would take a picture of a whole Mr. Johnson back to Little Rock.

20 He must have tired of being crippled, as prisoners tire of penitentiary bars and the guilty tire of blame. The high-topped shoes and the cane, his uncontrollable muscles and thick tongue, and the looks he suffered of either contempt or pity had simply worn him out, and for one afternoon, one part of an afternoon, he wanted no part of them.

21 I understood and felt closer to him at that moment than ever before or since.

Connecting to Culture and Experience: Self-Image

Angelou concludes her essay with an anecdote about the one time she saw Uncle Willie "pretend to himself and others that he wasn't lame" (paragraph 6). According to Angelou, Uncle Willie not only presented a different image of himself to the visiting strangers but also pretended to himself that he was different. Uncle Willie's actions suggest the possibility that when people present different images of themselves to others, these images can also influence how they see themselves.

Explore this possibility with other students in your class. Begin by telling each other about an occasion when you tried to project a different image of yourself—such as when you moved to a new neighborhood or city, started out in a new school, logged on to an Internet chatroom, or tried out for a new job or a team. The image you presented may have been only a little different, or it may have been radically different. In what ways did you act differently? How did people respond to you? How did acting differently or receiving different responses from others make you feel about yourself?

Analyzing Writing Strategies

1. At the beginning of this chapter, we make several generalizations about writing about remembered people. Consider which of these assertions are true of Angelou's essay:
   - It focuses on a person with whom the writer had a significant, rather than casual, relationship.

- It tries to convey the person's significance without oversimplifying or sentimentalizing.
- It vividly describes the person's appearance, mannerisms, ways of speaking, and typical behavior.
- It relates specific anecdotes that reveal important aspects of the person and of his or her relationship to the writer.

2. **Dialogue** is a key element in many essays about remembered people. To see how Angelou uses dialogue to give readers an understanding of Uncle Willie, reread paragraphs 9–15. Reflect on the importance of dialogue in the reading. What does it enable you to learn about Uncle Willie and about Angelou's feelings toward him?

For more on dialogue, see Chapter 14, pp. 635–36.

Commentary: A Vivid Portrait

Angelou presents a vivid portrait of Uncle Willie by using three **describing strategies**: naming, detailing, and comparing. Notice, for example, how this bit of description from paragraph 2 incorporates all three strategies:

For more on describing strategies, see Chapter 15, p. 643.

> Uncle Willie used to sit, *like a giant black Z* (he had been crippled as a child), and hear us testify to the Lafayette County Training Schools' abilities. His **face** pulled down on the left side, *as if a pulley had been attached to his lower teeth,* and his left **hand** was *only a mite bigger than Bailey's,* but on the second mistake or on the third hesitation his big overgrown right **hand** would catch one of us behind the collar, and in the same moment would thrust the culprit toward the dull red **heater**, which *throbbed like a devil's toothache.*

Angelou uses naming (shown here in **bold** type) to point to some notable features of Uncle Willie's appearance (his face and hands) as well as to an object in the room (the heater) that looms large in her memory. Detailing (underlined in the passage) combines with naming to particularize the description, to make it apply only to this one person, her uncle. The details identify what distinguishes Uncle Willie's face and hands: His face looks lopsided, and his hands are of unequal size. This combination of naming and detailing gives readers a vivid and memorable picture of Uncle Willie.

The third describing strategy—comparing (indicated by *italics* in the passage)—adds another important dimension to the picture. Angelou uses comparing, for example, when she describes her uncle's body as shaped "like a giant black Z." The comparison used here is a simile, an explicit comparison announced by the word *like* or *as*. Angelou also uses a metaphor, an indirect comparison, when she calls herself a "culprit" for making a math mistake. Skilled writers like Angelou employ similes and metaphors not to decorate their writing but to create vivid images that enable readers to understand the writer's feelings. The simile describing the heater throbbing "like a devil's toothache" associates Uncle Willie with the devil, an association that adds to the impression of him as all-powerful and threatening.

To create a vivid portrait, Angelou also uses an important narrating strategy—**specific narrative action**. Narrative action uses active verbs and modifying phrases

For more on specific narrative action, see Chapter 14, pp. 633–34.

and clauses to show a person's movements and gestures. Here is an example with the actions underlined:

> Uncle Willie was making his own way down the long shadowed aisle between the shelves and the counter—hand over hand, like a man climbing out of a dream. I stayed quiet and watched him lurch from one side, bumping to the other. . . . (paragraph 18)

These concrete narrative actions help readers visualize Uncle Willie's movements. As you write your own remembered-person essay, try to use specific narrative action to show the person's typical movements or special occasions when the person walked or gestured in a memorable way.

Considering Topics for Your Own Essay

Consider writing about an adult who has significantly influenced your life. Think about someone who is outside your immediate family—perhaps a grandparent, aunt or uncle, teacher, or coach. Begin by listing two or three possibilities. Choose one, and then consider the following questions: How might you engage your readers' interest and disclose the person's significance in your life? What details might you include? What anecdotes might you relate? If you have access to them, what photographs or other memorabilia might you include with your essay to help readers get a sense of the person and your relationship?

For more information on including memorabilia, see p. 112.

To use the Writing Guide Software to record your ideas, click on
▶ **Journal**

***Mary Karr**, the Jessee Truesdale Peck Professor of Literature at Syracuse University, is best known for her autobiographical writing, but she is also a distinguished poet. She has written two best-selling and critically acclaimed autobiographies—*The Liar's Club: A Memoir *(1995), about her early childhood in an East Texas oil refinery town, and* Cherry *(1998), about her tumultuous adolescence. She is a two-time winner of the Pushcart Prize for prose and poetry. Her poems have appeared in magazines such as the* New Yorker *and the* Atlantic Monthly *and have been published in three collections:* Abacus *(1991),* The Devil's Town *(1993), and* Viper Rum *(1998). Karr also writes essays about poetry, including an introduction to the Modern Library edition of T. S. Eliot's* The Waste Land and Other Poems *(2001).*

Even though her writing is often about her own experience, Karr has explained in an interview that writing for her is "an inefficient process" that takes time and effort but that ultimately helps her figure out what she has to say. She lets herself write "really badly" at first, then she rereads what she has written "to find the story within the story," or what she calls the significant or "resonant moment" that she can "work with" as she revises. As you read this excerpt from Cherry *about a childhood friend with whom Karr is still close, think about what part or parts of the essay resonate with meaning and feeling for you as a reader.*

Cherry

Mary Karr

Only one girl showed outlaw tendencies nearly as wild as mine: Clarice Fontenot, who at fourteen had three years on me, which discrepancy didn't seem to matter at first. The only obstacle to our spending every conceivable second together that summer was her Cajun daddy's tight rein on her, which consisted of seemingly innumerable chores and capricious rules he ginned out. 1

The Fontenots lived in a celery-green house on the corner that seemed to bulge at its seams with her wild-assed brothers. They all slicked back their hair on the sides and walked with a sexy, loose-hipped slouch. If they looked at you at all, the glance came from the sides of their faces. Like their tight-lipped father, they barely spoke, just radiated a sly disapproval. 2

Clarice's role in that Catholic household seemed to be serving their needs. While they ran the roads, she scrubbed and hung laundry and baby-sat a variety of black-eyed cousins whose faces (like hers) were spattered with freckles as if flicked from a paintbrush. Her blights and burdens put me in mind of Cinderella's, though Clarice rarely whined. Still, her circumstances defined her somehow, for her jittery, electric manner seemed to have formed itself solely to oppose both her station in life and her brothers' quiet surliness. 3

Clarice would have hung out at my house every day for the abundant food and the air conditioning if not my somewhat peculiar company. But her daddy's strictness was the stuff of neighborhood legend. A compact, steel-gray man, he was about the only guy on our block who didn't do refinery work (I think he worked for the gas company). That he wore a tie to work made him not exotic but peculiar. No one's daddy knew his schedule or ever heard him say more than a passing hey. Usually, Clarice could only play at my house an hour or so before she'd be called home for chores. I didn't take these partings lightly. 4

Once she was back home, I'd patrol the strip of road before her house, skateboarding past palmettos and the dog run and back again, trying all the while to predict her return by the advance of her work. Window by window, the glass she was washing would lose its grease smears and begin to give back blue sky and flickers of sun when I rolled by. Or I'd watch through those windows while Clarice unhooked each venetian blind. I'd try to measure how long it would take for her to lower those blinds into the Clorox-fuming bathtub, to wash each slat, then towel it off and reappear to hang the blind, giving me an exasperated wave before moving to the next. 5

Sometimes her daddy just summoned her home for no reason. Which infuriated me. She'd joke that his fun-meter had gone off, some invisible gauge he had that measured the extent of her good time and sought to lop it off. He'd insist she stay in her own yard, and forbid me to cross over the property line. I'd pace their yard's edge for an hour at a pop, or just sit cross-legged along their hurricane fence line reading while their deranged German shepherd loped and bayed and threatened to eat my face off. From my lap I'd 6 flip him the permanent bird using a Venus pencil to keep my fingers cocked in place. A few times, Clarice joined me in this border-holding action. She'd loiter in the heat on her side of the fence, glancing over her shoulder till her dad's gray face slid into a window or his gravelly voice shouted her in.

Doubtless her daddy meant this all as some kind of protection. Plenty of girls her age "got in trouble," and there were countless lowlife characters circling like sharks to pluck any unwatched female into libidinal activity in some hot rod or pickup truck. But my own parents were so lax about corralling me at all ("You can do anything you're big enough to do," Daddy liked to say) that I found Mr. Fontenot's strictures mind-boggling. In my head I engaged in long courtroom soliloquies about him, at the ends of which he and his feckless sons were led away shackled while a gavel banged and Clarice and I hugged each other in glee. 7

Clarice bridled against her daddy's limits but never actually broke the rules. She lacked both the self-pity and the fury I had in such abundance. She laughed in a foghorn-like blast that drew stares in public. She could belch on command loud enough to cause old ladies in restaurants to ask for far tables. I never mastered this. But thanks to her, I can whistle with my fingers, execute a diving board flip, turn a cartwheel, tie a slip knot, and make my eyeballs shiver like a mesmerist. While other people worried what would come of Clarice if she didn't calm down, for me she had the absolute power of someone who fundamentally didn't give a damn, which she didn't (other than toeing her father's line, which she seemed to do breezily enough). 8

My first memory of her actually comes long before that summer. It was from the bleached-out time before we'd passed through the school doors, so we had no grade levels by which to rank ourselves. 9

A cold sun was sliding down a gray fall sky. Some older boys had been playing tackle football in the field we took charge of every weekend. In a few years, they'd be called to Southeast Asia, some of them. Their locations would be tracked with pushpins in red, white, and blue on maps on nearly every kitchen wall. But that afternoon, they were quick as young deer. They leapt and dodged, dove from each other and collided in midair. Bulletlike passes flew to connect them. Or the ball spiraled in high arc across the frosty sky one to another. In short, they were mindlessly agile in a way that captured as audience every little kid within running distance of the yellow goalposts. 10

We could not help watching. Even after I stepped accidentally in a fire-ant nest and got a constellation of crimson bites on my ankles. Even after streetlights clicked on and our breaths began to spirit before us and to warm my hands I had to pull my arms from my sweatshirt sleeves, then tuck my fingers into my armpits so the sleeves flapped empty as an amputee's. In fact, even once the game had ended, when the big boys had run off to make phone calls or do chores, we stayed waiting to be called for supper. I can almost hear the melamine plates being slid from the various cupboards and stacked on tile counters. But having witnessed their game, we were loath to unloose ourselves from the sight of it. 11

It was before the time of stark hierarchies. Our family dramas were rumored, but the stories that would shape us had not yet been retold so often as to calcify our characters inside them. Our rivalries had not yet been laid down. No one was big enough to throw 12 a punch that required stitches or to shout an invective that would loop through your head at night till tears made your pillowcase damp. Our sexual wonderings seldom called us to touch each other, just stare from time to time at the mystery of each other's pale underpants or jockey shorts, which we sometimes traded looks at under a porch or in the blue dark of a crawl space. For years our names ran together like beads on a string, JohnandBobbieClariceandCindyandLittleMary (as opposed to Big Mary, who was Mary Ferrell). With little need to protect our identities from each other, we could still fall into great idleness together—this handful of unwatched kids with nowhere to be.

At some moment, Clarice figured out as none of us had before how to shinny up the goalpost. 13

That sight of her squiggling up the yellow pole magically yanks the memory from something far-off into a kind of 3-D present. I am alive in it. There's early frost on the grass, and my ant bites itch. Clarice's limbs have turned to rubber as she wraps round the pole. She's kicked off her Keds, so her bare feet on cold metal give purchase. About a foot at a time she scoots up, hauls herself by her hands, then slides her feet high. And again. She's weightless as an imp and fast. 14

At the top of the pole, she rises balletic, back arched like a trapeze artist. She flings one hand up: *Ta-da,* she says, as if she were sheathed in a crimson-spangled bathing suit with fishnet hose and velvet ballet slippers, then again *ta-da*. We cheer and clap, move back to the ten-yard line to take her in better. This is a wonder, for her to climb so far above us. And there we align ourselves with the forces of awe that permit new tricks to be dreamed up on chilly fall nights when nothing but suppers of fried meat and cream gravy await us, or tepid baths. 15

For a few minutes, Bobbie Stuart tries to weasel up the other pole, but he's too stiff. His legs jackknife out from under him, and his arms can't hold his long thin body. 16

Then Clarice does something wholly unexpected for which she will be forever marked. 17

She sticks her thumbs in the gathered waistband of her corduroy pants with the cowgirl lassos stitched around the pockets. With those thumbs, she yanks both her pants and her underpanties down around her bare feet. She then bends over and waggles her butt at us as I later learned strippers sometimes do. Screams of laughter from us. John falls over and rolls on the ground like a dog, pointing up and laughing at her bare white ass, which still holds a faint tan line from summer. 18

We've just about got used to the idea of her butt when she executes another move. She wheels around to face us and show us her yin-yang, a dark notch in her hairless pudendum. Her belly is round as a puppy's jutted forward. Then our howls truly take on hyena-like timbre. And there across the ditch, which marks the realm of adult civilization, appears the fast moving figure of Mrs. Carter through leaf smoke of a ditch fire. She's holding the spatula in her hand with which she intends to blister our asses, Clarice's most specifically. 19

But she's a grown-up, Mrs. Carter. Her steps on the muddy slope are tentative. Not wanting to funk up her shoes with mud, she hesitates before she leaps across. And in that interval, Clarice slithers down the yellow pole and tears off in a streak. And the rest of us flee like wild dogs. 20

Decades later, I asked Clarice point blank why she did it. We were in our forties then, living two thousand miles apart, and talking—oddly enough—on our car phones. Her voice was sandpaper rough with a cold, but it still carried the shimmer of unbidden amusement. I'd only seen her every two or three years—the occasional holiday, at my daddy's funeral, and after Mother's bypass surgery when she kept vigil with me. Still, there's no one who'd be less likely to tell me a flat-footed lie. Across the hissing static, I asked why she took her pants down that day, whether somebody had dared her to and I just didn't remember. 21

The answer that she gave remains the truest to who she was and who I then so much needed her to be: "Because I could, I guess," she said. "Wasn't anybody around to stop me." 22

Connecting to Culture and Experience: Retold Stories

Karr explains that she is writing about a time when "the stories that would shape us had not yet been retold so often as to calcify our characters inside them" (paragraph 12). She is referring here to a common phenomenon: the way certain stories are told and retold by one or more members of a group, such as a family or a circle of friends. Karr suggests that this retelling fixes the person in time and place, perhaps exaggerating certain personality traits or emphasizing particular aspects of the person's life. For example, in retelling the story about Clarice, one could say that Karr mythologizes her friend, representing her as a cross between Cinderella (dutifully doing endless chores while her brothers do whatever they wish) and Bart Simpson (playfully thumbing her nose at what is considered proper or respectable).

With two or three other students, discuss such retold stories. Identify one story told and retold over the years about one of your relatives or a long-time personal friend. It could even be a story about you. Tell this story briefly to the others; and then explain who among your family and friends usually tells it, to whom it is usually told, and what it shows about the person who is the subject of it or about the storytellers. Also tell them whether you think the story calcifies or mythologizes this person by exaggerating certain personal qualities. Then, as a group, speculate about how these stories took shape and why people enjoy retelling them.

Analyzing Writing Strategies

For more on these describing strategies, see Chapter 15, p. 643.

1. Karr uses the describing strategies of naming, detailing, and comparing. To analyze her use of these strategies, look closely at the following sentence from paragraph 2: "The Fontenots lived in a celery-green house on the corner that seemed to bulge at its seams with her wild-assed brothers." Karr uses **naming** to focus readers' attention on several objects and people: *Fontenots, house,* and *brothers.* She uses **detailing** selectively to single out the house, describing it in terms of

color *(celery-green)* and location *(on the corner)*. To convey to readers what she remembers most about the Fontenot house—that it could barely contain Clarice's rambunctious brothers—Karr uses **comparing** in the form of metaphor: *wild-assed* and *bulge at its seams*. She also uses simile, when she describes Clarice's cousins' faces "spattered with freckles as if flicked from a paintbrush" (paragraph 3). Whereas simile is an explicit comparison introduced by *as* or *like*, metaphor is an implied comparison such as *wild-assed* or *tight-lipped*.

Reread paragraphs 10 and 11, looking for and marking examples of naming, detailing, and comparing. Underline the names, put brackets around the details, and put parentheses around the comparisons. Then consider how Karr uses these describing strategies. Notice how much naming she uses, populating the scene with numerous objects and people. Make a rough count of the number of names that have descriptive details attached to them and how many names stand on their own. Of the detailing, note how often visual details are used instead of other sensory details (for example, hearing or smell). Finally, look at when Karr uses comparison. What is the dominant impression you get of the scene from Karr's naming, detailing, and comparing?

2. Remembered-person essays often include **anecdotes**, brief stories about onetime events that illustrate something important about the person's character and the writer's relationship with the person. Karr's portrait of Clarice focuses on one such anecdote, the story about the time Clarice climbed the goalpost and mooned her friends. The opening phrase of paragraph 9, "My first memory of her," lets readers know that a particular event is about to be narrated. Following the familiar conventions of storytelling, Karr opens the next paragraph with descriptive language that sets the scene, establishing the time of day, the season, and the place where the event took place: "A cold sun was sliding down a gray fall sky. Some older boys had been playing tackle football in the field we took charge of every weekend" (paragraph 10).

For more on narrating events, see Chapter 14.

Notice that Karr begins her narration in these sentences with the past tense *(was sliding, had been playing)*. Like setting the scene with description, narrating in the past tense is a familiar convention of autobiographical storytelling. But notice that with the opening sentence of paragraph 14, Karr shifts from the past to the present tense: *yanks, am, there's, itch, wraps, scoots, hauls, slides.* Review the following paragraphs, underlining the verbs, to see whether she continues in present tense until the end of the essay or to note where she reverts back to the past tense. Then speculate about why Karr chose to break with convention and tell this particular story in the present tense. What effect does her use of the present tense have on you as a reader?

3. To help readers imagine events and people, autobiographers rely on many sentence strategies. Prominent among them is a phrase based on a verb ending in *ing* and known as a participial phrase. Karr makes especially effective use of *ing* phrases. To understand one use she makes of them, analyze the role of five similar examples. Begin by underlining the phrase from *glancing* to the end of the last sentence in paragraph 6, the phrase from *being slid* to the end of the fifth sen-

For information on participial phrases in autobiography, turn to p. 119.

tence in paragraph 11, the phrase from *pointing up* to *white ass* in the last sentence of paragraph 18, and the two phrases beginning with *living* and *talking* in the second sentence of paragraph 21. Then analyze how these phrases relate to what comes before them in their sentences. What do they add? Assuming they make a similar contribution to their sentences, try to identify what it is.

Commentary: Autobiographical Significance

Writers convey a person's significance in their lives by communicating both their **remembered feelings and thoughts** and their **present perspective** as they write about their past experience. For example, Karr presents her remembered feelings when she says that Mr. Fontenot's habit of summoning Clarice home without reason "infuriated" her (paragraph 6) and her remembered thoughts when she tells us that Clarice's "blights and burdens put me in mind of Cinderella's" (paragraph 3). We can hear her child's voice when she describes herself as pacing "for an hour at a pop" or flipping the German shepherd "the permanent bird" (paragraph 6). In relating her remembered feelings when Clarice is called home to do chores, we can see Karr's childish selfishness and frustration at being deprived of her friend's company, how she would "patrol the strip of road before [Clarice's] house . . . trying all the while to predict her return by the advance of her work" (paragraph 5).

In addition to these remembered feelings and thoughts, we can also see in the essay places where the adult Karr expresses her present perspective. Sometimes she employs language that only an adult would use, such as *capricious* (paragraph 1), *libidinal activity* (7), *strictures* (7), and *pudendum* (19). At other times, she gives adult judgments, such as when she acknowledges that Clarice's father's *mind-boggling* strictures were probably well intentioned and possibly even realistic. Karr also offers adult insights when she characterizes Clarice: "her circumstances defined her somehow, for her jittery, electric manner seemed to have formed itself solely to oppose both her station in life and her brothers' quiet surliness" (paragraph 3). Finally, Karr gives her present perspective when she interprets Clarice's character and compares it to her own:

> Clarice bridled against her daddy's limits but never actually broke the rules. She lacked both the self-pity and the fury I had in such abundance. . . . While other people worried what would come of Clarice if she didn't calm down, for me she had the absolute power of someone who fundamentally didn't give a damn, which she didn't (other than toeing her father's line, which she seemed to do breezily enough). (paragraph 8)

The ending of Karr's essay underscores the fact that remembered-person essays are autobiographical as well as biographical. That is, in conveying the remembered person's significance in the writer's life, the writer not only presents the person but also inevitably presents herself as well. Karr's ending comment tells as much about Karr herself as about Clarice: "The answer that she gave remains the truest to who she was and who I then so much needed her to be" (paragraph 22).

Considering Topics for Your Own Essay

Consider writing about a person near your own age who influenced you during your childhood or early adolescence. List as many people as you can. Recall neighbors, classmates, friends from camp, teammates. The people on your list may be close friends or other people with whom you still keep in touch, as Karr and Clarice do, or people with whom you have lost contact. They might even be relatives—cousins or siblings. Choose one person from your list, and try to recall two or three specific times the two of you did something especially memorable together. List these anecdotes, and make notes about what each memory might reveal about the person and about your relationship.

To use the Writing Guide Software to record your ideas, click on
▶ **Journal**

***Amy Wu** wrote this essay when she was seventeen years old, just before becoming a student at New York University. A journalist and a recent fellow at the Scripps Howard New Media Workshop at Columbia University, Wu is on the staff of the* Monterey County Herald *in California. Her articles have appeared in* Time Asia, Wired News, ABCNews.com, *the* New York Times, *the* Los Angeles Times, Asia Week, *and other publications. This essay was published in* Chinese American Forum, *a quarterly magazine.*

As you read, notice the way Wu relies on contrasts between her mother and other kinds of mothers to help readers understand her special relationship with her mother.

A Different Kind of Mother

Amy Wu

My best friend once asked me what it was like being brought up by a Chinese mother. Surprisingly, I could find no answer. I found myself describing my mother's beauty—the way my mother's hair was so silky and black, how her eyes were not small and squinty, but shaped like perfect almonds. How her lips and cheeks were bright red even if she put on no makeup. 1

But unlike my friends, who see my mother as a Chinese mother, I see my mother as simply "my" mother. The language between any mother and daughter is universal. Beyond the layers of arguments and rhetoric, and beyond the incidents of humiliation and misunderstandings, there is a love that unites every mother and daughter. 2

I am not blind, however, to the disciplinary differences between a culture from the west and a culture from the east. Unlike American mothers, who encourage their young children to speak whatever is on their mind, my mother told me to hold my tongue. Once, when I was 5 or 6, I interrupted my mother during a dinner with her friends and told her that I disliked the meal. My mother's eyes transformed from serene pools of blackness 3

Amy Wu and her mother

into stormy balls of fire. "Quiet!" she hissed, "do you not know that silent waters run deep?" She ordered me to turn my chair to the wall and think about what I had done. I remember throwing a red-faced tantrum before my mother's friends, pounding my fists into the rug, and throwing my utensils at the steaming dishes. Not only did I receive a harsh scolding, but a painful spanking. By the end of that evening, I had learned the first of many lessons. I learned to choose my words carefully before I opened my undisciplined mouth.

Whenever my friends and I strike up conversations about our mothers in the cafeteria or at slumber parties, I find myself telling them this story. Nevertheless, they respond to my story with straight and pale faces. "How," one of my friends asked, "can a mother be so cruel?" "You mean she beat you in front of other people?" another asked. My best friend told me that her mother disciplined her children wisely instead of abusing them. She sat them on her lap, patiently explaining what they had done wrong. She didn't believe in beating children into submission. 4

What my American friends cannot understand, however, is how my mother's lessons have become so embedded within me, while my friends have easily forgotten their mother's words. My mother's eyes are so powerful, her fists so strong, that somehow I cannot erase her words of advice. To this day, I choose my words carefully before I speak, unlike so many of my friends whose words spill out aimlessly when they open their mouths. My mother says that American girls are taught to squabble like chickens, but a Chinese girl is taught how to speak intelligently. 5

Only lately have I also discovered that Chinese mothers show their love in different ways. Ever since I was a little girl, my mother has spent hours cooking intricate dishes. I remember Friday evenings she would lay out the precious china her mother had given her as a wedding present—how she laid down the utensils and glasses so meticulously, how she made sure there was not a crease in the tablecloth. 6

She would spend the entire day steaming fish, baking ribs, cutting beef into thin strips, and rolling dough to make dumplings. In the evening, her work of labor and art would be unveiled. My father and I and a few Chinese neighbors and friends would be invited to feast on my mother's work of art. 7

I remember how silent my mother was as she watched her loved ones devour her labor of love. She would sit back, with a small smile on her face. She would nibble at the food in her dish while urging others to eat more, to take seconds, and thirds and fourths. "Eat, eat!" she would order me. I dared not tell her I was too full. 8

She would fill my bowl with mounds of rice and my dish with endless vegetables, fish, and fried delicacies. A Chinese mother's love flows from the time and energy she puts into forming a banquet. A Chinese mother's love comes through her order to eat more. 9

My American friends laugh so hard that tears come out of their eyes, when I tell them how my Chinese mother displays her love. "So she wants you to get fat!" one screamed. They said that their mothers showed love by hugging them tightly, buying them clothes, and kissing them on the cheeks. 10

Deep inside, I know that my mother does show her love, except she does it when she thinks I am asleep. Every so often, she will tiptoe into my dark room, sit on the edge of my bed, and stroke my hair. When I am awake, however, she is like a professor constantly hounding her prize student and expecting only the best. All throughout my childhood, she drilled me on lessons of cleanliness and respect. 11

A few years ago at my Grandpa Du's 67th birthday party, I ran up to my grandfather and planted a wet, juicy kiss on his right cheek. To this day, I can easily remember the horrified looks on my relatives' faces. My grandfather turned pale for a second and then smiled meekly. He nodded his head and quickly sat down. 12

Later that evening, my mother cornered me against the wall. "Do you not know that respect to elderly is to bow!" she screamed. Her face turned bright purple. My excuses of "I didn't know . . ." were lost in her powerful words. 13

From that day on, I bowed to anyone Chinese and older than I. I have learned that respect for the elderly earns a young person a different kind of respect. These days, my grandfather points to me and tells my little cousins to follow my example. "She has been taught well," he tells them. 14

It saddens me that my Chinese mother is so often misunderstood. After she threw my friends out during my twelfth birthday party, because they refused to take off their shoes, they saw her as a callous, cruel animal. One of my friends went home and told her father that I had an abusive mother. Her father even volunteered to call the child welfare department. They never dared to step foot in my house again. 15

My mother has given me so many fine values and morals because of her way of teaching me. I choose words carefully before I speak. I am careful to speak and act toward the elderly a certain way. Without my mother's strong words and teachings, I believe that I would be a rather undisciplined person who didn't value life greatly. I would most likely have been spoiled and callous and ignorant. I have also learned that there is more than one definition of love between a mother and a daughter. 16

Connecting to Culture and Experience: Cultural Differences

Wu's essay suggests that ethnic differences may be especially apparent when we look at how parents raise their children—both in how they discipline and how they show their love. To her friends, for example, Wu's mother seems "callous" and "cruel" (paragraph 15). Wu's mother is similarly critical of the way her daughter's friends are being raised by their parents. Paragraph 15 probably presents the most graphic example of ethnic difference: Not only do Wu's friends refuse to respect Chinese tradition by taking off their shoes when entering the house, but a friend's father threatens to call the child welfare department to report Wu's mother as "abusive."

With other students in your class, discuss your reactions to the ethnic differences Wu writes about. You may want to begin by taking turns describing your family's cultural background, possibly including your own and your ancestors' nationalities, religious affiliations, regional backgrounds, and racial identifications. Then discuss some of your family's traditions and values to see if there are any notable cultural differences among the people in your class.

Analyzing Writing Strategies

1. To convey her mother's significance, Wu tells readers directly from her **present perspective** at the time she is writing what she thinks and feels about their relationship. For example, she begins and ends the opening anecdote by stating what she learned from the experience (paragraph 3). Reread the rest of the essay, looking for places where Wu expresses her present perspective and putting brackets around them. Then reflect on how effectively these present perspective comments help you understand Wu's relationship with her mother.
2. In addition to telling readers how she feels about her mother, Wu tries to create a vivid portrait so that readers can imagine what her mother looks like. Reread paragraphs 1, 3, and 5, where Wu **describes** her mother. Underline the features she names and the details she gives. For example, in paragraph 1, she calls attention to her mother's "hair" being "silky and black."

For more on strategies for description, see Chapter 15, p. 643.

Commentary: Anecdotes and Recurring Events

To present her mother, Wu uses two related but different narrating strategies—**anecdotes** (onetime events) and **recurring events**. In paragraph 3, for instance, Wu relates an anecdote that shows what happened the one time she told her mother she did not like the food prepared for dinner. Wu uses the temporal transition "Once" to signal readers that she is telling an anecdote. She uses another temporal transition ("when I was 5 or 6") to locate the event at a particular point in time. Wu presents the event in a simple chronological sequence of actions and reactions: The young Wu interrupts her mother to complain about the food, she is reprimanded and told to face the wall, she throws a tantrum, and she suffers the consequences of a scolding and spanking.

For more information on strategies of narration, turn to Chapter 14, p. 627.

In contrast, paragraphs 6–9 present a recurring event that takes place every Friday: banquets for family and friends. Wu uses the verb tense marker "would" to signal readers that her mother's activities are recurring and not onetime events ("Friday evenings she would lay out the precious china. . . . She would spend the entire day steaming fish. . . . She would fill my bowl. . . ."). The Friday banquet is an important family ritual—the same china and utensils set out in the same way, the same dishes prepared in the same way. The mother always behaves predictably, as does Wu. There is not a hint that anything unusual ever happened at one of these banquets. Nevertheless, this recurring event helps readers see what Wu ultimately came to appreciate: the nonverbal way her mother expresses her love for her family.

In addition to showing what happened through anecdotes and recurring events, Wu lets us hear what was said on these occasions. She reconstructs **dialogue**, to emphasize the words that were used ("'Quiet!,' she hissed . . .") (paragraph 3). She also summarizes conversations ("She ordered me to turn my chair to the wall . . .") (paragraph 3).

Dialogue reveals important aspects of Wu's relationship with her mother. Since effective dialogue captures the mood as well as the content of a conversation, it gives readers an immediate impression of the person's character and reveals how he or she relates to others. Since writers are unlikely to recall precisely what was said, they must invent or reconstruct dialogue.

For more information on writing dialogue, turn to Chapter 14, pp. 635–36.

Notice that Wu does not give us many of her mother's words, but what her mother does say—and especially how she says it—is revealing. We know how she sounds because Wu describes her mother's tone of voice: "she hissed." Writers tend to quote sparingly, choosing words that will leave a strong impression with readers. Seldom does a dialogue present a long speech unless the writer wants to emphasize the person's ideas or idiosyncratic way of talking.

Considering Topics for Your Own Essay

Consider writing about a parent, guardian, counselor, religious leader, or another older person who has influenced you deeply, for good or ill. Choose one person, and think for a few moments about what you would want readers to know about this person and your relationship. What details of appearance, style, or movement might you select? Which anecdotes would be memorable for readers and most revealing of your relationship with the person?

To use the Writing Guide Software to record your ideas, click on
▶ **Journal**

***Jan Gray** was a first-year college student when she wrote the following essay about her father, a man toward whom she has ambivalent but mostly angry feelings. As you read, notice how Gray uses description to convey these feelings.*

To see this essay with pop-up annotations in the software, click on
▶ **Remembering People**
▶ **Read**

Father

Jan Gray

1 My father's hands are grotesque. He suffers from psoriasis, a chronic skin disease that covers his massive, thick hands with scaly, reddish patches that periodically flake off, sending tiny pieces of dead skin sailing to the ground. In addition, his fingers are permanently stained a dull yellow from years of chain

smoking. The thought of those swollen, discolored, scaly hands touching me, whether it be out of love or anger, sends chills up my spine.

By nature, he is a disorderly, unkempt person. The numerous cigarette burns, food stains, and ashes on his clothes show how little he cares about his appearance. He has a dreadful habit of running his hands through his greasy hair and scratching his scalp, causing dandruff to drift downward onto his bulky shoulders. He is grossly overweight, and his pullover shirts never quite cover his protruding paunch. When he eats, he shovels the food into his mouth as if he hasn't eaten for days, bread crumbs and food scraps settling in his untrimmed beard. 2

Last year, he abruptly left town. Naturally, his apartment was a shambles, and I offered to clean it so that my mother wouldn't have to pay the cleaning fee. I arrived early in the morning anticipating a couple hours of vacuuming and dusting and scrubbing. The minute I opened the door, however, I realized my task was monumental: Old yellowed newspapers and magazines were strewn throughout the living room; moldy and rotten food covered the kitchen counter; cigarette butts and ashes were everywhere. The pungent aroma of stale beer seemed to fill the entire apartment. 3

As I made my way through the debris toward the bedroom, I tried to deny that the man who lived here was my father. The bedroom was even worse than the front rooms, with cigarette burns in the carpet and empty bottles, dirty dishes, and smelly laundry scattered everywhere. Looking around his bedroom, I recalled an incident that had occurred only a few months before in my bedroom. 4

I was calling home to tell my mother I would be eating dinner at a girlfriend's house. To my surprise, my father answered the phone. I was taken aback to hear his voice because my parents had been divorced for some time and he was seldom at our house. In fact, I didn't even see him very often. 5

"Hello?" he answered in his deep, scratchy voice. 6

"Oh, umm, hi Dad. Is Mom home?" 7

"What can I do for you?" he asked, sounding a bit too cheerful. 8

"Well, I just wanted to ask Mom if I could stay for dinner here." 9

"I don't think that's a very good idea, dear." I could sense an abrupt change in the tone of his voice. "Your room is a mess, and if you're not home in ten minutes to straighten it up, I'll really give you something to clean." Click. 10

Pedalling home as fast as I could, I had a distinct image of my enraged father. I could see his face redden, his body begin to tremble slightly, and his hands gesture nervously in the air. Though he was not prone to physical violence and always appeared calm on the outside, I knew he was really seething inside. The incessant motion of those hands was all too vivid to me as I neared home. 11

My heart was racing as I turned the knob to the front door and headed for my bedroom. When I opened my bedroom door, I stopped in horror. The dresser drawers were pulled out, and clothes were scattered across the floor. Everything on top of the dresser—a perfume tray, a couple of baskets of hair clips and earrings, and an assortment of pictures—had been strewn about. The dresser itself was tilted on its side, supported by the bed frame. As I stepped in and closed the door behind me, tears welled up in my eyes. 12

I hated my father so much at that moment. Who the hell did he think he was to waltz into my life every few months like this?

I was slowly piecing my room together when he knocked on the door. I choked back the tears, wanting to show as little emotion as possible, and quietly murmured, "Come in." He stood in the doorway, one hand leaning against the door jamb, a cigarette dangling from the other, flicking ashes on the carpet, very smug in his handling of the situation. 13

"I want you to know I did this for your own good. I think it's time you started taking a little responsibility around this house. Now, to show you there are no hard feelings, I'll help you set the dresser back up." 14

"No thank you," I said quietly, on the verge of tears again. "I'd rather do it myself. Please, just leave me alone!" 15

He gave me one last look that seemed to say, "I offered. I'm the good guy. If you refuse, that's your problem." Then he turned and walked away. I was stunned at how he could be so violent one moment and so nonchalant the next. 16

As I sat in his bedroom reflecting on what he had done to my room, I felt the utmost disgust for this man. There seemed to be no hope he would break his filthy habits. I could come in and clean his room, but only he could clean up the mess he had made of his life. But I felt pity for him, too. After all, he is my father—am I not supposed to feel some responsibility for him and to love and honor him? 17

Connecting to Culture and Experience: Ambivalence

Jan Gray admits that her disgust for her father is mixed with pity. Ambivalence—mixed feelings—is fundamental to our relationships with others. We normally do not feel only hatred toward other people. On the other hand, we usually do not feel only unqualified love and devotion, either. Our feelings tend to be influenced by our most recent or memorable interactions with the person as well as by our experiences with other people, which can affect our understanding of a relationship and alter our feelings about the person.

With students in your class, discuss ambivalence in human relationships. Identify someone for whom you have notably ambivalent feelings—a family member, a friend, an employer, or anyone else—someone you feel comfortable talking about with your classmates. Your feelings may be mainly negative, mainly positive, or evenly balanced. Take turns describing your relationship with the person you have chosen and speculating about how your ambivalent feelings emerged. Explain also how you have been able to sustain the relationship, if you have.

As a group, what can you conclude about ambivalence in relationships? On the basis of your individual experiences, does it seem that ambivalence is inevitable? Do you think that accepting ambivalence would make families more stable and people in general more tolerant? If so, try to explain how.

Analyzing Writing Strategies

1. Reread the **dialogue** in paragraphs 6–10 and 13–16, paying attention to what Gray's father says and how each conversation develops. Notice also how Gray comments on what her father says and how she shows his actions as he talks to her. Then consider these questions: What does each conversation reveal about the father and Gray's relationship with him? Do the conversations confirm what you learn about the father and the relationship elsewhere in the essay, or do they offer new information? If they offer something new, what do you think they reveal?

For more on dialogue, see Chapter 14, pp. 635–36.

2. Gray presents two **anecdotes** that take place at different times and places. Notice that instead of putting these anecdotes in a simple chronological order, one after the other, she embeds one anecdote within the other. She uses a narrating strategy called flashback, commonly used in movies and television. Find where each anecdote begins and ends. Note especially how Gray makes the transition from one time in the past to another time in the past. Then look at her overall purpose. What do you think Gray is trying to achieve with this anecdote within an anecdote?

For more anecdotes (one-time events), see Chapter 14, p. 630.

3. The Writer at Work section later in this chapter (pp. 126–31) presents the first draft of Gray's essay. Compare the two versions by making a scratch outline of the draft and the revision. How did Gray change the **organization**? Why do you think she made these changes, and what effect do they have?

Commentary: Autobiographical Significance

Instead of telling what she remembers feeling about her father or what she feels now about their relationship, Gray shows his significance through descriptive details and actions. For example, her description of his skin condition and personal slovenliness reveals how repulsive she finds him. The way he abandons his apartment shows how irresponsible he is. Most important, the way he threatens her and throws the contents of her dresser around her bedroom shows how cruel and violent he can be. Through description, anecdotes, and recurring activities, Gray creates a **dominant impression** that clearly conveys to readers what she thinks and feels about her father.

For more on creating a dominant impression, see Chapter 15, pp. 653–54.

Although Gray seeks to create an impression that is consistent throughout the essay, she expresses her contradictory feelings at the end. She admits that she "felt the utmost disgust for" her father, but at the same time she acknowledges that she also "felt pity for him." Her final sentence poses a rhetorical question, one that readers are not expected to answer and that she probably cannot answer either. She feels that she should and apparently wants very much "to love and honor" her father. But his behavior makes it nearly impossible for her to do so. One reason we choose, like Gray, to write about difficult relationships is to come to terms with our contradictory feelings. While the writing process may not resolve our ambivalence, it can help us to understand why we feel as we do.

Considering Topics for Your Own Essay

Imagine writing about someone with whom you have had a serious conflict. How would you present this person? Which anecdotes might be most revealing? What conversations might you reconstruct that would dramatize the conflict? What impression of this person would you attempt to convey to readers?

To use the Writing Guide Software to record your ideas, click on
▶ **Journal**

PURPOSE AND AUDIENCE

A writer of an essay about a remembered person may have several possible purposes in mind. Perhaps the most prominent is to gain a better understanding of the remembered person and of the writer's relationship with the person. To achieve this purpose, the writer needs to see the complexity of the relationship to avoid either demonizing or idealizing the person.

Another purpose is to entertain readers with a vivid portrait of an unusual or engaging person. To achieve this goal, writers present a remembered person through description, dialogue, recurring events, and anecdotes. All of these strategies are carefully coordinated to create a dominant impression that will enable readers to readily imagine the person and understand why he or she is significant for the writer. Writers hope that these insights will lead readers to reflect on people who have been important in their own lives.

BASIC FEATURES: REMEMBERING PEOPLE

A Vivid Portrait

At the center of an essay about a remembered person is a vivid portrait. Writers of remembered-person essays rely on the full range of descriptive strategies—naming, detailing, and comparing—to present a person to their readers. But they tend to be selective, choosing only one or two distinctive features of the person's appearance to emphasize. Maya Angelou, for example, uses naming, detailing, and comparing to describe Uncle Willie's lopsided face "pulled down on the left side, as if a pulley had been attached to his lower teeth" (paragraph 2). Similarly, Gray focuses attention on her father's "massive, thick hands with scaly, reddish patches that periodically flake off, sending tiny pieces of dead skin sailing to the ground" (paragraph 1).

Writers also use specific narrative action to describe people moving and gesturing. We saw how Angelou shows her uncle's labored movement: "Uncle Willie was making his own way down the long shadowed aisle between the shelves and the counter—hand over hand, like a man climbing out of a dream. I stayed quiet and watched him lurch from one side, bumping to the other . . ." (paragraph 18). Wu's description of her grandfather's reaction when she kisses him ("My grandfather turned pale for a second and then smiled meekly") (paragraph 12) is punctuated by her mother's contrasting reaction ("my mother cornered me against the wall . . . she screamed. Her face turned bright purple") (paragraph 13).

Besides presenting their subjects visually, writers let us hear their subjects speak. All the readings in this chapter include some dialogue. Angelou creates dialogue to present a stuttering, yet proud Uncle Willie ("I have an old m-m-mother and my brother's t-two children to l-look after") (paragraph 15). Karr reconstructs what Clarice said during her goalpost performance ("*Ta-da,* she says") (paragraph 15) and what she answered when Karr "asked why she took her pants down that day" (paragraph 21): "'Because I could, I guess' she said. 'Wasn't anybody around to stop me'" (paragraph 22).

Revealing Anecdotes and Recurring Events

In portraying significant relationships, writers may narrate anecdotes or recurring events. Many writers do both. In her brief essay about Uncle Willie, Angelou presents a onetime incident (when strangers came to the store) and a recurring event (doing math homework). Although she focuses on one anecdote, Karr also relates what typically occurred when Karr would wait impatiently for Clarice to finish her chores and when Clarice's father would make her stay in her own yard. Similarly, Wu shows us both what happened once when she complained about her mother's food and what happened every Friday at the ritual family banquets. Gray focuses on anecdotes depicting two specific events ("last year" when she cleaned her father's apartment and "a few months" earlier when he had wrecked her bedroom), but she also refers to recurring activities ("When he eats . . .").

Writers use the whole panoply of narrating strategies to present anecdotes and recurring events. To create the dynamic quality of time passing and to orient readers, for example, they use calendar and clock time *(next day, Friday evenings, 67th birthday party)*, temporal transitions *(when, used to, finally)*, and verb tense markers (*would*, to signal recurring activities).

An Indication of the Person's Significance

Portrait writers choose as their subjects people they consider significant, and they try to convey that autobiographical significance to their readers. Readers expect to understand the person's significance; however, they do not expect the essay to begin with the kind of explicit thesis statement typical of argumentative writing. Some writers begin their essays with statements about the person and their relationship, but these statements tell only part of what they have to say. The rest comes in the writers' comments and evaluations as they describe the person and narrate the events. In the opening sentence, Karr explains why Clarice was such an important person in her young life — because she validated Karr's own "outlaw tendencies." Wu frames her essay at the beginning and end with statements about love between mothers and daughters. But she also sprinkles insights throughout the essay. After the anecdote about interrupting her mother, Wu comments that she "had learned the first of many lessons" (paragraph 3). After describing her mother's banquet preparations, she observes that a "Chinese mother's love flows from the time and energy she puts into forming a banquet" (paragraph 9).

Whether or not writers state this significance explicitly, they show it through anecdotes, recurring events, dialogue, descriptive details, and narrative actions. For example, Angelou ends by commenting on what she understood after witnessing her uncle presenting a "whole Mr. Johnson" to the strangers from Little Rock.

The subjects writers choose are significant to them, but their feelings about those subjects often involve ambivalence. Angelou's relationship with Uncle Willie is highly ambivalent, for example, as is Gray's with her father. Neither writer tries to force a neat resolution by reducing deep and contradictory feelings to simple love or hate. They acknowledge the ambivalence and accept it. In many portraits, the significance seems to lie in this inevitable complexity of close relationships. Similarly, good writers avoid sentimentalizing their relationships, neither damning nor idealizing their subjects. Gray comes close to damning her father but stops just short of it by admitting her feelings of pity and responsibility. Angelou sympathizes with Uncle Willie's shame about his lameness and stuttering, but she does not present him as a long-suffering saint.

GUIDE TO WRITING
Remembering People

THE WRITING ASSIGNMENT

THE WRITING ASSIGNMENT

Write an essay about a person who has been important in your life. Strive to present a vivid portrait, one that will let your readers see the person's character and the significance of the relationship.

INVENTION

INVENTION

- Finding a Person to Write About
- Describing the Person
- Testing Your Choice
- Exploring Memorabilia
- Researching Remembered People
- Reflecting on the Person's Significance
- Defining Your Purpose for Your Readers
- Formulating a Tentative Thesis Statement

PLANNING AND DRAFTING

PLANNING & DRAFTING

- Seeing What You Have
- Setting Goals
- Outlining
- Drafting

CRITICAL READING GUIDE

CRITICAL READING GUIDE

- First Impression
- Description
- Anecdotes and Recurring Events
- Significance
- Organization

REVISING

REVISING

- Vivid Description
- Anecdotes and Recurring Events
- Autobiographical Significance
- Organization

EDITING AND PROOFREADING

EDITING & PROOFREADING

- Checking for Sentence Fragments
- Checking for Hyphens
- A Common ESL Problem

GUIDE TO WRITING

THE WRITING ASSIGNMENT

Write an essay about a person who has been important in your life. Strive to present a vivid portrait, one that will let your readers see the person's character and the significance of the relationship.

To use the Writing Guide Software for this assignment, click on
▶ **Remembering People**
▶ **Write**

INVENTION

The following activities will help you to choose a person, to describe this person, to explore your relationship, and to define the significance of the relationship. Each activity takes no more than a few minutes. Together, they enable you to search your memory and to think deeply about the person you choose to write about. Done one by one over several days' time, they provide a record of your thinking and put you in a strong position for drafting your essay.

Finding a Person to Write About

You may already have a person in mind. Even if you do, however, it is a good idea to consider other people in order to choose the best possible subject. The following activities will help you to make a good choice.

Listing People You Remember. *Make a list of people you could write about.* List only those people about whom you can recall specific details and stories. Include relatives, teachers, coaches, employers, friends, neighbors, and others. Also include people suggested by the Considering Topics for Your Own Essay activities following each reading in this chapter. Make your list as complete as you can, including people you knew for a long time and those you knew briefly, people you knew long ago and those you knew recently, people you liked and those you disliked. The following categories may give you some ideas:

- Anyone who had authority over you or, conversely, anyone over whom you had authority
- Anyone who helped you in difficult times or made life difficult for you
- Anyone whose advice or actions influenced you
- Anyone who taught you something important about yourself

- Anyone who inspired strong emotions in you—admiration, envy, disapproval, fascination, surprise, disappointment
- Anyone whose behavior or values led you to question your own

Listing People Related to Identity and Community. *Think about people who helped you to explore your own identity and sense of community.* List only people you remember vividly—people you knew very well over a period of time. Do not overlook the importance of people outside your immediate family.

- Someone who helped you develop a previously unknown side of yourself or play a role you had not played before
- Someone who led you to redefine your sense of identity, perhaps by making you think about your appearance, gender, age, financial status, cultural traditions, or family background
- Someone who caused you to reflect on whether you or anyone else can really change
- Someone who led you to question assumptions or stereotypes you had about other people
- Someone who made you feel you were part of a larger community or that you had something worthwhile to contribute or, conversely, someone who made you feel alienated, like an outsider

Listing People Related to Work and Career. The following categories should help you to recall people who have influenced your thoughts about work and career.

- Someone who competed with you at work or someone with whom you learned to work collaboratively
- Someone who served as a positive or negative role model, perhaps leading you to change your attitudes toward work, your willingness to be supervised, or your ability to lead others
- Someone who helped you reevaluate your attitudes about a career—for example, about the pursuit of money or happiness, about focusing all of your energy in one direction to increase your chances of success, or about the value of helping people or protecting the environment
- Someone who helped you evaluate your choice of a college major or your attitude toward school in light of your career goals

Choosing a Person. *Look over your list of possibilities, and choose one person you can describe vividly and whose significance in your life you feel comfortable sharing with your readers.* Your instructors and classmates will be your first readers, but it may help to identify a group of other potential readers—friends, family members, fellow workers, teammates—who would be interested in knowing about your relationship with this person. Remember that in writing about the person, you also are writing about yourself. Make the best choice you can for now. If you become uncomfortable with this choice as you explore your memory, you can make another choice later.

Describing the Person

The following activities will help you to recall specific information that you can use to describe the person. If you complete each activity thoughtfully, you will have a wealth of remembered detail to draw on in drafting your essay. Even after you start drafting, you can return to these lists to capture fleeting memories that can be incorporated as you need them.

Appearance. *Describe the person's appearance using naming, detailing, and comparing.* You might start at the top, with the person's hair and face, and work down to the feet. Or you might start with the person's typical way of dressing. Try to remember as much as you can.

Actions. *Describe with specific narrative actions the way the person looked while moving and gesturing.* Detail any habits or typical mannerisms you recall. Depict the person in action: talking, eating, driving, playing sports, and so on.

Anecdotes and Recurring Events. *List three or more anecdotes (onetime events) and recurring events that show something important about the person and your relationship.* For each anecdote or recurring event, write for several minutes telling what happened, who was there, what was said, and what you think it would show readers about the person and your relationship.

Dialogues. *Reconstruct one or two conversations you had with the person or with someone else about the person.* Think of the first, last, or most memorable thing the person said to you. You may not remember exactly what was said, but try to re-create the conversation so that readers can imagine what was going on. Include any memorable words or phrases the person typically used, and describe the person's tone of voice. Set up each conversation as a dialogue, with each person's words starting a new line.

Testing Your Choice

Now you need to decide whether you recall enough detail to give readers a vivid impression of this particular person. Reread your invention notes to see whether your memories seem promising. If you remember specific descriptions and stories you can use in an essay, then you have probably made a good choice. Consider also your intended readers and what you would want them to understand about the person and your relationship. As you go on to explore your feelings and thoughts, you will have to decide whether you still feel comfortable writing to these particular readers about this person. If at any point you lose confidence in your choice, return to your list, and choose another person to write about.

Testing Your Choice: A Collaborative Activity

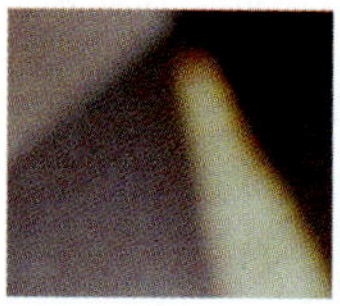

At this point, you may find it useful to get together with two or three other students and describe your remembered person. Your instructor may ask you to do this collaborative activity either in class or online, using a chatroom for your real-time discussion. This collaborative activity will help you determine whether you can present the person in a way that informs and interests others.

Presenters: Take turns briefly identifying the role the person played in your life. Give a few key details describing the person's appearance and manner, and relate an anecdote or recurring activity that reveals something important about the person and your relationship.

Listeners: After each presenter speaks, tell him or her what impression you got of the person and the relationship. Note one thing the presenter said that you found especially vivid or surprising.

Exploring Memorabilia

Memorabilia are visuals, sounds, and objects associated with the person you are writing about. Examples include photographs, homemade videos, postcards, songs, movie ticket stubs, souvenirs from trips or amusement parks, old clothes, and books. Memorabilia can help you remember details about the person. They might also be included—whole or in snippets—as visual or aural elements with your essay, multimedia presentation, or Web site.

For an illustration of memorabilia in a remembered-person essay and suggestions for designing your document, turn to pp. 131–32.

You may or may not know about any relevant memorabilia. If you can easily get access to any, take time now to do so. Add to your invention notes any details about the person the memorabilia suggest. Consider using one or more in your essay.

Researching Remembered People: An Online Activity

The World Wide Web provides a rich repository of information about individuals, both those who establish an online presence themselves and those who appear in—or are brought to mind by—sites created by others. As you think about the memories you have of your chosen person and the influence he or she has had on your life, try to make good use of the Web in the following ways:

- Investigate the person's site, if any, as well as sites of friends, family members, or others (especially people you both know) who have been important in the person's life.

- Look up sites related to places or activities you associate with the person, such as neighborhoods in which he or she has lived; schools or workplaces; favorite sports, hobbies, films and music, or restaurants.

Add to your invention notes any ideas, memories, or insights suggested by your online research. Download any visuals you might consider including in your essay—such as pictures of the person, you with the person, or other people important to the person, as well as pictures of places important in some anecdote you want to relate about the person. Also, be sure to download or record the information necessary to document each site from which you might decide to use any materials. If you do not find any information online relevant to the person you plan to write about, do not lose confidence in your choice. The Web may supplement what you know about the person, but memories of your own relationship with the person are the key to your success with this essay.

For information on acknowledging electronic sources, turn to Chapter 22, pp. 767–70.

Reflecting on the Person's Significance

Now you should consider what significance the person has had in your life. The following activities can help you discover this significance and find a way to share it with your readers.

Recalling Your Remembered Feelings and Thoughts. *Write for five minutes about your memories of the person.* Use the following questions to stimulate your memory:

If You Have Known This Person All or Most of Your Life

- What are my earliest memories of the person?
- What was our relationship like initially? What did we do together and say to each other?
- How did we influence each other at various stages of our relationship?
- What were my feelings about the person?

If You Knew This Person for a Limited Time

- What do I remember about our first meeting—the place, time, occasion, other people, words exchanged? What did I expect, and what was my first impression of the person?
- What did we do together and say to each other?
- How did we influence each other at various stages of our relationship?
- What were my feelings about the person?

Pause now to focus your thinking about your remembered feelings and thoughts. Add a couple of sentences, indicating what you most remember thinking and feeling about the person and your relationship.

Exploring Your Present Perspective. *Write for a few minutes reflecting on your relationship with this person.* Try to express your insights and feelings about the person's importance in your life. Use these questions to expand your ideas:

- Looking back on our relationship, in what ways do I understand it differently now than I did at the time?
- Would I have wanted the person to act differently toward me? How?
- How do I feel about the way I acted toward the person? Would I have behaved any differently had I known then what I know now? Why?
- If my feelings toward the person were ambivalent, how would I describe them? Were there any underlying tensions, outright disagreements, or unexpressed resentments?
- Do I see now that we differed in our values, attitudes, or goals?
- Did certain historical events in our community or in the country affect our relationship? Did differences between us (such as age, gender, cultural traditions, family background, or money) affect our relationship?
- Has looking at an old photograph or other memorabilia reminded me of anything about my relationship with the person?

Pause now to focus your thinking about your present perspective. Add two or three sentences describing what you think and feel now as you look back on your relationship with the person.

Defining Your Purpose for Your Readers

Write a few sentences, defining your purpose in writing about this particular person for your readers. Use these questions to focus your thoughts:

- Who are my readers? Remember that in choosing a person, you considered several possible readers: your instructors and classmates, friends, family members, fellow workers, teammates.
- What do my readers know about me?
- What, if anything, do they know about the person I am writing about?
- What do I want my readers to learn about the person and our relationship from reading my essay?
- What do I want to convey to readers about the person's significance in my life?

Formulating a Tentative Thesis Statement

Review what you wrote for Reflecting on the Person's Significance, and add another two or three sentences that will help you tell readers what you understand about the person and what the relationship means to you. Try to write sentences that do not summarize what you have written but that extend your insights and reflections. These sentences may be contradictory because they express ambivalent feelings. They also must necessarily be partial and speculative because you may never understand fully the person's significance in your life.

Keep in mind that readers do not expect you to begin your essay with the kind of explicit thesis statement typical of argumentative essays. If you decide to tell readers why the person was significant, you will most likely do so through interpretive or evaluative comments as you describe the person, present dialogue, and relate anecdotes and recurring activities. You are not obliged to tell readers the significance, but you should show it through the way you present the person and portray your relationship.

For more on thesis statements, see Chapter 13, pp. 611–13.

PLANNING AND DRAFTING

This section will help you review your invention writing and get started on your first draft.

If you are using the Writing Guide Software, click on
▶ **Planning and Drafting**

Seeing What You Have

You have now produced a lot of writing for this assignment: descriptions of the person's appearance and behavior, recollections of anecdotes and recurring events, memorable conversations with the person and with others about the person, reflections on the person's significance. If you have done your invention writing on the computer, you may have sentences or whole paragraphs that can be copied and pasted into your draft. Reread what you have written so far to see what you have. Watch for anecdotes, recurring events, specific narrative actions, vivid descriptive details, and choice bits of dialogue. Note also any language that resonates with feeling or that seems especially insightful. Highlight any writing you think could be used in your draft.

Then ask yourself the following questions:

- Do I remember enough specific details about the person to describe him or her vividly?
- Do I understand how the person was significant to me?
- Do my anecdotes, recurring events, and dialogues capture the person's character and portray our relationship effectively?
- Relationships tend to be complex. Will I be able to avoid sentimentality, oversimplifications, or stereotyping?

If your invention writing seems too general or superficial, or if you have discovered you feel uncomfortable writing about your relationship with this person, then choose another person to write about. As frustrating as it is to start over, it is far better to do so now than later.

If you get stuck at any stage of the writing process, the Writing Guide Software can give you some ideas for moving forward. At the top of the right-hand toolbar is a button labeled "This Stage." If you click on the Help link, the software will suggest some specific options for what to do. You can also click on Example to see another student's work at this stage.

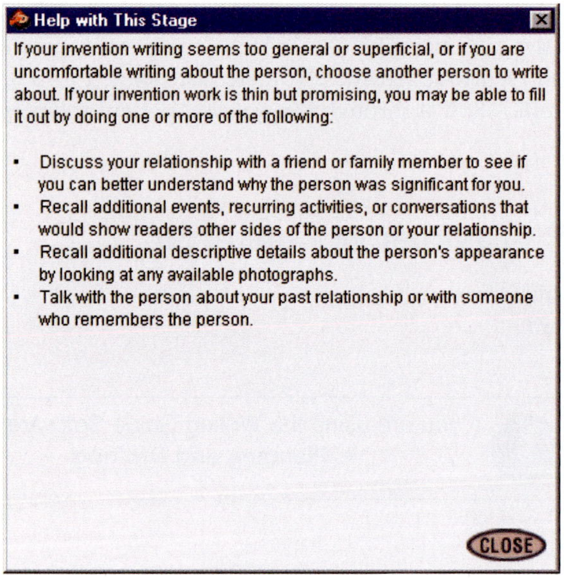

If your invention writing looks thin but promising, you may be able to fill it out by doing one or more of the following:

- Discuss your relationship with a friend or family member to see if you can better understand why the person was significant to you.
- Recall additional anecdotes, recurring events, or conversations that would show readers other sides of the person or your relationship.
- Look at photographs, letters, or other memorabilia to recall additional descriptive details about the person and your relationship.
- Talk with the person about your past relationship or with someone who remembers the person.

Setting Goals

Before actually beginning to draft, set goals to guide the decisions you will make as you draft and revise. Here are some questions that should help you set your goals:

Your Purpose and Readers

- How can I help readers to see the significance this person has for me?
- If my readers are likely to know someone like this person, how can I help them imagine the particular person I am writing about and avoid generalizing?
- If my readers are likely to be surprised by this person or by our relationship, how can I break through their preconceptions to get them to see the person as I do?

The Beginning

- What can I do in the opening sentences to awaken readers' interest? Should I begin with a surprising statement, as Karr and Wu do, or with an anecdote, as Angelou does? Should I first present myself, or should I let readers see the person right away, as Gray does?
- Should I provide some background or context, as Karr, Wu, and Gray do, or jump right into the action, as Angelou does?

Describing the Person

- Which descriptive details will give readers a strong visual image of the person? What impression will these details convey to readers? How can I use photographs, letters, or other memorabilia to help readers imagine the person?
- Which anecdotes, recurring events, and conversations will best convey the values, attitudes, and character traits I want to emphasize?
- To help readers understand my relationship with the person, what anecdotes or recurring events will show them about how we interacted with one another? What dialogues would best capture the way we spoke to one another?
- What will my stories and conversations reveal about my remembered thoughts and feelings and about my present perspective? Do I need to insert any direct statements about how I felt at the time or how I feel now?

The Ending

- What do I want the ending to accomplish? Should it sum things up? Fix a particular image in readers' minds? Provide a sense of completion? Open up new possibilities?
- How shall I end? With my present perspective, as Gray and Wu do? With the person's words or with speculation about the person's feelings, as Angelou and Karr do? With an anecdote?

Outlining

After you have set goals for your draft, you might want to make a scratch outline of your essay, indicating a tentative sequence for the material you will include. You could use the outlining function of your word processing program. Note briefly how you plan to begin; list in order possible anecdotes, recurring events, descriptions, and conversations; and note how you might end. As you draft, you may well diverge from your outline if you discover a better way to organize your essay.

Drafting

General Advice. Start drafting your essay, keeping in mind the goals you set while you were planning. As you write, try to describe your subject in a way that makes his or her importance in your life clear to your readers. Turn off your grammar checker and spelling checker at this stage if you find them distracting. Don't be afraid to skip around in your outline. Jump back and fill in a spontaneous idea, or leap ahead and write a later section first if you find that easier. If you get stuck while drafting, explore the problem by using some of the writing activities in the Invention section of this chapter. You may want to review the general drafting advice on p. 17.

As you read over your first draft, you may see places where you can add new material to reveal more about your relationship with the person. Or you may even decide that after this first draft, you can finally understand the complexity of the relationship, and you may set out to do so in a second draft.

Sentence Strategies. As you draft an essay about a remembered person, you must provide vivid, concise details to help readers imagine the person, other people, and places. Two effective ways to present such details in your sentences are by using adjectives, especially before the nouns they modify, and by using participial phrases.

Use adjectives before the nouns they modify to create vivid, concise details of people and places. Experienced writers of autobiography place very few of their adjectives after the nouns they modify. Instead, they tend to place them before the nouns, as in these examples from readings in this chapter (the adjectives are in italics, the nouns in bold):

> The lady laughed in a *soft Arkansas* **voice**. . . . (Maya Angelou, paragraph 12)

> A *compact, steel-gray* **man**, he was about the only guy on our block who didn't do *refinery* **work**. . . . (Mary Karr, paragraph 4)

If you place adjectives before nouns, where possible, your writing gains a conciseness and directness that may make it easier for your readers to imagine the people and places in your essay. Mary Karr uses single-word or compound adjectives before nouns 111 times in her essay. (Compound adjectives, like *steel-gray*, include two or more words that are usually separated by hyphens when they appear before nouns.) Yet in nearly every instance, Karr could have chosen instead to modify the noun with a less concise phrase or clause or even to move the modification into a separate sentence. In each of the following pairs, the first item is what Karr might have written, while the second is what she actually wrote:

> Only one girl showed tendencies *to be an outlaw* nearly as wild as mine.

> Only one girl showed *outlaw* tendencies nearly as wild as mine. (paragraph 1)

"Ta-da," she says, as if she were sheathed in a bathing suit *covered with crimson spangles.*

"Ta-da," she says, as if she were sheathed in a *crimson-spangled* bathing suit. (paragraph 15)

Passes *that were like bullets* flew to connect them.

Bulletlike passes flew to connect them. (paragraph 10)

Karr and the other writers in this chapter sometimes put adjectives after nouns, and they also make frequent use of adjective phrases and clauses following nouns. So will you. (In fact, it is unlikely that you could write a remembered-person essay without using adjective phrases and clauses.) Keep in mind, however, that experienced writers frequently choose the more concise and vivid adjective-noun combination.

When you write a first draft, you may find that you frequently see the need to modify a noun only after you have written it down, so you may tend to add on your adjectives in the form of phrases and clauses. As you review and revise your draft-in-progress, you can be on the lookout for phrase and clause modifiers to reduce to single-word or compound modifiers.

For more on placing adjectives in relation to nouns, go to www.bedfordstmartins.com/theguide and click on Sentence Strategies.

Use participial phrases to help readers imagine people and their actions and to relate your own thoughts. These phrases begin with verb forms called participles: either present participles, ending in *ing (being, longing, grasping, drinking),* or past participles, usually ending in *ed, d, en, n,* or *t (baked, found, driven, torn, sent).* Experienced writers of autobiography rely primarily on *ing* participles.

Participial phrases help you show simultaneous actions, make an image more specific or vivid, and relate what you were thinking at the time of an action.

To show simultaneous actions:

I stayed quiet and watched him lurch from one side, *bumping to the other,* until he reached the coal-oil tank. (Maya Angelou, paragraph 18)

He stood in the doorway, one hand *leaning against the door jamb,* a cigarette dangling from the other, flicking ashes on the carpet. . . . (Jan Gray, paragraph 13)

Looking around his bedroom, I recalled an incident that had occurred only a few months before in my bedroom. (Jan Gray, paragraph 4)

To make a previously mentioned action or image (in bold) more specific and vivid:

Once she was back home, **I'd patrol the strip of road before her house,** *skateboarding past palmettos and the dog run and back again. . . .* (Mary Karr, paragraph 5)

I remember **throwing a red-faced tantrum** before my mother's friends, *pounding my fists into the rug,* and *throwing my utensils at the steaming dishes.* (Amy Wu, paragraph 3)

When I am awake, however, she is like **a professor** *constantly hounding her prize student* and *expecting only the best.* (Amy Wu, paragraph 11)

The dresser itself was **tilted on the side,** *supported by the bed frame.* (Jan Gray, paragraph 12)

To relate what you were thinking at the time:

Once she was back home, I'd patrol the strip of road before her house, skateboarding past palmettos and the dog run and back again, *trying all the while to predict her return by the advance of her work.* (Mary Karr, paragraph 5)

I choked back the tears, *wanting to show as little emotion as possible,* and quietly murmured, "Come in." (Jan Gray, paragraph 13)

For more on using participial phrases, go to www.bedfordstmartins.com and click on Sentence Strategies.

Participial phrases are not required for a successful essay about a remembered person, yet they do provide writers an effective sentence option.

In addition to placing adjectives before the nouns they modify and to relying on participial phrases, you can strengthen your autobiographical writing with other kinds of sentences as well. You may want to review the discussions of short sentences (pp. 62–63) and of sentences that feature absolute phrases (p. 182). If you reconstruct conversations with your remembered person, you may want to preview the role of speaker tags in sentences with dialogue (pp. 181–82).

CRITICAL READING GUIDE

Now is the time to get a good critical reading of your draft. Writers usually find it helpful to have someone else read and comment on their drafts, and all writers know how much they learn about writing when they read other writers' drafts. Your instructor may schedule readings of drafts as part of your coursework—in class or online. If not, you can ask a classmate, friend, or family member to read your draft. You could also seek comments from a tutor at your campus writing center. The guidelines in this section can be used by anyone reviewing an essay about a remembered person. (If you are unable to have someone else read your draft, turn ahead to the Carrying Out Revisions section on p. 123, where you will find guidelines for reading your own draft critically.)

If you are using the Writing Guide Software, click on
▶ **Critical Reading Guide**

▶ **If You Are the Writer.** To provide focused, helpful comments, your reader must know your essay's intended audience, your purpose, and a problem in the draft that you need help solving. Briefly write out this information at the top of your draft.

- ***Readers:*** Identify the intended readers of your essay. How do you assume they will react to your writing?

- ***Purpose:*** What impression do you want readers of your essay to have of the person? What do you want them to understand about the person's significance in your life?
- ***Problem:*** Ask your draft reader to help you solve the most important problem you see with your draft. Describe this problem briefly.

▶ If You Are the Reader. The following guidelines can be useful for approaching a draft with a focused, questioning eye.

1. ***Read for a First Impression.*** Begin by reading the draft straight through to get a general impression. Read for enjoyment, ignoring spelling, punctuation, and usage errors for now. Try to imagine the person and to understand his or her significance for the writer.

   When you have finished this first quick reading, write a few sentences about your overall impression. Summarize the person's significance as you understand it. If you have any insights about the person or the relationship, write down these thoughts as well. Next, consider the problem the writer identified, and respond briefly to that concern now. (If you find that the problem is covered by one of the other guidelines listed below, respond to it in more detail there if necessary.)
2. ***Consider How Vividly the Person Is Described.*** Point out particularly effective descriptions as well as any descriptions that seem vague or that contradict the dominant impression of the person given by the rest of the essay. Note where naming, detailing, or comparing could be added to help describe the person's appearance or where specific narrative actions could show the person's typical ways of moving, gesturing, and talking. If visuals are included, let the writer know whether you think they add valuable information.
3. ***Consider the Effectiveness of Anecdotes and Recurring Events.*** Point out especially effective anecdotes and recurring events. Also point out ones that seem confusing or that do not contribute to your understanding of the person or the relationship. Identify dialogue that seems helpful, and identify dialogue that seems to be poorly written or not to add anything.
4. ***Assess Whether the Autobiographical Significance Is Clear.*** Point out the passages that help you understand the significance and any that do not aid your understanding. If you think the essay sentimentalizes the person or oversimplifies the relationship, tell the writer why you think so.
5. ***Analyze the Effectiveness of the Organization.*** Consider the overall plan, perhaps by making a scratch outline. Decide whether the writer might strengthen the essay by shifting parts around, changing the order of anecdotes, or moving the descriptions of the person.
   - Look again at the beginning of the essay to see whether it sets up the right expectations. Point out any description, anecdote, recurring event, or dialogue that might make a better beginning.

Making Comments Electronically
Most word processing software offers features that allow you to insert comments directly into the text of someone else's document. Many readers prefer to make their comments in this way because it tends to be faster than writing on a hard copy and space is virtually unlimited; from the writer's point of view, it also eliminates the problem of deciphering handwritten comments. Even where such special comment features are not available, simply typing comments directly into a document in a contrasting color can provide the same advantages.

- Look at the ending. Comment on its effectiveness, noting if it repeats what you already know or oversimplifies, trivializes, or sentimentalizes the relationship. Point out any description, anecdote, recurring event, or dialogue that would work better at the end.
- Look again at any memorabilia the writer has incorporated. Assess how well the memorabilia are integrated into the essay. Point to any items that do not help you visualize the person or understand the relationship.

REVISING

This section will help you get an overview of your draft and revise it accordingly.

If you are using the Writing Guide Software, click on
▶ **Revising**

Getting an Overview

Consider your draft as a whole, following these two steps:

1. ***Reread.*** If at all possible, put the draft aside for a day or two. When you do reread it, start by reconsidering your purpose. Then read the draft straight through, trying to see it as your intended readers will.
2. ***Outline.*** Make a quick scratch outline on paper, either with pen or pencil or by using the headings and outline or summary functions of your word processor.

Planning for Revision. Resist the temptation to dive in and start changing your text until after you have a comprehensive view of what needs to be done. Using your outline as a guide, move through the document, using the change-highlighting or commenting tools of your word processor to note comments received from others and problems you want to solve (or mark these on a hard copy if you prefer).

Analyzing the Basic Features of Your Draft. Turn to the Critical Reading Guide that begins on p. 120. Using this guide, reread the draft to identify problems you need to solve. Note the problems on your draft.

Studying Critical Comments. Review all of the comments you have received from other readers, and add to your notes any that you intend to act on. For each comment, look at your draft to determine what might have led the reader to make a particular point. Try to be objective about any criticism. Ideally, these comments will help you to see your draft as others see it (rather than as you hoped it would be) and to identify specific problems.

Carrying Out Revisions

Having identified problems in your draft, you now need to figure out solutions and—most important—to carry them out. Basically, you have three options for finding solutions:

1. Review your invention and planning notes for material you can add to your draft.
2. Do additional invention writing to provide material you or your readers think is needed.
3. Look back at the readings in this chapter to see how other writers have solved similar problems.

The following suggestions, which are organized according to the basic features on your revision chart, will get you started solving common writing problems.

Vivid Description

- ***Do you need more visual description?*** Try naming features of the person's appearance and style of dress and adding these details to help readers imagine what the person looked like. Think, for example, of Wu's mother's "silky and black" hair or Gray's father's "massive, thick hands with scaly, reddish patches" or Karr's friend Clarice's "foghorn-like blast" of a laugh and the way her legs "turned to rubber" as she shinnied up the yellow goalpost. Consider adding a vivid comparison, like Wu's metaphor describing her mother's eyes transforming "from serene pools of blackness into stormy balls of fire" or Angelou's simile visualizing Uncle Willie sitting "like a giant black Z." Look through your invention notes for descriptive language you might add to your draft. Remember that all the authors in this chapter gain both vividness and conciseness in their descriptions by placing single-word or compound adjectives before the nouns they modify.
- ***Can you add specific narrative actions?*** Look back at your invention notes to see what specific gestures or mannerisms you described. Show what the person looked like while in action—while arguing, laughing, or playing a game. Recall how effective participial phrases (beginning with *ing* or *ed* forms of verbs) can be presenting action and movement. For example, Gray describes her father in a doorway, "one hand leaning against the door jamb, a cigarette dangling from the other, flicking ashes on the carpet" (paragraph 13), and Wu remembers her mother "hounding her prize student and expecting only the best" (paragraph 11).
- ***Do any descriptions weaken the dominant impression?*** Omit extraneous descriptions, or reconsider the impression you want to make.

Checking Sentence Strategies Electronically
To check your draft for a sentence strategy especially useful in remembered-person essays, use your word processor's highlighting function to mark adjectives, including phrases and clauses that modify nouns. Then think about whether you could make your portrayal of people and places more vivid and concise and make it easier for readers to imagine them by moving any adjectives to precede the nouns they modify or by revising any of the phrases and clauses into single-word or compound adjectives. For more on placement of adjectives, see p. 118.

Anecdotes and Recurring Events

- ***Do any of the anecdotes or recurring events seem confusing?*** Try adding signals—such as clock time and transitional words—to clarify when each action occurred in relation to the other actions.
- ***Could the essay use more anecdotes or recurring events?*** Look over your invention notes for other onetime or recurring events worth telling about. Try to think of events that will help readers understand the person and your relationship.
- ***Does any dialogue seem irrelevant or poorly written?*** Eliminate any dialogue that does not help readers imagine the person or understand the relationship. Liven up quoted dialogue with the actual words and phrases that the person typically used. Summarize other parts of the conversation. Instead of relying on "he said" or "she said," describe the person's tone of voice or attitude with phrases like "she hissed" and "I said quietly, on the verge of tears."

Autobiographical Significance

- ***Do you need to clarify the significance this person has had in your life?*** Try to make the dialogues, anecdotes, and recurring events show readers something important about your relationship. Consider stating directly how you felt at the time or showing your feelings through description or by your actions. Also try letting readers know your present perspective by choosing words that convey a particular tone or by making direct statements. If any of the anecdotes, conversations, or descriptive details seem to contradict the overall impression you are trying to create, cut them, or reconsider the significance you are trying to show.
- ***Is your essay too sentimental or oversimplified?*** Consider acknowledging any ambivalent feelings you may have had or still have about the person or the relationship. Think of ways to introduce some complexity into your presentation—for example, by showing different, contradictory sides of the person's character or by showing lows as well as highs in the relationship.

Organization

- ***Is the beginning weak?*** See whether there is a better way to begin. Consider an engaging dialogue, an intriguing anecdote, or a colorful description. Try to find something that will capture readers' attention.
- ***Is the ending flat?*** Review your draft to see if there is a better place to end your essay. You might try ending with a question to leave readers with something to ponder. Or there might be something at the outset that you could refer to again at the end to frame the essay.
- ***If you have included memorabilia as part of your document's design, are the items well chosen and effectively integrated?*** Indicate where in the essay a bit of memorabilia could be described or mentioned. Think about what other memorabilia could be added.

EDITING AND PROOFREADING

Now is the time to check your revised draft for grammar, punctuation, and mechanics. According to our research, essays about remembered people frequently display problems with sentence fragments, missing hyphens in compound adjectives that precede nouns, and subject + pronoun repetition. The following guidelines will help you locate and correct these errors. This book's Web site also provides interactive online exercises to help you learn to identify and correct the first of these errors; to access these exercises, go to the URL listed in the margin next to that section of the guidelines.

If you are using the Writing Guide Software, click on
▶ **Editing and Proofreading**

A Note on Grammar and Spelling Checkers
These tools are good at catching certain types of errors, but currently there's no replacement for a good human proofreader. Grammar checkers in particular are extremely limited in what they can usually find, and often they only give you summary information that isn't helpful if you don't already understand the rule in question. They are also prone to give faulty advice for fixing problems and to flag correct items as wrong. Spelling checkers cause fewer problems but can't catch misspellings that are themselves words, such as *to* for *too*.

Checking for Sentence Fragments. A sentence fragment is a group of words that is punctuated as a sentence but that lacks some necessary sentence element, usually either a subject or a verb. Writing about a remembered person seems to encourage sentence fragments such as the following:

> **I felt sorry for Lucy. Not because of her weight problem but because of her own discomfort with herself.**

The first five words are a sentence, containing a subject *(I)* and a verb *(felt)*. The next fourteen words constitute a fragment; although they are punctuated like a sentence, beginning with a capital letter and ending with a period, they include neither a subject nor a verb. Sentence fragments seem to occur when writers try to present many specific details so that readers can imagine the person. The following examples have been edited to attach the fragment to the sentence preceding it.

For practice, go to bedfordstmartins.com/theguide/frag

▶ **I felt sorry for Lucy~~.~~; ~~Not~~ *not* because of her weight problem but because of her own discomfort with herself.**

▶ **Frank turned over the tarot cards one at a time~~.~~; ~~Each~~ *each* time telling me something about my future.**

▶ **There she stood at the door to our summer cabin~~.~~; ~~The~~ *the* spare, dimly lit space where we were to become closest friends and then bitter enemies.**

Checking for Hyphens. When you use a compound adjective (an adjective that is made up of more than one word and is not listed in a dictionary as a single entry), you have to decide whether you need to use a hyphen or hyphens between the words.

In general, you should hyphenate compound adjectives that precede a noun but not those that follow a noun.

> **Coach Braga was a feared but well-respected man.**
>
> **Coach Braga was feared but well respected.**

You may have used some compound adjectives as you were adding vivid details to your essay. Check your draft carefully to see that you have hyphenated compound adjectives correctly. Here are some more examples taken from student essays about remembered people:

- ▶ **The intruder turned out to be a fifteen-year-old runaway.**
- ▶ **One of my musician friends had a four-channel mixing board.**
- ▶ **I bought a high-powered Honda CRX.**

A Common ESL Problem. Unlike some other languages, English does not allow a subject to be repeated by a pronoun *(he, she, it, you, we, they)*.

- ▶ **Great-Aunt Sonia ~~she~~ taught me to pick mushrooms.**
- ▶ **The person I miss the most from my country ~~he~~ is Luis Paulo.**
- ▶ **In Rio, the rivalry between Flamengo and Fluminense ~~it~~ is as strong as the one here between the Yankees and the Red Sox.**

A WRITER AT WORK

REVISING A DRAFT AFTER A CRITICAL READING

In this section, we look at the way Jan Gray's essay about her father evolved from draft to revision. Included here are her first draft and the written critique of it that one of her classmates made. Read the draft and critique, and then reread her final version, "Father," printed on pp. 101–103.

The First Draft

Gray drafted her essay after spending a couple of hours on the invention and planning activities. She had no difficulty choosing a subject, since she had such strong feelings about and vivid memories of her father. On her word processor, she wrote the draft quickly in one sitting, not worrying about punctuation or usage.

My father is a large intelligent, overpowering man. He's well-respected in the food-processing trade for his clever but shrewd business tactics but I find his manipulative qualities a reflection of the maturity that he lacks. For as long as I can remember he's always had to be in control, decision-maker of the family and what he said was law. There was no compromising with this man and for that reason I've always feared him. 1

When I was little and he used to still live with us, every time he came home from work I avoided him as best I could. If he came in the kitchen I went in the living room and if he came into the living room I went upstairs to my bedroom just to avoid any confrontation. 2

Family trips were the worst. There was nowhere to go, I was locked up with him in a camper or motel for 1 week, 2 weeks or however long the vacation lasted. I remember one trip in particular. It was the summer after my 12th Birthday and the whole family (5 kids, 2 adults and one dog) were going to go "out west" for a month. We travelled through Wyoming, North and South Dakota, Colorado and other neighboring states were on the agenda. My father is the type who thinks he enjoys these family outings because as a loyal husband and father that's what he should do. Going to the state parks and the wilderness was more like a business trip than a vacation. He had made the agenda so no matter what we were to stick to it. That meant at every road sign like Yellowstone Nat'l Park we had to stop, one or more of the kids would get out stand by the sign and he'd take a picture just so he could say we've been there. Get in and get out as quick as possible was his motto to cover as much ground in as little time as he could. I hated having to take those pictures because it seemed so senseless--who cares about the dumb signs anyway? But dad is a very impatient man and any sign of non conformity was sure to put him in a rage. Not a physical violence, no, my father never did get violent but you always knew when he was boiling up inside. I could sense it in the tone of his voice and the reddish glaze that would cover his eyes. He would always stay very calm yet he was ready to explode. He never physically hurt anyone of us kids--sure we've all been spanked before 3 but only when we were younger. Although he constrained himself from inflicting harm on people he didn't hold back from damaging objects.

I remember one time I was calling my mother from a girlfriend's house to ask if I could stay over for dinner when my father unexpectedly answered the phone. "Hello?" he said, in his usually gruffy manner. 4

"Oh, hi dad. Is Mom around?" 5

"What can I do for you?" 6

"Well, I just wanted to ask her if I could eat dinner over here at Shana's." 7

"I don't think that's a very good idea. Your room is a shambles and if your not home in 10 minutes I'm really going to make a mess for you to clean up." Click. 8

I was in shock. I hadn't expected him to be there because at this time my parents were divorced but I knew he was serious so I jumped on my bike and pedalled home as fast as I could. I know I was there within ten minutes but apparently he didn't think so. I walked in the front door and headed straight for my room. When I opened my bedroom door I couldn't believe what I saw. My dresser drawers were all pulled out and clothes strewn about the room, the dresser was lying on its side and everything on top of the dresser had been cast aside in a fit of anger. I closed my door and tears began to well up in my eyes. I hated him so much at the moment. All those years of fear suddenly turned to anger and resentment. Who the hell was this man to do this when he didn't even live in the house anymore? I was slowly piecing my room back together when he knocked on the door. I choked back the tears because I didn't want him to know that his little outrage had gotten to me and quietly said, "Come in." 9

He opened the door and stood in the doorway one arm leaning on the door jamb and a cigarette with ashes falling on the carpet dangling from his other hand. 10

"I want you to know I did this for your own good" He said. "I think its time you started taking a little responsibility around this house. Now let me help you put the dresser back up." 11

"No thanks. I'd rather do it myself." 12

"Aw, come on. Let's not have any hard feelings now." 13

"Please, I said. I'd rather do it myself so would you please leave me alone." By this time I was shaking and on the 14 verge of breaking out in tears. He gave me one last look that seemed to say, "I offered, I did the right thing, I'm the good guy and she refused me so now it's her problem" and he walked out.

I was so upset that he could be so violent one moment 15
and then turn around and patronize me by offering to help clean up what he had done. That one incident revealed his whole character to me.

My father is a spiteful, manipulative, condescending, 16
malicious man and from that day on I knew I would never understand him or want to.

Gray opens her draft with a series of direct statements, describing her father's character and stating her feelings about him. The second paragraph illustrates what she tells us in the first. Paragraph 3 also serves as illustration, showing her father's domination over the family and concluding with a physical description and a suggestion of his potential for violence.

In paragraphs 4–15, Gray relates an anecdote. Though long, it is fast-paced and dramatic. She uses dialogue to show us her father's character and description to help us visualize the damage he did to her room. Then she ends as she began—with a series of statements explicitly disclosing her feelings.

Critical Comments

A classmate named Tom Schwartz read Gray's draft. He read it through once and quickly wrote down his general impression. Following the Critical Reading Guide in this chapter (pp. 120–22), Schwartz then reread the draft to analyze its features closely. It took him a little more than half an hour to complete a full written critique, which appears here. Note that each point corresponds to a step in the Critical Reading Guide.

1. Read for a First Impression

Your dad sure seems crazy. I can see he's impossible to live with. Because he's your dad, he's naturally significant. You say you hate him, and you call him a lot of names. But you also say he thought of himself as a loyal father. Was there anytime he was OK?

2. Consider How Vividly the Person Is Described

I can't picture him. What did he look like? I like the description of your messed up room. I'd like even more detail, like what clothes were thrown around and where. Did he break anything when he tipped the dresser? Was the whole room a wreck or just the dresser? Oh yeah, the detail of his cigarette ashes falling on the carpet is great. He's the one who's making the mess, not you.

You make a lot of statements. Most need illustration. I don't get it about there being no compromising with him. What do you expect him to do? My dad is pretty strict too. But he doesn't wreck my room.

3. Consider the Effectiveness of Anecdotes and Recurring Events

I don't get the vacation. Was it a birthday trip? Didn't you go to Yellowstone? Or did you just take pictures of signs? Sounds weird. The room anecdote is the best. It's really dramatic. The dialogue works as a frame, I think. He had some nerve offering to help pick up the dresser. How smug and self-satisfied. Patronizing is right. Great anecdote.

4. Assess Whether the Autobiographical Significance Is Clear

I just said you might have more feelings than you're admitting. You certainly have every reason to hate him. You say he never really hit you. But he certainly was violent, like you said.

I'm not sure why you wrote about your dad. Maybe you just feel strongly about him and need to figure him out. Maybe because he's colorful--unusual, unpredictable, not like other fathers, even divorced ones. I think he was a great choice for an essay. You disclose a lot of unpleasant stuff about your family. You certainly seem honest.

5. Analyze the Effectiveness of the Organization

The beginning doesn't lead me to expect the room anecdote. The stuff about his business seems out of place. You're writing about your relationship with him, not about his business. I don't have any suggestions.

The ending may be going too far, now that I think of it. Also, even though you say you don't want to understand him, here you are writing about him. Maybe there's more to it than you're admitting. You could end with the paragraph before. The anecdote sure does reveal his character.

This critique helped Gray a great deal in revising her draft. Reread her revision now to see what she changed (pp. 101–103). It is clear that many of her changes were suggested by Schwartz.

In writing about what she learned from writing this essay, Gray remarked:

> Tom's criticism helped me a lot. He warned me against making too many statements without illustrating them. He said I needed more showing and less telling. He also questioned the vacation anecdote. I guess it didn't have much of a point. And the incident with my room seemed to work so well I decided to add the part about my dad's apartment.

Gray realized that the heart of her essay was in the anecdote about her room. She also saw, from Schwartz's comments, that the opening paragraphs were not working. Responding to his request for more physical description of her father, Gray returned to the invention activity in which she listed important details about her father's appearance. From this exploration, she came up with the detailed description that opens her revised essay. As she was describing her father, she remembered the incident of cleaning his apartment and decided to use the description of his filthy apartment to frame the description of her own ransacked room.

Perhaps Schwartz's greatest contribution was to help Gray reexamine her father's real significance in her life. Specifically, Schwartz made her realize that her feelings were more complicated than she let on in her first draft. In writing about what she learned, Gray concluded, "The feelings I wanted to express didn't come across. I had a hard time writing the paper because I held back on a lot of things. I'm pretty ambivalent in my feelings toward my father right now." Gray discovered she could disclose her ambivalent feelings by showing her father, his room, and the confrontation over her room. Gray's portrait of her father turned out to be more sympathetic than her comments about him, expressing some ambivalence—pity as well as fury.

DESIGNING YOUR WORK

For the library display described earlier in this chapter (see p. 84), the volunteer and the waitress chose several artifacts to accompany their written narrative. They looked for photographs and objects that could be displayed in the space they had available—two glass cases and a bulletin board—and that would convey the flavor of the neighborhood during the years the diner and its owner played such an important role in the community. They chose a variety of items to accompany their written text, which provided the overall structure for the display. Enlarged photocopies of the typed document were cut apart, pasted on boards, and positioned so that viewers could easily read one section of the text, look at the artifacts, and then move on to the next part of the display.

Selecting Artifacts

Many of the artifacts that the volunteer and the waitress selected showed how the diner and the nearby high school had changed over time. Copies of menus, spanning over thirty years' time, showed that though many favorites on the menu had remained the same, prices had inevitably increased. Pennants from the high school football team showed different designs over the years but collectively reminded viewers about the many generations of teammates that had celebrated their winning games by eating at the diner afterward. Records from the jukebox showed how teenagers' tastes had changed. Yearbooks, opened to pages with student photographs (including the waitress in her high school days), illustrated how styles and attitudes changed during the decades the diner was open. In choosing these memorabilia, the volunteer and waitress contrasted the changes that come with time with the constant presence of the restaurant and the owner as part of the neighborhood. In this way, they illustrated the old adage, "The more things change, the more they stay the same."

Incorporating Letters and Other Primary Documents

The diner owner had saved a great many letters and postcards from former neighborhood children. The volunteer and the waitress included some of these often casual and conversational notes (along with a selection of informal snapshots) to show how many of the diner's patrons had considered the owner to be something of a friend and mentor. The writers clearly wanted to keep the owner apprised of the changes and advances in their lives because he had been such a friendly figure in their formative years.

Primary documents, which are original written materials rather than texts that reproduce or discuss other texts, often contain nuances and illustrate feelings that can be difficult to summarize. Reproducing the exact words used by speakers and writers is sometimes the best way to convey a sense of immediacy. Primary documents or sections of them can often speak for themselves when paraphrases or summaries are not enough to capture everything of importance. In the library display, the letters showed that many people felt affection toward the diner's owner and echoed the waitress's claims that he served as a significant mentor.

Layout showing the combination of text, photos, and other memorabilia used in part of the library display

THINKING CRITICALLY ABOUT WHAT YOU HAVE LEARNED

Now that you have spent considerable time reading and discussing essays about remembered people and then writing such an essay yourself, you should reflect on what you have learned. What problems did you have as a writer, and how did you solve them? How did reading other essays influence your own essay? What ideas do you have about the social and cultural dimensions of this kind of writing?

Reflecting on Your Writing

Write a one-page explanation, telling your instructor about a problem you encountered in writing your essay and how you solved it. Before you begin, gather all of your writing—invention and planning notes, drafts, critical comments, revising notes and plans, and final revision. Review these materials as you complete this writing task.

1. ***Identify one writing problem you needed to solve as you wrote about a remembered person.*** Do not be concerned with grammar and punctuation; concentrate on problems unique to developing an essay in this genre. For example: Did you puzzle over how to create a vivid portrait or present revealing anecdotes and scenes? Was it difficult for you to probe the significance of the relationship?
2. ***Determine how you came to recognize the problem.*** When did you first discover it? What called it to your attention? If someone else pointed out the problem to you, can you now see hints of it in your invention writings? If so, where specifically? When you first recognized the problem, how did you respond?
3. ***Reflect on how you went about solving the problem.*** Did you change the wording of a passage, cut or add details, or move paragraphs around? Did you reread one of the essays in this chapter to see how another writer handled a similar problem, or did you look back at the invention suggestions? If you talked about your writing problem with another student, a tutor, or your instructor, did talking about it help? How useful was the advice you received?
4. ***Write a brief explanation of the problem and your solution.*** Be as specific as possible in reconstructing your efforts. Quote from your invention notes or draft essay, others' critical comments, your revision plan, or your revised essay to show the various changes in your writing as you solved the problem. This is time well spent. If you can identify a particular problem, explain how you solved it, and understand what you learned from the experience, you will be able to solve future writing problems more easily.

Reviewing What You Learned from Reading

Write a page or two explaining to your instructor how the readings in this chapter influenced your final revision. Your own essay about a remembered person has been influenced to some extent by the essays in this chapter as well as by classmates' essays that you have read. These other essays may have helped you to choose your subject, suggested ideas for using anecdote and dialogue, shown you how to reveal ambivalence, or assisted you in some other way. Before you write, take some time to think about what you have learned from these selections.

1. ***Reread the final revision of your essay, and then look back at the selections you read before completing it.*** Do you see any specific influences? For example, if you were impressed with the way one of the readings avoided sentimentality, acknowledged ambivalent feelings, detailed a scene, or compared two people, look to see where you might have been striving for similar effects in your own writing. Also look for ideas you got

from your reading: writing strategies you were inspired to try, specific details you were led to include, or effects you sought to achieve.

2. ***Write an explanation of these influences.*** Did one selection have a particularly strong influence on your essay, or were several selections influential in different ways? Quote from the other essays and from your final revision to show how your portrait was influenced by the other selections. Finally, point out anything you would now do to improve your own essay, based on reviewing the reading selections again.

Considering the Social Dimensions of Essays about Remembered People

Writing about a person who played a significant role in your life can help you understand how you usually respond in certain types of relationships and what you need and expect from other people. Moreover, writing about significant people requires that you look at yourself as a participant in dynamic, reciprocal relationships. Thus, such writing encourages you to acknowledge that you are not solely responsible for all of your achievements or all of your failings. It shows you how others have helped as well as hindered you, taught as well as thwarted you.

Because they focus on interpersonal relationships, reading and writing essays about remembered people also can help us to understand other points of view. Maya Angelou, for example, writes about an incident that helped her to understand Uncle Willie's deepest feelings. When she senses his vulnerability, she begins to see him not simply in terms of how he treats her but also in terms of his own needs and frustrations. Her empathy allows her to feel closer to him, but it does not erase her other feelings of anger and resentment. Similarly, Amy Wu's essay shows us that how we understand and evaluate other people may depend on cultural expectations. Instead of seeing others as simple stereotypes, reading and writing about remembered people can help us to recognize people as complex human beings. Moreover, it can make us aware of the influences that help shape our thinking about other people and our assumptions about relationships.

These ideas about relationships lead to some basic questions about how we use writing about remembered people to understand others and ourselves. Following are two topics for discussion. Note your thoughts as you read the questions or discuss them in class. Then write a page or two for your instructor exploring your ideas and conclusions.

Ways of Understanding Other People. As we read and write essays about remembered people, we are influenced by other factors, such as whether we tend to understand people psychologically in terms of personal feelings, conflicts, and desires or more socially in terms of the public cultural, economic, and political conditions of our lives. You can understand these different perspectives by applying them to the selections in this chapter. For example, Maya Angelou's portrait of Uncle Willie could be understood psychologically, as demonstrating a child's resentment of a father figure or an adult's inability to show affection. But it also could be explained in terms of the larger social and political context. Uncle Willie's behavior toward Angelou and her brother might be connected to his position as an African American man living in the segregated South of the 1930s and 1940s. Or we could easily attribute his behavior to the fact that he lives with a marked physical disability in a society intolerant of physical differences. Depending on how you interpret behavior, you could see Uncle Willie's bullying of Angelou and her brother either as a neurotic assertion of power or as an effort to fulfill societal expectations that a substitute father should see that his children do their homework.

1. ***Consider how you have generally interpreted other people's essays about remembered people.*** Have you understood the essays primarily in personal, psychological terms? Or in more public—social, cultural, or political—terms? A little of both?
2. ***Consider how you thought of the person when you were writing about a significant person in your own life.*** Did you see the person as being motivated by certain personal needs or fears? Or did you see the person as being affected more by external social forces and pressures?

3. ***Reflect on what these two ways of understanding people make possible.*** What kinds of insights does psychological understanding of people lead to? What kinds of insights does social or political understanding of people lead to?

Views of the Self. If we assume that reading and writing about remembered people can contribute to self-discovery, we must consider how the "self" is defined and how it may be affected by significant relationships. Many people think that the self is formed early in life and remains basically unchanged by later circumstances. If you accept this view, then you are likely to see people as fundamentally unaffected by personal relationships. For example, you might see Jan Gray as emotionally independent of her father, secure in her own sense of herself: She seems neither to need his praise nor to care about his criticism. On the other hand, you may think of the self as more fluid and variable, believing that the various roles we play constitute different aspects of the self and that we change when we interact with other people. If you read Gray's essay from this perspective, you might see her relationship with her father as changing over time and Gray herself as different at various stages in the relationship. You might conclude that after her father wrecked her room, she was not the same person, that she was changed by the experience. You might also speculate that seeing her father's pathetic apartment was a turning point, enabling her to distance herself from him emotionally.

1. ***Draw some conclusions about the impact of relationships on the self.*** Do relationships provide an opportunity for us to act out who we already are? Or do they change us by giving us different roles to play?
2. ***Consider your own views of the Gray essay.*** Do you think Gray changes as her relationship with her father evolves, or do you see her as basically staying the same throughout? What in the essay makes you think so? (If you have read Gray's first draft in the Writer at Work section [pp. 126–29], think about what it reveals about her childhood.)
3. ***Think about your own essay in the same terms.*** Does it reveal a single, unified self or one that is marked by different perspectives and changes over time?

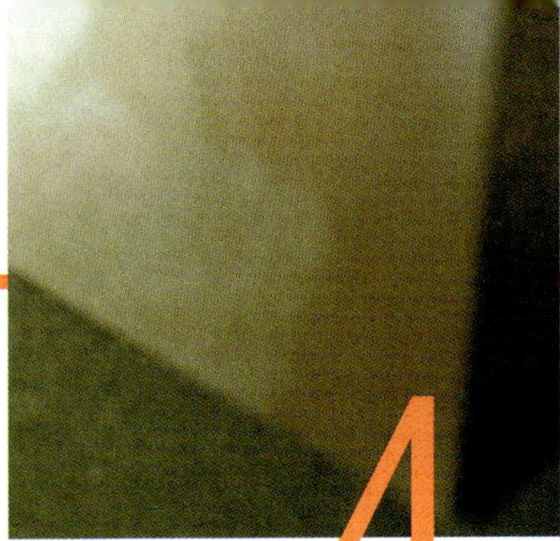

4

Writing Profiles

Profiles tell about people, places, and activities. Some profile writers try to reveal the unapparent inner workings of places or activities we considered familiar. Other profile writers introduce us to the exotic places or people—peculiar hobbies, unusual places of business, bizarre personalities.

Whatever their subject, profile writers strive most of all to enable readers to imagine the person, place, or activity that is the focus of the profile. Writers succeed only by presenting many specific and vivid details: how the person dresses, gestures, and talks; what the place looks, sounds, and smells like; what the activity requires of those who participate in it. Not only must the details be vivid, but they also must help to convey a writer's perspective—some insight, idea, or interpretation—on the subject.

Because profiles share many features with essays about remembered events and people—such as description, narration, and dialogue—you may use many of the strategies learned in Chapters 2 and 3 when you write your profile. Yet profiles differ from writing that reflects on personal experience in that profiles present newly acquired knowledge gained from your observations. In acquiring this knowledge, you practice observing, interviewing, and notetaking. These field-research activities are important in many areas of academic study, including anthropology, sociology, psychology, education, and business.

The scope of your profile may be large or small, depending on your assignment and your subject. You could attend a single event such as a parade, dress rehearsal for a play, or city council meeting and write your observations of the place, people, and activities. Or you might conduct an interview with a person who has an unusual occupation and write a profile based on your interview notes. If you have the time to do more extensive research, you might write a more complete profile based on several visits and interviews with various people.

Writing in Your Other Courses

- For an education course, a student who has been studying collaborative learning principles profiles a group of sixth-grade students working together on an Internet project. The student observes and takes extensive notes on the collaboration. To learn what the sixth graders think about working together, the student interviews them individually and as a group. She also talks with the classroom teacher about how students were prepared to do this kind of work and how their collaboration will be evaluated. She organizes the profile narratively, telling the story of one erratic but ultimately productive group meeting. She interweaves interpretive comments based on collaborative learning principles. From her descriptions and comments emerges a perspective that group work is unlikely to succeed unless the students together with the teacher frequently reflect on what they are learning and how they can work together more productively.

- For an anthropology assignment, a student plans to research and write an ethnography (somewhat like an in-depth profile) about the football program and team at a local high school. He interviews coaches, players, parents, a few teachers not directly involved in the football program, the school principal, and a sports reporter for the local newspaper. He attends several practices and games. His detailed description of the football program alternates observational details with his own perspective on what football means to this particular high school community, particularly the way it confers status on the players, their parents, and their friends.

Writing in the Community

- An art history student profiles a local artist recently commissioned to paint an outdoor mural for the city. The student visits the artist's studio and talks with him about the process of painting murals. The artist invites the student to spend the following day with a team of local art students and neighborhood volunteers working on the mural under his direction. This firsthand experience helps the student describe the process of mural painting almost from an insider's point of view. She organizes her profile around the main stages of this collaborative mural project, from conception to completion. As she describes each stage, she weaves in details about the artist, his helpers, and the site of their work, seeking to capture the civic spirit that pervades the mural project.
- For a small-town newspaper, a writer profiles a community activist who appears regularly at city council meetings to speak on various problems in his neighborhood. The writer interviews the activist as well as two of the council members. He also observes the activist speaking at one council meeting on the problem of trash being dumped in unauthorized areas. At this meeting, the activist describes an all-night vigil he made to capture on videotape a flagrant act of illegal dumping in an empty lot near his home. The writer uses the activist's appearance at this meeting as a narrative framework for the profile; he also integrates details of the activist's public life along with images from the videotape.

Writing in the Workplace

- To help a probation court judge make an informed decision about whether to jail a teenager convicted of a crime or return him to his family, a social worker prepares to write a report and make a recommendation to the court. She interviews the teenager and his parents and observes the interactions among the family members. Her report describes in detail what she saw and heard, concluding with a recommendation that the teenager be allowed to return to his parents' home.

- For a company newsletter, a public-relations officer profiles a day in the life of the new CEO. He follows the CEO from meeting to meeting—taking photographs, observing her interactions with others, and interviewing her between meetings about her management philosophy and her plans for handling the challenges facing the company. The CEO invites the writer to visit her at home and meet her family. He stays for dinner, helps clear the table, and then watches the CEO help her daughter with homework. He takes more photographs. The published profile is illustrated by two photographs, one showing the CEO engaged in an intense business conference and the other showing her helping her daughter with homework.

Practice Choosing a Profile Subject: A Collaborative Activity

The preceding scenarios suggest some occasions for writing profiles. Imagine that you have been assigned to write a profile of a person, a place, or an activity on your campus, in your community, or at your workplace. Think of subjects that you would like to know more about. Your instructor may schedule this collaborative activity as a classroom discussion or ask you to conduct an online discussion in a chatroom.

Part 1. List three to five subjects you are curious about. Choose subjects you can imagine yourself visiting and learning more about. If possible, name a specific subject—a particular musician, day-care center, or local brewery. Consider interesting *people* (for example, store owners, distinguished teachers, accomplished campus or community musicians or sports figures, newspaper columnists, public defenders, CEOs, radio talk show hosts), *places* (for example, a college health center or student newspaper office, day-care center, botanical garden, community police department, zoo, senior citizen center, farmer's market, artist's studio, museum or sculpture garden, historic building, public transportation center, or garage), and *businesses* or *activities* (for example, a comic-book store, wrecking company, motorcycle dealer, commercial fishing boat, local brewery or winery, homeless shelter, building contractor, dance studio, private tutoring service, or dog kennel).

Now get together with two or three other students, and take turns reading your lists of subjects to one another. The other group members will tell you which item on your list they personally find most interesting and why they chose that item and ask you any questions they have about it.

Part 2. After you have all read your lists and received responses, discuss these questions as a group:

- What surprised you most about group members' choices of interesting subjects from your list?
- If you were now choosing a subject from your list to write about, how would group members' comments and questions influence your choice?
- How might their comments and questions influence your approach to learning more about this subject?

READINGS

No two profiles are alike, and yet they share defining features. Together, the four readings in this chapter reveal a number of these features, so you will want to read as many of them as possible. If time permits, complete the activities in the Analyzing Writing Strategies section that follows each reading, and read the Commentary. Following the readings is a section called Basic Features: Profiles (p. 165), which offers a concise description of the features of profiles and provides examples from the four readings.

***John T. Edge** directs the Southern Foodways Symposium, which is part of the Center for the Study of Southern Culture at the University of Mississippi. He coordinates an annual conference on southern food. Food writer for the national magazine* Oxford American, *he has also written for* Cooking Light, Food & Wine, *and* Gourmet. *He has published several books, including* A Gracious Plenty: Recipes and Recollections from the American South *(1999);* Southern Belly *(2000), a portrait of southern food told through profiles of people and places; and, with photographer Robb Helfrick,* Compass Guide Georgia *(2001), a collection of new and archival photographs, literary excerpts, and practical travel information.*

This reading (and the photograph shown on p. 141) first appeared in a 1999 issue of Oxford American *and was reprinted in 2000 in* Utne Reader. *Edge profiles an unusual manufacturing business, Farm Fresh Food Supplier, in a small Mississippi town. He introduces readers to its pickled meat products, which include pickled pig lips. Like many other profile writers, Edge participates in his subject, in his case not by joining in the activities undertaken at Farm Fresh but by attempting to eat a pig lip at Jesse's Place, a nearby "juke" bar. You will see that the reading begins and ends with this personal experience.*

As you read, enjoy Edge's struggle to eat a pig lip, but notice also how much you are learning about this bar snack food as Edge details his discomfort in trying to eat it. Be equally attentive to the information he offers about the history and manufacturing of pig lips at Farm Fresh.

I'm Not Leaving Until I Eat This Thing

John T. Edge

It's just past 4:00 on a Thursday afternoon in June at Jesse's Place, a country juke 17 miles south of the Mississippi line and three miles west of Amite, Louisiana. The air conditioner hacks and spits forth torrents of Arctic air, but the heat of summer can't be kept at bay. It seeps around the splintered doorjambs and settles in, transforming the squat particleboard-plastered roadhouse into a sauna. Slowly, the dank barroom fills with grease-smeared mechanics from the truck stop up the road and farmers straight from the fields, the soles of their brogans thick with dirt clods. A few weary 1

souls make their way over from the nearby sawmill. I sit alone at the bar, one empty bottle of Bud in front of me, a second in my hand. I drain the beer, order a third, and stare down at the pink juice spreading outward from a crumpled foil pouch and onto the bar.

I'm not leaving until I eat this thing, I tell myself. 2

Half a mile down the road, behind a fence coiled with razor wire, Lionel Dufour, proprietor of Farm Fresh Food Supplier, is loading up the last truck of the day, wheeling case after case of pickled pork offal out of his cinder-block processing plant and into a semitrailer bound for Hattiesburg, Mississippi. 3

His crew packed lips today. Yesterday, it was pickled sausage; the day before that, pig feet. Tomorrow, it's pickled pig lips again. Lionel has been on the job since 2:45 in the morning, when he came in to light the boilers. Damon Landry, chief cook and maintenance man, came in at 4:30. By 7:30, the production line was at full tilt: six women in white smocks and blue bouffant caps, slicing ragged white fat from the lips, tossing the good parts in glass jars, the bad parts in barrels bound for the rendering plant. Across the aisle, filled jars clatter by on a conveyor belt as a worker tops them off with a Kool-Aid-red slurry of hot sauce, vinegar, salt, and food coloring. Around the corner, the jars are capped, affixed with a label, and stored in pasteboard boxes to await shipping. 4

Unlike most offal—euphemistically called "variety meats"—lips belie their provenance. Brains, milky white and globular, look like brains. Feet, the ghosts of their cloven hoofs protruding, look like feet. Testicles look like, well, testicles. But lips are different. 5

Loosed from the snout, trimmed of their fat, and dyed a preternatural pink, they look more like candy than like carrion.

6 At Farm Fresh, no swine root in an adjacent feedlot. No viscera-strewn killing floor lurks just out of sight, down a darkened hallway. These pigs died long ago at some Midwestern abattoir. By the time the lips arrive in Amite, they are, in essence, pig Popsicles, 50-pound blocks of offal and ice.

7 "Lips are all meat," Lionel told me earlier in the day. "No gristle, no bone, no nothing. They're bar food, hot and vinegary, great with a beer. Used to be the lips ended up in sausages, headcheese, those sorts of things. A lot of them still do."

8 Lionel, a 50-year-old father of three with quick, intelligent eyes set deep in a face the color of cordovan, is a veteran of nearly 40 years in the pickled pig lips business. "I started out with my daddy when I wasn't much more than 10," Lionel told me, his shy smile framed by a coarse black mustache flecked with whispers of gray. "The meatpacking business he owned had gone broke back when I was 6, and he was peddling out of the back of his car, selling dried shrimp, napkins, straws, tubes of plastic cups, pig feet, pig lips, whatever the bar owners needed. He sold to black bars, white bars, sweet shops, snowball stands, you name it. We made the rounds together after I got out of school, sometimes staying out till two or three in the morning. I remember bringing my toy cars to this one joint and racing them around the floor with the bar owner's son while my daddy and his father did business."

9 For years after the demise of that first meatpacking company, the Dufour family sold someone else's product. "We used to buy lips from Dennis Di Salvo's company down in Belle Chasse," recalled Lionel. "As far as I can tell, his mother was the one who came up with the idea to pickle and pack lips back in the '50s, back when she was working for a company called Three Little Pigs over in Houma. But pretty soon, we were selling so many lips that we had to almost beg Di Salvo's for product. That's when we started cooking up our own," he told me, gesturing toward the cast-iron kettle that hangs from the rafters by the front door of the plant. "My daddy started cooking lips in that very pot."

10 Lionel now cooks lips in 11 retrofitted milk tanks, dull stainless-steel cauldrons shaped like oversized cradles. But little else has changed. Though Lionel's father has passed away, Farm Fresh remains a family-focused company. His wife, Kathy, keeps the books. His daughter, Dana, a button-cute college student who has won numerous beauty titles, takes to the road in the summer, selling lips to convenience stores and wholesalers. Soon, after he graduates from business school, Lionel's younger son, Matt, will take over operations at the plant. And his older son, a veterinarian, lent his name to one of Farm Fresh's top sellers, Jason's Pickled Pig Lips.

11 "We do our best to corner the market on lips," Lionel told me, his voice tinged with bravado. "Sometimes they're hard to get from the packing houses. You gotta kill a lot of pigs to get enough lips to keep us going. I've got new customers calling every day; it's all I can do to keep up with demand, but I bust my ass to keep up. I do what I can for my family—and for my customers.

12 "When my customers tell me something," he continued, "just like when my daddy told me something, I listen. If my customers wanted me to dye the lips green, I'd ask, 'What shade?' As it is, every few years we'll do some red and some blue for the Fourth

of July. This year we did jars full of Mardi Gras lips—half purple, half gold," Lionel recalled with a chuckle. "I guess we'd had a few beers when we came up with that one."

Meanwhile, back at Jesse's Place, I finish my third Bud, order my fourth. *Now,* I tell myself, my courage bolstered by booze, *I'm ready to eat a lip.* 13

They may have looked like candy in the plant, but in the barroom they're carrion once again. I poke and prod the six-inch arc of pink flesh, peering up from my reverie just in time to catch the barkeep's wife, Audrey, staring straight at me. She fixes me with a look just this side of pity and asks, "You gonna eat that thing or make love to it?" 14

Her nephew, Jerry, sidles up to a bar stool on my left. "A lot of people like 'em with chips," he says with a nod toward the pink juice pooling on the bar in front of me. I offer to buy him a lip, and Audrey fishes one from a jar behind the counter, wraps it in tinfoil, and places the whole affair on a paper towel in front of him. 15

I take stock of my own cowardice, and, following Jerry's lead, reach for a bag of potato chips, tear open the top with my teeth, and toss the quivering hunk of hog flesh into the shiny interior of the bag, slick with grease and dusted with salt. Vinegar vapors tickle my nostrils. I stifle a gag that rolls from the back of my throat, swallow hard, and pray that the urge to vomit passes. 16

With a smash of my hand, the potato chips are reduced to a pulp, and I feel the cold lump of the lip beneath my fist. I clasp the bag shut and shake it hard in an effort to ensure chip coverage in all the nooks and crannies of the lip. The technique that Jerry uses—and I mimic—is not unlike that employed by home cooks mixing up a mess of Shake 'n Bake chicken. 17

I pull from the bag a coral crescent of meat now crusted with blond bits of potato chips. When I chomp down, the soft flesh dissolves between my teeth. It tastes like a flaccid cracklin', unmistakably porcine, and not altogether bad. The chips help, providing texture where there was none. Slowly, my brow unfurrows, my stomach ceases its fluttering. 18

Sensing my relief, Jerry leans over and peers into my bag. "Kind of look like Frosted Flakes, don't they?" he says, by way of descrbing the chips rapidly turning to mush in the pickling juice. I offer the bag to Jerry, order yet another beer, and turn to eye the pig feet floating in a murky jar by the cash register, their blunt tips bobbing up through a pasty white film. 19

Connecting to Culture and Experience: Gaining Firsthand Experience

Undoubtedly, Edge believed that he should visit a place where Farm Fresh Food Supplier's most popular product is consumed. He went further, however: He decided to experience the product firsthand by handling, smelling, and tasting it. Except for his own squeamishness, nothing prevented him from gaining the firsthand experience he sought. Aside from experiences in family and personal relationships, think about times when you have sought to gain firsthand experience and either succeeded or failed. Perhaps you yearned to sing but never took lessons, challenged yourself to go beyond watching basketball or soccer on television and won a spot on a school team, dreamed of an internship at a certain workplace but never could find the time to arrange it, imagined visiting a natural or historic site you had only read about and found a way to do so, or thought about joining others to protest a social injustice but never took action.

Identify one longed-for personal experience you missed out on and one you achieved, and think about why you failed in one case and succeeded in the other. At the time, how ready and able were you to gain access to the experience? What part did your personal decisiveness and effort play? Did you feel timid or bold about seeking what you wanted? Did you try to be accommodating, or did you have to be challenging or even disruptive? What roles did other people play? Who supported you, and who attempted to silence or exclude you? With whom did you have to negotiate? How did your gender or age affect the outcome? How important was money or other resources?

With two or three other students, discuss your attempts to gain longed-for personal experience. Begin by telling each other about one experience, explaining briefly what drew you to it, what happened, how you felt about the outcome, and why you think you succeeded or failed. Then, as a group, discuss what your stories reveal about what motivates and helps young Americans and what frustrates them as they try to gain longed-for experiences that may open new opportunities to them.

Analyzing Writing Strategies

1. The introduction to this chapter makes several generalizations about profile essays. Consider which of these assertions apply to Edge's essay:
   - It is based on the writer's newly acquired observations.
   - It takes readers behind the scenes of familiar places or introduces them to unusual places and people.
   - It is informative and entertaining.
   - It presents scenes and people vividly through description, action, and dialogue.
   - It suggests or asserts the writer's perspective on the subject—an idea about the subject or an insight into it.
2. Edge focuses on one of Farm Fresh's products, pickled pig lips. He probably assumes that most of his readers have never seen a pickled pig lip, much less eaten one. Therefore, he describes this product carefully. To see how he does so, underline in paragraphs 4, 5, 7, 14, and 18 every **detail** of a pickled pig lip's appearance, size, texture or consistency, smell, and taste. If you have never seen a pickled pig lip, what more do you need to know to imagine what it looks like? Which details make a lip seem appealing to you? Which ones make it seem unappealing? Edge scatters the details across the profile, rather than collecting them in one place. For you as one reader, how did this scattering help or hinder your attempts to fully understand what a pig lip is like?

For more on sensory descriptions, see Chapter 15, pp. 648–53.

3. To present their subjects, profile writers occasionally make use of a **sentence strategy** that relies on a sentence structure known as an *absolute phrase*. To discover what absolute phrases contribute, underline these absolutes in Edge's profile: in paragraph 1, sentence 4, from "the soles" to the end of the sentence, and sentence 6, from "one empty bottle" to the end; in paragraph 8, sentence 2, from "his shy smile" to the end; and in paragraph 19, sentence 3, from "their blunt tips" to the end. Make notes in the margin about how the absolute phrase seems to be related to what comes before it in the sentence. Given that Edge's goal is to help readers imagine what he observes, what does each absolute contribute toward that goal? How are these four absolutes alike and different in what they add to their sentences?

To learn more about how absolute phrases contribute to profiles, see Sentence Strategies, p. 182.

Commentary: A Topical Plan

A profile may be presented **narratively**, as a sequence of events observed by the writer during an encounter with the place, person, or activity; or it may be presented **topically**, as a series of topics of information gathered by the writer about the person, place, or activity. Though Edge **frames** (begins and ends) his profile with the narrative or story about attempting to eat a pig lip, he presents the basic information about Farm Fresh Food Supplier topically.

The following scratch outline of Edge's profile shows at a glance the topics he chose and how they are sequenced:

For more on scratch outlining, see Chapter 11, pp. 572–74.

loading meat products on a truck (paragraph 3)

an overview of the production process, with a focus on that day's pig lips (4)

pig lips' peculiarity in not looking like where they come from on the pig (5)

the origin of Farm Fresh's materials—shipped frozen from the Midwest (6)

some characteristics of a pig lip (7)

Lionel's introduction to marketing food products and services (8)

Lionel's resurrection of the family meatpacking business (9)

family involvement in the business (10)

Lionel's marketing strategy (11)

Lionel's relations with customers (12)

Reviewing his interview and observation notes taken while he was at Farm Fresh, Edge apparently decided to organize them not as a narrative in the order in which he took them but as topics sequenced to be most informative for readers. He begins with the finished product, with Lionel loading the truck for shipment. Then he outlines the production process and mentions the various products. From there, he identifies the source of the products and briefly describes a pig lip, his main interest. Then he offers a history of Farm Fresh and concludes with Lionel's approach to his business. When you plan your profile essay, you will have to decide whether to organize your first draft topically or chronologically.

Considering Topics for Your Own Essay

Consider writing about a place that serves, produces, or sells something unusual, perhaps something that, like Edge, you could try yourself for the purpose of further informing and engaging your readers. If such places do not come to mind, you could browse the Yellow Pages of your local phone directory. There are many possibilities: producer or packager of a special ethnic or regional food or a local café that serves it, licensed acupuncture clinic, caterer, novelty and toy balloon store, microbrewery, chain saw dealer, boat builder, talent agency, manufacturer of ornamental iron, bead store, nail salon, pet fish and aquarium supplier, detailing shop, tattoo parlor, scrap metal recycler, fly fishing shop, handwriting analyst, dog or cat sitting service, photo restorer, burglar alarm installer, Christmas tree farm, wedding specialist, reweaving specialist, wig salon. You need not evaluate the quality of the work provided at a place as part of your observational essay. Instead, keep the focus on informing readers about the service or product the place offers. Relating a personal experience with the service or product is a good idea but not a requirement for a successful essay.

To use the Writing Guide Software to record your ideas, click on
▶ **Journal**

***Trevor B. Hall** runs a Boston nonprofit company, The Call Academy, that provides enrichment programs for low-income urban high school students. Program participants study literature, practice the documentary arts (writing, video and film, photography), and take part in adventure travel.* DoubleTake, *a magazine for the documentary arts, published Hall's "A Documentary Classroom," a profile of one teacher's efforts to bring documentary into the English classroom, in 2001. The following profile was published in* DoubleTake *in 2000. As you read, notice how Hall goes about presenting the Edison Café as an irreplaceable social asset to Skagit Valley, Washington.*

The Edison Café

Trevor B. Hall

It is almost 6 A.M. in the town of Edison, Washington, 1
and Julie Martin's headlights are cutting through fog and darkness. Julie is the cook and owner of the Edison Café. When she pulls up behind the small, crooked, fire-engine-red building, her first customer is waiting for her. Few words are passed as she opens the doors and begins to ready the kitchen. Soon the local farmers will begin to pour in. They are tall, hearty men with weathered baseball caps or cowboy hats, earned dirt under every fingernail. Their entrance is always the same: the door creaks open; everyone looks at the new arrival, who swings around the lunch counter to the coffee machine.

"Mornin'," shouts Julie from the kitchen. 2

The new arrival quietly replies: "How-do?" The regulars each grab a mug, fill it, then top off everyone else's cup. It's an unwritten rule that no one's coffee gets low or cold. 3

Outside it's still pitch black, and the only light in Edison comes from the café—the fluorescent red EAT sign in the window and the dim yellow glow of the interior lights. Some mornings, there is playful banter; at times they all hold comfortable stares and listen quietly to the faux-antique, turquoise radio. 4

Edison is set in Washington State's Skagit Valley, some twenty-three thousand square acres of the most plush, fertile farmland one can imagine. The valley has the look of a dark-green down comforter, creased by the water that travels down from the Cascade Mountains on its way to the Pacific Ocean. Dotting the horizon to the west are the rounded San Juan Islands. Directly to the east, the ten-thousand-foot volcanic Mount Baker stands watch (when, on occasion, the winter clouds split to allow its appearance). It is from this mountain that rainwater begins the journey down through the foothills and into the Samish River and its tributaries, creating a wetlands on this valley floor. 5

The valley gives life to a wide variety of birds: waterfowl (mostly ducks), eagles, blue herons, huge flocks of sparrows, occasionally an exotic snowy egret or a mysterious Egyptian hawk. The valley is home to some of the best winter hawk-watching in the country. It is an active, lively place where nature and its doings are never far from the eye. 6

Most of Skagit Valley is farmland, and Edison is one of the only towns with remnants of a main street (though Edison is no longer officially recognized by a postal zip code of its own). Established in 1869 and named after the inventor Thomas Alva Edison, the town enjoyed a heyday in the late 1880s, when it boasted three hotels, two churches, three grocery stores, a hardware store, a bank, a cheese factory, and four thirst-quenching establishments. For the most part, individually owned farms have since been pushed out by larger industry, and the logging and fishing businesses have slowed to a near standstill. The town has learned to be grateful for its two remaining bars and, of course, the Edison Café. 7

Mt. Baker's clouds over Edison, 2000

Early-rise breakfast, 2000

As the day progresses, the café will see three waves of customers: the early-morning farmers; the gamy, dice-wielding "shakers and rollers"; and the Edison Elementary School's rear-window gang. 8

The first crew is mostly men (and two of their wives, Rosie and Lucille) in their fifties or sixties. They are people who have, in one way or another, worked the land of Skagit Valley: dairy farmers, potato farmers, fishermen, construction workers. The Edison Café is home for them—a combination dining room and kitchen. 9

One local asserts that while an estimated twenty-seven people have actually owned the café since its beginnings in 1944, life in the café hasn't changed much over the years. Some of the owners have tried to fancy the place up a bit, but the changes were always met with either indifference or outright scorn by its customers. Julie understands: "It needs to be a place where people can come in with cow dung on their boots. You can't change that." 10

Julie is an attractive woman in her early forties, her blond hair usually pulled back for cooking—a woman who knows what people around here like, to the point that almost no one actually places a food order. Customers sit down, chat with whoever is around, and eventually some food shows up—their meal, which is a day's selection of certain familiar possibilities: two pieces of bacon, a pancake, and a sausage; two eggs, a piece of bacon, and hash browns; an egg, two pancakes, and toast. The bill arrives on time. Everyone pays for the food (though some on mentally kept accounts), but if you're lucky, you can drink coffee for free. 11

"They roll me double or nothin' for the coffee," Julie declares. With five dice, in three rolls, you must get a six, a five, a four, then the highest total of the remaining two dice wins. Those are the basic rules, but time has built many nuances into this game. Before people head out the door, they call to Julie, "Come roll me for this coffee." Julie emerges from the kitchen, dries her hands on her white apron, straightens her shoulders, peers at her competition, and grabs the dented leather dice cup. When Julie is on one of her winning streaks, she gets her fair share of suspicious looks, but it's part of the deal. 12

"Now, don't you bad mouth me for that one," she gently warns a loser as she makes way back to the griddle. 13

By about 7:30 A.M., the first wave of customers is off to work, and the dice cup has moved to the corner table, where the next wave will hit. It's not the last Julie will see of the morning crew, though; most will return periodically throughout the day (some of them four or five times). A little bit of light comes into the valley, and Julie can step out back for a moment's break. 14

Other than the arrival of her two waitresses—the sharp-tongued Roxy and the charming woman known as Bear—or one of Julie's two high-school-aged daughters, the midmorning quiet lasts until about ten o'clock, when the shakers and rollers—a group of eight to ten local residents, mostly retired couples—show up, as they do every day, for The Game. The first half-hour or so is spent rolling for coffee, until someone rises to the top as the day's winner. That person then rolls one-on-one against Julie, double or nothing, for the entire table's coffee. Talk of the weather, the nation, and town gossip rumble through the café. Then, promptly at 10:45, the usual breakfasts are delivered for everyone. 15

Morning dice, 2000

The meals are the standard fare—eggs, toast, hash browns, bacon—except in the case of Peter Menth, who is in his late sixties and whose well-trimmed gray beard and black captain's hat give him the authority of a fishing-boat captain at sea. His meal commands an equally grand respect and even has its own name on the menu: the Peter Pan Hotcake. This is no ordinary hotcake, and is surely the mark of a man who "won't grow up." Simply put, it is huge—so big that Peter bought his own larger-than-life plate to accommodate it—but the hotcake still falls over the sides. Julie respectfully keeps the plate in back. 16

Yet the usual stack is nothing to ignore—especially when ordered as part of the farmer's breakfast special: two eggs, two sausage links, two strips of bacon, hash browns, and two pancakes, all for $7.25. Many adolescent appetites have made an attempt at this one and come close—until the pancakes arrived, thudding on the counter under their own weight. 17

In his book *Blue Highways*, William Least Heat-Moon offers that the measure of an American café can be taken by the number of calendars on its wall; five calendars earns his top rating. The Edison Café tops that by three, and I would add one twist to Least Heat-Moon's measuring stick: if one of the calendars features pictures of tractors . . . loosen your belt. This café offers such a calendar, and a meal for two, really, all for under $10; a customer is hard pressed to spend more than $5, and further pressed not to leave the Edison Café teetering, completely full. Nonetheless, at noon a gang of students from the Edison Elementary School certainly tries their hand at this. (The café sits on the school's property, always has, which is why the elementary-school students are allowed to run over for lunch.) One local, Duane, recalls the café's presence in his life during his days as a student in the late 1940s: "I remember being beat up in this café in 1947—by my dad," he says with a smile—then explains: "I brought a white-face bull right in the front door, did a one-eighty-degree turn with it, and headed out. They banned me for a month." The school cafeteria food soon helped him mend his ways, and today's students are quick to tell you that Julie's food is an "awesome" option. 18

The madness begins quietly enough as two of the students, Emma and Kyla, arrive before the crowds. Through good grades, they have earned the right to "work the window" and get a free lunch in exchange. Moments after their arrival, the rush is on. From the back window of the café, it looks like a mob running in panic from a fire: backpacks bouncing off of shoulders, sneakers squeaking across the wet pavement, eyes wide with anticipation. 19

"We keep them under control," Emma says. "They give us their order, we shout it out to Julie, then we make sure everyone gets the right food. It's not too hard, and we get a free lunch, which is great!" Julie loves her two helpers, referring to them as "my girls." 20

This last rush is usually over by twelve-thirty; then Julie can take a well-earned rest on the bench out back. The sun is most likely to show its face about this time of the day, and she leans against the café wall, her face aimed at the warmth. One of her waitresses likely joins her, and the gossip begins. If it's her daughter, she often prods, "Didn't I fire you this morning for being late?" Leaning on her mom's shoulder, the daughter shoots back, "Mom, you fire me every morning." 21

So it has gone for years and years—a community tradition born of the need for food, comfort, and ritual. Everyday service to others is willingly and eagerly offered as a café 22 owner's privilege—a service tendered with love, not because it promotes good corporate culture or because it will bolster profits, but because these are Julie's day husbands, her shakers and rollers, her girls. The Edison Café is a town's reliable home away from home, where personal politics and pettiness must be checked at the door. From the dark, foggy mornings to the breaks of sunshine in the afternoon, Julie knows that day in and day out, for better and for worse, in Edison, Washington, she "gets 'em fed."

Connecting to Culture and Experience: Community Social Life

You belong to several communities: your college, your neighborhood if you live off campus, perhaps a church or other spiritual community. You can see that communities are small-scale, local, and somewhat intimate, in that people at least recognize and greet each other and perhaps even talk casually. Besides these occasional brief, casual interactions, people in a community are likely to seek more substantial social interactions and look for places to find it, like the customers at the Edison Café.

Think about the communities you have belonged to or now belong to, and identify one place where you occasionally met or meet now to talk informally with others. These would be meetings, indoors or out, with two or more people you consider friends or perhaps only acquaintances. The meetings recur, at least for a few weeks. There is typically no agenda or purpose for the meeting, even though you might eat together, play cards, or watch a sports event on television. It may be scheduled, or it may occur spontaneously. There could be a different mix of people at each meeting.

With two or three other students, describe in turn this place, detailing where you meet, who typically shows up, how frequently and for how long you talk, and what you talk about. Then together explore the social meanings of these informal meetings. That is, what is your motive for meeting? What sustains your interest in meeting? What do you gain as individuals and as a group from these meetings? What do you think holds together groups like this, and what dissolves them?

Analyzing Writing Strategies

1. A profile writer attempts to convey a **perspective** on a subject—a point of view on it, an insight into it, an idea about it, an interpretation of it, or even a judgment about its worth. This perspective can be stated or implied, and all the details and information in the profile must be consistent with this perspective. Hall states his perspective quite directly in paragraph 22. In that paragraph, underline phrases that identify the role of the Edison Café in the community. Also underline relevant phrases in paragraphs 7, 9, and 15. From these various statements, write a sentence of your own that concisely expresses your understanding of Hall's perspective on his subject.
2. Photographs seem a natural partner to the written text of a profile. Hall includes three with his text. With film or digital camera, you can create visual images to

combine with the text of your profile. Any images you choose to include should complement the information your text offers and be consistent with your perspective on the subject.

Consider Hall's images in relation to his text, and make notes about what the images contribute to your understanding of the Edison Café. Try to think about the text without the images. What do the images add that you could not imagine or infer about the café from the text itself? How do the images support Hall's perspective on the café?

Commentary: A Role for the Writer

Depending on their subjects and personal inclinations, profile writers usually adopt one of two roles: **participant observer** or **detached observer**. In the participant-observer role, the writer reports his personal involvement and engagement in the subject. John T. Edge adopts this role in profiling Farm Fresh Food Supplier by narrating his personal experience with a real pig lip, oozing red-dyed vinegar and other unidentified juices, caked with soggy crushed potato chips, soft and yielding to the touch. He inserts himself in a vivid and humorous way into his profile. In contrast, Trevor B. Hall adopts the detached-observer role in profiling the Edison Café. He remains invisible, merely a reporter of what he observes. Although most readers would assume that Hall had eaten a meal at the café, he offers no clues that he did so. His chosen role as a writer may not correspond to his role as a researcher, however. Sitting quietly at the counter, sipping his coffee, not talking to anyone—only observing—he could have learned much of what he presents in the profile. He could have remained a cool observer of activities. Instead, it is evident that he interviewed owner Julie Martin, two or three of the adult customers, and two of the elementary-school students. It seems very likely that he ate at least one, maybe two, meals, since he was at the café from before 6 A.M. to after 12:30 P.M. Even though Hall almost certainly initiated conversations, drank many cups of coffee, and ordered a meal or two, he nevertheless adopts a detached-observer role in writing the profile.

Considering Topics for Your Own Essay

Consider writing about places or activities that fulfill a major—or even essential—social function in your community, just as the Edison Café does for many people who live in Edison, Washington. You might visit a place where people, perhaps of different ages, gather occasionally and informally, like a senior citizens' center, local park, bowling alley, campaign headquarters, public library reading room, coffee house, café, or bar. Or you might profile an activity with a community purpose, such as a parade, Little League game, church youth group, college informal study group, benefit walkathon or marathon, gallery opening, bake sale, or jazz festival.

To use the Writing Guide Software to record your ideas, click on
▶ **Journal**

***Peggy Orenstein** has been a managing editor of* Mother Jones, *a founding editor of the magazine* 7 days, *and a member of the editorial boards of* Esquire *and* Manhattan, inc. *Her essays have appeared in the* New York Times Magazine, *the* New Yorker, Vogue, *and other nationally known publications. Her 1994 book,* School Girls: Young Women, Self-Esteem, and the Confidence Gap, *won a* New York Times *Notable Book of the Year Award, and in 1996, the National Women's Political Caucus honored her for her contributions to literature and politics. She has since published* Flux: Women on Sex, Work, Kids, Love, and Life in a Half-Changed World *(2002).*

This profile, which takes place primarily in an eighth-grade math class, comes from the opening chapter of School Girls. *Orenstein undertook the extensive research for this book after reading a study conducted by the American Association of University Women in 1991, which identified a gender gap in the achievements of male and female students in America. Her research concentrated on the ways in which some schools and teachers—often unwittingly—may inhibit girls' classroom experiences and constrain their opportunities to participate. As you read the profile, think about whether the story it tells is one you have witnessed firsthand.*

The Daily Grind: Lessons in the Hidden Curriculum

Peggy Orenstein

Amy Wilkinson has looked forward to being an eighth grader forever—at least for the last two years, which, when you're thirteen, seems like the same thing. By the second week of September she's settled comfortably into her role as one of the school's reigning elite. Each morning before class, she lounges with a group of about twenty other eighth-grade girls and boys in the most visible spot on campus: at the base of the schoolyard, between one of the portable classrooms that was constructed in the late 1970s and the old oak tree in the overflow parking lot. The group trades gossip, flirts, or simply stands around, basking in its own importance and killing time before the morning bell. 1

At 8:15 on Tuesday the crowd has already convened, and Amy is standing among a knot of girls, laughing. She is fuller-figured than she'd like to be, wide-hipped and heavy-limbed with curly, blond hair, cornflower-blue eyes, and a sharply upturned nose. With the help of her mother, who is a drama coach, she has become the school's star actress: last year she played Eliza in Weston's production of *My Fair Lady.* Although she earns solid grades in all of her subjects—she'll make the honor roll this fall—drama is her passion, she says, because "I love entertaining people, and I love putting on characters." 2

Also, no doubt, because she loves the spotlight: this morning, when she mentions a boy I haven't met, Amy turns, puts her hands on her hips, anchors her feet shoulder width apart, and bellows across the schoolyard, "Greg! Get over here! You have to meet Peggy." 3

She smiles wryly as Greg, looking startled, begins to make his way across the schoolyard for an introduction. "I'm not exactly shy," she says, her hands still on her hips. "I'm bold." 4

Amy is bold. And brassy, and strong-willed. Like any teenager, she tries on and discards different selves as if they were so many pairs of Girbaud jeans, searching 5 ruthlessly for a perfect fit. During a morning chat just before the school year began, she told me that her parents tried to coach her on how to respond to my questions. "They told me to tell you that they want me to be my own person," she complained. "My mother *told* me to tell you that. I do want to be my own person, but it's like, you're interviewing me about who I am and she's telling me what to say—that's not my own person, is it?"

When the morning bell rings, Amy and her friends cut off their conversations, scoop up their books, and jostle toward the school's entrance. Inside, Weston's hallways smell chalky, papery, and a little sweaty from gym class. The wood-railed staircases at either end of the two-story main building are worn thin in the middle from the scuffle of hundreds of pairs of sneakers pounding them at forty-eight-minute intervals for nearly seventy-five years. Amy's mother, Sharon, and her grandmother both attended this school. So will her two younger sisters. Her father, a mechanic who works on big rigs, is a more recent Weston recruit: he grew up in Georgia and came here after he and Sharon were married. 6

Amy grabs my hand, pulling me along like a small child or a slightly addled new student: within three minutes we have threaded our way through the dull-yellow hallways to her locker and then upstairs to room 238, Mrs. Richter's math class. 7

The twenty-two students that stream through the door with us run the gamut of physical maturity. Some of the boys are as small and compact as fourth graders, their legs sticking out of their shorts like pipe cleaners. A few are trapped in the agony of a growth spurt, and still others cultivate downy beards. The girls' physiques are less extreme: most are nearly their full height, and all but a few have already weathered the brunt of puberty. They wear topknots or ponytails, and their shirts are tucked neatly into their jeans. 8

Mrs. Richter, a ruddy, athletic woman with a powerful voice, has arranged the chairs in a three-sided square, two rows deep. Amy walks to the far side of the room and, as she takes her seat, falls into a typically feminine pose: she crosses her legs, folds her arms across her chest, and hunches forward toward her desk, seeming to shrink into herself. The sauciness of the playground disappears, and, in fact, she says hardly a word during class. Meanwhile, the boys, especially those who are more physically mature, sprawl in their chairs, stretching their legs long, expanding into the available space. 9

Nate, a gawky, sanguine boy who has shaved his head except for a small thatch that's hidden under an Oakland A's cap, leans his chair back on two legs and, although the bell has already rung, begins a noisy conversation with his friend, Kyle. 10

Mrs. Richter turns to him, "What's all the discussion about, Nate?" she asks. 11

"*He's* talking to *me,*" Nate answers, pointing to Kyle. Mrs. Richter writes Nate's name on the chalkboard as a warning toward detention and he yells out in protest. They begin to quibble over the justice of her decision, their first—but certainly not their last—power struggle of the day. As they argue, Allison, a tall, angular girl who once told me, "My goal is to be the best wife and mother I can be," raises her hand to ask a question. Mrs. Richter, finishing up with Nate, doesn't notice. 12

"Get your homework out, everyone!" the teacher booms, and walks among the students, checking to make sure no one has shirked on her or his assignment. Allison, who 13 sits in the front row nearest both the blackboard and the teacher, waits patiently for another moment, then, realizing she's not getting results, puts her hand down. When Mrs. Richter walks toward her, Allison tries another tack, calling out her question. Still, she gets no response, so she gives up.

As a homework assignment, the students have divided their papers into one hun- 14
dred squares, color-coding each square prime or composite—prime being those numbers which are divisible only by one and themselves, and composite being everything else. Mrs. Richter asks them to call out the prime numbers they've found, starting with the tens.

Nate is the first to shout, "Eleven!" The rest of the class chimes in a second later. 15
As they move through the twenties and thirties, Nate, Kyle, and Kevin, who sit near one another at the back of the class, call out louder and louder, casually competing for both quickest response and the highest decibel level. Mrs. Richter lets the boys' behavior slide, although they are intimidating other students.

"Okay," Mrs. Richter says when they've reached one hundred. "Now, what do you 16
think of one hundred and three? Prime or composite?"

Kyle, who is skinny and a little pop-eyed, yells out, "Prime!" but Mrs. Richter turns 17
away from him to give someone else a turn. Unlike Allison, who gave up when she was ignored, Kyle isn't willing to cede his teacher's attention. He begins to bounce in his chair and chant, *"Prime! Prime! Prime!"* Then, when he turns out to be right, he rebukes the teacher, saying, "See, I told you."

When the girls in Mrs. Richter's class do speak, they follow the rules. When Allison 18
has another question, she raises her hand again and waits her turn; this time, the teacher responds. When Amy volunteers her sole answer of the period, she raises her hand, too. She gives the wrong answer to an easy multiplication problem, turns crimson, and flips her head forward so her hair falls over her face.

Occasionally, the girls shout out answers, but generally they are to the easiest, 19
lowest-risk questions, such as the factors of four or six. And their stabs at public recognition depend on the boys' largesse: when the girls venture responses to more complex questions, the boys quickly become territorial, shouting them down with their own answers. Nate and Kyle are particularly adept at overpowering Renee, who, I've been told by the teacher, is the brightest girl in the class. (On a subsequent visit, I will see her lay her head on her desk when Nate overwhelms her and mutter, "I hate this class.")

Mrs. Richter doesn't say anything to condone the boys' aggressiveness, but she 20
doesn't have to: they insist on—and receive—her attention even when she consciously tries to shift it elsewhere in order to make the class more equitable.

After the previous days' homework is corrected, Mrs. Richter begins a new lesson, 21
on the use of exponents.

"What does three to the third power mean?" she asks the class. 22

"I know!" shouts Kyle. 23

Instead of calling on Kyle, who has already answered more than his share of ques- 24
tions, the teacher turns to Dawn, a somewhat more voluble girl who has plucked her eyebrows down to a few hairs.

"Do you know, Dawn?" 25

Dawn hesitates, and begins "Well, you count the number of threes and. . . ." 26

"But I know!" interrupts Kyle. *"I know!"* 27

Mrs. Richter deliberately ignores him, but Dawn is rattled: she never finishes her 28
sentence, she just stops.

"I know! ME!" Kyle shouts again, and then before Dawn recovers herself he blurts, 29
"It's three times three times three!"

At this point, Mrs. Richter gives in. She turns away from Dawn, who is staring 30
blankly, and nods at Kyle. "Yes," she says. "Three times three times three. Does everyone get it?"

"YES!" shouts Kyle; Dawn says nothing. 31

Mrs. Richter picks up the chalk. "Let's do some others," she says. 32

"Let me!" says Kyle. 33

"I'll pick on whoever raises their hand," she tells him. 34

Nate, Kyle, and two other boys immediately shoot up their hands, fingers squeezed 35
tight and straight in what looks like a salute.

"Don't you want to wait and hear the problem first?" she asks, laughing. 36

They drop their hands briefly. She writes "8^4" on the board. "Okay, what would that 37
look like written out?"

Although a third of the class raises their hands to answer, including a number of stu- 38
dents who haven't yet said a word, she calls on Kyle anyway.

"Eight times eight times eight times eight," he says triumphantly, as the other stu- 39
dents drop their hands.

When the bell rings, I ask Amy about the mistake she made in class and the embar- 40
rassment it caused her. She blushes again.

"Oh yeah," she says. "That's about the only time I ever talked in there. I'll never do 41
that again."

Connecting to Culture and Experience: Gender Equality

The hidden curriculum, according to Orenstein, teaches girls that boys have more power and authority. Other writers have argued that schools are more agreeable places for girls than for boys. Think about this debate and about how your own experiences in middle school and high school contribute to it. You may have liked or disliked school in general, but try to recall specific events, teachers, classes, or activities that seemed unfairly and unjustifiably to favor boys or girls or that suggested boys or girls possessed some essential advantage over the other. Identify one example of this favoritism that you well remember.

With two or three other students, take turns describing the occasion you remembered where boys or girls were favored. Then, as a group, note any similarities and differences between your own experiences and what Orenstein observed.

Analyzing Writing Strategies

1. In profiles, **dialogue** functions, as it does in autobiography, to reveal people. Dialogue functions in another important way in profiles—to inform readers about a subject. To present the Weston students' interactions and the teacher's role in the eighth-grade math classroom, beginning in paragraph 11 Orenstein relies increasingly on dialogue. From paragraph 22 to the end, she relies mainly on dialogue. In paragraphs 22–41, underline the dialogue (the material within quotation marks), including the speaker tags *(she asks, shouts Kyle)*. Within the context of the entire profile, think about what you learn about the teacher and the students from this dialogue, and make notes about what you discover. (Keep in mind that Orenstein could have summarized this part of the class meeting without using any dialogue. For example, in paragraphs 22 and 23, she creates dialogue from the discussion she heard that day in Amy's math class: "'What does three to the third power mean?' she asks the class. 'I know!' shouts Kyle." Orenstein could have summarized instead: "She asks the class what three to the third power means, and Kyle shouts that he knows.")
2. Writers with information to share rely on **comparison and contrast**, among other strategies. Orenstein's profile reveals two basic and important contrasts: One is Amy outside math class and Amy inside math class; the other is the boys' behavior in the class and the girls' behavior in the class. Focusing on the first contrast, in paragraphs 2–5 and 7, underline any information that tells or shows what Amy is like outside of math class; and in paragraphs 9, 18, 40, and 41 underline any information that tells or shows what Amy is like in math class. Write a few sentences summarizing the contrast you find.

For more on comparison and contrast as writing strategies, see Chapter 18, p. 671.

Commentary: A Narrative Plan

Whereas John T. Edge relies on a topical plan to profile Farm Fresh Food Supplier (turn to p. 145 for a scratch outline and an explanation of the topical plan), Orenstein relies on a **narrative plan**. That is, she tells a story about one math class she observed. Except for the few minutes that Orenstein spends outside the school before the school day begins, the profile reports only a few selected activities that take place in one forty-eight-minute math class. Instead of categorizing interactions selected from different times in the class, Orenstein lines up the interactions just as they occurred in time from the beginning to the end of class. Here is a possible scratch outline of the profile:

outside the school (paragraph 1)

Amy as extrovert (2–5)

on the way to math class (6–7)

the students and teachers (8–9)

boys get the teacher's attention, girls are ignored (10–13)

boys dominate while homework is reviewed (14–20)

Amy seems embarrassed, boys shout down the girls (19–20)

Kyle duels Dawn as the new lesson begins (21–31)

teacher recognizes Kyle and ignores many other raised hands (32–39)

Amy as embarrassed, resigned student (40–41)

For Orenstein's purposes, this narrative plan is quite effective. It reveals how the boys dominate class discussion from beginning to end and how the teacher continually defers to their noisy persistence. Whether you choose a narrative or topical plan depends on the material you have to work with and on the perspective you hope to convey.

Considering Topics for Your Own Essay

Consider profiling a group of people who interact with each other for a specific purpose—such as a teacher and students interacting in a classroom to learn a specific concept or practice a skill; a group of actors rehearsing for a play; a basketball team practicing for an upcoming game; employees working collaboratively on a project; businesspeople or other citizens writing a proposal that they will present at a city council meeting (or a meeting of any other decision-making body) for questions, discussion, and action; or members of a club, sports team, or other interest group meeting to resolve a crisis.

To use the Writing Guide Software to record your ideas, click on
▶ **Journal**

***Brian Cable** wrote the following selection when he was a first-year college student. Cable's profile of a mortuary combines both seriousness and humor. He lets readers know his feelings as he presents information about the mortuary and the people working there. As you read, notice how Cable manages to inform you about the business of a mortuary while taking you on a guided tour of the premises. Notice also how he expresses his lack of seriousness about a serious place, a place of death and grief.*

To see this essay with pop-up annotations in the software, click on
▶ **Writing Profiles**
▶ **Read**

The Last Stop

Brian Cable

> Let us endeavor so to live that when we come to die even the undertaker will be sorry.
>
> —MARK TWAIN

Death is a subject largely ignored by the living. We don't discuss it much, not as children (when Grandpa dies, he is said to be "going away"), not as adults, not even as senior citizens. Throughout our lives, death remains intensely private. The death of a loved one can be very painful, partly because of the sense of loss but also because someone else's mortality reminds us all too vividly of our own. 1

Thus did I notice more than a few people avert their eyes as they walked past the dusty-pink building that houses the Goodbody Mortuaries. It looked a bit like a church—tall, with gothic arches and stained glass—and somewhat like an apartment complex—low, with many windows stamped out of red brick. 2

It wasn't at all what I had expected. I thought it would be more like Forest Lawn, serene with lush green lawns and meticulously groomed gardens, a place set apart from the hustle of day-to-day life. Here instead was an odd pink structure set in the middle of a business district. On top of the Goodbody Mortuaries sign was a large electric clock. "What the hell," I thought, "Mortuaries are concerned with time, too." 3

I was apprehensive as I climbed the stone steps to the entrance. I feared rejection or, worse, an invitation to come and stay. The door was massive, yet it swung open easily on well-oiled hinges. "Come in," said the sign. "We're always open." Inside was a cool and quiet reception room. Curtains were drawn against the outside glare, cutting the light down to a soft glow. 4

I found the funeral director in the main lobby, adjacent to the reception room. Like most people, I had preconceptions about what an undertaker looked like. Mr. Deaver fulfilled my expectations entirely. Tall and thin, he even had beady eyes and a bony face. A low, slanted forehead gave way to a beaked nose. His skin, scrubbed of all color, contrasted sharply with his jet black hair. He was wearing a starched white shirt, gray pants, and black shoes. Indeed, he looked like death on two legs. 5

He proved an amiable sort, however, and was easy to talk to. As funeral director, Mr. Deaver ("Call me Howard") was responsible for a wide range of services. Goodbody Mortuaries, upon notification of someone's death, will remove the remains from the hospital or home. They then prepare the body for viewing, whereupon features distorted by illness or accident are restored to their natural condition. The body is embalmed and then placed in a casket selected by the family of the deceased. Services are held in one of three chapels at the mortuary, and afterward the casket is placed in a "visitation room," where family and friends can pay their last respects. Goodbody also makes arrangements for the purchase of a burial site and transports the body there for burial. 6

All this information Howard related in a well-practiced, professional manner. It was obvious he was used to explaining the specifics of his profession. We sat alone in the lobby. His desk was bone clean, no pencils or paper, nothing—just a telephone. He did all his paperwork at home; as it turned out, he and his wife lived right upstairs. The phone rang. As he listened, he bit his lips and squeezed his Adam's apple somewhat nervously. 7

"I think we'll be able to get him in by Friday. No, no, the family wants him cremated." 8

His tone was that of a broker conferring on the Dow Jones. Directly behind him was a sign announcing "Visa and Master Charge Welcome Here." It was tacked to the wall, right next to a crucifix. 9

"Some people have the idea that we are bereavement specialists, that we can handle the emotional problems which follow a death: Only a trained therapist can do that. We provide services for the dead, not counseling for the living." 10

Physical comfort was the one thing they did provide for the living. The lobby was modestly but comfortably furnished. There were several couches, in colors ranging from earth brown to pastel blue, and a coffee table in front of each one. On one table lay some magazines and a vase of flowers. Another supported an aquarium. Paintings of pastoral scenes hung on every wall. The lobby looked more or less like that of an old hotel. Nothing seemed to match, but it had a homey, lived-in look. 11

"The last time the Goodbodys decorated was in '59, I believe. It still makes people feel welcome." 12

And so "Goodbody" was not a name made up to attract customers but the owner's family name. The Goodbody family started the business way back in 1915. Today, they do over five hundred services a year. 13

"We're in *Ripley's Believe It or Not*, along with another funeral home whose owners' names are Baggit and Sackit," Howard told me, without cracking a smile. 14

I followed him through an arched doorway into a chapel that smelled musty and old. The only illumination came from sunlight filtered through a stained glass ceiling. Ahead of us lay a casket. I could see that it contained a man dressed in a black suit. Wooden benches ran on either side of an aisle that led to the body. I got no closer. From the red roses across the dead man's chest, it was apparent that services had already been held. 15

"It was a large service," remarked Howard. "Look at that casket—a beautiful work of craftsmanship." 16

I guess it was. Death may be the great leveler, but one's coffin quickly reestablishes one's status. 17

We passed into a bright, fluorescent-lit "display room." Inside were thirty coffins, lids open, patiently awaiting inspection. Like new cars on the showroom floor, they gleamed with high-gloss finishes. 18

"We have models for every price range." 19

Indeed, there was a wide variety. They came in all colors and various materials. Some were little more than cloth-covered cardboard boxes, others were made of wood, and a few were made of steel, copper, or bronze. Prices started at $400 and averaged about $1,800. Howard motioned toward the center of the room: "The top of the line." 20

This was a solid bronze casket, its seams electronically welded to resist corrosion. Moisture-proof and air-tight, it could be hermetically sealed off from all outside elements. Its handles were plated with 14-karat gold. The price: a cool $5,000. 21

A proper funeral remains a measure of respect for the deceased. But it is expensive. In the United States the amount spent annually on funerals is about $2 billion. Among ceremonial expenditures, funerals are second only to weddings. As a result, practices are changing. Howard has been in this business for forty years. He remembers a time when everyone was buried. Nowadays, with burials costing $2,000 a shot, people often opt instead for cremation—as Howard put it, "a cheap, quick, and easy 22 means of disposal." In some areas of the country, the cremation rate is now over 60 percent. Observing this trend, one might wonder whether burials are becoming obsolete. Do burials serve an important role in society?

For Tim, Goodbody's licensed mortician, the answer is very definitely yes. Burials will remain in common practice, according to the slender embalmer with the disarming smile, because they allow family and friends to view the deceased. Painful as it may be, such an experience brings home the finality of death. "Something deep within us demands a confrontation with death," Tim explained. "A last look assures us that the person we loved is, indeed, gone forever." 23

Apparently, we also need to be assured that the body will be laid to rest in comfort and peace. The average casket, with its inner-spring mattress and pleated satin lining, is surprisingly roomy and luxurious. Perhaps such an air of comfort makes it easier for the family to give up their loved one. In addition, the burial site fixes the deceased in the survivors' memory, like a new address. Cremation provides none of these comforts. 24

Tim started out as a clerk in a funeral home but then studied to become a mortician. "It was a profession I could live with," he told me with a sly grin. Mortuary science might be described as a cross between pre-med and cosmetology, with courses in anatomy and embalming as well as in restorative art. 25

Tim let me see the preparation, or embalming, room, a white-walled chamber about the size of an operating room. Against the wall was a large sink with elbow taps and a draining board. In the center of the room stood a table with equipment for preparing the arterial embalming fluid, which consists primarily of formaldehyde, a preservative, and phenol, a disinfectant. This mixture sanitizes and also gives better color to the skin. Facial features can then be "set" to achieve a restful expression. Missing eyes, ears, and even noses can be replaced. 26

I asked Tim if his job ever depressed him. He bridled at the question: "No, it doesn't depress me at all. I do what I can for people and take satisfaction in enabling relatives to see their loved ones as they were in life." He said that he felt people were becoming more aware of the public service his profession provides. Grade-school classes now visit funeral homes as often as they do police stations and museums. The mortician is no longer regarded as a minister of death. 27

Before leaving, I wanted to see a body up close. I thought I could be indifferent after all I had seen and heard, but I wasn't sure. Cautiously, I reached out and touched the skin. It felt cold and firm, not unlike clay. As I walked out, I felt glad to have satisfied my curiosity about dead bodies, but all too happy to let someone else handle them. 28

Connecting to Culture and Experience: Death

"Death," Cable announces in his opening sentence, "is a subject largely ignored by the living. We don't discuss it much, not as children (when Grandpa dies, he is said to be 'going away'), not as adults, not even as senior citizens." Yet when a family member dies, every family is forced to mark death in some way.

With two or three other students, discuss how your families and friends prepare for and arrange a funeral or memorial service. Think of a funeral you have attended, or ask a family member to describe how your family traditionally marks the death of a loved one. Consider the following questions, for example: Is there a formal service? If so, where does it take place—in a house of worship, a funeral home, a private home, a cemetery, or somewhere else? Who typically attends? Do people dress formally or informally? Who speaks, and what kinds of things are said? What kind of music, if any, is played? Is the body cremated or buried? Is there usually a gathering after the formal service? If so, what is its purpose compared to the formal service?

Then, together, compare the different family traditions revealed in the services described by the members of your group. Try to answer these questions: What do you think the funeral or memorial service accomplishes for each family? What did it accomplish for you personally?

Analyzing Writing Strategies

1. How does the opening quotation from Mark Twain shape your expectations as a reader? Compare Cable's opening (the quotation and paragraphs 1 and 2) against the **openings** of the three other profile essays in this chapter. What can you conclude about the opening strategies of these profile writers? Given each writer's subject, materials, and purpose, which opening do you find most effective and why?
2. During his visit to the mortuary, Cable focuses on four rooms: the lobby (paragraph 11), the chapel where funeral services are conducted (15), the casket display room (18–21), and the embalming room (26). Reread Cable's **descriptions** of these four rooms, and then underline the details he uses to describe each room. What impression do you get of each room? What might Cable gain by contrasting them so sharply? How do these descriptions work together to convey Cable's **perspective** on the mortuary?

For more on describing, see Chapter 15, p. 643.

3. The Writer at Work section later in this chapter presents Cable's interview notes and preliminary interview write-up. Turn to pp. 190–95 to read these items now. Then consider how Cable integrates quotations from the interviews and descriptive details from his observations into his final essay. What do the quotations reveal about Cable's impressions of Howard and Tim? What do the descriptive details tell you about the effect that his visit to the mortuary had on him? How do the quotations and descriptive details shape your reaction to the essay?

Commentary: Conveying a Perspective

By deciding to present himself as a participant in his profile, Cable can readily **convey his perspective**, his ideas and insights, by telling readers directly what he thinks and feels about the mortuary and the people who work there. He begins with some general ideas about death and the way that people tend to deal with death basically by ignoring it. Then, in paragraphs 3 and 4, he discusses his expectations and confesses his apprehensions about the initial visit.

Cable quotes Howard and Tim and summarizes their words, describing them and commenting on what the funeral director and mortician said. His descriptions and comments express his insights into these people and the kinds of work they do. For example, when Cable introduces Howard Deaver, the funeral director, in paragraphs 5–10, he begins by comparing Deaver to his preconceptions about what an undertaker looks like. Then he describes Deaver, no doubt emphasizing his stereotypical features:

> Tall and thin, he even had beady eyes and a bony face. A low, slanted forehead gave way to a beaked nose. His skin, scrubbed of all color, contrasted sharply with his jet black hair. He was wearing a starched white shirt, gray pants, and black shoes. Indeed, he looked like death on two legs. (5)

The description creates an image that reinforces the stereotype of an undertaker. But that is apparently not the perspective he wants to convey because Cable quickly replaces this stereotype with a different one when he describes Howard's tone on the telephone with a client as "that of a broker conferring on the Dow Jones" (paragraph 9). To make sure readers get the idea that mortuaries are a big business, Cable points out that on the wall directly behind Howard "was a sign announcing 'Visa and Master Charge Welcome Here.'" Skillfully combining direct comment and concise description (sometimes called **telling** and **showing**), Cable conveys a perspective on mortuaries as efficient, profit seeking businesses that nevertheless understand that their services provide clients with what they want and need at a difficult time.

Considering Topics for Your Own Essay

Try to list at least two or three places or activities that you have strong preconceptions about, and add a few notes to each one describing the preconception. For example, you might think that fast-food places are popular because their customers have few other choices of places to eat, that counselors will put pressure on you to conform if you ask for help with a personal problem at the student counseling center, that car repair shops regularly perform unnecessary repairs and overcharge customers, or that college librarians are too busy to help students find sources for their essays. Choose one such place or activity, and think about how you would go about profiling it. How would you test your preconception? How might you use your preconception to heighten readers' interest in your profile?

To use the Writing Guide Software to record your ideas, click on
▶ **Journal**

PURPOSE AND AUDIENCE

A profile writer's primary purpose is to inform readers about the subject of the profile. Readers expect a profile to present information in an engaging way, however. Whether profiling people, places (a pig lip manufacturer, café, or mortuary), or activities (classroom interaction), the writer must engage as well as inform readers. Readers of profiles expect to be surprised by unusual subjects. If the subject is familiar, they expect it to be presented from an unusual perspective. When writing a profile, you will have an immediate advantage if your subject is a place, an activity, or a person that is likely to surprise and intrigue your readers. For example, the writer of "I'm Not Leaving Until I Eat This Thing" (pp. 140–43) has the triple advantage of being able to describe an unusual snack food, a little-known production process, and a colorful bar in which he can try out the unusual snack. Even when your subject is familiar, however, you can still engage your readers by presenting it in a way they have never before considered. For example, the writer of "The Last Stop" describes a mortuary owner as an ordinary, efficient businessman and not a "bereavement specialist."

A profile writer has one further concern: to be sensitive to readers' knowledge of a subject. Since readers must imagine the subject profiled and understand the new information offered about it, the writer must carefully assess what readers are likely to know already. For a profile of a pig-products processor, the decisions of a writer whose readers have likely never seen a pickled pig lip or foot will be quite different from those of a writer whose readers occasionally hang out in jukes and other bars where pickled pig products are always visible floating in a bottle of garish-colored vinegar. Given Edge's attention to detail, he is clearly writing for a general audience that has never before seen a pickled pig lip or foot, much less considered eating one.

Description of People and Places

Successful profile writers master the strategies of description. The profiles in this chapter, for example, evoke all the senses: **sight** ("the pink juice pooling on the bar in front of me," Edge, paragraph 15); **touch** ("slick with grease," Edge, 16; "the skin . . . felt cold and firm, not unlike clay," Cable, 28); **smell** ("hallways smell chalky, papery, and a little sweaty from gym class," Orenstein, 6); **taste** ("hot and vinegary," Edge, 7); **hearing** ("[plates] thudding on the counter under their own weight," Hall, 17; "sneakers squeaking across the wet pavement," Hall, 19); and **physical sensation** ("a gag that rolls from the back of my throat," Edge, 16); "my stomach ceases its fluttering," Edge, 18). **Similes** ("their legs sticking out of their shorts like pipe cleaners," Orenstein, 8; "elementary school students] like a mob running in panic from a fire," Hall, 19), and **metaphors** ("the air conditioner hacks and spits forth torrents of Arctic air," Edge, 1) appear occasionally.

Profile writers often describe people in graphic detail ("his shy smile framed by a coarse black mustache," Edge, 8; "beady eyes and a bony face," Cable, 5; "a ruddy, athletic woman with a powerful voice," Orenstein, 9; "wide-hipped and heavy-limbed with curly, blond hair," Orenstein, 2). They show people moving and gesturing ("he bit his lips and squeezed his Adam's apple," Cable, 7; "I poke and prod the six-inch arc of pink flesh," Edge, 14; "she crosses her legs, folds her arms across her chest, and hunches forward," Orenstein, 9). Writers rely on dialogue to reveal character ("Look at that casket—a beautiful work of craftsmanship," Cable, 16; "You gonna eat that thing or make love to it?," Edge, 14; "Greg! Get over here! You have to meet Peggy," Orenstein 3).

Information about the Subject

Profile writers give much thought to how and where to introduce information to their readers. After all, readers expect to be informed—to learn something surprising or useful. To meet this expectation, profile writers' basic strategy is to interweave information with descriptions of the subject (as Cable does profiling a mortuary) and with narratives of events (as Edge does when he struggles to eat a pig lip). Throughout their profiles, writers make good use of several strategies relied on by all writers of explanation: classification, example or illustration, comparison and contrast, definition, process narration, and cause and effect.

Edge **classifies** information about Farm Fresh when, in one part of his profile, he divides information about the business into four categories: rebirth of the family business, family involvement, marketing strategies, and customer relations. Hall gives several **examples** of the kinds of food served at the Edison Café. Orenstein **contrasts** Amy outside of class with Amy in class. Cable **defines** the terms "mortuary science" and "embalming fluid." Edge **narrates** the process of preparing and bottling pig lips and, after receiving instruction, of eating one. Edge presents the **causes**

of Farm Fresh's failure as a business and of its rebirth, and he discloses frankly the **effects** of his attempts to eat a pig lip.

A Topical or Narrative Plan

Profile writers rely on two basic plans for reporting their observations: **topical**, with the information grouped into topics; and **narrative**, with the information interwoven with elements of a story. The profiles by Hall, Orenstein, and Cable are all organized narratively. In all three, the narrative is a story of a single visit to a place. For Hall, the visit is a long morning from 6:30 A.M. to 12:30 P.M. spent at the Edison Café; even the long chunk of information about Skagit Valley that Hall presumably acquired at a different time (paragraphs 5–7) is inserted into the morning narrative. For Orenstein, the visit is a bit of time on the school playground followed by one meeting of Mrs. Richrer's math class. For Cable, the visit is one of indeterminate length, probably two or three hours, to Boodbody Mortuaries. (Some profile writers present information gathered from several visits as though it was learned in a single visit.)

In the central segment of his profile of a southern pig-products producer, Edge organizes the information topically: He creates topics out of the many bits of information he gathers on the tour of Farm Fresh led by the owner, Lionel Dufour, and then sequences them in the profile in a way that he thinks will be most informative to readers. Yet Edge frames the information about Farm Fresh with a narrative of his attempts to eat one of its products, illustrating that a profile can be organized topically in some parts and narratively in others. Usually, however, one plan or the other predominates. Which plan you adopt will depend on your subject, the kinds of information you collect, and your assessment of what might be most engaging and informative for your readers.

A Role for the Writer

Profile writers must adopt a role or stance for themselves when they present their subjects. There are two basic options: **detached observer** and **participant observer**. Hall remains a detached and invisible observer throughout his profile. There is no evidence that he participates in any of the activities or conversations at the Edison Café. Once she takes her seat in Amy's math classroom, Orenstein is a detached observer. She says nothing to the students or teacher, and she does not leave her chair, observing all the interactions from a fixed point of view. In the central part, of his profile, where he presents what he learned on his visit to Farm Fresh Food Supplier, Edge, too, is a detached observer. We can easily infer that he asked questions and made comments, but he decides not to report any of them; instead, he focuses unwaveringly on the equipment, canning process, workers, and Dufour family members. By contrast, Cable adopts a participant-observer role. Even before he enters the mortuary, he inserts himself personally into the profile, reflecting on death, expressing his disappointment in the appearance of the place, admitting his apprehension about entering, revealing his sense of humor. Readers know where he is at all times as his tour of the building proceeds, and he seems as much a participant in the narrative of his visit as Deaver and Tim are. Before he leaves the mortuary, he touches a corpse, to satisfy his curiosity. Both Edge and Orenstein also adopt a participant-observer role for relatively brief portions of their profiles—Edge when he tries to eat a pig's lip in the juke, Orenstein when she joins Amy and her friends on the playground at the start of the school day.

A Perspective on the Subject

Profile writers do not simply present their observations of a subject; they also offer insights into the person, place, or activity being profiled. They may convey a perspective on their subjects by stating it explicitly, by implying it through the descriptive details and other information they include, or both. Brian Cable shares his realization that Americans seem to capitalize on death as a way of coping with it. Peggy Orenstein conveys her perspective that girls' school achievements and life opportunities may be curtailed unless they get support for their efforts to participate in the classroom. Hall comes to understand that the warm, civil social interactions he observes at the Edison Café are more than merely pleasurable for the patrons: They are essential to social cohesion in Skagit Valley. Edge's perspective on pig products is less explicit, but perhaps, as a specialist in southern cooking, he hopes to convey the impression that regional foods remain important to many of the people who live in a region. In small southern towns, bar patrons are not satisfied by peanuts, pretzels, and packaged cheese and crackers. They want a soft, pink, vinegary pig lip shaken in a bag of crushed potato chips.

GUIDE TO WRITING
Profiles

THE WRITING ASSIGNMENT

THE WRITING ASSIGNMENT

Write an essay about an intriguing person, place, or activity in your community. Observe your subject closely, and then present what you have learned in a way that both informs and engages readers.

INVENTION AND RESEARCH

INVENTION & RESEARCH

- Finding a Subject to Write About
- Exploring Your Preconceptions
- Planning Your Project
- Posing Some Preliminary Questions
- Discovering a Perspective
- Considering Your Own Role
- Defining Your Purpose for Your Readers
- Formulating a Tentative Thesis Statement
- Considering Document Design

PLANNING AND DRAFTING

PLANNING & DRAFTING

- Seeing What You Have
- Setting Goals
- Outlining
- Drafting

CRITICAL READING GUIDE

CRITICAL READING GUIDE

- First Impression
- Organization
- The Writer's Role
- Description
- Quality and Presentation of Information
- The Writer's Perspective
- Final Thoughts

REVISING

REVISING

- A Description of People and Places
- Information about the Subject
- A Topical or Narrative Plan
- A Role for the Writer
- A Perspective on the Subject

EDITING AND PROOFREADING

EDITING & PROOFREADING

- Checking the Punctuation of Quotations
- A Common ESL Problem: Adjective Order

GUIDE TO WRITING

THE WRITING ASSIGNMENT

Write an essay about an intriguing person, place, or activity in your community. Observe your subject closely, and then present what you have learned in a way that both informs and engages readers.

To use the Writing Guide Software for this assignment, click on
▶ **Writing Profiles**
▶ **Write**

INVENTION AND RESEARCH

Preparing to write a profile involves several activities, such as finding a subject, exploring your preconceptions about it, planning your project, and posing some preliminary questions. Each step takes no more than a few minutes, yet together these activities will enable you to anticipate problems likely to arise in a complex project like a profile, to arrange and schedule your interviews wisely, and to take notes and gather materials in a productive way. There is much to learn about observing, interviewing, and writing about what you have learned, and these activities will support your learning.

Finding a Subject to Write About

When you choose a subject, you consider various possibilities, select a promising one, and check that particular subject's accessibility.

Listing Subjects. *Make a list of subjects to consider for your profile.* Even if you already have a subject in mind, take a few minutes to consider some other possibilities. The more possibilities you consider, the more confident you can be about your choice. Do not overlook the subjects suggested by the Considering Topics for Your Own Essay activities following each reading in this chapter.

Before you list possible subjects, consider realistically the time you have available and the amount of observing and interviewing you will be able to accomplish. Whether you have a week to plan and write up one observational visit or interview or a month to develop a full profile will determine what kinds of subjects will be appropriate for you. Consult with your instructor if you need help defining the scope of your profile project.

Here we present some ideas you might use as starting points for a list of subjects. Try to extend your list to ten or twelve possibilities. Consider every subject you can think of, even unlikely ones. People like to read about the unusual.

People

- Anyone with an unusual or intriguing job or hobby—a private detective, beekeeper, classic-car owner, or dog trainer
- A prominent local personality—a parent of the year, labor organizer, politician, consumer advocate, television or radio personality, or community activist
- A campus personality—a coach, distinguished teacher, or ombudsman
- Someone recently recognized for outstanding service or achievement—a volunteer, mentor, or therapist

Places

- A weight-reduction clinic, martial arts studio, body-building gym, or health spa
- A small-claims court, juvenile court, or consumer fraud office
- A used-car lot, old movie house, used-book store, antique shop, historic site, auction hall, flower or gun show, or farmers' or flea market
- A hospital emergency room, hospice, birthing center, or psychiatric unit
- A local diner; the oldest, biggest, or quickest restaurant in town; or a coffeehouse
- A campus radio station, computer center, agricultural research facility, student center, faculty club, museum, newspaper office, or health center
- A book, newspaper, or Internet publisher; florist shop, nursery, or greenhouse; pawnshop; boatyard; or automobile restorer or wrecking yard
- A recycling center; fire station; airport control tower; theater, opera, or symphony office; refugee center; orphanage; or convent or monastery

Activities

- A citizens' volunteer program—a voter registration service, public television auction, meals-on-wheels project, tutoring program, or election campaign
- A sports event—a marathon, Frisbee tournament, chess match, or wrestling or boxing meet
- A hobby—folk dancing, roller blading, rock climbing, or poetry reading

Listing Subjects Related to Identity and Community. Writing a profile about a person or a place in your community can help you learn more about particular individuals in your community and about institutions and activities fundamental to community life. By *community* we mean both geographic communities, such as towns and neighborhoods, and institutional and temporary communities, such as religious congregations, college students majoring in the same subject, volunteer organizations, and sports teams. The following suggestions will enable you to list several possible subjects.

People

- Someone who has made or is currently making an important contribution to a community

- Someone who is a prominent member of one of the communities you belong to and can help you define and understand that community
- Someone in a community who is generally tolerated but is not liked or respected, such as a homeless person, a gruff store owner, or an unorthodox church member, or someone who has been or is in danger of being shunned or exiled from a community
- Someone who has built a successful business, overcome a disability or setback, supported a worthy cause, served as a role model, or won respect from coworkers or neighbors

Places

- A facility that provides a needed service in a community, such as a legal advice bureau, child-care center, medical clinic, or shelter offering free meals
- A place where people of different ages, genders, ethnic groups, or some other attribute have formed a kind of ongoing community, such as a chess table in the park, political or social action headquarters, computer class, local coffeehouse, or barber or beauty shop
- A place where people come together because they are of the same age, gender, or ethnic group, such as a seniors-only housing complex, a boathouse for a men's crew team, a campus women's center, or an African American or Asian American student center
- An Internet site where people form a virtual community, such as a chat room, game parlor, or bulletin board

Activities

- A team practicing a sport or other activity (one you can observe as an outsider, not as a participant)
- A community improvement project, such as graffiti cleaning, tree planting, house repairing, church painting, or highway litter pickup
- A group of researchers working collaboratively on a project

Listing Subjects Related to Work and Career. The following categories will help you consider work- and career-related subjects. Writing a profile on one of these possibilities can help you learn more about your attitudes toward your own work and career goals by examining how others do their work and pursue their careers.

People

- A college senior or graduate student in a major you are considering
- Someone working in the career you are thinking of pursuing
- Someone who trains people to do the kind of work you would like to do

Places

- A place on campus where students work—the library, computer center, cafeteria, bookstore, office, or tutoring or learning center
- A place where you could learn more about the kind of career you would like to pursue—a law office, medical center, veterinary hospital, research institute, television station, newspaper, school, software manufacturer, or engineering firm
- A place where people do a kind of work you would like to know more about—a clothing factory, coal mine, dairy farm, racetrack, restaurant, bakery, commercial fishing boat, gardening nursery, nursing home, or delicatessen
- A place where people are trained for a certain kind of work or career—a police academy, cosmetology program, video repair course, or truck drivers' school

Activities

- The actual activities performed by someone doing a kind of work represented on television, such as that of a police detective, judge, attorney, newspaper reporter, taxi driver, novelist, or emergency room doctor
- The activities involved in preparing for a particular kind of work, such as a boxer preparing for a fight, an attorney preparing for a trial, a teacher or professor preparing a course, an actor rehearsing a role, or a musician practicing for a concert

Choosing a Subject. *Look over your list of possibilities, and choose a subject that you find you want to know more about and that your readers will find interesting.* Note, too, that most profile writers report the greatest satisfaction and the best results when they profile an unfamiliar person, place, or activity. If you choose a subject with which you are somewhat familiar, try to study it in an unfamiliar setting. For example, if you are a rock climber and decide to write a profile on rock climbing, do not rely exclusively on your own knowledge of and authority on the subject. Seek out other rock-climbing enthusiasts, even interview some critics of the sport to get another perspective, or visit a rock-climbing event or training class where you can observe without participating. By adopting an outsider's perspective on a familiar subject, you can make writing your profile a process of discovery for yourself as well as for your readers.

Stop now to focus your thoughts. *In a sentence or two, identify the subject you have chosen, and explain why you think it is a good choice for you and your readers.*

Checking on Accessibility. *Take steps to ensure that your subject will be accessible to you.* Having chosen a subject, you need to be certain you will be able to make observations and conduct interviews to learn more about it. Find out who might be able to give you information by making some preliminary phone calls. Explain that you need information for a school research project. You will be surprised how helpful people can be when they have the time. If you are unable to contact knowledgeable people or get access to the place you need to observe, you may not be able to write on this subject. Therefore, try to make these initial contacts early.

Exploring Your Preconceptions

Explore your initial thoughts and feelings about your subject in writing before you begin observing or interviewing. Write for a few minutes about your thoughts, using the following questions as a guide:

What I already know about this subject

- How can I define or describe it?
- What are its chief qualities or parts?
- Do I associate anyone or anything with it?
- What is its purpose or function?
- How does it compare with other, similar subjects?

My attitude toward this subject

- Why do I consider it intriguing?
- What about it most interests me?
- Do I like it? Respect it? Understand it?

My own and my readers' expectations

- How do my preconceptions of this subject compare with my readers'?
- What might be unique about my preconceptions?
- What attitudes about this subject do I share with my readers?
- How is this subject represented in the media?
- What values and ideas are associated with subjects of this kind?

Testing Your Choice: A Collaborative Activity

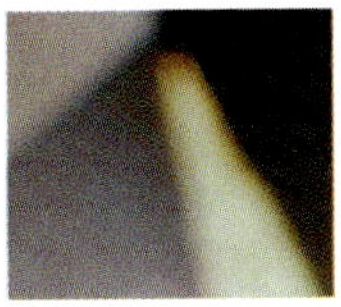

At this point, you will find it useful to get together with two or three other students and describe the subject you have chosen to profile. Your instructor may ask you to do this collaborative activity either in class or online, using a chat room for your real-time discussion. It will help you decide whether you have chosen a good subject to write about, one that will allow you to proceed confidently as you develop your profile.

Presenters: Take turns identifying your subjects. Explain your interest in the subject, and speculate about why you think it will interest your readers.

Listeners: Briefly tell each presenter what you already know about his or her subject, if anything, and what would make it interesting to readers.

Planning Your Project

Set up a tentative schedule for your observational and interview visits. Whatever the scope of your project—a single observation, an interview with one follow-up exchange, or multiple observations and interviews—you will want to get the most out of your time with your subject. Chapter 20 offers guidance in observing and interviewing and will give you an idea of how much time you will need to plan, carry out, and write up an observation or interview.

Take time now to consult Chapter 20. Figure out the amount of time you have to complete your essay, and then decide what visits you will need to make, whom you will need to interview, and what library or Internet research you might want to do, if any. Estimate the time necessary for each. You might use a chart like the following one:

Date	*Time Needed*	*Purpose*	*Preparation*
10/23	1 hour	Observe	Bring map, directions, paper
10/25	2 hours	Library research	Bring references, change or copycard for copy machine
10/26	45 minutes	Interview	Read brochure and prepare questions
10/30	3 hours	Observe and interview	Confirm appointment; bring questions and extra pen

You will probably have to modify your plan once you actually begin work, but it is a good idea to keep some sort of schedule in writing.

If you are developing a full profile, your first goal is to get your bearings. Some writers begin by observing; others start with an interview. Many read up on the subject before doing anything else to get a sense of its main elements. You may also want to read about other subjects similar to the one you have chosen. Save your notes.

Researching Your Profile Subject: An Online Activity

One way to get a quick initial overview of the information available on the subject of your profile is to search for the subject online. Use Google (http://google.com) or Yahoo! Directory (http://dir.yahoo.com) to discover possible sources of information about the subject:

- For example, if you are profiling a beekeeper, you could get some useful background information to guide you in planning your interview by entering "bee keeping."
- If you are profiling a person, enter the full name to discover whether he or she has a personal Web site. If you are profiling a business or institution, the chances are even better that it offers a site. Either kind of site would orient and inform you prior to your interview or first visit.

Bookmark or keep a record of promising sites. After your interview with or visit to the subject, download any materials, including visuals, you might consider including in your own essay. If you find little or no information about your subject online, do not lose confidence in your choice. All of the information you need to develop your profile can come from your observations and interviews when you visit your subject.

Posing Some Preliminary Questions

Write questions to prepare for your first visit. Before beginning your observations and interviews, try writing some questions for which you would like to find answers. These questions will orient you and allow you to focus your visits. As you work, you will find answers to many of these questions. Add to this list as new questions occur to you, and delete any that come to seem irrelevant.

Each subject invites its own special questions, and every writer has particular concerns. Consider, for example, how one student prepares interview questions for her profile of a local office of the Women's Health Initiative, a nationwide fifteen-year study of women's health established by the National Institutes of Health in 1991. After reading about the long-term health study in her local newspaper, the student calls the local WHI office to get further information. The administrator faxes her a fact sheet on the study and her office's special part in it. The student knows that she will need to mention the study in her profile of the local office and the people who work there. She also hopes to interview women who volunteer to participate in the research. Consequently, she devises the following questions to launch her research and prepare for her interview of the local director:

- Why has so little research been done until recently on women's health?
- How did the study come about, and what is the role of the National Institutes of Health?
- Why does the study focus only on women between the ages of fifty and eighty?
- Will women from all income levels be involved?
- Why will it take fifteen years to complete the study?
- When was this office established, and what role does it play in the national study?
- Does the office simply coordinate the study, or does it also provide health and medical advice to women participating in the study?
- Who works at the office, and what are their qualifications to work there?
- Will I be able to interview women who volunteer to participate in the research?
- Will I be permitted to take photographs at the office?
- Would it be appropriate to take photographs of the researchers and participants, if they give their consent?

Discovering a Perspective

After you have completed your observations and interviews, write for a few minutes, reflecting on what you now think is interesting and meaningful about the person, place, or activity you have chosen for your profile. Consider how you would answer these questions about your subject:

- What visual or other sensory impression is most memorable?
- What does this impression tell me about the person, place, or activity?
- What mood do I associate with my subject?
- What about my subject is most striking and likely to surprise or interest my readers?
- What is the most important thing I have learned about my subject? Why is it important?
- If I could find out the answer to one more question about my subject, what would that question be? Why is this question important?
- What about my subject says something larger about our culture and times?
- Which of my ideas, interpretations, or judgments do I most want to share with readers?

Considering Your Own Role

Decide tentatively whether you will adopt a detached-observer or participant-observer role to present your profile. As a detached observer, you would focus solely on the place and people, keeping yourself invisible to readers. As a participant-observer, you would insert yourself personally into the profile by reporting what you said or thought during interviews and commenting on the activities you observe.

Defining Your Purpose for Your Readers

Write a few sentences, defining your purpose in writing about this particular person, place, or activity for your readers. Use these questions to focus your thoughts:

- Who are my readers? Apart from my instructors and classmates, who would be interested in reading an essay about this particular subject? If I were to try to publish my essay, what magazine, newspaper, newsletter, or Web site might want a profile on this particular subject? Would people who work in a particular kind of business or who pursue certain kinds of hobbies or sports be interested in the essay?
- What do I want my readers to learn about the person, place, or activity from reading my essay?
- What insight can I offer my readers about the person, place, or activity?

Formulating a Tentative Thesis Statement

Review what you wrote for Discovering a Perspective (p. 176), and add another two or three sentences that will help you tell readers what you understand about the person, place, or activity on which you are focusing. Try to write sentences that extend your insights and interpretations and that do not simply summarize what you have already written.

Keep in mind that readers do not expect you to begin a profile essay with the kind of explicit thesis statement typical of argumentative essays. If you decide to tell readers your perspective on the person, place, or activity, you will most likely do so through interpretive or evaluative comments as you describe people and places, present dialogue, and narrate what you observed. You are not obliged to tell readers your perspective, but you should show it through the way you profile the subject.

Considering Document Design

Think about whether visual or audio elements—photographs, postcards, menus, or snippets from films, television programs, or songs—would strengthen your profile. These are not at all a requirement of an effective profile, but they sometimes are helpful. Consider also whether your readers might benefit from design features such as headings, bulleted or numbered lists, or other typographic elements that can make an essay easier to follow.

PLANNING AND DRAFTING

This section will help you review your invention writing and research notes and get started on your first draft.

> If you are using the Writing Guide Software, click on
> ▶ **Planning and Drafting**

Seeing What You Have

Read over your invention materials to see what you have. You probably have a great deal of material—notes from observational and interview visits or from library research, some idea of your preconceptions, a list of questions, and perhaps even some answers. You should also have a tentative perspective on the subject, some idea about it or insight into it. Your goals at this point are to digest all of the information you have gathered; to pick out the promising facts, details, anecdotes, and quotations; and to see how it all might come together to present your subject and your perspective on it to readers.

If you have done your invention writing on the computer, you may have sentences or whole paragraphs that can be copied and pasted into your draft. Whether your material is on screen or on paper, highlight key words, phrases, and sentences, and either make annotations in the margins or use your computer's annotating function.

As you sort through your material, try asking yourself the following questions to help clarify your focus and interpretation:

- How do my preconceptions of the subject contrast with my findings about it?
- Can I compare or contrast what different people say about my subject? Do I see any discrepancies between people's words and their behavior?
- How do my reactions compare with those of the people directly involved?
- How could I consider the place's appearance in light of the activity that occurs there?
- If I examine my subject as an anthropologist or archaeologist would, what evidence could explain its role in society at large?
- Could I use a visual or other graphic to complement the text?

Setting Goals

The following questions will help you establish goals for your first draft. Consider each question briefly now, and then return to them as necessary as you draft and revise.

Your Purpose and Readers

- Are my readers likely to be familiar with my subject? If not, what details do I need to provide to help them understand and visualize it?
- If my readers are familiar with my subject, how can I present it to them in a new and engaging way? What information do I have that is likely to be unfamiliar or entertaining to them?
- What design elements might make my writing more interesting or easier for readers to understand?

The Beginning

The opening is especially important in a profile. Because readers are unlikely to have any particular reason to read a profile, the writer must arouse their curiosity and interest. The best beginnings are surprising and specific; the worst are abstract. Here are some strategies you might consider:

- Should I open with a brief anecdote, as Edge does, an emphatic statement, as Orenstein does, or an intriguing epigraph, as Cable does?
- Should I simply begin at the beginning, as Hall does?
- Can I start with an amazing fact, anecdote, or question that would catch readers' attention?

Description of People and Places

- How might I give readers a strong visual image of people and places?
- Can I think of a simile or metaphor that would help me present an evocative image?
- Which bits of dialogue would convey information about my subject as well as a vivid impression of the speaker?
- What specific narrative actions can I include to show people moving and gesturing?

Information about the Subject

- How can I fully satisfy readers' needs for information about my subject?
- How can I manage the flow of information so that readers do not lose interest?
- What special terms will I need to define for my readers?
- Would comparisons or contrasts make the information clearer and more memorable?

A Narrative or Topical Plan

Profile writers use two basic methods of organizing information, arranging it narratively like a story or topically by grouping related materials.

If You Use a Narrative Plan

- How can I make the narrative interesting, perhaps even dramatic?
- What information should I present through dialogue, and what information should I interrupt the narrative to present?
- How much space should I devote to describing people and places and to telling what happened during a visit?
- If I have the option of including design elements, how might I use them effectively—to clarify the sequence of events, highlight a dramatic part of the narrative, or illustrate how the people and places in the profile changed over time?

If You Use a Topical Plan

- Which topics will best inform my readers and hold their interest?
- How can I sequence the topics to bring out significant comparisons or contrasts?
- What transitions will help readers make connections between topics?
- If I have the option of including design elements, are there ways I can use them effectively to reinforce the topical organization?

A Perspective on the Subject

- How can I convey a perspective on the subject that seems original or at least fresh?
- Should I state my perspective or leave readers to infer it from the details of my presentation?

The Ending

- Should I try to frame the essay by repeating an image or phrase from the beginning or by completing an action begun earlier in the profile?
- Would it be effective to end by stating or restating my perspective?
- Should I end with a telling image, anecdote, or bit of dialogue or with a provocative question or connection?

Outlining

If you plan to arrange your material narratively, plot the key events on a timeline. If you plan to arrange your material topically, you might use clustering or topic outlining to help you divide and group related information.

The following outline suggests one possible way to organize a narrative profile of a place:

Begin by describing the place from the outside.

Present background information.

Describe what you see as you enter.

Introduce the people and activities.

Tour the place, describing what you see as you move from one part to the next.

Fill in information, and comment about the place or the people.

Conclude with reflections on what you have learned about the place.

Here is a suggested outline for a topical profile about a person:

Begin with a vivid image of the person in action.

Use dialogue to present the first topic.

Narrate an anecdote or a procedure to illustrate the first topic.

Present the second topic.

Describe something related to it.

Evaluate or interpret what you have observed.

Present the third topic, etc.

Conclude with a bit of action or dialogue.

All of the material for these hypothetical essays would come from observations, interviews, and background reading. The plan you choose should reflect the possibilities in your material as well as your purpose and readers. At this point, your decisions must be tentative. As you begin drafting, you will almost certainly discover new ways of organizing your material. Once you have written a first draft, you and others may see better ways to organize the material for your particular audience.

Drafting

General Advice. Start drafting your essay, keeping in mind the goals you set while you were planning. As you write, try to describe your subject in a way that conveys your perspective on it. Turn off your grammar checker and spelling checker at this stage if you find them distracting. Don't be afraid to skip around in your draft. Jump back and fill in a spontaneous idea, or leap ahead and write a later section first if you find that easier. If you get stuck while drafting, explore the problem by using some of the writing activities in the Invention and Research section of this chapter (pp. 169–77).

As you read over your first draft, you may see places where you can add new material to reveal more about the person, place, or activity. You may even decide that after this first draft, you can finally understand the complexity of your subject and set out to convey it more fully in a second draft.

Sentence Strategies. As you draft a profile, you will need to present what people have said to you and others during your observations and interviews and to help your readers imagine the actions, people, and objects you have encountered. Two sentence strategies called *speaker tags* and *absolute phrases* are useful for these purposes.

Use general and specific speaker tags along with other words and phrases to present what people say. When you directly quote (rather than paraphrase or summarize) what someone has said, you will usually need to identify the speaker. The principal way to do so is to create what is called a **speaker tag**.

You may rely on a *general* or all-purpose speaker tag, using forms of *say* and *tell:*

> "We keep them under control," Emma *says.* (Trevor B. Hall, paragraph 20)
>
> "I'll pick on whoever raises their hand," she *tells* him. (Peggy Orenstein, paragraph 34)

Other speaker tags may be more *specific* or precise:

> Dawn *hesitates and begins* "Well, you count the number of threes and. . . ." (Peggy Orenstein, paragraph 26)
>
> "But I know!" *interrupts* Kyle. "I know!" (Peggy Orenstein, paragraph 27)
>
> "Mornin'," *shouts* Julie from the kitchen. (Trevor B. Hall, paragraph 2)

As you draft your profile, consider using specific speaker tags. They give readers more help with imagining speakers' attitudes and personal styles. In addition, to any speaker tag you may add a word or phrase to identify or describe the speaker or to reveal more precisely *how, where, when,* or *why* the speaker speaks:

> "We're in *Ripley's Believe It or Not,* along with another funeral home whose owners' names are Baggit and Sackit," Howard told me, *without cracking a smile.* (Brian Cable, paragraph 14)
>
> "We do our best to corner the market on lips," Lionel told me, *his voice tinged with bravado.* (John T. Edge, paragraph 11)
>
> "Don't you want to wait and hear the problem first?" she asks, *laughing.* (Peggy Orenstein, paragraph 36)

For more on using speaker tags in profiles, go to www.bedfordstmartins.com/theguide and click on Sentence Strategies.
For information on punctuating sentences with quotations, see p. 751.

Even though all of these sentence resources are available to help you make speaker tags more precise and revealing, keep in mind that experienced writers rely on general speaker tags using forms of *say* and *tell* without any added material for most of their sentences with quotations. Also keep in mind that some dialogue can be introduced without speaker tags, if it is likely the reader can infer from the context who is speaking. Turn to Brian Cable's essay for examples in paragraphs 8 and 10.

Use absolute phrases to help readers better imagine actions and people or objects. In profiling a subject, an unusual but very effective kind of sentence enables you to show simultaneous parts of a complex action or to detail observations of a person or object. Such a sentence relies on a grammatical structure known as an *absolute phrase,* which adds meaning to a sentence but does not modify any particular word in the rest of the sentence. (You need not remember its name or the grammatical explanation for it to use the absolute phrase effectively in your writing.) Here is an example, with the absolute phrase in italics:

> Some of the boys are as small and compact as fourth graders, *their legs sticking out of their shorts like pipe cleaners.* (Peggy Orenstein, paragraph 8)

Orenstein could have presented her observation of the boys' skinny legs in a separate sentence, but the sentence she actually wrote makes the general idea of the boys' smallness specific and concrete with a vivid image of their smallness, their pipe-cleaner–skinny legs. Absolute phrases nearly always are attached to the end of a main clause, adding various kinds of details to it to create a more complex, informative sentence. They are usually introduced by a noun or a possessive pronoun like *his* or *their.* Here are three further examples of absolute phrases from this chapter's readings:

> "I'm not exactly shy," she says, *her hands still on her hips.* (Peggy Orenstein, paragraph 4)

> This was a solid bronze casket, *its seams electronically welded to resist corrosion.* (Brian Cable, paragraph 21)

> Inside were thirty coffins, *lids open,* patiently awaiting inspection. (Brian Cable, paragraph 18)

> I offer the bag to Jerry, order yet another beer, and turn to eye the pig feet floating in a murky jar by the cash register, *their blunt tips bobbing up through a pasty white film.* (John T. Edge, paragraph 19)

For more on using absolute phrases in profiles, go to www.bedfordstmartins.com/theguide and click on Sentence Strategies.

Absolute phrases are certainly not required for a successful profile—experienced writers use them only occasionally—yet they do offer writers an effective sentence option. Try them out in your own writing.

In addition to using specific speaker tags and absolute phrases, you can strengthen your profile with other kinds of sentences as well, and you may want to review the discussions of sentences that use participial phrases (pp. 119–20) and that place references to time at the beginning (pp. 63–64) and adjectives before nouns (pp. 118–19).

CRITICAL READING GUIDE

Now is the time to get a good critical reading of your draft. Writers usually find it helpful to have someone else read and comment on their drafts, and all writers know how much they learn about writing when they read other writers' drafts. Your instructor may schedule readings of drafts as part of your coursework—in class or online. If not, you can ask a classmate, friend, or family member to read your draft. You could also seek comments from a tutor at your campus writing center. The guidelines in this section can be used by *anyone* reviewing a profile. (If you are unable to have someone else read your draft, turn ahead to the Carrying Out Revisions section on p. 186, where you will find guidelines for reading your own draft critically.)

The Writing Guide Software provides an electronic form of the Critical Reading Guide. To save yourself the work of copying the text of the guide, just insert your background information for your reader and (if necessary) the draft of your essay into the electronic form. Then, depending on your reader's preference, you can either send the form to the reader electronically or print it out for him or her.

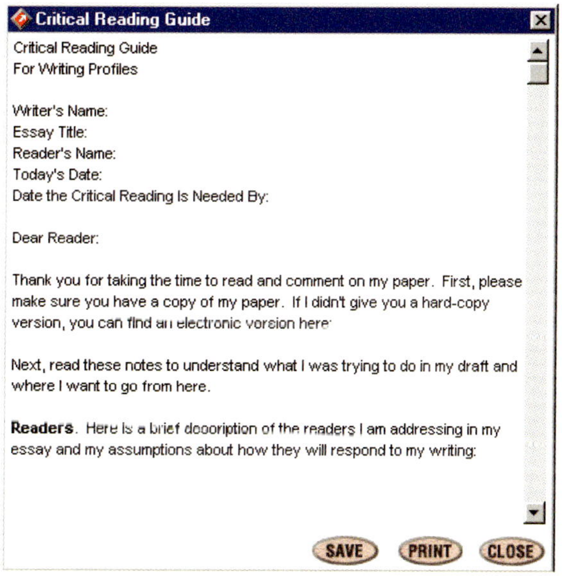
Critical Reading Guide

Critical Reading Guide
For Writing Profiles

Writer's Name:
Essay Title:
Reader's Name:
Today's Date:
Date the Critical Reading Is Needed By:

Dear Reader:

Thank you for taking the time to read and comment on my paper. First, please make sure you have a copy of my paper. If I didn't give you a hard-copy version, you can find an electronic version here:

Next, read these notes to understand what I was trying to do in my draft and where I want to go from here.

Readers. Here is a brief description of the readers I am addressing in my essay and my assumptions about how they will respond to my writing:

SAVE PRINT CLOSE

Making Comments Electronically
Most word processing software offers features that allow you to insert comments directly into the text of someone else's document. Many readers prefer to make their comments in this way because it tends to be faster than writing on a hard copy and space is virtually unlimited; from the writer's point of view, it also eliminates the problem of deciphering handwritten comments. Even where such special comment features are not available, simply typing comments directly into a document in a contrasting color can provide the same advantages.

▶ **If You Are the Writer.** To provide comments that are focused and helpful, your reader must know your essay's intended audience, your purpose, and a problem in the draft that you need help solving. Briefly write out this information at the top of your draft.

- ***Readers:*** Identify the intended readers of your essay.
- ***Purpose:*** What do you hope your readers will see and learn about your subject?
- ***Problem:*** Ask your draft reader to help you solve the most important problem you see with your draft. Describe this problem briefly.

▶ **If You Are the Reader.** The following guidelines can be useful for approaching a draft with a well-focused, questioning eye.

1. ***Read for a First Impression.*** Begin by reading the draft straight through to get a general impression. Read for enjoyment, ignoring spelling, punctuation, and other kinds of errors for now. Try to imagine the subject and to understand the perspective that the profile offers on its subject.

   When you have finished this first quick reading, write a few sentences about your overall impression. State the profile's perspective on its subject or main insight into it, as you best understand it. Next, consider the problem the writer identified, and respond briefly to that concern now. (If you find that the problem is covered by one of the other guidelines listed below, respond to it in more detail there if necessary.)

2. ***Analyze the Effectiveness of the Organization.*** Consider the overall plan, perhaps by making a scratch outline. Keep in mind that the plan may be narrative or topical or a combination of the two. If the plan narrates a visit (or visits) to a place, point out places where the narrative slows unnecessarily or shows gaps. Point out where time markers and transitions would help. Let the writer know whether the narrative arouses and holds your curiosity. Where does dialogue fall flat, and where does it convey immediacy and drama? If the plan is organized topically, note whether the writer presents too much or too little information for a topic and whether topics might be sequenced differently or connected more clearly. Finally, decide whether the writer might strengthen the profile by reordering any of the parts or the details.

   - ***Look again at the beginning*** of the essay to see whether it captures your attention. If not, is there a quotation, a fact, or an anecdote elsewhere in the draft that might make a better opening?
   - ***Look again at the ending*** to see whether it leaves you hanging, seems too abrupt, or oversimplifies the subject. If it does, suggest another way of ending, possibly by moving a part or a quotation from elsewhere in the essay.
   - ***Look again at any visuals.*** Tell the writer how well the visuals—headings, lists, tables, photographs, drawings, video—are integrated into the profile. Advise the writer about any visuals that seem misplaced or unnecessary.

3. ***Evaluate the Writer's Role.*** Decide whether the writer has adopted the participant-observer or detached-observer role or a combination of the two roles to present the profile subject. The writer has likely chosen one role or the other, but if both roles are visibly present, evaluate whether the writer really needs both roles or whether the alternation between the two is too frequent or confusing in any way. If the writer remains throughout in a participant-observer role, look for places where the writer is perhaps too prominent, dominating rather than featuring the subject. Point out where the writer-participant is most appealing and informative and also, perhaps, most distracting and tire-

some. If the writer remains throughout in the detached-observer role, notice whether the writer consistently directs you where and how to look at the subject, keeping you confidently moving through the profile.

4. ***Analyze the Description of People and Places.*** Begin by pointing out two or three places in the profile where the description of people, places, and activities or processes is most vivid for you, where your attention is held and you can readily imagine who or what is being described. Identify places where you would like more descriptive details. Also indicate where you need to see people in action—moving, talking, gesturing—to understand what is going on.
5. ***Assess the Quality and Presentation of the Information about the Subject.*** Show the writer where you learned something truly interesting, surprising, or useful. Point out where the information is too complex, coming at you too quickly, or incomplete. Ask for definitions of words you do not understand or clarification of definitions that do not seem immediately clear. Ask for a fuller description of any activity or process you cannot readily understand. Assess the clarity and informativeness of all visuals and design features. If there are parts of the information about the subject that you think could be better presented or complemented by visuals, let the writer know. Show the writer where the interweaving of description and information seems out of balance—too much of one or the other for too long.
6. ***Question the Writer's Perspective on the Subject.*** Begin by trying to state briefly what you believe to be the writer's perspective on the subject—some idea or insight the writer wants to convey. (This perspective statement may differ from the one you wrote at the beginning of your critical reading of this draft.) Then look for and underline one or two places where the writer explicitly states or implies a perspective. If the perspective is stated, tell the writer whether you fully understand or would welcome some elaboration. If the perspective is only implied, let the writer know whether you are content with the implication or whether you would prefer to have the perspective explicitly stated. With the writer's perspective in mind, skim the draft one last time looking for unneeded or extraneous description and information.
7. ***Give the Writer Your Final Thoughts.*** What is the draft's strongest part? What part is most memorable? What part is weakest or most in need of further work?

REVISING

This section will help you get an overview of your draft and revise it accordingly.

If you are using the Writing Guide Software, click on
▶ **Revising**

Getting an Overview

Consider your draft as a whole, following these two steps:

1. ***Reread.*** If at all possible, put the draft aside for a day or two. When you do reread it, start by reconsidering your purpose. Then read the draft straight through, trying to see it as your intended readers will.
2. ***Outline.*** Make a quick scratch outline on paper, or use the headings and outline/summary functions of your word processor.

Planning for Revision. Resist the temptation to dive in and start changing your text until after you have a comprehensive view of what needs to be done. Using your outline as a guide, move through the document, using the change-highlighting or commenting tools of your word processor to note comments received from others and problems you want to solve (or mark on a hard copy if you prefer).

Analyzing the Basic Features of Your Own Draft. Turn to the Critical Reading Guide on pp. 183–85. Using this guide, reread the draft to identify problems you need to solve. Note the problems on your draft.

Studying Critical Comments. Review all of the comments you have received from other readers. For each comment, look at the draft to determine what might have led the reader to make that particular point. Try to be objective about any criticism. Ideally, these comments will help you see your draft as others see it (rather than as you hoped it would be) and to identify specific problems. Add to your notes any problems readers have identified.

Carrying Out Revisions

Having identified problems in your draft, you now need to figure out solutions and carry them out. Basically, you have three options for finding solutions:

1. Review your observation or interview notes for other information and ideas.
2. Do additional observations or interviews to answer questions that you or other readers raised.
3. Look back at the readings in this chapter to see how other writers have solved similar problems.

The following suggestions, which are organized according to the basic features of profiles, will get you started solving some problems common to this kind of writing.

A Description of People and Places

- ***Can the description of the person who is the focus of the profile be improved?*** Add details to help readers see the person. Think, for example, of Orenstein's description of Amy's "curly, blond hair, cornflower-blue eyes, and . . . sharply upturned nose" (paragraph 2). Recall, for example, how after giving a wrong answer Amy "turns crimson, and flips her head forward so her hair falls over her face" (paragraph 18).

- *Should other people be described briefly?* Consider naming and detailing a few physical features of each person. Recall, for example, Orenstein's quick descriptive phrases: "Kyle, who is skinny and a little pop-eyed" (paragraph 17) and "Mrs. Richter, a ruddy, athletic woman with a powerful voice" (paragraph 9). Add comparisons, as Cable does when he says Howard Deaver "looked like death on two legs" (paragraph 5). Also consider adding specific narrative action. Think of Deaver again, on the phone: "As he listened, he bit his lips and squeezed his Adam's apple" (paragraph 7).
- *Can you enliven the description of the place?* Add other senses to visual description. Recall, for example, these sensory descriptions from the readings: sound (the clattering of a conveyer belt, a door creaking open), texture (a splintered door jamb, the soft flesh of a pig lip, a cold and firm cadaver), smell (a school hallway smelling of chalk, paper, and sweat), and taste (a pig lip that tastes porcine).
- *Do readers have difficulty seeing people in action or imagining what is involved in the activity?* Add specific narrative actions to show people moving, gesturing, or talking. For example, recall from Orenstein's profile Amy's confident poses outside of class and the boys' frantic gestures as they attempt to dominate classroom discussion. Remember that Orenstein makes use of absolute phrases to help readers better imagine the students' appearance and actions.

Information about the Subject

- *Do readers feel bogged down by information?* Look for ways to reduce information or to break up long blocks of informational text with description of scenes or people, narration of events, lists, or other design elements. Consider presenting information through dialogue, as Edge and Orenstein do.

A Topical or Narrative Plan

- *Does your narratively arranged essay seem to drag or ramble?* Try adding drama through dialogue or specific narrative action. Try using comparison and contrast, as Orenstein does.
- *Does your topically arranged essay seem disorganized or out of balance?* Try rearranging topics to see if another order makes more sense. Add clearer, more explicit transitions or topic sentences. Move or condense information to restore balance.
- *Does the opening fail to engage readers' attention?* Consider alternatives. Think of questions you could open with, or look for an engaging image or dialogue later in the essay to move to the beginning. Go back to your observation or interview notes for other ideas. Recall how the writers in this chapter open their profile essays: Cable combines a quote by Mark Twain with comments about how people try to ignore death, Edge sits at a juke bar staring at a pig lip, Hall stands in the dark outside the Edison Café waiting for Julie to arrive.

Checking Sentence Strategies Electronically

To check your draft for a sentence strategy especially useful in profiles, use your word processor's highlighting function to mark sentences that include direct quotations. Then look at each sentence to see whether and, if so, how you have identified the speaker. Where you have not identified the speaker, think about whether you need to do so by adding a speaker tag. Also consider whether you could help your readers better imagine speakers' attitudes and personal styles by making any speaker tags more specific, either by using a verb other than *say* or *tell* or by adding a phrase that tells how, where, when, or why the speaker spoke. For more on using speaker tags, see p. 181.

- ***Are transitions between stages in the narrative or between topics confusing or abrupt?*** Add appropriate words or phrases, or revise sentences to make transitions clearer or smoother.
- ***Does the ending seem weak?*** Consider ending at an earlier point or moving something striking to the end. Review your invention and research notes to see if you overlooked something that would make for a strong ending. Consider ending your essay with a quotation, as many of the writers in this chapter do.
- ***Are the design features effective?*** Consider adding textual references to any visual elements in your essay or positioning visuals more effectively. Think of other possible design features you might incorporate to enhance your profile. Use images, as do Hall and Edge.

A Role for the Writer

- ***Do readers want to see more of you in the profile?*** Consider revealing yourself participating in some part of the activity. Add yourself to one of the conversations you participated in, recreating dialogue for yourself.
- ***Do readers find your participation so dominant that you seem to eclipse other participants?*** Bring other people forward into more prominent view by adding material about them, reducing the material about yourself, or both.

A Perspective on the Subject

- ***Are readers unsure what your perspective is?*** Try stating it more directly. Be sure that the descriptive and narrative details reinforce the perspective you want to convey.
- ***Are your readers' ideas about the person, place, or activity being profiled different from yours?*** Consider whether you can incorporate any of their ideas into your essay or use them to develop your own ideas.
- ***Do readers point to any details that seem especially meaningful?*** Consider what these details suggest about your own perspective on the person, place, or activity.

A Note on Grammar and Spelling Checkers
These tools are good at catching certain types of errors, but currently there's no replacement for a good human proofreader. Grammar checkers in particular are extremely limited in what they can usually find, and often they only give you summary information that isn't helpful if you don't already understand the rule in question. They are also prone to give faulty advice for fixing problems and to flag correct items as wrong. Spelling checkers cause fewer problems but can't catch misspellings that are themselves words, such as *to* for *too.*

EDITING AND PROOFREADING

Now is the time to check your revised draft for errors in grammar, punctuation, and mechanics. Our research has identified several errors that occur often in profiles, including problems with the punctuation of quotations and the order of adjectives. The following guidelines will help you check your essay for these common errors. This book's Web site also provides interactive online exercises to help you learn to identify and correct each of these errors; to access the exercises for a particular error, go to the URL listed in the margin next to that section of the guidelines.

If you are using the Writing Guide Software, click on
▶ **Editing and Proofreading**

Checking the Punctuation of Quotations. Because most profiles are based in part on interviews, you probably have quoted one or more people in your essay. When you quote someone's exact words, you must enclose those words in quotation marks and observe strict conventions for punctuating quotations. Check your revised draft for your use of the following specific punctuation marks.

All quotations should have quotation marks at the beginning and the end.

► **"What exactly is civil litigation?" I asked.**

Commas and periods go *inside* quotation marks.

► **"I'm here to see Anna Post," I replied nervously.**

► **Tony explained, "Fraternity boys just wouldn't feel comfortable at the Chez Moi Café."**

Question marks and exclamation points go *inside* closing quotation marks if they are part of the quotation, *outside* if they are not.

For practice, go to bedfordstmartins.com/theguide/quote

► **After a pause, the patient asked, "Where do I sign?"**

► **Willie insisted, "You can *too* learn to play Super Mario!"**

► **When was the last time someone you just ticketed said to you, "Thank you, Officer, for doing a great job"?**

Use commas with speaker tags (*he said, she asked,* etc.) that accompany direct quotations.

► **"This sound system costs only four thousand dollars," Jorge said.**

► **I asked, "So where were these clothes from originally?"**

A Common ESL Problem: Adjective Order. In trying to present the subject of your profile vividly and in detail, you probably have included many descriptive adjectives. When you include more than one adjective in front of a noun, you may have difficulty sequencing them. For example, do you write *a large old ceramic pot* or *an old large ceramic pot?* The following list shows the order in which adjectives are ordinarily arranged in front of a noun.

1. ***Amount:*** a/an, the, a few, six
2. ***Evaluation:*** good, beautiful, ugly, serious
3. ***Size:*** large, small, tremendous
4. ***Shape, length:*** round, long, short
5. ***Age:*** young, new, old

6. ***Color:*** red, black, green
7. ***Origin:*** Asian, Brazilian, German
8. ***Material:*** wood, cotton, gold
9. ***Noun used as an adjective:*** computer (as in *computer program*), cake (as in *cake pan*)
10. ***The noun modified***

For practice, go to bedfordstmartins.com/theguide/order

A WRITER AT WORK

THE INTERVIEW NOTES AND WRITE-UP

Most profile writers take notes when interviewing people. Later, they may summarize their notes in a short write-up. In this section, you will see some of the interview notes and a write-up that Brian Cable prepares for his mortuary profile, "The Last Stop," printed on pp. 159–61.

Cable arranged to tour the mortuary and conduct interviews with the funeral director and mortician. Before each interview, he wrote out a few questions at the top of a sheet of paper and then divided it into two columns; he used the left-hand column for descriptive details and personal impressions and the right-hand column for the information he got directly from the person he interviewed. Following are Cable's notes and write-up for his interview with the funeral director, Howard Deaver.

Cable used three questions to guide his interview with Howard and then took brief notes during the interview. He did not concern himself too much with note-taking because he planned to spend a half-hour directly afterward to complete his notes. He focused his attention on Howard, trying to keep the interview comfortable and conversational and jotting down just enough to jog his memory and catch especially meaningful quotations. A typescript of Cable's interview notes follows.

The Interview Notes

QUESTIONS

1. How do families of the deceased view the mortuary business?
2. How is the concept of death approached?
3. How did you get into this business?

DESCRIPTIVE DETAILS & PERSONAL IMPRESSIONS	INFORMATION
weird-looking tall long fingers big ears low, sloping forehead Like stereotype--skin colorless	Howard Deaver, funeral director, Goodbody Mortuaries "Call me Howard" How things work: Notification, pick up body at home or hospital, prepare for viewing, restore distorted features--accident or illness, embalm, casket--family selects, chapel services (3 in bldg.), visitation room--pay respects, family & friends.
	Can't answer questions about death--"Not bereavement specialists. Don't handle emotional problems. Only a trained therapist can do that." "We provide services for dead, not counseling for the living." (great quote) Concept of death has changed in last 40 yrs (how long he's been in the business) Funeral cost: $500-$600, now $2,000
plays with lips blinks plays with Adam's apple desk empty--phone, no paper or pen	Phone call (interruption) "I think we'll be able to get him in on Friday. No, no, the family wants him cremated." Ask about Neptune Society--cremation
angry disdainful of the Neptune Society	Cremation "Cheap, quick, easy means of disposal." Recent phenomenon. Neptune Society--erroneous claim to be only one.

DESCRIPTIVE DETAILS & PERSONAL IMPRESSIONS	INFORMATION
	"We've offered them since the beginning. It's only now it's come into vogue." Trend now back toward burial. Cremation still popular in sophisticated areas 60% in Marin Co. and Florida Ask about paperwork--does it upstairs, lives there with wife, Nancy.
musty, old stained glass sunlight filtered	Tour around (happy to show me around) Chapel--large service just done, Italian.
man in black suit roses wooden benches	"Not a religious institution--a business." casket--"beautiful craftsmanship"--admires, expensive
contrast brightness fluorescent lights Plexiglas stands	Display room--caskets, about 30 of them Loves to talk about caskets "models in every price range" glossy (like cars in a showroom) cardboard box, steel, copper, bronze $400 up to $1,800. Top of line: bronze, electronically welded, no corrosion--$5,000

Cable's interview notes include many descriptive details of Howard as well as of various rooms in the mortuary. Though most entries are short and sketchy, much of the language found its way into the final essay. In describing Howard, for example, Cable noted that he fits the stereotype of the cadaverous undertaker, a fact that Cable emphasized in his essay.

He put quotation marks around Howard's actual words, some of them written in complete sentences, others in fragments. We will see how Cable filled these quotes in when he wrote up the interview. In only a few instances did he take down more than he could use. Even though profile writers want good quotes, they should not use quotes to present information that can be more effectively expressed in their own words. In profiles, writers use direct quotation both to provide information and to capture the mood or character of the person speaking.

As you can see, Howard was not able to answer Cable's questions about the families of the deceased and their attitudes toward death or mortuaries. The gap between these questions and Howard's responses led Cable to recognize one of his own misperceptions about mortuaries—that they serve the living by helping people adjust to the death of loved ones. This misperception would become an important theme of his essay.

Immediately after the interview, Cable filled in his notes with details while they were still fresh in his mind. Next, he took some time to reflect on what he had learned from his interview with Howard. Here are some of his thoughts:

> I was surprised by how much Howard looked like the undertakers in scary movies. Even though he couldn't answer some of my questions, he was friendly enough. It's obviously a business for him (he loves to talk about caskets and to point out all their features, like a car dealer kicking a tire). Best quote: "We offer services to the dead, not counseling to the living." I have to bring up these issues in my interview with the mortician.

The Interview Write-Up

Writing up an account of the interview a short time afterward helped Cable fill in more details and reflect further on what he had learned. His write-up shows him already beginning to organize the information he had gained from his interview with the funeral director.

> I. His physical appearance.
>
> Tall, skinny, with beady blue eyes embedded in his bony face. I was shocked to see that he looks just like the undertakers in scary movies. His skin is white and colorless, from lack of sunshine. He has a long nose and a low, sloping forehead. He was wearing a clean white shirt. A most unusual man--have you ever seen those Ames Home Loan commercials? But he was friendly, and happy to talk with me. "Would I answer some questions? Sure."
>
> II. What people want from a mortuary.
>
> A. Well first of all, he couldn't answer my second question, about how families cope with the loss of a loved one. "You'd have to talk to a psychologist about that," he said. He did tell me how the concept of death has changed over the last ten or so years.

B. He has been in the business for forty years(!). One look at him and you'd be convinced he'd been there at least that long. He told me that in the old times, everyone was buried. Embalmed, put in a casket, and paid final homage before being shipped underground forever. Nowadays, many people choose to be cremated instead. Hence comes the success of the Neptune Society and others specializing in cremation. You can have your ashes dumped anywhere. "Not that we don't offer cremation services. We've offered them since the beginning," he added with a look of disdain. It's just that they've become so popular recently because they offer a "quick, easy, and efficient means of disposal." Cheap too--I think it is a reflection of a "no nonsense" society. The Neptune Society has become so successful because it claims to be the only one to offer cremations as an alternative to expensive burial. "We've offered it all along. It's just only now come into vogue."

Sophisticated areas (I felt "progressive" would be more accurate) like Marin County have a cremation rate of over 60 percent. The phone rang. "Excuse me," he said. As he talked on the phone, I noticed how he played with his lips, pursing and squeezing them. He was blinking a lot, too. I meant to ask him how he got into this business, but I forgot. I did find out his name and title: Mr. Howard Deaver, funeral director of Goodbody Mortuaries (no kidding, that's the real name). He lives on the premises, upstairs with his wife. I doubt if he ever leaves the place.

III. It's a business!

Some people have the idea that mortuaries offer counseling and peace of mind--a place where everyone is sympathetic and ready to offer advice. "In some mortuaries, this is true. But by and large, this is a business. We offer services to the dead, not counseling to the living." I too had expected to feel an awestruck respect for the dead upon entering the building. I had also expected green lawns, ponds with ducks, fountains, flowers, peacefulness--you know, a "Forest Lawn" type deal. But it was only a tall, Catholic-looking building. "Mortuaries do not sell plots for burial," he was saying. "Cemeteries do that, after we embalm the body and select a casket. We're not a religious institution." He seemed hung up on caskets--though maybe he was just trying to impress upon me the differences between caskets. "Oh, they're very important. A good casket is a sign of respect. Sometimes if the family

```
doesn't have enough money, we rent them a nice one. People pay
for what they get just like any other business." I wondered
when you had to return the casket you rented.
     I wanted to take a look around. He was happy to give me
a tour. We visited several chapels and visiting rooms--places
where the deceased "lie in state" to be "visited" by family
and friends. I saw an old lady in a "fairly decent casket," as
Mr. Deaver called it. Again I was impressed by the simple
businesslike nature of it all. Oh yes, the rooms were elabo-
rately decorated, with lots of shrines and stained glass, but
these things were for the customers' benefit. "Sometimes we
have up to eight or nine corpses here at one time, sometimes
none. We have to have enough rooms to accommodate." Simple
enough, yet I never realized how much (trouble?) people were
after they died. So much money, time, and effort go into their
funerals.
     As I prepared to leave, he gave me his card. He'd be
happy to see me again, or maybe I could talk to someone else.
I said I was going to interview the mortician on another day.
I shook his hand. His fingers were long and his skin was warm.
```

Writing up the interview helped Cable probe his subject more deeply. It also helped him express a humorous attitude toward his subject. Cable's interview notes and write-up were quite informal; later, he integrated this material more formally into his full profile of the mortuary.

DESIGNING YOUR WORK

The education student working on a paper about collaborative learning principles (see pp. 137–38) published her paper on the Web so that her classmates and other interested people could read her work. Internet publishing is becoming an increasingly popular medium for students to share their work not just with their peers but with a wider audience as well. For this student, whose paper was based on her field research in a sixth-grade classroom, Web-based publishing allowed her to show her final product to the sixth graders and the teacher she had profiled.

Web documents can be more visually complex and interactive than most other written pieces. In her Web-based essay, the education student incorporated photographs, links, color highlights, and quotations to make the material both more interesting and helpful to her readers. As the accompanying illustration shows, she also took advantage of the multiple frames and navigational tools Web publishing provides. She also included the list of scholarly essays about collaborative learning that served as background reading for her own work in two formats: as a traditional works-cited list at the end of her essay and as a pop-up window—a multimedia equivalent of a sidebar. While the works-cited list lent credibility to her work academically, the window was designed to provide content and links that might immediately attract casual visitors and encourage them to read the student's own writing more closely. When writers publish on the Web, they are much less bound by space constraints than they are when they generate conventional print documents. Duplication of information is also less of a concern, as readers can be expected to skip around and view the site selectively. The student organized the information in a way that enabled her to provide several different points of entry into her site.

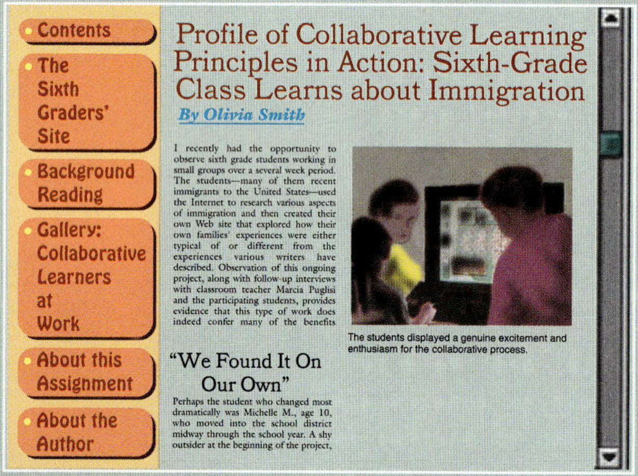

Opening page of student's paper published on the Web

In the main essay, the student writer included links to the sixth-grade class's Web site. Included on this site were the final projects that resulted from the Internet research she had watched the students perform. She encouraged readers to view the variety and quality of these projects as evidence of the significance of collaborative learning as a classroom tool.

The student decided to display one photograph of the sixth graders in action to give her readers a sense of what collaborative learning looks like and how the layout of the classroom she visited differed from the traditional setup. She included a button allowing readers to access other photos she had taken with her subjects' permission as part of her field research. By leaving viewing choices in her readers' hands, she helped ensure that they would not be forced to sit through a lengthy period of downloading.

At key points in her essay, the student writer also included quotes from the sixth graders themselves. She used these quotes as subtitles for individual sections of her essay, and to draw more attention to the quotes, she used a font larger than the body of the essay—a technique borrowed from print publishing. The availability of color, graphics, and animated or scrolling text in Web publishing has expanded the possibilities for creating visually exciting documents. In their capacity as Web page designers, however, writers must avoid bombarding readers with meaningless visual effects. In this example, the student made effective use of color and space on the Web page to help organize the key points she was making and to draw attention to the sixth graders' own voices and thoughts. In doing so, she clearly conveyed the students' love for school and made their quest for learning come alive.

THINKING CRITICALLY ABOUT WHAT YOU HAVE LEARNED

Now that you have spent several days discussing profiles and writing one of your own, take some time to reflect on what you have learned about this genre. What problems did you encounter while you were writing your profile, and how did you solve them? How did what you learned as a reader of profiles help you write your own profile? Finally, explore the social dimensions of profiles: In what ways do they influence your thinking about yourself and the society we live in?

Reflecting on Your Writing

Write a one-page explanation, telling your instructor about a problem you encountered in writing your profile and how you solved it. Before you begin, gather all of your writing invention material, planning and interview notes, drafts, critical comments, revision notes and plans, and final revision. Review these materials as you complete this writing task.

1. ***Identify one writing problem you needed to solve as you worked on your profile.*** Do not be concerned with grammar or punctuation; concentrate instead on problems unique to developing a profile. For example: Did you puzzle over how to organize your diverse observations into a coherent essay? Was it difficult to convey your own perspective? Did you have any concerns about presenting your subject vividly or controlling the flow of information?
2. ***Determine how you came to recognize the problem.*** When did you first discover it? What called it to your attention? If someone else pointed out the problem to you, can you now see hints of it in your invention writings? If so, where specifically? When you first recognized the problem, how did you respond?
3. ***Reflect on how you went about solving the problem.*** Did you work on the wording of a passage, cut or add details about your subject, or move paragraphs or sentences around? Did you reread one of the essays in this chapter to see how another writer handled a similar problem, or did you look back at the invention suggestions? If you talked about the problem with another student, your instructor, or someone else, did talking about it help? How useful was the advice you received?
4. ***Write a brief explanation of the problem and your solution.*** Reconstruct your efforts as specifically as possible. Quote from your invention notes or draft essay, others' critical comments, your revision plan, or your revised essay to show the various changes your writing underwent as you tried to solve the problem. When you have finished, consider how explaining what you have learned about solving this writing problem can help you solve future writing problems.

Reviewing What You Learned from Reading

Write a page or so explaining to your instructor how the readings in this chapter influenced your final essay. Before you write, take time to reflect on what you have learned from the readings in this chapter and how your reading has influenced your writing.

1. ***Reread the final revision of your profile essay; then look back at the selections you read before completing it.*** Do you see any specific influences? For example, if you were impressed with the way one of the readings presented a place through concrete details, made an ordinary activity seem interesting, focused all of the materials around a compelling and unexpected interpretation, or reconstructed dialogue from interview notes, look to see where you might have been striving to use the same writing strategies, include comparable details, or achieve similar effects in your own writing.

2. ***Write an explanation of these influences.*** Did one selection in particular influence you, or were you influenced by several readings in different ways? Quote from the readings and from your final revision to show how your profile essay was influenced by the selections in this chapter. Finally, now that you have reviewed the other readings again, point out any ways in which you might further improve your profile.

Considering the Social Dimensions of Profiles

Profiles offer some of the same pleasures as autobiographies, novels, and films: good stories, memorable characters, exotic places or familiar places viewed freshly, vivid images of people at work and play. They divert and entertain. They may even shock or fascinate. In addition, they offer information that may surprise and should interest readers. This special combination of entertainment and information makes profiles unique among all the kinds of reading and writing available to us.

Like travel writing and natural history, profiles nearly always take us to a particular place, usually a place we have never been. For example, Cable provides many visual details of Goodbody Mortuaries, with its gothic arches and stained glass, its hotel-like lobby with couches and coffee tables, aquarium, and pastoral paintings.

But the larger appeal of profiles is that they present real people that most readers will never have a chance to meet. Often, profiles present people the writer admires and assumes that readers will admire for their achievements, endurance, dedication, skill, or unselfishness. For example, Edge clearly admires Lionel Dufour for his persistence and success, and Hall admires Julie Martin for her warmth and sociability, as well as her skills in the kitchen at the Edison Café. Profiles also present less admirable people; these people may occasionally be shown as cruel, greedy, or selfish, but more often they are people, such as Amy Wilkinson, with whom we can empathize. The strongest profiles present us not with saints, monsters, or helpless victims but with people of mixed motives, human failings, and some resources even in dire situations. Orenstein suggests that Amy herself bears some responsibility for her lack of assertiveness in school.

Entertain Readers, or Show the Whole Picture? Profiles broaden our view of the world by entertaining and informing us with portraits of unusual people in particular places. It is important to recognize, however, that profiles sometimes offer a more limited view of their subjects than they seem to. For example, the impulse to entertain readers may lead a profile writer to focus exclusively on the dramatic, bizarre, colorful, or humorous aspects of a person, place, or activity, ignoring the equally important humdrum, routine, or even disturbing aspects. Imagine a profile that focuses on the free trips that a travel agent enjoys as part of the job but ignores the everyday demands of dealing with clients, the energy-draining precision required by computerized airline reservation systems, and the numbing routine of addressing envelopes and mailing tickets to clients. Such a profile would provide a limited and distorted picture of a travel agent's work.

In addition, by focusing on the dramatic or glamorous aspects of a subject, profile writers tend to ignore economic or social consequences and to slight supporting players. Profiling the highly praised chef in a trendy new restaurant, a writer might not ask whether the chef participates in the city's leftover-food-collection program for the homeless or find out who the kitchen workers and wait staff are, how the chef treats them, or how much they are paid. Profiling the campus bookstore, a writer might become so caught up in the details of ordering books for hundreds of courses and selling them efficiently to hordes of students during the first week of a semester that he or she could forget to ask about textbook costs, pricing policies, profit margins, and payback on used textbooks.

1. ***Consider whether any of the profiles you have read glamorize or sensationalize their subjects.*** Do they ignore less colorful but centrally important everyday activities? Is this a problem with your own profile?

2. ***Single out a profile you read that seems to overlook potential social or economic consequences.*** What is overlooked? Why do you think the writer omits these aspects?
3. ***Write a page or so explaining what the omissions signify.*** What do they suggest about the readers' desires to be entertained and the profile writer's reluctance to present the subject as boring or disturbing in some way?

Be Aware of the Writer's Viewpoint. Though profiles may seem impartial and objective, they inevitably reflect the views of their writers. The choice of subject, the details observed, the questions asked, the ultimate focus and presentation—all are influenced by the writer's interests and values, gender and ethnicity, and assumptions about social and political issues. For example, we would expect a vegetarian to write a very different profile of a cattle ranch than a beef lover would. Consequently, profiles should be read critically, particularly because the writer's values are likely to be unstated.

1. ***Consider the attitudes, values, and views of the profile writers in this chapter.*** Are their attitudes obvious or hidden? How can you tell?
2. ***Consider your own profile essay in the same terms.*** Are your attitudes obvious or hidden? If obvious, how did you make them so, and did you feel as though you were taking a risk? If hidden, why did you think it best to keep your personal views out of sight?
3. ***Write a page or so about how your viewpoint influenced your writing.*** How have your own assumptions, values, gender, ethnicity, or other characteristics influenced your choice of a subject to profile, your approach to learning about it, and your attitudes toward it?

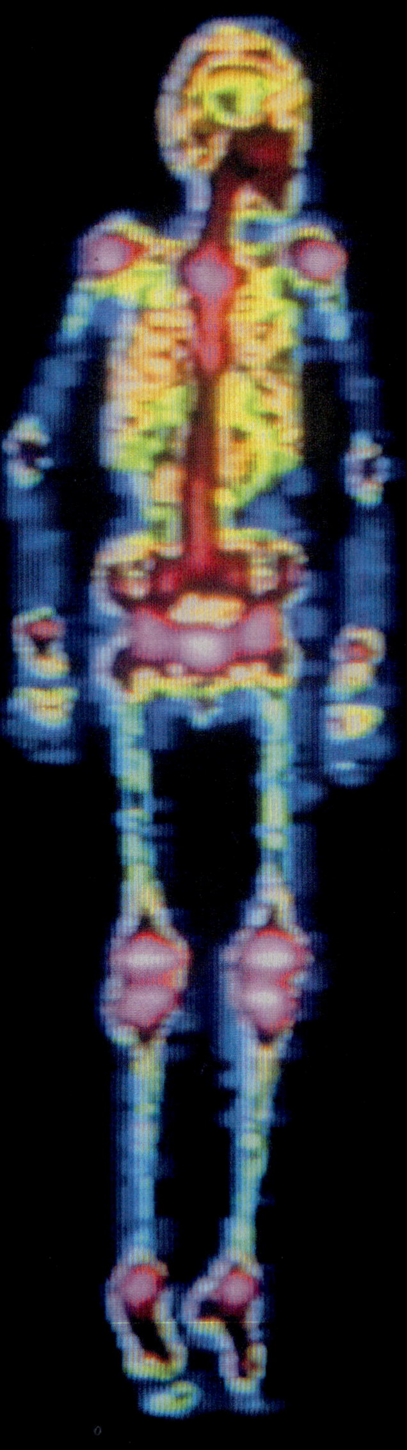

5

Explaining a Concept

Explanatory writing serves primarily to inform readers. Successful explanatory writing presents information confidently and efficiently, usually with the purpose of educating the reader about a subject. College students, however, are required to write explanations not primarily to teach others but to demonstrate what they have learned. Whether the explanation is researched or written from memory, the writer must analyze and evaluate a variety of kinds of information and then organize and synthesize the information to make a coherent presentation. This type of writing—which includes much of what we find in newspapers, magazines, and research reports—may be based on firsthand observations and interviews (as in Chapter 4) as well as on library and Internet research. Although writers of explanation may be experts on a subject, as in the essay by Randy Olson in this chapter, more often they are people who study what experts have discovered to convey that knowledge to others, as in the other essays in the chapter.

This chapter focuses on one important kind of explanatory writing—explanations of concepts. The chapter readings explain the concepts of romantic love, shifting baselines, indirect aggression, and cannibalism. These concepts name processes and phenomena like those you are studying in your college courses or using at work. Every field of study has its concepts: Physics has entropy, mass, and fission; literature has irony, romanticism, and postmodernism; music has harmony; art has perspective; mathematics has probability; and so on. You can see from this brief list that concepts are central to the understanding of virtually every subject. Moreover, when you begin to study a new field, you are expected to learn a new set of concepts. That is why introductory courses and their textbooks teach a whole new vocabulary of technical terms and specialized jargon. When you read the opening chapter of this textbook, for example, you were introduced to many concepts important to the study of writing, such as genre, writing process, invention, and revision.

Learning to explain a concept is especially important to you as a college student. It will help you read explanatory writing, a staple of academic discourse; it will prepare you to write a common type of exam and paper assignment; it will acquaint you with the basic strategies common to all types of explanatory writing—definition, classification, comparison and contrast, cause and effect, and process narration; and it will sharpen your skill in researching and using sources, abilities essential for success in college, whatever your major.

You will encounter writing that explains concepts in many different contexts, as the following examples suggest:

Writing in Your Other Courses

- For a linguistics course, a student writes a term paper tracing children's gradual control of sentences—or syntax, as linguists say—from about eighteen months to five or six years of age. The student first explains how researchers go about studying children's syntax, using several well-known studies as examples. Then he presents the widely accepted classification of stages that children go through as they gain control of syntax. As he presents each stage, he gives examples of children's syntax in their monologues and conversations in different situations, examples chosen from many possibilities in the published research studies. Even though he writes for his instructor, who is an expert in child language development, he carefully defines key terms to show that he understands what he is writing about.
- For a history of religion course, a student writes a research paper on religious fundamentalism. To explain this concept, she relies primarily on a book by a noted religious scholar. She follows the scholar's classification of the ways that fundamentalist religious groups are similar and organizes her paper around these similarities, which include a sense of threat and an organized reaction to the threat, a reliance on authoritative texts, a resistance to ambiguity and ambivalence, an inclination to behave aggressively toward unbelievers, an allegiance to a grand past, and a belief in a bright future. She illustrates each of these features of fundamentalism with examples from the beliefs and histories of fundamentalist groups around the world. She concludes by pointing out that religious fundamentalism began to be a major political force in the late twentieth century.

Writing in the Community

- Community policing has just been adopted by the police department in a midsized city, and a writer in the department's public relations division has been assigned to write and produce a brochure explaining the new approach. The brochure will be mailed to all homes in the city. The writer designs a small, foldout, six-panel, two-sided brochure that will feature both text and photographs. The text briefly explains the major features of community policing, including the involvement of neighborhood residents and businesses in police decisions about crime-control priorities, the long-term assignment of officers to particular neighborhoods, increased reliance on foot and bicycle patrols rather than on car patrols, and the establishment of neighborhood police mini-stations. Working with a photographer, the brochure writer arranges to have photographs taken that represent the different features of community policing explained in the text.
- As part of her firm's plan to encourage managers to volunteer in the community for a few hours each month, a manager at a marketing research firm has been

tutoring fifth-grade students in math. Learning about the manager's expertise in surveys, the teacher encourages her to plan a presentation to the class about surveying, an important research method in the social sciences. The manager agrees to do so and begins her lesson by having students fill out a brief questionnaire on their television-watching habits. She explains that she is not collecting data for marketing purposes but rather introducing them to surveys. With the students helping, she tabulates the results on a computer, separating the results by sex, time of week (weekdays or weekends), and kinds of television shows. Using a PowerPoint program, she projects the data onto a large screen so that everyone can see how the tables represent the survey results. The manager first guides a brief discussion of the survey and the results, helping students understand its purpose, form, and graphic representation. Then she shows them on the screen examples of questions from other surveys and explains who does such surveys, what they hope to learn, and how they report and use the results. She explains that the state tests that the students take every year are a form of survey. Finally, she passes out a short-answer quiz so that she and each student can find out how much has been learned about surveys.

Writing in the Workplace

- Returning from a small invitational seminar on the national security implications of satellite photography, the CEO of a space-imaging company prepares a report to his employees on the international debate about symmetrical transparency, the concept of using satellite photography to make everything on the planet visible to everyone on the planet at one-meter resolution—enough detail to reveal individual cars in parking lots, small airplanes on runways, backyard swimming pools, and individual shrubs and trees planted in parks. Aware of the financial implications for his company of the outcome of the debate, the executive carefully organizes his information and prepares a written text to read aloud to his employees, a one-page handout that lists key issues in the debate, and a transparency to project on a large screen during his presentation. He begins by reminding employees that the company's cameras already provide high-resolution images to government and corporate purchasers. Addressing the question of whether symmetrical transparency and the multinational monitoring that it makes possible compromise national security—or promise greater worldwide security and peace—the CEO gives a brief overview of key issues in the debate. These issues include how closed societies (like that of North Korea) will be affected differently from more open ones, whether global terrorism will be reduced or become more prevalent or more effective, and whether the chance of a nuclear standoff will be lessened. He concludes by pointing out that the big question for the U.S. government to answer soon is whether to attempt to control space or insist that it be open to everyone.
- Legislation in a western state defines a new concept in tourism—agritourism. To explain the concept, a state senator invites farmers, vineyard owners, and

ranchers in his part of the state to an informal meeting. To prepare for the meeting, he writes a four-page summary of the legislation and prepares a one-page list of the main points in his presentation for everyone to pick up and read before the meeting begins. Assuming that his listeners have all visited a bed and breakfast inn, the senator compares the rules in the new law with the rules governing B&Bs. He emphasizes that in agritourism, guests tour a farm or ranch and participate in supervised chores. Meals must be offered three times a day and prepared and served by people who have been certified through coursework at a community college. He also explains that the greatest beneficiaries of agritourism will be small and medium-sized farms and ranches, where income is relatively low and varies greatly from year to year.

Practice Explaining a Concept: A Collaborative Activity

The preceding scenarios suggest some occasions for writing about concepts. Think of concepts you are currently studying or have recently studied or concepts connected to a job, sport, or hobby you know a lot about. Here are some possibilities: hip-hop, squeeze play, critical thinking, ambition, hypertext, interval training, photosynthesis, civil rights, manifest destiny, postcolonialism. Your instructor may schedule this collaborative activity as a face-to-face in-class discussion or ask you to conduct an online real-time discussion in a chat room. Whatever the medium, here are some guidelines to follow:

Part 1. Choose one concept to explain to two or three other students. When you have chosen your concept, think about what others in the group are likely to know about it and how you can inform them about it in two or three minutes. Consider how you will define the concept and what other strategies you might use—description, comparison, and so on—to explain it in an interesting, memorable way.

Get together with two or three other students, and explain your concepts to one another. You might begin by indicating where you learned the concept and in what area of study or work or leisure it is usually used.

Part 2. When all group members have explained their concepts, discuss what you learned from the experience of explaining a concept. Begin by asking one another a question or two that elicits further information that you need to understand each concept more fully. Then consider these questions:

- How did you decide what to include in your explanation and what to leave out?
- What surprised you in the questions that readers asked about your presentation?
- If you were to repeat your explanation to a similar group of listeners, what would you add, subtract, or change?

READINGS

No two essays that explain concepts are much alike, and yet they share defining features. Together, the four readings in this chapter reveal a number of these features, so you will want to read as many of them as possible. If time permits, complete the activities in the Analyzing Writing Strategies section that follows each selection, and read the Commentary. Following the readings is a section called Basic Features: Explaining Concepts (p. 231), which offers a concise description of the features of concept explanations and provides examples from the four readings.

***Anastasia Toufexis** has been an associate editor of* Time*, senior editor of* Discover*, and editor in chief of* Psychology Today*. She has written major reports, including some best-selling cover stories, on subjects as diverse as medicine, health and fitness, law, environment, education, science, and national and world news. Toufexis received a bachelor's degree from Smith College in 1967 and spent several years reporting for medical and pharmaceutical magazines. She has won a number of awards for her writing, including a Knight-Wallace Fellowship at the University of Michigan and an Ocean Science Journalism Fellowship at Woods Hole Oceanographic Institution. She has also lectured on science writing at Columbia University, the University of North Carolina, and the School of Visual Arts in New York.*

The following essay was originally published in 1993 in Time *magazine. As you read, notice how Toufexis brings together a variety of sources of information to present a neurochemical perspective on love.*

Love: The Right Chemistry

Anastasia Toufexis

> Love is a romantic designation for a most ordinary biological—or, shall we say, chemical?—process. A lot of nonsense is talked and written about it.
>
> —Greta Garbo to Melvyn Douglas in *Ninotchka*

O.K., let's cut out all this nonsense about romantic love. 1
Let's bring some scientific precision to the party. Let's put love under a microscope.

When rigorous people with Ph.D.s after their names do that, what they see is not 2
some silly, senseless thing. No, their probe reveals that love rests firmly on the foundations of evolution, biology and chemistry. What seems on the surface to be irrational, intoxicated behavior is in fact part of nature's master strategy—a vital force that has helped humans survive, thrive and multiply through thousands of years. Says Michael Mills, a psychology professor at Loyola Marymount University in Los Angeles: "Love is our ancestors whispering in our ears."

It was on the plains of Africa about 4 million years ago, in the early days of the 3
human species, that the notion of romantic love probably first began to blossom or at least that the first cascades of neurochemicals began flowing from the brain to the bloodstream to produce goofy grins and sweaty palms as men and women gazed deeply into each other's eyes. When mankind graduated from scuttling around on all fours to

walking on two legs, this change made the whole person visible to fellow human beings for the first time. Sexual organs were in full display, as were other characteristics, from the color of eyes to the span of shoulders. As never before, each individual had a unique allure.

When the sparks flew, new ways of making love enabled sex to become a roman- 4
tic encounter, not just a reproductive act. Although mounting mates from the rear was, and still is, the method favored among most animals, humans began to enjoy face-to-face couplings; both looks and personal attraction became a much greater part of the equation.

Romance served the evolutionary purpose of pulling males and females into long- 5
term partnership, which was essential to child rearing. On open grasslands, one parent would have a hard—and dangerous—time handling a child while foraging for food. "If a woman was carrying the equivalent of a 20-lb. bowling ball in one arm and a pile of sticks in the other, it was ecologically critical to pair up with a mate to rear the young," explains anthropologist Helen Fisher, author of *Anatomy of Love.*

While Western culture holds fast to the idea that true love flames forever (the movie 6
Bram Stoker's Dracula has the Count carrying the torch beyond the grave), nature apparently meant passions to sputter out in something like four years. Primitive pairs stayed together just "long enough to rear one child through infancy," says Fisher. Then each would find a new partner and start all over again.

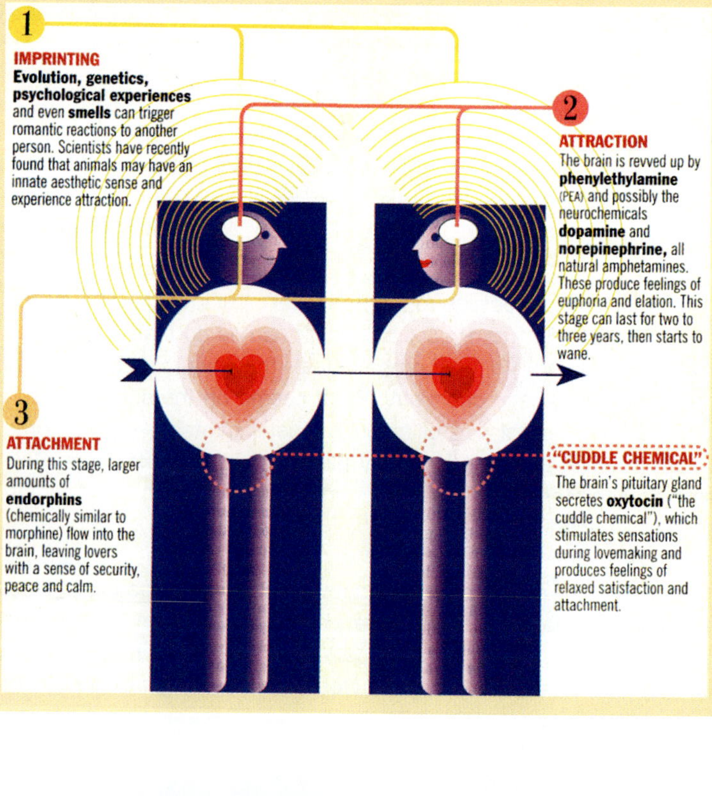

What Fisher calls the "four-year itch" shows up unmistakably in today's divorce statistics. In most of the 62 cultures she has studied, divorce rates peak around the fourth year of marriage. Additional youngsters help keep pairs together longer. If, say, a couple have another child three years after the first, as often occurs, then their union can be expected to last about four more years. That makes them ripe for the more familiar phenomenon portrayed in the Marilyn Monroe classic *The Seven-Year Itch.* 7

If, in nature's design, romantic love is not eternal, neither is it exclusive. Less than 5% of mammals form rigorously faithful pairs. From the earliest days, contends Fisher, the human pattern has been "monogamy with clandestine adultery." Occasional flings upped the chances that new combinations of genes would be passed on to the next generation. Men who sought new partners had more children. Contrary to common assumptions, women were just as likely to stray. "As long as prehistoric females were secretive about their extramarital affairs," argues Fisher, "they could garner extra resources, life insurance, better genes and more varied DNA for their biological futures. . . ." 8

Lovers often claim that they feel as if they are being swept away. They're not mistaken; they are literally flooded by chemicals, research suggests. A meeting of eyes, a touch of hands or a whiff of scent sets off a flood that starts in the brain and races along the nerves and through the blood. The results are familiar: flushed skin, sweaty palms, heavy breathing. If love looks suspiciously like stress, the reason is simple: the chemical pathways are identical. 9

Above all, there is the sheer euphoria of falling in love—a not-so-surprising reaction, considering that many of the substances swamping the newly smitten are chemical cousins of amphetamines. They include dopamine, norepinephrine and especially phenylethylamine (PEA). Cole Porter knew what he was talking about when he wrote, "I get a kick out of you." "Love is a natural high," observes Anthony Walsh, author of *The Science of Love: Understanding Love and Its Effects on Mind and Body.* "PEA gives you that silly smile that you flash at strangers. When we meet someone who is attractive to us, the whistle blows at the PEA factory." 10

But phenylethylamine highs don't last forever, a fact that lends support to arguments that passionate romantic love is short-lived. As with any amphetamine, the body builds up a tolerance to PEA; thus it takes more and more of the substance to produce love's special kick. After two to three years, the body simply can't crank up the needed amount of PEA. And chewing on chocolate doesn't help, despite popular belief. The candy is high in PEA, but it fails to boost the body's supply. 11

Fizzling chemicals spell the end of delirious passion; for many people that marks the end of the liaison as well. It is particularly true for those whom Dr. Michael Liebowitz of the New York State Psychiatric Institute terms "attraction junkies." They crave the intoxication of falling in love so much that they move frantically from affair to affair just as soon as the first rush of infatuation fades. 12

Still, many romances clearly endure beyond the first years. What accounts for that? Another set of chemicals, of course. The continued presence of a partner gradually steps up production in the brain of endorphins. Unlike the fizzy amphetamines, these are soothing substances. Natural pain-killers, they give lovers a sense of security, peace 13 and calm. "That is one reason why it feels so horrible when we're abandoned or a lover dies," notes Fisher. "We don't have our daily hit of narcotics."

Researchers see a contrast between the heated infatuation induced by PEA, along with other amphetamine-like chemicals, and the more intimate attachment fostered and prolonged by endorphins. "Early love is when you love the way the other person makes you feel," explains psychiatrist Mark Goulston of the University of California, Los Angeles. "Mature love is when you love the person as he or she is." It is the difference between passionate and compassionate love, observes Walsh, a psychobiologist at Boise State University in Idaho. "It's Bon Jovi vs. Beethoven." 14

Oxytocin is another chemical that has recently been implicated in love. Produced by the brain, it sensitizes nerves and stimulates muscle contraction. In women it helps uterine contractions during childbirth as well as production of breast milk, and seems to inspire mothers to nuzzle their infants. Scientists speculate that oxytocin might encourage similar cuddling between adult women and men. The versatile chemical may also enhance orgasms. In one study of men, oxytocin increased to three to five times its normal level during climax, and it may soar even higher in women. . . . 15

Chemicals may help explain (at least to scientists) the feelings of passion and compassion, but why do people tend to fall in love with one partner rather than a myriad of others? Once again, it's partly a function of evolution and biology. "Men are looking for maximal fertility in a mate," says Loyola Marymount's Mills. "That is in large part why females in the prime childbearing ages of 17 to 28 are so desirable." Men can size up youth and vitality in a glance, and studies indeed show that men fall in love quite rapidly. Women tumble more slowly, to a large degree because their requirements are more complex; they need more time to check the guy out. "Age is not vital," notes Mills, "but the ability to provide security, father children, share resources and hold a high status in society are all key factors." 16

Still, that does not explain why the way Mary walks and laughs makes Bill dizzy with desire while Marcia's gait and giggle leave him cold. "Nature has wired us for one special person," suggests Walsh, romantically. He rejects the idea that a woman or a man can be in love with two people at the same time. Each person carries in his or her mind a unique subliminal guide to the ideal partner, a "love map," to borrow a term coined by sexologist John Money of Johns Hopkins University. 17

Drawn from the people and experiences of childhood, the map is a record of whatever we found enticing and exciting—or disturbing and disgusting. Small feet, curly hair. The way our mothers patted our head or how our fathers told a joke. A fireman's uniform, a doctor's stethoscope. All the information gathered while growing up is imprinted in the brain's circuitry by adolescence. Partners never meet each and every requirement, but a sufficient number of matches can light up the wires and signal, "It's love." Not every partner will be like the last one, since lovers may have different combinations of the characteristics favored by the map. 18

O.K., that's the scientific point of view. Satisfied? Probably not. To most people—with or without Ph.D.s—love will always be more than the sum of its natural parts. It's a commingling of body and soul, reality and imagination, poetry and phenylethylamine. In our deepest hearts, most of us harbor the hope that love will never fully yield up its secrets, that it will always elude our grasp. 19

Connecting to Culture and Experience: Love Maps

The chemistry of love is easily summarized: Amphetamines fuel romance; endorphins and oxytocin sustain lasting relationships. As Toufexis makes clear, however, these chemical reactions do not explain why specific people are initially attracted to each other. Toufexis observes that an initial attraction occurs because each of us carries a "unique subliminal guide" or "love map" (paragraph 17) that leads us unerringly to a partner. Moreover, she explains that men look for maximal fertility, whereas women look for security, resources, status, and a willingness to father children.

Discuss these explanations for attraction between the sexes. Consider where your love map comes from and how much it may be influenced by your family, your ethnicity, or images in the media or advertising. Consider whether it is possible for an individual's love map to change over time—from adolescence to adulthood, for example.

Analyzing Writing Strategies

1. At the beginning of this chapter, we made several generalizations about essays explaining concepts. Consider which of these assertions are true of Toufexis's essay:
   - It seeks to inform readers about a specific subject.
   - It presents information confidently and efficiently.
   - It relies almost exclusively on established information.
2. To explain a concept, you have to **classify** the information; that is, group or divide it into meaningful categories. Otherwise, you struggle to write about a jumble of information, and your readers quickly give up trying to make sense of it. For example, a writer setting out to explain testing in American colleges to a college student in Thailand would first try to classify the subject by dividing it into categories like the following: short-answer, essay, multiple-choice, lab demonstration, artistic performance.

   To understand more about how Toufexis classifies her information, make a scratch outline of paragraphs 9–15, where she presents the centrally important information on specific chemicals. How is the information divided and sequenced in these paragraphs? What cues does Toufexis provide to help you follow the sequence? What do you find most and least successful about the division?

To learn more about classifying, turn to Chapter 17.

For more on scratch outlining, see Chapter 12, pp. 594–95.

Commentary: A Focused Concept and Careful Use of Sources

Unless they are writing entire books, writers explaining concepts must **focus** their attention on particular aspects of concepts. For instance, Toufexis focuses in her relatively brief magazine article on the chemistry of love between adult human heterosexual mates. She excludes homosexual love, parents' love for their children, dogs' love for their masters, views on love by various religions, the history of romance as revealed in literature, courtship rituals through time, and dozens of other possible subjects related to love. Toufexis holds to her chemical focus throughout the essay, except for a brief but relevant digression about "love maps" toward the end. When they finish the essay, readers have learned nothing new about love in general, but they are well informed about the neurochemistry of love. By keeping to this narrow focus, Toufexis is able to present information that is likely to be new to most readers and therefore is more likely to hold readers' attention.

Besides maintaining a focus on a specific aspect of a concept, concept explanations rely on authoritative, expert **sources**, on established material gleaned from reputable publications or interviews. Toufexis uses both these kinds of sources. She apparently arranged telephone or in-person interviews with six different professors specializing in diverse academic disciplines: psychology, anthropology, psychiatry, and sexology. (She does not immediately identify the discipline of one professor—Walsh, in paragraph 10—but from the title of his book, we might guess that he is a biochemist, and in paragraph 14 we are not surprised to learn that he is a psychobiologist.) We assume that Toufexis read at least parts of the two books she names in paragraphs 5 and 10, and perhaps she also read other sources, which may have led her to some of the professors she interviewed.

What is most notable about Toufexis's use of sources is that she does not indicate precisely where she obtained all the information she includes. For example, she does not cite the source of the anthropological information in paragraphs 3–5, although a reader might guess that she summarized it from *Anatomy of Love,* cited at the end of paragraph 5. We cannot be certain whether the quote at the end of paragraph 5 comes from the book or from an interview with its author. As long as she gives general indications of where her information comes from, Toufexis can safely assume that her readers will not fault her for failing to provide exact bibliographical information. These liberties in citing sources are expected by experienced readers of magazines and newspapers, including the leading ones that educated readers count on to keep them up to date on developments in various fields. Readers would be surprised to find footnotes or works cited lists in popular publications.

To learn more about avoiding plagiarism and documenting sources using MLA or APA styles, turn to Chapter 22.

In most college writing, however, sources must be cited. Moreover, college writers—whether students or professors—are expected to follow certain styles for citing and acknowledging their sources, such as MLA style in English and APA style in psychology. Academic writers cite sources because credit must be given to the authors of any work that contributes to a new piece of work.

Observing a third important requirement of essays that explain concepts, Toufexis provides several different kinds of **cues** to keep readers on track. In addition to paragraph-opening transitions, Toufexis carefully forecasts the topics and direction of her essay in her second paragraph: "their probe reveals that love rests firmly on the foundations of evolution, biology and chemistry." This forecast helps readers anticipate the types of scientific information Toufexis has selected for her special focus on love and the sequence that she will use to introduce them.

Considering Topics for Your Own Essay

Like Toufexis, you could write an essay about love or romance, but you could choose a different focus: on its history (how and when did it develop as an idea in the West?), its cultural characteristics (how is love regarded currently among different American ethnic groups or world cultures?), its excesses or extremes, its expression between parent and child, or the phases of falling in and out of love. Also consider writing about other concepts involving personal relationships, such as jealousy, codependency, idealization, stereotyping, or homophobia.

To use the Writing Guide Software to record your ideas, click on
▶ **Journal**

***Randy Olson** holds a Ph.D. in marine biology and an M.F.A. in film, a combination that enables him to teach biology at the University of Southern California and also to produce films on science. Olson's field work as a marine biologist focuses on the Great Barrier Reef of Australia, where he studies the ecology of starfish, corals, and sea squirts. In addition, he heads Prairie Starfish Productions, which has produced a music video about the sex life of barnacles, a documentary on scientists working in a deep-sea submersible, public-service announcements for television, and short films such as "Rediagnosing the Oceans."*

This film (which can be downloaded from http://www.OceanRx.org) is part of the Shifting Baselines Media Campaign, which Olson mentions in his essay and which he is collaborating on with Jeremy Jackson, director of the Geosciences Research Division of the Scripps Institution of Oceanography at the University of California at San Diego. Olson wrote this essay for the Los Angeles Times *in 2002 as the first stage in this media campaign. As you read, think about why Olson centers his essay on the concept of shifting baselines. If the ultimate purpose of the media campaign is to alert readers to the problems of overfishing in coastal ecosystems and the deteriorating coral reefs, why do you think Olson wants his readers to understand this concept?*

Shifting Baselines: Slow-Motion Disaster below the Waves

Randy Olson

There is a new term in the environmental movement. It 1
sounds esoteric, like the kind of thing you don't really need to understand, something you can leave to the more technical types.

The term is "shifting baselines," and you do need to 2
know it, because shifting baselines affect the quality-of-life decisions you face daily. Shifting baselines are the chronic, slow, hard-to-notice changes in things, from the disappearance of birds and frogs in the countryside to the increased drive time from L.A. to San Diego. If your ideal weight used to be 150 pounds and now it's 160, your baseline—as well as your waistline—has shifted.

The term was coined by fisheries biologist Daniel Pauly in 1995. It was a term we'd 3
apparently been needing, because it quickly spread to a variety of disciplines. It's been applied to analysis of everything from deteriorating cities to declining quality of entertainment.

4 Among environmentalists, a baseline is an important reference point for measuring the health of ecosystems. It provides information against which to evaluate change. It's how things used to be. It is the tall grass prairies filled with buffalo, the swamps of Florida teeming with bird life, and the rivers of the Northwest packed with salmon. In an ideal world, the baseline for any given habitat would be what was there before humans had much impact.

5 If we know the baseline for a degraded ecosystem, we can work to restore it. But if the baseline shifted before we really had a chance to chart it, then we can end up accepting a degraded state as normal—or even as an improvement.

6 The number of salmon in the Pacific Northwest's Columbia River today is twice what it was in the 1930s. That sounds great—if the 1930s are your baseline. But salmon in the Columbia River in the 1930s were only 10% of what they were in the 1800s. The 1930s numbers reflect a baseline that had already shifted.

7 This is what most environmental groups are now struggling with. They are trying to decide: What do we want nature to look like in the future? And more important: What did nature look like in the past?

8 These questions are particularly important to ask about oceans, my main research interest. Last year Jeremy Jackson of the Scripps Institution of Oceanography brought the problem into focus with a cover article in *Science* that was chosen by *Discover* magazine as the most important discovery of the year.

9 Jackson and his 18 co-authors pulled together data from around the world to make the case that overfishing had been the most important alteration to the oceans over the past millennium. Furthermore, humans have had such a strong effect on the oceans for so long that, in many locations, it is difficult to even imagine how full of life the oceans used to be.

10 One of scientists' biggest concerns is that the baselines have shifted for many ocean ecosystems. What this means is that people are now visiting degraded coastal environments and calling them beautiful, unaware of how they used to look.

11 People go diving today in California kelp beds that are devoid of the large black sea bass, broomtailed groupers, and sheephead that used to fill them. And they surface with big smiles on their faces because it is still a visually stunning experience to dive in a kelp bed. But all the veterans can think is, "You should have seen it in the old days."

12 Without the old-timers' knowledge, it's easy for each new generation to accept baselines that have shifted and make peace with empty kelp beds and coral reefs. Which is why it's so important to document how things are—and how they used to be.

13 For the oceans, there is disagreement on what the future holds. Some marine biologists argue that, as the desirable species are stripped out, we will be left with the hardiest, most undesirable species—most likely jellyfish and bacteria, in effect the rats and roaches of the sea. They point to the world's most degraded coastal ecosystems—places like the Black Sea, the Caspian Sea, even parts of the Chesapeake Bay. That's about all you find: jellyfish and bacteria.

14 We have already become comfortable with a new term, "jellyfish blooms," which is used to describe sudden upticks in the number of jellyfish in an area. The phenomenon has become sufficiently common that an international symposium was held on the subject in 2000. Meanwhile, other types of world fisheries are in steep decline.

15 It is easy to miss changes in the ocean. It's big and deep. But sometimes, if people have studied the same oceanic trends over time, we get a glimpse of a highly disturbing picture. The Scripps Institution's Jackson, for example, has documented the nearly complete disappearance of the ecosystem he built his career studying: the coral reefs of Jamaica. "Virtually nothing remains of the vibrant, diverse coral reef communities I helped describe in the 1970s," Jackson says. "Between overfishing, coastal development, and coral bleaching, the ecosystem has been degraded into mounds of dead corals covered by algae in murky water." Nothing you would want to make into a postcard.

16 Next year two major reports will be released on the state of the oceans: the Oceans Report from the Pew Charitable Trusts, and the report of the U.S. Oceans Commission. The advance word on both is that the news will not be good.

17 The last major U.S. report on the oceans was 30 years ago. That report warned that "there may be a risk some day of severely declining oceans." The inside word on the upcoming reports is that they will conclude that the oceans are today in severe decline.

18 The Ocean Conservancy, Scripps Institution, and the Surfrider Foundation are mounting a major media campaign for early next year to call attention to the overall fate of the oceans and the problem of shifting baselines. The solutions are already known: We must care more about the environment and work to prevent its decline. Hundreds of environmental groups have action plans to help achieve such goals. The only thing they are lacking is mass support.

19 The oceans are our collective responsibility. We all have to ask the questions: What did they used to look like? What are we putting into them? Where did these fish we are eating come from? Are my food preferences jeopardizing the health of the oceans?

20 And, in a more philosophical vein, we should consider the shifting baselines in our own lives, examining how and where have we lowered our standards to the point that we accept things that once would have been unacceptable. Our environment has clearly suffered from our increasing comfort with shifting baselines. I suspect our lives have suffered in other ways as well.

Connecting to Culture and Experience: Shifting Baselines in Our Lives

Olson suggests that the concept of shifting baselines could be applied productively to "examining how and where have we lowered our standards to the point that we accept things that once would have been unacceptable" (paragraph 20). With two or three other students, explore this idea.

Work together to list five or six examples of how you lowered your expectations by shifting a baseline. One of Olson's examples is the way that a person's ideal weight rises as time passes. Other examples of shifting baselines include a drive to work or school that increases from thirty minutes to sixty, a \$7.00 first-run movie ticket that seems reasonable even though you paid \$5.00 only a few years ago, the acceptance of the possibility of another terrorist attack on American soil after September 11, 2001, and the expectation that a couple will live together before they marry.

Choose at least two of the examples of shifting baselines you listed, and talk with two or three other students about how recognizing that the baseline has shifted could help someone decide what to do now or what to work toward in the future to solve a problem or improve a situation.

Analyzing Writing Strategies

1. Because he is writing this essay as part of his media campaign, Olson must find a way to **interest readers** in the concept of shifting baselines. Newspaper articles, as well as essays in magazines, often rely on an intriguing title to make the piece stand out in a field crowded with other titles and graphic images vying for readers' attention. The use of the word "disaster" in the original newspaper title, "Slow-Motion Disaster below the Waves," seems calculated to capture attention. Newspaper writers also typically compose a type of introduction that they call the "hook" because it is supposed to secure and hold readers' attention. To assess the effectiveness of Olson's opening strategy, look closely at the two opening paragraphs.

   You will see immediately that in the first paragraph Olson characterizes the concept (as a "new term" identified with "the environmental movement") and also describes his readers while speaking directly and informally to them (by using the pronoun "you" and acknowledging that they will think the concept probably "sounds" both "esoteric" and "technical"). To understand Olson's approach, ask yourself why he would talk about the concept and his readers in this way. What purpose does this strategy serve? Then look closely at the second paragraph to see how the first paragraph sets up the second. Finally, think about how well these opening paragraphs work to hook you.

2. In a sense, the entire essay explaining a concept is an extended **definition**. But at some point the writer must offer a clear—and relatively concise—**definition** of the key concept term. Olson offers a straightforward sentence definition of "shifting baselines" in paragraph 2, and in paragraph 4, he defines the word "baseline." Reread paragraphs 2 and 4, and underline the sentence definitions. Why do you think Olson chose to define one of his key words and not the other word, "shifting"?

   Now let us examine how Olson defines his terms. First, notice that he cues readers so that we know he is presenting a definition. For example, in paragraph 2, he uses the simple sentence structure—"Shifting baselines are"—to signal the beginning of a definition. Look at the sentences you underlined in paragraph 4 to see how he cues readers there.

   Then notice that Olson uses the common strategy of defining a new term with a second, more familiar term. This second term names a general class of things in which the first term fits. Review the sentences you underlined in paragraphs 2 and 4, and put brackets around the more general class terms used to define "shifting baselines" and "baseline." In paragraph 4, Olson provides more than one general class term to define "baseline." How well does this strategy of defining unfamiliar terms help you understand the concept of shifting baselines?

For more on sentence definitions, turn to Chapter 16.

Commentary: Using Examples to Explain a Concept

Examples play a central role in most concept explanations, helping to make the abstract concept more concrete and easier for readers to grasp. If examples are memorable, surprising, or connected to readers' experience, they can also help stimulate readers' interest in and understanding of the concept. Olson's essay demonstrates how writers often use examples—**brief examples** as well as **extended examples**.

We can find brief examples throughout Olson's essay. But the opening, especially paragraphs 2–4, is teeming with them. Most of these examples are used to support the definitions in paragraphs 2 and 4. In paragraph 2, Olson emphasizes the idea of change in defining shifting baselines by referring to the disappearance of birds and frogs, increased driving time, and higher ideal weight. Similarly, in paragraph 4, he offers the examples of the "tall grass prairies filled with buffalo, the swamps of Florida teeming with bird life, and the rivers of the Northwest packed with salmon" to define baseline as the "reference point" from which to measure change. In paragraph 3, Olson uses the examples of "deteriorating cities" and "declining quality of entertainment" to illustrate the broad range of subjects to which the concept of shifting baselines can be usefully applied.

In addition to brief examples, Olson uses two longer examples. In paragraph 6, he illustrates the importance of taking a historical perspective when using the concept of shifting baselines to study the ecology of Columbia River salmon. In paragraph 8, Olson introduces an even longer, more developed example of shifting baselines, the ocean example that extends to paragraph 19. Even within this extended example, he gives lists of brief examples, as in paragraph 11, where he lists some of the kinds of fish—such as black sea bass and sheephead—that are no longer found in California kelp beds, and in paragraph 13, where he lists the only two species that survive the degraded ecosystem: jellyfish and bacteria. This developed example of the ocean illustrates the devastating effects of shifting baselines and explains why it is so important to have what he calls in paragraph 12 "old-timers' knowledge"—hearsay that may be inaccurate but that has been instrumental in leading researchers to measure baselines accurately.

To complement these examples, Olson presents a **scenario** in paragraphs 10 and 11. A scenario is a generalized anecdote that is not about a particular person but about an experience that is typical of many people's experiences. In this scenario, Olson imagines the common experience of "people" who "go diving today in California kelp beds." He presents them moving, emoting ("they surface with big smiles on their faces"), and talking ("You should have seen it in the old days.").

Example and scenario help make Olson's concept explanation understandable. Their familiar detail may also help make readers sympathetic to his campaign to draw attention to the devastating ecological effects signaled by shifting baselines. When you plan your concept explanation, you will want to provide your readers, who will know less about the concept than you do, with enough familiar examples so that they too can understand the concept you are explaining and appreciate its importance.

Considering Topics for Your Own Essay

If, like Olson, you are interested in the environment, you might consider writing about such concepts as ecology, ecotourism, ecosystem, biodiversity, habitat, acid rain, deforestation, ecocriticism, biosphere, or conservation. You might even address the idea of nature itself or what we consider to be natural, as opposed to artificial or constructed by human beings. Here are some other concepts associated with nature that you might want to consider: Eden, Arcadia, frontier, wilderness, vegetarianism, vegan, animism, the great chain of being, xeroscape garden, subsistence farming, monoculture, enclosure, crop rotation, fallow land, bioengineering, extinct species, and the picturesque.

To use the Writing Guide Software to record your ideas, click on
▶ **Journal**

***Natalie Angier** studied English, physics, and astronomy in college and "dreamed of starting a popular magazine about science for intelligent lay readers who wanted to know more about what's going on across the great divide of C. P. Snow's two cultures"—the sciences and the humanities. At the age of twenty-two, she realized her dream when she joined the founding staff of* Discover *magazine. Since then, she has worked as a science writer for newspapers (winning a Pulitzer Prize for her* New York Times *writing on biology and medicine), magazines (such as* Time, *the* Atlantic Monthly, *and* Reader's Digest*), and television (Fox and the Canadian Broadcasting Corporation). In addition to the Pulitzer, Angier has won other distinguished honors for science writing, including the Lewis Thomas Award and recognition from the American Association for the Advancement of Science (AAAS). She also has taught science writing at New York University's Graduate Program in Science and Environmental Reporting and edited* The Best American Science and Nature Writing 2002. *Angier has written four books, including* Natural Obsessions: Striving to Unlock the Deepest Secrets of the Cancer Cell *(1988);* The Beauty of the Beastly: New Views on the Nature of Life *(1995); and* Woman: An Intimate Geography *(1999), a National Book Award finalist, from which the following selection explaining the concept of indirect aggression is excerpted.*

Like Toufexis writing for Time *magazine and Olson writing for the* Los Angeles Times *newspaper, Angier is writing for a popular audience, the "intelligent lay readers" she dreamed of writing for when she was still a college student. As an experienced popularizer or translator of scientific research, Angier knows that she needs to present information authoritatively and show readers that she has done her research so that they will have confidence in the credibility of the information she is presenting. As you read, consider how well she succeeds in convincing you to accept her authority.*

Indirect Aggression

Natalie Angier

This study has been done many times. If you take a group of babies or young toddlers and dress them in nondescript, non-sex-specific clothes—yellow is always a good color!—and make sure that their haircuts don't give them away, and if you put them in a room with a lot of adults watching, the adults will not be able to sex the children accurately. The adults will try, based on the behaviors of each child, but they will be right no more often than they would be if they flipped a coin. This has been shown again and again, but still we don't believe it. We think we can tell a boy or a girl by the child's behavior, specifically by its level of aggressiveness. If you show a person a videotape of a crying baby and tell her the baby is a boy, the observer will describe the baby as looking angry; if you tell the person the baby is a girl, she will say the child is scared or miserable. 1

I am at a party with my daughter, who is sixteen months old. A boy who is almost eighteen months comes into the room and takes a toy away from my daughter. I say something humorous to her about how she's got to watch out for those older kids, they'll always try to push you around. And the boy's mother says, "It's also because he's a boy." That's what happens at this age, she says. The boys become very boyish. A little while later, a girl who is almost eighteen months old takes my daughter's cup of milk away from her. The mother of the other girl doesn't say, "It's because she's a girl, she's becoming girlish." Of course she doesn't say that; it would make no sense, would it? An older girl taking a cup away from a younger girl has nothing to do with the girlness of either party. But taking the toy away is viewed as inherent to the older boy's boyness. 2

I felt very aggressive about the whole thing; alas, not being a toddler, I couldn't go and kick anybody in the kneecap. Which is the sort of thing that toddlers do, whatever their sex. They kick, they hit, they scream, they throw objects around, they act like pills past their expiration date. And we adults put up with it, and we subscribe to the myth of the helpless, innocent child, and it's a good thing we do and that children are cute, because otherwise we might well see the truth: that our children are born with astonishing powers, and with brains that seem by default to counsel aggression. 3

"Young children are like animals," says Kaj Björkqvist, of Turku Akademi University in Finland. "Before they have language, they have their bodies. And through their bodies they can be aggressive, and so that is what they do, that is how they are. They are physically aggressive—boys, girls, all of them." Björkqvist studies female aggression. He has done cross-cultural comparisons of children in Europe, North America, the Middle East, and Asia. Everywhere he has found that young children are physically aggressive, and that before the age of three, there are no significant differences between girl aggression and boy aggression. 4

We grow into our sex-specific aggressions. We own the code of aggression from birth, and we perfect its idiom through experience and experimentation. . . . When the mind comes into its own and the child starts speaking fluently, purposefully, adults become less tolerant of physical aggression. Today, in most cultures, acceptance of physical aggression declines as the child gets older; by the time a person reaches puberty, the tendency to use physical force to wrest a desired object or behavior from another is considered frankly pathological. This is true for both sexes, but particularly for 5 girls. Physical aggression is discouraged in girls in manifold and aggressive ways. Not only are they instructed against offensive fighting; they are rarely instructed in defensive fighting. Girls don't learn how to throw a punch. Humor is another form of aggression, and until recently humor has been used to squelch the very notion of a warrior female. Just the thought of a girl-fight, and people snicker and rub their hands with glee. Cat fight! Scratching, screeching, pulling hair, and falling on butt with skirt hiked in the air! Happily, the smirky parody of girl-fights has gotten a bit paunchy and dated of late, and instead we've been treated to images of GI Janes and bodiced Xenas wielding swords and Klingon women with brickbat fists, though whether the mass media's revisionist fighting female has been driven by attitudinal change or by the need to jolt a bored and distracted audience is unclear.

Whatever the media moment may be, girls still do not often engage in physical fights. The older children get, the less physically aggressive they become—though not always, and not everywhere—but the dropoff rate for the use of physical aggression in girls is much sharper than it is for boys. At least in the developed West, by the time girls and boys are in third grade, boys are about three times as likely as girls to kick or strike at somebody who makes them mad. What then do girls do with that aggressiveness, which in the bliss of preverbalism could speak through hands and feet? It does not go away. It finds a new voice. It finds words. Girls learn to talk hornet talk. Mastering curse words and barbed insults is an essential task of childhood. Girls also learn to use their faces as weapons. Expressions like sticking out your tongue or rolling your eyes or curling your lip all seem funny to adults, but studies show that they aren't funny to children, and that they can be effective in conveying anger and dislike or in ostracizing an undesirable. Aggression researchers initially thought that girls had the edge over boys in verbal aggression and that they were more likely than boys to belittle their peers with words and facial flexions, but a series of Finnish studies of eight- and eleven-year-olds suggested otherwise. The researchers sought to determine how children responded when they were angry. They asked the children to describe themselves and their reactions to being roused to rage; they asked teachers and parents to describe how the children reacted in conflict; and they asked children to talk about each other, to rate each other's rileability and behaviors in a squall. The scientists found that boys and girls were equally likely to use verbal aggression against their cohorts, to call them nasty names to their faces, to yell, to mock, to try to make the despised ones look stupid. And so boys kick and fight more than girls do, and the sexes argue and chide in equal amounts. We might then conclude, so boys are more aggressive, for they shout with their mouths and on occasion with their bodies, while the girls keep their fists to themselves. 6

There are other ways in which rage emerges among girls, though, ways that are roughly girl-specific. A girl who is angry often responds by stalking off, turning away, snubbing the offender, pretending she doesn't exist. She withdraws, visibly so, aggressively so. You can almost hear the thwapping of her sulk. Among eleven-year-olds, girls are three times more likely than boys to express their anger in the form of a flamboyant snub. In addition, girls at this age, more than boys, engage in a style of aggression called indirect aggression. 7

I'll admit up front that I dislike this form of aggression, and that to mention it is to reinforce clichés about female treachery and female conniving. Yet it is an aggression that we gals know, because we grew up as girls and we saw it and struggled against it and hated it and did it ourselves. Indirect aggression is anonymous aggression. It is backbiting, gossiping, spreading vicious rumors. It is seeking to rally others against the despised but then denying the plot when confronted. The use of indirect aggression increases over time, not just because girls don't generally use their fists to make their point, but because the effectiveness of indirect aggression is tied to the fluency of a person's social intelligence; the more sophisticated the person, the cleverer her use of the dorsal blade. In this sense, then, a girl's supposed head start over boys in verbal fluency may give her an edge in applying an indirect form of aggression. But the advantage, such as it is, doesn't last, for males catch up, and by the time we reach adulthood we have all become political animals, and men and women are, according to a number of studies, equally likely to express their aggression covertly. Despite rumors to the contrary, systematic eavesdroppings have revealed that men and women gossip an equal amount about their friends, families, colleagues, and celebrities. Adults of both sexes go to great lengths to express their antipathy toward one another indirectly, in ways that mask their hostile intent while still getting the jab done. For example, a person might repeatedly interrupt an opponent during an office meeting, or criticize the antagonist's work, rather than attacking his or her character—even though the source of the aggressor's ire has nothing to do with the quality of the opponent's performance. 8

Indirect aggression is not pretty, nor is it much admired. To the contrary it is universally condemned. When children and adults are asked to describe their feelings about the various methods of expressing anger, backstabbing behavior ranks at the bottom, below a good swift kick to the crotch. Yet there it is, with us, among us, not exclusively female by any means, but a recognizable hazard of girlhood. Part of the blame lies with the myth of the good-girl, for the more girls are counseled against direct forms of aggression and the more geniality of temperament is prized, the greater is the likelihood that the tart girls will resort to hidden machinations to get what they want. In cultures where girls are allowed to be girls, to speak up and out, they are in fact more verbally, directly aggressive and less indirectly aggressive than in cultures where girls and women are expected to be demure. In Poland, for example, a good smart mouth is considered a female asset, and girls there rag each other and pull no punches and report feeling relatively little threat of intragroup skullduggery. Among female Zapotec Indians in Mexico, who are exceedingly subordinate to men, indirect aggression prevails. Among the Vanatinai of Papua New Guinea, one of the most egalitarian and least stratified societies known to anthropologists, women speak and move as freely as they please, and they sometimes use their fists and feet to demonstrate their wrath, and there is no evidence of a feminine edge in covert operations. 9

Another reason that girls may resort to indirect aggression is that they feel such extraordinary aggression toward their friends—lashing, tumbling, ever-replenishing aggression. Girl friendships are fierce and dangerous. The expression "I'll be your best friend" is not exclusively a girl phrase, but girls use it a lot. They know how powerful the words are, how significant the offer is. Girls who become good friends feel a compulsion 10 to define the friendship, to stamp it and name it, and they are inclined to rank a close friend as a best friend, with the result that they often have many best friends. They think about their friends on a daily basis and try to figure out where a particular friend fits that day in their cosmology of friendships. Is the girl her best friend today, or a provisional best friend, pending the resolution of a minor technicality, a small bit of friction encountered the day before? The girl may want to view a particular girl as her best friend, but she worries how her previous best friend will take it—as a betrayal or as a potential benefit, a bringing in of a new source of strength to the pair. Girls fall in love with each other and feel an intimacy for each other that is hard for them to describe or understand.

When girls are in groups, they form coalitions of best friends, two against two, or 11
two in edgy harmony with two. A girl in a group of girls who doesn't feel that she has a specific ally feels at risk, threatened, frightened. If a girl who is already incorporated into the group decides to take on a newcomer, to sponsor her, the resident girl takes on a weighty responsibility, for the newcomer will view her as (for the moment) her best friend, her only friend, the guardian of her oxygen mask.

When girls have a falling-out, they fall like Alice down the tunnel, convinced that it 12
will never end, that they will never be friends again. The Finnish studies of aggression among girls found that girls hold grudges against each other much longer than boys do. "Girls tend to form dyadic relationships, with very deep psychological expectations from their best friends," Björkqvist said. "Because their expectations are high, they feel deeply betrayed when the friendship falls apart. They become as antagonistic afterwards as they had been bonded before." If a girl feels betrayed by a friend, she will try to think of ways to get revenge in kind, to truly hurt her friend, as she has been hurt. Fighting physically is an unsatisfactory form of punishing the terrible traitor. It is over too quickly. To express anger might work if the betrayer accepts the anger and responds to it with respect. But if she doesn't acknowledge her friend's anger or sense of betrayal, if she refuses to apologize or admit to any wrongdoing, or if she goes further, walking away or mocking or snubbing her friend, at that point a girl may aim to hurt with the most piercing and persistent tools for the job, the psychological tools of indirect, vengeful aggression, with the object of destroying the girl's position, her peace of mind, her right to be. Indirect aggression is akin to a voodoo hex, an anonymous but obsessive act in which the antagonist's soul, more than her body, must be got at, must be penetrated, must be nullified.

Connecting to Culture and Experience: Gender and Aggression

Angier makes the point that although both boys and girls use both direct and indirect aggression, adolescent boys are more likely to use direct aggression and girls of the same age are more likely to use indirect aggression. Try to recall one experience from your adolescent and teenage years of each kind of aggression—indirect and direct—when you were either the aggressor or the victim of aggression.

With two or three other students, discuss your experience with these two kinds of aggression. For each of the experiences you recall, tell what happened, who was involved, and what was said and done. Then discuss whether your experience supports the research Angier cites showing that adolescent boys use direct aggression more often than girls, and girls use indirect aggression more often than boys. Also discuss your attitudes toward these two kinds of aggression. Note that Angier states that she personally dislikes indirect aggression and that it is "universally condemned" (paragraph 9). Which kind of aggression, if any, do you think is more acceptable, and by whom? If you think that one kind of aggression tends to be preferred or relied on more than the other, how would you explain the preference?

Analyzing Writing Strategies

1. Reread paragraphs 1–3 to see how Angier begins this concept explanation. Focus first on paragraph 1. What is the point of this paragraph? Having already read the rest of the selection, how do you think this first paragraph prepares readers for the explanation that follows? What does it lead readers to expect will follow?

   Now focus on paragraphs 2 and 3. What is the point of these paragraphs? How do they prepare readers for the explanation that follows?

   Finally, speculate on why Angier chose to begin her essay with these two different openings. How effective for you is this way of beginning? If you were to choose, which opening would you keep, and why? If you think they work together well, comment on why you think so.

2. In paragraphs 9–12, Angier presents two causes for girls' apparent preference for indirect over direct aggression. Reread these paragraphs to identify the two causes and to notice that Angier is not arguing for her own speculations about why girls prefer indirect aggression (see Chapter 9, Speculating about Causes). Instead, she has decided that for readers to understand the concept of indirect aggression, they need to know what researchers have determined to be the causes for girls' reliance on indirect aggression. Therefore, she devotes several paragraphs to **reporting the causes** established by field and experimental research studies. Review these paragraphs, and highlight the passages where she is referring to sources she has read in the library and possibly on the Internet.

   Notice also that Angier explains one cause rather quickly but spends several paragraphs elaborating her explanation of the other cause. How well do you think she explains each of these causes? Why do you think she decided to go into more detail about one cause and not the other?

3. To explain indirect aggression, Angier makes effective use of a **sentence strategy** that relies on a grammatical structure known as an **appositive**. Underline these appositives: in paragraph 10, sentence 1, from *lashing* to the end; paragraph 10, sentence 8, from *bringing in* to the end; paragraph 11, sentence 1, from *two against two* to the end; paragraph 12, the second from last sentence, from *psychological* through *aggression;* paragraph 12, the last sentence, from *an anonymous* to the end. Now compare each appositive to what comes before in its

For more on sentence strategies important to writers explaining concepts, turn to Sentence Strategies, p. 245.

sentence. Make notes in the margin about how the appositive and what comes before seem to be related to each other. What does each appositive contribute? How are the five of them alike and different in what they add to the sentence?

Commentary: Using Comparison/Contrast to Explain Concepts

As a writer experienced in explaining new concepts, Angier knows that perhaps the best way to explain something unfamiliar is to relate it to something familiar. **Comparing and contrasting** seeks to make clear how the unfamiliar is like or unlike the familiar. In this selection, Angier sets up three kinds of comparisons: between indirect aggression and other kinds of aggression, between girls and boys, and between different age groups.

Let us look first at the comparison of indirect aggression to other types of aggression. Although her readers are unlikely to know what indirect aggression is, Angier can assume they will know other types of aggression with which she can compare it. In the opening paragraphs, she discusses the most common type of aggression—physical aggression. She lists many examples of physical aggression, including kicking, hitting, and throwing objects. In paragraph 6, she brings up a second type of aggression: "hornet talk" or verbal aggression. This kind of aggression is exemplified by cursing, belittling, insulting, yelling, and mocking, In paragraph 7, Angier introduces a third type of aggression, which she identifies at the end of the paragraph as "indirect aggression" and contrasts with the other kinds of aggression. In contrast to the confrontation and body contact associated with physical aggression, she tells us that indirect aggression involves withdrawing or turning away. In contrast to calling people "nasty names to their faces" (paragraph 6), which is typical of verbal aggression, indirect aggression includes backstabbing behaviors such as gossiping, spreading rumors, and plotting (paragraph 8). These contrasts help readers understand that indirect aggression has both physical and verbal elements but differs from physical and verbal aggression chiefly by being indirect or by masking its "hostile intent," as Angier explains in paragraph 8.

In addition to comparing indirect aggression to other types of aggression, Angier also compares boys and girls in terms of which type of aggression they use. At the same time, she compares aggressive behaviors at different ages. In paragraphs 1–3, she shows that people assume there is a difference between girls and boys as toddlers. In paragraph 4, however, she summarizes the research finding that "before the age of three, there are no significant differences between girl aggression and boy aggression." In paragraph 5, she makes explicit the idea that "sex-specific aggressions" change through time. This point is developed in subsequent paragraphs where she contrasts girls' and boys' preferences at different ages. She explains that as children grow older, girls become less physically aggressive and more verbally aggressive and boys become both more physically and more verbally aggressive. In paragraph 8, she explains that although girls develop indirect aggression earlier, by the time they are adults both sexes are equally adept at this covert form of aggression.

For more information on comparing and contrasting, see Chapter 18.

Comparison and contrast are important explanatory writing strategies that you may want to consider using in your own concept explanation.

Considering Topics for Your Own Essay

Angier mentions several concepts associated with behavior that you might consider explaining, such as hostility, aggression, obsession, grudge, coalition, friendship, intimacy, betrayal, and rileability. She also refers to kinds of communication such as gossip and rumor. Other kinds of communication you could write about include body language, metaphor, instant messaging, sign language, and semiotics.

To use the Writing Guide Software to record your ideas, click on
▶ **Journal**

Linh Kieu Ngo *wrote this essay as a first-year college student. In it, he defines a concept that is of importance in anthropology and of wide general interest—cannibalism, the eating of human flesh by other humans. Most Americans know about survival cannibalism—eating human flesh to avoid starvation—but Ngo also explains the historical importance of dietary and ritual cannibalism in his essay. As you read, notice how he relies on examples to illustrate the types.*

To see this essay with pop-up annotations in the software, click on
▶ **Explaining a Concept**
▶ **Read**

Cannibalism: It Still Exists

Linh Kieu Ngo

1 Fifty-five Vietnamese refugees fled to Malaysia on a small fishing boat to escape communist rule in their country following the Vietnam War. During their escape attempt, the captain was shot by the coast guard. The boat and its passengers managed to outrun the coast guard to the open sea, but they had lost the only person who knew the way to Malaysia, the captain.

2 The men onboard tried to navigate the boat, but after a week fuel ran out, and they drifted farther out to sea. Their supply of food and water was gone; people were starving, and some of the elderly were near death. The men managed to produce a small amount of drinking water by boiling salt water, using dispensable wood from the boat to create a small fire near the stern. They also tried to fish but had little success.

3 A month went by, and the old and weak died. At first, the crew threw the dead overboard, but later, out of desperation, they turned to human flesh as a source of food. Some people vomited as they attempted to eat it, while others refused to resort to

cannibalism and see the bodies of their loved ones sacrificed for food. Those who did not eat died of starvation, and their bodies in turn became food for others. Human flesh was cut out, washed in salt water, and hung to dry for preservation. The liquids inside the cranium were drunk to quench thirst. The livers, kidneys, hearts, stomachs, and intestines were boiled and eaten.

Five months passed before a whaling vessel discovered the drifting boat, looking like a graveyard of bones. There was only one survivor. 4

Cannibalism, the act of human beings eating human flesh (Sagan 2), has a long history and continues to hold interest and create controversy. Many books and research reports offer examples of cannibalism, but a few scholars have questioned whether it actually was ever practiced anywhere, except in cases of ensuring survival in times of famine or isolation (Askenasy 43–54). Recently, some scholars have tried to understand why people in the West have been so eager to attribute cannibalism to non-Westerners (Barker, Hulme, and Iversen). Cannibalism has long been a part of American popular culture. For example, Mark Twain's "Cannibalism in the Cars" tells a humorous story about cannibalism by well-to-do travelers on a train stranded in a snowstorm, and cannibalism is still a popular subject for jokes ("Cannibal Jokes"). 5

If we assume there is some reality to the reports about cannibalism, how can we best understand this concept? Cannibalism can be broken down into two main categories: exocannibalism, the eating of outsiders or foreigners, and endocannibalism, the eating of members of one's own social group (Shipman 70). Within these categories are several functional types of cannibalism, three of the most common being survival cannibalism, dietary cannibalism, and religious and ritual cannibalism. 6

Survival cannibalism occurs when people trapped without food have to decide "whether to starve or to eat fellow humans" (Shipman 70). In the case of the Vietnamese refugees, the crew and passengers on the boat ate human flesh to stay alive. They did not kill people to get human flesh for nourishment but instead waited until the people had died. Even after human carcasses were sacrificed as food, the boat people ate only enough to survive. Another case of survival cannibalism occured in 1945, when General Douglas MacArthur's forces cut supply lines to Japanese troops stationed in the Pacific Islands. In one incident, Japanese troops were reported to have sacrificed the Arapesh people of northeastern New Guinea for food in order to avoid death by starvation (Tuzin 63). The most famous example of survival cannibalism in American history comes from the diaries, letters, and interviews of survivors of the California-bound Donner Party, who in the winter of 1846 were snowbound in the Sierra Nevada Mountains for five months. Thirty-five of eighty-seven adults and children died, and some of them were eaten (Hart 116–117; Johnson). 7

Unlike survival cannibalism, in which human flesh is eaten as a last resort after a person has died, in dietary cannibalism humans are purchased or trapped for food and then eaten as a part of a culture's traditions. In addition, survival cannibalism often involves people eating other people of the same origins, whereas dietary cannibalism usually involves people eating foreigners. 8

In the Miyanmin society of the west Sepik interior of Papua, New Guinea, villagers do not value human life over that of pigs or marsupials because human flesh is part of 9 their normal diet (Poole 7). The Miyanmin people observe no differences in "gender, kinship, ritual status, and bodily substance"; they eat anyone, even their own dead. In this respect, then, they practice both endocannibalism and exocannibalism; and to ensure a constant supply of human flesh for food, they raid neighboring tribes and drag their victims back to their village to be eaten (Poole 11). Perhaps, in the history of this society, there was at one time a shortage of wild game to be hunted for food, and because people were more plentiful than fish, deer, rabbits, pigs, or cows, survival cannibalism was adopted as a last resort. Then, as their culture developed, the Miyanmin may have retained the practice of dietary cannibalism, which has endured as a part of their culture.

10 Similar to the Miyanmin, the people of the Leopard and Alligator societies in South America eat human flesh as part of their cultural tradition. Practicing dietary exocannibalism, the Leopard people hunt in groups, with one member wearing the skin of a leopard to conceal the face. They ambush their victims in the forest and carry their victims back to their village to be eaten. The Alligator people also hunt in groups, but they hide themselves under a canoelike submarine that resembles an alligator, then swim close to a fisherman's or trader's canoe to overturn it and catch their victims (MacCormack 54).

11 Religious or ritual cannibalism is different from survival and dietary cannibalism in that it has a ceremonial purpose rather than one of nourishment. Sometimes only a single victim is sacrificed in a ritual, while at other times many are sacrificed. For example, the Bangala tribe of the Congo River in central Africa honors a deceased chief or leader by purchasing, sacrificing, and feasting on slaves (Sagan 53). The number of slaves sacrificed is determined by how highly the tribe members revered the deceased leader.

12 Ritual cannibalism among South American Indians often serves as revenge for the dead. Like the Bangalas, some South American tribes kill their victims to be served as part of funeral rituals, with human sacrifices denoting that the deceased was held in high honor. Also like the Bangalas, these tribes use outsiders as victims. Unlike the Bangalas, however, the Indians sacrifice only one victim instead of many in a single ritual. For example, when a warrior of a tribe is killed in battle, the family of the warrior forces a victim to take the identity of the warrior. The family adorns the victim with the deceased warrior's belongings and may even force him to marry the deceased warrior's wives. But once the family believes the victim has assumed the spiritual identity of the deceased warrior, the family kills him. The children in the tribe soak their hands in the victim's blood to symbolize their revenge of the warrior's death. Elderly women from the tribe drink the victim's blood and then cut up his body for roasting and eating (Sagan 53–54). The people of the tribe believe that by sacrificing a victim, they have avenged the death of the warrior and the soul of the deceased can rest in peace.

13 In the villages of certain African tribes, only a small part of a dead body is used in ritual cannibalism. In these tribes, where the childbearing capacity of women is highly valued, women are obligated to eat small, raw fragments of genital parts during fertility rites. Elders of the tribe supervise this ritual to ensure that the women will be fertile. In the Bimin-Kuskusmin tribe, for instance, a widow eats a small, raw fragment of flesh from the penis of her deceased husband in order to enhance her future fertility and reproductive capacity. Similarly, a widower may eat a raw fragment of flesh from his deceased wife's vagina along with a piece of her bone marrow; by eating her flesh, he

hopes to strengthen the fertility of his daughters borne by his dead wife, and by eating her bone marrow, he honors her reproductive capacity. Also, when an elder woman of the village who has shown great reproductive capacity dies, her uterus and the interior parts of her vagina are eaten by other women who hope to benefit from her reproductive power (Poole 16–17).

Members of developed societies in general practice none of these forms of canni- 14
balism, with the occasional exception of survival cannibalism when the only alternative is starvation. It is possible, however, that our distant-past ancestors were cannibals who through the eons turned away from the practice. We are, after all, descended from the same ancestors as the Miyanmin, the Alligator, and the Leopard people, and survival cannibalism shows that people are capable of eating human flesh when they have no other choice.

Works Cited

Askenasy, Hans. *Cannibalism: From Sacrifice to Survival.* Amherst, NY: Prometheus, 1994.

Barker, Francis, Peter Hulme, and Margaret Iversen, eds. *Cannibalism and the New World.* Cambridge: Cambridge UP, 1998.

Brown, Paula, and Donald Tuzin, eds. *The Ethnography of Cannibalism.* Washington: Society of Psychological Anthropology, 1983.

"Cannibal Jokes." The Loonie Bin of Jokes. <http://www.looniebin.mb.ca/cannibal.html> (22 Sept. 1999).

Hart, James D. *A Companion to California.* Berkeley: U of California P, 1987.

Johnson, Kristin. "New Light on the Donner Party." (28 Sept. 1999) <http://www.metrogourmet.com/crossroads.KJhome.htm>.

MacCormack, Carol. "Human Leopard and Crocodile." Brown and Tuzin 54–55.

Poole, Fitz John Porter. "Cannibals, Tricksters, and Witches." Brown and Tuzin, 11, 16–17.

Sagan, Eli. *Cannibalism.* New York: Harper, 1976.

Shipman, Pat. "The Myths and Perturbing Realities of Cannibalism." *Discover* Mar. 1987: 70+.

Tuzin, Donald. "Cannibalism and Arapesh Cosmology." Brown and Tuzin 61–63.

Twain, Mark. "Cannibalism in the Cars." *The Complete Short Stories of Mark Twain.* Ed. Charles Neider. New York: Doubleday, 1957. 9–16.

Connecting to Culture and Experience: Taboos

The author of a respected book on the Donner Party has this to say about the fact that some members of the party ate other members after they had died:

> Surely the necessity, starvation itself, had forced them to all they did, and surely no just man would ever have pointed at them in scorn, or assumed his own superiority. . . . Even the seemingly ghoulish actions invoked in the story may be rationally explained. To open the bodies first for the heart and liver, and to saw apart the skulls for the brain were not acts of perversion. We must remember that these people had been liv-

ing for months upon the hides and lean meat of half-starved work oxen; their diet was lacking not only in mere quantity, but also in all sorts of necessary vitamin and mineral constituents, even in common salt. Almost uncontrollable cravings must have assailed them, cravings which represented a real deficiency in diet to be supplied in some degree at least by the organs mentioned.

–GEORGE R. STEWART, *Ordeal by Hunger*

With two or three other students, discuss this author's argument and his unwillingness to pass judgment on the Donner Party's cannibalism. Individually, are you inclined to agree or disagree with the author? Give reasons for your views. Keep in mind that no one, perhaps with one exception toward the very end of the Donner Party's isolation, was murdered to be eaten. Therefore, the issue is not murder but the eating of human flesh and body parts by other humans to remain alive. Humans do eat many other animals' flesh and body parts for nourishment. Where do you think the taboo against cannibalism comes from in our society? What are your views on whether the taboo should be observed in all circumstances? What do you think about extending the taboo to the consumption of animal flesh?

Analyzing Writing Strategies

1. At the end of paragraph 6, Ngo names three types of cannibalism, which he defines in the subsequent paragraphs. Find where these types are defined in paragraphs 7, 8, and 12, and underline the **definitions**. Some definitions are given in a single phrase, and others are made up of several phrases, not always contiguous. Exclude the examples from your underlining. Then look over the definitions you have underlined with the following questions in mind: What makes these definitions easy or hard for you to understand? In what ways does the example that begins the essay (paragraphs 1–4) prepare you to understand the definitions? How do the examples that follow the definitions help you understand each concise definition?

For more information on defining, see Chapter 16.

2. As he explains the different types of cannibalism, Ngo makes good use of **examples** in paragraphs 7–13. Choose one of the longer examples in paragraph 9, 12, or 13, and analyze how it is put together and how effective it is. What kinds of information does it offer? What sources does the writer rely on? What seems most memorable or surprising to you in the example? How does it help you understand the type of cannibalism being illustrated? In general, how effective does it seem to you in explaining the concept?
3. Read the Writer at Work section on p. 255 to see how Ngo **integrates information from sources** into his own writing. Study the example comparing Ngo's paragraph 9 with one of his sources, Poole's essay on "Cannibals, Tricksters, and Witches." Notice in this paragraph that Ngo cites Poole several times but quotes only one phrase.

   Now skim Ngo's essay looking for places where he cites sources to see when he has chosen to quote and when to paraphrase his sources. Notice how sparingly he quotes, apparently preferring to paraphrase his sources. Look closely at the

For more on paraphrasing and summarizing reading, see Chapter 12, pp. 595–97.

occasions when Ngo uses language from his sources (paragraphs 7 and 9)—including the example from the Writer at Work—and speculate about Ngo's reasons for quoting these particular words rather than using his own words in a paraphrase.

Commentary: A Logical Plan

For more information on classifying and its role in planning an essay, see Chapter 17.

Writers face special challenges in planning essays that explain concepts. First they gather a lot of information about a concept. Then they find a focus for the explanation. With the focus in mind, they research the concept further, looking for information to help them develop the focus. At this point, they have to find a way to arrange the information into logically related topics. This process is known formally as **classifying**. Sometimes, as in Ngo's research, one of the sources provides the classification, but sometimes the writer has to create it. This borrowing or creation allows writers to plan their essays to identify the topics in the order in which they will present them.

Ngo's explanation of cannibalism illustrates the importance of a **logical plan**. The following topical scratch outline of the essay will help you see Ngo's classification and plan:

- Narration of a specific recent incident of cannibalism (paragraphs 1–4)
- Context for the concept (5)
- Definition of cannibalism and introduction of its two main categories and three types (6)
- Definition of survival cannibalism, with two brief examples (7)
- Definition of dietary cannibalism (8)
- Two extended examples of dietary cannibalism (9–10)
- Definition of ritual cannibalism, with one brief example (11)
- Two extended examples of ritual cannibalism (12–13)
- Conclusion (14)

For more on scratch outlines, see Chapter 12, pp. 594–95.

Ngo presents the **classification** in paragraph 6. It has two levels. On the first level, the information is divided into exocannibalism and endocannibalism. On the second level, each of the first two divisions is divided into three parts: survival, dietary, and ritual cannibalism. That is, either outsiders or members of one's own group can be eaten in each type of cannibalism. Ngo relies on the three types of cannibalism to create a plan for his essay. First he explains survival cannibalism, then dietary cannibalism, and finally, ritual cannibalism. This plan may be considered logical in at least two ways: It moves from most to least familiar and from least to most complex. Perhaps Ngo assumes that his readers will know about the Donner Party, an unfortunate group of 1846 immigrants to California who were trapped high in the Sierra Nevada Mountains by early, heavy snowstorms and ended up practicing survival endocannibalism. Therefore, Ngo explains this type of cannibalism first and then moves on to the less familiar types, whose complex practice takes different forms around the world. Ngo devotes two or three times more space to explaining dietary and ritual cannibalism than he does to explaining survival cannibalism, and he presents detailed examples of these forms.

Ngo does more than adopt a classification and use it to plan his essay. He helps readers anticipate and follow the plan by **forecasting** it and then providing cues to the steps in the plan. At the end of paragraph 6, Ngo forecasts the types of cannibalism he will focus on: survival cannibalism, dietary cannibalism, and religious and ritual cannibalism. This forecast introduces the names or terms that Ngo will use consistently throughout the explanation and presents the types of cannibalism in the order that Ngo will discuss them. Readers are thereby prepared for the step-by-step plan of the explanation.

Ngo lets readers know when he is leaving one type of cannibalism and addressing the next type by constructing visible **transitions** at the beginnings of paragraphs. Here are the three key transition sentences:

> Survival cannibalism occurs when people trapped without food have to decide "whether to starve or to eat fellow humans. . . ." (paragraph 7)
>
> Unlike survival cannibalism, in which human flesh is eaten as a last resort after a person has died, in dietary cannibalism humans are purchased or trapped for food and then eaten as a part of a culture's traditions. (8)
>
> Religious or ritual cannibalism is different from survival and dietary cannibalism in that it has a ceremonial purpose rather than one of nourishment. (11)

You can feature these types of cues—forecasts and transitions—in your essay explaining a concept. Whereas forecasting is optional, transitions are essential; without them, your readers will struggle to follow your explanation and may throw up their hands in confusion and irritation.

For more information on forecasting and transition, see Chapter 12.

Considering Topics for Your Own Essay

Consider writing about some other well-established religious or cultural taboo such as murder, incest, or pedophilia. Or you might consider writing about a concept that tells something about current or historical social values, practices, or attitudes. To look at changing attitudes toward immigration, for example, think about concepts like assimilation, multiculturalism, the melting pot, and race. To look at changing attitudes toward dating, consider concepts like courtship, calling, and flirting.

To use the Writing Guide Software to record your ideas, click on
▶ **Journal**

PURPOSE AND AUDIENCE

Though it often seeks to engage readers' interests, explanatory writing gives prominence to facts about a subject. It aims to engage readers' intellects rather than their imaginations, to instruct rather than entertain or argue.

Setting out to teach readers about a concept is no small undertaking. To succeed, you must know the concept so well that you can explain it simply, without jargon or other confusing language. You must be authoritative without showing off or talking down. You must also estimate what your readers already know about the concept to decide which information will be truly new to them. You want to define unfamiliar words and pace the information carefully so that your readers are neither bored nor overwhelmed.

This assignment requires a willingness to cast yourself in the role of expert, which may not come naturally to you at this stage in your development as a writer. Students are most often asked to explain things in writing to readers who know more than they do—their instructors. When you plan and draft this essay, however, you will be aiming at readers who know less—maybe much less—than you do about the concept you will explain. Like Toufexis, Olson, and Angier, you could write for a general audience of adults who regularly read a newspaper and subscribe to a few magazines. Even though some of them may be highly educated, you can readily and confidently assume the role of expert after a couple of hours of research into your concept. Your purpose may be to deepen your readers' understanding of a concept they may already be familiar with. If you choose to write for upper elementary or secondary school students, you could introduce them to an unfamiliar concept, or if you write for your classmates, you could demonstrate to them that a concept in an academic discipline that they find forbidding can actually be made both understandable and interesting. Even if you are told to consider your instructor your sole reader, you can assume that your instructor is eager to be informed about nearly any concept you choose.

You have spent many years in school reading explanations of concepts: Your textbooks in every subject have been full of concept explanations. Now, instead of receiving these explanations, you will be delivering one. To succeed, you will have to accept your role of expert. Your readers will expect you to be authoritative and well informed; they will also expect that you have limited the focus of your explanation but that you have not excluded anything essential to their understanding.

A Focused Concept

The primary purpose for explaining a concept is to inform readers, but writers of explanatory essays do not hope to communicate everything that is known about a concept. Instead, they make choices about what to include, what to emphasize, and what to omit. Most writers focus on one aspect of the concept. Anastasia Toufexis focuses on the neurochemistry of love, Randy Olson focuses on shifting baselines in the ocean, Natalie Angier focuses on girls' preference for indirect aggression, and Linh Kieu Ngo focuses on three specific types of cannibalism.

An Appeal to Readers' Interests

Most people read explanations of concepts for work or study. Consequently, they expect the writing to be simply informative and not necessarily entertaining. Yet readers appreciate explanations that both identify the concept's importance and engage them with lively writing and vivid detail. The essays in this chapter show some of the ways in which writers may appeal to readers. For example, Toufexis uses humor and everyday language to attract readers' attention. She opens her essay with this direct address to readers: "O.K., let's cut out all this nonsense about romantic love." Calling romantic love "nonsense" arrests readers' attention as they thumb through the magazine in which the essay originally appeared. Randy Olson takes a less provocative tack. He tries to hook readers by announcing that the concept is "new" and important: "There is a new term in the environmental movement. It sounds esoteric, like the kind of thing you don't really need to understand, something you can leave to the more technical types. The term is 'shifting baselines,' and you do need to know it, because shifting baselines affect the quality-of-life decisions you face daily." He disarmingly acknowledges that readers are likely to assume that the concept is "esoteric" and for "technical types" rather than for them. But he goes on to say in a friendly yet assertive way that readers should pay attention because the concept is important to them personally. Opening strategies like these can do much to interest readers in the concept.

A Logical Plan

Since concept explanations present information that is new to readers and can therefore be hard to understand, writers need to develop a plan that presents new material step by step in a logical order. The most effective explanations are carefully organized and give readers all the obvious cues they need, such as forecasting statements, topic sentences, transitions, and summaries. In addition, the writer may try to frame the essay for readers by relating the ending to the beginning. We have seen these features repeatedly in the readings in this chapter. For example, Toufexis frames her essay with references to Ph.D.s, forecasts the three sciences from

which she has gleaned her information about the neurochemistry of love, and begins nearly all of her paragraphs with a transition sentence.

Good writers never forget that their readers need clear signals. Because writers already know the information and are aware of how their essays are organized, they can find it difficult to see the essay the way someone reading it for the first time would. That is precisely how it should be seen, however, to be sure that the essay includes all the necessary cues.

Clear Definitions

Essays explaining concepts depend on clear definitions. To relate information clearly, a writer must be sensitive to readers' knowledge; any key terms that are likely to be unfamiliar or misunderstood must be explicitly defined, as Toufexis defines *attraction junkies* (paragraph 12) and *endorphins* (paragraph 13) and as Ngo defines the *categories* of cannibalism (paragraph 6) and *types* of cannibalism (at the beginnings of paragraphs where he illustrates them). Olson defines both his concept term *shifting baselines* (paragraph 2) and the key term *baseline* (paragraph 4). In a sense, all the readings in this chapter are extended definitions of concepts, and all the authors offer relatively concise, clear definitions of their concepts at some point in their essays.

Appropriate Writing Strategies

Many writing strategies are useful for presenting information. The strategies that a writer uses are determined by the way he or she focuses the essay and the kind of information available. The following strategies are particularly useful in explaining concepts:

Classification. One way of presenting information is to divide it into groups and discuss the groups one by one. For example, Toufexis divides the chemicals she discusses into those associated with falling in love and those associated with lasting relationships. Ngo divides cannibalism into three types.

Process Narration. Process narration typically explains how something is done. Many concepts involve processes that unfold over time, such as the geologic scale, or over both time and space, such as bird migration. Process narration involves some of the basic storytelling strategies covered in Chapters 2 and 3: narrative time signals, actors and action, and connectives showing temporal relationships. For example, Ngo briefly narrates one process of ritual cannibalism (paragraph 12).

Comparison and Contrast. The comparison/contrast strategy is especially useful for explaining concepts because it helps readers understand something

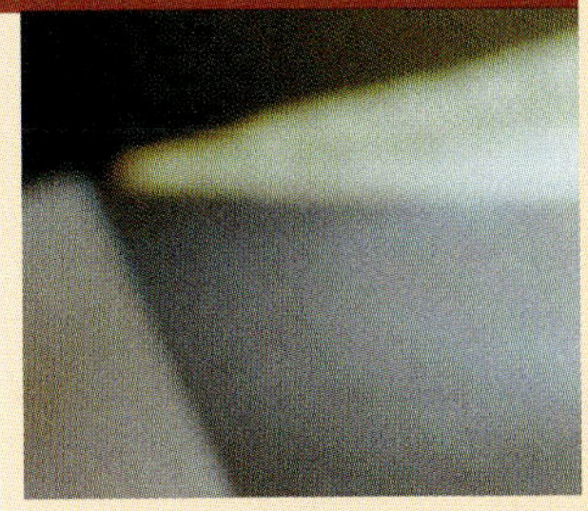

new by showing how it is similar to or different from things they already know. Every essayist in this chapter makes use of comparison and contrast. For example, Angier compares indirect aggression with physical and verbal aggression, girls with boys, and different age groups with one another. Ngo compares the three types of cannibalism as well as different cultures.

Cause and Effect. Another useful strategy for explaining a concept is to report its causes or effects. Toufexis explains the evolutionary benefits of romantic love, and Angier reports the causes established by research to explain why adolescent girls rely on indirect aggression. Note that writers of explanatory essays ordinarily either report established causes or effects or report others' speculated causes or effects as if they were established facts. They usually do not themselves speculate about possible causes or effects.

Careful Use of Sources

To explain concepts, writers usually draw on information from many different sources. Although they often draw on their own experiences and observations, they almost always do additional research into what others have to say about their subject. Referring to expert sources always lends authority to an explanation.

How writers treat sources depends on the writing situation. Certain formal situations, such as college assignments or scholarly papers, have rules for citing and documenting sources. Students and scholars are expected to cite their sources formally because readers judge their work in part by what the writers have read and how they have used their reading. Ngo's essay illustrates this academic form of citing sources. For more informal writing—magazine articles, for example—readers do not expect or want page references or publication information, but they do expect sources to be identified. This identification often appears within the text of the article, as illustrated in the selections by Toufexis and Olson, which were originally published in a magazine and a newspaper, respectively. Other nonacademic writing—popular books, for example—may be based on research, but those authors may choose not to impose on readers the formal documentation style of academic writing. Angier, for example, mentions in her preface that she interviewed hundreds of experts. She also includes a list of sources at the end of the book and identifies most of them in the text—such as Björkqvist in paragraph 12—so that her readers can find their names in the alphabetical list at the end.

GUIDE TO WRITING
Explaining Concepts

THE WRITING ASSIGNMENT

THE WRITING ASSIGNMENT
Write an essay about a concept that interests you and that you want to study further. When you have a good understanding of the concept, explain it to your readers, considering carefully what they already know about it and how your essay might add to what they know.

INVENTION AND RESEARCH

INVENTION & RESEARCH
- Finding a Concept to Write About
- Surveying Information about the Concept
- Focusing the Concept
- Testing Your Choice
- Researching Your Topic Focus
- Considering Explanatory Strategies
- Considering Document Design
- Defining Your Purpose for Your Readers
- Formulating a Tentative Thesis Statement

PLANNING AND DRAFTING

PLANNING & DRAFTING
- Seeing What You Have
- Setting Goals
- Outlining
- Drafting

CRITICAL READING GUIDE

CRITICAL READING GUIDE
- First Impression
- Clear Focus and Explanation of Concept
- Appropriate Content
- Organization
- Clarity of Definitions
- Use of Sources
- Effectiveness of Visuals
- Final Thoughts

REVISING

REVISING
- A Focused Concept
- An Appeal to Readers' Interests
- A Logical Plan
- Clear Definitions
- Appropriate Writing Strategies
- Careful Use of Sources

EDITING AND PROOFREADING

EDITING & PROOFREADING
- Checking the Punctuation of Adjective Clauses
- Checking for Commas around Interrupting Phrases

GUIDE TO WRITING

THE WRITING ASSIGNMENT

Write an essay about a concept that interests you and that you want to study further. When you have a good understanding of the concept, explain it to your readers, considering carefully what they already know about it and how your essay might add to what they know.

> To use the Writing Guide Software for this assignment, click on
> ▶ **Explaining a Concept**
> ▶ **Write**

INVENTION AND RESEARCH

The following guidelines will help you find a concept, understand it fully, select a focus that is appropriate for your readers, test your choice, and devise strategies for presenting your discoveries in a way that will be truly informative for your particular readers. Each activity is easy to do and takes only a few minutes. If you can spread out the activities over several days, you will have adequate time to understand the concept and decide how to present it. Keep a written record of your invention work to use when you draft the essay and later when you revise it. If you write on the computer, you may be able to copy and paste into your draft material from your invention and research notes.

Finding a Concept to Write About

Even if you already have a concept in mind, completing the following activities will help you to be certain of your choice.

Listing Concepts. *Make a list of concepts you could write about.* The longer your list, the more likely you are to find just the right concept for you. And should your first choice not work out, you will have a ready list of alternatives. Include concepts you already know something about as well as some you know only slightly and would like to research further. Also include concepts suggested by the Considering Topics for Your Own Essay activities following each reading in this chapter.

Your courses provide many concepts you will want to consider. Here are some typical concepts from a number of academic and other subjects. Your class notes or textbooks will suggest many others.

- ***Literature:*** irony, metaphysical conceit, semiotics, hero, dystopian novel, humanism, picaresque, the absurd, canon, representation, figurative language, modernism, identity politics, queering

- ***Philosophy:*** existentialism, nihilism, logical positivism, determinism, metaphysics, ethics, natural law, Zeno's paradox, epistemology, ideology
- ***Business management:*** autonomous work group, quality circle, cybernetic control system, management by objectives, zero-based budgeting, liquidity gap
- ***Psychology:*** metacognition, Hawthorne effect, assimilation/accommodation, social cognition, moratorium, intelligence, divergent/convergent thinking, operant conditioning, short-term memory, the Stroop effect, sleep paralysis
- ***Government:*** majority rule, minority rights, federalism, popular consent, exclusionary rule, political party, political machine, interest group, hegemony
- ***Biology:*** photosynthesis, mitosis, karyotype analysis, morphogenesis, ecosystem, electron transport, plasmolysis, phagocytosis, homozygosity, diffusion
- ***Art:*** cubism, Dadaism, surrealism, expressionism
- ***Math:*** polynomials, boundedness, null space, permutations and combinations, factoring, Rolle's theorem, continuity, derivative, indefinite integral
- ***Physical sciences:*** matter, mass, weight, energy, gravity, atomic theory, law of definite proportions, osmotic pressure, first law of thermodynamics, entropy
- ***Public health:*** alcoholism, seasonal affective disorder, contraception, lead poisoning, prenatal care, toxicology
- ***Environmental studies:*** acid rain, recycling, ozone depletion, toxic waste, endangered species
- ***Sports:*** squeeze play, hit and run (baseball); power play (hockey); nickel defense, wishbone offense (football); serve and volley offense (tennis); setup (volleyball); pick and roll, inside game (basketball)
- ***Personal finance:*** mortgage, budget, insurance, deduction, revolving credit, interest rates, dividend, bankruptcy
- ***Law:*** tort, contract, garnishment, double indemnity, reasonable doubt, class-action suits, product liability, lemon law
- ***Sociology:*** norm, deviance, role conflict, ethnocentrism, class, social stratification, conflict theory, action theory, acculturation, Whorf-Sapir hypothesis, machismo

Listing Concepts Related to Identity and Community. Many concepts are important in understanding identity and community. As you consider the following concepts, try to think of others in this category: self-esteem, character, personality, autonomy, individuation, narcissism, multiculturalism, ethnicity, race, racism, social contract, communitarianism, community policing, social Darwinism, identity politics, special-interest groups, diaspora, colonialism, public space, the other, agency, difference, yuppie, generation X.

Listing Concepts Related to Work and Career. Concepts like the following enable you to gain a deeper understanding of your work experiences and career aspirations: free enterprise, minimum wage, affirmative action, stock option, sweatshop, glass ceiling, downsizing, collective bargaining, service sector, market, entrepreneur, bourgeoisie, underclass, working class, middle class, division of labor, monopoly, automation, robotics, management style, deregulation, multinational corporation.

Choosing a Concept. *Look over your list of possibilities and select one concept to explore.* Pick a concept that interests you, one you feel eager to learn more about. Consider also whether it might interest others. You may know very little about the concept now, but the guidelines that follow will help you research it and understand it fully.

Surveying Information about the Concept

Your research efforts for a concept essay must be divided into two stages. First, you want to achieve quickly a far-reaching survey or overview of information about the concept you have chosen. Your goal in this first stage is to learn as much as you can from diverse sources so that you may decide whether you want to write about this topic and whether you can identify an aspect of it to focus on.

In the second stage, when you know what your focus will be, you begin in-depth research for information that will educate you about this focus. When Natalie Angier arrived at this stage, she would have been learning as much as possible about indirect aggression between girls, not aggression in general. When Linh Kieu Ngo arrived at this stage, he would have been digging for information on ways to classify the different types of cannibalism.

The activities that follow will guide you through this two-stage research process.

Discovering What You Already Know. *Before doing any research on your concept or even looking at any handy references, take a few minutes to write about what you already know about the concept.* Also say why you have chosen the concept and why you find it interesting and worth knowing about. Write quickly, without planning or organizing. Write phrases or lists as well as sentences. You could even add drawings or quick sketches or write down questions about the concept, questions that express your curiosity or uncertainty. If you find that you know very little about the concept, you still might want to write about it—out of personal motivation, which is not a bad reason to commit yourself to the study of an unfamiliar concept.

Sorting Through Your Personal Resources. *Check any materials you already have at hand that explain your concept.* If you are considering a concept from one of your academic courses, you will find explanatory material in your textbook or perhaps your lecture notes.

To acquire a comprehensive, up-to-date understanding of your concept, however, you will need to know how experts other than your textbook writer and instructor define and illustrate it. To find this information, you might locate relevant articles or books in the library, search for resources or make inquiries on the Internet, or consult experts on campus or in the community.

Going Online. *Keep a list of Web sites you find that invite more than a quick glance, sites that hold your attention and inform you about your concept. Bookmark each site, or record its name and URL. You might make a few brief notes about key contents or features of sites from which you learn the most. Also keep a list of possible focuses you discover.* Keep your goal for this stage in mind: to educate yourself quickly about the concept and look for a possible focus for your essay. It is too early to begin downloading a lot of material.

Going to the Library. *Keep a list of the most promising materials you discover in the library. Continue your other list of possible focuses, trying to come up with at least two or three possibilities.* Besides taking a quick look at relevant encyclopedias and disciplinary guides, look for your concept name in the subject headings of the *Library of Congress Subject Headings* and also in the library catalog, using the keyword search option. The library can give you access to special online resources; ask a librarian for advice. Remember that moving through your search quickly will give you a good overview of information about your concept. Consult Chapter 21, Library and Internet Research, for help with using the library productively.

Researching Concepts: An Online Activity

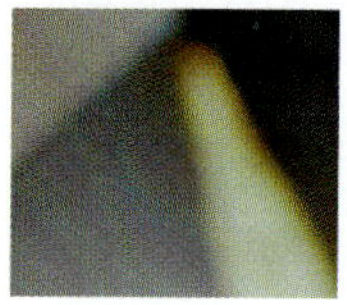

One way to get a quick initial overview of the information available on a concept is to search for the concept online. You can do this in several ways:

- Enter the name of your concept in a search tool such as Google (http://google.com) or Yahoo! Directory (http://dir.yahoo.com) to discover possible sources of information about the concept.
- Check an online encyclopedia in the field to which the concept belongs. Here are a few specialized encyclopedias that may be helpful:
  - *Encyclopedia of Psychology* http://www.psychology.org/
  - *The Internet Encyclopedia of Philosophy* http://www.utm.edu/research/iep/
  - *Webopedia* http://www.webopedia.com

Bookmark or keep a record of promising sites. When you proceed to a narrower search for information about your topic focus, you could then download any materials, including visuals, that you might consider including in your own essay.

Focusing the Concept

Once you have an overview of your concept, you must choose a focus for your essay. More is known about most concepts than you can include in an essay, and concepts can be approached from many perspectives (for example, history, definition, significance), so you must limit your explanation. Doing this will help you avoid the common problem of trying to explain too much. Because the focus must reflect both your special interest in the concept and your readers' likely knowledge and interest, you will want to explore both.

Exploring Your Own Interests. *Make a list of two or three aspects of the concept that could become a focus for your essay, and evaluate what you know about each focus. Leave some space after each item in the list.* Under each possible focus in your list, make notes about why it interests you and why it seems just the right size (not so small that it is trivial and not so large that it is overwhelming). Indicate whether you know enough to begin writing about that aspect of the concept, what additional questions you would need to answer, and what is important or interesting to you about that particular aspect.

Analyzing Your Readers. *Take a few minutes to analyze in writing your readers.* To decide what aspect of the concept to focus on, you also need to think about who your prospective readers are likely to be and to speculate about their knowledge of and interest in the concept. Even if you are writing only for your instructor, you should give some thought to what he or she knows and thinks about the concept.

The following questions are designed to help you with your analysis:

- Who are my readers, and what are they likely to know about this concept?
- What, if anything, might they know about the field of study to which this concept applies?
- What could I point out that would be useful for them to know about this concept, perhaps something that could relate to their life or work?
- What connections could I make between this concept and others that my readers are likely to be familiar with?

Choosing a Focus. *With your interests and those of your readers in mind, choose an aspect of your concept on which to focus, and write a sentence justifying its appropriateness.*

Testing Your Choice

Pause now to test whether you have chosen a workable concept and focused it appropriately. As painful as it may be to consider, starting fresh with a new concept is better than continuing with an unworkable one. The following questions can help you test your choice:

- Do I understand my concept well enough to explain it?
- Have I discovered a focus for writing about this concept?
- Do I think I can find enough information for an essay with such a focus?
- Do I see possibilities for engaging my readers' interest in this aspect of my concept?

If you cannot answer yes to all four questions, consider choosing another focus or selecting another concept to write about.

Testing Your Choice: A Collaborative Activity

Get together with two or three other students to find out what your readers are likely to know about your subject and what might interest them about it. Your instructor may ask you to complete this activity in class or online in a chat room.

Presenters: Take turns briefly explaining your concept, describing your intended readers, and identifying the aspect of the concept that you will focus on.

Listeners: Briefly tell the presenter whether the focus sounds appropriate and interesting for the intended readers. Share what you think readers are likely to know about the concept and what information might be especially interesting and memorable for them.

Researching Your Topic Focus

Now begins stage two of your research process. With a likely focus in mind, you are ready to mine both the Internet and the library for valuable nuggets of information. Your research becomes selective and deliberate, and you will now want to keep careful records of all sources you believe will contribute in any way to your essay. If possible, make photocopies of print sources, and print out sources you download from CD-ROMs or the Internet. If you must rely on notes, be sure to copy any quotations exactly and enclose them in quotation marks so that later you can quote sources accurately.

Since you do not know which sources you will ultimately use, keep a careful record of the author, title, publication information, page numbers, and other required information for each source you gather. Check with your instructor about whether you should follow the Modern Language Association (MLA) or American Psychological Association (APA) style of acknowledging sources. In this chapter, the Ngo essay follows the MLA style.

Going Online. *Return to online searching, with your focus in mind. Download and print out essential material if possible, or take careful notes. Record all of the details you will need to acknowledge sources in your essay, should you decide to use them.*

Going to the Library. *Return to the library to search for materials relevant to your focus. Photocopy, print out, or take notes on promising print and electronic materials. Keep careful records so that you can acknowledge your sources.*

Considering Explanatory Strategies

Before you move on to plan and draft your essay, consider some possible ways of presenting the concept. Try to answer each of the following questions in a sentence or two. Questions that you can answer readily may identify strategies that can help you explain your concept.

- What term is used to name the concept, and what does it mean? (definition)
- How is this concept like or unlike related concepts? (comparison and contrast)
- How can an explanation of this concept be divided into parts? (classification)
- How does this concept happen, or how does one go about doing it? (process narration)
- What are this concept's known causes or effects? (cause and effect)

Considering Document Design

Think about whether visual elements—tables, graphs, drawings, photographs—would make your explanation clearer. These are not a requirement of an essay explaining a concept, but they could be helpful. Consider also whether your readers might benefit from design features such as headings, bulleted or numbered lists, or other elements that would present information efficiently or make your explanation easier to follow. You could construct your own graphic elements, download materials from the Internet, copy images from television or other sources, or scan into your document visuals from books and magazines. Remember that you should cite the source of any visual you do not create yourself, and you should also request permission from the source of the visual if your paper is going to be posted on the Web.

Defining Your Purpose for Your Readers

Write a few sentences that define your purpose in writing about this particular concept for your readers. Remember that you have already identified and analyzed your readers and that you have begun to research and develop your explanation with these readers in mind. Given these readers, try now to define your purpose in explaining the concept to them. Use these questions to focus your thoughts:

- Are my readers familiar with the concept? If not, how can I overcome their resistance or puzzlement? Or, if so, will my chosen focus allow my readers to see the familiar concept in a new light?
- If I suspect that my readers have misconceptions about the concept, how can I correct the misconceptions without offending readers?
- Do I want to arouse readers' interest in information that may seem at first to be less than engaging?
- Do I want readers to see that the information I have to report is relevant to their lives, families, communities, work, or studies?

Formulating a Tentative Thesis Statement

Write one or more sentences that could serve as a thesis statement. State your concept and focus. You might also want to forecast the topics you will use to explain the concept.

Anastasia Toufexis begins her essay with this thesis statement:

> O.K., let's cut out all this nonsense about romantic love. Let's bring some scientific precision to the party. Let's put love under a microscope.
>
> When rigorous people with Ph.D.s after their names do that, what they see is not some silly, senseless thing. No, their probe reveals that love rests firmly on the foundations of evolution, biology and chemistry.

Toufexis's concept is love, and her focus is the scientific explanation of love—specifically the evolution, biology, and chemistry of love. In announcing her focus, she forecasts the order in which she will present information from the three most relevant academic disciplines—anthropology (which includes the study of human evolution), biology, and chemistry. These discipline names become her topics.

In his essay on cannibalism, Linh Kieu Ngo offers his thesis statement in paragraph 6:

> Cannibalism can be broken down into two main categories: exocannibalism, the eating of outsiders or foreigners, and endocannibalism, the eating of members of one's own social group (Shipman 70). Within these categories are several functional types of cannibalism, three of the most common being survival cannibalism, dietary cannibalism, and religious and ritual cannibalism.

Ngo's concept is cannibalism, and his focus is on three common types of cannibalism. He carefully forecasts how he will divide the information to create topics and the order in which he will explain each of the topics, the common types of cannibalism.

As you draft your own tentative thesis statement, take care to make the language clear and unambiguous. Although you may want to revise your thesis statement as you draft your essay, trying to state it now will give your planning and drafting more focus and direction. Keep in mind that the thesis in an explanatory essay merely announces the subject; it never asserts a position that requires an argument to defend it.

PLANNING AND DRAFTING

The following guidelines will help you get the most out of your invention notes, determine specific goals for your essay, and write a first draft.

> If you are using the Writing Guide Software, click on
> ▶ **Planning and Drafting**

Seeing What You Have

Reread everything you have written so far. This is a critically important time for reflection and evaluation. Before beginning the actual draft, you must decide whether your subject is worthwhile and whether you have sufficient information for a successful essay.

It may help, as you read, to annotate your invention writings. Look for details that will help you explain the concept in a way that your readers can grasp. Highlight key words, phrases, or sentences; make marginal notes or electronic annotations of any material you think could be useful. If you have done your invention writing on the computer, you may have sentences or whole paragraphs that can be copied and pasted into your draft.

Be realistic. If at this point your notes do not look promising, you may want to choose a different focus for your concept or select a different concept to write about. If your notes seem thin but promising, do further research to find more information before continuing.

Setting Goals

Successful writers are always looking beyond the next sentence to larger goals. Indeed, the next sentence is easier to write if you keep larger goals in mind. The following questions can help you set these goals. Consider each one now, and then return to them as necessary while you write.

Your Purpose and Readers

- How can I build on my readers' knowledge?
- What new information can I present to them?
- How can I organize my essay so that my readers can follow it easily?
- What tone would be most appropriate? Would an informal tone like Toufexis's or a formal one like Ngo's be more appropriate to my purpose?

The Beginning

- How shall I begin? Should I open with a provocative quotation, as Toufexis does? With an incident illustrating the concept, as Angier and Ngo do? With an explanation of why readers need to understand the concept, as Olson does? With a question?
- How can I best forecast the plan that my explanation will follow? Should I offer a detailed forecast, as Toufexis and Ngo do?

Writing Strategies

- What terms do I need to define? Can I rely on brief sentence definitions, or will I need to write extended definitions? Should I give a history of the concept term?
- Are there ways to classify the information?

- What examples can I use to make the explanation more concrete?
- Would any comparisons or contrasts help readers understand the information?
- Do I need to explain any processes or known causes or effects?

The Ending

- Should I frame the essay by relating the ending to the beginning, as Toufexis does?
- Should I end by suggesting what is special about the concept, as Angier does?
- Should I end with a speculation about the past, as Ngo does?
- Should I end by suggesting how my readers can apply the concept to their own lives, as Olson does?

Outlining

The goals that you have set should help you draft your essay, but first you might want to make a quick scratch outline to refocus on the basic story line. You could use the outlining function of your word processing program. In your outline, list the main topics into which you have divided the information about your concept. Use this outline to guide your drafting, but do not feel tied to it. As you draft, you may find a better way to sequence the action and integrate these features.

An essay explaining a concept is made up of four basic parts:

- An attempt to engage readers' interest
- The thesis statement, announcing the concept, its focus, and its topics
- An orientation to the concept, which may include a description or definition of the concept
- Information about the concept

Here is a possible outline for an essay explaining a concept:

An attempt to gain readers' interest in the concept
Thesis statement
Definition of the concept
Topic 1 with illustration
Topic 2 with illustration
(etc.)
Conclusion

An attempt to gain readers' interest could take as little space as two or three sentences or as much as four or five paragraphs. The thesis statement and definition are usually quite brief—sometimes only a few sentences. A topic illustration may occupy one or several paragraphs, and there can be few or many topics, depending on how the information has been divided up. A conclusion might summarize the information presented, give advice about how to use or apply the information, or speculate about the future of the concept.

Consider any outlining that you do before you begin drafting to be tentative. As you draft, be ready to revise your outline, shift parts around, or drop or add parts. If you use the outlining function of your word processing program, changing your outline will be simple, and you may be able to write the essay simply by expanding the outline.

Drafting

General Advice. Start drafting your essay, keeping in mind the goals you set while you were planning. Remember also the needs and expectations of your readers; organize, define, and explain with them in mind. Work to increase readers' understanding of your concept. Turn off your grammar checker and spelling checker at this stage if you find them distracting. Do not be afraid to skip around in your document. Jump back and fill in a spontaneous idea, or leap ahead and write a later section first if you find that easier. If you get stuck while drafting, try using some of the writing activities in the Invention and Research section of this chapter. You may want to review the general drafting advice on pp. 16–17.

Sentence Strategies. As you draft an essay explaining a concept, you must introduce library and Internet research sources and their authors within your sentences. You must also devise sentences that allow you to subordinate some information to other information and to introduce many examples or illustrations for readers to understand the concept. Precise verbs and a versatile sentence modifier called an **appositive** can help you achieve these goals.

Use informative, precise verbs to introduce sources and authors. Experienced writers of all kinds of explanatory and informational writing take great care in choosing verbs to introduce sources and authors, as these examples illustrate (the verbs are in italics):

> Lovers . . . are literally flooded by chemicals, research *suggests.* (Anastasia Toufexis, paragraph 9)

> The inside word on the upcoming reports is that they will *conclude* that the oceans are today in severe decline. (Randy Olson, paragraph 17)

> The scientists *found* that boys and girls were equally likely to use verbal aggression against their cohorts. . . . (Natalie Angier, paragraph 6)

> In one incident, Japanese troops *were reported* to have sacrificed the Arapesh people of northeastern New Guinea for food in order to avoid death by starvation. (Linh Kieu Ngo, paragraph 7)

When you explain a concept to readers unfamiliar with it, you usually are presenting information that is well established and currently considered reliable by experts on your topic. Because you are not making an argument either for or against your sources or authors, you need to introduce them to readers using somewhat neutral language—like the italicized verbs *suggests, conclude, found,* and *were reported* in the preceding examples. Yet there are important distinctions in meaning among these four verbs. *Found* connotes that Natalie Angier is merely reporting a research discovery or an earlier discovery newly confirmed. *Suggests* may indicate that Anastasia Toufexis is referring to broad implications of research rather than to findings. Randy Olson chooses *conclude* to refer to the conclusions or summaries of research findings from several reports, which he wishes readers to consider conclusive or decisive. Paraphrasing a source with *were reported,* Linh Kieu Ngo makes clear to readers that the writer relied on secondhand information.

As you refer to sources in your concept explanation, you will be able to choose carefully among a wide variety of precise verbs. Every writer in this chapter uses a great variety of verbs for this purpose—sometimes for the sake of variety, no doubt, but usually in an effort to help readers better understand how the writer is using a source. As you draft your essay, you may find this partial list of verbs from the readings helpful in selecting precisely the right verbs to introduce your sources:

For more on using informative, precise verbs to introduce sources and authors, go to bedfordstmartins.com/theguide and click on Sentence Strategies.

reveals	contends	questions
explains	brings into focus	tells
observes	pulls together	tries to understand
notes	documents	reports
shows	warns	finds
speculates	mounts	according to [name of author or source]
rejects	reveals	

Use appositives to identify people, define terms, and give examples and specifics. An appositive can be defined as a group of words, usually based on a noun or pronoun, that identifies or gives more information about another noun or pronoun just preceding it. Appositives come in many forms, as shown in these examples (the appositives are in italics):

> Says Michael Mills, *a psychology professor at Loyola Marymount University in Los Angeles:* "Love is our ancestors whispering in our ears." (Anastasia Toufexis, paragraph 2)

> Cannibalism, *the act of human beings eating human flesh* (Sagan 2), has a long history and continues to hold interest and create controversy. (Linh Kieu Ngo, paragraph 5)

In this chapter's four readings, appositives appear frequently: forty-one times, with a range of five to fifteen appearances per reading. Writers explaining concepts rely to such an extent on appositives because they serve so many purposes. Among the most common are the following:

- Identifying a thing or person, often to establish a source's authority

  "Love is a natural high," observes Anthony Walsh, *author of* The Science of Love: Understanding Love and Its Effects on Mind and Body. (Anastasia Toufexis, paragraph 10)

- Giving examples or more specific information

  They point to the world's most degraded coastal ecosystems—*places like the Black Sea, the Caspian Sea, even parts of the Chesapeake Bay.* (Randy Olson, paragraph 13)

  Girls who become good friends feel a compulsion to define the friendship, *to stamp it and name it.* . . . (Natalie Angier, paragraph 10)

- Introducing a new term

  Each person carries in his or her mind a unique subliminal guide to the ideal partner, *a "love map."* . . . (Anastasia Toufexis, paragraph 17)

Appositives accomplish these and other purposes very efficiently by enabling the writer to put related bits of information next to each other in the same sentence, thereby merging two potential sentences into one or shrinking a potential clause to a phrase. For example, Ngo, instead of making use of the appositive, could have written either of the following:

> Cannibalism can be defined as the act of human beings eating human flesh. It has a long history and continues to hold interest and create controversy.

> Cannibalism, which can be defined as the act of human beings eating human flesh, has a long history and continues to hold interest and create controversy.

Both of these versions are readable and clear. By using an appositive, however, Ngo saves four or five words, subordinates the definition of cannibalism to his main idea about history and controversy, and yet locates the definition exactly where readers need to see it.

For more on using appositives, go to bedfordstmartins/theguide and click on Sentence Strategies.

In addition to using precise verbs to introduce sources and examples and to relying on appositives, you can strengthen your concept explanation with other kinds of sentences as well, and you may want to review the information about sentences that express comparison and contrast (p. 432) and sentences that use conjunctions and phrases to indicate the logical relationships between clauses and sentences (pp. 310–11). If you frequently quote from sources, you may want to review the examples of integrating quoted material into your sentences (pp. 749–51).

CRITICAL READING GUIDE

Now is the time to get a good critical reading of your draft. Your instructor may arrange such a reading as part of your coursework—in class or online. If not, you can ask a classmate, friend, or family member to read your draft using this guide. If your campus has a writing center, you might ask a tutor there to read and comment on your draft. (If you are unable to have someone else review your draft, turn ahead to the Revision section for help reading your own draft with a critical eye.)

If you are using the Writing Guide Software, click on
▶ **Critical Reading Guide**

Making Comments Electronically
Most word processing software offers features that allow you to insert comments directly into the text of someone else's document. Many readers prefer to make their comments in this way because it tends to be faster than writing on a hard copy and space is virtually unlimited; from the writer's point of view, it also eliminates the problem of deciphering handwritten comments. Even where such special comment features are not available, simply typing comments directly into a document in a contrasting color can provide the same advantages.

▶ **If You Are the Writer.** To provide focused, helpful comments, your reader must know your essay's intended audience, your purpose, and a problem in the draft that you need help solving. Briefly write out this information at the top of your draft.

- ***Readers:*** To whom are you directing your concept explanation? What do you assume they know about the concept? How do you plan to engage and hold their interest?
- ***Purpose:*** What do you hope to achieve with your readers?
- ***Problem:*** Ask your reader to help you solve the most important problem you see in the draft. Describe this problem briefly.

▶ **If You Are the Reader.** Use the following guidelines to help you give constructive, helpful comments to others on essays explaining concepts.

1. ***Read for a First Impression.*** Read first to get a sense of the concept. Then briefly write out your impressions. What in the draft do you think will especially interest the intended readers? Where might they have difficulty in following the explanation? Next, consider the problem the writer identified, and respond briefly to that concern now. (If you find that the problem is covered by one of the other guidelines listed below, respond to it in more detail there if necessary.)
2. ***Assess Whether the Concept Is Clearly Explained and Focused.*** Restate, in one sentence, what you understand the concept to mean. Indicate any confusion or uncertainty you have about its meaning. Given the concept, does the focus seem appropriate, too broad, or too narrow for the intended readers? Can you think of a more interesting aspect of the concept on which to focus the explanation?
3. ***Consider Whether the Content Is Appropriate for the Intended Readers.*** Does it tell them all that they are likely to want to know about the concept? Can you suggest additional information that should be included? What unanswered questions might readers have about the concept? Point out any information that seems either superfluous or too predictable.
4. ***Evaluate the Organization.*** Look at the way the essay is organized by making a scratch outline. Does the information seem to be logically divided? If not, suggest a better way to divide it. Also consider the order or sequence of information. Can you suggest a better way of sequencing it?
   - Look at the *beginning*. Does it pull readers into the essay and make them want to continue? Does it adequately forecast the direction of the essay? If possible, suggest a better way to begin.
   - Look for obvious *transitions* in the draft. Tell the writer how they are helpful or unhelpful. Try to improve one or two of them. Look for additional places where transitions would be helpful.

- Look at the *ending*. Explain what makes it particularly effective or less effective than it might be, in your opinion. If you can, suggest a better way to end.

5. ***Assess the Clarity of Definitions.*** Point out any definitions that may be unclear or confusing to the intended readers. Identify any other terms that may need to be defined.
6. ***Evaluate the Use of Sources.*** If the writer has used sources, review the list of sources cited. Given the purpose, readers, and focus of the essay, does the list seem balanced, and are the selections appropriate? Try to suggest concerns or questions about sources that readers knowledgeable about the concept might raise. Then consider the use of sources within the text of the essay. Are there places where summary or paraphrase would be preferable to quoted material or vice versa? Note any places where the writer has placed quotations awkwardly into the text, and recommend ways to smooth them out.
7. ***Evaluate the Effectiveness of Visuals.*** If charts, graphs, tables, or other visuals are included, let the writer know whether they help you understand the concept. Suggest ideas you have for changing, adding, moving, or deleting visuals.
8. ***Give the Writer Your Final Thoughts.*** Which part needs the most work? What do you think the intended readers will find most informative or memorable? What do you like best about the draft essay?

REVISING

Now you are ready to revise your essay. Your instructor or other students may have given you advice on improving your draft. Nevertheless, you may have begun to realize that your draft requires not so much revision as rethinking. For example, you may recognize that the focus you chose is too broad to be explained adequately in a few pages, that you need to make the information more engaging or interesting for your intended readers, or that you need substantially more information to present the concept adequately. Consequently, instead of working to improve parts of the draft, you may need to write a new draft that radically reenvisions your explanation. It is not unusual for students—and professional writers—to find themselves in this situation. Seek your instructor's advice if you must plan a radical revision.

On the other hand, you may feel quite satisfied that your draft achieves most, if not all, of your goals. In that case, you can focus on refining specific parts of your draft. Very likely you have thought of ways to improve your draft, and you may even have begun improving it. This section will help you get an overview of your draft and revise it accordingly.

If you're using the Writing Guide Software, you can click on the Revision Checklist button to get a pop-up list of questions about your draft for you to consider. After you answer them, you'll see suggestions for revisions based on your answers.

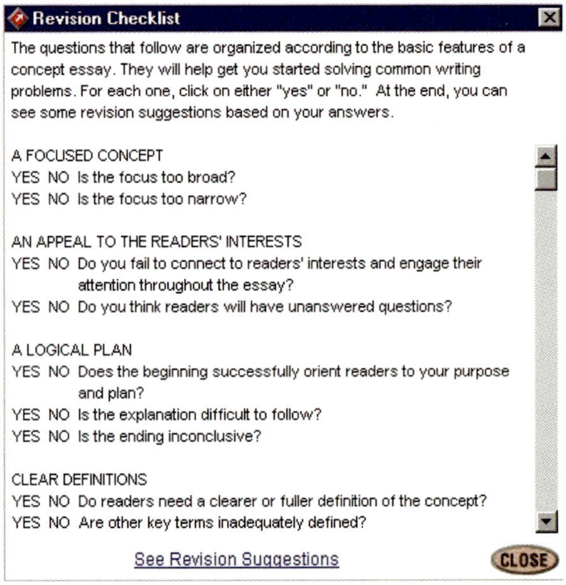

Getting an Overview

Consider your draft as a whole. It may help to do so in two steps:

1. ***Reread.*** If at all possible, put the draft aside for a day or two before rereading it. When you return to it, start by reconsidering your readers and purpose. Then read the draft straight through, trying to see it as your intended readers will.
2. ***Outline.*** Make a scratch outline to get an overview of the essay's development. Consider using the headings and outline/summary functions of your word processor.

Planning for Revision. Resist the temptation to dive in and start changing your text until after you have a clear view of the big picture. Using your outline as a guide, move through the document, using the highlighting or commenting tools of your word processor to note comments received from others and problems you want to solve (or mark on a hard copy if you prefer).

Analyzing the Basic Features of Your Own Draft. Using the Critical Reading Guide on the preceding pages, reread the draft to identify problems you need to solve. Note the problems on your draft.

Studying Critical Comments. Review all of the comments you have received from other readers, and add to your notes any that you intend to act on. Try not to react defensively. For each comment, look at the draft to determine what might have led the reader to make the comment. By letting you see how others respond to your draft, these comments provide valuable information about how you might improve it.

Carrying Out Revisions

Having identified problems in your draft, you now need to come up with solutions and—most important—to carry them out. Basically, there are three ways to find solutions:

1. Review your invention and planning notes and your sources for information and ideas to add to the draft.
2. Do further invention or research to answer questions your readers raised.
3. Look back at the readings in this chapter to see how other writers have solved similar problems.

The following suggestions, which are organized according to the basic features of explanatory essays, will get you started solving some writing problems common to them.

A Focused Concept

- ***Is the focus too broad?*** Consider limiting it further so that you can explain one part of the concept in more depth. If readers were uninterested in the aspect you focused on, consider focusing on some other aspect.
- ***Is the focus too narrow?*** You may have isolated too minor an aspect. Go back to your invention and research notes, and look for larger or more significant aspects.

An Appeal to Readers' Interests

- ***Do you fail to connect to readers' interests and engage their attention throughout the essay?*** Help readers see the significance of the information to them personally. Eliminate superfluous or too-predictable content. Open with an unusual piece of information that catches readers' interest.
- ***Do you think readers will have unanswered questions?*** Review your invention writing and sources for further information to answer them.

A Logical Plan

- ***Does the beginning successfully orient readers to your purpose and plan?*** Try making your focus obvious immediately. Forecast the plan of your essay.
- ***Is the explanation difficult to follow?*** Look for a way to reorder the parts so that the essay is easier to follow. Try constructing an alternative outline. Add transitions or summaries to help keep readers on track. Or consider ways you might classify and divide the information to make it easier to understand or provide a more interesting perspective on the topic.

- *Is the ending inconclusive?* Consider moving important information there. Try summarizing highlights of the essay or framing it by referring to something in the beginning. Or you might speculate about the future of the concept or assert its usefulness.

Clear Definitions

- *Do readers need a clearer or fuller definition of the concept?* Add a concise definition early in your essay, or consider adding a brief summary that defines the concept later in the essay (in the middle or at the end). Remove any information that may blur readers' understanding of the concept.
- *Are other key terms inadequately defined?* Supply clear definitions, searching your sources or checking a dictionary if necessary.

Appropriate Writing Strategies

- *Does the content seem thin or the definition of the concept blurred?* Consider whether any other writing strategies would improve the presentation.
  - Try comparing or contrasting the concept with a related one that is more familiar to readers.
  - Add some information about its known causes or effects.
  - See whether adding examples enlivens or clarifies your explanation. Remember that appositive phrases are a good way to introduce brief examples.
  - Tell more about how the concept works or what people do with it.
  - Add design features or visuals such as charts, headings, drawings, or photographs.

Checking Sentence Strategies Electronically
To check your draft for a sentence strategy especially useful in explaining concepts, use your word processor's highlighting function to mark places where you refer to sources and their authors. Then look at the verbs that you use to introduce each source or author, and think about whether changing any of them to a more precise, informative verb would help your readers to understand better how you are using the source. For more on using informative, precise verbs to introduce sources and authors, see p. 245.

Careful Use of Sources

- *Do readers find your sources inadequate?* Return to the library or the Internet to find additional ones. Consider dropping weak or less reliable sources. Make sure that your sources provide coverage in a comprehensive, balanced way.
- *Do you rely too much on quoting, summarizing, or paraphrasing?* Change some of your quotations to summaries or paraphrases, or vice versa.
- *Does quoted material need to be more smoothly integrated into your own text?* Revise to make it so. Remember to use precise verbs to introduce sources and authors.
- *Are there discrepancies between your in-text citations and the entries in your list of sources?* Compare each citation and entry against the examples given in Chapter 22 for the documentation style you are using. Be sure that all of the citations and entries follow the style exactly. Check to see that your list of sources has an entry for each source that you cite in the text.

EDITING AND PROOFREADING

Now is the time to check your revised draft carefully for errors in usage, punctuation, and mechanics and to consider matters of style. Our research on students' writing has identified several errors that are especially common in writing that explains concepts. The following guidelines will help you check and edit your essay for these errors. This book's Web site also provides interactive online exercises to help you learn to identify and correct each of these errors; to access the exercises for a particular error, go to the URL listed in the margin next to that section of the guidelines.

A Note on Grammar and Spelling Checkers
These tools are good at catching certain types of errors, but currently there's no replacement for a good human proofreader. Grammar checkers in particular are extremely limited in what they can usually find, and often they only give you summary information that isn't helpful if you don't already understand the rule in question. They are also prone to give faulty advice for fixing problems and to flag correct items as wrong. Spelling checkers cause fewer problems but can't catch misspellings that are themselves words, such as *to* for *too.*

If you are using the Writing Guide Software, click on
▶ **Editing and Proofreading**

Checking the Punctuation of Adjective Clauses. Adjective clauses include both a subject and a verb. They give information about a noun or a pronoun. They often begin with *who, which,* or *that.* Here is an example from a student essay explaining the concept of schizophrenia, a type of mental illness:

> **It is common for schizophrenics to have delusions *that they are being persecuted.***

Because adjective clauses add information about the nouns they follow—defining, illustrating, or explaining—they can be useful in writing that explains a concept. Adjective clauses may or may not need to be set off with a comma or commas. To decide, first you have to determine whether the clause is essential to the meaning of the sentence. Clauses that are essential to the meaning of a sentence should not be set off with a comma; clauses that are not essential to the meaning must be set off with a comma. Here are two examples from the student essay about schizophrenia:

ESSENTIAL **It is common for schizophrenics to have delusions *that they are being persecuted.***

The adjective clause defines and limits the word *delusions.* If the clause were removed, the basic meaning of the sentence would change, saying that schizophrenics commonly have delusions of all sorts.

NONESSENTIAL **Related to delusions are hallucinations, *which are very common in schizophrenics.***

The adjective clause gives information that is not essential to understanding the main clause *(Related to delusions are hallucinations).* Taking away the adjective clause *(which are very common in schizophrenics)* in no way changes the basic meaning of the main clause.

For practice, go to bedfordstmartins.com/theguide/comma and bedfordstmartins.com/theguide/uncomma.

To decide whether an adjective clause is essential or nonessential, mentally delete the clause. If taking out the clause changes the basic meaning of the sentence or makes it unclear, the clause is probably essential and should not be set off with commas. If the meaning of the main part of the sentence or the main clause does not change enormously, the clause is probably nonessential and should be set off with commas.

- **Postpartum neurosis, which can last for two weeks or longer, can adversely affect a mother's ability to care for her infant.**
- **The early stage starts with memory loss, which usually causes the patient to forget recent life events.**
- **Seasonal affective disorders are mood disturbances~~,~~ that occur with a change of season.**
- **The coaches~~,~~ who do the recruiting should be disciplined.**

Adjective clauses following proper nouns always require commas.

- **Nanotechnologists defer to K. Eric Drexler, who speculates imaginatively about the uses of nonmachines.**

For practice, go to bedfordstmartins.com/theguide/comma and bedfordstmartins.com/theguide/uncomma.

Checking for Commas around Interrupting Phrases. When writers are explaining a concept, they need to supply a great deal of information. They add much of this information in phrases that interrupt the flow of a sentence. Words that interrupt are usually set off with commas. Be especially careful with interrupting phrases that fall in the middle of a sentence. Such phrases must be set off with two commas, one at the beginning and one at the end:

- **People on the West Coast, especially in Los Angeles, have always been receptive to new ideas.**
- **Alzheimer's disease, named after the German neuropathologist Alois Alzheimer, is a chronic degenerative illness.**
- **These examples, though simple, present equations in terms of tangible objects.**

A WRITER AT WORK

SELECTING AND INTEGRATING INFORMATION FROM SOURCES

This section describes how student writer Linh Kieu Ngo selected information from a source and integrated it into one part of his essay on cannibalism.

One paragraph from Ngo's essay illustrates a sound strategy for integrating sources into your essay, relying on them fully—as you nearly always must do in explanatory writing—and yet making them your own. Here is paragraph 9 from Ngo's essay (the five sentences are numbered for ease of reference):

> (1) In the Miyanmin society of the west Sepik interior of Papua, New Guinea, villagers do not value human life over that of pigs or marsupials because human flesh is part of their normal diet (Poole 7). (2) The Miyanmin people observe no differences in "gender, kinship, ritual status, and bodily substance"; they eat anyone, even their own dead. (3) In this respect, then, they practice both endocannibalism and exocannibalism; and to ensure a constant supply of human flesh for food, they raid neighboring tribes and drag their victims back to their village to be eaten (Poole 11). (4) Perhaps, in the history of this society, there was at one time a shortage of wild game to be hunted for food, and because people were more plentiful than fish, deer, rabbits, pigs, or cows, survival cannibalism was adopted as a last resort. (5) Then, as their culture developed, the Miyanmin may have retained the practice of dietary cannibalism, which has endured as a part of their culture.

Most of the information in this paragraph comes from a twenty-six-page research report by an anthropologist, Fitz John Porter Poole. Given Ngo's purpose in this paragraph—to illustrate some forms of dietary cannibalism—he selects only a limited amount of information from small sections of text on two different pages of the Poole report. Notice first that Ngo quotes only once (sentence 2, a phrase that emphasizes what indiscriminate dietary cannibals the Miyanmin people are). Otherwise, Ngo paraphrases information from Poole. (When you **paraphrase**, you construct your own sentences and phrases but rely necessarily on the key words in your source.) For example, in his sentence 1, Ngo paraphrases this sentence: "For Miyanmin, they claim, humans do indeed become food in an ordinary sense and are seen as comparable to pigs and marsupials." Toward the end of sentence 3, Ngo again paraphrases Poole. By contrast, Ngo's sentences 4 and 5 seem to be his own speculations about the possible origins of Miyanmin cannibalism because this information does not appear in Poole.

The paragraph illustrates a careful balance between a writer's ideas and information gleaned from sources. Ngo is careful not to let the sources take over the explanation. The paragraph also illustrates judicious use of quotations and paraphrases. Ngo avoids stringing quotes together to illustrate an explanation.

DESIGNING YOUR WORK

In the successful presentation made by the marketing manager who volunteers to teach fifth graders about the concept of surveys (see the community writing project described on pp. 202–203), effective document design is an important factor. Much of the preparation the researcher makes beforehand involves creating a questionnaire for the students to fill out.

She recognizes that students will need to be interested in the questionnaire, not intimidated by its appearance, and able to fill it out quickly, without much thought. After first drafting the questionnaire so that it fits on a single page, she realizes that students will be able to fill it out more easily if each question has more space around it. She then refers to workbooks and other printed material designed for ten- and eleven-year-olds for guidance in deciding how much space they need to write out their answers. In this case, the convenience of her audience outweighs the time and expense of photocopying multiple pages.

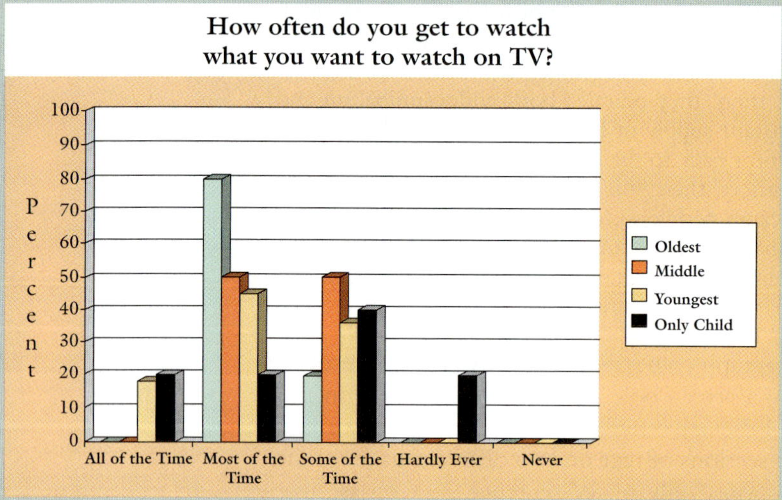

The appearance of the questionnaire itself is not her only design consideration, however. The marketing researcher is savvy enough to know that information from the questionnaire has to be easy to represent graphically, so that the students will understand and appreciate the results when they are projected on a large screen, and she keeps this goal in mind as she drafts the language for the questionnaire. For instance, by asking separate questions about television-watching habits on weekdays and weekends, the researcher ensures that she has two categories of data to tabulate.

For more on oral presentations, see Chapter 26.

Because of the time constraints and the need to maintain the audience's interest during an oral presentation, the researcher also makes sure that the questions are phrased in a way that will permit her to input some of the students' answers into the computer right there in the classroom. Thus she writes multiple-choice questions and short fill-ins.

Finally, the marketing researcher makes sure she knows how to use her PowerPoint program to display the results clearly.

THINKING CRITICALLY ABOUT WHAT YOU HAVE LEARNED

Now that you have read and discussed several essays that explain concepts and written one of your own, take some time to reflect on the act of reading and writing concept essays and to think critically about how explanations of concepts influence the way we think about ourselves and our culture.

Reflecting on Your Writing

Write a one-page explanation, telling your instructor about a problem you encountered in writing your essay and how you solved it. Before you begin, gather all of your writing—invention and planning notes, drafts, critical comments, revision notes and plans, and final revision. Review these materials, and refer to them as you complete this writing task.

1. ***Identify one writing problem you had to solve as you worked to explain the concept in your essay.*** Do not be concerned with grammar and punctuation; concentrate instead on problems unique to developing a concept explanation. For example: Did you puzzle over how to focus your explanation? Did you worry about how to appeal to your readers' interests or how to identify and define the terms that your readers would need explained? Did you have trouble integrating sources smoothly?
2. ***Determine how you came to recognize the problem.*** When did you first discover it? What called it to your attention? If you did not become aware of the problem until someone else pointed it out, can you now see hints of it in your invention writings? If so, where specifically? How did you respond when you first recognized the problem?
3. ***Reflect on how you went about solving the problem.*** Did you work on the wording of a particular passage, cut or add information, move paragraphs or sentences around, add transitions or forecasting statements, experiment with different writing strategies? Did you reread one of the essays in this chapter to see how another writer handled the problem, or did you look back at the invention suggestions? If you talked about the writing problem with another student, a tutor, or your instructor, did talking about it help? How useful was the advice you received?
4. ***Write a brief explanation of how you identified the problem and how you solved it.*** Be as specific as possible in reconstructing your efforts. Quote from your invention notes and draft essay, others' critical comments, your revision plan, or your revised essay to show the various changes your writing underwent as you tried to solve the problem. If you are still uncertain about your solution, say so. Thinking in detail about how you identified a particular problem, how you went about solving it, and what you learned from this experience can help you solve future writing problems more easily.

Reviewing What You Learned from Reading

Write a page or two explaining to your instructor how the readings in this chapter influenced your final draft. To some extent, your own essay has been influenced by the concept explanations that you have read in this chapter and by classmates' essays that you have read. Your reading may have helped you choose a topic, suggested that you needed to do research, or shown you how to structure your essay or how to use examples or comparisons. Before you write, take time to reflect on what you have learned about concept explanations from the readings in this chapter and how the readings have influenced your own writing.

1. ***Reread the final revision of your essay; then look back at the selections you read before completing your essay.*** Name any specific influences. For

example, if you were impressed by the way one of the readings described the origins or originators of the concept, organized the information, or connected to the reader's knowledge through analogy or comparison, look in your revised essay to see where you might have been striving for similar effects in your own writing. Also look for ideas you got from your reading: writing strategies you were inspired to try, specific details you were led to include, effects you sought to achieve.

2. ***Write an explanation of these influences.*** Did one reading have an especially strong influence on your essay, or were several readings influential in different ways? Quote from the readings and from your final revision to show how your essay explaining a concept was influenced by the readings in this chapter. Finally, based on this review of the chapter's readings, briefly explain any further improvements you would now make in your essay.

Considering the Social Dimensions of Concept Explanations

Concepts are the building blocks of knowledge, essential to its creation and acquisition. We use concepts to name and organize ideas and information in areas as diverse as snowboarding and psychiatry. Academic disciplines and most professions are heavily concept-based, enabling newcomers to be introduced efficiently, if abstractly, to the basic knowledge they need to begin learning.

The Nature of Knowledge. As you have learned from your reading, research, and writing for this chapter, writers explaining concepts present knowledge as established and uncontested. They presume to be unbiased and objective, and they assume that readers will not doubt or challenge the truth or the value of the knowledge they present. This stance encourages readers to feel confident about the validity of the explanation.

However, explanatory writing should not always be accepted at face value. Textbooks and reference materials, in particular, sometimes present a limited view of knowledge in an academic discipline. Because introductory textbooks must be highly selective, they necessarily leave out certain sources of information and types of knowledge.

1. ***Consider the claim that concept explanations attempt to present their information as uncontested truths.*** Identify a reading in this chapter that particularly seems to support this claim, and then think about how it does so. Do the same for a chapter or section in a textbook you are reading for another course.
2. ***Reflect on how concept explanations present established knowledge.*** How do you think knowledge gets established in academic disciplines such as biology, psychology, and history? How might the prominent researchers and professors in a discipline go about deciding what is to be considered established knowledge for now? How might they decide when that established knowledge needs to be revised? If possible, ask these questions of a professor in a subject you are studying.
3. ***Write a page or two explaining your initial assumptions about the knowledge or information you presented about a concept in your essay.*** When you were doing research on the concept, did you discover that some of the information was being challenged by experts? Or did the body of knowledge seem settled and established? Did you at any point think that your readers might question any of the information you were presenting? How did you decide what information might seem new or even surprising to readers? Did you feel comfortable in your roles as the selector and giver of knowledge?

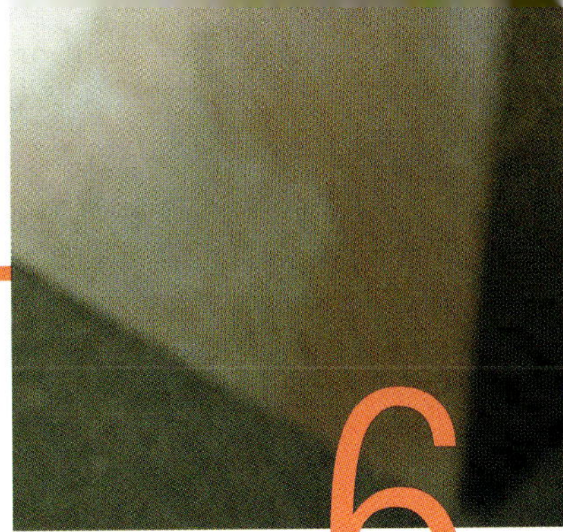

Arguing a Position

6

You may associate arguing with quarreling or with the in-your-face debating we hear so often on radio and television talk shows. These ways of arguing may let us vent strong feelings, but they seldom lead us to consider seriously other points of view or to look critically at our own thinking.

This chapter presents a more deliberative way of arguing that we call **reasoned argument** because it depends on giving reasons rather than raising voices. It demands that positions be supported rather than merely asserted. It also commands respect for the right of others to disagree with you as you may disagree with them. Reasoned argument requires more thought than quarreling but no less passion or commitment, as you will see when you read the essays in this chapter arguing about controversial issues.

Controversial issues are, by definition, issues about which people may have strong feelings. The issue may involve a practice that has been accepted for some time, like fraternity hazing, or it may concern a newly proposed or recently instituted policy, like the Peacekeepers school program. People may agree about goals but disagree about the best way to achieve them, as in the perennial debate over how to guarantee adequate health care for all citizens. Or they may disagree about fundamental values and beliefs, as in the debate over euthanasia or abortion.

As you can see from these examples, controversial issues have no obvious right answer, no truth that everyone accepts, no single authority on which everyone relies. Writers cannot offer absolute proof in debates about controversial issues because such issues are matters of opinion and judgment. Simply gathering information—finding the facts or learning from experts—will not settle disputes like these, although the more that is known about an issue, the more informed the positions will be.

Although it is not possible to prove that a position on a controversial issue is right or wrong, it is possible through reasoned argument to convince others to accept or reject a particular position. To be convincing, not only must an argument present convincing reasons and plausible support for its position, but it also should anticipate readers' likely objections and opposing arguments, conceding those that are reasonable and refuting those that are not. Vigorous debate that sets forth arguments and counterarguments on all sides of an issue can advance everyone's thinking.

Learning to make reasoned arguments on controversial issues and to think critically about our own as well as others' arguments is not a luxury; it is a necessity if our increasingly diverse society is to survive and flourish. As citizens in a democracy, we have a special duty to inform ourselves about pressing issues and to participate constructively in the public debate. Honing our thinking and arguing skills also has practical advantages in school, where we often are judged by our ability to write convincingly, and in the workplace, where we often need to recommend or defend controversial policy decisions.

You will encounter writing that argues a position in many different contexts, as the following examples suggest.

Writing in Your Other Courses

- For a sociology class, a student writes an essay on surrogate mothering. She finds several newspaper and magazine articles and checks the Internet for surrogate mothering Web sites. In her essay, she acknowledges that using *in vitro* fertilization and a surrogate may be the only way some couples can have their own biological children. Although she respects this desire, she argues that from a sociological perspective surrogate mothering does more harm than good. She gives two reasons: that the practice has serious emotional consequences for the surrogates and their families and that it exploits poor women by creating a class of professional breeders. She supports her argument with anecdotes from surrogates and their families as well as with quotations from sociologists and psychologists who have studied surrogate mothering.
- For a business course, a student writes an essay arguing that the glass ceiling that prevents women from advancing up the corporate ladder still exists at the highest executive levels. She acknowledges that in the nearly twenty years after the phrase "glass ceiling" was coined by a writer at the *Wall Street Journal* in 1986, the percentage of corporate officers who are women has grown. Nevertheless, she argues, the statistics are misleading. Because it is good business to claim gender equity, many companies define to their own advantage the positions counted as corporate officers. The student cites statistics from the Catalyst research group indicating that only 7 percent of the corporate officers in line positions—those responsible for the bottom line and therefore most likely to be promoted to chief executive positions—are women.

For a look at some of the decisions this student makes about document design, see pp. 322–23.

Writing in the Community

- For the campus newspaper, a student writes an editorial condemning the practice of fraternity hazing. He acknowledges that most hazing is harmless but argues that hazing can get out of hand and even be lethal. He refers specifically to two incidents reported in the national news in which one student died of alcohol poisoning after being forced to drink too much liquor and another student had a heart attack after being made to run too many laps around the school's track. To show that the potential for a similar tragedy exists on his campus, the writer recounts several anecdotes told to him by students there about their experiences pledging for fraternities. He concludes with a plea to the fraternities on campus to radically change—or at least, curtail—their hazing practices before someone is seriously hurt or killed.

- In a letter to the school board, parents protest a new Peacekeepers program that is being implemented at the local middle school. The writers acknowledge that the aim of the program—to teach students to avoid conflict—is worthwhile. But they argue that the program's methods unduly restrict students' freedoms. Moreover, they claim that the program teaches children to become passive and submissive rather than thinking adults who are willing and able to fight for what is right. To support their argument, they list some of the rules that have been instituted at the middle school: Students must wear uniforms to school, must keep their hands clasped behind their backs when walking down the halls, may not raise their voices in anger or use obscenities, and cannot play aggressive games like dodge ball or contact sports like basketball and football.

Writing in the Workplace

- For a business magazine, a corporate executive writes an essay arguing that protecting the environment is not only good citizenship, but also good business. She supports her position with examples of two companies that became successful by developing innovative methods of reducing hazardous wastes. She also reminds readers of the decisive actions taken in the late 1980s by established corporations to help solve the problem of ozone depletion, such as DuPont's decision to discontinue production of chlorofluorocarbons (CFCs) and McDonald's elimination of styrofoam cartons. Finally, she points out that *Fortune* magazine agrees with her position, noting that the eight deciding factors in its annual ranking of America's Most Admired Corporations include community and environmental responsibility alongside financial soundness.
- In a memo to the director of personnel, a loan company manager argues that written communication skills should be a more important factor in hiring. He acknowledges that math skills are necessary but tries to convince the director that mistakes in writing are too costly to ignore. To support his argument, he cites examples of bad writing in letters and memos that cost the company money and time. For additional examples and suggestions on solving the problem, he refers the personnel director to an ongoing discussion about writing on a listserv to which the manager subscribes.

Practice Arguing a Position: A Collaborative Activity

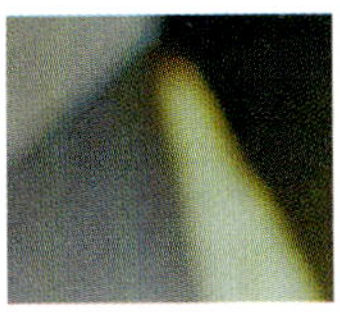

The preceding scenarios suggest some occasions for arguing a position. Your instructor may schedule this collaborative activity as a face-to-face in-class discussion or ask you to conduct an online real-time discussion in a chat room. Whatever the medium, here are some guidelines to follow:

To construct an effective argument, you must assert a position and offer support for it. This activity gives you a chance to practice constructing an argument with other students.

Part 1. Get together with two to three other students, and choose an issue. You do not have to be an expert on the issue, but you should be familiar with some of the arguments people typically make about it. If you do not have an issue in mind, the following list might help you think of possibilities.

- Should all students be required to wear uniforms in school?
- Should college athletes be paid a portion of the money the school gains from sports events?
- Should community service be a requirement for graduation from high school or college?

In your group, spend two to three minutes quickly exchanging your opinions, and then agree together to argue for the same position on the issue, whether you personally agree with the position or not. Also decide who you would want to read your argument and what you expect these readers to think about the issue. Choose someone in the group to write down the results of your discussion like this:

Issue: Should grades in college be abolished?

Position: Grades should be abolished.

Readers: Teachers who think grades measure learning accurately and efficiently.

Take another ten to fifteen minutes to construct an argument for your position, giving several reasons and noting the kinds of support you would need. Also try to anticipate one or two objections you would expect from readers who disagree with your position. Write down what you discover under the following headings: Reasons, Support Needed, and Likely Objections. Following is an example of this work for the position that grades should be abolished.

Reasons

1. Tests are not always the best way to judge students' knowledge because some students do poorly on tests even though they know the material.
2. Tests often evaluate only what is easily measurable, such as whether students remember facts, rather than whether students can use facts to support their ideas.

Support Needed

1. Research on testing anxiety
2. Anecdotes from students' experience with testing anxiety
3. Teachers' comments on why they rely on tests and how they feel about alternatives to testing (such as group projects)

Likely Objections

1. Tests are efficient for teachers and for students, especially in comparison with research papers.

2. Tests are evaluated strictly on what students have learned about the subject, not on how well they write or how well a group collaborates.

Part 2. Discuss for about five minutes what you did as a group to construct an argument:

Reasons: What did you learn about giving reasons? If you thought of more reasons than you needed, how did you choose? If you had difficulty thinking of reasons, what could you do?

Support: What did you learn about supporting an argument? How many different kinds of support (such as quotations, examples, or anecdotes) did you consider? Which reasons seemed the easiest to support? Which the hardest?

Objections: What did you learn about anticipating objections to your argument? How did you come up with these objections? Given your designated readers, was it easy or hard to think of their likely objections? How could you learn more about your readers' likely objections?

READINGS

No two essays taking a position are alike, and yet they share defining features. Together, the four readings in this chapter reveal a number of these features, so you will want to read as many of them as possible. If time permits, complete the activities in the Analyzing Writing Strategies section that follows each selection, and read the Commentary. Following the readings is a section called Basic Features: Arguing Positions (p. 294), which offers a concise description of the features of writing that takes a position and provides examples from the four readings.

Richard Estrada *was the associate editor of the* Dallas Morning News *editorial page and a syndicated columnist whose essays appeared regularly in the* Washington Post, *the* Los Angeles Times, *and other major newspapers. He was best known as a thoughtful, independent-minded commentator on immigration and social issues. Before joining the* Dallas Morning News *in 1988, Estrada worked as a congressional staff member and as a researcher at the Center for Immigration Studies in Washington, D.C. In the 1990s, he was appointed to the U.S. Commission on Immigration Reform. Following his death at the age of forty-nine in 1999, the Richard Estrada Fellowship in Immigration Studies was established in his honor.*

Estrada wrote this essay during the 1995 baseball World Series in which the Atlanta Braves played the Cleveland Indians. The series drew the public's attention to the practice of dressing team mascots like Native Americans on the warpath and encouraging fans to rally their team with gestures like the "tomahawk chop" and pep yells like the "Indian chant." The controversy over these practices revitalized a longstanding debate over naming sports teams with words associated with Native Americans. Several high schools and at least one university, Stanford, have changed the names of their sports teams because of this ongoing controversy. A coworker remarked that in his newspaper columns, Estrada "firmly opposed separating the American people into competing ethnic and linguistic groups." As you read this essay, think about his purpose in writing this position essay and how it seeks to bring different groups together.

Sticks and Stones and Sports Team Names

Richard Estrada

When I was a kid living in Baltimore in the late 1950s, there was only one professional sports team worth following. Anyone who ever saw the movie *Diner* knows which one it was. Back when we liked Ike, the Colts were the gods of the gridiron and Memorial Stadium was their Mount Olympus. 1

Ah, yes: The Colts. The Lions. Da Bears. Back when defensive tackle Big Daddy Lipscomb was letting running backs know exactly what time it was, a young fan could easily forget that in a game where men were men, the teams they played on were not invariably named after animals. Among others, the Packers, the Steelers and the distant 49ers were cases in point. But in the roll call of pro teams, one name in particular always discomfited me: the Washington Redskins. Still, however willing I may have been to go along with the name as a kid, as an adult I have concluded that using an ethnic group essentially as a sports mascot is wrong. 2

The Redskins and the Kansas City Chiefs, along with baseball teams like the Atlanta Braves and the Cleveland Indians, should find other names that avoid highlighting ethnicity. 3

By no means were such names originally meant to disparage Native Americans. The noble symbols of the Redskins or college football's Florida State Seminoles or the Illinois Illini are meant to be strong and proud. Yet, ultimately, the practice of using a people as mascots is dehumanizing. It sets them apart from the rest of society. It promotes the politics of racial aggrievement at a moment when our storehouse is running over with it. 4

The World Series between the Cleveland Indians and the Atlanta Braves re-ignited the debate. In the chill night air of October, tomahawk chops and war chants suddenly became far more familiar to millions of fans, along with the ridiculous and offensive cartoon logo of Cleveland's "Chief Wahoo." 5

The defenders of team names that use variations on the Indian theme argue that tradition should not be sacrificed at the altar of political correctness. In truth, the nation's No. 1 P.C. [politically correct] school, Stanford University, helped matters some when it changed its team nickname from "the Indians" to "the Cardinals." To be sure, Stanford did the right thing, but the school's status as P.C. without peer tainted the decision for those who still need to do the right thing. 6

Another argument is that ethnic group leaders are too inclined to cry wolf in alleging racial insensitivity. Often, this is the case. But no one should overlook genuine cases 7 of political insensitivity in an attempt to avoid accusations of hypersensitivity and political correctness.

The real world is different from the world of sports entertainment. I recently heard a father who happened to be a Native American complain on the radio that his child was being pressured into participating in celebrations of Braves baseball. At his kid's school, certain days are set aside on which all children are told to dress in Indian garb and celebrate with tomahawk chops and the like. 8

That father should be forgiven for not wanting his family to serve as somebody's mascot. The desire to avoid ridicule is legitimate and understandable. Nobody likes to be trivialized or deprived of their dignity. This has nothing to do with political correctness and the provocations of militant leaders. 9

Against this backdrop, the decision by newspapers in Minneapolis, Seattle and Portland to ban references to Native American nicknames is more reasonable than some might think. 10

What makes naming teams after ethnic groups, particularly minorities, reprehensible is that politically impotent groups continue to be targeted, while politically powerful ones who bite back are left alone. How long does anyone think the name "Washington Blackskins" would last? Or how about "the New York Jews"? 11

With no fewer than 10 Latino ballplayers on the Cleveland Indians' roster, the team could change its name to "the Banditos." The trouble is, they would be missing the point: Latinos would correctly object to that stereotype, just as they rightly protested against Frito-Lay's use of the "Frito Bandito" character years ago. 12

It seems to me that what Native Americans are saying is that what would be intolerable for Jews, blacks, Latinos and others is no less offensive to them. Theirs is a request not only for dignified treatment, but for fair treatment as well. For America to ignore the complaints of a numerically small segment of the population because it is small is neither dignified nor fair. 13

Connecting to Culture and Experience: Name-Calling

As children, we may say, "Sticks and stones will break my bones, but words will never hurt me." Most children, however, recognize the power of words, especially words that make them feel different or inferior.

Make a list of words that are used to refer to groups with which you identify. Try to think of words associated with your ethnicity, religion, gender, interests, geographic region, or any other factor. (Are you perhaps a redneck Okie good ole boy religious fanatic?) Which of the words on your list, if any, do you consider insulting? Why? Would you consider someone who called you these names insensitive?

With two or three other students, discuss your name-calling lists, giving examples from your list. Tell when, where, and by whom you or others in your group have been called these names. Speculate about motives of the name callers, and describe your reactions.

Analyzing Writing Strategies

1. At the beginning of this chapter, we discuss several **features** of essays that argue a position. Consider which of these is true of Estrada's essay:
   - It presents a controversial issue.
   - It asserts a clear position on the issue.
   - It argues for the position by presenting plausible reasons and support.
   - It anticipates readers' objections and arguments, either conceding or refuting them.
2. Reread paragraphs 11–13, where Estrada offers hypothetical **examples** of team names for ethnic groups, such as the "Washington Blackskins" and "the New York Jews." How do these examples support Estrada's argument? Given his readers, how convincing do you think they are likely to be? How effective are they for you, as one reader?

Commentary: Presenting the Issue and Plausible Reasons

Although the title of his essay implies its subject, Estrada does not identify the **issue** explicitly until the end of the second paragraph. He begins the essay by remembering his childhood experience as a football fan and explaining that, even as a child, he was made uncomfortable by the practice of naming sports teams for Native Americans. In paragraphs 2–4, he lists team names (Washington Redskins, Kansas City Chiefs, Atlanta Braves, Cleveland Indians, Florida State Seminoles, Illinois Illini) to remind readers how common the practice is. Then, in paragraph 8, he relates an anecdote about a father who not only feels uncomfortable but also feels personally ridiculed as a Native American when his son's school celebrates Braves' victories with Indian costumes and tomahawk chops. Estrada uses this anecdote to demonstrate that the issue is important and worth taking seriously.

Estrada presents the issue in this way to appeal to the readers of his column in the politically conservative *Dallas Morning News.* He apparently assumes that unless he can convince his readers that the issue of sports teams' names is significant, many readers would dismiss it as unimportant or as advancing a liberal agenda. Therefore, Estrada tries to make his readers empathize with what he calls a real-world issue, one that actually hurts kids (paragraph 8). When you present the issue in your own essay, you also may need to help readers understand why it is important and for whom. In the next reading, for example, you will notice that the primary purpose of Barbara Ehrenreich's essay is to make readers appreciate the seriousness of the issue she is addressing.

Presenting the issue is just a beginning. To convince readers, Estrada has to give the **reasons** that he believes naming sports teams for ethnic groups is detrimental. He gives two: because it treats people like team mascots and it singles out a politically weak group. Moreover, to be convincing, the reasons have to seem plausible to readers. The position (naming sports teams for Native Americans is wrong) has to follow logically from the reason: If readers accept the reason, then they also should accept the position. In other words, if readers are convinced by the support Estrada provides to show the effects of treating people like mascots, then they will be inclined to agree with Estrada that the practice is wrong. Similarly, if readers are convinced also that naming sports teams for Native Americans unfairly singles out a politically weak group, then they would be even more likely to agree with Estrada's conclusion.

Considering Topics for Your Own Essay

List some issues that involve what you believe to be unfair treatment of a marginalized minority group. For example, should a law be passed to make English the official language in this country, requiring that ballots and drivers' tests be printed only in English? Should elementary schools continue bilingual education to help non-English-speaking students learn subjects like math, science, and history while they are learning to read and write fluently in English? What is affirmative action, and should it be used in college admissions for underrepresented groups?

To use the Writing Guide Software to record your ideas, click on
▶ **Journal**

Barbara Ehrenreich published her first article in a science journal when she was a graduate student in biology. After earning her Ph.D., she chose a career as a writer instead of as a research scientist, but Ehrenreich believes that her science background has helped her to look at things both analytically and systematically, seeing the "ways things fit together." A prolific author, she has published essays in such journals as *Time*, the *Atlantic Monthly*, the *New York Times Magazine*, the *Nation*, and *Harper's*, for which she is also a contributing editor. Ehrenreich has researched and written more than a dozen books, including *The American Health Empire: Power, Profits, and Politics* (1970); *Fear of Falling: The Inner Life of the Middle Class* (1989), which was nominated for a National Book Critics' Award; and *Blood Rites: Origins and History of the Passions of War* (1997). For the critically acclaimed *Nickel and Dimed: On (Not) Getting By in America* (2001), from which this reading comes, Ehrenreich went "undercover" as a waitress, a maid, a nursing home aide, and a Wal-Mart sales associate. A chapter from *Nickel and Dimed* published in *Harper's* won the Sydney Hillman Award for Journalism, and Ehrenreich has also received a National Magazine Award for Excellence in Reporting, a Ford Foundation Award for Humanistic Perspectives on Contemporary Society, a Guggenheim Fellowship, and a John D. and Catherine T. MacArthur Foundation grant.

At the time Ehrenreich began her research in 1998, most Americans were enjoying unprecedented economic prosperity stimulated by the dot-com bubble that burst by the time her book was published in 2001. Controversial welfare reform that required single mothers to find jobs was considered a success because more than half of former welfare recipients were employed and the unemployment rate in general was at an all-time low. Nevertheless, reports like that of the Economic Policy Institute, which Ehrenreich refers to in the first paragraph of *this reading, indicated that the working poor were struggling just to keep their heads above water. Of course, economic conditions change, and when you read this essay, the situation for the working poor may be better or worse than it was when Ehrenreich completed her research. As you read the essay, think about your own economic situation and that of your family and friends.*

Nickel and Dimed

Barbara Ehrenreich

Many people earn far less than they need to live on. How much is that? The Economic Policy Institute recently reviewed dozens of studies of what constitutes a "living wage" and came up with an average figure of $30,000 a year for a family of one adult and two children, which amounts to a wage of $14 an hour. This is not the very minimum such a family could live on; the budget includes health insurance, a telephone, and child care at a licensed center, for example, which are well beyond the reach of millions. But it does not include restaurant meals, video rentals, Internet access, wine and liquor, cigarettes and lottery tickets, or even very much meat. The shocking thing is that the majority of American workers, about 60 percent, earn less than $14 an hour. Many of them get by by teaming up with another wage earner, a spouse or grown child. Some draw on government help in the form of food stamps, housing vouchers, the earned income tax credit, or—for those coming off welfare in relatively generous states—subsidized child care. But others—single mothers, for example—have nothing but their own wages to live on, no matter how many mouths there are to feed. 1

Employers will look at that $30,000 figure, which is over twice what they currently pay entry-level workers, and see nothing but bankruptcy ahead. Indeed, it is probably impossible for the private sector to provide everyone with an adequate standard of living through wages, or even wages plus benefits, alone: too much of what we need, such as reliable child care, is just too expensive, even for middle-class families. Most civilized nations compensate for the inadequacy of wages by providing relatively generous public services such as health insurance, free or subsidized child care, subsidized housing, and effective public transportation. But the United States, for all its wealth, leaves its citizens to fend for themselves—facing market-based rents, for example, on their wages alone. For millions of Americans, that $10—or even $8 or $6—hourly wage is all there is. 2

It is common, among the nonpoor, to think of poverty as a sustainable condition—austere, perhaps, but they get by somehow, don't they? They are "always with us." What is harder for the nonpoor to see is poverty as active distress: The lunch that consists of Doritos or hot dog rolls, leading to faintness before the end of the shift. The "home" that is also a car or a van. The illness or injury that must be "worked through," with gritted teeth, because there's no sick pay or health insurance and the loss of one day's pay will mean no groceries for the next. These experiences are not part of a sustainable lifestyle, even a lifestyle of chronic deprivation and relentless low-level punishment. They are, by almost any standard of subsistence, emergency situations. And that is how we should see the poverty of so many millions of low-wage Americans—as a state of emergency. . . . 3

Some odd optical property of our highly polarized and unequal society makes the poor almost invisible to their economic superiors. The poor can see the affluent easily 4 enough—on television, for example, or on the covers of magazines. But the affluent rarely see the poor or, if they do catch sight of them in some public space, rarely know what they're seeing, since—thanks to consignment stores and, yes, Wal-Mart—the poor are usually able to disguise themselves as members of the more comfortable classes. Forty years ago the hot journalistic topic was the "discovery of the poor" in their inner-city and Appalachian "pockets of poverty." Today you are more likely to find commentary on their "disappearance," either as a supposed demographic reality or as a shortcoming of the middle-class imagination.

In a 2000 article on the "disappearing poor," journalist James Fallows reports that, 5
from the vantage point of the Internet's nouveaux riches, it is "hard to understand people for whom a million dollars would be a fortune . . . not to mention those for whom $246 is a full week's earnings."[1] Among the reasons he and others have cited for the blindness of the affluent is the fact that they are less and less likely to share spaces and services with the poor. As public schools and other public services deteriorate, those who can afford to do so send their children to private schools and spend their off-hours in private spaces—health clubs, for example, instead of the local park. They don't ride on public buses and subways. They withdraw from mixed neighborhoods into distant suburbs, gated communities, or guarded apartment towers; they shop in stores that, in line with the prevailing "market segmentation," are designed to appeal to the affluent alone. Even the affluent young are increasingly unlikely to spend their summers learning how the "other half" lives, as lifeguards, waitresses, or housekeepers at resort hotels. The *New York Times* reports that they now prefer career-relevant activities like summer school or interning in an appropriate professional setting to the "sweaty, low-paid and mind-numbing slots that have long been their lot."[2]

Then, too, the particular political moment favors what almost looks like a "conspir- 6
acy of silence" on the subject of poverty and the poor. . . . Welfare reform itself is a factor weighing against any close investigation of the conditions of the poor. Both parties heartily endorsed it, and to acknowledge that low-wage work doesn't lift people out of poverty would be to admit that it may have been, in human terms, a catastrophic mistake. In fact, very little is known about the fate of former welfare recipients because the 1996 welfare reform legislation blithely failed to include any provision for monitoring their post-welfare economic condition. Media accounts persistently bright-side the situation, highlighting the occasional success stories and downplaying the acknowledged increase in hunger.[3] And sometimes there seems to be almost deliberate deception. In June 2000, the press rushed to hail a study supposedly showing that Minnesota's welfare-to-work program had sharply reduced poverty and was, as *Time* magazine put it, a "winner."[4] Overlooked in these reports was the fact that the program in question was a pilot project that offered far more generous child care and other subsidies than Minnesota's actual welfare reform program. Perhaps the error can be forgiven—the pilot project, which ended in 1997, had the same name, Minnesota Family Investment Program, as Minnesota's much larger, ongoing welfare reform program.[5]

You would have to read a great many newspapers very carefully, cover to cover, to 7
see the signs of distress. You would find, for example, that in 1999 Massachusetts food pantries reported a 72 percent increase in the demand for their services over the

previous year, that Texas food banks were "scrounging" for food, despite donations at or above 1998 levels, as were those in Atlanta.[6] You might learn that in San Diego the Catholic Church could no longer, as of January 2000, accept homeless families at its shelter, which happens to be the city's largest, because it was already operating at twice its normal capacity.[7] You would come across news of a study showing that the percentage of Wisconsin food-stamp families in "extreme poverty"—defined as less than 50 percent of the federal poverty line—has tripled in the last decade to more than 30 percent.[8] You might discover that, nationwide, America's food banks are experiencing "a torrent of need which [they] cannot meet" and that,[9] according to a survey conducted by the U.S. Conference of Mayors, 67 percent of the adults requesting emergency food aid are people with jobs.[10]

One reason nobody bothers to pull all these stories together and announce a widespread state of emergency may be that Americans of the newspaper-reading professional middle class are used to thinking of poverty as a consequence of unemployment. During the heyday of downsizing, in the Reagan years, it very often was, and it still is for many inner-city residents who have no way of getting to the proliferating entry-level jobs on urban peripheries. When unemployment causes poverty, we know how to state the problem—typically, "the economy isn't growing fast enough"—and we know what the traditional liberal solution is—"full employment." But when we have full or nearly full employment, when jobs are available to any job seeker who can get to them, then the problem goes deeper and begins to cut into that web of expectations that make up the "social contract." According to a recent poll conducted by Jobs for the Future, a Boston-based employment research firm, 94 percent of Americans agree that "people who work fulltime should be able to earn enough to keep their families out of poverty."[11] I grew up hearing over and over, to the point of tedium, that "hard work" was the secret of success: "Work hard and you'll get ahead" or "It's hard work that got us where we are." No one ever said that you could work hard—harder even than you ever thought possible—and still find yourself sinking ever deeper into poverty and debt. 8

When poor single mothers had the option of remaining out of the labor force on welfare, the middle and upper middle class tended to view them with a certain impatience, if not disgust. The welfare poor were excoriated for their laziness, their persistence in reproducing in unfavorable circumstances, their presumed addictions, and above all for their "dependency." Here they were, content to live off "government handouts" instead of seeking "self-sufficiency," like everyone else, through a job. They needed to get their act together, learn how to wind an alarm clock, get out there and get to work. But now that government has largely withdrawn its "handouts," now that the overwhelming majority of the poor are out there toiling in Wal-Mart or Wendy's—well, what are we to think of them? Disapproval and condescension no longer apply, so what outlook makes sense? 9

Guilt, you may be thinking warily. Isn't that what we're supposed to feel? But guilt doesn't go anywhere near far enough; the appropriate emotion is shame—shame at our own dependency, in this case, on the underpaid labor of others. When someone works for less pay than she can live on—when, for example, she goes hungry so that you can eat more cheaply and conveniently—then she has made a great sacrifice for you, she has made you a gift of some part of her abilities, her health, and her life. The "working 10 poor," as they are approvingly termed, are in fact the major philanthropists of our society. They neglect their own children so that the children of others will be cared for; they live in substandard housing so that other homes will be shiny and perfect; they endure privation so that inflation will be low and stock prices high. To be a member of the working poor is to be an anonymous donor, a nameless benefactor, to everyone else. As Gail, one of my restaurant coworkers put it, "you give and you give."

Someday, of course—and I will make no predictions as to exactly when—they are bound to tire of getting so little in return and to demand to be paid what they're worth. There'll be a lot of anger when that day comes, and strikes and disruption. But the sky will not fall, and we will all be better off for it in the end. 11

Notes

1. "The Invisible Poor," *New York Times Magazine,* March 19, 2000.
2. "Summer Work Is out of Favor with the Young," *New York Times,* June 18, 2000.
3. The *National Journal* reports that the "good news" is that almost six million people have left the welfare rolls since 1996, while the "rest of the story" includes the problem that "these people sometimes don't have enough to eat" ("Welfare Reform, Act 2," June 24, 2000: 1,978–93).
4. "Minnesota's Welfare Reform Proves a Winner," *Time,* June 12, 2000.
5. Center for Law and Social Policy, "Update," Washington, D.C., June 2000.
6. "Study: More Go Hungry since Welfare Reform," *Boston Herald,* January 21, 2000; "Charity Can't Feed All while Welfare Reforms Implemented," *Houston Chronicle,* January 10, 2000; "Hunger Grows as Food Banks Try to Keep Pace," *Atlanta Journal and Constitution,* November 26, 1999.
7. "Rise in Homeless Families Strains San Diego Aid," *Los Angeles Times,* January 24, 2000.
8. "Hunger Problems Said to Be Getting Worse," *Milwaukee Journal Sentinel,* December 15, 1999.
9. Deborah Leff, the president and CEO of the hunger-relief organization America's Second Harvest, quoted in the *National Journal,* "Welfare Reform, Act 2."
10. "Hunger Persists in U.S. despite the Good Times," *Detroit News,* June 15, 2000.
11. "A National Survey of American Attitudes toward Low-Wage Workers and Welfare Reform," Jobs for the Future, Boston, May 24, 2000.

Connecting to Culture and Experience: The American Dream

In paragraph 8, Barbara Ehrenreich writes about "that web of expectations that make up the 'social contract.'" She explains the essential feature of this social contract in these terms: "'hard work' was the secret of success: 'Work hard and you'll get ahead.'" What she is referring to here is the ideology of the American dream, a set of beliefs and values held by people in the United States and around the world. The American dream assumes that if you work hard enough, you—or at least your children—will be better off financially.

Make a list of the values and beliefs that you associate with the American dream. Then get together with two or three other students, and compare your lists. What do your lists say about the value and rewards of hard work?

Analyzing Writing Strategies

1. In arguing a position on a controversial issue, writers usually state their position in a **thesis statement**. At the end of paragraph 3, Ehrenreich asserts her thesis: "And that is how we should see the poverty of so many millions of low-wage Americans—as a state of emergency." For a position to be effective, it must be arguable. That is, it should not be a simple statement of fact that can be proven true or false. Nor should a thesis be a matter of faith. Instead, it should be an opinion about which others disagree. It also should be clear and unambiguous as well as appropriately qualified. Use these criteria—that the position be arguable, clear, and appropriately qualified—to decide how effectively Ehrenreich states her position.
2. Ehrenreich sprinkles her argument with **statistics**. For example, in the opening paragraph, she specifies $14 an hour as the "living wage" that a family of one adult and two children needs. In the same paragraph, she also writes that 60 percent of American workers earn less than this hourly wage. Statistics like these can carry a lot of weight if readers are confident that they come from a reliable source that collects data objectively and professionally. Writers usually cite their sources so that readers can decide for themselves whether the statistics can be believed. For example, if you did a Google search on the Economic Policy Institute, you would find the institute's Web site and learn about EPI's purpose; its corporate, academic, or other affiliations; and its membership. This information could help you judge with some confidence the source's credibility and whether you can count on its statistics.

   Underline the statistics Ehrenreich presents in paragraphs 7 and 8, and put brackets around the sources. Then check Ehrenreich's notes to see what information she gives about each source that could help you determine its credibility.

   (Notice that Ehrenreich does not follow either of the formal styles of documentation, MLA and APA, that are explained in this book; instead she uses a modified form of the *Chicago Manual of Style* system that is often used in books for a general audience. Instead of giving parenthetical citations in the text that are keyed to a list of works cited, she provides notes and does not include a list of works cited. She also does not systematically include page references. When you write a research paper for any of your classes, be sure to ask your instructor what style you should use.)

For more information on citing sources, see Chapter 22.

Commentary: Supporting Examples

In the book from which this selection comes, Ehrenreich has the luxury of space to present extended **examples** to show how particular individuals struggle every day to make ends meet. In this selection from the book's conclusion, however, she needs to make her point quickly with a few brief examples.

Notice how she gives examples in paragraph 3. She provides a list of three examples, and the list is framed by introductory and concluding sentences:

> It is common, among the nonpoor, to think of poverty as a sustainable condition—austere, perhaps, but they get by somehow, don't they? They are "always with us." What is harder for the nonpoor to see is poverty as active distress: The lunch that consists of Doritos or hot dog rolls, leading to faintness before the end of the shift. The "home" that is also a car or a van. The illness or injury that must be "worked through," with gritted teeth, because there's no sick pay or health insurance and the loss of one day's pay will mean no groceries for the next. These experiences are not part of a sustainable lifestyle, even a lifestyle of chronic deprivation and relentless low-level punishment. They are, by almost any standard of subsistence, emergency situations.

This set of examples provides vivid images of the "active distress" Ehrenreich is trying to help her readers to see. Each example refers to a fundamental human need: food, shelter, and health. By emphasizing needs such as these, she reinforces a point she makes at the beginning of her essay: The working poor lack basic necessities, not luxuries. Examples like these help readers to understand what Ehrenreich means by "active distress," and they can also help to convince readers that the problem she is trying to call attention to is serious indeed.

As a writer, you will want to notice not only that Ehrenreich uses examples to support her argument but also that she uses punctuation and sentence structure to present the examples in a way that emphasizes her point:

> What is harder for the nonpoor to see is poverty as active distress: The lunch that. . . . The "home" that. . . . The illness or injury that. . . .

Notice that she introduces the list with a colon, a punctuation mark that often precedes a series of examples. Notice also that Ehrenreich uses the same sentence structure for each example: beginning with *the* and a noun *(lunch, home, illness)* followed by a clause beginning with *that.* By consistently beginning each clause with a noun—*lunch, home,* and *illness*—Ehrenreich focuses readers' attention on the basic necessities that many of the working poor lack, thereby repeatedly stressing the point she is making in the paragraph. You might also note that the examples are not full sentences in themselves but are grammatical because they complete the first part of the sentence ("What is harder . . . is").

When you are writing your own argument, you may want to provide examples for your readers to help them appreciate your point. Following Ehrenreich, try to arrange your sentences in a way that will draw your readers' attention to what you think is most important for them to notice.

Considering Topics for Your Own Essay

You might want to write an essay arguing your own position on the issue that Ehrenreich addresses. If you agree with her that the working poor need help, you might want to argue that the minimum wage should be raised. (The federal minimum wage is currently $5.15 an hour, although some states have higher rates. The minimum wage for employees who earn tips is $2.13 an hour.) Or you might want to argue that citizens should be provided a better social safety net that guarantees quality health care, food stamps, housing subsidies, child care, or other support services. Consider any other social issues you might want to write about. Identify an issue on which you have a position, and think about how you would gather information to construct an argument for your position.

To use the Writing Guide Software to record your ideas, click on
▶ **Journal**

Jonathan Rauch *has been a newspaper reporter for the* Winston-Salem (North Carolina) Journal, *a correspondent for the international magazine the* Economist, *and a columnist for the* National Journal. *His writing now appears in many periodicals, including the* Wall Street Journal, *the* New Republic, Reason Online, *the* Atlantic Monthly, *and* Slate. *Rauch has published four books:* The Outnation: A Search for the Soul of Japan *(1992),* Kindly Inquisitors: The New Attacks on Free Thought *(1993),* Demosclerosis: The Silent Killer of American Government *(1994), and* Government's End: Why Washington Stopped Working *(1999). He has been a writer in residence at the Brookings Institution, a Poynter Fellow, and a Japan Society Fellow, and he was given an award for his coverage of the European Parliament in the* Economist.

Over a two-week period in 2001, Rauch participated with Stanley Kurtz in a multipart debate about same-sex marriage published by National Review Online *(http://www.nationalreview.com/full_coverage/gay-marriage.shtml). The online version of the following essay by Rauch, "Who's More Worthy?," the fifth in the series, has a link in its first sentence to Kurtz's essay "Point of No Return," which had been posted three days earlier. (The full text of Kurtz's essay appears on pp. 283–87.)*

In the final paragraphs of his essay, Rauch refers to various ways that same-sex marriage could be made legal: by congressional legislation; by "plebiscite," which in this context means by a vote of state legislatures to add another amendment to the U.S. Constitution; or by "judicial fiat," which means by a decision of the U.S. Supreme Court in which the justices decide that nothing in the Constitution prohibits same-sex marriage. Rauch also refers to a constitutional amendment that Kurtz favors called the Federal Marriage Amendment, which defines marriage as a union of a man and a woman.

Even though Rauch is writing for a popular online magazine, his vocabulary is rather sophisticated. As you read, look up unfamiliar words in the dictionary, and write their definitions in the margins. For example, in the first paragraph, you may need to look up mandating, liberalism, traduces, *and* federalism.

Who's More Worthy?

Jonathan Rauch

Thanks to Stanley Kurtz for another provocative and richly argued article. Shall we drill a little deeper? If I read him correctly, his argument boils down to something like this: 1

1) Marriage is rooted essentially in "the underlying dynamic of male-female sexuality." Nothing else can sustain marriage.
2) As a result, it is simply impossible for same-sex (especially male-male) couples to be good marital citizens. They may get married, but they won't act married, and society won't treat them as married.
3) Because homosexuals will do a bad job of "exemplifying modern marriage for the nation" and marriage is in bad enough shape already, homosexuals should not be allowed to marry.
4) Allowing same-sex marriage anywhere in America at any time is effectively the same as mandating it everywhere forever. So same-sex marriage must never be tried anywhere, ever. Or, to put it a bit coarsely: "I don't believe homosexuals can handle marriage responsibly. And they should never be allowed a chance to prove me wrong. Sorry, gay people, but that's life."

Kurtzism, as I'll take the liberty of calling this approach, gets four things wrong. It misanalyzes marriage. It misunderstands homosexuality. It sits crosswise with liberalism. And it traduces federalism. Other than that, no problem.

Start with Proposition 1. Kurtz argues that, whatever else marriage is about, ultimately and indispensably it's about "the underlying dynamic of male-female sexuality." I'm not sure exactly what this means beyond saying that marriage must be between a man and a woman, so I'm not sure how to address it specifically. Here is what I think marriage is indispensably about: the commitment to care for another person, for better or worse, in sickness and in health, till death do you part. 2

A marriage can and often does flourish long after the passion has faded, long after the children have gone, and (yes) long after infidelity; it can flourish without children and even without sex. A marriage is a real marriage as long as the spouses continue to affirm that caring for and supporting and comforting each other is the most important task in their lives. A golden anniversary is not a great event because both spouses have held up their end of a "dynamic of male-female sexuality" but because 50 years of devotion is just about the noblest thing that human beings can achieve. 3

I can't prove I'm right and Kurtz is wrong. But I think my view is much closer to what people actually think their marriages are fundamentally about, and also, by the way, to what marriage should be fundamentally about. Most married people I know regard themselves as more or less equal partners in an intricate relationship whose essential ingredient is the lifelong caregiving contract. Obviously, they'd agree that male-female sexual dynamics play an important role in their marriage; but then, they're male-female couples, so they would say that. If you told them that marriage is fundamentally about (in Kurtz's words) "a man's responsibilities to a woman," rather than a person's responsibilities to a person, they'd look at you funny. 4

5 Why is Kurtz so reluctant to put commitment instead of sex roles at the center of marriage? Because, I suspect, he knows homosexuals can form commitments. To cut off this pass, he claims that in practice homosexuals too often won't form commitments (Proposition 2). Same-sex couples, or in any case male same-sex couples, won't act married, and society won't be bothered if they don't, so marriage will become a hollow shell.

6 I've explained why I believe that a world where everyone, straight and gay, can grow up aspiring to marry will be a world where gays and straights and marriage are all better off. Kurtz has explained why he thinks otherwise. All of that is well and good, but it only gets us so far, because the key questions are all empirical. How would married gay couples behave? How would married heterosexuals react? Unfortunately, we have no direct evidence. One can say that in Vermont, which has a civil-union law, "the institution of marriage has not collapsed," as the governor recently said. One can say that gay men (no one seems worried about lesbians not taking marriage seriously) represent probably 3 percent of the population, and that it seems a stretch to insist that the 97 percent will emulate the 3 percent. But none of that proves anything. Absent some actual experience with same-sex marriage, everything is conjecture.

7 Still, I think Kurtz's conjecture is based on a view of homosexuality that is both misguided and at least unintentionally demeaning. His article contains this arresting phrase: "As the ultimate symbol of the detachment of sexuality from reproduction, homosexuality embodies the sixties ethos of sexual self-fulfillment." So there you are. My relationship with my partner Michael is about "sexual self-fulfillment," because, I guess, we can't have children. Let me gently but passionately say to Kurtz that this is an affront. It implies that a straight man's life partner is his wife, while a gay man's life partner is just his squeeze. Let me also gently but firmly instruct Kurtz on a point that I and other homosexuals are in a position to know something about. Our partners are not walking dildos and vibrators. Our partners are our companions, our soulmates, our loves.

8 I'm not familiar with the Stiers book he cites, and I couldn't get it on deadline, so I can't comment on it. I can say, though, that I wouldn't be the least surprised if right now, in 2001, grown gay men and women often regard marriage as a novelty or a convenient benefits package. What does Kurtz expect? These are people who grew up knowing they could never marry, who have structured their whole lives outside of marriage, and who have of necessity built their relationships as alternatives to marriage.

9 I don't expect that homosexuals will all flock to the altar the day after marriage is legalized. You don't take a culture that has been defined forever by exclusion from marriage and expect it to change overnight. I do think that, a few years after legalization, we'll see something new: A whole generation of homosexuals growing up knowing that they can marry, seeing successfully married gay couples out and about, and often being encouraged to marry by their parents and mentors. Making the closet culture the exception rather than the rule for young gay people was the work of one or maybe two generations. The shift to a normative marriage culture may happen just as fast.

10 I know, I know. Kurtz will simply insist that real, committed marriage will never be normative for homosexuals; gays just don't have that "dynamic of male-female sexuality" thing. Unfortunately, I don't think I can persuade him by telling him about all the gay

people I know who have committed their enduring love and care to each other. I doubt I could persuade him even by telling him about all the men I know who have fed and comforted and carried their dying partners, and covered their partners with their bodies to keep them warm, and held their hands at the end and then sobbed and sobbed. Who is more fit to marry, the homosexual who comes home every night to wipe the vomit from the chin of his wasting partner, or the heterosexual who serves his first wife with divorce papers while she is in the hospital with cancer so that he can get on with marrying his second wife? Alas, I think I know what Kurtz would say.

Kurtz cites figures on gay men's fidelity and attitudes toward monogamy. There are lots of problems with these kinds of numbers, but the more interesting question is: Just what does Kurtz think this kind of data proves? Exactly how monogamous do homosexuals have to be in order to earn the right to marry? I'd have thought that being better than 80 percent faithful would be pretty darn good. Would 90 percent satisfy him? Maybe 98.2 percent? And if a group's average fidelity is the qualification for marriage, shouldn't Kurtz let lesbians marry right now? And why are homosexuals the only class of people who are not allowed to marry until they prove, in advance, that they'll be good marital citizens? Last time I checked, heterosexual men were allowed to take a fifth wife, no questions asked, even if they beat their first, abandoned their second, cheated on their third, and attended orgies with their fourth. 11

For centuries, homosexuals have been barred from marrying and even from having open relationships. The message has been: Furtive, underground sex is all homosexuals deserve. And now Kurtz is insisting (Proposition 3) that homosexuals can't wed because we're not as sexually well-behaved as married heterosexuals? While also insisting that, no matter how badly heterosexuals behave, their right to marry will go unquestioned? Really, the gall! 12

Forgive my ill temper on that point. I understand that, to Kurtz and many other Americans, same-sex marriage seems a radical concept, an abuse of the term "marriage." What I think Kurtz and too many other opponents of gay marriage fail to appreciate is the radicalism of telling millions of Americans that they can never marry anybody they love. To be prohibited from taking a spouse is not a minor inconvenience. It is a lacerating deprivation. Marriage, probably more even than voting and owning property and having children, is the core element of aspiration to the good life. Kurtz would deprive all homosexuals of any shot at it lest some of them set a poor example. I think this is both inhumane and cuts against liberalism's core principle, which is that people are to be treated ends in themselves, not as means to some utilitarian social end. I am grateful to Kurtz for leaving the door open to domestic-partnership programs as a consolation prize; this is a good-hearted gesture, and I accept it as such. But surely he recognizes that domestic partnership is no substitute for matrimony. Surely, indeed, that is his point in offering it. 13

Same-sex marriage is too important to be approached thoughtlessly. I'm glad that Kurtz is thinking as strenuously about the possible downsides as I am about the possible upsides. Where he veers toward something like extremism is in his demand that homosexuals be denied any chance to prove his conjectures wrong (Proposition 4). "There is no such thing as an experiment in gay marriage," he says. "Rauch seems to think that if 14 his cost-free portrait of gay marriage turns out to be mistaken, we can simply call off the experiment. But by then it will surely be too late. Such effects take years to play out, decades more to measure, and even when measured, agreement on the meaning of such data is nearly impossible to achieve."

But pretty nearly all major social-policy reforms play out over years and decades, 15
and agreement on how to measure the results is never complete; Kurtz might just as well say that no state should be allowed to try welfare reform or charter schools or a "living wage" because the effects take years to play out, decades to measure, etc. The whole point of federalism is to allow states to try reforms that might not work, and to allow states' voters—not me or Stanley Kurtz—to decide for themselves what counts as working. In rejecting this principle root and branch, Kurtz emerges as a radical enemy not just of same-sex marriage but of federalism itself.

I don't have much new to say about his peculiar claim that, once any state adopts 16
same-sex marriage, every other state will have to follow, because Kurtz doesn't have anything new to say defending it. He simply re-asserts it. "Imagine a married couple, where one spouse is hospitalized after a car accident in another state, losing visiting rights or the right to make medical decisions, because their marriage isn't recognized in that state," he says, as if the situation is obviously untenable. OK, I've imagined it. That kind of arrangement would be perfectly manageable. Gay spouses in a state with same-sex marriage would understand that they will need a medical power of attorney that's valid out-of-state. None of these complexities is remotely thorny enough to force any state to recognize same-sex marriage against its will. It seems to me that what Kurtz really fears is that one state will adopt same-sex marriage and others will look at it and say, "Actually, that doesn't seem so bad—pretty good, even. We don't mind recognizing it even if we don't adopt it ourselves." What he really fears, in other words, is not a disastrous state experiment but a successful one.

Again Kurtz asserts that federal judges will high-handedly impose one state's same- 17
sex marriages on all the others. Again I say that there is—just as he says—plenty of room in the law for determined judges to decide this legal issue either way, but that any sane Supreme Court will be determined not to impose same-sex marriage on an unwilling nation. And if undemocratic judicial fiat is what worries Kurtz, why does he greet with silence my suggestion that a simple constitutional amendment—far easier to pass than the one he supports—would solve the problem?

But all of this stuff about states' being "forced" to accept same-sex marriage is 18
a red herring. Kurtz makes it clear that he is no happier if a state adopts same-sex marriage by legislation or plebiscite than by judicial fiat. His proposed constitutional amendment accordingly strips states, and not just judges, of the power to permit same-sex marriage, even if everybody in some state wants to try it. What I suspect Kurtz really knows and fears is that as more homosexuals form devoted and visible unions, and as more of the public accepts and honors those unions, same-sex marriage will seem ever less strange and radical, and ever more in harmony with Americans' core values—which it is. Although he fears that same-sex marriage will come to pass over the public's objections, he fears even more that it will come to pass with the public's assent.

Connecting to Culture and Experience: Marriage or Living Together

In paragraph 13, Rauch makes an impassioned appeal on behalf of marriage—gay or heterosexual: "To be prohibited from taking a spouse is not a minor inconvenience. It is a lacerating deprivation. Marriage, probably more even than voting and owning property and having children, is the core element of aspiration to the good life." When Rauch says in the same paragraph that "domestic partnership is no substitute for matrimony," he is making an important distinction between marriage and living together.

With two or three other students, discuss your views on marriage. If, like Rauch, you think there is something special about marriage, explain what it is. (Notice that Rauch prefers marriage to living together as an end in itself and not as a way to provide a stable home for children. He also talks about marriage in terms of the commitment of "enduring love and care to each other" (paragraph 10) rather than simply in terms of sexual attraction.

Analyzing Writing Strategies

1. When writers of position essays refer to what others have written on the issue, they use their own words to **summarize** their source's argument or they **quote** the actual language. Often, writers combine summary with quotation, quoting only those words or sentences that seem particularly significant. When writers, like Rauch, try to refute other writers, they have to be especially careful to represent the source accurately and fairly.

   Like Rauch's original *National Review Online* readers, you can easily check his source to see if he has misrepresented Kurtz's argument. Kurtz's essay is reprinted on pages 283–87. Find *one* place where Rauch summarizes or quotes Kurtz, and examine Kurtz's essay to see whether you think Rauch has done a good job of representing the argument. To help you compare the two essays, here is a key that shows where in Kurtz's essay Rauch found the language he summarizes or quotes. You might need to read the surrounding paragraphs in Kurtz's essay to get a complete understanding of the passage:

   - In paragraphs 2 and 4, Rauch refers to Kurtz's paragraph 2.
   - In paragraph 7, Rauch refers to Kurtz's paragraph 7.
   - In paragraph 8, Rauch refers to Kurtz's paragraph 10.
   - In paragraph 11, Rauch refers to Kurtz's paragraph 12.
   - In paragraph 14, Rauch refers to Kurtz's paragraph 13.
   - In paragraph 17, Rauch refers to Kurtz's paragraph 15.

   If Rauch quotes Kurtz, consider what seems significant about the language he chose to quote. If Rauch summarizes Kurtz's language, consider whether the summary captures the gist of Kurtz's argument fairly.

2. To see how Rauch makes his argument, choose *one* of the four points he lists in paragraph 1. Then reread the part of the essay where he counterargues this point:

   Point 1: paragraphs 2–3
   Point 2: paragraphs 4–11

Point 3: paragraphs 12–13
Point 4: paragraphs 14–18

If you completed the preceding analysis task, you have already thought about how well Rauch represents a bit of Kurtz's argument. Your focus now is on the effectiveness of Rauch's **counterargument**. Determine first whether Rauch concedes anything on the point you have chosen. Then look at the way he tries to refute Kurtz's argument on the point. Underline any reasons he gives for disagreeing with Kurtz, and put brackets around any supporting evidence he provides. Make notes about what you find most and least convincing about Rauch's counterargument.

For more on counterarguing, see Chapter 19.

Commentary: Anticipating Opposing Positions and Cueing Readers

When writers successfully counterargue, they nearly always show that they are aware of positions others have taken on the issue; and they respond in some way to these opposing positions as well as to readers' most likely objections to the writer's argument. Writers have three options for **counterarguing**: merely acknowledging other positions and objections, conceding valid points by accommodating or making room for them in their own argument, or trying to refute them.

How writers choose to counterargue depends on their readers and purpose. Writing this essay as part of a continuing debate, Rauch knew that his primary debate opponent, Stanley Kurtz, would scrutinize his every word. He also knew that he and Kurtz respect one another. In an earlier essay, Kurtz had described Rauch as "one of the wisest observers of the Washington scene," who believes that "same-sex marriage is a win-win-win proposition: good for homosexuals, good for heterosexuals, and good for marriage itself" ("Love and Marriage"). Consequently, in this essay, Rauch acknowledges Kurtz's "good-hearted gesture" even as he rejects it (paragraph 13). Although he is polite toward Kurtz, Rauch's primary strategy of counterarguing is to refute Kurtz's argument point by point.

Rauch begins his essay without explaining the issue or his position to readers, whom he can assume have been following the debate. Readers who are just tuning in can figure out by the end of the first paragraph what the issue is and where Rauch and Kurtz stand on the issue. Given this rhetorical situation, it is understandable that Rauch begins his essay by summarizing the four points of Kurtz's argument that he will refute. With this opening paragraph, Rauch **forecasts** for readers the plan of his essay. By repeating the phrase "Proposition 1" in paragraph 2, "Proposition 2" in paragraph 5, "Proposition 3" in paragraph 12, and "Proposition 4" in paragraph 14, Rauch makes it easy for readers to follow each step in his argument.

Rauch also uses certain key words and phrases in the numbered list in paragraph 1 and repeats them later in the essay in the paragraph where he takes up the point. For example, in paragraph 2, he repeats the words that he quotes from Kurtz's essay: "the underlying dynamic of male-female sexuality." Similarly in paragraph 5, referring to Proposition 2, Rauch repeats his own words: "Same-sex couples . . . won't act married." In paragraph 12, where he discusses Proposition 3, however, Rauch does not repeat either his own or Kurtz's language. Instead, he substitutes the phrase "not as sexually well-behaved" to refer to Kurtz's third point that "homosexuals will do a bad job of 'exemplifying modern marriage.'" For the fourth point, Rauch rewords a phrase that he uses in paragraph 1 ("never be allowed a chance to prove me wrong"); in paragraph 14, this phrase becomes "denied any chance to prove his conjectures wrong." When you are planning your own essay, you also may want to use some of these cueing devices to make it easy for readers to follow your argument.

For more information on forecasting, see Chapter 11.

Considering Topics for Your Own Essay

You might want to take your own position on the issue of same-sex marriage, possibly responding to Rauch and Kurtz. If you do further research on this issue, you could begin with the other essays listed at the *National Review Online* Web site (see the headnote to the Rauch essay for its URL). Rauch argues passionately that marriage is far superior to living together. Consider writing an argument on whether to wait until marriage to have sex or whether to move in with someone before or instead of getting married. Other sex- or gender-related issues include whether parental permission or a court's consent should be required before a doctor can give a minor the "abortion pill" RU-486 or perform an abortion, whether prostitution should be legalized or decriminalized, and whether neighbors should be informed when a convicted sex offender moves into a new neighborhood.

To use the Writing Guide Software to record your ideas, click on
▶ **Journal**

Stanley Kurtz *has a Ph.D. in social anthropology, taught in the Great Books program at Harvard, and was a Dewey Prize lecturer in the social sciences at the University of Chicago. He has been a fellow at the Hudson Institute and is currently a research fellow at the Stanford University's Hoover Institution and a contributing editor at* National Review Online. *His essays have also appeared in many periodicals, including the* Wall Street Journal, *the* Weekly Standard, Commentary, *and the* Chronicle of Higher Education.

Point of No Return

Stanley Kurtz

I thank Jonathan Rauch for his thoughtful and courteous 1
reply to my two earlier pieces, "Love and Marriage," and "The Right Balance." I have long admired Rauch's command of this issue (and of other issues) and value this opportunity for an exchange.

Rauch, it seems to me, has missed my central point in "Love and Marriage." It is 2
true that marriage itself, and not merely women and children, domesticates men. But my

point is that marriage is only able to do so by building upon the underlying dynamic of male-female sexuality. Marriage does indeed invoke public expectations of fidelity and mutual support through ritual gestures like weddings. But wedding or no, the public will not condemn a man who sleeps around on another man, or who fails to support his male partner financially. A wedding embodies and reinforces already existing public sentiments about man's responsibilities to a woman; it cannot create such sentiments out of thin air.

In an elegant little essay, "I Do?" David Blankenhorn, shows us why weddings don't always do what they used to do. Blankenhorn focuses on the vogue for ceremonies in which couples create their own vows. In the old view, the vow existed prior to the couple, and therefore embodied a set of public standards to which the couple could be held accountable. But in a world of self-created vows, the couple is prior to the promise, which can be made (or withdrawn) at will. 3

Rauch wants to invent, not merely some vows, but a whole new form of marriage (two actually—gay and lesbian), all the while assuming that the standards and expectations of the most traditional forms of heterosexual marriage will trail along for the ride. But those expectations have been attenuated, even for many heterosexual marriages. And the very same people who now see marriage as a subjective projection, rather than a shared social standard to which to aspire, are the people who favor gay marriage, the idea of which appeals to them precisely as a symbol of the infinite flexibility of social life. Rauch seems to be depending on the Left half of the country to enact gay marriage, while assuming that the Right half will enforce the traditional social expectations on gay couples. Rauch's intentions are admirable, but this simply will not happen. 4

Supporters of gay marriage keep telling us that the sky will not fall. What they do not understand is that, when it comes to marriage, the sky has already fallen. It is lying about our feet, and considerable effort will be required even to hoist it back a few yards over our heads. The trouble with gay marriage is that it forecloses that possibility. Personally, I neither seek, nor think possible, a complete restoration of the traditional system—when the expectations for marriage were so powerful that homosexuals felt compelled to wed heterosexually. 5

But gay marriage is a surpassingly radical attack on the very foundations of marriage itself. It detaches marriage from the distinctive dynamics of heterosexual sexuality, divorces marriage from its intimate connection to the rearing of children, and opens the way to the replacement of marriage by a series of infinitely flexible contractual arrangements. (For more on this last point, see my piece in the September 2000 issue of *Commentary.*) All this can only destroy the finely woven web of social expectations upon which Rauch wishes to depend. As I argued in "Love and Marriage," for example, once marriage has been divorced from heterosexuality, it will be impossible to induce even a partial restoration of traditional courtship. (And by the way, this subversive effect on the sexual complementarity so integral to marriage will derive every bit as much from lesbian marriages as from gay male marriages.) 6

For Rauch, our increased tolerance for homosexuality is of but trivial significance—in comparison with the cultural changes of the sixties and seventies—in bringing about the current weakening of marriage. But the point is, our increased tolerance for homo- 7 sexuality is inextricably bound up with the cultural changes of the sixties—and is by no means trivial in its effects. As the ultimate symbol of the detachment of sexuality from reproduction, homosexuality embodies the sixties ethos of sexual self-fulfillment. That, after all, is why it is such a hot-button issue in the culture wars. So changing social attitudes toward homosexuality cannot help but have a profound effect upon the social and moral significance of sexuality itself.

In the mainstream press, we hear often (and rightly so) from brilliant moderates like Jonathan Rauch. Yet radical gays—the writer Michael Bronski, for example—have argued at length (and correctly) that complete social equivalence between homosexuality and heterosexuality cannot help but undermine social restraints upon sexuality, thus ushering in the final triumph of the sixties ethos. Like Bronski, vast sections of the gay community support gay marriage, not on Rauch's "conservative" grounds, and not even simply as a road to social acceptance, but out of the entirely justified conviction that gay marriage will be a critical step in the undoing of marriage itself. These writings seldom find their way into the *Wall Street Journal,* yet they merit our attention. 8

Rauch claims that the effect of gay marriage on the larger institution is an empirical question. As it happens, we have some very important empirical evidence on the matter—all the more powerful because it was collected by a lesbian sociologist who writes as an advocate of gay marriage. That evidence paints a picture of gay marriage greatly at variance with Rauch's assurances. 9

Gretchen Stiers's 1999 study, *From This Day Forward,* makes it clear that while exceedingly few of even the most committed gay and lesbian couples believe that marriage will strengthen and stabilize their personal relationships, nearly half of those gays and lesbians who actually disdain traditional marriage (and even gay commitment ceremonies) will nonetheless get married. Why? For "the bennies"—the financial and legal benefits of marriage. 10

And as Stiers shows, many radical gays and lesbians who actually yearn to see marriage abolished (and multiple sexual unions legitimized) intend to marry, not only as a way of securing benefits, but as part of a self-conscious attempt to subvert the institution of marriage from within. 11

Stiers's study was focused on the very most committed gay couples. Yet even in a sample artificially weighted with nearly every gay male couple in Massachusetts who had gone through a commitment ceremony (and Stiers had to go out of her research protocol just to find enough male couples to balance out the committed lesbian couples) nearly 20 percent of the men questioned did not practice monogamy. Obviously, in a truly representative sample of gay male couples, that number would be vastly higher. More significantly, a mere 10 percent of even these most committed gay men mentioned monogamy as an important aspect of commitment (necessarily meaning that even many of those men in the sample who had undergone "union ceremonies" failed to identify fidelity with commitment). And these, the very most committed gay male couples, are theoretically the people who will be enforcing marital norms on their gay male peers, and exemplifying modern marriage for the nation. So concerns about the effects of gay marriage on the social ideal of marital monogamy seem more than justified. 12

13 Rauch seems to think that if his cost-free portrait of gay marriage turns out to be mistaken, we can simply call off the experiment. But by then it will surely be too late. Such effects take years to play out, decades more to measure, and even when measured, agreement on the meaning of such data is nearly impossible to achieve. Just think of the battle over the effects of day care. There is no such thing as an experiment in gay marriage. Once legalized, the damage will have been done, and reversal, if possible at all, would take decades.

14 Rauch persists in identifying federalism with variable practices among the states. But federalism is actually a careful balancing of national unity with state diversity. And as I argued in "The Right Balance," federalism has always demanded national commonality in the fundamental definition of marriage. The legal history of marriage demonstrates what should in any case be obvious, that traveling across country and finding out that you are no longer married is an entirely different matter than working up a will or taking a state bar exam. Imagine a married couple, where one spouse is hospitalized after a car accident in another state, losing visiting rights or the right to make medical decisions, because their marriage isn't recognized in that state. If even what was once experienced as the horror of miscegenation could not stand against that, how can we expect judges to sit still for it now?

15 Rauch appears to have abandoned his own and Andrew Sullivan's legal arguments and now rests his assurances on the matter of nationally imposed gay marriage upon a strictly political judgment. Naturally, at the moment, the Supreme Court would be loathe to impose gay marriage. But just wait until the practice is legalized in some state, or states, and the social and political chaos begins. At that point, the Court will take the case, and could easily go either way. (And that's just this Supreme Court. Remember, we're talking about future Supreme Courts as well.) At the time, the conventional wisdom was that the Supreme Court would turn *Bush v. Gore* back to Florida. But the specter of a national crisis goaded the Court into action.

16 So far as I can tell, Jonathan Rauch and Andrew Sullivan have welcomed the imposition of civil unions upon the Vermont state legislature by the Vermont state supreme court. Yet that action, which pretended to find a mandate for gay marriage buried in the state's constitution, was surely one of the most egregious violations of the principles of judicial restraint in this country's history.

17 The Federal Marriage Amendment not only guards against the nationalization of gay marriage by judicial fiat, it also guards against a state judiciary that has cast all democratic restraint to the wind and has taken the right to define and regulate marriage out of the hands of the people. Having broken faith with the principles of democracy, the nation's judiciary has left the public with little recourse.

18 The decision in Vermont was a direct result of a national campaign by gay rights activists to make an end run around legislatures and impose gay marriage upon the country through the courts. So far as I can tell, "conservative" advocates of gay marriage have been acting in concert with that campaign, not calling it to account for its undemocratic excesses. And now we are told to make DOMA constitutional, which would do nothing to prevent judicial usurpations of democracy such as we saw in Vermont.

Anyone awake to this issue understands that there is already a national culture war over the issue of gay marriage. The Federal Marriage Amendment did not start this war. Judicial arrogance in Vermont did that. But as I have argued, the Federal Marriage Amendment, by balancing a national definition of marriage with at least the possibility of differential state-by-state benefits packages, might lead to a workable, if imperfect, solution to this intractable problem. 19

Despite my differences with both Jonathan Rauch and Andrew Sullivan, I greatly admire them both for the brilliance, honor, and tenacity of their fight to legalize same-sex marriage. As I have said publicly, I personally do not see homosexuality as sinful, and do not wish to see a return to the fifties. This battle has an element of tragedy about it, for while I do not believe gay marriage will succeed in domesticating gay men, or even in entirely removing the stigma of homosexuality, I do believe that gay marriage would be received by a stigmatized group as a welcome sign of social approval. But I also believe that the price of that sign is too high—that gay marriage will be a major step in the further unstringing of our most fundamental—and most fundamentally threatened—social institution. And in the end, because we are all children first, gay marriage will hurt all of us far more than it will help. 20

Jessica Statsky *wrote the following essay about children's competitive sports for her college composition course. Before reading, recall your own experiences as an elementary student playing competitive sports, either in or out of school. If you were not actively involved yourself, did you know anyone who was? Looking back, do you think that winning was unduly emphasized? What value was placed on having a good time? On learning to get along with others? On developing athletic skills and confidence?*

To see this essay with pop-up annotations in the software, click on
▶ **Arguing a Position**
▶ **Read**

Children Need to Play, Not Compete

Jessica Statsky

Over the past three decades, organized sports for children have increased dramatically in the United States. And though many adults regard Little League Baseball and Peewee Football as a basic part of childhood, the games are not always joyous ones. When overzealous parents and coaches impose adult standards on children's sports, the result can be activities that are neither satisfying nor beneficial to children. 1

I am concerned about all organized sports activities for children between the ages of six and twelve. The damage I see results from noncontact as well as contact sports, 2 from sports organized locally as well as those organized nationally. Highly organized competitive sports such as Peewee Football and Little League Baseball are too often played to adult standards, which are developmentally inappropriate for children and can be both physically and psychologically harmful. Furthermore, because they eliminate many children from organized sports before they are ready to compete, they are actually counterproductive for developing either future players or fans. Finally, because they emphasize competition and winning, they unfortunately provide occasions for some parents and coaches to place their own fantasies and needs ahead of children's welfare.

One readily understandable danger of overly competitive sports is that they entice children into physical actions that are bad for growing bodies. Although the official Little League Web site acknowledges that children do risk injury playing baseball, they insist that severe injuries are infrequent, "far less than the risk of riding a skateboard, a bicycle, or even the school bus" ("What about My Child?"). Nevertheless, Leonard Koppett in *Sports Illusion, Sports Reality* claims that a twelve-year-old trying to throw a curve ball, for example, may put abnormal strain on developing arm and shoulder muscles, sometimes resulting in lifelong injuries (294). Contact sports like football can be even more hazardous. Thomas Tutko, a psychology professor at San Jose State University and coauthor of the book *Winning Is Everything and Other American Myths,* writes: 3

> I am strongly opposed to young kids playing tackle football. It is not the right stage of development for them to be taught to crash into other kids. Kids under the age of fourteen are not by nature physical. Their main concern is self-preservation. They don't want to meet head on and slam into each other. But tackle football absolutely requires that they try to hit each other as hard as they can. And it is too traumatic for young kids. (qtd. in Tosches A1)

As Tutko indicates, even when children are not injured, fear of being hurt detracts from their enjoyment of the sport. The Little League Web site ranks fear of injury as the seventh of seven reasons children quit ("What about My Child?"). One mother of an eight-year-old Peewee Football player explained, "The kids get so scared. They get hit once and they don't want anything to do with football anymore. They'll sit on the bench and pretend their leg hurts . . ." (qtd. in Tosches). Some children are driven to even more desperate measures. For example, in one Peewee Football game, a reporter watched the following scene as a player took himself out of the game: 4

> "Coach, my tummy hurts. I can't play," he said. The coach told the player to get back onto the field. "There's nothing wrong with your stomach," he said. When the coach turned his head the seven-year-old stuck a finger down his throat and made himself vomit. When the coach turned back, the boy pointed to the ground and told him, "Yes there is, coach. See?" (Tosches A33)

Besides physical hazards and anxieties, competitive sports pose psychological dangers for children. Martin Rablovsky, a former sports editor for the *New York Times,* says that in all his years of watching young children play organized sports, he has noticed very few of them smiling. "I've seen children enjoying a spontaneous prepractice scrimmage become somber and serious when the coach's whistle blows," Rablovsky says. "The spirit of play suddenly disappears, and sport becomes joblike" 5 (qtd. in Coakley 94). The primary goal of a professional athlete—winning—is not appropriate for children. Their goals should be having fun, learning, and being with friends. Although winning does add to the fun, too many adults lose sight of what matters and make winning the most important goal. Several studies have shown that when children are asked whether they would rather be warming the bench on a winning team or playing regularly on a losing team, about 90 percent choose the latter (Smith, Smith, and Smoll 11).

Winning and losing may be an inevitable part of adult life, but they should not be part of childhood. Too much competition too early in life can affect a child's development. Children are easily influenced, and when they sense that their competence and worth are based on their ability to live up to their parents' and coaches' high expectations—and on their ability to win—they can become discouraged and depressed. Little League advises parents to "keep winning in perspective" ("Your Role"), noting that the most common reasons children give for quitting, aside from change in interest, are lack of playing time, failure and fear of failure, disapproval by significant others, and psychological stress ("What about My Child?"). According to Dr. Glyn C. Roberts, a professor of kinesiology at the Institute of Child Behavior and Development at the University of Illinois, 80 to 90 percent of children who play competitive sports at a young age drop out by sixteen (Kutner). 6

This statistic illustrates another reason I oppose competitive sports for children: because they are so highly selective, very few children get to participate. Far too soon, a few children are singled out for their athletic promise, while many others, who may be on the verge of developing the necessary strength and ability, are screened out and discouraged from trying out again. Like adults, children fear failure, and so even those with good physical skills may stay away because they lack self-confidence. Consequently, teams lose many promising players who with some encouragement and experience might have become stars. The problem is that many parent-sponsored, out-of-school programs give more importance to having a winning team than to developing children's physical skills and self-esteem. 7

Indeed, it is no secret that too often scorekeeping, league standings, and the drive to win bring out the worst in adults who are more absorbed in living out their own fantasies than in enhancing the quality of the experience for children (Smith, Smith, and Smoll 9). Recent newspaper articles on children's sports contain plenty of horror stories. *Los Angeles Times* reporter Rich Tosches, for example, tells the story of a brawl among seventy-five parents following a Peewee Football game (A33). As a result of the brawl, which began when a parent from one team confronted a player from the other team, the teams are now thinking of hiring security guards for future games. Another example is provided by an *L.A. Times* editorial about a Little League manager who intimidated the opposing team by setting fire to one of their team's jerseys on the pitching mound before the game began. As the editorial writer commented, the manager showed his young team that "intimidation could substitute for playing well" ("The Bad News"). 8

Although not all parents or coaches behave so inappropriately, the seriousness of the problem is illustrated by the fact that Adelphi University in Garden City, New York, offers a sports psychology workshop for Little League coaches, designed to balance 9 their "animal instincts" with "educational theory" in hopes of reducing the "screaming and hollering," in the words of Harold Weisman, manager of sixteen Little Leagues in New York City (Schmitt). In a three-and-one-half-hour Sunday morning workshop, coaches learn how to make practices more fun, treat injuries, deal with irate parents, and be "more sensitive to their young players' fears, emotional frailties, and need for recognition." Little League is to be credited with recognizing the need for such workshops.

10 Some parents would no doubt argue that children cannot start too soon preparing to live in a competitive free-market economy. After all, secondary schools and colleges require students to compete for grades, and college admission is extremely competitive. And it is perfectly obvious how important competitive skills are in finding a job. Yet the ability to cooperate is also important for success in life. Before children are psychologically ready for competition, maybe we should emphasize cooperation and individual performance in team sports rather than winning.

11 Many people are ready for such an emphasis. In 1988, one New York Little League official who had attended the Adelphi workshop tried to ban scoring from six- to eight-year-olds' games—but parents wouldn't support him (Schmitt). An innovative children's sports program in New York City, City Sports for Kids, emphasizes fitness, self-esteem, and sportsmanship. In this program's basketball games, every member on a team plays at least two of six eight-minute periods. The basket is seven feet from the floor, rather than ten feet, and a player can score a point just by hitting the rim (Bloch). I believe this kind of local program should replace overly competitive programs like Peewee Football and Little League Baseball. As one coach explains, significant improvements can result from a few simple rule changes, such as including every player in the batting order and giving every player, regardless of age or ability, the opportunity to play at least four innings a game (Frank).

12 Authorities have clearly documented the excesses and dangers of many competitive sports programs for children. It would seem that few children benefit from these programs and that those who do would benefit even more from programs emphasizing fitness, cooperation, sportsmanship, and individual performance. Thirteen- and fourteen-year-olds may be eager for competition, but few younger children are. These younger children deserve sports programs designed specifically for their needs and abilities.

Works Cited

Bloch, Gordon B. "Thrill of Victory Is Secondary to Fun." *New York Times* 2 Apr. 1990, late ed.: C12.

"The Bad News Pyromaniacs?" Editorial. *Los Angeles Times* 16 June 1990: B6.

Coakley, Jay J. *Sport in Society: Issues and Controversies.* St. Louis: Mosby, 1982.

Frank, L. "Contributions from Parents and Coaches." Online posting. 8 July 1997. CYB Message Board. 14 May 1999 <http://members.aol.com/JohnHoelter/b-parent.html>.

Koppett, Leonard. *Sports Illusion, Sports Reality.* Boston: Houghton, 1981.

Kutner, Lawrence. "Athletics, through a Child's Eyes." *New York Times* 23 Mar. 1989, late ed.: C8.

Schmitt, Eric. "Psychologists Take Seat on Little League Bench." *New York Times* 14 Mar. 1988, late ed.: B2.

Smith, Nathan, Ronald Smith, and Frank Smoll. *Kidsports: A Survival Guide for Parents.* Reading: Addison, 1983.

Tosches, Rich. "Peewee Football: Is It Time to Blow the Whistle?" *Los Angeles Times* 3 Dec. 1988: A1+.

"What about My Child?" *Little League Online.* Little League Baseball, Incorporated. 1999. 30 June 1999 <http://www.littleleague.org/about/parents/yourchild.htm>.

"Your Role as a Little League Parent." *Little League Online.* Little League Baseball, Incorporated. 1999. 30 June 1999 <http://www.littleleague.org/about/parents/yourrole.htm>.

Connecting to Culture and Experience: Competition versus Cooperation

Statsky makes the point that competition is highly valued in our culture and that cooperation tends to be downplayed. With two or three other students, discuss some of the ways in which schools encourage competition, especially through courses, instruction, and testing; tutoring and counseling; and sports or other activities. Consider also how cooperation is encouraged. Think about whether, in your own experience, the schools you attended encouraged one more than the other.

If you believe that your schools preferred either competition or cooperation, reflect on why they might have done so. Who in society might benefit most from such a preference—men or women, the poor or the middle class or upper class, your school's administrators or teachers or students? Who loses most?

Analyzing Writing Strategies

1. **Anecdotes** can provide convincing support if they are clearly relevant to the point they support, believable, and vivid enough to enable readers to imagine what happened. In paragraph 4, Statsky presents one fully developed anecdote that includes dialogue and a detailed narrative. In paragraph 8, she offers two brief anecdotes that summarize rather than detail the events: One is about a brawl among parents, and the other about a team manager who set fire to a jersey of the opposing team. Locate and reread these anecdotes to find out what each one contributes to Statsky's argument and to judge how convincing they are likely to be for her readers.

For more on using anecdotes and authorities, see Chapter 19.

2. To support her argument, Statsky repeatedly quotes **authorities**, experts who agree with her position. Skim the essay, underlining each authority she cites. Note where she quotes whole sentences or individual words and phrases. Then pick one source you think adds something important to her argument, and briefly explain what it adds.

For more on quoting and summarizing, see Chapter 22.

3. Several times in her argument, Statsky adopts a strategy that is favored by writers taking positions on issues and that you can identify. To analyze two examples of the strategy, underline the second and third sentences of paragraph 1 and the

For more on sentence strategies important to writers taking positions, turn to Sentence Strategies, p. 308.

first sentence of paragraph 9. What do these two examples have in common? Begin by thinking about the relation of the opening "though" and "although" clauses to what follows in the sentences.

4. Read the Writer at Work section on pp. 319–21 to see how Statsky describes her prospective readers and **anticipates opposing positions**. Notice how in her invention work she begins to develop her counterargument with these readers in mind. Take time to compare the relevant paragraphs (5, 10, and 11) in the final revised essay.

For more on counterarguing, see Chapter 19.

Commentary: A Clear Position

Writers arguing a position must state their **position** clearly, but they also try not to overstate it. By avoiding absolute, unconditional language and carefully qualifying her position, Statsky makes clear her concerns without making enthusiasts of competitive sports overly defensive. Throughout the essay, she qualifies with words like *not always, can, maybe,* and *it would seem*—words that potentially have a major effect on readers, making Statsky's position seem reasonable without making her seem indecisive. Similarly, Statsky qualifies her position by focusing on a particular age group. To ensure that readers know the particular kind of sports she is talking about, she gives two familiar examples: Peewee Football and Little League Baseball.

Statsky's unambiguous word choice and appropriate qualification satisfy two of the three requirements for an effective **thesis**. The third requirement, that the position be arguable, is indicated clearly in paragraph 2, where Statsky forecasts the three reasons for opposing organized competitive sports for young children that she develops later in the essay:

1. Such sports are "both physically and psychologically harmful" (developed in paragraphs 3–6)
2. They are "counterproductive for developing either future players or fans" (developed in paragraph 7)
3. They allow adults "to place their own fantasies and needs ahead of children's welfare" (developed in paragraphs 8–9)

Inexperienced writers are sometimes reluctant to state a thesis and forecast their reasons as clearly and directly as Statsky does. They fear that being direct will oversimplify or give away their whole argument. But we can see from Statsky's essay that the effectiveness of her argument is enhanced, not diminished, by her directness. Nor does directness prevent her from advancing a complex and thoughtful argument on an issue that is certain to arouse strong feelings in many readers.

Considering Topics for Your Own Essay

Make a list of issues related to childhood and adolescence. For example, should elementary and secondary schools be on a year-round schedule? Should children have the right to divorce their parents? Should adolescents who commit serious crimes be tried as adults? Then choose an issue that you think you could write about. What position would you take?

To use the Writing Guide Software to record your ideas, click on
▶ **Journal**

PURPOSE AND AUDIENCE

Purpose and audience are closely linked when you write an essay arguing a position. In defining your purpose, you also need to anticipate your readers. Most writers compose essays arguing for a position because they care deeply about the issue. As they develop an argument with their readers in mind, however, writers usually feel challenged to think critically about their own as well as their readers' feelings and thoughts about the issue.

Writers with strong convictions seek to influence their readers. Assuming that logical argument will prevail over prejudice, they try to change readers' minds by presenting compelling reasons and support based on shared values and principles. Nevertheless, they also recognize that in cases where disagreement is profound, it is highly unlikely that a single essay will be able to change readers' minds, no matter how well written it is. When they are addressing an audience that is completely opposed to their position, most writers are satisfied if they can simply win their readers' respect for a different point of view. Often, however, all that they can do is to sharpen the differences.

BASIC FEATURES: ARGUING POSITIONS

A Focused Presentation of the Issue

Writers use a variety of strategies to present the issue and prepare readers for their argument. For current, hotly debated issues, the title may be enough to identify the issue. Estrada's allusion to the familiar children's chant in his title "Sticks and Stones and Sports Team Names" is enough to identify the issue for many readers. Statsky gives a brief history of the debate about competitive sports for children. Many writers provide concrete examples early on to make sure that readers can understand the issue. Statsky mentions Peewee Football and Little League Baseball as examples of the kind of organized sports she opposes. Ehrenreich opens her essay by detailing what would constitute a "living wage," noting how few American workers earn that amount.

How writers present the issue depends on what they assume readers already know and what they want readers to think about the issue. Therefore, they try to define the issue in a way that promotes their position. Estrada defines the issue of naming sports teams after Native Americans in terms of how it affects individuals, especially children, rather than in terms of liberal or conservative politics. Similarly, Ehrenreich presents the issue of a living wage in terms of its practical impact on society, and Rauch presents the issue of same-sex marriage in the context of his heterosexual readers' beliefs about opposite-sex marriage.

A Clear Position

Very often writers declare their position in a thesis statement early in the essay. This strategy has the advantage of letting readers know right away where the writer stands. Statsky places her thesis in the opening paragraph, whereas Estrada puts his in the second paragraph. Moreover, all of the writers in this chapter restate the thesis at places in the argument where readers could lose sight of the central point. And they reiterate the thesis at the end.

In composing a thesis statement, writers try to make their position unambiguous, appropriately qualified, and clearly arguable. For example, to avoid ambiguity, Estrada uses common words like *wrong*. But because readers may differ on what they consider to be wrong, Estrada demonstrates exactly what he thinks is wrong about naming teams for ethnic groups. To show readers he shares their legitimate concerns about hypersensitivity, Estrada qualifies his thesis to apply only to genuine cases of political insensitivity. Finally, to show that his position is not based solely on personal feelings, Estrada appeals to readers' common sense of right and wrong.

Plausible Reasons and Convincing Support

To argue for a position, writers must give reasons. Even in relatively brief essays, writers sometimes give more than one reason and state their reasons explicitly. Estrada, for instance, gives two reasons for his position that naming sports teams for ethnic groups is detrimental: It treats people like team mascots, and it singles out politically weak groups. Statsky gives three reasons for her opposition to competitive sports for children: They are harmful to the children, discourage most from participating, and encourage adults to behave badly.

Writers know they cannot simply assert their reasons. They must support them with examples, statistics, authorities, or anecdotes. We have seen all of these kinds of support used in this chapter. For instance, Statsky uses all of them in her essay—giving examples of common sports injuries that children incur, citing statistics indicating the high percentage of children who drop out of competitive sports, quoting authorities on the physical and psychological hazards of competitive sports for young children, and relating an anecdote of a child vomiting to show the enormous psychological pressure competitive sports put on some children. Ehrenreich depends primarily on examples and statistics to support her position that the working poor are living in a perpetual state of emergency that must be acknowledged and remedied.

Anticipating Opposing Positions and Objections

Writers also try to anticipate other widely held positions on the issue as well as objections and questions readers might raise to an argument. The writers in this chapter counterargue by either accommodating or refuting opposing positions and objections. Estrada does both, implying that he shares his readers' objection to political correctness but arguing that naming sports teams after ethnic groups is a genuine case of political insensitivity and not an instance of hypersensitivity.

Rauch takes up four different objections to his position that had been presented by his debate opponent, Stanley Kurtz, and devotes his argument to refuting them. For each, he first presents Kurtz's objection, summarizing or quoting Kurtz's essay. Then he counterargues briefly, questioning Kurtz's reasoning as well as his fairness.

Anticipating readers' positions and objections can enhance the writer's credibility and strengthen the argument. When readers holding an opposing position recognize that the writer takes their position seriously, they are more likely to listen to what the writer has to say. It can also reassure readers that they share certain important values and attitudes with the writer, building a bridge of common concerns among people who have been separated by difference and antagonism.

GUIDE TO WRITING
Arguing Positions

THE WRITING ASSIGNMENT

THE WRITING ASSIGNMENT

Write an essay on a controversial issue. Learn more about the issue, and take a position on it. Present the issue to readers, and develop an argument for the purpose of confirming, challenging, or changing your readers' views on the issue.

INVENTION AND RESEARCH

INVENTION & RESEARCH

- Finding an Issue to Write About
- Exploring the Issue
- Analyzing Potential Readers
- Testing Your Choice
- Developing Your Argument
- Anticipating Readers' Objections and Questions
- Anticipating Opposing Positions
- Considering Document Design
- Defining Your Purpose for Your Readers
- Formulating a Tentative Thesis Statement

PLANNING AND DRAFTING

PLANNING & DRAFTING

- Seeing What You Have
- Doing Further Research
- Setting Goals
- Outlining
- Drafting

CRITICAL READING GUIDE

CRITICAL READING GUIDE

- First Impression
- Presentation of the Issue
- Clear Statement of the Position
- Reasons and Support
- Treatment of Opposing Positions, Likely Objections
- Effectiveness of Organization
- Final Thoughts

REVISING

REVISING

- Presentation of the Issue
- A Clear Position
- Plausible Reasons and Convincing Support
- Anticipation of Opposing Arguments or Objections
- The Organization

EDITING AND PROOFREADING

EDITING & PROOFREADING

- Checking for Commas before Coordinating Conjunctions
- Checking the Punctuation of Conjunctive Adverbs
- A Common ESL Problem: Subtle Differences in Meaning

GUIDE TO WRITING

THE WRITING ASSIGNMENT

Write an essay on a controversial issue. Learn more about the issue, and take a position on it. Present the issue to readers, and develop an argument for the purpose of confirming, challenging, or changing your readers' views on the issue.

> To use the Writing Guide Software for this assignment, click on
> ▶ **Arguing a Position**
> ▶ **Write**

INVENTION AND RESEARCH

The following activities will help you find an issue, explore what you know about it, and do any necessary research to develop an argument and counterargument. Each activity is easy to do and in most cases takes only a few minutes. Spreading the activities over several days will help you think critically about your own as well as other people's positions on the issue. Keep a written record of your invention and research to use when you draft and revise your essay.

Finding an Issue to Write About

To find the best possible issue for your essay, list as many possibilities as you can. The following activities will help you make a good choice.

Listing Issues. *Make a list of issues you might consider writing about.* Begin your list now, and add to it over the next few days. Include issues on which you already have a position and ones you do not know much about but would like to explore further. Do not overlook the issues suggested by the Considering Topics for Your Own Essay activities following each reading in this chapter.

Put the issues you list in the form of questions, like the following examples:

- Should local school boards be allowed to ban books (like *The Adventures of Huckleberry Finn* and *Of Mice and Men*) from school libraries?
- Should teenagers be required to get their parents' permission to obtain birth-control information and contraceptives?
- Should public libraries and schools be allowed to block access to selected Internet sites?
- Should undercover police officers be permitted to pose as high school students to identify sellers and users of drugs?

- Should training in music performance or art (drawing, painting, sculpting) be required of all high school students?
- Should college admission be based solely on academic achievement in high school?
- Should colleges be required to provide child-care facilities for children of students taking classes?
- Should students attending public colleges be required to pay higher tuition fees if they have been full-time students but do not graduate within four years?
- Should elected state or national representatives vote primarily on the basis of their individual conscience, their constituents' interests, or the general welfare?
- Should scientists attempt to clone human beings as they have done with animals?
- Should more money be directed into research to cure [any disease you want to name]?

Listing Issues Related to Identity and Community. As the following suggestions indicate, many controversial issues will enable you to explore your understanding of identity and community. List issues that interest you.

- Should student athletes be required to maintain a certain grade point average to participate in college sports?
- Should parents be held responsible legally and financially for crimes committed by their children under age eighteen?
- Should students choose a college or courses that would confirm or challenge their beliefs and values?
- Should high schools or colleges require students to perform community service as a condition for graduation?
- Should children of immigrants who do not speak English be taught in their native language while they are learning English?
- Should all materials related to voting, driving, and income-tax reporting be written only in English or in other languages read by members of the community?
- Should the racial, ethnic, or gender makeup of a police force parallel the makeup of the community it serves?

Listing Issues Related to Work and Career. Many current controversial issues will allow you to explore work and career topics. Identify issues that you would consider writing about.

- Should businesses remain loyal to their communities, or should they move to wherever labor costs, taxes, or other conditions are more favorable?
- When they choose careers, should people look primarily for jobs that are well paid or for jobs that are personally fulfilling, morally acceptable, or socially responsible?

- Should the state or federal government provide job training or temporary employment to people who are unemployed but willing to work?
- Should the primary purpose of a college education be job training?
- Should drug testing be mandatory for people in high-risk jobs such as bus drivers, heavy-equipment operators, and airplane pilots?

Choosing an Interesting Issue. *Select an issue from your list that you think would be interesting to explore further.* You may already have an opinion on the issue, or you may have chosen it because you want to learn more about it.

Your choice may be influenced by whether you have time for research or whether your instructor requires you to do research. Issues that have been written about extensively make excellent topics for extended research projects. In contrast, you may feel confident writing about a local community or campus issue without doing much, if any, research.

Exploring the Issue

To explore the issue, you need to define it, determine whether you need to do research, and decide tentatively on your position.

Defining the Issue. *To begin thinking about the issue, write for a few minutes explaining how you currently understand it.* If you have strong feelings about the issue, briefly explain why, but do not try to present your argument at this time. Focus on clarifying the issue by considering questions like these:

- Who has taken a position on this issue, and what positions have they taken?
- How does the issue affect different groups of people? What is at stake for them?
- What is the issue's history? How long has it been an issue? Has it changed over time? What makes it important now?
- How broad is the issue? What other issues are related to it?

Doing Research. *If you do not know very much about the issue or the different views people have taken on it, do some research before continuing.* You can gather information by talking to others and by reading what others have written. Choosing one or two key terms of your issue, look for them in the subject headings of the *Library of Congress Subject Headings* and also in the library catalog, using the keyword search option. The library can also give you access to special online resources; check the library's Web site or ask a librarian for advice. Keep a list of the most promising materials you discover.

If you do not have time for research and lack confidence in your knowledge of the issue, you should switch to another issue about which you are better informed. Return to your list of possible issues, and start over.

Exploring Your Opinion. *Write for a few minutes exploring your current thinking on the issue.* What is your current position? Why do you hold this position? What other positions on the issue do you know about? As you develop your argument and learn more about the issue, you may change your mind. Your aim now is merely to record your thinking as of this moment.

Analyzing Potential Readers

Write several sentences describing the readers to whom you will be addressing your argument. Begin by briefly identifying your readers; then use the following questions to help you describe them.

- What position or positions will my readers take on this issue? How entrenched are these positions likely to be?
- What do my readers know about the issue? In what contexts are they likely to have encountered it? In what ways might the issue affect them personally or professionally?
- How far apart on the issue are my readers and I likely to be? What fundamental differences in worldview or experience might keep us from agreeing? Which of my readers' values might most influence their view of the issue?
- Why would I want to present my argument to these particular readers? What could I realistically hope to achieve—convincing them to adopt my point of view, getting them to reconsider their own position, confirming or challenging some of their underlying beliefs and values?

Testing Your Choice

Decide whether you should proceed with this particular issue. Review your invention notes to see whether you understand the issue well enough to continue working with it and whether you can feel confident that you will be able to construct a convincing argument for your prospective readers. To make these decisions, ask yourself the following questions:

- Have I begun to understand the issue and my own position well enough to begin constructing a well-reasoned, well-supported argument?
- Do I have a good enough sense of how my readers view this issue to begin formulating an argument that is appropriate for them?
- Do I now know enough about the issue, or can I learn what I need to know in the time I have remaining?

If you cannot answer these questions affirmatively at this point in the process, it might be wise to consider a different issue. Giving up on a topic after you have worked on it is bound to be frustrating, but if you have little interest in the issue and do not have any idea how you could address your readers, starting over may be the wisest course of action. The following collaborative activity may help you decide whether to go on with this issue or to begin looking for an alternative.

Testing Your Choice: A Collaborative Activity

At this point in your invention work, you will find it helpful to get together with two or three other students to discuss the issue you have tentatively chosen.

Arguers: In turn, each of you identify the issue you are planning to write about. Explain briefly why you care about it personally and why you think your intended readers might see it as important. Then tell the most important reason that you have taken your position on the issue.

Listeners: Tell the arguer what you know about the issue and what you think makes it worth arguing about. Then try to suggest one thing the arguer could say to make the favored reason most convincing to the intended readers.

Developing Your Argument

To construct a convincing argument, you need to list reasons for your position, choose the most plausible ones, and support them.

Listing Reasons. *Write down every reason you can think of for why you have taken your position.* You can discover reasons for your position by trying to come up with "because" statements—for example, "I believe that my college should provide day care for the young children of full-time students **because these students are most likely to drop out if they cannot count on reliable day care**." Given that few convincing arguments rely on only one reason, try to come up with at least two or three.

Choosing the Most Plausible Reasons. *Write several sentences on each reason to determine which reasons seem most plausible—that is, most likely to be convincing to your particular readers. Then identify your most plausible reasons.* If you decide that none of your reasons seems very plausible, you might need to reconsider your position, do some more research, or choose another issue.

Anticipating Readers' Objections and Questions

To construct a convincing argument, you also need to anticipate and decide how you will counterargue readers' objections and questions.

Listing Your Most Plausible Reasons. *Review the choices you made at the end of the preceding activity, and list your two or three most plausible reasons.*

Listing Objections and Questions. *Under each reason, list one or more objections to or questions about it that readers could raise.* You may know how readers will respond to some of your reasons. For others, you may need to be inventive. Imagining yourself as a critical reader, look for places where your argument is vulnerable to criticism. For example, think of an assumption that you are making that others might not accept or a value others might not share. Imagine how people in different situations—different neighborhoods, occupations, age groups, living arrangements—might react to your argument.

Accommodating a Legitimate Objection or Question. *Choose one objection or question that makes sense to you, and write for a few minutes on how you could accommodate it into your argument.* You may be able simply to acknowledge an objection or answer a question and explain why you think it does not negatively affect your argument. If the criticism is more serious, try not to let it shake your confidence. Instead, consider how you can accommodate it, perhaps by conceding the point and qualifying your position or changing the way you argue for it.

If the criticism seems so damaging that you cannot accommodate it into your argument, however, you may need to rethink your position or even consider writing on a different issue. If you arrive at such an impasse, discuss the problem with your instructor; do not abandon your issue unless it is absolutely necessary.

Refuting an Illegitimate Objection or Question. *Choose one objection or question that seems to challenge or weaken your argument, and write for a few minutes on how you could refute it.* Do not choose to refute only the weakest objection (to make what is sometimes called a **straw-man argument**) while ignoring the strongest one. Consider whether you can show that an objection is based on a misunderstanding or that it does not really damage your argument.

Anticipating Opposing Positions

Now that you have planned your argument and counterargument, you need to consider how you can respond to the arguments for other positions on the issue.

Considering Other Positions. *Identify one or more widely held positions other than your own that people take on the issue.* If you can, identify the individuals or groups who support the positions you list.

Researching Opposing Positions: An Online Activity

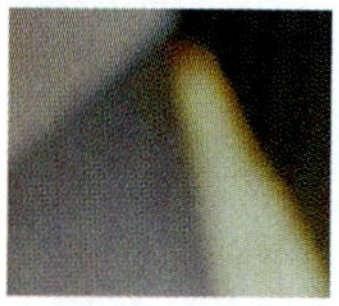

To learn more about opposing positions, search for your issue online. To do so, enter a key term—a word or brief phrase—of your issue into a search tool such as Google (http://www.google.com) or Yahoo! Directory (http://dir.yahoo.com). If possible, identify at least two positions different from your own. No matter how well argued, they need not weaken your confidence in your position. Your purpose is to understand opposing positions so well that you can represent one or more of them accurately and counterargue them effectively.

Bookmark or keep a record of promising sites. Download any materials that may help you represent and counterargue opposing positions.

Listing Reasons for the Opposing Position. *Choose the opposing position you think is likely to be most attractive to your particular readers, and list the reasons people give for it.* Given what you now know, try to represent the argument accurately and fairly. Later, you may need to do some research to find out more about this opposing position.

Accommodating a Plausible Reason. *Choose one reason that makes sense to you, and write for a few minutes on how you could accommodate it into your argument.* Consider whether you can accommodate the point and put it aside as not really damaging to your central argument. You may also have to consider qualifying your position or changing the way you argue for it.

Refuting an Implausible Reason. *Choose one reason that you do not accept, and write for a few minutes on how you will plan your refutation.* Do not choose to refute a position no one really takes seriously. Also be careful not to misrepresent other people's positions or to criticize people personally (sometimes called an **ad hominem attack**). Do try to get at the heart of your disagreement.

You may want to argue that the values on which the opposing argument is based are not widely shared or are just plain wrong. Or perhaps you can point out that the reasoning is flawed (for instance, showing that an example applies only to certain people in certain situations). Or maybe you can show that the argument lacks convincing support (for instance, that the opposition's statistics can be interpreted differently or that quoted authorities do not qualify as experts). If you do not have all the information you need, make a note of what you need and where you might find it. Later, you can do more research to develop this part of your argument.

Considering Document Design

Think about whether including visual or audio elements—cartoons, photographs, tables, graphs, or snippets from films, television programs, or songs—would strengthen your argument. These are not a requirement of an effective essay arguing a position, but they could be helpful. Consider also whether your readers might benefit from design features such as headings, bulleted or numbered lists, or other elements that would make your essay easier to follow. You could construct your own graphic elements, download materials from the Internet, tape images and sounds from television or other sources, or scan into your document visuals from books and magazines. If you do use visual or audio materials you did not create yourself, be sure to acknowledge your sources in your essay (and request permission from the sources if the essay will be posted on the Web).

Defining Your Purpose for Your Readers

Write a few sentences, defining your purpose in writing about your position on this issue for your particular readers. Remember that you already have analyzed your potential readers and developed your argument with these readers in mind. Given these readers, try now to define your purpose by considering the following possibilities and any others that might apply to your writing situation:

- If my readers are likely to be sympathetic to my point of view, what do I hope to achieve—give them reasons to commit to my position, arm them with ammunition to make their own arguments, or win their respect and admiration?
- If my readers are likely to be hostile to my point of view, what do I hope to accomplish—get them to concede that other points of view must be taken seriously, make them defend their reasons, show them how knowledgeable and committed I am to my position, or show them how well I can argue?
- If my readers are likely to take an opposing position but are not staunchly committed to it, what should I try to do—make them think critically about the reasons and the kinds of support they have for their position, give them reasons to change their minds, show them how my position serves their interests better, appeal to their values and sense of responsibility, or disabuse them of their preconceptions and prejudices against my position?

Formulating a Tentative Thesis Statement

Write several sentences that could serve as a thesis statement. Assert your position carefully. You might also forecast your reasons, listing them in the order in which you will take them up in your argument. In other words, draft a thesis statement that tells your readers simply and directly what you want them to think about the issue and why.

Estrada states his thesis at the end of the second paragraph: "Still, however willing I may have been to go along with the name as a kid, as an adult I have concluded that using an ethnic group essentially as a sports mascot is wrong." Perhaps the most explicit and fully developed thesis statement in this chapter's readings is Jessica Statsky's. She asserts her thesis at the end of the first paragraph and then qualifies it and forecasts her reasons in the second paragraph:

> When overzealous parents and coaches impose adult standards on children's sports, the result can be activities that are neither satisfying nor beneficial to children.
>
> I am concerned about all organized sports activities for children between the ages of six and twelve. The damage I see results from noncontact as well as contact sports, from sports organized locally as well as those organized nationally. Highly organized competitive sports such as Peewee Football and Little League Baseball are too often played to adult standards, which are developmentally inappropriate for children and can be both physically and psychologically harmful. Furthermore, because they eliminate many children from organized sports before they are ready to compete, they are actually counterproductive for developing either future players or fans. Finally, because they emphasize competition and winning, they unfortunately provide occasions for some parents and coaches to place their own fantasies and needs ahead of children's welfare.

As you formulate your own tentative thesis statement, pay attention to the language you use. It should be clear and unambiguous, emphatic but appropriately qualified, as well as arguable and based on plausible reasons. Although you will most probably refine this thesis statement as you work on your essay, trying now to articulate it will help give your planning and drafting direction and impetus.

PLANNING AND DRAFTING

You should now review what you have learned about the issue, do further research if necessary, and plan your first draft by setting goals and making an outline.

> If you are using the Writing Guide Software, click on
> ▶ **Planning and Drafting**

Seeing What You Have

Pause now to reflect on your invention and research notes. Reread everything carefully to decide whether you have enough plausible reasons and convincing support to offer readers and whether you understand the debate well enough to anticipate and respond to your readers' likely objections. It may help, as you read, to annotate your invention writings. If you have done your invention writing on the computer, you may have sentences or whole paragraphs that can be copied and pasted into your draft. Reread what you have written so far to identify the potentially useful material. Look for details that will help you clarify the issue for readers, present a strong argument for your position, and counterargue possible objections and alternative positions. Highlight key words, phrases, or sentences; make marginal notes or electronic annotations.

If your invention notes are skimpy, you may not have given enough thought to the issue or know enough at this time to write a convincing argument about it. You can do further research at this stage or begin drafting and later do research to fill in the blanks.

If you fear that you are in over your head, consult your instructor to determine whether you should make a radical change. For example, your instructor might suggest that you tackle a smaller, more doable aspect of the issue, perhaps one with which you have firsthand experience. It is also possible that your instructor will advise you to give up on this topic for the time being and to try writing on a different issue.

Doing Further Research

If you think you lack crucial information that you will need to plan and draft your essay, this is a good time to do some further research. Consider possible sources, including people you could interview as well as library materials and Internet sites. Then do your research, making sure to note down all the information you will need to cite your sources.

Setting Goals

Before you begin writing your draft, consider some specific goals for your essay. The draft will be easier to write and more focused if you have some clear goals in mind. The following questions will help you set them. You may find it useful to return to them while you are drafting, for they are designed to help you look at specific features and strategies of an essay arguing a position on a controversial issue.

Your Purpose and Readers

- Who are my readers, and what can I realistically hope to accomplish by addressing them?
- Should I write primarily to change readers' minds, to get them to consider my arguments seriously, to confirm their opinions, to urge them to do something about the issue, or to accomplish some other purpose?
- How can I present myself so that my readers will consider me informed, knowledgeable, and fair?

The Beginning

- What opening would capture readers' attention?
- Should I begin as if I were telling a story, with phrases like "When I was" (Estrada) or "Over the past three decades" (Statsky)?
- Should I open with a rhetorical question, an arresting quotation, or a surprising statistic? Ehrenreich combines all three in her opening sentences.
- Should I open by summarizing an opposing argument that I will refute, as Rauch does?
- Should I make clear at the outset exactly what my concerns are and how I see the issue, as Statsky does?

Presentation of the Issue

- Should I place the issue in a historical context or in a personal context, as Estrada does?
- Should I use examples—real or hypothetical—to make the issue concrete for readers, as Estrada does?
- Should I try to demonstrate that the issue is important by citing statistics, quoting authorities, or describing its negative effects, as Statsky and Ehrenreich do?

Your Argument and Counterargument

- How can I present my reasons so that readers will see them as plausible, leading logically to my position?
- If I have more than one reason, how should I sequence them?
- Should I forecast my reasons or counterarguments early in the essay, as Statsky and Rauch do?

- Which objections should I anticipate? Can I concede any objections without undermining my argument, as Estrada does?
- Which opposing positions should I anticipate? Can I counterargue by showing that the statistics offered by others are not relevant, as Rauch does? Can I support my position with anecdotes, as Estrada does?

The Ending

- How can I conclude my argument effectively? Should I reiterate my thesis?
- Should I try to unite readers with different allegiances by reminding them of values we share, as Estrada and Ehrenreich do?
- Could I conclude by looking to the future or by urging readers to take action or make changes, as Statsky does?

Outlining

An essay arguing a position on a controversial issue contains as many as four basic parts:

1. Presentation of the issue
2. A clear position
3. Reasons and support
4. Anticipating opposing positions and objections

These parts can be organized in various ways. If you expect some of your readers to oppose your argument, you might try to redefine the issue so that these readers can see the possibility that they may share some common values with you after all. To reinforce your connection to readers, you could go on to concede the wisdom of an aspect of their position before presenting the reasons and support for your position. You would conclude by reiterating the shared values on which you hope to build agreement. In this case, an outline might look like this:

Presentation of the issue
Accommodation of some aspect of an opposing position
Thesis statement
First reason with support
Second reason with support (etc.)
Conclusion

If you have decided to write primarily for readers who agree rather than disagree with you, then you might choose to organize your argument as a refutation of opposing arguments to strengthen your readers' convictions. Begin by presenting the issue, stating your position, and reminding readers of your most plausible reasons. Then take up each opposing argument, and try to refute it. You might conclude by calling your supporters to arms. Here is an outline showing what this kind of essay might look like:

Presentation of the issue
Thesis statement
Your most plausible reasons
First opposing argument with refutation
Second opposing argument with refutation
Conclusion

There are, of course, many other possible ways to organize an essay arguing for a position on a controversial issue, but these outlines should help you start planning your own essay.

Consider tentative any outlining you do before you begin drafting. Never be a slave to an outline. As you draft, you will usually see ways to improve on your original plan. Be ready to revise your outline, shift parts around, or drop or add parts as you draft. If you use the outlining function of your word processing program, changing your outline will be simple, and you may be able to write the essay simply by expanding the outline.

Drafting

General Advice. Start drafting your essay, keeping in mind the goals you set while you were planning. Remember also the needs and expectations of your readers; organize, define, and explain with them in mind. Turn off your grammar checker and spelling checker at this stage if you find them distracting. Don't be afraid to skip around in your draft; jump back and fill in a spontaneous idea, or leap ahead and write a later section first if you find that easier. If, as you draft, you find that you need more information, just make a note of what you have to find out and go on to the next point. When you are done drafting, you can search for the information you need. If you get stuck while drafting, explore the problem by using some of the writing activities in the Invention and Research section of this chapter. You may want to review the general drafting advice in Chapter 1.

As you draft, keep in mind that the basis for disagreement about controversial issues often depends on values as much as on credible support. Try to think critically about the values underlying your own as well as others' views so that your argument can take these values into account. Consider the tone of your argument and how you want to come across to readers.

Sentence Strategies. As you draft, you will need to move back and forth smoothly between direct arguments for your position and counterarguments for your readers' likely objections, questions, and preferred positions on the issue. One useful strategy for making this move is to concede the value of a likely criticism and then to attempt to refute it immediately, either in the same sentence or in the next one. You will also need to use conjunctions and similar phrases to indicate explicitly and precisely the logical relationships between your sentences.

Counterargue by conceding and then immediately refuting. How do you introduce brief concession followed by refutation into your argument? The following sentences from Jessica Statsky's essay illustrate several ways to do so (the concessions are in italics, the refutations in bold):

> The primary goal of professional athletes—winning—is not appropriate for children. Their goals should be having fun, learning, and being with friends. *Although winning does add to the fun,* **too many adults lose sight of what matters and make winning the most important goal.** (paragraph 5)

> *And it is perfectly obvious how important competitive skills are in finding a job.* **Yet the ability to cooperate is also important for success in life.** (10)

In both these examples from different stages in her argument, Statsky concedes the importance or value of some of her readers' likely objections, but then firmly refutes them. (Because these illustrations are woven into an extended argument, you may be better able to appreciate them if you look at them in context by turning to the paragraphs where they appear.) The following examples come from other readings in the chapter:

> *Guilt, you may be thinking warily. Isn't that what we're supposed to feel?* **But guilt doesn't go anywhere near far enough; the appropriate emotion is shame. . . .** (Barbara Ehrenreich, paragraph 10)

> *I'm glad that Kurtz is thinking as strenuously about the possible downsides as I am about the possible upsides.* **Where he veers toward something like extremism is in his demand that homosexuals be denied any chance to prove his conjectures wrong. . . .** (Jonathan Rauch, paragraph 14)

This important counterargument strategy sometimes begins not with concession but with acknowledgment; that is, the writer simply accurately restates part of an opponent's argument without conceding the wisdom of it. Here is an example:

> *Supporters of gay marriage keep telling us that the sky will not fall.* **What they do not understand is that, when it comes to marriage, the sky has already fallen.** (Stanley Kurtz, paragraph 5)

The concession-refutation move, sometimes called the "yes-but" strategy, is important in most arguments; in fact, it usually recurs, as it does in all the readings in this chapter. Following is an outline of some of the other language this chapter's authors rely on to introduce their concession-refutation moves:

Introducing the concession	*Introducing the refutation that follows*
I understand that	What I think is
I can't prove	But I think
I am grateful	But surely
Rauch claims that	As it happens
It is true that	But my point is
Another argument	But

And it is not difficult to imagine other concession-refutation pairings:

It has been argued that	Nevertheless,
We are told that	My own belief is
Proponents argue that	This argument, however,
This argument seems plausible	But experience and evidence show
One common complaint is	In recent years, however,
I'm not saying. . . . Nor am I saying	But I am saying
Activists insist	Still, in spite of their good intentions
A reader might ask	But the real issue

For more on using concession-refutation sentences in position papers, go to bedfordstmartins.com/theguide and click on Sentence Strategies.

Use conjunctions and phrases like them to indicate explicitly and precisely the logical relationships between clauses and sentences. In all writing, conjunctions serve to indicate the specific ways that clauses and sentences relate in meaning to each other, but reasoned arguments are especially dependent on these logical links. There are three main types of conjunctions: coordinating conjunctions like *and, but,* or *so;* subordinating conjunctions like *while, because,* and *although;* and, of special importance in arguments taking a position, conjunctive adverbs like *furthermore, consequently, however, nevertheless,* and *therefore.* Here is an example from a reading in this chapter, with the conjunctive adverb in italics:

> Highly organized competitive sports such as Peewee Football and Little League Baseball are too often played to adult standards, which are developmentally inappropriate for children and can be both physically and psychologically harmful. *Furthermore,* because they eliminate many children from organized sports before they are ready to compete, they are actually counterproductive for developing either future players or fans. (Jessica Statsky, paragraph 2)

Statsky chooses the conjunctive adverb *furthermore* because in the previous sentence she has given one reason that she opposes highly competitive organized sports for children and she wants readers to understand that she is about to give another one. In this situation, she might also have chosen *moreover, in addition,* or *at the same time.*

Now look at this example:

> Like adults, children fear failure, *and so* even those with good physical skills may stay away because they lack self-confidence. *Consequently,* teams lose many promising players who with some encouragement and experience might have become stars. (Jessica Statsky, paragraph 7)

Here Statsky uses *and so* to link the two main clauses in the first sentence and the conjunctive adverb *consequently* to link the second sentence to the first. In both cases, she is arguing that what comes after the conjunction is an unfortunate effect or consequence of what comes before it: Fear of failure causes staying away, which in turn causes the loss of promising players. Instead of *consequently,* she might have chosen *therefore, as a result,* or *in effect* to make this logical relationship explicit.

Notice that conjunctive adverbs seem somewhat formal. This level of formality would be appropriate in most arguments taking positions on public issues. Should you be writing for a familiar audience of peers or a publication aimed at a popular audience, however, you might want to adopt less formal conjunctions or phrases for indicating logical relationships between your clauses and sentences. For example, you could use *but* instead of *however, and* or *in addition* instead of *moreover, still* for *nevertheless,* or *so* instead of *consequently.* In this chapter's readings, the writers Barbara Ehrenreich and Stanley Kurtz consistently use informal conjunctions, Jessica Statsky mostly uses formal ones, and Jonathan Rauch mixes the two.

You might find the following list helpful when you are searching for precisely the right conjunctive adverb or phrase for the logical relationship you want to signal. If you are unsure about which one to choose, look up the most likely one in a dictionary or, better, a dictionary of synonyms. Keep in mind that these useful expressions serve only to *signal* a logical relationship; they cannot *create* such a relationship, which is determined by the content of the clauses or sentences they join. Your readers will not necessarily see the similarities between two things, for example, just because you have joined them with *similarly.*

To expand or add: *moreover, further, furthermore, in addition, at the same time, in the same way, by the same token, that is, likewise*

To reformulate or replace: *in other words, better, rather, again, alternatively, on the other hand*

To exemplify: *for example, as an example, thus, for instance*

To qualify: *however, nevertheless, on the other hand, at the same time*

To dismiss: *in any case, in either case, whichever way it is, anyhow, at any rate, however it is*

To show cause or effect: *therefore, consequently, as a result, in effect, for this reason, otherwise, in that case, accordingly, hence, thus*

To show comparison: *in comparison, by comparison, in the same way, similarly, likewise, in the same way*

To show contrast: *instead, on the contrary, rather, by contrast, in opposition, on the other hand*

To show emphasis: *indeed, again*

For more on using conjunctive adverbs for signaling logical relationships, go to bedfordstmartins.com/theguide and click on Sentence Strategies.

In addition to making the concession-refutation move and using conjunctions to signal logical relationships, you can strengthen your reasoned arguments with other kinds of sentence strategies as well, and you may want to study the discussions of sentences that feature appositives to identify or establish the authority of a source (pp. 246–47), signal the stages of an argument (pp. 490–91), and present supporting examples in parallel grammatical form (p. 491).

CRITICAL READING GUIDE

Now is the time to get a good critical reading of your draft. Your instructor may arrange such a reading as part of your coursework; if not, you can ask a classmate, friend, or family member to read it over. If your campus has a writing center, you might ask a tutor there to read and comment on your draft using this guide to critical reading. (If you are unable to have someone else review your draft, turn ahead to the Revising section for help reading your own draft with a critical eye.)

If you are using the Writing Guide Software, click on
▶ **Critical Reading Guide**

Making Comments Electronically
Most word processing software offers features that allow you to insert comments directly into the text of someone else's document. Many readers prefer to make their comments in this way because it tends to be faster than writing on a hard copy and space is virtually unlimited; from the writer's point of view, it also eliminates the problem of deciphering handwritten comments. Even where such special comment features are not available, simply typing comments directly into a document in a contrasting color can provide the same advantages.

▶ **If You Are the Writer.** To provide focused, helpful comments, your critical reader must know your essay's intended audience, your purpose, and a problem in the draft that you need help solving. Briefly write out this information at the top of your draft.

- ***Readers:*** To whom are you directing your argument? What do you assume they think about this issue? Do you expect them to be receptive, skeptical, resistant, antagonistic?
- ***Purpose:*** What effect do you realistically expect your argument to have on these particular readers?
- ***Problem:*** Ask your reader to help you solve the most important problem you see in your draft. Describe this problem briefly.

▶ **If You Are the Reader.** Use the following guidelines to help you give constructive, critical comments to others on their position papers.

1. ***Read for a First Impression.*** Tell the writer what you think the intended readers would find most and least convincing. If you personally think the argument is seriously flawed, share your thoughts. Then try to help the writer improve the argument for the designated readers.

   Next, consider the problem the writer identified, and respond briefly to that concern now. (If you find that the problem is covered by one of the other guidelines listed below, respond to it in more detail there if necessary.)
2. ***Analyze the Way the Issue Is Presented.*** Look at the way the issue is presented, and indicate whether you think that most readers would understand the issue differently. If you think that readers will need more information to grasp the issue and appreciate its importance, ask questions to help the writer fill in whatever is missing.
3. ***Assess Whether the Position Is Stated Clearly.*** Write a sentence or two summarizing the writer's position as you understand it from reading the draft. Then identify the sentence or sentences in the draft where the thesis is stated explicitly. (It may be restated in several places.) If you cannot find an explicit statement of

the thesis, let the writer know. Given the writer's purpose and audience, consider whether the thesis statement is too strident or too timid and whether it needs to be more qualified, more sharply focused, or more confidently asserted. If you think that the thesis, as presented, is not really arguable—for example, if it asserts a fact no one questions or a matter of personal belief—let the writer know.

4. ***Evaluate the Reasons and Support.*** Identify the reasons given for the writer's position. Have any important reasons been left out or any weak ones overemphasized? Indicate any contradictions or gaps in the argument. Point to any reasons that do not seem plausible to you, and briefly explain why. Then note any places where support is lacking or unconvincing. Help the writer think of additional support or suggest sources where more or better support might be found.
5. ***Assess How Well Opposing Positions and Likely Objections Have Been Handled.*** Identify places where opposing arguments or objections are mentioned, and point to any where the refutation could be strengthened or where shared assumptions or values offer the potential for accommodation. Also consider whether the writer has ignored any important opposing arguments or objections.
6. ***Consider Whether the Organization Is Effective.*** Get an overview of the essay's organization, perhaps by making a scratch outline. Point to any parts that might be more effective earlier or later in the essay. Point out any places where more explicit cueing—transitions, summaries, or topic sentences—would clarify the relationship between parts of the essay.
   - Reread the *beginning.* Will readers find it engaging? If not, see whether you can recommend something from later in the essay that might work better as an opening.
   - Study the *ending.* Does the essay conclude decisively and memorably? If not, suggest an alternative. Could something be moved to the end?
   - Assess the *design features and visuals.* Comment on the contribution of any headings, tables, or other design features and illustrations. Help the writer think of additional design features and illustrations that could make a contribution to the essay.
7. ***Give the Writer Your Final Thoughts.*** What is this draft's strongest part? What part is most in need of further work?

REVISING

Now you are ready to revise your essay. Your instructor or other students may have given you advice on improving your draft. Nevertheless, you may have begun to realize that your draft requires not so much revising as rethinking. For example, you may recognize that your reasons do not lead readers to accept your position, that you cannot adequately support your reasons, or that you have been unable to refute damaging objections to your argument. Consequently, instead of working to improve parts of the draft, you may need to write a new draft that radically reenvisions your argument. It is not unusual for students—and professional writers—to find themselves in this situation. Learning to make radical revisions is a valuable lesson for all writers.

On the other hand, you may feel quite satisfied that your draft achieves most, if not all, of your goals. In that case, you can focus on refining specific parts of your draft. Very likely you have thought of ways of improving your draft, and you may even have begun improving it. This section will help you get an overview of your draft and revise it accordingly.

If you are using the Writing Guide Software, click on
▶ **Revising**

Getting an Overview

Consider your draft as a whole, following these two steps:

1. ***Reread.*** If at all possible, put the draft aside for a day or two before rereading it. When you return to it, start by reconsidering your purpose. Then read the draft straight through, trying to see it as your intended readers will.
2. ***Outline.*** Make a scratch outline, indicating the basic features as they appear in the draft. Consider using the headings and outline/summary functions of your word processor.

Planning for Revision. Resist the temptation to dive in and start changing your text until after you have a clear view of the big picture. Using your outline as a guide, move through the document, using the highlighting or commenting tools of your word processor to note comments received from others and problems you want to solve (or mark on a hard copy if you prefer).

Analyzing the Basic Features of Your Own Draft. Using the questions presented in the Critical Reading Guide on pp. 312–13, reread your draft to identify specific problems you need to solve. Note the problems on your draft.

Studying Critical Comments. Review all of the comments you have received from other readers, and add to your notes any suggestions you intend to act on. For each comment, look at the draft to see what might have led the reader to make that particular point. Try to be receptive to any criticism. By letting you see how other readers respond to your draft, these comments provide valuable information about how you might improve it.

Carrying Out Revisions

Having identified problems in your draft, you now need to come up with solutions and—most important—to carry them out. Basically, you have three ways of finding solutions:

1. Review your invention and planning notes for information and ideas to add to your draft.
2. Do additional invention and research to provide material you or your readers think is needed.
3. Look back at the readings in this chapter to see how other writers have solved similar problems.

The following suggestions, which are organized according to the basic features of position papers, will help you get started solving some problems common to them.

Presentation of the Issue

- ***Do readers have difficulty summarizing the issue, or do they see it differently from the way you do?*** Try to anticipate possible misunderstandings or other ways of seeing the issue.
- ***Do readers need more information?*** Consider adding examples, quoting authorities, or simply explaining the issue further.
- ***Does the issue strike readers as unimportant?*** State explicitly why you think it is important and why you think your readers should think so, too. Try to provide an anecdote, facts, or a quote from an authority that would demonstrate its importance.

A Clear Position

- ***Do readers have difficulty summarizing your position or finding your thesis statement?*** You may need to announce your thesis statement more explicitly or rewrite it to prevent misunderstanding.
- ***Do any words seem unclear or ambiguous?*** Use other words, explain what you mean, or add an example to make your position more concrete.
- ***Do you appear to be taking a position that is not really arguable?*** Consider whether your position is arguable. If you believe in your position as a matter of faith and cannot provide reasons and support, then your position probably is not arguable. Consult your instructor about changing your position or topic.
- ***Could you qualify your thesis to account for exceptions or strong objections to your argument?*** Add language that specifies when, where, under what conditions, or for whom your position applies.

Plausible Reasons and Convincing Support

- ***Do readers have difficulty identifying your reasons?*** Announce each reason explicitly, possibly with topic sentences. Consider adding a forecast early in the essay so readers know what reasons to expect.
- ***Have you left out any reasons?*** Consider whether adding particular reasons would strengthen your argument. To fit in new reasons, you may have to reorganize your whole argument.

- ***Do any of your reasons seem implausible or contradictory?*** Either delete such reasons, or show how they relate logically to your position or to your other reasons.
- ***Does your support seem unconvincing or scanty?*** Where necessary, explain why you think the support should lead readers to accept your position. Review your invention notes, or do some more research to gather additional examples, statistics, anecdotes, or quotations from authorities.

Anticipation of Opposing Arguments or Objections

- ***Do readers have difficulty finding your responses to opposing arguments or objections?*** Add transitions that call readers' attention to each response.
- ***Do you ignore any important objections or arguments?*** Consider adding to your response. Determine whether you should replace a response to a relatively weak objection with a new response to a more important one.
- ***Are there any concessions you could make?*** Consider whether you should acknowledge the legitimacy of readers' concerns or accommodate particular objections. Show on what points you share readers' values, even though you may disagree on other points. Remember that all of the authors in this chapter concede and then attempt to refute, relying on useful sentence openers like *I understand that, What I think is,* and *It is true that . . ., but my point is. . . .*
- ***Do any of your attempts at refutation seem unconvincing?*** Try to strengthen them. Avoid attacking your opponents. Instead, provide solid support—respected authorities, accepted facts, and statistics from reputable sources—to convince readers that your argument is credible.

Checking Sentence Strategies Electronically
To check your draft for a sentence strategy especially useful in essays arguing a position, use your word processor's highlighting function to mark places where you are either making concessions to or trying to refute opposing arguments or objections that readers might have to your argument. Then look at each place, and think about whether you could strengthen your argument at that point by combining concession and refutation, either by moving or adding a concession just before a refutation or by moving or adding a refutation immediately following a concession. For more on the concession-refutation strategy, see p. 309.

The Organization

- ***Do readers have trouble following your argument?*** Consider adding a brief forecast of your main reasons at the beginning of your essay and adding explicit topic sentences and transitions to announce each reason as it is developed. As all the authors do in this chapter, consider signaling explicitly the logical relations between steps and sentences in your argument. Remember that they use both informal signals like *yet* and *still* and formal signals like *moreover, consequently,* and *therefore.*
- ***Does the beginning seem vague and uninteresting?*** Consider adding a striking anecdote or surprising quotation to open the essay, or find something in the essay you could move to the beginning.
- ***Does the ending seem indecisive or abrupt?*** Search your invention notes for a strong quotation, or add language that will reach out to readers. Try moving your strongest point to the ending.
- ***Can you add illustrations or any other design features to make the essay more interesting to read and to strengthen your argument?*** Consider incorporating a visual you came across in your research or one you can create on your own.

EDITING AND PROOFREADING

Now is the time to edit your revised draft for errors in grammar, punctuation, and mechanics and to consider matters of style. Our research has revealed several errors that are especially likely to occur in student essays arguing a position. The following guidelines will help you check and edit your draft for these common errors. This book's Web site also provides interactive online exercises to help you learn to identify and correct some of these errors; to access the exercises for a particular error, go to the URL listed in the margin next to that section of the guidelines.

A Note on Grammar and Spelling Checkers
These tools are good at catching certain types of errors, but currently there's no replacement for a good human proofreader. Grammar checkers in particular are extremely limited in what they can usually find, and often they only give you summary information that isn't helpful if you don't already understand the rule in question. They are also prone to give faulty advice for fixing problems and to flag correct items as wrong. Spelling checkers cause fewer problems but can't catch misspellings that are themselves words, such as *to* for *too*.

The Writing Guide Software gives you quick access to specific editing advice when you reach this stage of an essay. At the top of the right-hand toolbar is a button labeled "This Stage." If you click on the Help link, the software will show you a list of errors especially common in the type of essay you are writing. Just click on an error to see an explanation and examples.

Checking for Commas before Coordinating Conjunctions

An independent clause is a group of words that can stand alone as a complete sentence. Writers often join two or more such clauses with coordinating conjunctions (*and, but, for, or, nor, so, yet*) to link related ideas in one sentence.

The new immigration laws will bring in more skilled people but their presence will take jobs away from other Americans.

In this sentence, *but* is a coordinating conjunction that joins two independent clauses. When you join independent clauses, use a comma before the coordinating conjunction. For clarity in this sentence, insert a comma between *people* and *but*.

The new immigration laws will bring in more skilled people but their presence will take jobs away from other Americans.

In this sentence, *but* is a coordinating conjunction

Checking for Commas before Coordinating Conjunctions. An indep clause is a group of words that can stand alone as a complete sentence. Writ ca join two or more such clauses with coordinating conjunctions *(and, but,* *so, yet)* to link related ideas in one sentence. Look at one example Statsky's essay:

> Winning and losing may be an inevitable part of adult life, but they should not be part of childhood. (paragraph 6)

In this sentence, Statsky links two ideas: (1) that winning and losing may be part of adult life and (2) that they should not be part of childhood. In essays that argue a position, writers often join ideas in this way as they set forth the reasons and support for their positions.

When you join independent clauses, use a comma before the coordinating conjunction so that readers can easily see where one idea stops and the next one starts:

- ▶ **The new immigration laws will bring in more skilled people, but their presence will take jobs away from other Americans.**
- ▶ **Sexually transmitted diseases are widespread, and many students are sexually active.**

For practice, go to bedfordstmartins.com/theguide/comma and bedfordstmartins.com/theguide/uncomma.

Do not use a comma when the coordinating conjunction joins phrases that are not independent clauses:

- ▶ **Newspaper reporters have visited pharmacies~~,~~ and observed pharmacists selling steroids illegally.**
- ▶ **We need people with special talents~~,~~ and diverse skills to make the United States a stronger nation.**

Checking the Punctuation of Conjunctive Adverbs. When writers take a position, the reasoning they need to employ seems to invite the use of conjunctive adverbs (*consequently, furthermore, however, moreover, therefore, thus*) to connect sentences and clauses. Conjunctive adverbs that open a sentence should be followed by a comma:

- ▶ **Consequently, many local governments have banned smoking.**
- ▶ **Therefore, talented nurses will leave the profession because of poor working conditions and low salaries.**

For practice, go to bedfordstmartins.com/theguide/comma, bedfordstmartins.com/theguide/uncomma, and bedfordstmartins.com/theguide/semi.

If a conjunctive adverb joins two independent clauses, it must be preceded by a semicolon and followed by a comma:

- ▶ **The recent vote on increasing student fees produced a disappointing turnout~~,~~; moreover, the presence of campaign literature on ballot tables violated voting procedures.**
- **...ildren watching television recognize violence but not its intention; thus, ...become desensitized to violence.**

Conjunctive adverbs that fall in the middle of an independent clause are set off with commas:

▶ **Due to trade restrictions, however, sales of Japanese cars did not surpass sales of domestic cars.**

A Common ESL Problem: Subtle Differences in Meaning. Because the distinctions in meaning among some common conjunctive adverbs are subtle, nonnative speakers often have difficulty using them accurately. For example, the difference between *however* and *nevertheless* is small; each is used to introduce statements that contrast with what precedes it. But *nevertheless* emphasizes the contrast, whereas *however* softens it. Check usage of such terms in an English dictionary rather than a bilingual one. *The American Heritage Dictionary of the English Language* has special usage notes to help distinguish frequently confused words.

A WRITER AT WORK

ANTICIPATING OBJECTIONS

In this section, we look at how Jessica Statsky tried to anticipate opposing positions and respond to them.

To understand Statsky's thinking about her possible counterargument, look first at the invention writing she did while analyzing her potential readers.

> I think I will write mainly to parents who are considering letting their children get involved in competitive sports and to those whose children are already on teams and who don't know about the possible dangers. Parents who are really into competition and winning probably couldn't be swayed by my arguments anyway. I don't know how to reach coaches (but aren't they also parents?) or league organizers. I'll tell parents some horror stories and present solid evidence from psychologists that competitive sports can really harm children under the age of twelve. I think they'll be impressed with this scientific evidence.
>
> I share with parents one important value: the best interests of children. Competition really works against children's best interests. Maybe parents' magazines (don't know of any specific ones) publish essays like mine.

Notice that Statsky listed three potential groups of readers—parents, coaches, and league organizers. In her essay, she addressed concerns of coaches and organizers, but she focused primarily on parents. She divided parents into two camps: those who are new to organized sports and unaware of the adverse effects of competition and those who are really into winning. Statsky decided against trying to change the minds of parents who place great value on winning. But as you will see in the next excerpt from her invention writing, Statsky gave a lot of thought to the position these parents would likely favor.

Listing Reasons for the Opposing Position

Statsky lists the following reasons for the position that organized competitive sports teach young children valuable skills:

```
--Because competition teaches children how to succeed in later
  life
--Because competition--especially winning--is fun
--Because competition boosts children's self-esteem
--Because competition gives children an incentive to excel
```

This list appears to pose serious challenges to Statsky's argument, but she benefits considerably before she drafts her essay by considering the reasons her readers might give for opposing her position. By preparing this list, she gains insight into how she must develop her own argument in light of these predictable arguments, and she can begin thinking about which reasons she might accommodate and which she must refute. Her essay ultimately gains authority because she can demonstrate a good understanding of the opposing arguments that might be offered by her primary readers—parents who have not considered the dangers of competition for young children.

Accommodating a Plausible Reason

Looking over her list of reasons, Statsky decides that she can accommodate readers by conceding that competitive sports can sometimes be fun for children—at least for those who win. Here are her invention notes:

```
     It is true that children do sometimes enjoy getting
prizes and being recognized as winners in competitions adults
set up for them. I remember feeling very excited when our
sixth-grade relay team won a race at our school's sports day.
And I felt really good when I would occasionally win the candy
bar for being the last one standing in classroom spelling con-
```

tests. But when I think about these events, it's the activity itself I remember as the main fun, not the winning. I think I can concede that winning is exciting to six- to twelve-year-olds, while arguing that it's not as important as adults might think. I hope this will win me some friends among readers who are undecided about my position.

We can see this accommodation in paragraph 5 of Statsky's revised essay (p. 288), where she concedes that sports should be fun. She quotes an authority who argues even fun is jeopardized when competition becomes intense.

Refuting an Implausible Reason

Statsky recognizes that she must attempt to refute the other objections in her list. She chooses one and tries out the following refutation to the first reason in her list:

It irritates me that adults are so eager to make first and second graders go into training for getting and keeping jobs as adults. I don't see why the pressures on adults need to be put on children. Anyway, both my parents tell me that in their jobs, cooperation and teamwork are keys to success. You can't get ahead unless you're effective in working with others. Maybe we should be training children and even high school and college students in the skills necessary for cooperation, rather than competition. Sports and physical activity are important for children, but elementary schools should emphasize achievement rather than competition--race against the clock rather than against each other. Rewards could be given for gains in speed or strength instead of for defeating somebody in a competition.

This brief invention activity leads to the argument in paragraph 10 of the revised essay (p. 290), where Statsky acknowledges the importance of competition for success in school and work, but goes on to argue that cooperation is also important. To support this part of her argument, she gives examples in paragraph 11 of sports programs that emphasize cooperation over competition.

You can see from Statsky's revised essay that her refutation of this opposing argument runs through her entire essay. These invention activities advanced her thinking about her readers and purpose; they also brought an early, productive focus to her research on competition in children's sports.

DESIGNING YOUR WORK

In her essay arguing that the glass ceiling still exists for women in the corporate world (see the business course project described on p. 262), the student includes pie charts and a table comparing the percentages of women and men at the highest levels of corporate America. She decides to reinforce her written argument with the graphics because she believes her readers may have difficulty absorbing information from text that is densely packed with numerical data.

First, she considers downloading visuals from the Federal Glass Ceiling Commission Report (http://www.ilr.cornell.edu/library/e_archive/glassceiling/Executive Summary.pdf) but decides that its 1991 publication date makes its statistics too outdated. Then she tries the Catalyst Web site (http://www.catalystwomen.org), only to discover that she cannot access the report she's interested in without purchasing it. Eventually, she locates an article in *Business Week* (November 22, 1999) with several easy-to-read pie charts and tables.

She decides to include *Business Week*'s three pie charts showing the percentages of female and male corporate officers, corporate officers with line jobs, and top earners. The charts are simple because each compares only two items, women and men. But because she thinks the color helps readers easily distinguish between the two groups, she decides to make color photocopies at her local copy shop. Even though her essay acknowledges there has been some improvement in the representation of women in the corporate world, she keeps the title *Business Week* gave the charts because

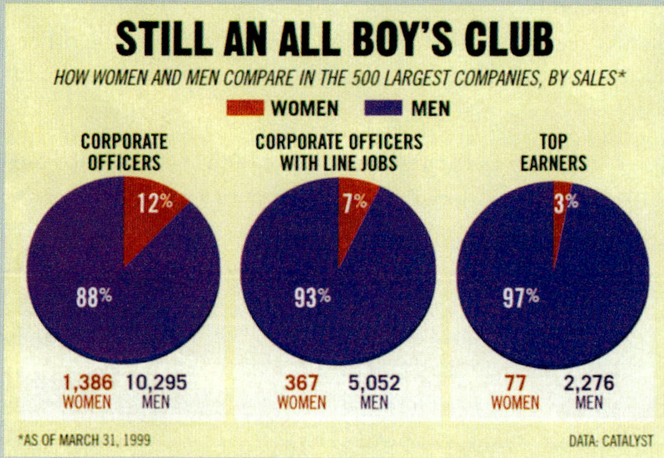

THINKING CRITICALLY ABOUT WHAT YOU HAVE LEARNED

Now that you have read and discussed several essays that argue a position on a controversial issue and written one of your own, take some time to think critically about what you have learned. What problems did you encounter as you were writing your essay, and how did you solve them? How did reading other essays that argue a position influence your own essay? How does this type of writing reflect cultural attitudes about public debate and controversy?

it reinforces her own position: "Still an All Boy's Club."

The *Business Week* article features two tables: "Power Titles: Who Has Them" and "Women in Power: A Score Card." Although the student incorporates information from the first table into her written argument, she decides against reproducing the first table in her essay because the titles of corporate officers vary so much from one company to another as to be virtually meaningless. She does include the second table from the article, however, because she thinks her readers will be interested in knowing which companies have a high percentage of women officers.

Another reason the student finds the *Business Week* graphics appealing is that they indicate the actual numbers of women and men so that readers can see at a glance the relatively small numbers of women who have made it into the upper echelons.

WOMEN IN POWER: A SCORE CARD

The top 51* companies based on their percentages of women corporate officers

COMPANY	TOTAL WOMEN OFFICERS	TOTAL OFFICERS	PERCENT WOMEN OFFICERS
US WEST	6	14	42.9%
PACIFICARE HEALTH SYSTEMS	15	35	42.9
LINCOLN NATIONAL	6	14	42.9
AVON PRODUCTS	9	21	42.9
NORDSTROM	15	36	41.7
FANNIE MAE	61	158	38.6
WASHINGTON MUTUAL	3	8	37.5
TIMES MIRROR	11	31	35.5
DAYTON HUDSON	8	23	34.8
VENATOR	8	23	34.8
PAINEWEBBER GROUP	2	6	33.3
SOUTHWEST AIRLINES	8	24	33.3
BJ'S WHOLESALE CLUB	2	6	33.3
KNIGHT-RIDDER	8	24	33.3
SLM HOLDING	4	12	33.3
CARDINAL HEALTH	7	22	31.8
MERCK	5	16	31.3
RYDER SYSTEM	5	16	31.3
MATTEL	5	16	31.3
PITNEY BOWES	5	16	31.3
PHILIP MORRIS	4	13	30.8
AMERITECH	10	33	30.3
CBS	3	10	30.0
TRANSAMERICA	6	20	30.0
HANNAFORD BROS.	8	27	29.6
ENRON	10	35	28.6
KELLY SERVICES	4	14	28.6%
NEW CENTURY ENERGIES	2	7	28.6
HUMANA	6	22	27.3
SBC COMMUNICATIONS	7	26	26.9
PNC BANK CORP.	4	15	26.7
NEW YORK TIMES	5	19	26.3
TEXTRON	6	24	25.0
EDISON INTERNATIONAL	3	12	25.0
GAP	5	20	25.0
WELLPOINT HEALTH NETWORKS	2	8	25.0
RALSTON PURINA	2	8	25.0
SOLECTRON	2	8	25.0
GPU	2	8	25.0
BRUNSWICK	4	16	25.0
BARNES & NOBLE	3	12	25.0
TRANS WORLD AIRLINES	5	21	23.8
JOHN HANCOCK MUTUAL LIFE INS.	22	93	23.7
SUPERVALU	4	17	23.5
SODEXHO MARRIOTT SERVICES	4	17	23.5
GANNETT	8	34	23.5
PECO ENERGY	7	30	23.3
CHASE MANHATTAN CORP.	6	26	23.1
COCA-COLA ENTERPRISES	6	26	23.1
UNICOM	3	13	23.1
3COM	12	52	23.1

*The list includes 51 companies because the last four companies are tied.

DATA FROM INFORMATION REPORTED BY THE 500 LARGEST PUBLIC CORPORATIONS, BASED ON REVENUE, IN 1998 ANNUAL REPORTS, PROXY STATEMENTS, AND 10-K STATEMENTS. ALL COMPANIES CONFIRMED INFORMATION BY MAIL, EXCEPT FOR SELECTRON AND COCA-COLA. REFLECTS OFFICERS AS OF MARCH 31, 1999, OR EARLIER.

Reflecting on Your Writing

Write a one-page explanation, telling your instructor about a problem you encountered in writing your essay and how you solved it. Before you begin, gather all of your invention and planning notes, drafts, critical comments, revision plan, and final revision. Review these materials as you complete this writing task.

1. ***Identify one writing problem you needed to solve as you worked on the essay.*** Do not be concerned with grammar and punctuation; concentrate instead on problems unique to developing an essay arguing for a position. For example: Did you puzzle over how to convince your readers that the issue is important? Did you have trouble asserting your position forcefully while acknowledging other points of view? Was it difficult to refute an important objection you knew readers would raise?
2. ***Determine how you came to recognize the problem.*** When did you first discover it? What called it to your attention? If you did not become aware of the problem until someone pointed it out to you, can you now see hints of it in your invention writings? If so, where specifically?

3. ***Reflect on how you went about solving the problem.*** Did you work on the wording of a passage, cut or add reasons or refutations, conduct further research, or move paragraphs or sentences around? Did you reread one of the essays in this chapter to see how another writer handled a similar problem, or did you look back at your invention writing? If you talked about the problem with another student, a tutor, or your instructor, did talking about it help? How useful was the advice you received?
4. ***Write a brief explanation of how you identified the problem and tried to solve it.*** Be as specific as possible in reconstructing your efforts. Quote from your invention notes and draft essay, others' critical comments, your revision plan, or your revised essay to show the various changes your writing—and thinking—underwent as you tried to solve the problem. If you are still uncertain about your solution, say so. Taking time to explain how you identified a particular problem, how you went about solving it, and what you learned from this experience can help you solve future writing problems more easily.

Reviewing What You Learned from Reading

Write a page or two explaining to your instructor how the readings in this chapter influenced your final essay. Your own essay has undoubtedly been influenced to some extent by one or more of the essays in this chapter as well as by classmates' essays that you may have read. These other essays may have helped you decide that you needed to do further research before you could argue responsibly for your position, that you could use a personal anecdote as part of your support, or that you should try to anticipate and effectively refute readers' objections. Before you write, take time to reflect on what you have learned from the readings and how they have influenced your own writing.

1. ***Reread the final revision of your essay; then look back at the selections you read before completing it.*** Do you see any specific influences? For example, did any reading influence how you decided to present the issue, use authorities, make concessions, or refute objections? Also look for ideas you got from your reading: writing strategies you were inspired to try, specific details you were led to include, and goals you sought to achieve.
2. ***Write an explanation of these influences.*** Did one selection have a particularly strong influence, or were several selections influential in different ways? Quote from the readings and from your final revision to show how your essay was influenced by the selections you read. Finally, based on your review of the chapter's readings, point out any further improvements you would now make in your essay.

Considering the Social Dimensions of Position Papers

Arguing positions on important social and political issues is essential in a democracy. Doing so gives us each a voice. Instead of remaining silent and on the margins, we can enter the ongoing debate. We can try to influence others, perhaps convincing them to change their minds or at least to take seriously our point of view. Airing our differences also allows us to live together in relative peace. Instead of brawling with each other at school board meetings, in legislative halls, on street corners, or in the classroom, we argue. We may raise our voices in anger and frustration, and our differences may seem insurmountable, but at least no one is physically hurt.

Anticipating the positions taken by our readers and their likely objections to our argument benefits us in another important way. It forces us to do more than merely assert our views; we must also give reasons that we think as we do. Anticipating readers' responses to our argument encourages us not only to think of reasons but also to think critically about our reasons so that we can defend them against potential criticism. To refute objections, we need to support our reasons in ways that ground our opinions in something other than personal belief—for example, in facts that can be verified, in the authority of experts, in anecdotal experiences with which others can identify. Ideally, then, writing position papers fosters the kind of reasonable debate that enables a diverse society like ours to hold together.

Yet even though reasoned argument about controversial social issues is a highly valued activity in our society, cautious readers and writers need to be aware that this way of presenting an argument for a position may have serious shortcomings and problems.

The Illusion of Objectivity. Part of what we value about reasoned argument is that it seems to allow us to transcend personal bias and narrow self-interest. In other words, it enables us to be—or at least appear—objective because we are not merely saying what we think but backing our opinions with reasons and support.

Many people, however, have begun to question this idea of objectivity. They suggest that objectivity is only an illusion because it is impossible to escape one's history and culture. Who we are and what we believe may be influenced by factors such as gender, ethnicity, family, religion, money, schooling, and exposure to the media (such as television, film, music, the Internet). Consequently, according to this point of view, the fact that we are able to give objective-sounding, seemingly logical reasons for our opinions does not guarantee that they are unbiased or even reasonable: What appears to be rational thought may be merely rationalization, a way of justifying fundamentally intuitive personal convictions. In other words, supporting a position with a well-reasoned argument may simply be a game we play to trick others—and ourselves—into believing that we are open-minded and our opinions are based on something other than personal bias.

1. ***As a reader of others' essays arguing a position, do you think you are swayed by objective-sounding arguments?*** Review the readings in this chapter to locate one reason you thought was objective or that seemed objective. What do you think makes this reason appear to be objective? What might lead readers to think it is?
2. ***Consider the entire essay and how it reflects some aspect of the writer's history and culture.*** Think of a factor that may have influenced the writer's point of view on the issue.
3. ***Reflect on the opposition between objectivity and personal bias.*** Do you think that reasoned argument should try to be objective? When you were writing your own position paper, were you trying to be objective? Which of your reasons would you now identify as objective-sounding, chosen because you thought your readers would find it convincing and not because you really believed it? If it is true that everyone has biases based on personal history and culture, does it necessarily follow that it is impossible to escape these biases or at least to set them aside? When Estrada anticipates the objection about political correctness, do you think he uses critical thinking to examine a bias he shares with readers, or do you think he's trying to trick readers and possibly also trick himself? Do any of the other writers in this chapter critically examine their underlying ideas or values? Did you do so in your own essay?
4. ***Write a page or two explaining your ideas about objectivity and bias in essays arguing a position.*** Connect your ideas to the readings in this chapter and to your own essay.

Suppressing Dissent. Some critics argue that society privileges reasoned argument over other ways of arguing in order to control dissent. Instead of expressing what may be legitimate outrage and inciting public concern through passionate language, dissenters are urged to be dispassionate and reasonable. They may even be encouraged to try to build their arguments on shared values even though they are arguing with people whose views they find repugnant. While it may help prevent violent confrontation, this emphasis on calmly giving reasons and support may also prevent an honest and open exchange of differences. In the end, trying to present a well-reasoned, well-supported argument may serve to maintain the status quo by silencing the more radical voices within the community.

1. ***In your own experience of writing an essay arguing a position on a controversial issue, did having***

to give reasons and support discourage you from choosing any particular issue or from expressing strong feelings? Reflect on the issues you listed as possible subjects for your essay and how you made your choice. Did you reject any issues because you could not come up with reasons and support for your position? When you made your choice, did you think about whether you could be dispassionate and reasonable about it?

2. ***Consider the readings in this chapter and the essays you read by other students in the class.*** Do you think any of these writers felt limited by the need to give reasons and support for their position? Which of the essays you read, if any, seemed to you to express strong feelings about the issue? Which, if any, seemed dispassionate?

3. ***Consider the kind of arguing you typically witness in the media—radio, television, newspapers, magazines, the Internet.*** We have said that society privileges reasoned argument, but in the media, have giving reasons and support and anticipating readers' objections been replaced with a more contentious, in-your-face style of arguing? Think of media examples of these two different ways of arguing. In the context of these examples, what can you conclude about reasoned argument stifling dissent?

4. ***Write a page or two explaining your ideas about whether the requirement to give reasons and support suppresses dissent.*** Connect your ideas to your own essay and to the readings in this chapter.

7 Proposing a Solution

Proposals are vital to a democracy. They inform citizens about problems affecting their well-being and suggest actions that could be taken to remedy these problems. People write proposals every day in business, government, education, and the professions. Proposals are a basic ingredient of the world's work.

As a special form of argument, proposals have much in common with position papers, described in Chapter 6. Both analyze a subject about which there is disagreement and take a definite stand on it. Both make an argument, giving reasons and support and acknowledging readers' likely objections or questions. Proposals, however, go further: They urge readers to take specific action. They argue for a proposed solution to a problem, and they succeed or fail by the strength of that argument.

Problem-solving is basic to most disciplines and professions. For example, scientists use the scientific method, a systematic form of problem solving; political scientists and sociologists propose solutions to troubling political and social problems; engineers employ problem-solving techniques in building bridges, automobiles, and computers; teachers make decisions about how to help students with learning problems; counselors devote themselves to helping clients solve personal problems; business owners and managers daily solve problems large and small.

Problem-solving depends on a questioning attitude—wondering about alternative approaches to bringing about change, puzzling over how a goal might be achieved, questioning why a process unfolds in a particular way, posing challenges to the status quo. In addition, it demands imagination and creativity. To solve a problem, you need to see it anew, to look at it from new angles and in new contexts.

Because a proposal tries to convince readers that its way of defining and solving the problem makes sense, proposal writers must be sensitive to readers' needs and expectations. Readers need to know details of the solution and to be convinced that it will solve the problem and can be implemented. If readers initially favor a different solution, knowing why the writer rejects it will help them decide whether to support or reject the writer's proposed solution. Readers may be wary of costs, demands on their time, and grand schemes.

As you plan and draft a proposal, you will have to determine whether your readers are aware of the problem and whether they recognize its seriousness, and you will have to consider their views on alternative possible solutions. Knowing what your readers know—their knowledge of the problem and willingness to make changes, their assumptions and biases, the kinds of arguments likely to appeal to them—is a central part of proposal writing.

The writing of proposals occurs in many different contexts, as the following examples suggest.

Writing in Your Other Courses

- For an economics class, a student writes an essay proposing a solution to the problem of inadequate housing for Mexican workers in the nearly three thousand maquiladora factories clustered along the Mexican side of the border with the United States. She briefly describes the binational arrangement that has produced over a million low-paying jobs for Mexican workers and increased profits for American manufacturers who own the assembly plants—along with job losses for thousands of American workers. She sketches the history of maquiladoras since the 1970s and then surveys some of the problems they have spawned. Focusing on inadequate housing, she argues that it, of all the problems, should be addressed first and is most amenable to modest, short-term solutions. The student argues that maquiladora owners must share with Mexican city and state governments the costs of planning and installing water delivery systems and minimal house plumbing installations, and provide low-interest loans to workers who want to buy indoor plumbing fixtures. Recognizing that this is only a first-stage solution to a major problem requiring long-term efforts, the student calls for an international competition to design entire maquiladora workers' communities, along with plans for adequate low-cost houses with plumbing and electricity.
- For an education class, a student researches the history of educational television production and programming for two- to thirteen-year-old children, beginning with the 1969 production of Children's Television Workshop's *Sesame Street*. He also researches children's television in Australia, Great Britain, and Japan and learns that these countries provide much more support for children's television programming than the United States does. For an assignment to write an essay proposing a solution, he proposes a plan to develop government support for children's programming. He presents the problem by comparing other countries' support for children's television to U.S. support. Influenced by a book by the founder of Children's Television Workshop, the student argues that television is the most efficient and effective way to teach pre-school-age children basic math and English skills. Arguing to support his proposal, the student concedes that attractive new programs continue to appear—for example, *Bill Nye, the Science Guy*—but argues that these are sporadic and cannot provide the amount or diversity of programming that is needed.

Writing in the Community

- A California high school junior enters an essay contest, "There Ought to Be a Law," sponsored by her state legislator. The goal of the contest is to encourage high school students to propose solutions to community problems. The student wins the contest with a proposal for a state law requiring school districts to replace textbooks every ten years. She presents the problem by describing her own battered, marked-up, dated textbooks, particularly a chemistry text published before she was born. To gain a better understanding of the problems caused by outdated textbooks, she talks with several other students and with teachers. Recognizing that she lacks the expertise to outline a legislative solution, she speculates about the probable obstacles, chief among them the costs of implementing her solution. The legislator drafts a law based on the student's proposal, invites the student to attend the opening of the next legislative session, and introduces the law at that session.

- A social services administrator in a large northeastern city becomes increasingly concerned about the rise in numbers of adolescents in jail for minor and major crimes. From his observations and the research studies he reads, he becomes convinced that a partial solution to the problem would be to intervene at the first sign of delinquent behavior in eight- to twelve-year-olds. In developing a proposal to circulate among influential people in the local police department, juvenile justice system, school system, and business and religious communities, the administrator begins by describing the long-term consequences of jailing young criminals. Trying to make the problem seem significant and worth solving, he focuses mainly on the costs and the high rate of return to criminal activity after release from jail. He then lists and discusses at length the major components of his early intervention program. These components include assigning mentors to young people who are beginning to fail in school, placing social workers in troubled families to help out daily before and after school, hiring neighborhood residents to work full-time on the streets to counter the influence of gangs, and encouraging businesses to hire high school students as paid interns. The administrator acknowledges that early intervention to head off serious criminal activity will require the cooperation of many city agencies. He offers to take the lead in bringing about this cooperation and in launching the program.

Writing in the Workplace

- Frustrated by what they see as the failure of schools to prepare students for the workplace, managers of a pharmaceuticals corporation in the Midwest decide to develop a proposal to move vocational and technical training out of ill-equipped high school vocational programs and onto the plant's floor. Seven division managers meet weekly for four months to develop a proposal for schools in the region. They are joined by one of the firm's experienced technical writers, who takes notes of discussions, writes progress reports, and eventually drafts the proposal. They define the problem as schools being unable to offer the cutting-edge teaching, modern equipment, motivation, or accountability of on-the-job training. They eventually propose a vocational track that would begin in grade 10, with all of the job training taking place in businesses and industries. Each year students would spend more time on the job, and by grade 12 they would work thirty-two hours a week and spend ten hours a week in school, mainly in courses in English (reading and writing) and advanced math. As the managers detail their solution, develop a timetable for implementing it, and speculate about how current school budgets could be reworked to support the program, they seek advice on early drafts of their proposal from business leaders, school board members, school administrators, representatives of teachers' unions, newspaper editorial boards, and key members of the state legislature. The final draft incorporates suggestions from these advisers and attempts to refute known arguments against the proposal.

- A woman in her sixties who has been hauling asphalt and gravel in a double-bottom dump truck for sixteen years writes a proposal for trucking company owners and managers, who face a continual shortage of well-qualified drivers for heavy diesel tractor-and-trailer trucks, suggesting that the companies focus on recruiting more women. As she plans her proposal, she talks to the owner of the company she drives for and to the few women drivers she knows. She begins the proposal by describing her work briefly and explaining how she got a lucky break when her brother taught her how to drive his truck. She then points out the problem: that few women ever get the chance to learn this skill. She proposes her solution to this problem: an in-house training program in which women recruits would be trained by company drivers on the job and after hours. Drivers would be paid for their after-hours training contributions, and the students would be paid a small stipend after agreeing to drive for the company for a certain number of months at a reduced salary. She argues that her proposal would succeed only if trucking companies sponsor a well-designed recruitment program relying on advertisements published on Web sites and in magazines read by working women, and she lists titles of several such publications. She attempts to refute the alternative solution of relying on already established truck-driving schools by arguing that many women cannot afford the tuition. Her proposal is first published in her company's internal newsletter and later, in slightly revised form, in a leading magazine read by trucking company owners and managers.

Practice Proposing a Solution to a Problem: A Collaborative Activity

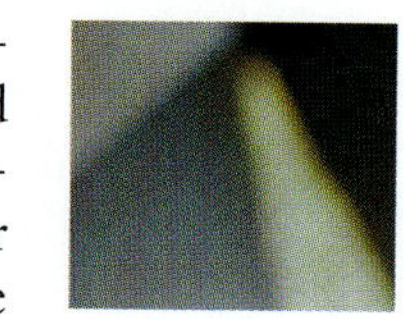

The preceding scenarios suggest some occasions for writing proposals to solve problems. To get a sense of the complexities and possibilities involved in proposing solutions, think through a specific problem, and try to come up with a feasible proposal. Your instructor may schedule this collaborative activity as a face-to-face in-class discussion or ask you to conduct an online real-time discussion in a chat room. Whatever the medium, here are some guidelines to follow:

Part 1. Form a group with two or three other students, and select one person to take notes during your discussion.

- First, identify two or three problems within your college or community, and select one that you all recognize and agree needs to be solved.

- Next, consider possible solutions to this problem, and identify one solution that you can all support. You need not all be equally enthusiastic for this solution.
- Finally, determine which individual or group has the authority to take action on your proposed solution and how you would go about convincing this audience that the problem is serious and must be solved and that your proposed solution is feasible and should be supported. Make notes also about questions this audience might have about your proposal and what objections the audience might raise.

Part 2. As a group, discuss your efforts at proposing a solution to a problem. What surprised or pleased you most about this activity? What difficulties did you encounter in coming up with arguments that the problem must be solved and that your proposed solution would solve it? How did the objections you thought of influence your confidence in your proposed solution?

READINGS

The four readings in this chapter illustrate a number of the features of essays that propose solutions to problems and many of the strategies that writers rely on to realize the features. No two proposals are alike, and yet they share defining features. Together, the four essays cover many of the possibilities of proposals, so you will want to read as many of them as possible. If time permits, complete the activities in the Analyzing Writing Strategies section that follows each selection, and read the Commentary. Following the readings is a section called Basic Features: Proposing Solutions (p. 360), which offers a concise description of the features of proposals and provides examples from the four readings.

***Mark Hertsgaard** is a journalist and a regular contributor to National Public Radio. His essays have appeared in numerous newspapers and magazines such as the* New York Times, *the* New Yorker, *the* Atlantic Monthly, Outside, Harper's, *and* Rolling Stone. *He also teaches nonfiction writing at Johns Hopkins University and has written five books, including* Nuclear, Inc.: The Men and Money behind Nuclear Energy *(1983),* A Day in the Life: The Music and Artistry of the Beatles *(1995), and* The Eagle's Shadow: Why America Fascinates and Infuriates the World *(2002). This proposal was originally published in* Time *magazine's special Earth Day edition in 2000, and it reflects the extensive research he did for his 1999 book* Earth Odyssey: Around the World in Search of Our Environmental Future.

Hertsgaard probably titled his proposal "A Global Green Deal" to remind readers of President Franklin D. Roosevelt's New Deal, which helped the United States recover from the Great Depression of the 1930s. Hertsgaard proposes that government encourage businesses to develop and use new, more efficient and environmentally friendly technologies. You will see that toward the end of his essay, Hertsgaard admits that his proposal is "no silver bullet" but argues that it will take us in the right direction and "buy us time to make the more deep-seated changes" that are needed (paragraph 16). As you read, notice how sensitive he is to readers who fear the problem is too daunting. Pay attention to the ways he tries to bolster readers' confidence that the problem can be solved while at the same time trying to be realistic about what his proposed solution can accomplish.

A Global Green Deal

Mark Hertsgaard

The bad news is that we have to change our ways— 1
and fast. Here's the good news: it could be a hugely profitable enterprise.

So what do we do? Everyone knows the planet is in 2
bad shape, but most people are resigned to passivity. Changing course, they reason, would require economic sacrifice and provoke stiff resistance from corporations and consumers alike, so why bother? It's easier to ignore the gathering storm clouds and hope the problem magically takes care of itself.

Such fatalism is not only dangerous but mistaken. For much of the 1990s I traveled 3
the world to write a book about our environmental predicament. I returned home sobered by the extent of the damage we are causing and by the speed at which it is occurring. But there is nothing inevitable about our self-destructive behavior. Not only could we dramatically reduce our burden on the air, water and other natural systems, we could make money doing so. If we're smart, we could make restoring the environment the biggest economic enterprise of our time, a huge source of jobs, profits and poverty alleviation.

What we need is a Global Green Deal: a 4
program to renovate our civilization environmentally from top to bottom in rich and poor countries alike. Making use of both market incentives and government leadership, a twenty-first-century Global Green Deal would do for environmental technologies what government and industry have recently done so well for computer and Internet technologies: launch their commercial takeoff.

Getting it done will take work, and before 5
we begin we need to understand three facts about the reality facing us. First, we have no time to lose. While we've made progress in certain areas—air pollution is down in the

U.S.—big environmental problems like climate change, water scarcity and species extinction are getting worse, and faster than ever. Thus we have to change our ways profoundly—and very soon.

Second, poverty is central to the problem. Four billion of the planet's 6 billion people face deprivation inconceivable to the wealthiest 1 billion. To paraphrase Thomas Jefferson, nothing is more certainly written in the book of fate than that the bottom two-thirds of humanity will strive to improve their lot. As they demand adequate heat and food, not to mention cars and CD players, humanity's environmental footprint will grow. Our challenge is to accommodate this mass ascent from poverty without wrecking the natural systems that make life possible. 6

Third, some good news: we have in hand most of the technologies needed to chart a new course. We know how to use oil, wood, water and other resources much more efficiently than we do now. Increased efficiency—doing more with less—will enable us to use fewer resources and produce less pollution per capita, buying us the time to bring solar power, hydrogen fuel cells and other futuristic technologies on line. 7

Efficiency may not sound like a rallying cry for environmental revolution, but it packs a financial punch. As Joseph J. Romm reports in his book *Cool Companies,* Xerox, Compaq and 3M are among many firms that have recognized they can cut their greenhouse-gas emissions in half—and enjoy 50 percent and higher returns on investment through improved efficiency, better lighting and insulation and smarter motors and building design. The rest of us (small businesses, homeowners, city governments, schools) can reap the same benefits. 8

Super-refrigerators use 87% less electricity than older, standard models while costing the same (assuming mass production) and performing better, as Paul Hawken and Amory and L. Hunter Lovins explain in their book *Natural Capitalism.* In Amsterdam the headquarters of ING Bank, one of Holland's largest banks, uses one-fifth as much energy per square meter as a nearby bank, even though the buildings cost the same to construct. The ING center boasts efficient windows and insulation and a design that enables solar energy to provide much of the building's needs, even in cloudy Northern Europe. 9

Examples like these lead even such mainstream voices as AT&T and Japan's energy planning agency, NEDO, to predict that environmental restoration could be a source of virtually limitless profit. The idea is to retrofit our farms, factories, shops, houses, offices and everything inside them. The economic activity generated would be enormous. Better yet, it would be labor intensive; investments in energy efficiency yield two to 10 times more jobs than investments in fossil fuel and nuclear power. In a world where 1 billion people lack gainful employment, creating jobs is essential to fighting the poverty that retards environmental progress. 10

But this transition will not happen by itself—too many entrenched interests stand in the way. Automakers often talk green but make only token efforts to develop green cars because gas-guzzling sport-utility vehicles are hugely profitable. But every year the U.S. government buys 56,000 new vehicles for official use from Detroit. Under the Global Green Deal, Washington would tell Detroit that from now on the cars have to be hybrid-electric or hydrogen-fuel-cell cars. Detroit might scream and holler, but if Washington 11 stood firm, carmakers soon would be climbing the learning curve and offering the competitively priced green cars that consumers say they want.

We know such government pump-priming works; it's why so many of us have computers today. America's computer companies began learning to produce today's affordable systems during the 1960s while benefiting from subsidies and guaranteed markets under contracts with the Pentagon and the space program. And the cyberboom has fueled the biggest economic expansion in history. 12

The Global Green Deal must not be solely an American project, however. China and India, with their gigantic populations and ambitious development plans, could by themselves doom everyone else to severe global warming. Already, China is the world's second largest producer of greenhouse gases (after the U.S.). But China would use 50% less coal if it simply installed today's energy-efficient technologies. Under the Global Green Deal, Europe, America and Japan would help China buy these technologies, not only because that would reduce global warming but also because it would create jobs and profits for workers and companies back home. 13

Governments would not have to spend more money, only shift existing subsidies away from environmentally dead-end technologies like coal and nuclear power. If even half the $500 billion to $900 billion in environmentally destructive subsidies now offered by the world's governments were redirected, the Global Green Deal would be off to a roaring start. Governments need to establish "rules of the road" so that market prices reflect the real social costs of clearcut forests and other environmental abominations. Again, such a shift could be revenue neutral. Higher taxes on, say, coal burning would be offset by cuts in payroll and profits taxes, thus encouraging jobs and investment while discouraging pollution. A portion of the revenues should be set aside to assure a just transition for workers and companies now engaged in inherently anti-environmental activities like coal mining. 14

All this sounds easy enough on paper, but in the real world it is not so simple. Beneficiaries of the current system—be they U.S. corporate-welfare recipients, redundant German coal miners, or cutthroat Asian logging interests—will resist. Which is why progress is unlikely absent a broader agenda of change, including real democracy: assuring the human rights of environmental activists and neutralizing the power of Big Money through campaign-finance reform. 15

The Global Green Deal is no silver bullet. It can, however, buy us time to make the more deep-seated changes—in our often excessive appetites, in our curious belief that humans are the center of the universe, in our sheer numbers—that will be necessary to repair our relationship with our environment. 16

None of this will happen without an aroused citizenry. But a Global Green Deal is in the common interest, and it is a slogan easily grasped by the media and the public. Moreover, it should appeal across political, class and national boundaries, for it would stimulate both jobs and business throughout the world in the name of a universal value: leaving our children a livable planet. The history of environmentalism is largely the story of ordinary people pushing for change while governments, corporations and other established interests reluctantly follow behind. It's time to repeat that history on behalf of a Global Green Deal. 17

Connecting to Culture and Experience: Acting to Create a More Livable Planet

Hertsgaard acknowledges in this proposal that his solution is "no silver bullet," but he hopes it will "buy us time to make the more deep-seated changes" that are needed (paragraph 16).

With two or three other students, discuss other actions that can be taken to buy us time and possibly also help to repair the environment. Begin by telling each other about conservation efforts you have made. For example, you may buy recycled paper, or your family may compost food remains. What other actions could you take? Then discuss whether helping the environment is a high priority for you. If you were buying a car, for instance, would getting an energy-efficient car be a high priority? If you have a choice between driving a car or taking public transportation to school or work, would you take public transportation to reduce energy costs and air pollution?

Analyzing Writing Strategies

1. At the beginning of this chapter, we make several generalizations about essays that propose solutions to problems. Consider which of these assertions are true of Hertsgaard's proposal:
   - It defines the problem and helps readers realize the seriousness of the problem.
   - It describes the proposed solution.
   - It attempts to convince readers that the solution will help solve the problem and can be implemented.
   - It anticipates readers' likely questions and objections.
   - It evaluates alternative solutions that readers may initially favor.
2. The most important part of a proposal is the solution. To be effective, the proposal has to **describe the solution** in a way that convinces readers that it can be implemented. Hertsgaard first presents his solution in paragraph 4, where he describes in broad terms the "Global Green Deal" he is proposing. But he does not describe how his solution to renovate the environment can be implemented until paragraphs 11–14. Reread these paragraphs to see how convincing he is in arguing that his solution can and should be implemented. Highlight in paragraphs 11 and 13–14 what would need to be done to implement the solution. Also look closely at paragraph 12 to see what it adds to his argument.

Commentary: Defining the Problem

Every proposal begins with a problem. Writers usually spend some time defining the problem—establishing that the problem exists and is serious enough to warrant action. What writers say about the problem and how much space they devote to it depend on what they assume their readers already know and think about it. In this proposal, Hertsgaard assumes the readers of *Time* magazine's special Earth Day edition know that "the planet is in bad shape," as he puts it in paragraph 2.

He identifies the problem more specifically at various points in the essay: "big environmental problems like climate change, water scarcity and species extinction" (5), "pollution" (7), and "global warming" (13). In paragraphs 5–9, Hertsgaard elaborates further by presenting "three facts about the reality" of the problem (5). The first two facts make the problem seem overwhelming, but the third is a ray of hope. He notes that we have made progress but that time is running out as developing countries become wealthier and place increasing pressures on the environment. The third fact, however, provides the "good news" that is an essential ingredient of his proposed solution: We already have the technological efficiency to make a difference.

Hertsgaard knows that many of his readers feel defeated by the enormity of the problem and that his proposal will fall on deaf ears if his readers do not believe that the steps he is proposing will do any good. Therefore, he tries to allay his readers' fears, in particular their feeling of "fatalism" (3). To reassure readers, he tries to be optimistic yet realistic. He tempers his own enthusiasm with language like this: "If we're smart, we could" (3) and "The Global Green Deal is no silver bullet. It can, however, buy us time to make the more deep-seated changes" (16). Ultimately, Hertsgaard tries to represent the problem as a "challenge" (6), something that "will take work" (5) but that can be done.

As you plan your proposal, you also will need to consider your readers' feelings as well as their knowledge. Remember that defining the problem is part of your argument. It should be designed to convince readers that you know what you are talking about and can be trusted. Hertsgaard builds his credibility with readers in part by referring to his extensive research (3, 8–9) but also by showing readers he understands the complexity of the problem.

Considering Topics for Your Own Essay

Hertsgaard's admittedly limited proposal might suggest to you other proposals to solve environmental problems. For example, you might consider writing a proposal for increasing the use of carpools on campus, reducing energy consumption in dormitories, or instituting a campus recycling program. You might interview people in your community about the feasibility of subsidizing alternative energy sources, such as solar-heating panels that could be installed in public buildings and parks. You might also research promising newer technologies for a proposal addressed to your college administration or local government.

To use the Writing Guide Software to record your ideas, click on
▶ **Journal**

***Mary Jo Bane**, an expert on public policy issues, currently is the Thornton Bradshaw Professor of Public Policy and Management in the Kennedy School of Government at Harvard University. She has also served in national and state government as assistant secretary for children and families at the U.S. Department of Health and Human Services (HHS) as well as commissioner of the New York State Department of Social Services. Among her many books are* Here to Stay: American Families in the Twentieth Century *(1976),* Who Will Provide? The Changing Role of Religion in American Social Welfare *(coedited with Brent Coffin and Ronald Thiemann, 2000), and* Lifting Up the Poor: A Dialogue on Religion, Poverty, and Welfare Reform *(with Lawrence M. Mead, 2003). Most of her articles have appeared in academic publications such as the* Journal of Human Resources, Journal of Policy Analysis and Management, *and the* Annals of the Society of Christian Ethics. *But she has also written essays for newspapers such as the* Boston Globe *and magazines published for and by Catholics such as* America *and* Commonweal, *in which this selection first appeared in March 2002. (We have added footnotes to explain some terms that may be unfamiliar to non-Catholics.)*

As a Catholic herself, Bane has been a vocal advocate for change. In paragraph 13, she anticipates an objection that people like her "are using the current crisis to advance their own agendas for church reform." As you read, notice how she responds to this criticism.

Boston's Priest-Pedophile Crisis

Mary Jo Bane

The Archdiocese of Boston[1] has been reeling for two months from continuing disclosures about pedophilia among priests, and from documentation of how members of the hierarchy,[2] up to and including Cardinal Bernard Law, attempted to mute the voices of the victims of abuse and protect the priest perpetrators. The *Boston Globe* ran a series of articles beginning January 6, many of them based on documents submitted to the court during the criminal child molestation trial of one of the priests, John Geoghan (now defrocked[3]). The *Globe* investigation made public a series of letters from the 1980s in which the hierarchy responded sympathetically to Geoghan and documents disclosing that Geoghan had been reassigned to parish[4] duties despite knowledge about his abuses. 1

Further investigative reporting by the *Globe* established that in the last ten years the hierarchy had settled cases of alleged abuse by at least seventy priests who had served in the archdiocese over a forty-year period. In response, Cardinal Law apologized to the victims, instituted a new zero-tolerance policy, agreed to refer all future allegations of abuse to criminal prosecutors and also, under pressure from the media and the state legislature, to refer past cases of abuse, going back forty years, for prosecution. As a result, the names of about eighty priests have been sent to prosecutors. (Currently there 2

[1] The jurisdiction of the archbishop of Boston, Cardinal Bernard Law.

[2] The organizational structure of the Catholic clergy within an archdiocese or other jurisdiction.

[3] No longer permitted to serve as a priest.

[4] A local church.

are about six hundred and fifty diocesan priests and seven hundred religious order priests in the archdiocese.)

The cardinal also assured the faithful that as a result of actions begun [in] the early 1990s, no priest against whom a credible accusation of abuse had been made was currently in active ministry. However, on February 2, two pastors were removed because of past accusations of pedophilia; since then, eight more priests have been removed. 3

Many Catholics in the archdiocese now question whether full disclosure has yet occurred, and see the cardinal's actions as too little too late. On February 8 the *Globe* reported a poll of a sample of about eight hundred Boston Catholics, in which 78 percent said they believed that church leaders have tried to cover up cases of abuse, and 64 percent said they believed church leaders care more about protecting priests who have abused children than protecting people. Only 24 percent expressed a favorable opinion of Cardinal Law. Forty-eight percent agreed that the cardinal should resign; 38 percent disagreed. A number of lay[5] Catholics, including me, called publicly, through op-eds and letters in the *Globe,* for the cardinal's resignation, and for changes in church policy to get at the deeper roots of the current crisis. 4

This crisis has focused attention on several important, broader issues: Are there cultural, structural, and policy practices in the church that generate or exacerbate such abuses? What reforms might address these problems while respecting the unique sacramental[6] nature of the church? What role can and should lay people play in reforming these practices? What means should lay people use? 5

One of the most devastating aspects of the disclosures has been the documentation of the closed, secret, and self-protecting nature of the decisions made by the hierarchy. The documents reveal a culture of secrecy and deference in which the top decision maker is surrounded by aides who seem to be more concerned with protecting their reputations and [those] of their allies than with the mission of the organization or the welfare of those it serves. They attempt to control information, prevent public disclosure, and silence dissent, even, in this case, the anguished cries of abused children and their families. 6

Cultures of this sort are not unknown; one thinks of recent corporate and governmental scandals. Tendencies toward centralization of power and control of information exist in all institutions. But over time organizational structures have been created by which governments, businesses, and nonprofit organizations curb some human abuses before they can result in serious harm. Well-governed institutions ensure full disclosure of information, institutionalize checks and balances on the exercise of power, and establish independent boards to advise and participate actively in choosing the chief executive officer. 7

The church is no ordinary institution. The great Vatican II[7] document, *Lumen gentium,* described the church as a sacrament, and as the People of God as well as a hier- 8

---

[5] Ordinary; not ordained as a priest. Lay people collectively are called *the laity.*

[6] Sacred or spiritual.

[7] A council held in the 1960s that modernized many church practices.

archically organized institution. The church is God's gathered people, guided by the Holy Spirit—a community in which God's saving work is accomplished and God's kingdom proclaimed. But the church is also a human institution, managed by humans with all their failings, including susceptibility to the corruptions of power and mistaken judgment.

It would seem to follow then that the church, consistent with its mission and its 9
sacramental nature, could make use of some of the practices adopted by secular[8] institutions to check inevitable human abuses. Three examples come to mind. One has to do with formal grievance and appeals procedures. Some of the most heart-wrenching testimony from abuse victims was their reports of having nowhere to turn when their priest was part of the problem, and of their attempts to engage others within the church which were ignored or rebuffed. Similarly, Catholics have no formal recourse when their pastors are insensitive or incompetent. Surely, a formal grievance and appeals process, with recourse to independent outside bodies, could serve the People of God well.

A second example comes in the area of financial management. The Archdiocese of 10
Boston conducts an annual appeal and is currently in the midst of a large capital campaign. The cardinal has said that no money from contributors has been or will be used for settlement payments or damages to abuse victims—which could easily have amounted already to tens of millions of dollars ($10 million seems to have been paid out in the Geoghan cases alone). Law's statement is simply incredible to anyone who realizes that money is fungible and that insurance is not free. But church funds are not subject to the disclosure and auditing rules that other organizations must adhere to, and there has been no voluntary disclosure of the detailed financial information that would allow contributors to exercise responsible stewardship. Financial disclosure and an independent expert board to oversee and account for archdiocesan spending are seemingly obvious practices that could help change the culture and restore trust.

A third example comes in the area of personnel policies. Pressures to reassign 11
rather than remove priests and to cover up both abuses and incompetence are certainly exacerbated by the serious shortage of priests. Many have suggested that the long-term solution to this problem can come only with the ordination of married men and of women. But even in the short term, creative solutions to the problem have been ignored. In Boston, for example, lay men and women are not permitted to administer parishes or encouraged to take responsibility for nonsacramental pastoral duties, leading to situations where parishes are closed or incompetent pastors retained simply because a priest must be in charge. Lay Catholics in Boston, as elsewhere, are well educated, talented, and eager to exercise church leadership. Here too, borrowing good practices from other sectors would suggest ways of using independent boards and expert groups to solve problems, ensure that abusive and unqualified priests are not exercising ministry, open up the institution, and allow the laity to use their gifts in the service of their church.

More openness, participation, and incorporation of good practices developed in 12
other institutional spheres would not, I am convinced, compromise the sacred character of the church. Should we not trust that the Holy Spirit is with the People of God and

[8] Nonreligious.

works in the church through many hands and voices, lay and clergy, and perhaps even through formal structures of participation and accountability?

There will no doubt be accusations that Boston's lay Catholics are using the current crisis to advance their own agendas for church reform, which is, of course, partly true. But Vatican II made very clear that we are all, lay and clergy, called to holiness and to ministry. Despite the long-ingrained tendency of lay men and women to defer to the hierarchy, lay people have both the right and the responsibility to make their voices heard. Many of us are now tragically aware of the consequences that follow from the concentration and misuse of power and lay deference to hierarchical authority. The proposals I offer here are responsive and responsible. Those who love the church grieve over what has happened to it in Boston but persist in hope for what it can become. 13

Connecting to Culture and Experience: Deference to Authority

When Bane refers in the final paragraph to "the long-ingrained tendency of lay men and women to defer to the hierarchy," she is making a point that could apply as well to secular institutions as well as religious ones.

With two or three other students, discuss your own tendency to defer to authority or your willingness to speak out and risk criticism. Begin by trying to recall an occasion when you were at odds with people in power—possibly on a team, in a school or a place of business, or in local or even national government. Tell each other what you disagreed about and what, if anything, you did or considered doing about it. If you spoke out or made a phone call or wrote an email or letter, what happened? If you decided not to speak out, why not? Then discuss why being in this position is so difficult.

Analyzing Writing Strategies

1. Bane **identifies the problem** in the title as "Boston's Priest-Pedophile Crisis," and in paragraphs 1–4 she gives readers a detailed chronology summarizing each revelation reported in the local newspaper. Nevertheless, in paragraphs 5–6, Bane defines the problem to which she proposes a solution in terms of what she calls "important, broader issues" (paragraph 5).

   First, reread paragraphs 1–6, and consider why she gives a play-by-play account of the *Boston Globe* investigation in the opening paragraphs. Then, consider why she focuses her proposal on what she calls in paragraph 6 the church's "culture of secrecy and deference." How effectively do you think she shifts the focus from the problem of sexual abuse to the broader problem of the "cultural, structural, and policy practices in the church that generate or exacerbate such abuses" (paragraph 5)?

2. At the end of paragraph 4, Bane explains that in addition to calling for Cardinal Law's resignation, she and other lay Catholics have proposed "changes in church policy to get at the deeper roots of the current crisis." Reread paragraphs 9–12

where she **describes the solution**. Underline the one sentence in each paragraph that best states the examples of secular practices that Bane says could improve the church. Then notice how she tries to convince readers of the plausibility of each example. How plausible do these examples seem to you as one reader?

3. Bane adopts a **sentence strategy** of asking rhetorical questions. (A rhetorical question is one the writer poses not to seek an answer but to achieve another purpose or effect.) In paragraph 5, Bane asks four of these questions in a row. Underline them, and within the context of the whole essay, decide what they contribute to Bane's proposal. Do they serve the same or different purposes? How could each one be changed to a meaningful statement? What advantages might these questions have over statements?

To learn more about rhetorical questions, turn to Sentence Strategies, p. 375.

Commentary: Anticipating Readers' Objections

Proposal writers try to present a strong argument for their solution, but they also usually try to anticipate and respond to readers' likely questions and objections. This anticipation and response is called **counterargument**. Writers have three strategies for counterarguing: they can simply acknowledge that they are aware of readers' concerns but do nothing else to respond; they can accommodate the criticism, modifying their argument by making concessions; or they can try to refute opposing arguments. Those seeking to convince readers to take action to solve a problem nearly always try to respond by accommodating or refuting readers' criticisms.

For more on these counterarguing strategies, see Chapter 19.

In paragraph 8, Bane does both—accommodates and refutes—in response to the objection that she is certain her Catholic *Commonweal* readers will make to the solution she has just presented at the end of paragraph 7. She knows that the comparisons she made in paragraph 7—between the church scandal and other "recent corporate and governmental scandals" and between "[w]ell-governed" secular institutions and the obviously not well-run archdiocese of Boston—would make many readers think that she was treating the church disrespectfully. To reassure readers that she respects and understands the special nature of the church, Bane has to acknowledge their concerns. Therefore, she begins paragraph 8 with a statement that she knows her readers will be relieved to hear from her: "The church is no ordinary institution." She knows that her readers would want her to concede this point because, as she makes clear in the following sentences, the spiritual nature of the church is crucial to church teaching. She invokes the authority of Vatican II to show that she accepts this point.

However, this concession does not end her counterargument. While on the one hand she tries to reassure readers, on the other hand she refutes their objection. She argues that the church is a secular organization as well as a spiritual one. It is the secular, nonreligious side of the church—what she calls "a human institution, managed by humans with all their failings"—that Bane proposes to change (8).

At the end of the essay, Bane also raises a second likely objection: "There will no doubt be accusations that Boston's lay Catholics are using the current crisis to advance their own agendas for church reform" (13). She concedes that this criticism "is, of course, partly true" (13). But she also refutes it. She knows that many of her readers will object to involving lay people in decision-making roles that have traditionally been the province of the church hierarchy. Although she tries to allay readers' concerns when she asserts that her proposal "would not . . . compromise the sacred character of the church" (12), she also criticizes lay people for not becoming involved. Again invoking the authority of Vatican II, she insists that churchgoers have "both the right and the responsibility" to speak out (13). In fact, she places part of the blame for the church's misuse of power on the passivity of churchgoers: "Many of us are now tragically aware of the consequences that follow from the concentration and misuse of power and lay deference to hierarchical authority" (13). Notice in this quotation that Bane uses the pronoun "us" to identify herself with her readers, with all lay Catholics "who love the church" and "grieve over what has happened to it in Boston."

Bane demonstrates that refutation need not be dismissive. As she refutes her readers' objections, she also tries to strengthen the bond of beliefs and values she shares with other Catholics. In planning and developing your own essay, your goals should be to anticipate a wide range of readers' inevitable questions and objections as well as to accommodate or refute these questions and objections convincingly but sensitively.

Considering Topics for Your Own Essay

Following Bane, consider making a proposal to improve the operation of an organization, business, or club to which you belong. For example, you might propose that your college keep administrative offices open in the evenings or on weekends to accommodate working students or that a child-care center be opened for students who are parents of young children. For a business, you might propose a system to handle customer complaints or a fairer way for employees to arrange their schedules. If you belong to a club that has a problem with the collection of dues, you might propose a new collection system or suggest alternative ways of raising money.

To use the Writing Guide Software to record your ideas, click on
▶ **Journal**

Katherine S. Newman *is the Malcolm Wiener Professor of Urban Studies at Harvard University; chair of the joint doctoral program in sociology, government, and social policy at Harvard's Kennedy School of Government; and dean of social science at the Radcliffe Institute for Advanced Studies. She has written many books, including* Declining Fortunes: The Withering of the American Dream *(1993),* No Shame in My Game: The Working Poor in the Inner City *(1999), and* A Different Shade of Gray: Mid-Life and Beyond in the Inner City *(2003). Her essays have appeared in popular newspapers and magazines such as the* New York Times *and* Newsweek *as well as in numerous scholarly journals such as the* American Anthropologist, *the* International Journal of Sociology and Social Policy, *and the* Brookings Review, *a* *journal concerned with public policy, in which "Dead-End Jobs: A Way Out" was originally published.*

This proposal resulted from Newman's research for No Shame in My Game, *a book that was awarded the Sidney Hillman Book Prize and the Robert F. Kennedy Book Award. As you read her proposal, notice her analysis of why the social networks that inner-city fast-food workers belong to fail to lead them to better jobs, and evaluate whether you think the proposed solution—an employer consortium (a group of cooperating employers)—"might re-create the job ladders that have disappeared," as Newman explained in an interview.*

Dead-End Jobs: A Way Out

Katherine S. Newman

Millions of Americans work full-time, year-round in jobs that still leave them stranded in poverty. Though they pound the pavement looking for better jobs, they consistently come up empty-handed. Many of these workers are in our nation's inner cities. 1

I know, because I have spent two years finding out what working life is like for 200 employees—about half African-American, half Latino—at fast-food restaurants in Harlem. Many work only part-time, though they would happily take longer hours if they could get them. Those who do work full-time earn about $8,840 (before taxes)—well below the poverty threshold for a family of four. 2

These fast-food workers make persistent efforts to get better jobs, particularly in retail and higher-paid service-sector occupations. They take civil service examinations and apply for jobs with the electric company or the phone company. Sometimes their efforts bear fruit. More often they don't. 3

A few workers make their way into the lower managerial ranks of the fast-food industry, where wages are marginally better. An even smaller number graduate into higher management, a path made possible by the internal promotion patterns long practiced by these firms. As in any industry, however, senior management opportunities are limited. Hence most workers, even those with track records as reliable employees, are locked inside a low-wage environment. Contrary to those who preach the benefits of work and persistence, the human capital these workers build up—experience in food production, inventory management, cash register operation, customer relations, minor machinery repair, and cleaning—does not pay off. These workers are often unable to move upward out of poverty. And their experience is not unusual. Hundreds of thousands of low-wage workers in American cities run into the same brick wall. Why? And what can we do about it? 4

Stagnation in the Inner City

Harlem, like many inner-city communities, has lost the manufacturing job base that once sustained its neighborhoods. Service industries that cater to neighborhood consumers, coupled with now dwindling government jobs, largely make up the local economy. With official jobless rates hovering around 18 percent (14 people apply for every minimum-wage fast-food job in Harlem), employers can select from the very top of the preference "queue." Once hired, even experienced workers have virtually nowhere to go. 5

One reason for their lack of mobility is that many employers in the primary labor market outside Harlem consider "hamburger flipper" jobs worthless. At most, employers credit the fast-food industry with training people to turn up for work on time and to fill out job applications. The real skills these workers have developed go unrecognized. However inaccurate the unflattering stereotypes, they help keep experienced workers from "graduating" out of low-wage work to more remunerative employment. . . . 6

As Harry Holzer, an economist at Michigan State University, has shown, "central-city" employers insist on specific work experience, references, and particular kinds of formal training in addition to literacy and numeracy skills, even for jobs that do not require a college degree. Demands of this kind, more stringent in the big-city labor markets than in the surrounding suburbs, clearly limit the upward mobility of the working poor in urban areas. If the only kind of job available does not provide the "right" work experience or formal training, many better jobs will be foreclosed. 7

Racial stereotypes also weaken mobility prospects. Employers view ghetto blacks, especially men, as a bad risk or a troublesome element in the workplace. They prefer immigrants or nonblack minorities, of which there are many in the Harlem labor force, who appear to them more deferential and willing to work harder for low wages. As Joleen Kirshenman and Kathryn Neckerman found in their study of Chicago workplaces, stereotypes abound among employers who have become wary of the "underclass." Primary employers exercise these preferences by discriminating against black applicants, particularly those who live in housing projects, on the grounds of perceived group characteristics. The "losers" are not given an opportunity to prove themselves. . . . 8

Social Networks

Social networks are crucial in finding work. Friends and acquaintances are far more useful sources of information than are want ads. The literature on the urban underclass suggests that inner-city neighborhoods are bereft of these critical links to the work world. My work, however, suggests a different picture: the working poor in Harlem have access to two types of occupational social networks, but neither provides upward mobility. The first is a homogeneous *lateral* network of age mates and acquaintances, employed and unemployed. It provides contacts that allow workers to move sideways in the labor market—from Kentucky Fried Chicken to Burger King or McDonald's—but not to move to jobs of higher quality. Lateral networks are useful, particularly for poor people who have to move frequently, for they help ensure a certain amount of portability in the low-wage labor market. But they do not lift workers out of poverty; they merely facilitate "churning" laterally in the low-wage world. 9

Young workers in Harlem also participate in more heterogeneous *vertical* networks with their older family members who long ago moved to suburban communities or better urban neighborhoods to become homeowners on the strength of jobs that were more widely available 20 and 30 years ago. Successful grandparents, great-aunts and uncles, and distant cousins, relatives now in their 50s and 60s, often have (or have retired from) jobs in the post office, the public sector, the transportation system, public utilities, the military, hospitals, and factories that pay union wages. But these industries are now 10 shedding workers, not hiring them. As a result, older generations are typically unable to help job-hunting young relatives.

Although little is known about the social and business networks of minority business owners and managers in the inner city, it seems that Harlem's business community, particularly its small business sector, is also walled off from the wider economy of midtown. Fast-food owners know the other people in their franchise system. They do business with banks and security firms inside the inner city. But they appear less likely to interact with firms outside the ghetto. 11

For that reason, a good recommendation from a McDonald's owner may represent a calling card that extends no farther than the general reputation of the firm and a prospective employer's perception—poor, as I have noted—of the skills that such work represents. It can move someone from an entry-level job in one restaurant to the same kind of job in another, but not into a good job elsewhere in the city. 12

Lacking personal or business-based ties that facilitate upward mobility, workers in Harlem's fast-food market find themselves on the outside looking in when it comes to the world of "good jobs." They search diligently for them, they complete many job applications, but it is the rare individual who finds a job that pays a family wage. Those who do are either workers who have been selected for internal promotion or men and women who have had the luxury of devoting their earnings solely to improving their own educational or craft credentials. Since most low-wage service workers are under pressure to support their families or contribute to the support of their parents' households, this kind of human capital investment is often difficult. As a result, the best most can do is to churn from one low-wage job to another. 13

The Employer Consortium

Some of the social ills that keep Harlem's fast-food workers at the bottom of a short job ladder—a poor urban job base, increasing downward mobility, discrimination, structural problems in the inner-city business sector—are too complex to solve quickly enough to help most of the workers I've followed. But the problem of poor social networks may be amenable to solution if formal organizations linking primary and secondary labor market employers can be developed. An "employer consortium" could help to move hard-working inner-city employees into richer job markets by providing the job information and precious referrals that "come naturally" to middle-class Americans. 14

How would an employer consortium function? It would include both inner-city employers of the working poor and downtown businesses or nonprofit institutions with higher-paid employees. Employers in the inner city would periodically select employees they consider reliable, punctual, hard-working, and motivated. Workers who have successfully completed at least one year of work would be placed in a pool of workers eligible for hiring by a set of linked employers who have better jobs to offer. Entry-level employers would, in essence, put their own good name behind successful workers as they pass them on to their consortium partners in the primary sector. 15

Primary-sector employers, for their part, would agree to hire from the pool and meet periodically with their partners in the low-wage industries to review applications and 16 follow up on the performance of those hired through the consortium. Employers "up the line" would provide training or educational opportunities to enhance the employee's skills. These training investments would make it more likely that hirees would continue to move up the new job ladders.

As they move up, the new hirees would clear the way for others to follow. First, their performance would reinforce the reputation of the employers who recommended them. Second, their achievements on the job might begin to lessen the stigma or fear their new employers may feel toward the inner-city workforce. On both counts, other consortium-based workers from the inner city would be more likely to get the same opportunities, following in a form of managed chain migration out of the inner-city labor market. Meanwhile, the attractiveness of fast-food jobs, now no better reputed among inner-city residents than among the rest of society, would grow as they became, at least potentially, a gateway to something better. 17

Advantages for Employers

Fast-food employers in Harlem run businesses in highly competitive markets. Constant pressure on prices and profit discourage them from paying wages high enough to keep a steady workforce. In fact, most such employers regard the jobs they fill as temporary placements: they *expect* successful employees to leave. And despite the simple production processes used within the fast-food industry to minimize the damage of turnover, sudden departures of knowledgeable workers still disrupt business and cause considerable frustration and exhaustion. 18

An employer consortium gives these employers—who *can't* raise wages if they hope to stay in business—a way to compete for workers who will stay with them longer than usual. In lieu of higher pay, employers can offer access to the consortium hiring pool and the prospect of a more skilled and ultimately better-paying job upon graduation from this real world "boot camp." . . . 19

Consortiums would also appeal to the civic spirit of minority business owners, who often choose to locate in places like Harlem rather than in less risky neighborhoods because they want to provide job opportunities for their own community. The big franchise operations mandate some attention to civic responsibility as well. Some fast-food firms have licensing requirements for franchisees that require demonstrated community involvement. 20

At a time when much of the public is voicing opposition to heavy-handed government efforts to prevent employment discrimination, employer consortiums have the advantage of encouraging minority hiring based on private-sector relationships. Institutional employers in particular—for example, universities and hospitals, often among the larger employers in East Coast cities—should find the consortiums especially valuable. These employers typically retain a strong commitment to workforce diversity but are often put off by the reputation of secondary-sector workers as unskilled, unmotivated, and less worthy of consideration. 21

The practical advantages for primary-sector managers are clear. Hirees have been vetted and tested. Skills have been assessed and certified in the most real world of 22 settings. A valuable base of experience and skills stands ready for further training and advancement. The consortium assures that the employers making and receiving recommendations would come to know one another, thus reinforcing the value of recommendations—a cost-effective strategy for primary-sector managers who must make significant training investments in their workers.

Minimal Government Involvement

Despite the evident advantages for both primary and secondary labor market employers, it may be necessary for governments to provide modest incentives to encourage wide participation. Secondary-sector business owners in the inner city, for example, might be deterred from participating by the prospect of losing some of their best employees at the end of a year. Guaranteeing these employers a lump sum or a tax break for every worker they promote into management internally or successfully place with a consortium participant could help break down such reluctance. 23

Primary-sector employers, who would have to provide support for training and possibly for schooling of their consortium employees, may also require some kind of tax break to subsidize their efforts at skill enhancement. Demonstration projects could experiment with various sorts of financial incentives for both sets of employers by providing grants to underwrite the costs of training new workers. 24

Local governments could also help publicize the efforts of participating employers. Most big-city mayors, for example, would be happy to shower credit on business people looking to boost the prospects of the deserving (read working) poor. 25

Government involvement, however, would be minimal. Employer consortiums could probably be assembled out of the existing economic development offices of U.S. cities, or with the help of the Chamber of Commerce and other local institutions that encourage private-sector activity. Industry- or sector-specific consortiums could probably be put together with the aid of local industry councils. 26

Moreover, some of the negative effects of prior experiments with wage subsidies for the "hard to employ"—efforts that foundered on the stigma assigned to these workers and the paperwork irritants to employers—would be reversed here. Consortium employees would be singled out for doing well, for being the cream of the crop. And the private-sector domination of employer consortiums would augur against extensive paperwork burdens. 27

Building Bridges

The inner-city fast-food workers that I have been following in Harlem have proven themselves in difficult jobs. They have shown that they are reliable, they clearly relish their economic independence, and they are willing to work hard. Still, work offers them no escape from poverty. Trapped in a minimum-wage job market, they lack bridges to the kind of work that can enable them to support their families and begin to move out of poverty. For reasons I have discussed, those bridges have not evolved naturally in our inner cities. But where they are lacking, they must be created and fostered. And we can begin with employer consortiums, to the benefit of everyone, workers and employers alike. 28

Connecting to Culture and Experience: The Value of Routine, Repetitive Work

Newman explains that one reason fast-food workers cannot find better jobs is that employers believe such workers learn only routine, repetitive skills that do not prepare them for other types of jobs.

With several students, discuss this possible limitation of fast-food jobs and other kinds of routine jobs. You may hold such a job now, or you may have held one in the past. Maybe you parked cars, delivered pizzas, ran a cash register, wiped down cars in a car wash, bagged and carried groceries or other merchandise, wrapped holiday packages, or did cleanup work. Tell each other about the routine jobs you have held. Then consider Newman's criticism of these jobs: that they only teach workers how to show up on time and follow rudimentary directions. Is this a fair criticism, do you think? Have critics overlooked certain important kinds of learning on these jobs? If so, what might these kinds of learning be? Or if you agree that these jobs are as limiting as the critics contend, what other kinds of low-paying work might teach more important skills?

Analyzing Writing Strategies

1. Reread paragraphs 1–8, where Newman **defines the problem** she believes needs to be solved. In a sentence or two, state what you understand the problem to be.

   At the end of paragraph 4, Newman asks why this problem continues. Underline the main reasons she gives in paragraphs 6–8. For her purpose and readers, how well does she define the problem? What questions might readers have about her presentation of the problem? Finally, how well does her proposed solution (employer consortiums) address the reasons the problem continues?

2. Readers are often aware of previous attempts to solve a problem, or they might think of solutions they believe are better than the one the writer is proposing. Writers who hope to win readers' support must **evaluate alternative solutions** that readers are likely to be aware of. To evaluate an alternative solution, writers usually either concede that it has some merit or refute it as meritless and not worth further consideration.

   Newman evaluates an alternative solution in paragraphs 9–13. How would you summarize this alternative to Newman's proposed solution of an employer consortium? What are the main reasons Newman gives for not taking this alternative solution seriously and encouraging readers to do the same? How well do you think she refutes this alternative to her proposed solution?

Commentary: Describing the Proposed Solution and Anticipating Objections

The heart of an essay proposing a solution to a problem is the proposed solution and the direct argument supporting the solution. Readers need to know exactly what is being proposed and how it can be implemented before they can decide whether it is feasible—cost-effective and likely to help solve the problem. Newman **describes her proposed solution** relatively fully. In paragraphs 14–17, she provides many details about the employer consortium. She begins paragraph 14 acknowledging the scope and complexity of the problem and admitting that the solution she is proposing focuses on only one aspect of the problem, "poor social networks." She ends the paragraph by explaining the goal of her proposed solution: to find better jobs for hard-working, ambitious fast-food workers. An "employer consortium," as she envisions it, would provide information about jobs and referrals to specific available jobs—the two main resources that inner-city fast-food employees lack.

Newman then describes in detail how easy it would be to implement or put into effect her solution (15–17). In explaining how an employer consortium would function, she outlines the responsibilities of the two key players in the consortium she envisions: the inner-city fast-food employers and the downtown employers with the better-paying jobs. Notice that she does not hesitate to specify criteria for eligible inner-city employees: They must be "reliable, punctual, hard-working, and motivated," and they must "have successfully completed at least one year of work" (15). To make it clear that inner-city employers will not be doing all the work, she describes how downtown employers would meet with fast-food employers, review workers' job applications, and pay attention to workers once they are on the job. The downtown employers would also be required to offer on-the-job training to prepare the new workers for better jobs (16).

She also points out some of the advantages of her solution for everyone involved. She argues that it offers inner-city employers a competitive edge without requiring them to raise wages (19). For other business owners and institutions, she argues that not only does her plan provide them with new employees who are well-trained, conscientious workers, but it also increases diversity in the workplace without government interference.

In addition to the direct argument for the solution, proposal writers usually try to **anticipate readers' likely objections**. To respond to the concern of inner-city employers that they would be continually giving up their best workers, Newman suggests that employers' reputations would be enhanced and the image of fast-food work would improve as the jobs came to be seen as a step to better jobs (17). She also argues that fast-food workers would presumably be more committed to doing a good job if the quality of their work could lead to a better job downtown—and their employers would benefit as a result. In addition, she acknowledges both that the loss of experienced workers would be a financial disadvantage to inner-city employers and that the costs of training employees would be an added burden to consortium employers. To accommodate these concerns, she adds to her proposal government subsidies to compensate employers (23–24).

When you plan your essay, you will need to develop an argument with your readers in mind, trying to convince them that your proposed solution makes sense and can be put into effect.

Considering Topics for Your Own Essay

Think of barriers or obstacles you have met or expect to meet in realizing your goals and dreams. You might want to think specifically about obstacles to preparing for and entering the career of your choice, but you need not limit yourself to career goals. Perhaps you are not able to get into an internship program that would give you some experience with the kind of work you hope to do. Perhaps your high school did not offer the courses you needed to prepare for the college major you want to pursue. Perhaps at some crucial point in your life you received inadequate medical care or counseling. Identify an obstacle you faced and think of it as a general problem to be solved; that is, assume that other people have confronted the same obstacle. How would you define the problem? How might you propose to solve it? To be more than a personal complaint about bad luck or mistreatment, your proposal would need to appeal to readers who have experienced a similar obstacle or who would be able to remove the obstacle or give sound advice on getting around it.

To use the Writing Guide Software to record your ideas, click on
▶ **Journal**

Patrick O'Malley *wrote the following proposal while he was a first-year college student. He proposes that college professors give students frequent brief examinations in addition to the usual midterm and final exams. After discussing with his instructor his unusual rhetorical situation—a student advising professors—he decided to revise the essay into the form of an open letter to professors at his college, a letter that might appear in the campus newspaper.*

O'Malley's essay may strike you as unusually authoritative. This tone of authority is due in large part to what O'Malley learned about the possibilities and problems of frequent exams as he interviewed two professors (his writing instructor and the writing program director) and talked with several students. As you read his essay, notice particularly how he anticipates professors' likely objections to his proposal and evaluates their preferred solutions to the problem he identifies.

To see this essay with pop-up annotations in the software, click on
▶ **Proposing a Solution**
▶ **Read**

More Testing, More Learning

Patrick O'Malley

It's late at night. The final's tomorrow. You got a C on the 1
midterm, so this one will make or break you. Will it be like the midterm? Did you study enough? Did you study the right things? It's too late to drop the course. So what

happens if you fail? No time to worry about that now—you've got a ton of notes to go over.

Although this last-minute anxiety about midterm and final exams is only too familiar to most college students, many professors may not realize how such major, infrequent, high-stakes exams work against the best interests of students both psychologically and intellectually. They cause unnecessary amounts of stress, placing too much importance on one or two days in the students' entire term, judging ability on a single or dual performance. They don't encourage frequent study, and they fail to inspire students' best performance. If professors gave additional brief exams at frequent intervals, students would be spurred to study more regularly, learn more, worry less, and perform better on midterms, finals, and other papers and projects. 2

Ideally, a professor would give an in-class test or quiz after each unit, chapter, or focus of study, depending on the type of class and course material. A physics class might require a test on concepts after every chapter covered, while a history class could necessitate quizzes covering certain time periods or major events. These exams should be given weekly or at least twice monthly. Whenever possible, they should consist of two or three essay questions rather than many multiple-choice or short-answer questions. To preserve class time for lecture and discussion, exams should take no more than 15 or 20 minutes. 3

The main reason professors should give frequent exams is that when they do and when they provide feedback to students on how well they are doing, students learn more in the course and perform better on major exams, projects, and papers. It makes sense that in a challenging course containing a great deal of material, students will learn more of it and put it to better use if they have to apply or "practice" it frequently on exams, which also helps them find out how much they are learning and what they need to go over again. A recent Harvard study notes students' "strong preference for frequent evaluation in a course." Harvard students feel they learn least in courses that have "only a midterm and a final exam, with no other personal evaluation." They believe they learn most in courses with "many opportunities to see how they are doing" (Light, 1990, p. 32). In a review of a number of studies of student learning, Frederiksen (1984) reports that students who take weekly quizzes achieve higher scores on final exams than students who take only a midterm exam and that testing increases retention of material tested. 4

Another, closely related argument in favor of multiple exams is that they encourage students to improve their study habits. Greater frequency in test taking means greater frequency in studying for tests. Students prone to cramming will be required—or at least strongly motivated—to open their textbooks and notebooks more often, making them less likely to resort to long, kamikaze nights of studying for major exams. Since there is so much to be learned in the typical course, it makes sense that frequent, careful study and review are highly beneficial. But students need motivation to study regularly, and nothing works like an exam. If students had frequent exams in all their courses, they would have to schedule study time each week and gradually would develop a habit of frequent study. It might be argued that students are adults who have to learn how to manage their own lives, but learning history or physics is more complicated than learning to drive a car or balance a checkbook. Students need coaching and practice in learning. The 5 right way to learn new material needs to become a habit, and I believe that frequent exams are key to developing good habits of study and learning. The Harvard study concludes that "tying regular evaluation to good course organization enables students to plan their work more than a few days in advance. If quizzes and homework are scheduled on specific days, students plan their work to capitalize on them" (Light, 1990, p. 33).

By encouraging regular study habits, frequent exams would also decrease anxiety 6 by reducing the procrastination that produces anxiety. Students would benefit psychologically if they were not subjected to the emotional ups and downs caused by major exams, when after being virtually worry-free for weeks they are suddenly ready to check into the psychiatric ward. Researchers at the University of Vermont found a strong relationship among procrastination, anxiety, and achievement. Students who regularly put off studying for exams had continuing high anxiety and lower grades than students who procrastinated less. The researchers found that even "low" procrastinators did not study regularly and recommended that professors give frequent assignments and exams to reduce procrastination and increase achievement (Rothblum, Solomon, & Murakami, 1986, pp. 393–394).

Research supports my proposed solution to the problems I have described. Com- 7 mon sense as well as my experience and that of many of my friends support it. Why, then, do so few professors give frequent brief exams? Some believe that such exams take up too much of the limited class time available to cover the material in the course. Most courses meet 150 minutes a week—three times a week for 50 minutes each time. A 20-minute weekly exam might take 30 minutes to administer, and that is one-fifth of each week's class time. From the student's perspective, however, this time is well spent. Better learning and greater confidence about the course seem a good trade-off for another 30 minutes of lecture. Moreover, time lost to lecturing or discussion could easily be made up in students' learning on their own through careful regular study for the weekly exams. If weekly exams still seem too time-consuming to some professors, their frequency could be reduced to every other week or their length to 5 or 10 minutes. In courses where multiple-choice exams are appropriate, several questions could be designed to take only a few minutes to answer.

Another objection professors have to frequent exams is that they take too much 8 time to read and grade. In a 20-minute essay exam, a well-prepared student can easily write two pages. A relatively small class of 30 students might then produce 60 pages, no small amount of material to read each week. A large class of 100 or more students would produce an insurmountable pile of material. There are a number of responses to this objection. Again, professors could give exams every other week or make them very short. Instead of reading them closely they could skim them quickly to see whether students understand an idea or can apply it to an unfamiliar problem; and instead of numerical or letter grades they could give a plus, check, or minus. Exams could be collected and responded to only every third or fourth week. Professors who have readers or teaching assistants could rely on them to grade or check exams. And the Scantron machine is always available for instant grading of multiple-choice exams. Finally, frequent exams could be given *in place of* a midterm exam or out-of-class essay assignment.

Since frequent exams seem to some professors to create too many problems, however, it is reasonable to consider alternative ways to achieve the same goals. One alternative solution is to implement a program that would improve study skills. While such a program might teach students how to study for exams, it cannot prevent procrastination or reduce "large test anxiety" by a substantial amount. One research team studying anxiety and test performance found that study skills training was not effective in reducing anxiety or improving performance (Dendato & Diener, 1986, p. 134). This team, which also reviewed other research that reached the same conclusion, did find that a combination of "cognitive/relaxation therapy" and study skills training was effective. This possible solution seems complicated, however, not to mention time-consuming and expensive. It seems much easier and more effective to change the cause of the bad habit rather than treat the habit itself. That is, it would make more sense to solve the problem at its root: the method of learning and evaluation. 9

Still another solution might be to provide frequent study questions for students to answer. These would no doubt be helpful in focusing students' time studying, but students would probably not actually write out the answers unless they were required to. To get students to complete the questions in a timely way, professors would have to collect and check the answers. In that case, however, they might as well devote the time to grading an exam. Even if it asks the same questions, a scheduled exam is preferable to a set of study questions because it takes far less time to write in class, compared to the time students would devote to responding to questions at home. In-class exams also ensure that each student produces his or her own work. 10

Another possible solution would be to help students prepare for midterm and final exams by providing sets of questions from which the exam questions will be selected or announcing possible exam topics at the beginning of the course. This solution would have the advantage of reducing students' anxiety about learning every fact in the textbook, and it would clarify the course goals, but it would not motivate students to study carefully each new unit, concept, or text chapter in the course. I see this as a way of complementing frequent exams, not as substituting for them. 11

From the evidence and from my talks with professors and students, I see frequent, brief in-class exams as the only way to improve students' study habits and learning, reduce their anxiety and procrastination, and increase their satisfaction with college. These exams are not a panacea, but only more parking spaces and a winning football team would do as much to improve college life. Professors can't do much about parking or football, but they can give more frequent exams. Campus administrators should get behind this effort, and professors should get together to consider giving exams more frequently. It would make a difference. 12

References

Dendato, K. M., & Diener, D. (1986). Effectiveness of cognitive/relaxation therapy and study-skills training in reducing self-reported anxiety and improving the academic performance of test-anxious students. *Journal of Counseling Psychology, 33,* 131–135.

Frederiksen, N. (1984). The real test bias: Influences of testing on teaching and learning. *American Psychologist, 39,* 193–202.

Light, R. J. (1990). *Explorations with students and faculty about teaching, learning, and student life.* Cambridge, MA: Harvard University Graduate School of Education and Kennedy School of Government.

Rothblum, E. D., Solomon, L., & Murakami, J. (1986). Affective, cognitive, and behavioral differences between high and low procrastinators. *Journal of Counseling Psychology, 33,* 387–394.

Connecting to Culture and Experience: Experience with Frequent Exams

O'Malley advocates frequent brief exams as a solution to the problems of midterm- and final-exam anxiety, poor study habits, and disappointing exam performance. With two or three other students, discuss O'Malley's proposal in light of your own experience. To what extent do your courses without frequent exams produce the problems he identifies? Which of your high school or college courses included frequent exams? Describe these courses and the kinds of exams they offered. When you were taking these courses, what effect did the frequent exams have on your study habits, anxiety level, and mastery of the coursework?

Analyzing Writing Strategies

1. O'Malley devotes almost a third of his essay to **anticipating readers' likely objections** to his proposal. This section of the essay begins in the middle of paragraph 5 (with the sentence "It might be argued . . .") and then resumes in paragraphs 7 and 8. Begin by underlining the three objections, one each in paragraphs 5, 7, and 8. Then make notes about how O'Malley **counterargues** these objections. Finally, evaluate how successful each counterargument seems to be for its intended readers—college professors. What seems most and least convincing in each counterargument?

For more on counterarguing, see Chapter 19.

2. Readers of proposals are nearly always aware of solutions different from the one the writer is proposing. Readers may know of alternatives to the writer's solution—a solution someone has already proposed or one that has been tried with mixed results. Or—as readers have a tendency to do—they may think of an alternative solution after learning about the writer's preferred one. Consequently, effective proposals try to evaluate one or more likely alternative solutions. O'Malley **evaluates alternative solutions** in paragraphs 9–10, a different one in each paragraph. Reread these counterarguments and notice two things: the strategies and resources that O'Malley relies on and the extent to which he either concedes that some good ideas can be found in each alternative or refutes alternatives as unworkable. How do you think his intended readers will react to these paragraphs? What might they find most and least convincing?

3. Turn to this chapter's Writer at Work section (pp. 384–85), where part of O'Malley's first draft appears. Compare the draft paragraph that begins "Lastly, with multiple exams . . ." with paragraph 4 of his final essay, and list specific changes he made from draft to revision. Knowing his purpose and readers, what advantages do you see in his changes?

Commentary: Supporting the Proposed Solution

O'Malley's essay demonstrates the importance of taking readers seriously. Not only does he interview both those who would carry out his proposal (professors) and those who would benefit from it (students), but he also features in his essay what he has learned from these interviews. Paragraphs 7–11 directly acknowledge professors' objections, their questions, and the alternative solutions they would probably prefer. These counterarguments, which may be essential to convincing readers to support a proposal, are only part of the overall argument, which centers on the writer's direct support of the proposed solution. Most of O'Malley's **direct argument** can be found in paragraphs 4–6, in which O'Malley presents three reasons that professors should give frequent exams: Students will (1) learn more and perform better on major exams, projects, and essays; (2) acquire better study habits; and (3) experience decreased anxiety and improved performance. He supports each reason with a combination of assertions based on his own experience and references to reputable research studies carried out at three universities. He quotes and paraphrases these studies.

For more on quoting and paraphrasing, see Chapter 22.

Argument and counterargument can be woven together in many different ways in an essay proposing a solution to a problem. Because O'Malley succeeds at balancing argument and counterargument, the organization of his proposal is worth noting. The following is a scratch **outline** of his essay:

opening: a scenario to introduce the problem (paragraph 1)
presentation of the problem and introduction of the solution (2)
details of the solution (3)
reason 1: improved learning and performance (4)
reason 2: improved study habits (5)
refutation of objection 1: students as adults (5)
reason 3: less procrastination and anxiety (6)
accommodation of objection 2: limited class time (7)
accommodation of objection 3: too much work (8)
refutation of alternative solution 1: study-skills training (9)
refutation of alternative solution 2: study questions (10)
accommodation of alternative solution 3: sample exam questions (11)
closing: reiteration of the proposed solution and advice on implementing it (12)

Except for a brief refutation in paragraph 5, O'Malley first presents the direct argument for frequent exams (paragraphs 4–6) and then counterargues (paragraphs

7–11). The outline reveals that counterargument takes up most of the space, not an unusual balance in proposals to solve problems. O'Malley might have counterargued first or counterargued as he presented his direct argument, as he does briefly in paragraph 5. The approach you take depends on what your readers know about the problem and their experience with other proposed solutions to it.

Considering Topics for Your Own Essay

Much of what happens in high school and college is predictable and conventional. Examples of conventional practices that have changed very little over the years are exams, group instruction, graduation ceremonies, required courses, and lowered admission requirements for athletes. Think of additional examples of established practices in high school or college; then select one that you believe needs to be improved or refined in some way. What changes would you propose? What individual or group might be convinced to take action on your proposal for improvement? What questions or objections should you anticipate? How could you discover whether others have previously proposed improvements in the practice you are concerned with? Whom might you interview to learn more about the practice and the likelihood of changing it?

You can use the electronic journal in the Writing Guide Software to record your thoughts about possible topics for your essay, as well as for other notes you make later in the writing process. The journal automatically records the date and the chapter for which the entry was written and allows you to sort entries by date, subject, or chapter.

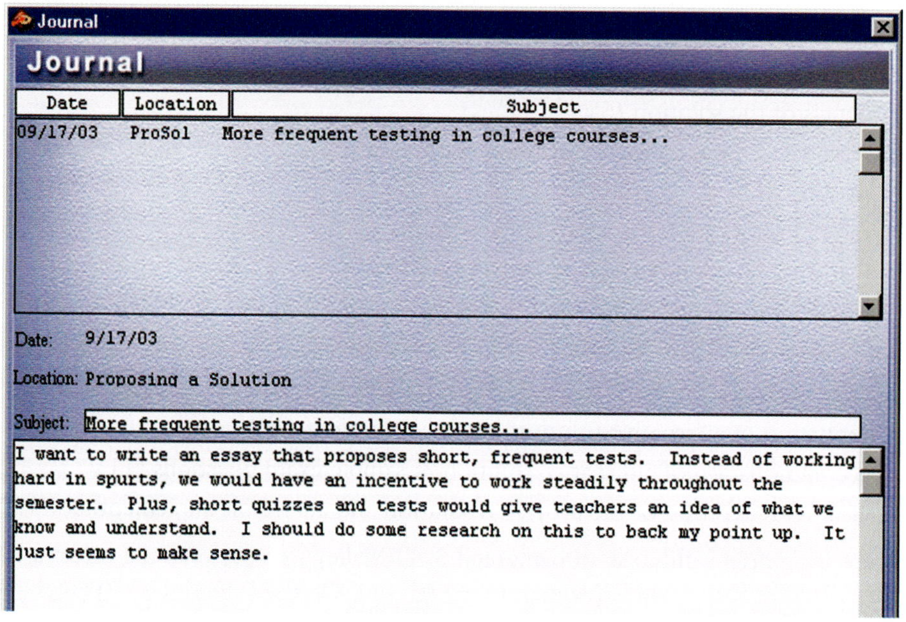

PURPOSE AND AUDIENCE

Most proposals are calls to action. Because of this clear purpose, a writer must anticipate readers' needs and concerns more when writing a proposal than in any other kind of writing. The writer attempts not only to convince readers but also to inspire them, to persuade them to support or implement the proposed solution. What your particular readers know about the problem and what they are capable of doing to solve it determine how you address them.

Readers of proposals are often unaware of the problem. In this case, your task is clear: to present them with evidence that will convince them of its existence. This evidence may include statistics, testimony from witnesses or experts, and examples, including the personal experiences of people involved with the problem. You can also speculate about the cause of the problem and describe its ill effects.

Sometimes readers recognize the existence of a problem but fail to take it seriously. When readers are indifferent, you may need to connect the problem closely to their own concerns. For instance, you might show how much they have in common with the people directly affected by it or how it affects them indirectly. However you appeal to readers, you must do more than alert them to the problem; you must also make them care about it. You want to touch readers emotionally as well as intellectually.

At other times, readers concerned about the problem may assume that someone else is taking care of it and that they need not become personally involved. In this situation, you might want to demonstrate that the people they thought were taking care of the problem have failed. Another assumption readers might make is that a solution they supported in the past has already solved the problem. You might point out that the original solution has proved unworkable or that new solutions have become available through changed circumstances or improved technology. Your aim is to rekindle these readers' interest in the problem.

Perhaps the most satisfying proposals are addressed to parties who can take immediate action to remedy the problem. You may have the opportunity to write such a proposal if you choose a problem faced by a group to which you belong. Not only do you have a firsthand understanding of the problem, but you also have a good idea of the kinds of solutions that other members of the group will support. (You might informally survey some of them before you submit your proposal to test your definition of the problem and your proposed solution.) When you address readers who are in a position to take action, you want to assure them that it is wise to do so. You must demonstrate that the solution is feasible—that it can be implemented and that it will work.

BASIC FEATURES: PROPOSING SOLUTIONS

A Well-Defined Problem

A proposal is written to offer a solution to a problem. Before presenting the solution, the writer must be sure that readers know and understand what the problem is. Patrick O'Malley, for example, devotes the first three paragraphs of his essay to defining the problem of infrequent course exams. It is wise to define the problem explicitly, as all the writers in this chapter do.

Stating the problem is not enough, however; the writer also must establish the problem as serious enough to need solving. Sometimes a writer can assume that readers will recognize the problem and its seriousness. For example, Hertsgaard assumes his readers understand the seriousness of the problem; his challenge is to help them overcome their feeling of fatalism so that they will pay attention to the solution he is proposing. At other times, readers may not be aware of the problem and will need to be convinced that it deserves their attention. Katherine S. Newman, for instance, does not assume that her readers will understand how difficult it is for inner-city fast-food workers to find better jobs.

In addition to defining the problem and establishing its seriousness for readers, a proposal writer may have to analyze the problem, exploring its causes, consequences, and history and past efforts at dealing with it.

A Clearly Described Solution

Once the problem is defined and its existence established, the writer must describe the solution so that readers can readily imagine what it would be like. Because O'Malley assumes that his readers know what brief exams are like, he runs little risk in not describing them. He does, however, identify their approximate lengths and possible forms—brief essay, short answer, or multiple choice. In contrast, because Newman cannot assume her readers will know what she means by an employer consortium, she describes it at length, focusing on who would be involved and the roles they would play.

A Convincing Argument in Support of the Proposed Solution

The main purpose of a proposal is to convince readers that the writer's solution will help to solve the problem. To this end, O'Malley gives three reasons why he thinks more brief exams will solve the problem and supports each reason with published research studies as well as his own experience. Similarly, Bane argues that the practices she proposes would counteract "the closed, secret, and self-protecting nature of the decisions" currently made by the church hierarchy (paragraph 6).

Writers must also argue that the proposed solution is feasible—that it can actually be implemented and that it will work. The easier it is to implement, the more likely it is to win readers' support. Therefore, writers sometimes set out the steps required to put the proposed solution into practice, an especially important strategy when the solution might seem difficult, time-consuming, or expensive to enact. All the writers in this chapter offer specific suggestions for implementing their proposals, though none outlines all the steps required. For example, O'Malley offers professors several specific ways to give their students frequent, brief exams; Hertsgaard explains how government pump priming would work; Bane suggests some of the practices that the church could adopt from secular organizations; and Newman offers many details about how an employer consortium would function.

An Anticipation of Readers' Objections and Questions

The writer arguing for a proposal must anticipate objections or reservations that readers may have about the proposed solution. Probably the greatest concern Hertsgaard anticipates is his readers' sense that the problem is too overwhelming to be solved. He accommodates or concedes the scope and seriousness of the problem but refutes his readers' hopelessness, arguing that we have already made progress in some areas and we possess the technology to make additional progress. Bane also combines accommodation with refutation, citing an authority (Vatican II) that she assumes her readers value as highly as she does.

An Evaluation of Alternative Solutions

Proposal writers sometimes try to convince readers that the proposed solution is preferable to other possible solutions. They may compare the proposed solution to other solutions readers may know about or ones they may think of themselves. O'Malley, for example, evaluates three alternative solutions—study-skills training, study questions, and sample exam questions as alternatives to frequent exams—and demonstrates what is wrong with each one. He rejects study-skills training because it is overly complicated, time-consuming, and expensive. He rejects study questions because, compared with exams, they would not save either students or professors any time or ensure that students each do their own individual work. He rejects the sample exam questions by arguing that it solves only part of the problem.

GUIDE TO WRITING
Proposing Solutions

THE WRITING ASSIGNMENT

THE WRITING ASSIGNMENT

Write an essay proposing a solution to a problem. Choose a problem faced by a community or group to which you belong, and address your proposal to one or more members of the group or to outsiders who might help solve the problem.

INVENTION AND RESEARCH

INVENTION & RESEARCH

- Finding a Problem to Write About
- Analyzing and Defining the Problem
- Identifying Your Readers
- Finding a Tentative Solution
- Defending Your Solution
- Testing Your Choice
- Offering Reasons for Your Proposal
- Considering Alternative Solutions
- Doing Research
- Considering Document Design
- Defining Your Purpose for Your Readers
- Formulating a Tentative Thesis Statement

PLANNING AND DRAFTING

PLANNING & DRAFTING

- Seeing What You Have
- Setting Goals
- Outlining
- Drafting

CRITICAL READING GUIDE

CRITICAL READING GUIDE

- First Impression
- Definition of the Problem
- Description of the Solution
- Convincing Argument in Support of Proposed Solution
- Anticipation of Readers' Objections, Questions
- Evaluation of Alternative Solutions
- Effectiveness of Organization
- Final Thoughts

REVISING

REVISING

- A Well-Defined Problem
- A Clearly Described Solution
- A Convincing Argument in Support of the Proposed Solution
- An Anticipation of Readers' Objections, Questions
- An Evaluation of Alternative Solutions
- The Organization

EDITING AND PROOFREADING

EDITING & PROOFREADING

- Checking for Ambiguous Use of *This* and *That*
- Checking for Sentences That Lack an Agent

GUIDE TO WRITING

THE WRITING ASSIGNMENT

Write an essay proposing a solution to a problem. Choose a problem faced by a community or group to which you belong, and address your proposal to one or more members of the group or to outsiders who might help solve the problem.

> To use the Writing Guide Software for this assignment, click on
> ▶ **Proposing a Solution**
> ▶ **Write**

INVENTION AND RESEARCH

The following activities will help you prepare to write a proposal. You will choose a problem you can write about, analyze and define the problem, identify your prospective readers, decide on and defend your proposed solution, test your choice, offer reasons and support for adopting your proposal, and consider readers' objections and alternative solutions, among other things. These activities are easy to complete. Doing them over several days will give your ideas time to ripen and grow. Be sure to keep a written record of your invention and research to use later when you draft and revise.

Finding a Problem to Write About

You may have already thought about a problem you could write about. Or you may have been drawn to one of the problems suggested by the Considering Topics for Your Own Essay activities following the readings in this chapter. Even so, you will want to consider several problems that need solving before making your final choice. The following activity will help you get started.

Listing Problems. *Make a list of problems you could write about.* Make a double-column chart like the following one. Divide a piece of paper or your computer screen into two columns. In the left-hand column, list communities, groups, or organizations to which you belong. Include as many communities as possible: college, neighborhood, hometown, and cultural or ethnic groups. Also include groups you participate in: sports, musical, work, religious, political, support, hobby, and so on. In the right-hand column, list any problems that exist within each group. Here is how such a chart might begin:

Community	*Problem*
My college	Poor advising or orientation Shortage of practice rooms in music building No financial aid for part-time students Lack of facilities for disabled students Lack of enough sections of required courses Class scheduling that does not accommodate working students or students with children
My neighborhood	Need for traffic light at dangerous intersection Unsupervised children getting into trouble Megastores driving away small businesses Lack of safe places for children to play

Listing Problems Related to Identity and Community. Writing a proposal can give you special insight into issues of identity and community by helping you understand how members of a community negotiate their individual needs and concerns. You may already have made a chart of communities to which you belong and problems in those communities. The following categories may help you think of additional problems in those or other communities that you could add to your list:

- Disagreement over conforming to community standards
- Conflicting economic, cultural, or political interests within the community
- Problems with equity or fairness between men and women, rich and poor, different ethnic groups
- Lack of respect or trust among the members of the community
- Struggles for leadership of the community

Listing Problems Related to Work and Career. Proposals are frequently written on the job and about the work people do. Based on your work experience, make a double-column chart like the following one. List the places you have worked in the left column and the problems you encountered on the job in the right column.

Workplace	*Problem*
Restaurant	Inadequate training Conflicts with supervisor Unfair shift assignments
Department store	Inadequate inventory Computer glitches Overcomplicated procedures
Office	Unfair workloads Changing requirements Inflexible work schedules Lack of information about procedures Difficulty in scheduling vacations Outdated technology

Choosing a Problem. *Choose one problem from your list that seems especially important to you, that concerns others in the group or community, and that seems solvable.* (You need not know the exact solution now.) The problem should also be one that you can explore in detail and are willing to discuss in writing.

Proposing to solve a problem in a group or community to which you belong gives you an inestimably important advantage: You can write as an expert, an insider. You know about the history of the problem, have felt the urgency to solve it, and perhaps have already thought of possible solutions. Equally important, you will know precisely to whom to address the proposal, and you can interview others in the group to get their views of the problem and to understand how they might resist your solution. From such a position of knowledge and authority comes confident, convincing writing.

Should you want to propose a solution for a social problem of national scope, concentrate on one with which you have direct experience and for which you can suggest a detailed plan of action. Even better, focus on unique local aspects of the problem. For example, if you would like to propose a solution to the lack of affordable child care for children of college students or working parents, you have a great advantage if you are a parent who has experienced the frustration of finding professional, affordable child care. Moreover, even though such a problem is national in scope, it may be solvable only campus by campus, business by business, or neighborhood by neighborhood.

Analyzing and Defining the Problem

Before you can begin to consider the best possible solution, you must analyze the problem carefully and then try to define it. Keep in mind that you will have to demonstrate to readers that the problem exists, that it is serious, and that you have a more than casual understanding of its causes and consequences. If you find that you cannot do so, you will want to select some other problem to write about.

Analyzing. *Start by writing a few sentences in response to these questions:*

- Does the problem really exist? How can I tell?
- What caused this problem? Can I identify any immediate causes? Any deeper causes? Is the problem caused by a flaw in the system, a lack of resources, individual misconduct or incompetence? How can I tell?
- What is the history of the problem?
- What are the bad effects of the problem? How does it harm members of the community or group? What goals of the group are endangered by the existence of this problem? Does it raise any moral or ethical questions?
- Who in the community or group is affected by the problem? Be as specific as possible: Who is seriously affected? Minimally affected? Unaffected? Does anyone benefit from its existence?
- What similar problems exist in this same community or group? How can I distinguish my problem from these?

Defining. *Write a definition of the problem, being as specific as possible.* Identify who or what seems responsible for it, and give one recent, telling example.

Identifying Your Readers

In a few sentences, describe your readers, stating your reason for directing your proposal to them. Then take a few minutes to write about these readers. Whom do you need to address—everyone in the community or group, a committee, an individual, an outsider? You want to address your proposal to the person or group who can help implement it. The following questions will help you develop a profile of your readers:

- How informed are my readers likely to be about the problem? Have they shown any awareness of it?
- Why would this problem be important to my readers? Why would they care about solving it?
- Have my readers supported any other proposals to solve this problem? If so, what do those proposals have in common with mine?
- Do my readers ally themselves with any group, and would that alliance cause them to favor or reject my proposal? Do we share any values or attitudes that could bring us together to solve the problem?
- How have my readers responded to other problems? Do their past reactions suggest anything about how they might respond to my proposal?

Finding a Tentative Solution

Solving problems takes time. Apparent solutions often turn out to be impossible. After all, a solution has to be both workable and acceptable to the community or group involved. Consequently, you should strive to come up with several possible solutions whose advantages and disadvantages you can weigh. You may notice that the most imaginative solutions sometimes occur to you only after you have struggled with a number of other possibilities.

Look back at the way you defined the problem and described your readers. Then with these factors in mind, list as many possible solutions to the problem as you can think of. You might come up with only two or three possible solutions; but at this stage, the more the better. To come up with different solutions, use the following problem-solving questions:

- What solutions to this problem have already been tried?
- What solutions have been proposed for related problems? Might they solve this problem as well?
- Is a solution required that would disband or change the community or group in some way?
- What solution might eliminate some of the causes of the problem?
- What solution would eliminate any of the bad effects of the problem?

- Is the problem too big to be solved all at once? Can I divide it into several related problems? What solutions might solve one or more of these problems?
- If a series of solutions is required, which should come first? Second?
- What solution would ultimately solve the problem?
- What might be a daring solution, arousing the most resistance but perhaps holding out the most promise?
- What would be the most conservative solution, acceptable to nearly everyone in the community or group?

Give yourself enough time to let your ideas percolate as you continue to add to your list of possible solutions and to consider the advantages and disadvantages of each one in light of your prospective readers. If possible, discuss your solutions with those members of the community or group who can help you consider the advantages and disadvantages of each one.

Choosing the Most Promising Solution. *In a sentence or two, state what you consider the best possible way of solving the problem.*

Determining Specific Steps. *Write down the major stages or steps necessary to carry out your solution.* This list of steps will provide an early test of whether your solution can, in fact, be implemented.

Defending Your Solution

Proposals have to be feasible—that is, they must be both reasonable and practical. Imagine that one of your readers strongly opposes your proposed solution and confronts you with the following statements. *Write a few sentences refuting each one.*

- It would not really solve the problem.
- I am comfortable with things as they are.
- We cannot afford it.
- It would take too long.
- People would not do it.
- Too few people would benefit.
- I do not even see how to get started on your solution.
- We already tried that, with unsatisfactory results.
- You support this proposal merely because it would benefit you personally.

Answering these questions should help you prepare responses to possible objections. If you feel that you need a better idea of how others are likely to feel about your proposal, talk with a few people who are directly involved with or affected by the problem. The more you know about your readers' concerns, the better you will be able to anticipate their reservations and preferred alternative solutions.

Testing Your Choice

Now examine the problem and your proposed solution to see whether you can write a strong proposal. Start by asking yourself the following questions:

- Is this a significant problem? Do other people in the community or group really care about it, or can they be persuaded to care?
- Will my solution really solve the problem? Can it be implemented?
- Can I answer objections from enough people in the community or group to win support for my solution?

As you plan and draft your proposal, you will probably want to consider these questions again. If at any point you decide that you cannot answer them with a confident yes, you may want to consider proposing a different, more feasible solution to the problem; if none exists, you may need to choose a different problem to write about.

Testing Your Choice: A Collaborative Activity

At this point, you will find it useful to get together with two or three other students and present your plans to one another. This collaborative activity will help you determine whether you can write this proposal in a way that will interest and convince others.

Presenters: Take turns briefly defining the problem you hope to solve, identifying your intended readers, and describing your proposed solution.

Listeners: Tell the presenter whether the proposed solution seems appropriate and feasible for the situation and intended readers. Suggest objections and reservations you believe readers may have.

Offering Reasons for Your Proposal

To make a convincing case for your proposed solution, you must offer your readers good reasons for adopting your proposal.

Listing Reasons. *Write down every plausible reason you could give that might persuade readers to accept your proposal.* These reasons should answer your readers' key question: Why is this the best possible solution?

Choosing the Strongest Reasons. *Put an asterisk next to the strongest reasons—the reasons most likely to be convincing to your intended readers.* If you do not consider at least two or three of your reasons strong, you will probably have difficulty developing a strong proposal and should reconsider your topic.

Evaluating Your Strongest Reasons. *Now look at your strongest reasons and explain briefly why you think each one will be effective with your particular readers, the members of the group or community you are addressing.*

Considering Alternative Solutions

List alternative solutions that members of the group or community might offer when they learn about your solution, and consider the advantages and disadvantages of each one relative to your solution. Even if members are likely to consider your proposal reasonable, they will probably want to compare your proposed solution with other possible solutions. You might find it helpful to chart the information as follows:

Possible Solutions	*Advantages*	*Disadvantages*
My solution		
Alternative solution 1		
Alternative solution 2		
Etc.		

Researching Alternative Solutions: An Online Activity

Searching the Web can be a productive way of learning about solutions other people have proposed or tried out. If possible, use your online research to identify at least two alternative solutions. Your purpose is to gain information about these solutions that will help you evaluate them fairly. Here are some specific suggestions for finding information about solutions:

- Enter keywords—words or brief phrases related to the problem or a solution—into a search tool such as Google (www.google.com) or Yahoo! (www.yahoo.com). For example, if you are concerned that many children in your neighborhood have no adult supervision after school, you could try keywords associated with the problem such as *latchkey kids,* or keywords associated with possible solutions such as *after-school programs.*
- If you think solutions to your problem may have been proposed by a government agency, you could try adding the word *government* to your keywords or searching on FirstGov.gov, the U.S. government's official Web portal. For example, you might explore the problem of latchkey children by following links at the Web site of the U.S. Department of Health & Human Services (www.hhs.gov). If you want to see whether the problem has been addressed in your state or local government, you can go to the Library of Congress Internet Resource Page on State and Local Governments (www.loc.gov/global/state/) and follow the links.

Add to your chart of the advantages and disadvantages of alternative solutions any information you find from your online research. Bookmark or keep a record of promising sites. You may want to download or copy information you could use in your essay, including visuals; if so, remember to record documentation information.

Doing Research

For guidelines on library and Internet research, see Chapter 21.

So far you have relied largely on your own knowledge and experience for ideas about solving the problem. You may now feel that you need to do some research to learn more about the causes of the problem and to find more technical information about implementing the solution.

If you are proposing a solution to a problem about which others have written, you will want to find out how they have defined the problem and what solutions they have proposed. You may need to acknowledge these solutions in your essay, either accommodating or refuting them. Now is a good time—before you start drafting—to get any additional information you need. If you are proposing a solution to a local problem, you will want to conduct informal interviews with several people who are aware of or affected by the problem. Find out whether they know anything about its history and current ill effects. Try out your solution on them. Discover whether they have other solutions in mind.

For more on interviewing, see Chapter 20.

Considering Document Design

Think about whether your readers might benefit from design features, such as headings, numbered lists, or other elements that would make your presentation of the problem easier to follow and your solution more convincing. Earlier in this chapter's readings, for instance, Katherine S. Newman uses headings to introduce the major sections of her proposal. Consider also whether visuals—drawings, photographs, tables, or graphs—would strengthen your argument. These are not required for essays proposing a solution, but they could be helpful. You may come across promising visuals in your research and either download them from the Internet or make photocopies from library materials. When you reproduce visuals, make sure to acknowledge their sources. If you are going to post your essay on the Web, you also need to ask the source for permission.

For more on document design, see Chapter 25. For guidelines on acknowledging the sources of visuals, see Chapter 22.

Defining Your Purpose for Your Readers

Write a few sentences defining your purpose in proposing a solution to a problem of concern to the particular readers you have in mind. Remember that you have already identified your readers in the group or community you are addressing and developed your proposal with these readers in mind. Given these readers, try now to define your purpose by considering the following questions:

- Do I seek incremental, moderate, or radical change? Am I being realistic about what my readers are prepared to do? How can I overcome their natural aversion to change of any kind?
- How can I ensure that my readers will not remain indifferent to the problem?
- Who can I count on for support, and what can I do to consolidate that support? Who will oppose my solution? Shall I write them off or seek common ground with them?

- What exactly do I want my readers to do? To take my proposed solution as a starting point for further discussion about the problem? To take action immediately to implement my solution? To commit themselves to take certain preliminary steps, like seeking funding or testing the feasibility of the solution? To take some other action?

Formulating a Tentative Thesis Statement

Write one or more sentences that could serve as your tentative thesis statement. In most essays proposing solutions to problems, the thesis statement is a concise assertion or announcement of the solution. Think about how emphatic you should make the thesis and whether you should include in it a forecast of your reasons.

For more on thesis and forecasting statements, see Chapter 13.

Review the readings in this chapter to see how other writers construct their thesis statements. For example, recall that Patrick O'Malley states his thesis early in his essay: "If professors gave additional brief exams at frequent intervals, students would be spurred to study more regularly, learn more, worry less, and perform better on midterms, finals, and other papers and projects" (paragraph 2). O'Malley's thesis announces his solution—brief, frequent exams—to the problems created for students in courses limited to anxiety-producing, high-stakes midterms and finals. The thesis lists the reasons students will benefit from the solution in the order in which the benefits appear in the essay. A forecast is not a requirement of a thesis statement, but it does enable readers to predict the stages of the argument, thereby increasing their understanding.

As you draft your own thesis statement, pay attention to the language you use. It should be clear and unambiguous, emphatic but appropriately qualified. Although you will probably refine your thesis statement as you draft and revise your essay, trying now to articulate it will help give your planning and drafting direction and impetus.

For more on asserting a thesis, see Chapter 19.

PLANNING AND DRAFTING

This section will help you review your invention writing and research notes, determine specific goals for your essay, prepare a rough outline, and get started on your first draft.

If you are using the Writing Guide Software, click on
▶ **Planning and Drafting**

Seeing What You Have

You have now produced a lot of writing for this assignment about a problem and why it needs attention, about alternative solutions, and about the solution you want to propose and why it is preferable to the other proposed solutions. If you have done your invention writing on the computer, you may have sentences or whole paragraphs that can be copied and pasted into your draft. Reread what you have written so far to identify the potentially useful material. Look for details that will help you present a convincing argument for your solution and a strong counterargument in response to readers' likely objections to your solution and their preference for alternative solutions. Highlight key words, phrases, or sentences; make marginal notes or electronic annotations.

If at this point you doubt the significance of the problem or question the success of your proposed solution, you might want to consider a new topic. If you are unsure about these basic points, you cannot expect to produce a convincing draft.

However, if your invention material seems thin but promising, you may be able to strengthen it with additional invention writing. Ask yourself the following questions:

- Can I make a stronger case for the seriousness of the problem?
- Can I think of additional reasons for readers to support my solution?
- Are there any other ways of refuting alternative solutions to or troubling questions about my proposed solution?

Setting Goals

Before beginning to draft, think seriously about the overall goals of your proposal. Not only will the draft be easier to write once you have clear goals, but it will almost surely be more convincing as well.

Here are some questions that will help you set goals now. You may find it useful to return to them while drafting, for they are designed to help you focus on exactly what you want to accomplish with this proposal.

Your Purpose and Readers

- What do my readers already know about this problem?
- Are they likely to welcome my solution or resist it?
- How can I anticipate any specific reservations or objections they may have?
- How can I gain readers' enthusiastic support? How can I get them to want to implement the solution?
- How can I present myself so that I seem both reasonable and authoritative?

The Beginning

- How can I immediately engage my readers' interest? Should I open with a dramatic scenario, as O'Malley does? With statistics that highlight the seriousness of the problem, as Newman does? With a recitation of facts or events, as Bane does? Or with a rhetorical question, anecdote, or quotation?
- What information should I give first? Next? Last?

Defining the Problem

- How much do I need to tell about the problem's causes or history?
- How can I show the seriousness of the problem? Should I stress negative consequences, as O'Malley does? Should I cite statistics, as Newman does?
- Is it an urgent problem? Should I emphasize its urgency, as Hertsgaard does?
- How much space should I devote to defining the problem? Only a little space (like Bane and O'Malley) or much space (like Hertsgaard and Newman)?

Describing the Proposed Solution

- How can I describe my solution so that it will look like the best way to proceed? Should I show how to implement it, as Hertsgaard and Newman do? Or should I focus on my reasons to support it, as O'Malley does?
- How can I make the solution seem easy to implement? Or should I acknowledge that the solution may be difficult to implement and argue that it will be worth the effort?

Anticipating Readers' Objections

- Should I acknowledge every possible objection to my proposed solution? How might I choose among these objections?
- Has anyone already raised these objections? Should I name the person?
- Should I accommodate certain objections and refute others, as O'Malley does?
- How can I support my refutation? Should I cite an authority my readers are likely to respect, as Bane does?
- How can I refute my readers' objections without seeming to attack anyone? Can I accommodate as well as refute objections, as Hertsgaard, Bane, and O'Malley do?

Evaluating Alternative Solutions

- How many alternative solutions do I need to mention? Which ones should I discuss at length? Should I indicate where each one comes from?
- How can I support my refutation of the alternative solutions? Can I argue that they are too expensive and time-consuming, as O'Malley does, or that they will not really solve the problem, as Newman does?
- How can I reject these other solutions without seeming to criticize their proponents? Newman and O'Malley, for example, succeed at rejecting other solutions respectfully.

The Ending

- How should I conclude? Should I end by restating the problem or by summarizing my solution and its advantages, as O'Malley and Newman do? Should I end with an inspiring call to action, as Hertsgaard and Newman do?

- Is there something special about the problem that I should remind readers of at the end?
- Should I end with a scenario suggesting the consequences of a failure to solve the problem?
- Might a shift to humor or satire provide an effective way to end?

Outlining

After setting goals for your proposal, you are ready to make a working outline—a scratch outline or a more formal outline using the outlining function of your word processing program. The basic outline for a proposal is quite simple:

The problem
The solution
The reasons for accepting the solution

This simple plan is nearly always complicated by other factors, however. In outlining your material, you must take into consideration many other details, such as whether readers already recognize the problem, how much agreement exists on the need to solve the problem, how many alternative solutions are available, how much attention must be given to these other solutions, and how many objections should be expected.

Here is a possible outline for a proposal where readers may not understand the problem fully and other solutions have been proposed:

Presentation of the problem
  Its existence
  Its seriousness
  Its causes
Consequences of failing to solve the problem
Description of the proposed solution
List of steps for implementing the solution
Reasons and support for the solution
  Acknowledgment of objections
  Accommodation or refutation of objections
Consideration of alternative solutions and their disadvantages
Restatement of the proposed solution and its advantages

See p. 357 for another sample outline.

Your outline will of course reflect your own writing situation. As you develop it, think about what your readers know and feel about your own writing goals. Once you have a working outline, you should not hesitate to change it as necessary while drafting and revising. For instance, you might find it more effective to hold back on presenting your own solution until you have dismissed other possible solutions. Or you might find a better way to order the reasons for adopting your proposal. The purpose of an outline is to identify the basic features of your proposal and to help you organize them effectively, not to lock you into a particular structure. If you use the outlining function of your word processing program, changing your outline will be simple and you may be able to write the essay simply by expanding the outline.

Most of the information you will need to develop each feature of a proposal can be found in your invention writing and research notes. How much space you devote to each feature is determined by the topic, not the outline. Do not assume that each entry on your outline must be given one paragraph. For example, each reason for supporting the solution may require a paragraph, but you might instead present the reasons, objections, and refutations all in one paragraph.

For more on outlining, see Chapter 11.

Consider tentative any outlining you do before you begin drafting. Never be a slave to an outline. As you draft, you will usually see ways to improve on your original plan. Be ready to revise your outline, shift parts around, or drop or add parts as you draft.

Drafting

General advice. Start drafting your proposal, keeping in mind the goals you set while you were planning and the needs and expectations of your readers; organize, define, and argue with them in mind. Also keep in mind the two main goals of proposals: (1) to establish that a problem exists and is serious enough to require a solution and (2) to demonstrate that your proposed solution is both feasible and the best possible alternative. Use your outline to guide you as you write, but do not hesitate to stray from it whenever you find that drafting takes you in an unexpected direction.

Turn off your grammar checker and spelling checker at this stage if you find them distracting. Don't be afraid to skip around in your document. Jump back and fill in a spontaneous idea, or leap ahead and write a later section first if you find that easier. If you get stuck while drafting, explore the problem by using some of the writing activities in the Invention and Research section of this chapter (p. 363). You may want to review the general drafting advice in Chapter 1 on p. 17.

Sentence Strategies. As you draft an essay proposing a solution to a problem, you will want to connect with your readers. You will also want readers to become concerned with the seriousness of the problem and thoughtful about the challenge of solving it. Sentences that take the form of rhetorical questions and sentences that feature either assertive or tentative language can help you achieve these goals.

Use rhetorical questions to engage your readers, orient them to reading a proposal, and forecast the plan of your proposal. A rhetorical question is conventionally defined as a sentence posing a question to which the writer expects no answer from the reader. (Of course, not being face to face with the writer, a reader could not possibly answer.) In proposals, however, rhetorical questions do important rhetorical work—that is, they assist a writer in realizing a particular purpose and they influence readers in certain ways. Here are three examples from Katherine S. Newman's proposal:

> Why? And what can we do about it? (paragraph 4)
>
> How would an employer consortium function? (15)

These questions help readers understand that they will be reading a proposal: Newman implies through the questions that she will be explaining why inner-city workers are trapped in low-wage jobs and outlining a proposal to solve the problem. In addition, she engages readers by sharing with them the questions behind her research project and voicing one of the specific questions they are likely to have about her proposed solution. Consequently, readers have confidence that she will answer the questions she has posed so boldly.

Other writers in this chapter use different kinds of rhetorical questions to achieve the same effects Newman seeks:

- Orienting readers to a proposal and forecasting the plan of the argument or parts of it

  So what do we do? (Mark Hertsgaard, paragraph 2)

  Why, then, do so few professors give frequent brief exams? (Patrick O'Malley, paragraph 7)

  What reforms might address these problems while respecting the unique sacramental nature of the church? (Mary Jo Bane, paragraph 5)

- Engaging readers by inviting their assent to a question even before the writer has answered it

  Are there cultural, structural, and policy practices in the church that generate or exacerbate such abuses? (Mary Jo Bane, paragraph 5)

For more on rhetorical questions in proposals, go to bedfordstmartins.com/theguide and click on Sentence Strategies.

All of the authors in this chapter use at least one carefully placed rhetorical question. One author uses five such questions. Nevertheless, rhetorical questions are not a requirement for a successful proposal; and when they are used, they appear only occasionally.

Present the problem assertively, and argue the solution tentatively. To stress the seriousness of the problem and the urgency of solving it, use assertive language freely. In contrast, to convince readers to join you in taking action to solve the problem, use tentative language. These language contrasts—assertiveness versus tentativeness—play out quite predictably in this chapter's readings, as in the following examples from Mary Jo Bane's and Katherine S. Newman's proposals:

- Asserting the seriousness of the problem and the urgency of solving it

  One of the *most devastating aspects* of the disclosures has been the documentation of the *closed, secret, and self-protecting* nature of the decisions made by the hierarchy. (Bane, paragraph 6)

  Millions of Americans work full-time, year-round in jobs that leave them *stranded in poverty.* (Newman, paragraph 1)

These sentences feature language that is blunt, unqualified, and attention-getting. Bane directly, unequivocally attacks and blames the Catholic hierarchy. Newman uses a familiar image of being stranded—isolated, alone, beyond reach of help—to dramatize the plight of low-paid full-time workers. Such language seems chosen to expose the failure of the status quo—of business as usual, of the way things have

why? Has the writer sought out common ground with readers who may advocate alternative solutions? Are such solutions accommodated or rejected without a personal attack on those who propose them? Try to think of other solutions that readers may prefer.

7. ***Consider the Effectiveness of the Organization.*** Evaluate the overall plan of the proposal, perhaps by outlining it briefly. Would any parts be more effectively placed earlier or later in the essay?
   - Look at the *beginning*. Is it engaging? If not, how might it be revised to capture readers' attention? Does it adequately forecast the main ideas and the plan of the proposal? Suggest other ways the writer might begin.
   - Look closely at the way the writer *orders the argument* for the solution—the presentation of the reasons and the accommodation or refutation of objections and alternative solutions. How might the sequence be revised to strengthen the argument? Point out any gaps in the argument.
   - Look at the *ending*. Does it frame the proposal by echoing or referring to something at the beginning? If not, how might it do so? Does the ending convey a sense of urgency? Suggest a stronger way to conclude.
   - Look at any *design elements and visuals* the writer has incorporated. Assess how well they are incorporated into the essay. Point to any items that do not strengthen either the presentation of the problem or the argument in support of the solution.
8. ***Give the Writer Your Final Thoughts.*** What is the draft's strongest part? What part is most in need of further work?

REVISING

Now you have the opportunity to revise your essay. Your instructor or other students may have given you advice on how to improve your draft. Or you may have begun to realize that your draft requires not so much revising as rethinking. For example, you may recognize that you are no longer convinced that the problem is serious, that you feel it is serious but cannot be solved now or anytime soon, that you cannot decide to whom to address the proposal, that you cannot come up with a set of convincing reasons that readers should support your solution, or that you have been unable to accommodate or refute readers' objections and questions or to evaluate alternative solutions. Consequently, instead of working to improve the various parts of your first draft, you may need to write a new draft that reshapes your argument. Many students—and professional writers—find themselves in this situation. Often a writer produces a draft or two and gets advice on them from others and only then begins to see what might be achieved.

If you feel satisfied that your draft mostly achieves what you set out to do, you can focus on refining the various parts of it. This section will help you get an overview of your draft and revise it accordingly.

If you are using the Writing Guide Software, click on
▶ **Revising**

Getting an Overview

Consider your draft as a whole, following these two steps:

1. ***Reread.*** If at all possible, put the draft aside for a day or two before rereading it. When you do go back to it, start by reconsidering your audience and purpose. Then read the draft straight through, trying to see it as your intended readers will.
2. ***Outline.*** Make a scratch outline, indicating the basic features as they appear in the draft. Consider using the headings and outline or summary functions of your word processor.

Planning for Revision. Resist the temptation to dive in and start changing your text until after you have a clear view of the big picture. Using your outline as a guide, move through the document, using the change-highlighting or commenting tools of your word processor to note comments received from others and problems you want to solve (or mark a hard copy if you prefer).

Analyzing the Basic Features of Your Own Draft. Turn to the Critical Reading Guide that begins on p. 377. Using this guide, reread the draft to identify problems you need to solve. Note the problems on your draft.

Studying Critical Comments. Review all of the comments you have received from other readers. For each comment, look at the draft to determine what might have led the reader to make that particular point. Try to be receptive to constructive criticism. Ideally, these comments will help you see your draft as others see it. Add to your notes any problems readers have identified.

Carrying Out Revisions

Having identified problems in your draft, you now need to find solutions and—most important—to carry them out. You have three ways of finding solutions:

1. Review your invention and planning notes for additional information and ideas.

2. Do further invention writing or research to provide material you or your readers think is needed.
3. Look back at the readings in this chapter to see how other writers have solved similar problems.

The following suggestions, which are organized according to the basic features of essays that propose solutions, will get you started solving some common writing problems. For now, focus on solving the problems identified in your notes. Avoid tinkering with grammar and punctuation; those tasks will come later, when you edit and proofread.

A Well-Defined Problem

- ***Is the definition of the problem unclear?*** Consider sketching out its history, including past attempts to deal with it, discussing its causes and consequences more fully, dramatizing its seriousness more vividly, or comparing it to other problems that readers may be familiar with. Remember that all the authors of the readings in this chapter use assertive language to stress the seriousness of the problem.

A Clearly Described Solution

- ***Is the description of the solution inadequate?*** Try outlining the steps or phases involved in its implementation. Help readers see how easy the first step will be, or acknowledge the difficulty of the first step.

A Convincing Argument in Support of the Proposed Solution

- ***Does the argument seem weak?*** Try to think of more reasons for readers to support your proposal.
- ***Is the argument hard to follow?*** Try to put your reasons in a more convincing order—leading up to the strongest one rather than putting it first, perhaps.

An Anticipation of Readers' Objections and Questions

- ***Does your refutation of any objection or question seem unconvincing?*** Consider accommodating it by modifying your proposal.
- ***Have you left out any likely objections to the solution?*** Acknowledge those objections and either accommodate or refute them. Remember that all the authors of the readings in this chapter use tentative language in arguing to support their solutions.

An Evaluation of Alternative Solutions

- ***Have you neglected to mention alternative solutions that some readers are likely to prefer?*** Do so now. Consider whether you want to accommodate or refute these alternatives. For each one, try to acknowledge its good points, but argue that it is not as effective a solution as your own. You may in fact want to strengthen your own solution by incorporating into it some of the good points from alternatives.

Checking Sentence Strategies Electronically
To check your draft for a sentence strategy especially useful in proposals, use your word processor's highlighting function to mark specific language where you present the problem and where you propose the solution. Then think about whether you could strengthen your proposal either by making the language about the problem more assertive, so that the problem seems more serious and urgent, or by making the language about the solution more tentative and cautious, so that readers are less likely to resist it. For more on assertive and tentative language in proposals, see p. 376.

The Organization

- ***Is the beginning weak?*** Think of a better way to start. Would an anecdote or an example of the problem engage readers more effectively?
- ***Is the ending flat?*** Consider framing your proposal by mentioning something from the beginning of your essay or ending with a call for action that expresses the urgency of implementing your solution.
- ***Would design elements make the problem or proposed solution easier to understand?*** Consider adding headings or visuals.

EDITING AND PROOFREADING

Now is the time to check your revised draft for errors in grammar, punctuation, and mechanics as well as to consider matters of style. Our research has identified several errors that are especially common in essays that propose solutions. The following guidelines will help you check and edit your essay for these common errors.

A Note on Grammar and Spelling Checkers
These tools are good at catching certain types of errors, but currently there's no replacement for a good human proofreader. Grammar checkers in particular are extremely limited in what they can usually find, and often they only give you summary information that isn't helpful if you don't already understand the rule in question. They are also prone to give faulty advice for fixing problems and to flag correct items as wrong. Spelling checkers cause fewer problems but can't catch misspellings that are themselves words, such as *to* for *too*.

If you are using the Writing Guide Software, click on
▶ **Editing and Proofreading**

Checking for Ambiguous Use of *This* and *That*. Using *this* and *that* vaguely to refer to other words or ideas can confuse readers. Because you must frequently refer to the problem and the solution in a proposal, you will often use pronouns to avoid the monotony or wordiness of repeatedly referring to them by name. Check your draft carefully for ambiguous use of *this* and *that*. Often the easiest way to edit such usage is to add a specific noun after *this* or *that*, as Patrick O'Malley does in the following example from his essay in this chapter:

> Another possible solution would be to help students prepare for midterm and final exams by providing sets of questions from which the exam questions will be selected or announcing possible exam topics at the beginning of the course. *This solution* would have the advantage of reducing students' anxiety about learning every fact in the textbook. . . .

O'Malley avoids an ambiguous *this* in the second sentence by repeating the noun *solution*. (He might just as well have used *preparation* or *action* or *approach*.)

The following sentences from proposals have been edited to avoid ambiguity:

▶ **Students would not resist a reasonable fee increase of about $40 a year. This** *increase* **would pay for the needed dormitory remodeling.**

▶ **Compared to other large California cities, San Diego has the weakest programs for conserving water. This** *neglect* **and our decreasing access to Colorado River water give us reason to worry.**

▶ **Compared to other proposed solutions to this problem, that** *one* **is clearly the most feasible.**

Checking for Sentences That Lack an Agent. A writer proposing a solution to a problem usually needs to indicate who exactly should take action to solve it. Such actors are called "agents." An agent is a person who is in a position to take action. Look at this sentence from O'Malley's proposal:

> To get students to complete the questions in a timely way, professors would have to collect and check the answers.

In this sentence, *professors* are the agents. They have the authority to assign and collect study questions, and they would need to take this action in order for this solution to be successfully implemented. Had O'Malley instead written "the answers would have to be collected and checked," the sentence would lack an agent. Naming an agent makes his argument convincing, demonstrating to readers that O'Malley has thought through one of the key parts of any proposal: who is going to take action.

The following sentences from student-written proposals illustrate how you can edit agentless sentences:

▶ *Your staff should plan a survey* ~~**A survey could be planned**~~ **to find out more about students' problems in scheduling the courses they need.**

▶ *The registrar should extend* ~~**Extending**~~ **the deadline to mid-quarter.** ~~**, would make sense.**~~

Sometimes it is appropriate to write agentless sentences, however. Study the following examples from O'Malley's essay:

> These exams should be given weekly, or at least twice monthly.
>
> Exams could be collected and responded to only every third or fourth week.
>
> Still another solution might be to provide frequent study questions for students to answer.

Even though these sentences do not name explicit agents, they are all fine because it is clear from the larger context who will perform the action. In each case, it is obvious that the action will be carried out by a professor.

A WRITER AT WORK

STRENGTHENING THE ARGUMENT

This section focuses on student writer Patrick O'Malley's successful efforts to strengthen his argument for the solution he proposes in his essay, "More Testing, More Learning." Read the following three paragraphs from his draft; then compare them with paragraphs 4–6 of his final essay on pp. 353–54. As you read, take notes on the differences you observe between the draft and final versions.

The predominant reason students perform better with multiple exams is that they improve their study habits. Greater regularity in test taking means greater regularity in studying for tests. Students prone to cramming will be forced to open their textbooks more often, keeping them away from long, "kamikaze" nights of studying. Regularity prepares them for the "real world" where you rarely take on large tasks at long intervals. Several tests also improve study habits by reducing procrastination. An article about procrastination from the <u>Journal of Counseling Psychology</u> reports that "students view exams as difficult, important, and anxiety provoking." These symptoms of anxiety leading to procrastination could be solved if individual test importance was lessened, reducing the stress associated with the perceived burden.

With multiple exams, this anxiety decrease will free students to perform better. Several, less important tests may appear as less of an obstacle, allowing the students to worry less, leaving them free to concentrate on their work without any emotional hindrances. It is proven that "the performance of test-anxious subjects varies inversely with evaluation stress." It would also be to the psychological benefit of students if they were not subjected to the emotional ups and downs of large exams where they are virtually worry-free one moment and ready to check into the psychiatric ward the next.

Lastly, with multiple exams, students can learn how to perform better on future tests in the class. Regular testing allows them to "practice" the information they learned, thereby improving future test scores. In just two exams, they are not able to learn the instructor's personal examination

```
style, and are not given the chance to adapt their study
habits to it. The American Psychologist concludes: "It is
possible to influence teaching and learning by changing the
type of tests."
```

One difference you may have noted between O'Malley's draft and revision paragraphs is the sequencing of specific reasons that readers should accept the solution and take action on it. Whereas the draft moves in three paragraphs from improving study habits to decreasing anxiety to performing better on future tests, the revision moves from learning more and performing better on major exams to improving study habits to decreasing anxiety. O'Malley made the change after a response from a classmate and a conference with his instructor helped him see that his particular readers (professors) would probably be most convinced by the improved quality of students' learning, not by improvements in their study habits and feelings. As he continued thinking about his argument and discovering further relevant research, he shifted his emphasis from the psychological to the intellectual benefits of frequent exams.

You may also have noticed that the paragraphs of the revision are better focused than in the draft. The psychological benefits (reduced anxiety as a result of less procrastination) are now discussed mainly in a single paragraph (the third), whereas in the draft they are mixed in with the intellectual benefits in the first two paragraphs. O'Malley also uses more precise language in his revision; for example, changing "future tests" to "major exams, projects, and papers."

Another change you may have noticed is that all of the quoted research material in the draft has been replaced in the revision. Extending his library research to support his argument, O'Malley discovered the very useful Harvard report. As he found a more logical sequence, more precise terms, and fuller elaboration for his argument, he saw different ways to use the research studies he had turned up initially and quoted in the draft.

A final difference is that in the revision, O'Malley argues his reasons more effectively. Consider the draft and revised paragraphs on improved study habits. In the draft paragraph, O'Malley shifts abruptly from study habits to procrastination to anxiety. Except for study habits, none of these topics is developed, and the quotation adds nothing to what he has already said. By contrast, the revised paragraph focuses strictly on study habits. O'Malley keeps the best sentences from the draft for the beginning of the revised paragraph, but he adds several new sentences to help convince readers of the soundness of his argument that frequent exams improve students' study habits. These new sentences serve several functions: They anticipate a possible objection ("It might be argued . . ."), note a contrast between complex academic learning and familiar survival skills, and assert claims about the special requirements of regular academic study. The quotation from the Harvard report provides convincing support for O'Malley's claims and an effective way to conclude the paragraph.

DESIGNING YOUR WORK

The truck driver who wrote the proposal for recruiting and training more women (in the Writing in the Workplace project described on page 332) drafted and designed her document on her personal computer. Although she did not want to spend a lot of time on design, she did recognize the importance of her document's overall appearance. Using one of her grandson's college research papers as a model, she used double-spaced type, conventional paragraph indents, and one-inch margins. She told her grandson she hoped this "term-paperish format" would help persuade readers of the seriousness of the problem and the value of her proposed solution.

The driver also incorporated graphs and tables, which she gathered from several trucking industry magazines and newsletters that she had access to, to support and strengthen her proposal. To stress that carriers must increase their fleets in order to remain competitive within the industry, she used a line graph showing how the skyrocketing demand for motor carriers in the next five years will greatly exacerbate the current driver shortage. She used a second graph to demonstrate that recruiting minority-group men alone was unlikely to provide enough new drivers to fill the new positions. To show how the trucking industry can attract women on the basis of salary, she included a table contrasting the amount of money a woman truck driver could earn after one year, after five years, and so on, to how much women in other fields could earn over the same periods of time. In addition, she countered readers' possible preferred solution, established truck-driving schools, with a list comparing tuition rates with income statistics from the local newspaper—a comparison that clearly illustrated how difficult it would be for the region's divorced and single women to afford such training. In the accompanying text, the driver explained that although the proposed after-hours training program would require participating companies to spend some money up front, this solution had the added benefit of helping the community.

The proposal incorporated photographs, such as this one, showing women truck drivers

Finally, she used photographs as a framing device. Toward the beginning of the proposal, she scanned in a snapshot showing her alongside the double-bottom dump truck that she first learned to drive, which helped establish her authority as a trucker. Toward the end of the proposal, she scanned in a variety of photographs showing women truck drivers competently performing their jobs; each of these images attested to the feasibility of her proposed solution.

THINKING CRITICALLY ABOUT WHAT YOU HAVE LEARNED

Now that you have worked extensively with essays that propose solutions to problems—reading them, talking about them, writing one of your own—take some time to reflect on what you have learned. What problems did you encounter while you were writing your essay, and how did you solve them? How did reading other essays proposing solutions influence your own essay? What ideas do you have about the social and cultural dimensions of this kind of writing?

Reflecting on Your Writing

Write a page or two telling your instructor about a problem you encountered in writing an essay that proposes a solution and how you solved it. Before you begin, gather all of your writing—invention and planning notes, drafts, critical comments, revision notes and plans, and final revision. Review these materials as you complete this writing task.

1. ***Identify one writing problem you had to solve as you worked on your proposal essay.*** Do not be concerned with grammar and punctuation; concentrate instead on problems unique to developing a proposal. For example: Did you puzzle over how to convince readers that your proposed solution would actually solve the problem you identified? Did you find it difficult to support the reasons you gave for recommending the solution? Did you have trouble coming up with alternative solutions that your readers might favor?
2. ***Determine how you came to recognize the writing problem.*** When did you first discover it? What called it to your attention? If someone else pointed out the problem to you, can you now see hints of it in your invention writings? If so, where specifically? When you first recognized the problem, how did you respond?
3. ***Reflect on how you went about solving the problem.*** Did you reword a passage, cut or add details about the problem or solution, or move paragraphs or sentences around? Did you reread one of the essays in this chapter to see how another writer handled a similar problem, or did you look back at the invention suggestions? If you discussed the writing problem with another student, a tutor, or your instructor, did talking about it help? How useful was the advice you received?
4. ***Write a page or so explaining the problem and your solution.*** Be as specific as possible in reconstructing your efforts. Quote from your invention notes, your draft essay, others' critical comments, your revision plan, and your revised essay to show the various changes your writing underwent as you tried to solve the problem. If you are still uncertain about your solution, say so. The point is not to prove that you have solved the problem perfectly but rather to show what you have learned about solving problems when writing proposals. Taking time to explain how you identified a particular problem, how you went about trying to solve it, and what you learned from this experience can help you solve future writing problems more easily.

Reviewing What You Learned from Reading

Write a page or two explaining to your instructor how the readings in this chapter influenced your final essay. Your own essay has probably been influenced to some extent by one or more of the proposals you have read in this chapter as well as by classmates' essays that you have read. These other proposals may have helped you decide how to show your readers the seriousness of the problem you focused on, or they may have suggested how you could convince readers that they should support your proposed solution and ignore alternative solutions. Before you write, take some time to reflect on what you have learned from these selections.

1. ***Reread the final revision of your essay; then look back at the selections you read before completing it.*** Do you see any specific influences? For example, if you were impressed with the way one of the readings defined the problem, built a bridge of shared concerns with readers, detailed the steps in implementing the solution, argued against an alternative solution, or demonstrated that the solution would not cost too much, look to see where you might have been striving for similar effects in your own writing. Also look for ideas you got from your reading: writing strategies you were inspired to try, specific details you were led to include, and effects you sought to achieve.
2. ***Write a page or two explaining these influences.*** Did one reading have a particularly strong influence on your essay, or were several readings influential in different ways? Quote from the readings and from your final revision to show how your proposal was influenced by the selections you read. Finally, based on your review of the chapter's readings, point out any further improvements you would now make in your essay.

Considering the Social Dimensions of Essays Proposing Solutions

Proposals to solve problems are essential to our society. Businesspeople, school administrators, and government officials especially depend on proposals to decide where to direct resources and energy. Proposals enable us as individuals and as a society to make things better. We probably value this kind of thinking and writing because it makes us feel effective. It convinces us that difficulties can be overcome, that we can make practical, material changes that will improve our lives and the lives of others. We tell ourselves that with a little time, hard work, and ingenuity, we can make a difference. And this attitude has produced many positive changes in our culture—improvements in civil rights, in gender equality, in business and applied sciences as diverse as bridge building and environmental protection. Even so, thorny problems persist in the very areas where the most gains have been accomplished.

Who Defines the Problem? First, when someone proposes a solution, that proposal shapes our thinking about some aspect of our own and others' lives by labeling it a problem. Yet the individuals most directly affected by the solution may not even accept this definition and may not want to see any change. For example, not all students regard infrequent testing as a problem, but O'Malley's proposed solution would affect them nonetheless.

This question of definition becomes particularly difficult when a relatively powerless constituency in our society—the homeless, illegal immigrants, unwed teenage mothers—is designated a problem by politicians and others in the mainstream. Writers (and readers) of proposals must exercise caution in such circumstances. For example, Newman proposes enabling inner-city fast-food workers to move to better-paying jobs downtown, but the workers remaining in the fast-food industry, especially those who prefer part-time work, would not want to be seen as working dead-end jobs.

1. ***How specifically would the proposals you have read and written actually make things better?*** Whose interests would be served by these solutions? Who would be affected without their own stated interests being served?
2. ***Do any of these proposals try to improve the status of a group that is not particularly powerful?*** If so, what do you think is motivating the proposal writer? Is there any evidence that the writer is a member of this group or has consulted members of the group? What gives the writer authority to speak for them?
3. ***Write a page or two explaining your ideas about defining social problems in essays that propose solutions to them.*** Connect your ideas to your own essay and to the readings in this chapter.

The Frustrations of Effecting Real Change. No matter how well researched and well argued, many proposals are simply never carried out. The head of a personnel department might spend weeks drawing up a persuasive and feasible proposal for establishing a company day-care center, only to have upper management decide not to commit the necessary resources. A team of educators and social scientists might spend several years researching and writing a comprehensive, book-length proposal for dealing with the nation's drastic illiteracy rate but never see their solutions carried out because of a lack of coordination among the country's various educational institutions and governing bodies. In fact, it might be argued that the most successful proposals often operate on the smallest scale. For example, a proposal suggesting ways for a single community to increase literacy rates would probably have a better chance of implementation and ultimate success than the more far-reaching national proposal. (Yet this observation does not rule out the value of the national proposal, on which the local proposal might, in fact, be based.)

Further, in choosing among competing alternative proposals, decision makers—who usually hold the power of the purse strings and necessarily represent a fairly conservative position—often go for the one that is cheapest, most expedient, and least disruptive. They may also choose small, incremental changes over more fundamental, radical solutions. While sometimes the most pragmatic choice, such immediately feasible solutions may also merely patch over a problem, failing to solve it structurally. They may even inadvertently maintain the status quo. Worse, they can cause people to give up all attempts to resolve a problem after superficial treatments fail.

1. ***Consider how proposals invite writers to select problems that are solvable and how they might inadvertently attempt to solve a minor problem that is actually only a small part of a major problem.*** Do any of the proposals you have read and written reveal this misdirection? If so, which ones, and what do you think is the major problem in each case? Do you think the minor problem is worth solving as a first step toward solving the major problem, or is it perhaps an unfortunate diversion?
2. ***Consider how the proposals you have read and written challenge the status quo.*** What existing situation do they challenge, and just how do they challenge it? What roadblocks might deter these challenges? Might the proposals be more successfully carried out on a local scale?
3. ***Reflect on commentators' argument that we should not try to solve fundamental social problems by "throwing money at them."*** Do you think this objection is a legitimate criticism of most proposals to solve social problems? Or is it a manipulative justification for allowing the rich and powerful to maintain the status quo? What else, besides money, is required to solve serious social problems? Where are these other resources to come from?
4. ***Write a page or two explaining your ideas about the frustrations of effecting real change.*** Connect your ideas to your own essay and to the readings in this chapter.

O'NEAL
34

8

Justifying an Evaluation

Evaluation involves making judgments. Many times each day, we make judgments about subjects as diverse as the weather, food, music, computer programs, sports events, politicians, and films. In everyday conversation, we often express judgments casually ("I like it" or "I don't like it"), only occasionally giving our reasons (for example, "I hate cafeteria food because it is bland and overcooked") or supporting them with specific examples ("Take last night's spaghetti. That must have been a tomato sauce because it was red, but it didn't have the tang of tomatoes. And the noodles were so overdone that they were mushy").

When we write an evaluation, however, we know most readers expect that instead of merely asserting a judgment, we will provide reasons and support for the judgment. We know that unless we argue convincingly, readers who disagree will simply dismiss our judgments as personal preferences.

Evaluators can argue convincingly in several ways. One way is by making the reasons for your judgment explicit and by providing specific examples to support your reasons. You can also demonstrate knowledge of the particular subject being evaluated and the general category to which the subject belongs. For example, in an evaluation of *The Matrix Revolutions,* you would want to reassure readers that you are judging this particular film against other action and science-fiction films, including the first two films in the *Matrix* trilogy, *The Matrix* and *The Matrix Reloaded.* Given the film's genre, readers will expect you to base your judgment on qualities such as special effects, action sequences, and ideas or themes. Showing readers you understand how your particular subject relates to other subjects in the same general category demonstrates that your judgment is based on standards that readers recognize as appropriate for judging that kind of subject. For example, most people would agree that taste and consistency are appropriate standards for judging spaghetti served in the school cafeteria, but they would reject the high noise level and uncomfortable seating in a cafeteria as appropriate reasons for evaluating cafeteria food (although these reasons would be appropriate for judging the cafeteria itself).

As you can see, writing evaluations contributes to your intellectual growth by teaching you to develop reasoned, well-supported arguments for your judgments. Evaluations also require you to look critically at the standards underlying your own judgments as well as those of other people. You will encounter evaluative writing in many different contexts, as the following examples suggest.

Writing in Your Other Courses

- For a film-study course, a student evaluates two films (*Emma* and *Clueless*) based on the Jane Austen novel *Emma*. The student reads the novel, watches both films on videotape, and takes extensive notes. He also does an Internet search for reviews of the films. In his evaluation, the student argues that *Emma*, a period piece that faithfully follows the novel, is less successful than *Clueless*, a loose adaptation set in contemporary Beverly Hills, in capturing the spirit and romance of the novel. He supports his judgment with examples from the films and the novel as well as a few quotations from the movie reviews.
- For a political science course, a student writes a research paper evaluating the two major presidential candidates' performances during the first of their scheduled televised debates. Before watching the debate, she researches newspaper and magazine reports on two previous presidential debates to see what standards others have used to evaluate televised debates. Then she watches the debate and records it so that she can review it later. As she views the debate, she makes notes evaluating each candidate's performance. Afterward, she copies the transcript of the debate from the newspaper and collects published, televised, and online reviews of the debate. She uses this material both to support her own judgment and to respond to opposing judgments. Her final multimedia research paper includes downloaded Internet materials and videotaped excerpts from the debate.

Writing in the Community

- For the travel section of a local newspaper, a motorcycle enthusiast writes an article called "Hog Heaven" evaluating a tour of the Harley-Davidson factory and museum in York, Pennsylvania. He argues that Harley fans will enjoy the two dozen antique bikes on display and that people interested in business will be fascinated by the Harley plant because it includes both a classic assembly line (in which each worker performs an isolated operation on the motorcycles as they move along a conveyor belt) and a Japanese-inspired assembly team (in which three workers assemble an entire motorcycle from beginning to end, following whatever procedure they think works best). He concludes by emphasizing that the free tour offers something for everyone.
- For a campus publication, a college student writes an evaluation of a history course. She explains that the course includes three one-hour lectures per week by the professor plus a one-hour-per-week discussion led by a teaching assistant (TA). She states her judgment that although the lectures are boring, hard to follow, and seemingly unrelated to the assigned reading, the TA-led discussions are stimulating and help students grasp important information in each week's lectures and readings. To support her judgment, she describes a typical lecture and contrasts it to a typical discussion. She praises the TA for his innovative "term game," in which two teams of students compete to identify important concepts brought up in the week's lectures and reading, and for reviewing essay drafts via email. She concludes by recommending the course even though she wishes the TA could conduct the lectures as well as the discussions.

Writing in the Workplace

- In a written review of the work of a probationary employee, a supervisor judges the employee's performance as being adequate overall but still needing improvement in two key areas: completing projects on time and communicating effectively with others. To support his judgment, the supervisor explains that in one instance the employee's lateness derailed a team of workers and tells how the employee's lack of tact and clarity in communicating with coworkers created serious misunderstandings during the six-month probation period.
- For a conference on innovations in education, an elementary school teacher evaluates *Schoolhouse Rock,* an animated educational television series developed in the 1970s and recently reissued in several new formats: books, CD-ROM learning games, and music CDs. She praises the series as an entertaining and inventive way of presenting information, giving two reasons why it is an effective teaching tool: Witty lyrics and catchy tunes make the information memorable, and cartoonlike visuals make the lessons painless. She supports each reason by showing and discussing videotaped examples of popular *Schoolhouse Rock* segments, such as "Conjunction Junction," "We the People," and "Three Is a Magic Number." She ends by expressing her hope that teachers and developers of multimedia educational software will learn from the example of *Schoolhouse Rock.*

Practice Evaluating a Subject: A Collaborative Activity

The preceding scenarios suggest some occasions for evaluating a subject. You can discover how much you already know about evaluating by completing the following collaborative activity. Your instructor may schedule it for an in-class discussion or ask you to conduct an online discussion in a chat room.

Part 1. Get together with two or three other students to choose a reading from an earlier chapter that you have all already read. Review the reading, and decide whether you think the reading was helpful or unhelpful to you in learning to write well in the genre of the reading. Everyone in the group does not have to share the same judgment.

- First, take turns telling the group whether the reading was helpful in learning to write in the genre and giving two reasons for that judgment. Do not try to convince the others that your judgment is right or your reasons are sound; simply state your judgment and reasons.
- Next, after each person gives a judgment and reasons, discuss briefly as a group whether the reasons seem appropriate for judging a reading in a writing course. Again, you do not have to agree about whether the reading was helpful or unhelpful; all you have to do is discover whether you can agree on the kinds of reasons that make sense when evaluating a reading in the context of a writing course.

Part 2. As a group, spend a few minutes discussing what happened when you tried to agree on appropriate reasons for evaluating the reading:

- Begin by focusing on the reasons your group found easiest to agree on. Discuss why your group found these reasons so easy to agree on.
- Then focus on the reasons your group found hardest to agree on. Discuss why your group found these particular reasons so hard to agree on.

What can you conclude about community standards for judging readings in a writing course?

READINGS

No two essays justifying an evaluation are alike, and yet they share defining features. Together, the four readings in this chapter reveal a number of these features, so you will want to read as many of the essays as possible. If time permits, complete the activities in the Analyzing Writing Strategies section that follows each selection, and read the Commentary. Following the readings is a section called Basic Features: Evaluations (p. 418), which offers a concise description of the features of evaluative essays and provides examples from the four readings.

Stephen Holden *is a film reviewer for the* New York Times *and member of the New York Film Critics Circle. He began his writing career as a freelance rock critic, and his music reviews have appeared in* Rolling Stone, *the* Village Voice, *and other major publications. He briefly was a record producer for RCA Records and later wrote a novel about the record industry entitled* Triple Platinum *(1979). Holden still occasionally writes evaluations of musical performances and recordings, but since 2000 he has been one of the* Times*'s primary film reviewers. He also wrote the introduction to a book based on a series of* Times *articles about the cultural significance of the television series* The Sopranos.

Like The Sopranos, *the film* Road to Perdition *is about the psychological and moral angst of mobsters and their families. In his review, "A Hell for Fathers and Sons," Holden mentions* The Sopranos *and argues that* Road to Perdition *is "a period gangster film that achieves the grandeur of a classic Hollywood western." Evaluations, as you will see, often make comparisons of this kind. As you read, notice how Holden develops the comparison, and think about why he uses the writing strategy of comparing and contrasting. What does it add to his evaluation?*

A Hell for Fathers and Sons

Stephen Holden

Early in *Road to Perdition,* a period gangster film that achieves the grandeur of a classic Hollywood western, John Rooney (Paul Newman), the crusty old Irish mob boss in a town somewhere outside Chicago, growls a lament that echoes through the movie like a subterranean rumble: "Sons are put on the earth to trouble their fathers." 1

Rooney is decrying the trigger-happy behavior of his corrupt, hot-headed son, Connor (Daniel Craig), who in a fit of paranoid rage impulsively murdered one of Rooney's loyal lieutenants. The ear into which Rooney pours his frustration belongs to Michael Sullivan (Tom Hanks), his personal hit man, who witnessed the killing. An orphan whom Rooney brought up as a surrogate son and who has married and fathered two boys, Sullivan is in some ways more beloved to Rooney than his own flesh and blood. He is certainly more trustworthy. 2

E1
B1 NE
FRIDAY, JULY 12, 2002

Weekend MOVIES PERFORMING ARTS

The New York Times

FILM REVIEW

A Hell for Fathers and Sons

An epic of murderous family values.

François Duhamel/DreamWorks Pictures and 20th Century Fox

Tom Hanks as Michael Sullivan, a Chicago hit man, ordering Michael Jr. (Tyler Hoechlin) to wait for him while he attends to business in "Road to Perdition," directed by Sam Mendes. The film opens today nationwide.

But as the film shows, Rooney's bitter observation about fathers and sons also works in reverse: fathers are eternal mysteries put on the earth to trouble their sons as well as teach them. The story is narrated by the older of Sullivan's two boys, 12-year-old Michael Jr. (Tyler Hoechlin), who in a prologue establishes the movie's tone and setting (most of the events take place over six weeks in the winter of 1931) and invites us to decide, once his tale has been told, whether his father was "a decent man" or "no good at all." 3

Road to Perdition, which opens today nationwide, is the second feature film directed by Sam Mendes, the British theatrical maestro who landed at the top of Hollywood's A-list with his cinematic debut, *American Beauty.* The new movie reteams him with Conrad L. Hall, the brilliant cinematographer responsible for that film's surreal classicist shimmer. With *Road to Perdition* they have created a truly majestic visual tone poem, one that is so much more stylized than its forerunners that it inspires a continuing and deeply satisfying awareness of the best movies as monumental "picture shows." 4

Because Sullivan is played by Mr. Hanks, an actor who invariably exudes conscientiousness and decency, his son's question lends the fable a profound moral ambiguity. *Road to Perdition* ponders some of the same questions as *The Sopranos,* a comparably great work of popular art, whose protagonist is also a gangster and a devoted family man. But far from a self-pitying boor lumbering around a suburban basement in his undershirt, Mr. Hanks's antihero is a stern, taciturn killer who projects a tortured nobility. Acutely aware of his sins, Sullivan is determined that his son, who takes after him temperamentally, not follow in his murderous footsteps. Yet when driven to the brink, Sullivan gives his son a gun with instructions to use it, if necessary, and enlists him to drive his getaway car. 5

In surveying the world through Michael Jr.'s eyes, the movie captures, like no film I've seen, the fear-tinged awe with which young boys regard their fathers and the degree to which that awe continues to reverberate into adult life. Viewed through his son's eyes, Sullivan, whose face is half-shadowed much of the time by the brim of his fedora, is a largely silent deity, the benign but fearsome source of all knowledge and wisdom. An unsmiling Mr. Hanks does a powerful job of conveying the conflicting emotions roiling beneath Sullivan's grimly purposeful exterior as he tries to save his son and himself from mob execution. It's all done with facial muscles. 6

Yet Sullivan is also beholden to his own surrogate father, who has nurtured and protected him since childhood. Mr. Newman's Rooney, with his ferocious hawklike glare, sepulchral rasp and thunderous temper, has the ultimate power to bestow praise and shame, to bless and to curse. The role, for which the 77-year-old actor adopts a softened Irish brogue, is one of Mr. Newman's most farsighted, anguished performances. 7

What triggers the movie's tragic chain of events is Michael Jr.'s worshipful curiosity about his father. Desperate to see what his dad actually does for a living, he hides in the back of the car that Sullivan drives to the fatal meeting at which Connor goes haywire. After the boy is caught spying, Connor, who hates and envies Sullivan, decides without consulting Rooney that the boy can't be trusted to keep silent and must die. He steals into Sullivan's house and shoots his wife, Annie (Jennifer Jason Leigh), and his other 8 son, Peter (Liam Aiken), mistaking Peter for Michael Jr., who returns on his bicycle as the murders are taking place.

Arriving home, Sullivan finds his surviving son sitting alone in the dark, and as the camera waits downstairs, Sullivan climbs to the second floor and discovers the bodies. As his world shatters, all we hear is a far-off strangled cry of grief and horror. Minutes later he is frantically packing Michael Jr. into a car, and the two become fugitives, making one deadly stop before heading toward Chicago where Sullivan hopes to work for Frank Nitti (Stanley Tucci), Al Capone's right-hand man. For the rest of the movie, Sullivan plots his revenge on Connor, who remains secreted in a Chicago hotel room, protected by Rooney. Sullivan's plan involves a Robin Hood-style scheme of robbing banks but stealing only mob money. 9

The film, adapted from a comic-book novel by Max Allan Collins with illustrations by Richard Piers Rayner, portrays the conflicts as a sort of contemporary Bible story with associations to Abraham and Isaac, and Cain and Abel. The very word *perdition,* a fancy term for hell, is meant to weigh heavily, and it does. 10

True to the austere moral code of classic westerns, the film believes in heaven and hell and in the possibility of redemption. In that spirit its characters retain the somewhat remote, mythic aura of figures in a western, and the movie's stately tone and vision of gunmen striding to their fates through an empty Depression-era landscape seems intentionally to recall *High Noon, Shane* and *Unforgiven.* When the characters speak in David Self's screenplay, their pronouncements often have the gravity of epigraphs carved into stone. 11

A scary wild card slithering and hissing like a coiled snake through the second half of the film is Maguire (Jude Law), a ghoulish hit man and photojournalist with a fanatical devotion to taking pictures of dead bodies. When he opens fire, his cold saucer-eyed leer and bottled-up volatility explode into frenzied seizures that suggest a demonically dancing puppet. And just when you have almost forgotten the character, he reappears like an avenging fury. 12

The look of the film maintains a scrupulous balance between the pop illustration of a graphic novel (Michael Jr. himself is shown reading one, *The Lone Ranger*) and Depression-era paintings, especially the bare, desolate canvases of Edward Hopper. The camera moves with serene, stealthy deliberation (nothing is rushed or jagged), while the lighting sustains a wintry atmosphere of funereal gloom. Mr. Hall embraces shadow as hungrily as Gordon Willis in the *Godfather* movies, but where the ruddy palette of *The Godfather* suggested a hidden, sensual, blood-spattered twilight, *Road to Perdition* comes in shades of gray fading to black. 13

Those shades are matched by Thomas Newman's symphonic score, which infuses a sweeping Coplandesque evocation of the American flatlands with Irish folk motifs. In the flashiest of many visually indelible moments, a cluster of gangsters silhouetted in a heavy rain are systematically mowed down on a Chicago street in a volley of machine-gun flashes that seem to erupt out of nowhere from an unseen assassin. But no shots or voices are heard. The eerie silence is filled by the solemn swell of Mr. Newman's score. It is one of many scenes of violence in which the camera maintains a discreet aesthetic distance from the carnage. 14

> 15 Although *Road to Perdition* is not without gore, it chooses its bloodier moments with exquisite care. The aftermath of another cold-blooded murder is seen only for an instant in the swing of a mirrored bathroom door. Another is shown as a reflection on a window overlooking an idyllic beach on which a boy frisks with a dog. Here the overlapping images evoke more than any words the characters' tragic apprehension of having to choose between two simultaneous, colliding worlds. One is a heaven on earth, the other hell.

Connecting to Culture and Experience: Parables and Fables

In evaluating *Road to Perdition,* Holden seems to think that the moral dilemma the film presents makes it interesting. He characterizes the comic-book novel from which the film is derived as "a sort of contemporary Bible story" (paragraph 10). Bible stories like those of Abraham and Isaac or Cain and Abel, to which Holden refers, are often parables or fables, simple stories that illustrate a moral or religious lesson—for example, "Thou shalt not kill." Holden calls *Road to Perdition* a fable with "a profound moral ambiguity" (paragraph 5).

With two or three other students, try to think of other films or television programs you have seen that also resemble parables or fables. If you can think of several examples, see whether you agree on what lessons they teach. If, on the other hand, you cannot think of any other examples, consider why contemporary media rarely presents moral lessons. Then discuss whether morality should be taken into account when evaluating films in general or only those films that, like *Road to Perdition,* try to make a point about morality.

Analyzing Writing Strategies

1. At the beginning of this chapter, we make several generalizations about evaluative essays. Consider which of these statements is true of Holden's essay:
   - It asserts an overall judgment.
   - It makes explicit the reasons for the judgment.
   - It provides specific support for the judgment.
   - It tries to demonstrate knowledge of the particular subject as well as the general category to which the subject belongs.
2. One reason Holden thinks highly of *Road to Perdition* is what he calls its "look" (paragraph 13), which is created by camera movements, lighting, sound, and silence. Reread paragraphs 13–14 to see how Holden uses **comparisons** to support his enthusiasm for the look of the film.

   Underline the comparisons. To what does Holden compare *Road to Perdition?* If any of these comparisons are familiar to you and you have seen *Road to Perdition,* explain how well they help you understand what Holden is saying about the look of the film. Also notice that for many of these comparisons, Holden adds descriptive language. In talking about lighting, for example, he

To write comparisons and similes, you have to rely on certain kinds of sentences. For more information on the sentences of comparison and contrast, turn to p. 432.

compares the use of shadow and color in *Road to Perdition* to that in the *Godfather* films (13). Explain how adding a little description helps readers, both those who are familiar with the comparison and those who are not.

3. Holden makes good use of another kind of comparison: the simile. There are three of them in paragraph 12, two beginning with *like* and one with *suggest*. Underline these similes. (Holden also uses metaphors: *wild card, ghoulish, saucer-eyed, explode*.) Explain how the similes help you imagine (or remember, if you have seen the film) the character Maguire.

For more about comparing and contrasting, see Chapter 18.

Commentary: Presenting the Subject and the Overall Judgment

Film reviews, like other evaluations, usually begin by **presenting the subject** and stating the writer's overall judgment. Stephen Holden identifies the movie by name in the first sentence, and in the first four paragraphs he categorizes it ("a period gangster film" [paragraph 1]), and tells where and when it takes place ("a town somewhere outside Chicago" [1], "six weeks in the winter of 1931" [3]), what the story is about, who the actors are and what characters they play, and who the director is.

Because they can usually assume their readers are trying to decide whether to see the film, reviewers have to think carefully about how much plot detail to include and why. At least in the opening paragraphs, Holden chooses to give information that is shown in the trailer used to advertise the film. Later, in paragraphs 8 and 9, he gives additional information but does not reveal the ending. In contrast, your instructor may want you to assume your readers have seen the film.

In addition to presenting the subject, writers of evaluation usually **state their overall judgment** early in the essay. In the first sentence, for example, Holden indicates his judgment is positive when he describes *Road to Perdition* as achieving "the grandeur of a classic Hollywood western." At the end of paragraph 4, after he has described the film and the people responsible for it, he reiterates this judgment in a clear, definitive thesis statement: "With *Road to Perdition* they have created a truly majestic visual tone poem, one that is so much more stylized than its forerunners that it inspires a continuing and deeply satisfying awareness of the best movies as monumental 'picture shows'" (4). This thesis statement has the three qualities expected of a good thesis: It is clear, arguable, and appropriately qualified. The key words *majestic* and *monumental* in this thesis sentence (like the words *grandeur* and *classic* in the first sentence) clearly express praise. The thesis is also obviously arguable since some viewers would very likely disagree with Holden's judgment.

For more information on thesis statements, see Chapter 19.

Because his is a rave review, Holden does not point out weaknesses of any kind. He does not qualify or limit his thesis. Most film reviews as well as other kinds of evaluations, however, combine praise and criticism. Rarely do critics find nothing to criticize. Even in highly positive evaluations, writers often acknowledge minor shortcomings to show readers that their evaluation is fair and balanced. Similarly, in negative reviews, the writer usually finds something to praise. As you read the next selection, you will see how a writer can express a positive overall judgment but still point out shortcomings.

Considering Topics for Your Own Essay

List several movies that you would enjoy reviewing, and choose one from your list that you recall especially well. Of course, if you were actually to write about this movie, you would need to see it at least twice to develop your reasons and find supporting examples. For this activity, however, you do not have to view your film again. Just be sure you have a strong overall judgment about it. Then consider how you would argue for your judgment. Specifically, what reasons do you think you would give your readers? Why do you assume that your readers would accept these reasons as appropriate for evaluating this particular film?

> To use the Writing Guide Software to record your ideas, click on
> ▶ **Journal**

Jonah Jackson *evaluates computer games for TechTV. He also writes reviews for* Computer Gaming World *and* Gamers.com. *This evaluation of a game called The Elder Scrolls III: Morrowind was initially published on the TechTV Web site and also aired on the TechTV show* Extended Play. *It was originally posted December 30, 2002, and modified on April 23, 2003, for a "best picks" program. Jackson gives the game five stars, TechTV's highest rating. According to TechTV, "Five-star games are a rarity. This is a landmark title that every gamer should consider owning. Even gamers who aren't fans of the genre will enjoy playing this game. It may have some slight flaws, but the ambition of the title and what the developer was able to successfully pull off more than make up for any shortcomings. If games are indeed art, these are masterpieces." As you read Jackson's review, notice that he points out the game's weaknesses as well as its strengths. Consider whether balancing the good with the bad in a review like this makes his argument more convincing or less so.*

The Elder Scrolls III: Morrowind

Jonah Jackson

Morrowind, the third title in Bethesda Softworks' Elder 1
Scrolls series, has hit the shelves. In this week's episode of *Extended Play* we sink our teeth into one of the largest and most richly detailed fantasy worlds ever to wear a set of polygons.[1] There are literally hundreds of hours of gameplay. A second CD that contains a construction set promises countless more hours of gameplay as gamers all over the world work hard on [your favorite mod here].[2] It's a good time to be a gamer.

---

[1] Polygons are used to create virtual three-dimensional space in video games.

[2] *Mod* is a modification of a computer game's technical features.

Outstanding Graphics

Morrowind would be worth the price of admission for the graphics alone. Building on past games, the island of Vvardenfell was meticulously created with dozens of climates and landscapes. Unique architectural detail differentiates cities and towns across the various regions. The sense of scope and grandeur is well maintained from the open canals of Vivec to the modest Ashlander yurt villages. Seeing the ruined ornate spires of an ancient city appear out of the mist as you walk through the countryside is something to behold. 2

Fog enshrouds the mountaintops, the water glistens and reflects landscape features, lightning, rain, and dust storms howl through the land, and night skies shine with stars. The Bethesda team has created a world that pulls you in with wide eyes from the moment you step off the slave boat onto the port of Seyda Neen. 3

Though the game is best played in the first person, there is a third-person camera position that's worth it if for nothing more than checking out the new duds you pick up in town. The few graphical quirks, such as shadows that get cast through walls and robe sleeves that obscure your ranged weapon targeting, are easy to forgive once you see your character reach up and shield his eyes while turning into the teeth of a windstorm. 4

Free to Explore

Morrowind begins with your arrival in Vvardenfell on an Imperial slave ship. After a short and clever character-generation segment disguised as a new-arrival check-in, you're off and running. Though you're given an initial task related to the game's main story, from the very beginning you're given the freedom to explore and adventure at your own pace. 5

Unlike many games that promise you the freedom to play however you want, Morrowind goes a long way toward meeting that promise. There are hundreds of side quests and locations to explore all over the map. You'll visit many of them and have a satisfying experience by simply following the main story. Alternatively, you can head into the countryside and make your way along a story line on your own. The sheer volume of quests and plot lines ensures that independent exploration will not hamper you when you want to return to the more traditional style of RPG[3] play. Plus it's downright fun to head into the nearest ancestral tomb to pick up a few goodies while walking down a nice country road. 6

Still, the best way to experience Morrowind is to attach yourself to a guild or two and start role-playing the quests you receive. While the ubiquitous fed-ex and find-my-lost-armor quests are well represented, many of your tasks will have more than one solution, depending on your skills, and you'll often find that the overlapping or conflicting interests of the guilds make the plot lines more interesting. The main story follows an engaging plot line as well and includes a huge back story that's interesting on its own. The island of Vvardenfell is a somewhat troubled section of the Empire. The native Dunmers or Dark Elves are at odds among themselves and with the Imperial presence. As the story unfolds you find that you play a larger and more important role in the future of Vvardenfell. 7

Quests and plots are revealed most often through interaction with the hundreds of characters found throughout Vvardenfell. Conversation is based on keywords and the interface[4] keeps track of questions and responses in a separate journal. Many of the generic townspeople do begin to look and sound alike after a while and the canned responses to certain questions do get old or even nonsensical. More than once townspeople seemed completely oblivious to world-changing events that had just taken place. 8

Customization

Every part of the game's design is implemented with an eye toward flexibility and customization to the player's desires. There are 10 races and 21 predefined classes, and you can create custom classes by choosing preferences from 27 skills among three specialization categories: Combat, Magic, and Stealth. 9

---

[3] *RPG* stands for *role-playing game*.

[4] *Interface* is the part of a program that presents information and allows user input.

10 Skills are improved through training or successful use of the skill. Level advancement is based on improving a combination of any skills a total of 10 times. Level advancement brings additional Health and the opportunity to assign additional points to your base attributes.

11 Any character class can improve any skill, although advancement is easier in the skills related to your class. The game has no time limit, though, so you can work to create a mighty sorcerer who's also the most skilled swordsman and deft pickpocket in the land.

12 With a few exceptions, all skills are useful and the game is well balanced. Playing a skilled orator and acrobat with limited combat skills is just as rewarding as hacking through the hordes with a barbarian warrior. Bethesda has done an excellent job writing a story that can be played through with many different character types.

Control

13 Navigation is similar to many FPS[5] titles and will be familiar to players of the first two Elder Scrolls games. The seamless combat interface is also easy to use, although the various types of weapon swing (slash, jab, and so on) are awkwardly related to your movement direction. A group of windowed menus is available with a simple click of the right mouse button. This pauses the game and lets you access inventory, map, magic items, and your character's detailed status. Basics such as health, mana, and spell effects, plus a minimap, are always available on screen. Some of the interface design is less than optimal. Your inventory, which you can sort by type, can become unwieldy as you collect a lot of potions or scrolls. It's especially difficult to manage all the potion-making ingredients if your character has the Alchemy skill.

14 The many quests you'll receive along the way are recorded in a chronological journal that's autoindexed as you go. This journal manages to record everything of importance, but it's missing the ability to sort or group items by quest. Nor does it separate completed quests and ongoing quests. Although the sheer volume of information is a bit much in later stages, the index feature does prevent the journal from becoming unusable.

Sound

15 Bethesda gave the music and sound effects the same care it gave the visuals. The grand scope of the story is served well by the basic theme music. Given 50-plus hours of game time, it was important to produce something that was unobtrusive enough to hear a few hundred times while still providing atmosphere. The combat music is a little flat, but it does provide important auditory clues about nearby enemies. The ambiance of the game is also helped by the carefully crafted sound of footsteps, creaking doors, howling wind, moaning spirits, unsheathing swords, rippling water, and dozens of other effects that really pull the game together.

[5] *FPS* refers to first-person shooter games, a multiplayer genre of computer games.

Summary

Morrowind is a flawed jewel, but flawed only because its scope is so grand. Beautiful graphics, compelling stories, a huge map to explore, engaging quests, and a simple interface all add up to a premier game. Its bugs and design quirks are more than compensated for by a core game that's just fantastic. It may have just missed the center of the bull's eye, but Bethesda gets five stars for hitting a target that no one else even dares aim for. 16

Connecting to Culture and Experience: Freedom of Play in Computer Games

According to Jonah Jackson, an important attraction of role-playing computer games is the freedom they give players to explore and play in any way they choose. In addition, computer game enthusiasts can also join online "mod communities" to modify their favorite games.

With two or three other students, discuss your experiences with role-playing computer games. Take turns describing what kinds of games you enjoy playing and what you like about playing these particular games. For example, how much do you value the freedom to play as you choose and the opportunity to be creative? Consider also how you feel about the game's rules. Do the rules restrict your enjoyment or contribute in some way to it? Does it matter to you—and do you think it should matter to Jackson—that what he calls freedom is really scripted?

Analyzing Writing Strategies

1. Writers of evaluations give readers a lot of information about the subject in the course of the essay. But they usually **present the subject** in the opening paragraph by identifying it in certain ways. Reread paragraph 1 to see how Jackson presents the subject he is evaluating. Underline the information he gives readers, and speculate about why you think he begins with this information.
2. Jackson indicates his **overall judgment** in the opening and then reasserts it as a thesis statement in the concluding paragraph. Reread paragraph 16 to see whether the thesis statement meets the three standards for a good thesis: that it be clear and unambiguous, arguable, and appropriately qualified.

Commentary: Giving Appropriate Reasons

The argument is probably the most important part of an evaluative essay. Writers argue by giving reasons and support for their overall judgment. In addition to this direct argument, writers also usually counterargue, anticipating and responding to readers' objections and alternative judgments. Here we focus on the way writers **give reasons for their judgment**.

Reasons in evaluative arguments are often statements praising or criticizing particular qualities of the subject. Jackson uses headings to focus attention on qualities such as graphics, customization, and control. Headings make his argument easy for readers to follow. They are especially useful for text posted online, as was the case with Jackson's original review, because reading long stretches of text onscreen can be difficult. Here is a scratch outline of Jackson's essay, including the headings:

For more on the use of headings, see Chapters 13 and 25.

Introduces the subject and states the judgment (paragraph 1)

Develops and supports the first reason: "Outstanding Graphics" (2–4)

Develops and supports the second reason: "Free to Explore" (5–8)

Develops and supports the third reason: "Customization" (9–12)

Develops and supports the fourth reason: "Control" (13–14)

Develops and supports the fifth reason: "Sound" (15)

Concludes and reiterates judgment (16)

Under each heading, Jackson presents his reason in topic sentences like these:

> ***Outstanding Graphics:*** Morrowind would be worth the price of admission for the graphics alone. Building on past games, the island of Vvardenfell was meticulously created with dozens of climates and landscapes. (paragraph 2)

> ***Free to Explore:*** Though you're given an initial task related to the game's main story, from the very beginning you're given the freedom to explore and adventure at your own pace. (5)

> ***Customization:*** Every part of the game's design is implemented with an eye toward flexibility and customization to the player's desires. (9)

He does not simply assert his reasons, he supports them with particular examples. Look at the way he specifies in paragraphs 2–4 what makes the graphics good. In his topic sentence, he claims that the graphics are praiseworthy because the island was "meticulously created with dozens of climates and landscapes" (2). He supports this assertion with numerous examples. In paragraph 2, he points out how each city and town—from "the ruined ornate spires of an ancient city" to "the open canals of Vivec" and "the modest Ashlander yurt villages"—is given its own look with "[u]nique architectural detail." In paragraph 3, he illustrates the different climates—fog, lightning, rain, dust storms, night skies—that the player encounters. In addition to praising the good graphics, Jackson points out the bad ones, what he calls a "few graphical quirks" (4). He gives examples of these "quirks": "shadows that get cast through walls and robe sleeves that obscure your ranged weapon targeting" (4). Supporting reasons with this kind of detail helps to convince readers that the writer is making an informed as well as a balanced evaluation. As you plan your argument, make sure that you support your reasons with specific examples.

Writers also sometimes need to argue that their **reasons are appropriate** because they are based on the kinds of standards that people knowledgeable about the subject normally use. Jackson, however, does not have to make this kind of argument because he can assume that his original TechTV audience of experienced computer game players agree that his reasons for evaluating a game are appropriate because they are based on important aesthetic and technical features of role-playing games. The order in which Jackson presents his reasons suggests that for this particular kind of game, graphics are the most important standard for judgment. Presumably, if something serious was wrong with the control interface, his review would have been much more negative, and he might have made control the first reason. Notice that he devotes eleven paragraphs to the first three reasons and only three paragraphs to the last two reasons. The Guide to Writing in this chapter (p. 421) will help you decide which reasons to present, how to support them, whether you need to argue for their appropriateness, and how to organize your essay.

Considering Topics for Your Own Essay

Like Jonah Jackson, you might have a favorite computer game. Or you might do a lot of digital photography and be able to evaluate digital cameras or a software program like Photoshop. Alternatively, you might be interested in evaluating a particular Web site you use regularly. Choose one particular game, software program, or Web site, and list its obvious strengths and weaknesses.

To use the Writing Guide Software to record your ideas, click on
▶ **Journal**

***Amitai Etzioni**, a sociologist, is University Professor at George Washington University, where he is director of the Institute for Communitarian Policy Studies. A former White House adviser on domestic affairs, he has served as the president of the American Sociological Association and the founding president of the international Society for the Advancement of Socio-Economics. He has written twenty-two books, including* The Spirit of Community: Rights, Responsibilities, and the Communitarian Agenda *(1993);* The New Golden Rule: Community and Morality in a Democratic Society *(1997), for which he won the Simon Wiesenthal Center's annual Tolerance Book Award;* The Limits of Privacy *(1999); and* My Brother's Keeper: A Memoir and a Message *(2003). Etzioni founded the journal* The Responsive Community, *and he also writes articles for general publications such as the* New York Times, *the* Washington Post, USA Today, *and the* Wall Street Journal.

This evaluative essay was first published in the Miami Herald. *According to the original headnote, Etzioni's teenage son Dari, one of his five children, helped him write it—although the headnote does not specify what Dari contributed. As you read the essay, notice that Etzioni also acknowledges learning from another of his children, Oren. Given that Etzioni is a respected professor and author, how do you think his credibility in this evaluation is affected by his admission that he got help from two of his children?*

Working at McDonald's

Amitai Etzioni

1 McDonald's is bad for your kids. I do not mean the flat patties and the white-flour buns; I refer to the jobs teen-agers undertake, mass-producing these choice items.

2 As many as two-thirds of America's high school juniors and seniors now hold down part-time paying jobs, according to studies. Many of these are in fast-food chains, of which McDonald's is the pioneer, trend-setter and symbol.

3 At first, such jobs may seem right out of the Founding Fathers' educational manual for how to bring up self-reliant, work-ethic-driven, productive youngsters. But in fact, these jobs undermine school attendance and involvement, impart few skills that will be useful in later life, and simultaneously skew the values of teen-agers—especially their ideas about the worth of a dollar.

4 It has been a longstanding American tradition that youngsters ought to get paying jobs. In folklore, few pursuits are more deeply revered than the newspaper route and the sidewalk lemonade stand. Here the youngsters are to learn how sweet are the fruits of labor and self-discipline (papers are delivered early in the morning, rain or shine), and the ways of trade (if you price your lemonade too high or too low . . .).

5 Roy Rogers, Baskin Robbins, Kentucky Fried Chicken, *et al.* may at first seem nothing but a vast extension of the lemonade stand. They provide very large numbers of teen jobs, provide regular employment, pay quite well compared to many other teen jobs and, in the modern equivalent of toiling over a hot stove, test one's stamina.

6 Closer examination, however, finds the McDonald's kind of job highly uneducational in several ways. Far from providing opportunities for entrepreneurship (the lemonade stand) or self-discipline, self-supervision and self-scheduling (the paper route), most teen jobs these days are highly structured—what social scientists call "highly routinized."

7 True, you still have to have the gumption to get yourself over to the hamburger stand, but once you don the prescribed uniform, your task is spelled out in minute detail. The franchise prescribes the shape of the coffee cups; the weight, size, shape and color of the patties; and the texture of the napkins (if any). Fresh coffee is to be made every eight minutes. And so on. There is no room for initiative, creativity, or even elementary rearrangements. These are breeding grounds for robots working for yesterday's assembly lines, not tomorrow's high-tech posts.

8 There are very few studies on the matter. One of the few is a 1984 study by Ivan Charper and Bryan Shore Fraser. The study relies mainly on what teen-agers write in response to questionnaires rather than actual observations of fast-food jobs. The authors argue that the employees develop many skills such as how to operate a food-preparation machine and a cash register. However, little attention is paid to how long it takes to acquire such a skill, or what its significance is.

9 What does it matter if you spend 20 minutes to learn to use a cash register, and then—"operate" it? What "skill" have you acquired? It is a long way from learning to work with a lathe or carpenter tools in the olden days or to program computers in the modern age.

10 A 1980 study by A. V. Harrell and P. W. Wirtz found that, among those students who worked at least 25 hours per week while in school, their unemployment rate four years

later was half of that of seniors who did not work. This is an impressive statistic. It must be seen, though, together with the finding that many who begin as part-time employees in fast-food chains drop out of high school and are gobbled up in the world of low-skill jobs.

Some say that while these jobs are rather unsuited for college-bound, white, middle-class youngsters, they are "ideal" for lower-class, "non-academic," minority youngsters. Indeed, minorities are "over-represented" in these jobs (21 percent of fast-food employees). While it is true that these places provide income, work and even some training to such youngsters, they also tend to perpetuate their disadvantaged status. They provide no career ladders, few marketable skills, and undermine school attendance and involvement. 11

The hours are often long. Among those 14 to 17, a third of fast-food employees (including some school dropouts) labor more than 30 hours per week, according to the Charper-Fraser study. Only 20 percent work 15 hours or less. The rest: between 15 and 30 hours. 12

Often the stores close late, and after closing one must clean up and tally up. In affluent Montgomery County, Md., where child labor would not seem to be a widespread economic necessity, 24 percent of the seniors at one high school in 1985 worked as much as five to seven days a week; 27 percent, three to five. There is just no way such amounts of work will not interfere with school work, especially homework. In an informal survey published in the most recent yearbook of the high school, 58 percent of seniors acknowledged that their jobs interfere with their school work. 13

The Charper-Fraser study sees merit in learning teamwork and working under supervision. The authors have a point here. However, it must be noted that such learning is not automatically educational or wholesome. For example, much of the supervision in fast-food places leans toward teaching one the wrong kinds of compliance: blind obedience, or shared alienation with the "boss." 14

Supervision is often both tight and woefully inappropriate. Today, fast-food chains and other such places of work (record shops, bowling alleys) keep costs down by having teens supervise teens with often no adult on the premises. 15

There is no father or mother figure with which to identify, to emulate, to provide a role model and guidance. The work-culture varies from one place to another: Sometimes it is a tightly run shop (must keep the cash registers ringing); sometimes a rather loose pot party interrupted by customers. However, only rarely is there a master to learn from, or much worth learning. Indeed, far from being places where solid adult work values are being transmitted, these are places where all too often delinquent teen values dominate. Typically, when my son Oren was dishing out ice cream for Baskin Robbins in upper Manhattan, his fellow teen-workers considered him a sucker for not helping himself to the till. Most youngsters felt they were entitled to $50 severance "pay" on their last day on the job. 16

The pay, oddly, is the part of the teen work-world that is most difficult to evaluate. The lemonade stand or paper route money was for your allowance. In the old days, apprentices learning a trade from a master contributed most, if not all, of their income to their parents' household. Today, the teen pay may be low by adult standards, but it is 17 often, especially in the middle class, spent largely or wholly by the teens. That is, the youngsters live free at home ("after all, they are high school kids") and are left with very substantial sums of money.

Where this money goes is not quite clear. Some use it to support themselves, especially among the poor. More middle-class kids set some money aside to help pay for college, or save it for a major purchase—often a car. But large amounts seem to flow to pay for an early introduction into the most trite aspects of American consumerism: flimsy punk clothes, trinkets and whatever else is the last fast-moving teen craze. 18

One may say that this is only fair and square; they are being good American consumers and spend their money on what turns them on. At least, a cynic might add, these funds do not go into illicit drugs and booze. On the other hand, an educator might bemoan that these young, yet unformed individuals, so early in life driven to buy objects of no intrinsic educational, cultural or social merit, learn so quickly the dubious merit of keeping up with the Joneses in ever-changing fads, promoted by mass merchandising. 19

Many teens find the instant reward of money, and the youth status symbols it buys, much more alluring than credits in calculus courses, European history or foreign languages. No wonder quite a few would rather skip school—and certainly homework—and instead work longer at a Burger King. Thus, most teen work these days is not providing early lessons in the work ethic; it fosters escape from school and responsibilities, quick gratification and a short cut to the consumeristic aspects of adult life. 20

Thus, parents should look at teen employment not as automatically educational. It is an activity—like sports—that can be turned into an educational opportunity. But it can also easily be abused. Youngsters must learn to balance the quest for income with the needs to keep growing and pursue other endeavors that do not pay off instantly—above all education. 21

Go back to school. 22

Connecting to Culture and Experience: Job Skills

Etzioni argues in this essay that "the McDonald's kind of job" does not teach the kinds of skills young people need to prepare for employment in a "high-tech" world, skills like entrepreneurship, self-discipline, and initiative (paragraphs 6–7).

With other students, discuss the skills you believe you need to learn for the kind of job or career you envision for yourself. Review the essay to make a complete list of the skills Etzioni mentions. Then discuss each skill to determine whether it is important to you. Add to Etzioni's list any other skills you think are important.

Analyzing Writing Strategies

1. To see how Etzioni **presents the subject**, working at McDonald's, reread the essay, underlining the factual details about who works at fast-food restaurants and what they do on the job. If you can, identify the source of Etzioni's information:

his own firsthand observation, conversations with fast-food workers (such as his sons), or published research. Then, based on your own knowledge of fast-food restaurants, report on which details you accept and which you think may be inaccurate or only partly true. Also, based on your knowledge of fast-food restaurants, consider what Etzioni may have left out and why: Indicate whether you think he left out certain facts because he assumes his readers already know them, because they are not important, or because they would not support his judgment.

2. Etzioni relies on two kinds of **support—examples and statistics**. Find and underline the examples he offers in paragraph 7 to support his assertion in paragraph 6 that jobs at McDonald's do not teach teenagers to become self-disciplined entrepreneurs. Then find and underline the statistics he offers in paragraphs 12 and 13 to support his assertion in paragraph 11 that such jobs undermine school attendance and involvement. Finally, speculate about whether these kinds of support are likely to be convincing for Etzioni's readers—parents who think that after-school jobs can teach teenagers valuable skills. How convincing are they for you?

For more on these ways of supporting an argument, see Chapter 19, pp. 681–83.

Commentary: Anticipating Readers' Alternative Judgments and Objections

Early in his essay, Etzioni acknowledges the **alternative judgment** he expects many of his readers to hold: that McDonald's-type jobs are good because they teach teenagers to become "self-reliant, work-ethic-driven, productive youngsters" (paragraph 3). Although he suggests that he shares with his readers these standards for evaluating jobs for teenagers, Etzioni makes clear that he disagrees with his readers' judgment about the type of fast-food jobs popularized by McDonald's.

In addition to anticipating readers' likely preference for the opposing judgment, Etzioni anticipates and counterargues readers' **possible objections** to his argument. For example, he acknowledges that Charper and Fraser's research finding that "employees develop many skills" (paragraph 8) directly contradicts his own claim that fast-food jobs "impart few skills that will be useful in later life" (paragraph 3). He handles this objection by accepting as fact Charper and Fraser's finding but counterarguing that the kinds of skills learned by fast-food workers are the wrong skills: They are "highly routinized" skills (paragraph 6) that prepare young people to work on "yesterday's assembly lines, not tomorrow's high-tech posts" (paragraph 7).

Similarly, Etzioni acknowledges as "impressive" Harrell and Wirtz's statistic showing that students who work a lot in high school may be employed four years later at a higher rate than those who do not work in high school (paragraph 10). But he then counterargues by noting that "many who begin as part-time employees in fast-food chains drop out of high school and are gobbled up in the world of low-skill jobs." He concludes this refutation by condemning McDonald's-type jobs because they "perpetuate" the status quo. He compares fast-food jobs to the school tracking system that separates "non-academic" and "college-bound" students (paragraph 11). Instead of providing minority youngsters with an opportunity to advance, he says,

McDonald's-type jobs "perpetuate their disadvantaged status," "provide no career ladders, few marketable skills, and undermine school attendance and involvement" (paragraph 11).

Etzioni has his readers very much in mind as he writes this essay. He anticipates how they are likely to evaluate the subject as well as how they might respond to his argument. Writers have three options in anticipating readers: They can simply acknowledge readers' concerns, they can accommodate them by making concessions, or they can try to refute them. Etzioni chooses this last option. As you plan your own essay, think about your readers and how you could anticipate and counterargue readers' concerns.

Considering Topics for Your Own Essay

In this essay, Etzioni evaluates a kind of job he thinks is inappropriate for high school students. List the kinds of jobs you know enough about to evaluate from personal experience. Then choose one job from your list, and consider the standards you would use to evaluate it. If you were to write an essay evaluating it, you could gather current information about it, should you need to do so, by going there to interview workers and customers, visiting its Web site, or going online or to the library to find out what people are currently saying about this kind of business. Unlike Etzioni, you would want to have had firsthand experience working at the job. If you worked at it recently or are working at it now, you could rely entirely on your personal knowledge as the basis for your evaluation.

To use the Writing Guide Software to record your ideas, click on
▶ **Journal**

Christine Romano *wrote the following essay when she was a first-year college student. In it she evaluates an argument essay written by another student, Jessica Statsky's "Children Need to Play, Not Compete," which appears in Chapter 6 of this book (pp. 287–91). Romano focuses not on the writing strategies or basic features of an essay arguing a position but rather on its logic—on whether the argument is likely to convince its intended readers. She evaluates the logic of the argument according to the standards presented in Chapter 12. You might want to review these standards on pp. 604–606 before you read Romano's evaluation. Also, if you have not already read Statsky's essay, you might want to do so now, thinking about what seems most and least convincing to you about her argument that competitive sports can be harmful to young children.*

To see this essay with pop-up annotations in the software, click on
▶ **Justifying an Evaluation**
▶ **Read**

"Children Need to Play, Not Compete," by Jessica Statsky: An Evaluation

Christine Romano

Parents of young children have a lot to worry about and to hope for. In "Children Need to Play, Not Compete," Jessica Statsky appeals to their worries and hopes in order to convince them that organized competitive sports may harm their children physically and psychologically. Statsky states her thesis clearly and fully forecasts the reasons she will offer to justify her position: Besides causing physical and psychological harm, competitive sports discourage young people from becoming players and fans when they are older and inevitably put parents' needs and fantasies ahead of children's welfare. Statsky also carefully defines her key terms. By *sports,* for example, she means to include both contact and noncontact sports that emphasize competition. The sports may be organized locally at schools or summer sports camps or nationally, as in the examples of Peewee Football and Little League Baseball. She is concerned only with children six to twelve years of age. 1

In this essay, I will evaluate the logic of Statsky's argument, considering whether the support for her thesis is appropriate, believable, consistent, and complete. While her logic *is* appropriate, believable, and consistent, her argument also has weaknesses. I will focus on two: Her argument seems incomplete because she neglects to anticipate parents' predictable questions and objections and because she fails to support certain parts of it fully. 2

Statsky provides appropriate support for her thesis. Throughout her essay, she relies for support on different kinds of information (she cites eleven separate sources, including books, newspapers, and Web sites). Her quotations, examples, and statistics all support the reasons she believes competitive sports are bad for children. For example, in paragraph 3, Statsky offers the reason that "overly competitive sports" may damage children's growing bodies and that contact sports, in particular, may be especially hazardous. She supports this reason by paraphrasing Koppett that muscle strain or even lifelong injury may result when a twelve-year-old throws curve balls. She then quotes Tutko on the dangers of tackle football. The opinions of both experts are obviously appropriate. They are relevant to her reason, and we can easily imagine that they would worry many parents. 3

Not only is Statsky's support appropriate, but it is also believable. Statsky quotes or summarizes authorities to support her argument in paragraphs 3–6, 8, 9, and 11. The question is whether readers would find these authorities credible. Since Statsky relies almost entirely on authorities to support her argument, readers must believe these authorities for her argument to succeed. I have not read Statsky's sources, but I think there are good reasons to consider them authoritative. First of all, the newspaper authors she quotes write for two of America's most respected newspapers, the *New York Times* and the *Los Angeles Times.* These newspapers are read across the country by political leaders and financial experts and by people interested in the arts and popular culture. Both have sports reporters who not only report on sports events but also take a critical look at sports issues. In addition, both newspapers have reporters who specialize in children's health and education. Second, Statsky gives background information about the authorities she quotes, which is intended to increase the person's believability in the eyes of parents of young children. In paragraph 3, she tells readers that Thomas Tutko is "a psychology professor at San Jose State University and coau- 4 thor of the book *Winning Is Everything and Other American Myths.*" In paragraph 5, she announces that Martin Rablovsky is "a former sports editor for the *New York Times,*" and she notes that he has watched children play organized sports for many years. Third, she quotes from two Web sites—the official Little League site and an AOL message board. Parents are likely to accept the authority of the Little League site and be interested in what other parents and coaches (most of whom are also parents) have to say.

In addition to quoting authorities, Statsky relies on examples and anecdotes to support the reasons for her position. If examples and anecdotes are to be believable, they must seem representative to readers, not bizarre or highly unusual or completely unpredictable. Readers can imagine a similar event happening elsewhere. For anecdotes to be believable, they should, in addition, be specific and true to life. All of Statsky's examples and anecdotes fulfill these requirements, and her readers would find them believable. For example, early in her argument, in paragraph 4, Statsky reasons that fear of being hurt greatly reduces children's enjoyment of contact sports. The anecdote comes from Tosches's investigative report on Peewee Football as does the quotation by the mother of an eight-year-old player who says that the children become frightened and pretend to be injured in order to stay out of the game. In the anecdote, a seven-year-old makes himself vomit to avoid playing. Because these echo the familiar "I feel bad" or "I'm sick" excuse children give when they do not want to go somewhere (especially school) or do something, most parents would find them believable. They could easily imagine their own children pretending to be hurt or ill if they were fearful or depressed. The anecdote is also specific. Tosches reports what the boy said and did and what the coach said and did. 5

Other examples provide support for all the major reasons Statsky gives for her position: 6

- That competitive sports pose psychological dangers—children becoming serious and unplayful when the game starts (paragraph 5)
- That adults' desire to win puts children at risk—parents fighting each other at a Peewee Football game and a coach setting fire to an opposing team's jersey (paragraph 8)
- That organized sports should emphasize cooperation and individual performance instead of winning—a coach banning scoring but finding that parents would not support him and a New York City basketball league in which all children play an equal amount of time and scoring is easier (paragraph 11)

All of these examples are appropriate to the reason they support. They are also believable. Together, they help Statsky achieve her purpose of convincing parents that organized, competitive sports may be bad for their children and that there are alternatives.

If readers are to find an argument logical and convincing, it must be consistent and complete. While there are no inconsistencies or contradictions in Statsky's argument, it is seriously incomplete because it neglects to support fully one of its reasons, it fails to anticipate many predictable questions parents would have, and it pays too little attention to noncontact competitive team sports. The most obvious example of thin support comes in paragraph 11, where Statsky asserts that many parents are ready for children's team sports that emphasize cooperation and individual performance. Yet the example of a Lit- 7 tle League official who failed to win parents' approval to ban scores raises serious questions about just how many parents are ready to embrace noncompetitive sports teams. The other support, a brief description of City Sports for Kids in New York City, is very convincing but will only be logically compelling to those parents who are already inclined to agree with Statsky's position. Parents inclined to disagree with Statsky would need additional evidence. Most parents know that big cities receive special federal funding for evening, weekend, and summer recreation. Brief descriptions of six or eight noncompetitive teams in a variety of sports in cities, rural areas, suburban neighborhoods—some funded publicly, some funded privately—would be more likely to convince skeptics. Statsky is guilty here of failing to accept the burden of proof, a logical fallacy.

Statsky's argument is also incomplete in that it fails to anticipate certain objections 8
and questions that some parents, especially those she most wants to convince, are almost sure to raise. In the first sentences of paragraphs 6, 9, and 10, Statsky does show that she is thinking about her readers' questions. She does not go nearly far enough, however, to have a chance of influencing two types of readers: those who themselves are or were fans of and participants in competitive sports and those who want their six- to twelve-year-old children involved in mainstream sports programs despite the risks, especially the national programs that have a certain prestige. Such parents might feel that competitive team sports for young children create a sense of community with a shared purpose, build character through self-sacrifice and commitment to the group, teach children to face their fears early and learn how to deal with them through the support of coaches and team members, and introduce children to the principles of social cooperation and collaboration. Some parents are likely to believe and to know from personal experience that coaches who burn opposing team's jerseys on the pitching mound before the game starts are the exception, not the rule. Some young children idolize teachers and coaches, and team practice and games are the brightest moments in their lives. Statsky seems not to have considered these reasonable possibilities, and as a result her argument lacks a compelling logic it might have had. By acknowledging that she was aware of many of these objections—and perhaps even accommodating more of them in her own argument, as she does in paragraph 10, while refuting other objections—she would have strengthened her argument.

Finally, Statsky's argument is incomplete because she overlooks examples of non- 9
contact team sports. Track, swimming, and tennis are good examples that some readers would certainly think of. Some elementary schools compete in track meets. Public and private clubs and recreational programs organize competitive swimming and tennis competitions. In these sports, individual performance is the focus. No one gets trampled. Children exert themselves only as much as they are able to. Yet individual performances are scored, and a team score is derived. Because Statsky fails to mention any of these obvious possibilities, her argument is weakened.

The logic of Statsky's argument, then, has both strengths and weaknesses. The sup- 10
port she offers is appropriate, believable, and consistent. The major weakness is incompleteness—she fails to anticipate more fully the likely objections of a wide range of readers. Her logic would prevent parents who enjoy and advocate competitive sports from taking her argument seriously. Such parents and their children have probably had positive experiences with team sports, and these experiences would lead them to believe that the

gains are worth whatever risks may be involved. Many probably think that the risks Statsky points out can be avoided by careful monitoring. For those parents inclined to agree with her, Statsky's logic is likely to seem sound and complete. An argument that successfully confirms readers' beliefs is certainly valid, and Statsky succeeds admirably at this kind of argument. Because she does not offer compelling counterarguments to the legitimate objections of those inclined not to agree with her, however, her success is limited.

Connecting to Culture and Experience: Competitive Team Sports and Social Cooperation

Romano reasons in paragraph 8 that some parents "feel that competitive team sports for young children create a sense of community with a shared purpose, build character through self-sacrifice and commitment to the group, teach children to face their fears early and learn how to deal with them through the support of coaches and team members, and introduce children to the principles of social cooperation and collaboration."

With two or three other students, discuss this view of the role that sports plays in developing a child's sense of social cooperation by giving children insights into how people cooperate in communities like neighborhoods, schools, workplaces, or even nations. Begin by telling one another about your own, your siblings', or your children's experiences with team sports between the ages of six and twelve. Explain how participating in sports at this young age did or did not teach social cooperation. If you think team sports failed to teach cooperation or had some other effect, explain the effect it did have.

Analyzing Writing Strategies

1. In paragaph 2, Romano **presents her overall judgment**. Underline the thesis statement, and evaluate it in terms of how well it meets the three standards for a good thesis: that it be clear and unambiguous, arguable, and appropriately qualified.
2. In addition to presenting her judgment in her thesis statement, Romano forecasts her reasons in paragraph 2. Reread Romano's essay, noting in the margin where she addresses each of these reasons. Then explain what you learn from the way Romano **presents her reasons**. Are they clear and easy to follow? Do you think her intended readers—her instructor and parents of young children (the same audience Statsky is trying to convince)—are likely to consider her reasons plausible? In other words, are these reasons appropriate for evaluating an essay that argues a position, based on standards her readers are likely to share? If you see a potential problem with any of the reasons she uses, explain the problem you see.
3. In paragraph 8, Romano observes that Statsky fails to anticipate certain objections and questions that her readers are almost sure to raise. Romano herself has analyzed her readers and tried to **anticipate their likely objections and questions** as well as the judgments they may be inclined to make of the subject. Turn to the Writer at Work section on pp. 441–42 to see how Romano uses the Guide to Writing in this chapter (pp. 421–40) to help her anticipate her readers' concerns. Note what Romano changes when she revises her draft.

Commentary: Presenting Convincing Support

For more on using textual evidence as support, see Chapter 19.

Because she is evaluating a written text, Romano uses textual evidence to support her argument. To provide textual evidence, writers can quote, paraphrase, or summarize passages from the text. Romano **quotes** selectively, usually brief phrases. In paragraph 4, for example, Romano supports her argument about the believability of Statsky's sources with a quote showing how Statsky presents authorities:

> In paragraph 3, she tells readers that Thomas Tutko is "a psychology professor at San Jose State University and coauthor of the book *Winning Is Everything and Other American Myths.*" In paragraph 5, she announces that Martin Rablovsky is "a former sports editor for the *New York Times.*"

In addition to quoting, Romano **paraphrases** and **summarizes** passages from Statsky's essay. A summary—a distillation of the main ideas—tends to be briefer than a paraphrase. Paraphrasing, in contrast, tries to capture the rich detail of the original. A good example of paraphrasing appears in the opening paragraph, where Romano represents Statsky's argument. Compare Romano's paraphrase to the original passage from Statsky's essay:

> ***Statsky's Original Version***
>
> Highly organized competitive sports such as Peewee Football and Little League Baseball are too often played to adult standards, which are developmentally inappropriate for children and can be both physically and psychologically harmful. Furthermore, because they eliminate many children from organized sports before they are ready to compete, they are actually counterproductive for developing either future players or fans. (paragraph 2)
>
> ***Romano's Paraphrase***
>
> Besides causing physical and psychological harm, competitive sports discourage young people from becoming players and fans when they are older and inevitably put parents' needs and fantasies ahead of children's welfare. (paragraph 1)

Notice that in the paraphrase, Romano mostly uses her own words, with a few significant exceptions for key terms like *physical* and *psychological, players* and *fans.*

Romano summarizes primarily to present parts of Statsky's argument, as in the following excerpt:

> ***Romano's Summary***
>
> [I]n paragraph 3, Statsky offers the reason that "overly competitive sports" may damage children's growing bodies and that contact sports, in particular, may be especially hazardous. She supports this reason by paraphrasing Koppett that muscle strain or even lifelong injury may result when a twelve-year-old throws curve balls. She then quotes Tutko on the dangers of tackle football. (paragraph 3)

If you compare this summary with Romano's paraphrase, you will notice another important distinction between summarizing and paraphrasing. When summarizing, writers usually describe what the author is doing in the passage. In the summarized passage, for instance, Romano uses Statsky's name and the pronoun *she* to relate the different strategic moves Statsky makes in the paragraph being summarized. When paraphrasing, however, writers typically leave out references to the author and his or her moves. Like Romano does in the preceding sample paraphrase, they simply restate what the author has written.

Especially when you write an evaluation of a written document, these are the strategies you need to employ for presenting textual evidence from the document itself.

For additional examples of paraphrasing and summarizing, see Chapter 22, pp. 753–56. For guidance on integrating quotations into your writing, see Chapter 22, pp. 749–51.

Considering Topics for Your Own Essay

List several written texts you would consider evaluating. For example, you might include in your list an essay from one of the chapters in this book. If you choose an argument from Chapters 6–10, you could evaluate its logic, its use of emotional appeals, or its credibility. You might prefer to evaluate a children's book that you read when you were young or that you now read to your own children, a magazine for people interested in a particular topic like computers or cars, a scholarly article you read for a research paper, or a short story from Chapter 10. You need not limit yourself to texts written on paper; also consider texts available online. Choose one possibility from your list, and come up with two or three reasons why it is a good or bad text.

To use the Writing Guide Software to record your ideas, click on
▶ **Journal**

PURPOSE AND AUDIENCE

When you evaluate something, you seek to influence readers' judgments and possibly their actions. Your primary aim is to convince readers that your judgment is well informed and reasonable and therefore that they can feel confident in making decisions based on it. Readers do not simply accept reviewers' judgments, however, especially on important subjects. More likely they read reviews to learn more about a subject so that they can make an informed decision themselves. Consequently, most readers care less about the forcefulness with which you assert your judgment than about the reasons and support you give for it.

Effective writers develop an argument designed for their particular readers. Given what you can expect your readers to know about your subject and the standards they would apply when evaluating this kind of subject, you decide which reasons to use as well as how much and what kind of support to give.

You may want to acknowledge directly your readers' knowledge of the subject, perhaps revealing that you understand how they might judge it differently. You might even let readers know that you have anticipated their objections to your argument. In responding to objections or different judgments, you could agree to disagree on certain points but try to convince readers that on other points you do share the same or at least similar standards.

BASIC FEATURES: EVALUATIONS

A Well-Presented Subject

The subject must be clearly identified if readers are to know what is being evaluated. Most writers name it explicitly. When the subject is a film, an essay, a video game, or a Web site, naming it is easy. When it is something more general, naming may require more imagination or just an arbitrary choice. Etzioni, for example, uses the name *McDonald's* to stand for the entire class of fast-food restaurant jobs he is evaluating.

Evaluations should provide only enough information to give readers a context for the judgment. However, certain kinds of evaluations—such as reviews of films, computer games, television programs, and books—usually require more information than others because reviewers have to assume that readers will be unfamiliar with the subject and are reading in part to learn more about it. Holden tells readers the names of the actors and director of *Road to Perdition*, the place and time in which the film's story unfolds, and a general outline of what happens to the main characters. For a recently released film, the writer must decide how much of the plot to reveal—trying not to spoil the suspense while explaining how well or poorly the suspense is managed. For a classic film or in certain classroom situations, reviewers need not worry about giving anything away.

A Clear Overall Judgment

Evaluation essays are built around an overall judgment—an assertion that the subject is good or bad or that it is better or worse than something else of the same kind. This judgment is the thesis of the essay. The thesis statement may appear in the first sentence, as it does in Etzioni's essay ("McDonald's is bad for your kids"), or elsewhere in the essay. Romano puts hers in the second paragraph. Holden asserts his thesis in the fourth paragraph. Writers also may restate the thesis at the end of the essay, summarizing their main points, as Jackson does. Wherever the thesis appears, it must satisfy three requirements: that it be clear and unambiguous, arguable, and appropriately qualified.

Although readers expect a definitive judgment, they also appreciate a balanced one. All of the writers in this chapter, except Holden, acknowledge both good and bad qualities of the subject they are evaluating. Romano praises the strengths and criticizes the weaknesses of Statsky's logic. Jackson gives the computer game his show's highest five-star rating, but he points out its shortcomings. Even Etzioni, who is highly critical of fast-food jobs, admits that fast-food chains do "provide very large numbers of teen jobs, provide regular employment," and "pay quite well compared to many other teen jobs" (paragraph 5).

Appropriate Reasons and Convincing Support

Writers assert the reasons for their judgment, often explain their reasons in some detail, and provide support for their reasons. For example, one of the reasons Etzioni gives for his judgment that McDonald's-type jobs are bad for teenagers is that they "impart few skills that will be useful in later life" (paragraph 3). He then specifies the skills that fast-food jobs teach young people and explains exactly why he thinks they are not useful later in life. Etzioni's argument hinges on the key terms *skills* and *useful,* both of which he defines and illustrates for readers.

For an argument to be convincing, readers have to accept the reasons as appropriate for evaluating the subject. Jackson, for example, assumes that his audience of computer game players will agree that his reasons are appropriate because they are based on standards that knowledgeable gamers apply when evaluating a game. Etzioni, on the other hand, argues that although fast-food workers do learn skills, they are not the kinds of skills young people need to succeed in a high-tech workplace.

Evaluators not only give reasons but must also support their reasons. They may use various kinds of support. Romano, for example, relies primarily on textual evidence to support her reasons, presenting it in quotations, paraphrases, and summaries. In evaluating a video game, Jackson supports his argument with examples and descriptions. Etzioni cites statistics and authorities.

Many writers also use comparisons to support an evaluative argument. For example, Holden refers to other films (such as *High Noon, Unforgiven,* and the *Godfather* movies), graphic novels (*The Lone Ranger*), Depression-era paintings (by artists like Edward Hopper), and music (by composers like Aaron Copland). Comparisons like these both support the argument and help to convince readers that the writer is an expert who knows the kinds of standards that knowledgeable people normally apply when evaluating this kind of film. Similarly, Jackson compares the video game he is reviewing to other role-playing games, and Etzioni compares McDonald's-type jobs to other jobs that teenagers in earlier generations have taken.

Anticipation of Readers' Objections and Alternative Judgments

Sometimes reviewers try to anticipate and respond to readers' possible objections and alternative judgments, but counterarguing is not as crucial for evaluation as is arguing directly for a judgment by giving reasons and support. When they do counterargue, reviewers may simply acknowledge that others perhaps disagree, may accommodate into their argument points others have made, or may try to refute objections and alternative judgments. Etzioni, for example, acknowledges that Harrell and Wirtz's research is impressive (paragraph 10). But he refutes it not by questioning the validity of their statistics but by arguing that working in fast-food restaurants in high school may guarantee employment four years later but not in the best jobs. Only going to college can guarantee the best jobs in the long run. Etzioni bases his counterargument on a standard he believes he shares with most readers: that having a job four years after graduating from high school is not as valuable as being able to get a higher-paying job after graduating from college.

GUIDE TO WRITING
Justifying an Evaluation

THE WRITING ASSIGNMENT

THE WRITING ASSIGNMENT

Write an essay evaluating a particular subject. Examine your subject closely, and make a judgment about it. Give reasons for your judgment, reasons based on widely recognized standards for evaluating a subject like yours. Support your reasons with examples and other details from your subject.

INVENTION AND RESEARCH

INVENTION & RESEARCH

- Finding a Subject to Write About
- Exploring Your Subject and Possible Readers
- Testing Your Choice
- Testing Your Choice: A Collaborative Activity
- Becoming an Expert on Your Subject
- Developing Your Evaluation
- Considering Document Design
- Defining Your Purpose for Your Readers
- Formulating a Tentative Thesis Statement

PLANNING AND DRAFTING

PLANNING & DRAFTING

- Seeing What You Have
- Setting Goals
- Outlining
- Drafting

CRITICAL READING GUIDE

CRITICAL READING GUIDE

- First Impression
- Presentation of the Subject
- Clear Judgment
- Reasons and Support
- Treatment of Readers' Objections, Questions, Alternative Judgments
- Effectiveness of the Organization
- Final Thoughts

REVISING

REVISING

- A Well-Presented Subject
- A Clear Overall Judgment
- Appropriate Reasons and Convincing Support
- Effective Counterargument
- The Organization

EDITING AND PROOFREADING

EDITING & PROOFREADING

- Checking Comparisons
- Combining Sentences

GUIDE TO WRITING

THE WRITING ASSIGNMENT

Write an essay evaluating a particular subject. Examine your subject closely, and make a judgment about it. Give reasons for your judgment, reasons based on widely recognized standards for evaluating a subject like yours. Support your reasons with examples and other details from your subject.

To use the Writing Guide Software for this assignment, click on
▶ **Justifying an Evaluation**
▶**Write**

INVENTION AND RESEARCH

The following activities will help you choose and explore a subject, consider your judgment, and develop your argument. These activities are easy to complete. Doing them over several days will give your ideas time to ripen and grow. Keep a written record of your invention and research to use later when you draft and revise.

Finding a Subject to Write About

You may already have a subject in mind and some ideas on how you will evaluate it. Even so, it is wise to take a few minutes to consider some other possible subjects. That way you can feel confident not only about having made the best possible choice but also about having one or two alternative subjects in case your first choice does not work. The following activities will help you make a good choice.

Listing Subjects. *Make a list of subjects you might be interested in evaluating.* Make your list as complete as you can, including, for example, the subjects suggested by the Considering Topics for Your Own Essay activity following each reading in this chapter. The following categories may give you some ideas.

- ***Culture:*** Television program, magazine or newspaper, computer game, band, songwriter, recording, film, actor, performance, dance club, coffeehouse, artist, museum exhibit, individual work of art
- ***Written work:*** Poem, short story, novel, Web site, magazine article, newspaper column, letter to the editor, textbook, autobiography, essay from this book
- ***Education:*** School, program, teacher, major department, library, academic or psychological counseling service, writing center, campus publication, sports team
- ***Government:*** Government department or official, proposed or existing law, agency or program, candidate for public office

- *Leisure:* Amusement park, museum, restaurant, resort, sports team, sports equipment, national or state park

Listing Subjects Related to Identity and Community. The following are ideas for an evaluative essay on issues of identity and community.

- Evaluate how well one of the following meets the needs of residents of your town or city: a community center, public library, health clinic, college, athletic team, festival, neighborhood watch or block parent program, meals-on-wheels program, theater or symphony, school or school program.
- Evaluate how well one of the following serves the members of your religious community: a religious school, youth or senior group, religious leader, particular sermon, bingo, revival meeting, choir, building and grounds.
- Evaluate how well one of the following aspects of local government serves the needs of the community: mayor, city council, police, courts, social services, park system, zoning commission.

Listing Subjects Related to Work and Career. Following are some suggestions for an evaluative essay on issues involving work and career.

- Evaluate a job you have had or currently have, or evaluate someone else you have observed closely, such as a coworker or supervisor.
- Evaluate a local job-training program, either one in which you have participated or one where you can observe and interview trainees.

Choosing a Subject. *Review your list, and choose the one subject that seems most promising.* Your subject should be one that you can evaluate with some authority, either one that you already know quite well or one that you can study closely over the next week or two.

Exploring Your Subject and Possible Readers

To explore the subject, you need to review what you now know about it, become more familiar with it, make a tentative judgment about it, and think seriously about who your readers may be before you proceed to study your subject in depth. You then will be in a good position to decide whether to stick with this subject for your essay or choose a different subject, making this initial brief period of invention work a very good investment of your time.

Reviewing What You Now Know about the Subject. *Write for a few minutes about what you already know about your subject right at this moment.* Focus your thinking by considering questions like these:

- Why am I interested in this subject?
- What do I like and dislike about this subject?

- What do I usually look for in evaluating a subject of this kind? What do other people look for?
- How can I arrange to become very familiar with my subject over the next week or two?

Familiarizing Yourself with the Subject. *Take notes about what you observe and learn as you get acquainted with your subject, notes that include the kinds of details that make your subject interesting and special.* Whatever your subject, you must now take the time to experience it. If you are evaluating a one-time performance, it must be scheduled within the next few days, and you must be exceedingly attentive to the one performance and take careful notes. If you plan to evaluate a film, it would be best if you could rent the video so that you can reexamine parts you need to refer to. If you are evaluating an agency, a service, or a program, observe and talk to people and make notes about what you see and hear.

Making a Tentative Judgment. *Review what you have written as you have been getting to know your subject; then write a few sentences stating your best current overall judgment of the subject.* Your judgment may be only tentative at this stage, or you may feel quite confident in it. Your judgment may also be mixed: You may have a high regard for certain aspects of the subject and, at the same time, a rather low assessment of other aspects. As you consider your overall judgment, keep in mind that readers of evaluative essays expect writers not only to balance their evaluation of a subject (by pointing out things they like as well as things they dislike) but also to state a definitive judgment, not a vague, wishy-washy, or undecided judgment.

Identifying and Understanding Potential Readers. *Write several sentences about possible readers, with the following questions in mind:*

- For what particular kinds of readers do I want to write this evaluation?
- What are my readers likely to know about my subject? Will I be introducing the subject to them (as in a film or book review)? Or will they already be familiar with it, and if so, how expert on the subject are they likely to be?
- How are my readers likely to judge my subject? What about it might they like, and what might they dislike?
- What reasons might they give for their judgment?
- On what standards is their overall judgment likely to be based? Do I share these standards or at least recognize their appropriateness?

Testing Your Choice

Pause now to decide whether you have chosen a subject about which you can make a convincing evaluative argument. Reread your invention notes to see whether you know enough about your subject or can get the information you need to write a convincing evaluation for the readers you have identified. Also consider whether you feel confident in your judgment.

As you develop your argument, you should become even more confident. If, however, you begin to doubt your choice, consider beginning again with a different subject selected from your list of possibilities. Before changing your subject, however, discuss your ideas with another student or your instructor to see whether they make sense to someone else.

Testing Your Choice: A Collaborative Activity

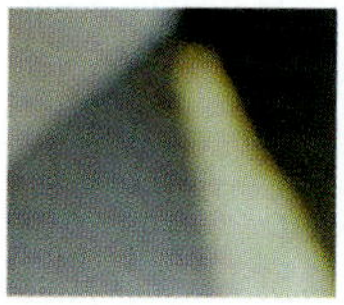

At this point in your invention work, you will find it helpful to get together with two or three other students to discuss your subjects and test ways of evaluating them.

Presenters: Each of you in turn briefly describe your subject without revealing your overall judgment.

Evaluators: Explain to each presenter how you would evaluate a subject of this kind. For example, would you judge a science-fiction film by the story, acting, ideas, special effects, or some other aspect of the film? Would you judge a lecture course by how interesting or entertaining the lectures are, how hard the tests are, how well the lectures are organized, or how well it succeeds in some other aspect of the class? In other words, tell the presenter what standards you would apply to his or her particular subject. (Presenters: Take notes about what you hear.)

Becoming an Expert on Your Subject

Now that you are confident about your choice of subject and have in mind some standards for judging it, you can confidently move ahead to become an expert on your subject. Over the next few days, you can immerse yourself in it to prepare to evaluate it confidently.

Immersing Yourself in Your Subject. *Take careful notes at every stage of gradually becoming thoroughly familiar with your subject.* If you are writing about a film, for example, you will need to view the film at least twice by attending screenings or renting a video or DVD. If you are evaluating the effectiveness of a public official, you will need to read recent public statements by the official and perhaps observe the official in action. If you decide to evaluate a local sports team, you will need to study the team, attend a game and if possible a practice, and review films of recent games. Consult with other students and your instructor about efficient strategies for becoming an expert on your subject. Your goal is to gather the details, facts, examples, or stories you will need to write an informative, convincing evaluation.

If you think you will need to do more research than time permits or you cannot view, visit, or research your subject to discover the details needed to support an evaluation of it, then you may need to consider choosing a different, more accessible subject.

Learning More about Standards for Judging Your Subject. *Make a list of prominent, widely recognized standards for judging your subject.* If you do not know the standards usually used to evaluate your subject, you could do some research. For example, if you are reviewing a film, you could read a few recent film reviews online or in the library, noting the standards that reviewers typically use and the reasons that they assert for liking or disliking a film. If you are evaluating a soccer team or one winning (or losing) game, you could read a book on coaching soccer or talk to an experienced soccer coach to learn about what makes an excellent soccer team or winning game. If you are evaluating a civic, governmental, or religious program, look for information online or in the library about what makes a good program of its type. If you are evaluating an essay in this book, you will find standards in the Purpose and Audience section and in the Basic Features section of the chapter where the essay appears. If you are evaluating an argument essay from Chapters 6–10, you will find additional standards in Evaluating the Logic of an Argument, Recognizing Emotional Manipulation, and Judging the Writer's Credibility, pp. 604–608.

Developing Your Evaluation

Now you are ready to discover how you might proceed to make a plausible, even convincing, argument to justify your judgment. Each of the following activities requires only a few minutes of your time spread out over a day or two, and they are all essential to your success in organizing and drafting your evaluation.

Listing Reasons. *Write down every reason you can think of to convince readers of your overall judgment.* Try stating your reasons like this: "My judgment is X because . . ." or "A reason I like (or dislike) X is that. . . ." Then look over your list to consider which reasons you regard as most important and likely to be most convincing to your readers. Highlight these reasons.

Finding Support. *Make notes about how to support your most promising reasons.* From your invention notes made earlier, select a few details, facts, comparisons, contrasts, or examples about your subject that might help you support each reason.

Anticipating Readers' Alternative Judgments, Questions, and Objections. *List a few questions your particular readers would likely want to ask you or objections they might have to your argument. Write for a few minutes responding to at least two of these questions or objections.* Now that you can begin to see how your argument might shape up, assume that some of your particular readers would judge your subject differently from the way you do. Remember that your responses—your counterargument—could simply acknowledge the disagreements, accommodate readers' views by conceding certain points, or refute readers' arguments as uninformed or mistaken.

Researching Alternative Judgments: An Online Activity

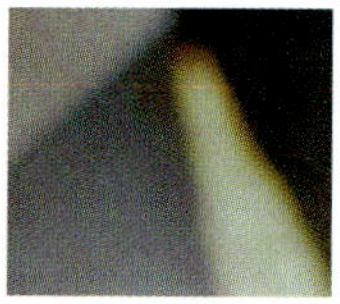

One way to learn more about judgments of your subject that differ from your own judgment is to search for reviews or evaluations of your subject online. You may even decide to incorporate quotations from or references to alternative judgments as part of your counterargument, although you need not do so in order to write a successful evaluation. Enter the name of your subject—movie title, restaurant name, compact disc title, title of a proposed law, name of a candidate for public office—in a search engine such as Google (google.com) or Yahoo! Directory (http://dir.yahoo.com). (Sometimes you can narrow the search usefully by including the keyword *review* as well.) Of course, not all subjects are conveniently searchable online, and some subjects—a local concert, a college sports event, a campus student service, a neighborhood program—will likely not have been reviewed by anyone but you.

Bookmark or keep a record of promising sites. Download any materials you might wish to cite in your evaluation, making sure you have all the information necessary to document the source.

Considering Document Design

Think about whether visual or audio elements—cartoons, photographs, tables, graphs, or snippets from films, television programs, or songs—would strengthen your argument. These are not at all a requirement of an effective evaluation essay, but they could be helpful. Consider also whether your readers might benefit by such design features as headings, bulleted or numbered lists, or other elements that would make your essay easier to follow. You could construct your own graphic elements, download materials from the Internet, tape images and sounds from television or other sources, or scan visuals into your document from books and magazines. If you do use visual or audio elements you did not create yourself, remember to document the sources in your essay (and request permission from the sources if the essay will be posted on the Web).

Defining Your Purpose for Your Readers

Write a few sentences defining your purpose in writing this evaluation for your readers. Remember that you already have analyzed your potential readers and developed your argument with these readers in mind. Given these readers, try now to define your purpose by considering the following possibilities and any others that might apply to your writing situation:

- If my readers are likely to agree with my overall judgment, should I try to strengthen their resolve by giving them well-supported reasons, helping them refute others' judgments, or suggesting how they might respond to questions and objections?

- If my readers and I share certain standards for evaluating a subject of this kind but we disagree on our overall judgment of this particular subject, can I build a convincing argument based on these shared standards or at least get readers to acknowledge the legitimacy of my judgment?
- If my readers use different standards of judgment, what should I try to do—urge them to think critically about their own judgment, to consider seriously other standards for judging the subject, or to see certain aspects of the subject they might have overlooked?

Formulating a Tentative Thesis Statement

Write several sentences that could serve as your thesis statement. Think about how you should state your overall judgment—how emphatic you should make it, whether you should qualify it, and whether you should include in the thesis a forecast of your reasons and support. Remember that a strong thesis statement should be clear, arguable, and appropriately qualified.

Review the readings in this chapter to see how other writers construct thesis statements. For example, recall that Etzioni abruptly begins his essay with a surprising overall judgment: "McDonald's is bad for your kids." He then qualifies this assertion in the next sentence to make clear that he is focusing on the types of jobs at McDonald's, not the food. Like Etzioni, Holden boldly asserts an overall judgment he knows will not be expected by his readers. His thesis statement is simple and direct: "With *Road to Perdition* they have created a truly majestic visual tone poem, one that is so much more stylized than its forerunners that it inspires a continuing and deeply satisfying awareness of the best movies as monumental 'picture shows'" (paragraph 4).

Romano uses the thesis statement to forecast her reasons as well as to express her overall judgment. She begins by indicating the standards she thinks are appropriate for evaluating her subject. Her thesis statement shows that she bases her reasons on these standards. In addition, it lets readers know in advance what she likes about the subject she is evaluating as well as what she does not like: "While [Statsky's] logic *is* appropriate, believable, and consistent, her argument also has weaknesses" (paragraph 2). In contrast to Etzioni, who states his thesis rather dramatically, Romano makes her thesis statement seem thoughtful and balanced. There is no ambivalence or confusion, however, about Romano's judgment. She is clear and emphatic, not vague or wishy-washy.

As you draft your own tentative thesis statement, think carefully about the language you use. It should be clear and unambiguous, emphatic but appropriately qualified. Although you will most probably refine your thesis statement as you draft and revise your essay, trying now to articulate it will help give direction and impetus to your planning and drafting.

PLANNING AND DRAFTING

This section will help you review what you have learned about evaluating your subject, determine specific goals for your essay, make a tentative outline, and get started on your first draft.

If you are using the Writing Guide Software, click on
▶ **Planning and Drafting**

Seeing What You Have

Pause now to reread your invention and research notes. Watch for language that describes the subject vividly, states your judgment clearly, presents your reasons and support convincingly, and counterargues objections to your argument or readers' alternative judgments. Highlight key words, phrases, and sentences; make marginal notes or electronic annotations. If you have done your invention writing on the computer, you may have sentences or whole paragraphs that can be copied and pasted into your draft.

If your invention notes seem skimpy, you may need to do further research at this stage, or you could begin drafting now and later do research to fill in the blanks.

If your confidence in your judgment has been shaken or if you are concerned that you will not be able to write an argument to support your judgment, consult your instructor to determine whether you should try evaluating a different subject.

Setting Goals

Before you begin drafting, set some specific goals to guide the decisions you will make as you draft and revise your essay. The draft will be easier to write and more focused if you start with clear goals in mind. The following questions will help you set goals. You may find it useful to return to them while you are drafting, for they are designed to help you focus on specific features and strategies of evaluative essays.

Your Purpose and Readers

- What do I want my readers to think about the subject after reading my essay? Do I want to show them how the subject that I am evaluating fails (as Etzioni does), how it succeeds (as Holden does), or how it includes both strengths and weaknesses (as Jackson and Romano do)?
- Should I assume that my readers are likely to have read other evaluations of the subject (perhaps like Holden and Jackson) or to have developed their own evaluation of it (like Etzioni and Romano)? Or should I assume that I am introducing readers to the subject?
- How should I present myself to my readers—as knowledgeable, balanced, or impassioned or in some other way?

The Beginning

- What opening would capture readers' attention? Should I open by stating my overall judgment, as Etzioni, Holden, and Jackson do? Or should I begin by giving readers a context for my evaluation, as Romano does?
- Should I try to make clear to readers at the outset the standards I will apply, as Romano does? Should I begin by comparing my subject with a subject more familiar to readers, as Jackson and Holden do?

The Presentation of the Subject

- How should I identify the subject? If it doesn't have a specific name, should I name it after something readers will recognize, as Etzioni does? Should I place it in a recognized category or genre, as Holden does when he refers to period gangster and classic western films?
- What about the subject should I describe? Can I use visuals to illustrate, as Holden and Jackson do?
- Should I place the subject historically, as Etzioni does when he compares delivering newspapers to working at McDonald's?
- If the subject has a story, how much of it should I tell? Should I simply set the scene and identify the characters, or should I give details of the plot, as Holden does?

Your Evaluative Argument

- How should I state my thesis? Should I forecast my reasons early in the essay, as Romano does? Should I place my thesis at the beginning or wait until after I have provided a context?
- How can I convince readers to consider my overall judgment seriously even if they disagree with it? Should I build my argument on shared standards (like Etzioni) or defend my standards (like Romano)? Should I try to present a balanced judgment by praising some things and criticizing others, as all the writers in this chapter but Holden do?
- How can I present my reasons? Should I explain the standards on which I base my reasons, as Romano does, or can I assume that my readers will share my standards, as Jackson does?
- If I have more than one reason, how should I order them? Should I begin with the ones I think are most important for judging a subject of this kind, as Jackson does? Or should I end with the strongest reason?
- How can I support my reasons? Can I find examples from the text to quote, paraphrase, or summarize, as Holden and Romano do? Can I call on authorities and cite statistics, as Etzioni does? Can I give examples, as Jackson does?
- What objections or alternative judgments should I anticipate? How should I respond—by merely acknowledging them, by conceding legitimate objections and qualifying my judgment, or by trying to refute objections I consider illegitimate or weak?

The Ending

- How should I conclude? Should I try to frame the essay by echoing something from the opening or from another part of the essay?
- Should I conclude by restating my overall judgment, as Romano and Jackson do?
- Should I end by making a recommendation, as Etzioni does?

Outlining

An evaluative essay contains as many as four basic parts:

1. A presentation of the subject
2. A judgment of the subject
3. A presentation of reasons and support
4. A consideration of readers' objections and alternative judgments

These parts can be organized in various ways. If, for example, you expect readers to disagree with your judgment, you could show them what you think they have overlooked or misjudged about the subject. You could begin by presenting the subject; then you could assert your thesis, present your reasons and support, and anticipate and refute readers' likely objections.

Presentation of the subject
Thesis statement (judgment)
First reason and support
Anticipation and refutation of objection
Second reason and support
Anticipation and accommodation of objection
Conclusion

If you expect some of your readers to disagree with your negative judgment even though they base their judgment on the same standard on which you base yours, you could try to show them that the subject really does not satisfy the standard. You could begin by reinforcing the standard you share and then demonstrate how the subject fails to meet it.

Establish shared standard
Acknowledge alternative judgment
State thesis (judgment) that subject fails to meet shared standard
First reason and support showing how subject falls short of standard
Second reason and support (etc.)
Conclusion

There are, of course, many other possible ways to organize an evaluative essay, but these outlines should help you start planning your own essay.

Consider tentative any outlining you do before you begin drafting. Never be a slave to an outline. As you draft, you will usually see ways to improve your original plan. Be ready to revise your outline, shift parts around, or drop or add parts as you draft. If you use the outlining function of your word processing program, changing your outline will be simple, and you may be able to write the essay simply by expanding the outline.

Drafting

General Advice. Start drafting your essay, keeping in mind the goals you set while you were planning. Remember also the needs and expectations of your readers; organize, define, and explain with them in mind. Turn off your grammar checker and spelling checker at this stage if you find them distracting. Don't be afraid to skip around in your draft; jump back and fill in a spontaneous idea, or leap ahead and write a later section first if you find that easier. If you discover that you need more information, just make a note of what you have to find out, and go to the next point. When you are done drafting, you can search for the information you need. If you get stuck while drafting, explore the problem by using some of the writing activities in the Invention and Research section of this chapter (pp. 421–27).

You may want to review the general drafting advice on pp. 16–17. In addition, keep in mind that in writing an evaluative argument, you must accept the burden of proof by offering reasons and support for your judgment. Remember, too, that the basis for judgment often depends on standards as much as reasons and support. Try to think critically about the standards on which you base your judgment as well as the standards that others apply to subjects of the kind you are evaluating.

If you're using the Writing Guide Software, you can click on a Sentence Strategies button at any step from Plan and Draft through Revise to get a brief explanation and some examples of strategies especially useful for the genre of writing you're doing. You can then click on a link to access a fuller discussion of these strategies and more examples, as well as discussions of other strategies that you may also find helpful.

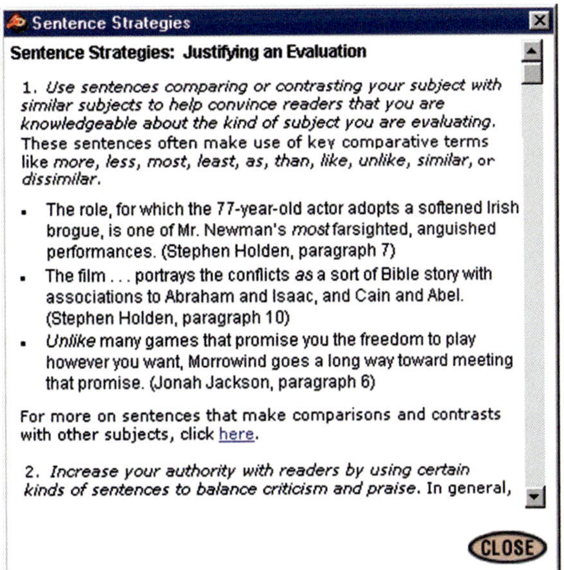

Sentence Strategies. As you draft an essay evaluating a subject, you may want to compare or contrast your subject with similar subjects to establish your authority with readers to evaluate a subject like yours. In addition, you are likely to want to balance the evaluation of your subject—by criticizing one or more aspects of the subject if you generally praise it or by praising one or more aspects of it if you generally criticize it. To do so, you will need to use sentences that clearly and efficiently express comparisons or contrasts, specifically ones that contrast criticism with praise and vice versa.

Use sentences comparing or contrasting your subject with similar subjects to help convince readers that you are knowledgeable about the kind of subject you are evaluating. These sentences often make use of key comparative terms like *more, less, most, least, as, than, like, unlike, similar,* or *dissimilar,* as readings in this chapter well illustrate:

> The role, for which the 77-year-old actor adopts a softened Irish brogue, is one of Mr. Newman's *most* farsighted, anguished performances. (Stephen Holden, paragraph 7)

In this sentence Holden compares Newman's performance in *Road to Perdition* to his performances in earlier movies, asserting that it is as good and perhaps even superior.

> The film . . . portrays the conflicts *as* a sort of contemporary Bible story with associations to Abraham and Isaac, and Cain and Abel. (Stephen Holden, paragraph 10)

In this sentence Holden compares the conflicts among the characters in the movie to the conflicts between father and son and between brother and brother in two memorable Bible stories: Abraham was willing to kill his son Isaac when commanded by God to do so (but was not required to actually kill the boy), and Cain killed his brother Abel out of jealous anger because God favored Abel's gift over Cain's. (Comparisons introduced by *like* or *as* are called *similes.*)

> *Unlike* many games that promise you the freedom to play however you want, Morrowind goes a long way toward meeting that promise. (Jonah Jackson, paragraph 6)

For more information on using sentences of comparison and contrast in evaluations, go to bedfordstmartins.com/theguide and click on Sentence Strategies. For illustrations of comparisons and contrasts in different kinds of writing, see Chapter 18, pp. 671–76.

In this sentence Jackson contrasts one feature of Morrowind with the corresponding feature of other computer games. Some comparisons or contrasts do not rely on an explicitly comparative term:

> *True to the austere moral code of classic westerns,* the film believes in heaven and hell and in the possibility of redemption. (Stephen Holden, paragraph 11)

> Roy Rogers, Baskin Robbins, Kentucky Fried Chicken, et al. may at first seem *nothing but a vast extension of the lemonade stand.* (Amitai Etzioni, paragraph 5)

Increase your authority with readers by using certain kinds of sentences to balance criticism and praise. The sentence strategies are similar for introducing criticism followed by praise and introducing praise followed by criticism, strategies we refer to in this chapter as **counterargument**. In general, these strategies rely on words expressing contrast, like *but, although, however, while,* and so on to set up the shift between the two responses.

Praise followed by criticism:

> *While* it is true that these places provide income, work and even some training to such youngsters, they also tend to perpetuate their disadvantaged status. (Amitai Etzioni, paragraph 11)
>
> This journal manages to record everything of importance, *but* it's missing the ability to sort or group items by quest. (Jonah Jackson, paragraph 14)
>
> . . . Statsky does show that she is thinking about her readers' questions. She does not go nearly far enough, *however,* to have a chance of influencing two types of readers. . . . (Christine Romano, paragraph 8)
>
> The seamless combat interface is also easy to use, *although* the various types of weapon swing (slash, jab, and so on) are awkwardly related to your movement direction. (Jonah Jackson, paragraph 13)
>
> *True,* you still have to have the gumption to get yourself over to the hamburger stand, *but* once you don the prescribed uniform, your task is spelled out in minute detail. (Amitai Etzioni, paragraph 7)

Criticism followed by praise:

> The combat music is a little flat, *but* it does provide important auditory clues about nearby enemies. (Jonah Jackson, paragraph 15)
>
> Its bugs and design quirks are *more than compensated for* by a core game that's just fantastic. (Jonah Jackson, paragraph 16)

For more on using sentences that balance criticism and praise in evaluations, go to bedfordstmartins.com/theguide and click on Sentence Strategies.

Notice that the last example does not use an explicitly comparative term to set up the contrast.

In addition to using sentences that make comparisons or contrasts with other subjects and sentences that balance criticism and praise, you can strengthen your evaluation with other kinds of sentences as well. You may want to review the information about using appositives (pp. 246–47), writing sentences introducing concession and refutation (pp. 308–10), and expressing logical relationships between sentences (pp. 310–11).

CRITICAL READING GUIDE

Now is the time to get a good critical reading of your draft. Writers usually find it helpful to have someone else read and comment on their drafts, and all writers know how much they learn about writing when they read other writers' drafts. Your instructor may arrange such a reading as part of your coursework—in class or online. If not, you can ask a classmate, friend, or family member to read your draft. You could also seek comments from a tutor at your campus writing center. (If you are unable to have someone else read your draft, turn ahead to the Revising section on p. 436, where you will find guidelines for reading your own draft critically.)

If you are using the Writing Guide Software, click on
▶ **Critical Reading Guide**

Making Comments Electronically
Most word processing software offers features that allow you to insert comments directly into the text of someone else's document. Many readers prefer to make their comments in this way because it tends to be faster than writing on a hard copy and space is virtually unlimited; from the writer's point of view, it also eliminates the problem of deciphering handwritten comments. Even where such special comment features are not available, simply typing comments directly into a document in a contrasting color can provide the same advantages.

▶ **If You Are the Writer.** To provide focused, helpful comments, your reader must know your essay's intended audience, your purpose, and a problem in the draft that you need help solving. Briefly write out this information at the top of your draft.

- ***Readers:*** Identify the intended readers of your essay. What do you assume that they think about your subject? Do you expect them to be receptive, skeptical, resistant, or antagonistic?
- ***Purpose:*** What effect do you realistically expect your argument to have on these particular readers?
- ***Problem:*** Ask your reader to help you solve the most important problem you see in your draft. Describe this problem briefly.

▶ **If You Are the Reader.** Use the following guidelines to help you give constructive, critical comments to others on evaluation essays:

1. ***Read for a First Impression.*** Tell the writer what you think the intended readers would find most and least convincing. If you personally think the evaluation is seriously flawed, share your thoughts. Then try to help the writer improve the argument for the designated readers. Next, consider the problem the writer identified, and respond briefly to that concern now. (If you find that the problem is covered by one of the other guidelines listed below, respond to it in more detail there if necessary.)
2. ***Analyze How Well the Subject Is Presented.*** Locate where in the draft the subject is presented, and ask questions that will help the writer strengthen the presentation. If you are surprised by the way the writer has presented the subject, briefly explain how you usually think of this particular subject or subjects of this kind. Also indicate whether any of the information about the subject seems unnecessary. Finally, and most important, let the writer know whether any of the information about the subject seems to you possibly inaccurate or only partly true.
3. ***Assess Whether the Judgment Is Stated Clearly.*** Write a sentence or two summarizing the writer's judgment as you understand it from reading the draft. Then identify the sentence or sentences in the draft where the judgment is stated explicitly. (It may be restated in several places.) If you cannot find an explicit statement of the judgment, let the writer know. Given the writer's purpose and audience, consider whether the judgment is arguable, clear, and appropriately qualified. If it seems indecisive or too extreme, suggest how the

writer might make it clearer or might qualify it by referring at least occasionally to the strengths of a criticized subject or the weaknesses of a praised subject.

4. ***Evaluate the Reasons and Support.*** Identify the reasons, and look closely at them and the support that the writer gives for them. If anything seems problematic, briefly explain what bothers you. For example, the reason may not seem appropriate for judging this kind of subject, you may not fully understand the reason or how it applies to this particular subject, the connection between a particular reason and its support may not be clear or convincing to you, the support may be too weak, or there may not be enough support to sustain the argument. Be as specific and constructive as you can, pointing out what does not work and also suggesting what the writer might do to solve the problem. For example, if the reason seems inappropriate, explain why you think so, and indicate what kinds of reasons you expect the intended readers to recognize as acceptable for judging this kind of subject. If the support is weak, suggest how it could be strengthened.

5. ***Assess How Well Readers' Objections, Questions, and Alternative Judgments Have Been Handled.*** Mark where the writer acknowledges, accommodates, or tries to refute readers' objections, questions, or alternative judgments. Point to any places where the counterargument seems superficial or dismissive, and suggest how it could be strengthened. Help the writer anticipate any important objections or questions that have been overlooked, providing advice on how to respond to them. Keep in mind that the writer may choose to acknowledge, accommodate, or refute opposing arguments.

6. ***Consider the Effectiveness of the Organization.*** Get an overview of the essay's organization, and point out any places where more explicit cueing—transitions, summaries, or topic sentences—would clarify the relationship between parts of the essay.
   - Look at the *beginning*. Do you think readers will find it engaging? If not, propose an alternative or suggest moving something from later in the essay that might work as a better opening.
   - Look at the *ending*. Does the essay conclude decisively and memorably? If not, suggest an alternative. Could something be moved to the end?
   - Look at the *design features*. Comment on the contribution of figures, headings, tables, and other design features. Indicate whether any visual or audio elements that have been included fail to support the evaluation effectively, and offer suggestions for improvement. Help the writer think of additional visual or audio elements that could make a contribution to the essay.

7. ***Give the Writer Your Final Thoughts.*** What is this draft's strongest part? What part is most in need of further work?

REVISING

Now you are ready to revise your essay. Your instructor or other students may have given you advice on improving your draft. Nevertheless, you may have begun to realize that your draft requires more rethinking than revising. For example, you may recognize that your reasons do not lead readers to accept your evaluation, that you cannot adequately support your reasons, or that you are unable to refute damaging objections to your argument. Consequently, instead of working to improve parts of the draft, you may need to write a new draft that radically reenvisions your argument. It is not unusual for students—and professional writers—to find themselves in this situation. Learning to make radical revisions is a valuable lesson for any writer.

If you feel satisfied that your draft achieves most, if not all, of your goals, you can focus on refining specific parts of it. Very likely you have thought of ways of improving your draft, and you may even have begun revising it. This section will help you get an overview of your draft and revise it accordingly.

If you are using the Writing Guide Software, click on
▶ **Revising**

Getting an Overview

Consider your draft as a whole, following these two steps:

1. ***Reread.*** If at all possible, put the draft aside for a day or two before rereading it. When you return to it, start by reconsidering your purpose. Then read the draft straight through, trying to see it as your intended readers will.
2. ***Outline.*** Make a scratch outline, indicating the basic features as they appear in the draft. Consider using the headings and outline/summary functions of your word processor.

Planning for Revision. Resist the temptation to dive in and start changing your text until after you have a solid grasp of the big picture. Using your outline as a guide, move through the document, using the change-highlighting or commenting tools of your word processor to note useful comments received from others and problems you want to solve (or mark on a hard copy if you prefer).

Analyzing the Basic Features of Your Own Draft. Using the Critical Reading Guide that begins on p. 433, identify problems that you now see in your draft.

Studying Critical Comments. Review all of the comments you have received from other readers, and add to your revision plan any that you intend to act on. For each comment, look at the draft to determine what might have led the reader to make that particular point. Try to be objective about any criticism. Ideally, these comments will help you see your draft as others see it, providing valuable information about how you can improve it.

Carrying Out Revisions

Having identified problems in your draft, you now need to come up with solutions and—most important—to carry them out. Basically, you have three ways of finding solutions:

1. Review your invention and planning notes for information and ideas to add to your draft.
2. Do additional invention and research to provide additional material that you or your readers think is needed.
3. Look back at the readings in this chapter to see how other writers have solved similar problems.

The following suggestions, which are organized according to the basic features of evaluation essays, will help you solve some common problems in this genre.

A Well-Presented Subject

- ***Is the subject unclear or hard to identify?*** Try to give it a name or to identify the general category to which it belongs. If you need more information about the subject, review your invention writing to see if you have left out any details you could now add. You may also need to revisit your subject or do further invention writing to answer questions that your classmates and instructor have raised or your intended readers might have.
- ***Is the subject presented in too much detail?*** Cut extraneous and repetitive details. If your subject is a film or book, consider whether you are giving away too much of the plot or whether your readers will expect you to give a lot of detail.
- ***Is any of the information inaccurate or only partly true?*** Reconsider the accuracy and completeness of the information you present. If any of the information will be surprising to readers, consider how you might reassure them that the information is accurate.

A Clear Overall Judgment

- ***Is your overall judgment hard to find?*** Announce your thesis more explicitly. If your judgment is mixed—pointing out what you like and do not like about the

Checking Sentence Strategies Electronically
To check your draft for a sentence strategy especially useful in evaluation essays, use your word processor's highlighting function to mark sentences where you praise or criticize various aspects of the subject. Then think about whether you could make your evaluation more authoritative and convincing to readers by making any of the sentences more balanced, either by praising something in an aspect that you have generally criticized or by criticizing something in an aspect that you have generally praised. For more on sentences that balance criticism and praise, see pp. 432–33.

subject—let readers know this from the beginning. Use sentences that balance praise and criticism, as most of the authors of this chapter's readings do.

- *Does your overall judgment seem indecisive or too extreme?* If your readers do not know what your overall judgment is or if they think you are either too positive or too negative, you may need to clarify your thesis statement or qualify it more carefully.

Appropriate Reasons and Convincing Support

- *Do any of the reasons seem inappropriate to readers?* Explain why you think the reason is appropriate, or show that your argument employs a standard commonly used for evaluating subjects of this kind.
- *Is any of the support thin or unconvincing?* To find additional support, review your invention writing, or reexamine the subject. Look closely again at your subject for more details that would support your reasons. As do all the authors of readings in this chapter, consider comparing or contrasting aspects of your subject with those of other subjects like yours.
- *Are any of your reasons and support unclear?* To clarify them, you may need to explain your reasoning in more detail or use examples and comparisons to make your ideas understandable. You may need to do some additional exploratory writing or research to figure out how to explain your reasoning. Consider also whether any of the reasons should be combined, separated, or cut.

Effective Counterargument

- *Do readers fail to recognize your counterargument?* Make your responses to readers' likely questions or objections or alternative judgments more explicit.
- *Are any important objections or questions overlooked?* Revisit your subject or invention notes to think more deeply about why and where readers might resist your argument. Try to imagine how a reader who strongly disagrees with your judgment (praising a movie or college program or restaurant for example) might respond to your evaluation.

The Organization

- *Does the essay seem disorganized or confusing?* You may need to add a forecasting statement, transitions, summaries, or topic sentences. You may also need to do some major restructuring, such as moving your presentation of the subject or reordering your reasons.
- *Is the beginning weak?* Review your notes to find an interesting quotation, comparison, image, or example to use in your first paragraph.
- *Is the ending weak?* See if you can restate your judgment, summarize your reasoning, or frame the essay by echoing a point made earlier.

- ***Can you add any visuals or design features to make the essay more interesting to read and to strengthen your argument?*** Consider taking features from your subject or creating visual or audio elements of your own.

EDITING AND PROOFREADING

Now is the time to check your revised draft for errors in grammar, punctuation, and mechanics and to consider matters of style. Our research has identified several errors that are especially likely to occur in evaluative writing. The following guidelines will help you proofread and edit your revised draft for these common errors.

A Note on Grammar and Spelling Checkers
These tools are good at catching certain types of errors, but currently there's no replacement for a good human proofreader. Grammar checkers in particular are extremely limited in what they can usually find, and often they only give you summary information that isn't helpful if you don't already understand the rule in question. They are also prone to give faulty advice for fixing problems and to flag correct items as wrong. Spelling checkers cause fewer problems but can't catch misspellings that are themselves words, such as *to* for *too*.

> If you are using the Writing Guide Software, click on
> ▶ **Editing and Proofreading**

Checking Comparisons. Whenever you evaluate something, you are likely to engage in comparison. You might want to show that a new recording is inferior to an earlier one, that one film is stronger than another, that this café is better than that one. Make a point of checking to see that all comparisons in your writing are complete, logical, and clear.

Editing to Make Comparisons Complete

▶ ***Jazz*** **is as good** ^*as*, **if not better than, Morrison's other novels.**

▶ **I liked the Lispector story because it's so different** ~~.~~ ^*from anything else I've ever read.*

Editing to Make Comparisons Logical

▶ **Will Smith's Muhammad Ali is more serious than any** ^*other* **role he's played.**

▶ **Ohio State's offense played much better than** ~~**Michigan.**~~ ^*Michigan's did.*

Check also to see that you say *different from* instead of *different than.*

▶ **Carrying herself with a confident and brisk stride, Katherine Parker seems different** ~~**than**~~ ^*from* **the other women in the office.**

▶ **Films like *Pulp Fiction* that glorify violence for its own sake are different ~~than~~** *from* **films like *Apocalypse Now* that use violence to make a moral point.**

Combining Sentences. When you evaluate something, you generally present your subject in some detail—defining it, describing it, placing it in some context. Inexperienced writers often give such details almost one by one, in separate sentences. Combining closely related sentences can make your writing more readable, helping readers to see how ideas relate.

▶ **In paragraph 5, the details provide a different impression, ~~It is~~ a comic or perhaps even pathetic impression, ~~This impression comes from~~** *based on* **the boy's attempts to dress up like a real westerner.**

From three separate sentences, this writer combines details about the "different impression" into one sentence, using two common strategies for sentence combining:

- Changing a sentence into an appositive phrase (a noun phrase that renames the noun or pronoun that immediately precedes it: "a comic or perhaps even pathetic impression")
- Changing a sentence into a verbal phrase (phrases with verbals that function as adjectives, adverbs, or nouns: "based on the boy's attempts to dress up like a real westerner")

Using Appositive Phrases to Combine Sentences

▶ **"Something Pacific" was created by Nam June Paik, ~~He is~~ a Korean artist who is considered a founder of video art.**

▶ **One of Dylan's songs** *, "Talkin' John Birch Paranoid Blues,"* **ridiculed the John Birch Society. ~~This song was called "Talkin' John Birch Paranoid Blues."~~**

Using Verbal Phrases to Combine Sentences

▶ **Spider-Man's lifesaving webbing sprung from his wristbands, ~~They carried~~** *carrying* **Mary Jane Watson and him out of peril.**

▶ **The coffee bar flanks the bookshelves, ~~It entices~~** *enticing* **readers to relax with a book.**

A WRITER AT WORK

ANTICIPATING READERS' OBJECTIONS AND QUESTIONS

In this section, we look at how Christine Romano tried to anticipate her readers' objections and questions. The final revision of Romano's evaluation essay appears in this chapter on pp. 411–15; Statsky's argument essay (which Romano evaluates) appears in Chapter 6 (pp. 287–91).

Because Romano was applying the standards for evaluating logical arguments that are presented in Chapter 12 of this textbook, she felt confident that the standards on which she based her overall judgment of Statsky's argument would also be important to her readers. Using the Exploring Your Subject and Possible Readers activity (pp. 422–23) in this chapter's Guide to Writing, she identified two kinds of readers: her instructor, who she assumed would approve of her using the textbook standards, and parents of young children, the same audience that Statsky addresses. Romano acknowledged that parents would not know the textbook standards, but she speculated that, like her, they also would be impressed by the way Statsky supports her position. Romano noted also that she expected parents to be sympathetic to Statsky's position because they would not want their children to be hurt playing sports.

After writing for a few minutes on the Testing Your Choice activity (pp. 423–24), Romano worked with a group of students in class on Testing Your Choice: A Collaborative Activity (p. 424). One of her group's members told her that he had been hurt playing in a Little League baseball game and had wanted to quit but that his dad had made him continue playing. He remembered crying and trying to get out of going to the next game. But looking back on the experience now, he said he was glad his father insisted because years later, when playing on the high school football team, he realized that being a serious athlete meant facing up to the fear and pain of injury. He said this was an important lesson, one that applied to everything in life, not just to playing sports. Therefore, the student told Romano, his standard for judging competitive sports for young children was based on how well the experience taught them to stick it out to conquer their pain and fear.

This student's choice of standards made Romano realize that Statsky's argument does not adequately address this compelling alternative judgment. When Romano planned and wrote her first draft, she tried to accommodate this student's point of view and others like it. In addition to praising the appropriateness, believability, and consistency of Statsky's argument, she criticized the argument for being incomplete: "[Statsky] neglects to anticipate parents' predictable questions and objections" (paragraph 2).

A few days later, Romano received some helpful advice from another student, who read her draft critically. Using the Critical Reading Guide in this chapter (p. 433–35), the student noted (in response to item 3 in the Guide) that she could not find a clear statement of the thesis (overall judgment) in the draft. She guessed that it might be hinted at in the final paragraph, but she was not sure what Romano's judgment was and urged Romano to state it clearly. Here is the draft version of Romano's final paragraph that the student reader commented on:

> I have been able to point out both strengths and weaknesses in the logic of Statsky's support for her argument. The strengths are appropriateness, believability, and consistency. The major weakness is incompleteness--a failure to anticipate more fully the likely objections of a wide range of readers. I have been able to show that her logic would prevent certain kinds of parents from taking her argument seriously, parents whose experience and whose children's experience of team sports lead them to believe that the gains are worth whatever risks may be involved and who believe that many of the risks Statsky points out can be avoided by careful monitoring. For parents inclined to agree with her, however, her logic is likely to seem sound and complete. An argument that successfully confirms readers' beliefs is certainly valid, and Statsky succeeds admirably at this kind of argument.

In response to item 4 in the Critical Reading Guide, the student reader noted that she thought Romano's draft essay was well supported by textual evidence and examples. She also said she found the praise of the strengths of Statsky's argument convincing but found the criticism of its weaknesses equally convincing. Therefore, she concluded by asking Romano to clarify her evaluation.

This request hit home because Romano had been trying to give Statsky's essay a mixed review but was not sure how well her own judgment was coming across. Romano was reassured by her critical reader's judgment that her argument was convincing, but she saw that she needed to clarify which standards carried the most weight for her. She revised the last paragraph, adding this final sentence to make her thesis more explicit and let readers see exactly which standards were most important in her evaluation of Statsky's argument:

> Because she does not offer compelling counterarguments to the legitimate objections of those inclined not to agree with her, however, her success is limited.

In his comparison of the films *Emma* and *Clueless,* the student author described on p. 392 of this chapter selected movie stills to accompany his written text. He collected a number of stills from each film and chose two contrasting images that would best illustrate his argument that *Emma,* the film, looks more like Austen's England, but that *Clueless* captures the satirical spirit of the novel.

The writer used the still from *Emma* of Emma and Knightley dancing to emphasize the film's attention to aesthetics and romance. Details such as the hanging garlands, the ornate woodwork, the women's similar pale-toned dresses, the style of dancing and the musicians in the background create an image of aristocratic wealth and elegance that, the student argues, satisfies audience expectations for a romantic period piece but obscures an important part of the novel's message.

To illustrate the flavor of *Clueless,* the student chose the picture of Cher descending the stairs in her minidress with shopping bags, water bottle in its holder, and cell phone. This over-the-top satiric image in *Clueless,* the student argued, was designed to emphasize the social and economic distinctions in the novel. The image captures the ridiculousness of Cher. While admired and well liked by her peers, she is also naïve and too well-off for her own good. Her interest in reforming Tai is a result of her confidence that she

Perrillo 3

Emma is, above all, a novel about class consciousness. Marriage is here, as in all of Austen's novels, a vehicle for exploring the rigidity of social class in nineteenth-century England. However, Emma the film (1996) is better at capturing the feel of the period than the intricacies of social dynamics. (See Fig. 1.) Though the characters come from a range of social classes, their homes and clothing look more similar than not. When Gwyneth Paltrow plays the occasionally lovable, occasionally irritating Emma, the focus on the heroine's failure at matchmaking overshadows the fact that she is obsessed not only with manners but also with wealth. For example, she has something that even her beloved Knightley does not, an estate that she will inherit from her father as long as she does not leave him. In the novel when Knightley agrees to live in the Woodhouse home after the two marry, he goes against traditional gender roles in order to make the most of the two characters' fortunes: his wealth and her property. As it does so many times, the film misses this cue, and instead focuses on Emma's emotional inability to leave her father. In the 1996 Emma, social distinctions get paved over for the audience's aesthetic expectations of a romance and of a period piece.

Fig. 1. This scene from Emma offers a typical example of the film's attention to aesthetics.

Perrillo 4

Clueless (1995), though it could not look less like Austen's England, better captures the spirit of the novel. Cher, who never leaves her cell phone at home and shops on Rodeo Drive, is both the consummate brat and the consummate charmer. (See Figure 2.) Cher does more than just try to find a suitable match for the obviously not as well-off or stylish Tai; she actually works on transforming her, much as Emma does with Harriet Smith in the novel. Cher encourages Tai to cut her hair, buy new clothes, exercise, and read more nonacademic books, and she takes pride in the new person that she has tried to create. In this way, the film parallels the novel's attention not only to Emma's preoccupation with social status but also to the way she tries to use Harriet to further elevate her own reputation.

Fig. 2. Clueless depicts Cher as a status-conscious consumer, echoing a significant theme in Austen's novel.

could help someone to become as stylish and savvy as herself. Just as the novel makes fun of Emma for her lack of critical self-awareness, the student argued, so does *Clueless* make fun of Cher.

THINKING CRITICALLY ABOUT WHAT YOU HAVE LEARNED

Now that you have read and discussed several evaluation essays and written one of your own, take some time to think critically about what you have learned. What problems did you encounter as you were writing your essay, and how did you solve them? How did reading other evaluation essays influence your own essay? How do evaluation essays in general reflect social or cultural attitudes about making judgments?

Reflecting on Your Writing

Write a one-page explanation, telling your instructor about a problem you encountered in writing your essay and how you solved it. Before you begin, gather all of your writing—invention and planning notes, drafts, critical comments, revision plan, and final revisions. Review these materials as you complete this writing task.

1. ***Identify one writing problem you needed to solve as you worked on the essay.*** Do not be concerned with grammar and punctuation problems; concentrate instead on problems unique to developing an evaluation essay. For example: Did you puzzle over how to present your subject? Did you have trouble acknowledging what you liked as well as what you disliked? Was it difficult to refute an important objection or answer a question you knew readers would raise?
2. ***Determine how you came to recognize the problem.*** When did you first discover it? What called it to your attention? If you did not become aware of the problem until someone else pointed it out to you, can you now see hints of it in your invention writings? If so, where specifically? When you first recognized the problem, how did you respond?
3. ***Reflect on how you went about solving the problem.*** Did you work on the wording of a passage, cut or add reasons or refutations, conduct further research, or move paragraphs or sentences around? Did you reread one of the essays in this chapter to see how another writer handled a similar problem, or did you look back at your invention writing? If you talked about the problem with another student, a tutor, or your instructor, did talking about it help? How useful was the advice you received?
4. ***Write a brief explanation of the problem and your solution.*** Be as specific as possible in reconstructing your efforts. Quote from your invention notes or draft essay, others' critical comments, your revision plan, or your revised essay to show the various changes that your writing—and thinking—underwent as you tried to solve the problem. If you are still uncertain about your solution, say so. Taking time to explain how you identified a particular problem, how you went about trying to solve it, and what you learned from this experience can help you solve future writing problems more easily.

Reviewing What You Learned from Reading

Write a page or two explaining to your instructor how the readings in this chapter influenced your final draft. Your own essay may have been influenced to some extent by one or more of the essays in this chapter as well as by classmates' essays that you have read. These other essays may have helped you decide that you needed to do further research before you could argue responsibly for your overall judgment, that you could use comparisons as part of your support, or that you should try to respond to readers' likely objections and questions. Before you write, take some time to reflect on what you have learned from these selections about writing evaluations.

1. ***Reread the final revision of your essay; then look back at the selections you read before completing it.*** Do you see any specific influences? For

example, did any reading influence how you decided to present the subject, balance your judgment, use examples or comparisons, or respond to readers' resistance to your evaluation? Also look for ideas you got from your reading: writing strategies you were inspired to try, types of sentences you relied on, or goals you sought to achieve.

2. ***Write an explanation of these influences.*** Did one reading have a particularly strong influence on your essay, or were several readings influential in different ways? Quote from the readings and from your final revision to show how your essay was influenced by other essays you read. Finally, based on your review of this chapter's readings, point out any further improvements you would now make in your essay.

Considering the Social Dimensions of Evaluations

The media or arts review—someone's judgment about the quality of movies, television programs, musical performances, books, and so forth—is a special kind of evaluation. We rely on such evaluations to help us decide what movies, computer games, or performances to see, what books to buy, and what exhibits to attend. They confirm or challenge our attraction to a particular television series or musical group. The best media reviewers develop impressive expertise. They come to be trusted by readers to set standards for movies, musical recordings, novels, or works of art. They educate readers, helping to shape their judgment and discrimination, building their confidence in recognizing a clumsy, a passable, or an outstanding work or performance. At their best, reviewers counterbalance advertising: Instead of enticing us to see every movie that comes to town, they help us choose among the advertised movies. A trusted media or arts reviewer for a local newspaper can come to influence a community's values—building a local consensus, for example, about what constitutes a successful musical performance and encouraging tolerance or even appreciation for new kinds of music.

Excluding and Silencing. By deciding what to review and what to ignore, media and arts reviewers determine what receives public attention and what remains invisible, and their decisions may often be based to a large extent on economic factors: Which review is likely to sell more newspapers or bring in more advertising? (In this sense, reviewers are part of a larger publicity apparatus; indeed, in our age of giant media conglomerates, a movie or music reviewer for a national magazine may well work for the same parent company that produced or distributed the film or the recording being reviewed—a situation that may not encourage the most objective evaluations.) Community theater or musical groups without money to advertise their performances may be given only a brief listing in the local newspaper; but unless they are reviewed, they will be unlikely to attract enough ticket buyers to survive (and the less mainstream their offerings, the less likely they are to be reviewed). Similarly, a new artist is simply not likely to be reviewed as widely as an established one.

For a long time, this sort of resistance to anything new and different kept many women and minority artists from being appreciated by reviewers—both in the universities and in the media—thus making it harder for them to earn a living by their work and effectively silencing their voices. This situation has changed in some ways, especially with the advent of the Internet, where people have wider access to reviews by professionals and by people who simply want to share their judgments with others. But reviewers who work for traditional media outlets such as newspapers and television still have great power to determine what is or is not considered a successful work of art.

1. ***Reflect on your own experience reading reviews on the Internet, in magazines, and in newspapers (including your college newspaper), as well as on the television or radio.*** Think of one film, television program, or live performance you decided to see because of a review you read or one recording, book, or DVD you purchased after reading a review of it. Recall how the review influenced you, and explain its influence.

2. ***Consider how you usually learn about new films, music, and books.*** Do you read reviews or get your information some other way? Does your information come mainly from the mainstream media, from word of mouth, from neighborhood or alternative newspapers, or from some other source? Where do you get information about nonmainstream music, books, computer games, or films?
3. ***Reflect on any media evaluations you read in connection with this assignment (Holden's and Jackson's reviews and others) in light of the ideas presented in the introduction to this section.*** Perhaps you wrote a media review yourself.
4. ***Write a page reflecting on the role played by media reviews in excluding or silencing new, innovative, or minority performers and artists.*** If possible, connect your ideas to the readings in this chapter and to your own essay.

Hidden Assumptions of Evaluators. Good evaluative writing provides readers with reasons and support for the writer's judgment. However, the writer's personal experiences, cultural background, and political ideology are also reflected in written evaluations. Even the most fair-minded evaluators write from the perspective of their particular ethnicity, religion, gender, age, social class, sexual orientation, academic discipline, and so on. Writers seldom make their assumptions explicit, however. Consequently, while the reasons for an evaluation may make it seem fair and objective, the writer's judgment may result from hidden assumptions that even the writer has not examined critically.

1. ***Choose one reading from this chapter, and try to identify one of the hidden assumptions of its writer.*** Think of a personal or cultural factor that may have influenced the writer's judgment of the subject. For example, how do you imagine that Romano's gender may have influenced her judgment of Statsky's essay on competitive sports for children? How do you think Etzioni's background as a college professor and a father of teenage sons might have influenced his negative evaluation of McDonald's-type jobs for teenagers?
2. ***Reflect on your own experience of writing an evaluation essay.*** How do you think factors such as gender, age, social class, ethnicity, religion, geographical region, or political perspective may have influenced your own evaluation? Recall the subjects that you listed as possibilities for your essay and how you chose one to evaluate. Also recall how you arrived at your overall judgment and how you decided which reasons to use and which not to use in your essay.
3. ***Write a page or two explaining your ideas about how hidden assumptions play a role in evaluation essays.*** Connect your ideas to the readings in this chapter and to your own essay.

Speculating about Causes

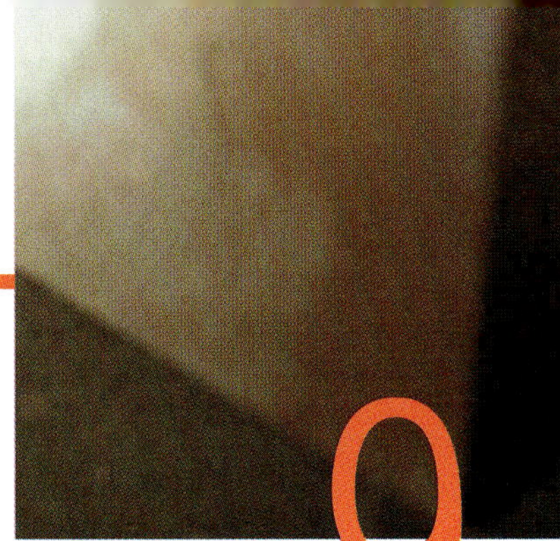

9

We all quite naturally try to explain causes. Because we assume that everything has a cause, we predictably ask "Why?" when we notice something new or unusual or puzzling.

Many things can be fully and satisfactorily explained. When children ask, "Why is the sky blue in the day and black at night?" parents can provide an answer. But we can answer other questions only tentatively: Why since the 1980s has the cost of a college education increased faster than the cost of living? Why have acts of violence by women increased? Why have SAT scores declined? Questions such as these often have only plausible, not definitive, explanations because we cannot design a scientific experiment to identify the cause conclusively. The decline in SAT scores, for example, has been attributed to the rise in television viewing among children. Although this contention is plausible, we cannot know for certain that television viewing is indeed responsible for the drop in scores.

Many of our questions can never be answered definitively but can only be speculated about based on the best available evidence and experience. *To speculate* means primarily "to examine or ponder something," but it also means "to question," "to be curious," and even "to take risks."

Writing that speculates about causes plays an important role in academic and professional life. Government specialists seek to understand the causes of unemployment or homelessness. Business executives study the reasons for increases in sales or declines in worker productivity. Educators look at why some teaching techniques work and others do not or how family problems affect students' performance in school.

This chapter presents several essays that speculate about the causes of a phenomenon or trend. A **phenomenon** is something notable about the human condition or social order—fear of failure, for example, or the high rate of intermarriage among ethnic and racial groups in the United States. A **trend** is a significant change that occurs over some period of time, generally months or years. It can be identified by an increase or a decrease—for example, a rise in the number of babies born with AIDS or a decline in the percentage of people who attend college right after graduating from high school.

When you speculate about causes, you describe your subject, propose some causes for it, and argue that one (or more) cause is the best available explanation. You do not have to prove that your explanation is right, but you must attempt to convince readers that it is plausible by supporting your explanation with examples, facts, statistics, or anecdotes. To make your argument convincing, you will probably need to anticipate readers' questions about or objections to it.

Speculating about why things are the way they are or why things change will develop your creativity as you identify possible causes. It will refine your judgment as you evaluate these causes and choose the most plausible ones. It will exercise your reasoning as you argue to support your speculations.

You will encounter writing that speculates about causes in many different contexts, as the following examples suggest.

Writing in Your Other Courses

- For an anthropology course, a student writes an essay speculating about the cause of the afternoon lull, the period of reduced activity after the midday meal. She cites research studies to reject two possible causes: the possibility that the lull is caused either by the biochemical effects of eating and digestion or by a change in body temperature. She also argues against the idea that the lull is due to laziness or a desire for diversion. She argues instead that it is most likely caused by a biological rhythm established during early human evolution in the tropics, where heat peaks in the early afternoon.
- For a biology course, a student writes a report describing the AIDS epidemic in the United States and sub-Saharan Africa and speculating about this question: Why is AIDS concentrated among homosexuals in this country but among heterosexuals in Africa? The student speculates that these differences could possibly be explained in part by such factors as sexual practices, attitudes toward courtship and marriage, and the impact of AIDS-prevention programs. The student relies on reports and speculations from hospice workers, medical doctors, and sociologists to support these speculations.

Writing in the Community

- For a report on her internship in a social agency, a nursing student interviews older people who have been abandoned or neglected by their relatives. She also reviews published studies of elder abuse and neglect. In her report, she describes the widespread and increasing trend of elder neglect and speculates about its possible causes. She recognizes early in her research that there is no widespread agreement on why relatives do not take responsibility for elder care. She speculates that there are possibly three major causes besides the obvious ones of caretakers' psychological or medical problems and poverty: Some caretakers must divide their efforts between caring for young children and an elder; some caretakers have long commutes to work, spend long hours on the job, and consequently do not have time to care adequately for an elder; and some caretakers have no helpful family members nearby and lack a neighborhood support network. The nurse intern supports her speculations with quotes from caretakers and elders she interviewed and with information from the reports she read.

- For a national newspaper, a science reporter writes an article speculating about the increasing intolerance in the United States of what she calls "boyish behavior." She describes various disorders that boys are being diagnosed with at a higher rate than girls and muses that a modern Tom Sawyer or Huckleberry Finn would be diagnosed with conduct disorder and attention-deficit hyperactivity disorder and put on Ritalin. She claims that biological differences between boys and girls cannot explain the increasing concern with "boyish behavior." Instead, she argues that changing cultural expectations best explain it. For example, because adults have become extremely fearful of crime, they attempt to stamp out any early signs of aggression in boys, such as rowdy playground behavior. In addition, because school classrooms are increasingly group-oriented, the individualist and the jokester are perceived as disruptive. Finally, boyish fidgetiness is seen as a threat to career success in an economy that increasingly values sitting still and concentrating for seven or more hours a day.

Writing in the Workplace

- Writing for a monthly journal read by other school administrators, a high school principal speculates about conditions that might make violence likely at a school site. She reviews a few recent examples of violence in high schools, focusing on conditions in those schools that allowed students to attack teachers and other students with guns, knives, or explosives. She argues that a major cause of school violence is that bathrooms, cafeterias, hallways, and recreational spaces used to be monitored by teachers, counselors, and administrators but now are monitored by people from the community who are not taken seriously by students. She also argues that lockers permit students to store weapons, ammunition, or explosives at school. Finally, she argues that reluctance to inspect everything that students carry into a school has contributed to violence. Recognizing that her analysis of the problem of violence in schools implies unpopular solutions—assigning teachers to monitor all school spaces, removing lockers, and installing backpack-screening equipment—she anticipates the reservations that other school principals will have to her reasoning. To support her causal argument, she quotes from educational research studies and from recent reports by other principals that agree or imply agreement with her speculations.
- The marketing executive of a large multistate supermarket chain needs to explain why an expensive advertising campaign has not attracted more customers to the stores' delicatessens. As he studies the analyses provided by the advertising firm, he realizes that he does not believe any of the reasons that it has advanced to explain the failure of the campaign. He makes notes about what he believes to be the most likely causes for the failure and plans an oral presentation accompanied by visuals for the next executive committee meeting. At the meeting, he uses computer-generated images to review the goals, costs, and results of the campaign. Then he reviews and refutes the advertising company's reasons for the campaign's failure. He argues that there are most likely two major causes: the advertising company's inexperience in coordinating multimedia campaigns and his own failure to discover the firm's inexperience before signing a contract with it.

Practice Speculating about Causes: A Collaborative Activity

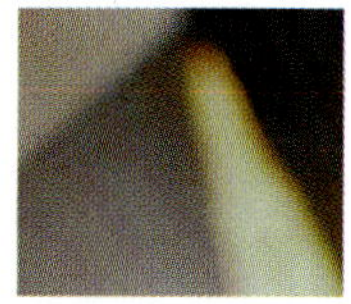

The preceding scenarios suggest some occasions for writing causal speculations. Your instructor may schedule this collaborative activity as an in-class discussion or ask you to conduct an online discussion in a chat room. Whatever the medium, here are some guidelines to follow.

To get a sense of this special kind of argument, choose a current trend, and speculate about its causes.

Part 1. Get together with two or three other students, and select one person to take notes.

1. Make a list of five or six trends—such as the decline in voter turnout in the United States, the increasing cost of a college education, or the increasing rate of smoking among young people. Choose one trend that interests all of you.
2. Together, list as many likely causes for this trend as you can in different areas, including economic, cultural, and psychological causes.
3. Select two or three causes that seem most likely to provide a partial explanation for the trend. Discuss how you might support each of these causes—that is, how you would convince others that these causes are plausible or likely explanations for the trend.

Part 2. When you have finished speculating, take a few more minutes to reflect on the process you have been engaged in.

- Where did your ideas about causes come from—reading, television, your own imagination?
- How did you differentiate among the causes, rejecting some and accepting others as most likely?
- What kinds of support did you come up with? Where do you think you might find further support?

READINGS

No two essays speculating about causes are alike, and yet they share defining features. Together, the four readings in this chapter reveal a number of these features, so you will want to read as many of them as possible. If time permits, complete the activities in the Analyzing Writing Strategies section that follows each selection, and read the Commentary. Following the readings is a section called Basic Features: Speculating about Causes (p. 474), which offers a concise description of the features of essays speculating about causes and provides examples from the four readings.

***Stephen King** is America's best-known writer of horror fiction. In 2003, he won a Lifetime Achievement Award from the Horror Writers Association, and he has also won the O'Henry Award, the Bram Stoker Award, the Hugo Award, and others. He is a prolific novelist and short-story writer. Thirty-three films and many TV movies have been based on his work, including* Carrie *(1974),* Misery *(1980),* The Shining *(1980),* Stand by Me *(1986), and* The Shawshank Redemption *(1994).*

In this essay excerpted from Playboy *magazine, King speculates about the popular appeal of horror movies. Before you begin reading, think about your own attitude toward horror films. Do you enjoy them? "Crave" them? Dislike them? Or are you indifferent? As you read, notice how assertively King presents his assumptions about people, such as the ones in the opening sentence. How does he try to get you to accept these assumptions? Is he successful?*

For more about Stephen King, check his official Web site: http://stephenking.com.

Why We Crave Horror Movies

Stephen King

I think that we're all mentally ill; those of us outside the asylums only hide it a little better—and maybe not all that much better, after all. We've all known people who talk to themselves, people who sometimes squinch their faces into horrible grimaces when they believe no one is watching, people who have some hysterical fear—of snakes, the dark, the tight place, the long drop . . . and, of course, those final worms and grubs that are waiting so patiently underground. 1

When we pay our four or five bucks and seat ourselves at tenth-row center in a theater showing a horror movie, we are daring the nightmare. 2

Why? Some of the reasons are simple and obvious. To show that we can, that we are not afraid, that we can ride this roller coaster. Which is not to say that a really good horror movie may not surprise a scream out of us at some point, the way we may scream when the roller coaster twists through a complete 360 or plows through a lake at the bottom of the drop. And horror movies, like roller coasters, have always been the special province of the young; by the time one turns 40 or 50, one's appetite for double twists or 360-degree loops may be considerably depleted. 3

We also go to re-establish our feelings of essential normality; the horror movie is innately conservative, even reactionary. Freda Jackson as the horrible melting woman in *Die, Monster, Die!* confirms for us that no matter how far we may be removed from the beauty of a Robert Redford or a Diana Ross, we are still light-years from true ugliness. 4

And we go to have fun. 5

Ah, but this is where the ground starts to slope away, isn't it? Because this is a very peculiar sort of fun, indeed. The fun comes from seeing others menaced—sometimes killed. One critic has suggested that if pro football has become the voyeur's version of combat, then the horror film has become the modern version of the public lynching. 6

It is true that the mythic, "fairy tale" horror film intends to take away the shades of gray. . . . It urges us to put away our more civilized and adult penchant for analysis and to become children again, seeing things in pure blacks and whites. It may be that horror movies provide psychic relief on this level because this invitation to lapse into simplicity, irrationality, and even outright madness is extended so rarely. We are told we may allow our emotions a free rein . . . or no rein at all. 7

If we are all insane, then sanity becomes a matter of degree. If your insanity leads you to carve up women like Jack the Ripper or the Cleveland Torso Murderer, we clap you away in the funny farm (but neither of those two amateur-night surgeons was ever caught, heh-heh-heh); if, on the other hand, your insanity leads you only to talk to yourself when you're under stress or to pick your nose on your morning bus, then you are left alone to go about your business . . . though it is doubtful that you will ever be invited to the best parties. 8

The potential lyncher is in almost all of us (excluding saints, past and present; but then, most saints have been crazy in their own ways), and every now and then, he has to be let loose to scream and roll around in the grass. Our emotions and our fears form their own body, and we recognize that it demands its own exercise to maintain proper muscle tone. Certain of these emotional muscles are accepted—even exalted—in civilized society; they are, of course, the emotions that tend to maintain the status quo of civilization itself. Love, friendship, loyalty, kindness—these are all the emotions that we applaud, emotions that have been immortalized in the couplets of Hallmark cards and in the verses (I don't dare call it poetry) of Leonard Nimoy. 9

When we exhibit these emotions, society showers us with positive reinforcement; we learn this even before we get out of diapers. When, as children, we hug our rotten little puke of a sister and give her a kiss, all the aunts and uncles smile and twit and cry, "Isn't he the sweetest little thing?" Such coveted treats as chocolate-covered graham crackers often follow. But if we deliberately slam the rotten little puke of a sister's fingers in the door, sanctions follow—angry remonstrance from parents, aunts, and uncles; instead of a chocolate-covered graham cracker, a spanking. 10

But anticivilization emotions don't go away, and they demand periodic exercise. We have such "sick" jokes as "What's the difference between a truckload of bowling balls and a truckload of dead babies?" (You can't unload a truckload of bowling balls with a pitchfork . . . a joke, by the way, that I heard originally from a ten-year-old.) Such a joke may surprise a laugh or a grin out of us even as we recoil, a possibility that confirms the thesis: If we share a brotherhood of man, then we also share an insanity of man. None of which is intended as a defense of either the sick joke or insanity but merely as an explanation of why the best horror films, like the best fairy tales, manage to be reactionary, anarchistic, and revolutionary all at the same time. 11

The mythic horror movie, like the sick joke, has a dirty job to do. It deliberately appeals to all that is worst in us. It is morbidity unchained, our most base instincts let free, our nastiest fantasies realized . . . and it all happens, fittingly enough, in the dark. For those reasons, good liberals often shy away from horror films. For myself, I like to see the most aggressive of them—*Dawn of the Dead,* for instance—as lifting a trap door in the civilized forebrain and throwing a basket of raw meat to the hungry alligators swimming around in that subterranean river beneath. 12

Why bother? Because it keeps them from getting out, man. It keeps them down there and me up here. It was Lennon and McCartney who said that all you need is love, and I would agree with that. 13

As long as you keep the gators fed. 14

Connecting to Culture and Experience: Media Violence

"The potential lyncher is in almost all of us," says Stephen King, ". . . and every now and then, he has to be let loose to scream and roll around in the grass" (paragraph 9). King seems to say that horror films perform a social function by allowing us to exercise (or possibly exorcise) our least civilized emotions.

Discuss this idea with two or three other students. Certain religious groups and politicians believe that the violence shown in films inspires people, especially the impressionable young, to commit violence—a belief quite different from King's. Do you believe that media violence exorcises or inspires violence? You may find that the members of your group disagree on this issue. What reasons can you give for your positions? If you believe that media violence inspires real violence, do you support censorship of movies, television programs, books, or magazines that portray violence? For children or adults or both? If you oppose censorship, do you support movie rating systems or the television V-chip, which gives parents some control over what their children watch?

Analyzing Writing Strategies

1. At the beginning of this chapter, we make several generalizations about essays that speculate about causes. Consider which of these assertions is true of King's essay:
   - It presents or describes its subject.
   - It proposes specific causes to explain the subject.
   - It argues that these causes are likely or plausible, though not definitive, explanations for the subject.
   - It tries to support each cause with examples, facts, statistics, or anecdotes.
   - It anticipates readers' questions about and objections to the causal argument.
2. King offers several kinds of support for the causes he proposes. For example, in paragraph 3, in the last sentence of paragraph 12, and in paragraphs 13 and 14, he provides **analogies**; in paragraph 4, an **example**; and in paragraph 6, a **comparison**. Analyze each kind of support: Notice what general statement King is trying to support in each case, and describe how the analogy, example, or comparison supports the general statement. Then evaluate whether the support is likely to be convincing for King's particular readers.

For more on supporting arguments, see Chapter 19, pp. 681–88.

Commentary: Plausible Causes and Logical Sequence of Causes

King proposes three **causes** of our craving for horror movies:

- We go to horror movies to prove that we can sit through them. (paragraphs 2–3)
- We go to reassure ourselves that we are normal. (4)
- We go because we enjoy seeing others in danger. (5–14)

Readers are likely to find the first cause plausible—likely, possible, or believable—because it seems obvious, but they may resist the other two, at least initially, because these causes are less predictable, even surprising. They are based on a popular theory that goes back to Aristotle and says we engage all of the arts, even horror movies, because they make us feel better. King's readers may not accept his theory, or they may find his less predictable causes implausible, but whatever their reaction, King has not bored them with causes so obvious that they could have predicted all of them before reading the argument.

King begins with a cause that seems obvious but is still worth mentioning: We go to horror films because we want to prove that we can sit through them, just as we ride roller coasters to show ourselves and others that we have the courage to do so (paragraph 3). We can surmise that King mentions this cause right away because he assumes that readers will be thinking of it. By connecting to a common experience of his readers and setting an obvious cause aside, he can move on to the not-so-obvious causes that are the heart of his argument.

King next entertains a very different cause: We go to horror movies "to re-establish our feelings of essential normality" (paragraph 4). This cause is much less predictable than the first. Although this cause is also plausible, it moves us from *obvious causes* toward the one *hidden* (unexpected, unlikely, risky) *cause* that King argues at length —that we "crave" horror movies (not just attend them casually) in order to manage our uncivilized emotions of fear, violence, and aggression.

In your own causal analysis essay, your first goal will be to speculate creatively about your subject so that you can come up with at least one not-so-obvious cause. Like King, you may want to place this cause last, after discussing other more obvious causes, and to argue for it at length and with ingenuity.

Considering Topics for Your Own Essay

Consider speculating about a popular cultural phenomenon that interests you. For instance, have you ever wondered why romance novels are so popular? Police shows or soap operas or MTV? Coffee houses or drive-through fast-food restaurants? You will think of other popular cultural phenomena. How might you present the phenomenon to your readers? What obvious and not obvious causes might you propose to explain the popularity of the phenomenon?

To use the Writing Guide Software to record your ideas, click on
▶ **Journal**

***David Brooks** is a contributing editor at* Newsweek *and the* Atlantic Monthly *and a senior editor at the* Weekly Standard. *He has written a book,* Bobos in Paradise: The New Upper Class and How They Got There *(2000), and edited the anthology* Backward and Upward: The New Conservative Writing *(1996). A widely read and respected spokesperson for politically conservative views, Brooks often appears as a commentator on* The News Hour with Jim Lehrer *on PBS,* Late Edition *on CNN, and National Public Radio. His essays have been published in many magazines and newspapers, including the* New Yorker, Commentary *and the* Wall Street Journal. *This essay was originally published in the* New York Times, *where Brooks has since become a regular columnist.*

In this essay, Brooks seeks to explain why so few people are politically hostile to the income and wealth of the richest Americans. The context for his discussion is that when Democrats have opposed recent Republican tax-cutting proposals on the grounds that they benefit mostly the rich, Republicans have accused them of waging "class warfare"—of trying to rouse the have-nots against the wealthy. Brooks claims that there is little resentment of the rich in the United States—and he attempts to explain why. As you read, keep in mind that economic class is related to both current income (salaries, business profits, interest and dividends, rental income) and accumulated wealth (real estate, other property, savings, and investments such as stocks and bonds). Low-income households are often defined as those having less than $30,000 a year for a family of four; middle-income households, $30,000 to $125,000; and upper-income households, $125,000 and up. Upper-income families, especially the top 1 percent that Brooks refers to in his essay, have not only high incomes but usually great wealth as well. Middle-income families are usually accumulating (or have already accumulated) some wealth by making payments on a house mortgage and contributing regularly to a retirement account. Lower-income families rarely possess any wealth.

Brooks frames the presentation of his subject with two questions: Why don't lower-income people vote their own self-interest, and why don't more lower-income Americans want to redistribute more wealth to people like themselves? By "self-interest" he refers to an interest in requiring upper-income people to pay more taxes to support public programs like schools and health care that benefit all the people. He begins his argument with two facts: that 19 percent of Americans believe they are among the top 1 percent in income and that another 20 percent expect eventually to join the top 1 percent. Before you read, decide how you would have answered the polling question that produced these results. Also identify your current income class or that of your family, and consider how much wealth you have accumulated.

The Triumph of Hope over Self-Interest

David Brooks

Why don't people vote their own self-interest? Every few years the Republicans propose a tax cut, and every few years the Democrats pull out their income distribution charts to show that much of the benefits of the Republican plan go to the richest 1 percent of Americans or thereabouts. And yet every few years a Republican plan wends its way through the legislative process and, with some trims and amendments, passes. 1

The Democrats couldn't even persuade people to oppose the repeal of the estate tax, which is explicitly for the mega-upper class. Al Gore, who ran a populist campaign, couldn't even win the votes of white males who didn't go to college, whose incomes have stagnated over the past decades and who were the explicit targets of his campaign. Why don't more Americans want to distribute more wealth down to people like themselves? 2

Well, as the academics would say, it's overdetermined.[1] There are several reasons. 3

[1] *Overdetermined* means having more than one determining factor or cause.

4 ***People vote their aspirations.***

5 The most telling polling result from the 2000 election was from a *Time* magazine survey that asked people if they are in the top 1 percent of earners. Nineteen percent of Americans say they are in the richest 1 percent and a further 20 percent expect to be someday. So right away you have 39 percent of Americans who thought that when Mr. Gore savaged a plan that favored the top 1 percent, he was taking a direct shot at them.

6 It's not hard to see why they think this way. Americans live in a culture of abundance. They have always had a sense that great opportunities lie just over the horizon, in the next valley, with the next job or the next big thing. None of us is really poor; we're just pre-rich.

7 Americans read magazines for people more affluent than they are (*W, Cigar Aficionado, The New Yorker, Robb Report, Town and Country*) because they think that someday they could be that guy with the tastefully appointed horse farm. Democratic politicians proposing to take from the rich are just bashing the dreams of our imminent selves.

8 ***Income resentment is not a strong emotion in much of America.***

9 If you earn $125,000 a year and live in Manhattan, certainly, you are surrounded by things you cannot afford. You have to walk by those buildings on Central Park West with the 2,500-square-foot apartments that are empty three-quarters of the year because their evil owners are mostly living at their other houses in L.A.

10 But if you are a middle-class person in most of America, you are not brought into incessant contact with things you can't afford. There aren't Lexus dealerships on every corner. There are no snooty restaurants with water sommeliers[2] to help you sort through the bottled *eau*[3] selections. You can afford most of the things at Wal-Mart or Kohl's and the occasional meal at the Macaroni Grill. Moreover, it would be socially unacceptable for you to pull up to church in a Jaguar or to hire a caterer for your dinner party anyway. So you are not plagued by a nagging feeling of doing without.

11 ***Many Americans admire the rich.***

12 They don't see society as a conflict zone between the rich and poor. It's taboo to say in a democratic culture, but do you think a nation that watches Katie Couric in the morning, Tom Hanks in the evening and Michael Jordan on weekends harbors deep animosity toward the affluent?

13 On the contrary. I'm writing this from Nashville, where one of the richest families, the Frists, is hugely admired for its entrepreneurial skill and community service. People don't want to tax the Frists—they want to elect them to the Senate. And they did.

14 Nor are Americans suffering from false consciousness.[4] You go to a town where the factories have closed and people who once earned $14 an hour now work for $8 an hour. They've taken their hits. But odds are you will find their faith in hard work and self-reliance undiminished, and their suspicion of Washington unchanged.

---

[2] A *sommelier* is a waiter who helps customers choose wines.

[3] *Eau* means *water* in French.

[4] *False consciousness* refers to a belief or idea that interferes with one's perception of reality.

Americans resent social inequality more than income inequality. 15

As the sociologist Jennifer Lopez[5] has observed: "Don't be fooled by the rocks that I got, I'm just, I'm just Jenny from the block." As long as rich people "stay real," in Ms. Lopez's formulation, they are admired. Meanwhile, middle-class journalists and academics who seem to look down on megachurches, suburbia and hunters are resented. If Americans see the tax debate as being waged between the economic elite, led by President Bush, and the cultural elite, led by Barbra Streisand, they are going to side with Mr. Bush, who could come to any suburban barbershop and fit right in. 16

Most Americans do not have Marxian categories in their heads. 17

This is the most important reason Americans resist wealth redistribution, the reason that subsumes all others. Americans do not see society as a layer cake, with the rich on top, the middle class beneath them and the working class and underclass at the bottom. They see society as a high school cafeteria, with their community at one table and other communities at other tables. They are pretty sure that their community is the nicest, and filled with the best people, and they have a vague pity for all those poor souls who live in New York City or California and have a lot of money but no true neighbors and no free time. 18

All of this adds up to a terrain incredibly inhospitable to class-based politics. Every few years a group of millionaire Democratic presidential aspirants pretends to be the people's warriors against the overclass. They look inauthentic, combative rather than unifying. Worst of all, their basic message is not optimistic. 19

They haven't learned what Franklin and Teddy Roosevelt and even Bill Clinton knew: that you can run against rich people, but only those who have betrayed the ideal of fair competition. You have to be more hopeful and growth-oriented than your opponent, and you cannot imply that we are a nation tragically and permanently divided by income. In the gospel of America, there are no permanent conflicts. 20

[5] Jennifer Lopez is an actress and a singer, not a sociologist.

Connecting to Culture and Experience: Attitudes about Class

Brooks believes Americans are more inclined to "see society as a high school cafeteria" than "as a layer cake" (paragraph 18). That is, he resists the idea that many middle- and low-income Americans feel that in this country the way wealth is distributed among the population does not fairly reflect the hard work and contributions of the majority of the people.

With two or three students, discuss these ideas. Do you share the attitudes Brooks claims are so common among Americans, or do you know people who share them? Where do you think attitudes like these come from? If you share these attitudes, did you get them from your parents? If you do not share these attitudes, what influences caused you to think as you do? Brooks concludes that attitudes like these may lead people to vote against their own self-interest but that they also reflect a fundamentally American feeling of hopefulness and optimism. Do you agree with this conclusion? Brooks seems to think it is a good outcome. Do you? Why or why not?

Analyzing Writing Strategies

1. Evaluate Brooks's **presentation of the subject**. In paragraphs 1–2, Brooks tries to interest readers in the subject by pointing to an irony about American voting patterns. How well does he explain the phenomenon and raise your curiosity about its causes?
2. For a causal argument to be convincing, it must be based on **plausible causes**. Review Brooks's five causes. Then choose one cause that seems plausible and one that seems less plausible, and explain what makes one more plausible to you than the other.

Commentary: Convincing Support

Brooks offers from one to four paragraphs of **support** for each of his five causes. This material needs to be both interesting and convincing. It also must be appropriate or relevant, believable, and consistent—that is, it should not contradict itself. Support is necessary in causal argument because the causes are likely or possible causes, not definitive ones, and therefore must be supported thoughtfully, creatively, and convincingly to seem plausible to readers. In addition to coming up with plausible causes, then, writers of causal arguments must offer convincing support for those causes.

For more on supporting arguments, see Chapter 19, pp. 681–88.

Brooks uses two different kinds of support, **examples** and **statistics**, to argue for his causes, but he relies primarily on examples. To support his first cause—that people do not vote their own self-interest because they vote their aspirations—he gives examples of magazines that Americans like to read (*W, Cigar Aficionado, the New Yorker, Robb Report, Town and Country*) that celebrate the lifestyles of the rich and famous (paragraph 7). To support his position that few Americans resent those with high incomes, he gives examples of ostentatious wealth that most middle-income Americans do not encounter on a daily basis, such as "2,500-square-foot apartments that are empty three-quarters of the year" because their owners live for part or most of the year in houses they own elsewhere (9), "Lexus dealerships on every corner," or "snooty restaurants with water sommeliers" (10). To support his proffered cause that "Many Americans admire the rich" (11), he lists examples of rich celebrities like Katie Couric, Tom Hanks, and Michael Jordan who are much admired (12).

In addition to examples, Brooks cites statistics. He supports his first cause by referring to a *Time* magazine opinion poll showing that a surprising number of Americans, 19 percent, "say they are in the richest 1 percent" of the population (paragraph 5).

When you plan and write your essay speculating about causes, you will need not only to think of plausible causes but also to discover ways to support each cause.

Considering Topics for Your Own Essay

Like Brooks, consider writing about the causes that lie behind people's political views and voting patterns. Why, for example, do certain voters routinely support bond issues to fund schools, vote to extend police and fire services, or oppose new taxes? Why do few people vote? Why do some people become politically active and others remain neutral or antagonistic toward politics?

To use the Writing Guide Software to record your ideas, click on
▶ **Journal**

***William S. Pollack** is an assistant clinical professor of psychology in the department of psychiatry at Harvard Medical School and director of the Centers for Men and Young Men and director of continuing education (psychology) at McLean Hospital. He is a past president of the Massachusetts Psychological Association and a founding member of the Society for the Psychological Study of Men and Masculinity, a division of the American Psychological Association. He has served as an adviser for the National Campaign against Youth Violence and is a consultant to the federal Department of Education's Safe Schools Initiative.*

Pollack coauthored In a Time of Fallen Heroes: The Re-Creation of Masculinity *(1993) and coedited* A New Psychology for Men *(1995) and* New Psychotherapy for Men *(1998). The following essay is excerpted from his most recent book,* Real Boys: Rescuing Our Sons from the Myths of Boyhood *(1999). About* Real Boys, *Pollack has written, "Through this book I would like to help families, communities, and boys themselves better understand what a real boy is and, most important, how to help boys flourish and succeed in our society."*

In this reading, Pollack focuses on the causes of depression in boys. As you read, notice that Pollack defines depression and describes its well-established biological causes before he speculates about its possible psychological causes. Read to understand how the biological and psychological causes of depression interact in boys and to evaluate the psychological causes that Pollack proposes.

Why Boys Become Depressed

William S. Pollack

The Many Faces of Depression

Depression affects boys in a variety of ways. It may make them feel sad, anxious, or numb. The depressed boy may act sullen and withdrawn or . . . may become agitated, overly aggressive, and full of rage. He may misbehave in school or become dependent on drugs or alcohol. Or he may just seem glum. 1

Depression in boys is a syndrome involving a whole range of behavioral difficulties and symptoms. While just about any adult who's been diagnosed with clinical depression will tell you that the experience is quite different from a "bad mood," it's essential, especially in the case of boys, to see depression as this kind of wide-ranging syndrome 2 with symptoms that fall along a continuum from mild to extreme. I believe that if we dwell merely on the most extreme—and obvious—instances of full-blown, or "clinical," depression, we risk failing to help boys cope with emotional states that, though less intense on the surface, are actually very painful for them, emotional states that without appropriate intervention may very well evolve into a major depression or provoke suicidal feelings. There's also a risk that by ignoring certain related behaviors, most notably irritable conduct and the abuse of substances, we may also fail to recognize the onset of a serious depression.

The Biology of Depression

We now know that in addition to psychological elements, depression can often be caused by biological factors, most notably by an imbalance in certain neurotransmitters, such as serotonin, that seem to directly affect emotional well-being. Medications that correct these imbalances—so-called SSRIs (selective serotonin reuptake inhibitors) such as Prozac (fluoxetine), Zoloft (sertraline), and Paxil (paroxetine)—have been shown to be helpful to many people, including children, suffering depression. But neurotransmitter levels are also affected by psychological phenomena, such as daily stress, loss of a loved one, or an early trauma, all of which may change the biological and chemical workings of the brain, leaving it vulnerable to depression. Exercise levels can change neurotransmitter levels in a different way, improving your mood and your biology. 3

We are just beginning to understand the complex interrelationships between the biological and psychological aspects of our emotional systems. As with the heart, some people are born with a genetic predisposition to heart disease; they inherit a weak heart, high blood pressure, or a tendency to atherosclerosis. Such individuals will have to work hard to prevent heart disease. But heart disease doesn't have to come about through genetics. If a previously strong heart receives enough abuse—a poor diet, chronic smoking, or a habitual lack of exercise—it will become vulnerable to a heart attack. Likewise, depression seems to run in some families, but a *vulnerability* to it can be created at any point, through early deprivation, a lack of healthy loving relationships, or repeated blows to one's self-esteem. 4

While I believe the biological, or "organic," components of clinical depression (and the medical treatments for them) are of paramount importance and need to be carefully studied, my primary focus here is on what other psychologists and I have discovered about *external* psychological factors that can lead boys toward serious sadness or depression—factors such as a boy's family life, how he's treated at school, the quality of his friendships, and what kind of emotional support he gets on a regular basis. 5

The Cost . . . of Society's Disconnection

In my view, so many of the symptoms of depression that boys experience are caused by gaps in how we, as a society, address the inner emotional worlds of our boys. . . . [B]oys are often pushed too early to be independent of those people—their parents—who have so far been their main source of comfort and nurturance. I believe that the pain of 6 being separated from and losing these people, in and of itself, is enough to depress just about any boy. While neither the trauma of premature separation nor "abandonment" leads all boys to become depressed, either may create a deep sadness in many boys, making them vulnerable to depression later, either as boys or as men.

Further, I believe that many boys become susceptible to depression because of the emotional scarring they receive through society's shame-based hardening process. No matter how healthy a boy's emotional system was when he started life, it quickly becomes compromised by the hardening he feels is necessary to avoid feelings of shame, and by his denial (because of shame) of vulnerable emotional states such as sadness, disappointment, and despair. Every boy needs to cry sometimes, to seek the comfort of loving arms, to tell someone how much he hurts and to have them respond with empathy. Yet because of the gender straitjacket that inhibits boys from ever completely *experiencing* these feelings (let alone expressing them) and insists that they don't need help, boys actively repress feelings of sadness in an unhealthy way that can lead them to feel lonely and frightened, or push them toward more severe forms of depression. 7

But the straitjacket also brings about sadness and depression in boys in yet another important way. . . . [O]ur gender-stereotyped myths about boys mislead us to believe that boys do not care much about their relationships with friends and families and that boys are generally tough, "cocky," and independent. Yet we've also learned that, in reality, most boys experience all sorts of insecurities, feel tremendously dependent on their friends and families, and in many areas (for example, at school or when dating) are prone to large fluctuations in self-esteem. Boys yearn for connection—they care a lot about their relationships and about how they are liked by others. But because we are so often confused by the old myths, we may tend not to pay attention to the emotional ups and downs in our sons' friendships and relationships and thus be unaware of the devastating feelings of shame our sons may experience when these friendships or relationships are not going well or have come to an end. Such shame in a boy, if no one detects it and explores it with him, can lead him to feel profoundly sad, afraid, and disconnected from the rest of the world, and even to become clinically depressed. 8

Depression over Relationships

Yet researchers have perennially doubted the intensity or basic emotional importance of boys' relationships and so have assumed that problems in them would be unlikely to cause boys to become sad or depressed. Thus a study on depression in adolescent boys and girls conducted by Joan Girgus and her colleagues at Princeton University hypothesized that "levels of depression in early adolescent girls are more closely related to their popularity with peers than in early adolescent boys"—an assumption based on "the frequent argument that women are more likely than men to base their self-esteem on their relationships with others and on the approval of others." But the results of the study were not as expected. "Surprisingly, the boys' depression scores were significantly correlated with both popularity and rejection, whereas the girls' depression scores were only significantly correlated with rejection. Thus, girls and boys are apparently equally vulnerable to depression as a function of poor peer relationships." 9

Another study, by Paul Rohde, John Seeley, and David Mace, in Eugene, Oregon, also found that boys suffer when they don't have healthy relationships. This study focused on the extent to which delinquent adolescents develop ideas about suicide, and it found that boys were more likely to think about suicide if they were suffering stressful life events and if they lacked social supports in situations such as when they were lonely and had few close relatives. The authors concluded that suicidal behavior for boys is closely linked to their social connections. 10

We now know that the opposite is also true—that strong relationships can prevent boys from sliding into depression or engaging in risky, self-destructive behaviors in the first place. The National Longitudinal Study on Adolescent Health . . . found that teenagers who felt connected to their families were less likely to experience emotional distress. They were also less likely to engage in violence, attempt suicide, or use harmful substances. The key factors were parents who shared activities with teens, who were physically present at key times during the day, and, most important, who expressed warmth, love, and caring. Also . . . Blake Bowden, at Cincinnati Children's Hospital Medical Center . . . found that teens who ate dinner with their parents at least five nights a week were significantly better adjusted than classmates who dined alone. 11

In my opinion, we simply must resist being fooled by a boy's mask. Boys are not Lone Rangers, and at all ages they need to be told that they're good, that they make good friends, that they're needed and loved. And, like all human beings, they particularly need caring support when their relationships are disrupted or come to an untimely end. 12

Connecting to Culture and Experience: Societal Expectations and Emotional Needs

Pollack argues that most people, including some psychologists who study adolescent development, wrongly believe that boys' relationships with family and friends are not as important to them as the same relationships are to girls. He also argues that most people believe boys need to be trained to be tough and independent. These arguments lead Pollack to conclude that too many people believe that boys' and girls' emotional lives and psychological needs are different, to the disadvantage of boys, whose emotional needs are widely ignored.

With two or three other students, discuss these ideas. Begin by describing a close, personal—but nonromantic—relationship you currently have with someone outside your family, and speculate about how this relationship affects the way you feel about yourself. Then describe a close personal relationship you once had that came to an end for some reason or another and reflect on how you felt about losing that relationship. How did you feel at the time about talking about this loss? What short- and long-term effects did losing this relationship have on your psychological well-being?

Now focus on the cultural or societal expectation that boys and girls, men and women, have—or should be trained to have—different emotional needs. Do you think most people have this expectation? Do you think Pollack correctly assesses the danger this expectation presents to boys?

Analyzing Writing Strategies

1. To analyze and evaluate Pollack's causes, make a scratch outline of paragraphs 6–8, where Pollack proposes three **causes** to explain why boys become depressed. In a phrase or sentence, identify the cause discussed in each of these paragraphs. Then decide whether each cause is likely to be considered plausible by Pollack's intended readers—parents and educators. Which cause is likely to be considered more or less plausible than the others? Why do you think so?

   Finally, analyze the logical sequence of these causes. How would you describe the relationship among the causes? Why do you think Pollack sequences them the way he does? If you believe the causes are sequenced meaningfully and logically, what evidence do you find for your view in the essay? What might make the sequence effective for the intended readers?

2. Unlike King, Pollack devotes a large part of his essay to a **presentation of the subject**—depression in boys. Reread paragraphs 1–5, noticing how Pollack presents the subject and evaluating how well he does so for his particular readers. What does he seem to be trying to accomplish in paragraphs 1 and 2? What would you say is the purpose of the last two sentences in paragraph 2, in light of the causal argument Pollack goes on to make? What contribution do paragraphs 3 and 4 make? Why might paragraph 5 be important to readers? Finally, how effective do you think Pollack's presentation of the subject is for his intended readers?

Commentary: Anticipating Readers' Objections and Alternative Causes

When you anticipate your readers' **objections and alternative causes**, you have three options: to merely acknowledge that you are aware of them, to accommodate or concede them by endorsing them or making them part of your own argument, or to refute them by trying to show that they are unimportant or implausible. While attempting to support his preferred causes for depression in boys in paragraphs 6–8, Pollack at least one time anticipates readers' objections. In the last sentence of paragraph 6, he anticipates what some readers will be thinking and concedes that neither abandonment nor premature separation leads all boys to become depressed. But he then goes on to insist that either may create a deep sadness in many boys, making them vulnerable to depression later. This strategy of conceding to the wisdom of part of an objection and refuting the rest is common in counterargument.

Pollack refutes another objection in paragraphs 9–11. He begins paragraph 9 by acknowledging that some researchers have always doubted that personal relationships are important to boys. Because this objection poses a serious challenge to his argument, Pollack must try to refute it convincingly. To do so, he draws support from four published studies. The first is especially useful because the researchers in the study assumed that boys would not be much influenced by their relationships. To the researchers' surprise—and, Pollack probably assumes, to some readers' surprise—boys who felt unpopular were just as vulnerable to depression as girls who felt the same way. Pollack devotes almost a third of his argument to counterargument—to conceding and refuting readers' likely objections to his own argument.

Considering Topics for Your Own Essay

For your own essay, you could, like Pollack, speculate about why a certain group behaves the way it does. For example, you might speculate about why boys of a certain age become interested in sports or video games, why girls are increasingly involved in competitive sports, why certain immigrant groups emphasize their children's education, or why certain groups of students begin but never complete college. You could rely on your personal experience to identify causes and argue to support them. In addition, you could research your subject in the library, on the Internet, or by interviewing experts. Try to move beyond obvious causes to hidden or unexpected causes. Consider both immediate and background causes for a group's behavior.

To use the Writing Guide Software to record your ideas, click on
▶ **Journal**

Sarah West *wrote this causal-speculation essay for her first-year college composition course. Unlike Stephen King, David Brooks, and William S. Pollack, who speculate about the causes of phenomena, West speculates about the causes of a trend: a sharp increase in reported incidents of workplace sexual harassment over a four-year period. She begins by establishing that the trend exists. Notice that her concern is not whether workplace sexual harassment is increasing but whether reports of incidents of it are increasing. (She recognized, during her invention and research, that it would be difficult to prove that actual acts of harassment are increasing or decreasing; she also recognized that such acts are likely decreasing as reported incidents increase and receive wide publicity.) West then launches her speculations about the causes for the increasing number of reports.*

As you read, keep in mind that the U.S. Supreme Court has defined illegal sexual harassment as "sufficiently severe or pervasive to alter the conditions of the victim's employment." In other words, it is not a casual or unthreatening one-time incident but several incidents that create a hostile work environment and undermine an employee's trust in a coworker and ability to work effectively.

The Rise of Reported Incidents of Workplace Sexual Harassment

Sarah West

To those students who recently graduated from high 1
school, it may sound like the Dark Ages, but it wasn't: Until 1964, an employee who refused to give in to his or her employer's sexual advances could be fired—legally. An employee being constantly humiliated by a coworker could be forced either to deal with the lewd comments, the stares, and the touching or just to quit

If you're using the Writing Guide Software, you can read a version of this essay (and of each of the other student essays in Chapters 2–9) with pop-up annotations that point out the different parts of the essay's structure and the ways the writer incorporated the basic features of that genre of writing and the sentence strategies especially useful for it.

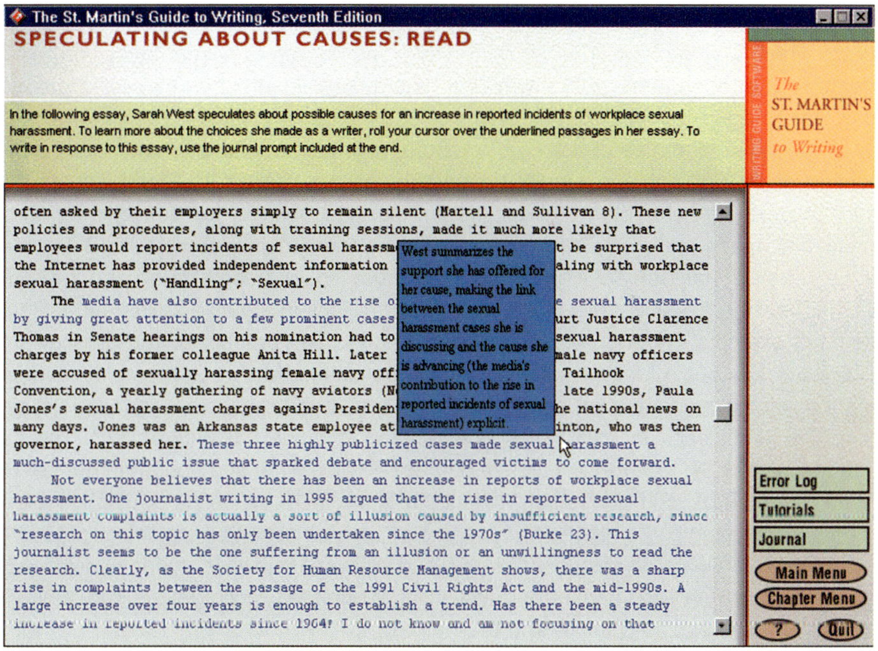

his or her job. It is truly strange to think that sexual harassment was perfectly legal in the United States until Congress passed the Civil Rights Act of 1964.

2 But even after 1964, sexual harassment still persisted. It was not widely known exactly what sexual harassment was or that federal laws against it existed. Often when an employee was sexually harassed on the job, he or she felt too alienated and humiliated to speak out against it (Martell and Sullivan 6). During the 1970s and 1980s, however, sexual harassment victims began coming forward to challenge their harassers. Then suddenly in the 1990s, the number of sexual harassment complaints and lawsuits sharply rose. According to a 1994 survey conducted by the Society for Human Resource Management, the percentage of human resource professionals who have reported that their departments handled at least one sexual harassment complaint rose from 35 percent in 1991 to 65 percent in 1994 *(Sexual)*. Why did this large increase occur in such a short amount of time? Possible answers to this question surely would include growing awareness of the nature of workplace sexual harassment, government action, efforts of companies to establish antiharassment policies and encourage harassed employees to come forward, and prominence given by the media to many cases of workplace harassment.

One significant cause of the rise in reported incidents of sexual harassment was most likely the increased awareness of what constitutes sexual harassment. There are two distinct types of sexual harassment, and although their formal names may be unfamiliar, the situations they describe will most certainly ring a bell. *Hostile environment* sexual harassment occurs when a supervisor or coworker gives the victim "unwelcome sexual attention" that "interferes with (his or her) ability to work or creates an intimidating or offensive atmosphere" (Stanko and Werner 15). *Quid pro quo* sexual harassment occurs when "a workplace superior demands some degree of sexual favor" and either threatens to or does retaliate in a way that "has a tangible effect on the working conditions of the harassment victim if he or she refuses to comply" (Stanko and Werner 15). 3

A fundamental cause of the rise in reports of workplace harassment was government action in 1964 and again in 1991. After the passage of the Civil Rights Act of 1991, which allowed, among other things, larger damage awards for sexually harassed employees, many more employees began coming forward with complaints. They realized that sexual harassment was not legal and they could do something about it. Suddenly, it became possible for a company to lose millions in a single sexual harassment case. For example, Rena Weeks, a legal secretary in San Francisco, sued the law firm of Baker & McKenzie for $3.5 million after an employee, Martin Greenstein, "dumped candy down the breast pocket of her blouse, groped her, pressed her from behind and pulled her arms back to 'see which one (breast) is bigger'" ("Workplace"). The jury awarded Weeks $7.1 million in punitive damages, twice what she sought in her lawsuit ("Workplace"). In addition, research revealed that the mere existence of sexual harassment in a company could lead to "hidden costs" such as absenteeism, lower productivity, and loss of valuable employees (Stanko and Werner 16). These "hidden costs" could add up to $6 or $7 million a year for a typical large company, according to one survey of Fortune 500 companies (Stanko and Werner 16). 4

Concerned about these costs, most companies decided to develop and publicize sexual harassment policies, making every employee aware of the problem and more likely to come forward as early as possible so that employers have a chance to remedy the situation before it gets out of hand. Prior to 1991, sexual harassment victims were often asked by their employers simply to remain silent (Martell and Sullivan 8). These new policies and procedures, along with training sessions, made it much more likely that employees would report incidents of sexual harassment. And we should not be surprised that the Internet has provided independent information to employees about dealing with workplace sexual harassment ("Handling"; "Sexual"). 5

The media have also contributed to the rise of reports of workplace sexual harassment by giving great attention to a few prominent cases. In 1991, Supreme Court Justice Clarence Thomas in Senate hearings on his nomination had to defend himself against sexual harassment charges by his former colleague Anita Hill. Later that same year, male U.S. Navy officers were accused of sexually harassing female navy officers at the infamous Tailhook Convention, a yearly gathering of navy aviators (Nelton 24). During the late 1990s, Paula Jones's sexual harassment charges against President Clinton dominated the national news on many days. Jones was an Arkansas state employee when, according to the charges, then-governor Clinton harassed her. These three highly 6 publicized cases made sexual harassment a much-discussed public issue that sparked debate and encouraged victims to come forward.

Not everyone believes that there has been an increase in reports of workplace sexual harassment. One journalist, writing in 1995, has argued that the rise in reported sexual harassment complaints is actually a sort of illusion caused by insufficient research, since "research on this topic has only been undertaken since the 1970s" (Burke 23). This journalist seems to be the one suffering from an illusion or an unwillingness to read the research. Clearly, as the Society for Human Resource Management shows, there was a sharp rise in complaints between 1991, when the Civil Rights Act was passed, and the mid-1990s. Has there been a steady increase in reported incidents since 1964? I do not know and am not focusing on that period. The noticeable increase in complaints from 1991 to 1994—from 35 percent to 65 percent *(Sexual)*—is enough to establish a trend. 7

It has also been suggested that the trend is the result of a greater percentage of women in the workplace (Martell and Sullivan 5). This may be a sufficient argument since women report sexual harassment in a significantly greater number of cases than men do (men report roughly one-tenth of what women report). It has been noted, however, that there recently has been a rise in sexual harassment complaints by male victims as well. According to the Equal Employment Opportunity Commission, the number of sexual harassment complaints filed annually by men more than doubled from 1989 to 1993 (Corey). Sexual harassment is by no means a new occurrence. It has most likely existed since workplace environments have existed. Yes, there are more women in the workplace today, which has likely increased the percentage of women workers who are being sexually harassed, but it is also very plausible that the rise in reported incidents of sexual harassment is because of increased awareness of sexual harassment and the steps that one can legally take to stop it. 8

It has taken thirty years, but American society seems to be making significant progress in bringing a halt to a serious problem. *Sexual harassment,* a phrase that was unfamiliar to most of us only a few years ago, is now mentioned almost daily on television and in newspapers. We can only hope that the problem will end if we continue to hear about, read about, and, most important, talk about sexual harassment and its negative consequences as we educate each other about sexual harassment. Then perhaps someday sexual harassment can be stopped altogether. 9

Works Cited

Burke, Ronald J. "Incidence and Consequences of Sexual Harassment in a Professional Services Firm." *Employee Counselling Today* Feb. 1995: 23–29.

Corey, Mary. "On-the-Job Sexism Isn't Just a Man's Sin Anymore." *Houston Chronicle* 30 Aug. 1993: D1.

"Handling Sexual Harassment Complaints." *Employer and Employee.* 1997. 8 Jan. 1998 <http://www.employer-employee.com/sexhar1.html>.

Martell, Kathryn, and George Sullivan. "Strategies for Managers to Recognize and Remedy Sexual Harassment." *Industrial Management* May-June 1994: 5–8.

Nelton, Sharon. "Sexual Harassment: Reducing the Risks." *Nation's Business* Mar. 1995: 24–26.

"Sexual Harassment: FAQ." *Employment: Workplace Rights and Responsibilities.* 1998. 8 Jan. 1998 <http://www.nolo.com/ChunkEMP/emp7.html>.

Sexual Harassment Remains a Workplace Problem, but Most Employers Have Policies in Place, SHRM Survey Finds. Alexandria: Society for Human Resource Management, 26 June 1994: 1.

Stanko, Brian B., and Charles A. Werner. "Sexual Harassment: What Is It? How to Prevent It." *National Public Accountant* June 1995: 14–16.

"Workplace Bias Lawsuits." *USA Today* 30 Nov. 1994: B2.

Connecting to Culture and Experience: Sexual Harassment or Romantic Relationship?

West speculates about possible causes for an increase in reported incidents of workplace sexual harassment. She does not mention consensual sex or romance in the workplace. And yet everyone knows that affairs and romances can begin at work. Sometimes they lead to marriage. Similarly, at college, romance can blossom, and lifetime partners may find each other. Moreover, as you are probably aware, colleges publish strict and punitive sexual harassment policies. What effects might workplace or college sexual harassment policies have on ordinary romantic relationships? Do such policies make trying to initiate a romantic relationship riskier? What if one party's advances are misinterpreted? What if a sour romance leads the rejected partner to recriminate by bringing false sexual harassment charges? If there is no well-defined or widely understood line between consent and harassment, might this uncertainty lead to misunderstandings, if not trouble?

Discuss with two or three other students the line between consent and harassment. First get a copy of your college's sexual harassment policies. If you work for an organization with a published sexual harassment policy, bring a copy to class. Decide whether these policies are clear and unambiguous. Do they mention consensual relationships or attempt to make a distinction between consent and harassment? How might they influence your attempts to start a relationship with someone at college or work?

Analyzing Writing Strategies

1. In paragraphs 3–6, West advances her causes for the increase in reports of sexual harassment in the workplace. She also attempts to **support** those causes—to argue for them so that readers will find them plausible. Analyze how she attempts to provide convincing support, and evaluate how successful she is.

   In each paragraph, find West's assertion of a cause early in the paragraph, and then look closely at the kind of support she provides. You will find that in different paragraphs she makes good use of definitions, examples, statistics, and other information she has gathered from published sources. Notice also the amount of space she devotes to support in these paragraphs.

Finally, evaluate how successful West is in providing convincing support for her particular readers. Consider whether her support is relevant and believable and whether her sources are reliable and authoritative. Where does the support seem most convincing and least convincing? Explain your judgments with examples from West's argument.

2. Reread paragraphs 7 and 8, where West **anticipates readers' objections and alternative causes**. In each paragraph, decide whether West is anticipating a reader's (or published author's) objection to her argument or anticipating a cause that a reader (or published author) might prefer. Then notice her strategy of counterargument. Does she acknowledge, accommodate, or refute? Finally, evaluate how convincing West's counterarguments are likely to be for her intended readers. Do they seem informed, responsible, and believable? Which parts seem most and least convincing—and why?

3. Underline the first sentence in each of paragraphs 3–6. Then analyze the role of each sentence in the paragraph that it begins and the role of the four first sentences as a group in the essay as a whole. What clues do these sentences offer that help you to understand their roles?

To learn more about the role of topic sentences, turn to Sentence Strategies, p. 490.

Commentary: Presenting the Subject

West **presents her subject** in paragraphs 1–3. She begins by trying to engage readers' interests and declaring the significance of her subject. She points out that protections from sexual harassment are surprisingly recent. For readers who are aware of the long history of efforts to guarantee all Americans basic personal rights and freedoms (beginning with the U.S. Constitution in 1787 and the Bill of Rights in 1791), West seems justified in her amazement that sexual harassment at work was not made illegal until the Civil Rights Act of 1964 was ratified. She singles out the Civil Rights Act of 1991 as the crucial event causing a sharp rise in the number of sexual harassment complaints.

Because West is presenting a **trend**, she has a special responsibility to document changes over time—in this case, an increase. She does so by relying on a report by a respected professional association of personnel managers who work in government and business, the Society for Human Resource Management. This report, which is listed in the works cited at the end of her essay, gives statistics supporting her claim that reports of sexual harassment on the job have increased sharply.

Notice that West makes readers aware that she intends to speculate not about an increase in workplace sexual harassment but about an increase in *reported incidents* of workplace sexual harassment. Perhaps no one knows whether workplace sexual harassment is increasing or decreasing. Because it is not always reported and for other reasons, it would be difficult to collect evidence that it is increasing or decreasing. West has solid evidence, however, that reports of harassment increased sharply between the early 1990s and the mid-1990s. Once she establishes that this trend exists, she turns to her defining question: "Why did this large increase occur in such a short amount of time?" (paragraph 2). Readers are then fully prepared for a causal argument.

Before beginning her causal argument, however, West orients readers to how her argument will unfold. In a forecast at the end of paragraph 2, she names the causes in the order she will take them up in her argument.

Considering Topics for Your Own Essay

West speculates about the causes of a trend (the rise of reported incidents of workplace sexual harassment), but she could have speculated about the phenomenon of sexual harassment itself—asking, for example, why there seems to be so much of it in the workplace. Following her lead, you could speculate about the causes of a trend or a phenomenon that influences how people live and work. Here are some examples: the increase in the number of students working part time or full time while in college; the increase in standardized testing requirements in public schools; the increase in the cost of a college education; the decline of neighborhood or community cohesion; the rising or declining influence of the political right; the growing gap in income and wealth between rich Americans and the rest of the population; or the increasing reliance by technology companies on workers trained in other countries.

To use the Writing Guide Software to record your ideas, click on
▶ **Journal**

PURPOSE AND AUDIENCE

The fundamental purpose of writing a causal argument is to engage readers in making sense of the world. The possible causes of puzzling phenomena or trends are worth thinking about and irresistibly interesting. Indeed, humans are probably unable *not* to speculate about causes, since so much of what we want to understand can never be known definitively.

If we assume that we can engage readers in our subject and our speculations about it, then our purpose becomes to help them understand their world better, to show them a new way to think about a subject. For example, like King, you might hope to lead readers to think about popular culture in new ways. Like Pollack, your purpose might be to subvert myths about human development. Or like Brooks or West, you might want readers to appreciate the significance of a major political phenomenon or social change.

The chief purpose of an essay speculating about causes is to convince readers that the proposed causes are plausible. Therefore, you must construct a coherent, logical, authoritative argument that readers will take seriously. Sometimes, like Brooks, you may want readers to look at a phenomenon in a new way or to go beyond obvious or familiar explanations. At other times, like Pollack and West, you may hope to influence policy decisions regarding a social problem.

Your audience will also affect your purpose. If you think that your readers are only mildly curious about the subject and know little about it, you might write partly to stimulate their interest in the subject itself. You could then concentrate on convincing them of the plausibility of your proposed causes. If you expect that readers will know a lot about the subject and oppose or be skeptical of your speculations, you could devote a lot of attention to conceding and refuting what you assume to be their preferred causes. If you believe that the distance between you and them is unbridgeable, you could even accentuate your differences, forcefully refuting their likely objections to your causes and refuting their preferred causes.

BASIC FEATURES: SPECULATING ABOUT CAUSES

A Presentation of the Subject

First, it is necessary to describe the subject. Depending on what readers know or need to know, writers sometimes devote a large portion of the essay to presenting the subject—describing it with specific details and examples and establishing that it actually exists (or existed) by citing statistics and statements by authorities.

In writing about a phenomenon he knows will be familiar to his readers, Stephen King simply asserts in his title that horror movies are widely popular. In contrast, William S. Pollack's less familiar and not-immediately engaging subject—depression in boys—requires considerable detail. Pollack devotes almost a third of his essay to describing how depression affects boys, how depression can be caused by biological factors, how biological and psychological factors interreact, and how important external psychological factors are in bringing on depression.

In an essay about a trend, a writer must always demonstrate that the trend exists. Sarah West, for example, demonstrates that the trend exists by citing statistics that document a dramatic four-year increase in reports of sexual harassment on the job. In some cases, a writer may have to show that the subject is an established, significant trend as opposed to a fad, a fluctuation, or a superficial change. For example, a new form of exercise might become a fad if many people try it out for a few months. This brief popularity would not make it a trend, but it might be part of a trend—a general increase in health consciousness, perhaps.

Plausible Causes

No matter how well presented the subject may be, a causal argument goes nowhere unless it offers plausible causes as a possible explanation. In many causal arguments, readers first encounter the writer's causes in a **forecast**—a list of causes in the order in which they will be taken up in the argument. Brooks uses a reader-friendly design by setting off his causes in italicized single-sentence paragraphs.

Speculating about the rise of reported incidents of workplace sexual harassment, Sarah West comes up with four plausible causes based on what she learned through research. The first cause is increased awareness and condemnation of sexual harassment following the passage of the landmark Civil Rights Act of 1964. The second cause is the sharp impetus given to the reporting of sexual harassment by the 1991 Civil Rights Act, which imposed severe penalties on businesses that failed to protect employees. The third cause is businesses' increased efforts to inform employees about their rights to do their jobs without being sexually harassed. Finally, the fourth cause is the increased attention paid by media to prominent cases of sexual harassment (not all of them proved). At first glance, even without West's arguments to support them, these causes seem likely and worth taking seriously. They do not immediately provoke readers' resistance or skepticism. They are, in short, plausible.

A Logical Sequence of Causes

Causes must be presented in a logical sequence. The reader needs to be aware of a meaningful step-by-step sequence of causes: The second cause follows from the first in some meaningful way, the third from the second, and so forth. Maybe an obvious cause prepares for a hidden cause, as in Stephen King's essay, or one cause creates a necessary condition for the next cause, as in William S. Pollack's essay, or every cause is a consequence of the preceding cause and predates the following cause, as in Sarah West's essay. West's logical sequence may seem complicated when it is outlined, but to readers making their way through the argument the sequence seems inevitable. Such a logical sequence is sometimes referred to as a **line of reasoning**.

Convincing Support

The support for every cause is the heart of causal speculation. A list of causes is not an argument. Writers of essays speculating about causes know that argument—or support—is required because a definitive, unarguable explanation for the subject is not available. Causal speculation is quintessentially argumentative; every cause must be argued for—or supported—if readers are going to be convinced that the explanation, though tentative, throws some light on the subject.

To provide convincing support for a cause requires both knowledge and creativity. Stephen King supports his causes with his understanding of psychology and his many years of writing horror novels and movies. David Brooks and Sarah West use examples, statistics, and authorities to support their arguments. Because she is writing for a college course, West cites and documents her sources.

A Consideration of Readers' Objections and Alternative Causes

Writers of causal speculation choose plausible causes and convincing support and sequence them logically in the essay. However, in nearly every writing situation requiring causal argument, writers must also imaginatively anticipate readers' objections and possible alternative causes and then acknowledge, accommodate, or refute these points in the counterargument. It is not enough simply to be aware that readers may have objections or alternative causes that they prefer over the writer's. These objections must be addressed within and become part of the argument, making it complete.

Stephen King anticipates that some readers will be skeptical that horror movies are popular because they appeal to and help us control the dark, dangerous side within us. He devotes roughly half of his essay to trying to convince readers that this cause is plausible. Similarly, William S. Pollack devotes about a third of his essay to refuting the widely held belief that relationships with family and friends are not as important to boys as they are to girls.

GUIDE TO WRITING
Speculating about Causes

THE WRITING ASSIGNMENT

THE WRITING ASSIGNMENT

Write an essay about an important or intriguing phenomenon or trend, and speculate about why it might have occurred. Describe your subject, demonstrate its existence, if necessary, and propose possible causes for it. Discover a way to sequence the causes logically. Then support or argue for the causes so that your readers will find them plausible.

INVENTION AND RESEARCH

INVENTION & RESEARCH

- Finding a Subject to Write About
- Exploring What You Know about Your Subject
- Considering Causes
- Researching Your Subject
- Considering Your Readers
- Testing Your Choice
- Testing Your Choice: A Collaborative Activity
- Researching Causes
- Developing Your Argument
- Anticipating Objections
- Anticipating Alternative Causes
- Considering Document Design
- Defining Your Purpose for Your Readers
- Formulating a Tentative Thesis Statement

PLANNING AND DRAFTING

PLANNING & DRAFTING

- Seeing What You Have
- Setting Goals
- Outlining
- Drafting

CRITICAL READING GUIDE

CRITICAL READING GUIDE

- First Impression
- Presentation of the Subject
- Convincing Causes and Support
- Anticipation of Readers' Objections, Questions
- Anticipation of Alternative Causes
- Effectiveness of Organization
- Final Thoughts

REVISING

REVISING

- A Presentation of the Subject
- Plausible Causes
- Convincing Support
- A Logical Sequence of Causes
- A Consideration of Readers' Objections and Questions
- Responses to Alternative Causes
- The Beginning and Ending

EDITING AND PROOFREADING

EDITING & PROOFREADING

- Checking Your Use of Numbers
- Checking for *Reason Is Because* Constructions

GUIDE TO WRITING

THE WRITING ASSIGNMENT

Write an essay about an important or intriguing phenomenon or trend, and speculate about why it might have occurred. Describe your subject, demonstrate its existence, if necessary, and propose possible causes for it. Discover a way to sequence the causes logically. Then support or argue for the causes so that your readers will find them plausible.

> To use the Writing Guide Software for this assignment, click on
> ▶ **Speculating about Causes**
> ▶**Write**

INVENTION AND RESEARCH

The following activities will help you find a subject, explore what you know about it, do any necessary research, and develop the parts of your causal argument. These activities are easy to complete. Doing them over several days will give your ideas time to ripen and grow. Be sure to keep a written record of your invention and research to use later when you draft and revise.

Finding a Subject to Write About

You may already have a subject in mind and some ideas about what might have caused it to occur. Even so, you should take some time to consider other possible subjects to ensure the best possible choice. Remember to consider both phenomena and trends as possible subjects for this writing assignment:

- A *phenomenon* is something notable about the human condition or the social order—fear of speaking to a group, for example, or opposition to gun-control legislation.
- A *trend* is a significant change extending over many months or years. It can be identified by an increase or a decrease—a rise in the birthrate, a decline in test scores.

Some subjects can be approached as either phenomena or trends. For example, you could speculate about the causes of the changing suicide rate among young people (a trend), or you could ignore the change and simply speculate about the causes of such suicides (a phenomenon).

The following activities will help you choose a subject for your essay. Make your lists of possible phenomena and trends as complete as possible, including, for example, the subjects suggested by the Considering Topics for Your Own Essay activity following each reading in this chapter.

Listing Phenomena. *Make a list of current phenomena that you could write about.* Here are some possibilities to consider. Start with a few of them, and see whether they bring to mind other topics of interest to you.

- ***College:*** A noisy library, insufficient parking, an instructor's skill or popularity, cheating on exams, a successful or an unsuccessful class or course, women as the majority of college students
- ***Personal life:*** Competitiveness, idealism, creativity, popularity, jealousy, laziness, workaholism, high achievement, contentiousness, rage
- ***Politics and government:*** Hostility toward politicians, low voter turnout, satisfactions of jury duty, stability of our system of government, negative campaigning, high percentage of minority inmates in U.S. prisons, the rise and fall in value of the dollar in relation to currency values in other countries
- ***Environment:*** Pollution, nuclear waste disposal, limited popularity of recycling programs, unsafe or borderline-safe food production
- ***Life stages:*** The "terrible twos," teenage alienation or rebellion, postponement of motherhood, midlife crisis, abrupt career changes
- ***The arts:*** Popularity of rap or jazz, decline of musical theater, impulse to censor the arts
- ***Culture:*** Continuing influence or popularity of a book, movie, actor, novelist, social activist, athlete, politician, religious leader, or television program; popularity of online and print catalog buying; limited appeal of movies with subtitles

Listing Trends. *Make a list of several trends, from the past as well as the present, that you would like to understand better.* Consider both trends you have studied and can research and ones you know about firsthand. Be sure that the possibilities you list are trends, not fads or short-term fluctuations. To start, consider the following possibilities:

- ***Shifting patterns in education:*** Increasing interest in teaching as a career, increases in home schooling or in community college enrollments, declining numbers of math and science majors, increase in the number of white students attending historically black colleges
- ***Changes in patterns of leisure or entertainment:*** Increasing consumption of fast food, declining interest in a particular style of music, increase in competitive cycling, increase or decrease in a magazine's circulation
- ***Shifts in religious practices:*** Declining church attendance, increasing incidence of women ministers or rabbis, increasing interest in Asian religions, increased membership in fundamentalist churches, growth of "megachurches"
- ***New patterns of political behavior:*** Increase in conservatism or liberalism, decline in support for legalized abortion, developing power of minorities and women, increase in support for same-sex marriage

- ***Societal changes:*** Increases in the number of working women with children, single-parent households, telecommuters, ethnic intermarriages, grandparents raising their grandchildren, vegetarians
- ***Changes in political or world affairs:*** Spreading influence of capitalism, increasing resistance to globalization, increasing numbers of women elected to political office, growing ethnic or religious conflicts, increasing numbers of women becoming suicide bombers
- ***Changes in economic conditions:*** Increasing cost of medical care, decline in real median wage for families and individuals since 1973, increasing gap between wealthiest and poorest Americans, decreasing family savings rate
- ***Historical emergence of noteworthy artistic movements or other trends:*** Rise of community colleges, comprehensive high schools, cities; emergence of Impressionism, pop art, arts and crafts movement; achievement of female suffrage; development of industrialization, unionization of labor, public health systems, a national highway system; settlement of the West

Listing Subjects Related to Identity and Community. These suggestions may bring to mind topics related to identity and community.

Phenomena

- A particular conflict in a community to which you belong
- The popularity of athletes or other groups of students in high school
- The lack of understanding and sympathy between the young and the old
- The obsession of many young women and men with their weight and body image
- The continued high numbers of pregnant teenagers despite widely available birth control
- The deterioration of children's attachment to one or both parents during adolescence
- The watching of more hours of TV than people say they would like
- The experience of high school as generally unpleasant by some students

Trends

- Increasing prejudice against new immigrants
- Increasing incidence of people abandoning or abusing aged relatives
- Increasing incidence of domestic violence against spouses or children
- Increasing popularity of twelve-step, self-help programs
- Increasing popularity of sororities and fraternities on college campuses
- Increasing sexual activity before age fifteen
- Increasing incidence of depression among young adolescents (ages thirteen to fifteen)

- Increasing obesity among children
- Increasing numbers of college athletes graduating from college
- Increasing use of plastic surgery to enhance self-image
- Increasing numbers of young people choosing to remain virgins until they marry
- Increasing rate of cigarette smoking among young people

Listing Subjects Related to Work and Career. The following suggestions will help you to think of subjects related to work and career.

Phenomena

- Students' expectations of less financial success than their parents
- A preference for self-employment even though people who own their own businesses work harder for more hours each day than do other workers
- College students who hold part-time jobs
- Business majors
- The importance or difficulty of arranging working internships while in college
- Older students who attend college

Trends

- Rising employment among young people
- Increasing numbers of full-time and part-time temporary or contingent workers
- Increasing types of service-related careers

Choosing a Subject. *Look over your list of possibilities, and choose one subject to write about.* Describe the subject in two or three sentences. You may or may not already have some ideas about why this phenomenon or trend occurred. As you analyze it in detail, you will have the opportunity to consider possible causes and to decide which ones are the most plausible.

Of the two types of subjects—a phenomenon or a trend—a trend may be more challenging to examine because you must nearly always do research to demonstrate that the phenomenon actually exists or that it has been increasing or decreasing over an extended period of time. (Usually one or two references will be adequate.) Since a trend begins at a specific point, you must take care that the causes you propose as the sources of the trend actually precede its onset. You may also need to differentiate between causes that launched the trend and those that perpetuate it.

It may help you in choosing a subject if you tentatively identify your ultimate readers. They could be either a general adult readership or adult readers who already have some special interest or stake in your subject. They could be instructors, administrators, coworkers, or employers. They could be members of a particular community or region.

Exploring What You Know about Your Subject

Write for several minutes about the subject you have chosen. Note everything you now know about it. (When you start writing, you may be surprised at how much you do know.) Try to describe why you are interested in this trend or phenomenon, and speculate about where you might find more information about it.

Considering Causes

Think now about what might have caused your selected phenomenon or trend to occur. List possible causes, and then analyze the most promising ones.

Listing Possible Causes. *Write down all the things you can think of that might have caused the phenomenon or trend.* Consider each of the following:

- Immediate causes (those responsible for making the phenomenon or trend begin when it did)
- Remote, background causes (those from before the phenomenon or trend began)
- Perpetuating causes (those that may have contributed to sustaining or continuing the phenomenon or trend)
- Obvious causes
- Hidden causes

Selecting the Most Promising Causes. *Review your list, and select five or six causes that seem to you to provide a plausible explanation of your subject.* Since you will next need to analyze these causes, it might be helpful to list them in table form. If you are writing on paper, skip five or six lines between each cause in your list.

Analyzing Promising Causes. *Below each cause in your list, explain why you think it is real and important.* Consider the following questions as you analyze each cause:

- Is it a necessary cause? Without it, could the phenomenon or trend have occurred anyway?
- Is it a sufficient cause? Could it alone have caused this phenomenon or trend?
- Would this cause affect everybody the same way?
- Would this cause always lead to phenomena or trends like this one?
- What particular anecdotes or examples might demonstrate the importance of the cause?
- Do you know of any authorities who have suggested that it is an important cause?
- Is it a remote or background cause or an immediate cause?
- Is it a perpetuating cause, sustaining the phenomenon or trend?
- Is it an obvious cause or a hidden cause?
- Could it actually be a *result* of the phenomenon or trend rather than a *cause*?

Researching Your Subject

In exploring your subject, you may have found that you already know enough to describe or define it adequately for your readers. If not, you will need to consult library and Internet sources or interview a faculty or community expert to learn more about the subject.

If you are speculating about the causes of a trend, you will also need to do some research to confirm that it actually is a trend and not just a fluctuation or a fad. To do so, you will need to find examples and probably statistics that show an increase or a decrease in the trend over time and that indicate the date when this change began. (For example, recall that Sarah West cites dates and statistics to demonstrate that reported incidents of sexual harassment on the job actually increased.) If you are unable to find evidence to confirm that a trend exists, then it is probably just a fad or short-term fluctuation. In this case, you will have to choose a different subject for your essay.

Researching the Phenomenon or Trend: An Online Activity

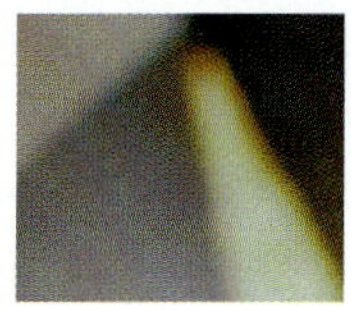

Searching the Web may help you establish the existence of the phenomenon or trend and provide information you can use in presenting it to your readers. Enter a key term describing your subject in a search engine such as Google (google.com) or Yahoo! Directory (dir.yahoo.com). Adding the word *trend* to your key term may help—for example, *religion trends* or *dieting trends.*

If you are interested in trends in education, you might find information at the National Center for Education Statistics Web site (http://nces.ed.gov/ssbr/pages/trends.asp). For other national trends, look for the relevant statistics link on the U.S. government Web site (http://firstgov.gov/).

Bookmark or keep a record of promising sites. Download any materials you might wish to cite in your evaluation, remembering to record the source information required to document them.

Considering Your Readers

Write a careful analysis of your readers. Because you will be trying to make a convincing case for some particular readers, you should know as much as possible about them. Only after you have analyzed your readers can you confidently decide how to present these causes in your essay—which causes you will emphasize, which causes will require the most convincing evidence, which causes will be obvious or not so obvious. Take a few minutes to answer the following questions:

- Who are my readers? (Describe them briefly.)
- What do my readers know about my subject? Will I have to prove its existence to them? How extensively will I have to define or describe it for them?

- What attitudes do my readers have about my subject? Do they care about it? Are they indifferent to it? Might they understand it differently from the way I understand it?
- What causes would they be most likely to think of?

Testing Your Choice

Now that you have explored your subject, considered its possible causes, and confirmed its existence, take some time to review your material and decide whether your subject is workable. Start by asking the following questions:

- Does the subject still interest me?
- Do I believe I can describe and define it in a way that will interest readers and show them that it is a phenomenon or a trend?
- Have I been able to come up with several possible causes?
- Do any of the causes I have come up with go beyond the obvious ones?
- Do I want to research the subject further?

If your subject does not seem promising, return to your list of possible subjects to select another.

Testing Your Choice: A Collaborative Activity

At this point, you will find it helpful to get together with two or three other students to discuss and get feedback on your subject and list of causes. This collaborative activity will help you determine whether you are ready to start developing your causal argument.

Presenters: Briefly identify your subject, and ask the listeners what causes immediately come to their minds as plausible explanations for your subject. Make a list of these causes as the listeners talk. Finally, tell the listeners the causes you propose to argue for, and ask them whether they accept these as likely or plausible. Take notes about their objections and questions. (When you plan and draft your essay, these lists and notes may suggest further causes you will want to argue for, and they will help you anticipate your readers' likely questions and objections to your proposed causes.)

Listeners: Respond imaginatively to the presenter's request for causes that you think initially explain the subject. When the presenter tells you the causes he or she proposes to argue for, praise those that seem plausible, but also ask all the questions and raise all the objections you can think of. In this way, you will help the presenter anticipate readers' likely questions and objections.

Researching Causes

Some causal arguments can be made fully and convincingly on the basis of your own knowledge and intuition. In fact, you may have to rely on your own ideas to explain very recent phenomena or emerging trends. Most subjects, however, will have already been noticed by others, and you will want to learn what they have said about the causes. Doing research can be helpful in several ways:

- To confirm or challenge your own ideas
- To identify further causes to add to your own explanation
- To provide support for causes that you want to argue for
- To identify causes that your readers may prefer more than the ones you find plausible
- To reveal some of the reservations that readers may have about the causes you suggest

As you discover causes others have proposed, add the most interesting or most plausible ones to your list. Analyze these as you did your own proposed causes. In your essay, you may want to accommodate them by integrating them in full or in part into your own argument.

As you gather evidence about causes, remember to record the information you will need to acknowledge your sources.

Developing Your Argument

Try out an argument in writing to support a key cause. Once you have figured out what to expect of your readers, review your list of causes and analyses, and make a new, shorter list of all the causes that you believe provide a plausible explanation of your subject. Then write a one-page argument for one cause that you think readers may find the most plausible or interesting or unexpected. Begin by identifying the cause. Then use some of the support you have found to make the cause seem plausible or likely to your readers. As part of your argument to support this cause, you may want to respond to readers' likely questions or objections.

Anticipating Objections

Try responding to the most likely objections to your causes. You should expect that readers will evaluate your essay critically by considering each cause and your support for it carefully before they decide that you have devised a plausible explanation. It would be wise, therefore, to account for any possible objections your readers could raise. Consider the two most likely objections, and think about how you would acknowledge, concede, or refute them. Write several sentences, trying out your response.

Anticipating Alternative Causes

Try responding to alternative causes that your readers may prefer to your own proposed causes. As they read your essay, your readers may think of other causes that seem more plausible to them than your causes. Try to think of two or three such causes now, and write several sentences about each one, explaining why you do not consider it important, why you specifically reject it, or why you think it is less plausible than your causes.

Considering Document Design

Think about whether your readers might benefit from design features, such as headings, numbered lists, or other elements that would make the development of your causal argument easier to follow. Consider also whether visuals—drawings, photographs, tables, or graphs—would strengthen your argument. These are not at all a requirement for an essay speculating about causes, but they could be helpful. You may come across promising visuals in your research and either download them from the Internet or make photocopies from library materials. Or you may find statistics that you can use to construct your own visuals, such as tables or graphs. If you do use visuals or statistics, be sure to document their sources and ask permission from the source if you want to post a visual on the Web.

Defining Your Purpose for Your Readers

Write a few sentences defining your purpose in devising this argument speculating about causes. Recall that in an earlier invention activity you identified your readers and considered what they know about your subject. Given these readers, try now to define your purpose by considering the following questions:

- How can I interest readers in my subject, establishing its significance for them personally, so that they will care about my speculations about its possible causes?
- Do I attempt to give my readers a fresh, new way of thinking about a phenomenon or trend that they may not have strong feelings about, or must I dissuade them from their present way of thinking about a phenomenon or trend that is already of significant concern to them?
- How much resistance should I expect from my readers to each of the causes I want to propose? Will the readers be largely receptive? Skeptical but convincible? Resistant and perhaps even antagonistic?
- How can I best respond to my readers' likely questions and objections and to the alternative causes they may prefer to my own? Shall I concede where I can or refute at every opportunity, and how can I refute without seeming dismissive of my readers' ideas?

Formulating a Tentative Thesis Statement

Write a sentence or two that could serve as your thesis statement. In an essay speculating about causes, the thesis statement focuses on the subject and announces the causes that are argued for in the piece. You will already have described the trend or phenomenon that is your subject. As readers approach your causal speculations, they need to know what causes you consider plausible and want them to take seriously and, though it is optional, would benefit from knowing how you have sequenced the causes.

Readings in this chapter illustrate effective thesis statements. For instance, Sarah West presents her thesis this way: "Why did this large increase [in reported incidents of workplace sexual harassment] occur in such a short amount of time? Possible answers to this question surely would include growing awareness of the nature of workplace sexual harassment, government action, efforts of companies to establish antiharassment policies and encourage harassed employees to come forward, and prominence given by the media to many cases of workplace harassment" (paragraph 2). West reiterates her subject and then lists all of the causes she believes best explain it. Furthermore, she lists the causes in exactly the order she will argue for them in the essay, helpfully forecasting for readers the sequence of the argument.

Similarly, after describing his subject—depression in boys—but before launching his causal speculations, William S. Pollack asserts his thesis: "While I believe the biological, or 'organic,' components of clinical depression (and the medical treatments for them) are of paramount importance and need to be carefully studied, my primary focus here is on what other psychologists and I have discovered about *external* psychological factors that can lead boys toward serious sadness or depression—factors such as a boy's family life, how he's treated at school, the quality of his friendships, and what kind of emotional support he gets on a regular basis" (paragraph 5). In clear and unambiguous language, Pollack announces that he intends to speculate about the psychological causes of boys' depression. He then forecasts the causes he believes to be most plausible.

PLANNING AND DRAFTING

This section will help you review your invention writing, determine specific goals for your essay, make a tentative outline, and get started on your first draft.

If you are using the Writing Guide Software, click on
▶ **Planning and Drafting**

Seeing What You Have

Pause now to reflect on your invention and research notes. Reread what you have written so far to see what you have. Watch for language that establishes the trend or phenomenon, argues convincingly for the causes you think are most plausible, and counterargues readers' likely objections to your causes as well as their alternative causes. Highlight key words, phrases, and sentences; make marginal notes or electronic annotations about any material you think could be useful. If you have done your invention writing on the computer, you may have sentences or whole paragraphs that can be copied and pasted into your draft.

Ask yourself the following questions:

- Could I research my subject more fully to make it seem more significant and worth speculating about?
- If I am speculating about the causes of a trend, do I have enough information to establish convincingly that the trend is (or was) increasing or decreasing over time?
- Will I be able to sequence my causes logically and argue for them convincingly?
- Have I been able to anticipate a wide range of readers' likely questions and objections?
- Have I been able to identify a few alternative causes readers may prefer over my causes?

Setting Goals

Before you begin drafting, set some specific goals to guide the decisions you will make as you draft and revise your essay. The draft will be easier to write and more convincing if you start with clear goals in mind. The following questions will help you set goals. You may find it useful to return to them while you are drafting, for they are designed to help you focus on specific elements of causal speculation essays.

Your Purpose and Readers

- What are my readers likely to know about my subject?
- How can I interest them in understanding its causes?
- How can I present myself so that my readers will consider me informed and authoritative?

The Beginning

- What opening would make readers take this subject seriously and really want to think about its causes? Should I declare its political significance, as David Brooks does? Assert its seriousness and importance, as William S. Pollack does? Provide a historical perspective, as Sarah West does?
- Should I personalize my subject by connecting it to my firsthand experience? Should I begin with an anecdote? Should I cite surprising statistics, as West does?

The Presentation of the Subject

- Do I need to demonstrate that my subject really exists, as Brooks, Pollack, and West do?
- If I am analyzing a trend, do I need to demonstrate that it is not just a fluctuation or a fad, as West does?
- How much and what kind of support do I need for these points?

The Causal Argument

- How many causes should I propose?
- How can I present my proposed causes in the most effective sequence? Should I arrange them from most to least important or vice versa, as Brooks does? From most obvious to least obvious, as Stephen King does, or vice versa? From immediate to remote or vice versa?
- Do I need to make other distinctions among causes, such as differentiating a cause that starts a trend from one that keeps it going?
- How much and what kind of support do I need to offer to make each cause plausible to my readers? Are any causes so obvious that support is unnecessary? Do I need to demonstrate to readers that all of my causes existed before the phenomenon or trend began?
- How can I anticipate readers' objections to my proposed causes? Should I just acknowledge the existence of some objections without responding to them? Concede other objections, as King does? Refute other objections, as Pollack and West do?
- How can I anticipate alternative causes readers might propose? Should I acknowledge one or more of these causes? Concede the plausibility of other causes, as West does? Refute other causes as not worth taking seriously, as Brooks and Pollack do?

The Ending

- How should I end my essay? Should I try to frame the essay by echoing something from the beginning, as West does?
- Should I summarize my causes or, as King and Pollack do, refocus on the key cause?
- Should I conclude with a conjecture about larger implications?

Outlining

A causal analysis may contain as many as four basic parts:

1. A presentation of the subject
2. Plausible causes, logically sequenced
3. Convincing support for each cause
4. A consideration of readers' questions, objections, and alternative causes

These parts can be organized in various ways. If your readers are not likely to think of any causes other than the ones you are proposing, you may want to begin by describing the subject and indicating its importance or interest. Then state your first proposed cause, supporting it convincingly and accommodating, conceding, or refuting readers' likely questions and objections. Follow the same pattern for any other causes you propose. Your conclusion could then mention—and elucidate—the lack of other explanations for your subject.

Presentation of the subject

First proposed cause with support and consideration of objections, if any

Second proposed cause with support and consideration of objections, if any (etc.)

Conclusion

If you need to account for alternative causes that are likely to occur to readers, you could discuss them first and give your reasons for conceding or rejecting them before offering your own proposed causes. Many writers save their own causes for last, hoping that readers will remember them best.

Presentation of the subject

Alternative causes and consideration of them

Proposed causes with support and consideration of objections, if any

Conclusion

Another option is to put your own causes first, followed by alternatives. This pattern helps you show the relative likelihood of your causes over the others. You might then end with a restatement of your causes.

Presentation of the subject

Proposed causes with support and consideration of objections, if any

Alternative causes compared with your causes

Concluding restatement of your proposed causes

There are, of course, many other possible ways to organize a causal analysis, but these outlines should help you start planning your own essay.

Consider any outlining you do before you begin drafting to be tentative. Never be a slave to an outline. As you draft, you will usually see ways to improve on your original plan. Be ready to revise your outline, shift parts around, or drop or add parts as you draft. If you use the outlining function of your word processing program, changing your outline will be simple, and you may be able to write the essay simply by expanding the outline.

Drafting

General Advice. Start drafting your essay, keeping in mind the goals you set while you were planning. Remember also the needs and expectations of your readers; organize, define, explain, and argue with them in mind. Turn off your grammar checker and spelling checker at this stage if you find them distracting. Don't be afraid to skip around in your draft; jump back and fill in a spontaneous idea, or leap ahead and write a later section first if you find that easier. If, as you draft, you discover that you need more information, make a note of what you need to find out, and go on to the next point. Later you can interview an expert, survey a group, or do further library or Internet research to get the information you need. If you get stuck while drafting, explore the problem by using some of the writing activities in the Invention and Research section of this chapter.

You may want to review the general drafting advice on pp. 16–17. These tips may also help you draft your essay:

- Remember that in writing about causes, you are dealing with probabilities rather than certainties. Therefore, resist the urge to claim that you have the final, conclusive answer; instead, simply assert that your explanation is plausible. Qualify your statements, and acknowledge readers' objections and alternative causes.
- Try to enliven your writing and to appeal to your readers' interests and concerns. Causal analysis is potentially rather dry.

Sentence Strategies. As you draft an essay speculating about the causes of a phenomenon or trend, you will want to ensure that your readers can readily recognize the stages of your argument and that they can easily understand the support you offer for each of your proposed causes. Two sentence strategies that can help you achieve these goals are using clear topic sentences, especially ones that are grammatically parallel, and using grammatically parallel sentences to present examples.

Signal the stages of your causal argument with easy-to-recognize topic sentences. Topic sentences are usually placed first or very early in a paragraph. They can announce a new cause, introduce counterargument (the writer's response to readers' likely questions or alternative causes), or identify different parts of the support for a cause or counterargument. They may include key terms that the writer has introduced in a thesis statement at the beginning of the essay, and they may take identical or similar sentence forms so that readers can recognize them more easily. Here are examples from Stephen King's essay. They identify what King believes to be the three main causes for many moviegoers' attraction to horror movies:

> Why? Some of the reasons are simple and obvious. To show that we can, that we are not afraid, that we can ride this roller coaster. (paragraph 3)
>
> We also go to re-establish our feelings of essential normality. (4)
>
> And we go to have fun. . . . The fun comes from seeing others menaced—sometimes killed. (5–6)

King assists readers in identifying each new stage of his argument by introducing the grammatical subject *we* in the first topic sentence and then repeating it to signal the next two stages: *we can, we also go, And we go.*

While King relies on topic sentences within paragraphs to signal the stages in his argument, as do William S. Pollack and Sarah West, David Brooks takes an unusual and effective approach: He signals his stages—the reasons that low- and middle-income Americans vote like upper-income people—with one-sentence paragraphs in bold italic type. That is, he separates each topic sentence from the paragraph that follows and calls attention to it with a design element (bold italic type). He also begins the last three topic sentences in grammatically parallel form, reinforcing his argument about how "Americans" think (or do not think) about issues of economic class.

> ***People vote their aspirations.*** (paragraph 4)
>
> ***Income resentment is not a strong emotion in much of America.*** (8)
>
> ***Many Americans admire the rich.*** (11)
>
> ***Americans resent social inequality more than income inequality.*** (15)
>
> ***Most Americans do not have Marxian categories in their heads.*** (17)

Do not hesitate to make your sequences of causes very visible and accessible to your readers. You need not set them off in bold italic type, as Brooks does, but keep in mind his example of exerting himself to help readers move comfortably from one stage of his causal argument to the next. Readers like to follow a logical, step-by-step argument. You can avoid frustrating their expectations by taking care to satisfy them—chiefly through the content of your argument, but also with visible signals.

For more on ways to signal the main stages of a causal argument, go to bedfordstmartins.com/the guide and click on Sentence Strategies.

Consider presenting examples supporting a cause in parallel grammatical form to help readers understand that the examples are related. Here is a sequence of two related examples from one paragraph in David Brooks's causal argument:

> There aren't Lexus dealerships on every corner. (paragraph 10)
>
> There are no snooty restaurants with water sommeliers. . . . (10)

In this case, the examples are introduced in forms that are not just grammatically similar but almost identical ("There aren't . . .," "There are no . . ."). In the next illustration, from a paragraph in Sarah West's argument, each example begins with a phrase identifying the year or years followed by the name of a person or group of people involved in sexual harassment charges. The repetition of grammatical form (along with the content of the sentences, of course) tells readers that the examples are related, making them not only easier to read but more convincing.

> In 1991, Supreme Court Justice Clarence Thomas in Senate hearings on his nomination. . . . (paragraph 6)
>
> Later that same year, male U.S. Navy officers were accused of sexually harassing female navy officers. . . . (6)
>
> During the late 1990s, Paula Jones's sexual harassment charges against President Clinton. . . . (6)

For more on relating examples to one another by repeating grammatical forms, go to bedfordstmartins.com/theguide and click on Sentence Strategies.

There are many ways to signal that a group of examples is related, and presenting them in the same grammatical form is certainly one effective way. All of the authors in this chapter do so at least twice.

In addition to using topic sentences that help readers follow the stages of your argument and using parallel grammatical form to present related examples, you can strengthen your causal argument with other kinds of sentences as well. You may want to review the information about sentences with appositives (pp. 246–47), strategies for indicating logical relationships between sentences (pp. 310–11), and sentences that introduce concession and refutation (pp. 309–10).

CRITICAL READING GUIDE

Now is the time to get a good critical reading of your draft. Writers usually find it helpful to have someone else read and comment on their drafts, and all writers know how much they learn about writing when they read other writers' drafts. Your instructor may arrange such a reading as part of your coursework—online or in class. If not, you can ask a classmate, friend, or family member to read your draft. You could also seek comments from a tutor at your campus writing center. (If you are unable to have someone else read your draft, turn ahead to the Revising section on pp. 494–96, where you will find guidelines for reading your own draft critically.)

If you are using the Writing Guide Software, click on
▶ **Critical Reading Guide**

Making Comments Electronically
Most word processing software offers features that allow you to insert comments directly into the text of someone else's document. Many readers prefer to make their comments in this way because it tends to be faster than writing on a hard copy and space is virtually unlimited; from the writer's point of view, it also eliminates the problem of deciphering handwritten comments. Even where such special comment features are not available, simply typing comments directly into a document in a contrasting color can provide the same advantages.

▶ **If You Are the Writer.** To provide focused, helpful comments, your reader must know your essay's intended audience, your purpose, and a problem in the draft that you need help solving. Briefly write out this information at the top of your draft.

- ***Readers:*** Identify the intended readers of your essay. What do you assume they already know and think about your subject and its causes? Do you expect them to be receptive, skeptical, resistant, or antagonistic?
- ***Purpose:*** What do you hope to accomplish with your readers?
- ***Problem:*** Ask your reader to help you solve the most important problem you see in your draft. Describe this problem briefly.

▶ **If You Are the Reader.** Reading a draft critically means reading it more than once—first to get a general impression and then to analyze its basic features. Use the following guidelines to assist you in giving critical comments to others on essays that speculate about the causes of phenomena or trends:

1. ***Read for a First Impression.*** Read the essay straight through. As you read, try to notice any words or passages that contribute to your first impression, and identify those that make weak contributions as well as strong ones.

   After you have finished reading the draft, write a few sentences describing your overall impression. Does the essay hold your interest? What in it most surprises you? What do you like best? Do you find the causal argument convincing? Next, consider the problem the writer identified, and respond briefly to that concern now. (If you find that the problem is covered by one of the other guidelines listed below, respond to it in more detail there if necessary.)
2. ***Evaluate How Well the Subject Is Presented.*** How well does the draft present the phenomenon or trend? Does it give enough information to make readers understand and care about the subject? Does it establish that the subject actually exists? If the subject is a trend, does the writer demonstrate a significant

increase or decrease over time? Where might additional details, examples, or statistics help?

3. ***Consider Whether the Causes and Support Are Convincing.*** Look first at the proposed causes, and list them. Do there seem to be too many? Too few? Do any seem either too obvious (not worth mentioning) or too obscure (remote in time or overly complicated)?

   Next, examine the support for each cause—anecdotes, examples, statistics, reference to authorities, and so on. Which support is most convincing? Which seems unconvincing? Where would more support or a different kind of support strengthen the argument?

   Check for errors in reasoning. Does the argument mistakenly take something for a cause just because it occurred before or at the start of the phenomenon or trend? Are any of the proposed causes of the subject actually *effects* of the subject?

4. ***Assess Whether Readers' Likely Objections and Questions Are Anticipated Adequately.*** Look for places where the writer acknowledges readers' possible objections to or questions about the proposed causes. How well are objections handled? Should any of them be taken more seriously? Help the writer see other ways of either accommodating or refuting objections. Do any of the refutations attack or ridicule the persons raising the objections? Try to think of other likely questions or objections the writer has overlooked.

5. ***Assess Whether Alternative Causes Are Adequately Anticipated.*** If alternative causes are acknowledged by the writer, are they presented fairly? Is it clear why they have been accommodated or rejected? Do the refutations seem convincing? Do any of the refutations attack or ridicule the persons proposing the alternative causes? Try to think of other plausible causes readers might prefer.

6. ***Consider Whether the Organization Is Effective.*** Given the expected readers, are the causes presented in an effective sequence? If not, suggest a more logical sequence.

   - *Look at the beginning.* Is it engaging? Imagine at least one other way to open the essay. Look for something later in the essay that could be moved to the beginning—an intriguing anecdote, for instance, or a surprising statistic.
   - *Look at the ending.* Is the ending decisive and memorable? Think of an alternative ending. Could something from earlier in the essay be moved to or restated at the end?
   - *Look again at any visuals the writer has incorporated.* Assess how well the visuals are integrated into the essay. Point to any items that do not provide support for the writer's argument.

7. ***Give the Writer Your Final Thoughts.*** What is this draft's strongest part? What about it is most memorable? What part is most in need of further work?

REVISING

Now you have the opportunity to revise your essay. Your instructor or other students may have given you advice on how to improve your draft. Or you may have begun to realize that your draft requires not so much revising as rethinking. For example, you may recognize that your causes are too obvious, that your causes lack a logical relationship to each other that would allow you to sequence them in a chain of reasoning, or that you have not anticipated readers' objections or alternative causes. Consequently, instead of working to improve the various parts of your first draft, you may need to write a new draft that radically reshapes your argument. Many students—and professional writers—find themselves in this situation. Often a writer produces a draft or two, gets advice on them from others, and only then begins to see what might be achieved.

If you feel satisfied that your draft mostly achieves what you set out to do, you can focus on refining the various parts of it. Very likely you have thought of ways to improve your draft, and you may even have begun improving it. This section will help you get an overview of your draft and revise it accordingly.

> If you are using the Writing Guide Software, click on
> ▶ **Revising**

Getting an Overview

Consider your draft as a whole, following these two steps:

1. ***Reread.*** If at all possible, put the draft aside for a day or two before rereading it. When you go back to it, start by reconsidering your audience and your purpose. Then read the draft straight through, trying to see it as your intended readers will.
2. ***Outline.*** Make a scratch outline, indicating the basic features as they appear in the draft. Consider using the headings and outline/summary functions of your word processor.

Planning for Revision. Resist the temptation to dive in and start changing your text until after you have a solid grasp of the big picture. Using your outline as a guide, move through the document, using the highlighting or commenting tools of your word processor to note comments received from others and problems you want to solve (or mark on a hard copy if you prefer).

Analyzing the Basic Features of Your Own Draft. Turn now to the Critical Reading Guide that begins on p. 492, and use it to identify problems in your draft. Note the problems on your draft.

Studying Critical Comments. Review all of the comments you have received from other readers. For each comment, look at the draft to determine what might have led the reader to make that particular point. Try to be objective about any criticism. Ideally, these comments will help you see your draft as others see it. Add to your notes any problems that you intend to act on.

Carrying Out Revisions

Having identified problems in your draft, you now need to find solutions and—most important—ways to implement them. Basically, you have three ways of finding solutions:

1. Review your invention and planning notes for other information and ideas.
2. Do additional invention writing or research to provide material that you or your readers think is needed.
3. Look back at the readings in this chapter to see how other writers have solved similar problems.

The following suggestions, which are organized according to the basic features of essays that speculate about causes, will get you started solving some problems that are common to them.

A Presentation of the Subject

- ***Is your subject unclear, or is its existence not clearly established?*** Discuss it in greater detail. Consider adding anecdotes, statistics, citations from authorities, or other details. If your subject is a trend, be sure you show evidence of a significant increase or decrease over an extended period.

Plausible Causes

- ***Do you propose too many causes?*** Clarify the role each one plays: Is it obvious? Hidden? Immediate, remote, or perpetuating? (You need not use these labels.) In addition, you may need to emphasize one or two causes or delete some that seem too obvious, too obscure, or relatively minor.
- ***Do you propose too few causes for a complex subject?*** Try to think of other possible causes, especially hidden or remote ones. Conduct further research if necessary.

Convincing Support

- ***Is your support skimpy or weak?*** Look for more or stronger types of support.
- ***Do you make errors in reasoning?*** Correct them. For example, if you cannot provide convincing support that a proposed cause occurred before the phenomenon or trend began and also contributed to it, you will have to delete that cause or at least present it more tentatively. If you have confused a cause with an effect, clarify their relationship.

Checking Sentence Strategies Electronically
To check your draft for a sentence strategy especially useful in essays speculating about causes, use your word processor's highlighting function to mark the sentences where you introduce each cause of the phenomenon or trend. Then look at whether each sentence indicates clearly to readers that you are moving on to a new stage in your causal argument. If any do not, think about how you could make the structure of the argument clearer, such as by repeating key terms from your thesis statement in these sentences or putting them into parallel grammatical form. For more on using topic sentences to signal the stages of a causal argument, see pp. 490–91.

A Logical Sequence of Causes

- ***Do your readers find the argument disorganized or hard to follow?*** Consider grouping related causes together, rearranging the causes in order of increasing or decreasing importance, or moving your refutations of alternative causes to precede your argument on behalf of the causes that you favor. Try to forge a logical chain of reasoning from cause to cause. Your plan may be more understandable if you forecast it at the beginning. Provide summaries, transitions, and other cues for readers. Remember that all the authors in this chapter signal clearly and visibly the stages of their arguments, especially where they introduce each separate cause for the phenomenon or trend.

A Consideration of Readers' Objections and Questions

- ***Are any of your refutations of possible objections to your proposed causes unconvincing?*** Try to provide stronger evidence. If you cannot do so, you may want to accommodate the objections.
- ***Do any refutations attack or ridicule people?*** Revise them to focus on the objections, not on the people who are making them.
- ***Do your readers raise questions about your argument that you have not considered or have not answered clearly?*** You may need to provide more information about your subject or more support for proposed causes.
- ***Do your readers make any objections that you have not considered or not taken seriously enough?*** Consider whether you can explain why they are wrong or should acknowledge their validity and incorporate them into your own argument.

Responses to Alternative Causes

- ***Do any of your refutations of alternative causes seem unconvincing?*** Try to provide a stronger counterargument, or consider accommodating the alternative causes.
- ***Do any refutations attack or ridicule people?*** Revise to focus on specific alternative causes that you believe to be implausible rather than on the people who are proposing these causes.
- ***Do your readers suggest any causes that you have not considered?*** Decide whether the causes are plausible and should be integrated into your argument. If they seem implausible, decide whether to mention and refute them.

The Beginning and Ending

- ***Is the beginning dull?*** Try opening with a surprising fact or an engaging anecdote or by emphasizing your subject's puzzling nature.
- ***Is the ending weak?*** Try to make it more emphatic or more interesting, perhaps by restating your main cause or causes, framing (referring to something mentioned at the beginning), or inviting readers to speculate further.

EDITING AND PROOFREADING

Now is the time to check your revised draft for errors in grammar, punctuation, and mechanics and to consider matters of style. Our research has identified several errors that are especially likely to occur in essays speculating about causes. The following guidelines are designed to help you check and edit your essay for these common errors.

> If you are using the Writing Guide Software, click on
> ▶ **Editing and Proofreading**

A Note on Grammar and Spelling Checkers
These tools are good at catching certain types of errors, but currently there's no replacement for a good human proofreader. Grammar checkers in particular are extremely limited in what they can usually find, and often they only give you summary information that isn't helpful if you don't already understand the rule in question. They are also prone to give faulty advice for fixing problems and to flag correct items as wrong. Spelling checkers cause fewer problems but can't catch misspellings that are themselves words, such as *to* for *too*.

Checking Your Use of Numbers. Whether they are indicating the scope of a phenomenon or citing the increase or decrease of a trend, writers who are speculating about causes often cite dates, percentages, fractions, and other numbers. Look, for example, at these sentences from Sarah West's essay:

> According to a 1994 survey conducted by the Society for Human Resource Management, the percentage of human resource professionals who have reported that their departments handled at least one sexual harassment complaint rose from 35 percent in 1991 to 65 percent in 1994.
>
> The jury awarded Weeks $7.1 million in punitive damages, twice what she sought in her lawsuit.

West follows the convention of spelling out numbers ("one") that can be written as one or two words and using a combination of numerals and words for a large number ("$7.1 million"). She could have used numerals for the large number: $7,100,000. She uses numerals for dates and percentages.

Conventions for presenting numbers in writing are easy to follow. The following sentences, taken from student essays that speculate about causes, have each been edited to demonstrate conventional ways of using numbers in academic writing.

Spelling Out Numbers and Fractions of One or Two Words

▶ **According to the World Health Organization, as many as ~~1~~ *one* person in every ~~50~~ *fifty* may be infected with HIV.**

▶ **Maybe ~~2/3~~ *two-thirds* of the smoke from a cigarette is released into the air.**

Using Figures for Numbers and Fractions of More than Two Words

▶ **That year the Japanese automobile industry produced only ~~four thousand eight hundred thirty-seven~~ *4,837* vehicles, mostly trucks and motorbikes.**

▶ This study shows that Americans spend an average of *5 1/3* ~~five and one-third~~ hours a day watching television.

Writing Percentages and Dates with Figures

▶ Comparing 1980 to 1960, we can see that time spent viewing television increased *28* ~~twenty-eight~~ percent.

Spelling Out Numbers That Begin a Sentence

▶ *Thirty* ~~30~~ percent of commercial real estate in Washington, D.C., is owned by foreigners.

Checking for *Reason Is Because* Constructions. When you speculate about causes, you need to offer reasons and support for your speculations. Consequently, essays that speculate about causes often contain sentences constructed around a *reason is because* pattern. Since *because* means "for the reason that," such sentences say essentially that "the reason is the reason."

REDUNDANT The *reason* we lost the war *is because* troop morale was down.

If you find this pattern in your writing, here are two ways to edit out the redundancy:

CLEAR The reason we lost the war is that troop morale was down.
CLEAR We lost the war because troop morale was down.

▶ Her research suggests that one reason women attend women's colleges is *that* ~~because~~ they want to avoid certain social pressures.

▶ *Older* ~~A reason older~~ Americans watch so much television ~~is~~ because they tend to be sedentary.

A WRITER AT WORK

ANALYZING CAUSES

When a writer is planning an essay that speculates about causes, identifying and analyzing possible causes are the most important parts of invention and research. Here we look at an invention table of causes and analyses that Sarah West developed for her essay, "The Rise of Reported Incidents of Workplace Sexual Harassment," which appears in this chapter on pp. 466–70.

West worked on this invention activity in stages, and her table of causes shows how her ideas about her subject evolved. When she began the activity, she assumed her subject would be a recent increase in workplace sexual harassment. Later, she modified her subject to focus on an increase in *reported incidents* of workplace sexual harassment, based on what she learned from doing library and Internet research. As you read through her invention table, notice how the causes and analyses reflect West's developing ideas about her subject. With her initial subject in mind, she entered the first three causes in the table and a partial analysis. Then, after she researched her subject and decided to focus on reported incidents, she added the other four causes and completed the analysis.

TABLE OF POSSIBLE CAUSES AND ANALYSES

Causes	Analyses
1. Women are not taken seriously at work by men	Background cause because sexist attitudes go back a long way. Definitely a cause that sustains the increase in sexual harassment. Obvious cause, I guess. My aunt was sexually harassed at work for a long time by her supervisor. She put up with it, and then the man left for a new job. Obviously men wouldn't harass women in any way if they took them seriously, so it's both a necessary and sufficient cause.
2. Men are unable to understand what sexual harassment feels like	If they understood, they wouldn't do it, making this a necessary cause. Maybe it's possible that some women don't mind or even encourage it, but most women must hate and resent it. Not a sufficient cause--men might still refrain from doing it even if they couldn't understand the effect it had. A few men probably are able to understand how sexual harassment makes women feel. Perpetuating and background cause because it comes from men's basic attitudes that are not easy to change. Not so obvious a cause as my first one.
3. Men are not worried about being reported	A necessary cause--if men feared the consequences of being caught, they wouldn't harass. They feel powerful and safe, proba-

Causes	Analyses
3. Men are not worried about being reported (continued)	bly because their bosses are men, who may play or have played the sexual harassment game themselves. A perpetuating cause, important, but maybe not too surprising to women. Can't see what would be the best order for these three causes. Need to find out what the experts have said about this trend.
4. Increased awareness	An immediate and perpetuating cause as well. Awareness of the 1964 Civil Rights Act and knowledge about the nature of sexual harassment at work has been recent and widespread among women. Researchers I read support this. Nearly all women workers had this information. But most business organizations continued to ignore the implications. And most men.
5. 1991 Civil Rights Act	This important legislation put in place penalties for businesses that did not have sexual harassment policies that protected women and punished men who got out of line. Well-documented and publicized cases cost some businesses a lot of money. An immediate cause that brought about the increase in reported cases of harassment. Both a necessary and sufficient cause because of the penalties. That's what caught everybody's attention. This cause wouldn't be obvious to readers who did not know about the 1991 Act. Use Stanko and Werner.
6. Company policies	Immediate, necessary, and sufficient cause. There were policies, manuals, training sessions for men and women. Probably the most immediate cause because women now had specific procedures to follow to report sexual harassment. Martell and Sullivan document these important changes. Also use "Handling" and "Sexual" and HRM report.
7. Media attention	Neither necessary nor sufficient cause, because media attention would not have

```
encouraged women to report harassment. It
was really the 1991 Act and the well-
publicized company policies. Could be an
effect, but I think it is a cause that sus-
tains what started with companies' new poli-
cies. Probably an obvious cause to readers,
who will recognize all the examples of media
attention I will use from my reading. Refer
to Nelton.
```

Once West had analyzed all these possible causes, she could decide how to use them to make the most convincing explanation of her subject. She decided to use all four of the causes she came up with from her research (causes 4–7). She thought her readers would find these causes plausible, and she knew she had enough statistics and examples to support them. Then she decided how to order the causes to produce the most logical argument. In addition, she considered potential objections to her argument and accommodations or refutations of them. She found one journalist who was skeptical that there was an increase in reported incidents of sexual harassment, and she tried her best to refute his argument (paragraph 7). Finally, she found one alternative cause for the increase, and she decided to concede part of it and try to refute the rest (paragraph 8).

DESIGNING YOUR WORK

The report that the biology student wrote about the possible causes of the AIDS epidemic in sub-Saharan Africa and North America (described on p. 450) was accompanied by several visuals, including a color map, downloaded from the Internet, that depicted areas of lesser and greater numbers of AIDS cases across the continent of Africa along with pie charts that showed the relationship between gender and AIDS infection in North America and in two regions in Africa. The student also incorporated several tables that presented statistics and other information that would have otherwise taken up unnecessary space and been difficult to grasp.

Making Use of Visuals

Maps, tables, graphs, charts, and diagrams are used to convey information in a way that is easy to read and comprehend. Readers can glean information from these visuals much more quickly and efficiently than they can from statistics that are contained only in written text. Color can be an important element in graphic design: Selecting colors to use to highlight your visuals can be much like selecting the most appropriate and effective words to convey your written ideas. In both cases, you want your choices to enhance readers' understanding of and interest in the argument you are making. Above all, visuals should be clearly designed and easy to read.

Visual aids cannot do all the work for the writer or for readers. Visuals can represent information but not interpret it. The writer must comment on the information illustrated in graphic aids, explain why the information they show is important, and suggest what the implications of such information might be. Consequently, when you consider integrating visuals into your work, be prepared to explain them carefully in your text. In addition, think about what types of visuals should be included in the text, where and how visuals will make the most sense to your readers, and what labels will need to accompany the visuals for clarity. These decisions will be influenced by whether you are presenting your work as hard copy, an oral presentation to a group, or a document on the Internet.

Selecting Visuals

For more on different types of visuals, see Chapter 25.

Visuals are used for specific purposes, and in many cases you will find that one type suits your purpose more effectively than the others. For example, maps can be an appropriate means of illustrating how multiple geographic areas experience some element similarly or differently. Different colors are often used to represent contrasts; one familiar example is the televised weather report, where a ranges of temperatures and of precipitation levels are mapped out. The biology student's map (see Figure 1) offers another example.

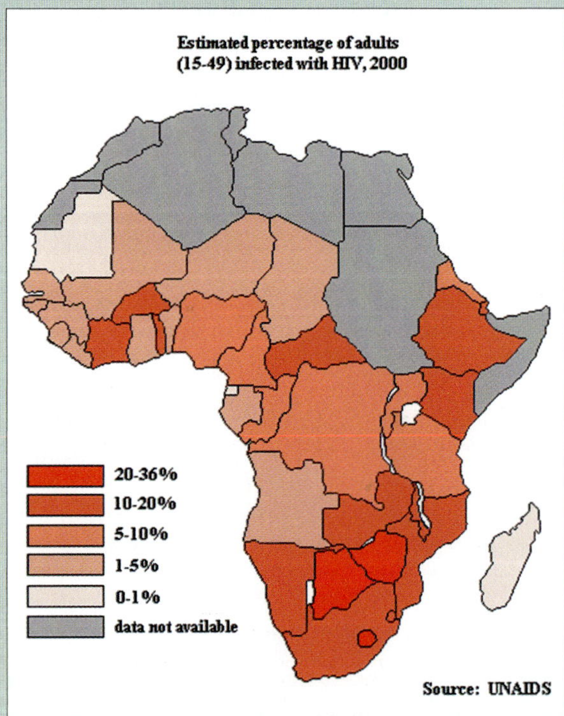

Figure 1. Spread of AIDS in Sub-Saharan Africa

Pie charts, such as the ones in the student's report (see Figure 2), show the relative percentages of the various parts making up a whole. Finally, diagrams most often illustrate physical relationships or show how things work. For example, the written instructions that come with many products we purchase are often accompanied by diagrams illustrating how to assemble or use the products.

For an example of an instructional process narrative containing diagrams, see Figure 14.3, p. 640.

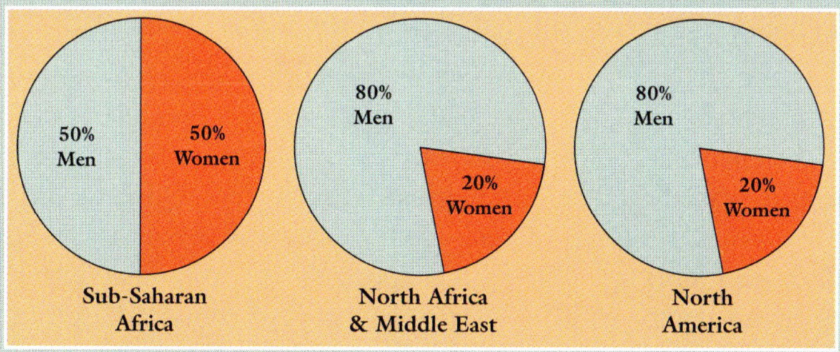

Figure 2. Proportion of Reported AIDS Cases by Gender

THINKING CRITICALLY ABOUT WHAT YOU HAVE LEARNED

Now that you have worked extensively with essays that speculate about causes—reading them, talking about them, writing one of your own—take some time to reflect on what you have learned about causal speculation. What problems did you encounter while you were writing your essay, and how did you solve them? How did reading other causal speculation essays influence your own essay? What ideas do you have about the social or cultural dimensions of this kind of writing?

Reflecting on Your Writing

Write an explanation of a page or two, telling your instructor about a problem you encountered in writing your essay and how you solved it. Before you begin, gather all of your writing—invention and planning notes, drafts, critical comments, revision notes and plans, and final revision. Review these materials as you complete this writing task.

1. ***Identify one writing problem you needed to solve as you worked on your essay.*** Do not be concerned with grammar and punctuation; concentrate instead on problems unique to developing an essay that speculates about causes. For example: Did you have trouble demonstrating that a trend exists? Was it difficult to decide on a logical sequence for presenting causes? Did you worry about the need to identify and address alternative causes?
2. ***Determine how you came to recognize the problem.*** When did you first discover it? What called it to your attention? If someone else pointed out the problem to you, can you now see hints of it in your invention writing? If so, where specifically?

When you first recognized the problem, how did you respond?

3. ***Reflect on how you went about solving the problem.*** Did you change the wording of a passage, cut or add causes or refutations, conduct further research, or move paragraphs or sentences around? Did you reread one of the essays in this chapter to see how another writer handled a similar problem, or did you look back at the invention suggestions? If you talked about the problem with another student, a tutor, or your instructor, did talking about it help? How useful was the advice you received?
4. ***Write an explanation of the problem and your solution.*** Be as specific as possible in reconstructing your efforts. Quote from your invention notes or draft essay, others' critical comments, your revision plan, or your revised essay to show the various changes your writing underwent as you tried to solve the problem. Taking time to explain how you identified a particular problem, how you went about trying to solve it, and what you learned from this experience can help you solve future writing problems more easily.

Reviewing What You Learned from Reading

Write a page or two explaining to your instructor how the readings in this chapter influenced your final essay. Your own essay has undoubtedly been influenced to some extent by one or more of the essays in this chapter as well as by classmates' essays that you have read. These other essays may have helped you decide on an appropriate subject, suggested the need to consider both immediate and background causes, or shown you how to accommodate or refute an important alternative cause. Before you write, take some time to reflect on what you have learned about writing causal speculation from these selections.

1. ***Reread the final revision of your essay; then look back at the selections you read before completing it.*** Do you see any specific influences? For example, if you were impressed with the way one of the readings established the existence of a trend, presented causes in a logical order, used authorities or personal experience and observation to support a cause, or argued convincingly against an alternative cause, look to see where you might have been striving for similar effects in your own writing. Also look for ideas you got from your reading: writing strategies you were inspired to try, specific details you were led to include, effects you sought to achieve.
2. ***Write an explanation of these influences.*** Did one selection have a particularly strong influence on your essay, or were several selections influential in different ways? Quote from the readings and from your final revision to show how your causal speculation essay was influenced by the selections you read. Finally, based on your review of this chapter's readings, point out any further improvement you would now make in your essay.

Considering the Social Dimensions of Causal Speculation

Persuasive writing, as we define it in this text, deals with probabilities and possibilities, not with certainties. Causal speculation is persuasive writing par excellence because it confronts aspects of social life that we do not yet understand and may never fully understand. Without this great social resource, we would feel helpless in the face of threatening social problems. They would seem like random acts of a chaotic universe. Instead, when confronted with the alarming evidence that the teenage suicide rate is high, we can start speculating about why many teenagers are ending their own lives. We can evaluate competing causes and decide which are the most plausible. Finally, we can take action, feeling reassured that our knowledge is sound, even though it is speculative and likely to change over time. Nevertheless, cautious readers and writers need to be aware of several problems posed by causal speculation.

The Power of Authority and Ideology. First, we need to keep in mind that what seems to be the best current explanation for the causes of a trend or phenomenon is not necessarily the only explanation. Speculating about causes tends to give greater voice to certain interests and to minimize or silence others.

Some analyses—particularly those of experts such as economists, psychologists, and popular authors—are often granted more authority than analyses favored by parents, teachers, community and religious leaders, and other persons most directly affected.

In addition, we need to remember that causal reasoning is always shaped by the analyst's ideology—the beliefs, values, and attitudes that determine a person's worldview. For example, Stephen King—a horror writer—has a real interest in establishing the horror movie as a legitimate literary and cinematic form; not surprisingly, then, he emphasizes the psychological benefits of horror movies. Conservative political analyst David Brooks is clearly pleased that relatively few Americans want to use government to redistribute wealth; an analyst who favors such redistribution might come up with a completely different explanation for this phenomenon than Brooks does.

Even the way we define a phenomenon or a trend can color our explanation of its causes. For example, when four white Los Angeles police officers were videotaped beating motorist Rodney King but acquitted of assault charges in the spring of 1992, many people took to the streets, starting fires, looting, and killing 55 people and injuring 2,383. While some observers called the disturbance a "riot," others used a more sympathetic term—"uprising." These two terms reflect two ways of understanding what happened in the city that spring, pointing to entirely different sets of possible causes. A great deal is at stake when society must decide whether the causes of violent crimes were linked to frustration with racism and unequal justice, on the one hand, or to lack of an adequate police "presence" and respect for the law, on the other hand.

1. ***Consider how the readings and your own essay are exercises in exerting authority.*** We have said that because causal speculation deals with possibilities instead of certainties, writers must be somewhat tentative about their speculations. However, if causal argument is to be convincing, it cannot be too timid. Writers who have studied a subject carefully may feel that they are justified in exerting their authority. Compare the William S. Pollack and Sarah West essays. Which seems more assertive? What accounts for your response? What seems to you assertive or unassertive about your own essay? Was it your knowledge or your ideology—your way of looking at the world—or both that gave you the confidence to be authoritative?
2. ***Consider how easy it is to accept a causal explanation.*** We have also said that if readers are not alert, they may begin to think that the explanation offered is the only possible one. Is either Pollack's or West's argument so seductive that you find yourself accepting it without question? Explain briefly.
3. ***Write a page or two explaining your ideas about authority and ideology in essays speculating about causes.*** Connect your ideas to your own essay and to the readings in this chapter.

Causes and Blame. Causal speculations sometimes become exercises in assigning blame. For example, not long ago, a woman's "provocative" attire could be cited in court as a cause (and possible justification) for her being raped. Similarly, women could be blamed for failing to be superwomen, and boys could be blamed for failing to keep a stiff upper lip and pull themselves out of their own depression. In cases like these, causal speculation can become a way for people to avoid confronting social responsibilities and put off working toward solving serious social problems.

1. ***Draw some conclusions about individual and social influences on behavior.*** Americans are often divided about whether individuals are primarily responsible for their circumstances or whether social, economic, and political conditions best explain people's difficulties and suffering. Where does Pollack position himself on this issue? Explore your own position as well. If you were to write about the causes of depression in boys, which kinds of causes—individual or social—would you emphasize? Why?
2. ***Write a page or two explaining your ideas on how essays speculating about causes can become exercises in assigning blame.*** Connect your ideas to your own essay and to the readings in this chapter.

10

Interpreting Stories

Stories have a special place in most cultures. Elders relate family and cultural history through stories; lessons are taught through moral fables and parables. The bonds of family and community are often strengthened by sharing stories.

Stories have the power to stimulate our feelings and imagination, allowing us to escape our everyday routine and become aware of the wider world around us. They can lead us to look at others with sensitivity and, for a brief time, to see the world through another person's eyes. They can also lead us to see ourselves differently, to gain insight into our innermost feelings and thoughts.

The stories you will read in this chapter may remind you of the essays about remembered events you read and wrote in Chapter 2. Like an autobiographical essay, a story succeeds largely on how well it conveys to readers the significance of an event. As you may remember, essays about remembered events convey significance primarily through vivid descriptive detail showing people in particular places engaged in some kind of dramatic action. Fictional stories work the same way, only the people are called the *characters,* places are called the *setting,* the dramatic action is called the *plot,* and the significance is called the *theme* or *meaning.*

In this chapter, you will be reading and writing essays interpreting a story. The essay interpreting a story is a special kind of academic writing—like the lab report in biology, the ethnography in anthropology, and the brief in law. College students can expect to write interpretive or analytical essays, as they are sometimes called, in English and film studies courses. Although the genre of essays interpreting stories is specialized, you do not have to be an English major to write a successful interpretive essay. Once you have learned the conventions of presenting an interpretive argument, you will be able to use your experience of listening to, viewing, reading, and telling stories to write insightfully about the fictional stories you read.

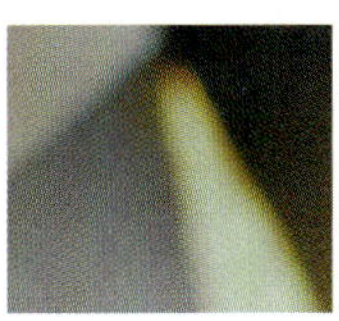

Practice Interpreting a Story: A Collaborative Activity

This activity invites you to practice arguing for your interpretation of a story. Get together with two or three other students to discuss your interpretations of a story you have all read. Your instructor may assign a story for your group or may invite you to choose one from this chapter, and he or she may schedule this collaborative activity as a face-to-face in-class discussion or ask you to conduct an online real-time discussion in a chat room. Whatever the medium, here are some guidelines to follow:

Part 1. Begin by picking a question for interpretation for your story from the list below. Members of your group may choose the same question or different ones.

Next take a few minutes to make notes of what you will say. Take turns telling the other group members your interpretation and your reasons for it. The others will react, indicating where they agree and disagree with your interpretation.

Questions for Interpretation

For "The Story of an Hour" (p. 509), how do you interpret the following?

1. The meaning of the final paragraph
2. What Mrs. Mallard feels "was approaching to possess her" and why she tries "to beat it back" in paragraph 10
3. Mrs. Mallard's thoughts in paragraph 14

For "Sunday in the Park" (p. 511), how do you interpret the following?

1. The portrayal of the other boy's father
2. Morton's threat to discipline Larry at the end of the story
3. The relationship between the speaker and her husband

For "The Use of Force" (p. 514), how do you interpret the following?

1. The doctor's ambivalence in paragraph 32 about his own actions
2. The doctor's attitude in paragraph 22 toward the girl and her parents
3. The girl's behavior

For "My Father's Chinese Wives" (p. 516), how do you interpret the following?

1. The relationship between the father and his daughters
2. The speaker's explanation in paragraphs 19–29 of why she was "bothered" by her father's decision to marry a "Chinese wife" (paragraph 1)
3. The speaker and Kaitlin's meeting with Zhou Ping

For "Araby" (p. 526), how do you interpret the following?

1. How the boy sees himself at the end of the story
2. Mangan's sister compared to the boy's representation of her
3. The changes the boy undergoes in the story

Part 2. After you have all presented your interpretations and gotten feedback from the group, use the following questions to explore what you learned about interpreting stories:

- What was most challenging for you: choosing a question, responding to it, or giving reasons for your interpretation?

- What one thing said by other members of your group, either in response to your interpretation or in presenting their own interpretations, might lead you to change your interpretation or how you argue for it?

AN ANTHOLOGY OF SHORT STORIES

Following are five short stories: "The Story of an Hour," by Kate Chopin; "Sunday in the Park," by Bel Kaufman; "The Use of Force," by William Carlos Williams; "My Father's Chinese Wives," by Sandra Tsing Loh; and "Araby," by James Joyce. Your instructor may invite the whole class or small groups to discuss one or more of these stories. You may also be asked to choose one of these stories for your interpretive essay.

***Kate Chopin** (1851–1904) was born in St. Louis and lived in Louisiana until her husband died in 1882, leaving her with six children. Encouraged by friends, Chopin wrote her first novel,* At Fault *(1890), when she was nearly forty years old. She wrote many short stories for popular magazines such as* Century, Harper's, *and* Vogue, *in which "The Story of an Hour" first appeared in 1894. She published two collections of stories and a second novel, her best-known work,* The Awakening *(1899).*

The Story of an Hour

Kate Chopin

Knowing that Mrs. Mallard was afflicted with a heart trouble, great care was taken to break to her as gently as possible the news of her husband's death. 1

It was her sister Josephine who told her, in broken sentences; veiled hints that revealed in half concealing. Her husband's friend Richards was there, too, near her. It was he who had been in the newspaper office when intelligence of the railroad disaster was received, with Brently Mallard's name leading the list of "killed." He had only taken the time to assure himself of its truth by a second telegram, and had hastened to forestall any less careful, less tender friend in bearing the sad message. 2

She did not hear the story as many women have heard the same, with a paralyzed inability to accept its significance. She wept at once, with sudden, wild abandonment, in her sister's arms. When the storm of grief had spent itself she went away to her room alone. She would have no one follow her. 3

There stood, facing the open window, a comfortable, roomy armchair. Into this she sank, pressed down by a physical exhaustion that haunted her body and seemed to reach into her soul. 4

5 She could see in the open square before her house the tops of trees that were all aquiver with the new spring life. The delicious breath of rain was in the air. In the street below a peddler was crying his wares. The notes of a distant song which some one was singing reached her faintly, and countless sparrows were twittering in the eaves.

6 There were patches of blue sky showing here and there through the clouds that had met and piled one above the other in the west facing her window.

7 She sat with her head thrown back upon the cushion of the chair, quite motionless, except when a sob came up into her throat and shook her, as a child who has cried itself to sleep continues to sob in its dreams.

8 She was young, with a fair, calm face, whose lines bespoke repression and even a certain strength. But now there was a dull stare in her eyes, whose gaze was fixed away off yonder on one of those patches of blue sky. It was not a glance of reflection, but rather indicated a suspension of intelligent thought.

9 There was something coming to her and she was waiting for it, fearfully. What was it? She did not know; it was too subtle and elusive to name. But she felt it, creeping out of the sky, reaching toward her through the sounds, the scents, the color that filled the air.

10 Now her bosom rose and fell tumultuously. She was beginning to recognize this thing that was approaching to possess her, and she was striving to beat it back with her will—as powerless as her two white slender hands would have been.

11 When she abandoned herself a little whispered word escaped her slightly parted lips. She said it over and over under her breath: "free, free, free!" The vacant stare and the look of terror that had followed it went from her eyes. They stayed keen and bright. Her pulses beat fast, and the coursing blood warmed and relaxed every inch of her body.

12 She did not stop to ask if it were or were not a monstrous joy that held her. A clear and exalted perception enabled her to dismiss the suggestion as trivial.

13 She knew that she would weep again when she saw the kind, tender hands folded in death; the face that had never looked save with love upon her, fixed and gray and dead. But she saw beyond that bitter moment a long procession of years to come that would belong to her absolutely. And she opened and spread her arms out to them in welcome.

14 There would be no one to live for her during those coming years; she would live for herself. There would be no powerful will bending hers in that blind persistence with which men and women believe they have a right to impose a private will upon a fellow-creature. A kind intention or a cruel intention made the act seem no less a crime as she looked upon it in that brief moment of illumination.

15 And yet she had loved him—sometimes. Often she had not. What did it matter! What could love, the unsolved mystery, count for in face of this possession of self-assertion which she suddenly recognized as the strongest impulse of her being!

16 "Free! Body and soul free!" she kept whispering.

17 Josephine was kneeling before the closed door with her lips to the keyhole, imploring for admission. "Louise, open the door! I beg; open the door—you will make yourself ill. What are you doing, Louise? For heaven's sake open the door."

18 "Go away. I am not making myself ill." No; she was drinking in a very elixir of life through that open window.

Her fancy was running riot along those days ahead of her. Spring days, and summer days, and all sorts of days that would be her own. She breathed a quick prayer that life might be long. It was only yesterday she had thought with a shudder that life might be long. 19

She arose at length and opened the door to her sister's importunities. There was a feverish triumph in her eyes, and she carried herself unwittingly like a goddess of Victory. She clasped her sister's waist, and together they descended the stairs. Richards stood waiting for them at the bottom. 20

Some one was opening the front door with a latchkey. It was Brently Mallard who entered, a little travel-stained, composedly carrying his gripsack and umbrella. He had been far from the scene of accident, and did not even know there had been one. He stood amazed at Josephine's piercing cry; at Richards' quick motion to screen him from the view of his wife. 21

But Richards was too late. 22

When the doctors came they said she had died of heart disease—of joy that kills. 23

***Bel Kaufman** (b. 1911) wrote* Up the Down Staircase *(1965), called by* Time *magazine "easily the most popular novel about U.S. public schools in history" and made into both a film and a play. Her story "Sunday in the Park" won the National Education Association/PEN Short Story Contest in 1983. The granddaughter of the great short-story writer Sholom Aleichem, Kaufman grew up in Russia and learned English after she came to the United States at age twelve.*

Sunday in the Park

Bel Kaufman

It was still warm in the late-afternoon sun, and the city noises came muffled through the trees in the park. She put her book down on the bench, removed her sunglasses, and sighed contentedly. Morton was reading the *Times Magazine* section, one arm flung around her shoulder; their three-year-old son, Larry, was playing in the sandbox: a faint breeze fanned her hair softly against her cheek. It was five-thirty of a Sunday afternoon, and the small playground, tucked away in a corner of the park, was all but deserted. The swings and seesaws stood motionless and abandoned, the slides were empty, and only in the sandbox two little boys squatted diligently side by side. *How good this is,* she thought, and almost smiled at her sense of well-being. They must go out in the sun more often; Morton was so city-pale, cooped up all week inside the gray factory like university. She squeezed his arm affectionately and glanced at Larry, delighting in the pointed little face frowning in concentration over the tunnel he was digging. The other boy suddenly stood up and with a quick, deliberate swing of his chubby arm threw a spadeful of sand at Larry. It just missed his head. Larry continued digging; the boy remained standing, shovel raised, stolid and impassive. 1

"No, no, little boy." She shook her finger at him, her eyes searching for the child's mother or nurse. "We mustn't throw sand. It may get in someone's eyes and hurt. We 2 must play nicely in the nice sandbox." The boy looked at her in unblinking expectancy. He was about Larry's age but perhaps ten pounds heavier, a husky little boy with none of Larry's quickness and sensitivity in his face. Where was his mother? The only other people left in the playground were two women and a little girl on roller skates leaving now through the gate, and a man on a bench a few feet away. He was a big man, and he seemed to be taking up the whole bench as he held the Sunday comics close to his face. She supposed he was the child's father. He did not look up from his comics, but spat once deftly out of the corner of his mouth. She turned her eyes away.

3 At that moment, as swiftly as before, the fat little boy threw another spadeful of sand at Larry. This time some of it landed on his hair and forehead. Larry looked up at his mother, his mouth tentative; her expression would tell him whether to cry or not.

4 Her first instinct was to rush to her son, brush the sand out of his hair, and punish the other child, but she controlled it. She always said that she wanted Larry to learn to fight his own battles.

5 "Don't *do* that, little boy," she said sharply, leaning forward on the bench. "You mustn't throw sand!"

6 The man on the bench moved his mouth as if to spit again, but instead he spoke. He did not look at her, but at the boy only.

7 "You go right ahead, Joe," he said loudly. "Throw all you want. This here is a *public* sandbox."

8 She felt a sudden weakness in her knees as she glanced at Morton. He had become aware of what was happening. He put his *Times* down carefully on his lap and turned his fine, lean face toward the man, smiling the shy, apologetic smile he might have offered a student in pointing out an error in his thinking. When he spoke to the man, it was with his usual reasonableness.

9 "You're quite right," he said pleasantly, "but just because this is a public place. . . ."

10 The man lowered his funnies and looked at Morton. He looked at him from head to foot, slowly and deliberately. "Yeah?" His insolent voice was edged with menace. "My kid's got just as good right here as yours, and if he feels like throwing sand, he'll throw it, and if you don't like it, you can take your kid the hell out of here."

11 The children were listening, their eyes and mouths wide open, their spades forgotten in small fists. She noticed the muscle in Morton's jaw tighten. He was rarely angry; he seldom lost his temper. She was suffused with a tenderness for her husband and an impotent rage against the man for involving him in a situation so alien and so distasteful to him.

12 "Now, just a minute," Morton said courteously, "you must realize. . . ."

13 "Aw, shut up," said the man.

14 Her heart began to pound. Morton half rose; the *Times* slid to the ground. Slowly the other man stood up. He took a couple of steps toward Morton, then stopped. He flexed his great arms, waiting. She pressed her trembling knees together. Would there be violence, fighting? How dreadful, how incredible. . . . She must do something, stop them, call for help. She wanted to put her hand on her husband's sleeve, to pull him down, but for some reason she didn't.

15 Morton adjusted his glasses. He was very pale. "This is ridiculous," he said unevenly. "I must ask you. . . ."

16 "Oh, yeah?" said the man. He stood with his legs spread apart, rocking a little, looking at Morton with utter scorn. "You and who else?"

17 For a moment the two men looked at each other nakedly. Then Morton turned his back on the man and said quietly, "Come on, let's get out of here." He walked awkwardly, almost limping with self-consciousness, to the sandbox. He stooped and lifted Larry and his shovel out.

18 At once Larry came to life; his face lost its rapt expression and he began to kick and cry. "I don't *want* to go home, I want to play better, I don't *want* any supper, I don't *like* supper. . . ." It became a chant as they walked, pulling their child between them, his feet dragging on the ground. In order to get to the exit gate they had to pass the bench where the man sat sprawling again. She was careful not to look at him. With all the dignity she could summon, she pulled Larry's sandy, perspiring little hand, while Morton pulled the other. Slowly and with head high she walked with her husband and child out of the playground.

19 Her first feeling was one of relief that a fight had been avoided, that no one was hurt. Yet beneath it there was a layer of something else, something heavy and inescapable. She sensed that it was more than just an unpleasant incident, more than defeat of reason by force. She felt dimly it had something to do with her and Morton, something acutely personal, familiar, and important.

20 Suddenly Morton spoke. "It wouldn't have proved anything."

21 "What?" she asked.

22 "A fight. It wouldn't have proved anything beyond the fact that he's bigger than I am."

23 "Of course," she said.

24 "The only possible outcome," he continued reasonably, "would have been—what? My glasses broken, perhaps a tooth or two replaced, a couple of days' work missed—and for what? For justice? For truth?"

25 "Of course," she repeated. She quickened her step. She wanted only to get home and to busy herself with her familiar tasks; perhaps then the feeling, glued like heavy plaster on her heart, would be gone. *Of all the stupid, despicable bullies,* she thought, pulling harder on Larry's hand. The child was still crying. Always before she had felt a tender pity for his defenseless little body, the frail arms, the narrow shoulders with sharp, winglike shoulder blades, the thin and unsure legs, but now her mouth tightened in resentment.

26 "Stop crying," she said sharply. "I'm ashamed of you!" She felt as if all three of them were tracking mud along the street. The child cried louder.

27 *If there had been an issue involved,* she thought, *if there had been something to fight for. . . . But what else could he possibly have done? Allow himself to be beaten? Attempt to educate the man? Call a policeman? "Officer, there's a man in the park who won't stop his child from throwing sand on mine. . . ."* The whole thing was as silly as that, and not worth thinking about.

28 "Can't you keep him quiet, for Pete's sake?" Morton asked irritably.

29 "What do you suppose I've been trying to do?" she asked.

30 Larry pulled back, dragging his feet.

31 "If you can't discipline this child, I will," Morton snapped, making a move toward the boy.

32 But her voice stopped him. She was shocked to hear it, thin and cold and penetrating with contempt. "Indeed?" she heard herself say. "You and who else?"

***William Carlos Williams** (1883–1963) is one of the most important poets of the twentieth century, best known for his long poem* Paterson *(1946–1958). He also wrote essays, plays, novels, and short stories. "The Use of Force" was published initially in* The Doctor Stories *(1933), a collection loosely based on Williams's experiences as a pediatrician.*

The Use of Force

William Carlos Williams

1 They were new patients to me, all I had was the name, Olson. Please come down as soon as you can, my daughter is very sick.

2 When I arrived I was met by the mother, a big startled-looking woman, very clean and apologetic, who merely said, Is this the doctor? and let me in. In the back, she added. You must excuse us, doctor, we have her in the kitchen where it is warm. It is very damp here sometimes.

3 The child was fully dressed and sitting on her father's lap near the kitchen table. He tried to get up, but I motioned for him not to bother, took off my overcoat and started to look things over. I could see that they were all very nervous, eyeing me up and down distrustfully. As often, in such cases, they weren't telling me more than they had to, it was up to me to tell them; that's why they were spending three dollars on me.

4 The child was fairly eating me up with her cold, steady eyes, and no expression to her face whatever. She did not move and seemed, inwardly, quiet; an unusually attractive little thing, and as strong as a heifer in appearance. But her face was flushed, she was breathing rapidly, and I realized that she had a high fever. She had magnificent blonde hair, in profusion. One of those picture children often reproduced in advertising leaflets and the photogravure sections of the Sunday papers.

5 She's had a fever for three days, began the father, and we don't know what it comes from. My wife has given her things, you know, like people do, but it don't do no good. And there's been a lot of sickness around. So we tho't you better look her over and tell us what is the matter.

6 As doctors often do I took a trial shot at it as a point of departure. Has she had a sore throat?

7 Both parents answered me together, No . . . No, she says her throat don't hurt her.

8 Does your throat hurt you? added the mother to the child. But the little girl's expression didn't change nor did she move her eyes from my face.

9 Have you looked?

10 I tried, said the mother, but I couldn't see.

As it happens we had been having a number of cases of diphtheria in the school to 11
which this child went during that month and we were all, quite apparently, thinking of that, though no one had as yet spoken of the thing.

Well, I said, suppose we take a look at the throat first. I smiled in my best profes- 12
sional manner and asking for the child's first name I said, come on, Mathilda, open your mouth and let's take a look at your throat.

Nothing doing. 13

Aw, come on, I coaxed, just open your mouth wide and let me take a look. Look, I 14
said opening both hands wide, I haven't anything in my hands. Just open up and let me see.

Such a nice man, put in the mother. Look how kind he is to you. Come on, do what 15
he tells you to. He won't hurt you.

At that I ground my teeth in disgust. If only they wouldn't use the word "hurt" I might 16
be able to get somewhere. But I did not allow myself to be hurried or disturbed but speaking quietly and slowly I approached the child again.

As I moved my chair a little nearer suddenly with one catlike movement both her 17
hands clawed instinctively for my eyes and she almost reached them too. In fact she knocked my glasses flying and they fell, though unbroken, several feet away from me on the kitchen floor.

Both the mother and father almost turned themselves inside out in embarrassment 18
and apology. You bad girl, said the mother, taking her and shaking her by one arm. Look what you've done. The nice man . . .

For heaven's sake, I broke in. Don't call me a nice man to her. I'm here to look at 19
her throat on the chance that she might have diphtheria and possibly die of it. But that's nothing to her. Look here, I said to the child, we're going to look at your throat. You're old enough to understand what I'm saying. Will you open it now by yourself or shall we have to open it for you?

Not a move. Even her expression hadn't changed. Her breaths however were com- 20
ing faster and faster. Then the battle began. I had to do it. I had to have a throat culture for her own protection. But first I told the parents that it was entirely up to them. I explained the danger but said that I would not insist on a throat examination so long as they would take the responsibility.

If you don't do what the doctor says you'll have to go to the hospital, the mother 21
admonished her severely.

Oh yeah? I had to smile to myself. After all, I had already fallen in love with the sav- 22
age brat, the parents were contemptible to me. In the ensuing struggle they grew more and more abject, crushed, exhausted while she surely rose to magnificent heights of insane fury of effort bred of her terror of me.

The father tried his best, and he was a big man, but the fact that she was his daugh- 23
ter, his shame at her behavior and his dread of hurting her made him release her just at the critical times when I had almost achieved success, till I wanted to kill him. But his dread also that she might have diphtheria made him tell me to go on, go on though he himself was almost fainting, while the mother moved back and forth behind us raising and lowering her hands in an agony of apprehension.

Put her in front of you on your lap, I ordered, and hold both her wrists. 24

But as soon as he did the child let out a scream. Don't, you're hurting me. Let go of my hands. Let them go I tell you. Then she shrieked terrifyingly, hysterically. Stop it! Stop it! You're killing me! 25

Do you think she can stand it, doctor! said the mother. 26

You get out, said the husband to his wife. Do you want her to die of diphtheria? 27

Come on now, hold her, I said. 28

Then I grasped the child's head with my left hand and tried to get the wooden tongue depressor between her teeth. She fought, with clenched teeth, desperately! But now I also had grown furious—at a child. I tried to hold myself down but I couldn't. I know how to expose a throat for inspection. And I did my best. When finally I got the wooden spatula behind the last teeth and just the point of it into the mouth cavity, she opened up for an instant but before I could see anything she came down again and gripping the wooden blade between her molars she reduced it to splinters before I could get it out again. 29

Aren't you ashamed, the mother yelled at her. Aren't you ashamed to act like that in front of the doctor? 30

Get me a smooth-handled spoon of some sort, I told the mother. We're going through with this. The child's mouth was already bleeding. Her tongue was cut and she was screaming in wild hysterical shrieks. Perhaps I should have desisted and come back in an hour or more. No doubt it would have been better. But I have seen at least two children lying dead in bed of neglect in such cases, and feeling that I must get a diagnosis now or never I went at it again. But the worst of it was that I too had got beyond reason. I could have torn the child apart in my own fury and enjoyed it. It was a pleasure to attack her. My face was burning with it. 31

The damned little brat must be protected against her own idiocy, one says to oneself at such times. Others must be protected against her. It is a social necessity. And all these things are true. But a blind fury, a feeling of adult shame, bred of a longing for muscular release are the operatives. One goes on to the end. 32

In a final unreasoning assault I overpowered the child's neck and jaws. I forced the heavy silver spoon back of her teeth and down her throat till she gagged. And there it was—both tonsils covered with membrane. She had fought valiantly to keep me from knowing her secret. She had been hiding that sore throat for three days at least and lying to her parents in order to escape just such an outcome as this. 33

Now truly she was furious. She had been on the defensive before but now she attacked. Tried to get off her father's lap and fly at me while tears of defeat blinded her eyes. 34

Sandra Tsing Loh *(b. 1962) is a writer and performer. Her books include* Depth Takes a Holiday: Essays from Lesser Los Angeles *(1996),* Aliens in America *(1997),* If You Lived Here, You'd Be Home by Now *(1997), and* A Year in Van Nuys *(2001). "My Father's Chinese Wives" won the Pushcart Prize for fiction in 1995. Loh's witty commentary can be heard on* The Loh Life *on public radio in Los Angeles, where she lives, and she is a frequent guest on National Public Radio's* Morning Edition.

My Father's Chinese Wives

Sandra Tsing Loh

1 My father doesn't want to alarm us. But then again, it would not be fair to hide anything either. The fact is, at 70, he is going to try and get married again. This time to a Chinese wife. He thinks this would be more suitable than to someone American, given his advanced age.

2 He has written his family in Shanghai, and is awaiting response. He is hoping to be married within six months.

3 Let us unpeel this news one layer at a time.

4 Question: At this point, is my father even what one would consider marriageable?

5 At age 70, my father—a retired Chinese aerospace engineer—is starting to look more and more like somebody's gardener. His feet shuffle along the patio in their broken sandals. He stoops to pull out one or two stray weeds, coughing phlegmatically. He wears a hideous old crew-neck tennis sweater. Later, he sits in a rattan chair and eats leathery green vegetables in brown sauce, his old eyes slitted wearily.

6 He is the sort of person one would refer to as "Old Dragon Whiskers." And not just because it is a picturesque Oriental way of speaking.

7 "I am old now," he started saying, about 10 years after my mother had died of cancer. "I'm just your crazy old Chinese father." He would rock backwards in his chair and sigh. "I am an old, old man . . ."

8 At times he almost seems to be over-acting this lizardy old part. He milks it. After all, he still does the same vigorous exercise regime—45 minutes of pull-ups, something that looks like the twist and much bellowing—he did 10 years ago. This always performed on the most public beaches possible, in his favorite Speedo—one he found in a dumpster.

9 "Crazy old Chinese father" is, in truth, a code word, a rationalization for the fact that my father has always had a problem . . . spending money. Why buy a briefcase to carry to work, when an empty Frosted Flakes Cereal box will do? Papers slip down neatly inside, and pens can be clipped conveniently on either side.

10 Why buy Bounty Paper Towels when, at work, he can just walk down the hall to the washroom, open the dispenser, and lift out a stack? They're free—he can bring home as many as we want!

11 If you've worn the same sweater for so many years that the elbows wear out, turn it around! Get another decade out of it! Which is why to this day, my father wears only crew neck, not V-neck sweaters . . .

12 Why drive the car to work when you can take the so-convenient RTD[1] bus? More time to read interesting scientific papers . . . and here they are, in my empty Frosted Flakes Box!

13 "Terrific!" is my older sister Kaitlin's response when I phone her with the news. Bear in mind that Kaitlin has not seen my father since the mid-'80s, preferring to nurse her bad memories of him independently, via a therapist. She allows herself a laugh, laying aside her customary dull hostility for a moment of more jocular hostility. "So who does he think would want to marry *him?*"

---

[1] The Los Angeles Rapid Transit District system.

"Someone Chinese," I answer. 14

"Oh good!" she exclaims. "That narrows down the field . . . to what? Half a billion? Nah, as always, he's doing this to punish us. 15

"Think about it," Kaitlin continues with her usual chilling logic. "He marries a German woman the first time around. It's a disaster. You and I represent that. Because he's passive aggressive and he's cheap. But no, to him, it's that rebellious Aryan[2] strain that's the problem. 16

"You take an Asian immigrant just off the boat, on the other hand. This is a person who has just fled a Communist government and a horrible life working in a bicycle factory for 10 cents a month and no public sanitation and repeated floggings every hour on the hour. After that, living with our father might seem like just another bizarre interlude. It could happen." 17

Kaitlin scores some compelling points, but nonetheless . . . 18

I'm bothered for a different reason . . . 19

Perhaps it is because in describing the potential new wife, he has used only that one adjective: *Chinese.* He has not said: "I'm looking for a smart wife," or even "a fat wife," he has picked "Chinese." It is meant to stand for so much. 20

Asian. Asian women. Asian *ladies.* 21

I think back to a college writing workshop I once attended. (No credit and perhaps that was appropriate.) It was long before my current "administrative assistant" job at Swanson Films. (Makers of the 10-minute instructional video "Laughterobics! Featuring Meredith Baxter Birney," among other fine titles.) 22

Anyway, the workshop contained 13 hysterical women—and one Fred. Fred was a wealthy Caucasian sixtysomething urologist; he was always serene and beautifully dressed and insistent upon holding the door open for me "because you're such a lovely lady." I always wore jeans and a USC sweatshirt, sometimes even sweatpants, so at first I did not know what he meant. 23

We women, on the other hand, were a wildly mixed group—writing anything from wintery Ann Beattie[3]–esque snippets to sci-fi romance/porn novels ("She would be King Zenothar's concubine,[4] whether she liked it or not"). We attacked each other's writing accordingly. People were bursting into tears every week, then making up by emotionally sharing stories about mutual eating disorders. 24

But there was one moment when all 13 women were of like minds. It was that moment when Fred would enter the classroom, laden with xeroxes, blushing shyly as a new bride. We would all look at each other as if to say, "Oh my God, Fred has brought in work *again.*" 25

As though springing from a murky bottomless well, each week new chapters would appear from this semi-epistolary novel Fred was penning about an elderly doctor named 26

---

[2] The blond-haired, blue-eyed ideal of Nazi Germany.

[3] A contemporary fiction writer known for her dry wit and penetrating family portraits.

[4] In some traditional societies, a live-in mistress.

Fred who goes on sabbatical for a year to Japan and there finds love with a 23-year-old Japanese medical student named Aku who smells of cherry blossoms.

There were many awkward scenes in which Fred and Aku were exploring each other's bodies as they lay—as far as I could gather—upon the bare floor, only a *tatami*[5] mat for comfort. (Fred would always italicize the Japanese words, as if to separate and somehow protect them from other, lesser words.) But it was all beautifully pure and unlike the urban squalor we find in America—the rock music, the drugs, the uncouth teenagers. 27

Anyway, I recall the one line that I have never since been able to blot from my mind. 28 I cannot think of it without a bit of a shiver. Nor the way he read it, in that hoarse tremulous voice . . .

"I put my hand in hers, and her little fingers opened like the petals of a moist flower." 29

It is a month later and, as in a dream, I sit at the worn formica family dining table 30 with my father, photos and letters spread before us.

Since my father has written to Shanghai, the mail has come pouring in. I have to 31 face the fact that my father is, well, hot. "You see?" he says. "Seven women have written! Ha!" He beams, his gold molar glinting. He is drinking steaming green tea from a beaker, which he handles with a Beauty and the Beast potholder.

Remarkably, my father doesn't make the least effort to mask his delight, no matter 32 how inappropriate. He is old now. *He can do whatever the hell he wants,* is how I now understand it. With a sigh, I turn to the photos. In spite of myself, I am wowed!

Tzau Pa, Ling Ling, Sui Pai, Chong Zhou . . . "28, administrative assistant," "47, 33 owner of a seamstress business," "39, freelance beautician." The words jump off the pages, both in English and Chinese translations. These women are dynamos, achievers, with black curly hair, in turtlenecks, jauntily riding bicycles, seated squarely on cannons before military museums, standing proudly with three grown daughters.

One thing unites them: they're all ready to leap off the mainland[6] at the drop of a 34 hat.

And don't think their careers and hobbies are going to keep them from being terrific 35 wives. Quite the opposite. Several already have excellent experience, including one who's been married twice already. The seamstress has sent him two shorts and several pairs of socks; there is much talk of seven-course meals and ironing and terrific expertise in gardening.

Super-achievement is a major theme that applies to all. And the biggest star of all 36 is my father. He clears his throat and gleefully reads from a letter by one Liu Tzun:

> Dr. Chow, your family has told me of your great scientific genius and of your many awards. I respect academic scholarship very highly, and would be honored to meet you on your next visit.

[5] The straw mat traditionally used in Japan as floor covering.

[6] China as opposed to Taiwan.

"You see?" my father chuckles. "They have a lot of respect for me in China. When 37
I go there, they treat me like President Bush! Free meals, free drinks . . . I don't pay for anything!"

"He had his chance. He got married once, for 25 years. He was a terrible husband 38
and a worse father."

Kaitlin is weighing in. All jokes are off. Her fury blazes away, further aggravated by 39
the fact that she is going through a divorce and hates her $50,000 a year job. Her monthly Nordstrom[7] bills are astronomical. MCI is positively crackling.

"He's a single man," I say. "Mum's been gone for 12 years now—" 40

"And now he gets a second try—just like that?" Kaitlin exclaims. "Clean slate? Start 41
right over? Buy a wife? It makes me sick. He is totally unqualified to sustain a marriage. A family structure of any kind collapses around him. Do you even remember one happy Christmas?"

Twinkling lights and tinsel suddenly swirl before me and looking deeper, through 42
green foliage, I see my mother looking beautiful and crisp in lipstick and pearls, her wavy auburn hair done . . . except for the fact that she is hysterical, and my father, his face a mask of disgust so extreme it is almost parodic, is holding his overpriced new V-necked tennis sweater from Saks[8] out in front of him like it is a dead animal —

"I try to block it out," is what I say. 43

"Well I was six years older than you so I can't." Kaitlin's pain is raw. "Why does he 44
deserve to be happy . . . now? He made Mama miserable in her lifetime—he was so cheap! I think she was almost glad to go as soon as she did! A $70 dress, leaving the heater on overnight, too much spent on a nice steak dinner—he could never let anything go! He could never just let it go! He just could . . . not . . . let . . . things . . . go!"

Meanwhile . . . 45

On its own gentle time clock, unsullied by the raging doubts of his two daughters . . . 46

My father's project bursts into flower. 47

And 47-year-old Liu—the writer of the magic letter—is the lucky winner! Within 48
three months, she is flown to Los Angeles. She and my father are married a week later.

I do not get to meet her right away, but my father fills me in on the stats. And I have 49
to confess, I'm a little surprised at how modern she is, how urban. Liu is a divorcee with, well, with ambitions in the entertainment business. Although she speaks no English, she seems to be an expert on American culture. The fact that Los Angeles is near Hollywood has not escaped her. This is made clear to me one Sunday evening, three weeks later, via telephone.

"I know you have friends in the entertainment business," my father declares. He has 50
never fully grasped the fact that I am a typist and that Swanson Films' clients include such Oscar contenders as Kraft Foods and Motorola.

---

[7] An upscale department store chain.

[8] An upscale department store chain.

"Aside from having knitted me a new sweater and playing the piano," my father con- 51
tinues, "you should know that Liu is an excellent singer—" Turning away from the phone, he and his new wife exchange a series of staccato reports in Mandarin,[9] which mean nothing to me.

"I'm sure that Liu is quite accomplished," I reply, "it's just that—" 52

"Oh . . . she's terr-ific!" my father exclaims, shocked that I may be calling Liu's musi- 53
cal talent into question. "You want to hear her sing? Here, here, I will put her on the phone right now . . ."

Creeping into my father's voice is a tremulous note that is sickeningly familiar. How 54
many times had I heard it during my childhood as I was being pushed towards the piano, kicking and screaming? How many times—

But that was 20 years ago. I gulp terror back down. I live in my own apartment now, 55
full of director's chairs, potted fici,[10] and Matisse[11] posters. I will be fine. My father has moved on to a totally new pushee . . .

Who picks up the phone, sighs—then bursts out triumphantly: 56

"Nee-ee hoo-oo man, tieh-hen see bau-hau jioo . . . !" 57

I have left you and taken the Toyota, Dr. Chow—so there!

Five weeks later, Liu just packs up her suitcase, makes some sandwiches, and 58
takes off in the family Toyota. She leaves her note on the same formica table at which she'd first won his heart.

My father is in shock. Then again, he is philosophical. 59

"Liu—she had a lot of problems. She said she had no one to talk to. There were no 60
other Chinese people in Tarzana.[12] She wanted me to give her gifts. She was bored. You know I don't like to go out at night. But I tell her, 'Go! See your friends in Chinatown.' But Liu does not want to take the bus. She wants to drive! But you know me, your cheap father. I don't want to pay her insurance. That Liu—she was a very bad driver—"

"Ha!" is Kaitlin's only comment. 61

Summer turns to fall in Southern California, causing the palm trees to sway a bit. 62
The divorce is soon final, Liu's settlement including $10,000, the microwave and the Toyota.

Never one to dwell, my father has picked a new bride: Zhou Ping, 37, home-maker 63
from Qang-Zhou province. I groan.

"But no . . . Zhou Ping is very good," my father insists. He has had several phone 64
conversations with her. "And she comes very highly recommended, not, I have to say, like Liu. Liu was bad, that one. Zhou Ping is sensible and hard-working. She has had a tough life. Boy! She worked in a coal mine in Manchuria[13] until she was 25. The winters

---

[9] The most widely spoken language or dialect in China.

[10] Ficus trees, a genus that includes the fig tree.

[11] The French painter Henri Matisse.

[12] A Los Angeles suburb.

[13] A region in northeast China.

there were very, very bitter! She had to make her own shoes and clothing. Then she worked on a farming collective, where she raised cattle and grew many different kinds of crops—by herself!"

65 "I'm sure she's going to fit in really well in Los Angeles," I say.

66 Zhou Ping is indeed a different sort. The news, to my astonishment, comes from Kaitlin. "I received . . ." her voice trails off, the very words seeming to elude her. "A *birthday card.* From Papa . . . and *Zhou Ping.*"

67 My sister continues in a kind of trance of matter-of-factness, as if describing some curious archaeological artifact. "Let's see, on the front is a picture with flowers on it. It's from Hallmark. Inside is gold lettering, cursive, that says, 'Happy Birthday!' At the bottom, in red pen, it says . . . 'Love, Zhou Ping and *your* Dad.'"

68 "Your 'Dad'?"

69 "I think Zhou Ping put him up to this. The envelope is not addressed in his handwriting. Nonetheless . . ." Kaitlin thinks it over, concurs with herself. "Yes. Yes. I believe this is the first birthday card I've ever received from him in my life. The first. It's totally bizarre."

70 A week later, Kaitlin receives birthday gifts in the mail: a sweater hand-knit by Zhou Ping, and a box of "mooncakes."[14] She is flipping out. "Oh no," she worries, "Now I really have to call and thank her. I mean, the poor woman probably has no friends in America. Who knows what he's having her do? We may be her only link to society!"

71 Kaitlin finally does call, managing to catch Zhou Ping when my father is on the beach doing his exercises (which he always does at 11 and at 3). Although Zhou Ping's English is very broken, she somehow convinces Kaitlin to fly down for a visit.

72 It will be Kaitlin's first trip home since our mother's passing. And my first meeting of either of my step-mothers.

73 I pull up the familiar driveway in my Geo. Neither Kaitlin nor I say anything. We peer out the windows.

74 The yard doesn't look too bad. There are new sprinklers, and a kind of irrigation system made by a network of ingenuously placed rain gutters. Soil has been turned, and thoughtfully. Cypresses have been trimmed. Enormous bundles of weeds flank the driveway, as if for some momentous occasion.

75 We ring the doorbell. Neither of us has had keys to the house in years.

76 The door opens. A short, somewhat plump Chinese woman, in round glasses and a perfect bowl haircut, beams at us. She is wearing a bright yellow "I hate housework!" apron that my mother was once given as a gag gift—and I think never wore.

77 "Kat-lin! Jen-na!" she exclaims in what seems like authentic joy, embracing us. She is laughing and almost crying with emotion.

---

[14] Traditional Chinese palm-sized round cakes that symbolize family unity and perfection.

In spite of myself, giggles begin to well up from inside me as if from a spring. I can't help it: I feel warm and euphoric. Authentic joy is contagious. Who cares who this woman is: no one has been this happy to see me in ages. 78

"Wel-come home," Zhou Ping says, with careful emphasis. She turns to Kaitlin, a shadow falling over her face. "I am glad you finally come home to see your Daddy," she says in a low, sorrowful voice. She looks over her shoulder. "He old now." 79

Then, as if exhausted by that effort, Zhou Ping collapses into giggles. I sneak a glance over at Kaitlin, whose expression seems to be straining somewhere between joy and nausea. Pleasantries lunge out of my mouth: "It's nice to finally meet you!" "How do you like America?" "I've heard so much about your cooking!" 80

My father materializes behind a potted plant. He is wearing a new sweater and oddly formal dress pants. His gaze hovers somewhere near the floor. 81

"Hul-lo," he declares, attempting a smile. "Long time no see!" he exclaims, not making eye contact, but in Kaitlin's general direction. 82

"Yes!" Kaitlin exclaims back, defiant, a kind of winged Amazon[15] in perfect beige Anne Klein II leisurewear. "It certainly is!" 83

My father stands stiffly. 84

Kaitlin blazes. 85

"It's good to see you!" he finally concludes, as though this were something he learned in English class. 86

Feeling, perhaps, that we should all leave well enough alone, the Chow family, such as we are, moves on through the house. It is ablaze with color—the sort of eye-popping combinations one associates with Thai restaurants and Hindu shrines. There are big purple couches, peach rugs, a shiny brass trellis and creeping charlies everywhere. 87

All this redecorating came at no great expense, though. "See this rug?" my father says proudly, while Zhou Ping giggles. "She found it in a dumpster. They were going to throw it away!" "Throw it away!" she exclaims. "See? It very nice." 88

Over their heads, Kaitlin silently mouths one word to me: "Help." 89

Beyond, the formica dining room table is set. Oddly. There are little rice bowls, chopsticks, and a sheet of plain white paper at each place setting. It is good to know some definite event has been planned. Kaitlin, my father and I are so unaccustomed to being in a room together that any kind of definite agenda—aka: "We'll eat dinner, and then we'll leave"—is comforting. 90

My father goes off to put some music on his new CD player. "That bad Liu made me buy it!" he explains. "But it's nice." Zhou Ping bustles into the kitchen. "Dinner ready—in five minute!" she declares. 91

Kaitlin waits a beat, then pulls me aside into the bathroom and slams the door. 92

"This is so weird!" she hisses. 93

We have not stood together in this bathroom for some 15 years. It seems different. I notice that the wallpaper is faded, the towels are new—but no, it's something else. On one wall is my mother's framed reproduction of the brown Da Vinci etching called *Pray-* 94

[15] A woman warrior in Greek mythology.

ing Hands which she had always kept in her sewing room. Right next to it, in shocking juxtaposition, is a green, red, blue and yellow "Bank of Canton" calendar from which a zaftig[16] Asian female chortles.

95 "I can't go through with this!" Kaitlin continues in stage whisper. "It's too weird! There are so many memories here, and not good ones!"

96 And like debris from a hurricane, the words tumble out:

97 "I go by the kitchen and all I can see is me standing before the oven clock at age five with tears in my eyes. He is yelling: 'What time is it? The little hand is most of the way to four and the big hand is on the eight! It was 3:18 twenty-two minutes ago—so what time is it now? What's eighteen plus twenty-two? Come on—you can do it in your head! Come on! Come on!'

98 "I go by the dining room and I see him hurling my Nancy Drew books[17] across the floor. They slam against the wall and I huddle against Mum, screaming. 'Why do you waste your time on this when your algebra homework isn't finished? You . . . good for nothing! You're nothing, nothing—you'll never amount to anything!'

99 "I go by the bedroom—"

100 "Please—" I have this sickening feeling like I'm going to cry, that I'm just going to lose it. I want to just sit down in the middle of the floor and roll myself into a ball. But I can't. Kaitlin's rage is like something uncontainable, a dreadful natural force, and I am the gatekeeper. I feel if I open the door, it will rush out and destroy the house and everyone in it. "Please," is what I end up whispering. "Please. Let's just eat. We'll be done in a hour. Then we can go home. I promise. You won't have to do this again for another 10 years—or maybe ever."

101 At dinner, endless plates of food twirl their way out of the kitchen, Zhou Ping practically dancing underneath. Spinach, teriyaki[18]-ish chicken, shrimp, some kind of egg thing with peas, dumplings packed with little pillows of pork.

102 And amazingly, there is no want of conversational material. Photos from Shanghai are being pulled out of envelopes and passed around, of her family, his family . . .

103 I do recognize three or four Chinese relatives—a cousin, an aunt, a grand-uncle? Their names are impossible for me to remember. We had met them in China during our last trip as a family. I was 15; it was right before our mother started to get sick.

104 Shanghai is a distant, confused memory for me, of ringing bicycle bells and laundry lines hanging from buildings. What I do remember is how curious my father's family had seemed about Kaitlin and me, his odd American experiment, oohing over our height and touching our auburn hair. There were many smiles but no intelligible conversation, at least to our ears. We probably won't see any of these people again before we die.

105 Zhou Ping, though, is determined to push through, to forge a bridge between us. She plunges ahead with her bad English, my father almost absent-mindedly correcting her.

---

[16] Yiddish for *pleasantly plump*.

[17] A popular series of mystery books featuring a teenage girl detective.

[18] A Japanese style of marinating and grilling.

Their lives are abuzz with activity. Zhou Ping is taking piano lessons at the com- 106
munity college. My father is learning Italian and French off the Learning Channel—he sets his alarm for four in the morning. "So early!" Zhou Ping hoots. They listen to Karl Haas' *Listening to Good Music* on the classical station at 10. "Mot-sart[19]—he very nice!" They have joined the Bahais,[20] a local quasi-religious group. "I must cook food all the time!" My father suddenly puts his spoon down. He is chewing slowly, a frown growing.

"This meat . . ." he shakes his head, "is very greasy." 107

He turns to Zhou Ping and the lines at both sides of his mouth deepen. His eyes 108
cloud. He says something to her in Chinese, with a certain sharp cadence that makes my spine stiffen . . .

Zhou Ping's face goes blank for a moment. Her eyes grow big. My stomach turns 109
to ice.

How will she respond? By throwing her napkin down, bursting into tears, running 110
from the room? Will she knock the table over, plates sliding after each other, sauces spilling, crockery breaking? Will we hear the car engine turn over as she drives off into the night, to leave us frightened and panicked?

It is none of these things. 111

Zhou Ping's head tilts back, her eyes crinkle . . . 112

And laughter pours out of her, peal after peal after peal. It is a big laugh, an enor- 113
mous laugh, the laugh of a woman who has birthed calves and hoed crops and seen harsh winters decimate countrysides. Pointing to our father, Zhou Ping turns to us with large glittering eyes and says words which sound incredible to our ears:

"Your Papa—he so funny!" 114

My jaw drops. No one has ever laughed out loud at this table, ever. We laughed 115
behind closed doors, in our bedrooms, in the bathroom, never before my father. We laughed sometimes with my mother, on those glorious days when he would be off on a trip—

But Kaitlin is not laughing. She is trembling; her face is turning red. 116

"Why were you always so angry?" Kaitlin cries out in a strangled voice. It is the 117
question that she has waited 30 years to ask. "Why were you so angry?"

There is shocked silence. My father looks weary and embarrassed. He smiles wanly 118
and shrugs his thin shoulders.

"No really," Kaitlin insists. "All those years. With Mama. Why?" 119

"I don't know," my father murmurs. "People get angry." 120

And I know, in that moment, that he doesn't have an answer. He literally doesn't. It's 121
as if anger was this chemical which reacted on him for 20 years. Who knows why, but like some kind of spirit, it has left him now. The rage is spent. He is old now. He is old.

Dusk has fallen, and long shadows fall across the worn parquet floor of the dining 122
room. After a moment of silence, my father asks Zhou Ping to sing a song. The hausfrau[21]

---

[19] The Austrian classical composer Wolfgang Amadeus Mozart.

[20] Members of Baha'i, a worldwide religion with more than five million followers.

[21] German for *housewife.*

from Qang Zhou opens her mouth and with an odd dignity, sings simply and slowly. My father translates.

From the four corners of the earth
My lover comes to me
Playing the lute
Like the wind over the water

He recites the words without embarrassment, almost without emotion. And why shouldn't he? The song has nothing to do with him personally: it is from some old Chinese fable. It has to do with missing someone, something, that perhaps one can't even define any more. 123

As Zhou Ping sings, everyone longs for home. But what home? Zhou Ping—for her bitter winters? My father—for the Shanghai he left 40 years ago? Kaitlin and I? We are even sitting in our home, and we long for it. 124

***James Joyce** (1882–1941), a native of Dublin, Ireland, is considered one of the most influential writers of the early twentieth century. "Araby," one of his most often anthologized stories, first appeared in the collection* Dubliners *in 1914. Like his novel* Portrait of the Artist as a Young Man, *published two years later, it relies on scenes from Joyce's own boyhood.*

Araby

James Joyce

North Richmond Street, being blind,[1] was a quiet street except at the hour when the Christian Brothers' School set the boys free. An uninhabited house of two storeys stood at the blind end, detached from its neighbours in a square ground. The other houses of the street, conscious of decent lives within them, gazed at one another with brown imperturbable faces. 1

The former tenant of our house, a priest, had died in the back drawing-room. Air, musty from having been long enclosed, hung in all the rooms, and the waste room behind the kitchen was littered with old useless papers. Among these I found a few paper-covered books, the pages of which were curled and damp: *The Abbot,* by Walter Scott, *The Devout Communicant* and *The Memoirs of Vidocq.*[2] I liked the last best because its leaves were yellow. The wild garden behind the house contained a central apple-tree and a few straggling bushes under one of which I found the late tenant's rusty bicycle-pump. He had been a very charitable priest; in his will he had left all his money to institutions and the furniture of his house to his sister. 2

[1] A dead end. The young Joyce in fact lived for a time on North Richmond Street in Dublin.

[2] *The Devout Communicant* is a collection of religious meditations. *The Abbot* is a historical romance set in the court of Mary, Queen of Scots, a Catholic, who was beheaded for plotting to assassinate her Protestant cousin, Queen Elizabeth I. *The Memoirs of Vidocq* is a collection of sexually suggestive stories about a French criminal turned detective.

When the short days of winter came dusk fell before we had well eaten our dinners. When we met in the street the houses had grown sombre. The space of sky above us was the colour of ever-changing violet and towards it the lamps of the street lifted their feeble lanterns. The cold air stung us and we played till our bodies glowed. Our shouts echoed in the silent street. The career of our play brought us through the dark muddy lanes behind the houses where we ran the gauntlet of the rough tribes from the cottages, to the back doors of the dark dripping gardens where odours arose from the ashpits, to the dark odorous stables where a coachman smoothed and combed the horse or shook music from the buckled harness. When we returned to the street light from the kitchen windows had filled the areas. If my uncle was seen turning the corner we hid in the shadow until we had seen him safely housed. Or if Mangan's sister came out on the doorstep to call her brother in to his tea we watched her from our shadow peer up and down the street. We waited to see whether she would remain or go in and, if she remained, we left our shadow and walked up to Mangan's steps resignedly. She was waiting for us, her figure defined by the light from the half-opened door. Her brother always teased her before he obeyed and I stood by the railings looking at her. Her dress swung as she moved her body and the soft rope of her hair tossed from side to side. 3

Every morning I lay on the floor in the front parlour watching her door. The blind was pulled down to within an inch of the sash so that I could not be seen. When she came out on the doorstep my heart leaped. I ran to the hall, seized my books and followed her. I kept her brown figure always in my eye and, when we came near the point at which our ways diverged, I quickened my pace and passed her. This happened morning after morning. I had never spoken to her, except for a few casual words, and yet her name was like a summons to all my foolish blood. 4

Her image accompanied me even in places the most hostile to romance. On Saturday evenings when my aunt went marketing I had to go to carry some of the parcels. We walked through the flaring streets, jostled by drunken men and bargaining women, amid the curses of labourers, the shrill litanies of shop-boys who stood on guard by the barrels of pigs' cheeks, the nasal chanting of street-singers, who sang a *come-all-you* about O'Donovan Rossa,[3] or a ballad about the troubles in our native land. These noises converged in a single sensation of life for me: I imagined that I bore my chalice safely through a throng of foes. Her name sprang to my lips at moments in strange prayers and praises which I myself did not understand. My eyes were often full of tears (I could not tell why) and at times a flood from my heart seemed to pour itself out into my bosom. I thought little of the future. I did not know whether I would ever speak to her or not or, if I spoke to her, how I could tell her of my confused adoration. But my body was like a harp and her words and gestures were like fingers running upon the wires. 5

One evening I went into the back drawing-room in which the priest had died. It was a dark rainy evening and there was no sound in the house. Through one of the broken panes I heard the rain impinge upon the earth, the fine incessant needles of water playing in the sodden beds. Some distant lamp or lighted window gleamed below me. I was thankful that I could see so little. All my senses seemed to desire to veil themselves and, 6

[3] A contemporary leader of an underground organization opposed to British rule of Ireland.

feeling that I was about to slip from them, I pressed the palms of my hands together until they trembled, murmuring: *"O love! O love!"* many times.

At last she spoke to me. When she addressed the first words to me I was so confused that I did not know what to answer. She asked me was I going to Araby. I forgot whether I answered yes or no. It would be a splendid bazaar, she said she would love to go.[4] 7

"And why can't you?" I asked. 8

While she spoke she turned a silver bracelet round and round her wrist. She could not go, she said, because there would be a retreat that week in her convent. Her brother and two other boys were fighting for their caps and I was alone at the railings. She held one of the spikes, bowing her head towards me. The light from the lamp opposite our door caught the white curve of her neck, lit up her hair that rested there and, falling, lit up the hand upon the railing. It fell over one side of her dress and caught the white border of a petticoat, just visible as she stood at ease. 9

"It's well for you," she said. 10

"If I go," I said, "I will bring you something." 11

What innumerable follies laid waste my waking and sleeping thoughts after that evening! I wished to annihilate the tedious intervening days. I chafed against the work of school. At night in my bedroom and by day in the classroom her image came between me and the page I strove to read. The syllables of the word *Araby* were called to me through the silence in which my soul luxuriated and cast an Eastern enchantment over me. I asked for leave to go to the bazaar on Saturday night. My aunt was surprised and hoped it was not some Freemason affair.[5] I answered few questions in class. I watched my master's face pass from amiability to sternness; he hoped I was not beginning to idle. I could not call my wandering thoughts together. I had hardly any patience with the serious work of life which, now that it stood between me and my desire, seemed to me child's play, ugly monotonous child's play. 12

On Saturday morning I reminded my uncle that I wished to go to the bazaar in the evening. He was fussing at the hallstand, looking for the hatbrush, and answered me curtly: 13

"Yes, boy, I know." 14

As he was in the hall I could not go into the front parlour and lie at the window. I left the house in bad humour and walked slowly towards the school. The air was pitilessly raw and already my heart misgave me. 15

When I came home to dinner my uncle had not yet been home. Still it was early. I sat staring at the clock for some time and, when its ticking began to irritate me, I left the room. I mounted the staircase and gained the upper part of the house. The high cold 16

---

[4] Traveling bazaars featured cafés, shopping stalls, and entertainment. Araby was the name of an English bazaar that visited Dublin when Joyce was a boy.

[5] The Freemasons is a secretive fraternal order that has a long history and that has traditionally been opposed by the Catholic Church.

empty gloomy rooms liberated me and I went from room to room singing. From the front window I saw my companions playing below in the street. Their cries reached me weakened and indistinct and, leaning my forehead against the cool glass, I looked over at the dark house where she lived. I may have stood there for an hour, seeing nothing but the brown-clad figure cast by my imagination, touched discreetly by the lamplight at the curved neck, at the hand upon the railings and at the border below the dress.

When I came downstairs again I found Mrs. Mercer sitting at the fire. She was an 17
old garrulous woman, a pawnbroker's widow, who collected used stamps for some pious purpose. I had to endure the gossip of the tea-table. The meal was prolonged beyond an hour and still my uncle did not come. Mrs. Mercer stood up to go: she was sorry she couldn't wait any longer, but it was after eight o'clock and she did not like to be out late, as the night air was bad for her. When she had gone I began to walk up and down the room, clenching my fists. My aunt said:

"I'm afraid you may put off your bazaar for this night of Our Lord." 18

At nine o'clock I heard my uncle's latchkey in the halldoor. I heard him talking to him- 19
self and heard the hallstand rocking when it had received the weight of his overcoat. I could interpret these signs. When he was midway through his dinner I asked him to give me the money to go to the bazaar. He had forgotten.

"The people are in bed and after their first sleep now," he said. 20

I did not smile. My aunt said to him energetically: 21

"Can't you give him the money and let him go? You've kept him late enough as it is." 22

My uncle said he was very sorry he had forgotten. He said he believed in the old 23
saying: "All work and no play makes Jack a dull boy." He asked me where I was going and, when I had told him a second time he asked me did I know *The Arab's Farewell to His Steed.* When I left the kitchen he was about to recite the opening lines of the piece to my aunt.

I held a florin tightly in my hand as I strode down Buckingham Street towards the 24
station. The sight of the streets thronged with buyers and glaring with gas recalled to me the purpose of my journey. I took my seat in a third-class carriage of a deserted train. After an intolerable delay the train moved out of the station slowly. It crept onward among ruinous houses and over the twinkling river. At Westland Row Station a crowd of people pressed to the carriage doors; but the porters moved them back, saying that it was a special train for the bazaar. I remained alone in the bare carriage. In a few minutes the train drew up beside an improvised wooden platform. I passed out on to the road and saw by the lighted dial of a clock that it was ten minutes to ten. In front of me was a large building which displayed the magical name.

I could not find any sixpenny entrance and, fearing that the bazaar would be closed, 25
I passed in quickly through a turnstile, handing a shilling to a weary-looking man. I found myself in a big hall girdled at half its height by a gallery. Nearly all the stalls were closed and the greater part of the hall was in darkness. I recognised a silence like that which pervades a church after a service. I walked into the centre of the bazaar timidly. A few people were gathered about the stalls which were still open. Before a curtain, over which

the words *Café Chantant*[6] were written in coloured lamps, two men were counting money on a salver. I listened to the fall of the coins.

Remembering with difficulty why I had come I went over to one of the stalls and 26
examined porcelain vases and flowered tea-sets. At the door of the stall a young lady was talking and laughing with two young gentlemen. I remarked their English accents and listened vaguely to their conversation.

"O, I never said such a thing!" 27

"O, but you did!" 28

"O, but I didn't!" 29

"Didn't she say that?" 30

"Yes. I heard her." 31

"O, there's a . . . fib!" 32

Observing me the young lady came over and asked me did I wish to buy anything. 33
The tone of her voice was not encouraging; she seemed to have spoken to me out of a sense of duty. I looked humbly at the great jars that stood like eastern guards at either side of the dark entrance to the stall and murmured:

"No, thank you." 34

The young lady changed the position of one of the vases and went back to the two 35
young men. They began to talk of the same subject. Once or twice the young lady glanced at me over her shoulder.

I lingered before her stall, though I knew my stay was useless, to make my interest 36
in her wares seem the more real. Then I turned away slowly and walked down the middle of the bazaar. I allowed the two pennies to fall against the sixpence in my pocket. I heard a voice call from one end of the gallery that the light was out. The upper part of the hall was now completely dark.

Gazing up into the darkness I saw myself as a creature driven and derided by van- 37
ity; and my eyes burned with anguish and anger.

---

[6] Literally, *singing café* (French), a music hall.

READINGS

The following two readings are essays written by students. Sally Crane and David Ratinov argue for different ways of understanding the ending of "Araby," the preceding short story by James Joyce. The Analyzing Writing Strategies section and the Commentary following each reading touch on a few features best illustrated by that essay, capturing its special qualities and strengths.

***Sally Crane** wrote this interpretive essay about James Joyce's "Araby" (p. 526) for her composition course. As her title suggests, Crane focuses on what the final scene tells about the boy's character. During class discussion, most of the other students said they thought the boy changes at the end of the story. In her essay, Crane argues that he is just as much in the dark at the end of the story as he was at the beginning. (*Note: *In citing paragraphs, Crane followed her instructor's special directions rather than MLA style.)*

Gazing into the Darkness

Sally Crane

Readers of "Araby" often focus on the final scene as the key to the story. They assume the boy experiences some profound insight about himself when he gazes "up into the darkness" (para. 37). I believe, however, that the boy sees nothing and learns nothing—about either himself or others. He's not self-reflective; he's merely self-absorbed. 1

The evidence supporting this interpretation is the imagery of blindness and the ironic point of view of the narrator. There can seem to be a profound insight at the end of the story only if we empathize with the boy and adopt his point of view. In other words, we must assume that the young boy is narrating his own story. But if the real narrator is the grown man looking back at his early adolescence, then it becomes possible to read the narrative as ironic and to see the boy as confused and blind. 2

The story opens and closes with images of blindness. The street is "blind" with an "uninhabited house . . . at the blind end" (para. 1). As he spies on Mangan's sister, from his own house, the boy intentionally limits what he is able to see by lowering the "blind" until it is only an inch from the window sash (para. 4). At the bazaar in the closing scene, "the light was out," and the upper part of the hall was "completely dark" (para. 36). The boy is left "gazing up into the darkness," seeing nothing but an inner torment that burns his eyes (para. 37). 3

This pattern of imagery includes images of reading, and reading stands for the boy's inability to understand what is before his eyes. When he tries to read at night, for example, the girl's "image [comes] between [him] and the page," in effect blinding him (para. 12). In fact, he seems blind to everything except this "image" of the "brown-clad figure cast by [his] imagination" (para. 16). The girl's "brown-clad figure" is also associated with the houses on "blind" North Richmond Street, with their "brown imperturbable faces" (para. 1). The houses stare back at the boy, unaffected by his presence and gaze. 4

The most important face he tries and fails to read belongs to Mangan's sister. His description of her and interpretation of the few words she says to him can be seen as further evidence of his blindness. He sees only what he wants to see, the "image" he has in his mind's eye. This image comes more from what he's read than from anything he's observed. He casts her simultaneously in the traditional female roles of angel and whore: 5

> While she spoke she turned a silver bracelet round and round her wrist. She could not go, she said, because there would be a retreat that week in her convent. . . . She held one of the spikes, bowing her head towards me. The light from the lamp opposite our door caught the white curve of her neck, lit up her hair that rested there and, falling,

> lit up the hand upon the railing. It fell over one side of her dress and caught the white border of a petticoat, just visible as she stood at ease. (para. 9)

Her angelic qualities are shown in her plans to attend a convent retreat and in her bowed head. Her whorish qualities come through in the way she flirtatiously plays with the bracelet, as if she were inviting him to buy her an expensive piece of jewelry at the bazaar. The "white curve of her neck" and the "white border of a petticoat" combine the symbolic color of purity, associated with the Madonna, with sexual suggestiveness (para. 9). The point is that there is no suggestion here or anywhere else in the story that the boy is capable of seeing Mangan's sister as a real person. She only exists as the object of his adoring gaze. In fact, no one seems to have any reality for him other than himself.

He is totally self-absorbed. But at the same time, he is also blind to himself. He says repeatedly that he doesn't understand his feelings: "Her name sprang to my lips at moments in strange prayers and praises which I myself did not understand. My eyes were often full of tears (I could not tell why)" (para. 5). His adoration of her is both "confused" and confusing to him. He has no self-understanding (para. 5). 6

The best insight we have into the boy comes from the language he uses. Much of his language seems to mimic the old priest's romantic books: "Her name was like a summons to all my foolish blood" (para. 4); "I imagined that I bore my chalice safely through a throng of foes" (para. 5); "my body was like a harp and her words and gestures were like fingers running upon the wires" (para. 5). Language like this sounds as though it comes out of a popular romance novel, something written by Danielle Steele perhaps. The mixing of romance with soft porn is unmistakable. Perhaps the boy has spent too much time reading the priest's sexually seductive stories from *The Memoirs of Vidocq* (para. 2). 7

I think this language is meant to be ironic, to point to the fact that the narrator is not the young boy himself but the young boy now grown and looking back at how "foolish" he was (para. 4). This interpretation becomes likely when you think of "Araby" as a fictionalized autobiography. In autobiographical stories, remembered feelings and thoughts are combined with the autobiographer's present perspective. The remembered feelings and thoughts in this story could be seen as expressing the boy's point of view, but we read them ironically through the adult narrator's present perspective. The romantic, gushy language the boy uses is laughable. It reveals the boy's blindness toward everyone, including himself. He sees himself as Sir Galahad, the chivalric hero on his own grail quest to Araby. The greatest irony comes at the end when his quest is exposed as merely a shopping trip and Araby as merely a suburban mall. 8

Most people interpret the ending as a moment of profound insight, and the language certainly seems to support this interpretation: "Gazing up into the darkness I saw myself as a creature driven and derided by vanity; and my eyes burned with anguish and anger" (para. 37). But here again we see the narrator using inflated language that suggests an ironic stance. So even in the moment of apparent insight, the boy is still playing a heroic role. He hasn't discovered his true self. He's just as self-absorbed and blind in the end as he was at the beginning. 9

Analyzing Writing Strategies

1. To see how interpretive essays develop and **support** their reasons, reread paragraph 5, where Crane argues that the boy cannot see the reality of Mangan's sister, only the two competing images of women he has learned from his religious training and romantic reading. To support this reason, Crane quotes a long passage from the story. Describe what she does in the rest of the paragraph following the indented quote.

For more on reasons and support, see Chapter 19, pp. 681–88.

2. One of the **reasons** Crane gives for her interpretation that the boy does not experience "some profound insight about himself" at the end of "Araby" is developed in paragraphs 6–8. Reread these paragraphs and summarize the argument.

Commentary: An Interesting and Clearly Stated Interpretation

Like position papers, evaluations, proposals, and causal speculations, essays interpreting stories make arguments. They state a thesis—asserting an idea about the story's meaning or significance—and try to convince readers that this interpretation is plausible. Like other arguments, the **thesis statement** of an interpretive essay must meet three basic standards: It must be arguable, clear, and appropriately qualified. In addition, the interpretation must be perceived by readers as interesting.

For more on thesis statements, see Chapter 19, pp. 677–81.

Sally Crane's thesis statement identifies itself as arguable by setting up a contrast between her interpretation of the story's ending and that of other readers:

> Readers of "Araby" often . . . assume the boy experiences some profound insight about himself when he gazes "up into the darkness." I believe, however, that the boy sees nothing and learns nothing—about either himself or others. He's not self-reflective; he's merely self-absorbed.
>
> The evidence supporting this interpretation is the imagery of blindness and the ironic point of view of the narrator. (paragraphs 1–2)

Crane summarizes the debate simply: Either the boy "experiences some profound insight" at the end, or as Crane herself argues, he "sees nothing and learns nothing."

As we pointed out in the headnote, Crane knew about this debate over the ending from class discussion. Because her essay continues the conversation, she can be confident that the readers of her essay—her instructor and classmates—will find her interpretation interesting, even if they disagree with it. To make her interpretation even more interesting, she uses critical approaches she has learned in English classes. Readers who are not conversant with concepts like *imagery*, *irony*, and *point of view* may not even understand what Crane is talking about, let alone find it interesting. Your instructor and the Suggestions for Interpreting (pp. 543–46) will help you develop an interpretation that is interesting as well as arguable.

In addition to being arguable and interesting, Crane's thesis statement is clear and appropriately qualified. Readers familiar with the concepts Crane uses are likely to understand her thesis statement, but some readers will probably think it is not appropriately qualified because she makes the broad generalization: "the boy sees nothing and learns nothing." To qualify a thesis statement, writers typically add limiting words like "usually" and "most" in place of absolutes like "nothing" and "all." However, writers who can offer readers convincing support for their generalizations do not hedge. They generalize confidently, letting readers decide for themselves whether the thesis statement is appropriate or needs to be qualified.

Not only does a good thesis statement assert the interpretation, but it also uses key terms to **forecast** the reasons and support that will be offered and to indicate the order in which they will come up in the essay. Crane's first key term, *sees nothing,* introduces the first reason she thinks the boy ultimately "learns nothing"—because throughout the story he cannot understand with any accuracy his own feelings and motivations or anyone else's. In the first sentence of paragraph 2, Crane forecasts that she will support this reason by showing how the story uses "imagery of blindness."

Writers with little experience reading and writing essays interpreting stories may think that stating the thesis at the beginning and forecasting the argument gives too much away. Although stories seldom state their meanings explicitly, essays interpreting stories are expected to do so. Interpretive arguments are most effective when readers have a clear sense of what they are arguing and why.

***David Ratinov** wrote the following essay about "Araby" (p. 526) for freshman composition. Like Sally Crane (p. 531), Ratinov is curious about what the boy's final statement might mean. But unlike Crane, Ratinov concludes that the boy does gain insight from seeing the hypocrisy of other characters as well as his own. As you read, notice how Ratinov's interpretation differs from Crane's. (*Note: *Like Crane, Ratinov cites paragraphs, following his instructor's directions rather than MLA style.)*

To see this essay with pop-up annotations in the software, click on
▶ **Interpreting Stories**
▶**Read**

From Innocence to Insight: "Araby" as an Initiation Story

David Ratinov

"Araby" tells the story of an adolescent boy's initiation 1
into adulthood. The story is narrated by a mature man reflecting on his adolescence and the events that forced him to face the disillusioning realities of adulthood. The minor characters play a pivotal role in this initiation process. The boy observes the hypocrisy of adults in the priest and Mrs. Mercer; and his vain, self-centered uncle introduces him to another disillusioning aspect of adulthood. The boy's infatuation with the girl ultimately ends in disillusionment, and Joyce uses the specific example of the boy's disillusionment with love as a metaphor for disillusionment with life itself. From the beginning, the boy deludes himself about his relationship with Mangan's sister. At Araby, he realizes the parallel between his own self-delusion and the hypocrisy and vanity of the adult world.

From the beginning, the boy's infatuation with Mangan's sister draws him away from 2
childhood toward adulthood. He breaks his ties with his childhood friends and luxuriates

in his isolation. He can think of nothing but his love for her: "From the front window I saw my companions playing below in the street. Their cries reached me weakened and indistinct and, leaning my forehead against the cool glass, I looked over at the dark house where she lived" (para. 16). The friends' cries are weak and indistinct because they are distant emotionally as well as spatially. Like an adult on a quest, he imagines he carries his love as if it were a sacred object, a chalice: "Her image accompanied me even in places the most hostile to romance. . . . I imagined that I bore my chalice safely through a throng of foes" (para. 5). Even in the active, distracting marketplace, he is able to retain this image of his pure love. But his love is not pure.

Although he worships Mangan's sister as a religious object, his lust for her is undeniable. He idolizes her as if she were the Virgin Mary: "her figure defined by the light from the half-opened door. . . . The light from the lamp opposite our door caught the white curve of her neck, lit up her hair that rested there and, falling, lit up the hand upon the railing" (paras. 3, 9). Yet even this image is sensual with the halo of light accentuating "the white curve of her neck." The language makes obvious that his attraction is physical rather than spiritual: "Her dress swung as she moved her body and the soft rope of her hair tossed from side to side" (para. 3). His desire for her is strong and undeniable: "her name was like a summons to all my foolish blood" (para. 4); "my body was like a harp and her words and gestures were like fingers running upon the wires" (para. 5). But in order to justify his love, to make it socially acceptable, he deludes himself into thinking that his love is pure. He is being hypocritical, although at this point he does not know it. 3

Hypocrisy is characteristic of the adults in this story. The priest is by far the most obvious offender. What is a man of the cloth doing with books like *The Abbot* (a romantic novel) and *The Memoirs of Vidocq* (a collection of sexually suggestive tales)? These books imply that he led a double life. Moreover, the fact that he had money to give away when he died suggests that he was far from saintly. Similarly, at first glance Mrs. Mercer appears to be religious, but a closer look reveals that she too is materialistic. Her church work—collecting used stamps for some "pious purpose" (presumably to sell for the church)—associates her with money and profit (para. 17). Even her name, Mercer, identifies her as a dealer in merchandise. In addition, her husband is a pawnbroker, a profession that the church frowns on. Despite being linked to money, she pretends to be pious and respectable. Therefore, like the priest, Mrs. Mercer is hypocritical. 4

The uncle, as the boy's only living male relative, is a failure as a role model and the epitome of vanity. He is a self-centered old man who cannot handle responsibility: When the boy reminds him on Saturday morning about the bazaar, the uncle brushes him off, devoting all his attention to his own appearance. After being out all afternoon the uncle returns home at 9:00, talking to himself. He rocks the hallstand when hanging up his overcoat. These details suggest that he is drunk. "I could interpret these signs" indicates that this behavior is typical of his uncle (para. 19). The uncle is the only character in the story the boy relies on, but the uncle fails him. Only after the aunt persuades him does the uncle give the boy the money he promised. From the priest, Mrs. Mercer, and his uncle, the boy learns some fundamental truths about adulthood, but it is only after his visit to Araby that he is able to recognize what he has learned. 5

Araby to the adolescent represents excitement, a chance to prove the purity of his love and, more abstractly, his hope; however, Araby fulfills none of these expectations. 6

Instead, the boy finds himself in utter disillusionment and despair. Araby is anything but exciting. The trip there is dreary and uneventful, lonely and intolerably slow—not the magical journey he had expected. When he arrives, Araby itself is nearly completely dark and in the process of closing. With his excitement stunted, he can barely remember why he came there (to prove the purity of his love by buying a gift for Mangan's sister).

The young lady selling porcelain and her gentleman friends act as catalysts, causing the boy to recognize the truth of his love for Mangan's sister. Their conversation is flirtatious—a silly lovers' game that the boy recognizes as resembling his own conversation with Mangan's sister. He concludes that his love for her is no different than the two gentlemen's love for this "lady" (para. 26). Neither love is pure. He too had only been playing a game, flirting with a girl and pretending that it was something else and that he was someone else. 7

His disillusionment with love is then extended to life in general. Seeing the last rays of hope fading from the top floors of Araby, the boy cries: "I saw myself as a creature driven and derided by vanity; and my eyes burned with anguish and anger" (para. 37). At last he makes the connection—by deluding himself, he has been hypocritical and vain like the adults in his life. Before these realizations he believed that he was driven by something of value (such as purity of love), but now he realizes that his quest has been in vain because honesty, truth, and purity are only childish illusions and he can never return to the innocence of childhood. 8

Analyzing Writing Strategies

For more on thesis statements, see Chapter 19, pp. 677–81.

1. Find the thesis statement in Ratinov's essay, and underline its key terms. Then find and circle where Ratinov uses these key terms in the rest of his essay. Are all of the key terms in the essay easy to find, or do any drop out of sight? Also determine whether Ratinov's key terms enable him to satisfy the standards of a well-written interpretive thesis statement: Is it interesting, arguable, clear, and appropriately qualified?

For more on topic sentence strategies, see Chapter 13, pp. 614–17.

2. Look closely at each opening sentence in paragraphs 2–8 to see if it functions as an effective **topic sentence**. Does it connect the preceding paragraph to the one it introduces? What other functions do these opening sentences have?

To learn more about commenting on quotations, turn to Sentence Strategies, p. 551.

3. In paragraph 2, underline the two quotations. Then analyze what Ratinov does before and after each quotation to provide a context for it and a comment on it. How does he prepare you to read each quote? How does he attempt to show you the relevance and point of each quote?

Commentary: Plausible Reasons and Convincing Support

Ratinov presents three interrelated reasons for his interpretation of the story's ending. His first reason is that the boy deludes himself by imagining his love for Mangan's sister to be noble. Second, he argues that the boy sees the adult characters in the story as hypocritical and self-centered. Finally, he argues that at the bazaar, the boy suddenly connects the adults' hypocrisy to his own. His self-delusion ends, thus completing his initiation into adulthood.

This chain of reasoning seems plausible. Whether readers accept it as such depends on how well Ratinov supports the argument. He supports it with **textual evidence**, primarily quotations of significant passages from the story. He may quote individual words (paragraph 7), short phrases (paragraph 4), a single sentence (paragraph 8), or strings of sentences (paragraph 2). Unlike Crane, who uses a block quotation (paragraph 5), Ratinov does not use any quotes long enough to require indentation—more than four lines, according to MLA style. Like Crane, Ratinov uses ellipsis marks (. . .) to indicate where he has omitted words from his quotation (paragraph 2). Both writers also parenthetically cite the paragraph numbers to indicate where the quotations can be found in the story. By citing paragraphs instead of the author and page number as MLA style dictates, these students are following their instructors' directions. Be sure to follow your instructor's preferred format for citing sources.

For more on textual evidence, see Chapter 19, pp. 686–88.

For more on MLA quotation style, see Chapter 22, pp. 758–61, and pp. 558–59 in this chapter.

Notice that, like Crane, Ratinov does more than merely quote words from the story. He tells readers what the words mean in the context of the argument he is making. In paragraph 2, for example, Ratinov makes an assertion, which he then supports by quoting two sentences. To make certain that readers understand how the quotation supports his assertion, Ratinov discusses two word choices and their implications.

PURPOSE AND AUDIENCE

When you write an essay interpreting a story, you cannot simply tell readers, who may have different interpretations, what you think and expect them to accept your interpretation or even to understand it fully. You need to show how you read the story. Ideally, your readers will see something new in the story after reading your essay. But even if they continue to read the story differently from the way you read it, they may still acknowledge that your interpretation reflects an imaginative, thoughtful reading of the story.

Interpreting a story, then, is not a competition for the "correct" interpretation. Your aim is to develop an interpretation that is insightful and interesting to readers who are already engaged in conversation with other readers about their different ways of reading the story. Readers do not require you to come up with a startling new idea, though they would be pleased if you did. Your readers will be disappointed, however, if your essay is unfocused, if the key terms in your thesis statement are unclear, if you do not give reasons for your interpretation or you do not support them with quotations from the story, or if your essay fails to provide the necessary cues to keep readers on track. Readers will be especially disappointed if they think you are retelling the story rather than developing your own interpretation of the story's meaning or significance.

BASIC FEATURES: INTERPRETING STORIES

An Appropriately Presented Subject

The essays interpreting stories in this chapter both focus on a specific subject—one particular story. When an interpretive essay responds to a class discussion or writing assignment, all the writer needs to do is identify the story by name. The readers—the instructor and other students in the class—already know who the author is and when the story was written. Both student writers in this chapter simply refer to "Araby" in the first few words of their opening sentence: "'Araby' tells the story . . ." (David Ratinov) and "Readers of 'Araby' . . ." (Sarah Crane).

Sometimes, students are asked to choose from a list of stories or to find a story on their own. On such occasions, you may need to give readers a little more information about the story—such as the name of the author and the date the story was originally published. To acquaint readers with the story, you also can briefly describe the situation. But avoid retelling the story in detail.

An Interesting and Clearly Stated Interpretation

An interpretation is an idea asserted about the meaning of the story. A good interpretation illuminates the story for readers by adding something interesting to the ongoing conversation in which readers are engaged. The main idea or thesis is usually presented explicitly in a thesis statement near the beginning of the essay and may be summarized again at the conclusion. In addition to being interesting, the thesis statement must be arguable, not a simple statement of fact that anyone who reads the story will know (such as stating that the boy in "Araby" lives in Dublin with his aunt and uncle). Nor should the thesis be obvious, a conclusion that most readers would make (the boy has a crush on Mangan's sister). A good thesis statement should also be clear, not vague or ambiguous, and appropriately qualified, not overgeneralized or exaggerated. Crane states her thesis in the second sentence of the opening paragraph: "I believe, however, that the boy sees nothing and learns nothing—about either himself or others." (The word *however* refers to the preceding sentence, which summarizes an opposing interpretation expressed by other students in her class.)

A good thesis statement forecasts the reasons the writer will use in the essay to develop and support the thesis. Inexperienced writers sometimes are afraid they are ruining the surprise by announcing their thesis and forecasting their argument at the beginning. But readers familiar with this kind of writing have come to expect writers to preview the argument in the opening paragraphs. Explicit forecasting is a convention of literary interpretation similar in purpose to the abstract that precedes many articles in scientific journals. Explicitness does not mean that you have to sacrifice subtlety or complexity in your interpretation. All it means is that you are striving to make your ideas as comprehensible as possible to readers.

Ratinov's opening paragraph provides a good example of explicit forecasting. He explains his main idea, beginning with his thesis, in the first sentence: "'Araby' tells the story of an adolescent boy's initiation into adulthood." Then, in the five sentences that follow, he previews his argument. Finally, in the last sentence of the opening paragraph, Ratinov provides a succinct summary of his reasons: "At Araby, he realizes the parallel between his own self-delusion and the hypocrisy and vanity of the adult world." Together with *initiation,* the key term in the opening sentence, the last sentence sets out three additional key terms: *self-delusion, hypocrisy,* and *vanity.* These additional key terms signal for readers the steps in Ratinov's argument, specifying what he means when he asserts that the boy's experience can be understood as an initiation story. For key terms to be useful to readers, they must be clear and consistent. Moreover, the reasons that the key terms stand for should be directly connected to the thesis and be well supported.

A Plausible Chain of Reasons with Convincing Support

Writers must argue for their interpretation. They can usually assume that their readers will be familiar with the story, but they can never assume that readers will understand or accept their interpretation.

Writers argue for their interpretation not so much to convince readers to adopt it but rather to convince them that it is plausible. An essential strategy writers typically follow is to show readers how they read the story. They do this by supporting their interpretation with textual evidence and explaining what they think these quotations mean in light of the thesis.

The primary source of support for your argument, then, is the story itself, particularly examples gleaned from it. Writers quote, summarize, and paraphrase passages from the story. They do more than just refer readers to a specific passage, however: They also explain the meaning of the passage and its relevance to their thesis. We can see an example of the way writers explain their textual support in the following passage from Ratinov's essay, where he describes what happens when the boy's uncle finally comes home from work, having forgotten that the boy was waiting for him:

> When the boy reminds him on Saturday morning about the bazaar, the uncle brushes him off, devoting all his attention to his own appearance. After being out all afternoon the uncle returns home at 9:00, talking to himself. He rocks the hallstand when hanging up his overcoat. These details suggest that he is drunk. "I could interpret these signs" indicates that this behavior is typical of his uncle. The uncle is the only character in the story the boy relies on, but the uncle fails him. (paragraph 5)

Notice that Ratinov summarizes the most important details, paraphrasing some of the language, and that he quotes sparingly—only one especially telling phrase. Everything else in this paragraph is Ratinov's commentary. Like Ratinov and Crane, you will want to combine explanatory commentary with quotation, summary, and paraphrase to support and develop your argument.

GUIDE TO WRITING
Interpreting Stories

THE WRITING ASSIGNMENT

THE WRITING ASSIGNMENT

Write an essay interpreting some aspect of a short story. Aim to convince readers that your view of the story is interesting and adds to the ongoing conversation among those who read stories and write about them. Back up your interpretation with reasons and support from the story.

INVENTION AND RESEARCH

INVENTION & RESEARCH

- Choosing a Story to Write About
- Analyzing the Story
- Writing to Explore Your Annotations
- Formulating a Tentative Thesis Statement
- Testing Your Choice
- Testing Your Choice: A Collaborative Activity
- Revising the Thesis Statement
- Finding Additional Support

PLANNING AND DRAFTING

PLANNING & DRAFTING

- Seeing What You Have
- Setting Goals
- Outlining
- Drafting

CRITICAL READING GUIDE

CRITICAL READING GUIDE

- First Impression
- Thesis Statement
- Support for Each Reason
- A Logical Chain of Reasons
- Organization
- Final Thoughts

REVISING

REVISING

- Your Purpose and Readers
- The Interpretation
- Reasons and Support
- The Organization

EDITING AND PROOFREADING

EDITING & PROOFREADING

- Checking for Parallelism in Your Writing
- Checking Your Use of Ellipsis Marks

GUIDE TO WRITING

THE WRITING ASSIGNMENT

Write an essay interpreting some aspect of a short story. Aim to convince readers that your view of the story is interesting and adds to the ongoing conversation among those who read stories and write about them. Back up your interpretation with reasons and support from the story.

> To use the Writing Guide Software for this assignment, click on
> ▶ **Interpreting Stories**
> ▶ **Write**

INVENTION AND RESEARCH

The following activities will help you choose a short story, analyze it, write to explore your annotations, formulate a tentative thesis statement, test your choice, revise your thesis statement, and find additional support in the story for your thesis. To make these activities as useful as possible, spread them out over several days, and keep a written record of your invention work.

Choosing a Story to Write About

Choose a story that fascinates, surprises, or puzzles you, one that will be worth spending time on because it excites your imagination. You may have chosen a story already, or your instructor may have assigned you one. If so, go on to the next section, Analyzing the Story.

If you need to choose a story on your own, read several stories before deciding on one to write about. Do not choose a story that seems obvious to you. Your instructor can help you decide whether you have made a good choice.

Considering Stories Related to Identity and Community. If you are studying the topic of identity and community, you will see immediately how the stories in this chapter relate to these concerns. Almost any story you choose to write about would allow you to think more about how people develop their individuality and their connections to others. Here are a few widely anthologized stories you might consider writing about:

"The Monkey Garden," by Sandra Cisneros

"The Open Boat," by Stephen Crane

"Fleur," by Louise Erdrich

"A Rose for Emily," by William Faulkner

"My Kinsman, Major Molineux," by Nathaniel Hawthorne

"A Clean, Well-Lighted Place," by Ernest Hemingway
"The Lottery," by Shirley Jackson
"The Metamorphosis," by Franz Kafka
"The Ones Who Walk away from Omelas," by Ursula Le Guin
"A Pair of Tickets," by Amy Tan
"Everyday Use," by Alice Walker

Considering Stories Related to Work and Career. "The Use of Force" (in this chapter) would be useful in writing about the topic of work and career. Here are some additional stories you might consider for exploring this topic:

"Sonny's Blues," by James Baldwin
"The Yellow Wallpaper," by Charlotte Perkins Gilman
"The Birthmark," by Nathaniel Hawthorne
"Reena," by Paule Marshall
"Shiloh," by Bobbie Ann Mason
"Bartleby the Scrivener," by Herman Melville
"Picasso," by Gertrude Stein
"The Catbird Seat," by James Thurber
"A&P," by John Updike
"Why I Live at the P.O.," by Eudora Welty

Finding a Story: An Online Activity

If your instructor has not assigned a story for you to write about, you may be able to find one that interests you by searching online. Simply entering the keyword *short stories* into a search engine such as Google (http://www.google.com) or Yahoo! Directory (http://dir.yahoo.com) will lead to Web sites with stories you could consider writing about. Many of these sites feature stories that have not been published in print, but others, such as the following, are collections of classic stories:

Twenty Great American Short Stories <http://www.americanliterature.com/SS/SSINDX.HTML>

Classic Short Stories <http://mbhs.bergtraum.k12.ny.us/cybereng/shorts/>

Classic Reader <http://www.classicreader.com/toc.php/sid.6/>

The Short Story Classics: The Best from the Masters of the Genre <http://www.geocities.com/short_stories_page/>

If your instructor needs to approve your choice, be sure to include information about the Web site along with the printout of the story you have chosen.

Analyzing the Story

To help you analyze the story, this section offers suggestions for interpreting that may help you annotate for potentially meaningful details. As you annotate the story, your goal will be to decide on a thesis, an idea about the story's meaning, for which you can develop a reasoned, well-supported argument.

Choosing a Suggestion for Interpreting. *Select one or more suggestions for interpreting that will help you focus on some aspects of the story that seem significant or about which you have questions.* For example:

- If on first reading the story you wondered why a character acts in a particular way, look at the suggestions for interpreting *character.*
- If you were struck by the language used to describe the scene, look at the suggestions for interpreting *setting.*
- If you noticed any kind of pattern in the events in the story, look at the suggestions for interpreting *plot structure.*
- If you had questions about the way the story is narrated, look at the suggestions for interpreting *point of view.*
- If you recognized a familiar motif (for example, a coming-of-age story) or theme (alienation), look at the suggestions for interpreting *literary motif* or *theme.*

You may want to read and annotate the story several times, keeping in mind the different suggestions for interpreting, before you decide on an idea you can use as a working thesis for your draft. Notice also that rereading the story with different suggestions in mind can help you to discover how different aspects of the story work together and can lead you to construct a more fully developed thesis.

Character

To interpret the character psychologically:

- Identify the character's motivations, inner conflicts, and doubts.
- Consider whether the character changes or learns anything in the course of the story.
- Focus on how the character relates to other characters, noting how the character deals with intimacy, commitment, and responsibility.
- Note whether the character seems depressed, manic, abusive, fearful, egotistical, or paranoid. Look for another character who may represent the character's alter ego—the "flip side" of the character's personality.

To interpret the character ethically or morally:

- Decide what you consider to be the character's virtues and/or vices.
- Consider what influences your judgment of the character—something in the story (such as what the narrator or another character says), something you bring

to the story (your views of right and wrong, based on your family upbringing or religious teachings), or something else.

- See whether any of the other characters have different moral values that could be compared and contrasted to the character's values.

To interpret the character from a social perspective:

- Consider how the character fits into and is defined by society—in terms of race, ethnicity, socioeconomic class, sexual orientation, age, or gender.
- Notice who in the story exercises power over whom, what causes the difference in power, what its effects are, and whether the balance of power changes during the story.

Setting

To interpret the setting in relation to the action, mood, or characters:

- Consider how the setting signals what is happening and whether it comments (possibly ironically) on the action.
- Notice how the setting affects the mood—for example, how it heightens suspense or foreboding.
- Look for cause-and-effect connections between the setting and what characters are thinking, doing, or feeling.

To interpret the setting historically or culturally:

- Think of how the historical period or cultural context in which the story is set might affect what happens and does not happen and why.
- Imagine how the meaning might be different if the historical time or cultural situation were different.

To interpret the setting metaphorically or symbolically:

- Assume that the setting is a projection of the thoughts and feelings of the narrator, and then consider what the setting tells you about the narrator's state of mind.
- Assume that the setting symbolizes the social relations among characters in the story, and then consider what the setting tells you about these relationships.
- Assume that the setting stands for something outside the characters' control (such as nature, God, or some aspect of society), and then consider what the setting tells you about the pressures and rules under which the characters function.

Plot Structure

To interpret the plot as realistic (as resembling real-life experience):

- Think of the story as a sequence of stages or steps leading somewhere, mark where each new stage begins, and consider how the sequence could be understood.

- Think of the story as having not only a main plot but also subplots that mirror, undercut, or comment in some way on the main plot.

To interpret the plot as surrealistic (as having symbolic rather than literal meaning):

- Think of the story as a series of images, more like a collage or a dream rather than a realistic portrayal of actual events, and look for ways of understanding the arrangement of these images.

Point of View

To interpret the point of view in terms of what the narrator can see:

- Consider whether the narrator is a character in the story or an all-knowing, disembodied voice who knows what every character thinks, feels, and does.
- Identify any important insights or ideas the narrator has.
- Consider how factors such as the narrator's gender, age, and ethnicity may influence what he or she notices as important.
- Consider what the narrator is not able to see or what the narrator distorts—for example, certain truths about himself or herself, about other characters, or about what happens in the story.

To interpret the point of view in terms of how the narrator represents what he or she sees:

- Characterize the narrator's tone at various points in the story—for example, as satirical, celebratory, angry, bitter, or optimistic.
- Infer what there is about the narrator (or about the situation) that could account for each tone you identify.
- Consider what special agenda or motive may have led the narrator to this particular way of describing characters and scenes or telling the story.
- Imagine how your interpretation might differ if the story were narrated from another character's point of view or by an all-knowing voice.

Literary Motif or Theme

To interpret the story in terms of a traditional story motif (or an ironic reversal of the tradition), consider whether it could be seen as:

- An initiation (or coming-of-age or rite-of-passage) story
- A heroic quest (for love, truth, fame, fortune, salvation of oneself or the community)
- A story about a character's disillusionment or fall from innocence
- A story about family or surrogate families
- A story about storytelling (or some other art) or about becoming a writer or an artist

To interpret the story in terms of a common literary theme, consider whether the following themes are found in the story:

- The American Dream
- Dynamics of Power
- Social Construction of Femininity or Masculinity
- Popular Culture
- Race Relations
- Alienation
- Imagination

For examples of Ratinov's annotations and invention writings, see the Writer at Work section on pp. 560–63.

Annotating with the Suggestions for Interpreting in Mind. *Annotate details in the story that relate to the focus you have chosen for your interpretation.* To annotate, simply underline, bracket, or highlight words and phrases that seem significant. Circle words to be defined, and write their definitions in the margins. Draw lines to connect related words and images. Make marginal notes indicating what you are learning about the story by annotating with the suggestions for interpreting in mind. Write down any further questions you have as you annotate.

Writing to Explore Your Annotations

Write at least a page exploring what you have discovered about the story from analyzing it with the suggestions for interpreting in mind. If you have reread the story several times with different suggestions for interpreting, you may be able to write several pages.

It may help to begin by reviewing the suggestions for interpreting you used and writing your thoughts about each suggestion. For example, if you focused on the suggestions to interpret the character psychologically, you could begin by explaining what you now think are the character's motivations, inner conflicts, and doubts. Then you could go on to discuss how the character changes—what precipitated the change, how it proceeded, how you can tell the character has changed, and why the change is significant.

You may also find it productive to write about patterns of words, figures of speech, characters, or events you found as you were annotating. For instance, when David Ratinov reflected on the annotations he had made using the suggestions for interpreting character, he discovered that several minor characters, in addition to the main character, were hypocritical.

Formulating a Tentative Thesis Statement

Using the suggestions for interpreting, you have annotated the story and explored your annotations. Your aim now is to list ideas you can support with details from the story, explore the connections among these ideas, and draft a tentative thesis statement.

Listing Ideas. *Write several sentences stating the ideas you have discovered using one or more of the suggestions for interpreting to annotate the story and to explore your annotations.* The only requirement is that you feel confident that you could find specific details and quotations in the story to support each idea. Do not worry about how these ideas relate to one another or even about whether they are contradictory. Simply write down every idea you can think of.

The suggestions for interpreting you used to annotate the story and explore your annotations should lead you, as they led Ratinov, to assert your ideas about the story. For example, writing about several of the characters in "Araby" convinced Ratinov that he could confidently assert the idea that "all the adult characters are hypocrites."

Writing to Develop Connections among Your Ideas. *Write for ten minutes contemplating how the ideas you listed can make a chain of reasons leading to a general conclusion or main idea about the story that would be your thesis.* As you write, you may decide to drop some of the ideas, reformulate others, or add new ideas. Focus your writing on these questions:

- What are the key terms in each idea? (For example, the key term in Ratinov's idea that "all the adult characters are hypocrites" is *hypocrite.*)
- Could any of these ideas be links in a chain of reasons leading to some new, main idea about the story I can make now? (For example, Ratinov links the idea that the boy in "Araby" is *self-deluded* and the idea that adults are *hypocrites* to the boy's discovery that he is a hypocrite too [key terms italicized].)

Drafting the Thesis Statement. *Now that you have asserted some ideas, thought about what their key terms enable you to say about the story, and considered how the terms could work together, write a few sentences stating your main idea or thesis and your reasons or supporting ideas.* Try completing the following sentence for each reason:

For more on thesis statements, see Chapter 13, pp. 611–13, and Chapter 19, pp. 677–81.

I think [main idea] about the story because [reason 1, 2, etc.].

Formulating a thesis statement (even one you know you will revise later) can be a challenge. It may help to review the thesis statements David Ratinov and Sally Crane wrote and to think about how they worded their key terms (italicized):

> "Araby" tells the story of an adolescent boy's *initiation* into adulthood . . . [by which] he realizes the parallel between his own *self-delusion* and the *hypocrisy* and *vanity* of the adult world. (Ratinov)
>
> I believe, however, that the boy *sees nothing* and *learns nothing*—about either himself or others. He's not self-reflective; he's merely *self-absorbed.* (Crane)

As you draft your own tentative thesis statement, pay attention to the language you use. It should be clear and unambiguous, emphatic but appropriately qualified. Although you will most probably refine your thesis statement as you draft and revise your essay, trying now to articulate it will help give your planning and drafting direction and impetus.

Testing Your Choice

Now that you have developed a tentative thesis statement, you need to be sure that it says what you want it to say, that your readers will find your interpretation interesting, and that you will be able to find support for it in the story. Review the key terms in your thesis to make sure you can find evidence for each point. Also consider whether your ideas still work together to form a logical chain of reasons. If your ideas still seem workable, you have probably made a good choice. However, if your ideas seem unworkable—that is, if you now think you cannot find examples in the story to support your ideas, or if your ideas seem too obvious or factual—you may need to return to Formulating a Tentative Thesis Statement or even to Analyzing the Story to develop your ideas or find new ones. You even may need to choose a different story and start over. If you are thinking of starting over, discuss the possibility with your instructor before doing so.

Testing Your Choice: A Collaborative Activity

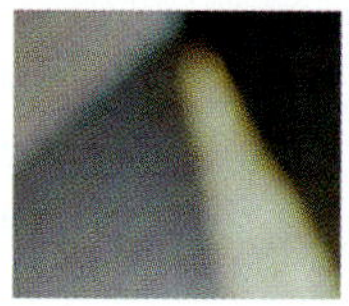

At this point, you will find it helpful to get together with two or three other students who have read your story and to get responses to one another's thesis statements. Your partners' feedback will help you determine whether your thesis or main idea is workable and whether you can construct a well-reasoned argument to support it.

Writers: Take turns reading your tentative thesis statement aloud. Then take notes as your partners tell you what your thesis statement leads them to expect from your essay.

Listeners: As the writer speaks, note down what you think are the key terms in the thesis statement. Remember that each of these key terms stands for an idea or a link in the chain of reasons arguing for the overall thesis. So tell the writer what the ideas are that you expect will be developed in the essay. Also indicate if you think the writer will have difficulty supporting any of these ideas, if you do not see how the ideas work together, or if you think any of the ideas are obvious or uninteresting. For example, if you were a member of David Ratinov's group, you might have said that his thesis statement led you to expect his essay to demonstrate three things: (1) the boy is *self-deluded,* (2) the adults are *hypocritical,* and (3) the boy ultimately realizes he has been self-deluded because of his *vanity,* and that this discovery completes his *initiation* into adulthood (key terms are italicized).

Revising the Thesis Statement

Try to improve your thesis statement. Consider whether you want to change your argument to alter the thesis statement or the reasons for it. Clear up any ambiguity or vagueness in your key terms, and qualify them more appropriately if necessary. Make explicit why you think your thesis is interesting and arguable by indicating how other readers disagree.

Finding Additional Support

If you do not have enough support for your reasons, reread the story, making additional annotations in passages where you find details you might be able to use. With your key terms in mind, evaluate the support you already have to determine whether it is sufficient to explain and illustrate each reason. Wherever support is lacking, fill it in by doing further annotating. If you cannot find any support for one of your reasons, you need to reconsider whether you should use that reason.

If you find details in the story that contradict any of your reasons, do not ignore the contradiction. Instead, analyze the details to see how you should modify your argument.

PLANNING AND DRAFTING

This section will help you review your invention notes, determine specific goals for your essay, make an outline, and get started on your first draft.

> If you are using the Writing Guide Software, click on
> ▶ **Planning and Drafting**

Seeing What You Have

Review your invention writing and annotated text. If some time has elapsed since you last read the story, you may want to reread it now. As you review what you have discovered about the story, consider whether your thesis is arguable and whether you have stated it clearly and directly. Also decide whether you have sufficient support and whether you might have overlooked anything important that could contradict or weaken your argument.

If you cannot find support for all of your reasons, you may not be ready to write a complete draft. You may, however, be ready to begin drafting the parts for which you do have support. Then you can return to the story to search for support for your other reasons. But if your ideas still seem obvious or not likely to be interesting to your readers, you may need to reconsider the direction in which you are going and possibly begin again.

Setting Goals

Before you start drafting, set some goals to guide the decisions you will make as you draft. Consider what you want to say about the story you are interpreting. Here are some questions that will help you set your goals and enable you to get across to your readers exactly what you want to tell them about the story:

Your Purpose and Readers

- Are my readers likely to know this story? If not, how much do I need to tell them about the story so that they can follow my argument? If so, how can I lead them to see my interpretation as interesting, whether or not they agree with it?
- Should I acknowledge readers' possible questions or differing interpretations, as Crane does?

The Interpretation

- How can I explicitly state my thesis and forecast my plan, as Crane and Ratinov do, without sounding stilted or mechanical?
- Which key terms will accurately forecast my reasons?

Reasons and Support

- How can I organize my reasons so that my readers will see how they interrelate or form a chain of reasoning, as Crane and Ratinov do?
- How can I integrate quotations smoothly into my writing?
- How can I connect quotations to my reasons so that readers will know why I have chosen these passages to quote?
- How can I make my argument sound authoritative and thoughtful?
- How much textual support must I include for my argument to be convincing?

The Ending

- Should I repeat my key terms, as Crane and Ratinov do?
- Should I reiterate my thesis statement?
- Should I end with a provocative question or with larger implications suggested by my interpretation?

Outlining

For more on outlining, see Chapter 12, pp. 592–95.

After setting goals for your essay, you are ready to make a working outline—a scratch outline or a formal outline using the outlining function of your word processing program. Remember that an outline is a tentative plan; you may change your plan as you make further discoveries while drafting.

Drafting

General Advice. Start drafting your essay, keeping in mind your purpose for writing and the goals you set while you were planning: You want to convince readers that your thesis is plausible. Explain your reasons fully and directly. Do not expect readers to guess at how a supporting quotation illustrates a reason; spell out the connections you want readers to see. Remember that your readers may have different ways of interpreting the passages to which you refer. Indicate exactly why you are citing specific details from the story and how you interpret the writer's choice of words.

If you get stuck while drafting, explore the problem by using some of the writing activities in the Invention and Research section of this chapter (pp. 541–49). Turn off your grammar checker and spelling checker at this stage if you find them distracting. Don't be afraid to skip around in your document. Jump back and fill in a spontaneous idea, or leap ahead and write a later section first if you find that easier. You may want to review the general drafting advice in Chapter 1 on pp. 16–17.

Sentence Strategies. As you draft an essay interpreting a short story, you will need to support your interpretation with quotations and paraphrases (restatements of quotations using mostly your own words) and with comments on them. Frequently quoting single words and brief phrases rather than whole sentences or passages and using language that refers directly to your quotations and paraphrases will help you achieve these goals.

Use short quotations frequently to support your interpretation of the story. Here are examples of short quotations from this chapter's two student essays:

> At the bazaar in the closing scene, "the light was out," and the upper part of the hall was "completely dark." (Sally Crane, paragraph 3)
>
> Her church work—collecting used stamps for some "pious purpose" (presumably to sell for the church)—associates her with money and profit. (David Ratinov, paragraph 4)

Crane and Ratinov do occasionally quote complete sentences—together they do so seven times—and one time Crane quotes several sentences in a row, set off as a block quotation (paragraph 5). The majority of their quotations, however, are brief phrases and single words from the stories they are interpreting. These additional examples illustrate the wide range of possibilities:

> The "white curve of her neck" and the "white border of a petticoat" combine the symbolic color of purity, associated with the Madonna, with sexual suggestiveness. (Sally Crane, paragraph 5)
>
> Yet even this image is sensual with the halo of light accentuating "the white curve of her neck." (David Ratinov, paragraph 3)
>
> He concludes that his love for her is no different than the two gentlemen's love for this "lady." (David Ratinov, paragraph 7)

Short word and phrase quotations like these will usually be part of the grammar of your own sentences—that is, they become the subjects, verbs, direct objects, and so on of your sentences. When you quote a complete sentence from a story, however, you will nearly always do so in a way that separates it from the grammar of your own sentence that introduces it, as in this example:

> Most people interpret the ending as a moment of profound insight, and the language certainly seems to support this interpretation: "Gazing up into the darkness I saw myself as a creature driven and derided by vanity; and my eyes burned with anguish and anger." (Sally Crane, paragraph 9)

For more on using short quotations to support your interpretation of a story, go to bedfordstmartins.com/theguide and click on Sentence Strategies.

Brief quotations are not in themselves superior to sentence and block quotations, but they allow you to sample more of the exact language of the story, making your argument more lively and interesting. They also enable you to bring together efficiently evidence from different parts of a story to support one part of your argument.

Comment directly on your quotations or paraphrases so that readers will understand their relevance to your interpretation of a story. The relevance, importance, or point of each of your quotations and paraphrases will rarely be obvious to your readers unless you provide a context for it, a comment in which you directly connect the quotation or paraphrase to the idea you are trying to support. Two prominent strategies that writers rely on in their comments are referring to quotations or paraphrases with *this* and *these* and repeating key nouns in them.

Referring to Quotations or Paraphrases with This and These

After mentioning images of looking, seeing, and blindness, Sally Crane comments, "*This pattern of imagery* includes images of reading, and reading stands for the boy's inability to understand what is before his eyes" (paragraph 4).

After quoting three of the boy's romantic thoughts about the girl, Sally Crane comments, "*Language like this* sounds as though it comes out of a popular romance novel, something written by Danielle Steele perhaps" (paragraph 7).

After paraphrasing the uncle's activities, David Ratinov comments, "*These details* suggest that he is drunk" (paragraph 5).

For more on using sentences that connect comments to quotations and paraphrases, go to bedfordstmartins.com/the guide and click on Sentence Strategies.

Referring to Quotations or Paraphrases by Repeating Key Nouns

After quoting the image of North Richmond Street houses with their "brown imperturbable faces," Sally Crane comments, "*The houses* stare back at the boy, unaffected by his presence and gaze" (paragraph 4).

After quoting three sentences that describe the boy's observations of his friends as they play in the street below his house, a quotation that mentions the friends' "cries," or shouts, David Ratinov comments, "*The friends' cries* are weak and indistinct because they are distant emotionally as well as spatially" (paragraph 2).

After paraphrasing information in the story about the priest, Mrs. Mercer, and the boy's uncle, David Ratinov comments, "From *the priest, Mrs. Mercer, and his uncle,* the boy learns some fundamental truths about adulthood, but it is only after his visit to Araby that he is able to recognize what he has learned" (paragraph 5).

There are many other ways to introduce comments on quotations and paraphrases, but using *this* and *these* and repeating key nouns are reliable and effective.

In addition to using frequent short quotations and commenting directly on your quotations and paraphrases, you can strengthen your interpretive writing with other kinds of sentences as well, and you may want to review the discussions of sentences that feature adjectives before nouns (pp. 118–19), specific speaker tags (pp. 181–82), and comparison and contrast (p. 432).

CRITICAL READING GUIDE

Now is the time to get a good critical reading of your draft. Most writers find it helpful to have someone else read and comment on their drafts, and all writers know how much they learn about writing when they read other writers' drafts. Your instructor may arrange such a reading as part of your coursework. If not, you can ask a classmate, friend, or family member to read your draft. You could also seek comments from a tutor at your campus writing center. The guidelines in this section can be used by *anyone* reviewing an essay interpreting a story. (If you are unable to have someone else read your draft, turn ahead to the Revising section, where you will find advice for reading your own draft critically.)

If you are using the Writing Guide Software, click on
▶ **Critical Reading Guide**

▶ **If You Are the Writer.** To provide focused, helpful comments, your reader must know your essay's intended audience, your purpose, and a problem in the draft that you need help solving. The reader must also have read the story you are writing about. Attach a copy of the story to your draft if you think your reader may not already have one, and write out brief answers to the following questions at the top of your draft:

- ***Readers:*** How do you think your interpretation builds on or contradicts the interpretations your readers are likely to have of the story?
- ***Purpose:*** What specifically do you want your readers to learn about the story from reading your essay?
- ***Problem:*** What is the most important problem you see in your draft?

▶ **If You Are the Reader.** Use the following guidelines to help you give critical comments to others on essays interpreting stories:

1. ***Read for a First Impression.*** Read first to grasp the writer's interpretation of the story. As you read, identify any passages that are particularly convincing as well as any that seem unclear or unsupported. Remember that even if you interpret the story differently, your goal now is to help the writer present his or her interpretation as effectively as possible.

   Write a one-sentence summary of the essay's thesis. Also indicate generally whether you think the writer's interpretation makes sense. Next, consider the problem the writer identified, and respond briefly to that concern now. (If you find that the problem is covered by one of the other guidelines listed below, respond to it in more detail there if necessary.)
2. ***Evaluate the Thesis Statement and How Well It Forecasts the Argument.*** Find the thesis statement, and highlight or underline its key terms. If you cannot find the thesis statement or cannot identify the key terms, let the writer

Making Comments Electronically
Most word processing software offers features that allow you to insert comments directly into the text of someone else's document. Many readers prefer to make their comments in this way because it tends to be faster than writing on a hard copy and space is virtually unlimited; from the writer's point of view, it also eliminates the problem of deciphering handwritten comments. Even where such special comment features are not available, simply typing comments directly into a document in a contrasting color can provide the same advantages.

know. Evaluate the thesis statement on the basis of whether it makes an interesting and arguable assertion (rather than a statement of fact or an obvious point), is clear and precise (neither ambiguous nor vague), and is appropriately qualified (neither overgeneralized nor exaggerated).

Then skim the rest of the essay, highlighting or underlining each key term as it is brought up. If you cannot find a key term later in the essay but you do see where the reason it stands for is developed and supported, let the writer know where it should be added. If a reason introduced by a key term in the thesis statement is left out of the essay altogether, tell the writer. Also note any important reasons that are developed in the essay but are not announced in the thesis statement.

3. ***Indicate Whether Each Reason Is Well Supported.*** Look closely at the sections where the reasons are developed. Note whether each reason is supported adequately with textual evidence such as quotations, paraphrases, or summaries. Indicate where support is lacking, and let the writer know if you do not understand how a particular quotation relates to the reason it is supposed to support. Point out any passages in the story that the writer could use to bolster this part of the argument or that undermine it.
4. ***Evaluate the Argument as a Chain of Reasons.*** Summarize briefly for the writer your understanding of how the reasons work together to argue for the thesis. If you do not see how a particular reason fits in, say so. Also note where logical connections linking the chain of reasons could be added, strengthened, or made more explicit.
5. ***Suggest How the Organization Could Be Improved.*** Consider the overall plan, perhaps by making a scratch outline. Note any places where the argument is hard to follow or where transitions are missing or do not work well.
   - Look again at the *beginning* to see if it adequately forecasts the rest of the essay.
   - Look at the *ending* to see if it is too abrupt, repetitive, or goes off in a new and surprising direction.
6. ***Give the Writer Your Final Thoughts.*** What is the draft's strongest part? What part is most in need of further work?

REVISING

This section will help you get an overview of your draft and revise it accordingly.

If you are using the Writing Guide Software, click on
▶ **Revising**

Getting an Overview

Consider your draft as a whole, following these two steps:

1. ***Reread.*** If at all possible, put the draft aside for a day or two. When you do reread, start by reconsidering your purpose. Then read the draft straight through, trying to see it as your intended readers will.
2. ***Outline.*** Make a scratch outline, indicating the basic features as they appear in the draft. Consider using the headings and outline/summary functions of your word processor.

For more on scratch outlining, see Chapter 12, pp. 594–95.

Planning for Revision. Resist the temptation to dive in and start changing your text until after you have a clear view of the big picture. Using your outline as a guide, move through the document, using the change-highlighting or commenting tools of your word processor to note comments received from others and problems you want to solve (or mark on a hard copy if you prefer).

Analyzing the Basic Features of Your Own Draft. Turn now to the Critical Reading Guide that begins on p. 553. Using this guide, identify problems you now see in your draft. Note the problems on your draft.

Studying Critical Comments. Review all of the comments you have received from other readers. For each comment, look at the draft to determine what might have led the reader to make that particular point. Try to be objective about any criticism. Ideally, these comments will help you see your draft as others see it. Add to your notes any problems readers have identified that you intend to act on.

Carrying Out Revisions

Having identified problems in your draft, you now need to figure out solutions and—most important—to carry them out. Basically, you have three ways of finding solutions:

1. Review your invention and planning notes for additional support and ideas.
2. Do further invention writing to answer questions your readers raised or to provide material you or your readers think is needed.
3. Look back at the student essays by Sarah Crane and David Ratinov to see how other writers have solved similar problems.

The following suggestions, which are organized according to the basic features of essays interpreting stories, will get you started solving some writing problems common in such essays.

Your Purpose and Readers

- Will readers recognize which story is the subject of this interpretation? State the title early on in the essay. Consider whether readers need to know the author or date of publication.

- Do readers need to be reminded about what happens in the story? If readers may not remember much about the story, briefly describe it for them, but avoid giving too much plot summary.

The Interpretation

- *Is your thesis statement hard for readers to find?* State explicitly at the beginning what your essay will demonstrate, announcing your thesis and forecasting the reasons you will use to argue for it.
- *Is your thesis statement perceived as unarguable or uninteresting?* Revise the thesis to make it clear that you are not stating a simple fact about the story or making an obvious point. Relate your interpretation to class discussion, as Crane does.
- *Are your key terms unclear or not appropriately qualified?* Revise your key terms to avoid ambiguity and vagueness. If you need to limit or qualify your thesis or reasons, add words like *some* or *usually.*
- *Are the key terms in the thesis statement not repeated later in the essay?* Delete any key term from the thesis statement that you do not discuss later in the essay or add language that develops and supports the reason for which this key term stands. If necessary, rewrite the paragraph's topic sentence using the key term.

Checking Sentence Strategies Electronically
To check your draft for sentence strategies especially useful in essays interpreting stories, use your word processor's highlighting function to mark quotations from the story. Then look at how many of the quotations are short (words and phrases) and how many are more extended (sentences and passages). If you have used mostly extended rather than short quotations, think about whether using more short ones (perhaps by using only words or phrases from some of the longer ones) would make your argument more lively and interesting. Also look to make sure that you have commented on each quotation, explaining its relevance to your interpretation of the story. For more on using quotations in literary interpretation, see pp. 551–52.

Reasons and Support

- *Does the thesis or do any of the reasons used to argue for it seem superficial or thin?* Try developing your reasons more fully by comparing or contrasting related reasons; classifying your reasons or dividing them into their subparts; or discussing the social, political, and cultural implications of your way of interpreting the story. Consider elaborating on your reasons by rereading the story with another related suggestion for interpreting in mind.
- *Does support seem lacking?* Add textual evidence by quoting, paraphrasing, or summarizing key passages. Focus your discussion more closely on the writer's choice of words, explaining what particular word choices mean in relation to your reasons. Consider using other kinds of support, such as information about the story's historical or cultural context.
- *Does the connection between a reason and its support seem vague?* Clarify your point by explaining why you think the support you have given illustrates the reason. Do not simply quote from the story. Explain how you interpret each quotation, which words seem significant, and how they demonstrate the point you are making. Remember that both Crane and Ratinov comment on the relevance or point of each quotation immediately after they introduce it.
- *Are there contradictions or gaps in your argument?* You may need to rewrite sections of your essay to eliminate contradictions or fill in gaps. Before cutting anything, consider whether the contradiction is real or apparent. If it is only apparent, explain more fully and clearly how your reasons relate logically to one another as well as to your thesis. To fill in gaps, you may have to lay out your train of thought more explicitly so that readers can more easily follow your logic.

The Organization

- ***Is the essay hard to follow?*** Provide more explicit cues: better forecasting, clear topic sentences, logical transitions, brief summaries.
- ***Does the opening fail to prepare readers for your argument?*** You may need to revise it to forecast your reasons more directly or to give readers a clearer context to help them understand your point.
- ***Does the ending seem abrupt?*** You may need to tie all the strands of the essay together, reiterate your thesis, or discuss its implications.

When you are using the Writing Guide Software, you can click on a Tutorials link to get a quick overview of more than twenty common problems writers have with paragraphs and sentences. In addition to an explanation and examples of the problem, most of the tutorials include suggestions and practice items for identifying and correcting it.

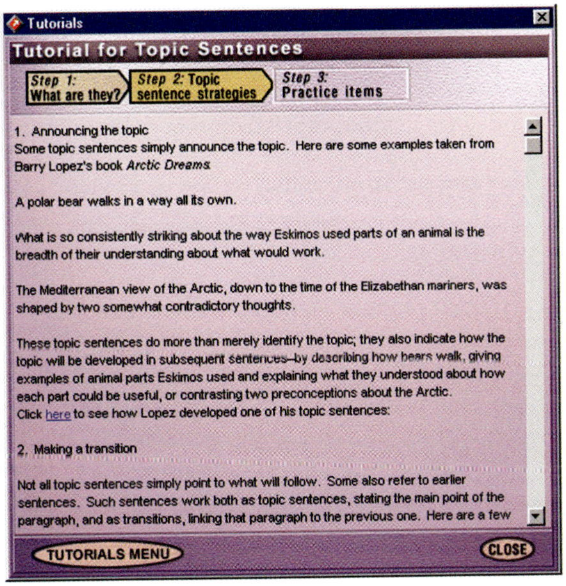

EDITING AND PROOFREADING

Now is the time to check your revised draft for problems in grammar, punctuation, and mechanics and to consider matters of style. It may help you to recognize problems if you study your draft in separate passes—first for paragraphs, then for sentences, and finally for words. Our research has identified several problems that occur often in essays interpreting stories: lack of parallel structure (a matter of style) and the misuse of ellipsis marks (a matter of punctuation). The following guidelines will help you check your draft for these common problems. This book's Web site also provides interactive online exercises to help you learn to identify and correct one of these errors; to access these exercises, go to the URL listed in the margin next to that section of the guidelines.

If you are using the Writing Guide Software, click on
▶ **Editing and Proofreading**

A Note on Grammar and Spelling Checkers
These tools are good at catching certain types of errors, but currently there's no replacement for a good human proofreader. Grammar checkers in particular are extremely limited in what they can usually find, and often they only give you summary information that isn't helpful if you don't already understand the rule in question. They are also prone to give faulty advice for fixing problems and to flag correct items as wrong. Spelling checkers cause fewer problems but can't catch misspellings that are themselves words, such as *to* for *too*.

Checking for Parallelism in Your Writing. When you present similar items together, you must present them in the same grammatical form. All items in a series should be parallel in form—all nouns, all prepositional phrases, all adverb clauses, and so on. Notice, for example, how Sally Crane edited her first-draft sentences to introduce parallel structure:

▶ **I believe, however, that the boy sees nothing and** *learns nothing—* ~~**is incapable of learning**~~ **about** *either* **himself or others.** *He's not self-reflective; he's merely* ~~**because he is so**~~ **self-absorbed.**

▶ **This image comes more from** *what he's read* ~~**his reading**~~ **than from anything he's observed.**

▶ **The greatest irony comes at the end when his quest is exposed as merely a shopping trip** *and Araby as merely a suburban mall.*

The parallelism makes Crane's sentences easier to read and helps her emphasize some of her points. The parallelism of "sees nothing" and "learns nothing" emphasizes the relationship between these two conditions in a way that the first-draft wording did not; the same is true of "what he's read" and "anything he's observed." In the final sentence, Crane added a parallel phrase as an ironic comment.

Following are several more examples from other student essays, each edited to show ways of making writing parallel.

For practice, go to bedfordstmartins.com/theguide/para.

▶ **To Kafka, loneliness,** *isolation,* ~~**being isolated,**~~ **and regrets are the price of freedom.**

▶ **Sarah really cares about her brother and** *values* ~~**to maintain**~~ **their relationship.**

She lets us know that she was injured by her mother's abuse but avoids saying what she felt after the incident, how others reacted to the incident, and *what* ~~**the**~~ **physical pain she endured.**

Checking Your Use of Ellipsis Marks. Ellipsis marks are three spaced periods. They are used to indicate that something has been omitted from quoted text. You will often quote other sources when you interpret a story, and you must be careful to use ellipsis marks to indicate places where you delete material from a quotation.

Look, for example, at the way Sally Crane uses ellipsis marks in quoting from "Araby."

ORIGINAL TEXT **North Richmond Street, being blind, was a quiet street except at the hour when the Christian Brothers' School set the boys free. An uninhabited house of two storeys stood at the blind end, detached from its neighbours in a square ground.**

QUOTED WITH ELLIPSIS MARKS **The street is "blind," with an "uninhabited house . . . at the blind end."**

These ellipsis marks indicate an omission in the middle of the sentence.

If you are using MLA style, follow these few simple rules about using ellipsis marks:

- When you delete words from the *middle of a quoted sentence,* add ellipsis marks, and leave a single space before and after each ellipsis point.
- When you delete words from the *end of a quoted sentence* and a grammatically complete sentence remains, add a period after the last word and then three ellipsis marks.
- Leave a single space after the period and the first two ellipsis points. Do not leave a space between the last point and the closing quotation mark.
- When you delete material from the middle of a passage of *two or more sentences,* use ellipsis marks where the text is omitted and a period after the preceding text if it is grammatically a complete sentence.
- When you delete words from the *beginning of a quoted sentence,* use ellipsis marks only if the remainder of the sentence begins with a capitalized word and is grammatically a complete sentence.
- Single words and brief phrases can be quoted without ellipsis marks.

For more on ellipsis marks, see Chapter 22, pp. 748–49.

The following sentences from other student essays interpreting "Araby" have been edited to correct problems with the use of ellipsis marks:

We learn that a former tenant of the boy's house, "... a priest, had died in the back drawing-room . . . He had been a very charitable priest; in his will he had left all his money to institutions and the furniture of his house to his sister."

The boys lived on "a quiet street . . ."

The light shone on "... the white border of a petticoat . . ."

A WRITER AT WORK

USING THE SUGGESTIONS FOR INTERPRETING TO ANALYZE A STORY

In this Writer at Work section, you will see some of the invention work that David Ratinov did for his essay interpreting "Araby," which appears earlier in this chapter (pp. 534–36). Using the Guide to Writing in this book, Ratinov chose the suggestions for interpreting character to guide his analysis of the story. As you will see, he annotated a portion of the story focusing on two characters (Mrs. Mercer and the boy's uncle), wrote to explore his annotations on the passages, and listed ideas for formulating his tentative thesis statement. You will be able to infer from his invention work how his ideas came to form the thesis he developed for his final essay.

Annotating

Ratinov annotated paragraphs 13–24 of "Araby" as he reread them with the suggestions for interpreting character in mind. The annotated passages are reproduced here. Notice the diversity of his annotations. In the text itself, he underlined key words, circled words to be defined, and connected related words and ideas. In the margin, Ratinov defined words, made comments, and posed questions. He also expressed his tentative insights, reactions, and judgments.

2nd mention of uncle fussing—vain? irritable? rude

On Saturday morning I reminded my uncle that I wished to go to the bazaar in the evening. He was fussing at the hallstand, looking for the hatbrush, and answered me curtly: 13

"Yes, boy, I know." 14

always unkind to the boy? uncle's effect on the boy

As he was in the hall I could not go into the front parlour and lie at the window. I left the house in bad humour and walked slowly towards the school. The air was pitilessly raw and already my heart misgave me. 15

uncle will be late

sudden change in mood; big contrast

liberated from uncle?

isolated from friends

romantic, even sensual

When I came home to dinner my uncle had not yet been home. Still it was early. I sat staring at the clock for some time and, when its ticking began to irritate me, I left the room. I mounted the staircase and gained the upper part of the house. The high cold empty gloomy rooms liberated me and I went from room to room singing. From the front window I saw my companions playing below in the street. Their cries reached me weakened and indistinct and, leaning my forehead against the cool glass, I looked over at the dark house where she lived. I may have stood there for an hour, seeing nothing but the brown-clad figure cast by my imagination, touched discreetly by the lamplight at the curved neck, at the hand upon the railings and at the border below the dress. 16

17 When I came downstairs again I found Mrs. Mercer sitting at the fire. She was an old garrulous woman, a pawnbroker's widow, who collected used stamps for some pious purpose. I had to endure the gossip of the tea-table. The meal was prolonged beyond an hour and still my uncle did not come. Mrs. Mercer stood up to go: she was sorry she couldn't wait any longer, but it was after eight o'clock and she did not like to be out late, as the night air was bad for her. When she had gone I began to walk up and down the room, clenching my fists. My aunt said:

merchandise
talkative
hypocritically religious
boy doesn't seem to like or trust the adults
uncle and Mercer both try to give a false impression

18 "I'm afraid you may put off your bazaar for this night of Our Lord."

aunt religious, but hypocritical?

19 At nine o'clock I heard my uncle's latchkey in the halldoor. I heard him talking to himself and heard the hallstand rocking when it had received the weight of his overcoat. I could interpret these signs. When he was midway through his dinner I asked him to give me the money to go to the bazaar. He had forgotten.

boy knows uncle is drunk
boy's fears are justified excuses

20 "The people are in bed and after their first sleep now," he said.

21 I did not smile. My aunt said to him energetically:

22 "Can't you give him the money and let him go? You've kept him late enough as it is."

aunt to the rescue

23 My uncle said he was very sorry he had forgotten. He said he believed in the old saying: "All work and no play makes Jack a dull boy." He asked me where I was going and, when I had told him a second time he asked me did I know *The Arab's Farewell to His Steed.* When I left the kitchen he was about to recite the opening lines of the piece to my aunt.

hypocritical
what a bore!
boy determined to go to bazaar to buy girl a gift

24 I held a florin tightly in my hand as I strode down Buckingham Street towards the station. The sight of the streets thronged with buyers and glaring with gas recalled to me the purpose of my journey. I took my seat in a third-class carriage of a deserted train. After an intolerable delay the train moved out of the station slowly. It crept onward among ruinous houses and over the twinkling river. At Westland Row Station a crowd of people pressed to the carriage doors; but the porters moved them back, saying that it was a special train for the bazaar. I remained alone in the bare carriage. In a few minutes the train drew up beside an improvised wooden platform. I passed out on to the road and saw by the lighted dial of a clock that it was ten minutes to ten. In front of me was a large building which displayed the magical name.

boy focused on his task
language shows boy's impatience
boy still isolated

As you can see, annotating this section of the story with the suggestions for interpreting character in mind led Ratinov to notice how negatively Mrs. Mercer and the uncle are portrayed by Joyce.

Exploratory Writing

Following the instructions in Writing to Explore Your Annotations in this chapter (p. 546), Ratinov discovered that the two characters are criticized primarily because of their hypocrisy. Here is what he wrote to explore this portion of his annotations:

> Mrs. Mercer may be a good neighbor to the boy's aunt, but the boy dislikes her. Joyce plants many clues that she is a hypocrite. She thinks of herself as a good religious Christian, but she is pious (an exaggerated Christian, not a believable one), she collects stamps to sell for charity instead of doing good works firsthand (my guess), and she gossips. Her husband got his money in an un-Christian way. Does the boy know all this or only the narrator much later? I'm sure the boy senses it. He says he has to endure Mrs. Mercer and her gossiping with his aunt. Now that I've looked over the evidence for the uncle's hypocrisy, it seems that his unguardianlike actions toward the boy--his irresponsibility toward him--are just as big a flaw as is his hypocrisy. He seems to be trying to hide something by drinking and being obsessive about his appearance--a failure to advance at work? He tries to impress people with a bigger house than he can afford. Says he believes in things that don't apply to his own actions. I think I can show that he's a hypocrite like Mrs. Mercer. Because the boy distrusts him, he must sense this hypocrisy.

As Ratinov wrote about the hypocrisy of Mrs. Mercer and the uncle, he became increasingly confident that he had not only an interesting idea, but one he could also find support for in the story.

Listing Ideas for the Thesis

Following the advice given in Formulating a Tentative Thesis Statement in this chapter (p. 546), Ratinov listed ideas he felt confident he could support. In all, he listed five ideas, but notice that the first one came from the exploratory writing he did about Mrs. Mercer and the uncle (shown above):

-- All the adult characters are hypocrites.

-- If this is just a story about romance, then all the adult characters wouldn't have to be so weak and flawed.

-- Mangan's sister is different from the adults, but through her the boy has to face up to what the adult world is all about.

-- The adults are initiating the boy into adulthood, but he doesn't see it until the end of the story.

-- Growing up means being able to see the world for what it actually is, not what you want it to be.

From these ideas about hypocrisy, romance, initiation into the adult world, and the connection between growing up and learning to see reality, Ratinov was able to devise the thesis statement he eventually used in his final essay.

THINKING CRITICALLY ABOUT WHAT YOU HAVE LEARNED

Now that you have read and discussed several essays interpreting a story and have written such an essay yourself, take some time to think critically about what you have learned. What problems did you encounter while you were writing your essay, and how did you solve them? How did reading other essays that interpret a story influence your own essay? What ideas do you have about the social and cultural dimensions of literary interpretation?

Reflecting on Your Writing

Write a one-page explanation, telling your instructor about a problem you encountered in writing your essay and how you solved it. Before you begin, gather all of your writing—invention and planning notes, drafts and critical comments, revision plan, and final revision. Review these materials as you complete this writing task.

1. ***Identify* one *significant writing problem you encountered while writing the essay.*** Do not be concerned with grammar and punctuation; focus instead on a problem specific to writing an interpretation. For example, were you uncertain about which suggestions for interpreting to use for analyzing the story? Did you puzzle over how best to state your thesis and forecast your argument? Did you have trouble deciding which passages from the story to use as support or whether to quote, summarize, or paraphrase them?
2. ***Determine how you came to recognize the problem.*** When did you first discover it—when you were trying to analyze the story, to find supporting evidence, or to sequence your reasons? If someone else pointed out the problem to you, can you now see signs of it in your invention work? If so, where specifically? When you first recognized the problem, how did you respond?
3. ***Reflect on how you went about solving the problem.*** Did you consider using a different suggestion for interpreting? Did you reread one of the essays in this chapter to see how another writer handled a similar problem, or did you do addi-

tional invention work such as rereading the story to fill in gaps in your original annotations? Did you reword, reorganize, or simply cut something that was problematic? If you talked about the problem with another student, a tutor, or your instructor, how did talking about it help?

4. ***Write a brief explanation of the problem and your solution.*** Be as specific as possible in reconstructing your efforts. Quote from your invention notes or draft essay, others' critical comments, your revision plan, and your final revision to show the various changes your writing and thinking underwent as you tried to solve the problem. If you are still uncertain about your solution, say so. Taking time to explain how you identified a particular problem, how you went about trying to solve it, and what you learned from this experience can help you solve future writing problems more easily.

Reviewing What You Learned from Reading

Write a page or so explaining to your instructor how the readings in this chapter influenced your final draft. Your own essay interpreting a story may have been influenced to some extent by the essays in this chapter—the two selections on "Araby"—and by classmates' essays that you have read. Before you write, take some time to reflect on what you have learned from these readings.

1. ***Reread the final revision of your essay; then look back at the essays you read before completing it.*** Do you see any specific influences? For example, did one of the essays influence the suggestions for interpreting you used or the organization you followed? If you were impressed by the way another writer stated a thesis clearly and emphatically, forecasted reasons, or used quotations as support, look to see where you might have been striving for similar effects in your own essay. Look for ideas you got from your reading: writing strategies you were inspired to try, details you were led to include, effects you sought to achieve.

2. ***Write an explanation of these influences.*** Did one selection have a particularly strong influence on your essay, or were parts of several selections influential in similar or different ways? Give examples from the readings and from your final revision to show how you built on what you have learned from other writers. Finally, based on your review of the chapter's readings, point out any further improvements you would now make in your essay.

Considering the Social Dimensions of Essays Interpreting Stories

Some genres, like position papers, have a broad general audience, composed of people whose knowledge of current controversial issues varies widely. Other genres, like essays interpreting stories, are highly specialized, read and written by a comparatively small group of people who share certain kinds of knowledge and interests. Students in English courses, whether they major in English or some other field, learn certain ways of reading and writing about stories. For example, they learn that interpretive essays are arguments, requiring arguable assertions, reasons, and supporting evidence.

But to write effectively in this genre, students also must learn what kinds of interpretations are likely to interest their particular readers—people engaged in an ongoing conversation about stories and other works of literature. They need to know some of the specialized vocabulary English majors use as well as the critical approaches to interpreting stories they find useful. English instructors determine which approaches their students need to become conversant with and they introduce these subjects in lecture and class discussion. They choose stories to read and assign essays to write that will give students opportunities to use these approaches.

The essays written by Sarah Crane and David Ratinov reflect the kinds of approaches students in English classes are likely to encounter. Both student writers are concerned with the character or character development of the boy in "Araby." They focus on what the boy says to himself at the end, the meaning of which is not obvious but requires interpretation. Their interpretations of the ending differ, but the kinds of interpretations they make fit comfortably within the usual conversation among English majors. Crane writes about the way the story is narrated, arguing that the boy is an unreliable narrator, unable to read others or himself accurately; therefore what he says is ironic, meaning the opposite of what it seems to say. Ratinov writes about a theme common to many stories, the theme of initiation. Crane and Ratinov also discuss images of women, although they emphasize different aspects of the boy's cultural background. Crane emphasizes the chivalric tradition about which the boy reads and Ratinov stresses his religious education. These subjects—irony, initiation, and images of women—are included in the suggestions for interpreting in the Guide to Writing because they represent some of the ways in which English majors understand stories.

1. List some of the subjects you and your classmates discussed in class and wrote about. Where did these subjects come from—class discussion, the suggestions for interpreting in the Guide to Writing, your instructor's questions or lecture, other English classes?
2. Consider whether any subjects were deemed by your instructor or other students as uninteresting or not appropriate for interpreting stories. How did you know they were out of line?
3. Write a page or two about your experience making interpretations in this and other English classes.

Part Two

CRITICAL THINKING STRATEGIES

11

A Catalog of Invention Strategies

Writers are like scientists: They ask questions, systematically inquiring about how things work, what they are, where they occur, and how more information can be learned about them. Writers are also like artists in that they use what they know and learn to create something new and imaginative.

The invention and inquiry strategies—also known as **heuristics**—described in this chapter are not mysterious or magical. They are available to all writers, and one or more of them may appeal to your common sense and experience. These techniques represent ways creative writers, engineers, scientists, composers—in fact, all of us—solve problems.

Once you have mastered these strategies, you can use them to tackle many of the writing situations you will encounter in college, on the job, and in the community. The best way to learn them is to use them as you write an actual essay. Chapters 2–10 show you when these strategies can be most helpful and how to make the most efficient use of them. The Guides to Writing in those chapters offer easy-to-use adaptations of these general strategies, adaptations designed to satisfy the special requirements of each kind of writing. You will learn how and when to use these strategies and see how to combine them to achieve your goals.

The strategies for invention and inquiry in this chapter are grouped into two categories:

> ***Mapping:*** A brief visual representation of your thinking or planning
>
> ***Writing:*** The composition of phrases or sentences to discover information and ideas and to make connections among them

These invention and inquiry strategies can be powerful tools for thinking about your topic and planning your writing. They will help you explore and research a topic fully before you begin drafting and then help you creatively solve problems as you draft and revise your draft. In this chapter, strategies are arranged alphabetically within each of the two categories.

MAPPING

Software-based Diagramming Tools
Software vendors have created a variety of electronic tools to help people working in business and technical fields better visualize complex projects. The features of these software packages allow you to enter, store, and rearrange information in a variety of visual formats such as flowcharts, webs, and outlines. For some types of complex writing assignments, these graphical depictions can make it easier for you (or your instructor) to see how to proceed on the project, where more information is needed, or other pitfalls that might not otherwise be apparent. If you are comfortable with any of these packages or if you are primarily a visual thinker, you may find the use of a diagramming tool helpful in the invention as well as later stages of your project.

Mapping strategies involve making a visual record of invention and inquiry. Many writers find that mapping helps them think about a topic. In making maps, they usually use key words and phrases to record material they want to remember, questions they need to answer, and new sources of information they want to check. The maps show the ideas, details, and facts they are examining. They also show possible ways to connect and focus materials. Maps might be informal graphic displays with words and phrases circled and connected by lines to show relationships, or they might be formal sentence outlines. Mapping can be especially useful for working in collaborative writing situations, for preparing oral presentations, and for creating visual aids for written or oral reports. Mapping strategies include clustering, listing, and outlining.

Clustering

Clustering is a strategy for revealing possible relationships among facts and ideas. Unlike listing (the next mapping strategy), clustering requires a brief period of initial preparation when you divide your topic into parts or main ideas. Clustering works as follows:

1. In a word or phrase, write your topic in the center of a piece of paper. Circle it.
2. Also in words or phrases, write down the main parts or ideas of your topic. Circle these, and connect them with lines to the topic in the center.
3. Next, think of facts, details, examples, or ideas related in any way to these main parts. Cluster these around the main parts.

Clustering can be useful for any kind of writing. You can use it in the early stages of planning an essay to find subtopics and organize information. You may try out and discard several clusters before finding one that is promising. Many writers use clustering to plan brief sections of an essay as they are drafting or revising. (A model of clustering is on the next page.)

Listing

Listing is a familiar activity. We make shopping lists and lists of errands to do or people to call. Listing can also be a great help in planning an essay. It enables you to recall what you already know about a topic and suggests what else you may need to find out. It is an easy way to get started with your invention writing, instead of just worrying about what you will write. A list rides along on its own momentum, the first item leading naturally to the next.

A basic activity for all writers, listing is especially useful to those who have little time for planning—for example, reporters facing deadlines and college students taking essay exams. Listing lets you order your ideas quickly. It can also serve as a first step in discovering possible writing topics.

Listing is a solitary form of brainstorming, a popular technique of problem solving in groups. When you work with a group to generate ideas for a collaborative

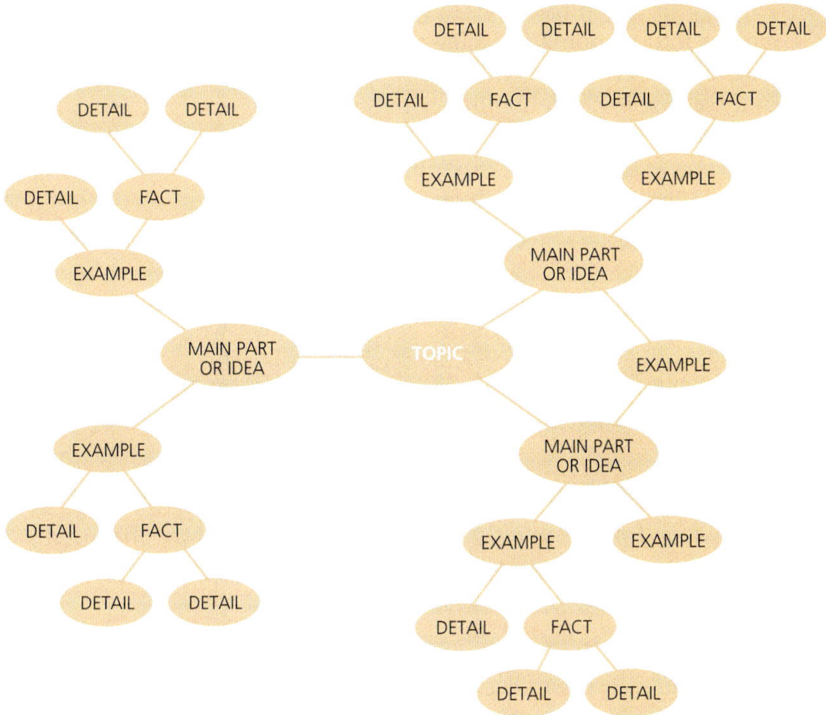

writing project, you are engaged in true brainstorming. Here is how listing works best for invention work:

1. Give your list a title that indicates your main idea or topic.
2. Write as fast as you can, relying on short phrases.
3. Include anything that seems at all useful. Try not to be judgmental at this point.
4. After you have finished or even as you write, reflect on the list, and organize it in the following way. This step is very important, for it may lead you to further discoveries about your topic.

   Put an asterisk next to the most promising items.
   Number key items in order of importance.
   Put items in related groups.
   Cross out items that do not seem promising.
   Add new items.

Outlining

Like listing and clustering, **outlining** is both a means of inventing what you want to say in an essay and a way of organizing your ideas and information. As you outline, you nearly always see new possibilities in your subject, discovering new ways of dividing or grouping information and seeing where you need additional information to develop your ideas. Because outlining lets you see at a glance where your essay's strengths and weaknesses lie, outlining can also help you read and revise your essay with a critical eye.

There are two main forms of outlining: informal scratch outlining and formal topic or sentence outlining. (Keep in mind that clustering is also a type of informal outlining.)

The Planning and Drafting sections of the Guides to Writing in Chapters 2–10 illustrate many different scratch outlines.

A *scratch outline* is considered an informal outline because it is little more than a list of the essay's main points. You have no doubt made scratch outlines many times—to plan essays or essay exams, to revise your own writing, and to analyze a difficult reading passage. Here are sample scratch outlines for two different kinds of essays. The first outlines Rick Bragg's essay in Chapter 2, and the second shows one way to organize a position paper (Chapter 6):

Scratch Outline: Essay about a Remembered Event

Turn to pp. 39–42 to compare this outline to Bragg's essay.

1. Gives background on his quest since boyhood for "a car built for speed"
2. Recalls the 1969 muscle car he bought the summer before his senior year of high school, how he paid for it, and his uncle's warning
3. Recalls how the car conveyed status to him among his peers
4. Recalls winning his first parking-lot race in the car and his subsequent thrill over speeding the car down country roads
5. Turns to specific incident two weeks after he got the car when, during a high-speed race through the country, he braked suddenly because he saw a police cruiser and flipped the car into ditch
6. Describes how, miraculously, he was relatively unhurt, hanging upside down and pinned in by the low adjustment of the steering wheel
7. Reflects on the inappropriateness of his initial mental response: to turn down the radio
8. Describes being pulled from the car by a state trooper and the trooper's comment that he should have been killed in the accident ("The Lord was riding with you, son")
9. Describes his mother's stunned reaction
10. Tells about the authorities' decision not to charge him
11. Remembers the sight of the crushed car once it had been flipped back over
12. Recalls the wrecker operator's echo of the trooper's comment
13. Ends with a reflection about an imagined newspaper headline that humorously summarizes his experience

Scratch Outline: Essay Arguing a Position

Presentation of the issue

Concession of some aspect of an opposing position

Thesis statement

First reason with support

Second reason with support (etc.)

Conclusion

Remember that the items in a scratch outline do not necessarily coincide with paragraphs. Sometimes two or more items may be developed in the same paragraph or one item may be covered in two or more paragraphs.

Chunking, a type of scratch outline commonly used by professional writers in business and industry and especially well suited to writing in the electronic age, consists of a set of headings describing the major points to be covered in the final document. What makes chunking distinctive is that the blocks of text—or "chunks"—under each heading are intended to be roughly the same length and scope. These headings can be discussed and passed around among several writers and editors before writing begins, and different chunks may be written by different authors, simply by typing notes or text on a word processor into the space under each heading. The list of headings is subject to change during the writing, and new headings may be added or old ones subdivided or discarded as part of the drafting and editing process.

The advantage of chunking in your own individual writing is that it breaks the large task of drafting into smaller tasks in a simple, evenly balanced way; once the headings are determined, the writing becomes just a matter of filling in the specifics that go in each chunk. Organization tends to improve as you get a sense of the weight of different parts of the document while filling in the blanks. Places where the essay needs more information or there is a problem with pacing tend to stand out because of the chunking structure, and the headings can either be taken out of the finished essay or left in as devices to help guide readers. If they are left in, they should be edited into parallel grammatical form like the items in a formal topic or sentence outline, as discussed below.

Topic and *sentence outlines* are considered more formal than scratch outlines because they follow a conventional format of numbered and lettered headings and subheadings:

I. (Main topic)
  A. (Subtopic of I)
  B.
    1. (Subtopic of I.B)
    2.
      a. (Subtopic of I.B.2)
      b.
        (1) (Subtopic of I.B.2.b)
        (2)
  C.
    1. (Subtopic of I.C)
    2.

Turn to pp. 287–91 to compare these outlines to Statsky's essay.

The difference between a topic and sentence outline is obvious: topic outlines simply name the topics and subtopics, whereas sentence outlines use complete or abbreviated sentences. To illustrate, here are two partial formal outlines of an essay arguing a position, Jessica Statsky's "Children Need to Play, Not Compete," from Chapter 6.

Formal Topic Outline

I. Organized sports harmful to children
   A. Harmful physically
      1. Curve ball (Koppett)
      2. Tackle football (Tutko)
   B. Harmful psychologically
      1. Fear of being hurt
         a. Little League Online
         b. Mother
         c. Reporter
      2. Competition
         a. Rablovsky
         b. Studies

Formal Sentence Outline

I. Highly organized competitive sports such as Peewee Football and Little League Baseball can be physically and psychologically harmful to children, as well as counterproductive for developing future players.
   A. Physically harmful because sports entice children into physical actions that are bad for growing bodies.
      1. Koppett claims throwing a curve ball may put abnormal strain on developing arm and shoulder muscles.
      2. Tutko argues that tackle football is too traumatic for young kids.
   B. Psychologically harmful to children for a number of reasons.
      1. Fear of being hurt detracts from their enjoyment of the sport.
         a. Little League Online ranks fear of injury seventh among the seven top reasons children quit.
         b. One mother says, "kids get so scared. . . . They'll sit on the bench and pretend their leg hurts."
         c. A reporter tells about a child who made himself vomit to get out of playing Peewee Football.

2. Too much competition poses psychological dangers for children.
   a. Rablovsky reports: "The spirit of play suddenly disappears, and sport becomes joblike."
   b. Studies show that children prefer playing on a losing team to "warming the bench on a winning team."

In contrast to an informal outline in which anything goes, a formal outline must follow many conventions. The roman numerals and capital letters are followed by periods. In topic and sentence outlines, the first word of each item is capitalized, but items in topic outlines do not end with a period as items in sentence outlines do. Every level of a formal outline except the top level (identified by the roman numeral *I*) must include at least two items. Items at the same level of indentation in a topic outline should be grammatically parallel—all beginning with the same part of speech. For example, *I.A.* and *I.B.* are parallel when they both begin with an adverb *(Physically harmful* and *Psychologically harmful)* or with a noun *(Harmful physically* and *Harmful psychologically)*; they would not be parallel if one began with an adverb *(Physically harmful)* and the other with a noun *(Harmful psychologically)*.

WRITING

Writing is itself a powerful tool for thinking. As you write, you can recall details, remember facts, develop your ideas, find connections in new information you have collected, examine assumptions, and critically question what you know.

Unlike most mapping strategies, **writing strategies** of invention invite you to produce complete sentences. Sentences provide considerable generative power. Because they are complete statements, they take you further than listing or clustering. They enable you to explore ideas and define relationships, bring ideas together or show how they differ, and identify causes and effects. Sentences can also help you develop a logical chain of thought.

Some of these invention and inquiry strategies are systematic, while others are more flexible. Even though they call for complete sentences that are related to one another, they do not require preparation or revision. You can use them to develop oral as well as written presentations.

These writing strategies include cubing, dialoguing, dramatizing, keeping a journal, looping, questioning, and quick drafting.

Cubing

Cubing is useful for quickly exploring a writing topic, probing it from six different perspectives. It is known as *cubing* because a cube has six sides. These are the six perspectives in cubing:

Describing: What does your subject look like? What size is it? What is its color? Its shape? Its texture? Name its parts.

Comparing: What is your subject similar to? Different from?

Associating: What does your subject make you think of? What connections does it have to anything else in your experience?

Analyzing: What are the origins of your subject? What are its parts or features? How are its parts related?

Applying: What can you do with your subject? What uses does it have?

Arguing: What arguments can you make for your subject? Against it?

Here are some guidelines to help you use cubing productively.

1. Select a topic, subject, or part of a subject. This can be a person, a scene, an event, an object, a problem, an idea, or an issue. Hold it in focus.
2. Limit your writing to three to five minutes for each perspective. The whole activity should take no more than half an hour.
3. Keep going until you have written about your subject from all six perspectives. Remember that cubing offers the special advantage of enabling you to generate multiple perspectives quickly.
4. As you write from each perspective, begin with what you know about your subject. However, do not limit yourself to your present knowledge. Indicate what else you would like to know about your subject, and suggest where you might find that information.
5. Reread what you have written. Look for bright spots, surprises. Recall the part that was easiest for you to write. Recall the part where you felt a special momentum and pleasure in the writing. Look for an angle or an unexpected insight. These special parts may suggest a focus or topic within a larger subject, or they may provide specific details to include in a draft.

Dialoguing

See pp. 71–72 for an example of dialogue used for invention.

A dialogue is a conversation between two or more people. You can use **dialoguing** to search for topics, find a focus, explore ideas, or consider opposing viewpoints. When you write a dialogue as an invention strategy, you need to make up all parts of the conversation (unless, of course, you are writing collaboratively—on a network, for example). To construct a dialogue by yourself, imagine two particular people talking, hold a conversation yourself with some imagined person, or simply talk out loud to yourself. To construct a dialogue independently or collaboratively, follow these steps:

1. Write a conversation between two speakers. Label the participants *Speaker A* and *Speaker B,* or make up names for them.
2. If you get stuck, you might have one of the speakers ask the other a question.
3. Write brief responses to keep the conversation moving fast. Do not spend much time planning or rehearsing responses. Write what first occurs to you, just as in a real conversation, where people take quick turns to prevent any awkward silences.

Dialogues can be especially useful with personal experience and persuasive essays because they help you remember conversations and anticipate objections.

Dramatizing

Dramatizing is an invention activity developed by the philosopher Kenneth Burke as a way of thinking about how people interact and as a way of analyzing stories and films.

Thinking about human behavior in dramatic terms can be very productive for writers. Drama has action, actors, setting, motives, and methods. Since stars and acting go together, you can use a five-pointed star to remember these five points of dramatizing: Each point on the star provides a different perspective on human behavior. We can think of each point independently and in combination. Let us begin by looking at each point to see how it helps us to analyze people and their interactions.

Action. An action is anything that happens, has happened, will happen, or could happen. Action includes events that are physical (running a marathon), mental (thinking about a book you have read), and emotional (falling in love). This category also refers to the results of activity (an essay).

Actor. The actor is involved in the action—either responsible for it or simply affected by it. (The actor does not have to be a person. It can be a force, something that causes an action. For example, if the action is a rise in the price of gasoline, the actor could be increased demand or short supply.) Dramatizing may also include a number of coactors working together or at odds.

Setting. The setting is the situation or background of the action. We usually think of setting as the place and time of an event, but it may also be the historical background of an event or the childhood of a person.

Motive. The motive is the purpose or reason for an action—the actor's intention. Actions may have multiple, even conflicting, motives.

Method. The method explains how an action occurs, including the techniques an actor uses. It refers to whatever makes things happen.

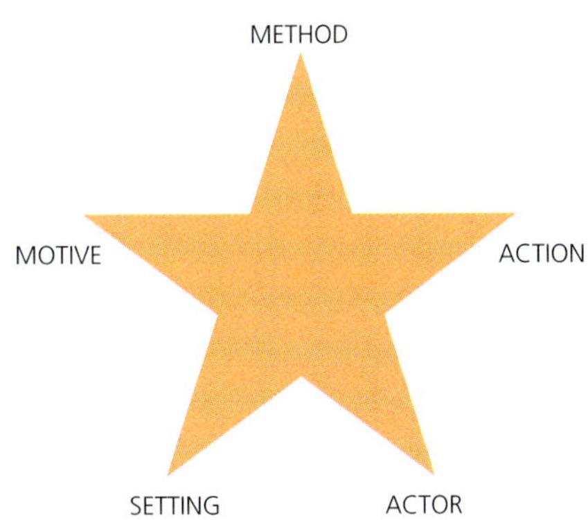

Each of these points suggests a simple invention question:

Action: What?

Actor: Who?

Setting: When and where?

Motive: Why?

Method: How?

This list looks like the questions reporters typically ask. But dramatizing goes further: It enables us to ask a much fuller set of invention questions that we generate by considering relations between and among these five elements. We can think about actors' motives, the effect of the setting on the actors, the relations between actors, and so on.

You can use this invention strategy to learn more about yourself or about other significant people in your life. You can use it, as well, to explore, analyze, or evaluate characters in stories or movies. Moreover, dramatizing is especially useful in analyzing the readers you want to inform or convince.

To use dramatizing, imagine the person you want to understand better in a particular situation. Holding this image in mind, write answers to any questions in the following list that apply. You may draw a blank on some questions, have little to say to some, and find a lot to say to others. Be exploratory and playful with the questions. Write responses quickly, relying on words and phrases, even drawings.

- What is the actor doing?
- How did the actor come to be involved in this situation?
- Why does the actor do what he or she does?
- What else might the actor do?
- What is the actor trying to accomplish?
- How do other actors influence—help or hinder—the main actor?
- What do the actor's actions reveal about him or her?
- What does the actor's language reveal about him or her?
- How does the event's setting influence the actor's actions?
- How does the time of the event influence what the actor does?
- Where does this actor come from?
- How is this actor different now from what he or she used to be?
- What might this actor become?
- How is this actor like or unlike the other actors?

Keeping a Journal

Professional writers often use **journals** to keep notes, and so might you. Starting a writer's journal is easy. Buy a special notebook, or open a new file on your computer, and start writing. Here are some possibilities:

- Keep a list of new words and concepts you learn in your courses. You could also write about the progress and direction of your learning in particular courses—

the experience of being in the course, your feelings about what is happening and what you are learning.

- Respond to your reading, both assigned and personal. As you read, write about your personal associations, reflections, reactions, and evaluations. Summarize or copy memorable or especially important passages, and comment on them. (Copying and commenting have been practiced by students and writers for centuries in special journals called *commonplace books.*)
- Write to prepare for particular class meetings. Write about the main ideas you have learned from assigned readings and about the relationship of these new ideas to other ideas in the course. After class, write to summarize what you have learned. List questions you have about the ideas or information discussed in class. Journal writing of this kind involves reflecting, evaluating, interpreting, synthesizing, summarizing, and questioning.
- Record observations and overheard conversations.
- Write for ten or fifteen minutes every day about whatever is on your mind. Focus these meditations on your new experiences as you try to understand, interpret, and reflect on them.
- Write sketches of people who catch your attention.
- Organize your time. Write about your goals and priorities, or list specific things to accomplish and what you plan to do.
- Keep a log over several days or weeks about a particular event unfolding in the news—a sensational trial, an environmental disaster, a political campaign, a campus controversy, the fortunes of a sports team.

You can use a journal in many ways. All of the writing in your journal has value for learning. You may also be able to use parts of your journal for writing in your other courses.

Looping

Looping is especially useful for the first stages of exploring a topic. As its name suggests, **looping** involves writing quickly to explore some aspect of a topic and then looping back to your original starting point or to a new starting point to explore another aspect. Beginning with almost any starting point, looping enables you to find a center of interest and eventually a thesis for your essay. The steps are simple:

1. Write down your area of interest. You may know only that you have to write about another person or a movie or a cultural trend that has caught your attention. Or you may want to search for a topic in a broad historical period or for one related to a major political event. Although you may wander from this topic as you write, you will want to keep coming back to it. Your purpose is to find a focus for writing.
2. Write nonstop for ten minutes. Start with the first thing that comes to mind. Write rapidly, without looking back to reread or to correct anything. *Do not stop writing. Keep your pencil moving.* Continuous writing is the key to looping. If

you get stuck for a moment, rewrite the last sentence. Trust the act of writing to lead you to new insights. Follow diversions and digressions, but keep returning to your topic.

3. After ten minutes, pause to reread what you have written. Decide what is most important—a single insight, a pattern of ideas, an emerging theme, a visual detail, anything at all that stands out. Some writers call this a "center of gravity" or a "hot spot." To complete the first loop, restate this center in a single sentence.
4. Beginning with this sentence, write nonstop for another ten minutes.
5. Summarize in one sentence again to complete the second loop.
6. Keep looping until one of your summary sentences produces a focus or thesis. You may need only two or three loops; you may need more.

Questioning

Asking **questions** about a subject is a way to learn about it and decide what to write. When you first encounter a subject, however, your questions may be scattered. Also, you are not likely to think right away of all the important questions you ought to ask. The advantage of having a basic list of questions for invention, like the ones for cubing and for dramatizing discussed earlier in this chapter, is that it provides a systematic approach to exploring a subject.

The questions that follow come from classical rhetoric (what the Greek philosopher Aristotle called *topics*) and a modern approach to invention called *tagmemics*. Based on the work of linguist Kenneth Pike, tagmemics provides questions about different ways we make sense of the world, the ways we sort and classify experience in order to understand it.

Here are the steps in using questions for invention:

1. In a sentence or two, identify your subject. A subject could be any event, person, problem, project, idea, or issue—in other words, anything you might write about.
2. Start by writing a response to the first question in the following list, and move right through the list. Try to answer each question at least briefly with a word or a phrase. Some questions may invite several sentences or even a page or more of writing. You may draw a blank on a few questions. Skip them. Later, when you have more experience with questions for invention, you can start anywhere in the list.
3. Write your responses quickly, without much planning. Follow digressions or associations. Do not screen anything out. Be playful.

What Is Your Subject?

- What is your subject's name? What other names does it have? What names did it have in the past?
- What aspects of the subject do these different names emphasize?
- Imagine a still photograph or a moving picture of your subject. What would it look like?

- What would you put into a time capsule to stand for your subject?
- What are its causes and results?
- How would it look from different vantage points or perspectives?
- What particular experiences have you had with the subject? What have you learned?

What Parts or Features Does Your Subject Have, and How Are They Related?

- Name the parts or features of your subject.
- Describe each one, using the questions in the preceding subject list.
- How is each part or feature related to the others?

How Is Your Subject Similar to and Different from Other Subjects?

- What is your subject similar to? In what ways are these subjects alike?
- What is your subject different from? In what ways are the subjects different?
- What seems to you most unlike your subject? In what ways are the two things unlike each other? Now, just for fun, note how they are alike.

How Much Can Your Subject Change and Still Remain the Same?

- How has your subject changed from what it once was?
- How is it changing now—moment to moment, day to day, year to year?
- How does each change alter your way of thinking about your subject?
- What are some different forms your subject takes?
- What does it become when it is no longer itself?

Where Does Your Subject Fit in the World?

- When and where did your subject originate?
- What would happen if at some future time your subject ceased to exist?
- When and where do you usually experience the subject?
- What is this subject a part of, and what are the other parts?
- What do other people think of your subject?

Quick Drafting

Sometimes you know what you want to say or have little time for invention. In these situations, **quick drafting** may be a good strategy. There are no special rules for quick drafting, but you should rely on it only if you know your subject well, have had experience with the kind of writing you are doing, and will have a chance to revise your draft. Quick drafting can help you discover what you already know about the subject and what you need to find out. It can also help you develop and organize your thoughts.

12 A Catalog of Reading Strategies

To become a thoughtful, effective writer, you must also become a critical reader. This chapter presents strategies to help you *read with a critical eye*. Reading critically means not just comprehending passively and remembering what you read but also scrutinizing actively and making thoughtful judgments about your reading. When you read a text critically, you need to alternate between understanding and questioning—on the one hand, striving to understand the text on its own terms; on the other hand, taking care to question its ideas and authority. You will benefit greatly from reading what others have written—and reading your own writing—in this way.

The strategies here complement and supplement reading strategies presented in Part One, Chapters 2–10. Critical reading is central to your success with the writing assignments in those chapters. The Connecting to Culture and Experience activity following each reading in Part One helps you think about the selection in light of your own experience and awareness of social issues, while the Analyzing Writing Strategies questions help you understand how the text works and evaluate how well it achieves its purpose with its readers. The Critical Reading Guide in each Part One chapter helps you read other students' drafts as well as your own to find out what is working and what needs improvement.

Reading is, after all, inextricably linked to writing, and the reading strategies in this chapter can help you enrich your thinking as a reader and participate in conversations as a writer. These strategies include the following:

- ***Annotating:*** Recording your reactions to, interpretations of, and questions about a text as you read it
- ***Taking inventory:*** Listing and grouping your annotations and other notes to find meaningful patterns
- ***Outlining:*** Listing the text's main ideas to reveal how it is organized
- ***Paraphrasing:*** Restating what you have read to clarify or refer to it
- ***Summarizing:*** Distilling the main ideas or gist of a text
- ***Synthesizing:*** Integrating into your own writing ideas and information gleaned from different sources
- ***Contextualizing:*** Placing a text in its historical and cultural contexts

- ***Exploring the significance of figurative language:*** Examining how metaphors, similes, and symbols are used in a text to convey meaning and evoke feelings
- ***Looking for patterns of opposition:*** Analyzing the values and assumptions embodied in the language of a text
- ***Reflecting on challenges to your beliefs and values:*** Critically examining the bases of your personal responses to a text
- ***Evaluating the logic of an argument:*** Determining whether a thesis is well reasoned and adequately supported
- ***Recognizing emotional manipulation:*** Identifying texts that unfairly and inappropriately use emotional appeals based on false or exaggerated claims
- ***Judging the writer's credibility:*** Considering whether writers represent different points of view fairly and know what they are writing about

These critical reading strategies can help you connect information from different sources and relate it to what you already know; distinguish fact from opinion; uncover and question assumptions; and subject other people's ideas as well as your own to reasoned argument. You can readily learn these strategies and apply them not only to a critical reading of the selections in Part One but also to your other college reading. Although mastering the strategies will not make critical reading easy, it can make your reading much more satisfying and productive and thus help you handle even difficult material with confidence. Critical reading strategies will, in addition, often be useful in your reading outside of school—for instance, these strategies can help you understand, evaluate, and comment on what political figures, advertisers, and other writers are saying.

ANNOTATING

Annotating Onscreen
Although this discussion of annotating assumes you are reading printed pages, you can also annotate many kinds of text on the computer screen by using your word processor's highlighting and commenting functions. Even if these functions are not available, you may be able to type annotations into the text using a different color or font. If electronic annotation is impossible, print out the text, and annotate by hand.

Annotations are the marks—underlines, highlights, and comments—you make directly on the page as you read. **Annotating** can be used to record immediate reactions and questions, outline and summarize main points, and evaluate and relate the reading to other ideas and points of view. Especially useful for studying and preparing to write, annotating is also an essential element of many other critical reading strategies. Your annotations can take many forms, such as the following:

Writing comments, questions, or definitions in the margins

Underlining or circling words, phrases, or sentences

Connecting ideas with lines or arrows

Numbering related points

Bracketing sections of the text

Noting anything that strikes you as interesting, important, or questionable

Most readers annotate in layers, adding further annotations on second and third readings. Annotations can be light or heavy, depending on the reader's purpose and the difficulty of the material. Your purpose for reading also determines how you use your annotations.

The following selection, excerpted from Martin Luther King Jr.'s "Letter from Birmingham Jail," is annotated to illustrate some of the ways you can annotate as you read. Add your own annotations, if you like.

Martin Luther King Jr. *(1929–1968) first came to national notice in 1955, when he led a successful boycott against the policy of restricting African American passengers to rear seats on city buses in Montgomery, Alabama, where he was minister of a Baptist church. He subsequently formed a national organization, the Southern Christian Leadership Conference, that brought people of all races from all over the country to the South to fight nonviolently for racial integration. In 1963, King led demonstrations in Birmingham, Alabama, that were met with violence; a bomb was detonated in a black church, killing four young girls. King was arrested for his role in organizing the protests, and while in prison, he wrote the famous "Letter from Birmingham Jail" to answer the criticism of local clergy and to justify to the nation his strategy of civil disobedience, which he called "nonviolent direct action."*

King begins his letter by discussing his disappointment with the lack of support he has received from white moderates, such as the group of clergy who published criticism in the local newspaper. As you read the following excerpt from his letter, try to infer from King's written response what the clergy's specific criticisms might have been. Also, notice the tone King uses to answer his critics. Would you characterize the writing as apologetic, conciliatory, accusatory, or in some other way?

An Annotated Sample from "Letter from Birmingham Jail"

Martin Luther King Jr.

¶1. White moderates block progress.

I must confess that over the past few years I have been gravely disappointed with the white moderate. I have almost reached the regrettable conclusion that the Negro's [great stumbling block in his stride toward freedom] is not the White Citizen's Counciler or the Ku Klux Klanner, but the white moderate, who is more devoted to "order" than to justice; who prefers a negative peace which is the absence of tension to a positive peace which is the presence of justice; who constantly says: "I agree with you in the goal you seek, but I cannot agree with your methods of direct action"; who paternalistically believes he can set the timetable for another man's freedom; who lives by a mythical concept of time 1

negative vs. positive

order vs. justice

ends vs. means

treating others like children

and who constantly advises the Negro to wait for a "more convenient season." Shallow understanding from people of good will is more frustrating than absolute misunderstanding from people of ill will. Lukewarm acceptance is much more bewildering than outright rejection.

¶12. Tension necessary for progress.

2 I had hoped that the white moderate would understand that law and order exist for the purpose of establishing justice and that when they fail in this purpose they become the [dangerously structured dams that block the flow of social progress.] I had hoped that the white moderate would understand that the present tension in the South is a necessary phase of the transition from an [obnoxious negative peace,] in which the Negro passively accepted his unjust plight, to a [substantive and positive peace,] in which all men will respect the dignity and worth of human personality. Actually, we who engage in nonviolent direct action are not the creators of tension. We merely bring to the surface the hidden tension that is already alive. We bring it out in the open, where it can be seen and dealt with. [Like a boil that can never be cured so long as it is covered up but must be opened with all its ugliness to the natural medicines of air and light, injustice must be exposed, with all the tension its exposure creates, to the light of human conscience and the air of national opinion before it can be cured.]

Tension already exists anyway.

True?

Simile: hidden tension is "like a boil"

¶13. Questions clergymen's logic: condemning his actions = condemning victims, Socrates, Jesus.

3 In your statement you assert that our actions, even though peaceful, must be condemned because they precipitate violence. But is this a logical assertion? Isn't this like condemning a robbed man because his possession of money precipitated the evil act of robbery? Isn't this like condemning Socrates because his unswerving commitment to truth and his philosophical inquiries precipitated the act by the misguided populace in which they

made him drink hemlock? Isn't this like condemning Jesus because his unique God-consciousness and never-ceasing devotion to God's will precipitated the evil act of crucifixion? We must come to see that, as the federal courts have consistently affirmed, it is wrong to urge an individual to cease his efforts to gain his basic constitutional rights because the question may precipitate violence. [Society must protect the robbed and punish the robber.]

Yes!

4 I had also hoped that the white moderate would reject the myth concerning time in relation to the struggle for freedom. I have just received a letter from a white brother in Texas. He writes: "All Christians know that the colored people will receive equal rights eventually, but it is possible that you are in too great a religious hurry. It has taken Christianity almost two thousand years to accomplish what it has. The teachings of Christ take time to come to earth." Such an attitude stems from a tragic misconception of time, from the strangely irrational notion that there is something in the very flow of time that will inevitably cure all ills. Actually, time itself is neutral; it can be used either destructively or constructively. More and more I feel that the people of ill will have used time much more effectively than have the people of good will. We will have to repent in this generation not merely for the [hateful words and actions of the bad people] but for the [appalling silence of the good people.] Human progress never rolls in on [wheels of inevitability;] it comes through the tireless efforts of men willing to be co-workers with God, and without this hard work, time itself becomes an ally of the forces of social stagnation. [We must use time creatively, in the knowledge that the time is always ripe to do right.] Now is the time to make real the promise of democracy and transform our pending [national

example of a white moderate

Silence is as bad as hateful words and actions.

metaphor

not moving

¶4. Time must be used to do right.

elegy] into a creative [psalm of brotherhood.] Now is the time to lift our national policy from the [quicksand of racial injustice] to the [solid rock of human dignity.]

metaphors

You speak of our activity in Birmingham as extreme. At first I 5
was rather disappointed that fellow clergymen would see my nonviolent efforts as those of an extremist. I began thinking about the fact that I stand in the middle of two opposing forces in the Negro community. One is a [force of complacency,] made up in part of Negroes who, as a result of long years of oppression, are so drained of self-respect and a sense of "somebodiness" that they have adjusted to segregation; and in part of a few middle-class Negroes, who because of a degree of academic and economic security and because in some ways they profit by segregation, have become insensitive to the problems of the masses. The other [force is one of bitterness and hatred,] and it comes perilously close to advocating violence. It is expressed in the various black nationalist [groups that are springing up] across the nation, the largest and best-known being Elijah Muhammad's Muslim movement. Nourished by the Negro's frustration over the continued existence of racial discrimination, this movement is made up of people who have lost faith in America, who have absolutely repudiated Christianity, and who have concluded that the white man is an incorrigible "devil."

King accused of being an extremist

¶5. King in middle of two extremes: complacent & angry.

Malcolm X?

I have tried to stand between these two forces, saying that 6
we need emulate neither the "do-nothingism" of the complacent nor the hatred and despair of the black nationalist. For there is the more excellent way of love and nonviolent protest. I am grateful to God that, through the influence of the Negro church, the way of nonviolence became an integral part of our struggle.

¶6. King offers better choice.

How did nonviolence become part of King's movement?

If this philosophy had not emerged, by now many streets of 7
the South would, I am convinced, be flowing with blood. And I am

¶7. King's movement prevented racial violence. Threat?

further convinced that if our white brothers dismiss as "rabble-rousers" and "outside agitators" those of us who employ nonviolent direct action, and if they refuse to support our nonviolent efforts, millions of Negroes will, out of frustration and despair, seek solace and security in black-nationalist ideologies—a development that would inevitably lead to a frightening racial nightmare.

Gandhi?

The church?

If . . . then . . .

comfort

8 Oppressed people cannot remain oppressed forever. The yearning for freedom eventually manifests itself, and that is what has happened to the American Negro. Something within has reminded him of his birthright of freedom, and something without has reminded him that it can be gained. Consciously or unconsciously, he has been caught up by the *Zeitgeist,* and with his black brothers of Africa and his brown and yellow brothers of Asia, South America and the Caribbean, the United States Negro is moving with a sense of great urgency toward the [promised land of racial justice.] If one recognizes this [vital urge that has engulfed the Negro community,] one should readily understand why public demonstrations are taking place. The Negro has many [pent-up resentments] and latent frustrations, and he must release them. So let him march; let him make prayer pilgrimages to the city hall; let him go on freedom rides—and try to understand why he must do so. If his repressed emotions are not released in nonviolent ways, they will seek expression through violence; this is not a threat but a fact of history. So I have not said to my people: "Get rid of your discontent." Rather, I have tried to say that this normal and healthy discontent can be [channeled into the creative outlet of nonviolent direct action.] And now this approach is being termed extremist.

worldwide uprising against injustice

spirit of the times

Not a threat?

¶8. Discontent is normal and healthy but must be channeled.

9 But though I was initially disappointed at being categorized as an extremist, as I continued to think about the matter

I gradually gained a measure of satisfaction from the label. Was not Jesus an extremist for love: "Love your enemies, bless them that curse you, do good to them that hate you, and pray for them which despitefully use you, and persecute you." Was not Amos an extremist for justice: "Let justice roll down like waters and righteousness like an ever-flowing stream." Was not Paul an extremist for the Christian gospel: "I bear in my body the marks of the Lord Jesus." Was not Martin Luther an extremist: "Here I stand; I cannot do otherwise, so help me God." And John Bunyan: "I will stay in jail to the end of my days before I make a butchery of my conscience." And Abraham Lincoln: "This nation cannot survive half slave and half free." And Thomas Jefferson: "We hold these truths to be self-evident, that all men are created equal. . . ." So the question is not whether we will be extremists, but what kind of extremists we will be. Will we be extremists for hate or for love? Will we be extremists for the preservation of injustice or for the extension of justice? In that dramatic scene on Calvary's hill three men were crucified. We must never forget that all three were crucified for the same crime—the crime of extremism. Two were extremists for immorality, and thus fell below their environment. The other, Jesus Christ, was an extremist for love, truth and goodness, and thereby rose above his environment. Perhaps the South, the nation and the world are in dire need of creative extremists.

Hebrew prophet

Christian apostle

English preacher

Founded Protestantism

No choice but to be extremists: But what kind?

¶9. Creative extremists are needed.

Disappointed in the white moderate

I had hoped that the white moderate would see this need. 10
Perhaps I was too optimistic; perhaps I expected too much. I suppose I should have realized that few members of the oppressor race can understand the deep groans and passionate yearnings of the oppressed race, and still fewer have the vision to see that [injustice must be rooted out] by strong, persistent and deter-

¶10. Some whites have supported King.

mined action. I am thankful, however, that some of our white brothers in the South have grasped the meaning of this social revolution and committed themselves to it. They are still all too few in quantity, but they are big in quality. Some—such as Ralph McGill, Lillian Smith, Harry Golden, James McBride Dabbs, Ann Braden and Sarah Patton Boyle—have written about our struggle in eloquent and prophetic terms. Others have marched with us down nameless streets of the South. They have languished in filthy, roach-infested jails, suffering the abuse and brutality of policemen who view them as "dirty nigger-lovers." Unlike so many of their moderate brothers and sisters, they have recognized the urgency of the moment and sensed the need for [powerful "action" antidotes] to combat the [disease of segregation.]

Who are they?

what they did

been left unaided

CHECKLIST: Annotating

1. Mark the text using notations like these:
   - Circle words to be defined in the margin.
   - Underline key words and phrases.
   - Bracket important sentences and passages.
   - Use lines or arrows to connect ideas or words.
2. Write marginal comments like these:
   - Number and summarize each paragraph.
   - Define unfamiliar words.
   - Note responses and questions.
   - Identify interesting writing strategies.
   - Point out patterns.
3. Layer additional markings on the text and comments in the margins as you reread for different purposes.

TAKING INVENTORY

An inventory is simply a list or grouping of items. **Taking inventory** helps you analyze your annotations for different purposes. When you take inventory, you make various kinds of lists to explore patterns of meaning you find in the text. For instance, in reading the annotated passage by Martin Luther King Jr., you might have noticed that many famous people are named or that certain similes and metaphors are used.

By listing the names (Socrates, Jesus, Luther, Lincoln, and so on) and then grouping them into categories (people who died for their beliefs, leaders, teachers, and religious figures) you could better understand why the writer refers to these particular people. Taking inventory of your annotations can be helpful in writing about a text you are reading.

CHECKLIST: Taking Inventory

1. Examine your annotations for patterns or repetitions such as recurring images, stylistic features, repeated words and phrases, repeated examples or illustrations, and reliance on particular writing strategies.
2. List and group the items in the pattern.
3. Decide what the pattern indicates about the reading.

OUTLINING

Outlining is an especially helpful critical reading strategy for understanding the content and structure of a reading. **Outlining**, which identifies the text's main ideas, may be part of the annotating process, or it may be done separately. Writing an outline in the margins of the text as you read and annotate makes it easier to find information later. Writing an outline on a separate piece of paper gives you more space to work with, and therefore such an outline usually includes more detail.

The key to outlining is distinguishing between the main ideas and the supporting material such as examples, quotations, comparisons, and reasons. The main ideas form the backbone, which holds the various parts and pieces of the text together. Outlining the main ideas helps you uncover this structure.

Making an outline, however, is not simple. The reader must exercise judgment in deciding which are the most important ideas. Because importance is relative, different readers can make different—and equally reasonable—decisions based on what interests them in the reading. Readers also must decide whether to use the writer's words, their own words, or a combination of the two. The words used in an outline reflect the reader's interpretation and emphasis. Reading is never a passive or neutral act; the process of outlining shows how constructive reading can be.

You may make either a formal, multileveled outline with roman (I, II) and arabic (1, 2) numerals together with capital and lowercase letters or an informal scratch outline that lists the main idea of each paragraph. A *formal outline* is harder to make and much more time consuming than a scratch outline. You might choose to make a formal outline of a reading about which you are writing an in-depth analysis or evaluation. For example, here is a formal outline a student wrote for a paper evaluating the logic of the King excerpt. Notice that the student uses roman numerals for the main ideas or claims, capital letters for the reasons, and arabic numerals for supporting evidence and explanation.

For more on the conventions of formal outlines, see pp. 574–75.

Formal Outline

I. "[T]he Negro's great stumbling block in his stride toward freedom is . . . the white moderate. . . "
  A. Because the white moderate is more devoted to "order" than to justice (paragraph 2)
    1. Law and order should exist to establish justice.
    2. Law and order compare to "dangerously structured dams that block the flow of social progress."
  B. Because the white moderate prefers a "negative peace" (absence of tension) to a "positive peace" (justice) (paragraph 2)
    1. The tension already exists.
    2. It is not created by nonviolent direct action.
    3. Society that does not eliminate injustice compares to a boil that hides its infections. Both can be cured only by exposure (boil simile).
  C. Because even though the white moderate agrees with the goals, he does not support the means to achieve them (paragraph 3)
    1. The argument that the means--nonviolent direct action--are wrong because they precipitate violence is flawed.
    2. An analogy compares black people to the robbed man who is condemned because he had money.
    3. Analogies compare black people with Socrates and Jesus.
  D. Because the white moderate paternalistically believes he can set a timetable for another man's freedom (paragraph 4)
    1. He rebuts the white moderate's argument that Christianity will cure man's ills and man must wait patiently for that to happen.
    2. He argues that "time itself is neutral" and that people "must use time creatively" for constructive rather than destructive ends.

II. Creative extremism is preferable to moderation.
  A. Classifies himself as a moderate (paragraphs 5-8)
    1. "I . . . stand between . . . two forces": the white moderate's complacency and the Black Muslim's rage.
    2. If nonviolent direct action were stopped, more violence, not less, would result.

```
      3. "[M]illions of Negroes will, out of frustration
         and despair, seek solace and security in black-
         nationalist ideologies. . ." (paragraph 7).
      4. Repressed emotions will be expressed--if not in non-
         violent ways, then through violence (paragraph 8).
   B. Redefines himself as a "creative extremist" (paragraph
      9)
      1. Extremism for love, truth, and goodness is creative
         extremism.
      2. He identifies himself with other extremists--Jesus,
         Amos, Paul, Martin Luther, John Bunyan, Abraham
         Lincoln, and Thomas Jefferson.
   C. Not all white people are moderates; some are committed
      to "this social revolution" (paragraph 10).
      1. He lists the names of white writers.
      2. He refers to other white activists.
```

Making a scratch outline takes less time than making a formal outline but still requires careful reading. A *scratch outline* will not record as much information as a formal outline, but it is sufficient for most critical reading purposes. To make a scratch outline, you first need to locate the topic of each paragraph in the reading. The topic is usually stated in a word or phrase, and it may be repeated or referred to throughout the paragraph. For example, the opening paragraph of the King excerpt (p. 585) makes clear that its topic is the white moderate.

After you have found the topic of the paragraph, figure out what is being said about it. To return to our example: King immediately establishes the white moderate as the topic of the opening paragraph and at the beginning of the second sentence announces the conclusion he has come to—namely, that the white moderate is "the Negro's great stumbling block in his stride toward freedom." The rest of the paragraph specifies the ways the white moderate blocks progress.

For each paragraph in the King excerpt, the annotations include a summary of the paragraph's topic. Here is an outline that lists those paragraph topics:

Paragraph Scratch Outline

```
¶1. white moderates block progress in the struggle for racial
    justice
¶2. tension necessary for progress
¶3. clergymen's criticism not logical
¶4. time must be used to do right
¶5. King is in the middle of two extremes: complacent and
    angry
¶6. King offers a better choice
```

¶7. King's movement has prevented racial violence

¶8. discontent normal and healthy but must be channeled

¶9. creative extremists needed

¶10. some whites have supported King

CHECKLIST: Outlining

1. Reread each paragraph, identifying the topic and the comments made about the topic. Do not include examples, specific details, quotations, or other explanatory and supporting material.
2. List the author's main ideas in the margin of the text or on a separate piece of paper.

PARAPHRASING

Paraphrasing is restating something you have read by using mostly your own words. As a critical reading strategy, paraphrasing can help you to clarify the meaning of an obscure or ambiguous passage. It is one of the three ways of integrating other people's ideas and information into your own writing, along with *quoting* (reproducing exactly the language of the source text) and *summarizing* (distilling the main ideas or gist of the source text) (p. 596). You might choose to paraphrase rather than quote when the source's language is not especially arresting or memorable. You might paraphrase short passages but summarize longer ones.

Following are two passages. The first is from paragraph 2 of the excerpt from King's "Letter." The second passage is a paraphrase of the first:

Original

I had hoped that the white moderate would understand that law and order exist for the purpose of establishing justice and that when they fail in this purpose they become the dangerously structured dams that block the flow of social progress. I had hoped that the white moderate would understand that the present tension in the South is a necessary phase of the transition from an obnoxious negative peace, in which the Negro passively accepted his unjust plight, to a substantive and positive peace, in which all men will respect the dignity and worth of human personality.

Paraphrase

King writes that he had hoped for more understanding from white moderates--specifically that they would recognize that law and order are not ends in themselves but means to the greater end of establishing justice. When law and order do not serve this greater end, they stand in the way of progress. King expected the white moderate to recognize that the current tense situation in the South is part of a transition process

> that is necessary for progress. The current situation is bad because although there is peace, it is an "obnoxious" and "negative" kind of peace based on blacks passively accepting the injustice of the status quo. A better kind of peace--one that is "substantive," real and not imaginary, as well as "positive"--requires that all people, regardless of race, be valued.

When you compare the paraphrase to the original, you can see that the paraphrase contains all the important information and ideas of the original. Notice also that the paraphrase is somewhat longer than the original, refers to the writer by name, and encloses King's original words in quotation marks. Although the paraphrase tries to be *neutral,* to avoid inserting the reader's opinions or distorting the original writer's ideas, it does inevitably express the reader's interpretation of the original text's meaning. Another reader might paraphrase the same passage differently.

CHECKLIST: Paraphrasing

1. Reread the passage to be paraphrased, looking up unfamiliar words in a college dictionary.
2. Translate the passage into your own words, putting quotation marks around any words or phrases you quote from the original.
3. Revise to ensure coherence.

SUMMARIZING

Summarizing is one of the most widely used strategies for critical reading because it helps the reader understand and remember what is most important in the reading. Another advantage of summarizing is that it creates a condensed version of the reading's ideas and information, which can be referred to later or inserted into the reader's own writing. Along with quoting and paraphrasing, summarizing enables you to refer to and integrate other writers' ideas into your own writing.

A summary is a relatively brief restatement, primarily in the reader's own words, of the reading's main ideas. Summaries vary in length, depending on the reader's purpose. Some summaries are very brief—a sentence or even a subordinate clause. For example, if you were referring to the excerpt from "Letter from Birmingham Jail" and simply needed to indicate how it relates to your other sources, your summary might focus on only one aspect of the reading. It might look something like this: "There have always been advocates of extremism in politics. Martin Luther King Jr., in 'Letter from Birmingham Jail,' for instance, defends nonviolent civil disobedience as an extreme but necessary means of bringing about racial justice." If, on the other hand, you were surveying the important texts of the civil rights movement, you might write a longer, more detailed summary that not only identifies the reading's main ideas but also shows how the ideas relate to one another.

Many writers find it useful to outline the reading as a preliminary to writing a summary. A paragraph-by-paragraph scratch outline (like the one on pp. 594–95) lists the reading's main ideas in the sequence in which they appear in the original. But summarizing requires more than merely stringing together the entries in an outline. It fills in the logical connections between the author's ideas. Notice also in the following example that the reader repeats selected words and phrases and refers to the author by name, indicating, with verbs like *expresses, acknowledges,* and *explains,* the writer's purpose and strategy at each point in the argument.

Summary

King expresses his disappointment with white moderates who, by opposing his program of nonviolent direct action, have become a barrier to progress toward racial justice. He acknowledges that his program has raised tension in the South, but he explains that tension is necessary to bring about change. Furthermore, he argues that tension already exists. But because it has been unexpressed, it is unhealthy and potentially dangerous.

He defends his actions against the clergy's criticisms, particularly their argument that he is in too much of a hurry. Responding to charges of extremism, King claims that he has actually prevented racial violence by channeling the natural frustrations of oppressed blacks into nonviolent protest. He asserts that extremism is precisely what is needed now--but it must be creative, rather than destructive, extremism. He concludes by again expressing disappointment with white moderates for not joining his effort as some other whites have.

A summary presents only ideas. While it may use certain key terms from the source, it does not otherwise attempt to reflect the source's language, imagery, or tone; and it avoids even a hint of agreement or disagreement with the ideas it summarizes. Of course, however, a writer might summarize ideas in a source like "Letter from Birmingham Jail" to show readers that he or she has read it carefully and then proceed to use the summary to praise, question, or challenge King's argument. In doing so, the writer might quote specific language that reveals word choice, imagery, or tone.

Checklist: Summarizing

1. Make a scratch outline of the reading.
2. Write a paragraph or more that presents the author's main ideas largely in your own words. Use the outline as a guide, but reread parts of the original text as necessary.
3. To make the summary coherent, fill in connections between ideas.

SYNTHESIZING

Synthesizing involves presenting ideas and information gleaned from different sources. As a critical reading strategy, synthesizing can help you see how different sources relate to one another—for example, offering supporting details or opposing arguments.

When you synthesize material from different sources, you construct a conversation among your sources, a conversation in which you also participate. Synthesizing contributes most to critical thinking when writers use sources not only to support their ideas, but to challenge and extend them as well.

In the following example, the reader uses a variety of sources related to the King passage (pp. 585–91). The synthesis brings the sources together around a central idea. Notice how quotation, paraphrase, and summary are all used to present King's and the other sources' ideas.

Synthesis

When King defends his campaign of nonviolent direct action against the clergymen's criticism that "our actions, even though peaceful, must be condemned because they precipitate violence" (King excerpt, paragraph 3), he is using what Vinit Haksar calls Mohandas Gandhi's "safety-valve argument" ("Civil Disobedience and Non-Cooperation" 117). According to Haksar, Gandhi gave a "non-threatening warning of worse things to come" if his demands were not met. King similarly makes clear that advocates of actions more extreme than those he advocates are waiting in the wings: "The other force is one of bitterness and hatred, and it comes perilously close to advocating violence" (King excerpt, paragraph 5). King identifies this force with Elijah Muhammad, and although he does not name him, King's contemporary readers would have known that he was referring also to Malcolm X who, according to Herbert J. Storing, "urged that Negroes take seriously the idea of revolution" ("The Case against Civil Disobedience" 90). In fact, Malcolm X accused King of being a modern-day Uncle Tom, trying "to keep us under control, to keep us passive and peaceful and nonviolent" (Malcolm X Speaks 12).

CHECKLIST: Synthesizing

1. Find and read a variety of sources on your topic, annotating the passages that give you ideas about the topic.
2. Look for patterns among your sources, possibly supporting or refuting your ideas or those of other sources.

3. Write a paragraph or more synthesizing your sources, using quotation, paraphrase, and summary to present what they say on the topic.

CONTEXTUALIZING

All texts were written sometime in the past and therefore may embody historical and cultural assumptions, values, and attitudes different from your own. To read critically, you need to become aware of these differences. **Contextualizing** is a critical reading strategy that enables you to make inferences about a reading's historical and cultural context and to examine the differences between its context and your own.

The excerpt from King's "Letter from Birmingham Jail" is a good example of a text that benefits from being read contextually. If you knew little about the history of slavery and segregation in the United States, Martin Luther King Jr., or the civil rights movement, it would be difficult to understand the passion for justice and impatience with delay expressed in this passage from King's writings. To understand the historical and cultural context in which King organized his demonstrations and wrote his "Letter from Birmingham Jail," you could do some library or Internet research. A little research would enable you to appreciate the intense emotions that swept the nation at the time. You would see that the threat of violence was all too real. Comparing the situation at the time King wrote the "Letter" in 1963 to situations with which you are familiar would help you understand some of your own attitudes toward King and the civil rights movement.

Here is what one reader wrote to contextualize King's writing:

Notes from a Contextualized Reading

1. I am not old enough to remember what it was like in the early 1960s when Dr. King was leading marches and sit-ins, but I have seen television documentaries showing demonstrators being attacked by dogs, doused by fire hoses, beaten and dragged by helmeted police. Such images give me a sense of the violence, fear, and hatred that King was responding to.

   The tension King writes about comes across in his writing. He uses his anger and frustration creatively to inspire his critics. He also threatens them, although he denies it. I saw a film on Malcolm X, so I could see that King was giving white people a choice between his own nonviolent way and Malcolm's more confrontational way.
2. Things have certainly changed since the sixties. Legal segregation has ended, but there are still racists like the detective in the O. J. Simpson trial. African Americans like General Colin Powell are highly respected and

```
powerful. The civil rights movement is over. So when I'm
reading King today, I feel like I'm reading history. But
then again, every once in a while there are reports of
police brutality because of race (think of Rodney King)
and of what we now call hate crimes.
```

CHECKLIST: Contextualizing

1. Describe the historical and cultural situation as it is represented in the reading and in other sources with which you are familiar. Your knowledge may come from other reading, television or film, school, or elsewhere. (If you know nothing about the historical and cultural context, you could do some library or Internet research.)
2. Compare the historical and cultural situation in which the text was written to your own historical and cultural situation. Consider how your understanding and judgment of the reading is affected by your own context.

EXPLORING THE SIGNIFICANCE OF FIGURATIVE LANGUAGE

Figurative language—metaphor, simile, and symbolism—enhances literal meaning by embodying abstract ideas in vivid images and by evoking feelings and associations.

Metaphor implicitly compares two different things by identifying them with each other. For instance, when King calls the white moderate "the Negro's great stumbling block in his stride toward freedom" (paragraph 1), he does not mean that the white moderate literally trips the Negro who is attempting to walk toward freedom. The sentence makes sense only if understood figuratively: The white moderate trips up the Negro by frustrating every effort to achieve justice.

Simile, a more explicit form of comparison, uses the word *like* or *as* to signal the relationship of two seemingly unrelated things. King uses simile when he says that injustice is "like a boil that can never be cured so long as it is covered up" (paragraph 2). This simile makes several points of comparison between injustice and a boil. It suggests that injustice is a disease of society as a boil is a disease of the body and that injustice, like a boil, must be exposed or it will fester and infect the entire body.

Symbolism compares two things by making one stand for the other. King uses the white moderate as a symbol for supposed liberals and would-be supporters of civil rights who are actually frustrating the cause.

How these figures of speech are used in a text reveals something of the writer's feelings about the subject. Exploring possible meanings in a text's figurative language involves (1) annotating and then listing the metaphors, similes, and symbols you find in a reading; (2) grouping the figures of speech that appear to express related feelings or attitudes, and labeling each group; and (3) writing to explore the meaning of the patterns you have found.

The following example shows the process of exploring figures of speech in the King excerpt.

Listing Figures of Speech

"stumbling block in his stride toward freedom" (paragraph 1)

"law and order . . . become the dangerously structured dams" (2)

"the flow of social progress" (2)

"Like a boil that can never be cured" (2)

"the light of human conscience and the air of national opinion" (2)

"the quicksand of racial injustice" (4)

Grouping Figures of Speech

Sickness: "like a boil" (2); "the disease of segregation" (10)

Underground: "hidden tension" (2); "injustice must be exposed" (2); "injustice must be rooted out" (10)

Blockage: "dams," "block the flow" (2); "Human progress never rolls in on wheels of inevitability" (4); "pent-up resentments" (8); "repressed emotions" (8)

Writing to Explore Meaning

The patterns labeled underground and blockage suggest a feeling of frustration. Inertia is a problem; movement forward toward progress or upward toward the promised land is stalled. The strong need to break through the resistance may represent King's feelings both about his attempt to lead purposeful, effective demonstrations and his effort to write a convincing argument.

The simile of injustice being "like a boil" links the two patterns of underground and sickness, suggesting something bad, a disease, is inside the people or the society. The cure is to expose or to root out the blocked hatred and injustice as well as to release the tension or emotion that has long been repressed. This implies that repression itself is the evil, not simply what is repressed. Therefore, writing and speaking out through political action may have curative power for individuals and society alike.

CHECKLIST: Exploring the Significance of Figurative Language

1. Annotate all the figures of speech you find in the reading—metaphors, similes, and symbols—and then list them.

2. Group the figures of speech that appear to express related feelings and attitudes, and label each group.
3. Write one or two paragraphs exploring the meaning of these patterns. What do they tell you about the text?

LOOKING FOR PATTERNS OF OPPOSITION

All texts carry within themselves voices of opposition. These **patterns of opposition** may echo the views and values of critical readers the writer anticipates or predecessors to whom the writer is responding in some way; they may even reflect the writer's own conflicting values. Careful readers look closely for such a dialogue of opposing voices within the text.

When we think of oppositions, we ordinarily think of polarities: *yes* and *no, up* and *down, black* and *white, new* and *old*. Some oppositions, however, may be more subtle. The excerpt from King's "Letter from Birmingham Jail" is rich in such oppositions: *moderate* versus *extremist, order* versus *justice, direct action* versus *passive acceptance, expression* versus *repression*. These oppositions are not accidental; they form a significant pattern that gives a critical reader important information about the essay.

A careful reading will show that King always values one of the two terms in an opposition over the other. In the passage, for example, *extremist* is valued over *moderate* (paragraph 9). This preference for extremism is surprising. The critical reader should ask why, when white extremists like members of the Ku Klux Klan have committed so many outrages against African Americans, King would prefer extremism. If King is trying to convince his readers to accept his point of view, why would he represent himself as an extremist? Moreover, why would a clergyman advocate extremism instead of moderation?

Studying the patterns of opposition enables you to answer these questions. You will see that King sets up this opposition to force his readers to examine their own values and realize that they are in fact misplaced. Instead of working toward justice, he says, those who support law and order maintain the unjust status quo. By getting his readers to think of white moderates as blocking rather than facilitating peaceful change, King brings them to align themselves with him and perhaps even embrace his strategy of nonviolent resistance.

Looking for patterns of opposition involves annotating words or phrases in the reading that indicate oppositions, listing the opposing terms in pairs, deciding which term in each pair is preferred by the writer, and reflecting on the meaning of the patterns. Here is a partial list of oppositions from the King excerpt, with the preferred terms marked by an asterisk:

Listing Patterns of Opposition

moderate	*extremist
order	*justice
negative peace	*positive peace

absence of justice	*presence of justice
goals	*methods
*direct action	passive acceptance
*exposed tension	hidden tension

CHECKLIST: Looking for Patterns of Opposition

1. Annotate the selection for words or phrases indicating oppositions.
2. List the pairs of oppositions. (You may have to paraphrase or even supply the opposite word or phrase if it is not stated directly in the text.)
3. For each pair of oppositions, put an asterisk next to the term that the writer seems to value or prefer over the other.
4. Study the patterns of opposition. How do they contribute to your understanding of the essay? What do they tell you about what the author wants you to believe?

REFLECTING ON CHALLENGES TO YOUR BELIEFS AND VALUES

To read critically, you need to scrutinize your own assumptions and attitudes as well as those expressed in the text you are reading. If you are like most readers, however, you will find that your assumptions and attitudes are so ingrained that you are not fully aware of them. A good strategy for getting at these underlying beliefs and values is to identify and reflect on the ways the text challenges you, how it makes you feel—disturbed, threatened, ashamed, combative, or some other way.

For example, here is what one student wrote about the King passage:

Reflections

In paragraph 1, Dr. King criticizes people who are "more devoted to 'order' than to justice." This criticism upsets me because today I think I would choose order over justice. When I analyze my feelings and try to figure out where they come from, I realize that what I feel most is fear. I am terrified by the violence in society today. I'm afraid of sociopaths who don't respect the rule of law, much less the value of human life.

I know Dr. King was writing in a time when the law itself was unjust, when order was apparently used to keep people from protesting and changing the law. But things are different now. Today, justice seems to serve criminals more than it serves law-abiding citizens. That's why I'm for order over justice.

CHECKLIST: Reflecting on Challenges to Your Beliefs and Values

1. Identify challenges by marking the text where you feel your beliefs and values are being opposed, citicized, or unfairly characterized.
2. Write a few paragraphs reflecting on why you feel challenged. Do not defend your feelings; instead, analyze them to see where they come from.

EVALUATING THE LOGIC OF AN ARGUMENT

An argument includes a thesis backed by reasons and support. The *thesis* asserts an idea, a position on a controversial issue, or a solution to a problem that the writer wants readers to accept. The *reasons* tell readers why they should accept the thesis, and the *support* (such as examples, statistics, authorities, and textual evidence) gives readers grounds for accepting it. For an argument to be considered logically acceptable, it must meet the three conditions of what we call the ABC test:

The ABC Test

For more on argument, see Chapter 19. For an example of the ABC test, see Christine Romano's essay in Chapter 8, pp. 411–15.

A. The reasons and support must be *appropriate* to the thesis.

B. The reasons and support must be *believable*.

C. The reasons and support must be *consistent* with one another as well as *complete*.

Testing for Appropriateness

As a critical reader, you must decide whether the argument's reasons and support are appropriate and clearly related to the thesis. To test for appropriateness, ask these questions: How does each reason or piece of support relate to the thesis? Is the connection between reasons and support and the thesis clear and compelling? Or is the argument irrelevant or only vaguely related to the thesis?

For more on analogy, see Chapter 18, pp. 675–76. For more on invoking authorities, see Chapter 19, pp. 684–85.

Readers most often question the appropriateness of reasons and support when the writer argues by analogy or by invoking authority. For example, in paragraph 2, King argues that when law and order fail to establish justice, "they become the dangerously structured dams that block the flow of social progress." The analogy asserts the following logical relationship: Law and order are to progress toward justice what a dam is to water. If you do not accept this analogy, the argument fails the test of appropriateness.

King uses both analogy and authority in the following passage: "Isn't this like condemning Socrates because his unswerving commitment to truth and his philosophical inquiries precipitated the act by the misguided populace in which they made him drink hemlock?" (paragraph 3). Not only must you judge the appropriateness of the analogy comparing the Greek populace's condemnation of Socrates to the white moderates' condemnation of King, but you must also judge whether it is appropriate to accept Socrates as an authority on this subject. Since Socrates is generally respected for his teaching on justice, his words and actions are likely to be considered appropriate to King's situation in Birmingham.

Testing for Believability

Believability is a measure of your willingness to accept as true the reasons and support the writer gives in defense of a thesis.

To test for believability, ask: On what basis am I being asked to believe this reason or support is true? If it cannot be proved true or false, how much weight does it carry?

In judging facts, examples, statistics, and authorities, consider the following points.

Facts are statements that can be proved objectively to be true. The believability of facts depends on their *accuracy* (they should not distort or misrepresent reality), their *completeness* (they should not omit important details), and the *trustworthiness* of their sources (sources should be qualified and unbiased). King, for instance, asserts as fact that the African American will not wait much longer for racial justice (paragraph 8). His critics might question the factuality of this assertion by asking, is it true of all African Americans? How much longer will they wait? How does King know what African Americans will and will not do?

Examples and *anecdotes* are particular instances that may or may not make you believe a general statement. The believability of examples depends on their *representativeness* (whether they are truly typical and thus generalizable) and their *specificity* (whether particular details make them seem true to life). Even if a vivid example or gripping anecdote does not convince readers, it usually strengthens argumentative writing by clarifying the meaning and dramatizing the point. In paragraph 5 of the King excerpt, for example, King supports his generalization that some African American nationalist extremists are motivated by bitterness and hatred by citing the specific example of Elijah Muhammad's Black Muslim movement. Conversely, in paragraph 9, he refers to Jesus, Paul, Luther, and others as examples of extremists motivated by love and Christianity. These examples support his assertion that extremism is not in itself wrong and that any judgment of extremism must be based on its motivation and cause.

Statistics are numerical data, including correlations. The believability of statistics depends on the *comparability* of the data (the price of apples in 1985 cannot be compared to the price of apples in 2003 unless the figures are adjusted to account for inflation), the *precision* of the methods employed to gather and analyze data (representative samples should be used and variables accounted for), and the *trustworthiness* of the sources (sources should be qualified, unbiased, and—except in historical contexts—as recent as possible).

Authorities are people to whom the writer attributes expertise on a given subject. Not only must such authorities be appropriate, as mentioned earlier, but they must be believable as well. The believability of authorities depends on their *credibility*, on whether the reader accepts them as experts on the topic at hand. King cites authorities repeatedly throughout his essay. He refers to religious leaders (Jesus and Luther) as well as to American political leaders (Lincoln and Jefferson). These figures are certain to have a high degree of credibility among King's readers.

Testing for Consistency and Completeness

In looking for consistency, you should be concerned that all the parts of the argument work together and that none of the reasons or support contradict any of the other reasons or support. In addition, the reasons and support, taken together, should be sufficient to convince readers to accept the thesis or at least take it seriously. To test for consistency and completeness, ask: Are any of the reasons and support contradictory? Do they provide sufficient grounds for accepting the thesis? Does the writer fail to counterargue (to acknowledge, accommodate, or refute any opposing arguments or important objections)?

For more on counterarguing, see Chapter 19, pp. 688–91.

A critical reader might regard as contradictory King's characterizing himself first as a moderate between the forces of complacency and violence and later as an extremist opposed to the forces of violence. King attempts to reconcile this apparent contradiction by explicitly redefining extremism in paragraph 9. Similarly, the fact that King fails to examine and refute every legal recourse available to his cause might allow a critical reader to question the sufficiency of his argument.

Checklist: Evaluating the Logic of an Argument

Use the ABC test:

A. *Test for appropriateness* by checking that the reasons and support are clearly and directly related to the thesis.

B. *Test for believability* by deciding whether you can accept the reasons and support as true.

C. *Test for consistency and completeness* by ascertaining whether the argument has any contradictions and whether any important objections or opposing arguments have been ignored.

RECOGNIZING EMOTIONAL MANIPULATION

Many different kinds of essays appeal to readers' emotions. Tobias Wolff's remembered-event essay (in Chapter 2) may be terrifying to some readers; John Edge's attempts to eat a pickled pig lip (in Chapter 4) may disgust some readers, especially vegetarians; and Richard Estrada's position paper (in Chapter 6) may be annoying to some readers because of his accommodating tone.

Writers often try to arouse emotions in readers to excite their interest, make them care, or move them to take action. There is nothing wrong with appealing to readers' emotions. What is wrong is manipulating readers with false or exaggerated appeals. As a critical reader, you should be suspicious of writing that is overly or falsely sentimental, that cites alarming statistics and frightening anecdotes, that demonizes others and identifies itself with revered authorities, or that uses symbols (flag waving) or emotionally loaded words (such as *racist*).

King, for example, uses the emotionally loaded word *paternalistically* to refer to the white moderate's belief that "he can set the timetable for another man's freedom" (paragraph 1). In the same paragraph, King uses symbolism to get an emotional reaction from readers when he compares the white moderate to the "Ku Klux Klanner." To get readers to accept his ideas, he also relies on authorities whose names evoke the greatest respect, such as Jesus and Lincoln. But some readers might object that comparing King's crusade to that of Jesus and other leaders of religious and political groups is pretentious and manipulative. A critical reader might also consider King's discussion of African American extremists in paragraph 7 to be a veiled threat designed to frighten readers into agreement.

Checklist: Recognizing Emotional Manipulation

1. Annotate places in the text where you sense emotional appeals are being used.
2. Assess whether any of the emotional appeals are unfairly manipulative.

JUDGING THE WRITER'S CREDIBILITY

Writers often try to persuade readers to respect and believe them. Because readers may not know them personally or even by reputation, writers must present an image of themselves in their writing that will gain their readers' confidence. This image cannot be made directly but must be made indirectly, through the arguments, language, and system of values and beliefs expressed or implied in the writing. Writers establish credibility in their writing in three ways:

By showing their knowledge of the subject

By building common ground with readers

By responding fairly to objections and opposing arguments

Testing for Knowledge

Writers demonstrate their knowledge through the facts and statistics they marshal, the sources they rely on for information, and the scope and depth of their understanding. As a critical reader, you may not be sufficiently expert on the subject yourself to know whether the facts are accurate, the sources are reliable, and the understanding is sufficient. You may need to do some research to see what others say about the subject. You can also check credentials—the writer's educational and professional qualifications, the respectability of the publication in which the selection first appeared, and reviews of the writer's work—to determine whether the writer is a respected authority in the field. For example, King brings with him the authority that comes from being a member of the clergy and a respected leader of the Southern Christian Leadership Conference.

Testing for Common Ground

One way writers can establish common ground with their readers is by basing their reasoning on shared values, beliefs, and attitudes. They use language that includes their readers *(we)* rather than excludes them *(they)*. They qualify their assertions to keep them from being too extreme. Above all, they acknowledge differences of opinion and try to make room in their argument to accommodate reasonable differences. As a critical reader, you want to notice such appeals.

King creates common ground with readers by using the inclusive pronoun *we,* suggesting shared concerns between himself and his audience. Notice, however, his use of masculine pronouns and other references ("the Negro . . . he," "our brothers"). Although King addressed his letter to male clergy, he intended it to be published in the local newspaper, where it would be read by an audience of both men and women. By using language that excludes women, a common practice at the time the selection was written, King misses the opportunity to build common ground with half of his readers.

Testing for Fairness

Writers reveal their character by how they handle opposing arguments and objections to their argument. As a critical reader, you want to pay particular attention to how writers treat possible differences of opinion. Be suspicious of those who ignore differences and pretend that everyone agrees with their viewpoints. When objections or opposing views are represented, consider whether they have been distorted in any way; if they are refuted, be sure they are challenged fairly—with sound reasoning and solid support.

One way to gauge the author's credibility is to identify the tone of the argument, for it conveys the writer's attitude toward the subject and toward the reader. Examine the text carefully for indications of tone: Is the text angry? Sarcastic? Evenhanded? Shrill? Condescending? Bullying? Do you feel as if the writer is treating the subject—and you, as a reader—with fairness? King's tone might be characterized in different passages as patient (he doesn't lose his temper), respectful (he refers to white moderates as "people of good will"), or pompous (comparing himself to Jesus and Socrates).

Checklist: Judging the Writer's Credibility

1. Annotate for the writer's knowledge of the subject, how well common ground is established, and whether the writer deals fairly with objections and opposing arguments.
2. Decide what in the essay you find credible and what you question.

Part Three

WRITING STRATEGIES

13

Cueing the Reader

Readers need guidance. To guide readers through a piece of writing, a writer can provide five basic kinds of **cues** or signals:

1. Thesis and forecasting statements, to orient readers to ideas and organization
2. Paragraphing, to group related ideas and details
3. Cohesive devices, to connect ideas to one another and bring about coherence and clarity
4. Connectives, to signal relationships or shifts in meaning
5. Headings and subheadings, to group related paragraphs and help readers locate specific information quickly

This chapter illustrates how each of these cueing strategies works.

ORIENTING STATEMENTS

To help readers find their way, especially in difficult and lengthy texts, you can provide two kinds of **orienting statements**: a thesis statement, which declares the main point, and a forecasting statement, which previews subordinate points, showing the order in which they will be discussed in the essay.

Thesis Statements

To help readers understand what is being said about a subject, writers often provide a thesis statement early in the essay. The **thesis statement** operates as a cue by letting readers know which is the most important general idea among the writer's many ideas and observations. Here are three thesis statements from essays in Part One:

> O.K., let's cut out all this nonsense about romantic love. Let's bring some scientific precision to the party. Let's put love under a microscope.
>
> When rigorous people with Ph.D.s after their names do that, what they see is not some silly, senseless thing. No, their probe reveals that love rests firmly on the foundations of evolution, biology and chemistry.
>
> –ANASTASIA TOUFEXIS, Chapter 5

> It seems to me that what Native Americans are saying is that what would be intolerable for Jews, blacks, Latinos and others is no less offensive to them. Theirs is a request not only for dignified treatment, but for fair treatment as well. For America to ignore the complaints of a numerically small segment of the population because it is small is neither dignified nor fair.
>
> –RICHARD ESTRADA, Chapter 6

> . . . I could not shake the idea that sooner or later I would get the rifle out again. All my images of myself as I wished to be were images of myself armed. Because I did not know who I was, any image of myself, no matter how grotesque, had power over me. This much I understand now. But the man can give no help to the boy, not in this matter nor in those that follow. The boy moves always out of reach.
>
> –TOBIAS WOLFF, Chapter 2

Most thesis statements, like Toufexis's, can be expressed in a single sentence; others may require two or more sentences, like Estrada's and Wolff's. Wolff's thesis explicitly states the point of a remembered event, but many autobiographical essays imply the thesis rather than state it directly.

Readers naturally look for something that will tell them the point of an essay, a focus for the many diverse details and ideas they encounter as they read. The lack of an explicit thesis statement can make this task more difficult. Therefore, careful writers keep readers' needs and expectations in mind when deciding how to state the thesis as clearly and directly as possible.

Another important decision is where to place the thesis statement. Most readers expect to find some information early on that will give them a context for reading the essay, particularly if they are reading about a new and difficult subject. Therefore, a thesis statement, like that of Toufexis, placed at the beginning of an essay enables readers to anticipate the content of the essay and helps them to understand the relationships among its various ideas and details.

Occasionally, however, particularly in fairly short, informal essays and in some autobiographical and argumentative essays, a writer may save a direct statement of the thesis until the conclusion, which is where Estrada and Wolff put theirs. Ending with the thesis brings together the various strands of information or supporting details introduced over the course of the essay and makes clear the essay's main idea.

Exercise 13.1

In the essay by Jessica Statsky in Chapter 6, underline the thesis statement, the last sentence in paragraph 1. Notice the key terms in this thesis, the words that seem to be essential to presenting Statsky's ideas: "overzealous parents and coaches," "impose adult standards," "children's sports," "activities . . . neither satisfying nor beneficial." Then skim the essay, stopping to read the sentence at the beginning of each paragraph. Also read the last paragraph.

Consider whether the idea in every paragraph's first sentence is anticipated by the thesis key terms. Consider also the connection between the ideas in the last paragraph and the thesis key terms. What can you conclude about how a thesis might assert the point of an essay, anticipate the ideas that follow, and help readers relate the ideas to each other?

Forecasting Statements

Some thesis statements include a **forecast**, which overviews the way a thesis will be developed. For example, note the role of the forecasting statement in this opening paragraph from an essay by William Langer on the bubonic plague:

> In the three years from 1348 through 1350 the pandemic of plague known as the Black Death, or, as the Germans called it, the Great Dying, killed at least a fourth of the population of Europe. It was undoubtedly the worst disaster that has ever befallen mankind. Today we can have no real conception of the terror under which people lived in the shadow of the plague. For more than two centuries plague has not been a serious threat to mankind in the large, although it is still a grisly presence in parts of the Far East and Africa. Scholars continue to study the Great Dying, however, as a historical example of human behavior under the stress of universal catastrophe. In these days when the threat of plague has been replaced by the threat of mass human extermination by even more rapid means, there has been a sharp renewal of interest in the history of the fourteenth-century calamity. With new perspective, students are investigating its manifold effects: demographic, economic, psychological, moral and religious.
>
> —WILLIAM LANGER, "The Black Death"

This introductory paragraph informs us that Langer's article is about the effects of the Black Death. His thesis (underlined) states that there is renewed interest in studying the social effects of the bubonic plague and that these new studies focus on five particular categories of effects. As a reader would expect, Langer then goes on to divide his essay into explanations of the research into these five effects, addressing them in the order in which they appear in the forecasting statement.

Exercise 13.2

Turn to Christine Romano's essay in Chapter 8, and underline the forecasting statement in paragraph 2. (After the first sentence, which states Romano's thesis, the remaining sentences offer a forecast of Romano's main points and the order in which she will address them.) Then skim the essay, pausing to read the first sentence in each paragraph. Notice whether Romano takes up every point she mentions in the forecasting statement and whether she sticks to the order she promises readers. What can you conclude about how a forecasting statement assists readers?

PARAGRAPHING

Paragraph cues as obvious as indentation keep readers on track. You can also arrange material in a paragraph to help readers see what is important or significant. For example, you can begin with a topic sentence, help readers see the relationship between the previous paragraph and the present one with an explicit transition, and place the most important information toward the end. This section illustrates these cues and others.

For additional visual cues for readers, see Headings and Subheadings on pp. 623–25.

Paragraph Cues

One **paragraph cue**—the indentation that signals the beginning of a new paragraph—is a relatively modern printing convention. Old manuscripts show that paragraph divisions were not always marked. To make reading easier, scribes and printers began to use the symbol ¶ to mark paragraph breaks, and later, indenting became common practice. Even that relatively modern custom, however, has been abandoned by most business writers, who now distinguish one paragraph from another by leaving a line of space above and below each paragraph. Writing on the Internet is also usually paragraphed in this way.

Paragraphing helps readers by signaling when a sequence of related ideas begins and ends. Paragraphing also helps readers judge what is most important in what they are reading. Writers typically emphasize important information by placing it at the two points where readers are most attentive—the beginning and the end of a paragraph. Many writers put information to orient readers at the beginning of a paragraph and save the most important information for last.

You can give special emphasis to information by placing it in its own paragraph.

Exercise 13.3

Turn to Patrick O'Malley's essay in Chapter 7, and read paragraphs 4–6 with the following questions in mind: Does all the material in each paragraph seem to be related? Do you feel a sense of closure at the end of each paragraph? Does the last sentence offer the most important or significant or weighty information in the paragraph?

Topic Sentence Strategies

A **topic sentence** lets readers know the focus of a paragraph in simple and direct terms. It is a cueing strategy for the paragraph, much as a thesis or forecasting statement is for the whole essay. Because paragraphing usually signals a shift in focus, readers expect some kind of reorientation in the opening sentence. They need to know whether the new paragraph will introduce another aspect of the topic or develop one already introduced.

Announcing the Topic. Some topic sentences simply announce the topic. Here are some examples taken from Barry Lopez's book *Arctic Dreams*:

> A polar bear walks in a way all its own.
>
> What is so consistently striking about the way Eskimos used parts of an animal is the breadth of their understanding about what would work.
>
> The Mediterranean view of the Arctic, down to the time of the Elizabethan mariners, was shaped by two somewhat contradictory thoughts.

These topic sentences do more than merely identify the topic; they also indicate how the topic will be developed in subsequent sentences—by describing how bears walk, giving examples of animal parts Eskimos used and explaining what they understood about how each part could be useful, or contrasting two preconceptions about the Arctic.

The following paragraph shows how one of Lopez's topic sentences (underlined) is developed:

> What is so consistently striking about the way Eskimos used parts of an animal is the breadth of their understanding about what would work. Knowing that muskox horn is more flexible than caribou antler, they preferred it for making the side prongs of a fish spear. For a waterproof bag in which to carry sinews for clothing repair, they chose salmon skin. They selected the strong, translucent intestine of a bearded seal to make a window for a snowhouse—it would fold up for easy traveling and it would not frost over in cold weather. To make small snares for sea ducks, they needed a springy material that would not rot in salt water—baleen fibers. The down feather of a common eider, tethered at the end of a stick in the snow at an angle, would reveal the exhalation of a quietly surfacing seal. Polar bear bone was used anywhere a stout, sharp point was required, because it is the hardest bone.
>
> –BARRY LOPEZ, *Arctic Dreams*

Exercise 13.4

Turn to David Ratinov's essay in Chapter 10. Underline the topic sentence (the first sentence) in paragraphs 3–5. Consider how these sentences help you anticipate the paragraph's topic and method of development.

Making a Transition. Not all topic sentences simply point to what will follow. Some also refer to earlier sentences. Such sentences work both as topic sentences, stating the main point of the paragraph, and as transitions, linking that paragraph to the previous one. Here are a few topic sentences from "Quilts and Women's Culture," by Elaine Hedges, that use specific transitions (underlined) to tie the sentence to a previous statement:

> Within its broad traditionalism and anonymity, however, variations and distinctions developed.
>
> Regionally, too, distinctions were introduced into quilt making through the interesting process of renaming.
>
> With equal inventiveness women renamed traditional patterns to accommodate to the local landscape.
>
> Finally, out of such regional and other variations come individual, signed achievements.
>
> Quilts, then, were an outlet for creative energy, a source and emblem of sisterhood and solidarity, and a graphic response to historical and political change.

Sometimes the first sentence of a paragraph serves as a transition, and a subsequent sentence states the topic. The underlined sentences in the following example illustrate this strategy:

> . . . What a convenience, what a relief it will be, they say, never to worry about how to dress for a job interview, a romantic tryst, or a funeral!
>
> Convenient, perhaps, but not exactly a relief. Such a utopia would give most of us the same kind of chill we feel when a stadium full of Communist-bloc athletes in identical sports outfits, shouting slogans in unison, appears on TV. Most people do not want to be told what to wear any more than they want to be told what to say. In

> Belfast recently four hundred Irish Republican prisoners "refused to wear any clothes at all, draping themselves day and night in blankets," rather than put on prison uniforms. Even the offer of civilian-style dress did not satisfy them; they insisted on wearing their own clothes brought from home, or nothing. Fashion is free speech, and one of the privileges, if not always one of the pleasures, of a free world.
>
> –ALISON LURIE, *The Language of Clothes*

Occasionally, whole paragraphs serve as transitions, linking one sequence of paragraphs with those that follow. This transition paragraph summarizes what went before (evidence of contrast) and sets up what will follow (evidence of similarity):

> Yet it was not all contrast, after all. Different as they were—in background, in personality, in underlying aspiration—these two great soldiers had much in common. Under everything else, they were marvelous fighters. Furthermore, their fighting qualities were really very much alike.
>
> –BRUCE CATTON, "Grant and Lee: A Study in Contrasts"

Exercise 13.5

Turn to the Stephen King essay in Chapter 9, and read paragraphs 8–12. As you read, underline the part of the first sentence in paragraphs 9–12 that refers to the previous paragraph, creating a transition from one to the next. Notice the different ways King creates these transitions. Consider whether they are all equally effective.

Positioning the Topic Sentence. Although topic sentences may occur anywhere in a paragraph, stating the topic in the first sentence has the advantage of giving readers a sense of how the paragraph is likely to be developed. The beginning of the paragraph is therefore the most common position for a topic sentence.

A topic sentence that does not open a paragraph is most likely to appear at the end. When a topic sentence concludes a paragraph, it usually summarizes or generalizes preceding information. In the following example, the topic is not stated explicitly until the last sentence.

> Even black Americans sometimes need to be reminded about the deceptiveness of television. Blacks retain their fascination with black characters on TV: Many of us buy *Jet* magazine primarily to read its weekly television feature, which lists every black character (major or minor) to be seen on the screen that week. Yet our fixation with the presence of black characters on TV has blinded us to an important fact that *Cosby,* which began in 1984, and its offshoots over the years demonstrate convincingly: There is very little connection between the social status of black Americans and the fabricated images of black people that Americans consume each day. The representation of blacks on TV is a very poor index to our social advancement or political progress.
>
> –HENRY LOUIS GATES JR., "TV's Black World Turns—but Stays Unreal"

When a topic sentence is used in a narrative, it often appears as the last sentence as a way to evaluate or reflect on events:

> A cold sun was sliding down a gray fall sky. Some older boys had been playing tackle football in the field we took charge of every weekend. In a few years, they'd be called

> to Southeast Asia, some of them. Their locations would be tracked with pushpins in red, white, and blue on maps on nearly every kitchen wall. But that afternoon, they were quick as young deer. They leapt and dodged, dove from each other and collided in midair. Bulletlike passes flew to connect them. Or the ball spiraled in a high arc across the frosty sky one to another. In short, they were mindlessly agile in a way that captured as audience every little kid within running distance of the yellow goalposts.
>
> –MARY KARR, *Cherry*

Mary Karr's essay is reprinted in Chapter 3.

It is possible for a single topic sentence to introduce two or more paragraphs. Subsequent paragraphs in such a sequence have no separate topic sentences of their own. Here is a two-paragraph sequence in which the topic sentence opens the first paragraph:

> Anthropologists Daniel Maltz and Ruth Borker point out that boys and girls socialize differently. Little girls tend to play in small groups or, even more common, in pairs. Their social life usually centers around a best friend, and friendships are made, maintained, and broken by talk—especially "secrets." If a little girl tells her friend's secret to another little girl, she may find herself with a new best friend. The secrets themselves may or may not be important, but the fact of telling them is all-important. It's hard for newcomers to get into these tight groups, but anyone who is admitted is treated as an equal. Girls like to play cooperatively; if they can't cooperate, the group breaks up.
>
> Little boys tend to play in larger groups, often outdoors, and they spend more time doing things than talking. It's easy for boys to get into the group, but not everyone is accepted as an equal. Once in the group, boys must jockey for their status in it. One of the most important ways they do this is through talk: verbal display such as telling stories and jokes, challenging and sidetracking the verbal displays of other boys, and withstanding other boys' challenges in order to maintain their own story—and status. Their talk is often competitive talk about who is best at what.
>
> –DEBORAH TANNEN, *That's Not What I Meant!*

Exercise 13.6

Consider the variety and effectiveness of the topic sentences in your most recent essay. Begin by underlining the topic sentence in each paragraph after the first one. The topic sentence may not be the first sentence in a paragraph, though often it will be.

Then double-underline the part of the topic sentence that provides an explicit transition from one paragraph to the next. You may find a transition that is separate from the topic sentence. You may not always find a topic sentence.

Reflect on your topic sentences, and evaluate how well they serve to orient your readers to the sequence of topics or ideas in your essay.

COHESIVE DEVICES

Cohesive devices guide readers, helping them follow your train of thought by connecting key words and phrases throughout a passage. Among such devices are pronoun reference, word repetition, synonyms, repetition of sentence structure, and collocation.

Pronoun Reference

One common cohesive device is **pronoun reference**. As noun substitutes, pronouns refer to nouns that either precede or follow them and thus serve to connect phrases or sentences. The nouns that come before the pronouns are called *antecedents*. In the following paragraph, the pronouns *(it* or *its)* form a chain of connection with their antecedent, *George Washington Bridge*.

> In New York from dawn to dusk to dawn, day after day, you can hear the steady rumble of tires against the concrete span of the George Washington Bridge. The bridge is never completely still. It trembles with traffic. It moves in the wind. Its great veins of steel swell when hot and contract when cold; its span often is ten feet closer to the Hudson River in summer than in winter.
>
> –GAY TALESE, "New York"

This example has only one pronoun-antecedent chain, and the antecedent comes first, so all the pronouns refer back to it. When there are multiple pronoun-antecedent chains with references forward as well as back, writers have to make sure that readers will not mistake one pronoun's antecedent for another's.

Word Repetition

To avoid confusion, writers often use **word repetition**. The device of repeating words and phrases is especially helpful if a pronoun might confuse readers:

> Some odd optical property of our highly polarized and unequal society makes the poor almost invisible to their economic superiors. The poor can see the affluent easily enough—on television, for example, or on the covers of magazines. But the affluent rarely see the poor or, if they do catch sight of them in some public space, rarely know what they're seeing, since—thanks to consignment stores and, yes, Wal-Mart—the poor are usually able to disguise themselves as members of the more comfortable classes.
>
> –BARBARA EHRENREICH, *Nickel and Dimed*

Barbara Ehrenreich's essay is reprinted in Chapter 6.

In the next example, several overlapping chains of word repetition prevent confusion and help the reader follow the ideas:

> Natural selection is the central concept of Darwinian theory—the fittest survive and spread their favored traits through populations. Natural selection is defined by Spencer's phrase "survival of the fittest," but what does this famous bit of jargon really mean? Who are the fittest? And how is "fitness" defined? We often read that fitness involves no more than "differential reproductive success"—the production of more surviving offspring than other competing members of the population. Whoa! cries Bethell, as many others have before him. This formulation defines fitness in terms of survival only. The crucial phrase of natural selection means no more than "the survival of those who survive"—a vacuous tautology. (A tautology is a phrase—like "my father is a man"—containing no information in the predicate ["a man"] not inherent in the subject ["my father"]. Tautologies are fine as definitions, but not as testable scientific statements—there can be nothing to test in a statement true by definition.)
>
> –STEPHEN JAY GOULD, *Ever Since Darwin*

Notice that Gould uses repetition to keep readers focused on the key concepts of "natural selection," "survival of the fittest," and "tautology." These key terms may vary in form—*fittest* becomes *fitness*, and *survival* changes to *surviving* and *survive*—but they serve as links in the chain of meaning.

Synonyms

In addition to word repetition, you can use **synonyms**, words with identical or very similar meanings, to connect important ideas. In the following example, the author develops a careful chain of synonyms and word repetitions:

> Over time, small bits of knowledge about a region accumulate among local residents in the form of stories. These are remembered in the community; even what is unusual does not become lost and therefore irrelevant. These narratives comprise for a native an intricate, long-term view of a particular landscape. . . . Outside the region this complex but easily shared "reality" is hard to get across without reducing it to generalities, to misleading or imprecise abstraction.
>
> –BARRY LOPEZ, *Arctic Dreams*

Note the variety of synonym sequences:

"particular landscape," "region"

"local residents," "community," "native"

"stories," "narratives"

"accumulate," "remembered," "does not become lost," "comprise"

"intricate, long-term view," "complex . . . reality," "without reducing it to generalities"

The result is a coherent paragraph that constantly reinforces the author's point.

Sentence Structure Repetition

Writers occasionally use **sentence structure repetition** to emphasize the connections among their ideas, as in this example:

> But the life forms are as much part of the structure of the Earth as any inanimate portion is. It is all an inseparable part of a whole. If any animal is isolated totally from other forms of life, then death by starvation will surely follow. If isolated from water, death by dehydration will follow even faster. If isolated from air, whether free or dissolved in water, death by asphyxiation will follow still faster. If isolated from the Sun, animals will survive for a time, but plants would die, and if all plants died, all animals would starve.
>
> –ISAAC ASIMOV, "The Case against Man"

From the third sentence to the last, Asimov repeats the same sentence structure—"If this . . . then that"—to show that the sentences or clauses are logically related; every one expresses a consequence of isolation.

Collocation

Collocation—the positioning of words together in expected ways around a particular topic—occurs quite naturally to writers and usually forms recognizable networks of meaning for readers. For example, in a paragraph on a high school graduation, a reader might expect to encounter such words as *valedictorian, diploma, commencement, honors, cap and gown,* and *senior class.* The paragraph that follows uses five collocation chains:

housewife, cooking, neighbor, home

clocks, calculated cooking times, progression, precise

obstinacy, vagaries, problem

sun, clear days, cloudy ones, sundial, cast its light, angle, seasons, sun, weather

cooking, fire, matches, hot coals, smoldering, ashes, go out, bed-warming pan

> The seventeenth-century housewife not only had to make do without thermometers, she also had to make do without clocks, which were scarce and dear throughout the sixteen hundreds. She calculated cooking times by the progression of the sun; her cooking must have been more precise on clear days than on cloudy ones. Marks were sometimes painted on the floor, providing her with a rough sundial, but she still had to make allowance for the obstinacy of the sun in refusing to cast its light at the same angle as the seasons changed; but she was used to allowing for the vagaries of sun and weather. She also had a problem starting her fire in the morning; there were no matches. If she had allowed the hot coals smoldering under the ashes to go out, she had to borrow some from a neighbor, carrying them home with care, perhaps in a bed-warming pan.
>
> –Waverly Root and Richard de Rouchement, *Eating in America*

Exercise 13.7

Now that you know more about pronoun reference, word repetition, synonyms, sentence structure repetition, and collocation, turn to Trevor B. Hall's essay in Chapter 4, and identify the cohesive devices you find in paragraphs 1–6. Underline each cohesive device you can find; there will be many devices. You might also want to connect with lines the various pronoun, related-word, and synonym chains you find. You could also try listing the separate collocation chains. Consider how these cohesive devices help you read and make sense of the passage.

Exercise 13.8

Choose one of your recent essays, and select any three contiguous paragraphs. Identify the cohesive devices you find in these three paragraphs. Underline every cohesive device you can find; there will be many devices. Try to connect with lines the various pronoun, related-word, and synonym chains you find. Also try listing the separate collocation chains.

You will be surprised and pleased at how extensively you rely on cohesive ties. Indeed, you could not produce readable text without cohesive ties. Consider these questions relevant to your development as a writer: Are all of your pronoun references clear? Are you straining for synonyms when repeated words would do? Do you ever repeat sentence structures to emphasize connections? Do you trust yourself to put collocation to work?

CONNECTIVES

A **connective** serves as a bridge to connect one paragraph, sentence, clause, or word with another. It also identifies the kind of connection by indicating to readers how the item preceding the connective relates to the one that follows it. Connectives help readers anticipate how the next paragraph or sentence will affect the meaning of what they have just read. There are three basic groups of connectives, based on the relationships they indicate: logical, temporal, and spatial.

Logical Relationships

Connectives help readers follow the **logical relationships** within an argument. How such connectives work is illustrated in this tightly and passionately reasoned paragraph by James Baldwin:

> The black man insists, by whatever means he finds at his disposal, that the white man cease to regard him as an exotic rarity and recognize him as a human being. This is a very charged and difficult moment, for there is a great deal of will power involved in the white man's naïveté. Most people are not naturally malicious, and the white man prefers to keep the black man at a certain human remove because it is easier for him thus to preserve his simplicity and to avoid being called to account for crimes committed by his forefathers, or his neighbors. He is inescapably aware, nevertheless, that he is in a better position in the world than black men are, nor can he quite put to death the suspicion that he is hated by black men therefore. He does not wish to be hated, neither does he wish to change places, and at this point in his uneasiness he can scarcely avoid having recourse to those legends which white men have created about black men, the most unusual effect of which is that the white man finds himself enmeshed, so to speak, in his own language which describes hell, as well as the attributes which lead one to hell, as being black as night.
>
> —James Baldwin, "Stranger in the Village"

Connectives Showing Logical Relationships

- ***To introduce another item in a series:*** first, second; in the second place; for one thing . . . , for another; next; then; furthermore; moreover; in addition; finally; last; also; similarly; besides; and; as well as
- ***To introduce an illustration or other specification:*** in particular; specifically; for instance; for example; that is; namely
- ***To introduce a result or a cause:*** consequently; as a result; hence; accordingly; thus; so; therefore; then; because; since; for
- ***To introduce a restatement:*** that is; in other words; in simpler terms; to put it differently

- ***To introduce a conclusion or summary:*** in conclusion; finally; all in all; evidently; clearly; actually; to sum up; altogether; of course
- ***To introduce an opposing point:*** but; however; yet; nevertheless; on the contrary; on the other hand; in contrast; still; neither; nor
- ***To introduce a concession to an opposing view:*** certainly; naturally; of course; it is true; to be sure; granted
- ***To resume the original line of reasoning after a concession:*** nonetheless; all the same; even though; still; nevertheless

Temporal Relationships

In addition to showing logical connections, connectives may indicate **temporal relationships**—a sequence or progression in time—as this example illustrates:

> That night, we drank tea and then vodka with lemon peel steeped in it. The four of us talked in Russian and English about mutual friends and American railroads and the Rolling Stones. Seryozha loves the Stones, and his face grew wistful as we spoke about their recent album, *Some Girls.* He played a tape of "Let It Bleed" over and over, until we could translate some difficult phrases for him; after that, he came out with the phrases at intervals during the evening, in a pretty decent imitation of Jagger's Cockney snarl. He was an adroit and oddly formal host, inconspicuously filling our teacups and politely urging us to eat bread and cheese and chocolate. While he talked to us, he teased Anya, calling her "Piglet," and she shook back her bangs and glowered at him. It was clear that theirs was a fiery relationship. After a while, we talked about ourselves. Anya told us about painting and printmaking and about how hard it was to buy supplies in Moscow. There had been something angry in her dark face since the beginning of the evening; I thought at first that it meant she didn't like Americans; but now I realized that it was a constant, barely suppressed rage at her own situation.
>
> –ANDREA LEE, *Russian Journal*

Connectives Showing Temporal Relationships

- ***To indicate frequency:*** frequently; hourly; often; occasionally; now and then; day after day; every so often; again and again
- ***To indicate duration:*** during; briefly; for a long time; minute by minute; while
- ***To indicate a particular time:*** now; then; at that time; in those days; last Sunday; next Christmas; in 2003; at the beginning of August; at six o'clock; first thing in the morning; two months ago; when
- ***To indicate the beginning:*** at first; in the beginning; since; before then
- ***To indicate the middle:*** in the meantime; meanwhile; as it was happening; at that moment; at the same time; simultaneously; next; then
- ***To indicate the end and beyond:*** eventually; finally; at last; in the end; subsequently; later; afterward

Spatial Relationships

Spatial relationships connectives orient readers to the objects in a scene, as illustrated in these paragraphs:

> On Georgia 155, I crossed Troublesome Creek, then went through groves of pecan trees aligned one with the next like fenceposts. The pastures grew a green almost blue, and syrupy water the color of a dusty sunset filled the ponds. Around the farmhouses, from wires strung high above the ground, swayed gourds hollowed out for purple martins.
>
> The land rose again on the other side of the Chattahoochee River, and Highway 34 went to the ridgetops where long views over the hills opened in all directions. Here was the tail of the Appalachian backbone, its gradual descent to the Gulf. Near the Alabama stateline stood a couple of LAST CHANCE! bars. . . .
>
> –WILLIAM LEAST HEAT MOON, *Blue Highways*

Connectives Showing Spatial Relationships

- ***To indicate closeness:*** close to; near; next to; alongside; adjacent to; facing
- ***To indicate distance:*** in the distance; far; beyond; away; there
- ***To indicate direction:*** up/down; sideways; along; across; to the right/left; in front of/behind; above/below; inside/outside; toward/away from

Exercise 13.9

Turn to Amy Wu's essay in Chapter 3. Relying on the lists of connectives just given, underline the *logical* and *temporal* connectives in paragraphs 1–5. Consider how the connectives relate the ideas and events from sentence to sentence. Do you see the need for further connectives to make the relationships clear?

Exercise 13.10

Select a recent essay of your own. Choose at least three paragraphs, and, relying on the lists of connectives given in the text, underline the logical, temporal, and spatial connectives. Depending on the kind of writing you were doing, you may find few, if any, connectives in one category or another. For example, an essay speculating about causes may not include any spatial connectives; writing about a remembered event might not contain connectives showing logical relationships.

Consider how your connectives relate the ideas from sentence to sentence. Comparing your connectives to those in the lists, do you find that you are making full use of the repertoire of connectives? Do you find gaps between any of your sentences that a well-chosen connective would close?

HEADINGS AND SUBHEADINGS

Headings and subheadings—brief phrases set off from the text in various ways—can provide visible cues to readers about the content and organization of a text. Headings can be distinguished from text in numerous ways, including the selective use of capital letters, bold or italic type, or different sizes of type. To be most helpful to readers, headings should be phrased similarly and follow a predictable system.

Heading Systems and Levels

In this chapter, the headings in the section Paragraphing, beginning on p. 613, provide a good example of a system of headings that can readily be outlined:

PARAGRAPHING

Paragraph Cues

Topic Sentence Strategies

Announcing the Topic.

Making a Transition.

Positioning the Topic Sentence.

To learn more about distinguishing headings from surrounding text and about setting up systems of headings, see Typography, pp. 821–24 in Chapter 25, Designing Documents.

Notice that in this example the heading system has three levels. The first-level heading sits on its own line, and all the letters are capitalized; this heading stands out most visibly among the others. (It is one of five such capitalized headings in this chapter.) The second-level heading also sits on its own line, but only the first letter in each word (except for articles and prepositions) is capitalized, and the others are lowercased. Like the heading in the first level, this second-level heading is aligned with the left margin. The first of these second-level headings has no subheadings beneath it, while the second has three. These third-level headings run into the paragraph they introduce, as you can see if you pause now to turn to pp. 614–16.

All of these headings are set apart from the surrounding text by the special use of capital letters or spacing or both. At each level, they follow a parallel grammatical structure: nouns at the first level, which you can confirm by skimming the chapter in order to look at the other four first-level heads; nouns at the second level ("cues" and "strategies"); and "-ing" nouns at the third level.

Headings and Genres

Headings may not be necessary in the short essays you will be writing for this composition course. Short essays offer readers thesis statements, forecasting statements, well-positioned topic sentences, and transition sentences so that they have all the cues they may need. Headings are rare in some genres, like essays about remembered events and people (Chapters 2 and 3) and essays profiling people and places (Chapter 4). Headings appear more frequently in genres such as concept explanations, position papers, public policy proposals, evaluations, and speculations about social problems (Chapters 5–9).

Frequency and Placement of Headings

Before dividing their essays into sections with headings and subheadings, writers need to make sure their discussion is detailed enough to support at least one heading at each level. The frequency and placement of headings depend entirely on the content and how it is divided and organized. Keep in mind that headings do not reduce the need for other cues to keep readers on track.

"Why Boys Become Depressed" by William S. Pollack in Chapter 9 uses four headings to cue readers, all of which are grammatically parallel (noun phrases):

The Many Faces of Depression

The Biology of Depression

The Cost of Society's Disconnection

Depression over Relationships

If you read or skim this essay, you will find that the text following the first heading defines depression in boys in terms of the kinds of symptoms they exhibit. The second heading begins a section that discusses the pharmaceutical treatment of depression based on research that shows that it can be caused by biological factors and that presents the writer's contention that external psychological factors should be taken into account as well. The third heading introduces a section in which the writer argues that depression among boys can be a result of societal gender stereotypes that encourage boys to deny or feel shame about their feelings of vulnerability, such as fear or loneliness. Finally, the fourth heading leads into a discussion of one of the writer's central points: that despite currently held misconceptions, satisfying relationships with others are crucially important for the emotional well-being of boys. A fairly equal amount of material (three to four paragraphs) is covered under the final three headings; the definition of depression under the first heading is somewhat briefer (two paragraphs).

Exercise 13.11

Turn to Katherine S. Newman's essay in Chapter 7, and survey that essay's system of headings. If you have not read the essay, read or skim it now. Also read Basic Features: Proposing Solutions at the end of the Chapter 7 Readings section (pp. 360–61) to familiarize yourself with the genre—proposing a solution. Consider how Newman's headings help readers anticipate what is coming and how the argument is organized. Analyze whether the headings substitute for or complement a strong system of other cues for keeping readers on track. Decide whether the headings guide readers through the particular stages of the genre. Finally, try to answer these questions: Do any of the headings suggest subheadings? Might fewer or more headings be helpful to readers? Are the headings grammatically parallel?

For more practice evaluating the effectiveness of headings, review "The Elder Scrolls III: Morrowind," in Chapter 8, pp. 400–4.

Exercise 13.12

Select one of your essays that might benefit from headings. Develop a system of headings, and insert them where appropriate. Be prepared to justify your headings in light of the discussion about headings in this section.

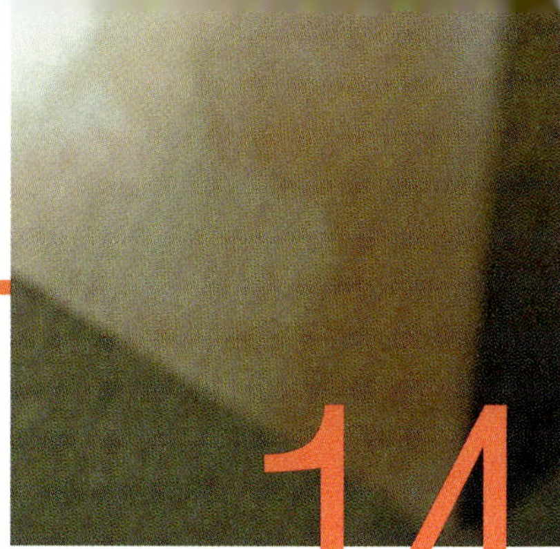

14 Narrating

Narrating is a basic writing strategy for representing action and events. As the term's Latin root, *gnarus* ("knowing"), implies, narrating also helps people make sense of events they are involved in, as well as events they observe or read about. From earliest childhood, we use narrating to help us reflect on what has happened, to explain what is happening, and to imagine what could happen.

Narrating is one of the most versatile writing strategies and serves many different purposes. It can be used to report on events, present information, illustrate abstract ideas, support arguments, explain procedures, and entertain with stories. This chapter begins by describing and illustrating five basic narrating strategies and concludes by looking at two types of process narrative—explanatory and instructional.

NARRATING STRATEGIES

Whether the purpose is to make clear exactly what happened or to dramatize events so that readers can imagine what the experience was like, writers use an array of narrating strategies. Strategies such as calendar and clock time, temporal transitions, verb tense, specific narrative action, and dialogue give narrative its dynamic quality, the sense of events unfolding in time. They also help readers track the order in which the events occurred and understand how they relate to one another.

Calendar and Clock Time

Presenting a clear sequence of action is essential to narrative. One of the simplest ways of constructing a clear time sequence is to place events on a timeline with years or precise dates and times clearly marked. Look, for example, at the chronology in Figure 14.1, which presents a series of events in the history of genetics. Chronologies like this one often appear in books and magazines as sidebars accompanying written narratives. A chronology is not itself a narrative, but it shares with narrative two basic elements: Events are presented in chronological order, and each event is marked (in this case, by year) so that readers can understand clearly when events occurred in relation to one another.

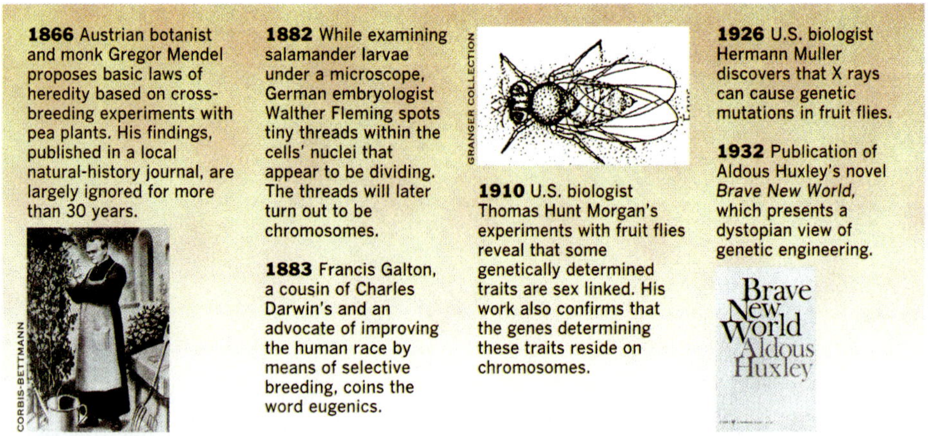

Figure 14.1 Chronology of Events in the History of Genetics
From *Time*, January 11, 1999, pp. 46–47.

Look now at a brief but fully developed narrative reconstructing the discovery of the bacterial cause of stomach ulcers. This narrative was written by Martin J. Blaser for *Scientific American*, a journal read primarily by nonspecialists interested in science. As you read, notice the same narrating strategies you saw in the chronology in Figure 14.1: sequencing events in chronological order and marking the passage of time by specifying when each event occurred (each time marker is underlined):

> In 1979 J. Robin Warren, a pathologist at the Royal Perth Hospital in Australia, made a puzzling observation. As he examined tissue specimens from patients who had undergone stomach biopsies, he noticed that several samples had large numbers of curved and spiral-shaped bacteria. Ordinarily, stomach acid would destroy such organisms before they could settle in the stomach. But those Warren saw lay underneath the organ's thick mucus layer—a lining that coats the stomach's tissues and protects them from acid. Warren also noted that the bacteria were present only in tissue samples that were inflamed. Wondering whether the microbes might somehow be related to the irritation, he looked to the literature for clues and learned that German pathologists had witnessed similar organisms a century earlier. Because they could not grow the bacteria in culture, though, their findings had been ignored and then forgotten.
>
> Warren, aided by an enthusiastic young trainee named Barry J. Marshall, also had difficulty growing the unknown bacteria in culture. He began his efforts in 1981. By April 1982 the two men had attempted to culture samples from 30-odd patients—all without success. Then the Easter holidays arrived. The hospital laboratory staff accidentally held some of the culture plates for five days instead of the usual two. On the fifth day, colonies emerged. The workers christened them *Campylobacter pyloridis* because they resembled pathogenic bacteria of the *Campylobacter* genus found in the intestinal tract. Early in 1983 Warren and Marshall published their first report, and within months scientists around the world had isolated the bacteria.
>
> –MARTIN J. BLASER, "The Bacteria behind Ulcers"

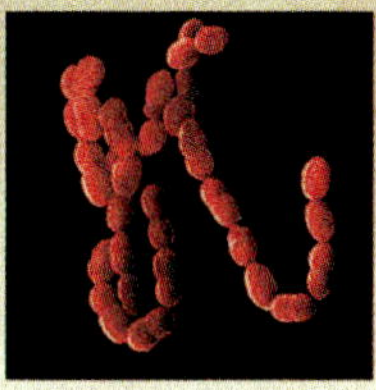
HANK MORGAN—SCIENCE SOURCE/PHOTORESEARCHERS

1944 Working with pneumococcus bacteria, Oswald Avery, Colin MacLeod and Maclyn McCarty prove that DNA, not protein, is the hereditary material in most living organisms.

1950 British physician Douglas Bevis describes how amniocentesis can be used to test fetuses for Rh-factor incompatibility. The prenatal test will later be used to screen for a battery of genetic disorders.

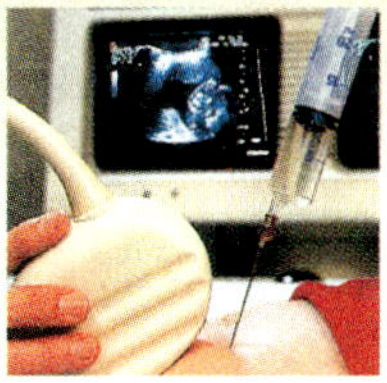
SATURN STILLS—SCIENCE PHOTO LIBRARY/PHOTORESEARCHERS

UPI/CORBIS-BETTMANN

1953 American biochemist James Watson and British biophysicist Francis Crick announce their discovery of the double-helix structure of DNA, the molecule that carries the genetic code.

1964 Stanford geneticist Charles Yanofsky and colleagues prove that the sequence of nucleotides in DNA corresponds exactly to the sequence of amino acids in proteins.

1969 A Harvard Medical School team isolates the first gene: a snippet of bacterial DNA that plays a role in the metabolism of sugar.

1970 University of Wisconsin researchers synthesize a gene from scratch.

1973 American biochemists Stanley Cohen and Herbert Boyer insert a gene from an African clawed toad into bacterial DNA, where it begins to work. Their experiment marks the beginning of genetic engineering.

KEN M. HIGHFILL—PHOTORESEARCHERS

Blaser cites specific years, months, days, and a holiday. These calendar markers convey the sense of time passing and indicate precisely when each event occurred and in what order. Calendar time also enables Blaser to emphasize the length of time it took to make the discovery (four years) and to draw attention to the fortunate accident that provided the dramatic turning point.

In addition to calendar time (years, months, days), writers sometimes also refer to clock time (hours, minutes, seconds). Here is a brief narrative from an essay profiling the emergency room at Bellevue Hospital in New York City:

> 9:05 P.M. An ambulance backs into the receiving bay, its red and yellow lights flashing in and out of the lobby. A split second later, the glass doors burst open as a nurse and an attendant roll a mobile stretcher into the lobby. When the nurse screams, "Emergency!" the lobby explodes with activity as the way is cleared to the trauma room. Doctors appear from nowhere and transfer the bloodied body of a black man to the treatment table. Within seconds his clothes are stripped away.
>
> –GEORGE SIMPSON, "The War Room at Bellevue"

In this example, we can see that references to clock time (underlined) not only help readers follow the sequence of actions but also contribute dramatic intensity by stressing the speed with which the actions were taken.

Exercise 14.1

Turn to the remembered-event essay "100 Miles per Hour, Upside Down and Sideways," by Rick Bragg, in Chapter 2, and underline the references to calendar time in paragraphs 2, 6, and 8. How do you think these calendar time markers function in the narrative? What do they tell you about the impression Bragg wants to create about his younger self?

Exercise 14.2

Read through "The Edison Café" by Trevor B. Hall, in Chapter 4, and underline any references to clock time that you find. In what way does Hall use clock time as the central organizing principle of his essay?

Temporal Transitions

For a more extensive list of connectives showing temporal relationships, see Chapter 13.

Whereas calendar and clock time tend to be used sparingly, writers regularly use **temporal transitions** such as *when, at that moment, before,* and *while.* Temporal transitions establish a clear sequence of actions in time. They are used to narrate both onetime and recurring events.

Onetime Events. Writers and readers rely on temporal transitions to show readers how events relate to one another, indicating which event came first, which event followed, and which events happened at the same time. To see how temporal transitions work, let us look at the concluding paragraphs of a remembered-event essay in which Russell Baker recounts what happened after his final flight test, his last chance to become a pilot. The "he" Baker refers to is the flight check pilot, T. L. (nicknamed "Total Loss") Smith.

> Back at the flight line, <u>when</u> I'd cut the ignition, he climbed out and tramped back toward the ready room <u>while</u> I waited to sign the plane in. <u>When</u> I got there he was standing at a distance talking to my regular instructor. His talk was being illustrated with hand movements, as pilots' conversations always were, hands executing little loops and rolls in the air. <u>After</u> he did the falling-leaf motion with his hands, he pointed a finger at my instructor's chest, said something I couldn't hear, and trudged off. My instructor, who had flown only with the pre-hangover Baker, was slack-jawed <u>when</u> he approached me.
>
> "Smith just said you gave him the best check flight he's ever had in his life," he said. "What the hell did you do to him up there?"
>
> "I guess I just suddenly learned to fly," I said.
>
> —RUSSELL BAKER, "Smooth and Easy"

In this brief narrative, we see how temporal transitions (underlined) show what Baker and Smith were each doing right after the test. For example, look closely at the two transitions in the first sentence. The word *when* presents actions in chronological order (first Baker stopped the plane, and then Smith got out). *While* performs a different function, showing that the next two actions occurred at the same time (Baker signed in as the instructor returned to the ready room). There is nothing complicated or unusual about this set of actions, but it would be hard to represent them in writing without temporal transitions.

Recurring Events. Temporal transitions also enable writers to show what recurring events typically happened over a longer period of time. In the following narrative by Monica Sone about her daily life in an internment camp for Japanese Americans during World War II, we can see how transitions (underlined) help the writer represent actions she routinely performed.

> First I typed on pink, green, blue and white work sheets the hours put in by the 10,000 evacuees, then sorted and alphabetized these sheets, and stacked them away in shoe boxes. My job was excruciatingly dull, but under no circumstances did I want to leave it. The Administration Building was the only place which had modern plumbing and running hot and cold water; in the first few months and every morning, after I had typed for a decent hour, I slipped into the rest room and took a complete sponge bath with scalding hot water. During the remainder of the day, I slipped back into the rest room at inconspicuous intervals, took off my head scarf and wrestled with my scorched hair. I stood upside down over the basin of hot water, soaking my hair, combing, stretching and pulling at it.
>
> —MONICA SONE, "Camp Harmony"

With the time marker *first,* Sone launches her narrative of the actions she typically took while working, such as typing and alphabetizing. In the third sentence, she introduces another set of routine actions she took surreptitiously "in the first few months and every morning."

Exercise 14.3

Turn to the remembered-event essay "On Being a Real Westerner," by Tobias Wolff, in Chapter 2. Underline the temporal transitions in paragraph 9, where Wolff relates a onetime event, and paragraph 5, where he presents recurring events. Notice the number of transitions he uses and how each one functions. What can you conclude about Wolff's use of temporal transitions from your analysis of these two paragraphs? How well do these transitions create a sense of time passing? How effectively do they help you follow the sequence of actions?

Exercise 14.4

Turn to "Love: The Right Chemistry," by Anastasia Toufexis, in Chapter 5. Read paragraph 3, underlining the temporal transitions Toufexis uses to present the sequence of evolutionary changes that may have contributed to the development of romantic love. How important are these transitions in helping you follow her narrative?

Verb Tense

In addition to time markers like calendar time and temporal transitions, writers use **verb tense** to represent action in writing and to help readers understand when each action occurred in relation to the other actions. Let us look at some of the ways writers use verb tense to narrate onetime and recurring events.

Onetime Events. Writers typically use the past tense to represent onetime events that began and ended at some time in the past. Here is a brief passage from a remembered-person essay by Amy Wu. In addition to the temporal transitions *once*

Amy Wu's essay is reprinted in Chapter 3.

and *when* in the opening sentence, which let readers know that this particular event occurred many years earlier, the writer also uses simple past-tense verbs (underlined):

> Once, when I was 5 or 6, I interrupted my mother during a dinner with her friends and told her that I disliked the meal. My mother's eyes transformed from serene pools of blackness into stormy balls of fire. "Quiet!" she hissed, "do you not know that silent waters run deep?"
>
> —AMY WU, "A Different Kind of Mother"

Verbs like *interrupted* and *hissed* show readers Wu's and her mother's actions. The simple past tense of these verbs signals to readers that the series of actions occurred in a straightforward sequence: The young Wu interrupted her mother, and then her mother got angry.

In the next example, by Chang-Rae Lee, we see how verb tense can be used to show more complicated relationships between past actions. Notice that Lee employs two different past tenses: the simple past *(amassed* and *moved)* and the past perfect *(had hoped)*:

> When Uncle Chul amassed the war chest he needed to open the wholesale business he had hoped for, he moved away from New York.
>
> —CHANG-RAE LEE, "Uncle Chul Gets Rich"

You do not have to know the names of these verb tenses to know that the hopes came before the money was amassed. In fact, most readers of English can understand complicated combinations of tenses without knowing their names.

Let us look at another verb tense combination used frequently in narrative: the simple past *(overheard)* and the past progressive *(was leaving)*.

> When Dinah Washington was leaving with some friends, I overheard someone say she was on her way to the Savoy Ballroom where Lionel Hampton was appearing that night—she was then Hamp's vocalist.
>
> —MALCOLM X, *The Autobiography of Malcolm X*

This combination of tenses plus the temporal transition *when* shows that the two actions occurred at the same time in the past. The first action ("Dinah Washington was leaving") continued during the period that the second action ("I overheard") occurred.

Occasionally, writers use the present instead of the past tense to narrate onetime events. Process narratives and profiles typically use the present tense to give the story a sense of "you are there" immediacy. The following excerpt from John T. Edge's profile of a rural Mississippi café that serves pickled pig lips (see Chapter 4) uses present-tense verbs (underlined) to give readers a sense that they are in the room with the writer:

> Slowly, the dank barroom fills with grease-smeared mechanics from the truck stop up the road and farmers straight from the fields, the soles of their brogans thick with dirt clods. A few weary souls make their way over from the nearby sawmill. I sit alone at the bar, one empty bottle of Bud in front of me, a second in my hand. I drain the beer,

order a third, and stare down at the pink juice spreading outward from a crumpled foil pouch and onto the bar.

I'm not leaving until I eat this thing, I tell myself.

–JOHN T. EDGE, "I'm Not Leaving Until I Eat This Thing"

Recurring Events. Verb tense, usually combined with temporal transitions, can also help writers narrate events that occurred routinely. In the following passage, for example, Willie Morris uses the helping verb *would* along with the temporal transitions *many times* and *often* to show recurring actions.

> Many times, walking home from work, I would see some unknowing soul venture across that intersection against the light and then freeze in horror when he saw the cars ripping out of the tunnel toward him. . . . Suddenly, the human reflex would take over, and the pedestrian would jackknife first one way, then another, arms flaying the empty air, and often the car would literally skim the man, brushing by him so close it would touch his coat or his tie. . . . On one occasion, feeling sorry for the person who had brushed against the speeding car, I hurried across the intersection after him to cheer him up a little. Catching up with him down by 32nd I said, "That was good legwork, sir. Excellent moves for a big man!" but the man looked at me with an empty expression in his eyes, and then moved away mechanically and trancelike, heading for the nearest bar.
>
> –WILLIE MORRIS, *North toward Home*

Notice also that Morris shifts to the simple past tense when he moves from recurring actions to an action that occurred only once. He signals this shift with the temporal transition *on one occasion.*

Exercise 14.5

Turn to the remembered-event essay "Calling Home," by Jean Brandt, in Chapter 2. Read paragraph 3, and underline the verbs, beginning with *got, took, knew,* and *didn't want* in the first sentence. Brandt uses verb tense to reconstruct her actions and reflect on their effectiveness. Notice also how verb tense helps you follow the sequence of actions Brandt took.

Specific Narrative Action

The narrating strategy we call **specific narrative action** uses active verbs and modifying phrases and clauses to present action vividly. Specific narrative action is especially suited to representing the intense, fast-moving, physical actions of sports events. The following example by George Plimpton shows how well specific narrative actions (underlined) work to show what happened during a practice scrimmage. Plimpton participated in the Detroit Lions football training camp while writing a book profiling professional football. This is what he experienced:

> Since in the two preceding plays the concentration of the play had been elsewhere, I had felt alone with the flanker. Now, the whole heave of the play was toward me, flooding the zone not only with confused motion but noise—the quick stomp of

feet, the creak of football gear, the strained grunts of effort, the faint *ah-ah-ah* of piston-stroke regularity, and the stiff calls of instruction, like exhalations. "Inside, inside! Take him inside!" someone shouted, tearing by me, his cleats thumping in the grass. A call—a parrot squawk—may have erupted from me. My feet splayed in hopeless confusion as Barr came directly toward me, feinting in one direction, and then stopping suddenly, drawing me toward him for the possibility of a buttonhook pass, and as I leaned almost off balance toward him, he turned and came on again, downfield, moving past me at high speed, leaving me poised on one leg, reaching for him, trying to grab at him despite the illegality, anything to keep him from getting by. But he was gone, and by the time I had turned to set out after him, he had ten yards on me, drawing away fast with his sprinter's run, his legs pinwheeling, the row of cleats flicking up a faint wake of dust behind.

–George Plimpton, *Paper Lion*

In this brief narrative, Plimpton uses active verbs *(erupted, leaned)*. But most of the action is expressed through modifying phrases and clauses. Here are some examples of the two most common kinds of modifiers that writers employ to present specific narrative action:

Participial phrases: *tearing by me, stopping suddenly, moving past me at high speed*

Absolute phrases: *his cleats thumping in the grass, his legs pinwheeling, the row of cleats flicking up a faint wake of dust behind*

As with verb tense, most English speakers know how to construct these phrases and clauses without knowing their grammatical names. By piling up specific narrative actions, Plimpton reconstructs for readers the texture and excitement of his experience on the football field. Combined with vivid sensory description *(the creak of football gear, the strained grunts of effort, the faint* ah-ah-ah *of piston-stroke regularity),* these specific narrative actions re-create the sights and sounds of people in motion.

Exercise 14.6

Turn to paragraph 18 of the remembered-person essay "Uncle Willie" by Maya Angelou, in Chapter 3. Underline any specific narrative actions you find in this brief paragraph. Then reflect on what they contribute to Angelou's narrative.

Exercise 14.7

Make a videotape of several brief—two- or three-minute—televised segments of a fast-moving sports competition such as a football or basketball game. Then review the tape, and choose one segment to narrate using specific narrative actions to describe in detail what you see.

If you cannot videotape a televised game, go to a place where there is action taking place (for example, where people are playing touch football, where a dog is catching a Frisbee, or where a skateboarder or inline skater is practicing a trick). As you watch the action, take detailed notes of what you see. Then, based on your notes, write a few sentences using specific narrative actions to describe the action you witnessed firsthand.

Dialogue

Dialogue reconstructs choice bits of conversation and does not try to present an accurate and complete record. It is most often used in narratives that dramatize events. In addition to showing people interacting, dialogue can give readers insight into character and relationships. Dialogue may be quoted to make it resemble the give-and-take of actual conversation, or it may be summarized to give readers the gist of what was said.

The following example from Gary Soto's *Living up the Street* shows how a narrative can combine quoted and summarized dialogue. In this passage, Soto recalls his first experience as a migrant worker in California's San Joaquin Valley.

> So it went. Two pans equaled one tray—or six cents. By lunchtime I had a trail of thirty-seven trays behind me while Mother had sixty or more. We met about halfway from our last trays, and I sat down with a grunt, knees wet from kneeling on dropped grapes. I washed my hands with the water from the jug, drying them on the inside of my shirt sleeve before I opened the paper bag for the first sandwich, which I gave to Mother. I dipped my hand in again to unwrap a sandwich without looking at it. I took a first bite and chewed it slowly for the tang of mustard. Eating in silence I looked straight ahead at the vines, and only when we were finished with cookies did we talk.
>
> "Are you tired?" she asked.
>
> "No, but I got a sliver from the frame," I told her. I showed her the web of skin between my thumb and index finger. She wrinkled her forehead but said it was nothing.
>
> "How many trays did you do?"
>
> I looked straight ahead, not answering at first. I recounted in my mind the whole morning of bend, cut, pour again and again, before answering a feeble "thirty-seven." No elaboration, no detail. Without looking at me she told me how she had done field work in Texas and Michigan as a child. But I had a difficult time listening to her stories. I played with my grape knife, stabbing it into the ground, but stopped when Mother reminded me that I had better not lose it. I left the knife sticking up like a small, leafless plant. She then talked about school, the junior high I would be going to that fall, and then about Rick and Debra, how sorry they would be that they hadn't come out to pick grapes because they'd have no new clothes for the school year. She stopped talking when she peeked at her watch, a bandless one she kept in her pocket. She got up with an "Ay, Dios," and told me that we'd work until three, leaving me cutting figures in the sand with my knife and dreading the return to work.
>
> –GARY SOTO, "One Last Time"

Quoted dialogue is easy to recognize, of course, because of the quotation marks. Notice that Soto uses signal phrases—*she asked* and *I told her*—in the first two quotations but that he leaves out the signal phrase in the third, possibly because it is clear from the context who is speaking. The fourth bit of quoted dialogue consists of only one word, *thirty-seven,* but is preceded by a fairly long narrative telling what he did and thought before speaking.

Summarized dialogue can be harder to identify. In this case, however, Soto embeds signal phrases *(she told me* and *she then talked)* in his narrative. He summarizes

For more on deciding when to quote, see Chapter 22.

what his mother talked about without going into detail or quoting words she might have used. Summarizing leaves out information the writer decides readers do not need. In this passage about a remembered event, Soto has apparently chosen to focus on his own feelings and thoughts rather than his mother's.

Exercise 14.8

Read the essay "A Different Kind of Mother" in Chapter 3, and consider Amy Wu's use of both direct quotation and summaries to report the speech of her mother, her friends, and her grandfather. Why might Wu have chosen at times to summarize speech and at other times to quote directly? Also look at the signal phrases the writer uses. Do these help readers clearly understand who is speaking? Do the instances of dialogue in the essay help to create specific impressions of the different speakers?

Exercise 14.9

If you wrote a remembered-event essay in Chapter 2 or wrote a bit of narrative in some other essay, reread your essay, looking for one example of each of the following narrating strategies: calendar or clock time, temporal transitions, past-tense verbs in onetime events, specific narrative action, and dialogue. Do not worry if you cannot find examples of all of the strategies. Pick one strategy you did use, and comment on what it contributes to your narrative.

NARRATING A PROCESS

Process narratives explain how something was done or instruct readers on how it could or should be done. Whether the purpose is explanatory or instructional, process narratives must convey clearly each necessary action and the exact order in which the actions occur. We will look at examples of both types of process narrative.

Explanatory Process Narratives

Explanatory process narratives often relate particular experiences or elucidate processes followed by machines or organizations. Let us begin with an excerpt from a remembered-event essay by Mary Mebane. She uses process narrative to let readers know what happened the first time she worked on an assembly line putting tobacco leaves on the conveyor belt.

> The job seemed easy enough as I picked up bundle after bundle of tobacco and put it on the belt, careful to turn the knot end toward me so that it would be placed right to go under the cutting machine. Gradually, as we worked up our tobacco, I had to bend more, for as we emptied the hogshead we had to stoop over to pick up the tobacco, then straighten up and put it on the belt just right. Then I discovered the hard part of the job: the belt kept moving at the same speed all the time and if the leaves were not placed on the belt at the same tempo there would be a big gap where your bundle should have been. So that meant that when you got down lower, you had to bend down, get the tobacco, straighten up fast, make sure it was placed knot end toward you, place it on the belt, and bend down again. Soon you were

bending down, up; down, up; down, up. All along the line, heads were bobbing—down, up; down, up—until you finished the barrel. Then you could rest until the men brought you another one.

—MARY MEBANE, "Summer Job"

In this passage, Mebane uses the basic narrating strategies of temporal transitions *(gradually, then, soon)* and simple past-tense verbs to place the actions in time. In addition, specific narrative actions *(bend down, get the tobacco, straighten up fast)* become a series of staccato movements *(down, up; down, up; down, up)* that emphasize the speed and machinelike actions she had to take to keep up with the conveyor belt.

The next example shows how a laser printer functions.

To create a page, the computer sends signals to the printer, which shines a laser at a mirror system that scans across a charged drum. Whenever the beam strikes the drum, it removes the charge. The drum then rotates through a toner chamber filled with thermoplastic particles. The toner particles stick to the negatively charged areas of the drum in the pattern of characters, lines, or other elements the computer has transmitted and the laser beam mapped.

Once the drum is coated with toner in the appropriate locations, a piece of paper is pulled across a so-called transfer corona wire, which imparts a positive electrical charge. The paper then passes across the toner-coated drum. The positive charge on the paper attracts the toner in the same position it occupied on the drum. The final phase of the process involves fusing the toner to the paper with a set of high-temperature rollers.

RICHARD GOLUB AND ERIC BRUS, *Almanac of Science and Technology*

Like Mebane's process narrative, this one sequences the actions chronologically from beginning ("the computer sends signals to the printer") to end ("fusing the toner to the paper"). Temporal transitions *(then, once, then, final),* present-tense verbs, and specific narrative actions *(sends, scans, shines, strikes)* convey the passage of time and place the actions clearly in this chronological sequence.

The major difference between this narrative and Mebane's is who is doing the action. Mebane performs the actions *(I picked up, I had to bend)* in her narrative; in this one, the actions are performed by different actors, all of them inanimate *(computer, drum, toner, paper).* Because the actors change from sentence to sentence, readers could easily become confused. Therefore, the writer must construct a clearly marked chain, introducing the actor's name in one sentence and repeating the name or using a synonym in the next sentence (underlined):

To create a page, the computer sends signals to the printer, which shines a laser at a mirror system that scans across a charged drum. Whenever the beam strikes the drum, it removes the charge. The drum then rotates through a toner chamber filled with thermoplastic particles. The toner particles . . .

Our last explanatory process narrative is a graphic sidebar of the type commonly used in magazines and books. This one comes from a *Newsweek* magazine feature on Matthew Scott, only the third person to receive a hand transplant. Figure 14.2 titled, "A Second Hand, A Second Chance," shows the process narrative.

A Second Hand, A Second Chance

It took a 17-member surgical team about 15 hours to complete Matthew Scott's hand transplant, the first in the United States. The operation is extremely complex. Unlike a solid organ transplant—a kidney, for example—a hand reattachment involves multiple tissues: skin, muscle, tendon, bone, nerves and blood vessels. At right, the procedure:

1 Skin and bones: Doctors give Scott general anesthesia. The flow of blood to his lower arm is restricted with a special tourniquet. Curved incisions (diagram A) are made in the forearm and (donor) wrist. Scott's radius and ulna bones are found and lined up with the donor hand's bones. Metal plates secure the bones together (B).

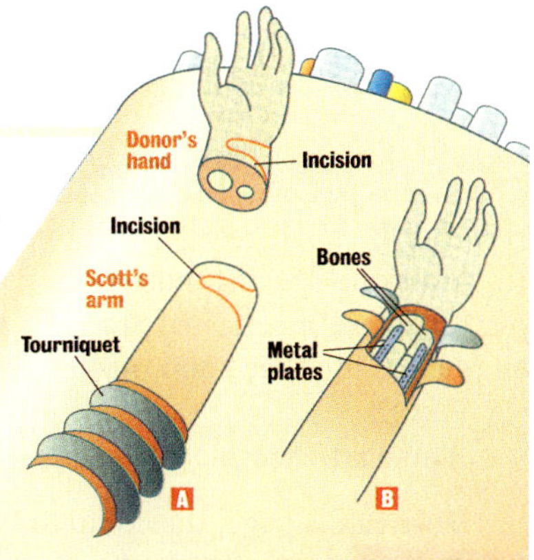

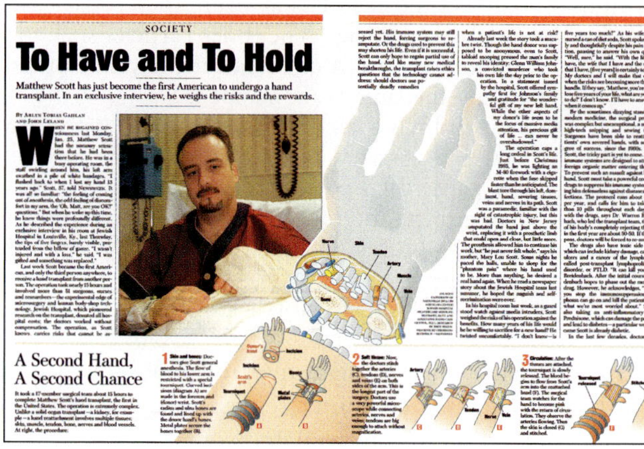
SOCIETY

To Have and To Hold

Matthew Scott has just become the first American to undergo a hand transplant. In an exclusive interview, he weighs the risks and the rewards.

A Second Hand, A Second Chance

Figure 14.2 Presentation of an Explanatory Process

The two-page layout reproduced here shows how "A Second Hand, A Second Chance" was designed as a sidebar accompanying a longer article, "To Have and to Hold." From *Newsweek,* February 8, 1999, pp. 50–51.

Notice that this process narrative integrates writing with graphics. The procedure is divided into three distinct steps, with each step clearly numbered and labeled *(1. Skin and bones)*. In each step, the figure captions refer to the graphics with letters—*Curved incisions (diagram A)*. The graphics themselves incorporate labels—*Donor's hand, Incision, Tourniquet released.* The writer uses some basic narrating strategies to present the actions and make clear the sequence in which they were taken: temporal transitions *(now, while, after)*, present-tense verbs, and specific narrative actions, mostly in the form of active verbs *(secure, stitch, watches)*. Much is left out, of course. Readers could not duplicate the procedure based on this narrative, but it does give *Newsweek* readers a clear sense of what was done during the fifteen hours of surgery.

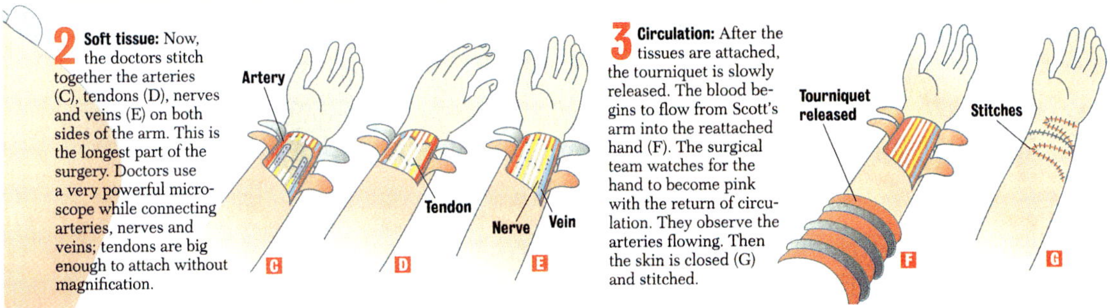

Exercise 14.10

In Chapter 4, read paragraph 6 of Brian Cable's profile of a local mortuary, "The Last Stop." Here Cable narrates the process that the company follows once it has been notified of a client's death. As you read, look for and mark the narrating strategies discussed in this chapter that Cable uses. Then reflect on how well you think the narrative presents the actions and their sequence.

Instructional Process Narratives

Unlike explanatory process narratives, **instructional process narratives** must include all of the information a reader needs to perform the procedure presented. Depending on the reader's experience, the writer might need to define technical terms, list tools that should be used, give background information, and account for alternatives or possible problems.

For guidelines on designing your own documents, see Chapter 25.

Figure 14.3 presents a detailed instructional process narrative from the Sunset *Home Repair Handbook* that gives readers directions for replacing a broken plug.

The instructions begin with general advice on when to replace a plug, followed by a classification of three common types of plugs that also are illustrated in the accompanying graphic. Notice that even though the graphic is not referred to explicitly in the text, readers are unlikely to be confused because the graphic is right next to the relevant paragraph and is clearly titled "Types of plugs."

Paragraphs 4 and 5 briefly explain the procedure for replacing two- and three-prong plugs. These procedures are spelled out in greater detail in the accompanying graphics titled "Replacing a plug with terminal screws" and "Replacing three special types of plugs." The first of these graphics includes four steps that are clearly numbered, illustrated, and narrated. Each step presents several actions to be taken, and its graphic shows what the plug should look like when these actions have been completed. We can identify the actions by looking at the verbs. Step 1 in "Replacing a plug with terminal screws," for example, instructs readers to take four separate

Replacing Plugs

Any plug with a cracked shell or loose, damaged, or badly bent contacts should be replaced. Also replace plugs that transmit power erratically or get warm when used. If a plug arcs when it's pushed into or pulled out of a receptacle, examine the wires; if they're not firmly attached to the terminal screws, tighten the connections.

The two kinds of common plugs are terminal-screw and self-connecting. In plugs with terminal screws, the wires are attached to screws inside the plug body. Self-connecting plugs clamp onto wires, making an automatic connection. These plugs, as well as two-prong plugs with terminal screws, are commonly used for lamps and small appliances. Three-prong grounding plugs are used for larger appliances and power tools. Detachable cords for small appliances have female plugs with terminal screws.

NOTE: Many old-style plugs with terminal screws have a removable insulating disc covering the terminals and wires. The NEC now requires "dead-front" plugs; such plugs have a rigid insulating barrier.

To replace a plug, cut off the old one plus at least an inch of the cord. For plugs that have terminal screws, split the cord insulation to separate the wires; then strip the insulation from the ends *(page 159)*.

When replacing a two-prong plug, connect the identified conductor to the silver-colored screw. For a three-prong grounding plug, attach the wires to the terminal screws as follows: white neutral wire to silver screw, black hot wire to brass screw, and green grounding wire to green terminal screw.

Types of plugs

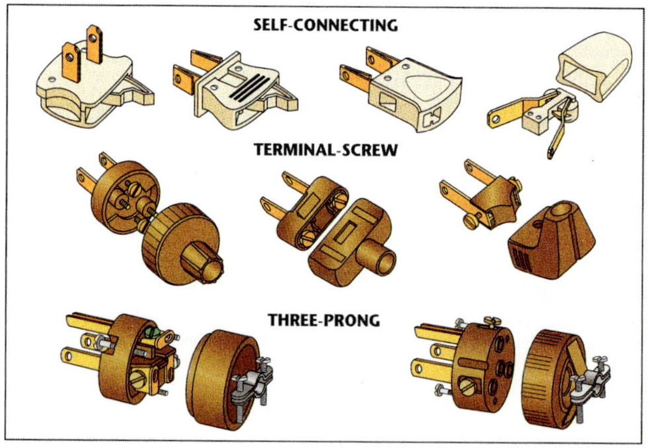

Replacing a plug with terminal screws

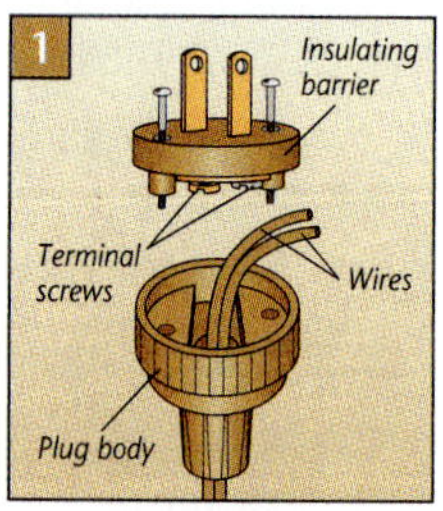

Unscrew and remove the new plug's insulating barrier. Using a utility knife, split the end of the cord to separate the wires; push the cord through the plug body.

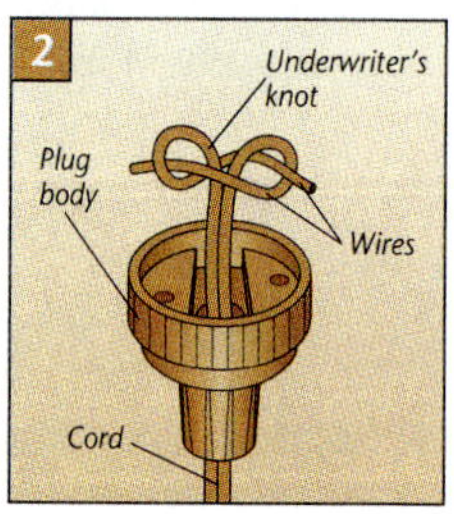

Make two loops with the wires, pass the loose ends of the wires through the loops, and pull to form an Underwriter's knot (to prevent strain on connections).

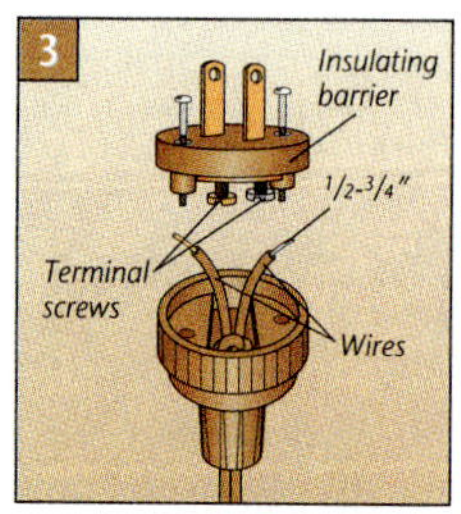

Strip 1/2 to 3/4 inch of insulation off the wire ends, being careful not to nick the wires *(page 159)*. Unscrew the terminal screws to allow space for the wires.

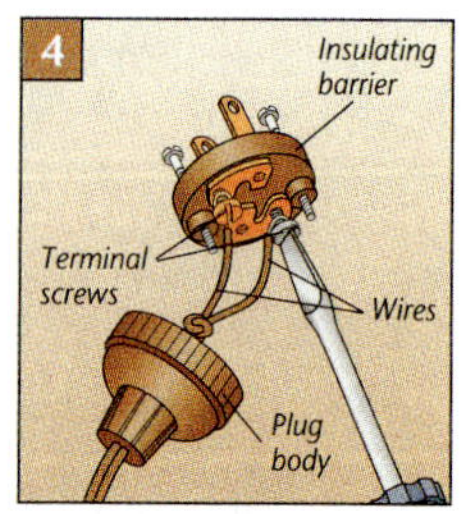

Form loops on wires and wrap them clockwise three-quarters of the way around screws. Tighten the screws, trim excess wire, and reattach the barrier to the body.

Replacing three special types of plugs

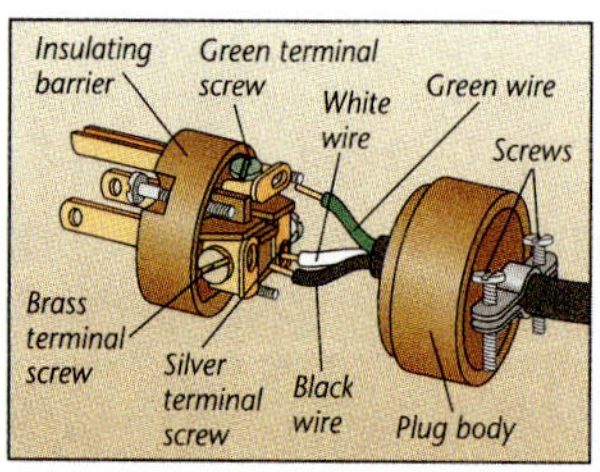

Three-prong grounding plug. Unscrew the insulating barrier; push stripped wires through the plug body into the correct terminal slots. Tighten the terminal screws and reassemble the plug.

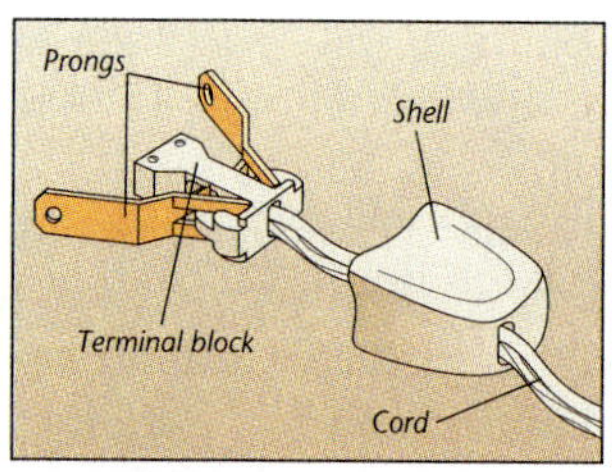

Self-connecting plug. Push the cord (don't strip it) through the shell and into the terminal block; squeeze the prongs together to grip the cord and slide into the shell.

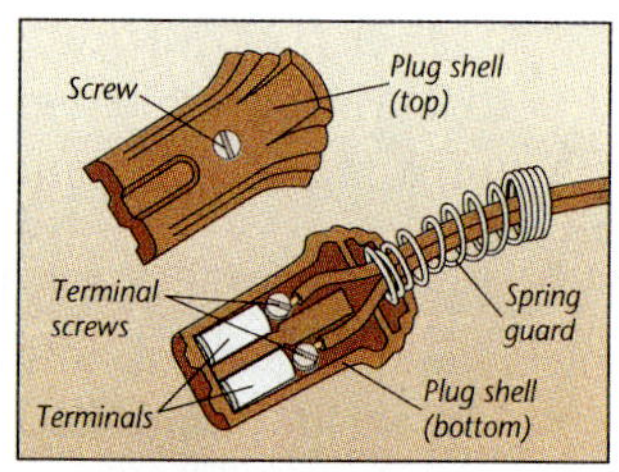

Female appliance plug. Unscrew the plug shell; feed the cord through the spring guard. Strip the wire ends *(page 159)*, wrap them clockwise around the terminal screws, and tighten; reassemble the plug.

Figure 14.3 Replacing Plugs

From *Home Repair Handbook* (Menlo Park, Calif.: Sunset, 1999), pp. 156–57.

actions, each signaled by the verb (italicized): "*Unscrew* and *remove* the new plug's insulating barrier. Using a utility knife, *split* the end of the cord to *separate* the wires; *push* the cord through the plug body." These are active verbs, and the sentences are in the form of clear and efficient commands.

The anonymous authors do not assume that readers know very much, especially on important safety matters. Paragraph 3, for example, presents a note explaining the National Electrical Code ("NEC") for old-style plugs. Also, readers are referred twice (in paragraph 4 and in step 3 of "Replacing a plug with terminal screws") to the explanation of how to strip wires safely, which appears on page 159 of the *Home Repair Handbook*.

Exercise 14.11

Write a one- to two-page instructional process narrative that tells readers how to make a peanut butter and jelly sandwich or perform some other equally simple procedure such as logging on to the Internet, shortening a pair of pants, separating egg whites from yolks, potting a plant, or filling a fountain pen. Address your narrative to readers who have never done the procedure before or to those who may know something about the procedure but would be interested in how you go about doing it.

15 Describing

Describing comes from the Latin *describere*, meaning "to sketch" or "to copy in writing." Written descriptions create images that help readers imagine what is being described. Readers often use the word *vivid* to characterize description that creates an intense, distinctive image, one that seems to bring the words on the page to life. Good description can also be evocative, calling up memories or suggesting feelings associated with the subject being described. Writers can use description for many purposes: to give readers an impression of a person or place, to illustrate abstract ideas, to make information memorable, or to support an argument. This chapter presents the three basic descriptive techniques of naming, detailing, and comparing; surveys the words writers of English typically use to evoke sense impressions that help to make description vivid; and examines how writers use description to create a dominant impression.

NAMING

Naming calls readers' attention to observable features of the subject being described. To describe a room, for example, you might name objects you see as you look around, such as a bed, pillows, blankets, dresser, clothes, books, a CD player, and CDs. These objects suggest what kind of room it is and begin to give readers an impression of what it is like to be in this particular room.

Look closely at the following passage describing a weasel that the writer, Annie Dillard, encountered in the woods. As you read, notice the underlined words (such as *face* and *chin*) that Dillard uses to name the weasel's most distinctive or memorable features:

> He was ten inches long, thin as a curve, a muscled ribbon, brown as fruitwood, soft-furred, alert. His face was fierce, small and pointed as a lizard's; he would have made a good arrowhead. There was just a dot of chin, maybe two brown hairs' worth, and then the pure white fur began that spread down his underside. He had two black eyes I didn't see, any more than you see a window.
>
> –ANNIE DILLARD, *Teaching a Stone to Talk*

With these names, readers can begin to put together a mental image of the animal Dillard is describing. She does not name one feature alone but gives readers names for different parts of the weasel. She also uses simple, everyday nouns to name the weasel's features. They are not technical words (like *maxilla* or *mandible,* words scientists might use to refer to its upper and lower jaw) but words like *chin* that all readers of English are likely to know. Words like *chin* are also concrete nouns that refer to specific, observable parts of a weasel's face. The piling up of names, combined with the simplicity and concreteness of the nouns, helps readers begin to imagine what the weasel looked like to Dillard.

Dillard's naming focuses on what she saw. Although writers most commonly name what they see, sight is not the only sense contributing to vivid descriptions. Here is a passage that illustrates some of the nouns writers can use to name smells *(stink),* sounds *(plunk),* tastes *(sweetness),* and touch *(rawness):*

> When the sun fell across the great white pile of the new Telephone Company building, you could smell the stucco burning as you passed; then some liquid sweetness that came to me from deep in the rings of the freshly cut lumber stacked in the yards, and the fresh plaster and paint on the brand-new storefronts. Rawness, sunshiny rawness down the end streets of the city, as I thought of them then—the hot ash-laden stink of the refuse dumps in my nostrils and the only sound at noon the resonant metal plunk of a tin can I kicked ahead of me as I went my way.
>
> —ALFRED KAZIN, *A Walker in the City*

Exercise 15.1

Go to a place where you can sit for a while, and observe the scene. It might be a landscape or a cityscape, indoors or outdoors, crowded or solitary. It could be a familiar or a new place. For five minutes, list everything in the scene that you can name using nouns. (A simple way to test if a word is a noun is to see if you can put the word *the, a,* or *an* in front of the word.) Remember, you can name objects you see *(dog, hydrant)* as well as impressions such as smells or sounds you experience at the place *(stench, hiss).*

Then write a page or so that describes the scene for someone who is not there with you. You could choose to write for readers who have been to the place but have not seen what you are seeing there now, or you could write for readers who have never been to this particular place to let them know what to expect when they get there.

Exercise 15.2

Turn to "Father," by Jan Gray, in Chapter 3. Read paragraph 12, and underline the names that Gray uses to describe her bedroom after her father punishes her for not getting home in time to clean her bedroom. Begin underlining with the words *heart, knob, door,* and *bedroom* in the opening sentence. How do you think the amount of naming Gray does, together with the words she chooses, contributes to the description's vividness—measured by your ability to imagine what her bedroom looked like?

DETAILING

Naming identifies the notable features of the subject being described; **detailing** makes the features more specific or particularized. Naming answers the questions "What is it?" and "What are its parts or features?" Detailing answers questions like these:

What size is it?

How many are there?

What is it made of?

Where is it located?

What is its condition?

How is it used?

Where does it come from?

What is its effect?

What is its value?

To add details to names, add modifiers—adjectives and adverbs, phrases and clauses. *Modifiers* make nouns more specific by supplying additional information. Notice how many modifying details (enclosed in brackets) about number, size, shape, color, texture, and value Dillard provides in her description of the weasel.

> He was [ten inches long], [thin] as a curve, a [muscled] ribbon, [brown] as fruitwood, [soft-furred], [alert]. His face was [fierce], [small] and [pointed] as a lizard's; he would have made a good arrowhead. There was just a dot of chin, maybe [two brown hairs'] worth, and then the [pure white] fur began that spread down his underside. He had [two black] eyes I didn't see, any more than you see a window.
>
> –Annie Dillard, *Teaching a Stone to Talk*

Dillard's details provide information that particularizes the weasel. In other words, readers recognize that she is describing what a specific weasel that she encountered looked like, not what a weasel is supposed to look like. Her weasel has certain qualities that make it an individual, such as its length *(ten inches long)* and color *(brown* and *pure white)*. Just as objective physical details like these help readers picture the weasel, other details convey subjective information about Dillard's thoughts and feelings during the encounter. For example, when Dillard writes that the weasel's "face was fierce," she is making a judgment and expressing her feelings. She uses details like this to make readers see the weasel as a wild animal, not a soft and cuddly pet.

In describing people, writers often combine physical details with details characterizing aspects of the individual's personality. These characterizations or evaluations let readers know something about the writer's feelings and thoughts about the person, as the following examples illustrate:

> My father, a [fat], [funny] man with [beautiful] eyes and a [subversive] wit . . .
>
> –Alice Walker, "Beauty: When the Other Dancer Is the Self"

> I was afraid of her [higharched bony] nose, her eyebrows [lifted in half-circles] above her [hooded], [brilliant] eyes, and of the [Kentucky] R's in her speech, and the [long] steps she took in her [hightop] shoes. I did nothing but fear her [bearing-down] authority. . . .
>
> –EUDORA WELTY, "Miss Duling"

Walker begins with a physical detail *(fat)* but then chooses details that express her evaluation *(funny, beautiful)* as well as her analysis of the type of humor her father uses *(subversive)*. Similarly, Welty combines physical description *(higharched bony nose)* with subjective judgment *(bearing-down authority)* to enable readers to understand why she feared her former schoolteacher.

Sometimes writers use physical details to symbolize a person's character or the writer's feelings toward that person. We can see, for example, in the following passage describing a first meeting with the swimming coach that author Brad Benioff perceives Rick as overwhelmingly powerful and threatening:

> Rick was [not a friendly looking] man. He wore only swim trunks, and his [short], [powerful] legs rose up to meet a [bulging] torso. His [big] belly was [solid]. His shoulders, as if to offset his front-heaviness, were [thrown back], creating a [deep] crease of [excess] muscle from his sides around the small of his back, a crease like a huge frown. His arms were [crossed], [two medieval] maces placed carefully on their racks, ready to be swung at any moment. His [round] cheeks and chin were [darkened] by traces of [black] whiskers. His hair was [sparse]. [Huge], [black], [mirrored] sunglasses replaced his eyes. Below his [prominent] nose was a [thin], [sinister] mustache. I couldn't believe this [menacing-looking] man was the [legendary jovial] Rick.
>
> –BRAD BENIOFF, "Rick"

Exercise 15.3

Return to the description you wrote in Exercise 15.1. Put brackets around the details you used to help describe the scene. Add any other details you think of now—details that indicate size, quantity, makeup, location, condition, use, source, effect, value, or any other quality that would make the description more specific and particularized for readers. Then reread your description. What do you think the detailing contributes to the description you wrote?

Exercise 15.4

Look again at paragraph 12 of Jan Gray's essay in Chapter 3. In Exercise 15.2, you underlined the names Gray used. Now put brackets around the details. You might begin, for example, with the modifiers *racing* and *front*. How do you think detailing contributes to Gray's description? How do these details help you imagine what Gray's bedroom looked like to her at that particular moment?

Exercise 15.5

Turn again to Jan Gray's essay in Chapter 3, this time to the opening paragraph. Read and put brackets around the words that detail the description of Gray's father.

If you have not read the entire essay, read it now, and consider how Gray uses her father's skin condition to symbolize her feelings about him. What do you think her father's skin condition represents to her? What does Gray's description of her father suggest to you about their relationship and her feelings toward him?

COMPARING

In addition to naming and detailing, writers sometimes use **comparing** to make their description more vivid for readers. Look again at Annie Dillard's description of a weasel, paying attention this time to the comparisons enclosed in parentheses:

> He was ten inches long, thin (as a curve), (a muscled ribbon), (brown as fruitwood), soft-furred, alert. His face was fierce, (small and pointed as a lizard's); (he would have made a good arrowhead). There was just a dot of chin, maybe two brown hairs' worth, and then the pure white fur began that spread down his underside. He had two black (eyes I didn't see, any more than you see a window).
>
> –ANNIE DILLARD, *Teaching a Stone to Talk*

Dillard uses two kinds of comparison in this description: simile and metaphor. Simile and metaphor point out similarities in things that are essentially dissimilar. A *simile* expresses the similarity directly by using the words *like* or *as* to announce the comparison. Dillard uses a simile when she writes that the weasel was "thin as a curve." A *metaphor,* by contrast, is an implicit comparison in which one thing is described as though it were the other. Dillard uses a metaphor when she calls the weasel "a muscled ribbon."

Similes and metaphors can add to the vividness of a description by giving readers additional information to help them picture the subject. For example, Dillard uses the word *thin* to detail the weasel's body shape. But *thin* is a relative term, leading readers to wonder, how thin? Dillard tries to anticipate this question by giving readers two images for comparison: a curve and a ribbon. Both of these comparisons help readers construct a fuller mental image of the weasel.

Comparing can also help convey to readers what the writer feels about the subject. Here is an example of comparing from Brad Benioff's description of Coach Rick that is suggestive of the writer's feelings: "His arms were crossed, two medieval maces placed carefully on their racks, ready to be swung at any moment." Sometimes the similes or metaphors writers use are suggestive but hard to pin down. What do you think Dillard means, for example, by comparing the weasel's eyes to a window: "He had two black eyes I didn't see, any more than you see a window"?

Exercise 15.6

Return to the description you wrote in Exercise 15.1 and may have added to in Exercise 15.3. Reread it, and mark any comparing you used. Try to add one or two more similes or metaphors to your description. How do you think your use of comparing may help readers imagine the subject or get a sense of what you feel about it?

Exercise 15.7

Look again at Jan Gray's essay in Chapter 3. Gray concludes paragraph 12 with a metaphor when she uses the word *waltz* to describe the way her father comes into her life every few months. Discuss with one or two classmates the comparison implied in the word *waltz*. What do you think it contributes, if anything, to Gray's description?

Look also at the comparison she uses in the sentence that opens paragraph 13: "I was slowly *piecing my room together* . . . " What does this comparison contribute to the image you have of Gray's bedroom and her feelings about her father?

USING SENSORY DESCRIPTION

When writers use **sensory description** to describe animals, people, or scenes, they usually rely on the sense of sight more than the other senses. Our vocabulary for reporting what we see is larger and more varied than our vocabulary for reporting other sense impressions. Quite a few nouns and verbs designate sounds; a smaller number of nouns, but few verbs, describe smells; and very few nouns or verbs convey touch and taste. It also seems easier to use naming to describe what we see. Nonvisual sense perceptions seem to be less readily divided into distinguishing features. For example, we have many names to describe the visible features of a car but few to describe the sounds a car makes. Nevertheless, writers can detail the qualities and attributes of nonvisual sensations—the loudness or tinniness or rumble of an engine, for instance. They can also use comparing to help readers imagine what something sounds, feels, smells, or tastes like.

The Sense of Sight

When people describe what they see, they identify the objects in their field of vision. Here are two brief examples of visual description. The first selection, by Amy Tan, depicts her mother's kitchen; the second passage, by Tracy Kidder, describes Mrs. Zajac, a grade school teacher.

> On Christmas Eve I saw that my mother had outdone herself in creating a strange menu. She was pulling black veins out of the backs of fleshy prawns. The kitchen was littered with appalling mounds of raw food: A slimy rock cod with bulging eyes that pleaded not to be thrown into a pan of hot oil. Tofu, which looked like stacked wedges of rubbery white sponges. A bowl soaking dried fungus back to life. A plate of squid, their backs crisscrossed with knife markings so they resembled bicycle tires.
>
> –Amy Tan, "Fish Cheeks"

> She was thirty-four. She wore a white skirt and yellow sweater and a thin gold necklace, which she held in her fingers, as if holding her own reins, while waiting for children to answer. Her hair was black with a hint of Irish red. It was cut short to the tops of her ears, and swept back like a pair of folded wings. She had a delicate cleft chin, and she was short—the children's chairs would have fit her. . . . Her hands kept very busy. They sliced the air and made karate chops to mark off boundaries. They extended straight out like a traffic cop's, halting illegal maneuvers yet to be perpe-

trated. When they rested momentarily on her hips, her hands looked as if they were in holsters.

—TRACY KIDDER, *Among Schoolchildren*

Exercise 15.8

Write a few sentences describing a teacher, friend, or family member. Do not rely on memory for this exercise; describe someone who is before you as you write so that you can describe in detail what you see. Later, when you are alone, reread what you have written, and make any changes you think will help make this visual description more vivid for your readers.

The Sense of Hearing

In reporting auditory impressions, writers seldom name the objects from which the sounds come without also naming the sounds themselves: the murmur of a voice, the rustle of the wind, the squeak of a hinge, the sputter of an engine. *Onomatopoeia* is the term for names of sounds that echo the sounds themselves: *squeak, murmur, hiss, boom, plink, tinkle, twang, jangle, rasp, chirr.* Sometimes writers make up words like *sweesh* and *cara-wong* to imitate sounds they wish to describe. Qualitative words like *powerful* and *rich* as well as relative terms like *loud* and *low* often specify sounds further. For detailing sounds, writers sometimes use the technique called *synesthesia*, applying words commonly used to describe one sense to another, such as describing sounds as *sharp* and *soft*.

To write about the sounds along Manhattan's Canal Street, Ian Frazier uses many of these describing and naming techniques. He also uses comparison when he refers metaphorically to the horns getting "tired and out of breath."

> The traffic on Canal Street never stops. It is a high-energy current jumping constantly between the poles of Brooklyn and New Jersey. It hates to have its flow pinched in the density of Manhattan, hates to stop at intersections. Along Canal Street, it moans and screams. Worn break shoes of semitrucks go "Ooohhhh nooohhhh" at stoplights, and the sound echoes in the canyons of warehouses and Chinatown tenements. People lean on their horns from one end of Canal Street to the other. They'll honk nonstop for ten minutes at a time, until the horns get tired and out of breath. They'll try different combinations: shave-and-a-hair-cut, long-long-long, short-short-short-long. Some people have musical car horns; a person purchasing a musical car horn seems to be limited to a choice of four tunes—"La Cucaracha," "Theme from *The Godfather*," "Dixie," and "Hava Nagila."
>
> —IAN FRAZIER, "Canal Street"

Exercise 15.9

Turn to paragraph 6 of Tobias Wolff's essay, "On Being a Real Westerner," in Chapter 2, and find the place where Wolff uses onomatopoeia to describe sound. Then look at paragraph 9, where Wolff describes the sound created by firing the rifle. What do you think these descriptions of sound contribute to this particular essay, which takes place mostly in the silence of Wolff's home?

Exercise 15.10

Find a noisy spot—a restaurant, a football game, a nursery school, a laundry room—where you can perch for about half an hour. Listen attentively to the sounds of the place, and make notes about what you hear. Then write a page or so describing the place through its sounds.

The Sense of Smell

The English language has a meager stock of words to express the olfactory sense. In addition to the word *smell,* fewer than a dozen commonly used nouns name this sensation: *odor, scent, vapor, fume, aroma, fragrance, perfume, bouquet, stench, stink.* Although there are other, rarer words like *fetor* and *effluvium,* few writers use them, probably for fear that their readers will not know them. Few verbs describe receiving or sending odors—*smell, sniff, waft*—but a fair number of detailing adjectives are available: *redolent, pungent, aromatic, perfumed, stinking, musty, rancid, putrid, rank, fetid, malodorous, foul, acrid, sweet,* and *cloying.*

Here is an example of how reporter Amanda Coyne uses smell to describe "convict moms" with their children in the prison visiting room:

> Occasionally, a mother will pick up her present and bring it to her nose when one of the bearers of the single flower—her child—asks if she likes it. . . . But most of what is being smelled today is the children themselves. While the other adults are plunking coins into the vending machines, the mothers take deep whiffs from the backs of their children's necks, or kiss and smell the backs of their knees, or take off their shoes and tickle their feet and then pull them close to their noses. They hold them tight and take in their own second scent—the scent assuring them that these are still their children and that they still belong to them.
>
> –AMANDA COYNE, "The Long Good-Bye: Mother's Day in Federal Prison"

In addition to using *smell* as a verb, Coyne describes the repeated action of bringing the object being smelled to the nose, an act that not only signifies the process of smelling but also underscores the intimacy of the act. To further emphasize intimacy, Coyne connects smelling with other intimate acts of kissing, tickling, pulling close, and holding tight.

Because she is not describing her own experience of smell, Coyne does not try to find words to evoke the effect the odor has. In the next passage, however, Frank Conroy uses comparing in addition to naming and detailing to describe how the smell of flowers affected him:

> The perfume of the flowers rushed into my brain. A lush aroma, thick with sweetness, thick as blood, and spiced with the clear acid of tropical greenery.
>
> –FRANK CONROY, *Stop-Time*

Naming the objects from which smells come can also be very suggestive.

> The odor of these houses was different, full of fragrances, sweet and nauseating. On 105th Street the smells were of fried lard, of beans and car fumes, of factory smoke and home-made brew out of backyard stills. There were chicken smells and goat

smells in grassless yards filled with engine parts and wire and wood planks, cracked and sprinkled with rusty nails. These were the familiar aromas: the funky earth, animal and mechanical smells which were absent from the homes my mother cleaned.

–LUIS J. RODRIGUEZ, *Always Running: Gang Days in L.A.*

Exercise 15.11

Turn to "Uncle Willie," by Maya Angelou, in Chapter 3, and read paragraph 2. Underline the words describing the sense of smell. How do you think this bit of sensory description helps readers imagine the scene?

Exercise 15.12

Choose a place with noticeable, distinctive smells where you can stay for ten or fifteen minutes. You may choose an eating place (a cafeteria, a doughnut shop), a place where something is being manufactured (a sawmill, a bakery), or some other place that has strong, identifiable odors (a fishing dock, a garden, a locker room). While you are there, take notes on what you smell, and then write a page or so describing the place primarily through its smells.

The Sense of Touch

Few nouns and verbs name tactile sensations besides words like *touch, feel, tickle, brush, scratch, sting, itch,* and *tingle*. Probably as a consequence, writers describing the sense of touch tend not to name the sensation directly or even to report the act of feeling. Nevertheless, a large stock of words describes temperature *(hot, warm, mild, tepid, cold, arctic)*, moisture content *(wet, dry, sticky, oily, greasy, moist, crisp)*, texture *(gritty, silky, smooth, crinkled, coarse, soft, leathery)*, and weight *(heavy, light, ponderous, buoyant, feathery)*. Read the following passages with an eye for descriptions of touch.

A small slab of roughly finished concrete offered a place to stand opposite a square of tar from which a splintered tee protruded.

–WILLIAM RINTOUL, "Breaking One Hundred"

The earth was moldy, a dense clay. No sun had fallen here for over two centuries. I climbed over the brick retaining wall and crawled toward the sound of the kitten. As I neared, as it sensed my presence was too large to be its mother, it went silent and scrabbled away from the reach of my hand. I brushed fur, though, and that slight warmth filled me with what must have been a mad calm because when the creature squeezed into a bearing wall of piled stones, I inched forward on my stomach.

–LOUISE ERDRICH, "Beneath the House"

Here is an example of a writer recalling a childish fantasy of aggression toward her younger sister. Notice the tactile description she uses.

She was baby-soft. I thought that I could put my thumb on her nose and push it bonelessly in, indent her face. I could poke dimples into her cheeks. I could work her face around like dough.

–MAXINE HONG KINGSTON, "The Quiet Girl"

Exercise 15.13

Do something with your hands, and then write a sentence or two describing the experience of touch. For example, you might pet a dog, dig a hole and put a plant into the earth, make a pizza, sculpt with clay, bathe a baby, scrub a floor, or massage a friend's back. As you write, notice the words you consider using to describe temperature, moisture content, texture, weight, or any other tactile quality.

Exercise 15.14

Turn again to "Uncle Willie," by Maya Angelou, in Chapter 3, and reread paragraph 2, this time looking at the way the writer describes her fear of touching the hot stove. Underline any language that describes the sense of touch. How do you think this sensory description helps readers imagine the scene?

The Sense of Taste

Other than *taste, savor,* and *flavor,* few words name gustatory sensations directly. Certain words do distinguish among types of tastes—*sweet (saccharine, sugary, cloying); sour (acidic, tart); bitter (acrid, biting); salty (briny, brackish)*—and several other words describe specific tastes *(piquant, spicy, pungent, peppery, savory, toothsome).*

In the following passage, M. F. K. Fisher describes the surprisingly "delicious" taste of tar:

> Tar with some dust in it was perhaps even more delicious than dirty chips from the iceman's wagon, largely because if we worked up enough body heat and had the right amount of spit we could keep it melted so that it acted almost like chewing gum, which was forbidden to us as vulgar and bad for the teeth and in general to be shunned. Tar was better than anything ever put out by Wrigley and Beechnut, anyway. It had a high, bright taste. It tasted the way it smelled, but better.
>
> –M. F. K. FISHER, "Prejudice, Hate, and the First World War"

Fisher identifies the taste of tar as "high" and "bright"—two words that are not typically associated with taste but might be suggestive to readers. Another way she tries to evoke the sense of taste is by comparing tar that acted like chewing gum to actual Wrigley and Beechnut chewing gum. More surprisingly, she compares the taste of tar to its smell.

Ernest Hemingway, in a more conventional passage, tries to describe taste primarily by naming the foods he consumed and giving details that indicate the intensity and quality of the tastes:

> As I ate the oysters with their strong taste of the sea and their faint metallic taste that the cold wine washed away, leaving only the sea taste and the succulent texture, and as I drank their cold liquid from each shell and washed it down with the crispy taste of the wine, I lost the empty feeling and began to be happy and to make plans.
>
> –ERNEST HEMINGWAY, *A Moveable Feast*

Notice that Hemingway combines taste and touch *(succulent texture* and *crispy taste).* Writers often use words like *juicy, chewy,* and *chunky* to evoke both the taste and the feel of food in the mouth.

Exercise 15.15

In the manner of Hemingway, take notes as you eat a particular food or an entire meal. Then write a few sentences describing the tastes you experienced.

Exercise 15.16

Turn to John T. Edge's "I'm Not Leaving Until I Eat This Thing" in Chapter 4, an essay about pickled pig's lips. Read paragraphs 7 and 18, underlining any language that describes or suggests the sense of taste. How well does this sensory description help you participate in the writer's experience?

CREATING A DOMINANT IMPRESSION

The most effective description creates a **dominant impression**, a mood or an atmosphere that reinforces the writer's purpose. Writers often attempt to create a dominant impression—for example, when they describe a place to set a scene and make readers aware of its atmosphere. Naming, detailing, comparing, and sensory language—all the choices about what to include and what to call things—come together to create this effect, as the following passage by Mary McCarthy illustrates. Notice that McCarthy directly states the idea she is trying to convey in the last sentence of the paragraph.

> Whenever we children came to stay at my grandmother's house, we were put to sleep in the sewing room, a bleak, shabby, utilitarian rectangle, more office than bedroom, more attic than office, that played to the hierarchy of chambers the role of a poor relation. It was a room seldom entered by the other members of the family, seldom swept by the maid, a room without pride; the old sewing machine, some cast off chairs, a shadeless lamp, rolls of wrapping paper, piles of pins, and remnants of material united with the iron folding cots put out for our use and the bare floor boards to give an impression of intense and ruthless temporality. Thin, white spreads, of the kind used in hospitals and charity institutions, and naked blinds at the windows reminded us of our orphaned condition and of the ephemeral character of our visit; there was nothing here to encourage us to consider this our home.
>
> –MARY MCCARTHY, *Memories of a Catholic Girlhood*

Everything in the room made McCarthy and her brothers feel unwanted, discarded, orphaned. The room itself is described in terms applicable to the children. (Like them, it "played to the hierarchy of chambers the role of a poor relation.") The objects she names, together with their distinguishing details—"cast-off chairs," "shadeless lamp," "iron folding cots," "bare floor boards," "naked blinds"—contribute to this overall impression, thus enabling McCarthy to convey her purpose to her readers.

Sometimes writers comment directly in a description. McCarthy, for instance, states that the sewing room gave "an impression of intense and ruthless temporality," everything serving to remind the children that they were orphans and did not live there. Often, however, writers want description to speak for itself. They *show* rather than tell, letting the descriptive language evoke the impression by itself. Such is the case in the following description by George Orwell of a room for hire:

> Hanging from the ceiling there was a heavy glass chandelier on which the dust was so thick that it was like fur. And covering most of one wall there was a huge hideous piece of junk, something between a sideboard and a hall-stand, with lots of carving and little drawers and strips of looking-glass, and there was a once-gaudy carpet ringed by the slop-pails of years, and two gilt chairs with burst seats, and one of those old-fashioned armchairs which you slide off when you try to sit on them. The room had been turned into a bedroom by thrusting four squalid beds in among the wreckage.
>
> —GEORGE ORWELL, *The Road to Wigan Pier*

Exercise 15.17

Return to Jan Gray's essay in Chapter 3, and read paragraphs 3 and 4 describing her father's abandoned apartment. What seems to you to be the dominant impression of this description? What do you think contributes most to this impression?

16

Defining

Defining is an essential strategy for all writing. Autobiographers, for example, must occasionally define objects, conditions, events, and activities for readers likely to be unfamiliar with particular terms. In the following example from Chapter 3, the definition is underlined.

> My father's hands are grotesque. He suffers from psoriasis, a chronic skin disease that covers his massive, thick hands with scaly, reddish patches that periodically flake off, sending tiny pieces of dead skin sailing to the ground.
>
> –JAN GRAY, "Father"

When writers share information or explain how to do something, they must often define important terms for readers who are unfamiliar with the subject. This example comes from Chapter 5.

> Shifting baselines are the chronic, slow, hard-to-notice changes in things, from the disappearance of birds and frogs in the countryside to the increased drive time from L.A. to San Diego.
>
> –RANDY OLSON, "Shifting Baselines: Slow-Motion Disaster below the Waves"

To convince readers of a position or an evaluation or to move them to act on a proposal, a writer must often define concepts important to an argument. This example comes from Chapter 6.

> You would come across news of a study showing that the percentage of Wisconsin food-stamp families in "extreme poverty"—defined as less than 50 percent of the federal poverty line—has tripled in the last decade to more than 30 percent.
>
> –BARBARA EHRENREICH, *Nickel and Dimed*

As these examples illustrate, there are many kinds of definitions and many forms that they can take. Some published essays and reports are concerned primarily with the definition of a little-understood or problematic concept or thing. Usually, however, definition is only a part of an essay. A long piece of writing, like a term paper, textbook, or research report, may include many kinds of brief and extended definitions, all of them integrated with other writing strategies.

This chapter illustrates various types of sentence definitions, the most common in writing. When writers use sentence definitions, they rely on various sentence patterns to provide concise definitions. The chapter also provides illustrations of multisentence extended definitions, including definition by word history, or etymology, and by stipulation.

SENTENCE DEFINITIONS

Every field of study, every institution, and every activity has its own unique concepts and terms. Coming to a new area for the first time, a participant or a reader is often baffled by the many unfamiliar names for objects and activities. In college, introductory courses in all the academic disciplines often seem like courses in definitions of new terms. In the same way, newcomers to a sport like sailing or rock climbing often need to learn much specialized terminology. In such cases, writers of textbooks and manuals rely on brief **sentence definitions**, involving a variety of sentence strategies.

Here are some sentence strategies from several widely used introductory college textbooks. These examples illustrate various sentence strategies an author may use to name and define terms for readers.

The most obvious sentence strategies simply announce a definition. (In each of the following examples, the word being defined is in italics, and the definition is underlined.)

> A *karyotype* is a graphic representation of a set of chromosomes.
>
> Then, within the first week, the cells begin to *differentiate*—to specialize in structure and function.
>
> *B lymphocytes* form in the bone marrow and release antibodies that fight bacterial infections.
>
> Geologists refer to the processes of mountain building as *orogenesis* (from the Greek *oro,* "mountain," and *genesis,* "birth").
>
> *Posthypnotic suggestions* (suggestions to be carried out after the hypnosis session has ended) have helped alleviate headaches, asthma, warts, and stress-related skin disorders.

All of these sentence strategies declare in a straightforward way that the writer is defining a term. Other strategies, signaled by certain sentence structures like clauses and appositives, are less direct but still quite apparent.

> During the *oral stage,* which lasts throughout the first 18 months, the infant's sensual pleasures focus on sucking, biting, and chewing.
>
> *Hemophilia* is called the bleeder's disease because the affected person's blood does not clot.

These sentence definitions—all of which appear in subordinate clauses—add details, express time and cause, or indicate conditions or tentativeness. In all these examples, however, the clauses play a specific defining role in the sections of the text where they appear.

Another common defining strategy is the appositive phrase. Here one word or phrase defines another word or phrase in a brief inserted phrase called an *appositive.* Sometimes the appositive contains the definition; other times it contains the word to be defined.

> *Taxonomy,* the science of classifying groups (taxa) of organisms in formal groups, is hierarchical.
>
> The actual exchange of gases takes place in small air sacs, the *alveoli,* which are clustered in branches like grapes around the ends of the smallest bronchioles.

Exercise 16.1

Look up any three of the following words or phrases in a dictionary. Define each one in a sentence. Try to use a different sentence pattern, like the ones just illustrated, for each of your definitions.

bull market	ecumenism	samba
carcinogen	edema	seasonal affective disorder
caricature	harangue	sonnet
clinometer	hyperhidrosis	testosterone
ectomorph	mnemonic	zero-based budgeting

Exercise 16.2

Turn to the essay in Chapter 5 titled "Cannibalism: It Still Exists" by student writer Linh Kieu Ngo, and analyze the sentence definitions in paragraphs 5, 6, 7, 8, and 11. Notice the different kinds of sentence patterns Ngo relies on. (You need not be able to analyze the sentences grammatically to examine their patterns.) Keeping in mind that Ngo's purpose is to introduce readers to the concept of cannibalism and its varieties, how helpful do you find these sentence definitions? How do they work with Ngo's use of examples?

EXTENDED DEFINITIONS

At times a writer may need to go further than a brief sentence definition and provide readers with a fuller, **extended definition** extending over several sentences. Here, for example, is how Janice Castro defines a new kind of worker in the U.S. economy, the "contingent" worker.

> Every day, 1.5 million temps are dispatched from agencies like Kelly Services and Manpower—nearly three times as many as 10 years ago. But they are only the most visible part of America's enormous new temporary work force. An additional 34 million people start their day as other types of "contingent" workers. Some are part-timers with some benefits. Others work by the hour, the day or the duration of a project, receiving only a paycheck without benefits of any kind. The rules of their employment vary widely and so do the attempts to label them. They are called short-timers, per-diem workers, leased employees, extra workers, supplementals,

> contractors—or in IBM's ironic computer-generated parlance, "the peripherals." They are what you might expect: secretaries, security guards, salesclerks, assembly-line workers, analysts and CAD/CAM designers. But these days they are also what you'd never expect: doctors, high school principals, lawyers, bank officers, X-ray technicians, biochemists, engineers, managers—even chief executives.
>
> –JANICE CASTRO, "Contingent Workers"

Castro begins by comparing contingent workers to the more familiar temporary workers ("temps") managed by temporary employment agencies. Then she gives examples of contingent workers' working arrangements and lists many names by which these workers are known. Finally, she identifies the various categories of contingent workers. These strategies—comparisons, examples, synonyms, and classification—are often found in extended definitions and in fact in all kinds of explanatory writing. Castro never concisely defines the word *contingent* in the phrase "contingent worker" because she assumes that readers can infer that it means roughly the opposite of permanent, continuing worker.

In this next example, Marie Winn offers an extended definition of television addiction. Like Janice Castro, Winn begins with a comparison. These two experienced writers know that comparison or contrast is often the most effective way to present an unfamiliar term or concept to readers. The key is to know your readers well enough to find a term nearly all of them will know to compare to the unfamiliar term.

> People often refer to being "hooked on TV." Does this, too, fall into the lighthearted category of cookie eating and other pleasures that people pursue with unusual intensity, or is there a kind of televison viewing that falls into the more serious category of destructive addiction? . . .
>
> Let us consider television viewing in the light of the conditions that define serious addictions.
>
> Not unlike drugs or alcohol, the television experience allows the participant to blot out the real world and enter into a pleasurable and passive mental state. The worries and anxieties of reality are as effectively deferred by becoming absorbed in a television program as by going on a "trip" induced by drugs or alcohol. And just as alcoholics are only inchoately aware of their addiction, feeling that they control their drinking more than they really do ("I can cut it out any time I want—I just like to have three or four drinks before dinner"), people similarly overestimate their control over television watching. Even as they put off other activities to spend hour after hour watching television, they feel they could easily resume living in a different, less passive style. But somehow or other while the television set is present in their homes, the click doesn't sound. With television pleasures available, those other experiences seem less attractive, more difficult somehow. . . .
>
> The self-confessed television addict often feels he "ought" to do other things—but the fact that he doesn't read and doesn't plant his garden or sew or crochet or play games or have conversations means that those activities are no longer as desirable as television viewing. In a way a heavy viewer's life is as imbalanced by his television "habit" as a drug addict's or an alcoholic's. He is living in a holding pattern, as it were, passing up the activities that lead to growth or development or a sense of accomplishment. This is one reason people talk about their television viewing so rue-

> fully, so apologetically. They are aware that it is an unproductive experience, that almost any other endeavor is more worthwhile by any human measure.
>
> Finally, it is the adverse effect of television viewing on the lives of so many people that defines it as a serious addiction. The television habit distorts the sense of time. It renders other experiences vague and curiously unreal while taking on a greater reality for itself. It weakens relationships by reducing and sometimes eliminating normal opportunities for talking, for communicating.
>
> And yet television does not satisfy, else why would the viewer continue to watch hour after hour, day after day? "The measure of health," writes Lawrence Kubie, "is flexibility . . . and especially the freedom to cease when sated." But the television viewer can never be sated with his television experiences—they do not provide the true nourishment that satiation requires—and thus he finds that he cannot stop watching.
>
> –MARIE WINN, "TV Addiction"

Besides comparing television addiction to drug or alcohol addiction, Winn describes the effects of television addiction and speculates about why addicts find it so hard to break the addiction.

Extended definitions may also include *negative definitions*—explanations of what the thing being defined is *not:*

> It's important to be clear about the reverse definition, as well: what dinosaurs are not. Dinosaurs are not lizards, and vice versa. Lizards are scaly reptiles of an ancient bloodline. The oldest lizards antedate the earliest dinosaurs by a full thirty million years. A few large lizards, such as the man-eating Komodo dragon, have been called "relics of the dinosaur age," but this phrase is historically incorrect. No lizard ever evolved the birdlike characteristics peculiar to each and every dinosaur. A big lizard never resembled a small dinosaur except for a few inconsequential details of the teeth. Lizards never walked with the erect, long-striding gait that distinguishes the dinosaurlike ground birds today or the birdlike dinosaurs of the Mesozoic.
>
> –ROBERT T. BAKKER, *The Dinosaur Heresies*

Exercise 16.3

Choose one term that names some concept or feature of central importance in an activity or a subject you know well. For example, if you sail, you know terms like *tacking* and *coming about.* If you are studying biology, you have probably encountered terms like *morphogenesis* and *ecosystem*. Choose a word with a well-established definition. Write an extended definition of several sentences for this important term. Write for readers your own age who will be encountering the term for the first time when they read your definition.

Exercise 16.4

As part of her explanation of indirect aggression in her essay in Chapter 5, Natalie Angier provides an extended definition of the term, beginning with the last sentence of paragraph 7 and continuing through the end of paragraph 8. How does Angier define *indirect aggression*? How does this definition fit in with Angier's larger purpose in this essay?

HISTORICAL DEFINITIONS

Occasionally, a writer will trace the history of a word, from its first use to its adoption into other languages to its shifting meanings over the centuries. Such a strategy can be a rich addition to an essay, bringing surprising depth and resonance to the definition of a concept. A **historical definition** may begin with the roots of a word but extends well beyond the word's origins to trace its history over a long period of time. Such a history should always serve a writer's larger purpose, as the example here shows.

In this example, from a special issue of *Time* magazine on the future uses of cyberspace and its potential impact on the economy, Philip Elmer-DeWitt provides a historical definition of the term *cyberspace*.

> It started, as the big ideas in technology often do, with a science-fiction writer. William Gibson, a young expatriate American living in Canada, was wandering past the video arcades on Vancouver's Granville Street in the early 1980s when something about the way the players were hunched over their glowing screens struck him as odd. "I could see in the physical intensity of their postures how *rapt* the kids were," he says. "It was like a feedback loop, with photons coming off the screens into the kids' eyes, neurons moving through their bodies and electrons moving through the video game. These kids clearly *believed* in the space the games projected."
>
> That image haunted Gibson. He didn't know much about video games or computers—he wrote his breakthrough novel *Neuromancer* (1984) on an ancient manual typewriter—but he knew people who did. And as near as he could tell, everybody who worked much with the machines eventually came to accept, almost as an article of faith, the reality of that imaginary realm. "They develop a belief that there's some kind of *actual space* behind the screen," he says. "Some place that you can't see but you know is there."
>
> Gibson called that place "cyberspace," and used it as the setting for his early novels and short stories. In his fiction, cyberspace is a computer-generated landscape that characters enter by "jacking in"—sometimes by plugging electrodes directly into sockets implanted in the brain. What they see when they get there is a three-dimensional representation of all the information stored in "every computer in the human system"—great warehouses and skyscrapers of data. He describes it in a key passage in *Neuromancer* as a place of "unthinkable complexity," with "lines of light ranged in the nonspace of the mind, clusters and constellations of data. Like city lights, receding. . . ."
>
> In the years since, there have been other names given to that shadowy space where our computer data reside: the Net, the Web, the Cloud, the Matrix, the Metaverse, the Datasphere, the Electronic Frontier, the information superhighway. But Gibson's coinage may prove the most enduring. By 1989 it had been borrowed by the online community to describe not some science-fiction fantasy but today's increasingly interconnected computer systems—especially the millions of computers jacked into the Internet.
>
> –PHILIP ELMER-DEWITT, "Welcome to Cyberspace"

Elmer-DeWitt begins with a story about how William Gibson created the name *cyberspace* for a strange phenomenon he observed—young people's intense concentration while playing video games. *Cybernetics* was already a familiar term used to describe computer-controlled processes like robots in factories. Gibson borrowed the *cyber* portion and combined it with *space* to reflect his imagined realm, the "place that you can't see but you know is there." Elmer-DeWitt also offers details about how Gibson imagined humans would gain access to cyberspace and how it was constructed. Finally, bringing the historical definition into the present, Elmer-DeWitt lists competing terms that have failed to supplant *cyberspace* as the term most people now use to identify the realm of computer data and electronic communication.

Exercise 16.5

Any good dictionary tells the origins of words. Historical, or etymological, dictionaries, however, give much more information, enough to trace changes in use of a word over long periods of time. The preeminent historical dictionary of our language is the *Oxford English Dictionary*. Less imposing is *A Dictionary of American English*, and more accessible still is *A Dictionary of Americanisms*. Look up the historical definition of any one of the following words in *A Dictionary of Americanisms*, and write several sentences on its roots and development.

basketball	bushwhack	gerrymander	rubberneck
bazooka	canyon	jazz	sashay
bedrock	carpetbag	lobbying	Scot-free
blizzard	dugout	pep	two-bit
bogus	eye-opener	picayune	
bonanza	filibuster	podunk	

STIPULATIVE DEFINITIONS

To stipulate means to seek or assert agreement on something. In a **stipulative definition**, the writer declares a certain meaning, generally not one found in the dictionary. Stipulative definitions have a variety of important functions, two of which are illustrated here.

In her autobiography, Annie Dillard defines *football* as she understood it as a nine-year-old.

> Some boys taught me to play football. This was fine sport. You thought up a new strategy for every play and whispered it to the others. You went out for a pass, fooling everyone. Best, you got to throw yourself mightily at someone's running legs. Either you brought him down or you hit the ground flat out on your chin, with your arms empty before you. It was all or nothing. If you hesitated in fear, you would miss and get hurt: you would take a hard fall while the kid got away, or you would get kicked in the face while the kid got away. But if you flung yourself wholeheartedly at the back of his knees—if you gathered and joined body and soul and pointed them diving fearlessly—then you likely wouldn't get hurt, and you'd stop the ball. Your fate, and your team's score, depended on your concentration and courage. Nothing girls did could compare with it.
>
> –ANNIE DILLARD, *An American Childhood*

For Dillard's complete essay, see Chapter 2.

There are recognizable elements of grown-up football in Dillard's definition. Her focus is less on rules and strategy, however, than on the "concentration and courage" required to make a successful tackle and, of course, on the sheer thrill of doing it. She stipulates this definition because it suits her purposes in telling a remembered incident about how she and her fellow football players were chased by a man whose car they had bombed with snowballs.

This next example illustrates how a newspaper columnist can create a stipulative definition of the term *environmentalism* to argue for a more realistic approach to protecting the environment.

> Ozone depletion and the greenhouse effect are human disasters. They happen to occur in the environment. But they are urgent because they directly threaten man. A sane environmentalism, the only kind of environmentalism that will win universal public support, begins by unashamedly declaring that nature is here to serve man. A sane environmentalism is entirely anthropocentric: it enjoins man to preserve nature, but on the grounds of self-preservation.
>
> A sane environmentalism does not sentimentalize the earth. It does not ask people to sacrifice in the name of other creatures. After all, it is hard enough to ask people to sacrifice in the name of other humans. (Think of the chronic public resistance to foreign aid and welfare.) Ask hardworking voters to sacrifice in the name of the snail darter, and, if they are feeling polite, they will give you a shrug.
>
> –Charles Krauthammer, "Saving Nature, but Only for Man"

Exercise 16.6

Look at the essays by Stanley Kurtz ("Point of No Return") and Jonathan Rauch ("Who's More Worthy?") in Chapter 6, in which the two writers debate the question of extending the right to marry to same-sex couples. Central to each argument is a stipulative definition of the concept of marriage. What is each writer's stipulative definition of *marriage?* How do their definitions differ? How does each definition function in the writer's overall argument?

Exercise 16.7

Write several sentences of a stipulative definition for one of the following.

1. Define in your own way game shows, soap operas, police dramas, horror movies, or some other form of entertainment. Try for a stipulative definition of what your subject is generally like. In effect, you will be saying to your readers—other students in your class who are familiar with these entertainments—"Let's for now define it this way."
2. Define in your own way some hard-to-define concept, such as "loyalty," "love," "bravery," "shyness," or "masculinity."
3. Think of a new development or phenomenon in contemporary romance, music, television, leisure, fashion, or eating habits, or in your line of work. Invent a name for it, and write a stipulative definition for it.

17 Classifying

Classifying is an essential writing strategy for thinking about and organizing ideas, information, and experience. The process of **classifying** involves either grouping or dividing. Writers group related items (such as *apples, oranges, bananas, strawberries, cantaloupes,* and *cherries*) and label the general class of items they grouped together *(fruit)*. Or they begin classifying with a general class (such as *fruit*) and then divide it into subclasses of particular types (*apples, oranges,* etc.).

This chapter shows how you can organize and illustrate a classification you have read about or constructed yourself.

ORGANIZING CLASSIFICATION

Classifying in writing serves primarily as a means of **organization**, of creating a framework for the presentation of information, whether in a few paragraphs of an essay or in an entire book. This section surveys several examples of classifying, ranging from a simple two-level classification to a complex multilevel system.

The simplest classification divides a general topic into two subtopics. Here is an example by Edward J. Loughram from a proposal to keep at-risk teenagers out of jail and help them lead productive lives. Before he can present his proposed solution, Loughram has to get readers to see that all juvenile offenders are not the same. He does this by explaining that although statistics show that the number of juvenile offenders is rising, they do not take into account the fact that there are two distinct groups (underlined) of young people getting into trouble. He classifies juvenile offenders into these two categories to argue that the problem of delinquency can be solved, at least in part, by interrupting the criminal paths of the second group.

> Two primary factors explain the growing numbers of juvenile offenders. First, there is indeed a rise in serious crime among young people, fueled by the steady stream of drugs and weapons into their hands. These dangerous offenders are committed—legitimately—to juvenile-correction agencies for long-term custody or treatment.
>
> But a second, larger group is also contributing to the increase. It consists of 11-, 12-, and 13-year-old first-time offenders who have failed at home, failed in school, and fallen through the cracks of state and community social-service agencies. These

> are not serious offenders, or even typical delinquents. But they are coming into the correctional system because we have ignored the warning signs among them.
>
> –EDWARD J. LOUGHRAM, "Prevention of Delinquency"

Loughram's is a simple classification with only two categories. Each category is discussed in its own paragraph and labeled clearly. The labels—*dangerous offenders* and *not serious offenders*—make explicit that the basis for Loughram's classification is the seriousness of the crimes.

From Loughram's essay, we see how a writer can use a simple two-category classification to advance an argument. The next example, excerpted from a concept explanation essay by Janice Castro, presents a somewhat more complicated classification system:

> Every day, 1.5 million temps are dispatched from agencies like Kelly Services and Manpower—nearly three times as many as 10 years ago. But they are only the most visible part of America's enormous new temporary work force. An additional 34 million people start their day as other types of "contingent" workers. Some are part-timers with some benefits. Others work by the hour, the day or the duration of a project, receiving only a paycheck without benefits of any kind. The rules of their employment vary widely and so do the attempts to label them. They are called short-timers, per-diem workers, leased employees, extra workers, supplementals, contractors—or in IBM's ironic computer-generated parlance, "the peripherals." They are what you might expect: secretaries, security guards, salesclerks, assembly-line workers, analysts and CAD/CAM designers. But these days they are also what you'd never expect: doctors, high school principals, lawyers, bank officers, X-ray technicians, biochemists, engineers, managers—even chief executives. . . .
>
> Already the temping phenomenon is producing two vastly different classes of untethered workers: the mercenary work force at the top of the skills ladder, who thrive; and the rest, many of whom, unable to attract fat contract fees, must struggle to survive.
>
> –JANICE CASTRO, "Contingent Workers"

Castro explains that "contingent" is only one of many labels used to identify this general class of part-time and temporary workers. In the second paragraph, she divides contingent workers into what she calls "two vastly different classes." Although Castro does not label these two types of contingent workers clearly, we can see that her basis for differentiating between these two groups is the amount of money they are paid. Members of one group "thrive," while those of the other "must struggle to survive." Therefore, we can label these groups *well-paid* and *low-paid*. Readers sometimes have to supply labels to clarify for themselves the categories in a classification.

So far, Castro's is a simple two-part classification system like Loughram's. It has two levels: the general class of contingent workers and two subclasses of well-paid and low-paid contingent workers. Castro, however, adds a third level to her classification by listing several types of jobs that fall under her two subclasses. Here is a tree diagram that graphically displays Castro's three-level classification:

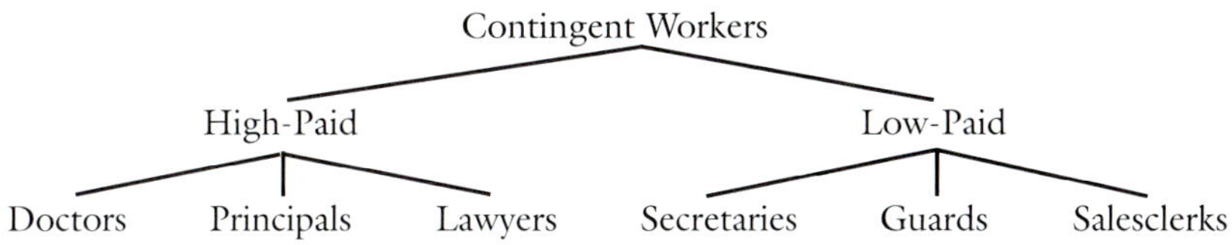

Later in the essay, Castro identifies another class of workers who are not contingent workers but are "a permanent cadre of 'core workers.'" To add this class of core workers to the tree diagram, we should also add a new general class at the top that includes all of the subclasses below it. We could label this most general class "corporate workers." Here is what the expanded tree diagram would look like:

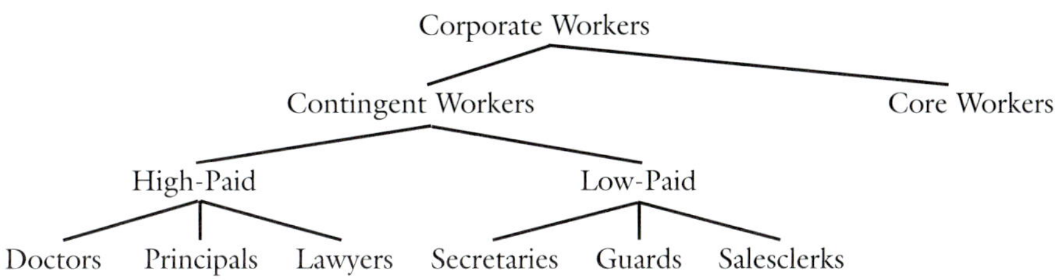

What the tree diagrams show at a glance is that in a classification system, some categories are on the same level, or *coordinate*. Some are on a higher level, *superordinate*. And some are on a lower level, *subordinate*. The highest level represents the most general category, and each lower level identifies increasingly specific types. If Castro took her classification to the most specific level, she would name individuals as examples of workers in each type of job. Whether you construct your own classification system or use someone else's, you want to make sure that each item is placed in an appropriate category on the proper level.

Exercise 17.1

Turn to the concept explanation in Chapter 5, "Cannibalism: It Still Exists," and make a tree diagram of the classification in paragraphs 5–12. What do you think is Linh Kieu Ngo's basis for classification? Does each item seem to be placed in an appropriate category and on the proper level?

Exercise 17.2

Review the essays you have written so far for this class or for another class, looking for an essay in which you used classifying. What was the purpose of your essay and your basis for classifying? Construct a tree diagram of your classification to see whether each item can be placed in an appropriate category and on the proper level.

ILLUSTRATING CLASSIFICATION

We used tree diagrams as an **illustration** of the categories and levels of Castro's classification of workers. Writers, however, sometimes integrate graphics into their own writing to make their classification easy for readers to see at a glance.

Here is an example from *Newsweek* magazine in which Sharon Begley and Martha Brant explain the problem of drug abuse by Olympic athletes. In this passage, the authors classify the performance-enhancing drugs athletes use into five categories (underlined) and present three kinds of information about each drug: what the drug does, how detectable it is, and what the health risks are. This organizational plan is graphically illustrated by the chart that accompanies the written text.

> If doping is, as [the head of IOC's Medical Commission Prince Alexandre] de Merode noticed, suddenly "an important problem," it is partly because the newest doping agents pose the risk of serious health problems, and even death. But the larger reason is that it is ridiculously easy to dope and not get caught. Doping and detection are like an arms race. First, trainers discover a performance-enhancing drug. Then, sports officials develop a test for it. Trainers retaliate by inventing a way to elude the detectors. So far, doping has stayed a lap ahead. "Undetectable drugs are 90 percent of estimated doping cases," says Hein Verbruggen, head of international cycling.
>
> Czech tennis pro Petr Korda tested positive for the steroid nandrolone after the Wimbledon quarterfinals last May, for instance. (Protesting that he did not know how the chemicals got into his system, he avoided the one-year suspension the International Tennis Association is supposed to impose.) But American pro Jim Courier charged that steroids are far from the worst abuse in tennis. "EPO is the problem," Courier told *Newsweek*. "I have pretty strong suspicions that guys are using it on the tour. I see guys who are out there week in and week out without taking rests. EPO can help you when it's the fifth set and you've been playing for four-and-a-half hours." Although the endurance-building effects of EPO last for about two weeks, its use can't be detected in urine at all or in blood for more than a day or so after the athlete stops taking it.
>
> EPO is only one weapon in a pharmaceutical arsenal of performance-enhancing substances flowing through sports. Stimulants like amphetamines, ephedrine and caffeine were the first substances to land on the IOC's list of banned agents, and they're still popular. They provide a quick pop of energy, and so are a favorite of sprinters, cyclists and swimmers. They are an ingredient of many asthma medications. Exercise-induced asthma has inexplicably stricken many Olympians, including 60 percent of the U.S. team in 1994, and medical use of stimulant inhalants is allowed. Are stimulants detectable? Sure, if your trainer's IQ matches his hat size. They clear the urine in hours, so all an athlete has to do is not take them too close to her event. If you've been using too soon before your race, there are always "masking agents." Probenecid, for one, inhibits substances from reaching the urine. And urine tests are all the IOC requires: blood tests, which can detect more substances, are deemed too invasive.
>
> Anabolic steroids, almost all of them derivatives of the hormone testosterone, are the mothers of all doping agents. They build muscles. By most estimates, an athlete can improve strength at least 5 percent by taking steroids either orally or through

Drug	What Does It Do?	Masking/ Detection	Risks
Human growth hormone (hGH)	Stimulates the intracellular breakdown of body fat, allowing more to be used for energy.	This is a natural hormone, so added amounts don't show up in blood or urine tests.	Muscle and bone disfigurement—jutting forehead, elongated jaw. Also: heart and metabolic problems.
Erythropoietin (EPO)	Increases the number of red blood cells without having to "dope" using one's own blood.	It's extremely difficult to detect because the extra blood cells are the athlete's own.	Extra cells can make blood the consistency of yogurt. This can lead to a clot, heart attack or stroke.
Testosterone	Used to build muscles. It lets the body recover quickly from strenuous exercise.	Rules allow up to five times the natural body level, giving athletes latitude.	Unnatural levels can cause heart disease, liver cancer and impotence.
Steroids/androstenedione	Anabolic steroids are incarnations of testosterone; androstenedione is a precursor molecule.	Water-based steroids (most common) are undetectable in urine after several weeks.	Synthetic testosterone carries the same risks as naturally occurring testosterone.
Stimulants	The first category that the IOC tested for. They delay the symptoms of fatigue.	Stimulants such as amphetamines can be detected; diuretics can dilute them in urine.	Fatigue is the body saying "stop"—overriding that message can be dangerous.

injection during high-intensity training. Drug-detection machines, such as the high-resolution mass spectrometer used at the Atlanta Games in 1996, can be tuned to detect any synthetic steroid; the Atlanta lab tested for 100 different types. But the Dr. Feelgoods of sport can tinker with the molecular structure of common steroids, so they slip through. "There are 72 banned steroids," says one American coach who says he developed drug regimes for athletes in Atlanta, "but the testosterone molecule is changeable in millions of ways. All you have to do is make a steroid not on the list." Or, simply by going cold turkey a few weeks before competition, an athlete can get the muscle-bulking effects without getting caught. If that seems too chancy, athletes can use a diuretic. These drugs, which are also banned, dilute the urine. That makes illicit substances virtually undetectable.

More and more athletes are turning to the source of all steroids: testosterone itself. Natural levels vary, so sports federations and the IOC try to detect doping indirectly. They measure the relative amounts of testosterone and another natural steroid called epitestosterone. In most people, testosterone levels are no more than twice epi levels. But to allow for individual variation, the IOC set the prohibited level at anything over 6 to 1. That means an athlete can dope himself up to, say, five times his normal testosterone levels, and get away with it. How much of an edge would that provide? A male athlete with a typical testosterone/epitestosterone ratio of 1.3 to 1 could boost that to 6 to 1, stay within the IOC limit and improve his performance at least 10 percent. Women, with a natural ratio of 2.5 to 1, could do even better, since they have less testosterone to begin with and so are more sensitive to added amounts. Testosterone can give women beards, deep voices and tough skin. It can make men's breasts swell and testicles shrivel.

The doping agents of choice today are substances that cannot be detected in urine: EPO and human growth hormone. Even though the performance-enhancing effects of hGH are unproved, many athletes believe it boosts energy. (Athletes dubbed the Atlanta Olympics "The Growth Hormone Games.") hGH can also cause grotesque skeletal deformations by stimulating abnormal bone growth. EPO, by increasing the production of red blood cells up to tenfold, can turn blood the consistency of yogurt, making it too thick to flow freely. The misuse of EPO has apparently killed at least 18 Dutch and Belgian cyclists since 1987.

–SHARON BEGLEY AND MARTHA BRANT, "The Real Scandal"

If you compare the chart to the written text, you will see that in some instances the chart simply repeats information that appears in the text but that more often the chart complements or adds to the text. For example, in the last paragraph of the text and in the "Risks" column of the chart, erythropoietin (EPO) is said to turn "blood the consistency of yogurt." The chart then adds to the text by explaining why thickening of the blood is dangerous: "This can lead to a clot, heart attack or stroke."

Although most readers would expect the chart to present the drugs in the order they appear in the essay, that is not the case here. In the essay, the drugs are discussed in this order: EPO, stimulants, steroids, testosterone, and human growth hormone (hGH). But in the chart, the order is hGH, EPO, testosterone, steroids, and stimulants. Except for EPO, the order in the chart reverses the order in the text. If you include a chart with your classification, be sure that your chart corresponds to the written text.

For more information on designing documents with graphics, see Chapter 25.

MAINTAINING CLARITY AND COHERENCE

The next example illustrates how writers can help readers follow a classification system by maintaining **clarity and coherence**—even when the subject is new and difficult. The passage comes from a book on physics by Gary Zukav. He uses classifying to explain the concept of mass. Simply defined, mass in physics is a measure of the matter in an object. How mass is calculated is the basis for Zukav's classification of two types of mass: gravitational and inertial.

As you read, notice the cues (underlined) the writer uses to help readers understand the classification.

There are two kinds of mass, which means that there are two ways of talking about it. The first is gravitational mass. The gravitational mass of an object, roughly speaking, is the weight of the object as measured on a balance scale. Something that weighs three times more than another object has three times more mass. Gravitational mass is the measure of how much force the gravity of the earth exerts on an object. Newton's laws describe the effects of this force, which vary with the distance of the mass from the earth. . . .

The second type of mass is inertial mass. Inertial mass is the measure of the resistance of an object to acceleration (or deceleration, which is negative acceleration). For example, it takes three times more force to move three railroad cars from a standstill to twenty miles per hour (positive acceleration) than it takes to move one railroad car from a standstill to twenty miles per hour. . . . Similarly, once they are moving, it takes three times more force to stop three cars than it takes to stop the single car. This is because the inertial mass of the three railroad cars is three times more than the inertial mass of the single railroad car.

–GARY ZUKAV, *The Dancing Wu Li Masters: An Overview of the New Physics*

From this passage, we can see some of the cues writers use to make a classification clear and coherent. Zukav begins by forecasting the classification he will develop *(There are two kinds of mass)*. He then introduces each category in its own paragraph, announced with the transition *(first* and *second)* and presented in the same sentence pattern *(The first is . . .* and *The second type of mass is . . .)*. Careful cueing like this can help make a classification clear to readers.

Exercise 17.3

Look back at the paragraphs from Linh Kieu Ngo's essay on cannibalism that you used to make a tree diagram in Exercise 17.1 or at the example by Begley and Brant earlier in this chapter, to examine the strategies these authors use to make their classifications clear and coherent. Notice how each category is introduced and the transitions used to help readers keep track of the categories. What conclusions can you draw about how writers maintain clarity and coherence from your analysis?

Exercise 17.4

Look back at the classification you examined in Exercise 17.2 to see how well you were able to maintain clarity and coherence in your classification. What changes would you make, if any, to improve clarity and coherence?

General strategies for coherence are discussed in Chapter 13.

18 Comparing and Contrasting

Comparing and contrasting make writing more memorable when you analyze and evaluate two or more things. You might compare two people you know well, two motorcycles you are considering buying for a cross-country tour, three Stephen King novels, four tomato plants being grown under different laboratory conditions, or two theories about the relationship between inflation and wages. But as soon as you begin to compare two things, you usually begin to contrast them as well, for rarely are two things alike in all respects. The contrasts, or differences, between the two motorcycles are likely to be more enlightening than the similarities, many of which may be so obvious as to need no analysis. Comparison, then, brings similar things together for examination, to see how they are alike. Contrast is a form of comparison that emphasizes differences.

The use of comparison and contrast is more than a writing strategy, of course. It is a way of thinking and learning. According to research on learning, we acquire new concepts most readily if we can see how they are similar to or different from concepts we already know.

Professional writers say that comparison and contrast is a basic strategy they would not want to be without. In some writing situations (like the ones we mentioned), it has no substitute. Indeed, some writing is essentially extended comparison. But for all kinds of writing situations, writers regularly alternate comparison and contrast with other writing strategies when they present information.

Chances are that you will confront many test questions and essay assignments asking you to compare and contrast—two poems, three presidents, four procedures. This strategy is popular in all academic disciplines, for it is one of the best ways to challenge students intellectually.

TWO WAYS OF COMPARING AND CONTRASTING

There are two ways to organize comparison and contrast in writing: in chunks and in sequence. In **chunking**, each object of the comparison is presented separately; in sequencing, the items are compared point by point. For example, a chunked comparison of two motorcycles would first detail all pertinent features of the Pirsig Z-1700 XL and then consider all features of the Kawazuki 1750XL, whereas a

sequenced comparison would analyze the Pirsig and the Kawazuki feature by feature. In a chunked comparison, the discussion is organized around each separate item being compared. In a sequenced comparison, it is organized around characteristics of the items being compared.

In the following example of chunked comparison, Jane Tompkins contrasts popular nineteenth-century "sentimental" novels with the "Western" novels that provided a reaction against them:

> The female, domestic, "sentimental" religion of the best-selling women writers—Harriet Beecher Stowe, Susan Warner, Maria Cummins, and dozens of others—whose novels spoke to the deepest beliefs and highest ideals of middle-class America, is the real antagonist of the Western.
>
> You can see this simply by comparing the main features of the Western with the sentimental novel. In these books . . . a woman is always the main character, usually a young orphan girl, with several other main characters being women too. Most of the action takes place in private spaces, at home, indoors, in kitchens, parlors, and upstairs chambers. And most of it concerns the interior struggles of the heroine to live up to an ideal of Christian virtue—usually involving uncomplaining submission to difficult and painful circumstances, learning to quell rebellious instincts, and dedicating her life to the service of God through serving others. In these struggles, women give one another a great deal of emotional and material support, and they have close relationships verging on what today we would identify as homosocial and homoerotic. There's a great deal of Bible reading, praying, hymn singing, and drinking of tea. Emotions other than anger are expressed very freely and openly. Often there are long, drawn-out death scenes in which a saintly woman dies a natural death at home. . . .
>
> The elements of the typical Western plot arrange themselves in stark opposition to this pattern, not just vaguely and generally but point for point. First of all, in Westerns (which are generally written by men), the main character is always a full-grown adult male, and almost all of the other characters are men. The action takes place either outdoors—on the prairie, on the main street—or in public places—the saloon, the sheriff's office, the barber shop, the livery stable. The action concerns physical struggles between the hero and a rival or rivals, and culminates in a fight to the death with guns. In the course of these struggles the hero frequently forms a bond with another man—sometimes his rival, more often a comrade—a bond that is more important than any relation he has with a woman and is frequently tinged with homoeroticism. There is very little free expression of the emotions. The hero is a man of few words who expresses himself through physical action—usually fighting. And when death occurs it is never at home in bed but always sudden death, usually murder.
>
> –JANE TOMPKINS, *West of Everything: The Inner Life of Westerns*

The two items being compared—sentimental novels and Westerns—are discussed separately, first one and then the other. Tompkins signals the shift from the first discussion to the contrasting one by a transitional sentence that begins a new paragraph. Each point of contrast is presented in the same order.

Schematically, a chunked comparison looks simple enough. As the preceding example shows, it is easy to block off such a discussion in a text and then provide a clean transition between the various parts. And yet it can in fact be more complicated for a writer to plan than a sequenced comparison. Sequenced comparison may be closer to the way people perceive and think about similarities or differences in things. For example, you may have realized all at once that two navy blazers are different, but you would identify the specific differences—buttons, tailoring, fabric—one at a time. A sequenced comparison would point to the differences in just this way, one at a time, whereas a chunked comparison would present all the features of one blazer and then do the same for the second. A writer using the chunked strategy, then, must organize all the points of comparison before starting to write and then be sure that the points of comparison are presented in the same order in the discussion of each item being compared. With sequencing, however, the writer can take up each point of comparison as it comes to mind.

Exercise 18.1

Identify the specific items contrasted in the example comparing sentimental novels and Westerns. Number in sequence each contrast, and underline both parts of the contrast. To get started, in the paragraph about sentimental novels, underline "a woman is always the main character, usually a young orphan girl," and number it "1" in the margin. In the paragraph about Westerns, underline "the main character is always a full-grown adult male," and number this "1" also to complete your identification of both parts of the comparison. Then look for contrast 2 and underline and number the contrasted items, and so on.

Look over your work and consider the pattern of these contrasts. Were they easy to identify? If so, what made them easy to identify? Was any contrast left incomplete? In general, how successful and informative do you find this set of contrasts?

In the next example, from a natural history of the earth, David Attenborough uses sequencing to contrast bird wings and airplane wings:

> Bird wings have a much more complex job to do than the wings of an aeroplane, for in addition to supporting the bird they must act as its engine, rowing it through the air. Even so the wing outline of a bird conforms to the same aerodynamic principles as those eventually discovered by man when designing his aeroplanes, and if you know how different kinds of aircraft perform, you can predict the flight capabilities of similarly shaped birds.
>
> Short stubby wings enable a tanager and other forest-living birds to swerve and dodge at speed through the undergrowth just as they helped the fighter planes of the Second World War to make tight turns and aerobatic manoeuvres in a dog-fight. More modern fighters achieve greater speeds by sweeping back their wings while in flight, just as peregrines do when they go into a 130 kph dive, stooping to a kill. Championship gliders have long thin wings so that, having gained height in a thermal up-current, they can soar gently down for hours and an albatross, the largest of flying birds, with a similar wing shape and a span of 3 metres, can patrol the ocean for hours in the same way without a single wing beat. Vultures and hawks circle at very slow speeds supported by a thermal and they have the broad rectangular wings that very slow flying aircraft have. Man has not been able to adapt wings to provide hovering flight. He has only achieved that with the whirling horizontal blades of a

helicopter or the downward-pointing engines of a vertical landing jet. Hummingbirds have paralleled even this. They tilt their bodies so that they are almost upright and then beat their wings as fast as 80 times a second producing a similar down-draught of air. So the hummingbird can hover and even fly backwards.

–DAVID ATTENBOROUGH, *Life on Earth*

In this example, note the limited, focused basis for the comparison: the shape of wings. Attenborough specifies this basis in the second sentence of the passage (underlined). Though birds and planes both fly, they have almost nothing else in common. They are so obviously different that it would even seem silly to compare them in writing. But Attenborough finds a valid—and fascinating—basis for comparison and develops it in a way that both informs and entertains his readers. A successful comparison always has these qualities: a valid basis for comparison, a limited focus, and information that will catch a reader's attention.

Exercise 18.2

Identify the specific items compared in the preceding selection comparing bird wings and aircraft wings. Underline both items, and number the pair in the margin. To get started, underline *tanager* and *fighter planes* in the first sentence of the second paragraph. In the margin, number this pair "1." Then identify pair 2 and so on.

Consider the pattern and ordering of the comparisons you have identified. Were the pairs of items easy to identify? If so, what made them easy to identify? Some comparisons begin by naming a bird, some by identifying a category of aircraft. Did this lack of predictability present problems for you? Do you see any possible justification for the writer's having given up the predictability of always beginning each comparison with either a bird or an aircraft? In general, how successful and informative did you find this comparison of birds' wings and aircrafts' wings?

Exercise 18.3

Write a page or so comparing or contrasting any one of the following subjects. Be careful to limit the basis for your comparison, and underline the sentence that states that basis. Use chunking or sequencing to organize the comparison.

Two ways of achieving the same goal (for example, travel by bus or subway or using flattery or persuasion to get what you want)

A good and bad job interview

Your relationship with two friends or relatives

Two or more forms of music, dance, film, or computer software

Two religions or congregations

Two methods of doing some task at home or on the job

Exercise 18.4

Read closely the specified comparisons in the following essays from Part One. How is each comparison organized? (It may or may not be neatly chunked or sequenced.)

Why do you think the writer organizes the comparison in that way? What is the role of the comparison in the whole essay? How effective is it?

"Love: The Right Chemistry," paragraph 14 (Chapter 5)

"Indirect Aggression," paragraphs 1–2 (Chapter 5)

"Dead-End Jobs: A Way Out," paragraphs 9–10 (Chapter 7)

ANALOGY

An **analogy** is a special form of comparison in which one part of the comparison is used simply to explain the other. See how John McPhee uses two different analogies—the twelve-month calendar and the distance along two widespread arms—to explain the duration of geologic time.

> In like manner, geologists will sometimes use the calendar year as a unit to represent the time scale, and in such terms the Precambrian runs from New Year's Day until well after Halloween. Dinosaurs appear in the middle of December and are gone the day after Christmas. The last ice sheet melts on December 31st at one minute before midnight, and the Roman Empire lasts five seconds. With your arms spread wide . . . to represent all time on earth, look at one hand with its line of life. The Cambrian begins in the wrist, and the Permian Extinction is at the outer end of the palm. All of the Cenozoic is in a fingerprint, and in a single stroke with a medium-grained nail file you could eradicate human history. Geologists live with the geologic scale. Individually, they may or may not be alarmed by the rate of exploitation of the things they discover, but, like the environmentalists, they use these repetitive analogies to place the human record in perspective—to see the Age of Reflection, the last few thousand years, as a small bright sparkle at the end of time.
>
> –John McPhee, *Basin and Range*

Analogies are not limited to abstract, scientific concepts. Writers often use analogies to make nontechnical descriptions and explanations more vivid or to make an imaginative point of comparison that serves a larger argument. For example, the following excerpt from Chapter 6 is from an essay arguing that a significant problem facing the United States today is the plight of the working poor, those members of society who work for low wages and without benefits. In it, the writer suggests, by analogy, that they are among society's "major philanthropists."

> But now that government has largely withdrawn its "handouts" [to the welfare poor], now that the overwhelming majority of the poor are out there toiling in Wal-Mart or Wendy's—well, what are we to think of them? Disapproval and condescension no longer apply, so what outlook makes sense?
>
> Guilt, you may be thinking warily. Isn't that what we're supposed to feel? But guilt doesn't go anywhere near far enough; the appropriate emotion is shame—shame at our own dependency, in this case, on the underpaid labor of others. When someone works for less pay than she can live on—when, for example, she goes hungry so that you can eat more cheaply and conveniently—then she has made a great sacrifice for you, she has made you a gift of some part of her abilities, her health, and

her life. The "working poor," as they are approvingly termed, are in fact the major philanthropists of our society. They neglect their own children so that the children of others will be cared for; they live in substandard housing so that other homes will be shiny and perfect; they endure privation so that inflation will be low and stock prices high. To be a member of the working poor is to be an anonymous donor, a nameless benefactor, to everyone else. As Gail, one of my restaurant coworkers put it, "you give and you give."

—BARBARA EHRENREICH, *Nickel and Dimed*

For Ehrenreich's complete essay, see Chapter 6.

Analogies are tricky. They can be useful, but analogies rarely are consistently accurate at all major points of comparison. For example, in the preceding analogy, the working poor can be seen as philanthropists in the sense that they have "made a great sacrifice" but not in the sense that they are selflessly sharing their wealth. Analogies can powerfully bring home a point, but skilled writers exercise caution with them.

Nevertheless, you will run across analogies regularly; indeed, it would be hard to find a book without at least one. For abstract information and in certain writing situations, analogy is often the writing strategy of choice.

Exercise 18.5

Write a one-paragraph analogy that explains a principle or process to a reader who is unfamiliar with it. Choose a principle or process that you know well. You might select a basic principle from the natural or social sciences, like morphogenesis, Federalism, or ethnocentrism; or you could consider a bodily movement, like running; a physiological process, like digestion; or a process from your job, like assembling a product. Look for something very familiar to compare it with that will help the reader understand the principle or process without a technical explanation.

19

Arguing

Arguing involves reasoning as well as making assertions. When you write an essay in which you assert a point of view, you are obliged to come up with reasons for your point of view and to find ways to support your reasons. In addition to arguing for your point of view, you must think carefully about what your readers know and believe to argue against—to **counterargue**—opposing points of view. If you ignore what your readers may be thinking, you will be unlikely to convince them to take your argument seriously.

This chapter presents the basic strategies for making assertions and reasoning about a writing situation. We focus on asserting a thesis, backing it up with reasons and support, and anticipating readers' questions and objections (counterarguing).

ASSERTING A THESIS

Central to any argument is the **thesis**—the point of view the writer wants readers to consider. The thesis statement may appear at the beginning of the essay or at the end, but wherever it is placed, its job is simple: to announce as clearly and straightforwardly as possible the main point the writer is trying to make in the essay.

There are five different kinds of argumentative essays in Part One of this book. Each of these essays requires a special kind of assertion and reasoning. Here we first define each type of assertion and suggest a question it is designed to answer. Then we illustrate each assertion and question with a thesis from a reading in Chapters 6–10:

Chapters 6–10 contain essays that argue for each of these kinds of assertions, along with guidelines for constructing an argument to support such an assertion.

- *Assertion of opinion:* What is your position on a controversial issue? (Chapter 6, "Arguing a Position")

  When overzealous parents and coaches impose adult standards on children's sports, the result can be activities that are neither satisfying nor beneficial to children.

  –JESSICA STATSKY, "Children Need to Play, Not Compete"

- *Assertion of policy:* What is your understanding of a problem, and what do you think should be done to solve it? (Chapter 7, "Proposing a Solution")

  Although this last-minute anxiety about midterm and final exams is only too familiar to most college students, many professors may not realize how such

> major, infrequent, high-stakes exams work against the best interests of students both psychologically and intellectually. . . . If professors gave additional brief exams at frequent intervals, students would be spurred to study more regularly, learn more, worry less, and perform better.
>
> –PATRICK O'MALLEY, "More Testing, More Learning"

- ***Assertion of evaluation:*** What is your judgment of a subject? (Chapter 8, "Justifying an Evaluation")

> Morrowind is a flawed jewel, but flawed only because its scope is so grand. Beautiful graphics, compelling stories, a huge map to explore, engaging quests, and a simple interface all add up to a premier game.
>
> –JONAH JACKSON, "The Elder Scrolls III: Morrowind"

- ***Assertion of cause:*** What do you think made a subject the way it is? (Chapter 9, "Speculating about Causes")

> The mythic horror movie, like the sick joke, has a dirty job to do. It deliberately appeals to all that is worst in us. It is morbidity unchained, our most base instincts let free, our nastiest fantasies realized . . . and it all happens, fittingly enough, in the dark.
>
> –STEPHEN KING, "Why We Crave Horror Movies"

- ***Assertion of interpretation:*** What does a story mean, or what is significant about it? (Chapter 10, "Interpreting Stories")

> "Araby" tells the story of an adolescent boy's initiation into adulthood. . . . From the beginning, the boy deludes himself about his relationship with Mangan's sister. At Araby, he realizes the parallel between his own self-delusion and the hypocrisy and vanity of the adult world.
>
> –DAVID RATINOV, "From Innocence to Insight: 'Araby' as an Initiation Story"

As these different thesis statements indicate, the kind of thesis you assert depends on the occasion for which you are writing and the question you are trying to answer for your readers. Whatever the writing situation, to be effective, every thesis must satisfy the same three standards: It must be *arguable, clear,* and *appropriately qualified.*

Arguable Assertions

Reasoned argument seems called for when informed people disagree over an issue or remain divided over how best to solve a problem, as is so often the case in social and political life. Hence the thesis statements in reasoned arguments make **arguable assertions**—possibilities or probabilities, not certainties. Argument becomes useful in situations in which there are uncertainties, situations in which established knowledge and facts cannot provide the answers.

Therefore, a statement of fact could not be an arguable thesis statement because facts are easy to verify—whether by checking an authoritative reference book, asking an authority, or observing the fact with your own eyes. For example, these statements assert facts:

Jem has a Ph.D. in history.

I am less than five feet tall.

Eucalyptus trees were originally imported into California from Australia.

Each of these assertions can be easily verified. To find out Jem's academic degree, you can ask him, among other things. To determine a person's height, you can use a tape measure. To discover where California got its eucalyptus trees, you can refer to a source in the library. There is no point in arguing over such statements (though you might question the authority of a particular source or the accuracy of someone's measurement). If a writer asserts something as fact and attempts to support the assertion with authorities or statistics, the essay is considered not an argument but a report of information.

Like facts, expressions of personal feelings are not arguable assertions. Whereas facts are unarguable because they can be definitively proved true or false, feelings are unarguable because they are purely subjective. Personal feelings can be explained, but it would be unreasonable to attempt to convince others to change their views or take action solely on the basis of your personal feelings.

You can declare, for example, that you love Ben & Jerry's Chunky Monkey ice cream or that you detest eight o'clock classes, but you cannot offer an argument to support such assertions. All you can do is explain why you feel as you do. Even though many people agree with you about eight o'clock classes, it would be pointless to try to convince others to share your feelings. If, however, you were to restate the assertion as "Eight o'clock classes are counterproductive," you could then construct an argument that does not depend solely on your subjective feelings, memories, or preferences. Your argument could be based on reasons and support that apply to others as well as to yourself. For example, you might argue that students' ability to learn is at an especially low ebb immediately after breakfast and provide scientific support, in addition, perhaps, to personal experience and interviews with your friends.

Clear and Precise Wording

The way a thesis is worded is as important as its arguability. The wording of a thesis, especially its key terms, must be clear and precise.

Consider the following assertion: "Democracy is a way of life." The meaning of this claim is uncertain, partly because the word *democracy* is abstract and partly because the phrase *way of life* is inexact. Abstract ideas like democracy, freedom, and patriotism are by their very nature hard to grasp, and they become even less clear with overuse. Too often, such words take on connotations that may obscure the meaning you want to emphasize. *Way of life* is fuzzy: What does it mean? Moreover, can a form of government be a way of life? It depends on what is meant by *way of life*. Does it refer to daily life, to a general philosophy or attitude toward life, or to something else?

Thus a thesis is vague if its meaning is unclear; it is ambiguous if it has more than one possible meaning. For example, the statement "My English instructor is mad" can be understood in two ways: The teacher is either angry or insane. Obviously, these are two very different assertions. You would not want readers to think you mean one when you actually mean the other.

Whenever you write argument, you should pay special attention to the way you phrase your thesis and take care to avoid vague and ambiguous language.

Appropriate Qualification

In addition to being arguable and clear, an argument thesis must make **appropriate qualifications** that suit your writing situation. If you are confident that your case is so strong that readers will accept your argument without question, state your thesis emphatically and unconditionally. If, however, you expect readers to challenge your assumptions or conclusions, you must qualify your statement. Qualifying a thesis makes it more likely that readers will take it seriously. Expressions like *probably, very likely, apparently,* and *it seems* all serve to qualify a thesis.

Exercise 19.1

Write an assertion of opinion that states your position on one of the following controversial issues:

Should English be the official language of the United States and the only language used in local, state, and federal government agencies in oral and written communications?

Should teenagers be required to get their parents' permission to obtain birth control information and contraceptives?

Should high schools or colleges require students to perform community service as a condition for graduation?

Should girls and boys be treated differently by their families or schools?

Should businesses remain loyal to their communities, or should they move wherever labor costs, taxes, or other conditions are more favorable?

These issues are complicated and have been debated for a long time. Constructing a persuasive argument would obviously require careful deliberation and research. For this exercise, however, all you need to do is construct a thesis on the issue you have chosen, a thesis that is arguable, clear, and appropriately qualified.

Exercise 19.2

Find the thesis in one of the argument essays in Chapters 6–10. Then decide whether the thesis meets the three requirements: that it be arguable, clear, and appropriately qualified.

Exercise 19.3

If you have written or are currently working on one of the argument assignments in Chapters 6–10, consider whether your essay thesis meets the three requirements: that it be arguable, clear, and appropriately qualified. If you believe it does not meet the requirements, revise it appropriately.

GIVING REASONS AND SUPPORT

Whether you are arguing a position, proposing a solution, justifying an evaluation, speculating about causes, or interpreting a story, you need to give **reasons and support** for your thesis.

Reasons can be thought of as the main points arguing for a thesis. Often they answer the question "Why do you think so?" For example, if you assert among friends that you value a certain movie highly, one of your friends might ask, "Why do you like it so much?" And you might answer, "*Because* it has challenging ideas, unusual camera work, and memorable acting." Similarly, you might oppose restrictions on students' use of offensive language at your college *because* they would make students reluctant to enter into frank debates on important issues, offensive speech is hard to define, and restrictions violate the free-speech clause of the First Amendment. These *because* phrases are your reasons. You may have one or many reasons, depending on your subject and your writing situation.

For your argument to succeed with your readers, you must not only give reasons but also provide support. The main kinds of support writers use are examples, statistics, authorities, anecdotes, and textual evidence. Following is a discussion and illustration of each kind, along with standards for judging the reliability of that particular type of support.

Examples

Examples may be used as support in all types of arguments. They are an effective way to demonstrate that your reasons should be taken seriously. For examples to be believable and convincing, they must be representative (typical of all the relevant examples you might have chosen), consistent with the experience of your readers (familiar and not extreme), and adequate in number (numerous enough to be convincing and yet selective and not likely to overwhelm readers).

The following illustration comes from a book on illiteracy in America by Jonathan Kozol, a prominent educator and writer. In these paragraphs, Kozol presents several examples to support a part of his argument that the human costs of illiteracy are high.

> Illiterates cannot read the menu in a restaurant.
>
> They cannot read the cost of items on the menu in the *window* of the restaurant before they enter.

> Illiterates cannot read the letters that their children bring home from their teachers. They cannot study school department circulars that tell them of the courses that their children must be taking if they hope to pass the SAT exams. They cannot help with homework. They cannot write a letter to the teacher. They are afraid to visit in the classroom. They do not want to humiliate their child or themselves.
>
> Illiterates cannot read instructions on a bottle of prescription medicine. They cannot find out when a medicine is past the year of safe consumption; nor can they read of allergenic risks, warnings to diabetics, or the potential sedative effect of certain kinds of nonprescription pills. They cannot observe preventive health care admonitions. They cannot read about "the seven warnings signs of cancer" or the indications of blood-sugar fluctuations or the risks of eating certain foods that aggravate the likelihood of cardiac arrest.
>
> –JONATHAN KOZOL, *Illiterate America*

These examples probably seem to most readers to be representative of all the examples Kozol collected in his many interviews with people who could neither read nor write. Though all of his readers are literate and have never experienced the frustrations of adult illiterates, Kozol assumes they can recognize that the experiences are a familiar part of illiterates' lives. Most readers will believe the experiences to be neither atypical nor extreme.

Exercise 19.4

Identify the examples in paragraphs 9 and 11 in Jessica Statsky's essay "Children Need to Play, Not Compete" in Chapter 6 and paragraphs 16–18 in Amitai Etzioni's essay "Working at McDonald's" in Chapter 8. If you have not read the essays, pause to skim them so that you can evaluate these examples within the context of the entire essay. How well do the examples individually and as a set meet the standards of representativeness, consistency with experience of readers, and adequacy in number? You will not have all the information you need to evaluate the examples—you rarely do unless you are an expert on the subject—but make a judgment based on the information available to you in the headnotes and the essays.

Statistics

In many kinds of arguments about economic, educational, or social issues, **statistics** may be essential. When you use statistics in your own arguments, you will want to ensure that they are up to date (they should be current, the best presently available facts on the subject), relevant (they should be appropriate for your argument), and accurate (they should not distort or misrepresent the subject). In addition, take care to select statistics from reliable sources and to use statistics from the sources in which they originally appeared if at all possible. For example, you would want to get medical statistics from a reputable and authoritative professional periodical like the *New England Journal of Medicine* rather than from a supermarket tabloid or an unaffiliated Web site. If you are uncertain about the most authoritative sources, ask a reference librarian or a professor who knows about your topic.

The following selection comes from an argument speculating about the decline of civic life in the United States. Civic life includes all of the clubs, organizations, and activities people choose to participate in. The author, a Harvard University professor, believes that since the early 1960s, Americans have participated less and less in civic life because they have been spending more and more time watching television. In these paragraphs, he uses statistics to support this possible causal relationship.

> The culprit is television.
>
> First, the timing fits. The long civic generation was the last cohort of Americans to grow up without television, for television flashed into American society like lightning in the 1950s. In 1950 barely 10 percent of American homes had television sets, but by 1959, 90 percent did, probably the fastest diffusion of a major technological innovation ever recorded. The reverberations from this lightning bolt continued for decades, as viewing hours grew by 17–20 percent during the 1960s and by an additional 7–8 percent during the 1970s. In the early years, TV watching was concentrated among the less educated sectors of the population, but during the 1970s the viewing time of the more educated sectors of the population began to converge upward. Television viewing increases with age, particularly upon retirement, but each generation since the introduction of television has begun its life cycle at a higher starting point. By 1995 viewing per TV household was more than 50 percent higher than it had been in the 1950s.
>
> Most studies estimate that the average American now watches roughly four hours per day (excluding periods in which television is merely playing in the background). Even a more conservative estimate of three hours means that television absorbs 40 percent of the average American's free time, an increase of about one-third since 1965. Moreover, multiple sets have proliferated: By the late 1980s three-quarters of all U.S. homes had more than one set, and these numbers too are rising steadily, allowing ever more private viewing. . . . This massive change in the way Americans spend their days and nights occurred precisely during the years of generational civic disengagement.
>
> –ROBERT D. PUTNAM, "The Strange Disappearance of Civic America"

These statistics come primarily from the U.S. Bureau of the Census, a nationwide count of the number of Americans and a survey, in part, of their buying habits, levels of education, and leisure activities. The Census reports are widely considered to be accurate and trustworthy. They qualify as original sources of statistics.

Exercise 19.5

In Chapter 6, identify the statistics in paragraphs 7 and 8 of Barbara Ehrenreich's essay and paragraphs 5 and 6 of Jessica Statsky's. Underline the statistics you find. If you have not read the essays, pause to skim them so that you can evaluate each writer's use of statistics within the context of the whole essay. How well do the statistics meet the standard of up-to-dateness, relevance, accuracy, and reliance on the original source? (If you find that you do not have all the information you need, base your judgments on whatever information is available to you.) Does the writer indicate where the statistics come from? What do the statistics contribute to the argument?

Chapter 21 provides help finding statistical data in the library.

Authorities

To support an argument, writers often cite experts on the subject who agree with their point of view. Quoting, paraphrasing, or even just referring to a respected **authority** can add to a writer's credibility. Authorities must be selected as carefully as facts and statistics. One qualification for authorities to support arguments is suggested by the way we refer to them: They must be authoritative—that is, trustworthy and reputable. They must also be specially qualified to contribute to the subject you are writing about. For example, a well-known expert on the American presidency might be a poor choice to support an argument on whether adolescents who commit serious crimes should be tried in the courts as adults. Finally, qualified authorities must have training at respected institutions or have unique real-world experiences, and they must have a record of research and publications recognized by other authorities.

The following example comes from a *New York Times* article about some parents' and experts' heightened concern over boys' behavior. The author believes that the concern is exaggerated and potentially dangerous to boys, and she wants to understand why it is increasing. In the full argument, she is particularly concerned about the number of boys who are being given Ritalin, a popular drug for treating attention-deficit hyperactivity disorder.

> Today, the world is no longer safe for boys. A boy being a shade too boyish risks finding himself under the scrutiny of parents, teachers, guidance counselors, child therapists—all of them on watch for the early glimmerings of a medical syndrome, a bona fide behavioral disorder. Does the boy disregard authority, make snide comments in class, push other kids around and play hooky? Maybe he has a conduct disorder. Is he fidgety, impulsive, disruptive, easily bored? Perhaps he is suffering from attention-deficit hyperactivity disorder, or ADHD, the disease of the hour and the most frequently diagnosed behavioral disorder of childhood. Does he prefer computer games and goofing off to homework? He might have dyslexia or another learning disorder.
>
> "There is now an attempt to pathologize what was once considered the normal range of behavior of boys," said Melvin Konner of the departments of anthropology and psychiatry at Emory University in Atlanta. "Today, Tom Sawyer and Huckleberry Finn surely would have been diagnosed with both conduct disorder and ADHD." And both, perhaps, would have been put on Ritalin, the drug of choice for treating attention-deficit disorder.
>
> —NATALIE ANGIER, "Intolerance of Boyish Behavior"

Notice the way the writer establishes the professional qualifications of the authority she quotes. She places him at a major research university (Emory University) and indicates by his department affiliations (anthropology and psychiatry) that he has special training to comment on how a culture treats its young men. Readers can infer from these two facts that he has almost certainly earned a doctorate in anthropology or psychiatry and that he has probably published research studies. This carefully selected quotation supports the writer's argument that there is a problem and that readers should care about it.

In this example, the writer relies on *informal* citation within her essay to introduce the authority she quotes. In newspapers, magazines, and some books, writers rely on informal citation, mentioning the title or author in the essay itself. In other books and in research reports, writers rely on a *formal* style of citation that allows them to refer briefly in an essay to a detailed list of works cited appearing at the end of the essay. This list provides the author, title, date, and publisher of every source of information referred to in the essay. To evaluate the qualifications of an authority in an argument relying on a list of works cited, you may have to rely solely on the information provided in the list.

For examples of two formal citation styles often used in college essays, see Chapter 22.

Exercise 19.6

Analyze how authorities are used in paragraphs 4 and 5 of Patrick O'Malley's essay "More Testing, More Learning" in Chapter 7 and in paragraphs 9–11 of William S. Pollack's essay "Why Boys Become Depressed" in Chapter 9. Begin by underlining the authorities' contributions to these paragraphs, whether through quotation, summary, or paraphrase. On the basis of the evidence you have available, decide to what extent each source is authoritative on the subject: qualified to contribute to the subject, trained appropriately, and recognized widely. How does the writer establish each authority's credentials? Then decide what each authority contributes to the argument as a whole. (If you have not read the essays, take time to read or skim them.)

Anecdotes

Anecdotes are brief stories about events or experiences, recounted in an engaging way. If they are relevant to the argument, well told, and true to life, they can provide convincing support. To be relevant, an anecdote must strike readers as more than an entertaining diversion; it must seem to make an irreplaceable contribution to an argument. If it is well told, the narrative or story is easy to follow, and the people and scenes are described memorably, even vividly. There are many concrete details that help readers imagine what happened. A true-to-life anecdote is one that seems to represent a possible life experience of a real person. It has to be believable, even if the experience is foreign to readers' experiences.

See Chapter 14, Narrating, and Chapter 2, Remembering Events, for more information about narrating anecdotes.

The following anecdote appeared in an argument taking a position on a familiar issue: gun ownership and control. The writer, an essayist, poet, and environmental writer who is also a rancher in South Dakota, always carries a pistol and believes that other people may have an urgent personal need to carry one and should have the right to do so. To support her argument, she tells several anecdotes, including this one:

> I was driving the half-mile to the highway mailbox one day when I saw a vehicle parked about midway down the road. Several men were standing in the ditch, relieving themselves. I have no objection to emergency urination, but I noticed they'd dumped several dozen beer cans in the road. Besides being ugly, cans can slash a cow's feet or stomach.
>
> The men noticed me before they finished and made quite a performance out of zipping their trousers while walking toward me. All four of them gathered around my small foreign car, and one of them demanded what the hell I wanted.

"This is private land. I'd appreciate it if you'd pick up the beer cans."

"What beer cans?" said the belligerent one, putting both hands on the car door and leaning in my window. His face was inches from mine, and the beer fumes were strong. The others laughed. One tried the passenger door, locked; another put his foot on the hood and rocked the car. They circled, lightly thumping the roof, discussing my good fortune in meeting them and the benefits they were likely to bestow upon me. I felt very small and very trapped and they knew it.

"The ones you just threw out," I said politely.

"I don't see no beer cans. Why don't you get out here and show them to me, honey?" said the belligerent one, reaching for the handle inside my door.

"Right over there," I said, still being polite, "—there, and over there." I pointed with the pistol, which I'd slipped under my thigh. Within one minute the cans and the men were back in the car and headed down the road.

I believe this incident illustrates several important principles. The men were trespassing and knew it; their judgment may have been impaired by alcohol. Their response to the polite request of a woman alone was to use their size, numbers, and sex to inspire fear. The pistol was a response in the same language. Politeness didn't work; I couldn't match them in size or number. Out of the car, I'd have been more vulnerable. The pistol just changed the balance of power.

–LINDA M. HASSELSTROM, "Why One Peaceful Woman Carries a Pistol"

Most readers would readily agree that this anecdote is well told. It has many concrete, memorable details. As in any good story, something happens: There is action, suspense, climax, resolution. There is even dialogue. It is about a believable, possible experience. Most important, as support for an argument, it is relevant to the writer's point, as she makes clear in the final paragraph.

Exercise 19.7

Analyze the way an anecdote is used in paragraph 2 of Natalie Angier's essay "Indirect Aggression" in Chapter 5. Consider whether the story is well told and true to life. Decide whether it seems to be relevant to the whole argument. Does the writer make the relevance clear? Do you find the anecdote convincing?

Textual Evidence

When you argue claims of value (Chapter 8) and interpretation (Chapter 10), **textual evidence** will be very important. In your other college courses, if you are asked to evaluate a controversial book, you must quote, paraphrase, or summarize passages so that readers can understand why you think the author's argument is or is not credible. If you are interpreting a novel for one of your classes, you must include numerous excerpts to show just how you arrived at your conclusion. In both situations, you are integrating bits of the text you are evaluating or interpreting into your own text and building your argument on these bits.

For these bits of textual evidence to be considered effective support for an argument of evaluation or interpretation, they must be carefully selected to be relevant to the argument's thesis and reasons. You must help readers see the connection between each piece of evidence and the reason it supports. Textual evidence must also be highly selective—that is, chosen from among all the available evidence to provide the support needed without overwhelming the reader with too much evidence or weakening the argument with marginally relevant evidence. Textual evidence usually has more impact if it is balanced between quotation and paraphrase from the text. For these selective, balanced choices of evidence to be comprehensible and convincing to readers, the evidence must be smoothly integrated into the sentences of the argument. Finally, the relevance of textual evidence is rarely obvious: The writer must ordinarily explain the link between the evidence and the writer's intended point.

The following example comes from a student essay in Chapter 10 in which the writer argues that the main character (referred to as "the boy") in the short story "Araby" by James Joyce is so self-absorbed that he learns nothing about himself or other people. These paragraphs offer the reasons that the writer believes readers should take her argument seriously. She attempts to support her reasons with textual evidence from the story.

You can read "Araby" in Chapter 10, pp. 526–30.

> The story opens and closes with images of blindness. The street is "blind" with an "uninhabited house . . . at the blind end." As he spies on Mangan's sister, from his own house, the boy intentionally limits what he is able to see by lowering the "blind" until it is only an inch from the window sash. At the bazaar in the closing scene, the "light was out," and the upper part of the hall was "completely dark." The boy is left "gazing up into the darkness," seeing nothing but an inner torment that burns his eyes.
>
> This pattern of imagery includes images of reading, and reading stands for the boy's inability to understand what is before his eyes. When he tries to read at night, for example, the girl's "image [comes] between [him] and the page," in effect blinding him. In fact, he seems blind to everything except this "image" of the "brown-clad figure cast by [his] imagination." The girl's "brown-clad figure" is also associated with the houses on "blind" North Richmond Street, with their "brown imperturbable faces." The houses stare back at the boy, unaffected by his presence and gaze.
>
> –SALLY CRANE, "Gazing into the Darkness"

Notice first how the writer quotes selected words and phrases about blindness to support her reasoning that the boy learns nothing because he is blinded. There are twelve quotations in these two paragraphs, all of them relevant and perhaps not so many as to overwhelm the reader. The writer relies not only on quotes but also on paraphrases of information in the story. The second and third sentences in paragraph 1 are largely paraphrases. The quotations in particular are integrated smoothly into the sentences so that readers' momentum is not blocked. Most important, the writer does not assume that the evidence speaks for itself; she comments and interprets throughout. For example, in the first paragraph, all the sentences except the fourth one offer some comment or explanation.

For more information on paraphrasing, see pp. 595–96 in Chapter 12.

Exercise 19.8

Analyze the use of evidence in paragraphs 2 and 3 of David Ratinov's essay "From Innocence to Insight: 'Araby' as an Initiation Story" in Chapter 10. If you have not read this essay, pause to skim or read it so that you can evaluate the effectiveness of the evidence in these paragraphs in the context of Ratinov's full argument. The quotes are easy to identify. The paraphrases you could identify with confidence only by reading the story, but you can probably identify some of them without doing so. Then try to identify the phrases or sentences that comment on or explain the evidence. Finally, consider whether Ratinov's evidence in these two paragraphs seems relevant to his thesis and reasons, appropriately selective, well balanced between quotes and paraphrases, integrated smoothly into the sentences he creates, and explained helpfully.

COUNTERARGUING

Asserting a thesis and backing it with reasons and support are essential to a successful argument. Thoughtful writers go further, however, by **counterarguing**—anticipating and responding to their readers' objections, challenges, and questions. To anticipate readers' concerns, try to imagine other people's points of view, what they might know about the subject, and how they might feel about it. Try also to imagine how readers would respond to your argument as it unfolds step by step. What will they be thinking and feeling? What objections would they raise? What questions would they ask?

To counterargue, writers rely on three basic strategies: acknowledging, accommodating or conceding, and refuting. Writers show they are aware of readers' objections and questions (acknowledge), modify their position to accept readers' concerns they think are legitimate (accommodate), or explicitly show why readers' objections are invalid or why their concerns are irrelevant (refute). Writers may use one or more of these three strategies in the same essay. According to research by rhetoricians and communications specialists, readers find arguments more convincing when writers have anticipated their concerns in these ways. Acknowledging readers' concerns and either accommodating or refuting them wins readers' respect, attention, and sometimes even agreement.

Acknowledging Readers' Concerns

When you **acknowledge** readers' questions or objections, you show that you are aware of their point of view and you take it seriously even if you do not agree with it. In the following example, Peter Marin directly acknowledges his readers' possible concerns. These are the opening paragraphs in an article arguing that some of America's homeless have chosen that way of life. Marin knows that readers may immediately doubt this surprising assertion. It seems inconceivable that people would choose to sleep on sidewalks and eat out of garbage cans. He acknowledges three different doubts his readers may have.

> The homeless, it seems, can be roughly divided into two groups: those who have had marginality and homelessness forced upon them and want nothing more than to escape them, and a smaller number who have at least in part chosen marginality, and now accept, or, in a few cases, embrace it.

> I understand how dangerous it can be to introduce the idea of choice into a discussion of homelessness. It can all too easily be used for all the wrong reasons by all the wrong people to justify indifference or brutality toward the homeless, or to argue that they are getting only what they deserve.
>
> And I understand, too, how complicated the notion can become: Many of the veterans on the street, or battered women, or abused and runaway children, have chosen this life only as the lesser of evils, and because, in this society, there is often no place else to go.
>
> And finally, I understand how much that happens on the street can combine to create an apparent acceptance of homelessness that is nothing more than the absolute absence of hope.
>
> Nonetheless we must learn to accept that there may indeed be people on the street who have seen so much of our world, or have seen it so clearly, that to live in it becomes impossible.
>
> –Peter Marin, "Go Ask Alice"

You might think that acknowledging readers' objections in this way—addressing readers directly, listing their possible objections, and discussing each one—would weaken an argument. It might even seem reckless to suggest objections that not all readers would think of. On the contrary, however, readers who expect writers to explore an issue thoroughly respond positively to this strategy because it makes the writer seem thoughtful and reasonable, more concerned with seeking the truth than winning an argument. By researching your subject and your readers, you will be able to use this strategy confidently in your own argumentative essays. And you will learn to look for it in arguments you read and use it to make judgments about the writer's credibility.

Exercise 19.9

Richard Estrada acknowledges readers' concerns in paragraphs 6 and 7 of his essay in Chapter 6, and Sarah West does so in paragraphs 7 and 8 of her essay in Chapter 9. How, specifically, do these authors attempt to acknowledge their readers' concerns? What do you find most and least successful in the two acknowledgments? How do the writers' acknowledgments affect your judgment of the writers' credibility?

Accommodating Readers' Concerns

To argue effectively, you must often take special care to **accommodate readers' concerns** by acknowledging their objections, questions, and alternative positions, causes, or solutions. Occasionally, however, you may have to go even further. Instead of merely acknowledging your readers' concerns, you may decide to accept some of them and incorporate them into your own argument. This strategy can be very disarming to readers. It is sometimes referred to as **concession**, for it seems to concede that opposing views have merit.

The following example comes from an essay enthusiastically endorsing email. After supporting his own reasons for this positive endorsement, the writer accommodates his readers' likely reservations by conceding that email poses certain problems.

> To be sure, egalitarianism has its limits. The ease and economy of sending email, especially to multiple recipients, makes us all vulnerable to any bore, loony, or commercial or political salesman who can get our email address. It's still a lot less intrusive than the telephone, since you can read and answer or ignore email at your own convenience. But as normal people's email starts mounting into the hundreds daily, which is bound to happen, filtering mechanisms and conventions of etiquette that are still in their primitive stage will be desperately needed.
>
> Another supposed disadvantage of email is that it discourages face-to-face communication. At Microsoft, where people routinely send email back and forth all day to the person in the next office, this is certainly true. Some people believe this tendency has more to do with the underdeveloped social skills of computer geeks than with Microsoft's role in developing the technology email relies on. I wouldn't presume to comment on that. Whether you think email replacing live conversation is a good or bad thing depends, I guess, on how much of a misanthrope you are. I like it.
>
> –MICHAEL KINSLEY, "Email Culture"

Notice that Kinsley's accommodation or concession is not grudging. He readily concedes that email brings users a lot of unwanted messages and may discourage conversation in the workplace.

Exercise 19.10

How does Patrick O'Malley attempt to accommodate readers in paragraphs 7 and 8 of his Chapter 7 essay arguing for more frequent exams? What seems successful or unsuccessful in his argument? What do his efforts at accommodation contribute to the essay?

Refuting Readers' Objections

Your readers' possible objections and views cannot always be accommodated. Sometimes they must be refuted. When you **refute readers' objections**, you assert that they are wrong and argue against them. Refutation does not have to be delivered arrogantly or dismissively, however. Writers can refute their readers' objections in a spirit of shared inquiry in solving problems, establishing probable causes, deciding the value of something, or understanding different points of view in a controversy. Differences are inevitable. Reasoned argument provides a peaceful and constructive way for informed, well-intentioned people who disagree strongly to air their differences.

In the following example, a social sciences professor refutes one argument for giving college students the opportunity to purchase lecture notes prepared by someone else. First, he concedes the possibility of accepting another viewpoint ("Now, it may well be argued . . . "), and then he suggests that he even agrees with this view in part ("The amphitheater lecture is indeed . . . scarcely to be idealized"). Ultimately, though, he refutes this objection ("Still . . . ").

> Now, it may well be argued that universities are already shortchanging their students by stuffing them into huge lecture halls where, unlike at rock concerts or basketball games, the lecturer can't even be seen on a giant screen in real time. If they're already

shortchanged with impersonal instruction, what's the harm in offering canned lecture notes?

The amphitheater lecture is indeed, for all but the most engaging professors, a lesser form of instruction, and scarcely to be idealized. Still, Education by Download misses one of the keys to learning. Education is a meeting of minds, a process through which the student educes, draws from within, a response to what the teacher teaches.

The very act of taking notes—not reading someone else's notes, no matter how stellar—is a way of engaging the material, wrestling with it, struggling to comprehend or take issue, but in any case entering into the work. The point is to decide, while you are listening, what matters in the presentation. And while I don't believe that most of life consists of showing up, education does begin with that—with immersing yourself in the activity at hand, listening, thinking, judging, offering active responses. A download is a poor substitute.

–TODD GITLIN, "Disappearing Ink"

As this selection illustrates, writers cannot simply dismiss readers' possible concerns with a wave of their hand. Gitlin states a potential objection fully and fairly but then goes on to refute it by claiming that students need to take their own lecture notes to engage and comprehend the material that is being presented to them.

Effective refutation requires a restrained tone and careful argument. Although you may not accept this particular refutation, you can agree that it is well reasoned and supported. You do not feel attacked personally because the writer disagrees with you.

Exercise 19.11

Analyze and evaluate the use of refutation in Jonathan Rauch's essay "Who's More Worthy?" (paragraphs 11 and 14) in Chapter 6. How does Rauch signal or announce the refutation? How does he support the refutation? What is the tone of the refutation, and how effective do you think the tone would be in convincing readers to take the writer's argument seriously?

LOGICAL FALLACIES

Fallacies are errors or flaws in reasoning. Although essentially unsound, fallacious arguments seem superficially plausible and often have great persuasive power. Fallacies are not necessarily deliberate efforts to deceive readers. Writers may introduce a fallacy accidentally by not examining their own reasons or underlying assumptions critically, by failing to establish solid support, or by using unclear or ambiguous words. Here is a summary of the most common logical fallacies (listed alphabetically):

- ***Begging the question:*** Arguing that a claim is true by repeating the claim in different words (sometimes called *circular reasoning*)
- ***Confusing chronology with causality:*** Assuming that because one thing preceded another, the former caused the latter (also called *post hoc, ergo propter hoc*—Latin for "after this, therefore because of this")

- ***Either-or reasoning:*** Assuming that there are only two sides to a question and representing yours as the only correct one
- ***Equivocating:*** Misleading or hedging with ambiguous word choices
- ***Failing to accept the burden of proof:*** Asserting a claim without presenting a reasoned argument to support it
- ***False analogy:*** Assuming that because one thing resembles another, conclusions drawn from one also apply to the other
- ***Hasty generalization:*** Offering only weak or limited evidence to support a conclusion
- ***Overreliance on authority:*** Assuming that something is true simply because an expert says so and ignoring evidence to the contrary
- ***Oversimplifying:*** Giving easy answers to complicated questions, often by appealing to emotions rather than logic
- ***Personal attack:*** Demeaning the proponents of a claim instead of refuting their argument (also called *ad hominem*—Latin for "against the man"—*attack*)
- ***Red herring:*** Attempting to misdirect the discussion by raising an essentially unrelated point
- ***Slanting:*** Selecting or emphasizing the evidence that supports your claim and suppressing or playing down other evidence
- ***Slippery slope:*** Pretending that one thing inevitably leads to another
- ***Sob story:*** Manipulating readers' emotions to lead them to draw unjustified conclusions
- ***Straw man:*** Directing the argument against a claim that nobody actually makes or that everyone agrees is very weak

Part Four

RESEARCH STRATEGIES

20

Field Research

In universities, government agencies, and the business world, field research can be as important as library research or experimental research. If you major in education, communication, or one of the social sciences, you will probably be asked to do writing based on your own observations, interviews, and questionnaire results. You will also read large amounts of information based on these methods of learning about individuals, groups, and institutions. You also might use observations or interviews to help you select or gain background for a service-learning project.

For more on service learning, see Chapter 28.

Observations and interviews are essential for writing profiles (Chapter 4). Interviewing could be helpful, as well, in documenting a trend or phenomenon and exploring its causes (Chapter 9): You might interview an expert or conduct a survey to establish the presence of a trend, for example. In proposing a solution to a problem (Chapter 7), you might want to interview people involved; or if many people are affected, you might find it useful to prepare a questionnaire. In writing to explain an academic concept (Chapter 5), you might want to interview a faculty member who is a specialist on the subject. As you consider how you might use such research most appropriately, ask your instructor whether your institution requires you to obtain approval for your field research.

OBSERVATIONS

This section offers guidelines for planning an observational visit, taking notes on your observations, writing them up, and preparing for follow-up visits. Some kinds of writing are based on observations from single visits—travel writing, social workers' case reports, insurance investigators' accident reports—but most observational writing is based on several visits. An anthropologist or a sociologist studying an unfamiliar group or activity might observe it for months, filling several notebooks with notes. If you are profiling a place (Chapter 4), you almost certainly will want to make more than one observational visit, some of them perhaps combined with interviews.

Second and third visits to observe further are important because as you learn more about a place from initial observations, interviews, or reading, you will discover new ways to look at it. Gradually, you will have more and more questions that can be answered only by follow-up visits.

Planning the Visit

To ensure that your observational visits are productive, you must plan them carefully.

Getting Access. If the place you propose to visit is public, you will probably have easy access to it. If everything you need to see is within view of anyone passing by or using the place, you can make your observations without any special arrangements. Indeed, you may not even be noticed. However, most observational visits require special access. Hence, you will need to arrange your visit, calling ahead or stopping by to introduce yourself, state your purpose, and get acquainted. Find out the times you may visit, and be certain you can gain access easily.

Announcing Your Intentions. State your intentions directly and fully. Say who you are, where you are from, and what you hope to do. You may be surprised at how receptive people can be to a college student on assignment for a class or a service-learning project. Not every place you wish to visit will welcome you, however. In addition, private businesses as well as public institutions place a variety of constraints on outside visitors. But generally, if people know your intentions, they may be able to tell you about aspects of a place or an activity you would not have thought to observe.

Taking Your Tools. Take a notebook with a firm back so that you will have a steady writing surface. Remember also to take a pen. Some observers dictate their observations into a tape recorder and transcribe their notes later. You might want to experiment with this method. We recommend, though, that you record your first observations in writing. Your instructor or other students in your class may want to see your notes, and transcribing a recording can take a lot of time.

Observing and Taking Notes

Here are some basic guidelines for observing and taking notes.

Observing. Some activities invite the observer to watch from multiple vantage points, whereas others may limit the observer to a single perspective. Take advantage of every perspective available to you. Come in close, take a middle position, and stand back. Study the scene from a stationary position, and then try to move around it. The more varied your perspectives, the more details you are likely to observe.

Your purposes in observing are twofold: to describe the activity or place and to analyze it. Therefore, you will want to look closely at the activity or place itself, and you will also want to discover the perspective you want to take on it and develop insights into it.

Try initially to be an innocent observer: Pretend that you have never seen anything like this activity or place before. Then consider your own and your readers' likely preconceptions. Ask yourself what details are surprising and what reinforces expectations.

Taking Notes. You will undoubtedly find your own style of notetaking, but here are a few pointers.

- Write on only one side of the page. Later, when you organize your notes, you may want to cut up the pages and file notes under different headings.
- Take notes in words, phrases, or sentences. Draw diagrams or sketches if they will help you see and understand the place or activity or recall details of it later on.
- Use abbreviations as much as you like, but use them consistently and clearly.
- Note any ideas or questions that occur to you.
- If you are expecting to see a certain behavior, try not to let this expectation influence what you actually do see.
- Use quotation marks around any overheard remarks or conversations you record.

Perhaps the most important advice about notetaking during an observational visit is to record as many details as possible about the place or activity and to write down your insights (ideas, interpretations, judgments) as they come to mind. Do not focus on taking notes in a systematic way. Be flexible. Later you will have the chance to reorganize your notes and fill in gaps. At the same time, however, you want to be sure to include details about the setting, the people, and your reactions.

The Setting. Describe the setting: Name or list objects you see there, and then record details of some of them—their color, shape, size, texture, function, relation to similar or dissimilar objects. Although your notes will probably contain mainly visual details, you might also want to record details about sounds and smells. Be sure to include some notes about the shape, dimensions, and layout of the place as a whole. How big is it? How is it organized?

The People. Note the number of people you observe, their activities, their movements and behavior. Describe their appearance or dress. Record parts of overheard conversations. Indicate whether you see more men than women, more members of one nationality or ethnic group than of another, more older than younger people. Most important, note anything surprising, interesting, or unusual about the people and how they interact with each other.

Your Personal Reactions. Write down your impressions, questions, ideas, or insights as they occur to you.

Reflecting on Your Observations

Immediately after your observational visit (within a few minutes, if possible), find a quiet place to reflect on what you saw, review your notes, and fill in any gaps with additional details or ideas. Give yourself at least a half-hour to add to your notes and to write a few sentences about your perspective on the place or activity. Ask yourself the following questions:

- What did I learn from my observational visit?
- How did what I observed fit my own or my readers' likely preconceptions of the place or activity?
- What perspective on the place do my notes seem to convey?
- What, if anything, seemed contradictory or out of place?

Writing Up Your Notes

Clustering is described in Chapter 11, pp. 570–71. Inventory-taking is described in Chapter 12, pp. 591–92.

Your instructor may ask you to write up your notes on the observational visit, as Brian Cable did after visiting the Goodbody mortuary for his profile essay. If so, review your notes, looking for a meaningful pattern in the details you have noted down. You might find clustering or taking inventory useful for discovering patterns in your notes.

Assume that your readers have never been to the place, and decide on the perspective of the place you want to convey to them. Choose details that will convey this. Then draft a brief description of the place. Your purpose is to select details from your notes that will help readers imagine the place and understand it.

See Chapter 15 for a full discussion of describing strategies.

Exercise 20.1

Arrange to meet with a small group (three or four students) for an observational visit somewhere on campus, such as the student center, campus gym, cafeteria or restaurant, or any other place where some activity is going on. Take notes by assigning each person in your group a specific task; one person can take notes on the appearance of the people, for example; another can take notes on their activities; another on their conversations; and another on what the place looks and smells like. Take about twenty to thirty minutes, and then report to each other on your observations. This will give you some good practice on what you will need to do when you observe on your own, and you will get to see some of the difficulties associated with observing people and places.

Preparing for Follow-Up Visits

Rather than repeat yourself in follow-up visits, try to build on what you have already discovered. You should probably do some interviewing and reading before another observational visit so that you will have a greater understanding of the subject when you observe it again. You might want to present your notes from your first visit to your instructor or to a small group from your class so that you could use their responses as well, especially if you are working on a specific assignment such as a profile. It is also important to develop a plan for your follow-up visits: questions to be answered, insights to be tested, types of information you would like to discover.

INTERVIEWS

Like making observations, interviewing tends to involve four basic steps: (1) planning and setting up the interview, (2) taking notes during the interview, (3) reflecting on the interview, and (4) writing up your notes.

Planning and Setting Up the Interview

The initial steps in interviewing involve choosing an interview subject and then arranging and planning for the interview.

Choosing an Interview Subject. First, choose someone to interview. If you are writing about some activity in which several people are involved, choose subjects representing a variety of perspectives—a range of roles, for example. For a profile of a single person, most or all of your interviews would be with that person. But for a service-learning project, for instance, you might interview several members of an organization to gain a more complete picture of its mission or activities. You should be flexible because you may be unable to speak with the person you initially targeted and may wind up interviewing someone else—the person's assistant, perhaps. Do not assume that this interview subject will be of little use to you. With the right questions, you might even learn more from the assistant than you would from the person you had originally expected to see.

Arranging an Interview. You may be nervous about calling up a busy person and asking for some of his or her time. Indeed, you may get turned down. But if so, it is possible that you will be referred to someone who will see you, someone whose job it is to talk to the public.

Do not feel that just because you are a student, you do not have the right to ask for people's time. You will be surprised at how delighted people are to be asked about themselves, particularly if you reach them when they are not feeling harried. Most people love to talk—about anything! And since you are a student on assignment, some people may feel that they are performing a public service by talking with you.

When introducing yourself to arrange the interview, give a short and simple description of your project. If you talk too much, you could prejudice or limit the interviewee's response. At the same time, it is a good idea to exhibit some sincere enthusiasm for your project. If you lack enthusiasm, the person may see little reason to talk with you.

Keep in mind that the person you want to interview will be donating valuable time to you. Be certain that you call ahead to arrange a specific time for the interview. Arrive on time. Dress appropriately. Bring all the materials you need. Express your thanks when the interview is over. Finally, try to represent your institution well, whether your interview is for a single course assignment or part of a larger service-learning project.

Planning for the Interview. The best interview is generally the well-planned interview. Making an observational visit and doing some background reading beforehand can be helpful. In preparation for the interview, you should consider your objectives and prepare some questions.

Think about your main objectives:

- Do you want an orientation to the place or your topic (the "big picture") from this interview?
- Do you want this interview to lead you to interviews with other key people?
- Do you want mainly facts or opinions?
- Do you need to clarify something you have heard in another interview, observed, or read?
- Do you want to learn more about the person, the place, or the activity through the interview—or all of these?

The key to good interviewing is flexibility. You may be looking for facts, but your interview subject may not have any to offer. In that case, you should be able to shift gears and go after whatever your subject is in a position to discuss. Be aware that the person you are interviewing represents only one point of view. You may need to speak with several people to get a more complete picture. Talking with more than one person may also help you discover contradictions or problems that could contribute to the significance you decide to emphasize.

Composing Questions. Take care in composing the questions you prepare in advance; they can be the key to a successful interview. Any question that places unfair limits on respondents is a bad question. Avoid forced-choice questions and leading questions.

Forced-choice questions impose your terms on respondents. If you are interviewing a counselor at a campus rape crisis center and want to know what he or she thinks is the motivation for rape, you could ask this question: "Do you think rape is an expression of passion or of power and anger?" But the counselor might not think that either passion or power and anger satisfactorily explain the motivation for rape. A better way to phrase the question would be as follows: "People often fall into two camps on the issue of rape. Some think it is an expression of passion, while others argue it is an expression of anger and insecurity. Do you think it is either of these? If not, what is your opinion?" Phrasing the question in this way allows the interviewee to react to what others have said but also gives the interviewee freedom to set the terms for his or her response.

Leading questions assume too much. An example of this kind of question is this: "Do you think the number of rapes has increased because women are perceived as competitors in a highly competitive economy?" This question assumes that there is an increase in the occurrence of rape, that women are perceived (apparently by rapists) as economic competitors, and that the state of the economy is somehow related to acts of rape. A better way of asking the question might be to make the assumptions more explicit by dividing the question into its parts: "Do you think the number of rapes has increased? What could have caused this increase? I've heard some people argue that the economy has something to do with it. Do you think so? Do you think rapists perceive women as competitors for jobs? Could the current economic situation have made this competition more severe?"

Good questions come in many different forms. One way of considering them is to divide them into two basic types: open and closed. **Open questions** give the respondent range and flexibility. They also generate anecdotes, personal revelations, and expressions of attitudes. **Closed questions** usually request specific information.

Suppose you are interviewing a small-business owner, for example. You might begin with a specific (closed) question about when the business was established and then follow up with an open-ended question such as, "Could you take a few minutes to tell me something about your early days in the business? I'd be interested to hear how it got started, what your hopes were, and what problems you had to face." Consider asking directly for an anecdote ("What happened when your employees threatened to strike?"), encouraging reflection ("What do you think has helped you most? What has hampered you?"), or soliciting advice ("What advice would you give to someone trying to start a new business today?"). Here are some examples of open and closed questions:

Open Questions

- What do you think about *(name a person or an event)*?
- Describe your reaction when *(name an event)* happened.
- Tell me about a time you were *(name an emotion)*.

Closed Questions

- How do you *(name a process)*?
- What does *(name a word or phrase)* mean?
- What does *(name a person, object, or place)* look like?
- How was it made?

The best questions encourage the subject to talk freely but to the point. If an answer strays too far from the point, you may need to ask a follow-up question to refocus the talk. Another tack you might want to try is to rephrase the subject's answer, to say something like "Let me see if I have this right" or "Am I correct in saying that you feel . . . ?" Often, a person will take the opportunity to amplify the original response by adding just the anecdote or quotable comment you have been looking for.

Bringing Your Tools. As for an observational visit, when you interview someone, you will need a notebook with a firm back so you can write in it easily without the benefit of a table or desk. You might find it useful to divide several pages into two columns by drawing a line about one-third of the width of the page from the left margin. Use the left-hand column to note details about the scene, the person, the mood

For an example of notes of this sort, see Chapter 4, pp. 190–92.

of the interview, and other impressions. Head this column *Details and Impressions.* At the top of the right-hand column, write several questions. You may not use them, but they will jog your memory. This column should be titled *Information.* In it, you will record what you learn from answers to your questions.

Taking Notes during the Interview

Because you are not taking a verbatim transcript of the interview (if you want a literal account, use a tape recorder or shorthand), your goals are to gather information and to record a few quotable bits of information, comments, and anecdotes. In addition, because the people you interview may be unused to giving interviews and so will need to know you are paying attention, it is probably a good idea to do more listening than notetaking. You may not have much confidence in your memory, but if you pay close attention, you are likely to recall a good deal of the conversation afterward. Take some notes during the interview: a few quotations; key words and phrases; details of the scene, the person, and the mood of the interview. Remember that how something is said is as important as what is said. Look for material that will give texture to your writing—gesture, verbal inflection, facial expression, body language, physical appearance, dress, hair, or anything that makes the person an individual.

Reflecting on the Interview

As soon as you finish the interview, find a quiet place to reflect on it and review your notes. This reflection is essential because so much happens in an interview that you cannot record at the time. Spend at least a half-hour adding to your notes and thinking about what you learned.

At the end of this time, write a few sentences about your main impressions from the interview. Ask yourself these questions:

- What did I learn?
- What seemed contradictory or surprising about the interview?
- How did what was said fit my own or my readers' likely expectations about the person, activity, or place?
- How can I summarize my impressions?

Writing Up Your Notes

Your instructor may ask you to write up your interview notes. If so, review them for useful details and ideas. Decide what perspective you want to make on this person. Choose details that will contribute to this perspective. Select quotations and paraphrases of information you learned from the person.

You might also review notes from any related observations or other interviews, especially if you plan to combine these materials in a profile, ethnographic study, or other project.

QUESTIONNAIRES

Questionnaires let you survey the opinions and knowledge of large numbers of people. You could carry out many face-to-face or phone interviews to get the same information, but questionnaires have the advantages of economy, efficiency, and anonymity. Some questionnaires, such as the ones you filled out when entering college, just collect demographic information: your name, age, sex, hometown, religious preference, intended major. Others, such as the Gallup and Harris polls, collect opinions on a wide range of issues. Before elections, we are bombarded with the results of such polls. Still other kinds of questionnaires, such as those used in academic research, are designed to help answer important questions about personal and societal problems.

This section briefly outlines procedures you can follow to carry out an informal questionnaire survey of people's opinions or knowledge and then write up the results. There are many good texts on designing questionnaires. A sample questionnaire appears in this section (Figure 20.1).

Focusing Your Study

A questionnaire survey usually has a limited focus. You might need to interview a few people to find this focus. Or you may already have a limited focus in mind. If you are developing a questionnaire as part of a service-learning project, discuss your focus with your supervisor or other staff members.

As an example, let us assume that you go to your campus student health clinic and have to wait over an hour to see a doctor. Sitting in the waiting room with many other students, you decide that this long wait is a problem that would be an ideal topic for a writing assignment you have been asked to do for your writing class, an essay proposing a solution to a problem (Chapter 7).

You do not have to explore the entire operation of the clinic to study this problem. You are not interested in how nurses and doctors are hired or in how efficient the clinic's system of ordering supplies is, for example. Your primary interests are how long students usually wait for appointments, what times are most convenient for students to schedule appointments, how the clinic accommodates students when demand is high, and whether the long wait discourages many students from getting the treatment they need. With this limited focus, you can collect valuable information using a fairly brief questionnaire. To be certain about your focus, however, you should talk informally with several students to find out whether they also think there is a problem with appointment scheduling at the clinic. You might want to talk with staff members, too, explaining your plans and asking for their views on the problem.

Whatever your interest, be sure to limit the scope of your survey. Try to focus on one or two important questions. With a limited focus, your questionnaire can be brief, and people will be more willing to fill it out. In addition, a survey based on a limited amount of information will be easier to organize and report on.

Writing Questions

The same two basic types of questions used for interviews, closed and open, are also useful in questionnaires. Figure 20.1 illustrates how these types of questions may be employed in the context of a questionnaire about the student health clinic problem. Notice that the questionnaire uses several forms of *closed questions* (in items 1–6): two-way questions, multiple-choice questions, ranking scales, and checklists. You will probably use more than one form of closed question in a questionnaire to collect different kinds of information. The sample questionnaire also uses several *open questions* (items 7–10) that ask for brief written answers. You may want to combine closed and open questions in your questionnaire because both offer advantages: Closed questions will give you definite answers, while open questions can elicit information you may not have anticipated as well as provide lively quotations for your essay explaining what you have learned.

Whatever types of questions you develop, try to phrase them in a fair and unbiased manner so that your results will be reliable and credible. As soon as you have a collection of possible questions, try them out on a few typical respondents. You need to know which questions are unclear, which seem to duplicate others, and which provide the most interesting responses. These tryouts will enable you to assess which questions will give you the information you need. Readers can also help you come up with additional questions.

Figure 20.1 Sample Questionnaire: Scheduling at the Student Health Clinic

This is a survey about the scheduling of appointments at the campus Student Health Clinic. Your participation will help determine how long students have to wait to use clinic services and how these services might be more conveniently scheduled. The survey should take only 3 to 4 minutes to complete. All responses are confidential. Thank you for your participation.

Two-way question

1. Have you ever made an appointment at the clinic? (Circle one.)

   Yes No

Multiple-choice questions

2. How frequently have you had to wait more than 10 minutes at the clinic for a scheduled appointment? (Circle one.)

   Always Usually Occasionally Never

3. Have you ever had to wait more than 30 minutes at the clinic for a scheduled appointment? (Circle one.)

   Yes No Uncertain

4. From your experience so far with the clinic, how would you rank its system for scheduling appointments? (Circle one.)

Ranking scale

0	1	2	3	4	5
no experience	inadequate	poor	adequate	good	outstanding

5. Given your present work and class schedule, when are you able to visit the clinic? (Check all applicable responses.)

_____ 8–10 A.M. _____ 1–3 P.M. — *Checklist*
_____ 10 A.M.–Noon _____ 3–5 P.M.
_____ 12–1 P.M.

6. Given your present work and class schedule, which times during the day (Monday through Friday) would be the most and least convenient for you to schedule appointments at the clinic? (Rank the four choices from *1* for most convenient time to *4* for least convenient time.)

_____ Morning (7 A.M.–Noon) _____ Dinnertime (5–7 P.M.) — *Ranking scale*
_____ Afternoon (12–5 P.M.) _____ Evening (7–10 P.M.)

7. How would you evaluate your most recent appointment at the clinic?

8. Based on your experiences with scheduling at the clinic, what advice would you give to other students about making appointments?

9. What do you believe would most improve the scheduling of appointments at the clinic?

10. If you have additional comments about scheduling at the clinic, please write them on the back of this page.

Open questions (questions 7–10)

Designing the Questionnaire

Begin your questionnaire with a brief, clear introduction stating the purpose of your survey and explaining how you intend to use the results. Give advice on answering the questions, and estimate the amount of time needed to complete the questionnaire (see Figure 20.1 for an example). You may opt to give this information orally if you plan to hand the questionnaire to groups of people and have them fill it out immediately. However, even in this case, your respondents will appreciate a written introduction that clarifies what you expect and helps keep them on track.

Select your most promising questions, and decide how to order them. Any logical order is appropriate. You might want to arrange the questions from least to most complicated or from general to specific. You may find it appropriate to group the questions by subject matter or format. Certain questions may lead to others. You might want to place open questions at the end (see Figure 20.1 for an example).

Design your questionnaire so that it looks attractive and readable. Make it look easy to complete. Do not crowd questions together to save paper. Provide plenty of space for readers to answer questions, especially open questions, and encourage them to use the back of the page if they need more space.

Testing the Questionnaire

Make a few copies of your first-draft questionnaire, and ask at least three readers to complete it. Time them as they respond, or ask them to keep track of how long they take to complete it. Discuss with them any confusion or problems they experience. Review their responses with them to be certain that each question is eliciting the information you want it to elicit. From what you learn, reconsider your questionnaire, and make any necessary revisions to your questions and design or format.

Administering the Questionnaire

Decide who you want to fill out your questionnaire and how you can arrange for them to do so. The more respondents you have, the better, but constraints of time and expense will almost certainly limit the number. You can mail or email questionnaires, distribute them to dormitories, or send them to campus or workplace mailboxes, but the return will be low. Half the people receiving questionnaires in the mail usually fail to return them. If you do mail the questionnaire, be sure to mention the deadline for returning it. Give directions for its return, and include a stamped, self-addressed envelope, if necessary. Instead of mailing the questionnaire, you might want to arrange to distribute it yourself to groups of people in class or around campus, at dormitory meetings, or at work.

Note that if you want to do a formal questionnaire study, you will need a scientifically representative group of readers (a random or stratified random sample). Even for an informal study, you should try to get a reasonably representative group. For example, to study satisfaction with appointment scheduling at the clinic, you would want to include students who have been to the clinic as well as those who have avoided it. You might even want to include a concentration of seniors rather than first-year students because, after four years, seniors would have made more visits to the clinic. If many students commute, you would want to be sure to have commuters among your respondents. Your essay will be more convincing if you demonstrate that your respondents represent the group whose opinions or knowledge you claim to be studying. As few as twenty-five respondents could be adequate for an informal study.

Writing Up the Results

Once you have the completed questionnaires, what do you do with them?

Summarizing the Results. Begin by tallying the results from the closed questions. Take an unused questionnaire, and tally the responses next to each choice. Suppose that you had administered the student health clinic questionnaire to twenty-five students. Here is how the tally might look for the checklist in question 5 of Figure 20.1.

5. Given your present work and class schedule, when are you able to visit the clinic? (Check all applicable responses.)

   _____ 8–10 A.M. ~~||||~~ ~~||||~~ ~~||||~~ ||| *(18)*   _____ 1–3 P.M. ||| *(3)*

   _____ 10 A.M.–Noon ~~||||~~ || *(7)*   _____ 3–5 P.M. ~~||||~~ |||| *(9)*

   _____ 12–1 P.M. ~~||||~~ ~~||||~~ ||| *(13)*

Each tally mark represents one response to that item. The totals add up to more than twenty-five because respondents were asked to check all the times when they could make appointments.

Next, consider the open questions. Read all respondents' answers to each question separately to see the kinds and variety of responses they gave. Then decide whether you want to code any of the open questions so that you can summarize results from them quantitatively, as you would with closed questions. For example, you might want to classify the types of advice given as responses to question 8 in the clinic questionnaire: "Based on your experiences with scheduling at the clinic, what advice would you give to other students about making appointments?" You could then report the numbers of respondents (of your twenty-five) who gave each type of advice. For an opinion question (for example, "How would you evaluate your most recent appointment at the clinic?"), you might simply code the answers as positive, neutral, or negative and then tally the results accordingly for each kind of response. However, the responses to most open questions are used as a source of quotations for your report or essay.

You can give the results from the closed questions as percentages, either within the text itself or in one or more tables. You can find table formats in texts you may be using or even in magazines or newspapers. Conventional table formats for the social sciences are illustrated in the *Publication Manual of the American Psychological Association*, 5th edition (Washington, DC: American Psychological Association, 2001).

Because readers' interests can be engaged more easily with quotations than with percentages, plan to use open responses in your essay. You can quote responses to the open questions within your text, perhaps weaving them into your discussion like quoted material from published sources. Or you can organize several responses into lists and then comment on them.

For strategies for integrating quoted material, see Chapter 22, pp. 747–53.

You can use computer spreadsheet programs to tabulate the results from closed questions and even print out tables or graphs that you can insert into your essay. For a small, informal survey, however, such programs will probably not save you much time.

Organizing the Write-up. In organizing your results, you might want to consider a plan that is commonly followed in the social sciences.

Reporting Your Survey

Statement of the problem

- Context for your study
- The question or questions you wanted to answer
- Need for your survey
- Brief preview of your survey and plan for your report

Review of other related surveys (if you know of any)

Procedures

- Questionnaire design
- Selection of participants
- Administration of the questionnaire
- Summary of the results

Results: Presentation of what you learned, with limited commentary or interpretation

Summary and discussion

- Brief summary of your results
- Brief discussion of their significance (commenting, interpreting, exploring implications, and possibly comparing to other related surveys)

21 *Library and Internet Research*

Research requires patience, careful planning, good advice, and even luck. The rewards are many, however. Each new research project leads you to unexplored regions of the library or of cyberspace. You may find yourself in a rare-book room reading a manuscript written hundreds of years ago or involved in a lively discussion on the Internet with people hundreds of miles away. One moment you may be keyboarding commands, and the next you may be threading a microfilm reader, viewing a videodisk, or squinting at the fine print in an index. You may breeze through an encyclopedia entry introducing you to a new subject or struggle with a just-published report of a highly technical research study on the same subject.

This chapter is designed to help you learn how to use the resources available in your college library and on the Internet. It gives advice on how to learn about the library and the Internet, develop efficient search strategies, keep track of your research, locate appropriate sources, and read them with a critical eye. Chapter 22 provides guidelines for using and acknowledging these sources in an essay. It also presents a sample research paper on home schooling that was written for an assignment on writing an essay speculating about the causes of a trend.

INTEGRATING LIBRARY AND INTERNET RESEARCH

Although this chapter includes separate sections on the library and the Internet, these two ways to find research information are closely intertwined. You can often use the Internet to access many of the library's resources—the catalog of books and other items, indexes to periodical articles, and other kinds of electronic databases—from your own computer in your home or dorm room. On the other hand, you will need or want to go through the library's computers rather than your own to access many Web-based resources, including those that charge fees for subscriptions or for downloading and printing out documents.

For most research topics, you will need to find source materials both in the library and on the Internet because each offers material not available from the other. The vast majority of books and articles published in print are not available online, and so you will almost certainly need to consult some of these print sources to avoid getting a skewed perspective on your topic, especially if it deals with events that occurred more than a few years ago. As discussed later in this chapter, print sources also tend to offer more reliable information than online ones. Likewise, though, very little online material ever appears in print, and especially for current topics, you will almost certainly want to check the Web for the latest developments or research findings. Compared with print sources, online sources usually take less time and effort both to find and to integrate into your own writing. So in some ways, they can help you do a more thorough job of research within the time available to you. Still, be careful not to rely too heavily on the Web just because it is easy to use.

ORIENTING YOURSELF TO THE LIBRARY

To conduct research in most college libraries, you will need to become familiar with a wide variety of resources. Public-access catalogs, almost all of them now electronic, provide information on books. Periodical indexes and abstracts, used to locate magazine and journal articles, are available both in print volumes and in various electronic forms: on CD-ROMs, through the library catalog, or through the World Wide Web. The materials you find may be in print, in reduced-size photographic formats like microfilm and microfiche that require special machines to read, or in electronic text files accessible through an electronic periodical index or library Web site.

Taking a Tour

Make a point of getting acquainted with your campus library. Your instructor may arrange a library orientation tour for your composition class. If not, you can join one of the regular orientation tours scheduled by the librarians or design your own tour (for suggestions, see Table 21.1). Because nearly all college libraries are more complex and offer more services than typical high school or public libraries, you will need to learn how your campus library's catalog and reference room are organized, how you can access computer catalogs and databases, whom to ask for help if you are confused, and where you can find books, periodicals, and other materials.

Nearly every college library offers a Web site and handouts describing its resources and services. Pick up copies of any available pamphlets and guidelines. Also look for a floor map of materials and facilities. See whether your library offers any research guidelines, special workshops, or presentations on strategies for locating resources. Many library Web sites offer tutorials for using the library's electronic resources.

Consulting a Librarian

Think of college librarians as instructors whose job is to help you understand the library and get your hands on sources you need to complete your research projects. Librarians at the information or reference desk are there to provide reference services, and most have years of experience answering the very questions you are likely to ask.

Table 21.1 Designing Your Self-Guided Library Tour

Here is a list of important locations or departments to look for in your college library.

Library Location	*What You Can Do at These Locations*
Loan desk	Obtain library cards, check out materials, place holds and recalls, pay fees or fines.
Reference desk	Obtain help from reference librarians to locate and use library resources.
Information desk	Ask general and directional questions.
Reserves desk	Gain access to books and journal articles that are on reserve for specific classes.
Interlibrary loan department	Request materials not available on site.
Public-access computers	Gain access to the library catalog, electronic periodical indexes and abstracts, the campus network, and the Internet.
Current periodicals	Locate unbound current issues of newspapers, journals, and magazines.
Directories of books and journals	Use directories to find the location of books and journals shelved by call numbers.
Reference collection	Find reference materials such as encyclopedias, dictionaries, handbooks, atlases, bibliographies, statistics, and periodical indexes and abstracts.
Government publications department	Locate publications from federal, state, and local government agencies.
Multimedia resources	Locate nonprint materials such as videos, CD-ROMs, and audiotapes.
Microforms	Locate materials on microfilm (reels) and microfiche (cards).
Special collections	Find rare and valuable materials not readily available in most library collections; in larger libraries only.
Archives	Find archival materials, collections of papers from important individuals and organizations that provide source material for original research (in larger libraries only).
Maps and atlases	Locate maps and atlases in a special location because of their size and format.
Copy service	Use self-service and special-function copiers.
Reading rooms	Read in quiet, comfortable areas.
Study rooms	Study in rooms reserved for individuals or small groups.

You should not hesitate to approach them with any questions you have about locating sources. Remember, however, that they can be most helpful when you can explain your research assignment clearly and ask questions that are as specific as possible. You need not do so face-to-face: Many library Web sites now offer "virtual reference" chat rooms that connect library users to a reference librarian who can offer advice, send electronic documents, and demonstrate electronic searches.

Knowing Your Research Task

Before you go to the library to start an assigned research project, learn as much as you can about the assignment. Ask your instructor to clarify any confusing terms and to define the purpose and scope of the project. Find out how you can narrow or focus the project once you begin the research. Asking a question or two in advance can prevent hours—or even days—of misdirected work. Should you need to ask a librarian for advice, have the assignment in writing. You should try to get to the library as soon as you understand the assignment. If many of your classmates will be working on similar projects, you may be competing with them for a limited number of books and other resources.

A LIBRARY SEARCH STRATEGY

For your library research to be manageable and productive, you will want to work carefully and systematically. Although specific search strategies may vary to fit the needs of individual research tasks, the general process presented in Figure 21.1 should help you get started, keep track of all your research, use library materials to get an overview of your subject, locate the sources you need, and read those sources with a critical eye. Remember that research is a recursive, repetitive process, not a linear one. You will be constantly refining and revising your research strategy as you find out more about your topic.

KEEPING TRACK OF YOUR RESEARCH

As you research your topic, you will want to keep a careful record of all the sources you locate by setting up a working bibliography. You will also want to take notes on your sources in some systematic way.

Keeping a Working Bibliography

A **working bibliography** is a preliminary, ongoing record of books, articles, Web sites—all the sources of information you discover as you research your subject. In addition, you can use your working bibliography to keep track of any encyclopedias, bibliographies, and indexes you consult, even though these general sources are not identified in an essay.

Each entry in a working bibliography is called a **bibliographic citation**. The information you record in each bibliographic citation will help you to locate the source in the library and then, if you end up using it in your paper, to *cite* or *document* it in the final **bibliography**—the list of references or works cited you provide at the end of an essay. Recording this information for each possible source as you identify it, rather than reconstructing it later, will save you hours of work. In addition to the bibliographic information, note the library location where the source is kept and any index or other reference work where you learned about it, just in case you

Know your research task.

- Keep a research journal.
- Keep a working bibliography.
- Take notes.

Get an overview of your topic.

- Look in encyclopedias and subject guides.
- Review textbooks.
- Explore newspapers, magazines, and Internet sites.
- Construct a list of key words and subject headings.
- Develop a preliminary topic statement.

Use subject guides to identify possible sources of information on specific topics.

Conduct a preliminary search for sources, using keywords and subject headings.

- Check the online catalog for books.
- Check periodical indexes for articles.
- Check Internet sites.

Evaluate and refine your search by asking yourself:

- Is this what I expected to find?
- Am I finding enough?
- Am I finding too much?
- Do I need to modify my key words?
- Do I need to recheck background sources?
- Do I need to modify my topic statement?

Refine your search based on the answers.

Locate sources.

- Books
- Magazine and journal articles
- Newspaper articles
- Internet sites
- Government and statistical sources
- Other sources appropriate to your topic

Read your sources with a critical eye.

- For information
- For relevance
- For accuracy
- For comprehensiveness
- For bias
- For currency

Continue to evaluate and refine your search strategy based on the research results.

Figure 21.1 Overview of an Information Search Strategy

have to track it down again. (See Figures 21.2 and 21.3 on p. 714 for guidelines on how to record bibliographic and other information for a book or a print article. For guidelines for Internet sources, see page 737.)

As you locate books in the library, record this information in your working bibliography for each book you look up.

Author: ______________________________

Title: ______________________________

Place of publication: ______________________________

Publisher: ______________________________

Date of publication: ______________________________

Library where book is located: ______________________________

Call number: ______________________________

Special location (such as in reference or government publications dept.): ______________

Is the book available or checked out?: ______________________________

Figure 21.2 Information for Working Bibliography—Books

As you locate articles in the library, record this information in your working bibliography for each article you look up.

Author of article: ______________________________

Title of article: ______________________________

Title of journal: ______________________________

Volume number: ______________ Issue number: ______________

Date of issue: ______________ Inclusive page numbers: ______________

Library and special location: ______________________________

Index where you found the article: ______________________________

Figure 21.3 Information for Working Bibliography—Periodical Articles

Confirm with your instructor which documentation style is required for your assignment so that you can follow that style for all the sources you put into your working bibliography. Chapter 22 presents two common documentation styles—one adopted by the Modern Language Association (MLA) and widely used in the humanities and the other advocated by the American Psychological Association (APA) and used in the social sciences. Individual disciplines often have their own preferred styles of documentation.

Practiced researchers keep their working bibliography on index cards, in a notebook, or in a computer file. Many researchers find index cards convenient because the cards are easy to arrange in the alphabetical order required for the list of works cited or references. Others find cards too easy to lose and prefer instead to keep everything—working bibliography, notes, and drafts—in one notebook. Researchers who use computers for their working bibliography can either record the information in a file in their word processing program or use one of the software programs that format the information according to a preset documentation style (such as MLA or APA) or a customized style created by the user. These programs can also create and insert the citations that are required—within the essay text or in footnotes or endnotes—and can format the final list of works cited. Some programs can even download source information from electronic indexes and other databases into a bibliographic file and then automatically format the information.

Whether you use index cards, a notebook, or a computer file for your working bibliography, your entries need to be accurate and complete. If the call number for a book is incomplete or inaccurate, for example, you will not be able to find the book in the stacks. If the author's name is misspelled, you may have trouble finding the book in the catalog. If the volume number for a periodical is incorrect, you may not be able to locate the article. If you get the bibliographic information from a catalog or index, check it when you examine the source directly.

Taking Notes

After you have identified some possible sources and found them in print or online, you will want to begin taking notes. If you can make a photocopy of the relevant parts or download them onto your computer, you may want to annotate on the page or on the screen. Otherwise, you should paraphrase, summarize, and outline useful information as separate notes. In addition, you will want to record quotations you might want to use in your essay.

Outlining, paraphrasing, and summarizing are discussed in Chapter 12, and quoting is discussed in Chapter 22.

You may already have a method of notetaking you prefer. Some researchers like to use index cards for notes as well as for their working bibliography. They use 3- by 5-inch cards for their bibliography and larger ones (4- by 6-inch or 5- by 7-inch) for notes, and some also use cards of different colors to organize their notes. Other people prefer to keep their notes in a notebook, and still others enter their notes into a computer file. Whatever method you use, be sure to keep accurate notes.

Careful notetaking is the most important way to minimize the risks of misquoting and of copying facts incorrectly. Another common error in notetaking is copying an author's words without enclosing them in quotation marks. This error leads easily to **plagiarism**, the unacknowledged and therefore improper use of another's words or ideas. Double-check all your notes, and be as accurate as you can.

For tips on avoiding plagiarism, see Chapter 22, p. 756.

You might consider photocopying materials from print sources that look especially promising. All libraries house photocopy machines or offer a copying service. Photocopying can facilitate your work, allowing you to reread and analyze important sources as well as to highlight material you may wish to quote, summarize, or paraphrase. However, because photocopying can be costly, you will want to be selective. Be sure to photocopy title pages or other publication information for each source you copy, or write this information on the photocopied text, especially if you are copying excerpts from several sources. Bring paper clips or a stapler with you to the library to help keep your photocopies organized.

For electronic sources you find in the library, download the material to a disk, and print it out if at all possible, especially if the source is on the Web. Downloading gives you the same options for rereading, highlighting, and annotating as photocopying does, and the printout serves as a "hard copy" in case the source changes or disappears. Be sure the printout or the working-bibliography entry includes all the information required by the documentation system you are using.

GETTING STARTED

"But where do I start?" That common question is easily answered. You first need an overview of your topic. If you are researching a concept or an issue in a course you are taking, a bibliography in your textbook or your course materials provides the obvious starting point. Your instructor can advise you about other sources that provide overviews of your topic. If your topic is currently in the news, you will want to consult newspapers, magazines, or Internet sites. For all other topics—and for background information—encyclopedias and disciplinary (subject) guides are often the place to start. They introduce you to diverse aspects of a subject that might lead you to find a focus for your research.

Consulting Encyclopedias

General encyclopedias, such as the *Encyclopaedia Britannica* and the *Encyclopedia Americana,* give basic information about many topics; however, general encyclopedias alone are not adequate resources for college research. Specialized encyclopedias cover topics in the depth appropriate for college writing. In addition to providing an overview of a topic, a specialized encyclopedia often includes an explanation of issues related to the topic, definitions of specialized terminology, and selective bibliographies of additional sources.

As starting points, specialized encyclopedias have two distinct advantages: (1) They provide a comprehensive introduction to key terms related to your topic, terms that are especially useful in identifying the subject headings used to locate material in catalogs and indexes, and (2) they provide a comprehensive presentation of a subject, enabling you to see many possibilities for focusing your research on one aspect of it.

The following list identifies some specialized encyclopedias in the major academic disciplines:

ART	*Dictionary of Art.* 34 vols. 1996.
BIOLOGY	*Concise Encyclopedia Biology.* 1995.
CHEMISTRY	*Concise Encyclopedia Chemistry.* 1993.
COMPUTERS	*Encyclopedia of Computer Science and Technology.* 45 vols. 1975.

ECONOMICS	*Fortune Encyclopedia of Economics.* 1993.
EDUCATION	*Encyclopedia of Educational Research.* 1992.
ENVIRONMENT	*Encyclopedia of the Environment.* 1994.
FOREIGN RELATIONS	*Encyclopedia of U.S. Foreign Relations.* 1997. *Encyclopedia of the Third World.* 1992.
HISTORY	*Encyclopedia USA.* 29 vols. 1983–. *New Cambridge Modern History.* 14 vols. 1957–1980, 1990–.
LAW	*Black's Law Dictionary.* 1990.
LITERATURE	*Encyclopedia of World Literature in the Twentieth Century.* 5 vols. 1981–1993. *Encyclopedia of Literature and Criticism.* 1990.
MUSIC	*New Grove Dictionary of Music and Musicians,* 2nd ed. 29 vols. 2001.
PHILOSOPHY	*Routledge Encyclopedia of Philosophy.* 10 vols. 1998.
PSYCHOLOGY	*Encyclopedia of Psychology.* 8 vols. 2000.
RELIGION	*Encyclopedia of Religion.* 16 vols. 1987.
SCIENCE	*McGraw-Hill Encyclopedia of Science and Technology.* 20 vols. 1997.
SOCIAL SCIENCES	*International Encyclopedia of the Social Sciences.* 19 vols. 1968–.
WOMEN'S STUDIES	*Women's Studies Encyclopedia,* Rev. ed. 3 vols. 1999.

You can locate any of these in the library by doing a title search in the online catalog and looking for the encyclopedia's call number. Find other specialized encyclopedias by looking in the catalog under the subject heading for the discipline, such as "psychology," and adding the subheading "encyclopedia" or "dictionary."

Three particular reference sources can help you identify other specialized encyclopedias covering your topic:

ARBA Guide to Subject Encyclopedias and Dictionaries, 2nd ed. (1997): Lists specialized encyclopedias by broad subject categories, with descriptions of coverage, focus, and any special features. Also available online.

Subject Encyclopedias: User Guide, Review Citations, and Keyword Index (1999): Lists specialized encyclopedias by broad subject categories and provides information about articles within them. By looking under the key terms that describe a topic, you can search for related articles in any of over four hundred specialized encyclopedias.

Kister's Best Encyclopedias: A Comparative Guide to General and Specialized Encyclopedias, 2nd ed. (1994): Surveys and evaluates more than a thousand encyclopedias, both print and electronic. Includes a title index and a topic index that you can use to find references to encyclopedias on special topics.

Consulting Disciplinary Guides

Once you have a general overview of your topic, you can consult one of the research guides within the discipline. The following guides can help you identify the major handbooks, encyclopedias, bibliographies, journals, periodical indexes, and computer databases in the various disciplines. You need not read any of these extensive works straight through, but you will find them to be valuable references. The *Guide to Reference Books,* 11th ed. (1996), edited by Robert Balay, will help you find disciplinary guides for subjects not listed here.

ANTHROPOLOGY	*Introduction to Library Research in Anthropology,* 2nd ed. 1998. By John M. Weeks.
ART	*Visual Arts Research: A Handbook.* 1986. By Elizabeth B. Pollard.
EDUCATION	*Education: A Guide to Reference and Information Sources,* 2nd ed. 2000. By Lois Buttlar and Nancy O'Brien.
FILM	*On the Screen: A Film, Television, and Video Research Guide.* 1986. By Kim N. Fisher.
GENERAL	*Guide to Reference Books,* 11th ed. 1996. Edited by Robert Balay.
HISTORY	*A Student's Guide to History,* 8th ed. 2001. By Jules R. Benjamin.
HUMANITIES	*The Humanities: A Selective Guide to Information Sources,* 5th ed. 2000. By Ron Blazek and Elizabeth S. Aversa. Also available online.
LITERATURE	*Reference Works in British and American Literature,* 2nd ed. 1998. By James K. Bracken. Also available online. *Literary Research Guide: An Annotated Listing of Reference Sources in English Literary Studies,* 3rd ed. 1998. By James L. Harner.
MUSIC	*Music: A Guide to the Reference Literature.* 1987. By William S. Brockman.
PHILOSOPHY	*Philosophy: A Guide to the Reference Literature,* 2nd ed. 1997. By Hans E. Bynagle. Also available online.
POLITICAL SCIENCE	*Political Science: A Guide to Reference and Information Sources.* 1990. By Henry York.
PSYCHOLOGY	*Library Use: A Handbook for Psychology,* 3rd ed. 2003.
SCIENCE AND TECHNOLOGY	*Information Sources in Science and Technology.* 1998. By Charlie Hurt.
SOCIAL SCIENCES	*The Social Sciences: A Cross-Disciplinary Guide to Selected Sources,* 3rd ed. 2002. By Nancy L. Herron. Also available online.
SOCIOLOGY	*Sociology: A Guide to Reference and Information Sources,* 2nd ed. 1997. By Stephen H. Aby.

WOMEN'S STUDIES *Introduction to Library Research in Women's Studies.* 1985. By Susan E. Searing.

Consulting Bibliographies

Like encyclopedias and disciplinary guides, bibliographies give an overview of what has been published on the subject. A **bibliography** is simply a list of publications on a given subject. Its scope may be broad or narrow. Some bibliographers try to be exhaustive, including every title they can find, but most are selective. To discover how selections were made, check the bibliography's preface or introduction. Occasionally, bibliographies are annotated with brief summaries and evaluations of the entries. Bibliographies may be found in a variety of places: in encyclopedias, in the library catalog, and in research guides. All specialized encyclopedias and disciplinary guides have bibliographies. Research articles include bibliographies to document their sources of information.

Even if you attend a large research university, your library is unlikely to hold every book or journal article that a bibliography might direct you to. The library catalog and serial record (a list of periodicals the library holds) will tell you whether the book or journal is available on site or through interlibrary loan.

IDENTIFYING SUBJECT HEADINGS AND KEYWORDS

To extend your research beyond encyclopedias, you need to find appropriate subject headings and keywords. **Subject headings** are specific words and phrases used in library catalogs, periodical indexes, and other databases to categorize the contents of books and articles so that people can look for materials about a particular topic. One way to begin your search for subject headings is to consult the *Library of Congress Subject Headings* (LCSH), which your library probably makes available both in print and online. This work lists the standard subject headings used in library catalogs. Here is an example from the LCSH:

Home schooling *(May Subd Geog)* ← Place names may follow heading

Here are entered works on the provision of compulsory education in the home by parents as an alternative to traditional public or private schooling. General works on the provision of education in the home by educational personnel are entered under Domestic Education.

Used for → UF Education, Home
Home-based education
Home education
Home instruction
Home teaching by parents
Homeschooling
Instruction, Home
Schooling, Home

Broader Term → BT Education

Related Term → RT Education—United States
Education—Parent participation

NT = Narrower term
SA = See also

This sample entry proved particularly useful because when the student researching this topic found nothing listed in the library catalog under "Home schooling," she tried the other headings until "Education—Parent participation" and "Education—United States" yielded information on three books. Note, too, that this entry explains the types of books that would be found under these headings and those that would be found elsewhere.

For an example of an online catalog reference to a periodical, see p. 734.

Instead of looking for likely headings in the LCSH, however, you can usually locate useful subject headings faster by searching the catalog or other database using **keywords**, words or phrases that you think describe your topic. As you read about your subject in an encyclopedia or other reference book, you should keep a list of keywords that may be useful. (Make sure you spell your keywords correctly. Computers are unforgiving of spelling errors.) As you review the results of a keyword search, look for the titles that seem to match most closely the topics that you are looking for. When you call up the detailed information for these titles, look for the section labeled "Subject" or "Subject Heading," which will show the headings under which the book or article is classified. (In the example that follows, this section is abbreviated as "Subj-lcsh.") In many computerized catalogs and databases, these subject headings are links that you can click on to get a list of other materials on the same subject. Keep a list in your working bibliography of all the subject headings you find that relate to your topic, so that you can refer to them each time you start looking for information. Here is an example of an online catalog listing for a book on home schooling:

The "imprint" line provides publication information.

The "description" is sometimes called the "physical description."

Subject headings

Title: Pathways to privatization in education / by Joseph Murphy . . . [et al.]
Imprint: Greenwich, Conn.: Ablex Pub. Corp., c1998

LOCATION	CALL NO	STATUS
MAIN	LB2806.36 .P38 1998	NOT CHCKD OUT

Description: xiii, 244 p.; 24 cm
Series: Contemporary studies in social and policy issues in education
Subj-lcsh **Privatization in education—United States**
Educational vouchers—United States
Home schooling—United States
Add author: Murphy, Joseph, 1949–
Note(s): Includes bibliographical references (p. 209–236) and index
ISBN: 1567503632 (cloth)
1567503640 (pbk.)

Determining the Most Promising Sources

As you follow a subject heading into the library catalog and periodical indexes, you will discover many seemingly relevant books and articles. How do you decide which ones to track down and examine? You may have little to go on but author, title, date, and publisher or periodical name, but these details actually provide useful clues. Look again, for example, at the online catalog reference to a book on home schooling (see p. 720). The title, *Pathways to Privatization in Education*, is the first clue to the subject coverage of the book. Note that the publication date, 1998, is fairly recent. From the subject headings, you can see that this book focuses on various aspects of the privatization of education, which includes home schooling, and that the geographic focus of the book is the United States. Finally, from the notes, you can see that the book includes an extensive bibliography that could lead you to other sources.

Now look at the following entry from *Education Index*, a periodical index:

For a discussion of periodical indexes, see p. 727.

Home schooling
Do children have to go to school? [Great Britain] C. Henson. *Child Educ (Engl)* v73 p68 Mr '96
Homegrown learning [Twin Ridges Elementary School District combines homeschooling with regular classroom instruction] D. Hill. il *Teach Mag* v7 p40-5 Ap '96
Should we open extracurriculars to home-schoolers? J. Watford; B. Dickinson. il *Am Teach* v80 p4 Mr '96

This entry lists articles that address different aspects of home schooling, briefly describing some of the articles. You can see that the first article deals with the issue from a British point of view, which might provide an interesting cross-cultural perspective for your essay. The title of the third article seems to indicate an argument on the issue; because it appears in a magazine for teachers, it might give you a sense of that profession's attitudes toward home schooling. Be careful, though, to stay focused on your specific research topic or thesis, especially if you are pressed for time and cannot afford to become distracted exploring sources that sound interesting but are unlikely to be useful.

In addition, each entry contains the information that you will need to locate it in a library. Going back to the first article, here is what each piece of information means.

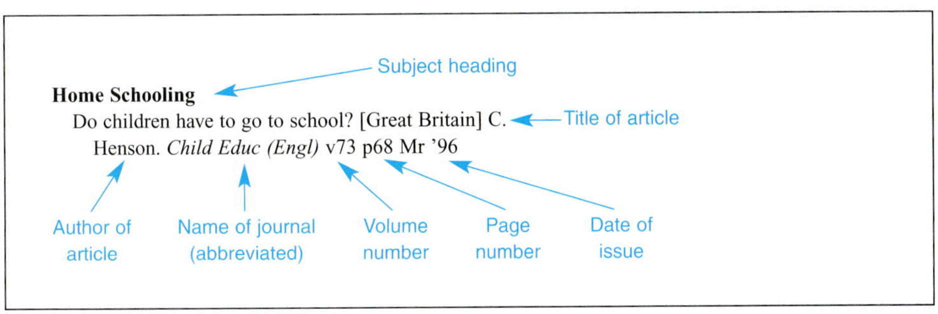

When you look in catalogs and indexes, consider the following points when deciding whether you should track down a particular source:

- ***Relevance to your topic:*** Do the title, subtitle, description, subject headings, and abstract help you determine how directly the particular source addresses your topic?

- ***Publication date:*** How recent is the source? For current controversies, emerging trends, and scientific or technological developments, you must consult recent material. For historical or biographical topics, you will want to start with present-day perspectives but eventually explore older sources that offer authoritative perspectives. You may also want or need to consult sources written at the time of the events or during the life of the person you are researching.
- ***Description:*** Does the length indicate a brief treatment of the topic or an extended treatment? Does the work include illustrations that may elaborate on concepts discussed in the text? Does it include a bibliography that could lead you to other works or an index that could give you an overview of what is discussed in the text? Does the abstract indicate the focus of the work?

From among the sources that look promising, select publications that seem by their titles to address different aspects of your topic or to approach it from different perspectives. Try to avoid selecting sources that are mostly by the same author, from the same publisher, or in the same journal. Common sense will lead you to an appropriate decision about diversity in source materials.

SEARCHING ONLINE LIBRARY CATALOGS AND DATABASES

Computerized library catalogs and other databases consist of thousands or millions of records, each representing an individual item such as a book, an article, or a government publication. The record is made up of different fields describing the item and allowing users to search for it and retrieve it from the database. Here is a record for a book from a library's online catalog, with the searchable fields in bold:

Author:	Gordon, William MacGuire, 1935–
Title:	The law of home schooling / William M. Gordon, Charles J. Russo, Albert S. Miles. Topeka, Kan.: National Organization on Legal Problems of Education, c1994.
Location:	Main
Call No:	JLL 74-383 no. 52
Description:	74 p.; 23 cm.
Series:	NOLPE monograph series no. 52.
Notes:	Includes bibliographical references and index.
Subjects:	Home schooling—Law and legislation—United States. Educational law and legislation—United States. Education—Parent participation—United States.
Other entries:	Russo, Charles J.

Using Different Search Techniques

Basic search strategies include author, title, and subject searches. When you request an **author search**, the computer looks for a match between the name you type and the names listed in the author field of all the records in the online catalog or other database. When you request a **title search** or a **subject search**, the computer looks for a match in the title field or the subject field, respectively. Computers are very literal. They try to match only the exact terms you enter, and most do not recognize variant or incorrect spellings. That is an incentive to become a good speller and a good typist. However, because most library catalogs and databases also offer the option of searching for titles and subjects by keywords, you need not enter the full exact title or subject heading. In addition, you can be flexible where the computer cannot. For instance, if you were researching the topic of home schooling, you could do a subject search not only for "home schooling" but also for "homeschooling" and "home-schooling." Table 21.2 on p. 724 describes some search capabilities commonly offered by library catalogs and databases.

Doing Advanced Searches and Using Boolean Operators

The real power of using an online catalog or other database is demonstrated when you need to look up books or articles using more than one keyword. For example, suppose you want information about home schooling in California. Rather than looking through an index listing all the articles on home schooling and picking out those that mention California, you can ask the computer to do the work for you by linking your two keywords. Many online catalogs and databases now offer the option of an **advanced search**, sometimes on a separate page from the main search page, that allows you to search for more than one keyword at a time, search for certain keywords while excluding others, or search for an exact phrase. Or you may be able to create this kind of advanced search yourself by using the **Boolean operators** AND, OR, and NOT along with quotation marks and parentheses.

To understand the operation of **Boolean logic** (developed by and named after George Boole, a nineteenth-century mathematician), picture one set of articles about home schooling and another set of articles about California. A third set is formed by articles that are about both home schooling and California. Figure 21.4 on p. 725 provides an illustration of how each Boolean operator works.

The search mechanisms for catalogs and databases usually require that the Boolean operators be typed in all capital letters. Some mechanisms use the plus sign (+) or the ampersand (&) instead of AND, the minus sign (–) instead of NOT, and the | sign instead of OR; check the Help page or home page for instructions if necessary.

You can also use quotation marks around a group of words to search for a phrase (with the words in the same order). And you can use parentheses to combine the Boolean operators: for example, *home schooling* NOT *(California* OR *Texas)* will retrieve all articles about home schooling except ones that mention California and ones that mention Texas.

Table 21.2 Common Search Capabilities Offered by Library Catalogs and Databases

Type of Search	*How the Computer Conducts the Search*	*Things to Know*
Author search (exact) • Individual (*Guterson, David*) • Organization (*U.S. Department of Education*)	Looks in the author field for the words entered	• Author searches generally are exact-match searches, so authors' names are entered *last name, first name* (for example, "Shakespeare, William"). If you enter "William Shakespeare," the computer will generate a list of authors whose last names are William. • Organizations can be considered authors. Enter the name of the organization in natural word order. • An exact-match author search is useful for finding books and articles by a particular author.
Title search (exact) • Book title • Magazine or journal title • Article title	Looks in the title field for words in the exact order you enter them	An exact-match title search is useful for identifying the location of known items, such as when you are looking for a particular journal or book.
Subject search (exact)	Looks in the subject heading or descriptor field for words in the exact order you enter them	An exact-match subject search is useful when you are sure about the subject heading.
Keyword search	Looks in the title, note, subject, abstract, and text fields for the words entered	A keyword search is the broadest kind you can use. It is useful during early exploration of a subject.
Title word search • Book title • Magazine or journal title • Article title	Looks in the title field of the record for the words entered and ignores word order	Since this is not an exact-match search, entering "home and schooling" will retrieve the same records as entering "schooling and home."
Subject word search	Looks in the subject heading or descriptor field of the record for the words entered and ignores word order	Since this is not an exact-match search, entering "education privatization" will retrieve the same records as "privatization education."

Using Truncation

Another useful search strategy employs **truncation**. With this technique, you drop the ending of a word or term and replace it with a symbol, which indicates you want to retrieve records containing any term that begins the same way as your term. For

AND

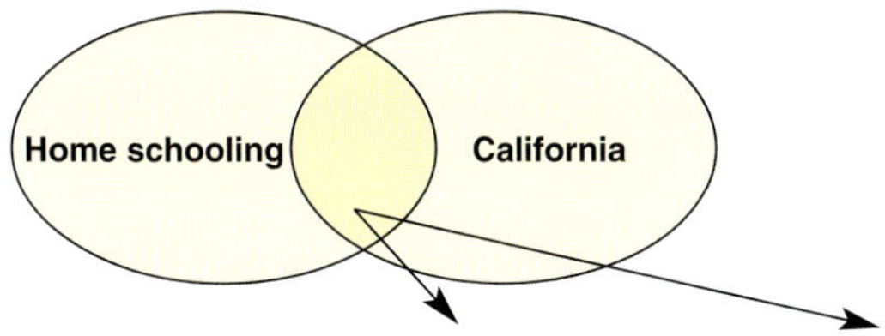

Returns references that contain both the term **home schooling** AND the term **California**

- Narrows the search
- Combines unrelated terms
- Is the default used by most online catalogs and databases

OR

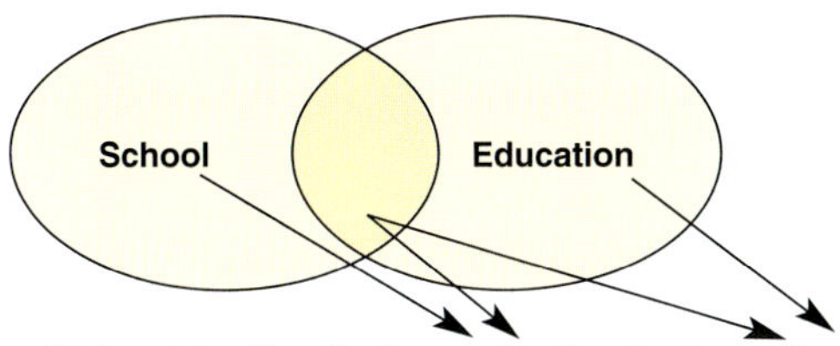

Returns all references that contain either the term **school** OR the term **education** OR both terms

- Broadens the search **("OR is more")**
- Is useful with synonyms and variant spellings: ("home schooling" and "homeschooling")

NOT

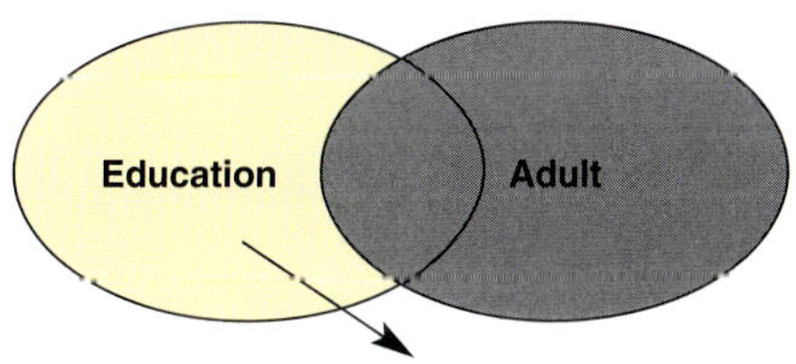

Returns references that include the term **education** but NOT the term **adult**

- Narrows the search
- May eliminate relevant material

Figure 21.4 The Boolean Operators: AND, OR, and NOT

example, by entering the term "home school#" you would retrieve all the records that have terms such as "home school," "home schooling," "home schools," "home schooled," or "home schoolers." Truncation is useful when you want to retrieve both the plural and singular forms of a word or any word for which you are not sure of the ending. Truncation symbols vary with the catalog or database. The question mark (?), asterisk (*), and pound sign (#) are frequently used.

Table 21.3 on p. 726 offers some suggestions for expanding or narrowing your electronic search.

Table 21.3 Electronic Search Tips

If You Find Too Many Sources on Your Topic:	*If You Find Insufficient Information on Your Topic:*
• Use a subject heading search instead of a keyword search. • Add a concept word to your search. • Use a more precise vocabulary to describe your topic.	• Use a keyword or title search instead of a subject heading search. • Eliminate unimportant words or secondary concepts from your search terms. • Try truncated forms of your keyword. • Use different words to describe your topic. • Check the spelling of each term you type.

LOCATING SOURCES

The following are guidelines for finding books, periodical articles, government documents and statistical information, and other types of sources.

Finding Books

Finding Books

1. Determine keywords or subject headings.
2. Enter terms in the online catalog.
3. Evaluate results.
4. Refine results if necessary.
5. Locate the books.

The primary source for books is the library's computerized catalog. Besides flexibly searching keywords and subject headings, the catalog may tell you whether a book is currently available or checked out. It also allows you to print out source information rather than having to copy the material by hand. However, the catalog will require correct spelling for searches and may contain only materials received and cataloged after a certain date.

Whether you search a library catalog by author, title, subject, or keyword, each record you find will provide the following standard information. You will need this information to enter the book in your working bibliography and to locate it in the library.

1. ***Call number:*** This number, which usually appears on a separate line in the computerized catalog record, is your key to finding the book in the library. Most college libraries use the Library of Congress call-number system, and most public libraries and some small college libraries use the Dewey system. The Library of Congress system uses both letters and numbers in the call number, and both are needed to locate a book. Call numbers serve two purposes: They provide an exact location for every book in the library, and because they are assigned according to subject classifications, they group together books on the same topic. When you go to the stacks to locate the book, therefore, always browse for other useful material on the shelves around it. Call numbers also give information about special collections of books kept in other library locations such as the reference room or government publications department. If the online catalog covers more than one library, the name of the library that has the book will also be included.

2. ***Author:*** The author's name usually appears last name first, followed by birth and death dates. For books with multiple authors, the record includes an author entry under each author's name.

Examples of records in online catalogs are shown on pp. 720 and 722.

3. ***Title:*** The title appears exactly as it does on the title page of the book, except that only the first word and proper nouns and adjectives are capitalized.
4. ***Publication information:*** The place of publication (usually just the city), the publisher, and the year of publication are listed. If the book was published simultaneously in the United States and abroad, both places of publication and both publishers are indicated.
5. ***Physical description:*** This section provides information about the book's page length and size. A roman numeral indicates the number of pages devoted to front matter (such as a preface, table of contents, and acknowledgments).
6. ***Notes:*** Any special features such as a bibliography or an index are listed here.
7. ***Subject headings:*** Assigned by the Library of Congress, these headings indicate how the book is listed in the subject catalog. They also provide useful links for finding other books on the same subject.

For more on the Library of Congress Subject Headings (LCSH), see pp. 719–20.

Finding Periodical Articles

The most up-to-date information on a subject is usually found not in books but in articles published in periodicals. A **periodical** is a publication such as a magazine, newspaper, or scholarly journal that is published on an ongoing basis, at regular intervals (for instance, daily, weekly, monthly, or annually), and with different content in each issue. Many print periodicals now publish online versions as well, although the contents may be somewhat different. In addition, some magazines and journals are published exclusively on the Web. Examples of periodicals include *Sports Illustrated* (magazine), the *New York Times* (newspaper), *Tulsa Studies in Women's Literature* (scholarly journal), *Kairos* (online journal), and *Slate* (online magazine).

Finding Periodical Articles

1. Select an appropriate periodical index or database.
2. Select a search option.
3. Display and evaluate the results of the search.
4. Refine your search strategy if necessary.
5. Interpret results to locate the articles.
6. Print, email, or download results for later use.

Articles in periodicals are usually not listed in the library catalog; to find them, you must use library reference works called **periodical indexes**. Some periodical indexes include **abstracts** or short summaries of articles. In the library, indexes may be available in print, in microform, on CD-ROM, through the computerized catalog, or as online databases. Many are available in both print and electronic formats, and some electronic indexes give you access to the full text of articles. Regardless of format, periodical indexes all serve the same basic function of leading the user to articles on a specific topic. If you understand how to use one, you will be able to use others.

Distinguishing Scholarly Journals and Popular Magazines

Although they are both called periodicals, journals and magazines have important differences. **Journals** publish articles written by experts in a particular field of study, frequently professors or researchers in academic institutions. Journals are usually specialized in their subject focus, research oriented, and extensively reviewed by specialists prior to publication. They are intended to be read by experts and students conducting research. **Magazines**, in contrast, usually publish general-interest articles written by journalists. The articles are written to entertain and educate the general public, and they tend to appeal to a much broader audience than journal articles.

Journals contain a great deal of what is called **primary literature**, reporting the results of original research. For example, a scientist might publish an article in a medical journal about the results of a new treatment protocol for breast cancer. **Secondary literature**, published in magazines, is intended to inform the general public about new and interesting developments in scientific and other areas of research. If a reporter from *Newsweek* writes an article about this scientist's cancer research, this article is classified as secondary literature. Table 21.4 summarizes some of the important differences between scholarly journals and popular magazines.

Selecting an Appropriate Periodical Index or Abstract

Periodical indexes and abstracts are of two types: general and specialized. Both provide you with information that will help you locate articles on a topic. In addition to the ones listed on pp. 729–32, check with a reference librarian to identify other indexes and abstracts that may be useful for your topic.

Table 21.4 How to Distinguish a Scholarly Journal from a Popular Magazine

Scholarly Journal	*Popular Magazine*
• The front or back cover lists the contents of the issue.	• The cover features a color picture.
• The title of the publication contains the word *Journal*.	• The title may be catchy as well as descriptive.
• You see the journal only at the library.	• You see the magazine for sale at the grocery store, in an airport, or at a bookstore.
• It does not include advertisements or advertises products such as textbooks, professional books, or scholarly conferences.	• It has lots of colorful advertisements in it.
• The authors of articles have *Ph.D.* or academic affiliations after their names.	• The authors of articles are journalists or reporters.
• Many articles have more than one author.	• Most articles have a single author but may quote experts.
• A short summary (abstract) of an article may appear on the first page.	• A headline or engaging description may precede the article.
• Most articles are fairly long, 5 to 20 pages.	• Most of the articles are fairly short, 1 to 5 pages.
• The articles may include charts, tables, figures, and quotations from other scholarly sources.	• The articles have color pictures and sidebar boxes.
• The articles have a bibliography (list of references to other books and articles) at the end.	• The articles do not include a bibliography.
• You probably would not read it at the beach.	• You might bring it to the beach to read.

General Indexes. These indexes are a good place to start your research because they cover a broad range of subjects. Most have separate author and subject listings as well as a list of book reviews. General indexes usually list only articles from popular magazines and newspapers, although some of them include listings from basic scholarly journals. Here is a list of the most common general indexes:

The Readers' Guide to Periodical Literature (1900–; online, 1983–; updated quarterly): Covers about two hundred popular periodicals and may help you launch your search for sources on general and current topics. Even for general topics, however, you should not rely on it exclusively. Nearly all college libraries house far more than two hundred periodicals, and university research libraries house twenty thousand or more. The *Readers' Guide* does not even attempt to cover the research journals that play such an important role in college writing. Here is an example of an entry for home education:

HOME EDUCATION
Home-school kids in public-school activities. D. Brockett. *The Education Digest* v61 p67–9 N '95
Pros and cons of home schooling. il *Parents* v70 p18 N '95
Why homeschooling is important for America [address, August 11, 1995] S. L. Blumenfeld. *Vital Speeches of the Day* v61 p763–6 O 1 '95

Magazine Index (on microfilm, 1988–; online as part of InfoTrac, 1973–; see below): Indexes over four hundred magazines.

InfoTrac (online): Time coverage varies by subscription. Includes three indexes: (1) the *General Periodicals Index,* which covers over twelve hundred general-interest publications, incorporating the *Magazine Index* and including the *New York Times* and the *Wall Street Journal*; (2) the *Academic Index,* which covers four hundred scholarly and general-interest publications, including the *New York Times*; and (3) the *National Newspaper Index,* which covers the *Christian Science Monitor, Los Angeles Times, New York Times, Wall Street Journal,* and *Washington Post.* Some entries also include abstracts of articles. This sample InfoTrac entry is from the *General Periodicals Index*:

```
AUTHOR(s):     Hawkins, Dana
TITLE(s):      Homeschool battles: clashes grow as some in the movement seek access
                 to public schools.
               illustration photograph

Summary:       An estimated 500,000 students in the US study at home, and there is an
                 increasing tension in some communities as some of the 'homeschoolers'
                 attempt to use the public schools on a limited basis. The parents of one
                 homeschooler in Oklahoma have sued the school district to gain access.

               U.S. News & World Report
               p57(2)
               Feb 12  1996  v120  n6

DESCRIPTORS:   Home schooling_Cases
               Public schools_Cases
               Education_Parent participation

more follows -- press <RETURN>  (Q to quit)
```

Alternative Press Index (1970–; online through Biblioline): Indexes alternative and radical publications.

Humanities Index (1974–; online, 1984–): Covers more than five hundred periodicals in archaeology, history, classics, literature, performing arts, philosophy, and religion.

Social Sciences Index (1974–; online, 1983–): Covers more than five hundred periodicals in economics, geography, law, political science, psychology, public administration, and sociology. The complete text of certain articles is available on the CD-ROM.

Public Affairs Information Service Bulletin (1915–; online, 1972–): Covers articles and other publications by public and private agencies on economic and social conditions, international relations, and public administration. Subject listings only.

Specialized Indexes and Abstracts. These publications list or summarize articles devoted to technical or scholarly research. As you learn more about your topic, you will turn to specialized indexes and abstracts to find references to scholarly articles. The following example from *Sociological Abstracts,* which indexes and summarizes articles from a wide range of periodicals that publish sociological research, is typical of entries found in specialized indexes:

> **91X2727**
> **Mayberry, Maralee & Knowles, J. Gary** (Dept Sociology U Nevada, Las Vegas 89154), **Family Unity Objectives of Parents Who Teach Their Children: Ideological and Pedagogical Orientations to Home Schooling,** UM *The Urban Review,* 1989, 21, 4, Dec, 209–225.
> ¶ The objectives of parents who teach their children at home are examined, using results from 2 qualitative studies: (1) a study conducted in Ore in 1987/88, consisting of interview & questionnaire data (N = 15 & 800 families, respectively); & (2) an ongoing ethnographic study being conducted in Utah (N = 8 families). Analysis suggests that while families have complex motives for teaching their children at home, most respondents felt that establishing a home school would allow them to maintain or further develop unity within the family. It is concluded that a family's decision to home school is often made in an attempt to resist the effects on the family unit of urbanization & modernization. Policy implications are discussed. 36 References. Adapted from the source document. (Copyright 1991, Sociological Abstracts, Inc., all rights reserved.)

When you compare this entry with the previous citations from the *Readers' Guide* and InfoTrac's *General Periodicals Index* (p. 729), you will see differences in the following features:

- The format of the citations
- The authors' qualifications
- The titles of the articles
- The titles of the publications where the articles appear

- The length of the articles
- The amount of information given about the content of the articles

Here is a list of specialized periodical indexes that cover various disciplines:

ABI/INFORM (1971–; online)
Accounting and Tax Index (1964–; online)
America: History and Life (1954–; CD-ROM, 1964–)
American Statistics Index (1973–)
Applied Science and Technology Index (1958–; online)
Art Index (1929–; online, 1983–)
Biological and Agricultural Index (1964–; online, 1983–)
Education Index (1929–; online, 1983–)
Engineering Index (1920–)
Historical Abstracts (1955–; online, 1982–)
Index Medicus (1961–; online as MEDLINE)
MLA International Bibliography of Books and Articles in the Modern Languages and Literature (1921–; online)
Music Index (1949–; online, 1981–)
Philosopher's Index (1957–; online)
Physics Abstracts (1898; online as INSPEC)
Psychological Abstracts (1927; online as PsycINFO; CD-ROM as PsycLIT)
Science Abstracts (1898)
Sociological Abstracts (1952; online as Sociofile)

Most periodical indexes and abstracts use their own system of subject headings. The print version of *Sociological Abstracts,* for example, has a separate volume for subject headings. Check the opening pages or, for an electronic index or abstract, the opening screen or home page to see how subjects are classified. Then look for periodicals or articles under your most useful subject heading from the LCSH or the heading that seems most similar to it. If you are using an electronic index, the items in the subject heading field for particular articles may function as links to lists of related materials.

Indexes to Periodicals Representing Particular Viewpoints. Some specialized periodical indexes tend to represent particular viewpoints and may help you identify different positions on an issue.

Chicano Index (1967–): An index to general and scholarly articles about Mexican Americans. Articles are arranged by subject with author and title indexes. (Before 1989, the title was *Chicano Periodical Index.*)

G. K. Hall Index to Black Periodicals (1999–); previously published as *Index to Black Periodicals* (1984–1998): An author and subject index to general and scholarly articles about African Americans.

Left Index (1982–; online only, 2000–): An author and subject index to over eighty periodicals with a Marxist, radical, or left perspective. Listings cover primarily topics in the social sciences and humanities.

Another useful source for identifying positions is *Editorials on File,* described on p. 735.

Full-Text Electronic Services. In addition to the electronic indexes and abstracts listed earlier, many libraries subscribe to other electronic database services that provide the full text of articles, often in particular subject areas. The text is available either in the database itself (so you can see it onscreen and download it or print it out) or by mail or fax for a fee. Subscriptions to these services tend to be expensive, so they may not be available in small college libraries, and the articles available may be limited to those in recent issues. Nevertheless, be sure to check with a librarian about what is available at your library. Some of these services include the following:

ERIC (Educational Resources Information Center) (online, 1966–): Indexes, abstracts, and provides some full texts of articles from 750 education journals.

Business Periodicals Ondisc (1988–) and ***ABI/INFORM*** (1988–): Provide full-text articles from business periodicals that can be printed on your library's laser printer.

PsycBooks (1987–): A CD-ROM database that indexes books and book chapters in psychology.

Ingenta (1998–; http://www.ingenta.com): An online document delivery service that lists articles from more than 5,400 online journals and 26,000 other publications. For a fee, you can receive the full text of the article, online or by fax.

LEXIS-NEXIS Academic Universe (time coverage varies by source; http://www.lexis-nexis.com/lncc/academic): Provides the full text of articles from academic journals and other sources containing legal, news, and government information and statistics.

JSTOR (http://www.jstor.org): Provides the full text of articles from older issues of more than three hundred journals in the humanities and social sciences.

Project Muse (1996–; http://muse.jhu.edu): Provides the full text of articles from more than two hundred journals in the humanities, social sciences, and mathematics from Johns Hopkins University Press and selected not-for-profit publishers.

Science Direct (1997–; http://www.sciencedirect.com): Provides the full text of articles from more than a thousand journals in science, technology, medicine, and the social sciences from Elsevier Press.

Interlibrary networks: Known by different names in different regions, these networks allow you to search in the catalogs of colleges and universities in your area and across the country. In many cases, you can request a book by interlibrary loan, although it may take several weeks to be delivered to your library. You can also request a copy of an article from a journal to which your own library does not subscribe. Most libraries do not lend their journals but will copy and forward articles for a fee.

Searching Electronic Periodical Databases

Although you can search an electronic periodical database by author or title, you will probably more often want to do subject searches using keywords. As with subject searches for books in the library catalog, make your keywords as precise as possible so that your search results in a manageable list of sources relevant to your topic. Most databases include a thesaurus of keywords and an advanced-search mechanism or set of guidelines for using Boolean operators or other keyword-combining procedures. In addition, many databases include a browse function. When you enter a keyword, this function automatically lists the terms that are close to the keyword alphabetically. If you enter a very general keyword, the function provides a list of subtopics that you can use to narrow your search before you ask the system to retrieve records.

Once you have typed your keywords, the computer searches the database and lists every reference to them that it finds. You can usually print the results or download the records to your own disk. Because online databases contain so much information, you may want to consult with a librarian to develop an efficient search strategy. Also keep in mind that most electronic indexes cover only the last ten to fifteen years; you may need to consult older printed versions of indexes as well.

Locating Periodicals in the Library

When you identify a promising magazine or journal article in a periodical index, you must go to the library's online catalog or periodicals database to learn whether the library subscribes to the periodical, whether the article is available in print or electronic form or both, and where you can find the magazine or journal issue you need. No library can subscribe to every periodical, so as you go through indexes and abstracts, be sure to identify more articles than you actually need. This will save you from having to repeat your catalog or database search later when you find out that your library does not subscribe to some of the magazines or journals that contain your possible sources.

Although every library arranges its print periodicals differently, recent issues are usually arranged alphabetically by title on open shelves. Older issues may be bound like books (shelved by call numbers or alphabetically by title) or filmed and available in microform. Ask a librarian at the reference desk how the periodicals in your library are arranged.

Suppose you want to look up an article on home schooling from the journal *Urban Review* that you found indexed in *Sociological Abstracts* (see p. 730). Here is a typical record for *Urban Review* from a library's online catalog or periodicals database. Notice that the title search refers to the title of the journal, not the title of the article.

You searched TITLE **Urban Review**

Title:	The Urban review	← Title of the journal
Imprint:	New York, Agathon Press [etc.]	← Where the journal is published
LOCATION:	MAIN-Latest in Curr Per	↓ Library where the journal is located and location of current (unbound) issues
	LC 5101 U75	← Call number
LIB. HAS:	B16-30(1984-98)	← Bound volumes and years the library owns
Latest Received:	June 1999 31:2	← Most recent issue received

In this instance, you would learn that the library does subscribe to *Urban Review* and that you could locate the 1989 article in one of the bound volumes in the library's collection.

Finding Newspaper Articles and Other News Sources

Newspapers provide useful information for many research topics in such areas as foreign affairs, economics, public opinion, and social trends. Libraries usually photograph newspapers and store them in miniature form on microfilm (reels) or microfiche (cards) that must be placed in viewing machines to be read. Newspaper indexes such as the *Los Angeles Times Index, New York Times Index,* and *London Times Index,* which are available online as well as in print, can help you locate specific articles on your topic. College libraries usually have indexes to local newspapers as well.

Your library may also subscribe to newspaper article and digest services, such as the following:

National Newspaper Index (microfilm, 1989–; online as part of InfoTrac, 1979–) (see p. 729): Indexes the *Christian Science Monitor, Los Angeles Times, New York Times, Wall Street Journal,* and *Washington Post*

NewsBank (microfiche and CD-ROM, 1970–): Full-text articles from five hundred U.S. newspapers; a good source of information on local and regional issues and trends

Newspaper Abstracts (1988–; online, 1989–): Indexes and gives brief abstracts of articles from nineteen major regional, national, and international newspapers

Facts on File (weekly; CD-ROM, 1980): A digest of U.S. and international news events arranged by subject, such as foreign affairs, arts, education, religion, and sports

Editorials on File (twice monthly): A digest of editorials from 150 U.S. and Canadian newspapers with brief descriptions of editorial subjects followed by fifteen to twenty editorials on the subject, reprinted from different newspapers

CQ Researcher (1991–; previously published since 1924 as Editorial Research Reports): Reports on current and controversial topics, including brief histories, statistics, editorials, journal articles, endnotes, and supplementary reading lists

Foreign Broadcast Information Service (FBIS) (1980–; online, 1990–): A digest of foreign broadcast scripts, newspaper articles, and government statements from Asia, Europe, Latin America, Africa, Russia, and the Middle East

Keesing's Record of World Events (1931–; also online): A monthly digest of events in all countries, compiled from British and other reporting services; includes speeches and statistics and chronological, geographic, and topical indexes

Finding Government and Statistical Information

Although college libraries still maintain large collections of print publications by government agencies, federal, state, and local governments are making many of their publications and reference services available through the World Wide Web. Ask a reference librarian for assistance in locating governmental sources in the library or on the Web. In particular, consider consulting the following sources for information on political subjects and national trends. Although these publications are not always listed in library catalogs or databases, they can usually be found in the reference area or the government documents department of college libraries. If these works are not listed in your library's catalog, ask for assistance in locating them.

Sources for Researching Political Subjects. Two publications that report developments in the federal government can be rich sources of information on political issues. Types of material they cover include congressional hearings and debates, presidential proclamations and speeches, U.S. Supreme Court decisions and dissenting opinions, and compilations of statistics.

Congressional Quarterly Almanac (annual): A summary of legislation that provides an overview of government policies and trends, including analysis as well as election results, records of roll-call votes, and the text of significant speeches and debates

CQ Weekly (online, 1998–; formerly published as *Congressional Quarterly Weekly Report*): A news service that includes up-to-date summaries of congressional committee actions, congressional votes, and executive branch activities as well as overviews of current policy discussions and other activities of the federal government

For guidance on developing an argument that speculates about the causes of a trend, see Chapter 9.

Sources for Researching Trends. Research can help you identify trends to write about and, most important, provide the statistical evidence you need to demonstrate the existence of a trend. The following resources can be especially helpful:

> ***Statistical Abstract of the United States*** (annual; some content online, http://www.census.gov/statab/www): A publication of the Bureau of the Census that provides a variety of social, economic, and political statistics, often covering several years, including tables, graphs, charts, and references to additional sources of information
>
> ***American Statistics Index*** (1974–; annual with monthly supplements): Attempts to cover all federal government publications containing statistical information of research significance and includes brief descriptions of references
>
> ***Statistical Reference Index*** (1980–): A selective guide to American statistical publications from sources other than the U.S. government, including economic, social, and political statistical sources
>
> ***World Almanac and Book of Facts*** (annual): Presents information on a variety of subjects drawn from many sources, including a chronology of the year, climatological data, and lists of inventions and awards
>
> ***The Gallup Poll: Public Opinion*** (1935–): A chronological listing of the results of public opinion polls, including information on social, economic, and political trends

In addition to researching the trend itself, you may want to research others' speculations about its causes. If so, the reports of federal government activities described in the preceding section may be helpful.

Finding Other Library Sources

Libraries hold vast amounts of useful materials other than books, periodicals, and government documents. Some of the following library sources and services may be appropriate for your research.

- ***Vertical files:*** Pamphlets and brochures from government and private agencies
- ***Special collections:*** Manuscripts, rare books, and materials of local interest
- ***Audio collections:*** Records, audiotapes, music CDs, readings, and speeches
- ***Video collections:*** Slides, filmstrips, videotapes, and DVDs
- ***Art collections:*** Drawings, paintings, and engravings
- ***Interlibrary loans:*** As noted above, many libraries can arrange to borrow books from other libraries or have copies of journal articles sent from other libraries as part of an interlibrary network program. Ask your librarian how long it will take to get the material you need (usually several weeks) and how to use the loan service (some libraries allow you to send an electronic request to the local interlibrary loan office).

- *Computer resources:* Interactive computer programs that combine text, video, and audio resources in history, literature, business, and other disciplines

USING THE INTERNET FOR RESEARCH

The **Internet** is a vast global computer network that enables users to store and share information quickly and easily. The **World Wide Web** is a network of sites on the Internet, each with its own **electronic address** (called a **URL**, or **uniform resource locator**). You can gain access to the Internet through your library or campus computer system or at home through a commercial **Internet service provider (ISP)**. To search the Web, you also need a **Web browser** such as Netscape or Internet Explorer. By now, most of you are familiar with searching the Internet. This section provides some basic background information about the Net and introduces you to some tools and strategies that will help you use it more efficiently to find information on a topic.

As you use the Internet for conducting research, keep the following concerns and guidelines in mind:

- ***The Internet has no central system of organization.*** On the Internet, a huge amount of information is stored on many different networks and servers and in many different formats, each with its own system of organization. The Internet has no central catalog, reference librarian, or standard classification system for the vast resources available there.
- ***Many electronic sources are not part of the Internet or require a paid subscription or other fees.*** Computerized library catalogs, electronic periodical indexes, full-text article databases, and other electronic resources are often stored on CD ROMs or on campus computer networks rather than on the Internet and so are available to students only through the library or other campus computers. Furthermore, some databases on the Web charge for a subscription or for downloading or printing out content. For these reasons (as well as the one discussed below), you should plan to use the library or campus computer system for much of your electronic research, since it will give you access to more material at a lower cost. You will not need to pay for subscriptions, and you may be able to download or print out material for free as well.
- ***Internet sources that you find on your own are generally less reliable than print sources or than electronic sources to which your library or campus subscribes.*** Because it is relatively easy for anyone to publish on the Internet, judging the reliability of online information is a special concern. Depending on your topic, purpose, and audience, the sources you find on the Internet may not be as credible or authoritative as print sources or subscription electronic sources, which have usually been screened by publishers, editors, librarians, and authorities on the topic. For some topics, most of what you find on the Internet may be written by highly biased or amateur authors, so you will need to balance or supplement these sources with information from your library or campus and print

sources. When in doubt about the reliability of an online source for a particular assignment, check with your instructor. (See Reading Sources with a Critical Eye on pp. 744–46 for more specific suggestions.)

- ***Internet sources are not as stable as print sources or as the electronic sources to which your library or campus subscribes.*** A Web site that existed last week may no longer be available today, or its content may have changed.
- ***Internet sources must be documented, and so you need to include them in your working bibliography.*** A working bibliography is an ongoing record of all the possible sources you discover as you research your subject. The working bibliography becomes the draft for the list of references or works cited at the end of your essay, even if you do not include all these sources in your final list. You will need to follow appropriate conventions for quoting, paraphrasing, summarizing, and documenting the online sources you use, just as you do for print sources. Because an Internet source can change or disappear quickly, be sure to record the infor-

Citing Internet sources using MLA style is discussed in Chapter 22, p. 767; APA style is discussed on p. 777.

As you locate potentially useful Internet sources, record this information (as much as applies) for each site:

Author(s) of work: ____________________

Title of work: ____________________

Title of site: ____________________

Editor(s) of site: ____________________

Sponsor of site: ____________________

Publication information for print version of work: ____________________

Range or total number of pages, paragraphs, screens, or other sections of the work, if numbering appears on screen: ____________________

Name of database and online service: ____________________

Date of electronic publication or latest update: ____________________

Date you accessed the source: ____________________

Electronic address (URL): ____________________

Keyword(s) or sequence of links you used to access the source: ____________________

____

Figure 21.5 Information for Working Bibliography—Internet Sources

mation for the working-bibliography entry when you first find the source. Whenever possible, download and print out the source to preserve it. Make sure your download or printout includes all the items of information required for the entry or at least all those you can find. Citation forms for Internet sources typically require more information than those for print sources, but the items are often harder (or impossible) to identify because Internet sources do not appear in the kinds of standard formats that print sources do. (See Figure 21.5 for an example of how to organize bibliographic information for an Internet source.)

NAVIGATING THE WEB

A **Web browser** is a software program that allows you to display and navigate Web pages on your computer. Web browsers have evolved from basic text-driven browsers such as Lynx into graphical, point-and-click interfaces such as Netscape Navigator and Microsoft Internet Explorer, which support not only text and hypertext links but also sound, images, animation, and video.

Understanding Home Pages

A particular Web site usually consists of multiple screens, or pages: a home page and other pages to which it is electronically linked. The **home page** is what you most often see first when you access a Web site; it typically provides a title heading, a brief introduction to or overview of the site, and a brief table of contents consisting of links to the information available at the site. In this way, it is like the opening pages of a book. Figure 21.6 on p. 740 shows the home page for *Home Education Magazine.* Web sites may be sponsored by companies, educational institutions, government agencies, private organizations, or individuals. The bottom of a home page usually includes the name of the group or person responsible for the site and an email address or other information about how to contact the sponsor or editor.

Using Links

On a Web page (and in other electronic documents, such as email), **links** to other pages, to other text on the same page, or to other Web sites are often indicated by underlined or boldface text. For example, the *Home Education Magazine* home page provides links to an online newsletter, a resource guide, and other material related to home schooling. Links can also appear as boxes, buttons, icons, or other graphic images. Each Web site has its own scheme for organizing and identifying links. In addition to sending your browser to another Web address, the links on a Web site can perform many other functions. For example, they may open a form to be filled out by the reader, start a video, play music or sounds, or launch a preaddressed email composition window.

Figure 21.6 Home Page for *Home Education Magazine*

Understanding URLs

Each Web page has its own address, called a **uniform resource locator** or **URL**, which allows people anywhere in the world to locate a particular Web page. The URL for the National Home Education Network follows the typical pattern: http://www.nhen.org.

- The first part of a URL usually consists of the abbreviation *http://* (meaning **hypertext transfer protocol**); it tells the sending and receiving computers how to transfer the information being sent.
- The second part of the URL usually includes the standard *www.*, to establish that the location being accessed is on the World Wide Web, and then identifies the institution, government agency, corporation, or organization that owns or sponsors the site. For example, home-ed-magazine.com indicates that the site is sponsored by *Home Education Magazine*. The three-letter suffix at the end of this part identifies what kind of site it is.

  .com = commercial site
  .edu = educational institution site
  .gov = government site
  .org = organization site
  .mil = military site
  .net = Internet service site

  If the owner or sponsor of the site is outside the United States, this part of the URL will also include a two-letter code indicating the country, such as *.ca* for Canada or *.uk* for the United Kingdom.
- Many URLs have a third part, which may be lengthy, identifying the part of the site where the page is found or the kind of computer language it is written in (as in *wlcm_hemnewsltr.html* for the *Home Education Magazine* newsletter).

When you type a URL into an address box to access a site, you generally need to follow the exact spacing and punctuation of the site's address. Sometimes, though, a browser or a site will not require the *http://* or the *www.* or will require that you omit them.

Creating Bookmarks

You can store the addresses of Web pages that you may want to visit again by creating **bookmarks** for them. In Netscape, you do this by clicking on a Bookmark button; in Internet Explorer, you click on Favorites and then on Add to Favorites. This stores the name of the page in a list that you can click on whenever you want to revisit the page. If you are not using your own computer, you will need to download your bookmarks onto a disk or email them to yourself to save them.

USING SEARCH TOOLS

Because the World Wide Web does not have a central directory that will point you to specific resources, **search tools** are important resources for searching the Web for information on your topic. Table 21.5 lists some of the most popular search tools. To use these tools effectively, you should understand their features, strengths, and limitations.

Most search tools now allow you to look for sources using both search engines and subject directories. **Search engines** are based on keywords. They are simply computer programs that scan the Web—or that part of the Web that is in the particular search engine's database—looking for the keyword(s) you have entered. **Subject directories** are based on categories, like the subject headings in a library catalog or periodical index. Beginning with a menu of general subjects, you click on increasingly narrow subjects (for example, going from Science to Biology to Genetics to DNA Mapping), until you reach either a list of specific Web sites or a point where you have to do a keyword search within the narrowest subject you have chosen. Search engines are useful whenever you have a good idea of the appropriate keywords for your topic or if you are not sure under what category the topic falls. But subject directories can help quickly narrow your search to those parts of the Web that are likely to be most productive and thus avoid keyword searches that produce hundreds or thousands of results.

Always click on the link called Help, Hints, or Tips on a search tool's home page to find out more about the recognized commands and advanced-search techniques for that specific search tool. Most search engines either allow searches using the Boolean operators discussed on pp. 723–26 or incorporate Boolean logic into an advanced-search page. Many also let you limit a search to specific dates, languages, or other criteria.

Table 21.5 Commonly Used Search Tools

Name	*URL*
Search Tools	
All the Web	http://www.alltheweb.com
AltaVista	http://www.altavista.com
Excite	http://www.excite.com
Google	http://www.google.com
HotBot	http://www.hotbot.com
Lycos	http://www.lycos.com
Teoma	http://www.teoma.com
Yahoo!	http://www.yahoo.com
Metasearch Tools (search multiple search engines and subject directories)	
Ixquick	http://www.ixquick.com
WebCrawler	http://www.webcrawler.com
ProFusion	http://www.profusion.com
Zworks	http://www.zworks.com

As with searches of library catalogs and databases, the success of a Web search depends to a great extent on the keywords you choose. Remember that many different words often describe the same topic. If your topic is ecology, for example, you may find information under the keywords *ecosystem, environment, pollution,* and *endangered species,* as well as a number of other related keywords, depending on the focus of your research. When you find a source that seems promising, be sure to create a bookmark for the Web page so that you can return to it easily later on.

USING EMAIL AND ONLINE COMMUNITIES FOR RESEARCH

You may find it possible to use your computer to do research in ways other than those already discussed in this chapter. In particular, if you can find out the email address of an expert on your topic, you may want to contact the person and ask whether he or she would agree to a brief online (or telephone) interview. In addition, several kinds of electronic communities available on the Internet may possibly be helpful. Many Web sites consist of or incorporate tools known as **bulletin boards** or **message boards**, in which anyone who registers may post messages to and receive them from other members. Older Internet servers known as news servers also provide access to bulletin boards or variants called **newsgroups**. Another kind of community, **mailing lists**, are groups of people who subscribe to receive email messages shared among all the members simultaneously. Finally, **chat rooms** allow users to meet together at the same time in a shared message space, using either a Web-based or generally available chat software application.

These different kinds of online communities often focus on a specific field of shared interest, and the people who frequent them are sometimes working professionals or academics with expertise in topics that are obscure or difficult to research otherwise. Such experts are often willing to answer both basic and advanced questions and will sometimes consent to an email or telephone interview. Even if they are not authorities in the field, online community members may stimulate your thinking about the topic in new directions or save you a large amount of research time by pointing you to a range of other available resources that might otherwise have taken you quite a while to uncover. Many communities provide some kind of indexing or search mechanism so that you can look for "threads" of postings related to your topic.

As with other sources, however, evaluate the credibility and reliability of online communities with a critical eye. Also be aware that while some communities and some members of them welcome guests and newcomers, others may perceive your questions as intrusive or unwanted. What may seem new and exciting to you may be old news for veterans. Finally, remember that some online communities are more active than others; survey the dates of posts and frequency of activity to determine whether a given group is still lively or has gone defunct.

You can probably access a variety of Usenet newsgroups related to your topic through your college library; go to www.groups.google.com to find a list. For mailing lists, you have to register for a subscription to the list. Remember that each subscription means you will be receiving a large amount of email, so think about the implications before you sign up.

READING SOURCES WITH A CRITICAL EYE

From the beginning of your search, you should evaluate potential sources to determine which ones you should take the time to examine more closely and then which of these you should use in your essay. Obviously, you must decide which sources provide information relevant to the topic. But you must also read sources with a critical eye to decide how credible or trustworthy they are. Just because a book or an essay appears in print or online does not necessarily mean that an author's information or opinions are reliable.

Selecting Relevant Sources

Begin your evaluation of sources by narrowing your working bibliography to the most relevant works. Consider them in terms of scope, date of publication, and viewpoint.

Scope and Approach. To decide how relevant a particular source is to your topic, you need to examine the source in depth. Do not depend on title alone, for it may be misleading. If the source is a book, check its table of contents and index to see how many pages are devoted to the precise subject you are exploring. In most cases, you will want an in-depth, not a superficial, treatment of the subject. Read the preface or introduction to a book or the abstract or opening paragraphs of an article and any biographical information given about the author to determine the author's basic approach to the subject or special way of looking at it. As you attend to these elements, consider the following questions:

- Does the source provide a general or specialized view? General sources are helpful early in your research, but then you need the authority or up-to-date coverage of specialized sources. Extremely specialized works, however, may be too technical.
- Is the source long enough to provide adequate detail?
- Is the source written for general readers? Specialists? Advocates? Critics?
- Is the author an expert on the topic? Does the author's way of looking at the topic support or challenge your own views? (The fact that an author's viewpoint challenges your own does not mean that you should reject the author as a source, as you will see from the discussion on multiple viewpoints.)
- Is the information in the source substantiated elsewhere? Does its approach seem to be comparable to, or a significant challenge to, the approaches of other credible sources?

Date of Publication. Although you should always consult the most up-to-date sources available on your subject, older sources often establish the principles, theories, and data on which later work is based and may provide a useful perspective for evaluating it. If older works are considered authoritative, you may want to become familiar with them. To determine which sources are authoritative, note the ones that are cited most often in encyclopedia articles, bibliographies, and recent works on the subject. If your source is on the Web, consider whether it has been regularly updated.

Viewpoint. Your sources should represent a variety of viewpoints on the subject. Just as you would not depend on a single author for all of your information, so you do not want to use only authors who belong to the same school of thought. For suggestions on determining authors' viewpoints, see the following Identifying Bias section.

Using sources that represent different viewpoints is especially important when developing an argument for one of the essay assignments in Chapters 6–10. During the invention work in those chapters, you may want to research what others have said about your subject to see what positions have been staked out and what arguments have been made. You will then be able to define the issue more carefully, collect arguments supporting your position, and anticipate arguments opposing it.

Identifying Bias

One of the most important aspects of evaluating a source is identifying any bias in its treatment of the subject. Although the word *bias* may sound accusatory, most writing is not neutral or objective and does not try or claim to be. Authors come to their subjects with particular viewpoints. In using sources, you must consider carefully how these viewpoints are reflected in the writing and how they affect the way authors present their arguments.

Although the text of the source will give you the most precise indication of the author's viewpoint, you can often get a good idea of it by looking at the preface or introduction or at the sources the author cites. When you examine a reference, you can often determine the general point of view it represents by considering the following elements.

Title. Does the title or subtitle indicate the text's bias? Watch for loaded words or confrontational phrasing.

Author. What is the author's professional title or affiliation? What is the author's perspective? Is the author in favor of something or at odds with it? What has persuaded the author to take this stance? How might the author's professional affiliation affect his or her perspective? What is the author's tone? Information on the author may be available in the book, article, or Web site itself or in biographical sources available in the library. You could also try entering the author's name into a search engine and see what you learn from the sites it finds.

Presentation of Argument. Almost every written work asserts a point of view or makes an argument for something the author considers important. To determine this position and the reason behind it, look for the main point. What evidence does

For more detail on these argumentative strategies, see Chapter 19.

the author provide as support for this point? Is the evidence from authoritative sources? Is the evidence persuasive? Does the author make concessions to or refute opposing arguments?

Publication Information. Is the book published by a commercial publisher, a corporation, a government agency, or an interest group? Is the Web site sponsored by a business, a professional group, a private organization, an educational institution, a government agency, or an individual? What is the publisher's or sponsor's position on the topic? Is the author funded by or affiliated with the publisher or sponsor?

Editorial Slant. What kind of periodical published the article—popular, academic, alternative? If you found the article on a Web site, is the site maintained by a commercial or academic sponsor? Does the article provide links to other Web resources? For periodicals, knowing some background about the publisher can help to determine bias because all periodicals have their own editorial slants. Where the periodical's name does not indicate its bias, reference sources may help you determine this information. Two of the most common are the following:

> ***Gale Directory of Publications and Broadcast Media*** (1990–, updated yearly): A useful source for descriptive information on newspapers and magazines. Entries often include an indication of intended audience and political or other bias. For example, the *San Diego Union* is described as a newspaper with a Republican orientation.
>
> ***Magazines for Libraries*** (1997): A listing of over 6,500 periodicals arranged by academic discipline. For each discipline, this book lists basic indexes, abstracts, and periodicals. Each individual listing for a periodical includes its publisher, the date it was founded, the places it is indexed, its intended audience, and an evaluation of its content and editorial focus. Here is an example of one such listing:

> 2605. ***Growing Without Schooling.*** [ISSN: 0745-5305] 1977. bi-m. $25. Susannah Sheffer. Holt Assocs., 2269 Massachusetts Ave., Cambridge, MA 02140. Illus., index, adv. Sample. Circ: 5,000.
>
> *Bk. rev:* 0–4, 400–600 words, signed. *Aud:* Ga, Sa.
>
> *GWS* is a journal by and for home schoolers. Parents and students share their views as to why they chose home schooling and what they like about it. While lesson plans or activities are not included, home schoolers could get ideas for interesting activities from articles chronicling their experiences ("Helping Flood Victims," "Legislative Intern"). "News and Reports" offers home schoolers information on legal issues while the "Declassified Ads" suggest resources geared toward home schoolers. This is an important title for public libraries and should be available to students and faculty in teacher preparation programs.

22

Using and Acknowledging Sources

In addition to your own firsthand observation and analysis, your writing in college will be expected to use and acknowledge secondary sources—readings, interviews, Web sites, computer bulletin boards, lectures, and other print and nonprint materials.

When you cite material from another source, you need to acknowledge the source, usually by citing the author and page or date (depending on the documentation system) in your text and including a list of works cited or references at the end of your paper. It is necessary to acknowledge sources correctly and accurately to avoid *plagiarism*, the act of using the words and ideas of others as if they were your own. By citing sources correctly, you give credit to the originator of the words and ideas you are using, give your readers the information they need to consult those sources directly, and build your own credibility.

This chapter provides guidelines for using sources effectively and acknowledging them accurately. It includes model citations for both the Modern Language Association (MLA) and American Psychological Association (APA) documentation styles and presents a sample research paper that follows the MLA format.

USING SOURCES

Writers commonly use sources by quoting directly, by paraphrasing, and by summarizing. This section provides guidelines for deciding when to use each of these three methods and how to do so effectively.

Deciding Whether to Quote, Paraphrase, or Summarize

As a general rule, quote only in these situations: (1) when the wording of the source is particularly memorable or vivid or expresses a point so well that you cannot improve it without destroying the meaning, (2) when the words of reliable and respected authorities would lend support to your position, (3) when you wish to highlight the author's opinions, (4) when you wish to cite an author whose opinions challenge or vary greatly from those of other experts, or (5) when you are going to discuss the source's choice of words. Paraphrase passages whose details you wish to note completely but whose language is not particularly striking. Summarize any long passages whose main points you wish to record selectively as background or general support for a point you are making.

Quoting

Quotations should duplicate the source exactly. If the source has an error, copy it and add the notation *sic* (Latin for "thus") in brackets immediately after the error to indicate that it is not your error but your source's:

> According to a recent newspaper article, "Plagirism [sic] is a problem among journalists and scholars as well as students" (Berensen 62).

However, you can change quotations (1) to emphasize particular words by underlining or italicizing them, (2) to omit irrelevant information or to make the quotation conform grammatically to your sentence by using ellipsis marks, and (3) to make the quotation conform grammatically or to insert information by using brackets.

Using Underlining or Italicizing for Emphasis. You may underline or italicize any words in the quotation that you want to emphasize, and add the words *emphasis added* (in regular type, not italicized or underlined) in brackets immediately after the words you want to emphasize.

> In his introduction, Studs Terkel (1972) claims that his book is about a search for "daily meaning as well as daily bread, for recognition as well as cash, for astonishment rather than torpor [emphasis added]; in short, for a sort of life rather than a Monday through Friday sort of dying" (p. xi).

Using Ellipsis Marks for Omissions. A writer may decide to leave certain words out of a quotation because they are not relevant to the point being made or because they add information readers will not need in the context in which the quotation is being used. When you omit words from within a quotation, you must use ellipsis marks—three spaced periods (. . .)—in place of the missing words. When the omission occurs within a sentence, include a space before the first ellipsis mark and after the closing mark. There should also be spaces between the three marks.

> Hermione Roddice is described in Lawrence's *Women in Love* as a "woman of the new school, full of intellectuality and . . . nerve-worn with consciousness" (17).

When the omission falls at the end of a sentence, place a sentence period *directly after* the final word of the sentence, followed by a space and three spaced ellipsis marks.

> But Grimaldi's commentary contends that for Aristotle rhetoric, like dialectic, had "no limited and unique subject matter upon which it must be exercised. . . . Instead, rhetoric as an art transcends all specific disciplines and may be brought into play in them" (6).

A period plus ellipsis marks can indicate the omission of the rest of the sentence as well as whole sentences, paragraphs, or even pages.

When a parenthetical reference follows the ellipsis marks at the end of a sentence, place the three spaced periods after the quotation, and place the sentence period after the final parenthesis:

> But Grimaldi's recent commentary on Aristotle contends that for Aristotle rhetoric, like dialectic, had "no limited and unique subject matter upon which it must be exercised. . . . Instead, rhetoric as an art transcends all specific disciplines . . ." (6).

When you quote only single words or phrases, you do not need to use ellipsis marks because it will be obvious that you have left out some of the original.

> More specifically, Wharton's imagery of suffusing brightness transforms Undine before her glass into "some fabled creature whose home was in a beam of light" (21).

For the same reason, you need not use ellipsis marks if you omit the beginning of a quoted sentence unless the rest of the sentence begins with a capitalized word and still appears to be a complete sentence.

Using Brackets for Insertions or Changes. Use brackets around an insertion or a change needed to make a quotation conform grammatically to your sentence, such as a change in the form of a verb or pronoun or in the capitalization of the first word of the quotation. In this example from an essay on James Joyce's "Araby," reprinted in Chapter 10, the writer adapts Joyce's phrases "we played till our bodies glowed" and "shook music from the buckled harness" to fit the grammar of her sentences:

> In the dark, cold streets during the "short days of winter," the boys must generate their own heat by "play[ing] till [their] bodies glowed." Music is "[shaken] from the buckled harness" as if it were unnatural, and the singers in the market chant nasally of "the troubles in our native land" (30).

You may also use brackets to add or substitute explanatory material in a quotation:

> Guterson notes that among Native Americans in Florida, "education was in the home; learning by doing was reinforced by the myths and legends which repeated the basic value system of their [the Seminoles'] way of life" (159).

Some changes that make a quotation conform grammatically to another sentence may be made without any signal to readers: (1) A period at the end of a quotation may be changed to a comma if you are using the quotation within your own sentence, and (2) double quotation marks enclosing a quotation may be changed to single quotation marks when the quotation is enclosed within a longer quotation.

Integrating Quotations

Depending on its length, a quotation may be incorporated into your text by being enclosed in quotation marks or set off from your text in a block without quotation marks. In either case, be sure to blend the quotation into your essay rather than dropping it in without appropriate integration.

In-Text Quotations. Incorporate brief quotations (no more than four typed lines of prose or three lines of poetry) into your text. You may place the quotation virtually anywhere in your sentence:

At the Beginning

"To live a life is not to cross a field," Sutherland quotes Pasternak at the beginning of her narrative (11).

In the Middle

Woolf begins and ends by speaking of the need of the woman writer to have "money and a room of her own" (4)—an idea that certainly spoke to Plath's condition.

At the End

In *The Second Sex,* Simone de Beauvoir describes such an experience as one in which the girl "becomes as object, and she sees herself as object" (378).

Divided by Your Own Words

"Science usually prefers the literal to the nonliteral term," Kinneavy writes, "—that is, figures of speech are often out of place in science" (177).

When you quote poetry within your text, use a slash (/) with spaces before and after to signal the end of each line of verse:

Alluding to St. Augustine's distinction between the City of God and the Earthly City, Lowell writes that "much against my will / I left the City of God where it belongs" (4–5).

Block Quotations. In the MLA style, use the block form for prose quotations of five or more typed lines and poetry quotations of four or more lines. Indent the quotation an inch (ten character spaces) from the left margin, as shown in the following example. In the APA style, use block form for quotations of forty words or more. Indent the block quotation five to seven spaces, keeping your indents consistent throughout your paper.

In a block quotation, double-space between lines just as you do in your text. *Do not* enclose the passage within quotation marks. Use a colon to introduce a block quotation, unless the context calls for another punctuation mark or none at all. When quoting a single paragraph or part of one in the MLA style, do not indent the first line of the quotation more than the rest. In quoting two or more paragraphs, indent the first line of each paragraph an extra quarter inch (three spaces). If you are using the APA style, the first line of subsequent paragraphs in the block quotation indents an additional five to seven spaces from the block quotation indent.

In "A Literary Legacy from Dunbar to Baraka," Margaret Walker says of Paul Lawrence Dunbar's dialect poems:

> He realized that the white world in the United States tolerated his literary genius only because of

```
his "jingles in a broken tongue," and they found the
old "darky" tales and speech amusing and within the
vein of folklore into which they wished to classify
all Negro life. This troubled Dunbar because he
realized that white America was denigrating him as a
writer and as a man. (70)
```

Introducing Quotations

Statements that introduce quotations take a range of punctuation marks and lead-in words. Here are some examples of ways writers typically introduce quotations.

Introducing a Quotation Using a Colon

A colon usually follows an independent clause placed before the quotation.

> As George Williams notes, protection of white privilege is critical to patterns of discrimination: "Whenever a number of persons within a society have enjoyed for a considerable period of time certain opportunities for getting wealth, for exercising power and authority, and for successfully claiming prestige and social deference, there is a strong tendency for these people to feel that these benefits are theirs 'by right'" (727).

Introducing a Quotation Using a Comma

A comma usually follows an introduction that incorporates the quotation in its sentence structure.

> Similarly, Duncan Turner asserts, "As matters now stand, it is unwise to talk about communication without some understanding of Burke" (259).

Introducing a Quotation Using that

No punctuation is generally needed with *that,* and no capital letter is used to begin the quotation.

> Noting this failure, Alice Miller asserts that "the reason for her despair was not her suffering but the impossibility of communicating her suffering to another person" (255).

Punctuating within Quotations

Although punctuation within a quotation should reproduce the original, some adaptations may be necessary. Use single quotation marks for quotations within the quotation:

Original from Guterson (16–17)

> E. D. Hirsch also recognizes the connection between family and learning, suggesting in his discussion of family background and academic achievement "that the significant part of our children's education has been going on outside rather than inside the schools."

Quoted Version

Guterson claims that E. D. Hirsch "also recognizes the connection between family and learning, suggesting in his discussion of family background and academic achievement 'that the significant part of our children's education has been going on outside rather than inside the schools'" (16–17).

If the quotation ends with a question mark or an exclamation point, retain the original punctuation:

"Did you think I loved you?" Edith later asks Dombey (566).

If a quotation ending with a question mark or an exclamation point concludes your sentence, retain the question mark or exclamation point, and put the parenthetical reference and sentence period outside the quotation marks:

Edith later asks Dombey, "Did you think I loved you?" (566).

Avoiding Grammatical Tangles

When you incorporate quotations into your writing, and especially when you omit words from quotations, you run the risk of creating ungrammatical sentences. Three common errors you should try to avoid are verb incompatibility, ungrammatical omissions, and sentence fragments.

Verb Incompatibility. When this error occurs, the verb form in the introductory statement is grammatically incompatible with the verb form in the quotation. When your quotation has a verb form that does not fit in with your text, it is usually possible to use just part of the quotation, thus avoiding verb incompatibility.

he describes seeing himself

▶ **The narrator suggests his bitter disappointment when ~~"I saw myself~~ ^ " as a creature driven and derided by vanity" (35).**

As this sentence illustrates, use the present tense when you refer to events in a literary work.

Ungrammatical Omission. Sometimes omitting text from a quotation leaves you with an ungrammatical sentence. Two ways of correcting the grammar are (1) adapting the quotation (with brackets) so that its parts fit together grammatically and (2) using only one part of the quotation.

▶ **From the moment of the boy's arrival in Araby, the bazaar is presented as a commercial enterprise: "I could not find any sixpenny entrance and . . .**

hand[ed]

^ ~~handing~~ a shilling to a weary-looking man" (34).

▶ **From the moment of the boy's arrival in Araby, the bazaar is presented as a commercial enterprise: ~~"I~~** *He* **"could not find any sixpenny entrance" and ~~. . .~~** *so had to pay a shilling to get in (34).* **~~handing a shilling to a weary looking man" (34).~~**

Sentence Fragment. Sometimes when a quotation is a complete sentence, writers neglect the sentence that introduces the quote—for example, by forgetting to include a verb. Make sure that the quotation is introduced by a complete sentence.

▶ **The girl's interest in the bazaar ~~leading~~** *leads* **the narrator to make what amounts to a sacred oath: "If I go . . . I will bring you something" (32).**

Paraphrasing and Summarizing

In addition to quoting sources, writers have the option of paraphrasing or summarizing what others have written.

Paraphrasing. In a **paraphrase**, the writer restates primarily in his or her own words all the relevant information from a passage, without any additional comments or any suggestion of agreement or disagreement with the source's ideas. A paraphrase is useful for recording details of the passage when the order of the details is important but the source's wording is not. Because all the details of the passage are included, a paraphrase is often about the same length as the original passage. Paraphrasing allows you to avoid quoting too much. Anyway, it is better to paraphrase than to quote ordinary material, where the author's way of expressing things is not worth special attention.

Here is a passage from a book on home schooling and an example of an acceptable paraphrase of it:

Original Source

Bruner and the discovery theorists have also illuminated conditions that apparently pave the way for learning. It is significant that these conditions are unique to each learner, so unique, in fact, that in many cases classrooms can't provide them. Bruner also contends that the more one discovers information in a great variety of circumstances, the more likely one is to develop the inner categories required to organize that information. Yet life at school, which is for the most part generic and predictable, daily keeps many children from the great variety of circumstances they need to learn well.

–David Guterson, *Family Matters: Why Homeschooling Makes Sense,* p. 172

Acceptable Paraphrase

According to Guterson, the "discovery theorists," particularly Bruner, have found that there seem to be certain conditions that help learning to take place. Because each indi-

> vidual requires different conditions, many children are not able to learn in the classroom. According to Bruner, when people can explore information in many different situations, they learn to classify and order what they discover. The general routine of the school day, however, does not provide children with the diverse activities and situations that would allow them to learn these skills (172).

Readers assume that some words in a paraphrase are taken from the source. Indeed, it would be nearly impossible for paraphrasers to avoid using any key terms from the source, and it would be counterproductive to try to do so because the original and paraphrase necessarily share the same information and concepts. Notice, though, that of the total of 86 words in the paraphrase, the paraphraser uses only a name *(Bruner)* and a few other key nouns and verbs *(discovery theorists, conditions, children, learn[ing], information, situations)* for which it would be awkward to substitute other words or phrases. If the paraphraser had wanted to use other kinds of language from the source—for example, the description of life at school as "generic and predictable"—these adjectives should have been enclosed in quotation marks.

In fact, the paraphraser puts quotation marks around only one of the terms from the source: "discovery theorists," a technical term likely to be unfamiliar to readers. The source of all the material in the paraphrase is identified by the author's name *(Guterson)* in the first sentence and by the page number *(172)* in the last sentence, which indicates where the paraphrased material appears in David Guterson's book. This source citation follows the style of the Modern Language Association (MLA). Notice that placing the citation information in this way indicates clearly to readers where the paraphrase begins and ends, so that they understand clearly where the text is expressing ideas taken from a source and where it is expressing the writer's own ideas (or ideas from a different source). Should readers want to check the accuracy or completeness of the paraphrase, they could turn to the alphabetically arranged list of works cited at the end of the essay in which the paraphrase appeared, look for Guterson's name, and find there all the information they would need to locate the book and check the source.

Although it is acceptable and often necessary to reuse a few key words or quote striking or technical language, paraphrasers must avoid borrowing too many words from a source and repeating the sentence structures of a source. Here is a paraphrase of the first sentence in the Guterson passage that repeats too many of the words and phrases in the source, making the paraphrase unacceptable.

Unacceptable Paraphrase: Too Many Borrowed Words and Phrases

> Apparently, some conditions, which have been illuminated by Bruner and other discovery theorists, pave the way for people to learn.

If you compare the source's first sentence and the paraphrase of it, you will see that the paraphrase borrows almost all of its key language from the source sentence, including the entire phrase *pave the way for.* Even if you cite the source, this heavy borrowing would be considered plagiarism, using the ideas and words of others as though they were your own.

Here is another paraphrase of the same sentence that too closely resembles the structure of the source sentence, again making the paraphrase unacceptable.

Unacceptable Paraphrase: Sentence Structure Repeated Too Closely

> Bruner and other researchers have also identified circumstances that seem to ease the path to learning.

If you compare the source's first sentence and this paraphrase of it, you will see that the paraphraser has borrowed the phrases and clauses of the source and arranged them in an identical sequence, simply substituting synonyms for most of the key terms: *researchers* for *theorists, identified* for *illuminated, circumstances* for *conditions, seem to* for *apparently,* and *ease the path to* for *pave the way for.* This paraphrase would also be considered plagiarism, even though most of the key terms have been changed and even if you cite the source.

Summarizing. Like a paraphrase, a **summary** may rely on key words from the source but is made up mainly of words supplied by the writer. It presents only the main ideas of a source, leaving out examples and details. Consequently, summaries allow you to bring concisely into your writing large amounts of information from source material.

Here is an example of a summary of five pages from the David Guterson book. You can see at a glance how drastically some summaries condense information, in this case from five pages to five sentences. Depending on the summarizer's purpose, the five pages could be summarized in one sentence, the five sentences here, or two or three dozen sentences.

> In looking at different theories of learning that discuss individual-based programs (such as home schooling) versus the public school system, Guterson describes the disagreements among "cognitivist" theorists. One group, the "discovery theorists," believes that individual children learn by creating their own ways of sorting the information they take in from their experiences. Schools should help students develop better ways of organizing new material, not just present them with material that is already categorized, as traditional schools do. "Assimilationist theorists," by contrast, believe that children learn by linking what they don't know to information they already know. These theorists claim that traditional schools help students learn when they present information in ways that allow children to fit the new material into categories they have already developed (171–75).

In this summary, the source of the summarized material is identified by the author's name in the first sentence and the page numbers of the material in the last sentence, following the citation style of the Modern Language Association. As with paraphrases, putting the citation information at the beginning and the end of the summary in this way makes clear to the reader the boundaries between the ideas in the source and the writer's own ideas (or the ideas in a different source).

Though this summarizer puts quotation marks around three technical terms from the original source, summaries usually do not include quotations: Their purpose is not to display the source's language but to present its main ideas. Longer summaries like this one are more than a dry list of main ideas from a source. They are instead a coherent, readable new text composed of the source's main ideas. Summaries provide balanced coverage of a source, following the same sequence of ideas and avoiding any hint of agreement or disagreement with them.

ACKNOWLEDGING SOURCES

Notice in the preceding examples of paraphrasing and summarizing that the source is acknowledged by name. Even when you use your own words to present someone else's information, you must acknowledge that you borrowed the information. The only types of information that do not require acknowledgment are common knowledge (John F. Kennedy was assassinated in Dallas), facts widely available in many sources (U.S. presidents used to be inaugurated on March 4 rather than January 20), well-known quotations ("To be or not to be. That is the question"), or material you created or gathered yourself, such as photographs that you took or data from surveys that you conducted. Remember that you need to acknowledge the source of any visual (photograph, table, chart, graph, diagram, drawing, map, screen shot) that you did not create yourself or of any information that you used to create your own visual. (You should also request permission from the source of a visual you want to borrow if your essay is going to be posted on the Web.) When in doubt about whether you need to cite a source for something, it is safer to do so.

The documentation guidelines later in this section present various styles for citing sources. Whichever style you use, the most important thing is that your readers be able to tell where words or ideas that are not your own begin and end. You can accomplish this most readily by taking and transcribing notes carefully, by placing parenthetical source citations correctly, and by separating your words from those of the source with **signal phrases** such as "According to Smith," "Peters claims," and "As Olmos asserts." (When you cite a source for the first time in a signal phrase, you may use the author's full name; after that, use just the last name.)

Avoiding Plagiarism

Writers—students and professionals alike—occasionally fail to acknowledge sources properly. The word **plagiarism**, which derives from the Latin word for "kidnapping," refers to the unacknowledged use of another's words, ideas, or information. Students sometimes get into trouble because they mistakenly assume that plagiarizing occurs only when another writer's exact words are used without acknowledgment. In fact, plagiarism applies to such diverse forms of expression as musical compositions and visual images as well as ideas and statistics. So keep in mind that, with the exceptions listed above, you must indicate the source of any borrowed information or ideas you use in your essay, whether you have paraphrased, summarized, or quoted directly from the source or have reproduced it or referred to it in some other way.

Remember especially the need to document electronic sources fully and accurately. Perhaps because it is so easy to access and distribute text and visuals online and to copy material from one electronic document and paste it into another, many students do not realize or forget that information, ideas, and images from electronic sources require acknowledgment in even more detail than those from print sources do (and are often easier to detect if they are not acknowledged).

Some people plagiarize simply because they do not know the conventions for using and acknowledging sources. This chapter makes clear how to incorporate sources into your writing and how to acknowledge your use of those sources. Others plagiarize because they keep sloppy notes and thus fail to distinguish between their own and their sources' ideas. Either they neglect to enclose their sources' words in quotation marks, or they fail to indicate when they are paraphrasing or summarizing a source's ideas and information. If you keep a working bibliography and careful notes, you will not make this serious mistake.

For more on keeping a working bibliography, see Chapter 21, pp. 712–15.

Another reason some people plagiarize is that they doubt their ability to write the essay by themselves. They feel intimidated by the writing task or the deadline or their own and others' expectations. If you experience this same anxiety about your work, speak to your instructor. Do not run the risk of failing a course or being expelled because of plagiarism. If you are confused about what is and what is not plagiarism, be sure to ask your instructor.

Understanding Documentation Styles

Although there is no universally accepted system for acknowledging sources, most documentation styles use parenthetical in-text citations keyed to a separate list of works cited or references. The information required in the in-text citations and the order and content of the works cited entries vary across academic disciplines. This section presents the basic features of two styles: the author-page system that is advocated by the Modern Language Association (MLA) and widely used in the humanities and the author-year system that is advocated by the American Psychological Association (APA) and widely used in the natural and social sciences.

In Part One of this book, you can find examples of student essays that follow the MLA style (Linh Kieu Ngo, Chapter 5; Jessica Statsky, Chapter 6; Sarah West, Chapter 9) and the APA style (Patrick O'Malley, Chapter 7). For more information about these documentation styles, consult the *MLA Handbook for Writers of Research Papers*, Sixth Edition (2003) or the *Publication Manual of the American Psychological Association*, Fifth Edition (2001).

Check with your instructor about which of these styles you should use or whether you should use some other style. A list of common documentation style manuals is provided in Table 22.1 on p. 758.

Table 22.1 Some Commonly Used Documentation Style Manuals

Subject	*Style Manual*	*Online Source*
General	*The Chicago Manual of Style.* 15th ed. 2003.	http://www.chicagomanualofstyle.org
	A Manual for Writers of Term Papers, Theses, and Dissertations. 6th ed. 1996.	—
Online Sources	*Columbia Guide to Online Style.* 1998.	http://www.columbia.edu/cu/cup/cgos/idx_basic.html
Biological Sciences	*Scientific Style and Format: The CBE Manual for Authors, Editors, and Publishers.* 6th ed. 1994.	http://www.councilscienceeditors.org/publications/style.cfm
Chemistry	*The ACS Style Guide.* 2nd ed. 1997.	http://www.pubs.acs.org/books/references.shtml
Government Documents	*The Complete Guide to Citing Government Documents.* Rev. ed. 1993.	http://www.lib.memphis.edu/gpo/citeweb.htm
Humanities	*MLA Handbook for Writers of Research Papers.* 6th ed. 2003.	http://www.mla.org
	MLA Style Manual and Guide to Scholarly Publishing. 2nd ed. 1998.	
Psychology/Social Sciences	*Publication Manual of the American Psychological Association.* 5th ed. 2001.	http://www.apastyle.org

The MLA System of Documentation

Citations in Text

The MLA author-page system generally requires that in-text citations include the author's last name and the page number of the passage being cited. There is no punctuation between author and page. The parenthetical citation should follow the quoted, paraphrased, or summarized material as closely as possible without disrupting the flow of the sentence.

> Dr. James is described as a "not-too-skeletal Ichabod Crane" (Simon 68).

Note that the parenthetical citation comes before the final period. With block quotations, however, the citation comes after the final period, preceded by a space (see pp. 750–51 for an example).

If you mention the author's name in your text, supply just the page reference in parentheses.

> Simon describes Dr. James as a "not-too-skeletal Ichabod Crane" (68).

A WORK WITH MORE THAN ONE AUTHOR

To cite a source by two or three authors, include all the authors' last names; for works with more than three authors, use all the authors' names or just the first author's name followed by *et al.,* meaning "and others," in regular type (not italicized or underlined).

Dyal, Corning, and Willows identify several types of students, including the "Authority-Rebel" (4).

The Authority-Rebel "tends to see himself as superior to other students in the class" (Dyal, Corning, and Willows 4).

The drug AZT has been shown to reduce the risk of transmission from HIV-positive mothers to their infants by as much as two-thirds (Van de Perre et al. 4–5).

TWO OR MORE WORKS BY THE SAME AUTHOR

Include the author's last name, a comma, a shortened version of the title, and the page number(s).

When old paint becomes transparent, it sometimes shows the artist's original plans: "a tree will show through a woman's dress" (Hellman, Pentimento 1).

A WORK WITH AN UNKNOWN AUTHOR

Use a shortened version of the title, beginning with the word by which the title is alphabetized in the works-cited list. ("Awash in Garbage" was the title in the following example.)

An international pollution treaty still to be ratified would prohibit all plastic garbage from being dumped at sea ("Awash" 26).

TWO OR MORE AUTHORS WITH THE SAME LAST NAME CITED IN YOUR ESSAY

In addition to the last name, include each author's first initial in the citation. If the first initials are also the same, spell out the authors' first names.

Chaplin's Modern Times provides a good example of montage used to make an editorial statement (E. Roberts 246).

A CORPORATE OR GOVERNMENT AUTHOR

In a parenthetical citation, give the full name of the author if it is brief or a shortened version if it is long. If you name the author in your text, give the full name even if it is long.

A tuition increase has been proposed for community and technical colleges to offset budget deficits from Initiative 601 (Washington State Board 4).

According to the Washington State Board for Community and Technical Colleges, a tuition increase . . . from Initiative 601 (4).

A MULTIVOLUME WORK

When you use two or more volumes of a multivolume work in your paper, include the volume number and the page number(s), separated by a colon and one space, in each citation.

According to Forster, modernist writers valued experimentation and gradually sought to blur the line between poetry and prose (3: 150).

If you cite only one volume, give the volume number in the works cited (see p. 764) and include only the page number(s) in the parenthetical citation.

A LITERARY WORK

For a novel or other prose work available in various editions, provide the page numbers from the edition used as well as other information that will help readers locate the quotation in a different edition, such as the part or chapter number.

In Hard Times, Tom reveals his utter narcissism by blaming Louisa for his own failure: "'You have regularly given me up. You never cared for me'" (Dickens 262; bk. 3, ch. 9).

For a play in verse, such as a Shakespearean play, indicate the act, scene, and line numbers instead of the page numbers.

At the beginning, Regan's fawning rhetoric hides her true attitude toward Lear: "I profess / myself an enemy to all other joys . . . / And find that I am alone felicitate / In your dear highness' love" (King Lear I.i.74–75, 77–78).

In the MLA style, act and scene numbers may instead be given in arabic numerals: (King Lear 1.1.74–75, 77–78).

For a poem, indicate the line numbers and stanzas or sections (if they are numbered), instead of the page numbers. If the source gives only line numbers, use the term *lines* in the first citation and give only the numbers in subsequent citations.

In "Song of Myself," Whitman finds poetic details in busy urban settings, as when he describes "the blab of the pave, tires of carts . . . the driver with his interrogating thumb" (8.153–54).

A RELIGIOUS WORK

For the Bible, indicate the book, chapter, and verse instead of the page numbers. Abbreviate books with names of five or more letters in your parenthetical citation, but spell out full names of books in your text.

She ignored the admonition "Pride goes before destruction, and a haughty spirit before a fall" (New Oxford Annotated Bible, Prov. 16.18).

A WORK IN AN ANTHOLOGY

Use the name of the author of the work, not the editor of the anthology, but use the page number(s) from the anthology.

In "Six Days: Some Rememberings," Grace Paley recalls that when she was in jail for protesting the Vietnam War, her pen and paper were taken away and she felt "a terrible pain in the area of my heart—a nausea" (191).

A QUOTATION FROM A SECONDARY SOURCE

Include the secondary source in your list of works cited. In your parenthetical citation, use the abbreviation *qtd. in* (in regular type, not italicized or underlined) to acknowledge that the original was quoted in a secondary source.

> E. M. Forster says "the collapse of all civilization, so realistic for us, sounded in Matthew Arnold's ears like a distant and harmonious cataract" (qtd. in Trilling 11).

AN ENTIRE WORK

Include the reference in the text without any page numbers or parentheses.

> In The Structure of Scientific Revolutions, Thomas Kuhn discusses how scientists change their thinking.

A WORK WITHOUT PAGE NUMBERS

If a work has no page numbers or is only one page long, you may omit the page number. If a work uses paragraph numbers instead, use the abbreviation *par(s)*, and use a comma after the author's name.

> The average speed on Montana's interstate highways, for example, has risen by only 2 miles per hour since the repeal of the federal speed limit, with most drivers topping out at 75 (Schmid).
>
> Whitman considered African American speech "a source of a native grand opera" (Ellison, par. 13).

TWO OR MORE WORKS CITED IN THE SAME PARENTHESES

When two or more different sources are used in the same passage of your essay, it may be necessary to cite them in the same parentheses. Separate the citations with a semicolon. Include any specific pages, or omit pages to refer to the whole work.

> A few studies have considered differences between oral and written discourse production (Scardamalia, Bereiter, and Goelman; Gould).

MATERIAL FROM THE INTERNET

Give enough information in the citation to enable readers to locate the Internet source in the list of works cited. If the author is not named, give the document title. Include page, section, paragraph, or screen numbers, if available.

> In handling livestock, "many people attempt to restrain animals with sheer force instead of using behavioral principles" (Grandin).

List of Works Cited

Providing full information for the citations in the text, the list of works cited identifies all the sources the writer uses. Entries are alphabetized according to the first author's last name or by the title if the author is unknown. Every source cited in the text must refer to an entry in the list of works cited. Conversely, every entry in the list of works cited must correspond to at least one in-text citation.

In the MLA style, multiple works by the same author (or same group of authors) are alphabetized by title. The author's name is given for the first entry only; in subsequent entries, three hyphens and a period are used.

```
Vidal, Gore. Empire. New York: Random, 1987.

---. Lincoln. New York: Random, 1984.
```

The information presented in a list of works cited follows this order: author, title, publication source, year, and (for an article) page range. The MLA style requires a "hanging indent," which means that the first line of a works-cited entry is not indented but subsequent lines of the entry are. The MLA specifies an indent of half an inch or five character spaces.

Books

Here is an example of a basic MLA-style entry for a book:

double-space

author, last name first | *title (and subtitle, if any), underlined*

```
Ehrenreich, Barbara. Nickel and Dimed: On (Not) Getting by in
     America. New York: Metropolitan, 2001.
```

indent one-half inch or 5 typewriter spaces | *publisher's city and name, year of publication*

A BOOK BY A SINGLE AUTHOR

```
Lamb, Sharon. The Secret Lives of Girls. New York: Free, 2002.
```

A BOOK BY AN AGENCY OR A CORPORATION

```
Association for Research in Nervous and Mental Disease. The
     Circulation of the Brain and Spinal Cord: A Symposium on
     Blood Supply. New York: Hafner, 1966.
```

A BOOK BY MORE THAN ONE AUTHOR

```
Saba, Laura, and Julie Gattis. The McGraw-Hill Homeschooling
     Companion. New York: McGraw, 2002.

Wilmut, Ian, Keith Campbell, and Colin Tudge. The Second
     Creation: Dolly and the Age of Biological Control. New
     York: Farrar, 2000.
```

A WORK BY MORE THAN THREE AUTHORS

The MLA lists all the authors' names *or* the name of the first author followed by *et al.* (in regular type, not italicized or underlined).

Hunt, Lynn, et al. The Making of the West: Peoples and Cultures. Boston: Bedford, 2001.

A BOOK BY AN UNKNOWN AUTHOR

Use the title in place of the author.

Rand McNally Commercial Atlas and Marketing Guide. Skokie: Rand, 2003.

A BOOK WITH AN AUTHOR AND AN EDITOR

If you refer to the author's text, begin the entry with the author's name.

Arnold, Matthew. Culture and Anarchy. Ed. J. Dover Wilson. Cambridge: Cambridge UP, 1966.

If you cite the editor in your paper, begin the entry with the editor's name.

Wilson, J. Dover, ed. Culture and Anarchy. By Matthew Arnold. 1869. Cambridge: Cambridge UP, 1966.

AN EDITED COLLECTION

Waldman, Diane, and Janet Walker, eds. Feminism and Documentary. Minneapolis: U of Minnesota P, 1999.

A WORK IN AN ANTHOLOGY OR A COLLECTION

Fairbairn-Dunlop, Peggy. "Women and Agriculture in Western Samoa." Different Places, Different Voices. Ed. Janet H. Momsen and Vivian Kinnaird. London: Routledge, 1993. 211-26.

TWO OR MORE WORKS FROM THE SAME ANTHOLOGY

To avoid repetition, you may create an entry for the collection and cite the collection's editor to cross-reference individual works to the entry.

Boyd, Herb, ed. The Harlem Reader. New York: Three Rivers, 2003.

Wallace, Michelle. "Memories of a Sixties Girlhood: The Harlem I Love." Boyd 243-50.

ONE VOLUME OF A MULTIVOLUME WORK

If only one volume from a multivolume set is used, indicate the volume number after the title.

Freud, Sigmund. The Complete Psychological Works of Sigmund Freud. Vol. 8. Trans. James Strachey. London: Hogarth, 1962.

TWO OR MORE VOLUMES OF A MULTIVOLUME WORK

Sandburg, Carl. Abraham Lincoln. 6 vols. New York: Scribner's, 1939.

A BOOK THAT IS PART OF A SERIES

Include the series title in regular type (not underlined or in quotation marks), followed by the series number and a period. If the word *Series* is part of the name, include *Ser.* before the number. Common abbreviations may be used for selected words in the series title.

Zigova, Tanya, et al. Neural Stem Cells: Methods and Protocols. Methods in Molecular Biology 198. Totowa: Humana, 2002.

A REPUBLISHED BOOK

Provide the original year of publication after the title of the book, followed by normal publication information for the edition you are using.

Alcott, Louisa May. An Old-Fashioned Girl. 1870. New York: Puffin, 1995.

A LATER EDITION OF A BOOK

Rottenberg, Annette T. The Structure of Argument. 2nd ed. Boston: Bedford, 1997.

A BOOK WITH A TITLE IN ITS TITLE

Do not underline a title normally underlined when it appears within the title of a book.

Hertenstein, Mike. The Double Vision of Star Trek: Half-Humans, Evil Twins, and Science Fiction. Chicago: Cornerstone, 1998.

O'Neill, Terry, ed. Readings on To Kill a Mockingbird. San Diego: Greenhaven, 2000.

Use quotation marks around a work normally enclosed in quotation marks when it appears within the title of a book.

> Miller, Edwin Haviland. Walt Whitman's "Song of Myself": A Mosaic of Interpretation. Iowa City: U of Iowa P, 1989.

A TRANSLATION

If you refer to the work itself, begin the entry with the author's name.

> Tolstoy, Leo. War and Peace. Trans. Constance Garnett. London: Pan, 1972.

If you cite the translator in your text, begin the entry with the translator's name.

> Garnett, Constance, trans. War and Peace. By Leo Tolstoy. 1869. London: Pan, 1972.

A DICTIONARY ENTRY OR AN ARTICLE IN A REFERENCE BOOK

> "Homeopathy." Webster's New World College Dictionary. 4th ed. 1999.

> Rowland, Lewis P. "Myasthenia Gravis." The Encyclopedia Americana. 2001 ed.

AN INTRODUCTION, PREFACE, FOREWORD, OR AFTERWORD

> Holt, John. Introduction. Better than School. By Nancy Wallace. Burnett: Larson, 1983. 9-14.

Articles

Here is an example of a basic MLA-style entry for an article in a periodical:

> Simon, Robin W. "Revisiting the Relationship among Gender, Marital Status, and Mental Health." American Journal of Sociology 107 (2002): 1065-96.

author, last name first

article title, in quotation marks

periodical title, underlined

double-space; indent one-half inch or 5 typewriter spaces

volume number

date, in parentheses, followed by colon

page numbers

If the article is not on a continuous sequence of pages, give the first page number followed by a plus sign, as in the following example.

AN ARTICLE FROM A DAILY NEWSPAPER

Peterson, Andrea. "Finding a Cure for Old Age." Wall Street Journal 20 May 2003: D1+.

AN ARTICLE FROM A WEEKLY OR BIWEEKLY MAGAZINE

Gross, Michael Joseph. "Family Life during Wartime." The Advocate 29 Apr. 2003: 42-48.

AN ARTICLE FROM A MONTHLY OR BIMONTHLY MAGAZINE

Stacey, Patricia. "Floor Time." Atlantic Monthly Jan./Feb. 2003: 127-34.

AN ARTICLE IN A SCHOLARLY JOURNAL WITH CONTINUOUS ANNUAL PAGINATION

The volume number follows the title of the journal.

Shan, Jordan Z., Alan G. Morris, and Fiona Sun. "Financial Development and Economic Growth: An Egg and Chicken Problem?" Review of International Economics 9 (2001): 443-54.

AN ARTICLE IN A SCHOLARLY JOURNAL THAT PAGINATES EACH ISSUE SEPARATELY

A period and the issue number follow the volume number.

Tran, Duke. "Personal Income by State, Second Quarter 2002." Current Business 82.11 (2002): 55-73.

AN EDITORIAL

"The Future Is Now." Editorial. National Review 22 Apr. 2002: 15-16.

A LETTER TO THE EDITOR

Orent, Wendy, and Alan Zelicoff. Letter. New Republic 18 Nov. 2002: 4-5.

A REVIEW

Cassidy, John. "Master of Disaster." Rev. of Globalization and Its Discontents, by Joseph Stiglitz. New Yorker 12 July 2002: 82-86.

If the review does not include an author's name, start the entry with the title of the review and alphabetize by that title. If the review is untitled, begin with the words *Rev. of* and alphabetize under the title of the work being reviewed.

AN UNSIGNED ARTICLE

Begin with the article title, alphabetizing the entry according to the first word after any initial *A*, *An*, or *The*.

"A Shot of Reality." U.S. News & World Report 1 July 2003: 13.

Electronic Sources

Electronic sources present special problems in documentation for several reasons. Their content frequently changes or disappears without notice; and because it is not organized in the kinds of standard ways that print books and periodicals are, finding the information needed for documentation is often difficult. If you cannot find some of this information, just include what you do find. You may also be able to get answers to some of your questions by going to www.mla.org.

Much of the information required in citations of electronic sources takes the same form as in corresponding kinds of print sources. For example, if you are citing an article from an online periodical, put the article title in quotation marks and underline or italicize the name of the periodical. If the source has been previously or simultaneously published in print, include the print publication information if it is available. You also should include information specific to electronic sources, where it is appropriate and available, including the following:

- The version number of the site, preceded by *Vers.*
- The date the source was published electronically or most recently updated
- The name of any institution or organization that sponsors the site (usually found at the bottom of the home page)
- The date you most recently accessed the source
- The URL, in angle brackets. Try to give the URL for the specific part of the source you are citing, but if this URL is very long or not provided, give the URL for the search page of the site, so that readers can find the source using the author or title. (In still other situations, the best URL you can give will be a site's home page.) In MLA style, a URL that will not fit on one line should be broken only after a slash. Do not use a hyphen at the break, and delete any hyphen added by your word processor.

Here is an example of a basic MLA-style entry for the most commonly cited kind of electronic source, a specific document from a Web site:

author, last name first · *title of document, in quotation marks* · *title of site, underlined*

Cuddy-Keane, Melba. "History of IVWS." The International Virginia Woolf Society Web Page. 23 June 2003. ← *date of most recent update*
International Virginia Woolf Society. 2 Aug. 2003
<http://www.utoronto.ca/IVWS>.

URL · *sponsor of site* · *date of access*

AN ENTIRE WEB SITE

Gardner, James Alan. A Seminar on Writing Prose. 2001. 15 Sept. 2002 <http://www.thinkage.ca/~jim/prose/prose.htm>.

If the author's name is not known, begin the citation with the title.

The International Virginia Woolf Society Web Page. 31 Aug. 2002. International Virginia Woolf Society. 20 Jan. 2003 <http://www.utoronto.ca/IVWS>.

For an untitled personal site, put a description such as *Home page* (in regular type, not underlined), followed by a period, in the position a title would normally be cited.

Chesson, Frederick W. Home page. 1 Apr. 2003. 7 July 2003 <http://pages.cthome.net/fwc>.

AN ONLINE SCHOLARLY PROJECT

For a complete project, provide the title, underlined, and the name of the editor, if given. Then give the electronic publication information—the version number (if any), the date of electronic publication or latest update, and the name of the sponsoring organization—followed by the date of access and the URL.

The Darwin Correspondence Project. Ed. Duncan Porter. 2 June 2003. Cambridge U Library. 13 July 2003 <http://www.lib.cam.ac.uk/Departments/Darwin/>.

A BOOK OR SHORT WORK WITHIN A SCHOLARLY PROJECT

Begin with the author's name and the title (underlined for a book or in quotation marks for an article, essay, poem, or other short work). Follow with the print publication information, if any, and the information about the project. Give the URL of the book or short work, not of the project, if they differ.

Corelli, Marie. The Treasure of Heaven. London: Constable, 1906. Victorian Women Writer's Project. Ed. Percy Willett. 10 July 1999. Indiana U. 3 Dec. 2002 <http://www.indiana.edu/~letrs/vwwp/corelli/treasure.html>.

Heims, Marjorie. "The Strange Case of Sarah Jones." The Free Expression Policy Project. 24 Jan. 2003. FEPP. 18 Apr. 2003 <http://www.fepproject.org/Commentaries/sarahjones.html>.

MATERIAL FROM A PERIODICALLY PUBLISHED DATABASE ON CD-ROM

Braus, Patricia. "Sex and the Single Spender." American Demographics 15.11 (1993): 28-34. ABI/INFORM. CD-ROM. UMI-ProQuest. 1993.

A NONPERIODICAL PUBLICATION ON A CD-ROM, MAGNETIC TAPE, OR DISKETTE

Picasso: The Man, His Works, the Legend. CD-ROM. Danbury: Grolier Interactive, 1996.

AN ARTICLE FROM AN ONLINE SUBSCRIPTION SERVICE

If you accessed the article through a personal subscription, after the date of publication give the name of the service, the date of access, and, if possible, the URL of the article or the service's search page. If the service supplies no URL that someone else could use to retrieve the article, end with either the word *Keyword,* a colon, and the keyword you used or the word *Path,* a colon, and the sequence of links you followed, with semicolons between the links.

Weeks, W. William. "Beyond the Ark." Nature Conservancy. Mar.-Apr. 1999. America Online. 2 Apr. 1999. Keyword: Ecology.

If you accessed the article through a library subscription, after the print publication information give the name of the database, underlined, if available; the name of the subscription service; the name of the library; the date of access; and the URL of the service's home page, if available. If the service provides only the first page number of the print version of the article, use a hyphen, a space, and a period after the number.

Hillenbrand, Laura. "A Sudden Illness: Personal History." New Yorker 7 July 2003: 56- . ProQuest. U of South Florida Main Lib. 10 July 2003 <http://www.proquest.umi.com>.

AN ARTICLE FROM AN ONLINE JOURNAL

Include the volume number and issue number, if given, after the title of the journal and the number of pages, paragraphs, or other sections, if given, after the date of publication.

Lankshear, Colin, and Michelle Knobel. "Mapping Postmodern Literacies: A Preliminary Chart." The Journal of Literacy and Technology 1.1 (2000). 10 Jan. 2002 <http://www.literacyandtechnology.org.v1n1/lk.html>.

A POSTING TO A DISCUSSION GROUP

For a posting to a newsgroup, include the author's name (if you know it), the title or subject line of the posting (in quotation marks), the identifying phrase *Online posting,* the posting date, and the access date. End with the newsgroup's name, preceded by the word *news:* and no space, in angle brackets.

Rostrum, Rich. "Did Jefferson Really Wish for the Abolishment of Slavery?" Online posting. 6 July 2003. 14 July 2003 <news:soc.hist.war.us-revolution>.

For a posting to a listserv, include the list's name after the posting date. For a listserv that archives postings at a Web site or listserv address, provide the URL, enclosed in angle brackets.

> Martin, Francesca Alys. "Wait--Did Somebody Say 'Buffy'?" Online posting. 8 Mar. 2000. Cultstud-l. 8 Mar. 2000. <http://lists.accomp.usf.edu/cgi-bin/lyris.pl?visit=cultstud-l&id=111011221>.

For a listserv with no Web site, provide the moderator's email address in place of a URL.

AN EMAIL MESSAGE

The subject line of the message is enclosed in quotation marks. Identify the persons who sent and received it and the date it was sent.

> Duffy, Lynn. "Re: Pet Therapy." Email to the author. 5 Nov. 2002.

SYNCHRONOUS COMMUNICATION

For a posting in a forum such as a MOO, MUD, or IRC, provide the name(s) of any specific speaker(s) you are citing and a description of the event, along with its date, the name of the forum, the date of access, and the URL, beginning with *telnet.* (If an archived version of the posting is available, cite the *http* address instead.)

> Patuto, Jeremy, Simon Fennel, and James Goss. Online discussion of "The Mytilene Debate." 9 May 1996. MiamiMOO. 28 Mar. 1998 <telnet://moo.cas.edu/cgi-bin/moo?look+4085>.

COMPUTER SOFTWARE

> <u>How Computers Work</u>. CD-ROM. Indianapolis: Que, 1998.

Other Sources

A LECTURE OR PUBLIC ADDRESS

> Birnbaum, Jack. "The Domestication of Computers." Keynote address. Conf. of the Usability Professionals Association. Hyatt Grand Cypress Resort, Orlando. 10 July 2002.

A GOVERNMENT DOCUMENT

If the author is known, the author's name may either come first or be placed after the title, introduced with the word *By.*

United States. Dept. of Health and Human Services. Building Communities Together: Federal Programs Guide 1999-2000. Washington: U.S. Dept. of Health and Human Services, 1999.

A PAMPHLET

Boat U.S. Foundation for Boating Safety and Clean Water. Hypothermia and Cold Water Survival. Alexandria, VA: Boat U.S. Foundation, 2001.

PUBLISHED PROCEEDINGS OF A CONFERENCE

If the name of the conference is part of the title of the publication, it need not be repeated. Use the format for a work in an anthology (see p. 763) to cite an individual presentation.

Duffett, John, ed. Against the Crime of Silence. Proc. of the Intl. War Crimes Tribunal, Nov. 1967, Stockholm. New York: Clarion-Simon, 1970.

A PUBLISHED DOCTORAL DISSERTATION

If the dissertation was published by University Microfilms International, add *Ann Arbor: UMI,* and the year. List the UMI number at the end of the entry.

Botts, Roderic C. Influences in the Teaching of English, 1917-1935: An Illusion of Progress. Diss. Northeastern U, 1970. Ann Arbor: UMI, 1971. 71-1799.

AN UNPUBLISHED DOCTORAL DISSERTATION

Bullock, Barbara. "Basic Needs Fulfillment among Less Developed Countries: Social Progress over Two Decades of Growth." Diss. Vanderbilt U, 1986.

A LETTER

Rogers, Katherine. Letter to the author. 22 Mar. 2003.

A MAP OR CHART

Mineral King, California. Map. Berkeley: Wilderness P, 1979.

A CARTOON OR COMIC STRIP

Provide the title (if given) in quotation marks directly following the artist's name.

Kaplan, Bruce Eric. Cartoon. New Yorker. 8 July 2002. 36.

AN ADVERTISEMENT

City Harvest "Feed the Kids" 2003. Advertisement. New York 26 May 2003: 15.

A WORK OF ART OR MUSICAL COMPOSITION

De Goya, Francisco. The Sleep of Reason Produces Monsters. Norton Simon Museum, Pasadena.

Beethoven, Ludwig van. Violin Concerto in D Major, op. 61.

Gershwin, George. Porgy and Bess.

If a photograph is not part of a collection, identify the subject, the name of the person who photographed it, and when it was photographed.

Washington Square Park, New York. Personal photograph by author. 24 June 1995.

A PERFORMANCE

Proof. By David Auburn. Dir. Daniel Sullivan. Perf. Mary-Louise Parker. Walter Kerr Theatre, New York. 9 Sept. 2001.

A TELEVISION PROGRAM

"Murder of the Century." American Experience. Narr. David Ogden Stiers. Writ. and prod. Carl Charlson. PBS. WEDU, Tampa. 14 July 2003.

A FILM OR VIDEO RECORDING

Space Station. Prod. and dir. Toni Myers. Narr. Tom Cruise. IMAX, 2002.

Casablanca. Dir. Michael Curtiz. Perf. Humphrey Bogart, Ingrid Bergman, and Paul Henreid. 1942. DVD. Warner Home Video, 2003.

A MUSIC RECORDING

Indicate the medium ahead of the name of the manufacturer for an audiocassette, audiotape, or LP; it is not necessary to indicate the medium for a compact disc.

Beethoven, Ludwig van. Violin Concerto in D Major, op. 61. U.S.S.R. State Orchestra. Cond. Alexander Gauk. David Oistrikh, violinist. Audiocassette. Allegro, 1980.

Springsteen, Bruce. "Dancing in the Dark." Born in the U.S.A. Columbia, 1984.

AN INTERVIEW

Lowell, Robert. "Robert Lowell." Interview with Frederick Seidel. Paris Review 25 (1975): 56-95.

Franklin, Ann. Personal interview. 3 Sept. 2002.

The APA System of Documentation

Citations in Text

AUTHOR INDICATED IN PARENTHESES

The APA author-year system calls for the last name of the author and the year of publication of the original work in the citation. If the cited material is a quotation, you also need to include the page number(s) of the original. If the cited material is not a quotation, the page reference is optional. Use commas to separate author, year, and page in a parenthetical citation. The page number is preceded by *p.* for a single page or *pp.* for a range. Use an ampersand (&) to join the names of multiple authors.

Dr. James is described as a "not-too-skeletal Ichabod Crane" (Simon, 1982, p. 68).

Racial bias does not necessarily diminish (Johnson & Tyree, 2001).

If you are citing an electronic source without page numbers, give the paragraph number if it is provided, preceded by the paragraph symbol (¶) or the abbreviation *para.* If no paragraph number is given, give the heading of the section and the number of the paragraph within it where the material appears, if possible.

The subjects were tested for their responses to various stimuli, both positive and negative (Simpson, 2002, para. 4).

AUTHOR INDICATED IN SIGNAL PHRASE

If the author's name is mentioned in your text, cite the year in parentheses directly following the author's name, and place the page reference in parentheses before the final sentence period. Use *and* to join the names of multiple authors.

Simon (1982) describes Dr. James as a "not-too-skeletal Ichabod Crane" (p. 68).

As Jamison and Tyree (2001) have found, racial bias does not diminish merely through exposure to individuals of other races (Conclusion section, para. 2).

SOURCE WITH MORE THAN TWO AUTHORS

To cite works with three to five authors, use all the authors' last names the first time the reference occurs and the last name of the first author followed by *et al.* subsequently. If a source has six or more authors, use only the last name of the first author and *et al.* (in regular type, not italicized or underlined) at first and subsequent references.

First Citation in Text

Dyal, Corning, and Willows (1975) identify several types of students, including the "Authority-Rebel" (p. 4).

Subsequent Citations

The Authority-Rebel "tends to see himself as superior to other students in the class" (Dyal et al., 1975, p. 4).

TWO OR MORE WORKS BY THE SAME AUTHOR

To cite one of two or more works by the same author or group of authors, use the author's last name plus the year (and the page, if you are citing a quotation). When more than one work being cited was published by an author in the same year, the works are alphabetized by title and then assigned lowercase letters after the date (1973a, 1973b).

When old paint becomes transparent, it sometimes shows the artist's original plans: "a tree will show through a woman's dress" (Hellman, 1973b, p. 1).

UNKNOWN AUTHOR

To cite a work listed only by its title, the APA uses a shortened version of the title.

An international pollution treaty still to be ratified would prohibit all plastic garbage from being dumped at sea ("Awash," 1987).

SECONDARY SOURCE

To quote material taken not from the original source but from a secondary source that quotes the original, give the secondary source in the reference list, and in your essay acknowledge that the original was quoted in a secondary source.

E. M. Forster says "the collapse of all civilization, so realistic for us, sounded in Matthew Arnold's ears like a distant and harmonious cataract" (as cited in Trilling, 1955, p. 11).

List of References

The APA follows this order in the presentation of information for each source listed: author, publication year, title, and publication source; for an article, the page range is given as well. Titles of books, periodicals, and the like should be italicized, if possible.

When the list of references includes several works by the same author, the APA provides the following rules for arranging these entries in the list:

- Same-name single-author entries precede multiple-author entries:

  Aaron, P. (1990).

  Aaron, P., & Zorn, C. R. (1985).

- Entries with the same first author and a different second author are alphabetized under the first author according to the second author's last name:

  Aaron, P., & Charleston, W. (1987).

  Aaron, P., & Zorn, C. R. (1991).

- Entries by the same authors are arranged by year of publication, in chronological order:

  Aaron, P., & Charleston, W. (1987).

  Aaron, P., & Charleston, W. (1993).

- Entries by the same authors with the same publication year should be arranged alphabetically by title (according to the first word after *A, An,* or *The*), and lowercase letters (*a, b, c,* and so on) are appended to the year in parentheses:

  Aaron, P. (1990a). *Basic* . . .

  Aaron, P. (1990b). *Elements* . . .

The APA recommends that the first line of each entry be indented five spaces in papers intended for publication but that student writers may use a hanging indent of five spaces. Ask your instructor which format is preferred. The following examples demonstrate a hanging indent of five spaces.

Books

A BOOK BY A SINGLE AUTHOR

Ehrenreich, B. (2001). *Nickel and dimed: On (not) getting by in America.* New York: Metropolitan.

A BOOK BY AN AGENCY OR A CORPORATION

Association for Research in Nervous and Mental Disease. (1966). *The circulation of the brain and spinal cord: A symposium on blood supply.* New York: Hafner.

A BOOK BY MORE THAN ONE AUTHOR

Saba, L., & Gattis, J. (2002). *The McGraw-Hill homeschooling companion.* New York: McGraw-Hill.

Hunt, L., Po-Chia Hsia, R., Martin, T. R., Rosenwein, B. H., Rosenwein, H., & Smith, B. G. (2001). *The making of the West: Peoples and cultures.* Boston: Bedford/St. Martin's.

If there are more than six authors, list only the first six followed by *et al.* (not italicized).

A BOOK BY AN UNKNOWN AUTHOR

Use the title in place of the author.

Rand McNally commercial atlas and marketing guide. (2003). Skokie: Rand McNally.

When an author is designated as "Anonymous," identify the work as "Anonymous" in the text, and alphabetize it as "Anonymous" in the reference list.

A BOOK WITH AN AUTHOR AND AN EDITOR

Arnold, M. (1966). *Culture and anarchy* (J. D. Wilson, Ed.). Cambridge: Cambridge University Press. (Original work published 1869)

AN EDITED COLLECTION

Waldman, D., & Walker, J. (Eds.). (1999). *Feminism and documentary.* Minneapolis: University of Minnesota Press.

A WORK IN AN ANTHOLOGY OR A COLLECTION

Fairbairn-Dunlop, P. (1993). Women and agriculture in western Samoa. In J. H. Momsen & V. Kinnaird (Eds.), *Different places, different voices* (pp. 211-226). London: Routledge.

A TRANSLATION

Tolstoy, L. (1972). *War and peace* (C. Garnett, Trans.). London: Pan Books. (Original work published 1869)

AN ARTICLE IN A REFERENCE BOOK

Rowland, R. P. (2001). Myasthenia gravis. In *Encyclopedia Americana* (Vol. 19, p. 683). Danbury, CT: Grolier.

AN INTRODUCTION, PREFACE, FOREWORD, OR AFTERWORD

Holt, J. (1983). Introduction. In N. Wallace, *Better than school* (pp. 9-14). Burnett, NY: Larson.

Articles

AN ARTICLE FROM A DAILY NEWSPAPER

Peterson, A. (2003, May 20). Finding a cure for old age. *The Wall Street Journal*, pp. D1, D5.

AN ARTICLE FROM A WEEKLY OR BIWEEKLY MAGAZINE

Gross, M. J. (2003, April 29). Family life during war time. *The Advocate*, 42-48.

AN ARTICLE FROM A MONTHLY OR BIMONTHLY MAGAZINE

Stacey, P. (2003, January/February). Floor time. *Atlantic Monthly*, *291*, 127-134.

AN ARTICLE IN A SCHOLARLY JOURNAL WITH CONTINUOUS ANNUAL PAGINATION

The volume number follows the title of the journal.

Shan, J. Z., Morris, A. G., & Sun, F. (2001). Financial development and economic growth: A chicken and egg problem? *Review of Economics*, *9*, 443-454.

AN ARTICLE IN A SCHOLARLY JOURNAL THAT PAGINATES EACH ISSUE SEPARATELY

The issue number appears in parentheses after the volume number.

Tran, Duke. (2002). Personal income by state, second quarter 2002. *Current Business*, *82*(11), 55-73.

AN ANONYMOUS ARTICLE

Communities blowing whistle on street basketball. (2003). *USA Today*, p. 20A.

A REVIEW

Cassidy, John. (2002, July 12). Master of disaster [Review of the book *Globalization and its discontents*]. *The New Yorker*, 82-86.

If the review is untitled, use the bracketed information as the title, retaining the brackets.

Electronic Sources

For more information on using the Internet for research, see Chapter 21, pp. 737–39.

While the APA guidelines for citing online resources are still something of a work in progress, a rule of thumb is that citation information must allow readers to access and

For answers to frequently asked questions on citing Internet sources in the APA style, go to http://www.apastyle.org/elecref/html.

retrieve the information cited. The following guidelines are derived from the *Publication Manual of the American Psychological Association,* Fifth Edition (2001), and the APA Web site.

For most sources accessed on the Internet, you should provide the following information:

- Name of author (if available)
- Date of publication or most recent update (in parentheses; if unavailable, use the abbreviation *n.d.*)
- Title of document
- Publication information, including volume and issue numbers for periodicals
- Retrieval information, including date of access and URL or path followed to locate the site

A WEB SITE

When you cite an entire Web site, the APA does not require an entry in the list of references. You may instead give the name of the site in your text and its Web address in parentheses. To cite a document that you have accessed through a Web site, follow these formats:

American Cancer Society. (2003). How to fight teen smoking. Retrieved June 3, 2003, from http://www.cancer.org/docroot/ped/content/ped_10_14_how_to_fight_teen_smoking.asp

Heims, M. (2003, January 24). The strange case of Sarah Jones. *The Free Expression Policy Project.* Retrieved April 18, 2003, from http://www.fepproject.org/commentaries/sarahjones.html

ARTICLE FROM A DATABASE

Follow the guidelines for a comparable print source, but conclude the retrieval statement with the name of the database. You do not need to indicate how you accessed the database.

Houston, R. G., & Toma, F. (2003). Home schooling: An alternative school choice. *Southern Economic Journal, 69*(4), 920-936. Retrieved July 15, 2003, from InfoTrac Onefile database.

Hillenbrand, L. (2003, July 10). A sudden illness: Personal history. *The New Yorker,* 56-66. Retrieved July 10, 2003, from ProQuest database.

AN ARTICLE FROM AN ONLINE PERIODICAL

If an article that you access through a periodical's Web site also exists in an identical print version, your citation can follow the format for the print article with the addition of "[Electronic version]" following the title of the article (before the period and without quotation marks). However, if you have any reason to believe that the format or content differs from the print version or if no page numbers are provided, then you need to include retrieval information.

Jauhar, S. (2002, July 15). A malady that mimics depression. *The New York Times*. Retrieved July 30, 2003, from http://www.nytimes.com/2003/07/15/health/15CASE.html?fta=y

Retrieval information is always required for periodicals that are published only online.

Lankshear, C., & Knobel, M. (2002). Mapping postmodern literacies: A preliminary chart. *The Journal of Literacy and Technology, 1*(1). Retrieved September 29, 2002, from http://www.literacyandtechnology.org/v1n1/lk.html

ONLINE POSTINGS

Include online postings in your list of references only if you can provide data that would allow retrieval of the source. Provide the author's name, the date of the posting, the subject line, and any other identifying information. For a message on a listserv, conclude the entry with the name of the list and complete retrieval information.

Gordon, M. (2003, January 29). Dialect mixing [Msg. 10]. Message posted to the American Dialect Society's ADS L electronic mailing list, archived at http://listserv.linguistlist.org/archives/ads-l.html

For a message posted to a newsgroup, conclude the entry with the newsgroup name. If the author is identified only by a screen name, use this name at the beginning of the citation.

Rostrum, Rich. (2003, July 14). Did Jefferson really wish for the abolishment of slavery? [Msg. 47]. Message posted to news://soc.history.war.us-revolution

AN EMAIL MESSAGE

In the APA style, it is not necessary to list personal correspondence, including email, in your reference list. Simply cite the person's name in your text, and in parentheses give the notation *personal communication* (in regular type, not underlined or italicized) and the date.

COMPUTER SOFTWARE

If an individual has proprietary rights to the software, cite that person's name as you would for a print text. Otherwise, cite as you would an anonymous print text.

How Computers Work [Computer software]. (1998). Indianapolis: Que.

Other Sources

A GOVERNMENT DOCUMENT

U.S. Department of Health and Human Services. (1999). *Building communities together: Federal programs guide 1999-2000.* Washington: Author.

AN UNPUBLISHED DOCTORAL DISSERATION

Bullock, B. (1986). *Basic needs fulfillment among less developed countries: Social progress over two decades of growth.* Unpublished doctoral dissertation, Vanderbilt University, Nashville, TN.

A TELEVISION PROGRAM

Charlsen, C. (Writer and producer). (2003, July 14). Murder of the century (Television series episode). In M. Samels (Executive producer), *American Experience.* Boston: WGBH.

A FILM OR VIDEO RECORDING

Myers, T. (Writer and producer). (2002). *Space station* [Film]. New York: IMAX.

A MUSIC RECORDING

If the recording date differs from the copyright date, the APA requires that it should appear in parentheses after the name of the label. If it is necessary to include a number for the recording, use parentheses for the medium; otherwise, use brackets.

Beethoven, L. van. (1806). Violin concerto in D major, op. 61 [Recorded by USSR State Orchestra]. (Cassette Recording No. ACS 8044). New York: Allegro. (1980)

Springsteen, B. (1984). Dancing in the dark. On *Born in the U.S.A.* [CD]. New York: Columbia.

AN INTERVIEW

When using the APA style, do not list personal interviews in your references list. Simply cite the person's name (last name and initials) in your text, and in parentheses give the notation *personal communication* (in regular type, not italicized or underlined) followed by a comma and the date of the interview. For published interviews, use the appropriate format for an article.

SOME SAMPLE RESEARCH PAPERS

As a writer, you will want or need to use sources on many occasions. You may be assigned to write a research paper, complete with formal documentation of outside sources. Several of the writing assignments in this book present opportunities to do library or field research—in other words, to turn to outside sources. Among the readings in Part One, the essays listed here cite and document sources. (The documentation style each follows is given in parentheses.)

"Cannibalism: It Still Exists," by Linh Kieu Ngo, Chapter 5, pp. 223–24 (MLA)

"Children Need to Play, Not Compete," by Jessica Statsky, Chapter 6, pp. 287–91 (MLA)

"More Testing, More Learning," by Patrick O'Malley, Chapter 7, pp. 352–56 (APA)

"The Rise of Reported Incidents of Workplace Sexual Harassment," by Sarah West, Chapter 9, pp. 466–70 (MLA)

AN ANNOTATED RESEARCH PAPER

On the following pages is a student research paper speculating about the causes of a trend—the increase in home schooling. The author cites statistics, quotes authorities, and paraphrases and summarizes background information and support for her argument. She uses the MLA documentation style.

1"

½"

Dinh 1

Double-spaced

Cristina Dinh
Professor Cooper
English XXX
15 November 2003

1"

Double-spaced

Title centered

Educating Kids at Home

Every morning, Mary Jane, who is nine, doesn't have to worry about gulping down her cereal so she can be on time for school. School for Mary Jane is literally right at her doorstep.

1"

Paragraphs indented five spaces

In this era of serious concern about the quality of public education, increasing numbers of parents across the United States are choosing to educate their children at home. These parents believe they can do a better job teaching their children than their local schools can. Home schooling, as this practice is known, has become a national trend over the past thirty years, and, according to education specialist Samuel L. Blumenfeld, it "is now the fastest-growing educational phenomenon in the United States" (1). A 1991 report by the U.S. Department of Education estimated that, nationwide, the number of home-schooled children rose from 15,000 in 1970 to between 250,000 and 350,000 during the 1990-91 school year (Lines 5). Today, that figure has grown to as much as 1.7 million, and current rates suggest that the number of home-schooled children increases by 15 percent each year (Cox 19). Some home-schooling advocates believe that even these numbers may be low because not all states require formal notification when parents decide to teach their children at home.

Author named in text; parenthetical page reference falls at end of subsequent sentence

Author named in parenthetical citation; no punctuation between name and page number

What is home schooling, and who are the parents choosing to be home-schoolers? David Guterson, a pioneer in the home-schooling movement, defined home schooling as "the attempt to gain an education outside of institutions" (5). Home-schooled children spend the majority of the conventional school day learning in or near their

Author named and identified to introduce quotation

1"

Dinh 2

homes rather than in traditional schools; parents or guardians are the prime educators. Former teacher and home-schooler Rebecca Rupp notes that home-schooling parents vary considerably in what they teach and how they teach, ranging from those who follow a highly traditional curriculum within a structure that parallels the typical classroom to those who essentially allow their children to pursue whatever interests them at their own pace (3). Home-schoolers commonly combine formal instruction with life skills instruction, learning fractions, for example, in terms of monetary units or cooking measurements (Saba and Gattis 89). While home-schoolers are also a diverse group politically and philosophically--libertarians, conservatives, Christian fundamentalists--most say they home school for one of two reasons: they are concerned about the way children are taught in public schools, or they are concerned about exposing their children to secular education that may contradict their religious beliefs (U.S. Department of Education).

Work by two authors cited

Work by government author cited

The first group generally believes that children need individual attention and the opportunity to learn at their own pace to learn well. This group says that one teacher in a classroom of twenty to thirty children (the size of typical public-school classes) cannot give this kind of attention. These parents believe they can give their children greater enrichment and more specialized instruction than public schools can provide. At home, parents can work one-on-one with each child and be flexible about time, allowing their children to pursue their interests at earlier ages. Many of these parents, like home-schooler Peter Bergson, believe that

> home schooling provides more of an opportunity to continue the natural learning process that's in evidence in all children. [In school,] you change the

Quotation of more than four lines typed as a block and indented ten spaces

Brackets indicate addition to quotation

Parenthetical citation of secondary source falls after period

Dinh 3

> learning process from self-directed to other-directed, from the child asking questions to the teacher asking questions. You shut down areas of potential interest. (qtd. in Kohn 22)

The second group, those who home school their children for religious reasons, is made up predominantly of Christian fundamentalists. Sociologist Mitchell L. Stevens, author of the first comprehensive study of home-schooling, cites a mailing sent out by Basic Christian Education, a company that markets home-schooling materials, titled "What Really Happens in Public Schools." This publication sums up the fears of fundamentalist home-schoolers about public schools: that they encourage high levels of teenage sexual activity and pregnancies "out of wedlock"; expose children to "violence, crime, lack of discipline, and, of course, drugs of every kind"; present positive portrayals of communism and socialism and negative portrayals of capitalism; and undermine children's Christian beliefs by promoting "New Age philosophies, Yoga, Transcendental Meditation, witchcraft demonstrations, and Eastern religions" (51).

What causes have contributed to the increasing number of parents in both groups choosing to home school their children? One cause for this trend can be traced back to the 1960s, when many people began criticizing traditional schools. Various types of "alternative schools" were created, and some parents began teaching their children at home (Friedlander 20). Parents like this mention several reasons for their disappointment with public schools and for their decision to home school. A lack of funding, for example, leaves children without new textbooks. A television news reporter recently found that students in Chattanooga public schools are using science and social studies textbooks that are ten to

Dinh 4

twelve years old and falling apart (Paige). Many schools also cannot afford to buy laboratory equipment and other teaching materials. At my own high school, the chemistry teacher told me that most of the lab equipment we used came from a research firm he worked for. In a 2002 Gallup poll, lack of proper financial support ranked first on the list of the problems in public schools (Oregon).

Shortened form of corporate author's name cited

Parents also cite overcrowding as a reason for taking their kids out of school. The more students in a classroom, the less learning that goes on, as Cafi Cohen discovered before choosing to home-school; after spending several days observing what went on in her child's classroom, she found that administrative duties, including disciplining, took up to 80 percent of a teacher's time with only 20 percent of the day devoted to learning (6). Moreover, faced with a large group of children, a teacher ends up gearing lessons to the students in the middle level, so children at both ends miss out. Gifted children and those with learning disabilities particularly suffer in this situation. At home, parents of these children say they can tailor the material and the pace for each child. Studies show that home-schooling methods seem to work well in preparing children academically. Lawrence Rudner, director of the ERIC Clearinghouse on Assessment and Evaluation at the University of Maryland and a researcher on home schooling, found that testing of home-schooled students showed them to be between one and three years ahead of public school students their age (xi). Home-schooled children have also made particularly strong showings in academic competitions; since the late 1990s, 10 percent of National Spelling Bee participants have been home-schooled, as have two National Spelling Bee and two National Geographic Bee winners (Lyman). More and more selective colleges are admitting, and even recruiting, home-schooled applicants (Cohen 149-51).

Dinh 5

In addition, home-schooling parents claim that their children are more well rounded than those in school. Because they don't have to sit in classrooms all day, home-schooled kids can pursue their own projects, often combining crafts or technical skills with academic subjects. Home schoolers participate in outside activities such as 4-H competitions, field trips with peers in home-school support groups, science fairs, musical and dramatic productions, church activities, and Boy Scouts or Girl Scouts (Saba and Gattis 59-62). In fact, they may even be able to participate to some extent in actual school activities. A 1999 survey conducted by the U.S. Department of Education's National Center for Educational Statistics found that 28 percent of public schools allowed home-schooled students to participate in extracurricular activities alongside enrolled students, and 20 percent allowed home-schooled students to attend some classes.

Many home-schooling parents believe that these activities provide the social opportunities kids need without exposing their children to the peer pressure they would have to deal with as regular school students. For example, many kids think that drinking and using drugs are cool. When I was in high school, my friends would tell me a few drinks wouldn't hurt or affect driving. If I had listened to them, I wouldn't be alive today. Four of my friends were killed under the influence of alcohol. Between 1992 and 2002, the number of high school seniors surveyed who had used any illicit drug in the last year climbed from 28 percent to over 40 percent (Johnston, O'Malley, and Bachman 7).

Work by three authors cited

Another reason many parents decide to home school their kids is that they are concerned for their children's safety. Samuel L. Blumenfeld notes that "physical risk" is an important reason many parents remove their children from public schools as

Dinh 6

"[m]ore and more children are assaulted, robbed, and murdered in school" and a "culture of violence, abetted by rap music, drug trafficking, . . . and racial tension, has engulfed teenagers" (4). Beginning in the mid-1990s, a string of school shootings--including the 1999 massacres in Littleton, Colorado, and Conyers, Georgia, and the 2001 massacre in Santee, California--has led to increasing fears that young people are simply not safe at school.

While all of the reasons mentioned so far are important, perhaps the single most significant cause of the growing home-schooling trend is Christian fundamentalist dissatisfaction with "godless" public schools. As early as 1988, Luanne Shackelford and Susan White, two Christian home-schooling mothers, were claiming that because schools expose children to "[p]eer pressure, perverts, secular textbooks, values clarification, TV, pornography, rock music, bad movies . . . [h]ome schooling seems to be the best plan to achieve our goal [to raise good Christians]" (160). As another mother more recently put it,

> I don't like the way schools are going. . . . What's wrong with Christianity all of a sudden? You know? This country was founded on Christian, on religious principles. [People] came over here for religious freedom, and now all of a sudden all religious references seem to be stricken out of the public school, and I don't like that at all. (qtd. in Stevens 67)

Although many nonfundamentalist home schoolers make some of these same criticisms, those who cite the lack of "Christian values" in public schools have particular concerns of their own. For example, home-schooling leader Raymond Moore talks of parents who are "'sick and tired of the teaching of

Brackets used to indicate changes in capitalization and addition to quotation for clarification

Ellipsis marks used to indicate words left out of quotations

Quotation cited in a secondary source

Single quotation marks indicate a quotation within a quotation

Citation placed close to quotation, before comma but after quotation marks

Internet source cited by shortened form of title; author's name and page numbers unavailable

Dinh 7

evolution in the schools as a cut-and-dried fact,' along with other evidence of so-called secular humanism" (Kohn 21), such as textbooks that contain material contradicting Christian beliefs. Moreover, parents worry that schools undermine their children's moral values. In particular, some Christian fundamentalist parents object to sex education in schools, saying that it encourages children to become sexually active early, challenging values taught at home. They see the family as the core and believe that the best place to instill family values is within the family. These Christian home-schooling parents want to provide their children not only with academic knowledge but also with a moral grounding consistent with their religious beliefs.

Still other home-schooling parents object to a perceived government-mandated value system that they believe attempts to override the values, not necessarily religious in nature, of individual families. For these parents, home schooling is a way of resisting what they see as unwarranted intrusion by the federal government into personal concerns (<u>Alliance</u>).

Armed with their convictions, parents such as those who belong to the Christian Home School Legal Defense Association have fought in court and lobbied for legislation that allows them the option of home schooling. In the 1970s, most states had compulsory attendance laws that made it difficult, if not illegal, to keep school-age children home from school. Today, home schooling is permitted in every state, with strict regulation required by only a few (Home School). As a result, Mary Jane is one of hundreds of thousands of American children who can start their school day without leaving the house.

1"

Dinh 8

Works cited begin on a new page, one inch from top margin

Works Cited

Title centered

Double-spaced

Entries in alphabetical order by authors' last names

Alliance for the Separation of School and State. 24 Oct. 2003 <http://www.sepschool.org>.

Blumenfeld, Samuel L. Homeschooling: A Parent's Guide to Teaching Children. Bridgewater: Replica, 1999.

Cohen, Cafi. And What about College?: How Homeschooling Leads to Admissions to the Best Colleges and Universities. Cambridge: Holt, 1997.

Cox, Craig. "School's Out." Utne Reader Jan./Feb. 2002: 18-22.

Friedlander, Tom. "A Decade of Home Schooling." The Home School Reader. Ed. Mark Hegener and Helen Hegener. Tonasket: Home Education, 1988.

Guterson, David. Family Matters: Why Homeschooling Makes Sense. San Diego: Harcourt, 1992.

Home School Legal Defense Association. State Action Map. 24 Oct. 2003 <http://www.hslda.org/hs/state/default.asp>.

Johnston, Lloyd D., Patrick M. O'Malley, and Jerald G. Bachman. Monitoring the Future: National Results on Adolescent Drug Use, Overview of Key Findings, 2002. Bethesda: National Institute on Drug Abuse, 2003. 20 Oct. 2003 <http://monitoringthefuture.org/pubs/monographs/overview2002.pdf>.

Kohn, Alfie. "Home Schooling." Atlantic Monthly Apr. 1988: 20-25.

Lines, Patricia. Estimating the Home School Education Population. Washington: U.S. Dept. of Education, 1991.

Lyman, Isabel. "Generation Two." The American Enterprise Oct./Nov. 2002: 48-49. InfoTrac OneFile. Sarasota Suncat Online. Sarasota County Lib. System, FL. 26 Oct. 2003 <http://infotrac.galegroup.com>.

Entry begins flush with left margin

Subsequent lines indent five spaces

URL enclosed by angle brackets

Period after author, after title, and at end of entry

Dinh 9

Oregon School Boards Association. "Gallup Poll: The Public's Attitudes toward Schools." 20 Aug. 2002. 29 Oct. 2003 <http://www.osba.org/commsvcs/surveys/pdkpoll.htm>.

Paige, Ashley. "Outdated Textbooks: Teachers Begging for New Materials." WEDF-TV News 12. WEDF, Chattanooga. 17 Apr. 2003. Transcript. 27 Oct. 2003 <http://www.wdef.com/news/MGBA04ELNED.html>.

Rudner, Lawrence. Foreword. The McGraw-Hill Homeschooling Companion. By Laura Saba and Julie Gattis. New York: McGraw, 2002.

Rupp, Rebecca. The Complete Home Learning Source Book. New York: Three Rivers, 1998.

Saba, Laura, and Julie Gattis. The McGraw-Hill Homeschooling Companion. New York: McGraw, 2002.

Shackleford, Luanne, and Susan White. A Survivor's Guide to Home Schooling. Westchester: Crossway, 1988.

Stevens, Mitchell L. Kingdom of Children: Culture and Controversy in the Homeschooling Movement. Princeton: Princeton UP, 2001.

United States. Department of Education. National Center for Education Statistics. Homeschooling in the United States: 1999. 2001. 25 Oct. 2003 <http://nces.ed.gov/pubs2001/HomeSchool/>.

Part Five

WRITING FOR ASSESSMENT

23 Essay Examinations

Essay exams are inescapable. Even though the machine-scorable multiple-choice test has sharply reduced the number of essay exams administered in schools and colleges, essay exams will continue to play a significant role in the education of liberal arts students. Many instructors—especially in the humanities and social sciences—still believe that an exam that requires you to write is the best way to find out what you have learned and, more important, help you consolidate and reinforce your learning. Instructors who give essay exams want to be sure you can sort through the large body of information covered in a course, identify what is important or significant, and explain your decision. They want to see whether you understand the concepts that provide the basis for a course and whether you can use those concepts to interpret specific materials, to make connections on your own, to see relationships, to draw comparisons and find contrasts, and to synthesize diverse information in support of an original assertion. They may even be interested in your ability to justify your own evaluations based on appropriate standards of judgment and to argue your own opinions with convincing reasons and supporting evidence. Remember that your instructors want to encourage you to think more critically and analytically about a subject; they feel, therefore, that a written exam provides the best demonstration that you are doing so.

As a college student, then, you will face a variety of essay exams, from short-answer identifications that require only a few sentences to take-home exams that may involve hours of planning and writing. You will find that the writing activities and strategies discussed in Parts One and Three of this book—particularly narrating, describing, defining, comparing and contrasting, classifying, and arguing—as well as the critical thinking strategies in Part Two will help you to do well on these exams. This chapter provides some more specific guidelines for you to follow in preparing for and writing essay exams and analyzes a group of typical exam questions to help determine which strategies will be most useful.

But you can also learn a great deal from your experiences with essay exams in the past—the embarrassment and frustration of doing poorly on one and the great pleasure and pride of doing well. Do you recall the best exam you ever wrote? Do you remember how you wrote it and why you were able to do so well? How can you be certain to approach such writing tasks confidently and to complete them successfully? Keep these questions in mind as you consider the following guidelines.

PREPARING FOR AN EXAM

First of all, essay exams require a comprehensive understanding of large amounts of information. Because exam questions can reach widely into the course materials—and in such unpredictable ways—the best way to ensure that you will do well on them is to keep up with readings and assignments from the very start of the course. Do the reading, go to lectures, take careful notes, participate in discussion sessions, and organize small study groups with classmates to explore and review course materials throughout the semester. Trying to cram weeks of information into a single night of study will never allow you to do your best.

Then, as an exam approaches, find out what you can about the form it will take. No question is more irritating to instructors than the pestering inquiry "Do we need to know this for the exam?" but it is generally legitimate to ask whether the questions will require short or long answers, how many questions there will be, whether you may choose which questions to answer, and what kinds of thinking and writing will be required of you. Some instructors may hand out study guides for exams or even lists of potential questions. However, you will often be on your own in determining how best to go about studying.

Try to avoid simply memorizing information aimlessly. As you study, you should be clarifying the important issues of the course and using these issues to focus your understanding of specific facts and particular readings. If the course is a historical survey, distinguish the primary periods, and try to see relations among the periods and the works or events that define them. If the course is thematically unified, determine how the particular materials you have been reading relate to those themes. If the course is a broad introduction to a general topic, concentrate on the central concerns of each study unit, and see what connections you can discover among the various units. Try to place all you have learned into perspective, into a meaningful context. How do the pieces fit together? What fundamental ideas have the readings, the lectures, and the discussions seemed to emphasize? How can those ideas help you digest the information the course has covered?

One good way to prepare yourself for an exam is by making up questions you think the instructor might ask and then planning answers to them with classmates. Returning to your notes and to assigned readings with specific questions in mind can help enormously in your process of understanding. The important thing to remember is that an essay exam tests more than your memory of specific information; it requires you to use specific information to demonstrate a comprehensive grasp of the topics covered in the course.

READING THE EXAM CAREFULLY

Before you answer a single question, read the entire exam so that you can apportion your time realistically. Pay particular attention to how many points you may earn in different parts of the exam; notice any directions that suggest how long an answer should be or how much space it should take up. As you are doing so, you may wish to make tentative choices of the questions you will answer and decide on the order in which you will answer them. If you have immediate ideas about how you would organize any of your answers, you might also jot down partial scratch outlines. But before you start to complete any answers, write down the actual clock time you expect to be working on each question or set of questions. Careful time management is crucial to your success on essay exams; giving some time to each question is always better than using up your time on only a few and never getting to others.

You will next need to analyze each question carefully before beginning to write your answer. Decide what you are being asked to do. Following your immediate impulse to cast about for ideas indiscriminately at this point might cause you to become flustered, to lose concentration, or even to go blank. But if you first look closely at what the question is directing you to do and try to understand the sort of writing that will be required, you can begin to recognize the structure your answer will need to take. This tentative structure will help you focus your attention on the particular information that will be pertinent to your answer. Consider this question from a sociology final:

> Drawing from lectures and discussions on the contradictory aspects of American values, the "bureaucratic personality," and the behaviors associated with social mobility, discuss the problems of attaining economic success in a relatively "open," complex, post-industrial society such as the United States.

Such a question can cause momentary panic, but you can nearly always define the writing task you face. Look first at the words that give you directions: *draw from* and *discuss*. The term *discuss* probably invites you to list and explain the problems of attaining economic success. The categories of these problems are already identified in the opening phrases: "contradictory . . . values," "bureaucratic personality," and "behaviors." Therefore, you would plan to begin with an assertion (or thesis) that included the key words in the final clause ("attaining economic success in a relatively open, complex, post-industrial society") and then take up each category of problem—and perhaps other problems you can think of—in separate paragraphs.

This question essentially calls for organization, recall, and clear presentation of facts from lectures and readings. Though the question looks confusing at first, once you sort it out, you will find that it contains the key terms for the answer's thesis, as well as the main points of development. The next section presents some further examples of the kinds of questions often found on essay exams. Pay particular attention to how the directions and the key words in each case can help you define the writing task involved.

SOME TYPICAL ESSAY EXAM QUESTIONS

Following are nine categories of exam questions, divided according to the sort of writing task involved and illustrated by examples. Although the wording of the examples in a category may differ, the essential directions are similar.

All of the examples are unedited and were written by instructors in six different departments in the humanities and social sciences at two different universities. Drawn from short quizzes, midterms, and final exams for a variety of first- and second-year courses, these questions demonstrate the range of writing you may be expected to do on exams.

Define or Identify

See Chapter 16 for more on defining.

Some questions require you to write a few sentences defining or identifying material from readings or lectures. Such questions almost always allow you only a few minutes to complete your answer.

You may be asked for a brief overview of a large topic, as in Question 23.1. This question, from a twenty-minute quiz in a literature course, was worth as much as 15 of the 100 points possible on the quiz.

Question 23.1

Name and describe the three stages of African literature.

Answering this question would simply involve following the specific directions. A student would probably *name* the periods in historical order and then *describe* each period in a separate sentence or two.

Other questions, like Question 23.2, supply a list of specific items to identify. This example comes from a final exam in a communication course, and the answer to each part was worth as much as 4 points on a 120-point exam.

Question 23.2

Define and state some important facts concerning each of the following:

A. demographics

B. instrumental model

C. RCA

D. telephone booth of the air

E. penny press

With no more than three or four minutes for each part, students taking this exam would offer a concise definition (probably in a sentence) and briefly expand the definition with facts relevant to the main topics in the course.

Sometimes the list of items to be identified can be complicated, including quotations, concepts, and specialized terms; it may also be worth a significant number of points. The next example contains the first five items in a list of fifteen that opened a literature final. Each item was worth 3 points, for a total of 45 out of a possible 130 points.

Question 23.3

Identify each of the following items:

1. projection
2. "In this vast landscape he had loved so much, he was alone."
3. Balducci
4. *pied noir*
5. the Massif Central

Although the directions do not say so specifically, a crucial aspect of this question is not just to identify each item but also to explain its significance in terms of the overall subject. In composing a definition or an identification, always ask yourself a simple question: Why is this item important enough to be on the exam?

Recall Details of a Specific Source

Sometimes instructors will ask for a straightforward summary or paraphrase of a specific source—for example, a report on a book or a film. To answer such questions, the student must recount details directly from the source and is not encouraged to interpret or evaluate. In the following example from a sociology exam, students were allowed about ten minutes and required to complete the answer on one lined page provided with the exam.

For more on paraphrasing and summarizing, see Chapter 12, pp. 595–97.

Question 23.4

In his article "Is There a Culture of Poverty?" Oscar Lewis addresses a popular question in the social sciences. What is the "culture of poverty"? How is it able to come into being, according to Lewis? That is, under what conditions does it exist? When does he say a person is no longer a part of the culture of poverty? What does Lewis say is the future of the culture of poverty?

The phrasing here invites a fairly clear-cut structure. Each of the five specific questions can be turned into an assertion and supported with illustrations from Lewis's article. For example, the first two questions could become assertions like these: "Lewis defines the culture of poverty as _______," and "According to Lewis, the culture of poverty comes into being through _______." The important thing in this case is to summarize accurately what the writer said and not waste time evaluating or criticizing his ideas.

Explain the Importance or Significance

Another kind of essay exam question asks students to explain the importance of something covered in the course. Such questions require specific examples as the basis for a more general discussion of what has been studied. This type of question often involves interpreting a literary or cinematic work by concentrating on a particular aspect of it, as in Question 23.5. This question was worth 10 out of 100 points and was to be answered in seventy-five to one hundred words.

Question 23.5

In the last scene of *The Paths of Glory*, the owner of a café brings a young German woman onto a small stage in his café to sing for the French troops, while Colonel Dax looks on from outside the café. Briefly explain the significance of this scene in relation to the movie as a whole.

In answering this question, a student's first task would be to reconsider the whole movie, looking for ways in which this one brief scene illuminates or explains larger issues or themes. Then, in a paragraph or two, the student would summarize these themes and point out how each element of the specific scene fits into the overall context.

You may also be asked to interpret specific information to show that you understand the fundamental concepts of a course. The following example from a Communications midterm was worth a possible 10 of 100 points and was allotted twenty minutes of exam time.

Question 23.6

Chukovsky gives many examples of cute expressions and statements uttered by small children. Give an example or two of the kinds of statements that he finds interesting. Then state their implications for understanding the nature of language in particular and communication more generally.

Here the student must start by choosing examples of children's utterances from Chukovsky's book. These examples would then provide the basis for demonstrating the student's grasp of the larger subject.

Questions like these are usually more challenging than definition and summary questions because you must decide for yourself the significance, importance, or implications of the information. You must also consider how best to organize your answer so that the general ideas you need to communicate are clearly developed.

Apply Concepts

See Chapter 5 for more on explaining a concept.

Very often, courses in the humanities and the social sciences emphasize significant themes, ideologies, or concepts. A common essay exam question asks students to apply the concepts to works studied in the course. Rather than providing specific information to be interpreted more generally, such questions present you with a general idea and require you to illustrate it with specific examples from your reading.

On a literature final, an instructor posed this writing task. It was worth 50 points out of 100, and students had about an hour to complete it.

Question 23.7

Many American writers have portrayed their characters or their poetic speaker as being engaged in a quest. The quest may be explicit or implicit, it may be external or psychological, and it may end in failure or success. Analyze the quest motif in the work of four of the following writers: Edwards, Franklin, Hawthorne, Thoreau, Douglass, Whitman, Dickinson, James, Twain.

On another literature final, the following question was worth 45 of 130 points. Students had about forty-five minutes to answer it.

Question 23.8

Several works studied in this course depict scapegoat figures. Select two written works and two films, and discuss how their authors or directors present and analyze the social conflicts that lead to the creation of scapegoats.

Question 23.7 instructs students to *analyze,* and Question 23.8 instructs them to *discuss;* yet the answers for both questions would be structured similarly. An introductory paragraph would define the concept—the *quest* or a *scapegoat*—and refer to the works to be discussed. Then a paragraph or two would be devoted to the works, developing specific support to illustrate the concept. A concluding paragraph would probably attempt to bring the concept into clearer focus, which is, after all, the point of answering these questions.

Comment on a Quotation

On essay exams, an instructor will often ask students to comment on a quotation they are seeing for the first time. Usually, such quotations will express some surprising or controversial opinion that complements or challenges basic principles or ideas in the course. Sometimes the writer being quoted is identified, sometimes not. In fact, it is not unusual for instructors to write the quotation themselves.

A student choosing to answer the following question from a literature final would have risked half the exam—in points and time—on the outcome.

Question 23.9

Argue for or against this thesis: "In *A Clockwork Orange,* both the heightened, poetic language and the almost academic concern with moral and political theories deprive the story of most of its relevance to real life."

The directions here clearly ask for an argument. A student would need to set up a thesis indicating that the novel either is or is not relevant to real life and then point out how its language and its theoretical concerns can be viewed in light of this thesis.

The next example comes from a midterm exam in a history course. Students had forty minutes to write their answers, which could earn as much as 70 points on a 100-point exam.

Question 23.10

"Some historians believe that economic hardship and oppression breed social revolt; but the experience of the United States and Mexico between 1900 and 1920 suggests that people may rebel also during times of prosperity."

Comment on this statement. Why did large numbers of Americans and Mexicans wish to change conditions in their countries during the years from 1900 to 1920? How successful were their efforts? Who benefited from the changes that took place?

Although here students are instructed to "comment," the three questions make clear that a successful answer will require an argument: a clear *thesis* stating a position on the views expressed in the quotation, specific *reasons* for that thesis, and *support* for the thesis from readings and lectures. In general, such questions do not require a "right" answer: Whether you agree or disagree with the quotation is not as important as whether you can argue your case reasonably and convincingly, demonstrating a firm grasp of the subject matter.

See Chapter 19 for more on these components of an argument.

Compare and Contrast

Instructors are particularly fond of essay exam questions that require a comparison and contrast of two or three principles, ideas, works, activities, or phenomena. To answer this kind of question, you need to explore fully the relations between things of importance in the course, analyze each thing separately, and then search out specific points of likeness or difference. Students must thus show a thorough knowledge of the things being compared, as well as a clear understanding of the basic issues on which comparisons and contrasts can be made.

Often, as in Question 23.11, the basis of comparison will be limited to a particular focus; here, for example, students are asked to compare two works in terms of their views of colonialism.

Question 23.11

Compare and analyze the views of colonialism presented in Memmi's *Colonizer and the Colonized* and Pontecorvo's *Battle of Algiers.* What are the significant differences between these two views?

Sometimes instructors will simply identify what is to be compared, leaving students the task of choosing the basis of the comparison, as in the next three examples from communication, history, and literature exams, respectively.

Question 23.12

In what way is the stage of electronic media fundamentally different from all the major stages that preceded it?

Question 23.13

What was the role of the United States in Cuban affairs from 1898 until 1959? How did its role there compare with its role in the rest of Spanish America during the same period?

Question 23.14

Write an essay on one of the following topics:

1. Squire Western and Mr. Knightley
2. Dr. Primrose and Mr. Elton

Whether the point of comparison is stated in the question or left for you to define for yourself, your answer needs to be limited to the aspects of similarity or difference that are most relevant to the general concepts or themes covered in the course.

See Chapter 18 for more on comparing and contrasting.

Synthesize Information from Various Sources

In a course with several assigned readings, an instructor may give students an essay exam question that requires them to pull together (synthesize) information from several or even all the readings.

For more on synthesizing, see Chapter 12, pp. 598–99.

The following example was one of four required questions on a final exam in a course in Latin American studies. Students had about thirty minutes to complete their answer.

Question 23.15

On the basis of the articles read on El Salvador, Nicaragua, Peru, Chile, Argentina, and Mexico, what would you say are the major problems confronting Latin America today? Discuss the major types of problems with references to particular countries as examples.

This question asks students to do a lot in thirty minutes. They must first decide which major problems to discuss, which countries to include in each discussion, and how to use material from many readings to develop their answers. To compose a coherent essay, a student will need a carefully developed forecasting statement.

For more on forecasting statements, see Chapter 13, p. 613.

Analyze Causes

In humanities and social science courses, much of what students study concerns the causes of trends, actions, and events. Hence, it is not surprising to find questions about causes on essay exams. In such cases, the instructor expects students to analyze causes from readings and lectures. These examples come from midterm and final exams in literature, sociology, cultural studies, and communication courses, respectively.

See Chapter 9 for more on analyzing causes.

Question 23.16

Why do Maurice and Jean not succumb to the intolerable conditions of the prison camp (the Camp of Hell) as most of the others do?

Question 23.17

Given that we occupy several positions in the course of our lives and given that each position has a specific role attached to it, what kinds of problems or dilemmas arise from those multiple roles, and how are they handled?

Question 23.18

Explain briefly the relationship between the institution of slavery and the emergence of the blues as a new African American musical expression.

Question 23.19

Analyze the way in which an uncritical promotion of the new information technology (computers, satellites, etc.) may support, unintentionally, the maintenance of the status quo.

Although these questions are presented in several ways ("what kinds of problems," "explain the relationship," "analyze the way"), they all require a list of causes in the answer. The causes would be organized under a thesis statement, and each cause would be argued and supported by referring to lectures or readings.

Criticize or Evaluate

See Chapter 8 for more on evaluation.

Occasionally, instructors will include essay exam questions that invite students to evaluate a concept or a work. Nearly always, they want more than opinion: They expect a reasoned, documented judgment based on appropriate standards of judgment. Such questions test students' ability to recall and synthesize pertinent information and to understand and apply criteria taught in the course.

On a final exam in a literature course, a student might have chosen one of the following questions about novels read in the course. Each would have been worth half the total points, with about an hour to answer it.

Question 23.20

Evaluate *A Passage to India* from a postcolonial critical standpoint.

Question 23.21

A Clockwork Orange and *The Comfort of Strangers* both attempt to examine the nature of modern decadence. Which does so more successfully?

To answer either of these questions, a student would have to be very familiar with the novels under discussion and would have to establish standards for evaluating works of literature. The student would initially have to make a judgment favoring one novel over the other (though not necessarily casting one novel as "terrible" and the other as "perfect"). The student would then give reasons for this judgment, with supporting quotations from the novels, and probably use the writing strategies of comparison and contrast to develop the argument.

See Chapter 18 for more on comparing and contrasting.

This next question was worth 10 of 85 points on a communication course midterm. Students were asked to answer "in two paragraphs."

Question 23.22

Eisenstein and Mukerji both argue that movable print was important to the rise of Protestantism. Cole extends this argument to say that print set off a chain of events that was important to the history of the United States. Summarize this argument, and criticize any part of it if you choose.

Here students are asked to criticize or evaluate an argument in several course readings. The instructor wants to know what students think of this argument and even though this is not stated, why they judge it as they do. Answering this unwritten "why" part of the question is the challenge: Students must come up with reasons and support appropriate to evaluating the argument.

PLANNING YOUR ANSWER

The amount of planning you do for a question will depend on how much time it is allotted and how many points it is worth. For short-answer definitions and identifications, a few seconds of thought will probably be sufficient. (Be careful not to puzzle too long over individual items like these. Skip over any you cannot recognize fairly quickly; often, answering other questions will help jog your memory.) For answers that require a paragraph or two, you may want to jot down several ideas and examples to focus your thoughts and give you a basis for organizing your information.

For longer answers, though, you will need to develop a much more definite strategy of organization. You have time for only one draft, so allow a reasonable period—as much as a quarter of the time allotted the question—for making notes, determining a thesis, and developing an outline. Jotting down pertinent ideas is a good way to begin; then you can plan your organization with a scratch outline (just a listing of points or facts) or a cluster.

For questions with several parts (different requests or directions, a sequence of questions), make a list of the parts so that you do not miss or minimize one part. For questions presented as questions (rather than directives), you might want to rephrase each question as a writing topic. These topics will often suggest how you should outline the answer.

For information on clustering and outlining, see Chapter 11, pp. 570–75.

You may have to try two or three outlines or clusters before you hit on a workable plan. But be realistic as you outline: You want a plan you can develop within the limited time allotted for your answer. Hence, your outline will have to be selective. It will contain not everything you know on the topic but rather what you know that can be developed clearly within the time available.

WRITING YOUR ANSWER

As with planning, your strategy for writing depends on the length of your answer. For short identifications and definitions, it is usually best to start with a general identifying statement and then move on to describe specific applications or explanations. Two sentences will almost always suffice, but make sure you write complete sentences.

For longer answers, begin by stating your forecasting statement or thesis clearly and explicitly. An essay exam is not an occasion for indirectness: You want to strive for focus, simplicity, and clarity. In stating your point and developing your answer, use key terms from the question; it may look as though you are avoiding the question unless you use key terms (the same key terms) throughout your essay. If the question does not supply any key terms, you will find that you have provided your own by stating your main point. Use these key terms throughout the answer.

If you have devised a promising outline for your answer, you will be able to forecast your overall plan and its subpoints in your opening sentences. Forecasting shows readers how your essay is organized and has the practical advantage of making your answer easier to read. You might also want to use briefer paragraphs than you ordinarily do and signal clear relations between paragraphs with transition phrases or sentences.

See Chapter 13 for more on forecasting and transitions.

As you begin writing your answer, freely strike out words or even sentences you want to change by drawing through them neatly with a single line. Do not stop to erase, and try not to be messy. Instructors do not expect flawless writing, but they are put off by unnecessary messiness.

As you continue to write, you will certainly think of new subpoints and new ideas or facts to include later in the essay answer. Stop briefly to make a note of these on your original outline. If you find that you want to add a sentence or two to sections you have already completed, write them in the margin or at the top of the page, with a neat arrow pointing to where they fit in your answer.

Do not pad your answer with irrelevancies and repetitions just to fill up space. You may have had an instructor who did not seem to pay much attention to what you wrote, but most instructors read exams carefully and are not impressed by the length of an answer alone. Within the time available, write a comprehensive, specific answer without padding.

Watch the clock carefully so that you do not spend too much time on one answer. You must be realistic about the time constraints of an essay exam, especially if you know the material well and are prepared to write a lot. If you write one dazzling answer on an exam with three required questions, you earn only 33 points, not enough to pass at most colleges. Being required to answer more than one question may seem unfair, but keep in mind that instructors plan exams to be reasonably comprehensive. They want you to write about the course materials in two or three or more ways, not just one way.

If you run out of time when you are writing an answer, jot down the remaining main ideas from your outline, just to show that you know the material and with more time could have continued your exposition.

Write legibly and proofread what you write. Remember that your instructor will likely be reading a large pile of exams. Careless scrawls, misspellings, omitted words, and missing punctuation (especially missing periods needed to mark the ends of sentences) will only make that reading difficult, even exasperating. A few minutes of careful proofreading can improve your grade.

MODEL ANSWERS TO SOME TYPICAL ESSAY EXAM QUESTIONS

Here we analyze several successful answers and give you an opportunity to analyze one for yourself. These analyses, along with the information we have provided elsewhere in this chapter, should greatly improve your chances of writing successful exam answers.

Short Answers

A literature midterm opened with ten items to identify, each worth 3 points. Students had about two minutes for each item. Here are three of Brenda Gossett's answers, each one earning her the full 3 points.

> Rauffenstein: He was the German general who was in charge of the castle where Boeldieu, Marical, and Rosenthal were finally sent in The Grand Illusion. He, along with Boeldieu, represented the aristocracy, which was slowly fading out at that time.
>
> Iges Peninsula: This peninsula is created by the Meuse River in France. It is there that the Camp of Hell was created in The Debacle. The Camp of Hell is where the French army was interned after the Germans defeated them in the Franco-Prussian War.
>
> Pache: He was the "religious peasant" in the novel The Debacle. It was he who inevitably became a scapegoat when he was murdered by Loubet, La Poulle, and Chouteau because he wouldn't share his bread with them.

The instructor said only "identify the following" but clearly wanted students both to identify the item and to indicate its significance to the work in which it appeared. Gossett does both and gets full credit. She mentions particular works, characters, and events. Although she is rushed, she answers in complete sentences. She does not misspell any words or leave out any commas or periods. Her answers are complete and correct.

Paragraph-Length Answers

One question on a weekly literature quiz was worth 20 points of the total of 100. With only a few minutes to answer the question, students were instructed to "answer in a few sentences." Here is the question and Camille Prestera's answer:

> In *Things Fall Apart,* how did Okonkwo's relationship with his father affect his attitude toward his son?

> Okonkwo despised his father, who was lazy, cowardly, and in debt. Okonkwo tried to be everything his father wasn't. He was hardworking, wealthy, and a great warrior and wrestler. Okonkwo treated his son harshly because he was afraid he saw the same weakness in Nwoye that he despised in his father. The result of this harsh treatment was that Nwoye left home.

Prestera begins by describing Okonkwo and his father, contrasting the two sharply. Then she explains Okonkwo's relationship with his son Nwoye. Her answer is coherent and straightforward.

Long Answers

Many final exams include at least one question requiring an essay-length answer. John Pixley had an hour to plan and write this essay for a final exam in a literature course in response to Question 23.7:

> Many American writers have portrayed their characters or their poetic speaker as being engaged in a quest. The quest may be explicit or implicit, it may be external or psychological, and it may end in failure or success. Analyze the quest motif in the work of four of the following writers: Edwards, Franklin, Hawthorne, Thoreau, Douglass, Whitman, Dickinson, James, Twain.

John Pixley's Answer

Key term, quest, *is mentioned in introduction and thesis.*

Americans pride themselves on being ambitious and on being able to strive for goals and to tap their potential. Some say that this is what the "American Dream" is all about. It is important for one to do and be all that one is capable of. This entails a quest or search for identity, experience, and happiness. Hence, the idea of the quest is a vital one in the United States, and it can be seen as a theme throughout American literature. 1

In eighteenth-century colonial America, Jonathan Edwards dealt with this theme in his autobiographical and personal writings. Unlike his fiery and hard-nosed sermons, these autobiographical writings present a sensitive, vulnerable man trying to find himself and his proper, satisfying place in the world. He is concerned with his spiritual growth, in being free to find and explore religious experience and happiness. For example, in Personal Narrative, he very carefully traces the stages of religious beliefs. He tells about periods of abandoned ecstasy, doubts, and rational revelations. He also notes that his best insights and growth came at times when he was alone in the wilderness, in nature. Edwards's efforts to find himself in relation to the world can also be seen in his "Observations of the Natural World," in which he relates various meticulously observed and described natural phenomena to religious precepts and occurrences. Here, he is trying to give the world and life, of which he is a part, some sense of meaning and purpose.

2 *First writer is identified immediately.*

Edwards's work and the details of his quest are presented.

Although he was a contemporary of Edwards, Benjamin Franklin, who was very involved in the founding of the United States as a nation, had a different conception of the quest. He sees the quest as being one for practical accomplishment, success, and wealth. In his Autobiography, he stresses that happiness involves working hard to accomplish things, getting along with others, and establishing a good reputation. Unlike Edwards's, his quest is external and bound up with society. He is concerned with his morals and behavior, but, as seen in part 2 of the Autobiography, he deals with them in an objective, pragmatic, even statistical way, rather than in sensitive pondering. It is also evident in this work that Franklin, unlike Edwards, believes so much in himself and his quest that he is able to laugh at himself. His concern with society can be seen in Poor Richard's Almanac, in which he gives practical advice on how to find success and happiness in the world, how to "be healthy, wealthy, and wise."

3 *Transition sentence identifies second writer. Key term* (quest) *is repeated.*

Contrast with Edwards adds coherence to essay.

Another key term from the question, external, *is used.*

Franklin's particular kind of quest is described.

Still another version of the quest can be seen in the mid-nineteenth-century poetry of Walt Whitman. The quest that he portrays blends elements of those of Edwards and Franklin. In "Song of Myself," which is clearly autobiographical, the speaker emphasizes the importance of finding, knowing, and enjoying oneself as part of nature and the human community. He says that one should come to realize that one is lovable, just

4 *Transition sentence identifies third writer. Key term is repeated.*

Comparison of Whitman to Edwards and Franklin sustains coherence of essay.

Whitman's quest is defined.

as are all other people and all of nature and life. This is a quest for sensitivity and awareness, as Edwards advocates, and for great self-confidence, as Franklin advocates. Along with Edwards, Whitman sees that peaceful isolation in nature is important; but he also sees the importance of interacting with people, as Franklin does. Being optimistic and feeling good--both in the literal and figurative sense--are the objects of this quest. Unfortunately, personal disappointment and national crisis (i.e., the Civil War) shattered Whitman's sense of confidence, and he lost the impetus of this quest in his own life.

Transition: Key term is repeated, and fourth writer is identified.

This theme of the quest can be seen in prose fiction as 5
well as in poetry and autobiography. One interesting example is "The Beast in the Jungle," a short story written by Henry James around 1903. It is interesting in that not only does the principal character, John Marcher, fail in his lifelong quest, but his failure comes about in a most subtle and frustrating way.

Quest of James character is described.

Marcher believes that something momentous is going to happen in his future. He talks about his belief to only one person, a woman named May. May decides to befriend him for life and watch with him for the momentous occurrence to come about, for "the beast in the jungle" to "pounce." As time passes, May seems to know what this occurrence is and eventually even says that it has happened; but John is still in the dark. It is only long after May's death that the beast pounces on him in his recognition that the "beast" was his failure to truly love May, the one woman of his life, even though she gave him all the encouragement that she possibly, decently could. Marcher never defined the terms of his quest until it was too late. By just waiting and watching, he failed to find feeling and passion. This tragic realization, as someone like Whitman would view it, brings about John Marcher's ruin.

Conclusion repeats key term.

As seen in these few examples, the theme of the quest is 6
a significant one in American literature. Also obvious is the fact that there are a variety of approaches to, methods used in, and outcomes of the quest. This is an appropriate theme for American literature seeing how much Americans cherish the right of "the pursuit of happiness."

Pixley's answer is strong for two reasons: He has the information he needs, and he has organized it carefully and presented it coherently.

Exercise 23.1

The following essay was written by Dan Hepler. He answered the same essay exam question as his classmate John Pixley. Analyze Hepler's essay to discover whether it meets the criteria of a good essay exam answer. Review the criteria mentioned earlier in this chapter in Writing Your Answer and in the annotated commentary of John Pixley's answer. Try to identify the features of Hepler's essay that contribute to or work against its success.

Dan Hepler's Answer

The quest motif is certainly important in American literature. By considering Franklin, Thoreau, Douglass, and Twain, we can see that the quest may be explicit or implicit, external or psychological, a failure or a success. Tracing the quest motif through these four authors seems to show a developing concern in American literature with transcending materialism to address deeper issues. It also reveals a drift toward ambiguity and pessimism. 1

Benjamin Franklin's quest, as revealed by his _Autobiography_, is for material comfort and outward success. His quest may be considered an explicit one because he announces clearly what he is trying to do: perfect a systematic approach for living long and happily. The whole _Autobiography_ is a road map intended for other people to use as a guide; Franklin apparently meant rather literally for people to imitate his methods. He wrote with the assumption that his success was reproducible. He is possibly the most optimistic author in American literature because he enjoys life, knows exactly _why_ he enjoys life, and believes that anyone else willing to follow his formula may enjoy life as well. 2

By Franklin's standards, his quest is clearly a success. But his _Autobiography_ portrays only an external, not a psychological, success. This is not to suggest that Franklin was a psychological failure. Indeed, we have every reason to believe the contrary. But the fact remains that Franklin _wrote_ only about external success; he never indicated how he really felt emotionally. Possibly it was part of Franklin's overriding optimism to assume that material comfort leads naturally to emotional fulfillment. 3

Henry David Thoreau presents a more multifaceted quest. His _Walden_ is, on the simplest level, the chronicle of 4

Thoreau's physical journey out of town and into the woods. But the moving itself is not the focus of Walden. It is really more of a metaphor for some kind of spiritual quest going on within Thoreau's mind. Most of the action in Walden is mental, as Thoreau contemplates and philosophizes, always using the lake, the woods, and his own daily actions as symbols of higher, more eternal truths. This spiritual quest is a success in that Thoreau is able to appreciate the beauty of nature and to see through much of the sham and false assumptions of town life and blind materialism.

Thoreau does not leave us with nearly as explicit a 5
"blueprint" for success as Franklin does. Even Franklin's plan is limited to people of high intelligence, personal discipline, and sound character; Franklin sometimes seems to forget that many human beings are in fact weak and evil and so would stand little chance of success similar to his own. But at least Franklin's quest could be duplicated by another Franklin. Thoreau's quest is more problematic, for even as great a mystic and naturalist as Thoreau himself could not remain in the woods indefinitely. This points toward the idea that the real quest is all internal and psychological; Thoreau seems to have gone to the woods to develop a spiritual strength that he could keep and take elsewhere on subsequent dealings with the "real world."

The quest of Frederick Douglass was explicit in that he 6
needed physically to get north and escape slavery, but it was also implicit because he sought to discover and redefine himself through his quest, as Thoreau did. Douglass's motives were more sharply focused than either Franklin's or Thoreau's; his very humanness was at stake, as well as his physical well-being and possibly even his life. But Douglass also makes it clear that the most horrible part of slavery was the mental anguish of having no hope of freedom. His learning to read, and his maintenance of this skill, seems to have been as important as the maintenance of his material comforts, of which he had very few. In a sense, Douglass's quest is the most psychological and abstract so far because it is for the very essence of freedom and humanity, both of which were mostly taken for granted by Franklin and Thoreau. Also, Douglass's quest is the most pessimistic of the three; Douglass concludes that physical violence is the only way out, as he finds with the Covey incident.

Finally, Mark Twain's <u>Huckleberry Finn</u> is an example of the full range of meaning that the quest motif may assume. Geographically, Huck's quest is very large. But again, there is a quest defined implicitly as well as one defined explicitly, as Huck (without consciously realizing it) searches for morality, truth, and freedom. Twain's use of the quest is ambiguous, even more so than the previous writers', because while he suggests success superficially (i.e., the "happily ever after" scene in the last chapter), he really hints at some sort of ultimate hopelessness inherent in society. Not even Douglass questions the good or evil of American society as deeply as Twain does; for Douglass, everything will be fine when slavery is abolished; but for Twain, the only solution is to "light out for the territories" altogether--and when Twain wrote, he knew that the territories were no more. 7

Twain's implicit sense of spiritual failure stands in marked contrast to Franklin's buoyant confidence in material success. The guiding image of the quest, however, is central to American values and, consequently, a theme that these writers and others have adapted to suit their own vision. 8

Exercise 23.2

Analyze the following essay exam questions to decide what kind of writing task they present. What is being asked of the student as a participant in the course and as a writer? Given the time constraints of the exam, what plan would you propose for writing the answer? Following each question is the number of points it is worth and the amount of time allotted to answer it.

1. Cortazar is a producer of fantastic literature. Discuss first what fantastic literature is. Then choose any four stories by Cortazar as examples, and discuss the fantastic elements in these stories. Refer to the structure, techniques, and narrative styles that he uses in these four stories. If you like, you may refer to more than four, of course. (Points: 30 of 100. Time: 40 of 150 minutes.)
2. During the course of the twentieth century, the United States has experienced three significant periods of social reform—the progressive era, the age of the Great Depression, and the decade of the 1960s. What were the sources of reform in each period? What were the most significant reform achievements of each period as well as the largest failings? (Points: 35 of 100. Time: 75 of 180 minutes.)
3. Since literature is both an artistic and ideological product, writers comment on their material context through their writing.
   a. What is Rulfo's perspective of his Mexican reality, and how is it portrayed through his stories?

b. What particular themes does he deal with, especially in these stories: "The Burning Plain," "Luvina," "They Gave Us the Land," "Paso del Norte," and "Tell Them Not to Kill Me"?
c. What literary techniques and structures does he use to convey his perspective? Refer to a specific story as an example.

(Points: 30 of 100. Time: 20 of 50 minutes.)

4. Why is there a special reason to be concerned about the influence of television watching on kids? In your answer, include a statement of the following:
   a. Your own understanding of the *general communication principles* involved for any television watcher.
   b. What is special about television and kids.
   c. How advertisers and producers use this information. (You should draw from the relevant readings as well as lectures.)

   (Points: 20 of 90. Time: 25 of 90 minutes.)
5. Analyze the autobiographical tradition in American literature, focusing on differences and similarities among authors and, if appropriate, changes over time. Discuss four authors in all. In addition to the conscious autobiographers—Edwards, Franklin, Thoreau, Douglass—you may choose one or two figures from among the following fictional or poetic quasi-autobiographers: Hawthorne, Whitman, Dickinson, Twain. (Points: 50 of 120. Time: 60 of 180 minutes.)
6. How does the system of (media) sponsorship work, and what, if any, ideological control do sponsors exert? Be specific and illustrative. (Points: 33 of 100. Time: 60 of 180 minutes.)
7. Several of the works studied in this course analyze the tension between myth and reality. Select two written works and two films, and analyze how their authors or directors present the conflict between myth and reality and how they resolve it, if they resolve it. (Points: 45 of 130. Time: 60 of 180 minutes.)
8. *Man's Hope* is a novel about the Spanish Civil War written while the war was still going on. *La Guerre Est Finie* is a film about Spanish revolutionaries depicting their activities nearly thirty years after the civil war. Discuss how the temporal relationship of each of these works to the civil war is reflected in the character of the works themselves and in the differences between them. (Points: 58 of 100. Time: 30 of 50 minutes.)
9. Write an essay on one of these topics: The role of the narrator in *Tom Jones* and *Pride and Prejudice* or the characters of Uncle Toby and Miss Bates. (Points: 33 of 100. Time: 60 of 180 minutes.)

Writing Portfolios

24

A writing portfolio displays your work. Portfolios for college composition courses usually include a selection of your writing for the course and an essay reflecting on your learning in the course. The contents of a portfolio will, of course, vary from writer to writer and from instructor to instructor. This chapter provides some advice for assembling a writing portfolio using the resources in *The St. Martin's Guide to Writing*.

THE PURPOSES OF A WRITING PORTFOLIO

Portfolios are widely used for many purposes, most generally to display an individual's accomplishments. Artists present portfolios of their work to gallery owners and patrons. Designers and architects present portfolios of their most successful and imaginative work to show potential clients what they can do. Some colleges request applicants to submit portfolios of high school writing; outstanding portfolios sometimes qualify students for college credit or placement in advanced courses. Graduating seniors may be asked to submit a portfolio of their best work for evaluation, sometimes leading to special recognition or rewards. Instructors applying for new positions or advancement may compile a portfolio to demonstrate excellence or innovation in their teaching. No matter what the specific purpose or occasion, a portfolio can present a rich opportunity to show what you can do.

Creating a portfolio for a composition course enables you to present your best, most representative, or most extensively revised writing and, to some extent, collaborate with your instructor in assessing your work. Your instructor will assign the final grade, but how you select the materials included in your portfolio and describe them in your introductory essay may have some influence on your instructor's judgment. Most important, selecting your work and composing a reflective essay gives you an opportunity to think critically about your learning in the course. Thinking critically, as we explain in Chapter 1, is a kind of metacognition that helps learners consolidate, reinforce, and therefore better remember and apply what they have learned. Putting together your portfolio, you reflect on what you have learned about the basic features of different genres, the writing strategies that help your writing achieve its purpose

For more on the process of thinking critically, see pp. 12–14.

for your particular readers, the composing strategies that enable you to manage complex and challenging writing assignments, and the reading and researching strategies that contribute to your success in college. In addition, reviewing your work can increase your satisfaction with your courses as you become more aware of the specific ways in which your knowledge is growing. Finally, it can give you insights into your own intellectual development, help you recognize your strengths and weaknesses, and discover your interests.

Whether or not you are asked to turn in a writing portfolio, you might want to consider keeping one as a valuable personal record of an important period in your intellectual development. You might even wish to update the portfolio each term, adding interesting work from all your courses or perhaps from all the courses in your major.

ASSEMBLING A PORTFOLIO FOR YOUR COMPOSITION COURSE

Some instructors give students free rein in deciding what to include in their portfolio, but most instructors specify what the portfolio should include. They usually ask students to select a certain number of the essays assigned in the course. They may specify that certain types of essays be included, such as one based on personal experience or observation and another based on library and Internet research, along with other materials like in-class writing or responses to readings. Many instructors also ask students to include materials that reflect their writing process for at least one of the essays (such as invention work, drafts, and critical responses). In addition to a selection of course materials, instructors usually require a reflective essay or letter that introduces the portfolio and evaluates the writer's own work.

Instructors who require portfolios often do not assign grades to individual drafts or revisions but wait until the end of the term to grade the entire portfolio. In such cases, instructors may ask students to submit a midterm portfolio for an in-progress course evaluation. A midterm portfolio usually includes plans for revising further one or more of the assigned essays.

There are many possible ways of assembling portfolios, and you will need to determine exactly what your instructor expects your portfolio to include. Here are some of the variables:

- Of the essays assigned in the course, how many should be included in the portfolio?
- How many of the essays assigned throughout the course may be revised further for the portfolio?
- What process work should be included?
- What other material written or collected for the course should be included (such as exercises, notes from collaborative activities, analyses of readings, downloaded Web pages)?

- What material from other courses, workplace projects, or service-learning projects may be included?
- Should the portfolio be introduced by a reflective essay or letter? If so, how long should it be? Are there any special requirements for this essay?
- How should the portfolio be organized? Should there be a table of contents? How should each entry be labeled and each page be numbered?
- Will the essays be graded when they are turned in, at midterm, or only at the end of the term when the final portfolio is submitted?

For more on service learning, see Chapter 28.

The following sections review specific resources in *The St. Martin's Guide to Writing* that can help you select work to include in your portfolio, reflect on what you have learned, and organize your portfolio.

Selecting Work

Your instructor will very likely specify a list of what to include in your portfolio. Whatever materials you include, you have some important decisions to make, and these decisions reveal a lot about you as a writer. Here are some suggestions to help you make selections:

- If you are asked to select only your best essays, you might begin by rereading your essays to see how well each one develops the basic features of its genre. Also review any critical responses you received from your instructor, classmates, writing center tutors, or other critical readers.
- If you are asked to make further revisions to one or more of your essays, you might begin by rereading the latest revision of each essay, using the Critical Reading Guide for that genre, or getting a critical response to each essay from your instructor, a classmate, or a writing center tutor. It may also help to review any critical responses you received on earlier drafts and the revision chart you made earlier to see what else you could do to improve the essay. Be sure to edit and proofread your essays carefully.
- If you are asked to select essays based on personal experience, you might choose from the remembering events and remembering people essays you wrote for Chapters 2 and 3. If you are asked for essays based on firsthand observation and analysis, look at what you wrote for the profile (Chapter 4), the story interpretation (Chapter 10), or the concept explanation (Chapter 5). If you are asked to include argument essays, review the writing you did for Chapters 6–9.
- If you are asked to select essays incorporating library or Internet research, look at the essays you wrote for Chapters 5–9.
- If you are asked to select essays with a range of different purposes and audiences, you might begin by reviewing the Purpose and Audience sections of the Part One chapters you used. Then reread your invention notes defining the particular purpose and audience for each essay you wrote.

- If you are asked to include examples of your writing process work, look in your process materials for your most imaginative invention work, for a first draft and one or more revisions showing significant rethinking or reorganization, for your critical reading response to another student's draft showing perceptive criticism and helpful suggestions, or for sentences you edited and the chart of your common errors.
- If you are asked to include a complete process for one essay, you might choose process materials that show the quality as well as quantity of work you have done. To reflect the quality of your work, look for examples of thoughtful invention and substantive revision you can point out in your reflective essay.
- If you are asked to select essays that show the progress you have made in the course, you may want to choose essays that underwent radical change through the term.

Reflecting on Your Work and Your Learning

Many instructors require a written statement in the form of an essay or letter introducing the portfolio. Some ask for a simple description of the work presented in your portfolio; others prefer an evaluation of your work; still others may want you to connect your learning in this course to other courses and to work you hope to do in the future. Keeping the following considerations in mind will help you write a thoughtful, well-organized statement to your instructor about what you have learned:

- ***Introduce and describe your work.*** Because you will need to refer to several works or parts of a work, name each item in your portfolio in a consistent way. In describing an essay, give its title, genre (using the title of the chapter in *The St. Martin's Guide*), purpose, audience, and topic.
- ***Justify your choices.*** When you justify what you see as your "best" work, you think critically about the standards you are using to evaluate good writing in each genre. *The St. Martin's Guide* sets forth clear criteria for each kind of writing in the Basic Features and Critical Reading sections in Chapters 2–10. Review these sections as you judge the success of your essay, and refer to them as you explain your choice.

If you need help writing an evaluation, review Chapter 8.

- ***Illustrate your growth as a writer with specific examples.*** You may have selected work to show how you have grown as a writer, but you should not assume your readers will read the portfolio as you do without some guidance. You need to show them where they can find evidence that supports your statements by citing relevant examples from the work included in your portfolio. Summarize or quote your examples and be sure to tell readers what you think the examples illustrate. Also refer to them in a way that will help readers locate them with ease—perhaps by page and paragraph number (see the next section for some suggestions for organizing your portfolio).
- ***Use* The St. Martin's Guide *to help you reflect on your learning.*** Your instructor may ask you to consider what you learned in writing and revising a particu-

lar essay as well as what you learned about the process of writing that essay. In either case, it will help you to anchor your reflections in the specific work you have done using this book. Consider what you have learned analyzing and discussing the readings, inventing and researching, participating in group inquiry, planning and drafting, getting and giving critical comments, and revising and editing. Look again at the Thinking Critically about What You Have Learned sections in Chapters 2–10. There you will find questions that will help you reflect on how you solved problems when revising an essay, how reading influenced your writing, and how your writing can be situated and understood in a larger social context. You may well be able to use material you have already written for these sections in your portfolio reflective essay.

Organizing the Portfolio

Some instructors prescribe the portfolio's design and organization, while others allow students to be creative. Portfolios may be presented in an inexpensive manila folder, a looseleaf, or on a Web site. Follow your instructor's specific guidelines. Here are some possibilities for organizing your portfolio:

- ***Include a cover or front page.*** The design of the front page may be left up to you. But be sure to indicate the class section number, the instructor's name, your own name, and the date.
- ***Include a table of contents.*** Portfolios, like books, need a table of contents so that readers can see at a glance what is included and where it is located. The table of contents should appear at the beginning of the portfolio, identify all of the parts of the portfolio, and specify the page on which each part begins. You may decide to renumber all of the pages in the portfolio consecutively even though some of the material already has page numbers. If you add new page numbers, consider using a different color, putting the new page numbers in a new place, or using a letter- or word-number sequence (such as *Event-1, Position-1*, etc.). Whatever you decide, be consistent.
- ***Include a reflective essay or letter.*** Most instructors want the reflective essay to be the first item in the portfolio following the table of contents. In this position, the reflective essay introduces the material in the portfolio. Your instructor may use your reflective essay as a guide, reading the sections of the portfolio you specifically refer to in your essay before skimming the rest of the material.
- ***Label each item.*** If your instructor does not specify how you should label your work, you need to develop a clear system on your own. You may need to explain your system briefly in a note on the table of contents or in your reflective essay where you refer to particular items in your portfolio. For example, you could use *The St. Martin's Guide* chapter number to identify each essay assignment. To indicate process materials, consider using the chapter number and title and the relevant heading from that chapter's Guide to Writing section (such as Chapter 2, Exploring Your Present Perspective). To identify different drafts, you could write on the top left margin of every page the chapter number, essay title, and

draft number. For drafts that received a critical reading, you might want to add the notation "Read by *S*." You should also date all of your work.

- ***Sequence the material.*** If your instructor does not indicate how you should order the work included in your portfolio, you will have to decide yourself. The sequence of materials should be consistent with the way you introduce your work in the reflective essay. If your instructor asks you to present two or more examples of your best work, you may want to begin with the essay you consider your very best. If your instructor asks you to show the progress you have made in the course, you could begin with your weakest essay and either show how you improved it or how later essays were stronger. If your instructor asks you to demonstrate growth, you might organize your work by the particular areas that improved. For example, you could show that you learned to revise substantively by presenting earlier and later revisions of an essay from early in the course and following them with a pair of revisions from a subsequent and more extensively reworked essay. Or to show that you learned to edit or altogether avoid certain sentence errors, you could give examples of a particular error being corrected in a revision and the same error being avoided in a later first draft.

Part Six

WRITING AND SPEAKING TO WIDER AUDIENCES

Designing Documents

25

This chapter introduces basic components of document design, discusses some common formats of paper and electronic documents you may be asked to create in your college courses or in the workplace, and offers guidelines for designing documents that many students, instructors, and business writers have found effective.

When you are required to use a particular document format such as the MLA or APA style for an academic writing assignment, you will not have many design choices. Your instructor will expect you to follow the MLA or APA rules for spacing, margins, heading formats, and so on. For writing assignments that do not require you to follow a particular academic format, you will have more flexibility.

For more on MLA or APA style, see Chapter 22.

ELEMENTS OF DOCUMENT DESIGN

Paper and electronic documents differ in important ways, but both employ basic principles of design, using typography, visuals, and white space to enhance readability. These principles have been developed over the centuries as increasing numbers of people have gained access to reading material, and designers today benefit not only from this accumulated knowledge but also from studies that have examined how the eye moves over the page, how readers actually read documents, and how reading takes place within different contexts.

Typography

Typography is the designer's term for the letters and symbols that make up the print on the page. You are already using important aspects of typography when you use capital letters, italics, boldface, or different sizes of type to signal a new sentence, identify the title of a book, or distinguish a heading from body text.

Word processing programs and personal computers now enable you to use dozens of different typefaces (fonts), bold and italic versions of these fonts, and a range of font sizes. Fortunately, you can rely on some simple design principles to make good typographic choices for your documents.

Choose Fonts That Are Easy to Read. A **font family** consists of the font in different sizes as well as in its boldface and italic forms. Not all fonts are suitable for extended pieces of writing.

Considering Font Style. Sentences and paragraphs printed in fonts that imitate ***calligraphy*** or handwriting are not only difficult to read but also informal in appearance. For most academic and business writing, you will probably want to choose a traditional font, such as `Courier` or Times New Roman, that is easy to read and does not call attention to itself. This book is set in Galliard.

Considering Font Size. To ensure that your documents can be read easily, you also need to choose an appropriate font size (traditionally measured in units called **points**). For most types of academic writing, a 12-point font is the standard size used for the main (body) text. However, for Web pages, you should consider using a larger font to compensate for the added difficulty of reading from a computer monitor. For overhead transparencies and computer-projected displays, you should use an even larger font size (such as 32-point) to ensure that the text can be read from a distance.

Combining Font Styles and Sizes. Although computers now make hundreds of font styles and sizes available to writers, you should avoid confusing readers with too many typographical features. Limit the fonts in a document to one or two font families. A common practice is to choose one font family for all titles and headings and another for the body text.

Use Boldface, Italics, and Font Size to Distinguish between Headings and Body Text. Titles and headings are often distinguished from body text by boldface, italics, or font size. These elements of typography are helpful in calling attention to certain parts or sections of a piece of writing, showing the hierarchy of its headings and subheadings as well as offering readers visual cues to its overall organization. However, you should always check with your instructor about the conventions for using (or not using) these elements in the particular discipline you are studying.

Distinguishing between Headings and Subheadings. Headings for major sections (level-one headings) must be visually distinct from headings that subdivide the major sections (level-two headings) and from headings that appear within the subdivisions (level-three headings). The most important headings should have more impact than any subheadings. The typography should reflect this hierarchy of the headings. Here is one possible system for distinguishing among three levels of headings:

LEVEL-ONE HEADING

Level-Two Heading

Level-Three Heading

Notice that the level-one and level-two headings are given the greatest prominence by the use of boldface and that they are distinguished from one another by the use of all capital letters for the major headings versus upper- and lowercase letters for the subheadings. The third-level heading, italicized but not boldfaced, is less prominent than the other two headings but can still be readily distinguished from body text. Whatever system you use to distinguish headings and subheadings, be sure to apply it consistently throughout the document.

For more on selecting appropriate headings and subheadings, see Chapter 13, pp. 623–25.

Positioning Headings Consistently. In addition to keeping track of the font size and style of headings, you need to position headings in the same way throughout a piece of writing. You will want to consider the spacing above and below headings and determine whether the headings should be aligned with the left margin, indented a fixed amount of space, or centered on the page.

Note: When you are required to observe the MLA or APA style of document design, you should center level-one headings (but do not add extra space above or below them), type headings in the same font and size used for the body text (do not use boldface or italics), and capitalize the important words in headings. While the MLA offers no specific guidelines for styling multiple levels of headings, the APA has specific formats for up to five levels of headings. For more information on the APA style for headings and subheadings, consult the *Publication Manual of the American Psychological Association* (5th edition, 2001) or the APA Web site at http://www.apastyle.org.

Using Type Size to Differentiate Headings from Text. In documents that do not need to observe the MLA or APA style, you may wish to use font size to help make headings visually distinct from the body of the text. If you do so, avoid using unnecessary space. To accompany 12-point body text, for instance, 14-point headings will suffice. The default settings for heading and body text styles on most word processing and desktop publishing programs are effective.

Consider Using Numbered and Bulleted Lists. Lists are often an effective way to present information in a logical and visually coherent way. Use a **numbered list** (1, 2, 3) to present the steps in a sequential process or to set forth items that readers will need to refer to easily (for instance, see Figure 25.12, p. 837). Use a **bulleted list** (marking each new item with a "bullet"—that is, a dash, circle, or box) to highlight key points when the order of the items is not significant (for instance, see Figure 25.10, p. 835).

Add Colors Sparingly and Systematically, If at All. Color printers, photocopiers, and online technology facilitate the use of color typography, but this technology does not necessarily make text easier to read. In most academic writing, the only color you should use is black. If you think using an additional color will increase your readers' understanding of what you have to say, experiment with a color that contrasts well with the black type and white background to see whether the mix of colors provides you with the flexibility you need. In addition, consider whether all members of your

Although you should avoid using color in most academic writing, in other writing situations color can help readers follow the organization of your document. For an example, notice the use of color to differentiate headings in one of the Guides to Writing in Chapters 2–10 of this book.

potential audience will have access to a full-color version of the document. Check with your instructor if you are not sure whether using more than one color would be appropriate in your writing for the class.

Visuals

Tables, graphs, charts, diagrams, drawings, photographs, maps, and screen shots add visual interest and are often more effective at conveying information than prose alone. Be certain, however, that each visual has a valid role to play in the document; if the visual is merely a decoration, leave it out.

You can create visuals on a computer, using the drawing tools of a word processing program, the charting tools of a spreadsheet program, or software specifically designed for creating visuals. You can also download visuals from the World Wide Web or photocopy or scan visuals from print materials.

If you want to borrow a visual for an essay that will be published, such as on a Web site or in the campus newspaper, you must obtain written permission from the copyright holder (usually the author, publisher, or organization holds the copyright). Write a letter asking permission to use the visual. Identify yourself and the visual you want to use, where you found the image, how you intend to use it, and where it will be published. Ask whether you need to use a particular credit line. Remember to enclose a photocopy of the visual with your permission request.

Choose the Appropriate Visual. Select the type of visual that best suits your purpose. The following list identifies various types of visuals, explains what they are best used for, and provides examples.

- ***Tables.*** A table is used to display numerical data and similar types of information. It usually includes several items as well as variables for each item. For example, Table 25.1 shows number and percentage changes in the population in the ten largest U.S. cities from 1990 to 2000.
- ***Bar graphs.*** A bar graph compares the values of two or more items, such as the ratio of men to women receiving bachelor's degrees over a period of four years. (See Figure 25.1.)
- ***Line graphs.*** A line graph shows change over time, such as the amount of government spending for low-income children between 1966 and 2002. (See Figure 25.2.)
- ***Pie charts.*** A pie chart shows the percentage of parts making up a whole. The whole (100 percent) in the chart shown in Figure 25.3 is the average annual number of deaths in the United States attributable to cigarette smoking; the parts are the various causes of death, such as lung cancer (31 percent) and coronary heart disease (20 percent).
- ***Flowcharts.*** A flowchart shows the stages in a process and their relationships. (See Figure 25.4 on p. 827.)

Table 25.1
Population Change for the Ten Largest U.S. Cities, 1990 to 2000

	Population		*Change, 1990 to 2000*	
City and State	*April 1, 2000*	*April 1, 1990*	*Number*	*Percentage*
New York, NY	8,008,278	7,322,564	685,714	9.4
Los Angeles, CA	3,694,820	3,485,398	209,422	6.0
Chicago, IL	2,896,016	2,783,726	112,290	4.0
Houston, TX	1,953,631	1,630,553	323,078	19.8
Philadelphia, PA	1,517,550	1,585,577	–68,027	–4.3
Phoenix, AZ	1,321,045	983,403	337,642	34.3
San Diego, CA	1,223,400	1,110,549	112,851	10.2
Dallas, TX	1,188,580	1,006,877	181,703	18.0
San Antonio, TX	1,144,646	935,933	208,713	22.3
Detroit, MI	951,270	1,027,974	–76,704	–7.5

Source: U.S. Census Bureau, Census 2000; 1990 Census, Population and Housing Unit Counts, United States (1990 CPH-2-1).

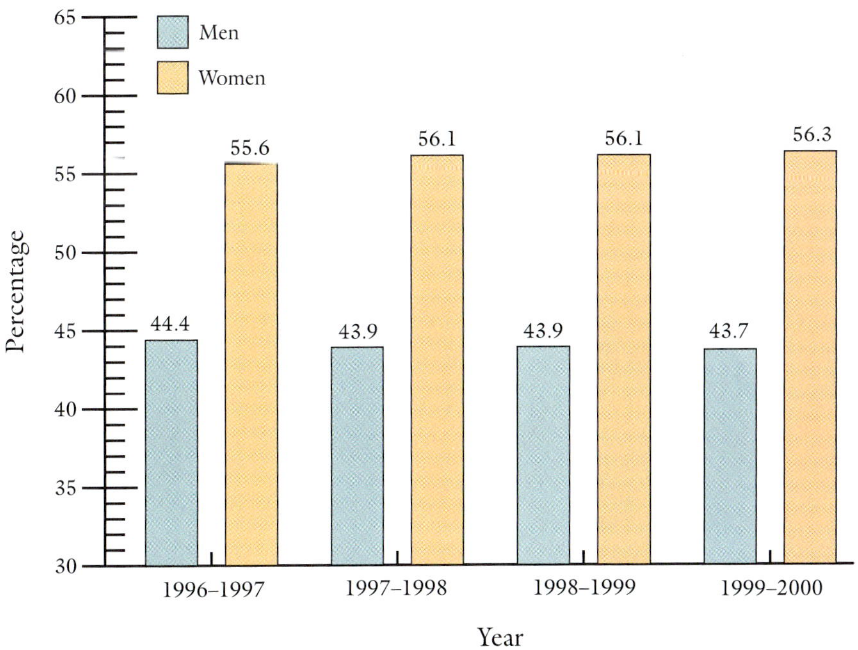

Figure 25.1. Bachelor's Degrees Conferred by Gender of Student
Source: U.S. Department of Education.

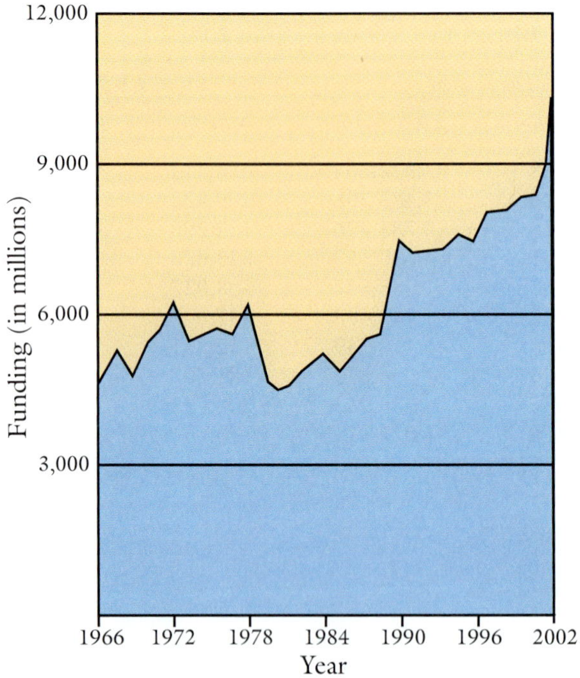

Figure 25.2. Title I Spending for Low-Income Children (in Constant Dollars)
Source: U.S. Department of Education.

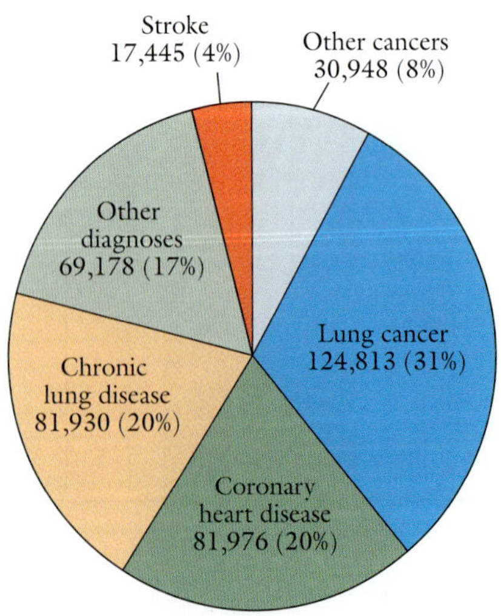

Figure 25.3. Average Annual U.S. Deaths Attributable to Cigarette Smoking, 1995–1999
Source: Data from U.S. Centers for Disease Control.
Note: Total annual average is 406,290 deaths.

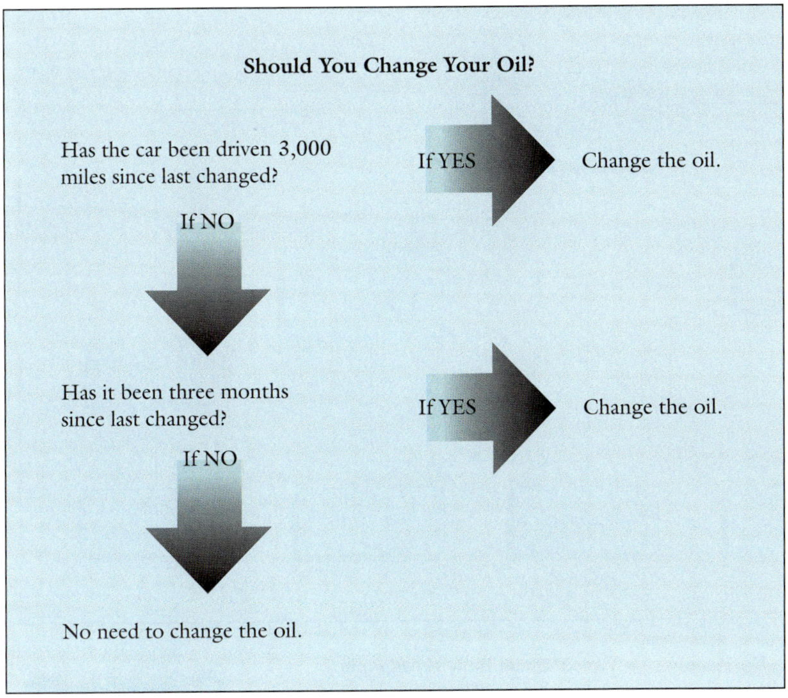

Figure 25.4. Oil-Changing Decision Process

- ***Organization charts.*** The lines of authority within a company or an organization—who reports to whom—are shown in an organization chart. (See Figure 25.5.)
- ***Diagrams.*** A diagram depicts an item or its properties, often using symbols. It is typically used to show relationships or how things function. (See Figure 25.6.)

For another example of a diagram, see Chapter 14, p. 640.

- ***Drawings.*** A drawing shows a simplified version or an artist's interpretation of an object. (See Figure 25.7.)
- ***Photographs.*** Although photographic images are generally assumed to duplicate what the eye sees, a photograph may, in fact, be manipulated in a variety of ways for special effects. Photographs that have been altered should be so identified. (See Figure 25.8.)
- ***Maps.*** A map may show geographical areas, lay out the spatial relationships of objects, or make a historical or political point. (See Figure 25.9.)
- ***Screen shots.*** A screen shot duplicates the appearance of a computer screen and is often used to reproduce a Web page in a print document. (See Figure 25.16 on p. 845 for an example.)

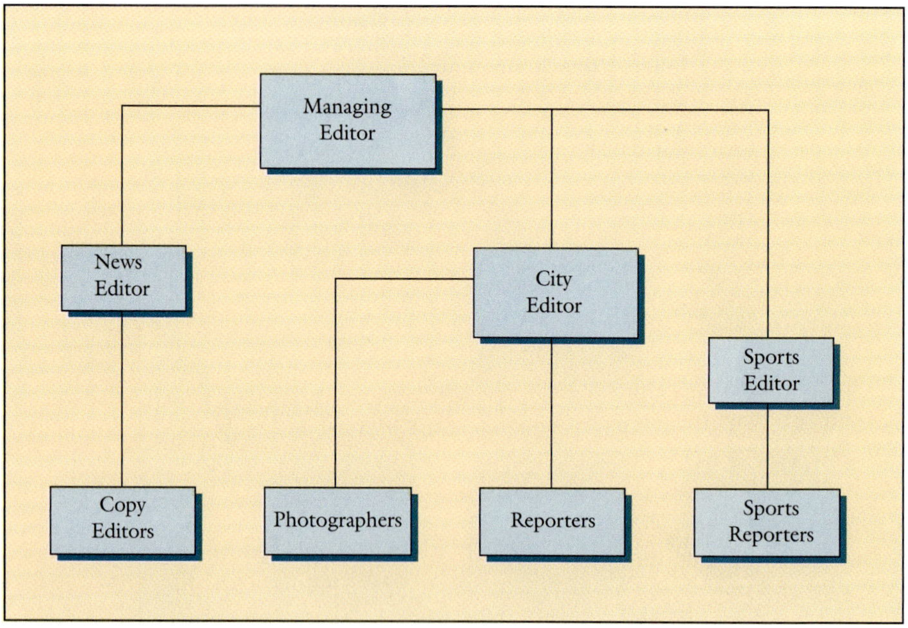

Figure 25.5. The Newsroom of a Typical Small Daily Newspaper

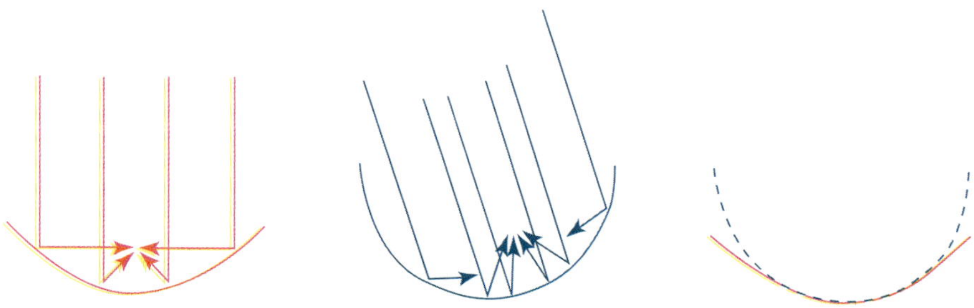

Parabolic: Perfectly focuses parallel rays but from one direction only; must be aimed.

Spherical: Focuses imperfectly but equally well from any direction; does not need to be aimed.

Together: Produces a circle of curvature that nearly coincides with the parabola near the vertex.

Figure 25.6. A Liquid Reflector Telescope
Source: Mare Frantz, Indiana University, Purdue University, Indianapolis.

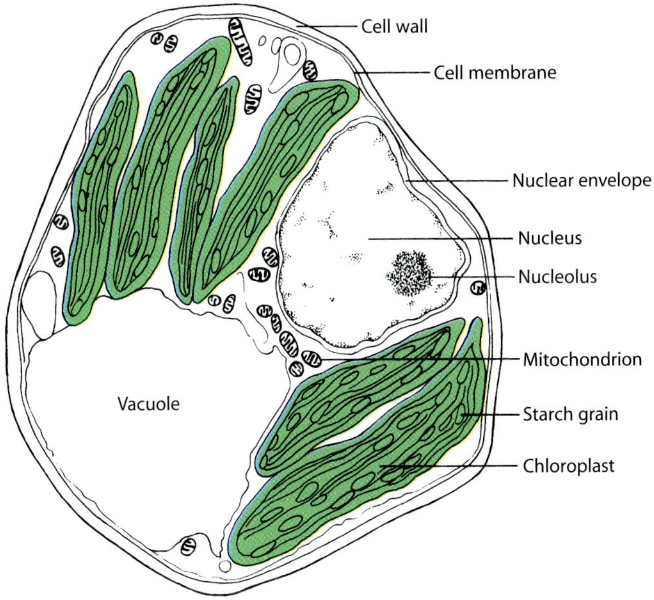

Figure 25.7. A Cell from the Leaf of a Corn Plant, Identifying Various Cellular Structures
Note: Compare with the photograph in Figure 25.8.

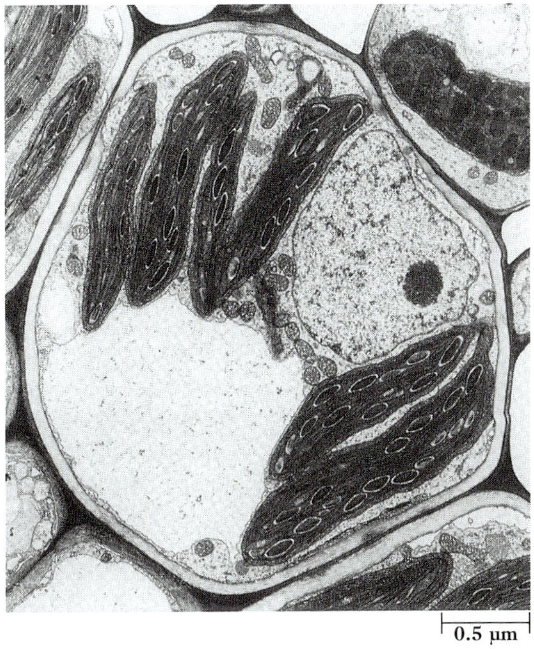

Figure 25.8. Electron Micrograph of Cells from the Leaf of a Corn Plant
Note: The measurement scale provided at the bottom right is a reminder that this image has been greatly magnified so that the parts of the cell can be distinguished by the human eye.

Figure 25.9. Western Relocation Authority Centers
During World War II, ethnic prejudice was strong, and although they posed no threat to national security, Japanese Americans were forced to go to "Western Relocation Authority" camps. As the map indicates, people were often taken a great distance from their homes.

Create Titles, Label the Parts, and Cite Your Sources. Number your visuals of the same type in sequential order and give each one a title or caption. Refer to tables as *Table 1, Table 2,* and so on, and to other types of visuals as *Figure 1, Figure 2,* and so on. (In a long work with chapters or sections, you may also need to include the chapter or section number *[Figure 25.1],* as is done in this chapter of this book). Make sure each title reflects both the subject of the visual (for example, income levels) and its purpose (to compare and illustrate changes in those income levels): *Figure 1. Percentage of U.S. Households in Three Income Ranges, 1990–2000.* Notice that MLA style requires that the title for a table be placed above the table and the title for a figure be placed below the figure.

To help readers understand a visual, clearly label all of its parts. In a table, for instance, give each column a heading; likewise, label each section of a pie chart with the percentage and the item it represents.

Finally, if you borrowed the visual from another document or created it from borrowed information, you must cite your source in a note (see Table 25.1 and Figure 25.1 for examples of source notes). In addition, be sure to document the source in your list of works cited or references.

Integrate the Visual into the Text. Visuals should facilitate, not disrupt, the reading of the body text. To achieve this goal, you first need to introduce and discuss the visual in your text and then insert the visual in an appropriate location.

Introducing the Visual. Ideally, you should introduce each visual by referring to it in your text, immediately *before* the visual appears. An effective textual reference answers the following questions:

- What is the number of the visual?
- Where is the visual located?
- What kind of information does it contain?
- What important point does the visual make or support?

Here is an example of an effective introduction for the line graph shown earlier (Figure 25.2):

> Note the sharp increase between 1990 and 2002 in federal spending for disadvantaged children (see Figure 25.2), which rose steadily over this period despite fluctuations in partisan control of Congress and the White House.

Placing the Visual in an Appropriate Location. MLA style requires and APA style recommends that you place a visual in the body of your text as soon after the discussion as possible, particularly when the reader will need to consult the visual. In APA style, visuals can also be gathered at the end of an essay if they contain supplemental information that may or may not be of interest to the reader or if the visuals take up multiple pages.

For more on overhead transparencies and computer-projected displays, see Chapter 26, pp. 849–50.

Design the Visual with Its Final Use in Mind. If you plan to incorporate a computer-generated visual into an overhead transparency or a computer-projected display, try to envision what you see on the computer screen as it would appear enlarged on a screen. Similarly, if you are designing the visual for use on a Web page, consider how the visual will appear when it is displayed on a computer screen (see p. 845 for an example).

Use Common Sense When Creating Visuals on a Computer. If you use a computer program to create visuals, keep this advice in mind:

- ***Make the decisions that your computer cannot make for you.*** A computer can automatically turn spreadsheet data into a pie chart or bar graph, but only you can decide which visual—or what use of color, if any—is most appropriate.
- ***Avoid "chart junk."*** Many computer programs provide an array of specific effects that can be used to alter visuals, including three-dimensional renderings, textured backgrounds, and shadowed text. Such special effects often detract from the message of the visual.
- ***Use clip art sparingly.*** Clip art consists of icons, symbols, and other simple, copyright-free drawings that identify recurring topics. Because clip art simplifies ideas, it is of limited use in conveying the complex information contained in most academic writing.

White Space

Another basic element of document design, white space, is simply the open space surrounding the text on a printed page or computer screen. You use white space typographically in your documents when you place a heading on its own line, when you set margins on the page, and even when you double-space between lines of text. In all of these cases, white space makes your document easier to read. When used generously, white space facilitates reading by keeping the pages of a document uncluttered and by helping the eye find and follow the text. Of course, "white" space can be any color that contrasts clearly with the text on the page.

Use "Chunking" to Break Up Dense Text. **Chunking**, the breaking up of text into smaller units, also facilitates reading. Paragraphing is a form of chunking that divides your text up into units of closely related information. In most academic essays and reports, the text is double-spaced, and paragraphs are distinguished by indenting the first line five character spaces.

For more on paragraphing, see Chapter 13, pp. 613–17.

In single-spaced text, you may want to facilitate easier reading by adding extra space between paragraphs, rather than indenting the first lines of paragraphs. This format is referred to as **block style** and is often used in memos, letters, and electronic documents. When creating electronic documents, especially Web pages, you might consider chunking your material into separate "pages" or screens, with links connecting the chunks.

For more on Web page design, see pp. 843–45.

Use Adequate Margins to Frame the Text on the Page. Adequate margins are an important component of white space and general readability. If your margins are too small, the page will seem cluttered. For academic essays, use one-inch margins on all sides unless your instructor (or the style manual you are following) advises differently. In general, you should turn off your word processor's justification and automatic hyphenation functions so that the width of the right margin will vary slightly (a format known as **ragged right**) but word spacing will be uniform. (Note, however, that justification and end-of-line hyphenation are acceptable options for students following the APA style.)

When your margins are too wide, readers may question their purpose. Some instructors, however, ask students to leave large margins to accommodate marginal comments. Multiple columns are an option you might consider, particularly if you are using type that is smaller than the conventional 10- or 12-point size, since smaller fonts require shorter lines for readability. However, multiple columns can be difficult to format.

For rules on formatting long quotations in the MLA and APA styles, see Chapter 22, pp. 750–51.

Consider Using White Space to Emphasize Selected Text Elements. To call attention to special text elements such as quotations, lists, and examples, you generally should put extra space to the left of the element. But be sure to check the relevant style manual for spacing conventions and requirements.

For special-purpose documents such as a flyer announcing an event, you may wish to experiment with colored papers as a background. If the background is dark, however, make sure the black type remains legible.

DESIGNING PAGE LAYOUT

The arrangement of text, visuals, and white space on a page—called the **page layout**—has a major impact on the readability of a document and may influence the reader's attitude about the document. A well-designed page is inviting to read and easy to scan.

Frequently, many of your major page-layout decisions will be predetermined by the kind of document you are preparing. Letters and memos, for example, have evolved through the years to meet the needs of readers. Because your readers will bring certain long-held expectations to these kinds of documents, altering an established format can cause confusion. Similarly, most aspects of the page design of an academic research paper are prescribed by the style manual used in the field of study, such as that of the MLA (humanities), APA (social sciences), or CBE (sciences). These styles have specific rules for margins, line spacing, headers, footers, bibliographies, and so on. Your instructor may have special format requirements as well. Always be sure to check whether your academic writing assignments have special format requirements.

Considering the Context in Which Your Document Will Be Read

When considering page design, you will want to analyze the context in which your document will be read. For instance, if you are writing an essay for a college course, your instructor will read it carefully. Your design decisions should make sustained reading as easy a process as possible; therefore, you will want to present a neat, clearly printed paper. Fonts that are too small to read easily or print that is too light to see clearly will make the reader's job unnecessarily difficult. Use double-spaced text and one-inch margins to leave your instructor room to write comments on the paper.

When you write for wider audiences, however, you cannot expect all readers to read your writing closely. Some readers may skim through an essay looking for key points or for information that is important specifically to them. For these readers, headings, bullets, and chunking are important design elements that help them "see" the main points of your writing as well as find the information that is of most interest to them. If readers are following written instructions to perform a task, they probably will be moving back and forth between reading and doing the task. In this context, you will need to design the document in a way that will make it easy for readers to find their place on the page as they move back and forth between text and task. Large fonts, informative headings, numbered lists, and substantial amounts of white space help readers find their place on the page with ease.

Analyzing the Context in Which Your Document Will Be Read

To analyze the context in which a document is read or used, ask yourself the following questions:

- ***Where will my document be read?*** Will the document be read in a well-lighted, spacious, quiet room? Or will it be read on a laptop computer screen on a noisy, lurching city bus?
- ***Do my readers have specific expectations for this kind of document?*** Am I writing a memo, letter, or report that my readers expect will follow certain design conventions?
- ***How will the information be used?*** Are my readers reading to learn, to be entertained, or to complete a task? Are they most likely to skim the document or to read it carefully?

SAMPLE DOCUMENTS

Earlier in this chapter you saw examples of various types of visuals; in this section you will take a look at various types of documents that you may be asked to prepare. Each sample document is accompanied by a discussion of appropriate design conventions. As you examine the documents, try also to analyze the way that typography, visuals, and white space are used to guide the reader's eye across the page. What design features make the documents easy to read? What features make finding specific information within the documents easy? What features make the document easy to use?

In addition to examining the sample documents with these questions in mind, look at the sample research paper in Chapter 22, pp. 782–90.

Memos

Memos, such as the one shown in Figure 25.10 on p. 834, are "internal" correspondence, often sent through email, between employees of the same organization (in contrast to business letters, which are sent to people outside the organization). The following conventions for writing a memo are well established and, in most cases, should not be altered. In addition, check to see whether your organization has specific guidelines for its memos (such as the use of preprinted letterhead or memo forms).

- ***Heading.*** A memo should carry the major heading *Memorandum* or *Memo.* If you are using letterhead stationery, position the heading just below the letterhead. The heading may be centered on the page or positioned at the left margin (depending on your organization's guidelines). In either case, the heading should be distinguished in some way from the rest of the body text, such as by a large font size, boldface type, or capital letters.
- ***Content headings.*** Just below the heading and separated by at least one line of space are the content headings: *Date, To, From,* and *Subject.* Place the content headings at the left margin and in the same size font as the body text.

SMITH AND KLEIN ASSOCIATES
MEMORANDUM

DATE: February 25, 2004
TO: Mary Reynolds, Vice President
FROM: Fred Rivera, Account Manager
SUBJECT: The Staley Pharmaceutical Presentation

[Subject line states clearly what the memo is about.]

The president and advertising director for Staley Pharmaceutical will review ideas and preliminary sketches on **Tuesday, March 9**. The presentation will be held in the ninth-floor conference room from **9:30 a.m. until noon**. We have prepared a complete campaign for their new cold tablet, including television and radio spots and print advertisements. We can expect them to raise the following issues during the meeting.

[Main point stated in the first sentence. Key information highlighted in bold.]

[Formal, businesslike tone.]

[Bulleted list.]

- **Budget:** Our proposed budget is significantly higher than the original estimate (see the figures attached). The higher numbers reflect their additional requests after the estimate was prepared.
- **Schedule:** Staley plans to bring the product to market on November 1. The advertising campaign is scheduled to begin in mid-October. This schedule will be tight, and we may not be able to meet our deadlines without increasing our costs.

Please let me know if you will be available to attend all or part of the meeting on March 9.

[Request for action.]

cc: Greg Miller, Senior Designer
Nora Katz, Sales Manager

["Copies" line identifies additional recipients of the memo.]

Figure 25.10. A Sample Memo

- ***Body text.*** The main text of a memo is usually presented in block style: single-spaced with an extra line of space between paragraphs. (Do not indent the first line of paragraphs in block style.) If you need to call attention to specific information, consider presenting it in a numbered or bulleted list, or highlight the information visually by using boldface or extra white space above and below it. In a memo announcing a meeting, for example, you might boldface the date, time, and place of the meeting so the reader can quickly find the information, or you might set off the date, time, and place on separate lines.

Letters

The **business letter** (exemplified in Figure 25.11) is the document most often used for correspondence between representatives of one organization and representatives of another (though email messages are increasingly being used in place of business letters). Like most other workplace documents, a business letter is written to obtain information about a company's products, to register a complaint, to respond to a complaint, or to introduce other documents (such as a proposal) that accompany the letter. As with the memo, the design conventions for letters are long established, although letters have more variations. Check to see whether there are specific business letter guidelines for your organization.

The heading of a business letter consists of the contact information for both the sender and receiver of the letter. Block style is the most commonly used format for business letters.

Be sure to state the purpose of your letter in the first few lines and to provide supporting information in the paragraphs that follow. Always maintain a courteous and professional tone throughout a business letter. Avoid using such stilted clichés as *enclosed herewith* and *as per your letter of Wednesday last*, but do include enough information to identify clearly any documents you refer to in the letter.

Email

Email, or electronic mail, is sent over a computer network from one user of the network to one or more other users. Increasingly, students and instructors rely on email to exchange information about assignments and schedules as well as to follow up on class discussions. (See Figure 25.12 on p. 837.) Email messages are usually concise, direct, relatively informal, formatted like paper memos, and limited to a single subject. Effective emails include a clear subject line.

Begin an email message by stating the main point; give additional information in subsequent paragraphs. If your email program enables you to do so, consider using headings to organize your material and bulleted or numbered lists to make your points stand out.

In many organizations, email messages are replacing handwritten or typed memos. When you send a memo electronically, make sure the headings automatically provided by the email program convey the same essential information as the content headings in a traditional memo. If you are part of a large or complex organization,

A letterhead providing information the recipient will need to communicate with the sender.

METROTYPE
409 South 8th Street
Pawkett, KY 45397
Phone: 502.555.1234 Fax: 502.555.4321 Email: type@micran.net

January 26, 2004

Full-block format: Each new line starts at the left margin.

Mr. Carl Boyer
Boyer Advertising Co.
1714 North 20th Street, Suite 16
Pawkett, KY 45397

Letter is single-spaced, with double-spacing between paragraphs and other major parts.

Dear Mr. Boyer:

The author refers to earlier correspondence to state purpose of the letter, a common and effective way to begin a business letter.

Thank you for your letter of January 16, 2004. You asked whether MetroType could provide one of your clients with mail-merged letters after first converting your client's files from WordPerfect to Microsoft Word. We certainly can. As I mentioned on the phone earlier today, creating mail-merge documents is one of our key services, and we frequently convert word processing files for customers who are moving from one program to another.

Elaboration, support, and detail.

Much of the file conversion is done automatically; however, we have noticed that some parts of a file (such as accented characters and graphics) aren't always converted accurately. For this reason, we will compare a printout of your client's original files to a printout of the converted files and then make whatever corrections are necessary. For an additional fee, we can also proofread the final documents. If your client is interested in having us proofread the documents, I would be happy to furnish you with a quote.

If you have any other questions, please call me at (502) 555-1234. In the meantime, I'll look forward to hearing from you again.

Sincerely yours,

Signature.

Trudy L. Philips

Trudy L. Philips
Owner/Director
TLP/dmp

Author's and typist's initials if typist is not author.

Figure 25.11. A Sample Business Letter

Date: Mon, 3 May 2004 16:00:45-0600
From: Paula Garrison@varnay.idbsu.edu
To: "Kevin S. Manderino" <kmand@varnay.idbsu.edu>
Subject: Suggested Questions for the Panelists Visiting SW-312
CC: "Kay Warner" <kwarn@varnay.idbsu.edu>, "Renee Peña" <rpena@varnay.idbsu.edu>

Computer-generated identifying information, formatted like a paper memo.

Accurate, informative subject line.

Hello, everyone.

Salutation (frequently omitted).

Just a reminder that Professor Haberer asked our group to come up with some questions for the three social workers who will be visiting SW-312. Since the next class is only a couple of days away, I thought I would get the discussion going by sending you some suggested questions. I took a quick look at the chapter on career opportunities and came up with the following questions:

Casual but professional tone.

1. What education and experience are necessary for the work you do?
2. What is a typical day on the job like for you?
3. What do you like best about the work you do? What do you like least?
4. What projects are you currently working on? What challenges or problems do those projects pose?
5. How has the work you do changed over the last few years? How do you expect it to change in the next few years?

Numbered list.

That's about all I can come up with. Feel free to add to the list or change these questions. Email me your suggestions, and I'll put together a final list. I think we'll need at least ten questions, but that's just a guess.

See you in class.

Figure 25.12. A Sample Email Message

you may want to repeat your name and add such information as your job title, division, and telephone extension in a "signature" at the end of the document.

Email is a broader medium of communication than the business memo. Nevertheless, in anything other than quick emails to friends, you should maintain a professional tone. Avoid sarcasm and humor, which may not come across as you intend, and be sure to proofread and spell-check your message before sending it. Also, because email messages are accessible to many people other than the person to whom you are writing, always be careful about what you write in an email message.

While email messages are among the simplest forms of electronic documents, new software programs allow you to attach files, insert hypertext links, and even insert pictures and graphics into your email documents. As a matter of courtesy, check to be sure that the recipient of your email message has the software to read these electronic documents before you include them with the message.

For information on Web pages, which are another common type of electronic document, see pp. 843–45.

Résumés

A **résumé** is used to acquaint a prospective employer with your work experience, education, and accomplishments. All résumés contain such basic information as your name, address, phone number, and email address (if you have one).

The format of résumés varies among disciplines and professions. Some professions require traditional formatting, while others allow for some flexibility in design. Be sure to research your field and the potential employers to see if a particular résumé format is preferred. Also see whether putting your résumé on a Web page might be advisable.

Résumés may also vary in terms of what is emphasized—educational or work experience, for example. A recent college graduate and a professional with years of experience would not benefit from using the same résumé format. Tailor your résumé to the job for which you are applying. If you have little work experience, focus your résumé on your grade point average, the courses you have taken, the projects you have completed, and the applicable skills and abilities you have acquired in college. (For an example of such a résumé, see Figure 25.13 on the next page.) If you have extensive, relevant, and continuous work experience, consider a chronological résumé, listing the jobs you have held (beginning with the most recent job) and describing the duties, responsibilities, and accomplishments associated with each one. If you have shifted directions during your adult life, consider organizing your résumé in a way that emphasizes the strengths and skills you have acquired and used in different settings—for instance, your experience speaking in front of groups, handling money, or working with machinery.

The résumé is a good example of why the context in which a document is read is so important. An employer may receive dozens of résumés for one position. Your résumé may not be read closely in a first screening. Consequently, your résumé should highlight your important qualifications visually so that the reader can quickly find the pertinent information by scanning the page.

Do not include such personal information as your height, weight, and age. Do mention personal interests or hobbies if they are relevant to the position. Finally, proofread your résumé carefully; it must be error-free. Your résumé is the first impression you make on a potential employer. Do everything you can to make a good first impression.

Job-Application Letters

A **job-application letter** (sometimes called a **cover letter**) is sent with a résumé when you apply for a job. One purpose of the job-application letter is to tell your reader why you have enclosed your résumé. However, its primary purpose is to persuade your reader that you are a qualified candidate for employment. For college students and recent graduates, most job-application letters (such as the one shown in Figure 25.14) consist of four paragraphs.

1. The *first paragraph* identifies which position you are applying for and how you became aware of its availability. If you are not applying for a particular position, the first paragraph expresses your desire to work for that particular organization.

Ample margins.

Kim Hua
Current Address: MS 1789, Union College, Union, PA 55342
Permanent Address: 702 Good Street, Borah, ID 83702
Phone: (412) 555-1234 Email: khua@mailer.union.edu

Contact information.

EDUCATION

Union College	Bachelor of Arts,	Anticipated May 2004
Union, PA	Child Development	GPA: 3.7

Relevant Courses: Lifespan Human Development, Infancy and Early Childhood, Parent-Child Relations, Fundamentals of Nutrition, Education of the Preschool Child

CHILD DEVELOPMENT WORK EXPERIENCE

- *Summer 2003, Union College Child-Care Center, Union College, Union, PA*

  Child Care Provider: Provided educational experiences and daily care for three 2-year-olds and four 3-year-olds.

Work experience begins with most current employment.

- *Summer 2002, St. Alphonsus Day Care Center, St. Alphonsus Hospital, Union, PA*

  Child Care Provider: Provided educational experiences and daily care for a group of nine children ages six through ten.

- *Fall 2001, Governor's Commission for the Prevention of Child Abuse, Union, PA*

  Intern: Located online resources relevant to the prevention of child abuse. Recommended which resources to include in the Web site of the Governor's Commission.

Relevant volunteer work.

OTHER WORK EXPERIENCE

2002 to present, Union Falls Bed & Breakfast, Union, PA

Payroll Manager: Maintained daily payroll records for all employees, compiled daily and weekly reports of payroll costs for the manager, and ensured compliance with all applicable state and federal laws governing payroll matters.

Other experience showing dependability and responsibility.

PROFESSIONAL AFFILIATIONS

Past President, Union College Child and Family Studies Club Student Member, American Society of Child Care Professionals Member, National Child Care Providers

Figure 25.13. A Sample Résumé

Modified block format: Your address, the date, and the signature block begin at the center of the page.

308 Fairmont Street
Warren, CA 07812
June 9, 2004

Ms. Ronda Green
Software Engineer
Santa Clara Technology
P.O. Box 679
Santa Clara, CA 09145

Dear Ms. Green:

Purpose of the letter.

I am responding to your February 11 post in the Usenet newsgroup comp .software.testing announcing that Santa Clara Technology is accepting résumés for an entry-level engineer position in the Quality Assurance Department. I think that my experience in quality assurance and my educational background qualify me for this position.

Education paragraph.

As my résumé states, I graduated this past May from the University of Southern California (USC) with a Bachelor of Science degree in Interdisciplinary Studies. The Interdisciplinary Studies program at USC allows students to develop a degree plan spanning at least two disciplines. My degree plan included courses in computer science, marketing, and technical communication. In addition to university courses, I have completed courses in team dynamics, project management, and C and C++ programming offered by the training department at PrintCom, a manufacturer of high-end laser printers.

Work-experience paragraph.

Throughout last summer, I worked as an intern in the quality-assurance department of PrintCom. I assisted quality-assurance engineers in testing printer drivers, installers, and utilities. In addition, I maintained a database containing the results of these tests and summarized the results in weekly reports. This experience gave me valuable knowledge of the principles of quality assurance and of the techniques used in testing software.

Concluding paragraph.

I would appreciate the opportunity to discuss further the education, skills, and abilities I could bring to Santa Clara Technology. You can reach me any workday after 3 p.m. (PDT) at (907) 555-1234 or by email at sstur17@axl.com.

Sincerely yours,

Shelley Sturman

Shelley Sturman

Enclosure: résumé

Figure 25.14. A Sample Job-Application Letter

2. The *second paragraph* briefly describes your education, focusing on specific achievements, projects, and relevant course work.
3. The *third paragraph* briefly describes your work experience, focusing on relevant responsibilities and accomplishments. (The second and third paragraphs should not merely restate what is in your résumé; rather, they should help persuade your reader that you are qualified for the job.)
4. The *fourth paragraph* expresses your willingness to provide additional information and to be interviewed at the employer's convenience.

Lab Reports

A **lab report** generally consists of the following five sections:

1. The *Introduction* provides background information: the hypothesis of the experiment, the question to be answered, how the question arose.
2. The *Methods* section describes how you conducted the research or performed the experiment.
3. The *Results* section describes what happened as a result of your research or experiment.
4. The *Discussion* section consists of your reasoning about your results.
5. The *References* section cites the sources you used in conducting the research, performing the experiment, or writing the lab report.

The content and format of a lab report may vary from discipline to discipline or from course to course. Before writing a lab report, be certain that you understand your instructor's requirements. The sample in Figure 25.15 shows excerpts from a lab report written by two students in a soils science course. It uses the documentation format advocated by the Council of Biology Editors (CBE).

Bulk Density and Total Pore Space

Joe Aquino and Sheila Norris
Soils 101
Lab Section 1
February 20, 2004

Introduction

Soil is an arrangement of solids and voids. The voids, called pore spaces, are important for root growth, water movement, water storage, and gas exchange between the soil and atmosphere. A medium-textured soil

Background information that the reader will need to understand the experiment.

Figure 25.15. A Sample Lab Report

(continued)

good for plant growth will have a pore-space content of about 0.50 (half solids, half pore space). The total pore space is the space between sand, silt, and clay particles (micropore space) plus the space between soil aggregates (macropore space).[1]

[The Introduction continues with a discussion of the formulas used to calculate bulk density, particle density, and porosity.]

Detailed explanation of the methods used.

Methods

To determine the bulk density[2] and total pore space of two soil samples, we hammered cans into the wall of a soil pit (Hagerstown silt loam). We collected samples from the Ap horizon and a Bt horizon. We then placed a block of wood over the cans so that the hammer did not smash them. After hammering the cans into the soil, we dug the cans, now full of soil, out of the horizons; we trimmed off any excess soil. The samples were dried in an oven at 105°C for two days and weighed. We then determined the volume of the cans by measuring the height and radius, as follows:

$$\text{volume} = {}^{1}/_{4}r^2h$$

We used the formulas noted in the Introduction to determine bulk density and porosity of the samples. Particle density was assumed to be 2.65 g/cm^3. The textural class of each horizon was determined by feel; that is, we squeezed and kneaded each sample and assigned it to a particular textural class.

Results

We found both soils to have relatively light bulk densities and large porosities, but the Bt horizon had greater porosity than the Ap. Furthermore, we determined that the Ap horizon was a silt loam, whereas the Bt was a clay (see Table 1).

Presents the results of the experiment, with a table showing quantitative data.

Table 1 Textural class, bulk density, and porosity of two Hagerstown soil horizons

Textural Class	Ap Silt Loam	Bt Clay
Bulk density (g/cm^3)	1.20	1.08
Porosity	0.55	0.59

[The Results section continues with sample calculations.]

Discussion

Both soils had bulk densities and porosities in the range we would have expected from the discussions in the lab manual and textbook. The Ap horizon is a medium-textured soil and is considered a good topsoil for plant growth, so a porosity around 0.5 is consistent with those facts. The Bt horizon is a fine-textured horizon (containing a large amount of clay), and the bulk density is in the predicted range.

Explains what was significant about the results of the research.

[The Discussion section continues with further discussion of the results.]

[The References section begins on a new page.]

References

1. Brady NC, Weil RR. The nature and properties of soils. 11th ed. New York: Prentice-Hall; 1996. 291 p.
2. Blake GR, Hartge KH. Bulk density. In: Klute A, editor. Methods of soil analysis. Part 1. 2nd ed. Agronomy 1986;9:363-376.

The references are in the format recommended by the Council of Biology Editors (CBE).

Electronic Documents: Web Pages

Electronic documents range from simple email messages to complex, interactive World Wide Web pages. While electronic documents often offer the potential for expanded use of color and visuals (including animation and video), the general principles of design used for paper documents can be applied to electronic documents with only minor modification. Here again you will want to analyze the context in which the document will be read. Will your reader be reading from a computer screen or printing the document on paper for reading? If the reading takes place on a computer screen, how big is the screen and how good is the resolution? Reading from a computer screen is more difficult, so you will want to avoid small fonts and confusing backgrounds that distract from the text.

The elements of print document design remain the same for Web pages and other electronic documents, with one important addition, **hypertext links** (also known as **hot links** or simply **links**). **Hypertext** is a system of codes that enables authors to link text or graphics on a particular section of the electronic document to additional text or graphics, to Web pages, or to short clips of video, animation, or sound. Readers navigate a hypertext in a nonlinear fashion, starting almost anywhere they like and branching off whenever a hypertext link piques their curiosity. Hypertext can make it easy for readers to access different sections of an electronic document. If an electronic document is long, for example, you can display an outline of its major headings and subheadings. These headings can then link to the text that accompanies them. The two most common types of electronic documents that you are likely to encounter as a writer are email and Web pages.

For a discussion of email and a sample document, see pp. 835–37.

A **World Wide Web page** is an electronic document stored on a **Web server**, a computer running special software and connected to the network of computers that makes up the World Wide Web. A Web server displays Web pages at the command of computer users accessing the server using a software program called a **Web browser**. Early on, most Web pages consisted of simple text on a gray background, and Web page authors needed to know **HTML (hypertext markup language)** programming to create a page. Today, increasingly sophisticated Web browsers allow for visual images, sounds, and other forms of interactive multimedia. Numerous software programs, called **HTML editors**, also provide those not familiar with HTML programming with an easy way to create Web pages, and most new word processing programs allow a document to be converted into HTML with the simple click of a button. Figure 25.16 shows a sample Web page.

A unique aspect of a Web page is its global audience. When you publish a Web page, you are writing to the world—or at least to people around the world who have access to the Web. Among other things, having a global audience means that you are writing to culturally diverse readers, many of whom may be unfamiliar with things you take for granted. For instance, if you refer to football on your Web page, many South American readers might first think of the sport Americans call soccer. Likewise, a visual that you find mildly humorous might strike readers from other cultures as blasphemous, insulting, or obscene. Therefore, to design an effective Web page, consider carefully who will be reading it and what you want it to convey to your global audience.

As you design a Web page, beware of letting fancy graphics and multimedia applications distract from your message. Yes, you can add a textured background to the screen that will make it look like marble or cloth, but will that background make reading the text easier? Will a sound file improve your communication, or are you adding sound simply because you can? Consider the following guidelines when designing a Web page:

- ***Make sure your text is easy to read.*** Many Web pages are difficult to read because of their textured and colored backgrounds. Keep the background of a Web page light in tone so that your text can be read with ease. Colored fonts can also be difficult to read. Always avoid vibrant colors for long blocks of text.
- ***Keep your Web pages short.*** Readers find it difficult to read a Web page that requires extensive scrolling on the screen. Break up long text blocks into separate Web pages that require no more than one or two screens of scrolling. Use hypertext links to connect the text blocks and to help readers navigate among the pages.
- ***Limit the file size of your Web pages.*** A Web page that is filled with visuals and sound files can be an annoyance to readers because the page may take several

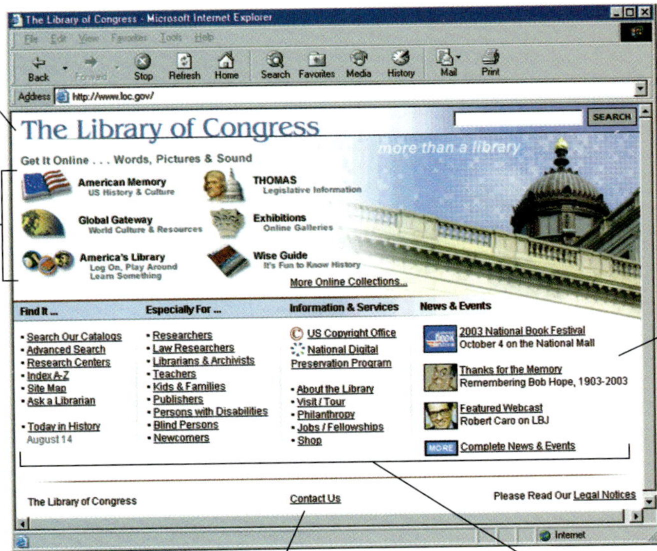

Figure 25.16. A Sample World Wide Web Page

minutes to load into a Web browser. Limiting your use of visuals and sound files so that your pages load quickly will help ensure that your document is read. This advice is especially important for the opening page of a Web site (also called a **home page**). You will encourage readers' interest in your Web site by making sure they do not have to wait too long to load the page and read your document.

- *Use hypertext links effectively.* Make sure that all of your links work correctly and that all pages of a Web site include a link back to your home page so readers can access it easily. You can make your text easier to read by judiciously limiting the number of links you embed in text. In addition to embedded text links, consider including a list of important links at one side of your document for readers' convenience.
- *Use the elements of document design.* Remember what you have learned in this chapter about typography, visuals, and white space when you create Web pages. Most principles of good paper document design apply to Web page design as well.

26

Oral Presentations

At some point in your academic career, you will probably be asked to give an oral presentation. In fact, you may give many oral presentations before you graduate, and you almost certainly will give oral presentations on the job. This chapter contains practical suggestions for preparing and giving effective oral presentations.

Be Ready

Many people are terrified at the thought of public speaking, particularly people who have little experience with it. Even experienced public speakers can become jittery before giving an oral presentation. The key to defeating nervousness and anxiety is to research and prepare. If you have researched your subject thoroughly and have planned your presentation in detail, then you should be able to relax. If you find that you are still anxious, take a few slow, deep breaths before starting your presentation. It is also helpful not to think of your presentation as a performance. Remember that you are communicating a message. Think of your presentation as simply talking to an audience.

Understand the Kind of Oral Presentation You Have Been Asked to Give

The list that follows identifies the four basic types of oral presentations.

- ***Impromptu presentation.*** An impromptu oral presentation is given without preparation. In a history class, for example, your instructor may call on you to explain briefly a concept you are studying, such as "manifest destiny." As best you can, you would recall what you have read and summarize the information. While impromptu presentations are given without preparation, they do require knowledge of the subject matter.
- ***Extemporaneous presentation.*** In an extemporaneous presentation, you prepare beforehand and speak from notes or an outline. For example, in a management class, you might prepare a report on a business that you recently visited. In most academic and business situations, extemporaneous talks are preferred because

they are informal yet well organized. Extemporaneous presentation often includes outlining your major points on a board or as a transparency for an overhead projector.

- ***Scripted presentation.*** Reading from a script is one way to ensure that you say exactly what you want to say—and that you take no more than the time you have been allotted. Because you read to your audience, a scripted presentation can be stiff and boring unless it is carefully planned and rehearsed. Scripted presentations also need to be written so that the audience can easily follow the presentation by just hearing it. Sentences often need to be shorter than in a document that is read. You will also need to provide more transitions and cues than in documents that are read. (See Use Cues to Orient Listeners on the next page.) A simple guideline to remember is that if your writing is difficult for you to read aloud, it will be difficult to hear as well.
- ***Memorized presentation.*** This type of oral presentation is written and committed to memory beforehand. For instance, at a sales meeting, you might evaluate a new product in relation to its competition. However, most people prefer scripted talks because of the difficulty of memorizing a lengthy oral presentation.

Assess Your Audience and Purpose

To give effective oral presentations you need to assess your audience and your purpose. Even for an impromptu presentation, you should take a few moments to think about whom you are speaking to and why. To assess your audience, ask the same questions you would ask about readers: Why are the members of my audience here? What do they already know about my subject? How do they feel about my topic? What objections might they have to my argument?

Define your purpose by completing the following statement: "In this oral presentation, I want to. . . ." For instance, you may want to speculate on the causes of the recent trend of companies' hiring numerous part-time and temporary contingent workers or argue your position on the ethics of this new hiring policy.

Determine How Much Information You Can Present in the Allotted Time

Your presentation should be exactly as long as the time allotted. Using substantially less time will make your presentation seem incomplete or superficial; using substantially more time may alienate your audience. Plan your presentation to allocate sufficient time for an introduction, concluding remarks, and follow-up questions (if a question-and-answer session is to be part of the presentation). If you are giving a scripted presentation, each double-spaced page of text will probably take two minutes to deliver. Time yourself to be sure.

Use Cues to Orient Listeners

Listening is one of the most difficult ways to comprehend information, in part because listeners cannot look back at previous information or scan forward, as readers can. To help your audience follow your oral presentation, use the same cues you would use to orient readers—but use them more frequently and overtly. Here are four basic cues that are especially helpful for listeners.

- ***Thesis and forecasting statements.*** Begin your presentation with thesis and forecasting statements that announce to audience members what you intend to communicate (your thesis) and the order in which you will present your material (your forecast). For instance, if you will present an argument about deregulation in the telecommunications industry, you can begin by asserting your position and preview the reasons you will offer to support your position.
- ***Transitions.*** Provide transitions when you move from one point to the next to help your audience follow the twists and turns of your presentation. For example, when you have finished discussing your first reason, state explicitly that you are now turning to your second reason.
- ***Summaries.*** End your oral presentation with a summary of the main points you have made. Also look for opportunities to use summaries throughout the presentation, particularly when you have spent a long time discussing something complicated. A brief summary that indicates the point you are making and its relation to your overall thesis can help listeners understand how the parts of your argument fit together to support your thesis.
- ***Visuals.*** Visual presentation of these cues will reinforce them. Your thesis, forecasting statements, transitions, and summaries can all be presented visually.

For further discussion and illustration of orienting cues, see Chapter 13.

Prepare Effective and Appropriate Visuals

For presentations that you plan ahead of time, you can use a variety of visuals—from simple lists and graphs to sophisticated computer demonstrations—to help both you and your audience. For instance, an overhead transparency or other projected image listing the major points of your presentation will help you make a forecasting statement that your listeners will pay attention to and remember. You can even leave the visual on display as you talk, referring to it to make a transition or adding to it as you answer questions.

Various technologies are available for displaying visuals. Writing on a board or flip chart has several advantages: low cost, high visibility, and simplicity for composing or altering on the spot. To present a long passage or detailed graphic, photocopied handouts are preferable, although they can be distracting.

Overhead transparencies are a popular way to display visuals during a presentation. An overhead transparency consists of text, graphics, or both printed on a sheet of 8½- by 11-inch film (see Figure 26.1 for an example). When illuminated by an overhead projector, the material is enlarged and projected on a screen. Overhead

Figure 26.1 Sample Overhead Transparency

transparencies can help your audience follow and remember your presentation. If you use them, think of them as integral to your presentation, not just decorative. They should be concise, easy to read, and uncluttered. You may use an overhead transparency to list the main points of your presentation, to signal transitions from one topic to another, and to summarize information you have presented.

Easy-to-use computer presentation software such as Microsoft PowerPoint is becoming increasingly widespread and extends the capabilities of the overhead transparency to include animation.

For more on designing documents, see Chapter 25.

As you prepare visuals, keep in mind that they must be legible to everyone in your audience, including people seated in the back of the room. Use a large, easy-to-read font and generous amounts of space around text.

Verify That You Will Have the Correct Equipment and Supplies

Well before your presentation is scheduled to begin, verify that the presentation room contains all of the equipment and supplies you will need. For example, if you plan to use an overhead projector, make sure it is in the room, placed correctly, and working well. Anticipating your needs (bring a marker) as well as potential problems (bring a spare bulb) will make your presentation go smoothly and help reduce your anxiety.

Rehearse Your Presentation

Rehearsing will help you to become more familiar with your material, to fit the material into the allotted time, and to feel more confident about speaking in public. If possible, rehearse in the same room in which you will give the presentation, using the same equipment. Also try to rehearse before an audience of colleagues or friends who can give you constructive criticism. Rehearsing a script or memorized presentation will enable you to plan your delivery. For a scripted talk, mark cues very selectively on your printed text to remind yourself when to pause or emphasize a word or phrase.

Deliver the Oral Presentation Professionally

Before your presentation, try to relax: Take a few deep breaths, drink some water, or step outside for some fresh air. If someone is to introduce you, give that person information about yourself and your presentation. Otherwise, begin by introducing yourself and your title or topic.

These guidelines will help you make a professional impression:

- As you speak, try to make eye contact with the people in the room.
- Use your hands to gesture as you would in a conversation; your hands should be neither clamped rigidly at your sides nor doing something distracting such as playing with your jewelry.
- If you are behind a lectern, avoid slouching, leaning on it, or gripping it tightly throughout the presentation.
- If you are using visuals, be careful not to block the audience's view of them. After introducing a new visual, resume making eye contact with audience members; talk to the audience, not the visual.
- Try to avoid distracting vocal mannerisms, such as repeatedly saying "uh," "like," or "you know."
- Speak loudly enough so that all members of the audience can hear you, and speak clearly and distinctly. Nervousness may cause you to speak too rapidly, so watch your pace.
- Do not speak in a monotone. Instead, let the pitch of your voice rise and fall naturally, especially when giving a scripted presentation.
- Dress appropriately for your audience and the formality of the situation in which you are speaking. The focus should be on your message, not on how you are dressed.

End Your Presentation Graciously

If no question-and-answer session is scheduled to follow your presentation, end the presentation by thanking your audience for giving you the opportunity to speak. If appropriate, offer to answer any questions in a private conversation or in a follow-up correspondence.

If a question-and-answer session follows your presentation, politely invite questions by saying something like, "If you have any questions, I would be happy to try to answer them now."

Working with Others

27

Although writing usually requires a solitary, individual effort, writers often seek advice and feedback from friends, colleagues, or mentors on their own *individual writing projects.* For instance, they may ask the advice of a librarian about researching their subject in the library or on the Internet, try out their argument on a coworker or fellow student, seek help to improve a draft, or get someone to check for grammar errors. On some occasions, writers also work together in small groups or teams to research, plan, and compose written reports—what we call *joint writing projects.*

Working with others is often referred to as *collaboration,* a term that we use throughout this chapter to mean working cooperatively with others to make writing better. Because collaborating with others on individual projects and especially on joint writing projects can be challenging and sometimes difficult, the following advice will help you anticipate the difficulties so that you can realize the full potential of collaboration.

WORKING WITH OTHERS ON YOUR INDIVIDUAL WRITING PROJECTS

From the very beginning of your work on an assignment in this book, you are collaborating with others to write the best essay you possibly can. Your instructor is a collaborator, as are other students in your class. For instance, their comments about the readings will help you understand more about the genres you will be writing, and their responses to your invention work and to drafts of your essays will give you many ideas. Of course, you yourself collaborate with other students when you give them your insights on the readings and on their writing.

In every assignment chapter, four special activities enable you to collaborate with other students in a purposeful way. Chapter 6, Arguing a Position, for example, has these activities:

Practice Arguing a Position: A Collaborative Activity. In this activity toward the beginning of the chapter, you work with two or three other students to try out a brief argument and discover how much you already know about this genre.

Connecting to Culture and Experience. This activity, following each of the readings, invites you to examine with other students some of the important ideas and underlying assumptions of the reading. In small-group discussion, you can explore your responses and develop your understanding.

Testing Your Choice: A Collaborative Activity. Partway through the invention work, at a point where you need to assess realistically whether you have made a wise topic choice, this activity guides you in presenting your topic to a few other students and getting their response and advice. From discovering what you have to say about your topic in this first public tryout and from reflecting on what other students have to say, you can decide whether you have chosen a topic you can write about convincingly.

Critical Reading Guide. Once you have a draft of your essay, anyone using the Critical Reading Guide can give you a comprehensive evaluation of your draft, and you can do likewise for others with their drafts. Because in Chapter 6 the Critical Reading Guide reflects the particular requirements of a successful essay arguing a position on a controversial issue, anyone using it to evaluate your draft will be able to give you focused, relevant advice. When you use the guide to evaluate another student's draft, you will be learning how to evaluate position essays, including your own.

In these four formal activities, you collaborate with others to develop your individual writing projects by discovering what you may know about a project before you get very far into it, assessing your progress after a period of initial work, and evaluating your first attempts to draft a complete essay. There are many other occasions for fruitful collaboration in the assignment chapters. You may use the activities informally with another student, or your instructor may ask you to do them in class or on your own time. For instance, in Chapter 6 you might work with other students to complete the Analyzing Writing Strategies tasks that follow every reading. You and another student might exchange revisions of your essays to help each other with final editing and proofreading. Or you might meet or exchange email messages with two or three other students to work on the challenging task, Considering the Social Dimensions of Position Papers, that concludes the chapter. These activities may seem easier or more enjoyable if you work on them with other students. But collaborative activities very likely will also be more productive, increasing your understanding of writing that takes positions on issues through the exchange of many more ideas than you might have come up with on your own.

Collaboration on your individual projects need not always be so purposeful and organized. It continues usefully in the most casual, brief encounter on or off campus with a classmate. You might lament the upcoming deadline for a first draft of the essay, telling each other what you still have to accomplish in the little time remaining. You might talk about what happened when you tried one of the book's collaborative activities. You might continue a discussion of a reading that began in class. You might describe the most formidable problem you must solve before you can complete your draft. If you are both doing library research on the same or a similar issue, you might tell each other about useful sources you have discovered.

Following are guidelines for successful collaboration on individual writing projects. These guidelines apply to formal, planned meetings to improve writing itself—from invention work through planning and revising:

- Whenever you read someone else's writing, have the writer inform you about his or her purpose and readers. Collaboration is always more effective when writers focus on helping other writers achieve their purposes for their particular readers. If a writer is explaining a concept to readers who know nothing about it, as might be the case in Chapter 5, Explaining a Concept, your comments are likely to be unhelpful if you assume the essay is addressed to someone who shares your understanding of the concept.
- Know the genre the writer is working in. If a writer is proposing a solution to a problem and you are evaluating the writing as though it were an essay arguing a position, your advice is likely to be off the mark.
- When you evaluate another writer's work, be sure you know the stage of its development. Is it a set of tentative notes for a first draft? A partial draft? A complete draft? A revision? If it is a draft, you want to focus on helping the writer develop and organize ideas; whereas if it is a revision, you might focus exclusively on cueing and coherence or editing and proofreading.
- When you evaluate someone's writing, be helpful and supportive but also frank and specific. You do a writing partner no favor if you shrink from criticizing and giving advice. If your criticism seems grounded in the purpose, audience, and genre, it will probably not seem arbitrary or personal to your partner.
- Bring as much writing as possible to a scheduled meeting with other writers. The further along your writing is the more you can learn from the collaboration, and your partners will feel that their time has been well spent.
- Try to be receptive to criticism. Later, you can decide whether to change your essay, and how.

WORKING WITH OTHERS ON JOINT WRITING PROJECTS

In addition to collaborating with others on your individual writing projects, your instructor may give you the opportunity to write an essay with other students—a joint project in which you collaborate to produce a single essay. For instance, in Chapter 6, Arguing a Position, you could collaborate to construct a persuasive argument for a position you share with two or three other students on a controversial issue. In Chapter 5, Explaining a Concept, you could work with a few other students to research and explain a concept, perhaps using graphics or hands-on activities to help others grasp the concept and its implications. In Chapter 7, Proposing a Solution, you have an opportunity to practice researching and writing proposals, by far the most common type of joint writing project in college, business, and the community.

Look, for example, at the workplace writing example on p. 331. A pharmaceuticals company decided to invest time and money in finding a solution to a problem the company saw as damaging to its business as well as to the community. The company assigned a team of seven division managers and a technical writer, gave them a budget to pay for outside consultants, and asked them to present a written proposal to the state legislature and local school board in six months' time.

The pharmaceuticals team divided the project into a series of research and writing tasks like those outlined in the Guide to Writing in Chapter 7. The team members scheduled due dates for each task and progress reports to identify problems as they arose. They assigned responsibility for each task either to individuals or small groups and identified which tasks might need consultation with outside experts.

When people collaborate on large writing projects like that of the pharmaceutical company, they usually divide up the work. For example, they might divide responsibilities according to the expertise of different group members. Someone who knows the problem firsthand might work on developing ways to explain the problem to those who have not experienced it directly. People who have experience making forecasts and planning budgets or hiring and managing people might be assigned to research and draft those aspects of the proposal. Everyone in the group might read and suggest revisions in the draft, and individuals may be assigned parts to strengthen and clarify. When a final draft seems near, one person might be assigned the job of improving cueing and coherence, while another might be in charge of editing and proofreading, and a third might work on document design.

Writing collaboratively on a joint project certainly has benefits. Collaboration not only draws on the expertise and energy of different people but can also be synergistic, creating an outcome that is greater than the sum of its parts. One difficulty of collaborative writing projects, however, is that learning how to work effectively with others takes time and effort. Writers working on a joint project need to spend a lot of time communicating with one another. They must learn to anticipate conflicts and resolve them constructively. They should be realistic in scheduling and do their assigned tasks responsibly. They have to be flexible in their writing processes and open to different points of view.

Your instructor may decide how large your group should be and may even assign students to particular groups. If you are unhappy being in a particular group, discuss the situation with your instructor as soon as possible. To help group members work together constructively on joint writing projects, here are some ground rules you will want to discuss and implement:

- Begin by establishing clear and easy means of communicating with one another. Exchange email addresses or establish a listserv, but also exchange phone numbers in case servers go down.
- Expect to spend a lot of time planning the project together and discussing who will do what and when. Discuss how the group should divide responsibilities. To decide how best to collaborate, you will need to plan the project so that you know what needs to be accomplished and in what order. Remember, however, to remain flexible and keep lines of communication open to deal with problems as they arise.
- Set a schedule of regular meetings. The meetings can take place in person, over the Internet, or by telephone. Agree on how to run the meetings. For example, should someone lead each discussion and should the role of discussion leader

rotate? Should notes or minutes be taken at each meeting and then reviewed subsequently to make sure that nothing important has been left out or misunderstood? Should each meeting have an agenda and, if so, how and when should it be developed for each subsequent meeting? Should votes be taken or should everything be decided by consensus?

- Try to treat each other with respect and consideration, but do not be surprised by disagreements and personality conflicts. Arguing can stimulate thinking—inspiring creativity as well as encouraging each person to explain ideas clearly and systematically. But arguing can also encourage aggressiveness in some people and withdrawal in others. Recognize that people interact differently in groups and have different ways of contributing. If there is a problem in the way the group interacts, address it immediately, perhaps by calling a special meeting to work out a solution. Try to avoid placing blame. Consider, for example, whether taking turns would ensure that everyone contributes to the discussion and no one dominates. Urge everyone to refrain from characterizing other people and instead to speak only about what they themselves think and feel by making "I" rather than "you" statements.
- Keep track of everyone's progress. Consider creating a chart so that all members can see at a glance what they need to do and when. Schedule regular progress reports so that any problems can be identified immediately. If someone is having difficulty completing a particular task, other group members should volunteer to help so that the project is not stalled.
- If the group will make an oral presentation of the written proposal, plan it carefully, giving each person a role. Rehearse the presentation as a group to make sure it satisfies the time limit and other requirements of the assignment.

For more on oral presentations, see Chapter 26.

After setting its ground rules, the pharmaceuticals team divided its work in much the same way as that suggested in the Guide to Writing a proposal in Chapter 7. Here are some highlights of the team's researching and writing process:

- To answer the kinds of questions listed on p. 365 of the Guide to Writing, under Analyzing and Defining the Problem (such as what caused the problem? what is its history? what are its bad effects?), the team assigned a small group to conduct library and Internet research. From this initial research, a specialist in the field of vocational training was interviewed and subsequently hired as a consultant by the team.
- As their attempts to analyze the problem continued, the team members turned to the next task in the Guide to Writing, Identifying Your Readers (p. 366). They assigned several small groups to do field research: to observe and conduct interviews at local high schools, to interview school board members and others in the community, and to interview state legislators who would be involved eventually in judging the proposal.
- They turned next to finding a solution. In researching the problem, they had collected many different ideas on how the problem might be solved as well as

criticisms of each possible solution. The whole team reviewed this material and after lengthy discussion agreed on several principles a good solution to this problem would need to have: (1) Students would have to begin vocational training as early as the tenth grade; (2) equipping area high schools and hiring specialized teachers would be too expensive; and (3) on-site training would not only make modern equipment and specialized teachers readily available to students, but would also motivate students and help them learn efficiency and accountability.

- Before figuring out how to implement these principles, the team members tested their ideas by consulting with a variety of people, many of whom they had interviewed earlier. This research helped them anticipate objections to their proposed solution and consider the specific steps necessary to implement their solution. Half of the team focused on drafting arguments to defend the solution, while the other half focused on drafting the implementation section. Leaders of the two groups kept in close communication.
- When they had a coherent argument for their solution and a plan for implementation worked out, the team members met to review the entire draft. They identified some problems and asked the drafting groups to do some revision.
- They showed the revised draft to a wide array of people, including business leaders, school board members, parent groups, representatives of teachers' unions, and interested students. They then categorized the problems and suggestions for revision offered by these critical readers and sent the draft back to the original drafting groups for another revision.
- The final revised draft was reviewed for clarity, coherence, and mechanics before being submitted to the company's board of directors and, after minor revisions, distributed to the state legislature and the local school board. It was also published in local newspapers and business magazines and on the company's Web site.

If you collaborate with other students to develop a proposal, you will not have as many outside resources as the pharmaceuticals company team in this model. The decisions this team made, however, mirror the kinds of decisions you and your fellow students will have to make.

28

Writing in Your Community

Service learning combines classroom education with life experience. Through partnerships with community organizations, colleges and universities can offer students ways to see how the knowledge that they are gaining in school can be put to work beyond the campus. Research and experience show that such programs provide valuable service to those who need it and also help students learn and retain course content. Students also often discover that their skills and knowledge can help others. If your composition class has a service-learning component, you will have an opportunity to learn more about your community, to become an active participant in that community, and to apply your writing skills to your community experience.

In service-learning programs, students are most often placed in off-campus positions with government bureaus such as local parks and recreation departments or nonprofit organizations that offer community support services such as care for the homeless. In these positions students apply what they are studying in class. Here are a few examples:

- Nursing students teach expectant mothers about prenatal and infant care.
- Chemistry students tour local elementary schools demonstrating the fun of science.
- Botany students teach fourth graders about plants native to their region.
- Zoology students help gather samples for a study of local amphibian populations.
- Political science students work with the local government to increase voter turnout.
- English students tutor grade school children who are having trouble learning to read and write.

Whatever form your service-learning experience takes, it can serve as a valuable resource for your writing. While you will probably find much to write about in your service experience, you may also find writing is a part of your service. When writing is part of your service, you move beyond having classmates and instructors as your primary audience, and enter the realm of public discourse.

USING YOUR SERVICE EXPERIENCE AS SOURCE MATERIAL

Finding a Topic

College students frequently find topic selection a difficult part of the writing process. One of the many advantages of service learning is that it can make finding an engaging subject for your writing much easier and more rewarding. The service experience should present numerous issues that might be fruitfully explored through your writing. Simply paying attention to the issues that come to bear on your service experience should help you generate a substantial list of ideas. You might ask yourself some simple questions:

- Who is most affected by the situation, and how are these people affected?
- How long has this situation existed?
- What are the results of this situation?
- What forces shape the situation? Can anything be done to alter these forces?
- How have other organizations successfully handled this issue? How else might the situation be improved?
- What common perceptions do people hold about this situation? What are my own perceptions?
- Are these perceptions inaccurate? How might they be changed?

For example, if your service experience includes working at a clinic that serves low-income families without health insurance, you might write about the long-term effects on children of insufficient medical care. You might also write a proposal to address the problem faced by people who have little or no medical coverage. Or perhaps you are interested in writing an argument advocating universal health care coverage. There are dozens of possible essay topics in any service experience.

Gathering Sources

In traditional college writing settings, research is often limited, by time and availability, to what one can find in the library or on the Internet. A service-learning environment can provide field research sources that would otherwise be difficult to tap. The most significant of these potential sources is the people who run the organization in which you are doing your service. If you have focused your writing on the kinds of issues that are relevant to your service, these people can serve as experts. Many of the people you work with will have years of experience and specialized training and probably will have researched the subject themselves. Take advantage of your opportunity to tap their knowledge. When approached courteously, people are often more than willing to discuss their thoughts on something important to them.

Depending on the situation, your service site might also be a good place to circulate a questionnaire or conduct a survey to help you gather information about your subject. Of course, your own observations and experiences as you perform your service will prove to be valuable as well. You might consider keeping a daily journal in which you record your experiences and observations as you perform your service. When you are ready to begin writing, you will already have done some early invention work.

For suggestions on making observations, conducting interviews, and creating questionnaires, see Chapter 20.

The service organization itself might also be a good source of information. Such organizations often collect and produce literature that is relevant to their mission. Your organization might even maintain its own small library of resource materials that you could borrow or use. Frequently such organizations are also part of a network of similar groups that share their expertise through newsletters, trade journals, Web sites, or online discussion groups. Explore these unique resources.

Keep in mind the ethical considerations that are involved. Many service-learning environments, such as those that involve counseling, tutoring, or teaching, can give you access to information that should be kept confidential, especially if you are working with minors. Be sure that you are open about your information-gathering and that everyone whom you might use as a source knows your intentions. Any questionnaires should include a disclosure stating what you intend to do with the information gathered. Any information gained from interviews should be properly attributed, but you should consider carefully maintaining the anonymity of anyone whom you use for examples in your writing, unless you have your subjects' explicit permission to use their names. Err on the side of caution and consideration, and ask your instructor if you have any questions about how to treat sensitive material.

Writing *about* Your Service Experience

Writing in a service-learning program is really no different from other writing situations. You still must identify for yourself the kind of writing you are doing, generate ideas through invention, and refine those ideas into a finished product through a process of drafting and revision. Service learning, however, may put you in a position to write for a nonacademic audience. For example, you might write an editorial for your campus or local newspaper in which you argue for increased support for your service organization or project. You might craft a letter to local government officials or even representatives to the national legislature suggesting a solution to a particular problem. When you do such writing, pay particular attention to your audience and purpose. Ask yourself how you might best appeal to the needs of your audience and how you can present your position in a convincing way. Remember that writing is action, and as such it can be a powerful tool.

The service-learning experience can provide you with subject matter for many of the academic writing activities discussed in Part One of this textbook. While you can no doubt generate your own list of ideas, here are some to consider:

Chapter 2: Remembering Events

- Write about your first day of service. What happened? How did you feel? What did you learn? How did it differ from what you expected to learn?

- Write about a particularly difficult day. Why was it difficult? How did you handle the situation? What would you do differently? What did you learn from the experience?

Chapter 3: Remembering People

- Write about one of the people you are working with. What makes this person special or distinctive? How does he or she act? What have you learned from this person?
- Write about someone you were able to help in some way. What kind of assistance did you give? How did this person respond to your help? How did you feel afterward?

Chapter 4: Writing Profiles

- Write about the place where you are doing your service. What does it look like? How does it make you feel? How does the location reflect or affect what goes on there? What does go on there?
- Write about one of the people you have met doing your service. What is he or she like? How is he or she typical (or atypical) of the people in the same position? What makes this person special or different?

Chapter 5: Explaining a Concept

- Write about a concept with which you were unfamiliar before you did your service. What does the concept mean? How is it important in the context of your service experience? How does what you learned about this concept make you think differently now?
- Write about a concept that you knew but now understand differently because of your service. How has your understanding of the concept changed? What caused that change? How might you explain that change to someone who does not share your experience?

Chapter 6: Arguing a Position

- Write an argument in support of the service organization you are working with. Why should people support it? How can they support it? Why is it a worthwhile endeavor?
- Write an argument about the value of service learning. What have you gained from this experience? Who should participate? What are the advantages of service learning to individuals and the community?

Chapter 7: Proposing a Solution

- Write about a process or procedure within or affecting the organization you are working with that you think needs to be improved. Why does it need to be improved? How might it be improved? What would the effect of the improvements be?

- Write about a policy, law, or practice that you think should be eliminated or revised because it negatively affects the organization you are working with. What would be the benefit of eliminating or revising it? Why was it created or instituted in the first place? What additional steps, if any, would need to be taken in order to remedy the problem?

Chapter 8: Justifying an Evaluation

- Write about how effectively the organization you are working with satisfies its objectives. How do you measure its effectiveness? In what ways does it succeed? In what ways does it fail?
- Write about your school's service-learning program. In what ways is it most successful? In what ways could it be improved?

Chapter 9: Speculating about Causes

- Write about the causes for a problem or situation that you have encountered through your service-learning experience. What brought the problem about? What circumstances perpetuate it?
- Write about why service-learning programs have become common. What function do they serve that traditional education models do not? What demand do they meet? Why are so many colleges and universities involved in such partnerships?

Writing *for* Your Service Organization

Some service-learning situations will put you in a position not just to write *about* your service experience but also to write *as part of* your service experience. You might be asked to create flyers, brochures, press releases, or Web pages for a community organization. You might help craft presentations or reports. While these may not be academic writing activities, they are still writing activities, and the strategies presented in this text still apply. You might be asked, for example, to help write a brochure that explains the purpose and function of the organization. In effect, you would be writing a profile of the organization, and you would need to keep in mind the basic features of profiles outlined in Chapter 4.

Such writing situations give you an opportunity to practice recognizing the kinds of writing you are asked to do. While in class you might be asked to select a topic and write an essay in which you argue a position (Chapter 6) or propose a solution (Chapter 7), in your service experience you might simply be asked to create a flyer that explains the importance of a no-kill animal shelter or a brochure that urges people to carpool as a way of cutting down traffic congestion. By identifying what kind of writing activity you are being asked to do, you can identify what basic features your readers will expect to find.

Writing in organizations is frequently a collaborative process. Everyone involved in the process is expected to do his or her part. When your written document will be used to represent your organization in any way, respect the expertise of the staff, especially when their assessment of the audience differs from your own. In some situations, your service writing may be heavily edited—or not used at all. Make sure your instructor and service-learning program administrators are aware of any instances in which you and members of the organization are having difficulty reaching a consensus.

For suggestions on how to make such collaboration run smoothly and successfully, see Chapter 27.

Finally, remember that nonacademic writing often requires greater attention to presentation than most kinds of academic writing. One-inch margins and double-spaced text simply are not enough when you are trying to create eye-catching documents such as brochures and press releases. Document design can not only make a piece of writing more visually attractive and thereby stimulate readers' interest, but can also help readers with different needs identify which parts of the document they will find most relevant. Therefore, carefully consider the layout and configuration of your document, and take advantage of the flexibility that even a simple word processing program can give you.

For more on document design, see Chapter 25.

Handbook

INTRODUCTION

Use this Handbook to help you correct errors in grammar and punctuation. Use it as well when you need advice about how to write clearer, more effective sentences. Finally, when you need to know whether to capitalize a word or whether to underline a title or put quotation marks around it, this Handbook is the first place to check. Because the Handbook is based on extensive research and is designed to be used efficiently, you can rely on it to enhance your command of standard edited English.

You may use the Handbook on your own when you edit your essays, or your instructor may guide you in using the Handbook to correct certain errors in your writing. If you are using the Handbook on your own, check the Handbook Contents on the next page, or look in the index for the category of error you are concerned about—for example, "pronoun reference," "commas," "quotation marks," or "parallelism." If you cannot identify the relevant category of error or locate the information you need, ask your instructor or another student for advice.

Your instructor may use the Handbook's letter-and-number system to lead you directly to the page where you can learn how to correct the error. For example, the code "P1-b" indicates that a comma is needed after an introductory word, phrase, or clause. Referring to the Detailed Handbook Contents inside the back cover, you would discover that P1-b is on or near p. H-58 in the Handbook. As an alternative, you can find P1-b by flipping through the text and looking at the orange tabs at the tops of the pages. Each tab indicates the section code for that page. The orange tabs on each page also include an abbreviation or a symbol for the topic covered on that page. If your instructor indicates errors in your sentences with conventional correction symbols such

HANDBOOK CONTENTS

as *cap*, *frag*, or *ww*, you can find the section where the error is covered by checking the chart of correction symbols near the back of this book.

When you locate the Handbook section that will help you correct an error or make a sentence more concise or more graceful, you will find a brief explanation and a sentence or two illustrating correct usage. The section also provides several hand-corrected sentences so that you can see immediately how to edit your own sentence. Most of these sample sentences come from student essays written for assignments in this book. Grammatical terms are defined in the margin. In addition, below the heading of each major Handbook section is a URL that you can use to access interactive online exercises for practice in the topics covered in that section.

To design a handbook that would provide an efficient quick reference for students, we carried out extensive research. Ten college writing instructors and four professional editors worked together to identify errors* in more than five hundred student essays from colleges across the country. All of the essays were written in first-year composition courses by students using *The St. Martin's Guide to Writing*. We used this research to determine the error categories listed in the Handbook Contents. The errors are listed below in order of descending frequency and can guide you in editing your own writing. The numbers in bold following each error indicate where in this Handbook you can find help with understanding and correcting each error.

1. Wordiness **W1-a–W1-c**
2. Misused word **W2-a, W2-e**
3. Incorrect or ambiguous pronoun reference **G1**
4. Verb tense errors **G5-a, G5-b**
5. Missing comma between independent clauses **P1-a**
6. Problems with hyphens between compound adjectives **M1-a**
7. Missing comma after introductory elements **P1-b**
8. Capitalization of proper or common nouns **M2-a**
9. Unnecessary comma between compound elements **P2-a**
10. Incorrect spacing **M3**
11. Missing words **E1-a–E1-d**
12. Missing comma with nonrestrictive word groups **P1-c**
13. Comma splice or fused sentence **S1, S2**
14. Problems in using quotation marks with other punctuation **P6-b**
15. Missing or unnecessary hyphens in compound nouns **M1-b**
16. Missing comma with transitional and parenthetical expressions, absolute phrases, and contrasted elements **P1-d**

---

* Spelling errors were not included.

17. Problems of pronoun-antecedent agreement **G2**
18. Incorrect preposition **W2-b, L3**
19. Misuse of *who, which,* or *that* **G3**
20. Unnecessarily complex sentence structure **W1-b**
21. Spelling out or using figures for numbers incorrectly **M4**
22. Problems with apostrophes in possessive nouns **P7-a**
23. Sentence fragment **S3**
24. Missing comma in items in a series **P1-e**
25. Unnecessary comma with restrictive word groups **P2-b**

This list of the top twenty-five errors can be categorized into the following five major patterns of errors. You may find it useful to keep these patterns in mind as you edit your work.

1. Missing or unnecessary commas **(P1-a–P1-d, P2-a–P2-g)**
2. Errors in word choice **(W1-a–W1-d, W2-a–W2-d)**
3. Errors in pronoun reference, agreement, or use **(G1, G2, G3)**
4. Verb tense errors **(G5-a, G5-b)**
5. Errors in recognizing and punctuating sentences—comma splices, fused sentences, fragments **(S1, S2, S3)**

KEEPING A RECORD OF YOUR OWN ERRORS

In addition to checking your work for the errors college students usually make, you will find it useful to keep a record of the errors that *you* usually make. Recording errors in your writing can help you discover your own most frequent errors and error patterns. You can then work toward avoiding them.

To use the Record of Errors form on p. H-5, note the name and section number of each error you make in the left-hand column. (See the Handbook Contents on p. H-2 or the list of correction symbols at the back of the book for the names of errors.) For example, if in your first essay your instructor or another student marks a vague use of the pronoun *this* at the beginning of two of your sentences, locate the section that provides help in correcting this error (G1), and enter the error name in the left column along with the section number: Vague use of *this, that,* and *which,* G1. Then under *Essay 1* and next to the name of the error, enter the number *2* to indicate how many times you made this error. As you edit subsequent essays, you can easily review this section in the Handbook to make sure you have avoided this pronoun problem.

By your second or third essay, you should begin to see patterns in the errors you make and to understand how to recognize and correct them.

RECORD OF ERRORS

Name of Error and Section Number in the Handbook	FREQUENCY						
	Essay 1	*Essay 2*	*Essay 3*	*Essay 4*	*Essay 5*	*Essay 6*	*Essay 7*

The Writing Guide Software includes an Error Log that you can use to keep track of your error patterns electronically. If you're using the software to write an essay, you'll be directed to check your Error Log when you get to the Editing and Proofreading stage of the process.

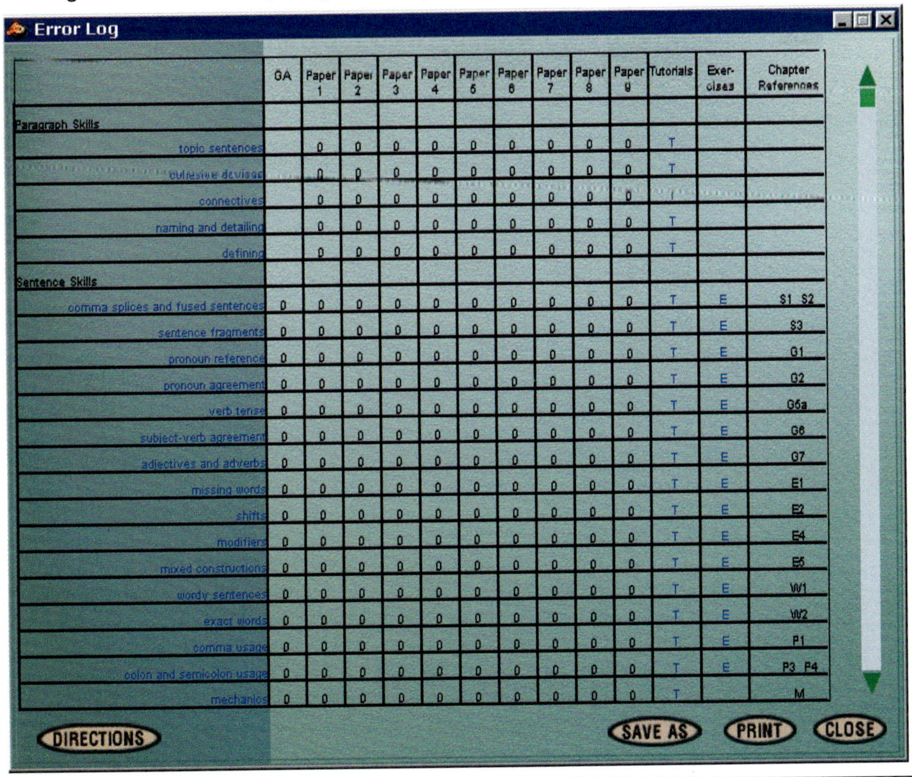

Error Log

	GA	Paper 1	Paper 2	Paper 3	Paper 4	Paper 5	Paper 6	Paper 7	Paper 8	Paper 9	Tutorials	Exercises	Chapter References
Paragraph Skills													
topic sentences		0	0	0	0	0	0	0	0	0	T		
cohesive devices		0	0	0	0	0	0	0	0	0	T		
connectives		0	0	0	0	0	0	0	0	0	T		
naming and detailing		0	0	0	0	0	0	0	0	0	T		
defining		0	0	0	0	0	0	0	0	0	T		
Sentence Skills													
comma splices and fused sentences	0	0	0	0	0	0	0	0	0	0	T	E	S1 S2
sentence fragments	0	0	0	0	0	0	0	0	0	0	T	E	S3
pronoun reference	0	0	0	0	0	0	0	0	0	0	T	E	G1
pronoun agreement	0	0	0	0	0	0	0	0	0	0	T	E	G2
verb tense	0	0	0	0	0	0	0	0	0	0	T	E	G6a
subject-verb agreement	0	0	0	0	0	0	0	0	0	0	T	E	G6
adjectives and adverbs	0	0	0	0	0	0	0	0	0	0	T	E	G7
missing words	0	0	0	0	0	0	0	0	0	0	T	E	E1
shifts	0	0	0	0	0	0	0	0	0	0	T	E	E2
modifiers	0	0	0	0	0	0	0	0	0	0	T	E	E4
mixed constructions	0	0	0	0	0	0	0	0	0	0	T	E	E5
wordy sentences	0	0	0	0	0	0	0	0	0	0	T	E	W1
exact words	0	0	0	0	0	0	0	0	0	0	T	E	W2
comma usage	0	0	0	0	0	0	0	0	0	0	T	E	P1
colon and semicolon usage	0	0	0	0	0	0	0	0	0	0	T	E	P3 P4
mechanics	0	0	0	0	0	0	0	0	0	0	T		M

DIRECTIONS SAVE AS PRINT CLOSE

S Sentence Boundaries

S1 Comma Splices

For practice, go to bedfordstmartins.com/theguide/csplice

independent (main) clause A word group with a subject and a predicate that can stand alone as a separate sentence. (A predicate is the part of a clause that includes a complete verb and says something about the subject.)

In a comma splice, two **independent clauses** are improperly joined by a comma.

COMMA SPLICE — [INDEPENDENT CLAUSE] I know what to do, [INDEPENDENT CLAUSE] I just don't know how to do it.

Because a comma splice can be edited in many ways, first consider how the ideas in the two independent clauses relate. For example, are they equally important, or does one depend on or explain the other? Then select the strategy below that will best clarify this relationship for a reader. To edit the example just given, for example, the writer might change the comma to a period.

▶ **I know what to do~~,~~. I just don't know how to do it.**

subordinating conjunction A word or phrase (such as *although, because, since,* or *as soon as*) that introduces a dependent clause and relates it to an independent clause.

Add a subordinating conjunction to one of the clauses, rewording as necessary.

▶ **^After ~~T~~the New York City police began to crack down on minor offenders, a significant decrease in major crime resulted as well.**

▶ **^Though *Midnight Cowboy*^, ~~was~~ rated X in the early 1970s, ~~it~~ contained one scene that was considered "sexually explicit," ~~yet~~ the movie was tastefully done and could not be considered pornographic by today's standards.**

dependent (subordinate) clause A word group that has a subject, a predicate, and a subordinating word (such as *because*) at the beginning; it cannot stand by itself as a sentence but must be connected to an independent (main) clause.

By beginning a clause with a subordinating conjunction, you indicate that the clause is subordinate to—and dependent on—the main clause. Usually, the **dependent clause** explains or qualifies the **independent clause.** Select the subordinating conjunction carefully so that it tells the reader how the ideas in the dependent clause relate to the ideas in the independent clause.

coordinating conjunction A word that joins comparable and equally important sentence elements: *for, and, or, but, nor, yet,* or *so.*

Separate the independent clauses with a comma and a coordinating conjunction.

▶ **On the album *Other People's Songs,* Erasure has produced an eclectic collection of cover treatments, ^and the result highlights the group's strengths and weaknesses throughout its thirty-year recording career.**

▶ By 1988, the average American car had achieved a high of 26 mpg, ^but by 2003 that figure had fallen to less than 21 mpg.

The coordinating conjunction tells the reader that the ideas in the two clauses are closely related and equally important.

Separate the independent clauses with a semicolon.

▶ The tattoo needle appeared to be like an extension of his arm; the needle was his brush, and the human body, his canvas.

▶ Nate was very lucky; he lived to see his hundredth birthday.

The semicolon tells the reader that the ideas in the two clauses are closely connected, but it implies the connection rather than stating it. Occasionally, a colon may be used to introduce a second independent clause (see P4-a).

Separate the independent clauses with a semicolon or a period, and add a conjunctive adverb or a transitional phrase such as *for example* or *in other words.*

conjunctive adverb A word or phrase (such as *finally, however,* or *therefore*) that tells how the ideas in two sentences or independent clauses are connected.

▶ He doesn't need the map right now; instead, he just follows the direction Kiem pointed out to him before and checks it with the compass.

▶ He doesn't need the map right now. Instead, he just follows the direction Kiem pointed out to him before and checks it with the compass.

The semicolon tells the reader that the ideas in the two clauses are closely connected, and the conjunctive adverb describes the connection. The period shows a stronger break. Conjunctive adverbs are used more frequently in formal than in informal writing.

Note: A subordinating conjunction always begins a clause, but a conjunctive adverb can appear in other positions within a clause. If the conjunctive adverb appears in the middle of one clause rather than between two clauses, the semicolon is still placed between the clauses, not before the adverb.

subordinating conjunction A word or phrase (such as *although, because, since,* or *as soon as*) that introduces and relates a dependent clause to the independent clause on which it depends.

▶ The importance of English as a link between those who have little else in common is clear; the true controversy, in fact, lies in other issues.

Turn the independent clauses into separate sentences.

▶ At high noon we were off, paddling down the Potomac River~~,~~. ~~we~~ We were two to a canoe, leaving space in the middle for our gear.

▶ Unfortunately, not many people realize how much scientific research with animals means to the medical world~~,~~. ~~only~~ Only the scientists themselves and the diseased patients who suffer and hope for new cures can fully understand the importance of animal testing.

The period at the end of the first independent clause tells the reader that one complete sentence is ending and another is beginning.

Turn one independent clause into a phrase that modifies the other.

▶ At high noon we were off, paddling down the Potomac River, ~~we were~~ two to a canoe with space in the middle for our gear.

Eliminating the subject and verb in the second clause turns this clause into a **modifying phrase,** reducing the number of words and closely connecting the ideas.

modifying phrase A word group that serves as an adjective or adverb.

S2 Fused Sentences

For practice, go to bedfordstmartins.com/theguide/fused

A fused or run-on sentence consists of two **independent clauses** run together with no punctuation.

independent (main) clause A word group with a subject and a predicate that can stand alone as a separate sentence. (A predicate is the part of a clause that includes a complete verb and says something about the subject.)

FUSED SENTENCE [INDEPENDENT CLAUSE] Her mood was good [INDEPENDENT CLAUSE] I took the opportunity to ask if she had a few minutes to answer some questions.

Because a fused sentence can be edited in many ways, first consider how the ideas in the two independent clauses are related, and then select the most appropriate strategy below. In the example just given, the writer might emphasize the causal relationship between the clauses.

▶ ~~Her~~ Because her mood was good, I took the opportunity to ask if she had a few minutes to answer some questions.

Make one of the clauses subordinate to the other by adding a subordinating conjunction and rewording as necessary.

> **subordinating conjunction** A word or phrase (such as *although, because, since,* or *as soon as*) that introduces a dependent clause and relates it to an independent clause.

▶ Kids can be so cruel to each other *that* it is a wonder we all make it through childhood.

▶ *Although kids can be extremely* ~~Kids can be so~~ cruel to each other, ~~it is a wonder~~ *amazingly,* we all make it through childhood.

By beginning a clause with a subordinating conjunction, you indicate that the clause is subordinate to—and dependent on—the main clause. Usually, the **dependent clause** explains or qualifies the independent clause. Choose the subordinating conjunction carefully so that it tells the reader how the dependent clause relates to the independent clause.

> **dependent (subordinate) clause** A word group that has a subject, a predicate, and a subordinating word (such as *because*) at the beginning; it cannot stand by itself as a sentence but must be connected to an independent (main) clause.

Add a comma and a coordinating conjunction to separate the independent clauses.

> **coordinating conjunction** A word that joins comparable and equally important sentence elements: *for, and, or, but, nor, yet,* or *so.*

▶ The beast was upon me*, and* I could feel his paws pressing down on my chest.

The coordinating conjunction tells the reader that the ideas in the two clauses are equally important.

Separate the independent clauses with a semicolon.

▶ I looked around at the different monitors; most were large color monitors, many of which were connected to the supercomputer.

The semicolon tells the reader that the ideas in the two clauses are closely connected, but it implies the connection rather than stating it. Occasionally, a colon may be used to introduce a second independent clause (see P4-a).

Separate the independent clauses with a semicolon or a period, and add a conjunctive adverb or a transitional phrase such as *for example* or *in other words.*

> **conjunctive adverb** A word or phrase (such as *finally, however,* or *therefore*) that tells how the ideas in two sentences or independent clauses are connected.

▶ Most students do not do their homework during the day*; instead,* they do it in the evening.

▶ Most students do not do their homework during the day*. Instead,* they do it in the evening.

The semicolon indicates that the ideas in the two clauses are closely connected, and the conjunctive adverb explains the connection. The period indicates a stronger break. Conjunctive adverbs appear more frequently in formal than in informal writing.

Note: A **subordinating conjunction** always *introduces* a clause, but a conjunctive adverb can occupy different positions within a clause. If the conjunctive adverb appears in the middle of one clause rather than between two clauses, the semicolon is still placed between the clauses, not before the adverb.

▶ **Most students do not do their homework during the day they do it in the evening.** [edit: ; instead, inserted after "it"]

Turn the independent clauses into separate sentences.

▶ **He was only eight. ~~his~~ His life hadn't even started.**

▶ **I couldn't believe it. I had fallen in a puddle of mud.**

The period at the end of the first independent clause tells the reader that one complete sentence is ending and another is beginning.

Turn one independent clause into a phrase that modifies the other.

▶ **The beast was upon me, ~~I could feel~~ his paws pressing down on my chest.**

Eliminating the subject and verb in the second clause turns this clause into a **modifying phrase,** reducing the number of words and closely linking the ideas.

modifying phrase A word group that serves as an adjective or adverb.

subject The part of a clause that identifies who or what is being discussed: At the checkpoint, *we* unloaded the canoes.

predicate The part of a clause that includes a complete verb and says something about the subject: At the checkpoint, we *unloaded the canoes.*

dependent (subordinate) clause A word group that has a subject, a predicate, and a subordinating word (such as *because*) at the beginning; it cannot stand by itself as a sentence but must be connected to an independent (main) clause: *Although it was raining,* we loaded our gear onto the buses.

S3 Sentence Fragments

For practice, go to bedfordstmartins.com/theguide/frag

A fragment is either an incomplete sentence, lacking a complete **subject** or **predicate,** or a **dependent clause** punctuated as a sentence. Even though a fragment begins with a capital letter and ends with a period, it cannot stand alone as a sentence.

FRAGMENT Tonight it's my turn. *A ride-along with Sergeant Rob Nether of the Green Valley Police Department.*

Because a fragment can often be edited in several ways, begin by considering what the fragment lacks and how its ideas relate to those in the sentences before and after it. Then use one of the following strategies to change the fragment into a complete sentence. To edit the fragment in the example, the writer might connect it to the preceding sentence.

▶ **Tonight it's my turn ~~. A~~ for a ride-along with Sergeant Rob Nether of the Green Valley Police Department.**

Connect the fragment to a complete sentence.

▶ Frank turned the tarot cards one at a time~~.~~, ~~Each~~ each time telling me something about my future.

▶ A unique design has the distinct advantage of becoming associated with its role~~.~~; ~~For~~ for example, the highly successful Coke bottle shape, which is now associated with soft drinks.

Eliminate the subordinating word or words that make a clause dependent.

▶ The world that I was born into demanded continuous work. ~~Where nobody~~ Nobody got ahead, and everyone came home tired.

Add or complete the verb or the subject to change a fragment into a complete sentence.

▶ The crowd in the lounge is basically young. The teenage and early twenties generation~~.~~ gathers there.

▶ Children are brought up in different ways. Some~~,~~ grow up around violence.

Note: Sometimes writers use fragments intentionally for emphasis or special effect.

> The bare utility of the clock echoes the simplicity of the office. No sign of a large hardwood desk or a pillowy leather chair or even a wall with shelves filled with imposing law books.

Use intentional fragments cautiously. Especially in academic writing, many readers may perceive them as errors, regardless of your intentions. In the example above, for instance, the same impact might also be achieved by using a colon or dash.

G Grammatical Sentences

G1 Pronoun Reference

For practice, go to bedfordstmartins.com/theguide/pref

pronoun A word that replaces a specific noun (such as *she, it, his, they, them, yours, ours, myself, whose,* or *which*), points out a specific noun (such as *this, these,* or *that*), or refers to an unspecified person or object (such as *each* or *everybody*).

antecedent The word or words that a pronoun replaces and to which it refers.

Make sure that each **pronoun** clearly refers to one specific **antecedent.**

The elderly and children are victims when no one bothers to check on *them.*

In this example, the pronoun *them* refers to a specific antecedent, *the elderly and children.*

Rewrite to eliminate vague uses of *they, it,* or *you.*

▶ Lani explained that everything is completely supported by individual contributions. ~~They receive~~ ^*The organization receives* no tax support.

▶ Often, a guest such as Caroline Kennedy or Kevin Costner may appear more than once. Although ~~it~~ ^*having the same guest return* seems repetitious, it actually is not because the guest discusses different topics each time.

▶ Parents argue that beginning the program in the sixth grade is too early. ^*They say that* ~~By~~ exposing teens to sex education early~~,~~ ~~you encourage~~ ^*encourages* them to go out and have sex.

Add a noun, change the pronoun to a noun, or revise the sentence to eliminate vague uses of *this, that,* or *which.*

▶ Researchers have noticed that men interrupt women more than women interrupt men. This ^*finding* may explain why women sometimes find it difficult to start and sustain conversations with men.

▶ I was an *A* student, and I thought ~~that~~ ^*good grades* should have been enough for any teacher.

▶ The brevity of the first story prevents the reader from dwelling on the plot and caring about the outcome. *Because these* ~~These~~ faults are not present in "The Soft Voice of the Serpent," ~~which makes~~ it *is* much more fulfilling to read.

Add a missing antecedent, or eliminate a pronoun with no clear antecedent.

▶ In addition to the cars your tenants actually drive, five or six vehicles are always on and around the property. As a result, not only do *your tenants* ~~they~~ park ~~some of them~~ in front of their neighbors' homes, but their questionable visitors park up and down the street as well.

Adding an antecedent (specifying *your tenants* instead of *they*) and eliminating a pronoun (reducing *park some of them* to *park*) simplify and clarify the sentence.

Identify a specific antecedent if a pronoun refers vaguely to a clause or a whole sentence.

▶ After the long ride, we reached the place for our expedition at Pine Heaven Forest in western Virginia. At my age, *the trip* ~~it~~ seemed to take forever.

Rewrite to eliminate an ambiguous reference to two possible antecedents.

▶ Students may now sue *if* their schools ~~if they~~ are underperforming.

▶ Students may now sue their *underperforming* schools. ~~if they are underperforming.~~

Rewrite to eliminate an implied reference.

▶ *In this* ~~This~~ song, tells about being carefree and going through life without any worries. Years later, though, *the singer* he starts to remember his past, and things do not seem so problem-free anymore.

In this example, adding *the singer* specifies an antecedent for *he*.

Note: Sometimes the implied noun may be present in another form, such as a possessive *(Mary's* for *Mary)* or as part of another word *(child* in *childhood).*

► **Radaker~~'s arguments~~ irritated everyone at the lecture because he failed to support ~~them~~ *his arguments* with examples or evidence.**

G2 Pronoun Agreement

For practice, go to bedfordstmartins.com/theguide/pagree

Make sure that a **pronoun** and its **antecedent** agree in **number,** in **person,** and in **gender.** In the following examples, the arrows connect the pronouns and their antecedents.

The *scientists* did not know what *they* were creating.

I **thought about Punita's offer while watching the movie. *My* curiosity won.**

After we went back to the lab, *Punita* started concentrating on *her* work.

The form of the antecedent and the form of the pronoun must correspond—agree—so that a reader is not troubled by inconsistencies or confused about how many, who, or which gender you mean.

pronoun A word that replaces a specific noun (such as *she, it, his, they, them, yours, ours, myself, whose,* or *which*), points out a specific noun (such as *this, these,* or *that*), or refers to an unspecified person or object (such as *each* or *everybody*).

antecedent The word or words that a pronoun replaces and to which it refers.

number The form of a word that shows whether it refers to one thing (singular) or more than one (plural): *parent, parents; child, children.*

person The form of a word that shows whether it refers to *I* or *we* (first person), to *you* (second person), or to *he, she, it,* or *they* (third person).

gender The form of a word that shows whether it refers to a male *(he)* or a female *(she).*

G2-a Use either singular or plural forms consistently for both a pronoun and its antecedent.

If the antecedent of a pronoun is singular, the pronoun must be singular so that both agree in number. Likewise, if the antecedent is plural, the pronoun must be plural.

The *shelter* gets most of *its* cats and dogs from *owners* who cannot keep *their* pets.

When the pronoun and its antecedent do not agree, change one or the other so that both are singular or both are plural, or rewrite the sentence to eliminate the inconsistency. See also E2-b.

Change either the pronoun or its antecedent so that both are singular or plural.

► **The patient is fully aware of the decision that ~~they are~~ *he or she is* making.**

► **~~The patient is~~ *Patients are* fully aware of the decision that they are making.**

Note: As an alternative, you may be able to eliminate the pronoun.

▶ The patient is fully aware of ~~the~~ *each* decision. ~~that they are making.~~

Revise the sentence to eliminate the inconsistency.

▶ Roommates get agitated at always being told to clean, and the roommate doing the yelling gets tired of ~~hearing their own voice complain.~~ *complaining.*

Use a singular pronoun to refer to a singular indefinite pronoun, or reword the sentence.

indefinite pronoun A pronoun that does not refer to a particular person or object, such as *anybody, anyone, each, everyone, everything, somebody, something, neither, none,* or *nobody* (which take the singular); *few, many,* and *several* (which take the plural); and *all, most,* and *some* (which can take either the singular or plural).

▶ Whether student, teacher, faculty member, graduate, or parent, each wants ~~their~~ *his or her* school to be the one that remains open.

▶ *All students, teachers, faculty members, graduates, and parents want* ~~Whether student, teacher, faculty member, graduate, or parent, each wants~~ their school to be the one that remains open.

▶ This event would be a good chance for ~~everyone~~ *students* to come out, socialize, and enjoy themselves.

▶ This event would be a good chance for everyone to come out, socialize, and enjoy ~~themselves.~~ *a relaxing afternoon.*

Consider the level of formality of your writing as you choose among your options. Participants in a casual conversation may not mind if an indefinite pronoun and its antecedent do not agree, but such errors are not acceptable in most formal writing.

Use a singular pronoun in most cases if the antecedent is a collective noun.

collective noun A noun (such as *class* or *family*) that refers to a group as a unit and is usually considered singular.

▶ The Santa Barbara School District has a serious problem on ~~their~~ *its* agenda.

A collective noun may sometimes be considered plural if it refers to the group members as individuals: The *couple* decided it was time to consolidate *their* bank accounts.

See also G6-b.

antecedent The word or words that a pronoun replaces and to which it refers.

gender The form of a word that shows whether it refers to a male *(he)* or a female *(she)*.

G2-b Use masculine, feminine, or gender-free forms to match a pronoun with its antecedent.

Match a masculine pronoun with a masculine antecedent and a feminine pronoun with a feminine antecedent so that the pronoun and its antecedent agree in **gender.**

I first met *Mark* the day *he* was hired.

If an antecedent might be either masculine or feminine, avoid using a pronoun that stereotypes by gender. See also W3-c.

Match a plural antecedent with a plural pronoun to include both sexes.

▶ Many people believe that ~~a boy or girl is~~ ^*children are* better off with a family that is able to provide for all of their needs than with a poverty-stricken parent.

Use a phrase that includes both masculine and feminine singular pronouns (such as *his or her*) to refer to both sexes.

▶ Many people believe that a child is better off with a family that is able to provide for all of ~~their~~ ^*his or her* needs than with a poverty-stricken parent.

Note: If repeating a phrase such as *his or her* seems cumbersome or repetitious, try using plural forms or eliminating the pronouns altogether, as the following strategy suggests.

Rewrite to eliminate unneeded or awkward pairs of masculine and feminine pronouns when you are referring to both men and women.

▶ This solution, of course, assumes that the bus ~~driver~~ ^*drivers* will be where ~~he/she is~~ ^*they are* supposed to be; boredom sometimes inspires ~~a driver~~ ^*drivers* to make up new and exciting variations on ~~his or her~~ ^*the* designated routes.

Note: Avoid using *he/she* in all but the most informal writing situations.

relative pronoun A pronoun (such as *who, whom, whose, which,* or *that*) that introduces an adjective clause (a clause that modifies a noun or pronoun).

G3 Relative Pronouns

For practice, go to bedfordstmartins.com/theguide/relp

Use personal **relative pronouns** to refer to people: *who, whom, whoever, whomever,* and *whose.*

This reaction is unlike the response of the boys, *who* had trouble focusing on a subject.

Use nonpersonal relative pronouns to refer to things: *which, whichever, whatever,* and *whose* (*whose* can be used as a nonpersonal relative pronoun as well as a personal one).

These interruptions, 75 percent of *which* come solely from males, disrupt conversations.

Use *that* for general references to things and groups.

Sensory modalities are governed by the side of the brain *that* is not damaged.

See also G6-e.

G3-a Select *who* for references to people, *which* for nonrestrictive references to things, and *that* for restrictive references to groups and things.

nonrestrictive clause A clause, set off by commas, that provides extra or nonessential information and could be eliminated without changing the meaning of the noun or pronoun it modifies.

restrictive clause A clause, not set off by commas, that provides information essential to defining or identifying the noun or pronoun it modifies.

My attention focused on a little dark-haired boy *who* was crying.

The tournament, *which* we had worked for all year, was the most prestigious event of the season.

Save Our Sharks tried to promote a bill *that* would forbid the killing of certain sharks.

Change *that* to *who* to refer to a person.

▶ Illness phobics have countless examinations despite the reassurance of each physician ~~that~~ ^*who* examines them.

▶ It was his parents ~~that~~ ^*who* made him run for student council, play the piano, and go out for sports.

Note: Rewriting a sentence to simplify its structure sometimes eliminates a problem with pronouns.

▶ ~~It was his~~ ^*His* parents ~~that~~ made him run for student council, play the piano, and go out for sports.

See also G3-b for information on *who* and *whom.*

nonrestrictive clause A clause, set off by commas, that provides extra or nonessential information and could be eliminated without changing the meaning of the noun or pronoun it modifies.

Change *that* to *which* when a nonrestrictive clause supplies extra, nondefining information.

▶ Caroline had the prettiest jet-black hair, ~~that~~ *which* went down to the middle of her back.

(See P1-c on using commas with nonrestrictive word groups.)

restrictive clause A clause, not set off by commas, that provides information essential to defining or identifying the noun or pronoun it modifies.

Change *which* to *that* when a restrictive clause supplies essential information defining a thing or a group.

▶ From the moment we are born, we come into a society ~~which~~ *that* assimilates us into its culture.

▶ In addition to the equipment and technology ~~which~~ *that* fill the trauma room, a team of experts assembles before the patient arrives.

(See P2-b on unnecessary commas with restrictive word groups.)

Note: Which is usually used only in nonrestrictive clauses, but sometimes writers use it in restrictive clauses as well.

object The part of a clause that receives the action of the verb (At the checkpoint, we unloaded *the canoes*) or the part of a phrase that follows a preposition (We dragged them to *the river*).

preposition A word (such as *between, in,* or *of*) that always appears as part of a phrase and indicates the relation between a word in a sentence and the object of the preposition: The water splashed *into* the canoe.

G3-b Use *who* as a subject and *whom* as an object.

Two strategies can help you to figure out which word to use.

1. Mark the phrase or clause, and then arrange its words in subject-verb-object order or preposition-object order. In this standard order, a subject *(who)* is followed by a verb, but an object *(whom)* follows a subject and verb or follows a preposition.
2. Look for the subject of the clause. If the verb in the clause has another subject, use *whom;* if the verb in the clause has no other subject, use *who.*

SUBJECT We remember [*who* tips well] and [*who* doesn't].

OBJECT OF VERB Mr. Scott is someone [*whom* I will always admire]. (*I will always admire whom.*)

OBJECT OF PREPOSITION The university employs a large number of foreign teaching assistants [for *whom* English is a second language].

Change *who* to *whom* when the pronoun is an object within another clause that has a subject and a verb.

▶ He has the ability to attract guests ~~who~~ *whom* people want to hear.

Change *who* to *whom* when the pronoun is the object of a preposition.

▶ He also met his wife, ~~who~~ *whom* he was married to for fifty-two years.

▶ He also met his wife, ~~who~~ *to whom* he was married ~~to~~ for fifty-two years.

Change *whom* to *who* when the pronoun is the subject of a clause, followed by a verb.

▶ The libraries are staffed by professionals ~~whom~~ *who* have instituted methods to keep students informed of new materials.

G4 Pronoun Case

For practice, go to bedfordstmartins.com/theguide/pcase

A pronoun can take different forms or cases, depending on its role in a sentence.

- Subject or **subject complement:** *I, we, you, he, she, it, they* (subjective form)

  "*You*'d better be careful," *she* said.

  It is *we* you owe the money to.

- Object of a verb or a **preposition:** *me, us, you, him, her, it, them* (objective form)

  This realization spurred *me* to hasten the search.

  Her dog, Peter the Great, went with *her* on the excavation in southern Siberia.

- Possession or ownership: *mine, ours, yours, his, hers, theirs, my, our, your, his, her, its, their* (possessive form)

  I trusted *his* driving.

  I finished putting *my* gear on and rolled over backward into the ocean.

  See R2-a for more on pronouns.

subject complement A word or word group that follows a linking verb (such as *seems, appears,* or *is* and other forms of *be*) and describes or restates the subject: The tents looked *old and dirty.*

Replace a reflexive pronoun that does not refer to another noun or pronoun in the clause.

▶ Kyle and ~~myself~~ *I* went upstairs to see how she was doing.

A reflexive pronoun does not belong in this sentence because *myself* does not refer to a preceding *I.*

reflexive pronoun A pronoun such as *myself* or *ourselves* that refers to a noun or a personal pronoun in the same clause.

compound subject Two or more words acting as a subject and linked by *and.*

Change a pronoun to the subjective form if it is part of a compound subject.

▶ Even though Annie and ~~me~~ I went through the motions, we didn't understand the customs of our host.

compound object Two or more words acting as an object and linked by *and.*

Change a pronoun to the objective form if it is an object (or part of a compound object) of a preposition or a verb.

▶ There was an invisible wall between ~~she~~ her and ~~I.~~ me.

gerund A verb form that is used as a noun and ends in *-ing: arguing, throwing.*

Change a pronoun to the possessive form when it modifies a gerund.

▶ One of the main reasons for ~~me~~ my wanting to stay home with my children until they enter grade school is that I would miss so much.

Change the form of a pronoun to fit the implied or understood wording of a comparison using *than* or *as.*

▶ I was still faster than ~~her~~ she.

Test whether a pronoun form fits by filling in the implied wording.

INCORRECT PRONOUN	I was still faster than *her* [was fast].
CORRECT PRONOUN	I was still faster than *she* [was fast].

Use *we* to precede a subject or *us* to precede an object.

We is the subjective form, and *us* is the objective form. Select the form that matches the role of the noun in the sentence.

▶ Whenever ~~us~~ we neighborhood kids would go out and play, I would always be goalie.

Test your choice of pronoun by reading the sentence with the noun left out.

INCORRECT PRONOUN	Whenever *us* would go out and play, I would always be goalie.
CORRECT PRONOUN	Whenever *we* would go out and play, I would always be goalie.

G5 Verbs

For practice, go to bedfordstmartins.com/theguide/verbs

Use standard verb forms in the appropriate **tense, mood,** and **voice.**

tense The form of a verb that shows the time of the action or state of being.

mood The form of a verb that shows the writer's attitude toward a statement.

voice The form of a verb that indicates (active) or deemphasizes (passive) the performer of the action.

G5-a Select the appropriate verb tense to place events in past, present, and future time.

Most of the time you will probably choose the correct verb tense without thinking about it. (See R2-a for a review of the basic verb tenses.) In a few situations, however, you will need to pay special attention to conventional usage or to the relationships among different verbs within the context of your essay.

> For ESL Writers
>
> See L2 for advice on how to use the correct tense in conditional clauses, two-word verbs, and helping (auxiliary) verbs and whether to use a gerund or infinitive form after a verb.

Change verbs from the past tense to the present when discussing events in a literary work or film, general truths, ongoing principles, and facts.

- **In the "Monkey Garden," the girl ~~knew~~ *knows* it ~~was~~ *is* time to grow up but still ~~wanted~~ *wants* to play with the other kids in her make-believe world.**
- **In the film, Virginia Woolf (Nicole Kidman) ~~was~~ *is* an intensely neurotic woman whose diet ~~seemed~~ *seems* to consist entirely of cigarettes.**

Academic readers expect this use of the present tense in a literary analysis, as if the action in a work is always present and ongoing. Readers also expect general truths, facts, and ongoing principles to be stated in the present tense. See also E2-a.

GENERAL TRUTH	**The family *is* the foundation for a child's education.**
ONGOING PRINCIPLE	**Attaining self-sufficiency *is* one of the most important priorities of our energy policy.**
FACT	**The earth *is tilted* at an angle of 23 degrees.**

Note: Some style guides make different recommendations about verb tense, depending on the field and its conventions. The style guide of the American Psychological Association (APA), for example, recommends using the past tense for past studies and past research procedures but using the present tense for research implications and conclusions.

APA STYLE Davidson *stated* that father absence *is* more than twice as common now as in our parents' generation.

Change the verb from the past tense to the past perfect (using *had*) to show that one past action already had taken place before another past action occurred.

▶ **The victim's roommate also claimed that she ^*had* called the dorm office two days prior to the suicide attempt.**

The past action identified by the verb *had called* occurred before the past action identified by the verb *claimed*.

progressive tense A tense that shows ongoing action, consisting of a form of *be* plus the *-ing* form of the main verb: I *am waiting.*

For ESL Writers

Certain verbs—ones that indicate existence, states of mind, and the senses of sight, smell, touch, and so on—are rarely used in the **progressive tense.** Such verbs include *appear, be, belong, contain, feel, forget, have, hear, know, mean, prefer, remember, see, smell, taste, think, understand,* and *want.*

▶ **I ~~am belonging~~ ^*belong* to the campus group for foreign students.**

G5-b Use the correct verb endings and verb forms.

The five basic forms of regular verbs (such as *talk*) follow the same pattern, adding *-s, -ed,* and *-ing* as shown here. The forms of irregular verbs (such as *speak*) do not consistently follow this pattern in forming the past and the past participle. (See R2-a.)

- Infinitive or base: *talk* or *speak*

  Every day I *talk* on the phone and *speak* to my friends.

- Third-person singular present (*-s* form): *talks* or *speaks*

  He *talks* softly, and she *speaks* slowly.

- Past: *talked* or *spoke*

  I *talked* to my parents last week, and I *spoke* to Jed on Tuesday.

- Present participle (*-ing* form): *talking* or *speaking*

  She is *talking* on the phone now, and he is *speaking* to a friend.

- Past participle (*-ed* form): *talked* or *spoken*

I have *talked* to her many times, but she has not *spoken* to him yet.

> For ESL Writers
>
> Choosing the correct verb form is sometimes complicated by English expressions. For example, *used to* followed by the base form of the verb does not mean the same as *get used to* followed by a gerund.
>
> **In the United States, most people *used to live* in rural areas. [This situation existed in the past but has changed.]**
>
> **My daughter *is getting used to going* to school every day. [She is getting in the habit of attending school.]**
>
> (For more on choosing correct word forms, see W2.)

Add an *-s* or *-es* ending to a verb when the subject is in the third-person singular (*he, she, it,* or a singular noun).

▶ The national drug control policy ~~treat~~ ^*treats* drug abuse as a law enforcement problem.

▶ This group ~~account~~ ^*accounts* for more than 10 percent of the total U.S. population.

Delete an *-s* or *-es* ending from a verb when the subject is in the first person *(I, we),* second person *(you),* or third-person plural *(they).*

▶ Because I didn't tell you about the movie, I really ~~suggests~~ ^*suggest* that you go see it.

Add a *-d* or an *-ed* ending to a regular verb to form the past tense or the past participle.

▶ This movie was filmed in New Orleans because it resembles the city where the story is ~~suppose~~ ^*supposed* to take place.

▶ As we walked through the library, she ~~explain~~ ^*explained* the meaning of the yellow signs.

Check to be sure you have used the correct form of an irregular verb.

If you are uncertain about a verb form, refer to the list of irregular verbs in R2-a or check your dictionary.

▶ The hostess greeted us and ~~lead~~ *led* us to our seats.

▶ We could tell our food had just ~~came~~ *come* off the grill because it still sizzled.

Note: Some verbs with different meanings are confusing because they have similar forms. For example, the verb *lie (lie, lay, lain, lying)* means "recline," but the verb *lay (lay, laid, laid, laying)* means "put or place." Check such verbs in the Glossary of Frequently Misused Words at the end of this Handbook or in a dictionary to make sure that you are using the correct forms of the word you intend.

▶ I thought everyone was going to see my car ~~laying~~ *lying* on its side.

indicative mood The verb form that is ordinarily used for statements and questions.

imperative mood The verb form used for commands or directions.

subjunctive mood The verb form that is used for wishes, suggestions, and conditions that are hypothetical, impossible, or unlikely.

base form The uninflected form of a verb: I *eat;* to *play.*

G5-c Choose the correct form of a verb to show the indicative, imperative, or subjunctive mood.

INDICATIVE There *was* Ward, the perfect father, who *served* as sole provider for the family.

Where *are* the Cleavers today?

IMPERATIVE *Take* me to the mall.

SUBJUNCTIVE If it *were* to rain on the day of the picnic, we would simply bring everything indoors.

The subjunctive is often used in clauses with *if* or *that.* Always use the base form of the verb for the present subjunctive (see G5-b). For the past tense of the verb *be,* the subjunctive form is *were,* not *was.*

▶ Even if this claim ~~was~~ *were* true, it would raise a very controversial issue.

▶ It was as if he ~~was~~ *were* stretching his neck to pick leaves or fruit out of a high tree.

active voice The verb form that shows the subject in action: The cat *caught* the mouse.

passive voice The verb form that shows something happening to the subject: The mouse *was caught* by the cat.

G5-d Use verbs primarily in the active voice.

The active voice calls attention to the actor performing an action. By contrast, the passive voice emphasizes the recipient of the action or the action itself while omitting or deemphasizing the actor.

ACTIVE The monkey *lived* in the garden.

PASSIVE The story *is told* by a girl as she reflects on her own childhood.

Change passive verbs to active in most writing situations.

Straightforward and direct, the active voice creates graceful, clear writing that emphasizes actors.

▶ The ~~story is told by the girl~~ *girl tells the story* as she reflects on her own childhood.

▶ ~~Physicians are attracted by the~~ *The* monetary rewards of high-tech research *attract physicians.*

Rewrite to eliminate awkward, unnecessary passive verbs.

▶ The guests cluster like grapes ~~as similar interests are sought.~~ *, seeking others with similar interests.*

Note: The passive is sometimes useful if you want to shift information to the end of a sentence. It is also frequently used in impersonal writing that focuses on an action rather than an actor, as in a scientific research report.

> **When the generator *is turned on,* water *is forced* down the tunnel, and the animals swim against the current. Their metabolism *is measured.* They have participated in this experiment before, and the results from that run and this new one *will be compared.***

G6 Subject-Verb Agreement

For practice, go to bedfordstmartins.com/theguide/svagree

Use **subjects** and **verbs** that agree in **person** and **number.** Agreement problems often occur when a sentence has a complicated subject or verb, especially when the subject and verb are separated by other words.

▶ **The large amounts of money that are associated with sports ~~is~~ *are* not the problem.**

The plural subject, *amounts,* requires a plural verb, *are.* See also R2-a to check the correct forms of *be* and other irregular verbs.

subject The part of a clause that identifies who or what is being discussed: At the checkpoint, *we* unloaded the canoes.

verb A word or phrase that expresses action or being and, along with a subject, is a basic component of a sentence: At the checkpoint, we *unloaded* the canoes.

person The form of a word that shows whether it refers to *I* or *we* (first person), to *you* (second person), or to *he, she, it,* or *they* (third person).

number The form of a word that shows whether it refers to one thing (singular) or more than one (plural): *parent, parents; child, children.*

G6-a Make sure the subject and verb agree even if they are separated by other words.

The *relationship* between artists and politicians *has become* a controversial issue.

First identify the subject and the verb; then change one to agree with the other.

▶ **The pattern of echoes from these sound waves ~~are~~ *is* converted by computer into a visual image.**

▶ **The ~~pattern of~~ echoes from these sound waves are converted by computer into a visual image.**

collective noun A noun (such as *class* or *family*) that refers to a group as a unit and is usually considered singular.

G6-b Use a singular verb with a subject that is a collective noun.

The *association distributes* information on showing bison, selling bison, and marketing bison meat.

Change the verb to a singular form if the subject is a collective noun.

▶ **If a military team ~~fight~~ *fights* without spirit and will, it will probably lose.**

Note: A collective noun is generally considered singular because it treats a group as a single unit. If it refers to the members of the group as individuals, however, it may be considered plural.

SINGULAR (GROUP AS A UNIT)	**The *staff is* amiable.**
PLURAL (INDIVIDUAL MEMBERS)	**The *staff exchange* greetings and small talk as *they begin* putting on *their* surgical garb.**

G6-c Use a verb that agrees with a subject placed after it.

In most sentences, the subject precedes the verb, but some sentences are inverted. For example, sentences beginning with *there is* and *there are* reverse the standard order, putting the subject after the verb.

VERB — SUBJECT
There *are no busy lines and brushstrokes* in the paintings.

VERB — SUBJECT
There *is interaction* between central and peripheral visual fields.

In inverted sentences, change the verb so that it agrees with the subject that follows it, or rewrite the sentence.

▶ **The next morning, there ~~was~~ *were* Mike and Cindy, acting as if nothing had happened.**

▶ **The next morning, ~~there was~~ Mike and Cindy~~,~~ *were* acting as if nothing had happened.**

G6-d Use a plural verb with a compound subject.

compound subject Two or more words acting as a subject and linked by *and.*

SUBJECT — VERB

She and her husband have a partnership with her in-laws.

Two subjects joined by *and* require a plural verb.

▶ Dust and dirt ~~accumulates,~~ accumulate; bathrooms get mildewy, and kitchens get greasy.

Note: If two subjects are joined by *or* or *nor,* the verb should agree with the subject that is closer to it.

Most nights, my daughter or my sons *start* dinner.

G6-e Use a verb that agrees with the antecedent of the pronoun *who, which,* or *that.*

antecedent The word or words that a pronoun replaces and to which it refers.

Its staff consists of nineteen *people* who *drive* to work in any kind of weather to make sure the station comes through for its listeners.

To check agreement, identify the antecedent of the pronoun.

▶ Within the ordered chaos of the trauma room are diagnostic tools, surgical devices, and X-ray equipment, which ~~is~~ are required for Sharp to be designated a trauma center.

▶ The males choose topics that enable them to establish dominance over others in the group, while the females tell personally moving stories that ~~encourages~~ encourage others to show their feelings.

Note: With the phrase *one of the* followed by a plural noun, use a verb that agrees with the noun.

One of the *features* that *make* the monitor different is that it doubles as a television.

G6-f Use a singular verb with an indefinite pronoun.

indefinite pronoun A pronoun that does not refer to a particular person or object, such as *anybody, each, one, everyone, everything, somebody, something, neither, none,* or *nobody* (which take the singular); *few, many,* and *several* (which take the plural); and *all, most,* and *some* (which can take either the singular or plural).

Everything on the playground *is* child friendly.

During informal conversation, people sometimes treat indefinite pronouns as plural forms. In formal writing, however, an indefinite pronoun usually refers to a single person or object and agrees with a singular verb.

▶ **There are two alternatives to this solution, and neither ~~seem~~ *seems* feasible.**

Note: If an indefinite pronoun such as *all, none,* or *some* refers to a plural noun, use a plural form of the verb. If it refers to a singular noun, use a singular form.

Some manage **to find jobs that fit their schedule, the surf schedule.**

Most are **respectable people.**

All **of the money** ***is*** **missing.**

subject complement A word or word group that follows a linking verb (such as *seems, appears,* or *is* and other forms of *be*) and describes or restates the subject: The tents looked *old and dirty.*

G6-g Use a verb that agrees with the subject rather than a subject complement.

The shark's favorite ***diet is*** **elephant seals and sea lions.**

When either the subject or the subject complement names a group or category, the choice between a singular or plural verb becomes confusing. Make sure that the verb agrees with the actual subject. If necessary, rewrite the sentence.

▶ **Big blocks of color in a simple flat shape ~~is~~ *are* his artistic trademark.**

▶ *He favors big* **~~Big~~ blocks of color in a simple flat shape. ~~is his artistic trademark.~~**

adjective A word that modifies a noun or a pronoun, adding information about it.

adverb A word that modifies a verb, an adjective, or another adverb, often telling when, where, why, how, or how often.

modifier A word, phrase, or clause functioning as an adjective or adverb that adds information and detail about a noun, a verb, or another word.

G7 Adjectives and Adverbs

For practice, go to bedfordstmartins.com/theguide/adjadv

Distinguish **adjectives** from **adverbs** so that you select the correct forms of these **modifiers.** See also R2-a.

ADJECTIVES **Because** ***angry*** **drivers are** ***dangerous*** **drivers, it is** ***imperative*** **that the county implement** ***a*** **solution.**

ADVERB **Installing traffic lights would** ***quickly*** **alleviate three important aspects of the problem.**

G7-a Select an adverb, not an adjective, to modify an adjective, another adverb, or a verb.

Often ending in *-ly,* adverbs tell how, when, where, why, and how often.

Despite a *very* busy work schedule, Caesar finds time in the afternoon to come *directly* to the high school and work as a volunteer track coach.

Change an adjective that modifies another adjective, an adverb, or a verb to an adverb form.

▶ **This man yelled at me so ~~loud~~ *loudly* that I began to cry.**

Note: Adjective forms that are common in informal conversation should be changed to adverb forms in more formal writing.

SPOKEN **The day was going *slow,* and I repeatedly caught my lure on the riverbed or a tree limb.**

WRITTEN **The day was going *slowly,* and I repeatedly caught my lure on the riverbed or a tree limb.**

G7-b Select an adjective, not an adverb, to modify a noun or a pronoun.

I am enamored of the *cool* motor, the *massive* boulder in the middle of the lake, and the sound of the wake *splashing* against the side of the two-seater.

Change an adverb that modifies a noun or a pronoun to an adjective.

▶ **Working within a ~~traditionally~~ *traditional* chronological plot, Joyce develops the protagonist's emotional conflict.**

An adjective generally appears immediately before or after the word it modifies. When an adjective acts as a **subject complement,** however, it is separated from the word it modifies by a **linking verb.**

My grandfather is *amazing.*

Note: Some verbs act as linking verbs only in certain contexts. When one of these verbs connects a subject and its complement, use an adjective form: She looked *ill.* When the verb is modified by the word that follows it, however, use an adverb: She looked *quickly.*

subject complement A word or word group that follows a linking verb (such as *seems, appears,* or *is* and other forms of *be*) and describes or restates the subject: The tents looked *old and dirty.*

linking verb *Be, seem, appear, become, taste,* or another verb that connects a subject with a subject complement that describes or modifies it: The chips *taste* salty.

For ESL Writers

ESL writers sometimes have trouble choosing between past and present participles *(looked, looking)* used as adjectives. See L6 for help in selecting the correct form.

G7-c Select the correct forms of adjectives and adverbs to show comparisons.

Add *-er* or *-est* to short words (usually of one or two syllables), or use *more, most, less,* and *least* with longer words and all *-ly* adverbs.

The southern peninsula's *smallest* kingdom was invaded continually by its two *more powerful* neighbors.

Use *-er, more* or *less* (the comparative form) to compare two things.

I had always been a little bit *faster* than she was.

Use *-est, most,* or *least* (the superlative form) to compare three or more.

An elite warrior corps grew that soon gained the respect of even its *most bitter* foes.

Change the forms of adjectives and adverbs to show comparison precisely.

▶ **She has clearly been the ~~least~~ less favored child in the sense that she is not as beautiful or as intelligent as her sister.**

E Effective Sentences

E1 Missing Words

For practice, go to bedfordstmartins.com/theguide/mword

To write effective prose, you need to supply all words necessary for clarity, completeness, and logic.

> For ESL Writers
>
> If English is not your native language, you may have special trouble with omitted words. See also L4.

E1-a Supply small words such as prepositions, conjunctions, infinitive parts, articles, and verb parts needed for clarity and completeness.

When you forget to include these small words, the reader may be puzzled or have to pause momentarily to figure out what you mean. Proofread your essays carefully, even out loud, to catch these omitted words.

Insert missing prepositions.

preposition A word (such as *between, in,* or *of*) that always appears as part of a phrase and indicates the relation between a word in a sentence and the object of the preposition: The water splashed *into* the canoe.

- ▶ **The car began to skid ^*in* the other direction.**
- ▶ **He graduated ^*from* high school at the top of his class.**
- ▶ **A child his age shouldn't be playing outside ^*at* that time of night.**

> For ESL Writers
>
> If you are not a native speaker of American English, prepositions may be especially difficult for you because they are highly idiomatic. In other words, native speakers of English use prepositions in ways that do not translate directly into other languages. The best way to understand when prepositions are needed in English sentences is to read widely and study the work of other writers. See also L3.

Insert missing conjunctions.

conjunction A word that relates sentence parts by coordinating, subordinating, or pairing elements, such as *and, because,* or *either . . . or.*

- ▶ **Most families and patients will accept the pain, inconvenience, ^*and* financial and emotional strain as long as the patient can achieve a life "worth living."**

▶ The heads of these golf clubs can be made of metal, wood, ^or graphite and often have special inserts in the part of the club that hits the ball.

A conjunction is generally needed to connect the final item in a series, such as *financial and emotional strain* in the first example and *graphite* in the second.

infinitive A verb form consisting of the word *to* plus the base form of the verb: *to run, to do.*

Restore the *to* omitted from an infinitive if it is needed for clarity.

▶ They decided ^to start the following Monday morning.

▶ I noticed how he used his uncanny talent for acting ^to make a dreary subject come alive.

article An adjective that precedes a noun and identifies a definite reference to something specific *(the)* or an indefinite reference to something less specific *(a* or *an).*

Insert missing articles.

▶ This incident ruined the party, but it was only ^the beginning of the worst.

▶ But such ^a condition could be resolved by other means.

> For ESL Writers
>
> Nonnative speakers of English sometimes have trouble understanding when and when not to use the articles *a, an,* and *the.* For more advice on the use of articles, see L1.

Insert other missing words that help clarify or complete a sentence.

▶ Malaria was once a widespread disease^, and ^it may become so again.

▶ In these scenes, women are often ^shown with long, luxurious hair.

▶ Finally, and I'm embarrassed to admit ^it, I pushed Cindy against the wall.

E1-b Insert the word *that* if it is needed to prevent confusion or misreading.

CONFUSING I would like to point out golf is not just a game for rich old men in ugly pants.

CLEARER I would like to point out *that* golf is not just a game for rich old men in ugly pants.

Without *that,* the reader may think at first that the writer is pointing out golf and have to double back to understand the sentence. In the revised sentence, *that* tells the reader exactly where the **dependent clause** begins.

dependent (subordinate) clause A word group that has a subject, a predicate, and a subordinating word at the beginning; it cannot stand by itself as a sentence but must be connected to an independent (main) clause.

► **Dryer says, [that] as people grow older, they may find themselves waking up early, usually at dawn.**

► **Another problem parents will notice is [that] the child leaves out certain words.**

Note: If the meaning of a sentence is clear without *that,* it may be left out.

E1-c Add enough words to a comparison to show that the items are of the same kind and to make the comparison logical, clear, and complete.

Because a comparison, by definition, connects two or more things for the reader, you should name both things and state the comparison fully. In addition, the items you are comparing should be of the same kind. For example, compare a person with another person, not with an activity or a situation.

The old student center has a *general store* that carries *as many books or supplies as* the *Saver Center.*

This sentence compares two stores, which are entities of the same kind. See also E7-c.

Reword a comparison to specify comparable items of the same kind.

► **Five-foot-five-inch Maria finds climbing to be more challenging ~~than~~ [for her than it is for] her six-foot-five-inch companions, who can reach the handholds more easily.**

The original version of this sentence says that climbing is more challenging than companions (illogically comparing an activity to people). The edited sentence says that climbing is more challenging for Maria than it is for her companions (logically comparing one person to other people).

Reword a comparison to identify clearly and completely all items being compared.

► **Danziger's article is interesting and lightly laced with facts, definitely more entertaining, [than Solomon's article.]**

Note: In some types of comparative sentences, standard English requires the conventional use of *as.*

Millie is *as* coordinated *as,* if not more coordinated than, Margot.

- ▶ **Students opting for field experience credits would learn as much, as, or more, than, students who take only classes.**

compound structure A sentence element, such as a subject or a verb, that consists of two or more items linked by *and* or another conjunction.

E1-d Supply all words needed to clarify the parts of a compound structure.

Although words may be left out of compound structures to avoid unnecessary repetition, these omitted words must fit in each part of the compound.

Women tend to express feelings *in the form of* requests, whereas men tend to express them *in* [*the form of*] commands.

When the same words do not fit in each part, you need to supply the missing words even if they are simply different forms of the same word.

- ▶ **Water buffalo meat has been gaining popularity in America and is being sold to the public.**

- ▶ **Observable behaviors that relate to classroom assault can be dealt with prior, to, during, and after an attack.**

E2 Shifts

For practice, go to bedfordstmartins.com/theguide/shifts

Follow the same pattern throughout a sentence or passage to avoid a shift in tense, person, number, mood, voice, or type of discourse.

tense The form of a verb that shows the time of the action or state of being.

E2-a Use one verb tense consistently in a sentence or passage unless a tense change is needed to show a time change.

- ▶ **The nurse tried to comfort me by telling jokes and explaining that the needle wouldn't hurt. With a slight push, the long, sharp needle ~~pierces~~ pierced through my skin and ~~finds~~ found its way to the vein.**

If you tend to mix verb tenses as you draft, perform a special edit of your entire essay, concentrating on this one issue.

Change the tense of any verbs that do not follow the established tense in a passage unless they show logical time changes.

▶ I noticed much activity around the base. Sailors and chiefs ~~are~~ *were* walking all over the place. At 8:00 A.M., all traffic, foot and vehicle, halted. Toward the piers, the flag ~~is rising~~ *rose* up its pole. After the national anthem ~~ends,~~ *ended;* salutes ~~are~~ *were* completed, and people ~~go~~ *went* on with what they ~~are~~ *had been* doing.

Change verbs to the present tense to discuss events in literature, general truths, facts, and other ongoing principles.

▶ In 2003, the Supreme Court ruled that antisodomy laws are unconstitutional because such laws ~~went~~ *go* against "our tradition [that] the state is not omnipresent in our homes."

▶ In the story, when the boy ~~died,~~ *dies;* Kathy ~~realized~~ *realizes* that it ~~was~~ *is* also time for her childhood to die, and so she ~~returned~~ *returns* to her South African home as an adult.

Note: The conventional use of the present tense for events in literary works and for enduring facts and principles may require tense shifts in a sentence or text. See also G5-a.

PRESENT TENSE	When Dr. Full *is introduced* in the story, he *is* very poor and dependent on alcohol.
PRESENT TENSE WITH LOGICAL SHIFT TO FUTURE	Each cell *has* forty-six chromosomes that *carry* the genetic traits the individual *will have* when he or she *is* born.

E2-b Change the nouns and pronouns in a passage to a consistent person and number.

▶ Lynn informs all the members of helpful programs for ~~you and your pet.~~ *them and their pets.*

▶ Lynn informs ~~all the members~~ *you* of helpful programs for you and your pet.

In casual conversation, people often shift between singular and plural nouns and pronouns or between the third person and the second (or even the first). In writing, however, such shifts may be confusing or may make the essay writing poorly focused.

person The form of a word that shows whether it refers to *I* or *we* (first person), to *you* (second person), or to *he, she, it,* or *they* (third person).

number The form of a word that shows whether it refers to one thing (singular) or more than one (plural): *parent, parents; child, children.*

Note: Besides making sure that the nouns and pronouns are consistent in person and number within a sentence or series of sentences, consider how your choice of person suits the tone or approach of your essay. The first or second person, for example, will usually strike a reader as less formal than the third person.

mood The form of a verb that shows the writer's attitude toward a statement.

voice The form of a verb that indicates (active) or deemphasizes (passive) the performer of the action.

E2-c Establish a consistent mood and voice in a passage.

▶ **Each time I entered his house, I ~~could~~ always ~~know~~ *knew* when he was home.**

The original sentence shifts from the indicative mood *(I entered),* used for statements and questions, to the subjunctive mood *(I could know),* used to indicate hypothetical, impossible, or unlikely conditions.

▶ **I stepped out of the car with my training permit, a necessary document ~~for the test to be taken.~~ *to take the test.***

Although mood and voice may need to change to fit the context of a sentence, unneeded shifts may seem inconsistent. See also G5-c on mood, G5-d on voice, and L2-a on conditional clauses.

Change the verbs in a conditional clause or passage to a consistent mood.

▶ **If the mother should change her mind and keep the child, the couple ~~will~~ *would* be reimbursed for their expenses.**

▶ **If the mother ~~should change~~ *changes* her mind and ~~keep~~ *keeps* the child, the couple will be reimbursed for their expenses.**

Change the verbs in a passage to a consistent voice, preferably the active voice.

▶ **I will judge the song according to the following criteria: the depth with which the lyrics treat each issue and the clarity with which ~~each issue is presented in the music.~~ *the music presents each issue.***

See also G5-d and W1-b.

E2-d Use either direct or indirect quotation without mixing the two.

Writers use direct quotation to present statements or questions in a speaker's or another writer's own words; they use indirect quotation to present the person's words without quoting directly.

▶ "Do whatever ~~they wanted to her~~ [you want to me]," she cried, "but don't harm Reza."

▶ ~~Do~~ [They could do] whatever they wanted to her, she cried, but ~~don't~~ [they shouldn't] harm Reza.

To avoid shifts between direct and indirect quotation, make sure that your pronouns are consistent in **person** (see G2) and your verbs are consistent in **mood** (see G5-c).

person The form of a word that shows whether it refers to *I* or *we* (first person), to *you* (second person), or to *he, she, it,* or *they* (third person).

mood The form of a verb that shows the writer's attitude toward a statement.

E3 Noun Agreement

For practice, go to bedfordstmartins.com/theguide/nagree

In most instances, use nouns that agree in **number** when they refer to the same topic, person, or object.

number The form of a word that shows whether it refers to one thing (singular) or more than one (plural): *parent, parents; child, children.*

> The treatment consists of *injections* of minimal *doses* of the *allergens* given at regular *intervals.*

Sometimes, however, the context calls for both singular and plural nouns.

> *Students* who want to make the most of *their* college years should pursue *a major course of study* while choosing *electives* or *a few minor courses of study* from the liberal arts.

Note: When you use a noun with a plural possessive such as *their,* the thing possessed can be expressed as a singular noun if each individual could possess only one item.

> By the time the *calves* reach two months of age, *their coat* has turned dark brown.

E3-a Select corresponding singular or plural forms for related references to a noun.

When several nouns are used to develop a topic, they may describe and expand the characteristics of a key noun, act as synonyms for one another, or develop related points in the discussion. A sentence or passage that includes such nouns will generally be clearer and more effective if the nouns agree in number.

▶ Many people tend to "take their jobs to bed" with them and stay awake thinking about what needs to be done the next day. They also worry about ~~a~~ ~~promotion, a layoff, or a shift~~ [promotions, layoffs, or shifts] in responsibilities.

E3-b Decide whether a noun should be singular or plural on the basis of its relationship to other words in the sentence and the meaning of the sentence as a whole.

A noun may need to agree with another word in the sentence or may need to be singular or plural to fit the context or idiomatic usage.

> ***Minnows* are basically inedible because *they* have very little meat on *their* *bodies.***

In this sentence the writer consistently uses plural forms *(they, their,* and *bodies)* to refer to the minnows but also uses *meat,* which conventionally takes a singular form in a context like this one.

Note: Nouns such as *kind, type,* or *sort* are singular, although they have plural forms *(kinds, types)*. Use *this* and *that* instead of *these* and *those* to modify the singular forms of these and similar words. Expressions with *kind of* or *sort of* are usually singular.

▶ **To comprehend ~~these~~ *this* type of ~~articles,~~ *article,* it helps to have a strong background in statistics.**

▶ **RAs are allowed to choose what kind of ~~programs~~ *program* they want to have.**

indefinite adjective A word that modifies a noun or another adjective and indicates an unspecific quantity, such as *few, many,* or *some.*

Change a noun to singular or to plural to agree with a preceding indefinite adjective.

▶ **Under some ~~circumstance,~~ *circumstances,* parents aren't there to supervise their kids.**

Consider changing a noun to singular or to plural to reflect its context in the sentence.

Sometimes it is customary to treat an abstract quality (such as *justice* or *power*) as a singular noun. In other cases, a noun should be singular or plural to fit with the grammar or logic of the rest of the sentence.

▶ **As soon as immigrants get to the United States, they realize that to get ~~a better job~~ *better jobs* and better living conditions, they need to learn English.**

Note: Some common idiomatic expressions mix singular and plural forms.

IDIOMATIC WORDING **The penalties set for offenders might be enough to help them see *the error of their ways* and eventually help them reform their social habits.**

E4 Modifiers

For practice, go to bedfordstmartins.com/theguide/mod

Put a **modifier** next to or very close to the particular word that it modifies so that the connection between the two is clear.

modifier A word, phrase, or clause functioning as an adjective or adverb that adds information and detail about a noun, a verb, or another word.

Fourteen teenage idealists *with nervous stomachs* waited *for their moment in front of the onlookers.*

We had raised all the money *that we needed for the five-day trip.*

A modifier's position in a sentence generally tells the reader what word the modifier qualifies.

E4-a Place a word, phrase, or clause next to or close to the word that it modifies.

My *frozen* smile faltered as my chin quivered.

The flurry *of fins, masks, weights, and wet suits* continued.

Beyond the chairs loomed the object *that I feared most*—*a beautiful, black Steinway grand* piano *that gleamed under the bright stage lights.*

If a modifier is too far away from the word it modifies, a reader may assume that it modifies another word closer to it. As a result, a *misplaced modifier* can create confusion, ambiguity, or even unintended humor.

Move a modifier closer to the word it modifies.

▶ The ~~attempted~~ number of ^*attempted* suicides this semester was four.

▶ The women have to do all the hard work, ^*needed to maintain the family,* especially in subsistence cultures. ~~needed to maintain the family.~~

▶ He and the other people start to look ^*as hard as they can* for any sign of a boat, an island, or an oil platform. ~~as hard as they can.~~

Rewrite to clarify the sentence.

▶ ^*In organizing meetings open to all neighbors, community* ~~Community~~ leaders should ~~organize meetings open to all neighbors at~~ ^*select* convenient times and locations.

- ▶ We were friends until I *turned eighteen and* became too popular and obnoxious for anyone to stand. ~~when I turned eighteen.~~

E4-b Place a modifier so that it qualifies the meaning of a particular word in the sentence instead of dangling.

A phrase that does not modify a specific word is called a *dangling modifier.* A dangling modifier usually occurs at the beginning of a sentence and is likely to be a **participial phrase** or a **prepositional phrase.**

- ▶ By far the best song on the album, *"Don't Know Why" has a* ~~the~~ vocal performance and musical arrangement ~~of "Don't Know Why"~~ *that* create a perfect harmony.

Rewrite the sentence, placing a word that could logically be modified immediately after the modifying phrase.

- ▶ Rather than receiving several painful shots in the mouth before a cavity is filled, *a patient may find that* hypnosis can work just as effectively.
- ▶ After surveying the floor on which I live, *I concluded that* the residents of my dorm don't care much for floor programs.

Rewrite the sentence by changing the modifying phrase into a dependent clause.

Unlike a phrase, a clause includes both a **subject** and a **predicate.** By changing a phrase to a clause, you can correct a dangling modifier by supplying the information or connection that is missing. Be sure to add words and rewrite so that both the subject and the predicate are clearly stated and the clause fits the rest of the sentence.

- ▶ *If the school board decides to close* ~~By closing~~ Dos Pueblos, the remaining high schools *will* ~~would~~ have larger student bodies and increased budgets.
- ▶ After *I concluded* ~~concluding~~ my monologue on the hazards of partying, she smiled broadly and said, "OK, Mom, I'll be more careful next time."

E4-c Place a limiting modifier just before the word it modifies to avoid ambiguity.

A limiting modifier creates confusion or ambiguity when it is misplaced because it often could modify several words in the same sentence.

participial phrase A group of words that begins with a present participle *(dancing, freezing)* or a past participle *(danced, frozen)* and modifies a noun or a pronoun: We boarded the bus, *expecting to leave immediately.*

prepositional phrase A group of words that begins with a preposition and indicates the relation between a word in a sentence and the object following the preposition: Her sunglasses slid *under the seat.*

dependent (subordinate) clause A word group that has a subject, a predicate, and a subordinating word (such as *because*) at the beginning; it cannot stand by itself as a sentence but must be connected to an independent (main) clause.

subject The part of a clause that identifies who or what is being discussed: At the checkpoint, *we* unloaded the canoes.

predicate The part of a clause that includes a complete verb and says something about the subject: At the checkpoint, we *unloaded the canoes.*

limiting modifier A modifier such as *almost, just,* or *only* that should directly precede the word or word group it limits.

▶ Landfills in Illinois are going to be filled to capacity by 2015, and some experts ~~even~~ say ^even sooner.

When *even* precedes *say* in the example above, the sentence suggests that the experts are "even saying," not that the date will be even sooner.

E4-d Keep the two parts of an infinitive together.

infinitive A verb form consisting of the word *to* plus the base form of the verb: *to run, to do.*

When other words follow the *to,* they "split" the infinitive, separating *to* from the base form of the verb. These other words can usually be moved elsewhere in the sentence. Be especially alert to **limiting modifiers** that split infinitives. See also E4-c.

▶ His stomach ^always seemed to ~~always~~ hang over his pants.

Note: Occasionally, moving intervening words creates a sentence more awkward than the version with the split infinitive. In such cases, leaving the split infinitive may be the better choice.

E5 Mixed Constructions

For practice, go to bedfordstmartins.com/theguide/mix

The beginning and ending of a sentence must match, and its parts should fit together. If a sentence changes course in the middle or its parts are mixed up, a reader will have to guess at the pattern or connection you intend.

E5-a Begin and end a sentence with the same structural pattern to avoid a mixed construction.

A sentence is mixed if it combines several grammatical patterns. You usually need to rewrite a mixed construction so that its parts fit together.

▶ ^If we save ~~The~~ more oil ~~that we save~~ now^, ~~means~~ ^we will have much more in the future.

Choose one of the grammatical patterns in a mixed sentence, and rewrite to use it consistently throughout the sentence.

▶ School is another ^place where ~~resource for~~ children who don't have anyone to talk to can get educated about the problem of teen pregnancy.

▶ School^, ~~is~~ another resource for children who don't have anyone to talk to^, can ^provide information ~~get educated~~ about the problem of teen pregnancy.

Rewrite a mixed sentence if neither part supplies a workable pattern for the whole.

- ▶ ~~This is something the~~ *The* shelter prides itself on ~~and is~~ always looking for new volunteers and ideas. ~~for the shelter.~~

- ▶ The ~~next part of the~~ essay *next detailed* ~~was where~~ the results of the study ~~were detailed~~ and *concluded with* ~~finally included~~ a commentary section. ~~concluding the article.~~

> **subject** The part of a clause that identifies who or what is being discussed.

> **predicate** The part of a clause that includes a complete verb and says something about the subject.

E5-b Match the subject and the predicate in a sentence so that they are compatible.

You can solve the problem of a logically mismatched subject and predicate—called *faulty predication*—by rewriting either the subject or the predicate so that the two fit together.

- ▶ *Students attending schools* ~~Schools~~ that prohibited paddling behaved as well as *those at* schools that permitted corporal punishment.

To test a sentence for faulty predication, ask yourself whether the subject can do what the predicate says: For example, do schools behave? If not, revise the sentence.

Revise the subject so that it can perform the action described in the predicate.

- ▶ Bean's service is top notch, and *the staff* is striving continually to meet student needs.

Revise the predicate so that it fits logically with the subject.

- ▶ Ironically, the main character's memory of Mangan's sister on the porch step *always includes* ~~cannot recall the image without~~ the lamplight.

E5-c Order words logically so that the meaning of the sentence will be clear.

- ▶ *Entering traffic* ~~Traffic entering~~ will be dispersed into a perimeter pattern of flow.

E5-d Eliminate the phrase *is where, is when,* or *the reason is because,* and then rewrite the sentence so that it is clear and logical.

Often you can replace an *is where* or *is when* phrase with a noun specifying a category or type.

▶ This ~~is where~~ *part makes* the irony ~~seems to be~~ *seem* most evident.

▶ An absolutist position is ~~when someone~~ *a stance taken by someone who* strongly opposes any restrictions on speech.

To eliminate *the reason is because,* rewrite the sentence, or use *the reason is that* or *because* instead.

▶ ~~Another reason~~ *In addition,* radio stations should not play songs with sexually explicit lyrics ~~is~~ because children like to sing along.

▶ Another reason radio stations should not play songs with sexually explicit lyrics is ~~because~~ *that* children like to sing along.

E6 Integrated Quotations, Questions, and Thoughts

For practice, go to bedfordstmartins.com/theguide/int

When you use sources or write dialogue, merge your quotations, questions, and thoughts smoothly into your text so that the reader can tell who is speaking, thinking, or providing information.

The expense of being a teenager has caused many youths to join the workforce just because "they were offered a job" (Natriello 60).

"Hello," I replied, using one of the few words I knew.

I told myself, Don't move.

Use introductory phrases to link ideas and provide necessary background and context. Refer to the source or the speaker in the sentence, varying your words to avoid repeating *says* or *states.* See also P6, P10, and pp. 181–82.

E6-a Introduce, connect, and cite source material with grammatically correct and logical wording when you integrate a direct quotation into a sentence.

direct quotation A speaker's or writer's exact words, which are enclosed in quotation marks.

Writers often introduce quotations by mentioning the name of the person being quoted. Although *says* and *states* are acceptable, consider using more precise verbs and phrases that establish exact logical connections and provide variety. Examples include *agrees, asserts, charges, claims, confirms, discusses, emphasizes,* and *suggests.*

In the words of American Motors President M. Paul Tippitt, "The cardinal rule of the new ballgame is change" (Sobel 259).

Readers expect quotations and text to fit gracefully so that the writer's ideas and the material from supporting sources are unified and coherent. See also E2-d.

Rewrite to cite a source smoothly, without jumping from sentences of text to quotation.

Identifying the author of your source in the main part of your sentence often supplies the context a reader needs.

► Most people are not even aware of the extent to which television plays a role

As Mitroff and Bennis point out,

in their lives. ^ "Television defines our problems and shapes our actions; in

(xi).

short, how we define our world" ^ ~~(Mitroff and Bennis xi).~~

Mitroff and Bennis assert that most

► ~~Most~~ people are not even aware of the extent to which ~~television plays a role~~

"television *" (xi).*

~~in their lives. "Television~~ defines our problems and shapes our actions~~; in~~

~~short, how we define our world" (Mitroff and Bennis xi).~~

If you were writing for a magazine or newspaper, you would usually include a publication name and date in your sentence. In academic writing, however, you should cite the author's name and the date of the publication in your text and provide full publication information in a list of works cited (see Chapter 22).

FOR A MAGAZINE Andrew DePalma's 2003 *New York Times* article, "Preparing to 'Tell Us about Yourself,'" explains this point clearly.

FOR AN ACADEMIC ESSAY OR A SCHOLARLY PUBLICATION Andrew DePalma (2003) explains this point clearly.

Rewrite the text that introduces or integrates the quotation, and reselect the words you are quoting if necessary.

► The average American child ~~who~~ is "exposed to violence from every medium"

and

~~. . . in addition listens to~~ "music that advocates drug use" (Hollis 624).

E6-b Integrate a question so that its source is clear.

Enclose a **direct quotation** in quotation marks, identifying the speaker and using his or her exact words. Do not use quotation marks for an **indirect quotation** or a question that you address to the reader.

direct quotation A speaker's or writer's exact words, which are enclosed in quotation marks.

indirect quotation A reworded statement or question that presents a speaker's or writer's ideas without quoting directly or using quotation marks.

DIRECT QUOTATION	"Can you get my fins?" he asked.
INDIRECT QUOTATION	Without much hesitation, I explained my mission to her and asked whether she would help me out.
QUESTION ADDRESSED TO READER	Should sex education be a required class in public schools?

As in any dialogue, begin a new paragraph to show each change of speaker.

▶ "The refrigeration system is frozen solid. Come back later," ~~Once~~ *he said; once* again turning his back to me. ~~I asked~~

I asked, "When would it be best for me to come back?"

E6-c Integrate thoughts so that they are clearly identified and consistently punctuated.

If you supply the exact words that you or someone else thinks, follow the guidelines for direct quotations. Quotation marks are optional, but be consistent throughout an essay.

Go eighty feet for thirty minutes, she reminded herself.

▶ 'Wife and kids?' I thought.

▶ "Wife and kids?" I thought.

E7 Parallelism

For practice, go to bedfordstmartins.com/theguide/para

Use parallel grammatical form to present items as a pair or in a series.

Imagine that you and your daughter are *walking* in the mall or *eating* in a popular restaurant.

By implementing this proposal, administrators could enhance the reputation of the university with quality *publications*, *plays*, *concerts*, and *sports teams*.

> An interruption has the potential *to disrupt turns at talk*, *to disorganize the topic of conversation*, and *to violate the current speaker's right to talk.*

The grammatical similarity of the items in the pair or series strongly signals the reader that they are equally important, similar in meaning, and related in the same way to the rest of the sentence.

E7-a Rewrite any item in a series that does not follow the same grammatical pattern as the other items.

Items in a series are usually linked by *and* or *or.* Each item should be parallel to the others, presented as a **noun,** an **infinitive,** a **gerund,** or another grammatical form.

noun A word that names a specific or general thing, person, place, concept, characteristic, or other idea.

infinitive A verb form consisting of the word *to* plus the base form of the verb: *to run, to do.*

gerund A verb form that is used as a noun and ends in *-ing: arguing, throwing.*

- ▶ The children must deal with an overprotective parent, sibling rivalry, and ~~living~~ ^*life* in a single-parent home.
- ▶ Drivers destined for Coronado can choose to turn left, ^*turn* right, or ^*proceed* ~~proceeding~~ straight into the city.

E7-b Rewrite one item in a pair so that both follow the same grammatical pattern.

Items in a pair are usually linked by *and* or *or.*

- ▶ While Simba is growing up, he is told of things he should do and things ^*he should* not ~~to~~ do.

E7-c Rewrite one item in a comparison using *than* or *as* so that it matches the other in grammatical form.

- ▶ They feel that using force is more comprehensible to the children than ^*threatening* abstract consequences.

E7-d Use parallel form for items joined by correlative conjunctions.

correlative conjunctions Word pairs that link sentence elements; the first word anticipates the second: *both . . . and, either . . . or, neither . . . nor, not only . . . but also.*

- ▶ At that time, the person is surprised not only about where he is but also ^*about* ~~unable to account for~~ what has happened.

Besides presenting the word pairs in parallel form, position the conjunctions so that each introduces a comparable point.

E8 Coordination and Subordination

For practice, go to bedfordstmartins.com/theguide/cosu

Use coordination and subordination to indicate the relationships among sentence elements.

E8-a Use coordination to join sentence elements that are equally important.

The sheriff's department lacks both the *officers* and the *equipment* to patrol every road in the county.

Most of us would agree with the evil queen's magic mirror that this Disney girl, with her *skin as white as snow, lips as red as blood,* and *hair as black as ebony,* is indeed, "the fairest one of all."

Writers use coordination to bring together in one sentence two or more elements of equal importance to the meaning. These elements can be words, phrases, or clauses, including **independent clauses** within the same sentence.

The sport of windsurfing dates back only to 1969, but *it already has achieved full status as an Olympic event.*

Children like to sing along with songs they hear on the radio; consequently, *radio stations should not play songs with language that demeans women.*

E8-b Use subordination to indicate that one sentence element is more important than other elements.

After Dave finished his mutinous speech, the corners of Dan's mouth slowly formed a nearly expressionless grin.

Political liberals, *who trace their American roots to the Declaration of Independence,* insist that the federal government should attempt to reduce inequalities of income and wealth.

Writers frequently subordinate information within a single sentence. The most important information appears in an independent clause, and the less important or subordinate information appears in words, **phrases,** or **dependent clauses** attached to the independent clause or integrated into it. (Often, the most important information in a sentence will be information that is new to a reader.)

independent (main) clause A word group with a subject and a predicate that can stand alone as a separate sentence. (A predicate is the part of a clause that includes a complete verb and says something about the subject: At the checkpoint, we *unloaded the canoes.*)

phrase A group of words that does *not* contain both a subject and a verb and is always part of an independent clause. Common types of phrases include *prepositional* (*After a flash of lightning,* I saw a tree split in half) and *verbal* (*Blinded by the flash,* I ran into the house).

dependent (subordinate) clause A word group that has a subject, a predicate, and a subordinating word (such as *because*) at the beginning; it cannot stand by itself as a sentence but must be connected to an independent (main) clause: *Although it was raining,* we loaded our gear onto the buses.

W Word Choice

Effective language is concise, exact, and appropriate for the context.

> **Tears stream down James's face as he sits scrunched up in the corner of the shabby living room, wishing that he had anyone else's life.**
>
> **We need traffic signals for this dangerous intersection.**

Well-chosen words engage the reader, conveying impressions or claims clearly and convincingly.

W1 Concise Sentences

For practice, go to bedfordstmartins.com/theguide/csent

Sentences with redundant phrasing, repetitive wording, wordy expressions, and unnecessary intensifiers are tiresome to read and may be difficult to understand. Concentrate on choosing words well, simplifying sentence stucture, and avoiding words that are unnecessary or evasive.

▶ ~~In many cases, this~~ [This] situation may ~~be due to the fact that~~ [occur because] these women [have had no] ~~were not given the~~ opportunity to work.

Note: Even though you may need to add detail or examples to clarify your ideas, cutting out useless words will make your writing more focused and precise.

W1-a Eliminate redundancies and repetition.

Redundant phrasing adds unnecessary words to a sentence. Repetitive wording says the same thing twice.

Eliminate or rewrite redundant expressions that repeat the same point in different words.

The phrase *blue in color* is redundant because it repeats obvious information, adding a category name to a description. The following phrases do the same: *large-sized, a reluctant manner, to an extreme degree, a helpless state, a crisis-type situation, the area of population control,* and *passive kind of behavior.* In addition, expressions such as *past memories, advance planning,* and *mix together* include modifiers that repeat information already provided in the word modified. After all, all memories are of the past, planning is always done in advance, and *mix* means "put together."

Other expressions such as *the fact is true, bisect in half,* and *in my opinion, I believe* are redundant because they contain obvious implications: *Truth* is implied by *fact, bisect* means "to divide in half," and *in my opinion* says the same thing as *I believe.* Pare down these and any similar expressions.

▶ Many machines in the drilling area need to be *modernized.* ~~updated to better and more modern equipment.~~

▶ All these recommendations are interconnected. ~~to one another.~~

▶ *California* ~~The~~ colleges ~~in the state of California~~ rely too much on the annual income of a student's parents and not enough on the parents' true financial situation.

Delete extra words from a redundant or repetitive sentence.

▶ In addition, there is a *convenient* customer service center. ~~for the convenience of the customers.~~

▶ Student volunteers will no longer be *exhausted* ~~overworked, overburdened, and overexhausted~~ from working ~~continuously at the jobs~~ without ~~any~~ breaks because of the *labor* shortage. ~~of labor.~~

W1-b Eliminate words that do not add to the meaning of a sentence.

Rewrite a wordy sentence to reduce the number of clauses and phrases.

Concentrate on turning clauses into phrases or replacing phrases, especially strings of prepositional phrases, with individual words. Sometimes you can even consolidate a series of sentences into one.

prepositional phrase A group of words that begins with a preposition and indicates the relation between a word in a sentence and the object following the preposition: Her sunglasses slid *under the seat.*

▶ *Michael Jordan is an excellent recent example* ~~One of the best examples in recent times~~ of an *overexposed* athlete. ~~being completely overexposed is that of Michael Jordan.~~

▶ *This* ~~It is this~~ exaggeration *provides the characters'* ~~that serves to provide the~~ comic appeal. ~~of the characters.~~

▶ *No single alternative will solve the problem of teen pregnancy; and all the possible solutions have disadvantages.* ~~There are many other possible alternative solutions to teen pregnancy. One solution is not going to work alone to solve the problem. But there are disadvantages that come along with them.~~

Eliminate wordy expressions, or replace them with fewer words.

Extra, empty words can creep into a sentence in many ways.

► **Demanding Eldridge's resignation ~~at this point in time~~ *now* will not solve the problem.**

► **However, in most neighorhoods, the same ~~group of~~ people who write the newsletters ~~are the ones who~~ *also* organize and participate in the activities.**

Here are examples of a few common wordy phrases and clearer, more concise alternatives.

Wordy Phrases	*More Concise Alternatives*
due to the fact that in view of the fact that the reason for for the reason that this is why in light of the fact that on the grounds that	for, because, why, since
despite the fact that regardless of the fact that	although, though
as regards in reference to concerning the matter of where . . . is concerned	concerning, about, regarding
it is necessary that there is a need for it is important that	should, must
has the ability to is able to is in a position to	can
in order to for the purpose of	to
at this point in time	now
on the subject of	on, about
as a matter of fact	actually
aware of the fact that	know
to the effect that	that
the way in which	how
in the event that	if, when

Rewrite a wordy sentence to simplify its structure.

Watch particularly for *there is* or *there are* at the beginning of a sentence or for a verb in the passive voice. These indirect structures have their uses. Often, however, you can express your ideas more directly and forcefully by editing to eliminate *there is* or *there are* or by changing from the passive to the active voice.

- ▶ ~~There are always five~~ *Five* or six spots *are always* open at the ends of the rows.
- ▶ ~~The topic is initiated by a~~ *A* member who has nothing to gain by the discussion *initiates* ~~of~~ the topic.

Note: Often, as in these examples, the verb *be* is far less precise than another verb might be. Whenever possible, replace *am, are, is, was,* and other forms of *be* with a stronger verb that clearly defines an action.

W1-c Rewrite a sentence to eliminate unnecessary intensifiers or hedges.

- ▶ Your choice could ~~very possibly~~ make the difference between a saved or lost life.

Delete unnecessary intensifiers such as *very, really, clearly, quite,* and *of course.*

Although intensifiers can strengthen statements, eliminating them or substituting more forceful words is often more effective.

- ▶ The plot of this movie is ~~really great.~~ *thrilling.*

Some intensifiers are unnecessary because the words they modify are already as strong as possible, such as *very unique.* (Something either is or is not unique; it cannot be *very* or *slightly* unique.)

- ▶ The *unique* arrangement of the plain blocks ~~is so unique that it~~ makes the sculpture seem textured.

Eliminate unnecessary hedges.

Writers use hedges such as *apparently, seem, perhaps, possibly, to a certain extent, tend,* and *somewhat* to avoid making claims that they cannot substantiate. Hedges add subtlety to their prose, appear careful and thoughtful, and acknowledge the possibility of important exceptions. Too many hedges, however, make writing tentative and uncertain.

▶ **~~In most cases, realistic~~ *Realistic* characteristics ~~tend to~~ *often* undermine comedy's primary function of making us laugh at exaggerated character traits.**

preposition A word (such as *between, in* or *of*) that always appears as part of a phrase and indicates the relation between a word in a sentence and the object of the preposition: The water splashed *into* the canoe.

W1-d Eliminate unnecessary prepositions.

▶ **I went to the hospital so the clerk could admit me ~~in~~.**

If the word following a preposition is the object of a verb, the preposition may be unnecessary.

▶ **Nothing happened, and my doctor ordered ~~for~~ them to stop inducing labor.**

▶ **Consequently, student volunteers will not be inclined to leave and seek ~~for~~ smaller hospitals with less intense shifts.**

Note: Another alternative is to change the verb.

▶ **Consequently, student volunteers will not be inclined to leave and ~~seek~~ *look* for smaller hospitals with less intense shifts.**

For ESL Writers

Prepositions also combine with verbs to form two- or three-word (or phrasal) verbs whose meaning cannot be understood literally *(handed in, longed for)*. When a preposition is part of a two- or three-word verb, it is called a *particle*. See L2-b.

W2 Exact Words

For practice, go to bedfordstmartins.com/theguide/eword

Effective writers choose words carefully, paying attention to meaning, form, idiomatic phrasing, and freshness.

The central library stands like a giant concrete mushroom, towering above the surrounding eucalyptus groves. The strong, angular lines are softened by a few well-placed, sweeping curves on the stabilizing pylons and the shrouds around the low windows.

W2-a Replace incorrect words with the exact words you intend, or omit incorrect words if they are unnecessary.

Check a dictionary when you are uncertain of the meaning of a word. Watch for incorrect words and for words similar in meaning or sound. See also the Glossary of Frequently Misused Words.

▶ Louis kicked him into a river ~~invested~~ *infested* with crocodiles.

▶ How do we stop offshore oil drilling and yet offer an alternative to ~~appease~~ *alleviate* the energy crisis?

▶ Some universities have chosen to go ~~literately~~ *literally* underground to avoid public scrutiny.

W2-b Use correct prepositions.

preposition A word (such as *between, in,* or *of*) that always appears as part of a phrase and indicates the relation between a word in a sentence and the object of the preposition: The water splashed *into* the canoe.

Short as they generally are, prepositions define crucial relationships for the reader.

> **The levels increase *in* width *from* the scrawny third floor *up to* the immense sixth story (*over* two hundred feet across).**

> **A building's beauty must be determined *by* the harmony *of* its design.**

If prepositions are a problem in your writing, note how other writers use them.

▶ Unlike many of the other pieces of art ~~about~~ *on* campus, the statues seemed to fit well.

> **For ESL Writers**
>
> If you find prepositions difficult, pay special attention to them as you read. For a review of the meanings of some common prepositions, see L3.

W2-c Use standard idioms, the conventional expressions generally used in American English.

idiom An expression whose meaning cannot be determined from its parts but must be learned (*call off* for "cancel"; *look after* for "take care of").

Read and listen carefully to get a sense of standard idioms, especially the ones that consist of small words, such as prepositions, and verb forms.

▶ The most serious problems of many developing countries stem ~~to~~ *from* lack of educational and economic opportunity.

For ESL Writers

Idiomatic two- and three-word verbs *(put down, set up)* and combinations of verbs or adjectives and prepositions *(look for, afraid of)* can be especially troublesome for writers whose first language is not English. See L2-b for more help with these expressions.

cliché An overused expression that has lost its original freshness, such as *hard as a rock.*

W2-d Eliminate or rewrite clichés or overused expressions.

Readers prefer lively, original expressions to familiar, overused phrases.

▶ **During ~~the thick of~~ the night, he must walk alone with only a flashlight for company.**

▶ **The audience ~~is on pins and needles,~~ wondering whose plan will falter first.** [inserted: *erupts in gasps and nervous giggles,*]

W2-e Select the correct form of the word that fits the context of your essay and conveys the meaning you intend.

If you are learning to use an unfamiliar word or are struggling to find a word whose meaning fits, you may use the wrong form of the word you intend. If so, change the word to the correct form when you discover your mistake or a reader notes it for you. Proofread your essays carefully for words written incorrectly. A good dictionary can help you determine which form of a word fits your context.

▶ **The phrase "you know" ~~is an introductory to~~ someone's opinion.** [inserted: *introduces*]

▶ **I found out that becoming a ~~manicure~~ is increasingly popular because it takes only a few months of training.** [inserted: *manicurist*]

figures of speech Images such as similes and metaphors that suggest a comparison (or analogy) between objects that are generally unlike each other.

simile A direct comparison that uses *like* or *as: like a tree bending in the strong wind.*

metaphor An indirect comparison that refers to or describes one thing as if it were the other: *The mob sharpened its claws.*

W2-f Use appropriate figures of speech.

Figures of speech, such as **similes** and **metaphors,** are vivid and original means of expressing comparisons. They help a reader perceive a similarity, often creating a striking image or a surprising but engaging idea.

> **Our dog Tiger rolls around in the warm mud and sinks his head into the soft ground like a hippo basking in the African sun.**

> **If you think of the *Journal of the American Medical Association* article as a two-hour documentary on PBS, the *American Health* essay is a thirty-second sound bite.**

A figure of speech can make a complex idea easier to understand or bring a scene or character to life for your readers. Make sure that any figure of speech that you use is clear, appropriate, and consistent.

INACCURATE METAPHOR **The children would jump from car to car *as if they were mushrooms.* [Mushrooms cannot jump.]**

Also avoid **mixed metaphors,** as in the following example, in which the soul is compared to both a criminal defendant and a plant.

mixed metaphor An inconsistent metaphor, one that mixes several images rather than completing one.

MIXED METAPHOR **Karma is an inorganic process of development in which the soul not only *pays the price* for its misdeeds but also *bears the fruit* of the *seeds sown* in former lives.**

W3 Appropriate Words

For practice, go to bedfordstmartins.com/theguide/aword

When you choose words carefully, your writing will have the appropriate level of formality, without slang, biased wording, or stuffy, pretentious language. Taken from a profile of a large city's trauma system, the following sentences illustrate how appropriate words can convey a sense of the environment.

At 6:50 P.M., the hospital's paging system comes alive.

Lying on the table, the unidentified victim can only groan and move his left leg.

All the components are in place: a countrywide trauma system, physicians and staff who care and are willing to sacrifice, and private hospitals serving the community.

Readers appreciate appropriate language choices that produce smooth, integrated writing, without sudden jumps from formal to informal language.

W3-a Use the level of formality expected in your writing situation.

Many problems with appropriate language occur when writers use language accepted in informal conversation in a more formal writing situation. For example, a phone conversation or email exchange with your friend will be more informal than a memo to your employer or a report for your political science class.

LESS FORMAL **One cool morning in May, I stood on the edge of Mount Everest, or at least that's what it seemed like to me.**

MORE FORMAL Mistreatment of the elderly is an unusually sensitive problem because it involves such value-laden ideas as *home* and *family.*

Taking into account the kind of essay you are writing, reword as necessary to avoid shifts in the level of formality.

- ▶ What makes an excellent church, auditorium, or theater makes a ~~lousy~~ *poor* library.
- ▶ The average cost to join a gymnasium ~~can run you~~ *is* around $40 a month~~, and that's only~~ when you sign a membership contract. ~~I bet~~ *Even if* you thought you ~~couldn't~~ *could not* afford a membership~~; Well,~~ you can.

slang Informal language that tends to change rapidly.

W3-b Limit the use of slang in formal writing situations.

Although slang may be appropriate to define a character or a situation in a narrative or description, it is likely to be out of place in more formal academic writing.

APPROPRIATE SLANG "This weather is *awesome* for peeling out. You *oughta* try it sometime." [appropriate for the dialogue in an essay about a remembered event]

INAPPROPRIATE SLANG Parties are an excellent way to *blow off steam* and take a break from the pressures of college. [too informal in a proposal addressed to college administrators]

Replace inappropriate slang expressions with more formal words.

- ▶ We shouldn't ~~dis~~ *criticize* these girls.
- ▶ The cast of the movie was ~~awesome.~~ *impressive.*

Replace slang with precise, more descriptive words.

- ▶ The cast of the movie ~~was awesome.~~ *vividly embodied the historical characters.*

nonsexist language Language that describes people without using words that make assumptions about gender or imply acceptance of gender-based stereotypes.

W3-c Use nonsexist language that includes rather than excludes.

Avoid using masculine pronouns (such as *he* or *his*) to refer to people who might be either men or women. Also avoid using words referring to men to represent people in general. See also G2-b.

Revise a sentence that uses masculine pronouns to represent people in general.

Use plural forms, eliminate the pronouns, or use both masculine and feminine pronouns.

▶ ~~A student's~~ *Students'* eligibility for alternative loans is based on whether or not ~~his~~ *their* school decides ~~he is~~ *they are* entitled to financial aid.

▶ Abstract expressionism is art that is based on the artist's spontaneous feelings at the moment when he *or she* is creating ~~his~~ *a* work.

Replace masculine nouns used to represent people in general with more inclusive words.

▶ Oligarchies have existed throughout ~~the history of man.~~ *human history.*

▶ Every individual has his *or her* rightful place in the social hierarchy.

▶ Every individual has ~~his~~ *a* rightful place in the social hierarchy.

Rewrite language that implies or reinforces stereotypes or discrimination.

▶ Oligarchies were left to ~~barbaric tribesmen~~ *the tribes* and herders ~~who were beyond the reach of civilization.~~ *outside the empire.*

▶ A doctor who did not keep up with his *or her* colleagues would be forced to update ~~his~~ procedures.

W3-d Replace pretentious language with simpler, more direct wording.

pretentious language Fancy or wordy language used primarily to impress.

Using impressive words is sometimes part of the pleasure of writing, but such words may be too elaborate for the situation or may seem to be included for their own sake rather than the reader's understanding. Use words that best express your idea, and balance or replace distractingly unusual words with simpler, more familiar choices.

▶ Perhaps ~~apprehension toward instigating~~ *fear of* these changes stems from financial concern.

▶ Expanded oil exploration may seem relatively innocuous, but this proposal is a deplorable suggestion to all but the most ~~pernicious, specious entities.~~ *deceptive, destructive groups.*

P Punctuation

P1 Commas

For practice, go to bedfordstmartins.com/theguide/comma

Use a comma to set off and separate sentence elements.

independent (main) clause A word group with a subject and a predicate that can stand alone as a separate sentence.

coordinating conjunction A word that joins comparable and equally important sentence elements: *for, and, or, but, nor, yet,* or *so.*

P1-a Add a comma between independent clauses joined by a coordinating conjunction.

INDEPENDENT CLAUSE — INDEPENDENT CLAUSE

Perhaps my father had the same dream, and perhaps my grandfather did as well.

When independent clauses are joined by a coordinating conjunction, a comma is required to tell the reader that another independent clause follows the first one.

- ▶ **In 2002, women's ice hockey became a full Olympic medal sport^, and the Canadian team brought home the gold.**
- ▶ **Researchers have studied many aspects of autism^, but they readily acknowledge that they have much more to learn.**

Note: If the independent clauses are brief and unambiguous, a comma is not required, though it is never wrong to include it.

The attempt fails and Spiderman must let go.

Note: When a coordinating conjunction joins two elements other than independent clauses, no comma is needed (see P2-a).

P1-b Place a comma after an introductory word, phrase, or clause.

Sentences often begin with words, phrases, or clauses that precede the independent clause and modify an element within it.

Naturally, **this result didn't help him any.**

With a jerk, **I lofted the lure in a desperate attempt to catch a fish and please my dad.**

When we entered the honeymoon suite, **the room smelled of burnt plastic and was the color of Pepto Bismol.**

The comma following each introductory element lets the reader know where the modifying word or phrase ends and the main clause begins.

► In a poor family with no father, a boy can find the gangs more appealing than the tough life of poverty.

► When I picked up the receiver, I heard an unfamiliar voice.

► Forgetting my mission for a moment, I took time to look around.

Note: If an introductory phrase or clause is brief—four words or fewer—the comma may be omitted unless it is needed to prevent misreading.

Without hesitation I dived into the lake.

P1-c Use commas to set off a nonrestrictive word group.

To test whether a word group is *nonrestrictive* (supplemental, nondefining, and thus nonessential) or *restrictive* (defining and thus essential), read the sentence with and without the word group. If the sentence is less informative but essentially unchanged in meaning without it, the word group is nonrestrictive. Use commas to set it off. Conversely, if omitting the word group changes the meaning of the sentence by removing a definition or limitation, it is restrictive. In this case, do not use commas.

NONRESTRICTIVE **The oldest fishermen, *grizzly sea salts wrapped in an aura of experience,* led the way.**

RESTRICTIVE **Blood and violence can give video games a sense of realism *that was not previously available.***

In the first sentence, the commas tell the reader that the word group presents extra information. The sentence would be essentially unchanged without the word group: *The oldest fishermen led the way.* In the second sentence, the word group is not set off with commas because it provides essential information about the realism of video games. The sentence would not have the same meaning without it.

Insert a comma to set off a nonrestrictive (nonessential) word group at the end of a sentence.

► We all stood, anxious and prepared for what he was about to say.

► The next period is the preoperational stage, which begins at age two and lasts until age seven.

► He was learning useful outdoor skills, such as how to tie knots and give first aid.

Insert a pair of commas to set off a nonrestrictive (nonessential) word group in the middle of a sentence.

- ▶ The most common moods are happiness, when the music is in a major key, or sadness, when the music is in a minor key.
- ▶ Laura, our neighbor and best friend, appeared at the kitchen window.
- ▶ My dog, Shogun, was lying on the floor doing what he does best, sleeping.

The last example illustrates the importance of context for deciding what is essential in a sentence. Here, the writer has only one dog, so the dog's name is nonrestrictive (nonessential) information and is placed between commas. If the writer had more than one dog, however, the name would be essential to identify which dog and would not be set off by commas.

See also P2-b.

P1-d Use commas to set off a transitional, parenthetical, or contrasting expression or an absolute phrase.

Often used to begin sentences, *transitional expressions* help the reader follow a writer's movement from point to point, showing how one sentence is related to the next. *Parenthetical comments* interrupt a sentence with a brief aside. *Contrasting expressions* generally come at the end of a sentence, introduced by *not, no,* or *nothing. Absolute phrases,* which can appear anywhere within a sentence, modify the whole clause and often include a past or present **participle** as well as modifiers.

participle A verb form showing present tense *(dancing, freezing)* or past tense *(danced, frozen)* that can also act as an adjective. In a participial phrase, a group of words begins with a present or past participle and modifies a noun or pronoun: We boarded the bus, *expecting to leave immediately.*

TRANSITIONAL *Besides,* it is summer.

PARENTHETICAL These are all indications, *I think,* of Jan's drive for power and control.

CONTRASTING Nick is the perfect example of a young, hungry manager trying to climb to the top, *not bothered by the feelings of others.*

ABSOLUTE "Did I ever tell you about the time I worked with Danny Kaye at Radio City Music Hall?" she asked, *her eyes focusing dreamily into the distance.*

By using commas to set off such expressions, you signal that they are additions, supplementing or commenting on the information in the rest of the sentence.

Insert a comma to set off a transitional, parenthetical, or contrasting expression or an absolute phrase that begins or ends a sentence.

- ▶ For example, in our society a wedding gown is worn by the bride only once, on her wedding day.

▶ We had an advantage, thanks to P.T.'s knowledge.

▶ My uncle talked to me as if I were a person, not a child.

▶ "Well, well," he'd grin, his crooked mouth revealing his perfect white teeth.

Insert a pair of commas to set off a transitional, parenthetical, or contrasting expression or an absolute phrase that falls in the middle of a sentence.

▶ Students, therefore, often complain about their TA's inability to speak English.

▶ At every response, I defended those innocent people and emphasized that no one, absolutely no one, can decide whether or not a person is worthy of living.

▶ He uttered his famous phrase, "If you don't have time to do something right, you definitely don't have time to do it over," for the first, but not the last, time.

▶ I followed her, both of us barefoot and breathing white mist, out the door into the blood-reddened snow.

Note: If a transitional element, such as a conjunctive adverb, links two independent clauses within one sentence, add a semicolon between the clauses to avoid a comma splice. (See P3-d and S1.)

▶ One can see how delicate he is, yet this fragility does not detract from his masculinity; instead, it greatly enhances it.

conjunctive adverb A word or phrase (such as *finally, however,* or *therefore*) that tells how the ideas in two sentences or independent clauses are connected.

independent (main) clause A word group with a subject and a predicate that can stand alone as a separate sentence.

comma splice The improper joining of two independent clauses with only a comma.

P1-e Use a comma to separate three or more items in a series, placing the final comma before the conjunction.

He was wearing a camouflage hat, a yellow sweatshirt, and a pair of blue shorts.

The commas in a series separate the items for the reader.

▶ He always tells me about the loyalty, honor, and pride he feels as a Marine.

▶ Our communities would get relief from the fear and despair that come from having unremitting violence, addiction, and open-air drug markets in their midst.

Note: Sometimes the comma preceding the conjunction is omitted when the items are brief and the relationship clear, but including it prevents misreading and keeps punctuation consistent in an essay.

POSSIBLE OPTION She was beautiful, smart and popular.

PREFERRED She was beautiful, smart, and popular.

Occasionally, a writer will separate the last two items in a series with a comma but omit *and*. Or a writer may join all the items in a series with *and* or *or* and thus need no commas at all. Use such alternatives sparingly.

In her, I found a woman with character, integrity, intelligence.

participial phrase A group of words that begins with a present participle *(dancing, freezing)* or a past participle *(danced, frozen)* and modifies a noun or a pronoun.

nonrestrictive word group A group of words, set off by commas, that provides extra or nonessential information and could be eliminated without changing the meaning of the noun or pronoun it modifies.

independent (main) clause A word group with a subject and a predicate that can stand alone as a separate sentence.

P1-f Use a comma before a trailing nonrestrictive participial phrase.

Participial phrases are generally **nonrestrictive word groups.** When they follow the **independent (main) clause** in a sentence, they should be set off with commas. (See P1-c.)

PARTICIPIAL PHRASE **The plane lifted off as he opened the package, *expecting to find cookies and a mushy love letter.***

The comma before the phrase signals the end of the main clause and sets off the important modifying phrase.

► **Every so often, a pelican agilely arcs high over the water, twisting downward gracefully to catch an unsuspecting mackerel.**

► **I sat down, confused and distraught.**

Note: If the participial phrase is restrictive, providing essential information, do not use a comma. (See P1-c and P2-b.)

Now at our disposal were the essential elements of life: the snow, Julie, me, and an entire pantry *stocked with food.*

I noticed his tiny form amid the crowd of vacationers *emerging from the terminal gate.*

Both participial phrases define or limit the nouns they modify, telling readers what kind of pantry and what kind of crowd. Consequently, they are not set off by commas.

direct quotation A speaker's or writer's exact words, which are enclosed in quotation marks.

P1-g Place a comma between a complete direct quotation and the text identifying the speaker.

I answered, "Okay, let me grab the ladder."

"Discipline is effective if you get the students to adopt your values," explained Fathman.

The comma, along with the quotation marks, helps the reader determine where the quotation begins and ends. See also P6.

▶ **So I asked her, "Momma, who you talkin' to?"**

▶ **"It will be okay," Coach reassured me, as he motioned for the emergency medical technicians to bring a board.**

▶ **Dr. Carolyn Bailey says, "I view spanking as an aggressive act."**

P1-h Add a comma (or pair of commas in the middle of a sentence) to set off expressions commonly included in dialogue.

Use commas to set off the name of a person **directly addressed** by a speaker, words such as *yes* and *no,* and mild **interjections.** Also use a comma to set off a question added to the end of a sentence.

direct address Words that are spoken directly to someone else who is named.

interjection An exclamatory word that indicates strong feeling or attempts to command attention: *Shhh! Oh! Ouch!*

"Chadan, you're just too compassionate."

"Yes, sir," replied Danny.

Boy, did we underestimate her.

That's not very efficient, is it?

A comma marks the division between the main part of the sentence and a comment that precedes or follows it:

▶ **"Well, son, what are you doing?"**

▶ **"No, sir."**

▶ **So, this is to be a battle of wills, is it? Fine, I'll play.**

▶ **"Besides, it'll be good for me."**

P1-i Use a comma between coordinate adjectives.

coordinate adjectives Two or more adjectives that modify a noun equally and independently: the *large, red* hat.

If you can change the order of a series of adjectives or add *and* between them without changing the meaning, they are coordinate and should be separated with a comma.

There are reasons for her *erratic, irrational* behavior.

The comma signals that the adjectives are equal, related in the same way to the word modified.

If the adjectives closest to the noun cannot logically be rearranged or linked by *and,* they are **noncoordinate adjectives** (also called *cumulative adjectives*) and should not be separated by commas.

noncoordinate adjectives Two or more adjectives that do not modify a noun equally. Instead, one or two of the adjectives closest to the noun form a noun phrase that the remaining adjectives modify: *colorful hot-air* balloons.

I pictured myself as a *professional race car* driver.

Once you have determined that adjectives are coordinate, add a comma between them.

▶ **I can still remember the smell of his cigar and his old, oily clothing.**

▶ **Professionals who use this five-step, systematic approach are less likely to injure or be injured during an assault.**

Note: The same rule applies to coordinate adjectives that follow the noun they modify or are otherwise separated from it in the sentence.

Skippy was a good-looking guy, *tall, blond,* and *lean.*

P1-j Add commas where needed to set off dates, numbers, and addresses.

When you include a full date (month, day, and year), use a pair of commas to set off the year.

▶ **In the July 8, 2002, issue of the *New Yorker,* Elizabeth Kolbert described Sidney Hook as "one of the most prominent public intellectuals of his generation" (23).**

If you present a date in reverse order (day, month, and year), do not add commas.

▶ **In the ~~July 8,~~ 8 July 2002 issue of the *New Yorker,* Elizabeth Kolbert described Sidney Hook as "one of the most prominent public intellectuals of his generation" (23).**

If a date is partial (month and year only), do not add commas.

This intriguing article appeared in the *April 2003* issue of *Personnel Journal.*

In large numbers, separate groups of three digits (thousands, millions, and so forth) with commas.

▶ **As of 2000, there were about 900,000 speakers of Korean in the United States.**

When you write out an address, add commas between the parts, setting off the street address, the city, and the state with the zip code. When an address or place name is embedded in a complete sentence, add a comma after the last element.

▶ **Mrs. Wilson relocated to Bowie, Maryland, after moving from Delaware.**

P1-k Add a comma if needed for clarity when a word is omitted, is repeated twice, or might be grouped incorrectly with the next words.

Such instances are rare. Check the guidelines in P1 and P2 so that you do not add unnecessary or incorrect commas.

▶ The statistics reveal that in 1997, 648,000 Hispanic students (48 percent of all Hispanic students) were enrolled in Hispanic-Serving Institutions (HSIs).

P2 Unnecessary Commas

For practice, go to bedfordstmartins.com/theguide/uncom

Because commas are warranted in so many instances, it is easy to use them unnecessarily or incorrectly, particularly with compound sentence elements, with restrictive elements, and between verbs and subjects or verbs and objects.

P2-a Omit the comma when items in a pair joined by *and* or another coordinating conjunction are not independent clauses.

Many word pairs can be joined by *and* or another coordinating conjunction, including compound predicates, compound objects, and compound subjects. None of these pairs should be interrupted by a comma.

COMPOUND PREDICATE *I grabbed my lunchbox* and *headed out to the tree.*

COMPOUND OBJECT As for me, I wore *a pink short set with ruffles* and *a pair of sneakers.*

COMPOUND SUBJECT My *father* and *brother* wore big hiking boots.

Two independent clauses joined by a coordinating conjunction require a comma (see P1-a). The comma shows the reader where one independent clause ends and the other begins. Using a comma in other situations thus sends the wrong signal.

▶ According to Ward, many Custer fans believe that Custer was a "hero," and "represents certain endangered manly virtues."

▶ The school district could implement more programs at both the junior high and the high school, and thus could offer the students more opportunities.

▶ I was running out of time, and patience.

▶ Culture is not what we do, but how we do things, and why we do them in a particular way.

coordinating conjunction A word that joins comparable and equally important sentence elements: *for, and, or, but, nor, yet,* or *so.*

independent (main) clause A word group with a subject and a predicate that can stand alone as a separate sentence.

compound predicate Two or more verbs or verb phrases linked by *and.*

compound object Two or more words acting as an object and linked by *and.*

compound subject Two or more words acting as a subject and linked by *and.*

P2-b Omit any comma that sets off a restrictive word group.

Use commas to set off a nonrestrictive word group but not a restrictive word group. A *restrictive word group* distinguishes the noun it modifies from similar nouns or precisely defines its distinguishing characteristics. A *nonrestrictive word group* provides extra or nonessential information.

RESTRICTIVE **She demonstrates this shortcoming in her story *"Is There Nowhere Else We Can Meet?"***

NONRESTRICTIVE **The supercomputer center, *which I had seen hundreds of times,* still held many mysteries for me.**

The context helps to determine which information is necessary and which is extra. In the first example, *"Is There Nowhere Else We Can Meet?"* identifies a specific story, distinguishing it from other stories by the same writer. In the second, *which I had seen hundreds of times* adds supplementary information, but the reference to the mysteries of the supercomputer center would be the same without this addition.

A comma signals that a word group is not essential to the meaning of the sentence. If a comma incorrectly sets off a restrictive word group, it undermines the meaning, suggesting to the reader that essential information is not important. See also P1-c.

► **The ten people from the community would consist of three retired people, over the age of sixty, three middle-aged people, between the ages of twenty-five and sixty, and four teenagers.**

► **Although divorce is obviously a cause of the psychological problems, a child will face, the parents need to support their child through the anxiety and turmoil.**

P2-c Omit any commas that unnecessarily separate the main elements of the sentence—subject and verb or verb and object.

subject The part of a clause that identifies who or what is being discussed.

verb A word or phrase that expresses action or being and, along with a subject, is a basic component of a sentence.

object The part of a clause that receives the action of the verb: At the checkpoint, we unloaded *the canoes.*

Even in a complicated sentence, a reader expects the core elements—**subject, verb,** and **object**—to lead directly from one to the other. A comma that separates two of these elements confuses matters by suggesting that some other material has been added, such as an introductory or trailing element or a transitional or parenthetical expression.

Delete a comma that unnecessarily separates a subject and its verb.

► ***Bilateral,*** **means that both the left and the right sides of the brain are involved in processing a stimulus.**

► **This movie's only fault, is that it does not set a good example for younger children.**

Delete a comma that unnecessarily separates a verb and its object.

► **Now the voters must decide, the issue of term limits.**

▶ Unlike Kaoma, many other groups or solo singers try without success to incorporate in their works, music from different cultures.

P2-d Omit a comma that separates the main part of the sentence from a trailing adverbial clause.

adverbial clause A clause that nearly always modifies a verb, indicating time, place, condition, reason, cause, purpose, result, or another logical relationship.

When an adverbial clause appears at the beginning of a sentence, it is usually set off by a comma because it is an introductory element. When the clause appears at the end of a sentence, however, a comma is ordinarily not needed.

When Pirates of the Caribbean _finally reaches its climax_, the ending is a doozy.

Depp shows his charm _when Sparrow seduces the governor's daughter._

Omitting this unnecessary comma makes the sentence flow more smoothly.

▶ I found the tables turned, when he interviewed me about the reasons for my tattoo.

P2-e Leave out any comma that separates noncoordinate adjectives.

noncoordinate adjectives Two or more adjectives that do not modify a noun equally. Instead, one or two of the adjectives closest to the noun form a noun phrase that the remaining adjectives modify: *colorful hot-air* balloons.

coordinate adjectives Two or more adjectives that modify a noun equally and independently: the *large, red* hat.

If you cannot rearrange the adjectives before a noun or add *and* between them, they are probably noncoordinate adjectives (sometimes called *cumulative adjectives*). Such adjectives are not equal elements; do not separate them with a comma. In contrast, coordinate adjectives should be separated by commas (see P1-i).

COORDINATE ADJECTIVES

Wearing a pair of jeans, _cutoff, bleached,_ and _torn_, with an embroidered blouse

NONCOORDINATE ADJECTIVES

and _soft leather_ sandals, she looked older and more foreign than Julie.

Leather modifies *sandals,* and *soft* modifies *leather sandals* as a unit. Thus the meaning is cumulative, and a comma would interrupt the connection between the adjectives and the noun.

▶ Huge, neighborhood parties could bring the people in our community together.

P2-f Omit any comma that appears before or after a series of items.

Although commas should be used to separate the items in a list, they should not be used before the first item or after the final one.

▶ Race, sex, religion, financial situation, or any other circumstance beyond the control of the applicant, should not be considered.

See also P1-e.

P2-g Omit or correct any other unnecessary or incorrect commas.

Check your essays carefully for the following typical comma problems.

coordinating conjunction A word that joins comparable and equally important sentence elements: *for, and, or, but, nor, yet,* or *so.*

Omit a comma that follows a coordinating conjunction.

A comma is needed *before* a coordinating conjunction if it links two independent clauses but not if it links a pair of other sentence elements. A comma is never needed *after* a coordinating conjunction, however. Be especially alert to this unnecessary comma when *but* or *yet* appears at the beginning of a sentence.

- **But, since sharks are not yet classified as endangered species, the members of Congress were not very sympathetic, and the bill was not passed.**

Note: A conjunction may or may not be needed for transition or dramatic effect, depending on the context of the sentence in your essay.

- **~~But, since~~ Since sharks are not yet classified as endangered species, the members of Congress were not very sympathetic, and the bill was not passed.**

Omit a comma following a coordinating conjunction joining two independent clauses, even if the conjunction is followed by a transitional or introductory expression.

- **The ominous vision of the piano wavered before my eyes, and, before I knew it, I was at the base of the steps to the stage, steps that led to potential public humiliation.**
- **I had finally felt the music deep in my soul, and, when I sang, I had a great feeling of relief knowing that everything was going to be all right.**

dependent (subordinate) clause A word group that has a subject, a predicate, and a subordinating word at the beginning; it cannot stand by itself as a sentence but must be connected to an independent (main) clause.

subordinating conjunction A word or phrase that introduces a dependent clause and relates it to an independent clause.

Omit a comma after the word that introduces a dependent clause.

Watch for words such as *who, which, that, whom, whose, where, when, although, because, since, though,* and other subordinating conjunctions.

- **This trend was evident as I entered a college where, the first-year enrollment had been rising.**
- **The drinking age should be raised because, drunk driving has become the leading cause of death among young people between the ages of fifteen and twenty-five.**

Omit a comma preceding *that* when it introduces an indirect quotation.

Unlike a direct quotation, an indirect quotation is not set off by a comma or quotation marks.

▶ After looking at my tests, the doctor said, that I had calcification.

Omit a comma immediately following a preposition.

A comma may follow a complete prepositional phrase at the beginning of a sentence, but a comma should not follow the preposition or interrupt the phrase.

▶ Despite, multiple recruitment and retention problems, the number of public school teachers increased by 27 percent between 1986 and 1999.

Omit unnecessary commas that set off a prepositional phrase in the middle of a sentence.

When a prepositional phrase appears in the middle of a sentence or at the end, it is usually not set off by commas. When it acts as an introductory element, however, it is generally followed by a comma.

▶ "I've seen the devil b'fore," he grumbled, in a serious tone, with his blue eyes peering into mine.

▶ The children's trauma team gathers in the Resuscitation Room, at the same time that John Doe is being treated.

indirect quotation A reworded statement or question that presents a speaker's or writer's ideas without quoting directly or using quotation marks.

preposition A word (such as *between, in,* or *of*) that always appears as part of a phrase and indicates the relation between a word in a sentence and the object of the preposition: The water splashed *into* the canoe.

prepositional phrase A group of words that begins with a preposition and indicates the relation between a word in a sentence and the object following the preposition: Her sunglasses slid *under the seat.*

Rewrite a sentence that is full of phrases and commas to simplify both the sentence structure and the punctuation.

▶ ~~The researchers could monitor, by~~ *By* looking through a porthole window, *the researchers could monitor* how much time ~~was spent, by Noah,~~ *Noah spent* in the dome.

P3 Semicolons

For practice, go to bedfordstmartins.com/theguide/semi

Use semicolons to join closely related independent clauses and to make long sentences with commas easier to read.

independent (main) clause A word group with a subject and a predicate that can stand alone as a separate sentence.

P3-a Use a semicolon to join independent clauses if the second clause restates or sets up a contrast to the first.

In fact, she always had been special; we just never noticed.

Although two independent clauses could be separated by a period, the semicolon tells the reader that they are closely related, emphasizing the restatement or sharpening the contrast.

► **Davie was not an angel~~,~~; he was always getting into trouble with the teachers.**

Note: When the independent clauses are linked by *and, but,* or another coordinating conjunction, use a comma rather than a semicolon (see P1-a) unless the independent clauses include internal punctuation (see P3-c).

P3-b Use semicolons to separate items in a series when they include internal commas.

Studies of gender differences in conversational interaction include an Elizabeth Aries article titled "Interaction Patterns and Themes of Male, Female, and Mixed Groups," a study conducted in a research laboratory setting; a Pamela Fishman article titled "Interaction: The Work Women Do," a study researched by naturalistic observation; and an article by Candace West and Don Zimmerman titled "Small Insults: A Study of Interruptions in Cross-Sex Conversation between Unacquainted Persons," a study conducted in a research laboratory setting.

Because the reader expects items in a series to be separated with commas, other commas within items can be confusing. The solution is to leave the internal commas as they are but to use a stronger mark, the semicolon, to signal the divisions between items.

► **Appliances that use freon include air conditioners, small models as well as central systems~~,~~; refrigerators~~,~~; and freezers, both home and industrial types.**

P3-c Use a semicolon to join a series of independent clauses when they include other punctuation.

Sometimes independent clauses include elements set off by internal punctuation. In such cases, use semicolons between the independent clauses if the other punctuation is likely to confuse a reader or make the sentence parts difficult to identify.

► **He was the guide~~,~~; and he was driving us in this old Ford sedan, just the two of us and him~~,~~; and I had noticed early on that the car didn't have a gas cap.**

Independent clauses like these could also be separated by periods, but semicolons let the reader know that the information in each clause is part of a continuing event.

P3-d Use a semicolon to join two independent clauses when the second clause contains a conjunctive adverb or a transitional expression.

Because a semicolon shows a strong relationship between independent clauses, writers often use it to reinforce the connection expressed by the adverb or transition. Always place the semicolon between the two clauses, no matter where the conjunctive adverb or transitional expression appears. Place the semicolon *before* the conjunctive adverb or transition if it begins the second independent clause. See also P1-d.

▶ **Ninety-five percent of Americans recognize the components of a healthy diet, ; however, they fail to apply their nutritional IQ when selecting foods.**

independent (main) clause A word group with a subject and a predicate that can stand alone as a separate sentence.

conjunctive adverb A word or phrase (such as *finally, however,* or *therefore*) that tells how the ideas in two sentences or independent clauses are connected.

transitional expression A word or group of words that expresses the relationship between one sentence and the next.

P3-e Omit or correct a semicolon used incorrectly to replace a comma or other punctuation mark.

Use semicolons to join two independent clauses or to separate the items in a series when they include other punctuation, but do not use semicolons in place of other punctuation.

Replace a semicolon with a comma to link an independent clause to a phrase or to set off an appositive.

▶ **The threat of a potentially devastating malpractice suit promotes the practice of defensive medicine; , doctors ordering excessive and expensive tests to confirm a diagnosis.**

appositive A word or word group that identifies or gives more information about a noun or pronoun that precedes it.

Replace a semicolon with a comma to join two independent clauses linked by a coordinating conjunction.

▶ **The ashtrays would need to be relocated to that area; , and it could then become an outdoor smoking lounge.**

See also P1-a.

coordinating conjunction A word that joins comparable and equally important sentence elements: *for, and, or, but, nor, yet,* or *so.*

Replace a semicolon with a colon to introduce a list.

▶ **Our county ditches fill up with old items that are hard to get rid of; : old refrigerators, mattresses, couches, and chairs, just to name a few.**

Note: For introducing an in-text list as in this example, a dash (see P5-b) is a less formal and more dramatic alternative to the colon (see P4-a).

P4 Colons

For practice, go to bedfordstmartins.com/theguide/colon

Besides introducing specific sentence elements, colons conventionally appear in works cited or bibliography entries, introduce subtitles, express ratios and times, and follow the salutations in formal letters.

P4-a Use a colon to introduce a list, an appositive, a quotation, a question, or a statement.

appositive A word or word group that identifies or gives more information about a noun or pronoun that precedes it.

independent (main) clause A word group with a subject and a predicate that can stand alone as a separate sentence.

Usually, a colon follows an **independent clause** that makes a general statement; after the colon, the rest of the sentence often supplies specifics—a definition, a quotation or question, or a list (generally in grammatically parallel form; see E7).

> **Society's hatred, violence, and bigotry take root here: the elementary school playground.**

Use the colon selectively to alert readers to closely connected ideas, a significant point, a crucial definition, or a dramatic revelation.

Note: Because a colon follows but does not interrupt an independent clause, it is not used after words such as *is, are, consists of, including, such as, for instance,* and *for example* (see P4-b).

Consider using a colon to introduce a list.

You can use a colon to introduce a list if the list is preceded by an independent clause. Be careful not to interrupt the clause in the middle (see P4-b).

▶ **Most young law school graduates become trial lawyers in one of three ways~~,~~: by going to work for a government prosecutor's office, by working for a private law firm, or by opening private offices of their own.**

Consider using a colon to emphasize an appositive.

Although you can always use commas to set off an appositive, try using a colon occasionally when you need special emphasis.

▶ **The oldest fishermen are followed by the younger generation of middle-aged fathers, excited by the chance to show their sons what their fathers once taught them. Last to arrive are the novices~~,~~: the thrill seekers.**

Consider using a colon to introduce a formal quotation, a question, a statement, or another independent clause.

▶ **We learn that the narrator is a troublemaker in paragraph twelve~~,~~: "I got thrown out of the center for playing pool when I should've been sewing."**

▶ I ran around the office in constant fear of his questions,: What do you have planned for the day? How many demonstrations are scheduled for this week? How many contacts have you made?

▶ Both authors are clearly of the same opinion,: recycling scrap tires is no longer an option.

▶ I guess the saying is true,: Absence does make the heart grow fonder.

Do not capitalize the first word following a colon that introduces an incomplete sentence. However, when the first word following a colon introduces a complete sentence, you can either capitalize the word or not, depending on your preference (see M2-b). Whichever choice you prefer, be consistent. When you introduce a quotation with a colon, always capitalize the word that begins the quotation. See also P6-b.

P4-b Delete or correct an unnecessary or incorrect colon.

As you proofread your writing, watch out for the following incorrect uses of the colon.

Omit a colon that interrupts an independent clause, especially after words such as *is, are, include, composed of, consists of, including, such as, for instance,* and *for example.*

independent (main) clause A word group with a subject and a predicate that can stand alone as a separate sentence.

▶ The tenets include: courtesy, integrity, perseverance, self-control, indomitable spirit, and modesty.

Replace an inappropriate colon with the correct punctuation mark.

▶ As I was touring the different areas of the shop, I ran into Christy, one of the owners:. "Hi, Kim," she said with a smile on her face.

P5 Dashes

For practice, go to bedfordstmartins.com/theguide/dashes

A dash breaks the rhythm or interrupts the meaning of a sentence, setting off information with greater emphasis than another punctuation mark could supply. Writers often use dashes to substitute for other punctuation in quick notes and letters to friends. In many kinds of published writing, dashes are an option used sparingly—but often to good effect.

P5-a Type, space, and position a dash correctly.

Type a dash (—) as two hyphens (--) in a row with no spaces before or after. Use one dash before a word or words set off at the end of the sentence. Use two dashes—one at the beginning and one at the end—if the word or words are in the middle of the sentence.

```
The rigid structure and asymmetrical arrangements of the
sculpture blend well with three different surroundings--the
trees, the library building, and the parking lots.
```

Retype a dash using two hyphens and no spaces.

▶ `Of all public stations in Maryland, WBJC reaches the largest audience -- almost 200,000 listeners per week.`

▶ `And of course, the trees in the sculpture were more than just imitation -- they spoke!`

Note: Most word processing programs will allow you to insert a solid dash (—) instead of two hyphens (--).

Use a pair of dashes, not just one, to mark the beginning and end of a word group that needs emphasis.

▶ I could tell that the people in the room work in uncomfortable conditions—they all wear white lab coats, caps, and gloves~~,~~—but they joke or laugh while building the guns.

If the word group includes commas or other internal punctuation, the dashes tell the reader exactly where the expression that is being set off begins and ends.

P5-b Consider using a dash to set off material from the rest of the sentence.

That smell completely cut off the outside world—the smell of the ocean, the soft breeze, the jubilation of young people under the sun.

Because the dash marks a strong break, it alerts the reader to the importance of the material that follows it.

Consider inserting a dash or pair of dashes to emphasize a definition, a dramatic statement, a personal comment, or an explanation.

▶ Binge eating~~,~~—larger than normal consumption of high-calorie foods~~,~~—starts with emotional distress and depression.

▶ But unlike the boys, the girls often turn to something other than violence~~,~~—motherhood.

▶ In many cases it may be more humane—and I personally believe it is much more humane—to practice euthanasia than to cause the patient prolonged suffering and pain.

Consider inserting a dash or pair of dashes to emphasize a list.

If the list appears in the middle of the sentence, use one dash at the beginning and another at the end to signal exactly where the list begins and ends.

▶ Another problem is that certain toy figures—The Hulk, Spiderman, and the X-Men, to name just a few~~,~~—are characters from movies that portray violence.

P5-c Rewrite a sentence that uses the dash inappropriately or excessively.

Use dashes purposefully; avoid relying on them instead of using other punctuation marks or developing clear sentences and transitions.

▶ Finally the TV people were finished with their interviewing *and* ~~—now they~~ wanted to do a shot of the entrance to the restaurant.

If you are not sure whether you have used a dash or pair of dashes appropriately, try removing the material that is set off. If the sentence does not make logical and grammatical sense, one or both of the dashes are misused or misplaced.

▶ That's a tall order—and a reason to start ~~—~~ amassing some serious capital soon.

P6 Quotation Marks

For practice, go to bedfordstmartins.com/theguide/quote

Use double quotation marks, always in pairs, to indicate direct quotations, to set off special uses of words, and to mark some types of titles. Proofread carefully to be sure that you have added quotation marks at both the beginning and the end of each quotation.

direct quotation A speaker's or writer's exact words, which are enclosed in quotation marks.

indirect quotation A reworded statement or question that presents a speaker's or writer's ideas without quoting directly or using quotation marks.

P6-a Set off direct quotations with quotation marks.

A direct quotation is set off by a pair of quotation marks and by an initial capital letter. **Indirect quotations,** however, do not use quotation marks or capital letters.

> "Mary," I finally said, "I can't keep coming in every weekend."

> Field Marshall Viscount Montgomery stated, "A good beating with a cane can have a remarkable sense of awakening on the mind and conscience of a boy" (James, 1963, p. 13).

> Ms. Goldman is saying that it's time to face the real issues.

When a phrase such as *she said* interrupts the quotation, do not capitalize the first word after the phrase unless the word actually begins a new quoted sentence.

▶ The commissioners came to the conclusion that alcohol prohibition was, in the words of Walter Lippman, "a helpless failure."

Note: In a research paper, indent a long quotation as a block, double spaced, and omit quotation marks. If you are following **MLA style,** indent a long quotation (five typed lines or more) ten spaces, or an inch from the left margin. If you are following **APA style,** indent a long quotation (forty words or more) five spaces.

MLA style Conventions set forth in the guidelines of the Modern Language Association for preparing research papers and documenting sources. See Chapter 22.

APA style Conventions set forth in the guidelines of the American Psychological Association for preparing research papers and documenting sources. See Chapter 22.

```
The mother points out the social changes over Dee's and her
lifetime, contrasting the two time periods.
          Who can even imagine me looking a strange white man
          in the eye? It seems to me I have talked to them
          always with one foot raised in flight, with my head
          turned in whichever way is farthest from them. Dee,
          though. She would always look anyone in the eye.
          (Walker 49)
```

P6-b Follow convention in using punctuation at the end of a quotation, after a phrase such as *he said* or *she said,* and with other punctuation in the same sentence.

Using other punctuation with quotation marks can be tricky at times.

Place a comma or a period inside the closing quotation mark.

▶ Fishman also discusses utterances such as "umm," "oh," and "yeah."

▶ Grandpa then said, "I guess you haven't heard what happened."

▶ "At that point I definitely began to have my doubts, but I tried to go on with my 'normal life.'"

In a research paper following either MLA style or APA style, the closing quotation mark should follow the last quoted word, but the period at the end of the sentence should follow the parentheses enclosing the citation.

▶ **Senator Gabriel Ambrosio added that “an override would send a terrible message, particularly to the young people ”(Schwaneberg 60).”**

Note: Place a colon or semicolon outside the closing quotation mark.

The doctor who tells the story says that the girl is “furious”; she shrieks “terrifyingly, hysterically” as he approaches her.

Follow an introductory phrase such as *he said* with either a comma or the word *that.*

▶ **I looked down and said, “I was trying on your dress blues.”**

▶ **Eberts and Schwirian bluntly point out that, “control attempts aimed at constraining or rehabilitating individual criminals or at strengthening local police forces are treating the symptoms or results of social conditions” (98).**

When you introduce a formal quotation with an independent clause, you can instead follow the introduction with a colon. (See P4-a.)

Place a question mark or an exclamation point inside the closing quotation mark if it is part of the quotation or outside if it is part of your own sentence.

▶ **My father replied, “What have I ever done to you?”?**

▶ **How is it possible that he could have kept repeating to our class, “You are too dumb to learn anything?”?**

Note: You do not need to add a period if a question mark or an exclamation point concludes a quotation at the end of the sentence.

▶ **Miriam produces a highlighter from her bookbag with an enthusiastic “Voilà!”.**

Supply a closing quotation mark at the end of a paragraph to show that a new quotation begins in the next paragraph.

In a dialogue, enclose each speaker’s words in quotation marks, and begin a new paragraph every time the speaker changes.

► “Come on, James,” Toby said. “Let’s climb over the fence.” new ¶ “I don’t think it’s a good idea!” I replied.

Omit the closing quotation mark if a quotation continues in the next paragraph.

If a quotation from a speaker or writer continues from one paragraph to the next, omit the closing quotation mark at the end of the first paragraph, but begin the next paragraph with a quotation mark to show that the quote continues.

► “. . . I enjoy waiting on these people because they also ask about my life, instead of treating me like a servant.”

“However, some customers can be rude and very impatient. . . .”

P6-c Consider using double quotation marks to set off words being defined.

Set off words sparingly (see P6-f), using quotation marks only for those you define or use with a special meaning. You may also use underlining or italics rather than quotation marks to set off words. (See M5-b.)

► The two most popular words in the state statutes are “reasonable” and “appropriate,” used to describe the manner of administration.

Note: Occasionally, quotation marks identify words used ironically. In general, keep such use to a minimum. (See P6-f.)

P6-d Enclose titles of short works (such as articles, chapters, essays, short stories, short poems, episodes in a television program, and songs) in quotation marks.

Note: Titles of longer works are underlined or italicized. (See M5-a.)

► The short story “The Use of Force,” by William Carlos Williams, is an account of a doctor’s unpleasant experience with his patient.

► Charlene Marner Solomon, author of “Careers under Glass,” writes an excellent, in-depth article on obstacles working women encounter when trying to move up the corporate ladder.

Place the quotation marks around the exact title of the work mentioned.

▶ The "Use of Force," by William Carlos Williams, is at first just another story of a doctor's visit.

Note: When you supply your own title at the beginning of your own essay, do not enclose it in quotation marks.

P6-e Use single quotation marks inside double quotation marks to show a quotation within a quotation.

Single quotation marks indicate that the quoted words come from another source or that the source added quotation marks for emphasis.

▶ Flanagan and McMenamin say, "Housing values across the United States have acted more like a fluctuating stock market than the "sure" investment they once were."

P6-f Omit or correct quotation marks used excessively or incorrectly.

Avoid using quotation marks unnecessarily to set off words or incorrectly with direct or indirect quotations.

Omit unneeded quotation marks used for emphasis, irony, or distance.

Avoid using quotation marks just to emphasize certain words, to show irony, or to distance yourself from slang, clichés, or trite expressions. Reserve quotation marks for words that you define or use with a special meaning. (See P6-c.)

▶ Environmental groups can wage war in the hallways of Washington and Sacramento and drive oil companies away from our "sacred" shores.

Add quotation marks to show direct quotations, and omit them from indirect quotations, rewording as necessary to present material accurately.

▶ To start things off, he said, ~~"While~~ *that "while* farming in Liberty, Texas, at the age of eighteen, the spirit of God ~~came to him to go to Houston."~~ *" inspired his move to Houston.*

Whenever you quote a written source or a person you have interviewed, check your notes to make sure that you are using quotation marks to enclose only the speaker's or writer's exact words.

slang Informal language that tends to change rapidly.

cliché An overused expression that has lost its original freshness, such as *hard as a rock*.

direct quotation A speaker's or writer's exact words, which are enclosed in quotation marks.

indirect quotation A reworded statement or question that presents a speaker's or writer's ideas without quoting directly or using quotation marks.

P7 Apostrophes

For practice, go to bedfordstmartins.com/theguide/apo

possessive form The form that shows that a thing belongs to someone or to something.

Use an apostrophe to mark the **possessive form** of nouns and some pronouns, the omission of letters or figures, and the plural of letters or figures.

P7-a Use an apostrophe to show the possessive form of a noun.

The form of a possessive noun depends on whether it is singular (one item) or plural (two or more items).

Add *-'s* to a singular noun to show possession.

a student's parents   the rabbit's eye   Ward's essay

Be sure to include the apostrophe and to place it before the *-s* so that the reader does not mistakenly think that the noun is plural.

▶ **The ~~apartments~~ [apartment's] design lacks softening curves to tame the bare walls.**

▶ **Mrs. Johnson says that 90 percent of the ~~libraries~~ [library's] material is on the first floor.**

Indicate shared or joint possession by adding *-'s* to the final noun in a list; indicate individual possession by adding *-'s* to each noun.

father and mother's room (joint or shared possession)

father's and mother's patterns of conversation (individual possession)

Indicate possession by adding *-'s* to the last word in a compound.

mother-in-law's

Note: Even if a singular noun ends in *s,* add an apostrophe and *-s.* If the second *s* makes the word hard to pronounce, it is acceptable to add only an apostrophe.

Louis's life   Williams's narrator   Cisneros's story   Sophocles' plays

To show possession, add only an apostrophe to a plural noun that ends in *s* but *-'s* if the plural noun does not end in *s.*

their neighbors' homes   other characters' expressions

the children's faces   the women's team

▶ **Males tend to interrupt ~~females~~ [females'] conversations.**

Note: Form the plural of a family name by adding *-s* without an apostrophe (the Harrisons); add the apostrophe only to show possession (the Harrisons' house).

P7-b Add an apostrophe to show where letters or figures are omitted from a contraction.

▶ "~~Lets~~ Let's go back inside and see if you can do it my way now."

▶ Many people had cosmetic surgery in the ~~80s.~~ '80s.

Note: The possessive forms of **personal pronouns** do not have apostrophes *(yours, its, hers, his, ours, theirs)* but are sometimes confused with contractions (such as *it's* for *it is*).

▶ A huge 10- by 4-foot painting of the perfect wave in all ~~it's~~ its glorious detail hangs high up on the wall of the surfing club.

personal pronoun A pronoun that refers to a specific person or object and changes form depending on its function in a sentence, such as *I, me, my, we, us,* and *our.*

P7-c Add *-'s* to form the plural of a number, a letter, or an abbreviation.

perfect 10's mostly *A*'s and *B*'s training the R.A.'s

▶ The participants were shown a series of ~~3s~~ 3's that configured into a large 5.

To show that a date refers to a decade, add *-s* without an apostrophe.

Women have come a long way in the business world since the *1950s.*

Note: Some style guides, such as the MLA guide, prefer no apostrophes with plural abbreviations: *ATMs.*

P7-d Add *-'s* to form the possessive of an indefinite pronoun.

▶ Everyone knows that good service can make or break ~~ones~~ one's dining experience.

Note: The possessive forms of **personal pronouns,** however, do not have apostrophes: *my, mine, your, yours, hers, his, its, our, ours, their, theirs.*

indefinite pronoun A pronoun that does not refer to a particular person or object, such as *all, anybody, anywhere, each, enough, every, everyone, everything, one, somebody, something, either, more, most, neither, none,* or *nobody.*

P7-e Omit unnecessary or incorrect apostrophes.

Watch for an apostrophe incorrectly added to a plural noun ending in *s* when the noun is not a possessive.

▶ Autistic ~~patient's~~ patients can be high, middle, or low functioning.

personal pronoun A pronoun that refers to a specific person or object and changes form depending on its function in a sentence, such as *I, me, my, we, us,* and *our.*

Also remove an apostrophe added to a possessive **personal pronoun** *(yours, its, hers, his, ours, theirs),* watching especially for any forms confused with contractions (such as *it's* for *it is*). See also P7-b.

▶ **That company does not use animals to develop ~~it's~~ *its* products.**

P8 Parentheses

For practice, go to bedfordstmartins.com/theguide/paren

Parentheses are useful for enclosing material—a word, a phrase, or even a complete sentence—that interrupts a sentence. Place words in parentheses anywhere after the first word of the sentence as long as the placement is appropriate and relevant and the sentence remains easy to read.

P8-a Add parentheses to enclose additions to a sentence.

acronym A word formed from the first letters of the phrase that it abbreviates, such as *BART* for *Bay Area Rapid Transit.*

Parentheses are useful for enclosing citations of research sources (following the format required by your style guide); for enclosing an **acronym** or abbreviation at first mention; for adding dates, definitions, illustrations, or other elaborations; and for numbering or lettering a list (always using a pair of marks).

▶ **Americans are not utilizing their knowledge, and as a result, their children are not benefiting (*American Dietetic Association*, 1990, p. 582~~.~~).**

▶ ***People for the Ethical Treatment of Animals* (PETA) is a radical animal liberation group.**

▶ **The bill ~~called~~ (S-2232) was introduced to protect people who smoke off the job against employment discrimination.**

▶ **Signals would (1) prevent life-threatening collisions, (2) provide more efficient and speedy movement of traffic, and (3) decrease frustration and loss of driver judgment.**

Note: Use commas to separate the items in a numbered list. If the items include internal commas, use semicolons. (See P3-b.)

P8-b Correct the punctuation used with parentheses, and omit unnecessary parentheses.

When you add information in parentheses, the basic pattern of the sentence should remain logical and complete, and the punctuation should be the same as it would be if the parenthetical addition were removed. Delete any comma *before* a parenthesis mark.

▶ **As I stood at the salad bar, a young lady asked if the kitchen had any cream cheese, (normally served only at breakfast).**

Parentheses are unnecessary if they enclose information that could simply be integrated into the sentence.

▶ **He didn't exhibit the uncontrollable temper and the high-velocity swearing (typical of many high school coaches).**

P9 Brackets

For practice, go to bedfordstmartins.com/theguide/brack

Use brackets to insert editorial notes into a quotation and to enclose parenthetical material within text that is already in parentheses. In a quotation, the brackets tell the reader that the added material is yours, not the original author's. See also P10.

▶ **"'The gang is your family,' he [(Hagan)] explains."**

If the original quotation includes a mistake, add [sic], the Latin word for "so," in brackets to tell the reader that the error occurs in the source. Often you can reword your sentence to omit the error.

Replace inappropriate brackets with parentheses.

▶ **The American Medical Society has linked "virtual" violence ([violence in the various media]) to real-life acts of violence (Hollis 623).**

P10 Ellipsis Marks

For practice, go to bedfordstmartins.com/theguide/ellip

Use ellipsis marks to indicate a deliberate omission within a quotation or to mark a dramatic pause in a sentence. Type ellipsis marks as three spaced periods (. . .), with a space before the first period and following the last period.

Aries also noticed this reaction in her research: "The mixed group setting seems to benefit men more than women . . . allowing men more variation in the ways they participate in discussions" (32).

If you omit the end of a quoted sentence or if you omit a sentence or more from the middle of a quoted passage, add a sentence period and a space before the first ellipsis mark. (If a quotation that ends with ellipsis marks is followed by a parenthetical citation, put the sentence period at the very end—after the closing quotation mark and the citation.)

Do not use opening or closing ellipsis marks if the quotation is clearly only part of a sentence.

▶ **According to the environmental group Earthgreen, U.S. oil reserves "... will be economically depleted by 2018 at the current consumption rate..." (Miller 476).**

See pp. 558–59 and pp. 748–49 for more on ellipsis marks.

P11 Slashes

For practice, go to bedfordstmartins.com/theguide/slash

Use a slash to separate quoted lines of poetry and to separate word pairs that present options or opposites.

In "A Poison Tree," William Blake gives the same advice: "I was angry with my friend: / I told my wrath, my wrath did end."

Note: When you use a slash to show the lines in poetry, leave a space before and after the mark. If you quote four lines or more, omit the quotation marks and slashes and present the poetry as a block quotation, double spaced. Following **MLA style,** indent each line of a block quotation ten spaces or an inch from the left margin. See also P6-a.

MLA style Conventions set forth in the guidelines of the Modern Language Association for preparing research papers and documenting sources. See Chapter 22.

P12 Periods

For practice, go to bedfordstmartins.com/theguide/period

Use a period to mark the end of a **declarative sentence,** an **indirect question,** or an abbreviation.

declarative sentence A sentence that makes a statement rather than asking a question or exclaiming.

indirect question A statement that tells what a question asked without directly asking the question.

▶ **Another significant use for clinical hypnosis would be to replace anesthesia.**

▶ **She asked her professor why he was not as tough on her as he was on the male students?.**

▶ **Mrs. Drabin was probably one of the smartest people I knew.**

Note: Some abbreviations do not include periods (see M6); always check your dictionary to be sure. In addition, many specialized professional and academic fields have their own systems for handling abbreviations.

P13 Question Marks

For practice, go to bedfordstmartins.com/theguide/quest

Add a question mark after a direct question.

▶ **Did they even read my information sheet.?**

Avoid using question marks to express irony or sarcasm. Use them sparingly to question the accuracy of a preceding word or figure.

P14 Exclamation Points

For practice, go to bedfordstmartins.com/theguide/excl

Use an exclamation point to show strong emotion or emphasis.

He fell on one knee and exclaimed, "Marry me, my beautiful princess!"

Use exclamation points sparingly. Replace inappropriate or excessive exclamation points with periods.

▶ **If parents know which disciplinary methods to use, they can effectively protect their children!.**

M Mechanics

M1 Hyphens

compound word A word formed from two or more words that function together as a unit.

Hyphens are used to form **compound words** and to break words at the end of a line. Depending on the word and its position in a sentence, a compound may be written as two separate words with no hyphen between them, as one word with no space or hyphen between the parts, or as a hyphenated word.

moonshine	postmaster	shipboard
vice versa	place kick	highly regarded
like-minded	once-over	all-around
father-in-law	take-it-or-leave-it	mid-December

compound adjective An adjective formed from two or more words that function as a unit.

M1-a Use a hyphen to join the parts of a compound adjective when it precedes a noun but not when it follows a noun.

Before Noun	*After Noun*
after-school activities	activities after school
well-known athlete	athlete who is well known
fast-growing business	business that is fast growing

When a compound adjective precedes a noun, the hyphen clarifies that the compound functions as a unit.

▶ **People usually think of locusts as hideous-looking creatures that everyone dislikes and wants to squash.**

▶ **I was a nineteen-year-old, second-semester sophomore.**

▶ **People are becoming increasingly health/conscious.**

When two different prefixes or initial words are meant to go with the same second word, use a hyphen and a space at the end of the first prefix or word.

Over twenty people crowd the small trauma room, an army of green- and blue-hooded medical personnel.

Note: Some compound adjectives are nearly always hyphenated, before or after a noun, including those beginning with *all-* or *self-*.

all-inclusive fee | self-sufficient economy
fee that is all-inclusive | economy that is self-sufficient

▶ The use of ethanol will be a self-perpetuating trend.

A compound with an *-ly* adverb preceding an adjective or a participle is always left as two words.

brilliantly clever scheme   rapidly growing business   highly regarded professor

adverb A word that modifies a verb, an adjective, or another adverb, often telling when, where, why, how, or how often.

adjective A word that modifies a noun or a pronoun, adding information about it.

participle A verb form showing present tense *(dancing, freezing)* or past tense *(danced, frozen)* that can also act as an adjective.

compound noun A noun formed from two or more words that function as a unit.

M1-b Present a compound noun as one word, as separate words, or as a hyphenated compound.

If you are not certain about a particular compound noun, look it up in your dictionary. If you cannot find it, spell it as separate words.

Close up the parts of a compound noun spelled as one word.

▶ Another road in our county now looks like an appliance grave yard.

Omit hyphens in a compound noun spelled as separate words.

▶ First, make the community aware of the problem by writing a letter-to-the-editor.

Add any hyphens needed in a hyphenated compound noun.

Hyphenate fractions, compound numbers (up to ninety-nine), and other nouns that are hyphenated in your dictionary.

▶ Almost two-thirds of women who marry before age eighteen end up divorced, twice the number of women who marry at twenty-one or older.

Note: Some compound words have more than one acceptable spelling (*workforce* and *work force,* for example); if you use such a compound, choose one spelling and use it consistently. If you are unsure about whether to use a hyphen, check your dictionary, or follow the common usage of professional publications in that field.

M1-c Spell words formed with most prefixes (including *anti-, co-, mini-, multi-, non-, post-, pre-, re-, sub-,* and *un-*) as one word with no hyphen.

antismoking	coauthor	multicultural	nonviolent
postwar	repossess	submarine	unskilled

▶ This possibility is so rare as to be non-existent.

Note: Insert a hyphen in a compound noun beginning with *ex-*, *great-*, or *self-* (unless it is followed by a suffix, as in *selfish*) or ending in *-elect* or *-in-law.* Check your dictionary in case of a question.

ex-husband self-motivated secretary-elect

▶ **Self-sufficiency is not the only motivation.**

Note: Use a hyphen in a word that includes a prefix and a **proper name.**

proper name The capitalized name of a specific person, group, place, or thing.

un-American anti-American pro-American

M1-d Use a hyphen when necessary to avoid ambiguity.

Sometimes a hyphen is necessary to prevent a reader from confusing a word with a prefix *(re-cover* or *re-creation)* with another word *(recover* or *recreation)* or from stumbling over a word in which two or three of the same letters fall together *(anti-inflammatory, troll-like)*.

While yelling feverishly, I wondered what compelled me to lie on this wet grass, pretending foolishly to *re-enact* the adventures of another time and place.

M1-e Insert a hyphen between syllables to divide a word at the end of a line.

If you must divide a word, look for a logical division, such as between syllables, between parts of a compound word, or between the root and a prefix or suffix. If you are uncertain about where to divide a word, check your dictionary.

go-ing	height-en	mus-cu-la-ture	back-stage
dis-satis-fied	com-mit-ment	honor-able	philos-ophy

Although many word processors will automatically divide words, writing is easier to read without numerous broken words. Check with your instructor or consult the style manual used in a specific field for advice about whether to use the hyphenation function.

M2 Capitalization

Capitalize proper names, the first word in a sentence or a quotation that is a sentence, and the main words in a title.

M2-a Capitalize proper names but not common nouns.

common noun The general name of a person, place, or thing.

Capitalize specific names of people, groups, places, streets, events, historical periods, monuments, holidays, days, months, and directions that refer to specific geographic areas.

World War II	the Great Depression	Lincoln Memorial
Independence Day	Passover	Ramadan
Monday	January	Colorado College
the Northeast	Native Americans	Magnolia Avenue

▶ **It is difficult for ~~a~~A mericans to comprehend the true meaning of freedom.**

When a reference is general, use a common noun (uncapitalized) rather than a proper one (capitalized). Do not capitalize general names of institutions, seasons, compass directions, or words that you want to emphasize.

summer vacation	last winter	university requirements
church service	southern exposure	western life

▶ **The ~~F~~f ederal institutions never even review the student's real financial situation.**

▶ **I work in a ~~L~~l aw ~~O~~o ffice that specializes in settling accident cases.**

Note: Adjectives derived from proper nouns should be capitalized: *Mexican, Napoleonic.* Common nouns such as *street* and *river* are capitalized only when they are part of a proper name: *Main Street, the Mississippi River.*

M2-b Capitalize the word that begins a sentence.

▶ **~~t~~T he garden was their world.**

If a sentence appears within parentheses and is not part of a larger sentence, capitalize the first word.

Note: When you use a colon to introduce an **independent clause**—usually a dramatic or emphatic statement, a question, or a quotation—you may either capitalize the first word of the clause or not capitalize it, but be consistent within an essay. When you use a colon to introduce any other type of clause, phrase, or word, as in a list, do not capitalize the first word. (See P4-a.)

independent (main) clause A word group with a subject and a predicate that can stand alone as a separate sentence.

M2-c Capitalize the first word in a quotation unless it is integrated into your own wording or continues an interrupted quotation.

Lucy Danziger says, "Forget about the glass ceiling" (81).

Marilyn describes the adult bison as having an "ugly, shaggy, brown coat."

Writers often incorporate short quotations and quotations introduced by *that* into their sentences; neither needs an initial capital letter. When a phrase such as *she said* interrupts a quotation, capitalize the first word in the quotation but not the first word after the phrase unless it begins a new sentence. See also P6.

▶ **Toby said, “~~t~~Trust me—we won’t get caught.”**

▶ **“~~r~~Renting,” she insists, “deprives you of big tax breaks.”**

Note: If you quote from a poem, capitalize words exactly as the poet does.

M2-d Capitalize the first and last words in a title and subtitle plus all other words except for articles, coordinating conjunctions, and prepositions.

article An adjective that precedes a noun and identifies a definite reference to something specific *(the)* or an indefinite reference to something less specific *(a* or *an).*

coordinating conjunction A word that joins comparable and equally important sentence elements: *for, and, or, but, nor, yet,* or *so.*

preposition A word (such as *between, in,* or *of*) that always appears as part of a phrase and that indicates the relation between a word in a sentence and the object of the preposition: The water splashed *into* the canoe.

War and Peace *Stranger in a Strange Land* *The Grand Canyon Suite*
Tragedy: Vision and Form “On First Looking into Chapman’s Homer”

Titles of short works are placed in quotation marks (see P6-d), and titles of long works are underlined or italicized (see M5-a).

▶ **In her article “The Gun ~~I~~in ~~T~~the Closet,” Straight tells of booming Riverside, California, a city east of Los Angeles.**

M2-e Capitalize a title that precedes a person’s name but not one that follows a name or appears without a name.

Professor John Ganim	Aunt Alice
John Ganim, my professor	Alice Jordan, my favorite aunt

▶ **At the state level, Reverend Green is ~~P~~president of the State Congress of Christian Education and ~~M~~moderator of the Old Landmark Association.**

Note: References to the President (of the United States) and other major public figures are sometimes capitalized in all contexts.

M2-f Avoid overusing capitalization for emphasis.

Although in some writing situations a word that appears entirely in capital letters can create a desired effect, you should limit this use of capital letters to rare occasions.

The powerful SMACK of the ball on the rival’s thigh brings an abrupt, anticlimactic end to the rising tension.

In most cases, follow the conventions for capitalizing described in this section.

▶ **The principles are called the ~~TENETS OF TAE KWON DO.~~** *tenets of Tae Kwon Do.*

M3 Spacing

Allow standard spacing between words and punctuation marks. Writers have traditionally left two spaces after a period at the end of a sentence and one after a comma. Style guides such as APA now recommend leaving one space after a sentence period. MLA and APA also supply specific directions about spacing source citations.

APA style Conventions set forth in the guidelines of the American Psychological Association for preparing research papers and documenting sources. See Chapter 22.

MLA style Conventions set forth in the guidelines of the Modern Language Association for preparing research papers and documenting sources. See Chapter 22.

M3-a Supply any missing space before or after a punctuation mark.

Although spell-checkers can help identify some misspelled words, they do not indicate spacing errors unless the error links two words or splits a word. Even if you write on a word processor, proofread carefully for spacing errors around punctuation marks.

▶ My curiosity got the best of me,|so I flipped through the pages to see what would happen.

▶ "I found to my horror, "|Nadine later wept, "that I was too late!"

▶ "I would die without bread!" Roberto declared.|"In my village, they made fresh bread every morning."

▶ Pet adoption fees include the cost of spaying or neutering all dogs and cats four months old or older|(if needed).

M3-b Close up any unnecessary space between words and punctuation marks.

▶ Karl did not know why this war was considered justifiable by the U.S. government .

▶ The larger florist shops require previous experience , but the smaller , portable wagons require only a general knowledge of flowers.

▶ Do you remember the song " The Wayward Wind" ?

M4 Numbers

Conventions for the treatment of numbers vary widely. In the humanities, writers tend to spell out numbers as recommended here, but in the sciences and social sciences, writers are far more likely to use numerals.

one out of ten	1 out of 10

M4-a Spell out whole numbers *one* through *ninety-nine,* numbers that begin sentences, and very large round numbers in most nonscientific college writing.

Five or six vehicles, in various states of disrepair, are on the property.

Forty-eight percent of students enrolling in bachelor's programs at public colleges fail to graduate.

There are more than eleven thousand regular parking spaces and almost a thousand metered spaces.

Spell out whole numbers *one* through *ninety-nine* in most nonscientific college writing.

▶ A hefty $7,000 is paid to Wells Fargo Security for ~~4~~ *four* guards who patrol the grounds ~~24~~ *twenty-four* hours a day.

▶ Only ~~15~~ *fifteen* years ago, it was difficult to find any public figures who were openly gay.

Note: Depending on the type of writing that you do and the conventions of your field, you may decide to spell out only numerals up to ten. Either rule is acceptable. Just be sure to follow it consistently.

Be consistent also in expressing related numbers. The following sentence expresses a range as "5 to 17." Ordinarily, *five* and *seventeen* would be spelled out, but because they appear in context with larger numbers expressed as numerals, they too are presented as numerals.

The dentists examined the mouths of 42,500 children, aged 5 to 17, at 970 schools across the nation.

Note: If two numbers occur in succession, use a combination of spelled-out words and numerals for clarity.

eight 20-cent stamps   ten 3-year-olds

Spell out a number that begins a sentence, or rewrite so that the number is no longer the first word.

▶ ~~41,000~~ *Forty-one thousand* women die from breast cancer each year.

▶ As many as 41,000 women die from breast cancer each year.

Spell out very large round numbers, or use a combination of numerals and words.

3.5 million dollars *or* $3.5 million   nearly 14 million
five thousand   a billion

M4-b Use numerals for numbers over a hundred, in fractions and percentages, with abbreviations and symbols, in addresses and dates, and for page numbers and sections of books.

99% 73 percent	3 cm 185 lbs.	5 A.M. 10:30 P.M.	$200
175 Fifth Avenue	May 6, 1970	the 1980s	18.5 1/2
page 44	chapter 22	volume 8	289 envelopes

▶ A woman with the same skills as her coworkers may earn an additional ~~eight~~ 8 to ~~twenty~~ 20 percent just by being well groomed.

Note: Either the word *percent* or the % symbol is acceptable as long as it is used consistently throughout a paper.

▶ The movie *Midnight Cowboy* was rated X in the late ~~nineteen sixties.~~ 1960s.

M5 Underlining (Italics)

When they are printed, underlined words appear in the slanted type called *italics.* Most word processors now include an italics option, but your instructor may prefer that you continue to underline.

M5-a Underline or italicize titles of long or self-contained works.

Titles of books, newspapers, magazines, scholarly journals, pamphlets, long poems, movies, videotapes, television and radio programs, long musical compositions, plays, comic strips, and works of art are underlined.

Hemingway's novel *The Sun Also Rises*   *Beowulf*   *Citizen Kane*
the *Washington Post*   *60 Minutes*   *Pride and Prejudice*

I found that the article in the *Journal of the American Medical Association* had more information and stronger scientific proof than the article in *American Health.*

Note: The Bible and its divisions are not underlined.

Titles of short works or works contained in other works, such as chapters, essays, articles, stories, short poems, and individual episodes of a television program, are not underlined but are placed in quotation marks. See also P6-d.

▶ **The hit Reese Witherspoon film "Legally Blond" was based on a novel by Amanda Brown, whose most recent book is "Family Trust."**

▶ **The original "Star Trek" series "The Trouble with Tribbles" was hugely popular.**

M5-b Underline or italicize words used as words and letters and numbers used as themselves.

the word *committed* three *7*'s a *q* or a *g*

▶ **Rank order is a term that Aries uses to explain the way that some individuals take the role as the leader and the others fall in behind.**

M5-c Underline or italicize names of vehicles (airplanes, ships, and trains), foreign words that are not commonly used in English, and occasional words that need special emphasis.

Lindbergh's *Spirit of St. Louis* Amtrak's *Silver Star*

Resist the temptation to emphasize words by putting them in bold type. In most writing situations, underlining provides enough emphasis.

▶ **Upon every table is a vase adorned with a red carnation symbolizing amore (the Italian word for "love").**

▶ **This situation could exist because it is just that, reverse socialization.** (no bold)

M5-d Underline or italicize when appropriate but not in place of or in addition to other conventional uses of punctuation and mechanics.

Eliminate any unusual uses of underlining or italics.

UNUSUAL The commissioner of the NFL, Paul Tagliabue, said, *"I do not believe playing [football] in Arizona is in the best interests of the NFL."*

APPROPRIATE The commissioner of the NFL, Paul Tagliabue, said, "I do not believe playing [football] in Arizona is in the best interests of the NFL."

M6 Abbreviations

Although abbreviations are more common in technical and business writing than in academic writing, you may sometimes want to use them to avoid repetition. Use the full word in your first reference, followed by the abbreviation in parentheses. Then use the abbreviation in subsequent references.

San Diego Humane Society (SDHS)   prisoners of war (POWs)

Abbreviations composed of all capital letters are generally written without periods or spaces between letters. When capital letters are separated by periods, do not skip a space after the period, except for the initials of a person's name, which should be spaced.

USA   CNN   UPI   B.A.   Ph.D.   T. S. Eliot

M6-a Use abbreviations that your readers will recognize for names of agencies, organizations, countries, and common technical terms.

FBI   IRS   CBS   NATO   NOW   DNA   GNP   CPM

The SDHS is an independently run nonprofit organization.

Note: Do not abbreviate geographic names in formal writing unless the areas are commonly known by their abbreviations *(Washington, D.C.)*.

M6-b Use A.M., P.M., *No.*, $, B.C., and A.D. only with specific numerals or dates.

7:15 a.m. *or* 7:15 A.M.   10:30 p.m. *or* 10:30 P.M.
$172.18 *or* $38   No. 18 *or* no. 18 [item or issue number of a source]
72 B.C. [before Christ]   72 B.C.E. [before the Common Era]
A.D. 378 [*anno Domini*]   378 C.E. [Common Era]

Note: A.D., for *anno Domini* ("in the year of our Lord"), is placed before the date, not after it.

M6-c Use commonly accepted abbreviations for titles, degrees, and Latin terms.

Change a title or a degree to an accepted abbreviation. Avoid duplication by using a title before a person's name or a degree after the name but not both.

Rev. Jesse Jackson	Mr. Roger Smith	Ms. Martina Navratilova
Diana Lee, M.D.	Dr. Diana Lee	James Boyer, D.V.M.
Ann Hajek, Ph.D.	Ring Lardner Jr.	Dr. Albert Einstein

According to Dr. Ira Chasnoff of Northwestern Memorial, cocaine produces a dramatic fluctuation in blood pressure.

Reserve Latin terms primarily for source citations or comments in parentheses rather than using them in the text of your essay.

c. (*or* ca.)	"circa" or about (used with dates)
cf.	compare
e.g.	for example
et al.	and others (used with people)
etc.	and so forth
i.e.	that is
vs. (*or* v.)	versus (used with titles of legal cases)

Some adult rights (e.g., the right to vote) clearly should not be extended to children.

***Roe v. Wade* is still the law of the land.**

M6-d Use abbreviations when appropriate, but do not use them to replace words in most writing.

In formal writing, avoid abbreviating units of measurement or technical terms (unless your essay is technical), names of time periods (months, days, or holidays), course titles or department names, names of states or countries (unless the abbreviation is the more common form), names of companies, and parts of books.

▶ **The Pets for People program gives older people the companionship they need,** *especially* **~~esp.~~ if they live alone.**

▶ **I called the closest site on Hancock** *Street* **~~St.~~ to ask for a tour.**

▶ **The walkout followed an incident on** *September* **~~Sept.~~ 27.**

M7 Titles and Headings

Use an appropriate title and headings that follow the format required for an essay or research paper. Consult your instructor or a style guide in your field to determine whether you are expected to supply a title page, running heads, text headings, or other design features.

M7-a Place your heading and title on the first page of a research paper, following MLA style.

MLA style Conventions set forth in the guidelines of the Modern Language Association for preparing research papers and documenting sources. See Chapter 22.

If you are following MLA style, do not include a title page. Instead, begin your first page with a double-spaced heading one inch from the top of the page and aligned with the left margin. In the heading, list your name, your instructor's name, the class name and number, and the date on separate, double-spaced lines. Double-space again and center your title, following the rules for capitalizing titles (see M2) but omitting the quotation marks.

Then begin the first paragraph of your text, indenting it and all other paragraphs five spaces or one-half inch and double-spacing every part of the text (including references to sources and quotations). Throughout your paper, leave one-inch margins on all four sides of the text, except for the **running head** with the page number (see M7-b). If your computer program has a feature that aligns the right margin (called "right justification"), turn this function off because it may produce odd spaces in your text and make it hard to read. Also turn off the "auto-hyphenation" feature. You may want to refer to the format of the sample paper in Chapter 22 (p. 781). See M7-b and M8-a for other MLA requirements.

running head (header) A heading at the top of a page that usually includes the page number and other information.

If you are following **APA style,** supply a title page (see M7-c), a brief abstract, and text headings (see M7-d).

APA style Conventions set forth in the guidelines of the American Psychological Association for preparing research papers and documenting sources. See Chapter 22.

M7-b Use an appropriate running head to number the pages of a research paper.

If you are following **MLA style,** provide a running head on each page, starting on page 1, that includes your last name and the page number. Position this heading one-half inch below the top of the page, aligned with the right margin. (Most word processing programs have a feature that will allow you to print a running head automatically on each page.) See the sample paper in Chapter 22 (p. 782). Other style guides recommend different running heads—such as the shortened title with the page number required by **APA**—so follow any directions carefully.

M7-c Prepare a title page for your essay or research paper if required.

Supply a separate title page if it is customary in a particular field or expected by your instructor. (If you are following MLA style, a separate title page is not required; see M7-a.) If you have not been given guidelines by your instructor, center your title about halfway down the page. Beginning about three inches up from the bottom of the page, list your name, your teacher's name, the class name and number, and the date, each on a separate line, centered and double-spaced.

M7-d Use text headings if required to identify the sections of a research paper.

In many fields, a research paper or report is expected to follow a particular structure and to include section headings so that a reader can easily identify the parts of the discussion. The APA, for example, recommends preparing an abstract or a closing summary, an introduction, and separate sections on the method, results, and implications of the study's findings (see p. 708). References and appendixes conclude the paper. Follow whatever guidelines your instructor or department provides.

Even if specific headings are not required, a long essay may be easier for a reader to follow if headings are supplied for each section. Such headings, however, cannot replace adequate transitions within your text, and they need to reflect your audience and purpose. A heading may be centered or aligned with the left margin of the paper. It may be spaced so that it is set off from the text or be followed directly by text on the same line. Follow your instructor's advice, and be consistent so that comparable headings are set up the same way—same type size and style, same capitalization, and same position on the page. Such consistency lets the reader know that sections are of similar weight or that one section is subsidiary to another.

M8 Special Design Features

Because computers make it easy to use different typefaces, type sizes, margin widths, and indents in your documents, you may be tempted to impose an elaborate design on a simple essay and fill it with variations and special features. Resist this temptation unless your instructor specifically encourages such experimentation. Use conventional design features and layouts to make your essay easy to follow, easy to read, and easy to understand.

M8-a Prepare your essay following any required conventions.

If you are required to follow a standard style, such as **MLA** or **APA,** check with your instructor about its requirements for margins, type size, and so forth. If you have not been given specific requirements, follow a fairly conservative style, like the MLA, to avoid excessive formatting that may not appeal to academic readers.

However you prepare your essay, most college instructors will hold you responsible if it should be lost. Always print a second copy, save the file on a backup disk, duplicate a typed or handwritten copy, or keep drafts so that you can replace a lost essay. Some instructors, especially in composition, require that you hand in planning materials and drafts or submit a complete portfolio at the end of the term. Keep any materials that may be needed later in the term.

MLA style Conventions set forth in the guidelines of the Modern Language Association for preparing research papers and documenting sources. See Chapter 22.

APA style Conventions set forth in the guidelines of the American Psychological Association for preparing research papers and documenting sources. See Chapter 22.

For an MLA-style essay or research paper, use only one side of plain, white, nonerasable paper (8½- by 11-inch sheets). If your final version looks messy from corrections or smudges, hand in a clean duplicate made on a good copier. Make sure your printer is in good condition so that your final drafts are neat with dark, readable type. If your instructor will accept a handwritten essay or research paper, prepare it neatly, writing clearly in black or blue ink on only one side of each page. See M7-a for directions about MLA margin widths and other spacing.

M8-b Use bold, italic, or unusual type styles or sizes sparingly.

A typical word-processor setting for text is double-spaced 12-point type. If you want to use bold or italic type, unusual fonts, or special sizes of type, check first with your instructor. Most college instructors prefer simplicity, although some might allow you to use slightly larger (14-point) type for the title, bold section headings in a long essay, additional spacing between sections, or slightly smaller (10-point) type in a crowded chart. Even so, use only features that will make your text easy to read and easy to follow. Be clear and consistent. Dramatic type variations are more suitable for a newsletter or brochure than an academic essay or report.

In **MLA style,** as in the style guides for other academic fields, the use of different type styles is essentially limited to underlining certain titles and words (see M5).

MLA style Conventions set forth in the guidelines of the Modern Language Association for preparing research papers and documenting sources. See Chapter 22.

UNUSUAL She finally let out a laughing smile and said, ***"I am so happy, Shellah."***

APPROPRIATE She finally let out a laughing smile and said, "I am so happy, Shellah."

UNUSUAL The effect is the same: **Any violent behavior will not be tolerated.**

APPROPRIATE The effect is the same: Any violent behavior will not be tolerated.

M8-c Use extra capital letters, icons, symbols, or other atypical features sparingly.

Although you may occasionally capitalize all of the letters in a word for emphasis, most college instructors will expect you to follow the standard conventions for capitalization (see M2). If you are preparing special tables, charts, boxes, or other visual materials, ask your instructor's advice about variations in capitalization, type size and style, special symbols, and so forth.

▶ When all of these components are pulled together, the lyrics become powerful, as proven by De Garmo ~~&~~ *and* Key.

M9 Spelling

Try several (or all) of the following suggestions for catching and correcting your spelling errors.

- Proofread your writing carefully to catch transposed letters *(becuase* for *because),* omitted letters *(becaus),* and other careless errors *(then* for *than).* When you proofread for spelling, read the text backward, beginning with the last word. (This strategy keeps you from reading for content and lets you focus on each word.)
- Check a good dictionary for any words you are uncertain about. When you are writing and doubt the spelling of a word, put a question mark by the word but wait to check it until you have finished drafting. (Check a misspeller's dictionary if you are unsure of the first letters of the word.)
- Keep a list of words you often misspell so that you can try to pinpoint your personal patterns. Although misspellings nearly always follow a pattern, you are not likely to misspell every word of a particular type, or you may spell the same word two different ways in the same essay.

prefix A word part, such as *pre-, anti-,* or *bi-,* that is attached to the beginning of a word to form another word: *preconceived, unbelievable.*

suffix A word part, such as *-ly, -ment,* or *-ed,* that is added to the end of a word to change the word's form *(bright, brightly)* or tense *(call, called)* or to form another word *(govern, government).*

M9-a Study the spelling rules for adding prefixes and suffixes to words.

Although English has a large number of words with unusual spellings, many follow the patterns that spelling rules describe.

Add a prefix to a root without doubling or dropping letters.

distrust   misbehave   unable
dissatisfy   misspell   unnatural

Add a suffix beginning with a vowel (such as *-ing*) in accord with the form of the root word.

Double the final consonant if the word has a single syllable that ends in a single consonant preceded by a single vowel.

begging   hidden   fitting

Do the same if the word has a final stressed syllable that ends in a single consonant preceded by a single vowel.

beginning   occurrence

The final consonant does not double if the word ends in a double consonant or has a double vowel.

acting   parted   seeming   stooped

In some cases, the stress shifts to the first syllable when a suffix is added. When it does, do not double the final consonant.

prefér:	preférring, preférred
	préference, préferable

Add a suffix that begins with *y* or a vowel by dropping a final silent *e*.

achieving	icy	location
grievance	lovable	continual

Note: Keep the final silent *e* to retain a soft *c* or *g* sound, to prevent mispronunciation, or to prevent confusion with other words.

changeable	courageous	noticeable
eyeing	mileage	canoeist
dyeing	singeing	

Add a suffix that begins with a consonant by keeping a final silent *e*.

achievement	discouragement	sincerely

Exceptions: acknowledgment, argument, awful, judgment, truly, wholly.

Form the plural of a singular noun in accord with its form.

If a singular noun ends in a consonant followed by *y*, change *y* to *i* and add *-es*.

baby, babies	cry, cries

Note: Simply add *-s* to proper names: her cousin *Mary,* both *Marys.*

If a singular noun ends in a vowel followed by *y*, add *-s*.

trolley, trolleys	day, days

If a singular noun ends in a consonant and *o*, add *-es*.

potato, potatoes	echo, echoes	veto, vetoes

Exceptions: autos, dynamos, pianos, sopranos.

If a singular noun ends in a vowel and *o*, add *-s*.

video, videos	rodeo, rodeos	radio, radios

If a singular noun ends in *s, ss, sh, ch, x,* or *z*, add *-es*.

Jones, Joneses	hiss, hisses	bush, bushes
match, matches	suffix, suffixes	buzz, buzzes

Note: The plural of *fish* is *fish;* the plural of *thesis* is *theses.*

Check the dictionary for the plural of a word that originates in another language.

criterion, criteria   datum, data

medium, mediums *or* media

hors d'oeuvre, hors d'oeuvres *or* hors d'oeuvre

M9-b Study the spelling rules (and the exceptions) that apply to words you routinely misspell.

Add *i* before *e* except after *c*.

Most people remember this rule because of the jingle "Write *i* before *e* / Except after *c* / Or when sounded like *ay* / As in *neighbor* and *weigh*." *Exceptions:* either, foreign, forfeit, height, leisure, neither, seize, weird.

Spell most words ending in the sound "seed" as *-cede*.

precede   recede   secede   intercede

Exceptions: proceed, succeed, supersede.

> For ESL Writers
>
> If you have learned Canadian or British English, you may have noticed some differences in the way that words are spelled in U.S. English.
>
> | *U.S. English* | *Canadian or British English* |
> |---|---|
> | color | colour |
> | realize | realise (*or* realize in Canadian English) |
> | center | centre |
> | defense | defence |

M9-c Watch for words that are often spelled incorrectly because they sound like other words.

In English, many words are not spelled as they sound. The endings of some words may be dropped in speech but need to be included in writing. For example, speakers often pronounce *and* as *an'* or drop the *-ed* ending on verbs. Other common words sound the same but have entirely different meanings. Watch carefully for words such as the following.

already ("by now": He is *already* in class.)

all ready ("fully prepared": I'm *all ready* for the test.)

an (article: Everyone read *an* essay last night.)
and (conjunction: The class discussed the problem *and* the solution.)

its (possessive pronoun: The car lost *its* shine.)
it's ("it is": *It's* too cold to go for a walk.)

maybe ("perhaps": *Maybe* we should have tacos for dinner.)
may be (verb showing possibility: They *may be* arriving tonight.)

than (conjunction showing comparison: The house was taller *than* the tree.)
then (adverb showing time sequence: First she knocked and *then* she opened the door.)

their (possessive pronoun: They decided to sell *their* old car.)
there (adverb showing location: The car dealer is located *there* on the corner.)
they're ("they are": *They're* going to pick up the new car tonight.)

your (possessive pronoun: I can see *your* apartment.)
you're ("you are": Call me when *you're* home.)

For distinctions between other words such as *affect/effect, principal/principle,* and *to/too,* see the Glossary of Frequently Misused Words.

Watch for and correct misspelled words that sound the same as other words.

▶ **I started packing my gear, still ~~vary~~ *very* excited about the trip.**

▶ **The campfire had ~~burn~~ *burned* down to a sizzle.**

▶ **I just ~~new~~ *knew* it was a bear, and I was going to be its dinner.**

▶ **As students pay ~~there~~ *their* fees, part of this money goes toward purchasing new books and materials.**

▶ **Pushing off from Anchovy Island, the boat sets its ~~coarse~~ *course*.**

M9-d Watch for words that are often misspelled.

Check your essays for the following words, which are often spelled incorrectly. Look up any other questionable words in a dictionary, and keep a personal list of words that you tend to misspell.

absence	accommodate	achievement	acquaintance
accidentally	accomplish	acknowledge	acquire

against	conscience	heroes	preparation
aggravate	conscious	immediately	privilege
all right	convenient	incredible	probably
a lot	criticize	indefinitely	proceed
although	definitely	interesting	professor
analyze	dependent	irrelevant	quiet
apparently	desperate	knowledge	quite
appearance	develops	loose	receive
appropriate	disappear	lose	recommend
argument	eighth	maintenance	reference
arrangement	eligible	maneuver	referred
attendance	embarrass	mischievous	roommate
basically	emphasize	necessary	schedule
before	environment	noticeable	separate
beginning	especially	occasion	similar
believe	every day	occur	studying
benefited	exaggerated	occurred	succeed
business	exercise	occurrences	success
businesses	exercising	particularly	successful
calendar	experience	performance	therefore
cannot	explanation	phenomena	thorough
categories	finally	phenomenon	truly
changeable	foreign	physically	unnecessarily
choose	forty	playwright	until
chose	fourth	practically	usually
coming	friend	precede	whether
commitment	government	preference	without
committed	harass	preferred	woman
competitive	height	prejudice	women

L ESL Troublespots

This section provides advice about problems of grammar and standard usage that are particularly troublesome for speakers of English as a second language (ESL).

L1 Articles

For practice, go to bedfordstmartins.com/theguide/art

The rules for using articles *(a, an,* and *the)* are complicated. Your choice depends on whether the article appears before a **count, noncount,** or **proper noun.** An *article* is used before a common noun to indicate whether the noun refers to something specific (*the* moon) or whether it refers to something that is one among many or has not yet been specified (*a* planet, *an* asteroid). In addition, for some nouns, the absence of an article indicates that the reference is not specific.

count noun A noun that names people and things that can be counted: one *teacher,* two *teachers;* one *movie,* several *movies.*

noncount noun A noun that names things or ideas that are not or cannot be counted: *thunder, money, happiness.*

proper noun The capitalized name of a specific person, group, place, or thing.

L1-a Select the correct article to use with a count noun.

- Use *a* or *an* with nonspecific singular count nouns.
- Use no article with nonspecific plural count nouns.
- Use *the* with specific singular and plural count nouns.

Note: The article *a* is used before a consonant and *an* before a vowel; exceptions include words beginning with a long *u,* such as *unit.*

Use *a* or *an* before a singular count noun when it refers to one thing among many or something that has not been specifically identified.

► We, as ^*a* society, have to educate our youth about avoiding teen pregnancy.

► ~~Darkroom~~ ^*A darkroom* is a room with no light where photographs are developed.

Use *the* before a singular or plural count noun when it refers to one or more specific things.

After you have used *a* or *an* with a count noun, subsequent references to the noun become specific and are marked by *the.*

> When I walked into the office, *a* woman in her mid-forties was waiting to be called. As I sat down, I looked at *the* woman.

Exceptions include a second reference to one among many.

> I was guided to *a* classroom. It was *a* bright room, filled with warm rays of Hawaiian sunlight.

Note: In most situations, use *the* with a count noun modified by a superlative adjective.

the most frightening moment   the smallest person

But: He gave *a* most unusual response.

Nouns such as *sun* generally refer to unique things; for instance, the only sun visible in the sky. Nouns such as *house* and *yard* often refer to things that people own. A writer may talk about *the yard* meaning his or her own yard. In most situations, both types of nouns can be preceded by the definite article *the.*

Don't look directly at *the sun.* [Only one sun could be meant.]

I spent Saturday cleaning *the house.* [The reader will infer that the writer is referring to his or her own house.]

Note: You can also introduce count nouns referring to specific entities with possessive nouns or pronouns (*Maya's* friends) or demonstrative pronouns (*these* friends). Indefinite count and noncount nouns can also be introduced by words that indicate amount (*few* friends, *some* sand).

COUNT NOUN	**She stayed with *her* eight children.**
NONCOUNT NOUN	**Her family wanted *some* happiness.**

Delete any article before a plural count noun when it does not refer to something specific.

▶ ~~The people~~ *People* **like Dee cannot forget their heritage.**

noncount noun A noun that names things or ideas that are not or cannot be counted: *thunder, money, happiness.*

L1-b Select the correct article to use with a noncount noun.

The many kinds of noncount nouns include the following.

Natural phenomena: *thunder, steam, electricity*

Natural elements: *gold, air, sunlight*

Manufacturing materials: *steel, wood, cement*

Fibers: *wool, cotton, rayon*

General categories made up of a variety of specific items: *money, music, furniture*

Abstract ideas: *happiness, loyalty, adolescence, wealth*

Liquids: *milk, gasoline, water*

Some nouns naming foodstuffs are always noncount *(pork, rice, broccoli)*; others are noncount when they refer to food as it is eaten *(We ate barbecued chicken and fruit)* but count when they refer to individual items or varieties *(We bought a plump chicken and various fruits).*

Delete any article before a noncount noun when it refers to something general.

▶ What is needed is ~~a~~ reasonable and measured legislation.

▶ The destruction of the war drew artists away from ~~the~~ reality, which is painful and cruel, and toward ~~the~~ abstract art that avoids a sense of despair.

Use *the* before a noncount noun when it refers to something specific or when it is specified by a prepositional phrase or an adjective clause.

The coffee is probably cold by now.

The water on the boat has to be rationed.

The water that we have left has to be rationed.

Note: You can also introduce noncount nouns referring to specific things with possessive nouns or pronouns (*her* money) or demonstrative pronouns (*that* money). Indefinite noncount nouns can also be introduced by words that indicate amount (*some* money).

prepositional phrase A group of words that begins with a preposition and indicates the relation between a word in a sentence and the object following the preposition: Her sunglasses slid *under the seat*.

adjective clause A clause that modifies a noun or pronoun and is generally introduced by a relative pronoun (such as *that* or *which*).

L1-c Select the correct article to use with a proper noun.

proper noun The capitalized name of a specific person, group, place, or thing.

Most plural proper nouns require *the: the* United States, *the* Philippines, *the* Black Hills, *the* Clintons, *the* Los Angeles Dodgers. Exceptions include business names (Hillshire Farms, Miller Auto Sales).

Delete any article before most singular proper nouns.

In general, singular proper nouns are not preceded by an article: Dr. Livingston, New York City, Hawaii, Disneyland, Mount St. Helens, Union Station, Wrigley Field.

▶ ~~The~~ Campus Security is a powerful deterrent against parties because if you are written up twice, you can lose your housing contract.

Note: The is used before proper noun phrases that include *of* (*the* Rock of Gibraltar, *the* Gang of Four). *The* is also required before proper nouns that name the following things:

1. Bodies of water, except when the generic part of the name precedes the specific name: *the* Atlantic Ocean, *the* Red River, but Lake Erie
2. Geographic regions: *the* West Coast, *the* Sahara, *the* Grand Canyon
3. Vehicles for transportation: *the Concorde*
4. Named buildings and bridges: *the* World Trade Center, *the* Golden Gate Bridge
5. National or international churches: *the* Russian Orthodox Church

6. Governing bodies preceded by a proper adjective: *the* British Parliament
7. Titles of religious and political leaders: *the* Dalai Lama, *the* president
8. Religious and historical documents: *the* Bible, *the* Magna Carta
9. Historical periods and events: *the* Gilded Age, *the* Civil War

L2 Verbs

For practice, go to bedfordstmartins.com/theguide/everb

Section R2-a reviews the basic English verb forms and includes a list of common irregular verbs. As you edit your writing, pay particular attention to conditional clauses, two-word verbs, helping (auxiliary) verbs, and gerund or infinitive forms after verbs.

independent (main) clause A word group with a subject and a predicate that can stand alone as a separate sentence.

L2-a Select verb tenses carefully in main clauses and conditional clauses.

Conditional clauses beginning with *if* or *unless* generally indicate that one thing causes another (a factual relationship); predict future outcomes or possibilities; or speculate about the past, present, future, or impossible events or circumstances.

[CONDITIONAL CLAUSE: If we *use* television correctly,] [MAIN CLAUSE: it *can give* us information and entertainment.]

[CONDITIONAL CLAUSE: If we *use* television incorrectly,] [MAIN CLAUSE: it *will control* our families and our community.]

Change both verbs to the same tense (generally present or past) to express general or specific truths or actions that happen together habitually.

► When we moved to America, my family ~~has~~ *had* good communication.

Change the verb in the main clause to the future and the verb in the conditional clause to the present to express future possibilities or predictions.

► If you ask in any of her restaurants, the manager ~~would~~ *will* tell you about working with her all these years.

base form The uninflected form of a verb: I *eat;* to *play.*

Change the verb in the main clause to *would, could,* or *might* plus the base form and change the verb in the *if* conditional clause to the past tense to speculate about events or conditions that are unreal, improbable, or contrary to fact.

Use *were* rather than *was* in an *if* clause.

▶ Some people believe that if the Health Department ~~gives~~ *were to give* out clean needles, the number of people using drugs would increase.

Change the verb in the main clause to *would have, might have, could have,* or *should have* plus the past participle, and change the verb in the *if* clause to the past perfect to speculate about actions in the past that did not in fact occur.

participle A verb form showing present tense *(dancing, freezing)* or past tense *(danced, frozen)* that can also act as an adjective.

▶ If the computer lab *had* added more hours during finals week, students would not have had to wait to use a computer.

Note: Do not add *would have* to the *if* clause.

L2-b Learn the meanings of the idiomatic two- and three-word verbs used in English.

Idiomatic two- or three-word (or phrasal) verbs usually combine a verb with a word that appears to be a preposition or an adverb (called a *particle*). The combined meaning cannot be understood literally, and similar expressions often have very different meanings.

hand in means "submit"
hand out means "distribute"
look into means "investigate"
look out for means "watch carefully"
run away means "leave without warning"
run into means "meet by chance"
walk out on means "abandon"
want out means "desire to be free of responsibility"

Native speakers of English will notice misuses of these idiomatic verbs even though they use the verbs without thinking about their literal meanings. When you are unsure of the meaning or usage of such verbs, consult a dictionary designed for nonnative speakers of English, or ask a native speaker.

L2-c Use the correct verb forms after helping verbs.

After the helping (auxiliary) verbs *do, does,* and *did,* always use the base form of the main verb. After the helping verbs *have, has,* and *had,* always use the past participle form of the main verb. (See R2-a and G5.)

base form The uninflected form of a verb: I *eat;* to *play.*

▶ They do not ~~cooperated~~ *cooperate* with the police.

▶ They have ~~doing~~ *done* these things for a long time.

▶ They have *been* doing these things for a long time.

Note: A modal such as *will* sometimes precedes *have, has,* or *had.*

By Friday I *will have finished* this project.

Following the helping verbs *be, am, is, are, was, were,* and *been* (forms of *be*), use the present participle to show ongoing action (progressive tense).

▶ The president is ~~given~~ *giving* a speech on all major networks.

Note: Use one of the modal verbs with *be.* Use *have, has,* or *had* with *been.*

Terence *could be making* some calls while I go out.

I *have been* working hard.

After the helping verbs *am, is, are, was,* and *were* (forms of *be*), use the past participle to form the **passive voice.**

passive voice The verb form that shows something happening to the subject: The mouse *was caught* by the cat.

▶ Regular programming is ~~cancel~~ *canceled* for tonight.

To form the passive, *be, being,* and *been* need another helping verb in addition to the past participle.

Tonya *will be challenged* in graduate school this fall.

After a **modal,** use the **base form.**

modals The helping verbs *can, could, may, might, must, shall, should, will,* and *would,* which must be used in conjunction with another (main) verb: I *may go* to the bank.

base form The uninflected form of a verb: I *eat;* to *play.*

The Senate *might* vote on this bill next week.

L2-d Follow verbs with gerunds or infinitives, depending on the verb and your meaning.

gerund A verb form that is used as a noun and ends with *-ing: arguing, throwing.*

infinitive A verb form consisting of the word *to* plus the base form of the verb: *to run, to do.*

1. Verbs that can be followed by either a gerund or an infinitive with no change in meaning

begin	continue	like	prefer
can't stand	hate	love	start

The roof *began leaking.*

The roof *began to leak.*

2. Verbs that change their meaning, depending on whether a gerund or an infinitive follows

forget	remember	stop	try

Salam *remembered going* to the park on Saturday. [Salam recalled a weekend visit to a park.]

Salam *remembered to go* to the park on Saturday. [Salam remembered that he had to go to the park on Saturday.]

3. Verbs that can be followed by a gerund but not an infinitive

admit	deny	keep	recall
appreciate	discuss	miss	resist
avoid	dislike	postpone	risk
can't help	enjoy	practice	suggest
consider	finish	put off	tolerate
delay	imagine	quit	

▶ **I recall ~~to see~~ *seeing* Michel there.**

Note: Not or *never* can separate the verb and the gerund.

We discussed *not* having a party this year.

4. Verbs that can be followed by an infinitive but not a gerund

agree	expect	need	refuse
ask	fail	offer	venture
beg	have	plan	wait
choose	hope	pretend	want
claim	manage	promise	wish
decide	mean		

▶ **Children often only pretend ~~eating~~ *to eat* food they dislike.**

Note: In a sentence with a verb followed by an infinitive, the meaning changes depending on the placement of a negative word such as *not* or *never.*

I *never* promised to eat liver. [I did not make the promise.]

I promised *never* to eat candy. [I promised not to do it.]

5. Verbs that must be followed by a noun or pronoun and an infinitive

advise	encourage	order	teach
allow	force	persuade	tell
cause	instruct	remind	urge
command	invite	require	warn
convince	need		

Magda taught *her parrot to say* a few words.

Note: Use an infinitive, not *that,* following a verb such as *want* or *need.*

▶ **José wants ~~that~~ his new car ~~stays~~ to stay in good condition.**

6. The verbs *let, make* ("force"), and *have* ("cause") must be followed by a noun or pronoun and the **base form** of the verb (not the infinitive)

base form The uninflected form of a verb: I *eat;* to *play.*

He *let me borrow* the car.

The drill sergeant *makes the recruits stand* at attention.

I *had the children draw* in their notebooks.

preposition A word (such as *between, in,* or *of*) that always appears as part of a phrase and indicates the relation between a word in a sentence and the object of the preposition: The water splashed *into* the canoe.

L3 Prepositions

For practice, go to bedfordstmartins.com/theguide/prep

Use the prepositions *in, on,* and *at* to indicate location and time.

Location

- *In* usually means *within a geographic place or enclosed area* (*in* Mexico, *in* a small town, *in* the park, *in* my bedroom, *in* a car).
- *On* means *on top of* (*on* the shelf, *on* a hill, *on* a bicycle); it is also used with modes of mass transportation (*on* a train, *on* the subway), streets (*on* Broadway), pages (*on* page 5), floors of buildings (*on* the tenth floor), and tracts of private land (*on* a farm, *on* the lawn).
- *At* refers to specific addresses and named locations (*at* 1153 Grand Street, *at* Nana's house, *at* Macy's), to general locations (*at* work, *at* home, *at* the beach), and to locations that involve a specific activity (*at* the mall, *at* the gym, *at* a party, *at* a restaurant).

Time

- *In* is used with months (*in* May), years (*in* 1999), and seasons (*in* the fall), as well as with *morning, afternoon,* and *evening* (*in* the morning).
- *On* is used with days of the week (*on* Wednesday) and dates (*on* June 2, 2000).

- *At* is used with specific times (*at* 7:30, *at* noon, *at* midnight) and with *night* (*at* night).

Change any incorrect prepositions so that *in, on,* and *at* convey time and location correctly.

▶ People are driving at 55 or 60 miles per hour ~~in~~ *on* the highway.

Change any incorrect prepositions to idiomatic usage.

▶ Is life worse in the refugee camps or in Vietnam? You would find answers ~~from~~ *in* his article.

▶ Williams gives readers insight ~~to~~ *into* the doctor's insecurity.

L4 Omitted or Repeated Words

For practice, go to bedfordstmartins.com/theguide/oword

In English, every sentence, with rare exceptions, should have both a **subject** and a **verb.** If your native language allows you to omit either subject or verb, check your drafts carefully to be sure that you include both in your writing.

subject The part of a clause that identifies who or what is being discussed.

verb A word or phrase that expresses action or being and, along with a subject, is a basic component of a sentence.

SUBJECT — VERB
My brother has been very successful in his job.

Supply both a subject and a verb in each sentence, but do not repeat the subject or other words that duplicate grammatical functions.

Add a missing subject.

▶ On the contrary, *the compliments* increase his irritability.

Add a missing verb.

▶ Mr. Yang *is* a man who owns a butcher shop.

Supply a missing expletive (*there* or *it*) if the subject follows the verb.

▶ ~~Are~~ *There are* many ways to help poor people get jobs.

Delete a repeated subject.

▶ The elderly woman ~~she~~ must have an eye infection.

Delete other words that repeat grammatical functions.

▶ **People say that the cost of insurance ~~has~~ never goes down anymore.**

▶ **Only a few people ~~that~~ are rich.**

L5 Adjective Order

For practice, go to bedfordstmartins.com/theguide/order

Adjectives generally appear in the following order in English sentences.

1. Article, pronoun, or other determiner: *a, an, the, that, his, their, Janine's*
2. Evaluation or judgment: *beautiful, ugly, elegant, magnificent, impressive*
3. Size or dimension: *short, tall, long, large, small, big, little*
4. Shape: *round, rectangular, square, baggy, circular, octagonal*
5. Age: *new, young, old, aged, antique*
6. Color: *pink, turquoise, gray, orange*
7. History or origin (country and religion): *Asian, Norwegian, Thai, American, Protestant, Mongolian, Buddhist, Muslim, Catholic, Jewish*
8. Material: *copper, cotton, plastic, oak, linen*
9. Noun used as a descriptive adjective: *kitchen* (sink), *bedroom* (lamp)

When you use several adjectives to modify a noun, arrange them in the order expected in English.

1 2 4 6	1 3 5
***a beautiful, round, turquoise* stone**	***her skinny, young* cousin**

participile A verb form showing present tense *(dancing, freezing)* or past tense *(danced, frozen)* that can also act as an adjective.

L6 Participles

For practice, go to bedfordstmartins.com/theguide/part

Use the present form of the participle *(-ing)* if it describes someone or something *causing* or *producing* a mental state. Use the past form *(-ed)* if it describes someone or something *experiencing* the mental state. Problem participles include the following pairs.

annoying/annoyed	exhausting/exhausted
boring/bored	pleasing/pleased
confusing/confused	surprising/surprised
disappointing/disappointed	terrifying/terrified
exciting/excited	tiring/tired

The class was *confused* by the *confusing* directions.

The teacher was *surprised* by the *surprising* number of questions.

Change a participle to its present form *(-ing)* if it describes someone or something causing or producing a situation.

▶ Parents must not accept the ~~frightened~~ ^frightening behavior that their children learn in gangs.

Change a participle to its past form *(-ed)* if it describes someone or something experiencing a situation.

▶ I was not ~~pleasing~~ ^pleased with the information about religion in this article.

R Review of Sentence Structure

As you write, your primary concern will be with rhetoric, not parts of speech or sentence structure. You will focus on learning how to develop ideas, illustrate general statements, organize an argument, and integrate information. Yet sentence structure is important. Writing clear and correct sentences is part of being a competent writer. This and the other sections in the Handbook will help you achieve that goal.*

R1 Basic Sentence Structure

This review of basic sentence structure will look first at the elements that make up simple sentences and then at how simple sentences produce compound and complex sentences.

R1-a Words, Phrases, and Clauses

The basic building blocks of sentences are, of course, words, which can be combined into discrete groupings or *phrases.*

Words and phrases are further combined to create clauses. A *clause* is a group of at least two words that both names a topic and makes some point about that topic; every clause can be divided into a subject and a predicate. The *subject* identifies the topic or theme of the sentence—what is being discussed—while the *predicate* says something about the subject and is the focus of information in the clause. A clause can be either *independent* (that is, a complete idea in itself) or *dependent* (combined with an independent clause to create a complete idea). Dependent (or subordinate) clauses are discussed in R2-b.

R1-b Sentence Units

To introduce the principles of sentence structure, it is useful to consider *simple sentences,* those with only a single independent clause made up of a subject and a predicate.

Subject	*Predicate*
Native Americans	introduced baked beans to the New England settlers.
The Native Americans	cooked their beans in maple sugar and bear fat.

---

*English sentence structure has been described with scientific precision by linguists. This brief review is based on an extraordinary sentence grammar, *A Grammar of Contemporary English* (New York: Harcourt, 1972). Two of its authors, Sir Randolph Quirk and Sidney Greenbaum, have written a shorter version, *A Concise Grammar of Contemporary English* (New York: Harcourt, 1973), which you might wish to consult for elaboration on any of the points discussed here.

Subject	*Predicate*
The settlers	used molasses and salt pork instead.
Both baked-bean dishes	were essentially the same.

The subject and the predicate may each be a single word or a group of words. In addition to its verb, the predicate may include **objects, complements,** and **adverbial modifiers.** Simple sentences, then, are composed of some combination of these basic units: subject, verb, direct object, indirect object, subject complement, object complement, and adverbial modifier.

Of these seven units, two—subject and verb—are required in every sentence. Note that the subject determines whether the verb in the predicate is singular or plural: In the last of the preceding examples, the plural subject *dishes* requires the plural verb *were*.

The basic sentence units can be defined as follows.

object The part of a clause that receives the action of the verb (At the checkpoint, we unloaded *the canoes*) or the part of a phrase that follows a preposition (We dragged them to *the river*).

complement A word or word group that describes or restates a subject or an object.

adverbial modifier A word or word group that modifies a verb, an adjective, or another adverb.

Subjects. The simplest subject can be a single noun or pronoun, but a subject may also commonly consist of a noun phrase (including adjectives and other sentence elements) or even a noun clause. Subjects may also be *compound* when two or more nouns or pronouns are linked by a conjunction. (See R2 for definitions and examples of these various elements.)

Verbs. These can be classified as *transitive,* when they occur with an object, or *intransitive,* when they occur without an object. Intransitive verbs that occur with complements are often called *linking verbs.* Like subjects, verbs may be compound.

Objects. These include *direct* and *indirect* objects, which, like subjects, can be nouns, noun phrases, noun clauses, or pronouns. Objects usually follow the subject and verb.

Complements. These are either subject complements or object complements: *Subject complements* refer to the subject, *object complements* to an object. Like subjects and objects, complements can be nouns or pronouns, noun phrases or noun clauses (sometimes referred to as *predicate nominatives*). Complements can also be adjectives or adjective phrases (sometimes called *predicate adjectives*). Like objects, complements usually follow the subject and verb. They also follow any objects.

Adverbials. These are modifiers that refer to the verb in the sentence. They can be adverbs, adverb phrases, or adverb clauses.

R1-c Types of Simple Sentences

The basic sentence elements listed in R1-b can be put together in various ways to produce seven general types of simple sentences. The basic units are subject (S), verb (V), direct object (DO), indirect object (IO), subject complement (SC), object complement (OC), and adverbial modifier (A).

S	(INTRANSITIVE) V
Pizza	bubbles.

S	(TRANSITIVE) V	DO
Americans	love	pizza.

S	(TRANSITIVE) V	IO	DO
Some people	serve	their guests	pizza.

S	(LINKING) V	(ADJECTIVE) SC	S	(LINKING) V	(NOUN) SC
Pizza	is	delicious.	It	is	an inexpensive meal.

S	(INTRANSITIVE) V	A
The best pizza	comes	from a local restaurant.

S	(TRANSITIVE) V	DO	OC
Vegetarians	consider	pepperoni pizza	unhealthy.

S	(TRANSITIVE) V	DO	A
They	prefer	cheese pizza	any day.

R1-d Combinations and Transformations

The simple sentence patterns shown in R1-c can be combined and transformed to produce all of the sentences writers of English need. Two or more clauses may be combined with a coordinating conjunction (such as *and* or *but*) or a pair of correlative conjunctions (such as *either . . . or*) to create a *compound sentence*. Writers create *complex sentences* by combining independent clauses with a subordinating conjunction (such as *although* or *because*) or by linking two clauses with a relative pronoun (such as *which* or *who*); clauses that contain subordinating conjunctions or relative pronouns are *dependent clauses* and can no longer stand on their own as simple sentences. Clauses can also be combined to produce *compound-complex sentences* (compound sentences that contain dependent clauses). Conjunctions and dependent clauses are discussed in more detail in R2.

COMPOUND **Pizza is delicious, and it is an inexpensive meal. Either Americans love pizza, or they consider it junk food.**

COMPLEX **Vegetarians consider pepperoni pizza unhealthy**

DEPENDENT CLAUSE
because it is high in saturated fat.

DEPENDENT CLAUSE
People who want to please their guests serve them pizza.

DEPENDENT CLAUSE
Because pizza is inexpensive, Americans love it.

DEPENDENT CLAUSE

COMPOUND-COMPLEX **Even though pepperoni pizza is unhealthy, it is a delicious meal, and Americans love it.**

All of the sentences listed so far have been *declarative* statements. Simple sentences may also be transformed into *questions, commands,* and *exclamations.* In addition, sentences that are in the *active voice* can generally be transformed into the *passive voice* if they have transitive verbs and objects.

QUESTION	**Why is pizza popular?**
COMMAND	**Bake the pizza in a brick oven.**
EXCLAMATION	**This pizza is delicious!**
PASSIVE	**Pepperoni pizza is considered unhealthy by vegetarians.**

R2 Basic Sentence Elements

This section reviews the parts of speech and the types of clauses and phrases.

R2-a Parts of Speech

There are ten parts of speech: nouns, pronouns, adjectives, adverbs, verbs, prepositions, conjunctions, articles, demonstratives, and interjections.

Nouns. Nouns function in sentences or clauses as **subjects, objects,** and **subject complements.** They also serve as objects of various kinds of **phrases** and as **appositives.** They can be proper *(Burger King, Bartlett pear, Julia Child, General Foods)* or common *(tomato, food, lunch, café, waffle, gluttony).* Common nouns can be abstract *(hunger, satiation, indulgence, appetite)* or concrete *(spareribs, soup, radish, champagne, gravy).* Nouns can be singular *(biscuit)* or plural *(biscuits);* they may also be collective *(food).* They can be marked to show possession *(gourmet's choice, lambs' kidneys).* Nouns take determiners *(that lobster, those clams),* quantifiers *(many hotcakes, several sausages),* and articles *(a milkshake, the eggnog).* They can be modified by adjectives *(fried chicken),* adjective phrases *(chicken in a basket),* and adjective clauses *(chicken that is finger-licking good).* See also E3.

Pronouns. Pronouns come in many different forms and have a variety of functions in clauses and phrases.

Personal pronouns function as replacements for nouns and come in three case forms:

1. Subjective, for use as subjects or subject complements: *I, we, you, he, she, it, they.*
2. Objective, for use as objects of verbs and prepositions: *me, us, you, him, her, it, them.*

subject The part of a clause that identifies who or what is being discussed: At the checkpoint, *we* unloaded the canoes.

object The part of a clause that receives the action of the verb (At the checkpoint, we unloaded *the canoes*) or the part of a phrase that follows a preposition (We dragged them to *the river*).

subject complement A word or word group that follows a linking verb (such as *seems, appears,* or *is* and other forms of *be*) and describes or restates the subject: The tents looked *old and dirty.*

phrase A group of words that does *not* contain both a subject and a verb and is always part of an independent clause.

appositive A word or word group that identifies or gives more information about a noun or pronoun that precedes it.

3. Possessive: *mine, ours, yours, his, hers, theirs.* Possessive pronouns also have a determiner form for use before nouns: *my, our, your, his, her, its, their.*

Calvin Trillin says the best restaurants in the world are in Kansas City, but *he* was born there.

If *you* ever have the spareribs and french-fried potatoes at Arthur Bryant's, *you* will never forget *them*.

***Your* memory of that lunch at Bryant's is clearer than *mine*.**

Personal pronouns come in three persons (first person: *I, me, we, us;* second person: *you;* third person: *he, him, she, her, it, they, them*), three genders (masculine: *he, him;* feminine: *she, her;* neuter: *it*), and two numbers (singular: *I, me, you, he, him, she, her, it;* plural: *we, us, you, they, them*).

Reflexive pronouns, like personal pronouns, function as replacements for nouns, nearly always replacing nouns or personal pronouns in the same clause. Reflexive pronouns include *myself, ourselves, yourself, yourselves, himself, herself, oneself, itself, themselves.*

Aunt Odessa prided *herself* on her chocolate sponge cake.

Reflexive pronouns may also be used for emphasis.

Barry baked the fudge cake *himself*.

Indefinite pronouns do not refer to a specific person or object: *each, all, everyone, everybody, everything, everywhere, both, some, someone, somebody, something, somewhere, any, anyone, anybody, anything, anywhere, either, neither, none, nobody, many, few, much, most, several, enough.*

Not *everybody* was enthusiastic about William Laird's 1698 improvement on apple cider—Jersey lightning applejack.

In the Colonies, *most* preferred rum.

Taverns usually served *both*.

adjective clause A clause that modifies a noun or pronoun and is generally introduced by a relative pronoun (such as *that* or *which*).

Relative pronouns introduce adjective (or relative) clauses. They come in three forms: personal, to refer to people *(who, whom, whose, whoever, whomever)*, nonpersonal *(which, whose, whichever, whatever)*, and general *(that)*.

In 1846, Nancy Johnson invented a small hand-operated machine, *which* was the forerunner of today's portable ice-cream freezer.

It was Jacob Fussell of Baltimore *who* established the first wholesale ice-cream business in 1851.

The fact *that* we had to wait until 1896 for someone to invent the ice-cream cone is surprising.

Interrogative pronouns have the same forms as relative pronouns but have different functions. They serve to introduce questions.

***Who* invented the ice-cream sundae?**

Of chocolate and vanilla ice cream, *which* do you prefer?

The waiter asked, "*Whose* chocolate walnut sundae is this?"

Demonstrative pronouns are pronouns used to point out particular persons or things: *this, that, these, those.*

***This* dish is what Mandy likes best for brunch: pecan waffles with blueberry syrup.**

Of everything on the menu, *these* must be most fattening.

See also G1–G4.

Adjectives. Adjectives modify nouns and pronouns. Adjectives often occur immediately before or after nouns they modify. As subject complements (sometimes called predicate adjectives), they may be separated by the verb from nouns or pronouns they modify.

subject complement A word or word group that follows a linking verb (such as *seems, appears,* or *is* and other forms of *be*) and describes or restates the subject: The tents looked *old and dirty.*

***Creole* cooking can be found in *many* diners along the Gulf of Mexico.**

Gumbo is a *spicy* soup.

Jambalaya tastes *delicious,* and it is *cheap.*

Some adjectives change form in comparisons.

Gumbo is *spicier* than crawfish pie.

Gumbo is the *spiciest* Creole soup.

Some words can be used as both pronouns and adjectives; nouns are also sometimes used as adjectives.

ADJ. *Many* people love ADJ. *crawfish* pie, and PRON. *many* prefer gumbo.

See also G7-b.

Adverbs. Adverbs modify verbs *(eat well),* adjectives *(very big appetite),* and other adverbs *(extremely well done).* They often tell when, how, where, why, and how often.

A number of adverbs are formed by adding *-ly* to an adjective *(hearty* appetite, eat *heartily)*.

Walter Jetton started the charcoal fires *early.* [when]

He basted the sizzling ribs *liberally* with marinade. [how]

Pots of beans simmered *nearby.* [where]

Like adjectives, adverbs can change form for comparison.

He ate the buttermilk biscuits *fast.* [*faster* than Bucky ate his biscuits, *fastest* of all the hungry diners]

With adverbs that end in *-ly,* the words *more* and *most* are used when making comparisons.

Junior drank the first cold lemonade *quickly.* [*more quickly* than Billy Joe, *most quickly* of all those at the table]

The *conjunctive adverb* (or simply the *connective*) is a special kind of adverb used to connect the ideas in two sentences or independent clauses. Familiar connectives include *consequently, however, therefore, similarly, besides,* and *nevertheless.*

The inspiration for Tex-Mex food came from Mexico. *Nevertheless,* it is considered a native American cuisine.

Finally, adverbs may evaluate or qualify the information in a sentence.

***Barbecue* comes from *barbacoa,* a word the Spaniards *probably* picked up from the Arawak Indians.**

See also G7-a.

Verbs. Verbs tell what is happening in a sentence by expressing action *(cook, stir)* or a state of being *(be, stay)*. Depending on the structure of the sentence, a verb can be **transitive** *(Jerry bakes cookies)* or **intransitive** *(Jerry bakes for a living);* an intransitive verb that is followed by a **subject complement** *(Jerry is a fine baker, and his cookies always taste heavenly)* is often called a **linking verb.**

Nearly all verbs have several forms (or principal parts), many of which may be irregular rather than follow a standard pattern. In addition, verbs have various forms to indicate *tense* (time of action or state of being), *voice* (performer of action), and *mood* (statement, command, or possibility). Studies have shown that because verbs can take so many forms, the most common errors in writing involve verbs. See also G5.

transitive verb A verb that needs an object—something that receives the action of the verb—to make its meaning complete.

intransitive verb A verb that does not need an object to make its meaning complete.

subject complement A word or word group that follows a linking verb (such as *seems, appears,* or *is* and other forms of *be*) and describes or restates the subject: The tents looked *old and dirty.*

linking verb *Be, seem, appear, become, taste,* or another verb that connects a subject with a subject complement that describes or modifies it: The chips *taste* salty.

Verb Phrases. Verbs divide into two primary groups: (1) *main (lexical) verbs* and (2) *auxiliary (helping) verbs* that combine with main verbs to create verb phrases. The three primary auxiliary verbs are *do, be,* and *have,* in all their forms.

do: does, did, doing, done

be: am, is, are, was, were, being, been

have: has, had, having

These primary auxiliary verbs can also act as main verbs in sentences. Other common auxiliary verbs *(can, could, may, might, shall, should, will, would, must, ought to, used to),* however, cannot be the main verb in a sentence but are used in combination with main verbs in verb phrases. The auxiliary verb works with the main verb to indicate tense, mood, and voice.

A favorite cheese in the United States *has* always been cheddar.

When the cheese curd forms, it *must* be separated from the whey.

After cheddar cheese is shaped into a block, it *should* be aged for at least several months.

By the year 2011, Americans *will have been* eating cheese for four hundred years.

Principal Parts of Verbs. All main verbs (as well as the primary auxiliary verbs *do, be,* and *have*) have five forms. The forms of a large number of verbs are regular, but many verbs have irregular forms.

Form	***Regular***	***Irregular***
Infinitive or base	sip	drink
Third-person singular present (*-s* form)	sips	drinks
Past	sipped	drank
Present participle (*-ing* form)	sipping	drinking
Past participle (*-ed* form)	sipped	drunk

The past and past participle for most verbs in English are formed by simply adding *-d* or *-ed (posed, walked, pretended, unveiled).* However, a number of verbs have irregular forms, most of which are different for the past and the past participle.

For regular verbs, the past and past participle forms are the same: *sipped.* Even though regular verbs have predictable forms, they pose certain spelling problems, having to do mainly with dropping or doubling the last letter of the base form before adding *-ing, -d,* or *-ed.* (See M9-a.) All new verbs coming into English have regular forms: *format, formats, formatted, formatting.*

Irregular verbs have unpredictable forms. (Dictionaries list the forms of irregular verbs under the base form.) Their *-s* and *-ing* forms are generally predictable, just like those of regular verbs, but their past and past participle forms are not. In particular, be careful to use the correct past participle form of irregular verbs.

Listed here are the principal parts of fifty-three commonly troublesome irregular verbs. Check your dictionary for a more complete listing.

Base	*Past Tense*	*Past Participle*
be: am, is, are	was, were	been
beat	beat	beaten
begin	began	begun
bite	bit	bitten
blow	blew	blown
break	broke	broken
bring	brought	brought
burst	burst	burst
choose	chose	chosen
come	came	come
cut	cut	cut
deal	dealt	dealt
do	did	done
draw	drew	drawn
drink	drank	drunk
drive	drove	driven
eat	ate	eaten
fall	fell	fallen
fly	flew	flown
freeze	froze	frozen
get	got	got (gotten)
give	gave	given
go	went	gone
grow	grew	grown
have	had	had
know	knew	known
lay	laid	laid
lead	led	led
lie	lay	lain
lose	lost	lost
ride	rode	ridden

Base	*Past Tense*	*Past Participle*
ring	rang	rung
rise	rose	risen
run	ran	run
say	said	said
see	saw	seen
set	set	set
shake	shook	shaken
sink	sank	sunk
sit	sat	sat
speak	spoke	spoken
spring	sprang (sprung)	sprung
steal	stole	stolen
stink	stank	stunk
swear	swore	sworn
swim	swam	swum
take	took	taken
teach	taught	taught
tear	tore	torn
throw	threw	thrown
wear	wore	worn
win	won	won
write	wrote	written

Tense. Native speakers of English know the **tense** system and use it confidently. They comprehend time as listeners and readers. As talkers, they use the system in combination with adverbs of time to identify the times of actions. As writers, however, even native speakers may find it difficult to put together sentences that express time clearly through verbs: Time has to be expressed consistently from sentence to sentence, and shifts in time perspective must be managed smoothly. In addition, certain conventions permit time to be expressed in unusual ways: History can be written in present time to dramatize events, or characters in novels may be presented as though their actions are in present time. The following examples of verb tense provide only a partial demonstration of the complex system indicating time in English.

tense The form of a verb that shows the time of the action or state of being.

Present. There are three basic types of present time: timeless, limited, and instantaneous. Timeless present-tense verbs express habitual action.

Some Americans *grow* their own fruits and vegetables.

Limited present-tense verbs express an action in process and of limited duration.

The neighbors *are preparing* watermelon rind preserves this week.

Instantaneous present-tense verbs express action being completed at the moment.

Laura *is eating* the last ripe strawberry.

Present-tense verbs can also be emphatic.

I certainly *do enjoy* homemade strawberry preserves in the middle of winter.

Past. There are several kinds of past time. Some actions must be identified as having taken place at a particular time in the past.

While he *was waiting,* Jake *ordered* a ham sandwich on whole wheat bread.

In the *present perfect tense,* actions may be expressed as having taken place at no definite time in the past or as occurring in the past and continuing into the present.

Jake *has eaten* more ham sandwiches than he can count.

The Downtown Deli *has sold* delicious ham sandwiches on homemade bread for as long as he can remember.

Action can even be expressed as having been completed in the past prior to some other past action or event (the *past perfect tense*).

Before he *had taken* a bite, Jake dropped his sandwich on the floor.

Future. The English verb system offers writers several different ways of expressing future time. Future action can be indicated with the modal auxiliary *will.*

Fast-food restaurants *will grow* in popularity.

A completed future action can even be viewed from some time farther in the future *(future perfect tense).*

Within a decade or two, Americans *will have given up* cooking their own meals.

Continuing future actions can be expressed with *will be* and the *-ing* form of the verb.

Americans *will* soon *be eating* every second meal away from home.

The right combination of verbs with *about* can express an action in the near future.

Jeremiah *is about to eat* his third hamburger.

Future arrangements, commands, or possibilities can be expressed.

Junior and Mary Jo *are to be married* at McDonald's.

You *have to be* there by noon to get a good table.

If Junior *is to lose* weight, he must give up french fries.

Voice. A verb is in the *active* voice when it expresses an action taken by the subject. A verb is said to be in the *passive* voice when it expresses something that happens to the subject.

In sentences with active verbs, it is apparent who is performing the action expressed in the verb.

The chef *disguised* the tasteless broccoli with a rich cheese sauce.

In sentences with passive verbs, it may not be clear who is performing the action.

The tasteless broccoli *was disguised* with a rich cheese sauce.

The writer could reveal the performer by adding a phrase *(by the chef),* but the revision would also create a clumsy sentence. Graceful, clear writing relies on active, rather than passive, verbs. Passive forms do fulfill certain purposes, however, such as expressing the state of something.

The broccoli *is disguised.*

The restaurant *was closed.*

Passives can give prominence to certain information by shifting it to the end of the sentence.

Who* closed this restaurant? It was closed by *the Board of Health.

Writers also use passives to make sentences more readable by shifting long **noun clauses** to the end.

noun clauses Word groups that can function like nouns, acting as subjects, objects, or complements in independent clauses.

ACTIVE	***That the chef disguised the tasteless broccoli* with a cheese sauce disgusted Elvira.**
PASSIVE	**Elvira was disgusted *that the chef disguised the tasteless broccoli* with a cheese sauce.**

Mood. Mood refers to the writer's attitude toward a statement. There are three moods: indicative, imperative, and subjunctive. Most statements or questions are in the *indicative mood.*

The chuck wagon *fed* cowboys on the trail.

***Did* cowboys ever *tire* of steak and beans?**

Commands or directions are given in the *imperative mood.*

***Eat* those beans!**

The *subjunctive mood* is used mainly to indicate hypothetical, impossible, or unlikely conditions.

If I *were* you, I'd compliment the cook.

***Had* they *been* here yesterday, they would have had hot camp bread.**

phrase A group of words that does *not* contain both a subject and a verb and is always part of an independent clause. Common types of phrases include *prepositional* (*After a flash of lightning,* I saw a tree split in half) and *verbal* (*Blinded by the flash,* I ran into the house).

object The part of a clause that receives the action of the verb (At the checkpoint, we unloaded *the canoes*) or the part of a phrase that follows a preposition (We dragged them to *the river*).

objective case The form a pronoun takes when it is an object (receiving the action of the verb): We helped *him.*

Prepositions. Prepositions occur in **phrases,** followed by **objects.** (The uses of prepositional phrases are explained in R2-c.) Most prepositions are single words *(at, on, by, with, of, for, in, under, over, by),* but some consist of two or three words *(away from, on account of, in front of, because of, in comparison with, by means of).* They are used to indicate relations—usually of place, time, cause, purpose, or means—between their objects and some other word in the sentence.

I'll meet you *at* El Ranchero *for* lunch.

The enchiladas are stuffed *with* cheese.

You can split an order *with* [Georgette and me].

Objects of prepositions can be single or compound nouns or pronouns in the **objective case** (as in the preceding examples) or phrases or clauses acting as nouns.

Herman began making nachos *by* [grating the cheese].

His guests were happy *with* [what he served].

Conjunctions. Like prepositions, conjunctions show relations between sentence elements. There are coordinating, subordinating, and correlative conjunctions.

Coordinating conjunctions *(and, but, for, nor, or, so,* or *yet)* join logically comparable sentence elements.

Guacamole is made with avocados, tomatoes, onions, *and* chiles.

You may add a little lemon or lime juice, *but* be careful not to add too much.

dependent (subordinate) clause A word group that has a subject, a predicate, and a subordinating word (such as *because*) at the beginning; it cannot stand by itself as a sentence but must be connected to an independent (main) clause.

Subordinating conjunctions *(although, because, since, though, as though, as soon as, rather than)* introduce **dependent clauses.**

***As soon as* the waitress came, Susanna ordered an iced tea.**

She dived into the salsa and chips *because* she was too hungry to wait for her combination plate.

Correlative conjunctions come in pairs, with the first element anticipating the second *(both . . . and, either . . . or, neither . . . nor, not only . . . but also).*

Charley wanted to order *both* the chile relleno *and* the enchiladas verdes.

Articles. There are only three articles in English: *the, a,* and *an. The* is used for definite reference to something specific; *a* and *an* are used for indefinite reference to something less specific. *The Mexican restaurant in Westbury* is different from *a Mexican restaurant in Westbury.*

Demonstratives. *This, that, these,* and *those* are demonstratives. Sometimes called demonstrative adjectives, they are used to point to something specific.

Put one of *these* maraschino cherries at each end of the banana split.

The accident left pineapple milkshake all over the front seat of *that* pickup truck.

Interjections. Interjections indicate strong feeling or an attempt to command attention: *phew, shhh, damn, oh, yea, yikes, ouch, boo.*

R2-b Dependent Clauses

Like independent clauses, all dependent clauses have a **subject** and a **predicate** (which may also have objects, complements, and adverbial modifiers). Unlike independent clauses, however, dependent clauses cannot stand by themselves as complete sentences; they always occur with independent clauses as part of either the subject or the predicate.

subject The part of a clause that identifies who or what is being discussed: At the checkpoint, *we* unloaded the canoes.

predicate The part of a clause that includes a complete verb and says something about the subject: At the checkpoint, we *unloaded the canoes.*

INDEPENDENT **Ribbon-shaped pasta is popular in northern Italy.**

DEPENDENT **. . . , while tubular-shaped pasta is popular in southern Italy.**

. . . , which is generally made by hand, . . .

Although it originally comes from China, . . .

There are three types of dependent clauses: adjective, adverb, and noun.

Adjective Clauses. Also known as *relative clauses,* adjective clauses modify nouns and pronouns in independent clauses. They are introduced by relative pronouns *(who, whom, which, that, whose)* or adverbs *(where, when),* and most often they immediately follow the noun or pronoun they modify. Adjective clauses can be either *restrictive* (essential to defining the noun or pronoun they modify) or *nonrestrictive* (not essential to understanding the noun or pronoun); nonrestrictive clauses are set off by commas, and restrictive clauses are not (see P1-c and P2-b).

subject The part of a clause that identifies who or what is being discussed: At the checkpoint, *we* unloaded the canoes.

object The part of a clause that receives the action of the verb (At the checkpoint, we unloaded *the canoes*) or the part of a phrase that follows a preposition (We dragged them to *the river*).

subject complement A word or word group that follows a linking verb (such as *seems, appears,* or *is* and other forms of *be*) and describes or restates the subject: The tents looked *old and dirty.*

independent (main) clause A word group with a subject and a predicate that can stand alone as a separate sentence. (A predicate is the part of a clause that includes a complete verb and says something about the subject: At the checkpoint, we *unloaded the canoes.*)

relative pronoun A pronoun (such as *who, whom, whose, which,* or *that*) that introduces an adjective clause (a clause that modifies a noun or pronoun).

dependent (subordinate) clause A word group that has a subject, a predicate, and a subordinating word (such as *because*) at the beginning; it cannot stand by itself as a sentence but must be connected to an independent (main) clause: *Although it was raining,* we loaded our gear onto the buses.

Vincent bought a package of agnolotti, *which is a pasta used in soup.*

We went back to the restaurant *where they serve that delicious veal.*

Everyone *who likes Italian cooking* knows Romano cheese well.

Adverb Clauses. Introduced by subordinating conjunctions (such as *although, because,* and *since*), adverb clauses nearly always modify verbs in independent clauses, although they may occasionally modify other elements (except nouns). Adverb clauses are used to indicate a great variety of logical relations with their independent clauses: time, place, condition, concession, reason, cause, circumstance, purpose, result, and so on. They are generally set off by commas.

***Although the finest olive oil in Italy comes from Lucca,* good-quality olive oil is produced in other regions of the country. [concession]**

***When the tomato sauce comes to a boil,* reduce the heat and simmer. [time]**

***If you know mushrooms,* you probably prefer them fresh. [condition]**

Ken carefully watches the spaghetti *because he does not like it to be overcooked.* [reason]

Noun Clauses. Like nouns, noun clauses can function as **subjects, objects,** or **complements** (or predicate nominatives) in independent clauses. They are thus essential to the structure of the **independent clause** in which they occur and so, like restrictive adjective clauses, are not set off by commas. A noun clause usually begins with a **relative pronoun,** but the introductory word may sometimes be omitted.

SUBJECT
***That we preferred the sausage* surprised us.**

OBJECT
Harold did not know for sure *whether baloney came from Bologna.*

SUBJECT COMPLEMENT
He assumed *that it did.*

DIRECT OBJECT
Hillary claims *no one eats pizza in Italy.* [relative pronoun *that* dropped]

PREP. OBJECT OF PREPOSITION
Gnocchi may be flavored with *whatever fresh herbs are available.*

R2-c Phrases

Like **dependent clauses,** phrases can function as either nouns, adjectives, or adverbs in sentences. However, unlike clauses, phrases do not contain both a subject and a verb. (A phrase, of course, cannot stand on its own but occurs as part of an **independent clause.**) The six most common types of grammatical phrases are *prepositional, appositive, participial, gerund, infinitive,* and *absolute.*

Prepositional Phrases. Prepositional phrases always begin with a **preposition** and function as either an adjective or adverb.

> **preposition** A word (such as *between, in,* or *of*) that always appears as part of a phrase and indicates the relation between a word in a sentence and the object of the preposition: The water splashed *into* the canoe.

Food *in Hunan* is noticeably different from that *in Sichuan*.
ADJECTIVE PHRASE (in Hunan); ADJECTIVE PHRASE (in Sichuan)

The perfect egg roll is crisp *on the outside* and crunchy *on the inside*.
ADVERB PHRASE (on the outside); ADVERB PHRASE (on the inside)

Appositive Phrases. Appositive phrases identify or give more information about a noun or pronoun just preceding. They take several forms. A single noun may also serve as an appositive.

The baguette, *the most popular bread in France*, is a loaf about two feet long.

The king of the breakfast rolls, *the croissant*, is shaped like a crescent.

The baker *Marguerite* makes superb croissants.

Participial Phrases. Participles are verb forms used to indicate certain tenses (present: *sipping;* past: *sipped*). They can also be used as verbals—words derived from verbs—and function as adjectives.

At breakfast, we were first served *steaming* coffee and a simple *buttered* roll.

A participial phrase is an adjective phrase made up of a participle and any complements or modifiers it might have. Like participles, participial phrases modify nouns and pronouns in sentences.

Two-thirds of the breakfasts *consumed in the diner* included sausage and eggs.

***Prepared in the chef's personal style*, the vegetable omelets are served with a cheese sauce *flavored with garlic and herbs*.**

***Mopping up the cheese sauce with the last of his roll*, Mickey thought to himself, I could get used to this.**

Gerund Phrases. Like a participle, a gerund is a verbal. Ending in *-ing,* it even looks like a present participle, but it functions as a noun, filling any noun slot in a clause. Gerund phrases include **complements** and any modifiers of the gerund.

> **complement** A word or word group that describes or restates a subject or an object.

SUBJECT (Roasting)
***Roasting* is the quickest way to cook a turkey.**

SUBJECT (Preparing a stuffed turkey)
***Preparing a stuffed turkey* takes several hours.**

You begin by *mixing the dressing*.
OBJECT OF PREPOSITION (mixing the dressing)

Infinitive Phrases. Like participles and gerunds, infinitives are verbals. The infinitive is the base form of the verb, preceded by *to: to simmer, to broil, to fry.* Infinitives and infinitive phrases function as nouns, adjectives, or adverbs.

Tamales can be complicated *to prepare.*
ADVERB

***To assemble the tamales,* begin by cutting the kernels off the corncobs.**
ADVERB

NOUN
Remembering *to save the corn husks* is important.
OBJECT OF GERUND PHRASE

Anyone's first tamale dinner is a meal *to remember for a long time.*
ADJECTIVE

Absolute Phrases. The absolute phrase does not modify or replace any particular part of a clause; it modifies the whole clause. An absolute phrase includes a noun or pronoun and often includes a past or present participle as well as modifiers. Nearly all modern prose writers rely on absolute phrases. Some style historians consider them a hallmark of modern prose.

> ***Her eyes glistening,* Lucy checked out the cases of doughnuts at Krispy Kreme Doughnuts.**
>
> **She stood patiently in line, *her arms folded to control her hunger, her book pack hanging off one shoulder.***
>
> **She walked slowly to a table, *each hand bearing a treasure.***

GL Glossary of Frequently Misused Words

Sometimes writers choose a word that is incorrect, imprecise in meaning, pronounced the same as the correct word (a homophone), or used widely but unacceptable in formal writing situations. In addition, problems can arise with idiomatic phrases, common everyday expressions that may or may not fit, or words whose denotations or connotations do not precisely suit the context of a particular sentence. In general, you should avoid imprecise popular usages in formal writing.

accept/except *Accept* is a verb ("receive with favor"). *Except* may be a verb ("leave out") but is more commonly used as a preposition ("excluding"). Other forms: *acceptance, acceptable; exception.*

None of the composition instructors will *accept* late papers, *except* Mr. Siu.

Her *acceptance* of the bribe *excepts* her from consideration for the position.

adapt/adopt *Adapt* means "adjust to make more suitable." *Adopt* means "take as one's own." Other forms: *adaptable, adaptation; adoption.*

To *adopt* an older child, parents must be willing to *adapt* themselves to the child's needs.

advice/advise *Advice* is a noun; *advise* is a verb. Other forms: *advisable, adviser.*

Everyone *advised* him to heed the expert's *advice.*

affect/effect *Affect* is commonly used as a verb, most often meaning "influence"; in psychology, the noun *affect* is a technical term for an emotional state. *Effect* is generally a noun ("result or consequences"); it is only occasionally used as a verb ("bring about"), although the adjective form *(effective)* is common.

Researchers are studying the *effect* of stress.

How does stress *affect* the human body?

all right *All right* is the preferred spelling, rather than *alright,* which many people regard as unacceptable.

a lot A common expression meaning "a large number," *a lot* is always written as two words. Because it is vague and informal, avoid it in college writing.

among/between Use *among* when you are referring to more than two objects; limit *between* to references to only two objects.

It is hard to choose one winner *among* so many highly qualified candidates for the scholarship.

***Between* the two extreme positions lies a vast middle ground.**

amount/number *Amount* refers to the quantity of a unit ("amount of water," "amount of discussion"), whereas *number* refers to the quantity of individual items ("number of papers," "number of times"). In general, use *amount* only with a singular noun.

anxious/eager *Anxious* means "nervous" or "worried"; *eager* means "looking forward [impatiently]." Avoid using *anxious* to mean *eager*.

The students were *eager* to learn their grades.

They were *anxious* they wouldn't pass.

between/among See **among/between.**

capital/capitol *Capital* is the more common word and has a variety of meanings, among them the principal city in a state or country; *capitol* refers only to a government building.

cite/sight/site *Cite* as a verb means "refer to as proof" or "summon to appear in court." *Site* is a noun meaning "place or location." *Sight* may be a verb or a noun and always refers to seeing or what is seen ("a sight for sore eyes").

Can you *cite* your sources for these figures?

A new dormitory will be built at this *site*.

When she *sighted* the speeding car, the officer *cited* the driver for recklessness.

complement/compliment *Complement* refers to completion, the making of a satisfactory whole, whereas *compliment* indicates admiration or praise; both can be used as either nouns or verbs. *Complementary* means "serving to complete" or "contrasting in color"; *complimentary* means "given free."

The dean *complimented* the school's recruiters on the full *complement* of students registered for the fall.

The designer received many *compliments* on the way the elements of the room *complemented* one another.

Buy a new refrigerator and receive a *complimentary* ice maker in a *complementary* color.

could of/should of/would of In standard speech, "could have," "should have," and "would have" sound very much like "could of," "should of," and "would of"; however, substituting *of* for *have* in this construction is too casual for written work. The same holds true for "might of," "must of," and "will of."

council/counsel *Council* is a noun ("an assembly of people who deliberate or govern"). *Counsel* is a verb meaning "advise" or a noun meaning "advice." Other forms: *councilor* ("member of a council"); *counselor* ("one who gives advice").

The *council* on drug abuse has issued guidelines for *counseling* troubled students.

Before voting on the important fiscal issue, City *Councilor* Lopez sought the *counsel* of her constituents.

desert/dessert As a noun or an adjective, *desert* (dez´ ert) means "a dry, uncultivated region"; as a verb, *desert* (di zurt´) means "abandon." A *dessert* is a sweet dish served at the end of a meal.

The hunters were alone in the arid *desert, deserted* by their guides.

After a heavy meal, sherbet is the perfect *dessert.*

eager/anxious See **anxious/eager.**

effect/affect See **affect/effect.**

emigrant/immigrant An *emigrant* moves out of a country; an *immigrant* moves into a country. Other forms: *emigrate, emigration, émigré; immigrate, immigration.*

Congress passed a bill to deal with illegal *immigrants* living in the United States.

Members of her family *emigrated* from Cuba to Miami and Madrid.

etc. An abbreviation of the Latin words *et cetera* ("and other things"), *etc.* should never be preceded by *and* in English. Also be careful to spell the abbreviation correctly (*not* "ect."). In general, use *etc.* sparingly, if at all, in college writing.

except See **accept/except.**

fewer/less Use *fewer* when referring to **count nouns;** reserve *less* for amounts you cannot count.

The new cookies have *fewer* calories than the other brand because they contain *less* sugar.

count noun A noun that names people and things that can be counted: one *teacher,* two *teachers;* one *movie,* several *movies.*

fortuitous/fortunate Often used incorrectly, the adjective *fortuitous* means "by chance" or "unplanned" and should not be confused with *fortunate* ("lucky").

Because the two candidates wished to avoid each other, their *fortuitous* meeting in the parking lot was not a *fortunate* event for either party.

hisself/theirselves In nonstandard speech, "hisself" is sometimes used for *himself* and "theirselves" for *themselves,* but such usage is not acceptable in written work.

hopefully In conversation, *hopefully* is often used as a convenient shorthand to suggest that some outcome is generally to be hoped for ("Hopefully, our nominee will win the election"); this usage, however, is not acceptable in most written work. Better substitutes include *I hope, let's hope, everyone hopes,* and *it is to be hoped,* depending on your meaning. The adverb *hopefully* ("full of hope") should always modify a specific verb or adverb.

I *hope* my brother will win the election.

We should all *hope* his brother will win the election.

Her sister is *hopeful* that she will win the election.

The candidate inquired *hopefully* about the results.

immigrant See **emigrant/immigrant.**

its/it's *Its* is a possessive pronoun; *it's* is the contraction of *it is.*

This job has *its* advantages.

When *it's* well grilled, there's nothing like a steak.

transitive verb A verb that needs an object—something that receives the action of the verb—to make its meaning complete.

intransitive verb A verb that does not need an object to make its meaning complete.

lay/lie The verb *lay,* meaning "put, place," is transitive (forms of *lay* are *lay, laid, laid*). The verb *lie,* meaning "recline," is intransitive (forms of *lie* are *lie, lay, lain*). Writers may incorrectly use *laid* as the past tense of *lie,* or *lay* as the present tense of *lie.* Other forms: *laying, lying.*

The lion *lies* in wait for the approach of its prey.

Joseph *laid* down his shovel, took a shower, and *lay* down for a nap.

less/fewer See **fewer/less.**

literally *Literally* means "exactly as stated, actually" and is often used to suggest that a cliché has in fact come true. However, to say, "The movie made my hair literally stand on end" is to misuse the word (although a person who suffered a fatal heart attack brought on by a fearful shock might correctly be said to have *literally* died of fright).

loose/lose *Lose* is a verb ("mislay, fail to maintain"); *loose* is most often used as an adjective ("not fastened tightly").

A *loose* board may make someone *lose* his or her balance.

number/amount See **amount/number.**

persecute/prosecute *Persecute* means "mistreat or oppress"; *prosecute* most often means "bring a legal suit or action against."

A biased majority can easily *persecute* minority groups.

The law may *prosecute* only those who are indicted.

prejudice/prejudiced *Prejudice* is a noun or a verb. When used adjectivally, it should take the form of the past tense of the verb: *prejudiced.*

We should fight *prejudice* wherever we find it.

He was *prejudiced* against the candidate because she spoke with an accent.

principal/principle *Principal* implies "first in rank, chief," whether it is used as an adjective ("the principal cities of the Midwest") or a noun ("the principal of a midwestern high school"). *Principle* is generally a noun meaning "a basic law or truth."

In *principle*, you are correct.

The *principle* of free speech will be the *principal* topic of discussion.

prosecute/persecute See **persecute/prosecute.**

sensual/sensuous Both *sensual* and *sensuous* suggest the enjoyment of physical pleasure through the senses. However, *sensual* generally implies self-indulgence, particularly in terms of sexual activity; *sensuous* has a more positive meaning and suggests the ability to appreciate intellectually what is received through the senses. Other forms: *sensuality; sensuousness.*

When drunk, the emperor gave himself up to brutal *sensuality.*

Anyone can enjoy a *sensuous* spring night.

set/sit The difference between the verbs *sit* and *set* is similar to that between *lie* and *lay: Sit* is generally intransitive ("rest on one's buttocks"), and *set* is transitive ("put [something] in a certain place"). *Set* also has a number of uses as a noun. The past tense and past **participle** forms of *sit* are both *sat;* these forms for *set* are both *set.*

participle A verb form showing present tense *(dancing, freezing)* or past tense *(danced, frozen)* that can also act as an adjective.

He would rather *sit* than stand and would rather lie than *sit.*

He *set* his suitcase on the ground and then *sat* on it.

should of See could of/should of/would of.

sight/site See cite/sight/site.

stationary/stationery *Stationary* is an adjective meaning "fixed, remaining in one place" ("Concrete will make the pole stationary"). *Stationery* refers to writing paper. One way to keep the distinction in mind is to associate the *er* in *paper* with that in *stationery.*

subordinating conjunction A word or phrase (such as *although, because, since,* or *as soon as*) that introduces a dependent clause and relates it to an independent clause.

restrictive word group A group of words, not set off by commas, that provides information essential to defining or identifying the noun or pronoun it modifies.

nonrestrictive word group A group of words, set off by commas, that provides extra or nonessential information and could be eliminated without changing the meaning of the noun or pronoun it modifies.

that/which When used as a **subordinating conjunction,** *that* always introduces a **restrictive word group;** *which* is generally used for **nonrestrictive word groups.** Although it is acceptable to use *which* before a restrictive word group, *that* is generally preferred to make it clear that the clause is restrictive. (See the discussion of restrictive and nonrestrictive word groups in P1-c and P2-b, and the review of sentence structure and sentence elements on p. H-129.)

Her first bid for the Senate was the only election *that* she ever lost.

Her first bid for the Senate, *which* was unsuccessful, brought her to prominence.

The Senate election *that* resulted in her defeat took place in 1968.

their/there/they're *Their* is a possessive pronoun; *there* specifies a place or functions as an expletive; and *they're* is a contraction of *they are.*

The coauthors say *there* are no copies of *their* script in their office, but *they're* not telling the truth.

theirselves See hisself/theirselves.

to/too/two *To* is a preposition, *too* is an adverb, and *two* is generally an adjective. The most common error here is the substitution of *to* for *too.*

It is *too* early *to* predict either of the *two* scores.

unique To be precise, *unique* means "one of a kind, like no other." Careful writers do not use it loosely to mean simply "unusual or rare." Nor can it correctly take a comparative form ("most unique"), although advertisers sometimes use it this way.

Her generosity is not *unique,* although today it is increasingly rare.

This example of Mayan sculpture is apparently *unique;* none other like it has so far been discovered.

used to In colloquial speech, *used to* often sounds like "use to." However, *used to* is the correct form for written work.

My grandfather *used to* be a Dodgers fan until the team moved to Los Angeles.

weather/whether *Weather* is a noun ("atmospheric conditions"); *whether* is a conjunction.

The *weather* forecast indicates *whether* there will be sun or rain.

which See **that/which.**

who's/whose *Who's* is the contraction of *who is* or *who has; whose* is a possessive pronoun.

***Who's* up next?**

She's the only student *who's* done her work correctly.

***Whose* work is this?**

The man *whose* job I took has retired.

would of See **could of/should of/would of.**

User's Guide for the Writing Guide Software

SYSTEM REQUIREMENTS

Here are the minimum system requirements for PC and Macintosh platforms:

PC

- Intel Pentium processor or compatible and Windows 95, 98, 2000, NT 4, or later
- 30 MB available RAM (not including RAM required to open word processor, browser software, or Excel)
- 16-bit color monitor (1024 × 768 pixels display setting recommended), keyboard, mouse
- Microsoft Word 6.0 or above or Corel WordPerfect 7.0 or above or Notepad
- Netscape 4.0 or above or Internet Explorer 4.0 or above (optional)
- Microsoft Excel 6.0 or above (optional)

Macintosh

- PowerPC, System 7.6.1, or later
- 30 MB available RAM (not including RAM required to open word processor, browser software, or Excel)
- 16-bit color monitor, keyboard, mouse
- AppleWorks 6.0 or SimpleText
- Netscape 4.0 or above or Internet Explorer 4.0 or above (optional)
- Microsoft Excel 6.0 or above (optional)

Installation

Installation is easy and takes only a few minutes. After inserting the CD into your computer's CD-ROM drive, follow these steps:

PC

- Go to the Start menu, and choose Run.

- Type [drive letter]:\Setup.exe, where "[drive letter]" is the letter assigned to your CD-ROM drive. Don't include the brackets. For example, D:\Setup.exe.
- Click OK, and follow the easy directions.

Macintosh

- Double-click on the CD-ROM icon that appears on your desktop.
- Double-click on Writing Guide Installer, and follow the instructions.

CONTENTS

WRITING GUIDE SOFTWARE: AN INTRODUCTION

The Writing Guide Software for *The St. Martin's Guide to Writing*, Seventh Edition, offers two types of learning environments: Chapters and Writer's Resources.

Chapters offer content and activities from Chapters 2 through 10 of your textbook. In each chapter, you can read an annotated sample student essay or use the Writing Guide to compose your own essay. The Writing Guide works with your own word processing program, placing most of the same advice and examples that are in your book on your computer screen, so that as you write, help for every stage of the writing process is just a click away.

Writer's Resources include Sentence Strategies, which provide explanations and examples of some strategies that are especially useful for the genre of writing you are doing; an electronic Journal, where you can respond to readings, take notes, and generate ideas for your writing; a Grammar Assessment, which identifies your strengths and weaknesses in key sentence skills; an Error Log, where you can track patterns in your problems with grammar, style, punctuation, and paragraphing; and Tutorials, which function as an interactive handbook. The Grammar Assessment results are automatically stored in the Error Log, and the Error Log contains links to the Tutorials as well as to Exercise Central, an online collection of more than four thousand interactive grammar, punctuation, and style exercises.

Logging In

When you start the program, the title screen loads, and then the log-in box soon appears (see Figure 1). Enter your first and last names and a password that is easy to remember. The name and password functions are case-sensitive, so be sure to capitalize carefully. When you have entered the information, click the arrow button in the lower right-hand corner to proceed.

When you log in for the first time, you will see the message "No record exists with this name. Do you want to create a new record?" (see Figure 2). You can click Cancel to start over or New to record your name and password.

After you have logged in for the first time, you must use the same first and last names and password whenever you return to the software. If you lose your password, you can create a new record, but your lost password and your prior work cannot be retrieved. It is a good idea to choose a password that is easy to remember and also to write it down for future reference.

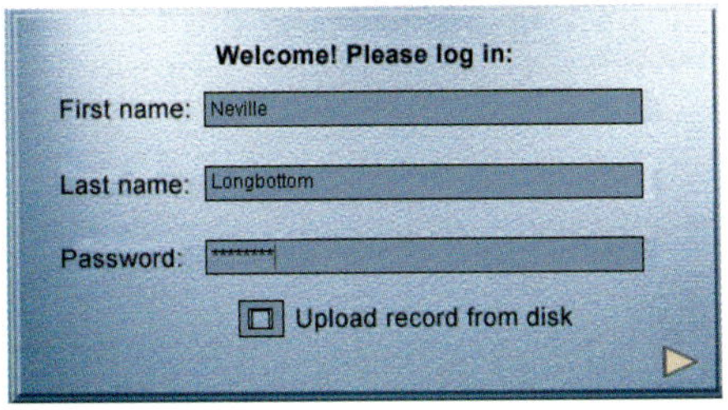

Figure 1

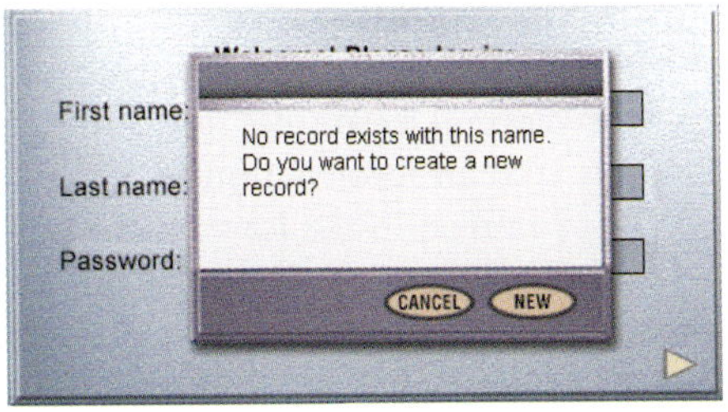

Figure 2

Loading from a Disk

Note that the log-in screen lets you select Upload record from disk. When you exit the Writing Guide Software using the program's Quit button, you are given the option to save to a floppy disk any work you have done in the Journal, Grammar Assessment (if you do not complete it in one session), and Error Log. If you use the Writing Guide Software on a computer other than your own, such as in the library, in class, or in the writing center or the learning lab, it is a good idea to save your work in these Writer's Resources to a disk so that you can move from one computer to another with the most up-to-date version of your work.

Navigating the Main Menu

After you have logged in, the main menu opens (see Figure 3).

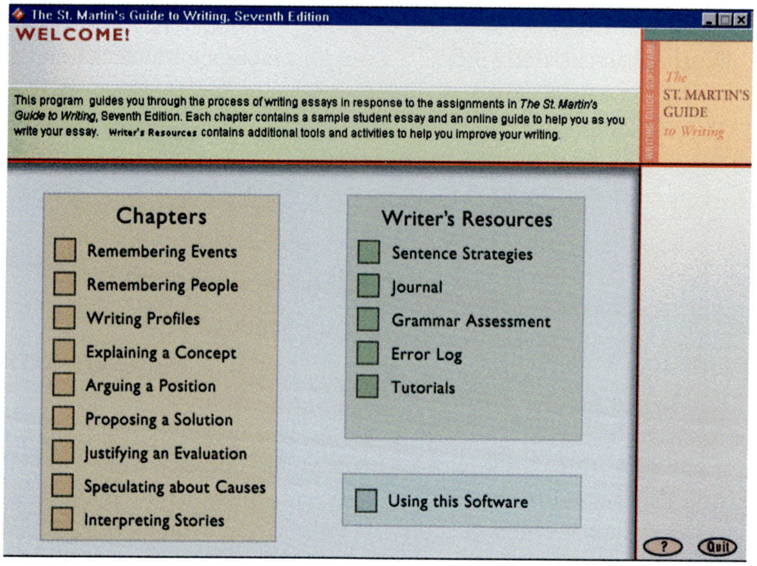

Figure 3

Several groups of buttons are displayed here. On the left are buttons for chapter titles in *The St. Martin's Guide to Writing;* clicking on one of these buttons takes you to the material for that chapter, including the Writing Guide. On the right are buttons for Writer's Resources, tools to help you with your writing. Using This Software contains contact information for technical support.

The ? button in the lower right-hand corner of the screen provides access to help for each element of the Writing Guide Software. No matter where you are within the software, this button remains in the same location, and you are able to access its contents. Use the Quit button if you wish to leave the program and save any work you have done in the Journal, Grammar Assessment, or Error Log to a floppy disk.

USING THE CHAPTERS

Select a chapter by clicking on the button next to its title. When you click on a chapter, you are shown the opening menu for that chapter and a brief description of the type of writing it covers.

On each chapter's opening menu, you are provided with two options (see Figure 4). You can read an annotated sample student essay (click on Read), or you can write your own essay using the Writing Guide (click on Write). Every chapter offers the same menu, but the contents are tailored to the type of writing the chapter explores. Note also that when you are in any of the chapters, the Error Log, Tutorials, and Journal are always available in the menu to the right.

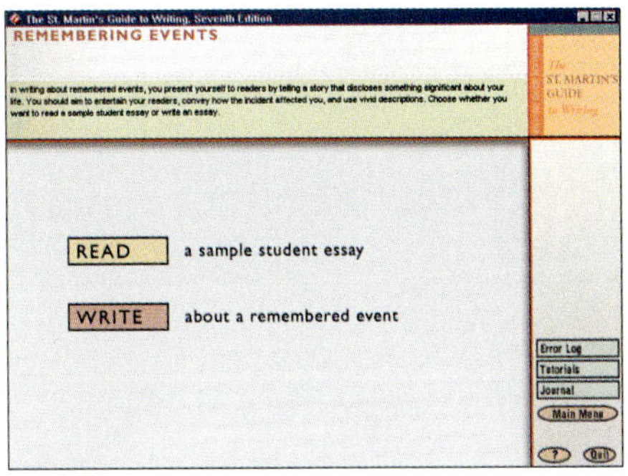

Figure 4

Reading Sample Student Essays

If you click on the Read button on the opening menu for any chapter, you are taken to an annotated student essay (see Figure 5). Each student essay's key elements are highlighted. When you roll your cursor over the highlighted text, an annotation appears describing that element's role in the essay. These annotations help you see how another student constructed his or her essay.

Using the Writing Guides

If you click on the Write button on the opening menu for any chapter, you are taken to that chapter's Writing Guide (see Figure 6). The Writing Guides are the heart of the Writing Guide Software and were designed to help you compose effective essays. Each chapter's Guide covers the type of writing covered by that chapter in the book. It offers advice and instruction tailored to that type of writing and takes you through a five-stage writing process: Invent, Plan and Draft, Read Critically, Revise, and Edit and Proofread. Some of these five stages incorporate substeps; for example, Figure 6 shows substep b (out of four substeps) in the Invent stage for the Remembering Events chapter. So that you don't accidentally skip over a substep as you move through the Writing Guides, you should use the forward and back arrows in the upper right-hand corner of the screen to move from one stage or substep to another.

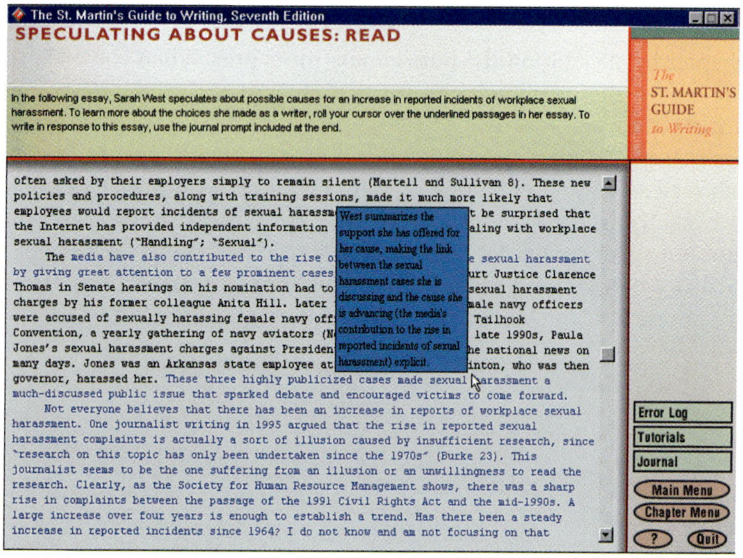

Figure 5

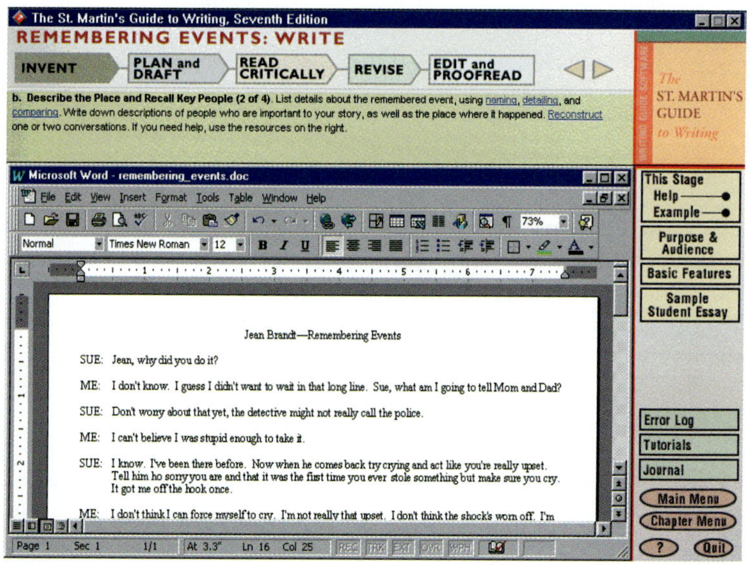

Figure 6

In the right-hand frame for each stage, you can find several buttons. In the This Stage box, you can click on Help to find advice specific to that stage, and Example to see a student writer's work at that stage. The frame also features links to helpful references that you can access at any stage to see what is required of you for that genre of writing. These references include Purpose and Audience, which explains why a writer would use that genre and what an audience's expectations are for that type of writing; Basic Features, which lists the essential characteristics of the genre; and the Sample Student Essay, which provides a complete model of the genre, written by a real student. Other buttons in the right-hand frame provide access to the Error Log, Tutorials, and Journal from anywhere inside a Writing Guide.

Additionally, when you click on any underlined term in blue in the instructions near the top of the screen, a pop-up box with a definition of the term appears.

Using Your Computer's Word Processing Program

When you open a chapter's Writing Guide (by clicking on Write on the chapter's opening menu), the computer's word processing program opens automatically inside the frame of the Writing Guide Software. *(Note: The word processing program must be closed before you open a Writing Guide.)* Everything you write while using a Writing Guide is in the computer's word processing program, and the program's standard features—Spell check, Save, Print, and so on—work as they usually do. *Save your work in the word processing program often so that you do not inadvertently lose anything you have written. Also make sure to remember the name of your file and where you save it (either on your hard drive or on a disk).* It may take a few sessions to complete an essay; when you return to the Writing Guide after having saved your work and closed your file, use your word processor's File and Open commands (not the Upload record from disk button on the log-in screen) to retrieve your essay.

Additional Resources

At the Plan and Draft stage, the Read Critically stage, and the Revise stage, you can click on a button in the right-hand frame to access a pop-up box with brief explanations and some examples of Sentence Strategies that are especially useful for that type of writing (see Figure 7). You can then click on links to access fuller discussions of these strategies and more examples, as well as discussions of other strategies you might also find helpful for that genre.

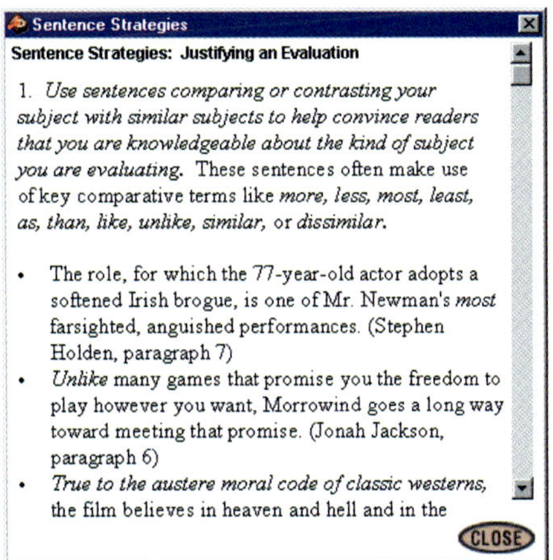

Figure 7

At the Read Critically stage, you can access an onscreen version of the Critical Reading Guide, which provides a list of questions that someone reviewing your draft should consider as well as a form for you to fill out to provide the reviewer with background information (see Figure 8). The Critical Reading Guide can be printed out. It can also be customized by first saving it as a file on your computer and then by adding, deleting, or revising questions.

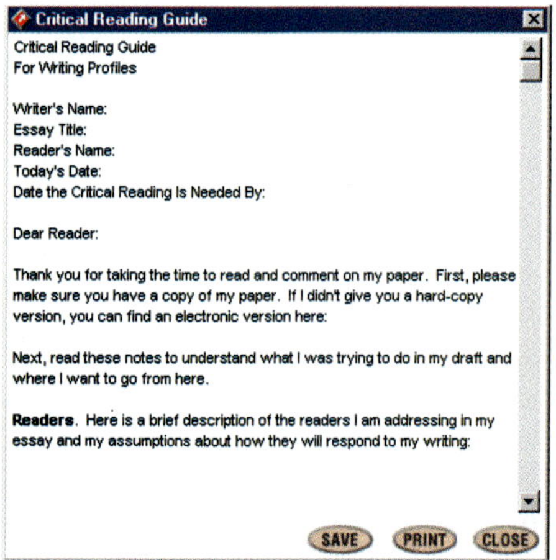

Figure 8

At the Revise stage, you are able to access the Revision Checklist, which asks you questions about your draft and provides automatic feedback with revision suggestions (see Figures 9 and 10). You can print out the revision suggestions or save them as a file on your computer.

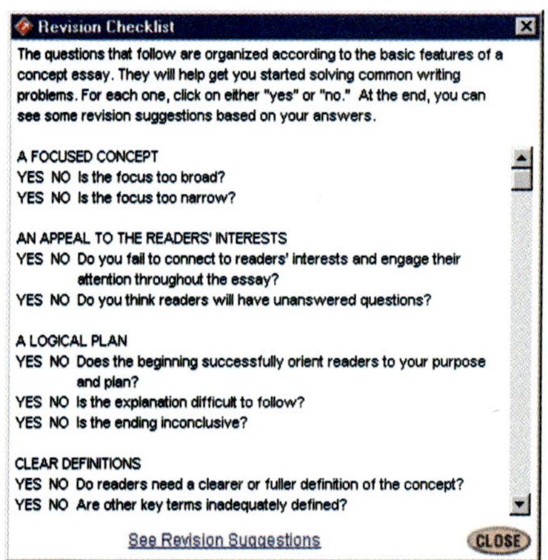

Figure 9

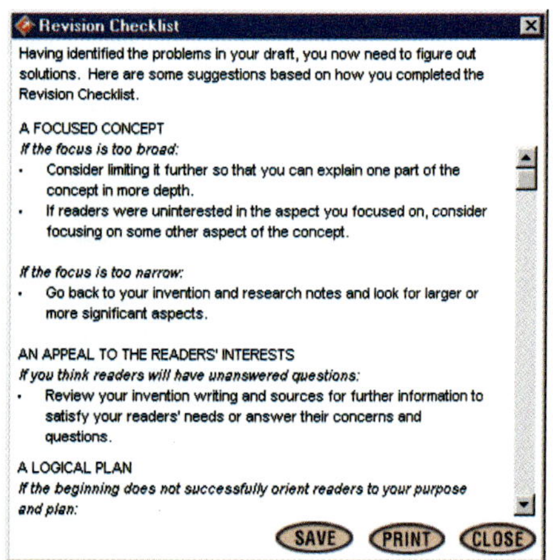

Figure 10

USING THE WRITER'S RESOURCES

In addition to the chapter-by-chapter Writing Guides, the Writing Guide Software offers a collection of Writer's Resources that you can use at your own or your instructor's discretion. All of these tools are accessible from the main menu (see Figure 3). The Error Log, Tutorials, and Journal can also be accessed from the frame on the right wherever you are in the Writing Guide Software (see Figures 4, 5, and 6).

Using the Sentence Strategies

The Sentence Strategies provide practical help with the nuts and bolts of drafting by showing you two useful sentence strategies for a given genre, explaining their advantages, providing examples from the readings in *The St. Martin's Guide to Writing,* and linking to discussions of other strategies you might also find helpful for that genre (see Figure 11). When you click on the Sentence Strategies button on the main menu (see Figure 3), a screen opens that lists each chapter and a brief description of the strategies presented for that type of writing. Click on a chapter title to open that chapter's Sentence Strategies. (Brief versions of each chapter's Sentence Strategies are accessible at the Plan and Draft stage, the Read Critically stage, and the Revise stage of the Writing Guide.)

Using the Journal

The Journal is a useful place for you to respond to readings, take notes, or generate ideas for your writing. The Journal works like many e-mail interfaces: You specify a subject and then type in text in the main box below (see Figure 12). After you have composed a journal entry, you then have seven options at the bottom of the screen—E-mail, Save As, New, Delete, Save, Print, and Close.

The E-mail button opens the e-mail program on your computer. It automatically pastes your journal entry's subject line into the e-mail's subject line and your journal

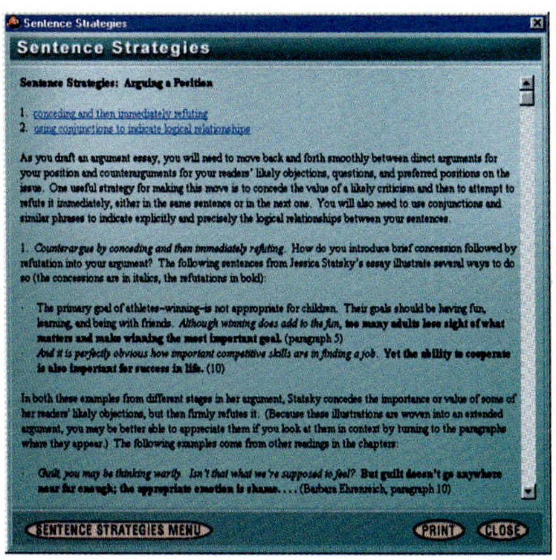

Figure 11

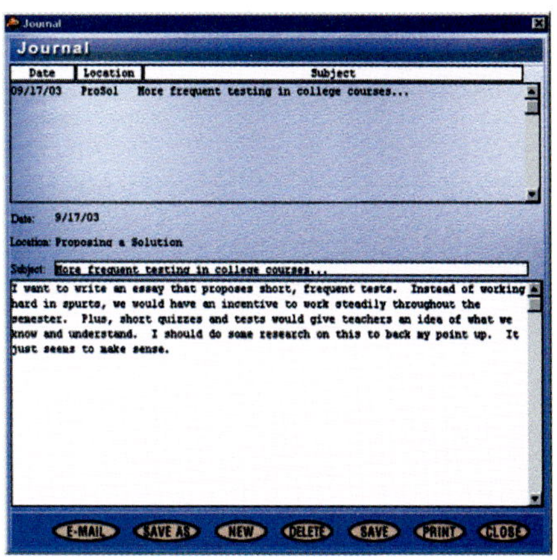

Figure 12

entry's text into the e-mail's body. You can then insert any e-mail addresses you choose and share your journal entry electronically with your instructor, a classmate, or a class e-mail discussion list.

The Save As button lets you save your journal entry as a file on your computer or a floppy disk.

The New button lets you start a new journal entry. When you click on the Journal button anywhere in the software, the most recent entry you have written is opened automatically. You can edit or expand on that entry or click New to start a new one.

The Save button lets you save the entry on which you are working. As with a word processor, you should save regularly as you write in your Journal so that longer entries are not lost if your computer crashes or you lose power. Each saved entry is listed in the top window of the Journal under Date, Location, and Subject.

The Delete button lets you remove an entry. When you click a saved entry in the list at the top of the Journal screen to delete it, the message you select appears in your Journal window, giving you a chance to look it over before deleting. You cannot recover deleted entries, so be sure you want to remove an entry before deleting it.

The Print button lets you print the entry. You can print only one entry at a time, so if your instructor asks you to hand in an entire Journal in print format, you might want to print each entry as you complete it and save the printouts in a folder until you need to turn them in.

Using the Grammar Assessment

The Grammar Assessment feature is a diagnostic test that helps you understand more about your grammar skills and problems. It takes you through a series of questions and then provides feedback, prompting you to answer a total of forty-four items.

The Grammar Assessment opens with directions on the first screen. Follow them to begin. All questions are multiple choice; to record an answer, click on your choice (the text for that choice turns blue when you click on it). You can change your mind by clicking on a different choice. An answer is not recorded until you click on the forward arrow at the bottom of the screen or hit the Enter key on your keyboard, either of which takes you to the next item in the assessment. If you cannot finish the Grammar Assessment in one session, use the Close button to exit. When you come back, click on the Resume button on the first screen to pick up where you left off.

Once you complete the Grammar Assessment, your results are presented as a grid that lists Skill, Score, and Review Recommendations (see Figure 13). You can print these results or save them as a file on your computer or a floppy disk. In the Take Tutorial column of the results grid, you can click on the T icon to view a Tutorial for that particular writing problem, or you can click on the E icon in the Go to Exercise Central column to open your Web browser and go to the Exercise Central quizzes for that problem. If you are using the hardcover version of *The St. Martin's Guide to Writing,* you should refer to the Read chapter column for the appropriate Handbook sections to learn more about a particular skill.

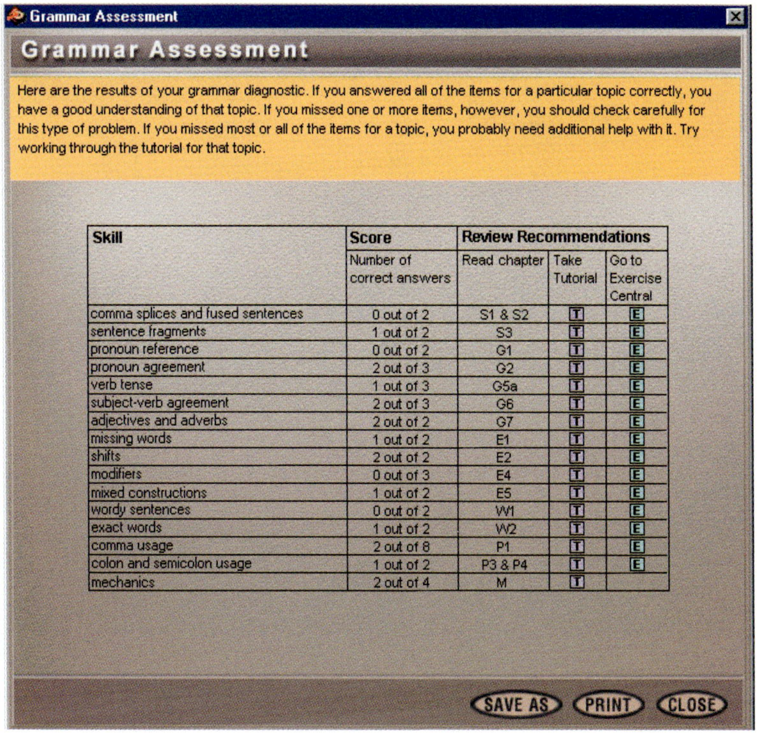
Grammar Assessment

Here are the results of your grammar diagnostic. If you answered all of the items for a particular topic correctly, you have a good understanding of that topic. If you missed one or more items, however, you should check carefully for this type of problem. If you missed most or all of the items for a topic, you probably need additional help with it. Try working through the tutorial for that topic.

Skill	Score	Review Recommendations		
	Number of correct answers	Read chapter	Take Tutorial	Go to Exercise Central
comma splices and fused sentences	0 out of 2	S1 & S2	T	E
sentence fragments	1 out of 2	S3	T	E
pronoun reference	0 out of 2	G1	T	E
pronoun agreement	2 out of 3	G2	T	E
verb tense	1 out of 3	G5a	T	E
subject-verb agreement	2 out of 3	G6	T	E
adjectives and adverbs	2 out of 2	G7	T	E
missing words	1 out of 2	E1	T	E
shifts	2 out of 2	E2	T	E
modifiers	0 out of 3	E4	T	E
mixed constructions	1 out of 2	E5	T	E
wordy sentences	0 out of 2	W1	T	E
exact words	1 out of 2	W2	T	E
comma usage	2 out of 8	P1	T	E
colon and semicolon usage	1 out of 2	P3 & P4	T	E
mechanics	2 out of 4	M	T	

SAVE AS PRINT CLOSE

Figure 13

The Grammar Assessment is a study guide, and you can take it as many times as you like. If you start the Grammar Assessment again, the results grid is cleared; however, a copy of your results is automatically transferred to your Error Log (see Figure 14) in the column labeled GA. Very often students will retake the Assessment to see how they have improved after working on some of their weaknesses. If you print or save your results, you can track your progress through multiple assessments taken over time.

Using the Error Log

The Error Log is a tool that allows you to track and learn about specific errors you are making in your writing as the term progresses.

The first column, headed GA, reflects the results of your Grammar Assessment, listing the number of incorrect answers you gave for each of the writing problems. This information is filled in automatically, and you cannot change these numbers unless you retake the Grammar Assessment. Most of the rest of the Error Log can be

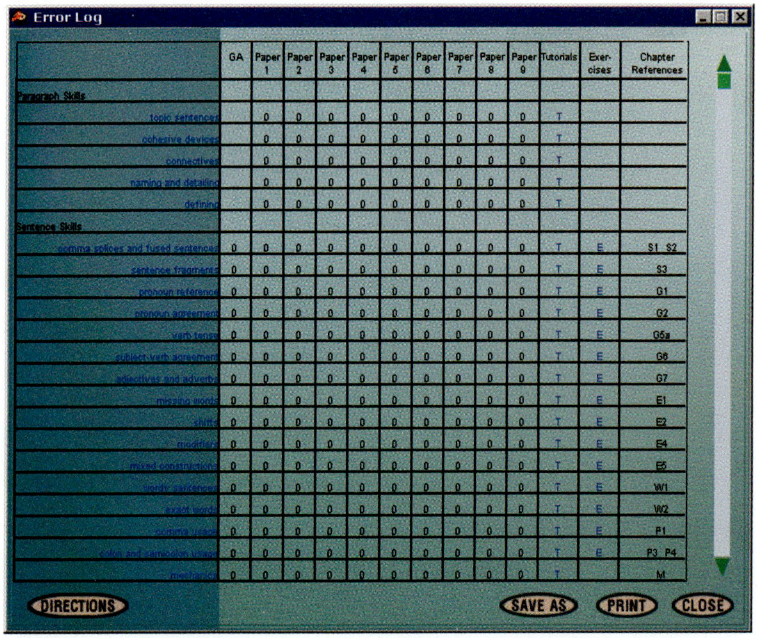

Figure 14

customized. Whenever your instructor returns a graded or corrected paper, use your log to record the types of errors and the number of times your instructor pointed them out. For example, if you have three unintentional sentence fragments in your first paper, click on the zero at the intersection of the Sentence fragments row and the Paper 1 column; when the zero turns red, press the number 3 on your keyboard. You can also rename the column headings with labels that remind you of the assignment *(Event),* the date *(9/16),* or the title of your paper *(Interview).* In addition, at the bottom of the Error Log are four rows where you can add writing problems that you would like to track but are not listed in the first column of the Log.

You may also access the Tutorial or Exercise Central quizzes for a particular skill by clicking on the T or E icons in the Tutorials and Exercises columns. If you are using the hardcover version of *The St. Martin's Guide to Writing,* refer to the Chapter References column for the appropriate Handbook sections to learn more about a particular skill.

If you save your Error Log to your computer or a floppy disk, the content is saved as an Excel file. Double-clicking on this file opens it in Excel, with all formatting correct. If your computer does not have Excel, you can access this file by opening your word processing program first and then opening the error log.xls file from within that word processing program. Changing the page layout to landscape and the font size to 8 gives the best possible alignment of the data.

Using the Tutorials

The Tutorials outline specific issues in writing—from grammar to mechanics to organization—and enable you to learn more about these issues.

The Tutorials for paragraph skills cover topic sentences, cohesive devices, connectives, naming and detailing, and defining. All of them have at least two steps (explaining what the skill is and providing practice using that skill), and some also have a third or fourth step (see Figure 15).

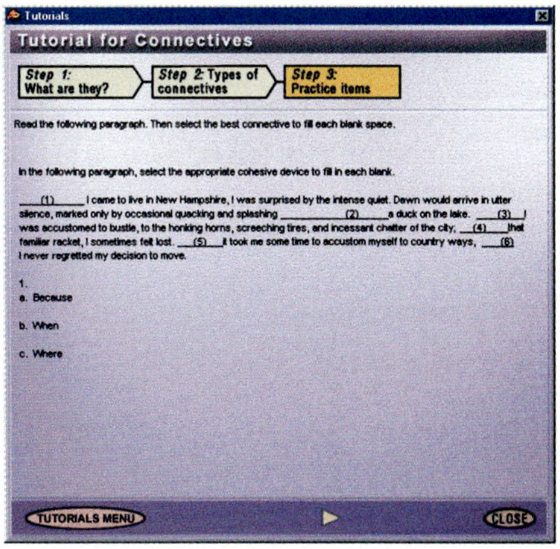

Figure 15

The Tutorials for sentence skills work in four steps (see Figure 16):

Step 1 explains what the issue is.

Step 2 provides tips on how to spot problems with this issue in your writing.

Step 3 gives advice on how to correct the problems.

Step 4 provides practice for correcting the problems.

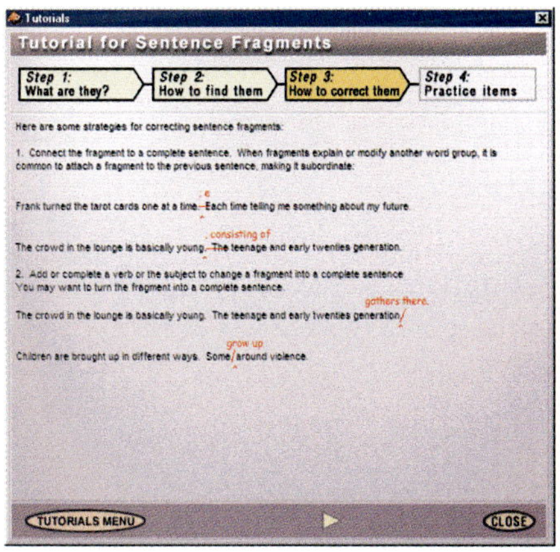

Figure 16

At the final step, you will always find a link to Exercise Central, where you can get further practice.

To move from one step to another in a tutorial, click on the buttons at the top of the screen. Other tutorials can be accessed by clicking on the Tutorials Menu button in the lower left-hand corner of the screen.

TROUBLESHOOTING

Handling Memory Problems

The Writing Guide Software for *The St. Martin's Guide to Writing* allows you to work simultaneously in the software and in your own word processing program. Also, you may at times choose a link from the software to Exercise Central (using your Web browser) or open a saved Error Log (using Excel).

To run all programs at once, your computer must have enough available memory. Difficulty in opening a component of the Writing Guide Software may be related to a shortage of memory, which is likely to occur only with older computers.

Handling Network Problems

For the Writing Guide Software for *The St. Martin's Guide to Writing* to work correctly in a networked environment, clients must have write access to the software's directory on the server.

If you are a Novell network user, note the following. After installing the Writing Guide Software, go to the Network folder on the CD-ROM and copy ela.exe and errorloga.dxr into the installation directory, replacing the two files with the same names. This corrects some errors that occur only on Novell networks with these two files.

In a networked environment, if users encounter an error message when trying to go to a Tutorial from the Error Log, the error can be corrected by having all users exit from the program and then deleting the file jump.txt or tempel.txt from the program directory.

Contacting Technical Support

If you have additional questions, please e-mail Technical Support at techsupport@bfwpub.com.

Acknowledgments

Text Credits

Maya Angelou. "Uncle Willie." From *I Know Why the Caged Bird Sings.* Copyright © 1969 and renewed 1997 by Maya Angelou. Reprinted with the permission of Random House, Inc.

Natalie Angier. "Indirect Aggression." From *Woman: An Intimate Geography.* Copyright © 1999 by Natalie Angier. Excerpted with the permission of Houghton Mifflin Company. All rights reserved.

Mary Jo Bane. "Boston Priest-Pedophile Crisis." Originally titled "Law and Disorder: Boston's Priest-Pedophile Crisis" from *Commonweal,* March 8, 2001, pp. 11–12. Copyright © 2002 by Commonweal Foundation. Reprinted with permission. For Subscriptions, www.commonwealmagazine.org.

Rick Bragg. "100 Miles per Hour, Upside Down and Sideways." From *All Over But the Shoutin'.* By Rick Bragg. Copyright © 1997 by Rick Bragg. Used with permission of Pantheon Books division of Random Books, Inc.

David Brooks. "The Triumph of Hope Over Self-Interest." From *The New York Times,* January 12, 2003, Op-Ed. Copyright © 2003, The New York Times. Reprinted by permission.

Annie Dillard. "A Chase." From *An American Childhood.* Copyright © 1987 by Annie Dillard. Reprinted by permission of HarperCollins Publishers, Inc.

John T. Edge. "I'm Not Leaving Until I Eat This Thing." From *The Oxford American,* September/October 1999. Copyright © 1999 by John T. Edge. Reprinted with the permission of the author. Photo of the pig by Shannon Brinkman. Reproduced by permission.

Barbara Ehrenreich. Excerpt from"Evaluation" from *Nickel and Dimed: On (Not) Getting By in America.* Copyright © 2001 by Barbara Ehrenreich. Reprinted with the permission of Henry Holt and Company LLC.

Richard Estrada. "Sticks and Stones and Sports Team Names." From *The Los Angeles Times,* October 29, 1995. Copyright © 1995, The Washington Post Syndicate. Reprinted with permission.

Amitai Etzioni. "Working at McDonald's." Copyright © 1986 by Amitai Etizioni, author of *The Spirit of Community.* Director, George Washington University Center for Communitarian Policy Studies. Reprinted with the permission of the author.

Trevor B. Hall. "The Edison Café." From *Doubletake,* Fall 2000. Copyright © 2000. Reprinted with permission of the author. Photos by Michael Coles. Reprinted by permission.

Mark Hertsgaard. "A Global Green Deal." From *Time,* April/May 2000. Copyright © 2000 Time, Inc. Reprinted by permission. *Globe* illustration by David Bowers. Reproduced by permission of the artist.

Stephen Holden. "A Hell for Fathers and Sons." From *The New York Times,* July 12, 2002. (with movie still). Copyright © 2002 The New York Times Company. Reprinted by permission.

Home Education Magazine. Screen shot of *Home Education Magazine* home page. www.hone-ed-magazine.com.

Jonah Jackson. "The Elder Scrolls III: Morrowind." Review from www.techtv.com. Reprinted by permission. (Images shown) from *The Elder Scrolls III: Morrowind* ™ © 2002 Bethesda Softworks LLC, a ZeniMax Media Company. The Elder Scrolls, Morrowind, Bethesda Softworks and ZeniMax are registered trademarks of ZeniMax Media Inc. All rights reserved.

Mary Karr. Excerpt from *Cherry.* Copyright © 1998 by Mary Karr. Used with the permission of Viking Penguin, a division of Penguin Group (USA) Inc.

Bel Kaufman. "Sunday in the Park." From The Available Press/PEN Short Story Collection (New York: Ballantine Books, 1985). Copyright © 1985 by Bel Kaufman. Reprinted with the permission of the author.

Stephen King. "Why We Crave Horror Movies." Copyright © Stephen King. Originally appeared in *Playboy* (1982). Reprinted with permission.

Ronnie D. Lankford, Jr. "American Roots Music." From www.documentaryfilms.net. Copyright © 2003 by Ronald D. Lankford, Jr. Reprinted with permission of the author.

Sandra Tsing Loh. "My Father's Chinese Wives." First appeared in *Quarterly West* (1994). Copyright © 1994 by Sandra Tsing Loh. Reprinted by permission.

Katherine S. Newman. "Dead-End Jobs: A Way Out." From *The Brookings Review* (Fall 1995). Copyright © 1995 by Katherine S. Newman. Reprinted with permission.

Randy Olson. "Shifting Baselines." Originally published in the *Los Angeles Times,* November 17, 2002. Copyright © 2002 by Randy Olson. Reprinted with the permission of the author.

Peggy Orenstein. "The Daily Grind: Lessons in the Hidden Curriculum." From *Schoolgirls: Young Women, Self-Esteem and the Confidence Gap.* Copyright © 1994 by Peggy Orenstein and the American Association of University Women. Used by permission of Doubleday, a division of Random House, Inc.

William S. Pollack. "Why Boys Become Depressed." From *Real Boys: Our Sons from the Myths of Boyhood.* Copyright © 1998 by William Pollack. Used by permission of Random House, Inc.

Jonathan Rauch. "Conservatives Should Support Same-Sex Marriage." From *National Review Online,* August 3, 2001. Reprinted by permission of United Feature Syndicate, Inc. Published as "The Marrying Kind" in *The Atlantic Monthly,* May 2002.

Anastasia Toufexis. "Love: The Right Chemistry." From *Time,* February 15, 1993. Copyright © 1993 by Time, Inc. Reprinted with permission.

William Carlos Williams. "The Use of Force." From *The Collected Stories of William Carlos Williams.* Copyright © 1938 by William Carlos Williams. Reprinted with the permission of New Directions Publishing Corporation.

Tobias Wolff. "On Being a Real Westerner." [editor's title] From *This Boy's Life.* Copyright © 1989 by Tobias Wolff. Reprinted with the permission of Grove/Atlantic, Inc.

Amy Wu. "A Different Kind of Mother." From *Chinese American Forum* 9, p. 26. Copyright © Amy Wu. Reprinted by permission of the author.

Picture Credits

24 (left), Frank Siteman; (right) Barbara Rios/Photo Researchers; **77** Photo: Dorothea Lange/Farm Security Administration—Office of War Information Photograph Collection/ Library of Congress Prints and Photographs Division; **82** (left) George Shelley/Corbis; (right) Edward Lettau/Photo Researchers; **98** Courtesy of Chinese American Forum, Vol. 9, No. 1. July, 1993; **136** (left) Bill Stormont/Corbis; (right) Enrico J. Azzato/Imagestate; **141** Photo by Shannon Brinkman. Reproduced by permission. **147** and **149** Photos by Michael Coles. Reprinted with permission. **196**; **200** (left) Alexander Tsiaras/Science Source/Photo Researchers; (right) Painting: *Portrait of Dora Maar* (detail) by Pablo Picasso, © 2004 Estate of Pablo Picasso/Artists Rights Society (ARS), New York/Photo Bridgeman-Giraudon/Art Resource; **206** Copyright 1993 by Time, Inc. Reprinted with permission. **256** Maria Burwell; **260** (left) Russell D. Curtis/ Photo Researchers; (right) Mitch Jacobson/AP/Wide World Photos; **322** and **323** "Still an All Boy's Club" & "Women in Power: A Score Card" from *Business Week*, November 22, 1999. © 1999 Business Week, Inc. Reprinted with permission. **328** (left) Sie SRL/Corbis; (right) Julie Nicholls/Corbis; **334** *Globe* illustration by David Bowers. Reproduced by permission of the artist. **386** Gabe Palmer/Corbis; **390** (left) Pat Sullivan/AP/Worldwide Photos; (right) Riccardo Marcialis © Photri, Inc./Corbis; **395** Publicity shot from *Road to Perdition.* Dreamworks/20th Century Fox. Published in *The New York Times.* **401** and **402** from *The Elder Scrolls III: Morrowind*™ © 2002 Bethesda Softworks LLC, a ZeniMax Media Company. The Elder Scrolls, Morrowind, Bethesda Softworks, and ZeniMax are registered trademarks of ZeniMax Media Inc. All rights reserved. **443** and **444** Photofest; **448** (left) Nigel Cook/*Daytona Beach News-Journal*/Corbis/Sygma; (right) Vincent Laforet/*The New York Times*; **506** (left) Bill Binzen/Corbis; (right) Kenfre, Inc./Imagestate; **628** and **629** (1866) Bettman/Corbis; (1910) The Granger Collection; (1944) Hank Morgan-Science Source/Photo Researchers; (1950) Saturn Stills—Science Photo Library/Photo Researchers; (1953) UPI/ Bettman/Corbis; (1973) Ken M. Highfill/Photo Researchers; (chart) © 1999 Time Inc. Reprinted by permission. **638** and **639** Diagram by Christoph Blumrich, © 1999 Newsweek, Inc. All Rights Reserved. Reprinted by permission; photo by Jeanne Friebert, SIPA Press. **640** from *Sunset's Home Repair Handbook*, © 1999. Sunset Publishing Corporation, Menlo Park, CA 94025; **665** and **667** © 1999 Newsweek, Inc. All rights reserved. Reprinted by permission. **740** Courtesy of *Home Education Magazine*; **829** (left) Illustration by Shirley Baty. From *Biology* 5e by Helena Curtis & N. Sue Barnes. © 1989 by Worth Publishers. Reprinted by permission. (right) Photo courtesy of Michael A. Walsh.

Author and Title Index

Index for ESL Writers

Agreement Form

I hereby transfer to Bedford/St. Martin's all rights to my essay,

(tentative title), subject to final editing by the publisher. These rights include copyright and all other rights of publication and reproduction. I guarantee that this essay is wholly my original work, and that I have not granted rights to it to anyone else.

Student's signature X: ____________________

Please type

Name: ____________________

Address: ____________________

____

____

Phone: ____________________

Please indicate the reader or publication source you assumed for your essay:

____

Write a few sentences about the purpose or purposes of your essay. What did you hope to achieve with your reader?

____

____

____

____

Bedford/St. Martin's representative: ____________________

Submitting Papers for Publication

To Students and Instructors

We hope that we'll be able to include essays from more colleges and universities in the next edition of *The Guide* and our accompanying anthology, *Sticks and Stones and other student essays.* Please let us see essays written using *The St. Martin's Guide* you'd like us to consider. Send them with this Paper Submission Form and the Agreement Form on the back to *The Guide,* Bedford/St. Martin's, 33 Irving Place, New York, NY 10003.

PAPER SUBMISSION FORM

Instructor's Name ______________________________

School ______________________________

Address ______________________________

Department ______________________________

Student's Name ______________________________

Course ______________________________

Writing activity the paper represents ______________________________

This writing activity appears in chapter(s) ______________________________
of *The St. Martin's Guide to Writing*